THE
DOLPHIN
READER

THE
DOLPHIN
READER

SECOND EDITION

DOUGLAS HUNT

University of Missouri

HOUGHTON MIFFLIN COMPANY   BOSTON

DALLAS   GENEVA, ILLINOIS   PALO ALTO

PRINCETON, NEW JERSEY

ACKNOWLEDGMENTS

JAMES BALDWIN: "Autobiographical Notes," "Stranger in the Village," "Notes of a Native Son" from *Notes of a Native Son* by James Baldwin. Copyright © 1955, renewed 1983 by James Baldwin. Reprinted by permission of Beacon Press. "Fifth Avenue, Uptown" reprinted from *Nobody Knows My Name* by James Baldwin. Copyright © 1960 by Esquire, Inc. Copyright renewed 1988 by Gloria Baldwin Kareta-Smart. Used by arrangement with the James Baldwin Estate.

TONI CADE BAMBARA: From *Gorilla, My Love*, by Toni Cade Bambara. Copyright © 1972 by Toni Cade Bambara. Reprinted by permission of Random House, Inc.

DAVE BARRY: "Lost in the Kitchen" originally entitled "Most Men Lost in Kitchen," Knight-Ridder Newspapers, May 2, 1986. Reprinted by permission of the author.

Acknowledgments continue following Author/Title Index.

COVER: Adapted from cover illustration by the late Stephen Harvard.

Printed in the U.S.A.

Library of Congress Catalog Card Number: 89-80942

ISBN: 0-395-43214-6

BCDEFGHIJ-A-96543210

CONTENTS

Note: An asterisk (*) denotes fiction or drama. Annotated Contents *may be found in the* Previews *that begin each unit.*

PREFACE

The opportunity to publish a second edition, like the opportunity to revise an essay, is both a blessing and a curse. The pain of undoing is at first greater than the pleasure of redoing. In the case of *The Dolphin Reader,* it was fairly clear what babies should not be thrown out with the bath water. Users of the first edition had told me that they were pleased with the way that the thematic units focused on central human questions, ones equally relevant to the lives of students and to the disciplines they study in college. They had also said that they appreciated the balance of views in the *Reader,* which encouraged students to see that the questions raised allowed for lively disagreement. More than one user of the first edition advised me to change as little as possible in the second edition, an invitation I was tempted to accept.

Once into the project, I realized that even the first edition's strengths could be strengthened. Its focus and balance had insured users that the essays would not stand as isolated examples of "good writing," as disengaged from one another as strangers in an elevator. But in the second edition I have tried to make the connections between selections tighter still. The ideal would be a book of essays and stories so rich in associations with each other that even a casual browser would be drawn into the conversational web.

When I was a boy I saw an educational film in which the idea of a chain reaction was illustrated by filling a room with mousetraps, placing a ping-pong ball on the bail of each trap, and then throwing a final ball into the room. Within a couple of seconds, the rattle of the traps sounded like an explosion and the air was white with ping-pong balls. I won't claim that each essay in this edition leads to all others in quite so dramatic a way, but the interconnection of ideas is very strong and transcends the boundaries between units. My eye falls, for example, on a passage in the opening paragraph of Melissa Greene's "No Rms, Jungle Vu": "We evolved over millions of years in the wild, where survival depended on our awareness of the landscape, the weather, and the animals. We haven't been domesticated long enough to have lost those senses." Pitch that idea into the room, and every selection in the *Nature and Civilization* unit throws up its ping-pong ball immediately, some in hearty agreement, some in alarm. Sooner or later one of them lands on Brigid Brophy's "Women," with its intense resistance to the idea that we are handcuffed by biology: "What distinguishes human from all other animal nature is the ability to be unnatural." This ball bounces onto Nathaniel Hawthorne's "The Birthmark," where an attempt to transcend nature proves disastrous. But by now, Konrad Lorenz's "The Biological Basis of Human Aggression" has launched a suggestion that letting nature take its course is also dangerous. This idea triggers in turn the entire *Aggression* unit, which triggers *Insiders and Outsiders,* which triggers *Having and Having Not,* and the whole business becomes, as Elaine Morgan puts it, "the kind of rumpus where anybody can join in."

Besides being more tightly connected to each other, the selections in the second edition are more tightly connected to the present. The units retain their historical depth, always beginning with essays at least a half-century old and giving students a sense of ideas changing over time. But 30 of the 105 essays and stories were published since 1980 and 50 since 1970. The *Femininity and Masculinity* unit, for example, begins with Virginia Woolf's classic "Professions for Women" (1930) and ends (chronologically) with Leonard Riskin's essay published on Superbowl Sunday, 1989.

In the first edition, a few authors were represented by more than one piece, giving students the opportunity to compare works and trace dominant themes. In the second edition, this feature has been strengthened and systematized by the addition of *Three Essayists,* a unit containing four essays each by George Orwell, James Baldwin, and Joan Didion. Also represented by at least two works are Brigid Brophy, Perri Klass, Annie Dillard, E. M. Forster, Patricia Hampl, C. S. Lewis, Konrad Lorenz, William Manchester, Lewis Thomas, E. B. White, Alice Walker, and Virginia Woolf—a group almost as diverse as it is talented.

Three other units are new in this edition, though they contain key essays from similar units of the first edition. *Experiments with Truth* shows good minds from various fields and with various purposes searching for elusive truths: what emerges is one of the fundamental assumptions of rhetoric—that the writer must make a truth from the material the world provides. *The Span of Life* includes some of the finest writing in the *Reader,* including essays in which young authors look at old people, middle-aged authors look forward and back, and Malcolm Cowley gives us "The View from Eighty."

The *Aggression* unit will be particularly welcomed by those who see the composition class as an introduction to the discourse and debate of the academic world. It presents essays that converge from various disciplines and philosophies on four interlocked questions: Are humans inherently aggressive? What makes some societies particularly inclined to violence and warfare? What is the role of the warrior in the twentieth century? How should the individual deal with a world in which we have "explosives above our heads as well as beneath our feet"?

At the suggestion of some users of the first edition, we have made changes in the apparatus. Key quotations from each selection had appeared as an "Annotated Table of Contents" at the front of the book. Now they appear as a "Preview" at the beginning of each section, followed immediately by an "Overview" that discusses the connections between essays and suggests topics for writing. Each selection is now preceded by a headnote that gives the reader a sense of who is talking.

The *Instructor's Guide to The Dolphin Reader* has been significantly improved by the addition of an index that points to discussions of the rhetorical qualities of the essays (thesis, style, organization, etc.) and also traces connections of ideas among the essays. For help with the *Instructor's Guide*, I once again thank Melody Richardson Daily, who not only wrote her half of the commentary but gave me many ideas for my own half. For scores of research missions, large and small, I thank Carolyn Perry.

Thanks also to my supportive editors at Houghton Mifflin, to dozens of teachers who have made suggestions in person, by phone, and by mail, and especially to the following colleagues, who reviewed the new edition in one or another of its several incarnations:

Nancy K. Barry, The University of Iowa
Earle V. Bryant, University of New Orleans, LA
Lou Camp, Bucks County Community College, PA
Sharon G. Carson, Kent State University, OH
Ian Cruickshank, St. Louis Community College at Florissant
    Valley, MO
Denise Dinwiddie, Diablo Valley College, CA
Betty L. Dixon, Rancho Santiago College, CA
Suzanne O. Edwards, The Citadel, SC
David R. Evans, University of Virginia
Susan Gavell, Southern Connecticut State University
Jennifer M. Ginn, North Carolina State University
Sandra J. Haecker, The University of Texas at San Antonio

Jerry Herron, Wayne State University, MI
Maureen Hoag, Wichita State University, KS
Michael J. Hogan, The University of New Mexico
Dianne Luce, Midlands Technical College, SC
Thomas F. MacMillan, Mendocino College, CA
Gary Nagy, Long Beach City College, CA
Frank G. Novak, Jr., Pepperdine University, CA
Judith K. Powers, University of Wyoming
Marian Price, University of Central Florida
Compton Rees, The University of Connecticut
Jeffrey L. Spear, New York University
Thomas R. Smith, Penn State University
Linda Thomas, Irvine Valley College, CA
Thomas T. Tuggle, Gainesville Junior College, GA
Verne V. Wehtje, Pacific Union College, CA
Elizabeth Williams, Pratt Institute, NY
Chris Higgins-Young, University of Central Florida
Laura W. Zlogar, University of Wisconsin-River Falls

DOUG HUNT

THE
DOLPHIN
READER

Introduction: *About Essays and Essayists*

Ask most people what an essay is, and they will tell you what it is not: not a whole book, not a short story, not a poem, not a play. A more positive definition is difficult because the essay resembles other forms of writing and mingles with them freely. A poem looks like a poem, with plenty of white space on the page and lines of irregular length; a play looks like a play. Flannery O'Connor begins "Revelation" like this:

> The doctor's waiting room, which was very small, was almost full when the Turpins entered and Mrs. Turpin, who was very large, made it look even smaller by her presence. . . . Her little bright black eyes took in all the patients as she sized up the seating situation.

We hear the machinery of fiction—setting, character, and point of view—humming smoothly in the background, and we settle down to read a short story. But very often we are well into an essay before we recognize it for what it is. It may look like just another letter, textbook chapter, book review, encyclopedia entry, lecture, or magazine article. Indeed, it probably *will* be one of these things: Martin Luther King, Jr.'s "Letter from Birmingham Jail"—a widely admired essay—was an open letter addressed to eight clergymen. Adrienne Rich's "Claiming an Education" was a speech to university students. Joan Didion's "Marrying Absurd" was a column for *The Saturday Evening Post*, written, as columns always are, against a deadline and specification of length. The essay was once a genteel literary form; today it has put on street clothes and sensible shoes and got itself a job.

But beneath even the most modern exterior, every essayist is a good deal like Montaigne, the Frenchman who christened the form four hundred years ago. He called his writings *essais* (French for "attempts") because they were not reports of objective truth but explorations of his own attitudes and thoughts on such subjects as cannibals, war, women, and hatred. Essayists in every era have been drawn to subjects where the facts do not speak for themselves, but must be measured against some personal frame of reference. The writer of a news story often gives us bare information: the journalistic formula is "who, what, where, when, why, and how?" But the essayist reserves a good deal of attention for other questions: "So what? Why should I care? What does this tell us about how we should live, or about how we do?" These are "moral" questions, not in the sermonizing sense, but in a broader sense. They are concerned with our *mores*—the customs, habits, and preoccupations that give life its shape. Some essayists state a "moral" thesis at the outset, as Charles Murray does in "What's So Bad about Being Poor?": ". . . there is nothing so terrible about poverty *per se*." Others, like C. S. Lewis in "The Inner Ring," provide a ladder on which we climb toward the thesis, rung by rung. Still others, like Annie Dillard and Edward Hoagland, seem to accumulate meaning as they wander through a series of anecdotes and observations. Finally, though, we see that the writer has led us to a statement of values.

Questions of value must always be referred to the individual head and heart. They cannot be approached in a purely objective way. As G. K. Chesterton once pointed out, we can learn a good deal about entomology without being insects, but if we want to understand humanity, we have to be human ourselves and project our understanding from the inside out. Facts, figures, charts, diagrams, quantifiable experiments—these can sometimes be useful, but they can't tell us how we should react on the day that the Supreme Court orders the desegregation of public schools, or men land on the moon, or the United States invades Cambodia, or an oil spill fouls the beaches of an Alaskan bay. They can't help us sort out the enigma of our own identities. They certainly can't help us order our minds when we face some personal tragedy. To think well about such things, a person needs a *perspective*, an intellectual and emotional place to stand. Perspective transforms an article into an essay.

This talk about perspective sounds obscure enough to need an example. Samuel Johnson—the eighteenth-century essayist—was half-blind and scarred from infancy by a skin disease, and for the first half of his life was poor and nearly friendless. The weight of this personal experience was behind his grim observation that "human life is everywhere a state in which much is to be endured and little to be enjoyed." All around him Johnson saw lives following a familiar trajectory—rising from unhappiness to the pursuit of some unreachable pleasure and sinking once more into unhappiness. His essays and sometimes even his individual sentences are shaped by this trajectory. "Hope is itself a species of happiness," he once began, and then let the air out of the balloon by adding, ". . . perhaps, the chief happiness which this world affords." This pessimism goes further than most of us are willing to be taken, but the perspective it provided made Johnson a formidable essayist and conversationalist. No one could size up a situation more quickly. When he had to explain the significance of the Great Pyramid, he pronounced it "a monument to the insufficiency of human enjoyments," evidence that even the Pharaohs were unhappy and had to "amuse the tediousness" of life by forcing slaves to lay stone upon stone for no reason. When he heard that a friend had remarried, he said that it was "the triumph of hope over experience"—one of the better lines in the history of black humor. When he wrote an essay on the dangers of affectation, he compared the pleasure of an inflated reputation to the ice palace raised by the Empress of Russia: "It was for a time splendid and luminous, but the first sunshine melted it away."

Not every essayist is so gloomy, thank goodness, or writes from a conviction about life that is as sweeping, but we can see in Johnson's case one of the defining characteristics of the essay: the writer uses a particular topic (like the Great Pyramid) as a way of expressing an insight of general interest (the insufficiency of human enjoyments). Assign three competent encyclopedists the task of describing the Grand Canyon in 500 words, and you'll get three articles that are more or less interchangeable. Ask three essayists what they did on their summer vacations and, if you are very, very lucky, you'll get "The Way to Rainy Mountain," "On a Greek Holiday," and "Once More to the Lake." Scott Momaday will reflect on the fate of his Kiowa ancestors, Alice Bloom on the thinness of the tourist's experience, and E. B. White on the sweetness of life and its shortness. An essayist approaches a topic the way a carpenter approaches an old barn, estimating the board feet it will provide toward some project already forming in his or her mind.

No insight, no essay: this is an uncomfortable truth for people of ordinary humility. When you sit down to write an essay, you may wish that you had Charles Murray's experience as a Peace Corps volunteer in Thailand. You may wish that you had Daniel Boorstin's knowledge of history or Lewis Thomas's background as a physician. You may even wish for a moment that you had led a life as miserable as Johnson's. Then, when it came to insight, you would have some cards to play.

In fact, all of us have three good cards. First, our lives—however ordinary they may seem to us—are unlike the lives of others. Our experiences touch at different points on the large issues that affect all lives. Perhaps you grew up in a small prairie town and have seen issues of race and class from an angle no New Yorker ever knew. Perhaps you attended a parochial school and watched the sisters react to feminism. Perhaps you have been a victim and have a statement to make on crime, or you are a technophile irritated by the technophobes around you. Whatever you are, it is one card you have to play.

Your second card is that you live in a remarkably communicative culture. The airwaves are so crowded with songs, advertisements, soap operas, and news programs that scientists working on sensitive electronic measurements have to sit in wire cages to cut out extraneous signals. Your campus is probably buzzing with conversations about movies, books, politics, sex, teachers, clothes, and careers. At the state school for the deaf near my home hands are constantly in motion. College and university libraries are so crowded that books sometimes lie in boxes waiting for new shelf space. The sheer mass of what is being said and written can help you find a subject, but it can also be overwhelming—a seemingly random barrage of messages in which it is hard to find dominant themes. One goal of *The Dolphin Reader* is to help sharpen your eye for some of the central questions around which thousands of conversations spin. The selections are not chosen solely because they are classics or because they have achieved some special brilliance of execution, but because they actively contribute to one of these perennial conversations. All the essays in the Progress section, for instance, are part of a familiar argument: X claims that technology is creating more problems than it is solving; Y claims that X is a hyprocritical romantic who wouldn't dream of giving up his blow dryer or computer or nuclear deterrent; Z says that both have a point, but both need to define their terms more carefully. A political debate on defense or energy policy is often little more than a remote branch of this conversation. The discussion of whether to take a camping vacation or fly to San Francisco may be another. So may a professorial dispute over the relative merits of Henry James and Jay McInerney. The Progress section explores still other branches, but, more important, it traces the conversation to its trunk. Grasp the trunk, and you can shake all the branches.

Your third card is time. Listen to the "man-on-the-street" interviews on the local news if you need to be reminded how hard it is to talk extemporaneously on a subject more complex than the weather. A very few people sound coherent and informed; most mumble whatever banalities and catch phrases come readily to mind and are embarrassed, I'm sure, when they hear the broadcast. Some of our best writers interview terribly. Bruce Lee of *Newsweek* once interviewed E. B. White and found him polite, dull, and uncommunicative. The next day White sent Lee two typed pages of crisp answers to the interview questions and a short note of apology: "I do not have the gift of oral expression, and am almost helpless except when running paper through a typewriter. . . ." Writing gives you time to draft, revise, attack the topic from a different angle, ask for opinions and advice, read what other people have said. If you ransack your brain at first and don't *find* an insight you can apply to your topic, you have time to *make* one (never as much time as you would like, of course). This opportunity—or necessity—of furnishing the mind is one of the rewards of writing an essay. Cardinal Newman once wrote that a university education "gives a man a clear conscious view of his own opinions and judgments, a truth in developing them, an eloquence in expressing them, and a force in urging them." That's a rather grand goal even for the whole of an education, but every hour spent struggling with an essay should bring you a little closer to it.

THE EVOLUTION OF AN ESSAY

That struggle, that *essaying* to clarify the writer's views, should really be included in the definition of an essay. Try to imagine essays in this expanded form. An essay like Melissa Greene's "No Rms, Jungle Vu," for example, would swell from its seventeen printed pages to encompass many hours of library research, interviews, and reading, many struggles to decide what to include and what to leave out, and many drafts and revisions. Greene told me that she worked on the essay off and on for about four months. We might all benefit from hearing a tape of what passed through her head as she wrote, but few of us would have four months to listen to it.

We can, however, examine the evolution of a short "comment" written by E. B. White. Comments are unsigned essays in miniature: in *The New Yorker* they are often written using the "editorial *we*," a practice that tends to make the writer sound like a Siamese twin. White began writing comments in 1927, and so had more than forty years of experience with them by 1969. Nonetheless, when the magazine asked him to comment on the moon landing that year, it was a particularly difficult assignment. The deadline pressure was intense: Neil Armstrong took his small step to the lunar surface at 10:56 P.M. on July 20, and the television broadcast of the moon walk lasted until 1:00 A.M.; White, who lived on a farm in Maine, had to cable his comment to New York in time for a press run at noon.

There were other difficulties. He was a little out of sympathy with the topic. The general response to the moon landing was a burst of pride, but White was not inclined to sound a fanfare in honor of the technological advance. Much of his best writing aims to "keep Man in a mood of decent humility." One of the observations on the pages he mailed to Bruce Lee was this:

> I am pessimistic about the human race because it is too ingenious for its own good. Our approach to nature is to beat it into submission. We

would stand a better chance of survival if we accommodated ourselves to this planet and viewed it appreciatively instead of skeptically and dictatorially. Never dictate to a swamp, or assume that it has no merit until drained.

He didn't share the nationalistic pride that the landing stirred in many Americans. Having seen nationalism cause two world wars, he was an advocate of the United Nations. These concerns were clearly on his mind when he sat down to run a first draft through the typewriter.

> Planning a trip to the moon differs in no essential respect from planning a trip to the beach. You have to decide what to take along, what to leave behind. Should the thermos jug go? The child's rubber horse? The dill pickles? These are sometimes fateful decisions on which the success or failure of the whole outing turns. Something goes along that spoils everything because it is always in the way. Something gets left behind that spoils everything because it is desperately needed for comfort or safety. The men who had to decide what to take along to the moon must have pondered long and hard, drawn up many a list. We're not sure they planned well, when they included the little telescoped flagpole and the American flag, artificially stiffened so that it would fly to the breeze that didn't blow. As we watched the Stars and Stripes planted on the surface of the moon, we experienced the same sensations of pride that must have filled the hearts of millions of Americans. But the emotion soon turned to   This was our great chance, and we muffed it. The men who stepped out onto the surface of the moon are in a class by themselves—pioneers of what is universal. They saw the earth whole—just as it is, a round ball in a   But they colored the moon red, white, and blue —good colors all—but out of place in that setting. The moon still influences the tides, and the tides lap on every shore, right around the globe. The moon still belongs to lovers, and lovers are everywhere— not just in America. What a pity we couldn't have planted some emblem that precisely expressed this unique, this incredible occasion, even if it were nothing more than a white banner, with the legend: "At last!"

Judged as a finished product by a writer of White's caliber, this is a dismal performance. Over the years, I've offered several right arms in exchange for a fragment of White's talent, so it reassures me to see that his first draft sounds flat and sometimes awkward. But of course he never imagined that this draft would be good. Notice, for instance, that he twice began sentences that he couldn't end. *What* exactly did our emotions turn to? A round ball in a *what?* Having no adequate answers, White left spaces and went on. His aim here was to discover the general shape of the comment, to see what he had to say. He may not have found the results very encouraging. The comparison to the family outing in the first seven sentences attempted to reduce the event to human scale, keeping us in a "mood of decent humility," but it was far-fetched. If White was going to get his readers to accept the analogy, he'd have to come up with some details that make moon-trip planning seem more ordinary and domestic. And didn't the passage about "experiencing the same sensation of pride" sound like a press release from the White House? Readers would surely be suspicious of a writer who parroted the official good cheer, then turned sharply around to say that we had "muffed" our chance. The draft had an uncharitable tone. It was a self-righteous condemnation of the space program at its moment of triumph. It had some good parts—the stiffened flag, the windless moon, the association of the moon with tides and lovers—but principally it helped White see what he should be thinking about. What *did* "our" emotions turn to? What did they start out as? Was he being a spoilsport?

In writing the second draft, White reconsidered both the moon landing and the paragraph, measuring them against his own values of charity, humility, and good humor. He kept the first seven sentences, but changed the rest substantially:

> The men who drew up the moon list for the astronauts planned long and hard and well. (Should the vacuum cleaner go to suck up moon-dust and save the world?) Among the items they sent along, of course, was the little jointed flagpole and the flag that could be stiffened to the breeze that didn't blow. It is traditional among explorers to plant the flag. Yet the two men who stepped out on the surface of the moon were in a class by themselves: they were of a new race of men, those who had seen the earth whole. When, following instructions, they colored the moon red, white, and blue, they were stepping out of character—or so it seemed to us who watched, trembling with awe and admiration and pride. This was the last scene in the long book of nationalism, and they followed the book. But the moon still holds the key to madness, which is universal, still controls the tides, that lap on every shore everywhere, and blesses lovers that kiss in every land, under no particular banner. What a pity we couldn't have played the scene as it should have been played; planting, perhaps, a simple white handkerchief, symbol of the common cold, that, like the moon, belongs to all and recognizes no borders.

This draft was *truer* than the first—truer to White's feelings and to the event. It had been silly to say that the planners "muffed" the moon trip. Now he gave them their due, acknowledging that they planned "long and hard and well." However much White may have wished that they had not brought along the flag, they had reasons for doing so: the precedent of former explorers, the "long book of nationalism." And if planting the flag was a mistake, the astronauts certainly couldn't be blamed; they were "following instructions." By making these changes, White avoided the sourness of the first draft. By adding madness to the list of the things associated with the moon in the next-to-last sentence, he went beyond the moon-spoon-June-croon formula of sentimental songs.

But the most important revision was in the last sentence. James Thurber once noted that the challenge of writing a comment is "to make something that was ground out sound as if it were dashed off." The closing sentence of the first draft, with its talk about "this unique, this incredible occasion" and its "white banner with the legend: 'At last!'," labored under the burden of its serious political intent. By converting the banner to a handkerchief, White lightened the tone, retained the political note, and kept us "in a mood of decent humility"—all in one seemingly effortless phrase.

He must have felt encouraged at this point in the evolution of his paragraph, but he also saw some flaws. The addition of the vacuum cleaner made the analogy between the family outing and the moon trip a little more credible, but the "save the world" part of the sentence was a feeble joke. And the final sentence, good as it was, trailed loosely off and lost some of its impact. At this point White typed a draft to correct these faults.

> Planning a trip to the moon differs in no essential respect from planning a trip to the beach. You have to decide what to take along, what to leave behind. Should the thermos jug go? The child's rubber horse? The dill pickles? These are the sometimes fateful decisions on which the success or failure of the whole outing turns. Something goes along that spoils everything because it is always in the way; something gets left behind that is desperately needed for comfort or for safety. The men who drew up the moon list for the astronauts planned long and hard and well. (Should the vacuum cleaner go to suck up moondust?) Among the items they sent along, of course, was the little jointed flagpole and the flag that could be stiffened to the breeze that did not blow. (It is traditional among explorers to plant the flag.) Yet the two men who stepped out on the surface of the moon were in a class by themselves and should have been equipped accordingly: they were of the new breed of men, those who had seen the earth whole. When, following instructions, they colored the moon red, white, and blue, they were fumbling with the past—or so it seemed to us who watched, trembling with awe and admiration and pride. This was the last chapter in the long book of nationalism, one that could well have been omitted. But the moon still holds the key to madness, which is universal, still controls the tides that lap on shores everywhere, and guards lovers that kiss in every land, under no banner but the sky. What a pity we couldn't have forsworn our little Iwo Jima scene and planted

instead a banner acceptable to all—a simple white handkerchief, perhaps, symbol of the common cold, which, like the moon, affects us all.

This paragraph had a finished look, and White, considering it
finished, cabled it to *The New Yorker*. When the heat of composition
cooled, however, he began to see faults. His attempt to absolve the
astronauts of blame by saying that they were "following instructions" was shaky ethically and awkward stylistically. The expression about coloring the moon red, white, and blue was flashy
nonsense. The talk about "trembling" with pride was overblown
and hackneyed; the reader would doubt that a generally level-
headed writer spends much time trembling. The lead, the first
seven sentences, was a mistake. The whole comparison to the family outing was unconvincing, inappropriate, belittling; and with the
last sentences in the paragraph now doing all that is necessary to
"keep Man in a mood of decent humility," it was superfluous.
Time was very short, but even now White wasn't content to mend
faults. An enthusiastic sailor, he remembered the doctrine of freedom of the seas. He found a way to add impact to the last sentence.
He took the paragraph through three more drafts. Then he sent
another cable saying that the comment was "no good as is" and
offering to dictate over the phone "a shorter one on the same
theme but different in tone." Here is the result as it appeared on
page one of *The New Yorker*:

> The moon, it turns out, is a great place for men. One-sixth gravity
> must be a lot of fun, and when Armstrong and Aldrin went into their
> bouncy little dance, like two happy children, it was a moment not only
> of triumph but of gaiety. The moon, on the other hand, is a poor place
> for flags. Ours looked stiff and awkward, trying to float on the breeze
> that does not blow. (There must be a lesson here somewhere.) It is
> traditional, of course, for explorers to plant the flag, but it struck us, as
> we watched with awe and admiration and pride, that our two fellows
> were universal men, not national men, and should have been
> equipped accordingly. Like every great river and every great sea, the
> moon belongs to none and belongs to all. It still holds the key to
> madness, still controls the tides that lap on shores everywhere, still
> guards the lovers that kiss in every land under no banner but the sky.
> What a pity that in our moment of triumph we couldn't have forsworn
> the familiar Iwo Jima scene and planted instead a device acceptable to
> all: a limp white handkerchief, perhaps, symbol of the common cold,
> which, like the moon, affects us all, unites us all.

This is certainly not the best comment White ever wrote, but like
all his comments it is compact and lively. Of the 305 words of
the original draft, 15 survive to the final draft. This is a fairly
low survival rate, but hardly unique. The journalist James Fallows

estimates his survival rate for a long essay at about one percent. Joan Didion, the novelist and essayist, says that there is a point in the writing of a new piece where she sits in a room "literally papered with false starts." What is important here is not the survival rate but the rethinking. It isn't merely White's *recording* of his reaction to the moon landing that changes from first draft to last: the reaction itself changes to something more generous and complete.

READING TO WRITE

As the evolution of E. B. White's comment shows us, the essay—however smooth its surface when finished—grows out of tensions and indecisions. It is the product of a mind wrestling with itself, in White's case a mind divided between delight in a great human accomplishment and alarm about a display of nationalism, between distrust of technology and admiration of scientists and astronauts, between the desire to amuse his readers and the need to admonish them. From the writer's point of view, an essay is the product of difficult decisions between opposing impulses. White might almost have been talking about the writer's situation when he developed the analogy of the trip to the beach: "Should the thermos jug go? The child's rubber horse? The dill pickles? These are the sometimes fateful decisions on which the success or failure of the whole outing turns." To the writer, slight decisions about the essay's surface may be inseparable from the large choices made in the essay's depths. Joan Didion once praised a fellow writer as a man for whom the placement of a comma could be a question of considerable importance. Writers grow acutely aware of the choices they face, great and small.

Most creative activities in art or business or private life involve hard choices, and people who are successful at them learn to thrive on the horns of a dilemma. In fact, they learn to relish difficulties, to seek our productive tensions. Walter Ong, a brilliant scholar and avid trout fisherman, once told me that when he begins to argue with himself, he knows he has come to the place where the big fish are.

Productive reading of essays, particularly those you will eventually respond to with essays of your own, is also a creative act that requires you to make decisions, not a dash from the first word to the last in search of the "main idea." An alert reader brings *at least* two minds to what he or she reads and learns to enjoy the friction between them. Mind One acts as a wide-eyed innocent, a true believer, inclined to accept anything it is told, share any enthusiasms or prejudices that the author may express. It submerges its identity in the author's. It is like the sympathetic listener who sits in the front row at a speech, leaning forward, smiling or laughing at all the appropriate places, and nodding appreciatively whenever the speaker clinches a point or introduces an example. Mind Two is a far less agreeable creature. Its impulse is to say no, to resign, as Henry David Thoreau once put it, from all the societies it has never joined. When the author argues, Mind Two argues back, challenging assumptions and re-interpreting data. When the author presents an example, it scrambles to think of a counter-example. When the author describes an experience, it doubts that the description is accurate or complete and comes up with experiences of its own that contradict the author's. Mind Two is pure cussedness; it feels its strength in opposition.

To have Minds One and Two wrangling in your skull while you try to read can be very difficult: it is hard to be sympathetic and skeptical at the same time. Some people have a talent for it, but I do not, and so have learned to read an essay twice before I can call it truly read. In fact, two readings may not be enough. Having read the essay once to make sure I got it and once to make sure it didn't get me instead, I can relax to read for pure pleasure. It is often during these pleasure cruises through essays that reading bears unexpected fruit. No longer worried about agreeing or disagreeing with the author, I get passages into my head that will never come out: Annie Dillard's comparison of the slide toward old age to a girl's downhill ride on a bicycle, William Manchester's description of H. L. Mencken's hands lying in his lap "like weapons put to rest," Martin Luther King's long, long sentence cataloguing the evils of segregation and ending in the icy politeness of "I hope, sirs, you can understand our legitimate and unavoidable impatience." Some passages are worth reading and re-reading until, without ever intending to, you have got them by heart.

But the sympathetic and the skeptical reading come first, working together like scissor blades. The first allows you to expand your thinking by being receptive to new ideas and attitudes. If you dig in your heels from the beginning and refuse to go an inch along the author's path, you miss an opportunity to grow and change. But to change constantly is to lose your identity. The skeptical reading keeps you from being so open-minded that you are finally empty-headed. Finding an honest way to balance the impulse to believe and the impulse to doubt is one of the marks of a person whose education has meant more than the collection of credit hours. It is in this moment of balance that your reading begins to tell you what you *must* write.

EXPERIMENTS
WITH TRUTH

Experiments with Truth: Preview

reflects . . . neither objective reality, nor an accurate picture of the past, nor a group of rigorously tested observations about human behavior.

That night, I realized that no matter how good I became in the manipulation of symbols, I could never hope to move anyone without allowing myself to be moved, that I could reveal only slight truths unless I was willing to reveal the truths about myself.

There may be no more pressing intellectual need in our culture than for people to become sophisticated about the function of memory. The political implications of the loss of memory are obvious. The authority of memory is a personal confirmation of selfhood. To write one's life is to live it twice. . . .

SHERIFF. Well, can you beat the women? Held for murder and worryin' about her preserves.
COUNTY ATTORNEY. I guess before we're through she may have something more serious than preserves to worry about.
HALE. Well, women are used to worrying over trifles.

"I am not," she said tearfully, "a wart hog. From hell." But the denial had no force. The girl's eyes and her words, even the tone of her voice, low but clear, directed only to her, brooked no repudiation. She had been singled out for the message . . .

Overview and Ideas for Writing

"Now, what I want is, Facts. Teach these boys and girls nothing but Facts. Facts alone are wanted in life. Plant nothing else, and root out everything else. You can only form the minds of reasoning animals upon Facts: nothing else will ever be of service to them. This is the principle on which I bring up my own children, and this is the principle on which I bring up these children. Stick to the Facts, sir!"

Never has a philosophy of education been more succinctly stated than Thomas Gradgrind's in the opening lines of Charles Dickens's novel *Hard Times* (1854). It is a robust philosophy that has lived essentially unchanged into our own time: E. D. Hirsch's *Cultural Literacy: What Every American Needs to Know* was one of the best-sellers of the 1980s. Gradgrindism is present in a somewhat diluted form in most attempts to define a "core curriculum" for primary, secondary, and college education. The Governor's Task Force on Basic Education (or some equally impressive body) will announce that every sixth-grader should be able to name the seven colors of the spectrum, left to right, and tests will be instituted to make sure that this happens. Whatever the defects of a curriculum based strictly on the learning of facts, it is easily implemented and monitored.

But to what end? Gradgrind's favorite pupil is a pale boy named Bitzer, whose definition of a horse is a series of facts, repeated by rote and without any hint of emotion or insight: "Quadruped. Gramnivorous. Forty teeth, namely twenty-four grinders, four eye-teeth, and twelve incisive. Sheds coat in the spring; in marshy country, sheds hoofs, too. Hoofs hard, but requiring to be shod by iron. Age known by marks in the mouth." We suspect from the start that Bitzer will come to a bad end: he looks and sounds like a person whose blood has been drained. If the ten writers in this unit are united by anything, it is by their resistance to Gradgrindism. Like Dickens's contemporary John Henry Newman, they hope for some insight that will "leaven the dense mass of facts" as yeast leavens bread. The leavenings are various: metaphor, memory, skepticism, faith, irony, self-scrutiny, even bullsterism.

As an eleventh writer for the unit, you should have experience that will allow you to contribute to the discussion. You have, after all, had several years of education in school and out. Like David Bradley and the protagonist of "Revelation," you may have had a long-standing assumption overturned by a moment of insight. You will have had experiences in the classroom that can be measured against the standards of learning proposed by William G. Perry, Jr., Adrienne Rich, and Jacob Bronowski. You may, like David L. Rosenhan and Susan Glaspell, have discovered situations where different viewers will see different "facts." Your memory should contain the germ of a good essay.

If you want to extend your experience with some research, you are in an ideal setting to do so: the college or university campus is a ready-made laboratory. You might locate an official statement of your college's educational goals and report on how those goals shape students' experience (or fail to shape it). You might use interviews and observation to compare the view faculty members take of education with the view students take. Or you might use the library to investigate the truth of some of the authors' controversial assertions: Rosenhan's statement that psychiatrists cannot reliably distinguish between the sane and the insane, Rich's statement that the truth taught in the academic world is shaped by the consciousness of white males, Robert Frost's statement that scientific knowledge is largely metaphorical, Joseph Wood Krutch's statement that most magazine articles are "machine made."

There is, of course, the possibility that you will have to write a dissent. The authors represented here would probably be pleased to have you disagree with them. They are not looking for more Bitzers, bloodless and mechanical. They want a livelier thinker, a tougher customer.

ROBERT FROST

Education by Poetry

Robert Frost (1874–1963), now thought of as the archetypal New England poet, knew very little success until the publication of *A Boy's Will* (1913) won him a readership in England. Thereafter he enjoyed a popularity that very few poets achieve in their lifetimes. He won the Pulitzer Prize for poetry four times, for *New Hampshire* (1923), *Collected Poems* (1930), *A Further Range* (1936), and *A Witness Tree* (1942). Frost's interests were not confined to literature. Sometimes a teacher, sometimes a farmer, and throughout his life an accomplished botanist, Frost had a knack for discovering a point of interest in whatever he encountered. He was fascinated by scientific and philosophical thought, and he was quite capable of writing a poem alluding to the second law of thermodynamics ("West-running Brook") or answering the argument that the design of the universe indicates a creator ("Design"). "Education by Poetry" is based on a talk Frost delivered at Amherst College in 1931.

I am going to urge nothing in my talk. I am not an advocate. I am 1
going to consider a matter, and commit a description. And I am going to describe other colleges than Amherst. Or, rather say all that is good can be taken as about Amherst; all that is bad will be about other colleges.

I know whole colleges where all American poetry is barred— 2
whole colleges. I know whole colleges where all contemporary poetry is barred.

I once heard of a minister who turned his daughter—his poetry- 3
writing daughter—out on the street to earn a living, because he said there should be no more books written; God wrote one book, and that was enough. (My friend George Russell, "Æ", has read no literature, he protests, since just before Chaucer.)

That all seems sufficiently safe, and you can say one thing for it. 4
It takes the onus off the poetry of having to be used to teach children anything. It comes pretty hard on poetry, I sometimes think,—what it has to bear in the teaching process.

Then I know whole colleges where, though they let in older 5
poetry, they manage to bar all that is poetical in it by treating it as something other than poetry. It is not so hard to do that. Their reason I have often hunted for. It may be that these people act from a kind of modesty. Who are professors that they should attempt to

deal with a thing as high and as fine as poetry? Who are *they?* There is a certain manly modesty in that.

That is the best general way of settling the problem; treat all poetry as if it were something else than poetry, as if it were syntax, language, science. Then you can even come down into the American and into the contemporary without any special risk.

There is another reason they have, and that is that they are, first and foremost in life, markers. They have the marking problem to consider. Now, I stand here a teacher of many years' experience and I have never complained of having had to mark. I had rather mark anyone for anything—for his looks, carriage, his ideas, his correctness, his exactness, anything you please,—I would rather give him a mark in terms of letters, A, B, C, D, than have to use adjectives on him. We are all being marked by each other all the time, classified, ranked, put in our place, and I see no escape from that. I am no sentimentalist. You have got to mark, and you have got to mark, first of all, for accuracy, for correctness. But if I am going to give a mark, that is the least part of my marking. The hard part is the part beyond that, the part where the adventure begins.

One other way to rid the curriculum of the poetry nuisance has been considered. More merciful than the others it would neither abolish nor denature the poetry, but only turn it out to disport itself, with the plays and games—in no wise discredited, though given no credit for. Any one who liked to teach poetically could take his subject, whether English, Latin, Greek, or French, out into the nowhere along with the poetry. One side of a sharp line would be left to the rigorous and righteous; the other side would be assigned to the flowery where they would know what could be expected of them. Grade marks where more easily given, of course, in the courses concentrating on correctness and exactness as the only forms of honesty recognized by plain people; a general indefinite mark of *X* in the courses that scatter brains over taste and opinion. On inquiry I have found no teacher willing to take position on either side of the line, either among the rigors or among the flowers. No one is willing to admit that his discipline is not partly in exactness. No one is willing to admit that his discipline is not partly in taste and enthusiasm.

How shall a man go through college without having been marked for taste and judgment? What will become of him? What will his end be? He will have to take continuation courses for college graduates. He will have to go to night schools. They are having night schools now, you know, for college graduates. Why? Because they have not been educated enough to find their way around in contemporary literature. They don't know what they may safely like in the libraries and galleries. They don't know how to judge an editiorial when they see one. They don't know how to judge a political campaign. They don't know when they are being fooled by a metaphor, an analogy, a parable. And metaphor is, of course, what we are talking about. Education by poetry is education by metaphor.

Suppose we stop short of imagination, initiative, enthusiasm, 10 inspiration and originality—dread words. Suppose we don't mark in such things at all. There are still two minimal things, that we have got to take care of, taste and judgment. Americans are supposed to have more judgment than taste, but taste is there to be dealt with. That is what poetry, the only art in the colleges of arts, is there for. I for my part would not be afraid to go in for enthusiasm. There is the enthusiasm like a blinding light, or the enthusiasm of the deafening shout, the crude enthusiasm that you get uneducated by poetry, outside of poetry. It is exemplified in what I might call "sunset raving." You look westward toward the sunset, or if you get up early enough, eastward toward the sunrise, and you rave. It is oh's and ah's with you and no more.

But the enthusiasm I mean is taken through the prism of the 11 intellect and spread on the screen in a color, all the way from hyperbole at one end—or overstatement, at one end—to understatement at the other end. It is a long strip of dark lines and many colors. Such enthusiasm is one object of all teaching in poetry. I heard wonderful things said about Virgil yesterday, and many of them seemed to me crude enthusiasm, more like a deafening shout, many of them. But one speech had range, something of overstatement, something of statement, and something of understatement. It had all the colors of an enthusiasm passed through an idea.

I would be willing to throw away everything else but that: en- 12 thusiasm tamed by metaphor. Let me rest the case there. Enthusiasm tamed to metaphor, tamed to that much of it. I do not think anybody ever knows the discreet use of metaphor, his own and other people's, the discreet handling of metaphor, unless he has been properly educated in poetry.

Poetry begins in trivial metaphors, pretty metaphors, "grace" 13 metaphors, and goes on to the profoundest thinking that we have. Poetry provides the one permissible way of saying one thing and meaning another. People say, "Why don't you say what you mean?" We never do that, do we, being all of us too much poets. We like to talk in parables and in hints and in indirections— whether from diffidence or some other instinct.

I have wanted in late years to go further and further in making 14 metaphor the whole of thinking. I find some one now and then to agree with me that all thinking, except mathematical thinking, is metaphorical, or all thinking except scientific thinking. The mathematical might be difficult for me to bring in, but the scientific is easy enough.

Once on a time all the Greeks were busy telling each other what   15
the All was—or was like unto. All was three elements, air, earth, and water (we once thought it was ninety elements; now we think it is only one). All was substance, said another. All was change, said a third. But best and most fruitful was Pythagoras' comparison of the universe with number. Number of what? Number of feet, pounds, and seconds was the answer, and we had science and all that has followed in science. The metaphor has held and held, breaking down only when it came to the spiritual and psychological or the out of the way places of the physical.

The other day we had a visitor here, a noted scientist, whose   16
latest word to the world has been that the more accurately you know where a thing is, the less accurately you are able to state how fast it is moving. You can see why that would be so, without going back to Zeno's problem of the arrow's flight. In carrying numbers into the realm of space and at the same time into the realm of time you are mixing metaphors, that is all, and you are in trouble. They won't mix. The two don't go together.

Let's take two or three more of the metaphors now in use to live   17
by. I have just spoken of one of the new ones, a charming mixed metaphor right in the realm of higher mathematics and higher physics: that the more accurately you state where a thing is, the less accurately you will be able to tell how fast it is moving. And, of course, everything is moving. Everything is an event now. Another metaphor. A thing, they say, is an event. Do you believe it is? Not quite. I believe it is almost an event. But I like the comparison of a thing with an event.

I notice another from the same quarter. "In the neighborhood of   18
matter space is something like curved." Isn't that a good one! It seems to me that that is simply and utterly charming—to say that space is something like curved in the neighborhood of matter. "Something like."

Another amusing one is from—what is the book?—I can't say it   19
now; but here is the metaphor. Its aim is to restore you to your ideas of free will. It wants to give you back your freedom of will. All right, here it is on a platter. You know that you can't tell by name what persons in a certain class will be dead ten years after graduation, but you can tell actuarially how many will be dead. Now, just so this scientist says of the particles of matter flying at a screen, striking a screen; you can't tell what individual particles

will come, but you can say in general that a certain number will
strike in a given time. It shows, you see, that the individual particle
can come freely. I asked Bohr about that particularly, and he said,
"Yes, it is so. It can come when it wills and as it wills; and the
action of the individual particle is unpredictable. But it is not so of
the action of the mass. There you can predict." He says, "That gives
the individual atom its freedom, but the mass its necessity."

Another metaphor that has interested us in our time and has   20
done all our thinking for us is the metaphor of evolution. Never
mind going into the Latin word. The metaphor is simply the
metaphor of the growing plant or of the growing thing. And somebody very brilliantly, quite a while ago, said that the whole universe, the whole of everything, was like unto a growing thing. That
is all. I know the metaphor will break down at some point, but it
has not failed everywhere. It is a very brilliant metaphor, I acknowledge, though I myself get too tired of the kind of essay that
talks about the evolution of candy, we will say, or the evolution of
elevators—the evolution of this, that, and the other. Everything is
evolution. I emancipate myself by simply saying that I didn't get up
the metaphor and so am not much interested in it.

What I am pointing out is that unless you are at home in the   21
metaphor, unless you have had your proper poetical education in
the metaphor, you are not safe anywhere. Because you are not at
ease with figurative values: you don't know the metaphor in its
strength and its weakness. You don't know how far you may expect to ride it and when it may break down with you. You are not
safe in science; you are not safe in history. In history, for instance—
to show that [it] is the same in history as elsewhere—I heard
somebody say yesterday that Aeneas was to be likened unto (those
words, "likened unto"!) George Washington. He was that type of
national hero, the middle-class man, not thinking of being a hero
at all, bent on building the future, bent on his children, his descendants. A good metaphor, as far as it goes, and you must know how
far. And then he added that Odysseus should be likened unto
Theodore Roosevelt. I don't think that is so good. Someone visiting
Gibbon at the point of death, said he was the same Gibbon as of
old, still at his parallels.

Take the way we have been led into our present position mor-   22
ally, the world over. It is by a sort of metaphorical gradient. There is
a kind of thinking—to speak metaphorically—there is a kind of
thinking you might say was endemic in the brothel. It is always
there. And every now and then in some mysterious way it becomes
epidemic in the world. And how does it do so? By using all the
good words that virtue has invented to maintain virtue. It uses

honesty, first,—frankness, sincerity—those words; picks them up,
uses them. "In the name of honesty, let us see what we are." You
know. And then it picks up the word joy. "Let us in the name of
joy, which is the enemy of our ancestors, the Puritans . . . Let us in
the name of joy, which is the enemy of the kill-joy Puritan . . ." You
see. "Let us," and so on. And then, "In the name of health . . ."
Health is another good word. And that is the metaphor Freudian-
ism trades on, mental health. And the first thing we know, it has us
all in up to the top knot. I suppose we may blame the artists a good
deal, because they are great people to spread by metaphor. The
stage too—the stage is always a good intermediary between the
two worlds, the under and the upper,—if I may say so without
personal prejudice to the stage.

In all this I have only been saying that the devil can quote   23
Scripture, which simply means that the good words you have lying
around the devil can use for his purposes as well as anybody else.
Never mind about my morality. I am not here to urge anything.
I don't care whether the world is good or bad—not on any particu-
lar day.

Let me ask you to watch a metaphor breaking down here be-   24
fore you.

Somebody said to me a little while ago, "It is easy enough for me   25
to think of the universe as a machine, as a mechanism."

I said, "You mean the universe is like a machine?"   26

He said, "No. I think it is one . . . Well, it is like . . ."   27

"I think you mean the universe is like a machine."   28

"All right. Let it go at that."   29

I asked him, "Did you ever see a machine without a pedal for the   30
foot, or a lever for the hand, or a button for the finger?"

He said, "No—no."   31

I said, "All right. Is the universe like that?"   32

And he said, "No. I mean it is like a machine, only . . ."   33

". . . it is different from a machine," I said.   34

He wanted to go just that far with that metaphor and no further.   35
And so do we all. All metaphor breaks down somewhere. That is
the beauty of it. It is touch and go with the metaphor, and until you
have lived with it long enough you don't know when it is going.
You don't know how much you can get out of it and when it will
cease to yield. It is a very living thing. It is as life itself.

I have heard this ever since I can remember, and ever since I   36
have taught: the teacher must teach the pupil to think. I saw a
teacher once going around in a great school and snapping pupils'
heads with thumb and finger and saying, "Think." That was when

thinking was becoming the fashion. The fashion hasn't yet quite
gone out.

We still ask boys in college to think, as in the nineties, but we   37
seldom tell them what thinking means; we seldom tell them it is
just putting this and that together; it is just saying one thing in
terms of another. To tell them is to set their feet on the first rung of
a ladder the top of which sticks through the sky.

Greatest of all attempts to say one thing in terms of another is the   38
philosophical attempt to say matter in terms of spirit, or spirit in
terms of matter, to make the final unity. That is the greatest attempt
that ever failed. We stop just short there. But it is the height of
poetry, the height of all thinking, the height of all poetic thinking,
that attempt to say matter in terms of spirit and spirit in terms of
matter. It is wrong to call anybody a materialist simply because he
tries to say spirit in terms of matter, as if that were a sin. Materialism is not the attempt to say all in terms of matter. The only
materialist—be he poet, teacher, scientist, politician, or statesman—is the man who gets lost in his material without a gathering
metaphor to throw it into shape and order. He is the lost soul.

We ask people to think, and we don't show them what thinking   39
is. Somebody says we don't need to show them how to think; bye
and bye they will think. We will give them the forms of sentences
and, if they have any ideas, then they will know how to write
them. But that is preposterous. All there is to writing is having
ideas. To learn to write is to learn to have ideas.

The first little metaphor . . . Take some of the trivial ones. I would   40
rather have trivial ones of my own to live by than the big ones of
other people.

I remember a boy saying, "He is the kind of person that wounds   41
with his shield." That may be a slender one, of course. It goes a
good way in character description. It has poetic grace. "He is the
kind that wounds with his shield."

The shield reminds me—just to linger a minute—the shield re-   42
minds me of the inverted shield spoken of in one of the books of
the "Odyssey," the book that tells about the longest swim on record. I forget how long it lasted—several days, was it?—but at last
as Odysseus came near the coast of Phaeacia, he saw it on the
horizon "like an inverted shield."

There is a better metaphor in the same book. In the end Odys-   43
seus comes ashore and crawls up the beach to spend the night
under a double olive tree, and it says, as in a lonely farmhouse
where it is hard to get fire—I am not quoting exactly—where it is
hard to start the fire again if it goes out, they cover the seeds of fire

with ashes to preserve it for the night, so Odysseus covered himself with the leaves around him and went to sleep. There you have something that gives you character, something of Odysseus himself. "Seeds of fire." So Odysseus covered the seeds of fire in himself. You get the greatness of his nature.

But these are slighter metaphors than the ones we live by. They 44
have their charm, their passing charm. They are as it were the first steps toward the great thoughts, grave thoughts, thoughts lasting to the end.

The metaphor whose manage we are best taught in poetry—that 45
is all there is of thinking. It may not seem far for the mind to go but it is the mind's furthest. The richest accumulation of the ages is the noble metaphors we have rolled up.

I want to add one thing more that the experience of poetry is to 46
anyone who comes close to poetry. There are two ways of coming close to poetry. One is by writing poetry. And some people think I want people to write poetry, but I don't; that is, I don't necessarily. I only want people to write poetry if they want to write poetry. I have never encouraged anybody to write poetry that did not want to write it, and I have not always encouraged those who did want to write it. That ought to be one's own funeral. It is a hard, hard life, as they say.

(I have just been to a city in the West, a city full of poets, a city 47
they have made safe for poets. The whole city is so lovely that you do not have to write it up to make it poetry; it is ready-made for you. But, I don't know—the poetry written in that city might not seem like poetry if read outside of the city. It would be like the jokes made when you were drunk; you have to get drunk again to appreciate them.)

But as I say, there is another way to come close to poetry, fortu- 48
nately, and that is in the reading of it, not as linguistics, not as history, not as anything but poetry. It is one of the hard things for a teacher to know how close a man has come in reading poetry. How do I know whether a man has come close to Keats in reading Keats? It is hard for me to know. I have lived with some boys a whole year over some of the poets and I have not felt sure whether they have come near what it was all about. One remark sometimes told me. One remark was their mark for the year; had to be—it was all I got that told me what I wanted to know. And that is enough, if it was the right remark, if it came close enough. I think a man might make twenty fool remarks if he made one good one some time in the year. His mark would depend on that good remark.

The closeness—everything depends on the closeness with which 49
you come, and you ought to be marked for the closeness, for noth-

ing else. And that will have to be estimated by chance remarks, not by question and answer. It is only by accident that you know some day how near a person has come.

The person who gets close enough to poetry, he is going to know   50 more about the word *belief* than anybody else knows, even in religion nowadays. There are two or three places where we know belief outside of religion. One of them is at the age of fifteen to twenty, in our self-belief. A young man knows more about himself than he is able to prove to anyone. He has no knowledge that anybody else will accept as knowledge. In his foreknowledge he has something that is going to believe itself into fulfilment, into acceptance.

There is another belief like that, the belief in someone else, a   51 relationship of two that is going to be believed into fulfilment. That is what we are talking about in our novels, the belief of love. And the disillusionment that the novels are full of is simply the disillusionment from disappointment in that belief. That belief can fail, of course.

Then there is a literary belief. Every time a poem is written, every   52 time a short story is written, it is written not by cunning, but by belief. The beauty, the something, the little charm of the thing to be, is more felt than known. There is a common jest, one that always annoys me, on the writers, that they write the last end first, and then work up to it; that they lay a train toward one sentence that they think is pretty nice and have all fixed up to set like a trap to close with. No, it should not be that way at all. No one who has ever come close to the arts has failed to see the difference between things written that way, with cunning and device, and the kind that are believed into existence, that begin in something more felt than known. This you can realize quite as well—not quite as well, perhaps, but nearly as well—in reading as you can in writing. I would undertake to separate short stories on that principle; stories that have been believed into existence and stories that have been cunningly devised. And I could separate the poems still more easily.

Now I think—I happen to think—that those three beliefs that I   53 speak of, the self-belief, the love-belief, and the art-belief, are all closely related to the God-belief, that the belief in God is a relationship you enter into with Him to bring about the future.

There is a national belief like that, too. One feels it. I have been   54 where I came near getting up and walking out on the people who thought that they had to talk against nations, against nationalism, in order to curry favor with internationalism. Their metaphors are all mixed up. They think that because a Frenchman and an

American and an Englishman can all sit down on the same
platform and receive honors together, it must be that there is no
such thing as nations. That kind of bad thinking springs from a
source we all know. I should want to say to anyone like that:
"Look! First I want to be a person. And I want you to be a person,
and then we can be as interpersonal as you please. We can pull
each other's noses—do all sorts of things. But, first of all, you have
got to have the personality. First of all, you have got to have the
nations and then they can be as international as they please with
each other."

I should like to use another metaphor on them. I want my 55
palette, if I am a painter, I want my palette on my thumb or on my
chair, all clean, pure, separate colors. Then I will do the mixing on
the canvas. The canvas is where the work of art is, where we make
the conquest. But we want the nations all separate, pure, distinct,
things as separate as we can make them; and then in our thoughts,
in our arts, and so on, we can do what we please about it.

But I go back. There are four beliefs that I know more about from 56
having lived with poetry. One is the personal belief, which is a
knowledge that you don't want to tell other people about because
you cannot prove that you know. You are saying nothing about it
till you see. The love belief, just the same, has that same shyness. It
knows it cannot tell; only the outcome can tell. And the national
belief we enter into socially with each other, all together, party of
the first part, party of the second part, we enter into that to bring
the future of the country. We cannot tell some people what it is we
believe, partly, because they are too stupid to understand and
partly because we are too proudly vague to explain. And anyway it
has got to be fulfilled, and we are not talking until we know more,
until we have something to show. And then the literary one in
every work of art, not of cunning and craft, mind you, but of real
art; that believing the thing into existence, saying as you go more
than you even hoped you were going to be able to say, and coming
with surprise to an end that you foreknew only with some sort of
emotion. And then finally the relationship we enter into with God
to believe the future in—to believe the hereafter in.

JOSEPH WOOD KRUTCH

No Essays, Please

Joseph Wood Krutch (1893–1970), born in Knoxville, took a
B.A. in science from the University of Tennessee and then

changed directions sharply, studying the history of drama and taking a Ph.D. in English from Columbia University. He never gave up his initial interest in biology, however, and once remarked that he knew "more about botany than any other New York critic, and more about the theatre than any other botanist." What prevented Krutch from pursuing a professional scientific career was his discomfort with the close link between science and technology: "Man's humanity is threatened by an almost exclusively technological approach to social, political, and economic thought." Not surprisingly, two of Krutch's best-known academic books are about Samuel Johnson and Henry David Thoreau—an eighteenth-century champion of free will and a nineteenth-century admirer of nature. Krutch was himself a significant twentieth-century essayist, a frequent contributor to such periodicals as *Atlantic Monthly, Harper's, The Saturday Review,* and *Natural History.* The following essay first appeared in *The Saturday Review,* March 10, 1951.

Every now and then someone regrets publicly the passing of the 1 familiar essay. Perhaps such regretters are usually in possession of a recent rejection slip; in any event there are not enough of them to impress editors. The very word "essay" has fallen into such disfavor that it is avoided with horror, and anything which is not fiction is usually called either an "article," a "story," or just a "piece." When *The Atlantic Monthly,* once the last refuge of a dying tradition, now finds it advisable to go in for such "articles" as its recent "What Night Playing Has Done to Baseball" it is obvious that not merely the genteel tradition but a whole literary form is dead.

I am sure that the books on how to become a writer in ten easy 2 lessons have been stressing this fact for a long time now. If *I* were writing such a book I certainly should, and I think that I could give some very practical advice. To begin with I should say something like the following:

Suppose that you have drawn a subject out of your mental box 3 and you find that it is "Fish." Now if you were living in the time of Henry Van Dyke and Thomas Bailey Aldrich,[1] your best lead would be: "Many of my friends are ardent disciples of Isaak Walton." That would have had the appropriate personal touch and the requisite not too recondite literary allusion. But today of course no live-wire editor would read any further, not because this sounds like a dull familiar essay but simply because it sounds like *a* familiar essay. But "Fish" is still a perfectly usable subject provided you remember that salable nonfiction "pieces" almost invariably fall into one of three categories: the factual, the polemic, and what we

1. Two genial American writers of the late nineteenth century.

now call—though I don't know why we have to deviate into French—*reportage.*

If you decide to be factual a good beginning would be: "Four 4 million trout flies were manufactured last year by the three leading sports-supply houses." That is the sort of thing which makes almost any editor sit up and take notice. But it is no better than certain other possible beginnings. The polemic article ought to start: "Despite all the efforts of our department of wild life conservation, the number of game fish in American lakes and streams continues to decline steadily." Probably this kind of beginning to this kind of article is best of all because it sounds alarming and because nowadays (and for understandable reasons) whatever sounds alarming is generally taken to be true. However, if you want to go in for the trickier *reportage* start off with a sentence something like this: " 'Cap' Bill Hanks, a lean, silent, wryly humorous down-Easterner, probably knows more about the strange habits of the American fisherman than any man alive."

Of course, no one will ever inquire where you got your statistics 5 about the trout flies, whether the fish population really is declining, or whether "Cap" Bill Hanks really exists. In fact, one of the best and lengthiest "Profiles" *The New Yorker* ever ran turned out to be about a "character" at the Fulton Fish Market who didn't. Whatever looks like official fact or on-the-spot reporting is taken at face value and will be widely quoted. The important thing is that the editor first and the reader afterward shall get the feeling that what he is being offered is not mere literature but the real low-down on something or other—whether that something or other is or is not anything he cares much about.

Fling your facts around, never qualify anything (qualifications 6 arouse distrust), and adopt an air of jolly omniscience. Remember that "essays" are written by introverts, "articles" by extroverts, and that the reader is going to resent anything which comes between him and that low-down which it is your principal function to supply. "Personalities," the more eccentric the better, are fine subjects for *reportage.* Manufacture or get hold of a good one and you may be able to do a "profile." But no one wants any personality to show in the magazine writer, whose business it is to be all-knowing, shrewd, and detached almost to the point of nonexistence. This means, of course, that your style should have no quality which belongs to you, only the qualities appropriate to the magazine for which you are writing. The most successful of all the magazines functioning in America today seldom print anything which is not anonymous and apparently owe a considerable part of their success to the fact that nearly everything which appears in them achieves the manner of *Life*, *Time*, or *Fortune*, as the case may be, but never by any chance any characteristic which would enable the most sensitive analyst of style to discover who had written it.

The ideal is obviously a kind of writing which seems to have 7 been produced not by a man but by some sort of electronic machine. Perhaps in time it will actually be produced that way, since such machines now solve differential equations and that is harder to do than to write the average magazine article. Probably if Vannevar Bush[2] were to put his mind to the problem, he could replace the whole interminable list of editors, assistant editors, and research assistants employed by the Luce publications[3] with a contraption less elaborate than that now used to calculate the trajectory of a rocket. Meanwhile the general effect of mechanical impersonality can be achieved by a system of collaboration in the course of which such personalities as the individual collaborators may have are made to cancel one another out.

This system works best when these collaborators are divided into 8 two groups called respectively "researchers" and "writers"—or, in other words, those who know something but don't write and those who don't know anything but do. This assures at the very outset that the actual writers shall have no dangerous interest in or even relation to what they write and that any individuality of approach which might tend to manifest itself in one of them will be canceled out by the others. If you then pass the end-result through the hands of one or more senior editors for further regularization, you will obviously get finally something from which every trace of what might be called handwork has disappeared. One might suppose that the criticism of the arts would be a department in which some trace of individuality would still be considered desirable, but I am reliably informed that at least at one time (and for all I know still) it was the custom to send an "editor" along with the movie critic to see every film so that this editor could tell the critic whether or not the film should be reviewed. This disposed of the possibility that the review might in some way reflect the critic's taste.

Obviously, few publications can afford the elaborate machinery 9 which the Luce organization has set up. However, a great many strive to achieve something of the same effect by simpler means, and they expect their contributors to cooperate by recognizing the

2. American engineer and physicist (1890–1974); he invented one of the earliest forms of the computer and directed the development of the first atomic bomb.
3. Magazines published by Henry Robinson Luce (1898–1967), among them *Time*, *Life*, *Fortune*, and *Sports Illustrated*.

ideal and by coming as close to the realization of it as is possible for an individual to come. The circulations achieved by these publications seem to indicate how wise from one point of view their policy is. Those which still permit or even encourage a certain amount of individuality in their writers—even those which still offer a certain amount of nonfiction which is to some extent personal and reflective as opposed to the factual and the bleakly expository—must content themselves with relatively small circulations. Moreover, since they also print a good deal of the other sort of thing they create the suspicion that they survive in spite of rather than because of their limited hospitality to the man-made as opposed to the machine-made article.

No doubt the kind of essay which *The Atlantic* and the old *Century* once went in for died of anemia. It came to represent the genteel tradition at its feeblest. No one need be surprised that it did not survive. But what is significant is the fact that, whereas the genteel novel was succeeded by novels of a different sort and genteel poetry by poetry in a different manner, the familiar essay died without issue, so that what disappeared was a once important literary form for which changed times found no use. And the result is that there disappeared with it the best opportunity to consider in an effective way an area of human interest.

Because the "article" is impersonal it can deal only with subjects which exist in an impersonal realm. If its subject is not ominous, usually it must be desperately trivial; and just as the best-selling books are likely to have for title either something like *The World in Crisis* or *My Grandmother Did a Strip Tease,* so the magazine articles which are not heavy are very likely to be inconsequential. I doubt that anyone was ever quite as eccentric as almost every subject of a *New Yorker* "Profile" is made to seem; but if a topic cannot be made "devastating" the next best thing is "fabulous."

Perhaps what disappeared with the familiar essay was not merely a form, not merely even an attitude, but a whole subject matter. For the familiar essay affords what is probably the best method of discussing those subjects which are neither obviously momentous nor merely silly. And, since no really good life is composed exclusively of problems and farce, either the reading of most people today does not actually concern itself with some of the most important aspects of their lives or those lives are impoverished to a degree which the members of any really civilized society would find it difficult to understand. Just as genuine conversation—by which I mean something distinguishable from disputation, lamentation, and joke-telling—has tended to disappear from social gatherings, so anything comparable to it has tended to disappear from the printed page. By no means all of the Most-of-My-Friends essays caught it. But the best of them caught something which nowadays hardly gets into print at all.

Somehow we have got into the habit of assuming that even the   13
so-called "human problems" are best discussed in terms as inhuman as possible. Just how one can profitably consider dispassionately so passionate a creature as man I do not know, but that seems to be the enterprise to which we have committed ourselves. The magazines are full of articles dealing statistically with, for example, the alleged failure or success of marriage. Lawyers discuss the law, sociologists publish statistics, and psychologists discuss case histories. Those are the methods by which we deal with the behavior of animals since animals can't talk. But men can—or at least once could—communicate, and one man's "familiar essay" on love and marriage might get closer to some all-important realities than any number of "studies" could.

No one is, to take another example, naïve enough to suppose   14
that all the current discussions of the welfare state are actually as "objective" as most of them pretend to be. Personal tastes, even simple self-interest, obviously influence most of them but only insofar as they introduce distortions between the lines. Everybody who writes for or against the competitive society tries to write as though he did not live in it, had had no personal experience of what living in it is like, and was dealing only with a question in which he had no personal interest. This is the way one talks about how to keep bees or raise Black Angus. It is not the way either the bees or the Black Angus would discuss the good life as it affected them, and it is a singularly unrealistic way of considering anything which would affect us. Even the objective studies would be better and more objective if their authors permitted themselves freely to express elsewhere their "familiar" reaction to conditions and prospects instead of working in these feelings disguised as logical argument or scientific deduction.

All the sciences which deal with man have a tendency to deper-   15
sonalize him for the simple reason that they tend to disregard everything which a particular science cannot deal with. Just as medicine confessedly deals with the physical man and economics confessedly deals not with Man but with the simplification officially designated as The Economic Man, so psychiatry deals with a fictitious man of whom there would be nothing more to be said if he were "normal," and one branch of psychology deals with what might be called the I.Q. man whose only significant aspect is his ability to solve puzzles.

Literature is the only thing which deals with the whole complex   16
phenomenon at once, and if all literature were to cease to exist the
result would probably be that in the end whatever is not considered by one or another of the sciences would no longer be taken
into account at all and would perhaps almost cease to exist. Then
Man would no longer be—or at least no longer be observed to be—
anything different from the mechanical sum of the Economic man,
the I.Q. man, and the other partial men with whom the various
partial sciences deal. Faced with that prospect, we may well look
with dismay at the disappearance of any usable literary form and
wonder whether or not we have now entered upon a stage during
which man's lingering but still complex individuality finds itself
more and more completely deprived of the opportunity not only to
express itself in living but even to discover corresponding individ-
ualities revealing themselves in the spoken or the written word.

That the situation could be radically altered by the cultivation of   17
the familiar essay I am hardly prepared to maintain. Its disappearance is only a minor symptom. Or perhaps it is just a little bit more
than that. At least there are a number of subjects which might
profitably be discussed by fewer experts and more human beings.
They might achieve a different kind of understanding of certain
problems and they might lead to more humanly acceptable conclusions. "Most of my friends seem to feel that . . ."

JACOB BRONOWSKI

The Creative Mind

Jacob Bronowski (1908–1974), born in Poland, took his Ph.D. in
mathematics at Cambridge University, and then published a
number of books about the very unmathematical poet William
Blake. Like many brilliant young people in the 1930s, Bronowski
(pronounced Bron-*off*-ski) had his life shattered by Hitler's rise to
power: "I suddenly realized that being happy, being human,
being a scientist, being with friends was not enough." As a member of a scientific team studying the effects of the atomic bombing
of Japan, Bronowski was once more jolted into a higher level of
concern about the times he was living in: he "knew that we had
dehumanized the enemy and ourselves at one blow." From 1945
forward, Bronowski labored to help his readers see that science
and technology—so deeply implicated in the horrors of World
War II—also had a human face. "The Creative Mind," originally

delivered as a lecture at the Massachusetts Institute of Technology in 1953, became chapter one of Bronowski's impressive short book *Science and Human Values* (1956). Wider fame came to Bronowski with the broadcast of his thirteen-part television series *The Ascent of Man*, which was published as a collection of essays in 1977.

1

On a fine November day in 1945, late in the afternoon, I was landed on an airstrip in southern Japan. From there a jeep was to take me over the mountains to join a ship which lay in Nagasaki Harbor. I knew nothing of the country or the distance before us. We drove off; dusk fell; the road rose and fell away, the pine woods came down to the road, straggled on and opened again. I did not know that we had left the open country until unexpectedly I heard the ship's loudspeakers broadcasting dance music. Then suddenly I was aware that we were already at the center of damage in Nagasaki. The shadows behind me were the skeletons of the Mitsubishi factory buildings, pushed backwards and sideways as if by a giant hand. What I had thought to be broken rocks was a concrete power house with its roof punched in. I could now make out the outline of two crumpled gasometers; there was a cold furnace festooned with service pipes; otherwise nothing but cockeyed telegraph poles and loops of wire in a bare waste of ashes. I had blundered into this desolate landscape as instantly as one might wake among the craters of the moon. The moment of recognition when I realized that I was already in Nagasaki is present to me as I write, as vividly as when I lived it. I see the warm night and the meaningless shapes; I can even remember the tune that was coming from the ship. It was a dance tune which had been popular in 1945, and it was called "Is You Is Or Is You Ain't Ma Baby?"

These essays, which I have called *Science and Human Values*, were born at that moment. For the moment I have recalled was a universal moment; what I met was, almost as abruptly, the experience of mankind. On an evening like that evening, some time in 1945, each of us in his own way learned that his imagination had been dwarfed. We looked up and saw the power of which we had been proud loom over us like the ruins of Nagasaki.

The power of science for good and for evil has troubled other minds than ours. We are not here fumbling with a new dilemma; our subject and our fears are as old as the toolmaking civilizations. Men have been killed with weapons before now: what happened at Nagasaki was only more massive (for 40,000 were killed there by a flash which lasted seconds) and more ironical (for the bomb exploded over the main Christian community in Japan). Nothing happened in 1945 except that we changed the scale of our indifference to man; and conscience, in revenge, for an instant became immediate to us. Before this immediacy fades in a sequence of televised atomic tests, let us acknowledge our subject for what it is: civilization face to face with its own implications. The implications are both the industrial slum which Nagasaki was before it was bombed, and the ashy desolation which the bomb made of the slum. And civilization asks of both ruins, "Is You Is Or Is You Ain't Ma Baby?"

2

The man whom I imagine to be asking this question, wrily with a   4
sense of shame, is not a scientist; he is civilized man. It is of course more usual for each member of civilization to take flight from its consequences by protesting that others have failed him. Those whose education and perhaps tastes have confined them to the humanities protest that the scientists alone are to blame, for plainly no mandarin[1] ever made a bomb or an industry. The scientists say, with equal contempt, that the Greek scholars and the earnest cataloguers of cave paintings do well to wash their hands of blame; but what in fact are they doing to help direct the society whose ills grow more often from inaction than from error?

This absurd division reached its *reductio ad absurdum*, I think,   5
when one of my teachers, G. H. Hardy, justified his great life work on the ground that it could do no one the least harm—or the least good. But Hardy was a mathematician; will humanists really let him opt out of the conspiracy of scientists? Or are scientists in their turn to forgive Hardy because, protest as he might, most of them learned their indispensable mathematics from his books?

There is no comfort in such bickering. When Shelley pictured   6
science as a modern Prometheus[2] who would wake the world to a wonderful dream of Godwin,[3] he was alas too simple. But it is as pointless to read what has happened since as a nightmare. Dream or nightmare, we have to live our experience as it is, and we have to live it awake. We live in a world which is penetrated through and through by science, and which is both whole and real. We cannot turn it into a game simply by taking sides.

1. *Mandarin* is sometimes used to mean a person influential in intellectual or literary circles.
2. One of the Titans of Greek mythology, he gave humans the gift of fire.
3. William Godwin, a utopian socialist, dreamed of a world of perfect personal freedom in small, self-sufficient communities.

And this make-believe game might cost us what we value most: 7
the human content of our lives. The scholar who disdains science
may speak in fun, but his fun is not quite a laughing matter. To
think of science as a set of special tricks, to see the scientist as the
manipulator of outlandish skills—this is the root of the poison
mandrake which flourishes rank in the comic strips. There is no
more threatening and no more degrading doctrine than the fancy
that somehow we may shelve the responsibility for making the
decisions of our society by passing it to a few scientists armored
with a special magic. This is another dream, the dream of H. G.
Wells, in which the tall elegant engineers rule, with perfect benevolence, a humanity which has no business except to be happy. To
H. G. Wells, this was a dream of heaven—a modern version of the
idle, harp-resounding heaven of other childhood pieties. But in fact
it is the picture of a slave society, and should make us shiver
whenever we hear a man of sensibility dismiss science as someone
else's concern. The world today is made, it is powered by science;
and for any man to abdicate an interest in science is to walk with
open eyes towards slavery.

My aim in this book is to show that the parts of civilization make 8
a whole: to display the links which give society its coherence, and,
more, which give it life. In particular, I want to show the place of
science in the canons of conduct which it has still to perfect.

This subject falls into three parts. The first is a study of the nature 9
of the scientific activity, and with it of all those imaginative acts of
understanding which exercise "The Creative Mind." After this it is
logical to ask what is the nature of the truth, as we seek it in science
and in social life; and to trace the influence which this search for
empirical truth has had on conduct. This influence has prompted
me to call the second part "The Habit of Truth." Last I shall study
the conditions for the success of science, and find in them the
values of man which science would have had to invent afresh if
man had not otherwise known them: the values which make up
"The Sense of Human Dignity."

This, then, is a high-ranging subject which is not to be held in 10
the narrow limits of a laboratory. It disputes the prejudice of the
humanist who takes his science sourly and, equally, the petty view
which many scientists take of their own activity and that of others.
When men misunderstand their own work, they cannot understand the work of others; so that it is natural that these scientists
have been indifferent to the arts. They have been content, with the
humanists, to think science mechanical and neutral; they could
therefore justify themselves only by the claim that it is practical. By
this lame criterion they have of course found poetry and music and

painting at least unreal and often meaningless. I challenge all these judgments.

3

There is a likeness between the creative acts of the mind in art   11
and in science. Yet, when a man uses the word science in such a
sentence, it may be suspected that he does not mean what the
headlines mean by science. Am I about to sidle away to those
riddles in the Theory of Numbers which Hardy loved, or to the
heady speculations of astrophysicists, in order to make claims for
abstract science which have no bearing on its daily practice?

I have no such design. My purpose is to talk about science as it is,   12
practical and theoretical. I define science as the organization of our
knowledge in such a way that it commands more of the hidden
potential in nature. What I have in mind therefore is both deep and
matter of fact; it reaches from the kinetic theory of gases to the
telephone and the suspension bridge and medicated toothpaste. It
admits no sharp boundary between knowledge and use. There are
of course people who like to draw a line between pure and applied
science; and oddly, they are often the same people who find art
unreal. To them, the word useful is a final arbiter, either for or
against a work; and they use this word as if it can mean only what
makes a man feel heavier after meals.

There is no sanction for confining the practice of science in this   13
or another way. True, science is full of useful inventions. And its
theories have often been made by men whose imagination was
directed by the uses to which their age looked. Newton turned
naturally to astronomy because it was the subject of his day, and it
was so because finding one's way at sea had long been a practical
preoccupation of the society into which he was born. It should be
added, mischievously, that astronomy also had some standing because it was used very practically to cast horoscopes. (Kepler used
it for this purpose; in the Thirty Years' War he cast the horoscope of
Wallenstein which wonderfully told his character, and he predicted
a universal disaster for 1634 which proved to be the murder of
Wallenstein.)

In a setting which is more familiar, Faraday worked all his life to   14
link electricity with magnetism because this was the glittering
problem of his day; and it was so because his society, like ours, was
on the lookout for new sources of power. Consider a more modest
example today: the new mathematical methods of automatic control, a subject sometimes called cybernetics, have been developed
now because this is a time when communication and control have
in effect become forms of power. These inventions have been directed by social needs, and they are useful inventions; yet it was

not their usefulness which dominated and set light to the minds of those who made them. Neither Newton nor Faraday, nor yet Norbert Wiener, spent their time in a scramble for patents.

What a scientist does is compounded of two interests: the interest of his time and his own interest. In this his behavior is no different from any other man's. The need of the age gives its shape to scientific progress as a whole. But it is not the need of the age which gives the individual scientist his sense of pleasure and of adventure, and that excitement which keeps him working late into the night when all the useful typists have gone home at five o'clock. He is personally involved in his work, as the poet is in his, and as the artist is in the painting. Paints and painting too must have been made for useful ends; and language was developed, from whatever beginnings, for practical communication. Yet you cannot have a man handle paints or language or the symbolic concepts of physics, you cannot even have him stain a microscope slide, without instantly waking in him a pleasure in the very language, a sense of exploring his own activity. This sense lies at the heart of creation. 15

4

The sense of personal exploration is as urgent, and as delightful, to the practical scientist as to the theoretical. Those who think otherwise are confusing what is practical with what is humdrum. Good humdrum work without originality is done every day by everyone, theoretical scientists as well as practical, and writers and painters too, as well as truck drivers and bank clerks. Of course the unoriginal work keeps the world going; but it is not therefore the monopoly of practical men. And neither need the practical man be unoriginal. If he is to break out of what has been done before, he must bring to his own tools the same sense of pride and discovery which the poet brings to words. He cannot afford to be less radical in conceiving and less creative in designing a new turbine than a new world system. 16

And this is why in turn practical discoveries are not made only by practical men. As the world's interest has shifted, since the Industrial Revolution, to the tapping of new springs of power, the theoretical scientist has shifted his interests too. His speculations about energy have been as abstract as once they were about astronomy; and they have been profound now as they were then, because the man loved to think. The Carnot cycle[4] and the dynamo grew equally from this love, and so did nuclear physics and the 17

4. The cycle of heat and work exchanges in an ideal steam engine, conceived by the nineteenth-century French engineer Sadi Carnot.

German V⁵ weapons and Kelvin's interest in low temperatures. Man does not invent by following either use or tradition; he does not invent even a new form of communication by calling a conference of communication engineers. Who invented the television set? In any deep sense, it was Clerk Maxwell who foresaw the existence of radio waves, and Heinrich Hertz who proved it, and J. J. Thomson who discovered the electron. This is not said in order to rob any practical man of the invention, but from a sad sense of justice; for neither Maxwell nor Hertz nor J. J. Thomson would take pride in television just now.

Man masters nature not by force but by understanding. This is why science has succeeded when magic failed: because it has looked for no spell to cast over nature. The alchemist and the magician in the Middle Ages thought, and the addict of comic strips is still encouraged to think, that nature must be mastered by a device which outrages her laws. But in four hundred years since the Scientific Revolution we have learned that we gain our ends only *with* the laws of nature; we control her only by understanding her laws. We cannot even bully nature by any insistence that our work shall be designed to give power over her. We must be content that power is the byproduct of understanding. So the Greeks said that Orpheus played the lyre with such sympathy that wild beasts were tamed by the hand on the strings. They did not suggest that he got this gift by setting out to be a lion tamer.

5

What is the insight with which the scientist tries to see into nature? Can it indeed be called either imaginative or creative? To the literary man the question may seem merely silly. He has been taught that science is a large collection of facts; and if this is true, then the only seeing which scientists need do is, he supposes, seeing the facts. He pictures them, the colorless professionals of science, going off to work in the morning into the universe in a neutral, unexposed state. They then expose themselves like a photographic plate. And then in the darkroom or laboratory they develop the image, so that suddenly and startlingly it appears, printed in capital letters, as a new formula for atomic energy.

Men who have read Balzac and Zola⁶ are not deceived by the claims of these writers that they do no more than record the facts. The readers of Christopher Isherwood do not take him literally when he writes "I am a camera." Yet the same readers solemnly

18

19

20

5. The rockets with which Hitler bombarded England in World War II.
6. Literary realists.

carry with them from their schooldays this foolish picture of the scientist fixing by some mechanical process the facts of nature. I have had of all people a historian tell me that science is a collection of facts, and his voice had not even the ironic rasp of one filing cabinet reproving another.

It seems impossible that this historian had ever studied the be- 21 ginnings of a scientific discovery. The Scientific Revolution can be held to begin in the year 1543 when there was brought to Copernicus, perhaps on his deathbed, the first printed copy of the book he had finished about a dozen years earlier. The thesis of this book is that the earth moves around the sun. When did Copernicus go out and record this fact with his camera? What appearance in nature prompted his outrageous guess? And in what odd sense is this guess to be called a neutral record of fact?

Less than a hundred years after Copernicus, Kepler published 22 (between 1609 and 1619) the three laws which described the paths of the planets. The work of Newton and with it most of our mechanics spring from these laws. They have a solid, matter of fact sound. For example, Kepler says that if one squares the year of a planet, one gets a number which is proportional to the cube of its average distance from the sun. Does anyone think that such a law is found by taking enough readings and then squaring and cubing everything in sight? If he does, then as a scientist, he is doomed to a wasted life; he has as little prospect of making a scientific discovery as an electronic brain has.

It was not this way that Copernicus and Kepler thought, or that 23 scientists think today. Copernicus found that the orbits of the planets would look simpler if they were looked at from the sun and not from the earth. But he did not in the first place find this by routine calculation. His first step was a leap of imagination—to lift himself from the earth, and put himself wildly, speculatively into the sun. "The earth conceives from the sun," he wrote; and "the sun rules the family of stars." We catch in his mind an image, the gesture of the virile man standing in the sun, with arms outstretched, overlooking the planets. Perhaps Copernicus took the picture from the drawings of the youth with outstretched arms which the Renaissance teachers put into their books on the proportions of the body. Perhaps he had seen Leonardo's drawings of his loved pupil Salai. I do not know. To me, the gesture of Copernicus, the shining youth looking outward from the sun, is still vivid in a drawing which William Blake in 1780 based on all these: the drawing which is usually called *Glad Day*.

Kepler's mind, we know, was filled with just such fanciful 24 analogies; and we know what they were. Kepler wanted to relate the speeds of the planets to the musical intervals. He tried to fit the five regular solids into their orbits. None of these likenesses worked, and they have been forgotten; yet they have been and they remain the stepping stones of every creative mind. Kepler felt for his laws by way of metaphors, he searched mystically for likenesses with what he knew in every strange corner of nature. And when among these guesses he hit upon his laws, he did not think of their numbers as the balancing of a cosmic bank account, but as a revelation of the unity of all nature. To us, the analogies by which Kepler listened for the movement of the planets in the music of the spheres are farfetched. Yet are they more so than the wild leap by which Rutherford and Bohr in our own century found a model for the atom in, of all places, the planetary system?

6

No scientific theory is a collection of facts. It will not even do to   25
call a theory true or false in the simple sense in which every fact is either so or not so. The Epicureans held that matter is made of atoms two thousand years ago and we are now tempted to say that their theory was true. But if we do so we confuse their notion of matter with our own. John Dalton in 1808 first saw the structure of matter as we do today, and what he took from the ancients was not their theory but something richer, their image: the atom. Much of what was in Dalton's mind was as vague as the Greek notion, and quite as mistaken. But he suddenly gave life to the new facts of chemistry and the ancient theory together, by fusing them to give what neither had: a coherent picture of how matter is linked and built up from different kinds of atoms. The act of fusion is the creative act.

All science is the search for unity in hidden likenesses. The   26
search may be on a grand scale, as in the modern theories which try to link the fields of gravitation and electromagnetism. But we do not need to be browbeaten by the scale of science. There are discoveries to be made by snatching a small likeness from the air too, if it is bold enough. In 1935 the Japanese physicist Hideki Yukawa wrote a paper which can still give heart to a young scientist. He took as his starting point the known fact that waves of light can sometimes behave as if they were separate pellets. From this he reasoned that the forces which held the nucleus of an atom together might sometimes also be observed as if they were solid pellets. A schoolboy can see how thin Yukawa's analogy is, and his teacher would be severe with it. Yet Yukawa without a blush calculated the mass of the pellet he expected to see, and waited. He was right; his meson was found, and a range of other mesons,

neither the existence nor the nature of which had been suspected before. The likeness had borne fruit.

The scientist looks for order in the appearance of nature by exploring such likenesses. For order does not display itself of itself; if it can be said to be there at all, it is not there for the mere looking. There is no way of pointing a finger or a camera at it; order must be discovered and, in a deep sense, it must be created. What we see, as we see it, is mere disorder.   27

This point has been put trenchantly in a fable by Karl Popper. Suppose that someone wished to give his whole life to science. Suppose that he therefore sat down, pencil in hand, and for the next twenty, thirty, forty years recorded in notebook after notebook everything that he could observe. He may be supposed to leave out nothing: today's humidity, the racing results, the level of cosmic radiation and the stockmarket prices and the look of Mars, all would be there. He would have compiled the most careful record of nature that has ever been made; and, dying in the calm certainty of a life well spent, he would of course leave his notebooks to the Royal Society. Would the Royal Society thank him for the treasure of a lifetime of observation? It would not. The Royal Society would treat his notebooks exactly as the English bishops have treated Joanna Southcott's box.[7] It would refuse to open them at all, because it would know without looking that the notebooks contain only a jumble of disorderly and meaningless items.   28

7

Science finds order and meaning in our experience, and sets about this in quite a different way. It sets about it as Newton did in the story which he himself told in his old age, and of which the schoolbooks give only a caricature. In the year 1665, when Newton was twenty-two, the plague broke out in southern England, and the University of Cambridge was closed. Newton therefore spent the next eighteen months at home, removed from traditional learning, at a time when he was impatient for knowledge and, in his own phrase, "I was in the prime of my age for invention." In this eager, boyish mood, sitting one day in the garden of his widowed mother, he saw an apple fall. So far the books have the story right; we think we even know the kind of apple; tradition has   29

7. Joanna Southcott (1750–1814) claimed to have transcribed divinely inspired messages concerning the Second Coming of Christ. At her death she left a locked box, instructing that it should be opened in the presence of all the bishops in a time of national emergency. It was opened, in the presence of one bishop, in 1928; nothing in it was deemed of interest, which further convinced the English religious establishment that she was merely a crank.

it that it was a Flower of Kent. But now they miss the crux of the story. For what struck the young Newton at the sight was not the thought that the apple must be drawn to the earth by gravity; that conception was older than Newton. What struck him was the conjecture that the same force of gravity, which reaches to the top of the tree, might go on reaching out beyond the earth and its air, endlessly into space. Gravity might reach the moon: this was Newton's new thought; and it might be gravity which holds the moon in her orbit. There and then he calculated what force from the earth (falling off as the square of the distance) would hold the moon, and compared it with the known force of gravity at tree height. The forces agreed; Newton says laconically, "I found them answer pretty nearly." Yet they agreed only nearly: the likeness and the approximation go together, for no likeness is exact. In Newton's sentence modern science is full grown.

It grows from a comparison. It has seized a likeness between two   30 unlike appearances; for the apple in the summer garden and the grave moon overhead are surely as unlike in their movements as two things can be. Newton traced in them two expressions of a single concept, gravitation: and the concept (and the unity) are in that sense his free creation. The progress of science is the discovery at each step of a new order which gives unity to what had long seemed unlike. Faraday did this when he closed the link between electricity and magnetism. Clerk Maxwell did it when he linked both with light. Einstein linked time with space, mass with energy, and the path of light past the sun with the flight of a bullet; and spent his dying years in trying to add to these likenesses another, which would find a single imaginative order between the equations of Clerk Maxwell and his own geometry of gravitation.

8

When Coleridge tried to define beauty, he returned always to   31 one deep thought: beauty, he said, is "unity in variety." Science is nothing else than the search to discover unity in the wild variety of nature—or more exactly, in the variety of our experience. Poetry, painting, the arts are the same search, in Coleridge's phrase, for unity in variety. Each in his own way looks for likenesses under the variety of human experience. What is a poetic image but the seizing and the exploration of a hidden likeness, in holding together two parts of a comparison which are to give depth each to the other? When Romeo finds Juliet in the tomb, and thinks her dead, he uses in his heartbreaking speech the words,

Death that hath suckt the honey of thy breath.

The critic can only haltingly take to pieces the single shock which this image carries. The young Shakespeare admired Marlowe, and Marlowe's Faustus had said of the ghostly kiss of Helen of Troy that it sucked forth his soul. But that is a pale image; what Shakespeare has done is to fire it with the single word honey. Death is a bee at the lips of Juliet, and the bee is an insect that stings; the sting of death was a commonplace phrase when Shakespeare wrote. The sting is there, under the image; Shakespeare has packed it into the word honey; but the very word rides powerfully over its own undertones. Death is a bee that stings other people, but it comes to Juliet as if she were a flower; this is the moving thought under the instant image. The creative mind speaks in such thoughts.

The poetic image here is also, and accidentally, heightened by the tenderness which town dwellers now feel for country ways. But it need not be; there are likenesses to conjure with, and images as powerful, within the man-made world. The poems of Alexander Pope belong to this world. They are not countrified, and therefore readers today find them unemotional and often artificial. Let me then quote Pope: here he is in a formal satire face to face, towards the end of his life, with his own gifts. In eight lines he looks poignantly forward towards death and back to the laborious years which made him famous.

> Years foll'wing Years, steal something ev'ry day,
> At last they steal us from our selves away;
> In one our Frolicks, one Amusements end,
> In one a Mistress drops, in one a Friend:
> This subtle Thief of Life, this paltry Time,
> What will it leave me, if it snatch my Rhime?
> If ev'ry Wheel of that unweary'd Mill
> That turn'd ten thousand Verses, now stands still.

The human mind had been compared to what the eighteenth century called a mill, that is to a machine, before; Pope's own idol Bolingbroke had compared it to a clockwork. In these lines the likeness goes deeper, for Pope is thinking of the ten thousand Verses which he had translated from Homer: what he says is sad and just at the same time, because this really had been a mechanical and at times a grinding task. Yet the clockwork is present in the image too; when the wheels stand still, time for Pope will stand still for ever; we feel that we already hear, over the horizon, Faust's defiant reply to Mephistopheles, which Goethe had not yet written—"let the clock strike and stop, let the hand fall, and time be at an end."

Werd ich zum Augenblicke sagen:
Verweile doch! du bist so schön!
Dann magst du mich in Fesseln schlagen,
Dann will ich gern zugrunde gehn!
Dann mag die Totenglocke schallen,
Dann bist du deines Dienstes frei,
Die Uhr mag stehn, der Zeiger fallen,
Es sei die Zeit für mich vorbei![8]

I have quoted Pope and Goethe because their metaphor here is not poetic; it is rather a hand reaching straight into experience and arranging it with new meaning. Metaphors of this kind need not always be written in words. The most powerful of them all is simply the presence of King Lear and his Fool in the hovel of a man who is shamming madness, while lightning rages outside.[9] Or let me quote another clash of two conceptions of life, from a modern poet. In his later poems W. B. Yeats was troubled by the feeling that in shutting himself up to write, he was missing the active pleasures of life; and yet it seemed to him certain that the man who lives for these pleasures will leave no lasting work behind him. He said this at times very simply, too:

The intellect of man is forced to choose
Perfection of the life, or of the work.

This problem, whether a man fulfills himself in work or in play, is of course more common than Yeats allowed; and it may be more commonplace. But it is given breadth and force by the images in which Yeats pondered it.

Get all the gold and silver that you can,
Satisfy ambition, or animate
The trivial days and ram them with the sun,
And yet upon these maxims meditate:
All women dote upon an idle man
Although their children need a rich estate;
No man has ever lived that had enough
Of children's gratitude or woman's love.

8. "If ever I say to the passing moment: Stay a while! Thou art so fair! Then may you cast me into chains. Then will I gladly perish. Then may the death-bell toll. Then are you freed from my service. Let the clock strike and stop, let the hand fall, and time be at an end."
9. In Act III, scene iv of Shakespeare's *King Lear*, psychological, moral, familial, and political disorder all find a metaphor in the storm that batters these three vulnerable men.

The love of women, the gratitude of children: the images fix two philosophies as nothing else can. They are tools of creative thought, as coherent and as exact as the conceptual images with which science works: as time and space, or as the proton and the neutron.

9

The discoveries of science, the works of art are explorations— 34 more, are explosions, of a hidden likeness. The discoverer or the artist presents in them two aspects of nature and fuses them into one. This is the act of creation, in which an original thought is born, and it is the same act in original science and original art. But it is not therefore the monopoly of the man who wrote the poem or who made the discovery. On the contrary, I believe this view of the creative act to be right because it alone gives a meaning to the act of appreciation. The poem or the discovery exists in two moments of vision: the moment of appreciation as much as that of creation; for the appreciator must see the movement, wake to the echo which was started in the creation of the work. In the moment of appreciation we live again the moment when the creator saw and held the hidden likeness. When a simile takes us aback and persuades us together, when we find a juxtaposition in a picture both odd and intriguing, when a theory is at once fresh and convincing, we do not merely nod over someone else's work. We re-enact the creative act, and we ourselves make the discovery again. At bottom, there is no unifying likeness there until we too have seized it, we too have made it for ourselves.

How slipshod by comparison is the notion that either art or 35 science sets out to copy nature. If the task of the painter were to copy for men what they see, the critic could make only a single judgment: either that the copy is right or that it is wrong. And if science were a copy of fact, then every theory would be either right or wrong, and would be so for ever. There would be nothing left for us to say but this is so, or is not so. No one who has read a page by a good critic or a speculative scientist can ever again think that this barren choice of yes or no is all that the mind offers.

Reality is not an exhibit for man's inspection, labelled "Do not 36 touch." There are no appearances to be photographed, no experiences to be copied, in which we do not take part. Science, like art, is not a copy of nature but a re-creation of her. We re-make nature by the act of discovery, in the poem or in the theorem. And the great poem and the deep theorem are new to every reader, and yet are his own experiences, because he himself re-creates them. They are the mark of unity in variety; and in the instant when the mind seizes this for itself, in art or in science, the heart misses a beat.

WILLIAM G. PERRY

Examsmanship and the Liberal Arts

William G. Perry, Jr. (1913–   ) served for many years with the Bureau of Study Counsel at Harvard University, where he advised students and studied the relation between education and the development of personality. "Examsmanship and the Liberal Arts" grew out of a five-year study in which Perry interviewed students to learn why some thrived in Harvard's intellectual climate and others of equal intelligence struggled unsuccessfully and unhappily. First published in *Examining at Harvard College* (1967), the essay suggests the general outline of Perry's answer: a university environment is essentially hostile to a simple black-and-white view of the world, and students who are willing to see the difficulty of finding *the* truth do better than their more rigid classmates. The essay, originally written for other members of the Harvard faculty, contrasts two epistemologies, or theories of knowledge—one based on what Perry calls "bull" and one based on what he calls "cow." A more complete account of these epistemologies and their importance in education can be found in Perry's book *Forms of Intellectual and Ethical Development in the College Years: A Scheme* (1970).

"But sir, I don't think I really deserve it, it was mostly bull, really." This disclaimer from a student whose examination we have awarded a straight "A" is wondrously depressing. Alfred North Whitehead invented its only possible rejoinder: "Yes sir, what you wrote is nonsense, utter nonsense. But ah! Sir! It's the right *kind* of nonsense!"

Bull, in this university, is customarily a source of laughter, or a problem in ethics. I shall step a little out of fashion to use the subject as a take-off point for a study in comparative epistemology. The phenomenon of bull, in all the honor and opprobrium with which it is regarded by students and faculty, says something, I think, about our theories of knowledge. So too, the grades which we assign on examinations communicate to students what these theories may be.

We do not have to be out-and-out logical-positivists[1] to suppose that we have something to learn about "what we think knowledge is" by having a good look at "what we do when we go about measuring it." We know the straight "A" examination when we see it, of course, and we have reason to hope that the student will understand why his work receives our recognition. He doesn't always. And those who receive lesser honor? Perhaps an understanding of certain anomalies in our customs of grading good bull will explain the students' confusion.

I must beg patience, then, both of the reader's humor and of his morals. Not that I ask him to suspend his sense of humor but that I shall ask him to go beyond it. In a great university the picture of a bright student attempting to outwit his professor while his professor takes pride in not being outwitted is certainly ridiculous. I shall report just such a scene, for its implications bear upon my point. Its comedy need not present a serious obstacle to thought.

As for the ethics of bull, I must ask for a suspension of judgment. I wish that students could suspend theirs. Unlike humor, moral commitment is hard to think beyond. Too early a moral judgment is precisely what stands between many able students and a liberal education. The stunning realization that the Harvard Faculty will often accept, as evidence of knowledge, the cerebrations of a student who has little data at his disposal, confronts every student with an ethical dilemma. For some it forms an academic focus for what used to be thought of as "adolescent disillusion." It is irrelevant that rumor inflates the phenomenon to mythical proportions. The students know that beneath the myth there remains a solid and haunting reality. The moral "bind" consequent on this awareness appears most poignantly in serious students who are reluctant to concede the competitive advantage to the bullster and who yet feel a deep personal shame when, having succumbed to "temptation," they themselves receive a high grade for work they consider "dishonest."

I have spent many hours with students caught in this unwelcome bitterness. These hours lend an urgency to my theme. I have found that students have been able to come to terms with the ethical problem, to the extent that it is real, only after a refined

1. Logical positivists like Bertrand Russell insist that philosophical speculation be tightly checked by reference to the "positive" date of experience. This position links them to the psychological behaviorists.

study of the true nature of bull and its relation to "knowledge." I shall submit grounds for my suspicion that we can be found guilty of sharing the student's confusion of moral and epistemological issues.

I

I present as my "premise," then, an amoral *fabliau*. Its hero-   7
villain is the Abominable Mr. Metzger '47. Since I celebrate his virtuosity, I regret giving him a pseudonym, but the peculiar style of his bravado requires me to honor also his modesty. Bull in pure form is rare; there is usually some contamination by data. The community has reason to be grateful to Mr. Metzger for having created an instance of laboratory purity, free from any adulteration by matter. The more credit is due him, I think, because his act was free from premeditation, deliberation, or hope of personal gain.

Mr. Metzger stood one rainy November day in the lobby of   8
Memorial Hall. A junior, concentrating in mathematics, he was fond of diverting himself by taking part in the drama, a penchant which may have had some influence on the events of the next hour. He was waiting to take part in a rehearsal in Sanders Theatre, but, as sometimes happens, no other players appeared. Perhaps the rehearsal had been canceled without his knowledge? He decided to wait another five minutes.

Students, meanwhile, were filing into the Great Hall opposite,   9
and taking seats at the testing tables. Spying a friend crossing the lobby toward the Great Hall's door, Metzger greeted him and extended appropriate condolences. He inquired, too, what course his friend was being tested in. "Oh, Soc. Sci. something-or-other." "What's it all about?"asked Metzger, and this, as Homer remarked of Patroclus, was the beginning of evil for him.

"It's about Modern Perspectives on Man and Society and All   10
That," said his friend. "Pretty interesting, really."

"Always wanted to take a course like that," said Metzger. "Any   11
good reading?"

"Yeah, great. There's this book"—his friend did not have time to   12
finish.

"Take your seats please" said a stern voice beside them. The idle   13
conversation had somehow taken the two friends to one of the tables in the Great Hall. Both students automatically obeyed; the proctor put blue books before them; another proctor presented them with copies of the printed hour-test.

Mr. Metzger remembered afterwards a brief misgiving that was   14
suddenly overwhelmed by a surge of curiosity and puckish glee. He

wrote "George Smith" on the blue book, opened it, and addressed the first question.

I must pause to exonerate the Management. The Faculty has a 15 rule that no student may attend an examination in a course in which he is not enrolled. To the wisdom of this rule the outcome of this deplorable story stands witness. The Registrar, charged with the enforcement of the rule, has developed an organization with procedures which are certainly the finest to be devised. In November, however, class rosters are still shaky, and on this particular day another student, named Smith, was absent. As for the culprit, we can reduce his guilt no further than to suppose that he was ignorant of the rule, or, in the face of the momentous challenge before him, forgetful.

We need not be distracted by Metzger's performance on the 16 "objective" or "spot" questions on the test. His D on these sections can be explained by those versed in the theory of probability. Our interest focuses on the quality of his essay. It appears that when Metzger's friend picked up his own blue book a few days later, he found himself in company with a large proportion of his section in having received on the essay a C. When he quietly picked up "George Smith's" blue book to return it to Metzger, he observed that the grade for the essay was A. In the margin was a note in the section man's hand. It read "Excellent work. Could you have pinned these observations down a bit more closely? Compare . . . in . . . pp. . . ."

Such news could hardly be kept quiet. There was a leak, and the 17 whole scandal broke on the front page of Tuesday's *Crimson*. With the press Metzger was modest, as becomes a hero. He said that there had been nothing to it at all, really. The essay question had offered a choice of two books, Margaret Mead's *And Keep Your Powder Dry* or Geoffrey Gorer's *The American People*. Metzger reported that having read neither of them, he had chosen the second "because the title gave me some notion as to what the book might be about." On the test, two critical comments were offered on each book, one favorable, one unfavorable. The students were asked to "discuss." Metzger conceded that he had played safe in throwing his lot with the most laudatory of the two comments, "but I did not forget to be balanced."

I do not have Mr. Metzger's essay before me except in vivid 18 memory. As I recall, he took his first cue from the name Geoffrey, and committed his strategy to the premise that Gorer was born into an "Anglo-Saxon" culture, probably English, but certainly "English speaking." Having heard that Margaret Mead was a social

anthropologist, he inferred that Gorer was the same. He then entered upon his essay, centering his inquiry upon what he supposed
might be the problems inherent in an anthropologist's observation
of a culture which was his own, or nearly his own. Drawing in part
from memories of table-talk on cultural relativity[2] and in part from
creative logic, he rang changes on the relation of observer to observed, and assessed the kind and degree of objectivity which might
accrue to an observer through training as an anthropologist. He
concluded that the book in question did in fact contribute a considerable range of " 'objective', and even 'fresh'," insights into the
nature of our culture. "At the same time," he warned, "these
observations must be understood within the context of their generation by a person only partly freed from his embeddedness in the
culture he is observing, and limited in his capacity to transcend
those particular tendencies and biases which he has himself developed as a personality in his interaction with this culture since his
birth. In this sense the book portrays as much the character of
Geoffrey Gorer as it analyzes that of the American people." It is my
regrettable duty to report that at this moment of triumph Mr. Metzger was carried away by the temptations of parody and added, "We
are thus much the richer."

In any case, this was the essay for which Metzger received his   19
honor grade and his public acclaim. He was now, of course, in
serious trouble with the authorities.

I shall leave him for the moment to the mercy of the Administra-   20
tive Board of Harvard College and turn the reader's attention to the
section man who ascribed the grade. He was in much worse trouble. All the consternation in his immediate area of the Faculty and
all the glee in other areas fell upon his unprotected head. I shall
now undertake his defense.

I do so not simply because I was acquainted with him and feel a   21
respect for his intelligence; I believe in the justice of his grade!
Well, perhaps "justice" is the wrong word in a situation so mani-
festly absurd. This is more a case in "equity." That is, the grade is
equitable if we accept other aspects of the situation which are
equally absurd. My proposition is this: if we accept as valid those C
grades which were accorded students who, like Metzger's friend,
demonstrated a thorough familiarity with the details of the book
without relating their critique to the methodological problems of

---

2. "An important part of Harvard's education takes place during meals in
the Houses." An Official Publication. [author's note] Houses are dormitories
for upperclassmen.

social anthropology, then "George Smith" deserved not only the same, but better.

The reader may protest that the C's given to students who showed evidence only of diligence were indeed not valid and that both these students and "George Smith" should have received E's. To give the diligent E is of course not in accord with custom. I shall take up this matter later. For now, were I to allow the protest, I could only restate my thesis: that "George Smith's" E would, in a college of liberal arts, be properly a "better" E.

At this point I need a short-hand. It is a curious fact that there is no academic slang for the presentation of evidence of diligence alone. "Parroting" won't do; it is possible to "parrot" bull. I must beg the reader's pardon, and, for reasons almost too obvious to bear, suggest "cow."

Stated as nouns, the concepts look simple enough:

cow (pure): data, however relevant, without relevancies.
bull (pure): relevancies, however relevant, without data.

The reader can see all too clearly where this simplicity would lead. I can assure him that I would not have imposed on him this way were I aiming to say that knowledge in this university is definable as some neuter compromise between cow and bull, some infertile hermaphrodite. This is precisely what many diligent students seem to believe: that what they must learn to do is to "find the right mean" between "amounts" of detail and "amounts" of generalities. Of course this is not the point at all. The problem is not quantitative, nor does its solution lie on a continuum between the particular and the general. Cow and bull are not poles of a single dimension. A clear notion of what they really are is essential to my inquiry, and for heuristic purposes I wish to observe them further in the celibate state.

When the pure concepts are translated into verbs, their complexities become apparent in the assumptions and purposes of the students as they write:

To cow (v. intrans.) or the act of cowing:
    To list data (or perform operations) without awareness of, or comment upon, the contexts, frames of reference, or points of observation which determine the origin, nature, and meaning of the data (or procedures). To write on the assumption that "a fact is a fact." To present evidence of hard work as a substitute for understanding, without any intent to deceive.

To bull (v. intrans.) or the act of bulling:
    To discourse upon the contexts, frames of reference and points of

observation which would determine the origin, nature, and meaning
of data if one had any. To present evidence of an understanding of
form in the hope that the reader may be deceived into supporting a
familiarity with content.

At the level of conscious intent, it is evident that cowing is more   27
moral, or less immoral, than bulling. To speculate about unconscious intent would be either an injustice or a needless elaboration
of my theme. It is enough that the impression left by cow is one of
earnestness, diligence, and painful naiveté. The grader may feel
disappointment or even irritation, but these feelings are usually
balanced by pity, compassion, and a reluctance to hit a man when
he's both down and moral. He may feel some challenge to his
teaching, but none whatever to his one-ups-manship. He writes in
the margin: "See me."

We are now in a position to understand the anomaly of custom: 28
As instructors, we always assign bull an E, *when we detect it;*
whereas we usually give cow a C, *even though it is always obvious.*

After all, we did not ask to be confronted with a choice between   29
morals and understanding (or did we?). We evince a charming
humanity, I think, in our decision to grade in favor of morals and
pathos. "I simply *can't* give this student an E after he has *worked* so
hard." At the same time we tacitly express our respect for the
bullster's strength. We recognize a colleague. If he knows so well
how to dish it out, we can be sure that he can also take it.

Of course it is just possible that we carry with us, perhaps from   30
our own school-days, an assumption that if a student is willing to
work hard and collect "good hard facts" he can always be taught to
understand their relevance, whereas a student who has caught
onto the forms of relevance without working at all is a lost scholar.

But this is not in accord with our experience.   31

It is not in accord either, as far as I can see, with the stated values   32
of a liberal education. If a liberal education should teach students
"how to think," not only in their own fields but in fields outside
their own—that is, to understand "how the other fellow orders
knowledge," then bulling, even in its purest form, expresses an
important part of what a pluralist university holds dear, surely a
more important part than the collecting of "facts that are facts"
which schoolboys learn to do. Here then, good bull appears not as
ignorance at all but as an aspect of knowledge. It is both relevant
and "true." In a university setting good bull is therefore of more
value than "facts," which, without a frame of reference, are not
even "true" at all.

Perhaps this value accounts for the final anomaly: as instructors,   33
we are inclined to reward bull highly, *where we do not detect its*

intent, to the consternation of the bullster's acquaintances. And
often we do not examine the matter too closely. After a long evening of reading blue books full of cow, the sudden meeting with a
student who at least understands the problems of one's field provides a lift like a draught of refreshing wine, and a strong disposition toward trust.

This was, then, the sense of confidence that came to our unfor-   34
tunate section man as he read "George Smith's" sympathetic
considerations.

II

In my own years of watching over students' shoulders as they   35
work, I have come to believe that this feeling of trust has a firmer
basis than the confidence generated by evidence of diligence alone.
I believe that the theory of a liberal education holds. Students who
have dared to understand man's real relation to his knowledge
have shown themselves to be in a strong position to learn content
rapidly and meaningfully, and to retain it. I have learned to be less
concerned about the education of a student who has come to
understand the nature of man's knowledge, even though he has
not yet committed himself to hard work, than I am about the
education of the student who, after one or two terms at Harvard, is
working desperately hard and still believes that collected "facts"
constitute knowledge. The latter, when I try to explain to him, too
often understands me to be saying that he "doesn't *put in enough
generalities.*" Surely he has "put in *enough* facts."

I have come to see such quantitative statements as expressions of   36
an entire, coherent epistemology. In grammar school the student is
taught that Columbus discovered America in 1492. The *more* such
items he gets "right" on a given test the more he is credited with
"knowing." From years of this sort of thing it is not unnatural to
develop the conviction that knowledge consists of the accretion of
hard facts by hard work.

The student learns that the more facts and procedures he can get   37
"right" in a given course, the better will be his grade. The more
courses he takes, the more subjects he has "had," the more credits
he accumulates, the more diplomas he will get, until, after graduate
school, he will emerge with his doctorate, a member of the community of scholars.

The foundation of this entire life is the proposition that a fact is a   38
fact. The necessary correlate of this proposition is that a fact is
either right or wrong. This implies that the standard against which
the rightness or wrongness of a fact may be judged exists *some-
place*—perhaps graven upon a tablet in a Platonic world outside

and above *this* cave of tears. In grammar school it is evident that the tablets which enshrine the spelling of a word or the answer to an arithmetic problem are visible to my teacher who need only compare my offerings to it. In high school I observe that my English teachers disagree. This can only mean that the tablets in such matters as the goodness of a poem are distant and obscured by clouds. They surely exist. The pleasing of befuddled English teachers degenerates into assessing their prejudices, a game in which I have no protection against my competitors more glib of tongue. I respect only my science teachers, authorities who *really know.* Later I learn from them that "this is only what we think *now.*" But eventually, surely. . . . Into this epistemology of education, apparently shared by teachers in such terms as "credits," "semester hours" and "years of French" the student may invest his ideals, his drive, his competitiveness, his safety, his self-esteem, and even his love.

College raises other questions: by whose calendar is it proper to   39 say that Columbus discovered America in 1492? How, when, and by whom was the year 1 established in this calendar? What of other calendars? In view of the evidence for Leif Ericson's previous visit (and the American Indians), what historical ethnocentrism is suggested by the use of the word "discover" in this sentence? As for Leif Ericson, in accord with what assumptions do you order the evidence?

These questions and their answers are not "more" knowledge.   40 They are devastation. I do not need to elaborate upon the epistemology, or rather epistemologies, they imply. A fact has become at last "an observation or an operation performed in a frame of reference." A liberal education is founded in an awareness of frame of reference even in the most immediate and empirical examination of data. Its acquirement involves relinquishing hope of absolutes and of the protection they afford against doubt and the glib-tongued competitor. It demands an ever widening sophistication about systems of thought and observation. It leads, not away from, but *through* the arts of gamesmanship to a new trust.

This trust is in the value and integrity of systems, their varied   41 character, and the way their apparently incompatible metaphors enlighten, from complementary facets, the particulars of human experience. As one student said to me: "I used to be cynical about intellectual games. Now I want to know them thoroughly. You see I came to realize that it was only when I knew the rules of the game cold that I could tell whether what I was saying was tripe."

We too often think of the bullster as cynical. He can be, and not   42 always in a light-hearted way. We have failed to observe that there can lie behind cow the potential of a deeper and more dangerous despair. The moralism of sheer work and obedience can be an ethic that, unwilling to face a despair of its ends, glorifies its means. The implicit refusal to consider the relativity of both ends and means leaves the operator in an unconsidered proprietary absolutism. History bears witness that in the pinches this moral superiority has no recourse to negotiation, only to force.

A liberal education proposes that man's hope lies elsewhere: in the negotiability that can arise from an understanding of the integrity of systems and of their origins in man's address to his universe. The prerequisite is the courage to accept such a definition of knowledge. From then on, of course, there is nothing incompatible between such an epistemology and hard work. Rather the contrary. 43

I can now at last let bull and cow get together. The reader knows best how a productive wedding is arranged in his own field. This is the nuptial he celebrates with a straight A on examinations. The masculine context must embrace the feminine particular, though itself "born of woman." Such a union is knowledge itself, and it alone can generate new contexts and new data which can unite in their turn to form new knowledge. 44

In this happy setting we can congratulate in particular the Natural Sciences, long thought to be barren ground to the bullster. I have indeed drawn my examples of bull from the Social Sciences, and by analogy from the Humanities. Essay-writing in these fields has long been thought to nurture the art of bull to its prime. I feel, however, that the Natural Sciences have no reason to feel slighted. It is perhaps no accident that Metzger was a mathematician. As part of my researches for this paper, furthermore, a student of considerable talent has recently honored me with an impressive analysis of the art of amassing "partial credits" on examinations in advanced physics. Though beyond me in some respects, his presentation confirmed my impression that instructors of Physics frequently honor on examinations operations structurally similar to those requisite in a good essay. 45

The very qualities that make the Natural Sciences fields of delight for the eager gamesman have been essential to their marvelous fertility. 46

III

As priests of these mysteries, how can we make our rites more precisely expressive? The student who merely cows robs himself, without knowing it, of his education and his soul. The student who only bulls robs himself, as he knows full well, of the joys of inductive discovery—that is, of engagement. The introduction of frames 47 of reference in the new curricula of Mathematics and Physics in the schools is a hopeful experiment. We do not know yet how much of these potent revelations the very young can stand, but I suspect they may rejoice in them more than we have supposed. I can't believe they have never wondered about Leif Ericson and that word "discovered," or even about 1492. They have simply been too wise to inquire.

Increasingly in recent years better students in the better high 48 schools and preparatory schools are being allowed to inquire. In fact they appear to be receiving both encouragement and training in their inquiry. I have the evidence before me.

Each year for the past five years all freshmen entering Harvard 49 and Radcliffe have been asked in freshman week to "grade" two essays answering an examination question in History. They are then asked to give their reasons for their grades. One essay, filled with dates, is 99% cow. The other, with hardly a date in it, is a good essay, easily mistaken for bull. The "official" grades of these essays are, for the first (alas!) C "because he has worked so hard," and for the second (soundly, I think) B. Each year a larger majority of freshmen evaluate these essays as would the majority of the faculty, and for the faculty's reasons, and each year a smaller minority give the higher honor to the essay offering data alone. Most interesting, a larger number of students each year, while not overrating the second essay, award the first the straight E appropriate to it in a college of liberal arts.

For us who must grade such students in a university, these de- 50 velopments imply a new urgency, did we not feel it already. Through our grades we describe for the students, in the showdown, what we believe about the nature of knowledge. The subtleties of bull are not peripheral to our academic concerns. That they penetrate to the center of our care is evident in our feelings when a student whose good work we have awarded a high grade reveals to us that he does not feel he deserves it. Whether he disqualifies himself because "there's too much bull in it," or worse because "I really don't think I've worked that hard," he presents a serious educational problem. Many students feel this sleaziness; only a few reveal it to us.

We can hardly allow a mistaken sense of fraudulence to under- 51 mine our students' achievements. We must lead students beyond their concept of bull so that they may honor relevancies that are really relevant. We can willingly acknowledge that, in lieu of the date 1492, a consideration of calendars and of the word "discovered," may well be offered with intent to deceive. We must insist that this does not make such considerations intrinsically immoral, and that, contrariwise, the date 1492 may be no substitute for them. Most of all, we must convey the impression that we grade understanding qua understanding. To be convincing, I suppose we must concede to ourselves in advance that a bright student's understanding is understanding even if he achieved it by osmosis rather than by hard work in our course.

These are delicate matters. As for cow, its complexities are not 52 what need concern us. Unlike good bull, it does not represent partial knowledge at all. It belongs to a different theory of knowledge entirely. In our theories of knowledge it represents total ignorance, or worse yet, a knowledge downright inimical to understanding. I even go so far as to propose that we award no more C's for cow. To do so is rarely, I feel, the act of mercy it seems. Mercy lies in clarity.

The reader may be afflicted by a lingering curiosity about the fate 53 of Mr. Metzger. I hasten to reassure him. The Administrative Board of Harvard College, whatever its satanic reputation, is a benign body. Its members, to be sure, were on the spot. They delighted in Metzger's exploit, but they were responsible to the Faculty's rule. The hero stood in danger of probation. The debate was painful. Suddenly one member, of a refined legalistic sensibility, observed that the rule applied specifically to "examinations" and that the occasion had been simply an hour-test. Mr. Metzger was merely "admonished."

DAVID L. ROSENHAN

On Being Sane in Insane Places

David L. Rosenhan (1929–   ) took a Ph.D. in psychology from Columbia University in 1958 and began an academic career that has focused partly on the problem of establishing truth in areas where much depends on subjective impressions. During the 1960s he was an associate professor at Princeton and a consultant with the Educational Testing Service, which is in the business of quantifying the elusive quality of "scholastic aptitude." In 1970, Rosenhan became a professor at Stanford University, where he has increasingly turned his attention to the psychology of law— both the psychology of law breakers and the psychology of the jurors who must establish guilt or innocence. Rosenhan is the author of textbooks on abnormal psychology and social psychology. "On Being Sane in Insane Places" appeared in *Science* on January 19, 1973. It explores the difficult question of how a psychiatrist can distinguish between the sane and the insane and raises disturbing questions about the effects of psychological labels.

If sanity and insanity exist, how shall we know them?   1

The question is neither capricious nor itself insane. However   2
much we may be personally convinced that we can tell the normal from the abnormal, the evidence is simply not compelling. It is commonplace, for example, to read about murder trials wherein eminent psychiatrists for the defense are contradicted by equally eminent psychiatrists for the prosecution on the matter of the defendant's sanity. More generally, there are a great deal of conflicting data on the reliability, utility, and meaning of such terms as "sanity," "insanity," "mental illness," and "schizophrenia." Finally, as early as 1934, Benedict suggested that normality and abnormality are not universal. What is viewed as normal in one culture may be seen as quite aberrant in another. Thus, notions of normality and abnormality may not be quite as accurate as people believe they are.

To raise questions regarding normality and abnormality is in no   3
way to question the fact that some behaviors are deviant or odd. Murder is deviant. So, too, are hallucinations. Nor does raising such questions deny the existence of the personal anguish that is often associated with "mental illness." Anxiety and depression exist. Psychological suffering exists. But normality and abnormality, sanity and insanity, and the diagnoses that flow from them may be less substantive than many believe them to be.

At its heart, the question of whether the sane can be distin-   4
guished from the insane (and whether degrees of insanity can be distinguished from each other) is a simple matter: do the salient characteristics that lead to diagnoses reside in the patients themselves or in the environments and contexts in which observers find them? From Bleuler,[1] through Kretschmer,[2] through the formulators of the recently revised *Diagnostic and Statistical Manual* of the American Psychiatric Association, the belief has been strong that patients present symptoms, that those symptoms can be

---

1. Eugen Bleuler (1857–1939), the Swiss psychologist who introduced the term "schizophrenia" and identified various schizophrenic types.
2. Ernst Kretschmer (1888–1964), the German psychiatrist who correlated body build with mental constitution.

categorized, and, implicitly, that the sane are distinguishable from
the insane. More recently, however, this belief has been questioned. Based in part on theoretical and anthropological considerations, but also on philosophical, legal, and therapeutic ones, the
view has grown that psychological categorization of mental illness
is useless at best and downright harmful, misleading, and pejorative at worst. Psychiatric diagnoses, in this view, are in the minds of
the observers and are not valid summaries of characteristics displayed by the observed.

Gains can be made in deciding which of these is more nearly   5
accurate by getting normal people (that is, people who do not
have, and have never suffered, symptoms of serious psychiatric
disorders) admitted to psychiatric hospitals and then determining
whether they were discovered to be sane and, if so, how. If the
sanity of such pseudopatients were always detected, there would
be prima facie evidence that a sane individual can be distinguished
from the insane context in which he is found. Normality (and
presumably abnormality) is distinct enough that it can be recognized wherever it occurs, for it is carried within the person. If, on
the other hand, the sanity of the pseudopatients were never discovered, serious difficulties would arise for those who support traditional modes of psychiatric diagnosis. Given that the hospital staff
was not incompetent, that the pseudopatient had been behaving as
sanely as he had been outside of the hospital, and that it had never
been previously suggested that he belonged in a psychiatric hospital, such an unlikely outcome would support the view that psychiatric diagnosis betrays little about the patient but much about the
environment in which an observer finds him.

This article describes such an experiment. Eight sane people   6
gained secret admission to 12 different hospitals. Their diagnostic
experiences constitute the data of the first part of this article; the
remainder is devoted to a description of their experiences in psychiatric institutions. Too few psychiatrists and psychologists, even
those who have worked in such hospitals, know what the experience is like. They rarely talk about it with former patients, perhaps
because they distrust information coming from the previously insane. Those who have worked in psychiatric hospitals are likely to
have adapted so thoroughly to the settings that they are insensitive
to the impact of that experience. And while there have been occasional reports of researchers who submitted themselves to psychiatric hospitalization, these researchers have commonly remained
in the hospitals for short periods of time, often with the knowledge
of the hospital staff. It is difficult to know the extent to which they
were treated like patients or like research colleagues. Nevertheless,

their reports about the inside of the psychiatric hospital have been valuable. This article extends those efforts.

PSEUDOPATIENTS AND THEIR SETTINGS

The eight pseudopatients were a varied group. One was a psychology graduate student in his 20's. The remaining seven were older and "established." Among them were three psychologists, a pediatrician, a psychiatrist, a painter, and a housewife. Three pseudopatients were women, five were men. All of them employed pseudonyms, lest their alleged diagnoses embarrass them later. Those who were in mental health professions alleged another occupation in order to avoid the special attentions that might be accorded by staff, as a matter of courtesy or caution, to ailing colleagues. With the exception of myself (I was the first pseudopatient and my presence was known to the hospital administrator and chief psychologist and, so far as I can tell, to them alone), the presence of pseudopatients and the nature of the research program was not known to the hospital staffs.

The settings were similarly varied. In order to generalize the findings, admission into a variety of hospitals was sought. The 12 hospitals in the sample were located in five different states on the East and West coasts. Some were old and shabby, some were quite new. Some were research-oriented, others not. Some had good staff-patient ratios, others were quite understaffed. Only one was a strictly private hospital. All of the others were supported by state or federal funds or, in one instance, by university funds.

After calling the hospital for an appointment, the pseudopatient arrived at the admissions office complaining that he had been hearing voices. Asked what the voices said, he replied that they were often unclear, but as far as he could tell they said "empty," "hollow," and "thud." The voices were unfamiliar and were of the same sex as the pseudopatient. The choice of these symptoms was occasioned by their apparent similarity to existential symptoms. Such symptoms are alleged to arise from painful concerns about the perceived meaninglessness of one's life. It is as if the hallucinating person were saying, "My life is empty and hollow." The choice of these symptoms was also determined by the *absence* of a single report of existential psychoses in the literature.

Beyond alleging the symptoms and falsifying name, vocation, and employment, no further alterations of person, history, or circumstances were made. The significant events of the pseudopatient's life history were presented as they had actually occurred. Relationships with parents and siblings, with spouse and children, with people at work and in school, consistent with the aforementioned exceptions, were described as they were or had been. Frustrations and upsets were described along with joys and satisfactions. These facts are important to remember. If anything, they strongly biased the subsequent results in favor of detecting sanity, since none of their histories or current behaviors were seriously pathological in any way.

Immediately upon admission to the psychiatric ward, the 11 pseudopatient ceased simulating *any* symptoms of abnormality. In some cases, there was a brief period of mild nervousness and anxiety, since none of the pseudopatients really believed that they would be admitted so easily. Indeed, their shared fear was that they would be immediately exposed as frauds and greatly embarrassed. Moreover, many of them had never visited a psychiatric ward, even those who had, nevertheless had some genuine fears about what might happen to them. Their nervousness, then, was quite appropriate to the novelty of the hospital setting, and it abated rapidly.

Apart from that short-lived nervousness, the pseudopatient be- 12 haved on the ward as he "normally" behaved. The pseudopatient spoke to patients and staff as he might ordinarily. Because there is uncommonly little to do on a psychiatric ward, he attempted to engage others in conversation. When asked by staff how he was feeling, he indicated that he was fine, that he no longer experienced symptoms. He responded to instructions from attendants, to calls for medication (which was not swallowed), and to dining-hall instructions. Beyond such activities as were available to him on the admissions ward, he spent his time writing down his observations about the ward, its patients, and the staff. Initially these notes were written "secretly," but as it soon became clear that no one much cared, they were subsequently written on standard tablets of paper in such public places as the dayroom. No secret was made of these activities.

The pseudopatient, very much as a true psychiatric patient, en- 13 tered a hospital with no foreknowledge of when he would be discharged. Each was told that he would have to get out by his own devices, essentially by convincing the staff that he was sane. The psychological stresses associated with hospitalization were considerable, and all but one of the pseudopatients desired to be discharged almost immediately after being admitted. They were, therefore, motivated not only to behave sanely, but to be paragons of cooperation. That their behavior was in no way disruptive is confirmed by nursing reports, which have been obtained on most of the patients. These reports uniformly indicate that the patients were "friendly," "cooperative," and "exhibited no abnormal indications."

THE NORMAL ARE NOT DETECTABLY SANE

Despite their public "show" of sanity, the pseudopatients were   14
never detected. Admitted, except in one case, with a diagnosis of
schizophrenia, each was discharged with a diagnosis of schizophrenia "in remission." The label "in remission" should in no way be
dismissed as a formality, for at no time during any hospitalization
had any question been raised about any pseudopatient's simulation. Nor are there any indications in the hospital records that the
pseudopatient's status was suspect. Rather, the evidence is strong
that, once labeled schizophrenic, the pseudopatient was stuck with
that label. If the pseudopatient was to be discharged, he must naturally be "in remission"; but he was not sane, nor, in the institution's view, had he ever been sane.

The uniform failure to recognize sanity cannot be attributed to   15
the quality of the hospitals, for although there were considerable
variations among them, several are considered excellent. Nor can it
be alleged that there was simply not enough time to observe the
pseudopatients. Length of hospitalization ranged from 7 to 52 days,
with an average of 19 days. The pseudopatients were not, in fact,
carefully observed, but this failure clearly speaks more to traditions
within psychiatric hospitals than to lack of opportunity.

Finally, it cannot be said that the failure to recognize the pseudo-   16
patients' sanity was due to the fact that they were not behaving
sanely. While there was clearly some tension present in all of them,
their daily visitors could detect no serious behavioral consequences—nor, indeed, could other patients. It was quite common
for the patients to "detect" the pseudopatients' sanity. During the
first three hospitalizations, when accurate counts were kept, 35 of a
total of 118 patients on the admissions ward voiced their suspicions, some vigorously. "You're not crazy. You're a journalist, or a
professor [referring to the continual note-taking]. You're checking
up on the hospital." While most of the patients were reassured by
the pseudopatient's insistence that he had been sick before he came
in but was fine now, some continued to believe that the pseudopatient was sane throughout his hospitalization. The fact that the
patients often recognized normality when staff did not raises important questions.

Failure to detect sanity during the course of hospitalization may   17
be due to the fact that physicians operate with a strong bias toward
what statisticians call the type 2 error. This is to say that physicians
are more inclined to call a healthy person sick (a false positive, type
2) than a sick person healthy (a false negative, type 1). The reasons
for this are not hard to find: it is clearly more dangerous to misdiag-

nose illness than health. Better to err on the side of caution, to suspect illness even among the healthy.

But what holds for medicine does not hold equally well for psychiatry. Medical illnesses, while unfortunate, are not commonly pejorative. Psychiatric diagnoses, on the contrary, carry with them personal, legal, and social stigmas. It was therefore important to see whether the tendency toward diagnosing the sane insane could be reversed. The following experiment was arranged at a research and teaching hospital whose staff had heard these findings but doubted that such an error could occur in their hospital. The staff was informed that at some time during the following 3 months, one or more pseudopatients would attempt to be admitted into the psychiatric hospital. Each staff member was asked to rate each patient who presented himself at admissions or on the ward according to the likelihood that the patient was a pseudopatient. A 10-point scale was used, with a 1 and 2 reflecting high confidence that the patient was a pseudopatient. [18]

Judgments were obtained on 193 patients who were admitted for psychiatric treatment. All staff who had had sustained contact with or primary responsibility for the patient—attendants, nurses, psychiatrists, physicians, and psychologists—were asked to make judgments. Forty-one patients were alleged, with high confidence, to be pseudopatients by at least one member of the staff. Twenty-three were considered suspect by at least one psychiatrist. Nineteen were suspected by one psychiatrist *and* one other staff member. Actually, no genuine pseudopatient (at least from my group) presented himself during this period. [19]

The experiment is instructive. It indicates that the tendency to designate sane people as insane can be reversed when the stakes (in this case, prestige and diagnostic acumen) are high. But what can be said of the 19 people who were suspected of being "sane" by one psychiatrist and another staff member? Were these people truly "sane," or was it rather the case that in the course of avoiding the type 2 error the staff tended to make more errors of the first sort—calling the crazy "sane"? There is no way of knowing. But one thing is certain: any diagnostic process that lends itself so readily to massive errors of this sort cannot be a very reliable one. [20]

THE STICKINESS OF PSYCHODIAGNOSTIC LABELS

Beyond the tendency to call the healthy sick—a tendency that accounts better for diagnostic behavior on admission than it does for such behavior after a lengthy period of exposure—the data speak to the massive role of labeling in psychiatric assessment. Having once been labeled schizophrenic, there is nothing the [21] pseudopatient can do to overcome the tag. The tag profoundly colors others' perceptions of him and his behavior.

From one viewpoint, these data are hardly surprising, for it has long been known that elements are given meaning by the context in which they occur. Gestalt psychology made this point vigorously, and Asch (1946) demonstrated that there are "central" personality traits (such as "warm" versus "cold") which are so powerful that they markedly color the meaning of other information in forming an impression of a given personality. "Insane," "schizophrenic," "manic-depressive," and "crazy" are probably among the most powerful of such central traits. Once a person is designated abnormal, all of his other behaviors and characteristics are colored by that label. Indeed, that label is so powerful that many of the pseudopatients' normal behaviors were overlooked entirely or profoundly misinterpreted. Some examples may clarify this issue. 22

Earlier I indicated that there were no changes in the pseudopatient's personal history and current status beyond those of name, employment, and, where necessary, vocation. Otherwise, a veridical description of personal history and circumstances was offered. Those circumstances were not psychotic. How were they made consonant with the diagnosis of psychosis? Or were those diagnoses modified in such a way as to bring them into accord with the circumstances of the pseudopatient's life, as described by him? 23

As far as I can determine, diagnoses were in no way affected by the relative health of the circumstances of a pseudopatient's life. Rather, the reverse occurred: the perception of his circumstances was shaped entirely by the diagnosis. A clear example of such translation is found in the case of a pseudopatient who had had a close relationship with his mother but was rather remote from his father during his early childhood. During adolescence and beyond, however, his father became a close friend, while his relationship with his mother cooled. His present relationship with his wife was characteristically close and warm. Apart from occasional angry exchanges, friction was minimal. The children had rarely been spanked. Surely there is nothing especially pathological about such a history. Indeed, many readers may see a similar pattern in their own experiences, with no markedly deleterious consequences. Observe, however, how such a history was translated in the psychopathological context, this from the case summary prepared after the patient was discharged. 24

> This white 39-year-old male . . . manifests a long history of considerable ambivalence in close relationships, which begins in early childhood. A warm relationship with his mother cools during his

adolescence. A distant relationship to his father is described as becoming very intense. Affective stability is absent. His attempts to control emotionality with his wife and children are punctuated by angry outbursts and, in the case of the children, spankings. And while he says that he has several good friends, one senses considerable ambivalence embedded in those relationships also. . . .

The facts of the case were unintentionally distorted by the staff to ²⁵ achieve consistency with a popular theory of the dynamics of a schizophrenic reaction. Nothing of an ambivalent nature had been described in relations with parents, spouse, or friends. To the extent that ambivalence could be inferred, it was probably not greater than is found in all human relationships. It is true the pseudopatient's relationships with his parents changed over time, but in the ordinary context that would hardly be remarkable—indeed, it might very well be expected. Clearly, the meaning ascribed to his verbalizations (that is, ambivalence, affective instability) was determined by the diagnosis: schizophrenia. An entirely different meaning would have been ascribed if it were known that the man was "normal."

All pseudopatients took extensive notes publicly. Under ordi- ²⁶ nary circumstances, such behavior would have raised questions in the minds of observers, as, in fact, it did among patients. Indeed, it seemed so certain that the notes would elicit suspicion that elaborate precautions were taken to remove them from the ward each day. But the precautions proved needless. The closest any staff member came to questioning these notes occurred when one pseudopatient asked his physician what kind of medication he was receiving and began to write down the response. "You needn't write it," he was told gently. "If you have trouble remembering, just ask me again."

If no questions were asked of the pseudopatients, how was their ²⁷ writing interpreted? Nursing records for three patients indicate that the writing was seen as an aspect of their pathological behavior. "Patient engages in writing behavior" was the daily nursing comment on one of the pseudopatients who was never questioned about his writing. Given that the patient is in the hospital, he must be psychologically disturbed. And given that he is disturbed, continuous writing must be a behavioral manifestation of that disturbance, perhaps a subset of the compulsive behaviors that are sometimes correlated with schizophrenia.

One tacit characteristic of psychiatric diagnosis is that it locates ²⁸ the sources of aberration within the individual and only rarely within the complex of stimuli that surrounds him. Consequently, behaviors that are stimulated by the environment are commonly misattributed to the patient's disorder. For example, one kindly nurse found a pseudopatient pacing the long hospital corridors. "Nervous, Mr. X?" she asked. "No, bored," he said.

The notes kept by pseudopatients are full of patient behaviors   29 that were misinterpreted by well-intentioned staff. Often enough, a patient would go "berserk" because he had, wittingly or unwittingly, been mistreated by, say, an attendant. A nurse coming upon the scene would rarely inquire even cursorily into the environmental stimuli of the patient's behavior. Rather, she assumed that his upset derived from his pathology, not from his present interactions with other staff members. Occasionally, the staff might assume that the patient's family (especially when they had recently visited) or other patients had stimulated the outburst. But never were the staff found to assume that one of themselves or the structure of the hospital had anything to do with a patient's behavior. One psychiatrist pointed to a group of patients who were sitting outside the cafeteria entrance half an hour before lunchtime. To a group of young residents he indicated that such behavior was characteristic of the oral-acquisitive nature of the syndrome. It seemed not to occur to him that there were very few things to anticipate in a psychiatric hospital besides eating.

A psychiatric label has a life and an influence of its own. Once   30 the impression has been formed that the patient is schizophrenic, the expectation is that he will continue to be schizophrenic. When a sufficient amount of time has passed, during which the patient has done nothing bizarre, he is considered to be in remission and available for discharge. But the label endures beyond discharge, with the unconfirmed expectation that he will behave as a schizophrenic again. Such labels, conferred by mental health professionals, are as influential on the patient as they are on his relatives and friends, and it should not surprise anyone that the diagnosis acts on all of them as a self-fulfilling prophecy. Eventually, the patient himself accepts the diagnosis, with all of its surplus meanings and expectations, and behaves accordingly.

The inferences to be made from these matters are quite simple.   31 Much as Zigler and Phillips have demonstrated that there is enormous overlap in the symptoms presented by patients who have been variously diagnosed (1961), so there is enormous overlap in the behaviors of the sane and the insane. The sane are not "sane" all of the time. We lose our tempers "for no good reason." We are occasionally depressed or anxious, again for no good reason. And we may find it difficult to get along with one or another person— again for no reason that we can specify. Similarly, the insane are not always insane. Indeed, it was the impression of the pseudopatients while living with them that they were sane for long periods of time—that the bizarre behaviors upon which their diagnoses were allegedly predicated constituted only a small fraction of their total behavior. If it makes no sense to label ourselves permanently depressed on the basis of an occasional depression, then it takes better evidence than is presently available to label all patients insane or schizophrenic on the basis of bizarre behaviors or cognitions. It seems more useful, as Mischel (1968) has pointed out, to limit our discussions to *behaviors*, the stimuli that provoke them, and their correlates.

It is not known why powerful impressions of personality traits, 32 such as "crazy" or "insane," arise. Conceivably, when the origins of and stimuli that give rise to a behavior are remote or unknown, or when the behavior strikes us as immutable, trait labels regarding the *behaver* arise. When, on the other hand, the origins and stimuli are known and available, discourse is limited to the behavior itself. Thus, I may hallucinate because I am sleeping, or I may hallucinate because I have ingested a peculiar drug. These are termed sleep-induced hallucinations, or dreams, and drug-induced hallucinations, respectively. But when the stimuli to my hallucinations are unknown, that is called craziness, or schizophrenia—as if that inference were somehow as illuminating as the others.

THE EXPERIENCE OF PSYCHIATRIC HOSPITALIZATION

The term "mental illness" is of recent origin. It was coined by 33 people who were humane in their inclinations and who wanted very much to raise the station of (and the public's sympathies toward) the psychologically disturbed from that of witches and "crazies" to one that was akin to the physically ill. And they were at least partially successful, for the treatment of the mentally ill *has* improved considerably over the years. But while treatment has improved, it is doubtful that people really regard the mentally ill in the same way that they view the physically ill. A broken leg is something one recovers from, but mental illness allegedly endures forever. A broken leg does not threaten the observer, but a crazy schizophrenic? There is by now a host of evidence that attitudes toward the mentally ill are characterized by fear, hostility, aloofness, suspicion, and dread. The mentally ill are society's lepers.

That such attitudes infect the general population is perhaps not 34 surprising, only upsetting. But that they affect the professionals— attendants, nurses, physicians, psychologists, and social workers— who treat and deal with the mentally ill is more disconcerting, both because such attitudes are self-evidently pernicious and because they are unwitting. Most mental health professionals would insist that they are sympathetic toward the mentally ill, that they are neither avoidant nor hostile. But it is more likely that an exquisite ambivalence characterizes their relations with psychiatric patients, such that their avowed impulses are only part of their entire attitude. Negative attitudes are there too and can easily be detected. Such attitudes should not surprise us. They are the natural offspring of the labels patients wear and the places in which they are found.

Consider the structure of the typical psychiatric hospital. Staff   35 and patients are strictly segregated. Staff have their own living space, including their dining facilities, bathrooms, and assembly places. The glassed quarters that contain the professional staff, which the pseudopatients came to call "the cage," sit out on every dayroom. The staff emerge primarily for caretaking purposes—to give medication, to conduct a therapy or group meeting, to instruct or reprimand a patient. Otherwise, staff keep to themselves, almost as if the disorder that afflicts their charges is somehow catching.

So much is patient-staff segregation the rule that, for four public   36 hospitals in which an attempt was made to measure the degree to which staff and patients mingle, it was necessary to use "time out of the staff cage" as the operational measure. While it was not the case that all time spent out of the cage was spent mingling with patients (attendants, for example, would occasionally emerge to watch television in the dayroom), it was the only way in which one could gather reliable data on time for measuring.

The average amount of time spent by attendants outside of the   37 cage was 11.3 percent (range, 3 to 52 percent). This figure does not represent only time spent mingling with patients, but also includes time spent on such chores as folding laundry, supervising patients while they shave, directing ward clean-up, and sending patients to off-ward activities. It was the relatively rare attendant who spent time talking with patients or playing games with them. It proved impossible to obtain a "percent mingling time" for nurses, since the amount of time they spent out of the cage was too brief. Rather, we counted instances of emergence from the cage. On the average, daytime nurses emerged from the cage 11.5 times per shift, including instances when they left the ward entirely (range, 4 to 39 times). Late afternoon and night nurses were even less available, emerging on the average 9.4 times per shift (range, 4 to 41 times). Data on early morning nurses, who arrived usually after midnight and departed at 8 A.M., are not available because patients were asleep during most of this period.

Physicians, especially psychiatrists, were even less available.   38 They were rarely seen on the wards. Quite commonly, they would be seen only when they arrived and departed, with the remaining time being spent in their offices or in the cage. On the average, physicians emerged on the ward 6.7 times per day (range, 1 to 17 times). It proved difficult to make an accurate estimate in this regard, since physicians often maintained hours that allowed them to come and go at different times.

The hierarchical organization of the psychiatric hospital has been   39 commented on before (Stanton & Schwartz, 1954), but the latent meaning of that kind of organization is worth noting again. Those with the most power have least to do with patients, and those with the least power are most involved with them. Recall, however, that the acquisition of role-appropriate behaviors occurs mainly through the observation of others, with the most powerful having the most influence. Consequently, it is understandable that attendants not only spend more time with patients than do any other members of the staff—that is required by their station in the hierarchy—but also, insofar as they learn from their superiors' behavior, spend as little time with patients as they can. Attendants are seen mainly in the cage, which is where the models, the action, and the power are.

I turn now to a different set of studies, these dealing with staff   40 response to patient-initiated contact. It has long been known that the amount of time a person spends with you can be an index of your significance to him. If he initiates and maintains eye contact, there is reason to believe that he is considering your requests and needs. If he pauses to chat or actually stops and talks, there is added reason to infer that he is individuating you. In four hospitals, the pseudopatient approached the staff member with a request which took the following form: "Pardon me, Mr. [or Dr. or Mrs.] X, could you tell me when I will be eligible for grounds privileges?" (or ". . . when I will be presented at the staff meeting?" or ". . . when I am likely to be discharged?"). While the content of the question varied according to the appropriateness of the target and the pseudopatient's (apparent) current needs the form was always a courteous and relevant request for information. Care was taken never to approach a particular member of the staff more than once a day, lest the staff member become suspicious or irritated. In examining these data, remember that the behavior of the pseudopatients was neither bizarre nor disruptive. One could indeed engage in good conversation with them.

The data for these experiments are shown in Table 1, separately   41 for physicians (column 1) and for nurses and attendants (column 2). Minor differences between these four institutions were overwhelmed by the degree to which staff avoided continuing contacts

Table 1. Self-initiated contact by pseudopatients with psychiatrists and nurses and attendants, compared to contact with other groups.

	Psychiatric hospitals	
Contact	(1) Psychiatrists	(2) Nurses and attendants
Responses		
Moves on, head averted (%)	71	88
Makes eye contact (%)	23	10
Pauses and chats (%)	2	2
Stops and talks (%)	4	0.5
Mean number of questions answered (out of 6)	*	*
Respondents (No.)	13	47
Attempts (No.)	185	1283

*Not applicable.

that patients had initiated. By far, their most common response consisted of either a brief response to the question, offered while they were "on the move" and with head averted, or no response at all.

The encounter frequently took the following bizarre form: (pseudopatient) "Pardon me, Dr. X. Could you tell me when I am eligible for grounds privileges?" (physician) "Good morning, Dave. How are you today?" (Moves off without waiting for a response.)   42

It is instructive to compare these data with data recently obtained at Stanford University. It has been alleged that large and eminent universities are characterized by faculty who are so busy that they have no time for students. For this comparison, a young lady approached individual faculty members who seemed to be walking purposefully to some meeting or teaching engagement and asked them the following six questions.   43

1) "Pardon me, could you direct me to Encina Hall?" (at the medical school: ". . . to the Clinical Research Center?").   44

2) "Do you know where Fish Annex is?" (there is no Fish Annex at Stanford).   45

3) "Do you teach here?"   46

Table 1 (continued)

University campus (nonmedical)	University medical center		
	Physicians		
(3) Faculty	(4) "Looking for a psychiatrist"	(5) "Looking for an internist"	(6) No additional comment
0	0	0	0
0	11	0	0
0	11	0	10
100	78	100	90
6	3.8	4.8	4.5
14	18	15	10
14	18	15	10

4) "How does one apply for admission to the college?" (at the
medical school: ". . . to the medical school?").

5) "Is it difficult to get in?"

6) "Is there financial aid?"

Without exception, as can be seen in Table 1 (column 3), all of
the questions were answered. No matter how rushed they were, all
respondents not only maintained eye contact, but stopped to talk.
Indeed, many of the respondents went out of their way to direct or
take the questioner to the office she was seeking, to try to locate
"Fish Annex," or to discuss with her the possibilities of being
admitted to the university.

Similar data, also shown in Table 1 (columns 4, 5, and 6), were
obtained in the hospital. Here too, the young lady came prepared
with six questions. After the first question, however, she remarked
to 18 of her respondents (column 4), "I'm looking for a psychiatrist," and to 15 others (column 5), "I'm looking for an internist."
Ten other respondents received no inserted comment (column 6).
The general degree of cooperative responses is considerably higher
for these university groups than it was for pseudopatients in psychiatric hospitals. Even so, differences are apparent within the
medical school setting. Once having indicated that she was looking

for a psychiatrist, the degree of cooperation elicited was less than when she sought an internist.

POWERLESSNESS AND DEPERSONALIZATION

Eye contact and verbal contact reflect concern and individua-   52
tion; their absence, avoidance, and depersonalization. The data I have presented do not do justice to the rich daily encounters that grew up around matters of depersonalization and avoidance. I have records of patients who were beaten by staff for the sin of having initiated verbal contact. During my own experience, for example, one patient was beaten in the presence of other patients for having approached an attendant and told him, "I like you." Occasionally, punishment meted out to patients for misdemeanors seemed so excessive that it could not be justified by the most radical interpretations of psychiatric canon. Nevertheless, they appeared to go unquestioned. Tempers were often short. A patient who had not heard a call for medication would be roundly excoriated, and the morning attendants would often wake patients with, "Come on, you m-----f------s, out of bed!"

Neither anecdotal nor "hard" data can convey the overwhelm-   53
ing sense of powerlessness which invades the individual as he is continually exposed to the depersonalization of the psychiatric hospital. It hardly matters *which* psychiatric hospital—the excellent public ones and the very plush private hospital were better than the rural and shabby ones in this regard, but, again, the features that psychiatric hospitals had in common overwhelmed by far their apparent differences.

Powerlessness was evident everywhere. The patient is deprived   54
of many of his legal rights by dint of his psychiatric commitment (Wexler & Scoville, 1971). He is shorn of credibility by virtue of his psychiatric label. His freedom of movement is restricted. He cannot initiate contact with the staff, but may only respond to such over-tures as they make. Personal privacy is minimal. Patient quarters and possessions can be entered and examined by any staff member, for whatever reason. His personal history and anguish is available to any staff member (often including the "grey lady" and "candy striper" volunteer) who chooses to read his folder, regardless of their therapeutic relationship to him. His personal hygiene and waste evacuation are often monitored. The water closets may have no doors.

At times, depersonalization reached such proportions that   55
pseudopatients had the sense that they were invisible, or at least unworthy of account. Upon being admitted, I and other pseudopa-

tients took the initial physical examinations in a semipublic room, where staff members went about their own business as if we were not there.

On the ward, attendants delivered verbal and occasionally serious physical abuse to patients in the presence of other observing patients, some of whom (the pseudopatients) were writing it all down. Abusive behavior, on the other hand, terminated quite abruptly when other staff members were known to be coming. Staff are credible witnesses. Patients are not. [56]

A nurse unbuttoned her uniform to adjust her brassiere in the presence of an entire ward of viewing men. One did not have the sense that she was being seductive. Rather, she didn't notice us. A group of staff persons might point to a patient in the dayroom and discuss him animatedly, as if he were not there. [57]

One illuminating instance of depersonalization and invisibility occurred with regard to medications. All told, the pseudopatients were administered nearly 2100 pills, including Elavil, Stelazine, Compazine, and Thorazine, to name but a few. (That such a variety of medications should have been administered to patients presenting identical symptoms is itself worthy of note.) Only two were swallowed. The rest were either pocketed or deposited in the toilet. The pseudopatients were not alone in this. Although I have no precise records on how many patients rejected their medications, the pseudopatients frequently found the medications of other patients in the toilet before they deposited their own. As long as they were cooperative, their behavior and the pseudopatients' own in this matter, as in other important matters, went unnoticed throughout. [58]

Reactions to such depersonalization among pseudopatients were intense. Although they had come to the hospital as participant observers and were fully aware that they did not "belong," they nevertheless found themselves caught up in and fighting the process of depersonalization. Some examples: a graduate student in psychology asked his wife to bring his textbooks to the hospital so he could "catch up on his homework"—this despite the elaborate precautions taken to conceal his professional association. The same student, who had trained for quite some time to get into the hospital, and who had looked forward to the experience, "remembered" some drag races that he had wanted to see on the weekend and insisted that he be discharged by that time. Another pseudopatient attempted a romance with a nurse. Subsequently, he informed the staff that he was applying for admission to graduate school in psychology and was very likely to be admitted, since a graduate [59] professor was one of his regular hospital visitors. The same person began to engage in psychotherapy with other patients—all of this as a way of becoming a person in an impersonal environment.

THE SOURCES OF DEPERSONALIZATION

What are the origins of depersonalization? I have already men-   60
tioned two. First are attitudes held by all of us toward the mentally ill—including those who treat them—attitudes characterized by fear, distrust, and horrible expectations on the one hand, and benevolent intentions on the other. Our ambivalence leads, in this instance as in others, to avoidance.

Second, and not entirely separate, the hierarchical structure of   61
the psychiatric hospital facilitates depersonalization. Those who are at the top have least to do with patients, and their behavior inspires the rest of the staff. Average daily contact with psychiatrists, psychologists, residents, and physicians combined ranged from 3.9 to 25.1 minutes, with an overall mean of 6.8 (six pseudopatients over a total of 129 days of hospitalization). Included in this average are time spent in the admissions interview, ward meetings in the presence of a senior staff member, group and individual psychotherapy contacts, case presentation conferences, and discharge meetings. Clearly, patients do not spend much time in interpersonal contact with doctoral staff. And doctoral staff serve as models for nurses and attendants.

There are probably other sources. Psychiatric installations are   62
presently in serious financial straits. Staff shortages are pervasive, staff time at a premium. Something has to give, and that something is patient contact. Yet, while financial stresses are realities, too much can be made of them. I have the impression that the psychological forces that result in depersonalization are much stronger than the fiscal ones and that the addition of more staff would not correspondingly improve patient care in this regard. The incidence of staff meetings and the enormous amount of record-keeping on patients, for example, have not been as substantially reduced as has patient contact. Priorities exist, even during hard times. Patient contact is not a significant priority in the traditional psychiatric hospital, and fiscal pressures do not account for this. Avoidance and depersonalization may.

Heavy reliance upon psychotropic medication tacitly contributes   63
to depersonalization by convincing staff that treatment is indeed being conducted and that further patient contact may not be necessary. Even here, however, caution needs to be exercised in understanding the role of psychotropic drugs. If patients were powerful rather than powerless, if they were viewed as interesting individ-

uals rather than diagnostic entities, if they were socially significant rather than social lepers, if their anguish truly and wholly compelled our sympathies and concerns, would we not *seek* contact with them, despite the availability of medications? Perhaps for the pleasure of it all?

THE CONSEQUENCES OF LABELING AND DEPERSONALIZATION

Whenever the ratio of what is known to what needs to be known approaches zero, we tend to invent "knowledge" and assume that we understand more than we actually do. We seem unable to acknowledge that we simply don't know. The needs for diagnosis and remediation of behavioral and emotional problems are enormous. But rather than acknowledge that we are just embarking on understanding, we continue to label patients "schizophrenic," "manic-depressive," and "insane," as if in those words we had captured the essence of understanding. The facts of the matter are that we have known for a long time that diagnoses are often not useful or reliable, but we have nevertheless continued to use them. We now know that we cannot distinguish insanity from sanity. It is depressing to consider how that information will be used. 64

Not merely depressing, but frightening. How many people, one wonders, are sane but not recognized as such in our psychiatric institutions? How many have been needlessly stripped of their privileges of citizenship, from the right to vote and drive to that of handling their own accounts? How many have feigned insanity in order to avoid the criminal consequences of their behavior, and, conversely, how many would rather stand trial than live interminably in a psychiatric hospital—but are wrongly thought to be mentally ill? How many have been stigmatized by well-intentioned, but nevertheless erroneous, diagnoses? On the last point, recall again that a "type 2 error" in psychiatric diagnosis does not have the same consequences it does in medical diagnosis. A diagnosis of cancer that has been found to be in error is cause for celebration. But psychiatric diagnoses are rarely found to be in error. The label sticks, a mark of inadequacy forever. 65

Finally, how many patients might be "sane" outside the psychiatric hospital but seem insane in it—not because craziness resides in them, as it were, but because they are responding to a bizarre setting, one that may be unique to institutions which harbor neither people? Goffman (1961) calls the process of socialization to such institutions "mortification"—an apt metaphor that includes the processes of depersonalization that have been described here. And while it is impossible to know whether the pseudopatients' 66

responses to these processes are characteristic of all inmates—they
were, after all, not real patients—it is difficult to believe that these
processes of socialization to a psychiatric hospital provide useful
attitudes or habits of response for living in the "real world."

SUMMARY AND CONCLUSIONS

It is clear that we cannot distinguish the sane from the insane   67
in psychiatric hospitals. The hospital itself imposes a special environment in which the meanings of behavior can easily be
misunderstood. The consequences to patients hospitalized in
such an environment—the powerlessness, depersonalization,
segregation, mortification, and self-labeling—seem undoubtedly
counter-therapeutic.

I do not, even now, understand this problem well enough to   68
perceive solutions. But two matters seem to have some promise.
The first concerns the proliferation of community mental health
facilities, of crisis intervention centers, of the human potential
movement, and of behavior therapies that, for all of their own
problems, tend to avoid psychiatric labels, to focus on specific problems and behaviors, and to retain the individual in a relatively non-
pejorative environment. Clearly, to the extent that we refrain from
sending the distressed to insane places, our impressions of them are
less likely to be distorted. (The risk of distorted perceptions, it
seems to me, is always present, since we are much more sensitive
to an individual's behaviors and verbalizations than we are to the
subtle contextual stimuli that often promote them. At issue here is
a matter of magnitude. And, as I have shown, the magnitude of
distortion is exceedingly high in the extreme context that is a psychiatric hospital.)

The second matter that might prove promising speaks to the   69
need to increase the sensitivity of mental health workers and researchers to the *Catch 22* position of psychiatric patients. Simply
reading materials in this area will be of help to some such workers
and researchers. For others, directly experiencing the impact of
psychiatric hospitalization will be of enormous use. Clearly, further
research into the social psychology of such total institutions will
both facilitate treatment and deepen understanding.

I and the other pseudopatients in the psychiatric setting had   70
distinctly negative reactions. We do not pretend to describe the
subjective experiences of true patients. Theirs may be different from
ours, particularly with the passage of time and the necessary process of adaptation to one's environment. But we can and do speak
to the relatively more objective indices of treatment within the
hospital. It could be a mistake, and a very unfortunate one, to

consider that what happened to us derived from malice or stupidity on the part of the staff. Quite the contrary, our overwhelming impression of them was of people who really cared, who were committed, and who were uncommonly intelligent. Where they failed, as they sometimes did painfully, it would be more accurate to attribute those failures to the environment in which they, too, found themselves than to personal callousness. Their perceptions and behavior were controlled by the situation, rather than being motivated by a malicious disposition. In a more benign environment, one that was less attached to global diagnosis, their behaviors and judgments might have been more benign and effective.

REFERENCES[3]

Asch, S. E. (1946). Forming impressions of personality. *Journal of Abnormal and Social Psychology*, **41**, 258–90.

Benedict, R. (1934). Anthropology and the abnormal. *Journal of General Psychology*, **10**, 59–79.

Goffman, E. (1961). *Asylums.* Garden City, N.Y.: Doubleday.

Mischel, W. (1968). *Personality and Assessment.* New York: Wiley.

Stanton, A. H., & Schwartz, M. S. (1954). *The mental hospital: a study of institutional participation in psychiatric illness and treatment.* New York: Basic.

Wexler, D. B., & Scoville, S. E. (1971). The administration of psychiatric justice. *Arizona Law Review*, **13**, 1–259.

Zigler E., & Phillips, L. (1961). Psychiatric diagnosis and symptomology. *Journal of Abnormal and Social Psychology*, **63**, 69–85.

ADRIENNE RICH

Claiming an Education

Adrienne Rich (1929–   ) is one of the foremost poets of our time and one who has changed most over the course of her poetic career. Her first volume of poetry, *A Change of World* (1951), which won the Yale Series of Younger Poets award, was filled with formal, cautious verse that allowed her to handle her emotions, as she later said, with asbestos gloves. Thirteen years later her ninth volume, *Diving into the Wreck* (1973), won the National

3. Rosenhan's original list of references and notes, compiled for a scholarly publication, was much longer than this. We are reprinting the key references only.

Book Award and contributed to a storm of controversy surrounding the author, who had become one of America's most
influential and outspoken feminists. It is typical of Rich that she
refused to accept the award as an individual, but accepted it on
behalf of women everywhere and contributed the stipend to
charity. Rich continues to publish, lecture, and teach very actively. Her recent volumes include *Your Native Land, Your Life*
(1986) and *Blood, Bread, and Poetry: Selected Prose 1979–1986*
(1986). "Claiming an Education" was originally a speech delivered to the students of Douglass College, Rutgers University, in
1977.

For this convocation, I planned to separate my remarks into two   1
parts: some thoughts about you, the women students here, and
some thoughts about us who teach in a women's college. But
ultimately, those two parts are indivisible. If university education
means anything beyond the processing of human beings into expected roles, through credit hours, tests, and grades (and I believe
that in a women's college especially it *might* mean much more), it
implies an ethical and intellectual contract between teacher and
student. This contract must remain intuitive, dynamic, unwritten;
but we must turn to it again and again if learning is to be reclaimed
from the depersonalizing and cheapening pressures of the present-
day academic scene.

The first thing I want to say to you who are students, is that you   2
cannot afford to think of being here to *receive* an education; you
will do much better to think of yourselves as being here to *claim*
one. One of the dictionary definitions of the verb "to claim" is: *to
take as the rightful owner; to assert in the face of possible contradiction.*
"To receive" is *to come into possession of; to act as receptacle or container
for; to accept as authoritative or true.* The difference is that between
acting and being acted-upon, and for women it can literally mean
the difference between life and death.

One of the devastating weaknesses of university learning, of the   3
store of knowledge and opinion that has been handed down
through academic training, has been its almost total erasure of
women's experience and thought from the curriculum, and its exclusion of women as members of the academic community. Today,
with increasing numbers of women students in nearly every
branch of higher learning, we still see very few women in the upper
levels of faculty and administration in most institutions. Douglass
College itself is a women's college in a university administered
overwhelmingly by men, who in turn are answerable to the state
legislature, again composed predominantly of men. But the most

significant fact for you is that what you learn here, the very texts you read, the lectures you hear, the way your studies are divided into categories and fragmented one from the other—all this reflects, to a very large degree, neither objective reality, nor an accurate picture of the past, nor a group of rigorously tested observations about human behavior. What you can learn here (and I mean not only at Douglass but any college in any university) is how *men* have perceived and organized their experience, their history, their ideas of social relationships, good and evil, sickness and health, etc. When you read or hear about "great issues," "major texts," "the mainstream of Western thought," you are hearing about what men, above all white men, in their male subjectivity, have decided is important.

Black and other minority peoples have for some time recognized   4 that their racial and ethnic experience was not accounted for in the studies broadly labeled human; and that even the sciences can be racist. For many reasons, it has been more difficult for women to comprehend our exclusion, and to realize that even the sciences can be sexist. For one thing, it is only within the last hundred years that higher education has grudgingly been opened up to women at all, even to white, middle-class women. And many of us have found ourselves poring eagerly over books with titles like: *The Descent of Man; Man and His Symbols; Irrational Man; The Phenomenon of Man; The Future of Man; Man and the Machine; From Man to Man; May Man Prevail?; Man, Science and Society;* or *One-Dimensional Man*—books pretending to describe a "human" reality that does not include over one-half the human species.

Less than a decade ago, with the rebirth of a feminist movement   5 in this country, women students and teachers in a number of universities began to demand and set up women's studies courses—to *claim* a woman-directed education. And, despite the inevitable accusations of "unscholarly," "group therapy," "faddism," etc., despite backlash and budget cuts, women's studies are still growing, offering to more and more women a new intellectual grasp on their lives, new understanding of our history, a fresh vision of the human experience, and also a critical basis for evaluating what they hear and read in other courses, and in the society at large.

But my talk is not really about women's studies, much as I   6 believe in their scholarly, scientific, and human necessity. While I think that any Douglass student has everything to gain by investigating and enrolling in women's studies courses, I want to suggest that there is a more essential experience that you owe yourselves, one which courses in women's studies can greatly enrich, but which finally depends on you, in all your interactions with yourself and your world. This is the experience of *taking responsibility toward yourselves*. Our upbringing as women has so often told us that this should come second to our relationships and responsibilities to other people. We have been offered ethical models of the self-denying wife and mother; intellectual models of the brilliant but slapdash dilettante who never commits herself to anything the whole way, or the intelligent woman who denies her intelligence in order to seem more "feminine," or who sits in passive silence even when she disagrees inwardly with everything that is being said around her.

Responsibility to yourself means refusing to let others do your 7 thinking, talking, and naming for you; it means learning to respect and use your own brains and instincts; hence, grappling with hard work. It means that you do not treat your body as a commodity with which to purchase superficial intimacy or economic security; for our bodies and minds are inseparable in this life, and when we allow our bodies to be treated as objects, our minds are in mortal danger. It means insisting that those to whom you give your friendship and love are able to respect your mind. It means being able to say, with Charlotte Brontë's *Jane Eyre:* "I have an inward treasure born with me, which can keep me alive if all the extraneous delights should be withheld or offered only at a price I cannot afford to give."

Responsibility to yourself means that you don't fall for shallow 8 and easy solutions—predigested books and ideas, weekend encounters guaranteed to change your life, taking "gut" courses instead of ones you know will challenge you, bluffing at school and life instead of doing solid work, marrying early as an escape from real decisions, getting pregnant as an evasion of already existing problems. It means that you refuse to sell your talents and aspirations short, simply to avoid conflict and confrontation. And this, in turn, means resisting the forces in society which say that women should be nice, play safe, have low professional expectations, drown in love and forget about work, live through others, and stay in the places assigned to us. It means that we insist on a life of meaningful work, insist that work be as meaningful as love and friendship in our lives. It means, therefore, the courage to be "different"; not to be continuously available to others when we need time for ourselves and our work; to be able to demand of others—parents, friends, roommates, teachers, lovers, husbands, children—that they respect our sense of purpose and our integrity as persons. Women everywhere are finding the courage to do this, more and more, and we are finding that courage both in our study of women in the past who possessed it, and in each other as we look to other women for comradeship, community, and challenge. The difference between a life lived actively, and a life of passive drifting and dispersal of energies, is an immense difference. Once we begin to feel committed to our lives, responsible to ourselves, we can never again be satisfied with the old, passive way.

Now comes the second part of the contract. I believe that in a women's college you have the right to expect your faculty to take you seriously. The education of women has been a matter of debate for centuries, and old, negative attitudes about women's role, women's ability to think and take leadership, are still rife both in and outside the university. Many male professors (and I don't mean only at Douglass) still feel that teaching in a women's college is a second-rate career. Many tend to eroticize their women students—to treat them as sexual objects—instead of demanding the best of their minds. (At Yale a legal suit [*Alexander* v. *Yale*] has been brought against the university by a group of women students demanding a stated policy against sexual advances toward female students by male professors.) Many teachers, both men and women, trained in the male-centered tradition, are still handing the ideas and texts of that tradition on to students without teaching them to criticize its antiwoman attitudes, its omission of women as part of the species. Too often, all of us fail to teach the most important thing, which is that clear thinking, active discussion, and excellent writing are all necessary for intellectual freedom, and that these require *hard work*. Sometimes, perhaps in discouragement with a culture which is both antiintellectual and antiwoman, we may resign ourselves to low expectations for our students before we have given them half a chance to become more thoughtful, expressive human beings. We need to take to heart the words of Elizabeth Barrett Browning, a poet, a thinking woman, and a feminist, who wrote in 1845 of her impatience with studies which cultivate a "passive recipiency" in the mind, and asserted that "women want to be made to *think actively:* their apprehension is quicker than that of men, but their defect lies for the most part in the logical faculty and in the higher mental activities." Note that she implies a defect which can be remedied by intellectual training; *not* an inborn lack of ability.

I have said that the contract on the student's part involves that you demand to be taken seriously so that you can also go on taking yourself seriously. This means seeking out criticism, recognizing that the most affirming thing anyone can do for you is demand that you push yourself further, show you the range of what you *can* do. It means rejecting attitudes of "take-it-easy," "why-be-so-serious," "why-worry-you'll-probably-get-married-anyway." It means assuming your share of responsibility for what happens in the classroom, because that affects the quality of your daily life here. It means that the student sees herself engaged *with* her teachers in an active, ongoing struggle for a real education. But for her to do this, her teachers must be committed to the belief that women's minds and experience are intrinsically valuable and indispensable to any civilization worthy the name; that there is no more exhilarating and intellectually fertile place in the academic world today than a women's college—*if* both students and teachers in large enough numbers are trying to fulfill this contract. The contract is really a pledge of mutual seriousness about women, about language, ideas, methods, and values. It is our shared commitment toward a world in which the inborn potentialities of so many women's minds will no longer be wasted, raveled-away, paralyzed, or denied.

DAVID BRADLEY

The Faith

David Bradley (1950–   ), after graduating summa cum laude from the University of Pennsylvania, moved to London to study the United States from a British perspective. He received an M.A. from King's College in London in 1974 and is currently a professor of English at Temple University and a frequent contributor to such magazines as *Esquire, Signature, Savvy,* and the *New York Arts Journal.* Bradley is best known as the author of *The Chaneyville Incident* (1981), a meticulously researched documentary novel based on a discovery made by his mother, Harriet M. Bradley. While doing research for the 1970 celebration of the bicentennial of Bedford, Massachusetts, Mrs. Bradley learned that shortly before the Civil War thirteen slaves escaping via the Underground Railroad had been intercepted in nearby Chaneyville. The slaves had refused to return to their owners and had been murdered by their captors. Bradley struggled with this story for eleven years before publishing a book that hovers between history and fiction. "The Faith," first published in 1983, shows us some of the ways that Bradley connects fact and fiction, personal truth and historical truth.

One evening not long ago I found myself sitting on a stage in   1
front of a live audience, being asked questions about life and art. I was uncomfortable, as I always am in such circumstances. Still,

things were going pretty well on this occasion, until the interviewer noted that my father had been a minister, and asked what influence religion, the church, and the faith of my father, had had on my development as a writer. After a moment of confusion, I responded that since I had, at various times and with more than a modicum of accuracy, been labeled a heretic, a pagan, a heathen, and a moral degenerate, all things considered, the faith of my father had had very little to do with my writing. Which was, depending on how cynical you want to be, either a total lie or as close as I could get to the truthful answer—which would have been: "Practically everything."

The history of my relationship to religion cannot be stated so   2
simply as "My father was a minister." In fact, I am descended from a long line of ministers. The first was my great-grandfather, a freedman named Peter Bradley, who, in the early part of the nineteenth century, was licensed to preach by the African Methodist Episcopal Zion Church, one of two denominations formed at that time by blacks who were tired of the discrimination they were forced to endure in the regular Methodist Church. Peter's son, Daniel Francis, followed in his father's footsteps and then went a step further, becoming a presiding elder with administrative and spiritual responsibility over a number of churches in western Pennsylvania and Ohio. Daniel Francis's son, David, followed his father's footsteps, and then added a step of his own: he was elected a general officer of the denomination (a rank just below that of bishop), with the dual responsibility of traveling the country to run conferences and workshops in Christian education and of publishing the church's quasi-academic journal, the *A. M. E. Zion Quarterly Review*, tasks he performed without interruption for nearly thirty years. Since David was my father, it would seem reasonable to expect that I would carry on the family tradition. That I did not was a fact that was viewed with great relief by all those who knew me—including David senior. Nevertheless, my apostasy had its origins in the church. For because of my father's editorial functions, I grew up in a publishing house.

My earliest memories of excitement, bustle, and tension center   3
on the process of mailing the 1,400- or 1,500-copy press run of the *Quarterly Review*. The books came in sweet-smelling and crisp from the printer, were labeled, bundled, and shipped out again in big gray-green musty mailbags labeled with the names of far-off states, a process that was sheer heaven to a three- or four-year-old and sheer hell for everybody else, especially my mother, who did the bulk of the work and had to give up a chunk of her house to the process.

In fact, the work of publishing the *Review* took up the whole   4 house most of the time; it was just that work usually went on at a less frenetic rate. While my father was away, my mother, who was the subscription and shipping department, spent some time cleaning the lists (a constant task, since ministers, the main subscribers, were regularly being moved around) and typing names and addresses onto labels. When my father returned home, the tempo picked up. He spent a good bit of time in the study, writing to other ministers and prominent lay people to solicit articles and publishable sermons, and editing those that had already arrived. At that same time, he would be writing a bit himself, composing the two or three editorials that graced each issue.

The _Review_, while it was called a quarterly, was not published   5
every three months, but rather four times a year; my father took it to the printer when he was home long enough to get it ready, and when the printer had time to do the work. The date for that was sometimes fixed only a week or so in advance, and once it was set, the tempo became fairly furious; my father spent more and more time in the study, selecting cover art, editing the late-arriving articles, rewriting the press releases from the National Council of Churches that he used for filler. Then, on the date designated, with the copy in one hand, and my hand in the other, my father would go to the printer.

I looked forward to going to the printer with my father, in part   6
because of the printer himself, a venerable gentleman named George, the perfect image of a chapelman all the way down to his ink-stained knuckles and honest-to-God green eyeshade. The chapel over which he presided was no mere print shop, but the printing plant of the local daily, a dark cavern with an ink-impregnated wood floor and air that smelled of hot metal and chemicals, crowded with weirdly shaped machines. On the left a bank of linotypes spewed hot type and spattered molten lead onto the floor. On the right were machines to do the tasks that at home I saw done by hand—address labels, tie bundles, stuff envelopes. At the back, dominating the entire scene, was the great press on which the paper was printed, a big, black, awkward-looking thing that towered to the ceiling and descended into the bowels of the earth. Once George invited my father to bring me down at night to see the press roll, a sight that proved to be so exciting I could not tell if all the shaking was due to the awesome turning of the rollers or to the weakness in my knees; but usually we went to the printer during the day, and the big press was simply a silent presence.

During the visits to the printer, my father and George would be   7
closeted in the little cubbyhole that served as George's office, while

I had the run of the chapel. It was on one of those occasions, I believe, that any chance I would follow in the family footsteps was lost. For on this one day, while George and my father muttered of ems and ens, one of the linotype operators paused in his work and invited me to write my name on a scrap of paper, and after I had done so, let me watch as he punched my name out in hot lead. I think that was the moment when my personal die was cast.

Of course, it might have had no lasting effect had not my father, at about the same time, inadvertently introduced me to the corrupting pleasure of having written a book. 8

A few years before I was born, my father abandoned his studies at New York University, where he had been working for a Ph.D. in history. Five years later, for no reason other than desire, he took up the writing of what would have been his dissertation: "A History of the A. M. E. Zion Church." 9

I do not remember what it was like being around him while he wrote—I was, after all, less than five. I recall his methodology, which was to write a fairly detailed outline in a flowing longhand on lined paper, which he would store in a big loose-leaf binder until he was ready to turn it into a messy typescript which a typist—often my mother—later rendered as clean copy. (For one reason or another, this is the method I now use to write nonfiction.) I believe there was a certain heightening of tension during the time he was sending the typescript off to publishers; I know that he eventually entered into a cooperative arrangement with a press in Tennessee, a measure which forced him to take out a second mortgage—something I know he felt guilty about, since years later he would explain that we were not in better financial shape because of the book, but something he did not really regret, since he did it again in order to publish the second volume. 10

At the time the first volume was published, I was only six, but already I was in love with books. I had my own card at the public library, and I had read everything they had that was suitable for a child my age, and a lot that was not. Moreover, I had reread much of it many times, and the characters and stories had become so familiar, that my imagination was no longer a participant in the process; as a result, I had taken to imagining the people behind the characters. I was not old enough for literary biographies (the biographies written for children at that time went heavy on Clara Barton and Thomas Alva Edison and the like, and concentrated on the time when they were children; I loathed the things). And so I made up my own, based on bits of story I had picked up here and there. I was fascinated with Herman Melville and Richard Henry Dana, Jr., both of whom my mother said had actually gone to sea. 11

And I was captivated by Jack London, who, my father told me, had really gone hunting gold in the frozen Yukon.

But even though I was taken with these people, I felt removed   12
from them; they were not real—not as real, anyway, as the characters about whom they wrote. For I could imagine myself standing before the mast or trekking the frozen tundra, but I simply could not imagine myself writing a book.

But then one day a big tractor-trailer pulled up in the driveway   13
and began to unload cartons, and my father, normally not an impulsive or a demonstrative man, took the first carton and ripped it open and pulled out a book that had his name stamped on the front board in gold foil, and suddenly the men behind the books I'd read were as real to me as my father. And suddenly I began to see that slug of type, which I had kept safe, mounted and inked, imprinting my name on a book.

I have always been uncertain about the importance of some of   14
the things that have happened to me, suspecting that if one thing had not pushed me in the direction of writing, then probably something else would have. But I know the importance of that moment. For time and time again, people have said to me that the writing of a book is an impossible task, even to comprehend. For me, though, it was not only comprehensible, it was visible. And so, by the age of six or seven, I had firmly turned away from the family tradition. Ironically enough, at about the same time I began to discover the majesty and beauty of the Christian worship service.

When I was four or five, my father had started taking me with   15
him on some of his travels, usually in the summer, when his work took him mostly to the Southeast. The first place I went with him— and it became a regular trip—was Dinwiddie, Virginia, where, in an aging ramshackle three-story building, the church operated an "Institute"—a combination Christian education workshop, summer camp, and revival meeting.

The Institute ran for three weeks—a week each for children,   16
teenagers (what the church called "young people"), and adults. The format for all was basically the same: a day of classes punctuated by morning and noon chapel services, an afternoon recreation period, and three meals of good plain food—corn bread, grits, chicken, pork, greens—and climaxed by evening worship. The morning and afternoon worship services were short and pretty plain affairs. The evening service was pageantry, if for no other reason than that it was the focal point of everybody's day. My father's involvement was primarily with the "young people," and so I spent more time at the Institute when they were there. Evening worship was important to them because it was the closest they

could get to a dating situation, and they made the most of it. It was important to the ministers, who shared the various offices of the service on a rotating basis, competing eagerly for the choice assignments, preaching and praying. It was important to the people in the community, who used the evening worship as a kind of camp meeting. And it was important to me, because the Institute was not equipped with a radio or a TV, and worse, had a limited number of books. (I was so desperate for reading matter I practically memorized the begats.) For me, evening worship was a source of entertainment.

It began with the arrival of the audience, the scrubbed youths 17 and their chaperones, followed closely by the people from the community: the older ladies in out-of-fashion but immaculate dresses and toilet water; the men, seeming all of an age, with big rough hands poking out of the cuffs of suit coats worn awkwardly; the younger girls, in light dresses, casting flirtatious glances at the young men at the Institute (who were usually from cities, and therefore seen as sophisticated) and sharp challenging looks at the Institute's young women (who were also usually from the city, and therefore seen as probably a little wild). They would all troop into the dilapidated auditorium, filling the rows of ragtag seating— trestle benches, tip-up seats from abandoned theaters, folding chairs mended with cardboard, even a couple of mismatched church pews—and wait impatiently for the ministers.

The ministers entered from the front, moving more or less in 18 time to the sound that came from an off-key, beaten-up piano. They were not unfamiliar figures—they were around all day, teaching classes, arguing points of theology and church politics, and playing Chinese checkers beneath the trees. Now they were solemn and dignified in black suits and clerical collars, each intent on performing his role, no matter how minor, with as much style as he could muster.

Performance was the word, for the service was high drama, from 19 the solemnly intoned ritual invocation, to the rolling hymns sung by a hundred people who needed no hymnals, in passionate voices that overpowered the doubtful leadership of the gap-toothed piano, to the hucksterish importunings over the collection plate, as a minister would announce the total and then proceed to cajole, shame, or bully the audience into bringing it higher. There was no applause, of course, but the performance of each minister was rewarded with responses from the worshipers; the preaching and praying being applauded with a spontaneous chorus of "Amen, amen," "Yes, yes, yes," and the ultimate accolade, "Preach on, preach on." Which they did, sometimes until midnight.

I was overwhelmed by the worship services, not because I was   20
religious, but because there was something innately compelling
about the form and pacing and order of it: the slow, solemn beginning, the rhythms of song and responsive reading, the spontaneous
lyricism, the sense of wholeness and cohesion and abandon when
a preacher really got going, the perfection of catharsis when the
end of the service flowed swiftly and smoothly to the benediction.

I have often wondered why my initial emotional response did   21
not manifest itself as some kind of visible expression of faith—why,
while I sang the hymns and was moved by the pageantry, I never
gave myself over to witnessing or even made a journey to the altar
to accept Jesus as my savior. I believe this was due to the example
of my father, who found emotional religious expression embarrassing, and took an intellectual approach to religion, to anything. In
any case, my love of worship expressed itself in an analytical
way—I began to see it as a critical paradigm. The order of service,
with its variations in pacing and mood, its combination of poetic
and prosaic elements, of mysticism and hucksterism, became, to
me, the model of what a dramatic experience should be. This led to
my development of a critical consciousness: I began to judge worship services as good, or not so good. More important, from the
point of view of a writer, I saw enough services that were not so
good to develop an editorial sense, a feeling for when the prayer
was becoming repetitive, when the hymn was wrong, when the
minister failed to create a sermon that expanded upon the text. But
more important than even that, I learned that the analytical, critical
approach, while a useful means, was not, for me, an end.

For I had on a very few occasions seen a preacher, sometimes   22
not a usually good preacher, create, perhaps with the aid of divine
inspiration, a service or a sermon that defied criticism. Once I saw it
happen to my father.

The year was 1965. By that time, our summer travels had taken   23
my father and me beyond Virginia into North and South Carolina.
Nevertheless, the format of the Christian education conventions we
attended was the same as that at the Dinwiddie Institute. In one
place, that year, they asked my father to preach.

I was not overly excited by the prospect, since I had heard him   24
preach two or three hundred times, and had always found his
sermons to be rather dry, tending, as he tended, to focus on the
head rather than the heart. The text was Isaiah 30:21: "And thine
ears shall hear a word behind thee, saying, This *is* the way, walk ye
in it," and as my father read it, I realized that I had heard the
sermon he was beginning at least four times, liking it less each
time. When he began to speak I expected the textual analysis and

explication by definition that marked his style. But this night he
abandoned that—something got hold of him. He followed the
reading of the text with the telling of a tale.

He had, he said, been in high school, sitting in a classroom,   25
when a man had come to the school asking for volunteers to go up
to fight a forest fire that raged on a nearby mountain. My father
and some others agreed to go, and were taken up by wagon, then
went on foot a mile or two farther, to a point where they had been
told to dig a firebreak. The fire, my father said, seemed a long way
away; not sensing the danger, they allowed themselves to become
absorbed in their task. When finally they looked up from it, they
found that the fire had swept about them—they were surrounded
by flames.

They reacted as one would have expected. My father told of his   26
panic, how he had at first cried hysterically, then begun to curse,
using words he had not realized he knew, had finally collapsed into
desperate prayer, all, it seemed, to no avail. But then, when the
smoke was at its thickest, when he was about to lose sight of his
companions, when the very sound of their wailing was lost in the
roaring of the flames, there came a voice calling to them to follow.
They followed that voice, escaping with its guidance through what
must have been the last gap in the fire. Afterward they asked who
it had been who risked himself to save them, but no one could tell
them who it was.

From the tale my father moved to the obvious but eloquent   27
equation, exchanging that unknown savior for a known one, who
called the same message, and who led all who followed him clear
of the flames. And then, almost abruptly, and far sooner than
anyone expected, he stopped. And he brought down the house.

That sermon shocked me. Because I knew my father, knew that   28
he had hidden that story for forty years, had kept it out of previous
versions of the same sermon because he was the kind of man who
hated to admit weakness, or indecision, or helplessness. I knew
that to relive that time on the mountainside had cost him greatly,
and to admit his own helplessness had cost him even more. But I
realized that the sermon had been something beyond that which
was usual for him, and I believed, for no reason I could express, but
nevertheless believed, that it was the paying of the price that had
made the sermon possible. I believed that in confessing his own
weakness he had found access to a hidden source of power inside,
or perhaps outside, himself—in any case, a source of power that
was magical, mystical.

Until that night I had not understood what it meant to write. I   29
had known that the writer's goal was to reveal truths in words

manipulated so effectively as to cause a movement in the minds and hearts of those who read them. But I had not understood that it would cost anything. I had believed that I could do those things while remaining secure and safe in myself—I had even believed that writing fiction was a way to conceal my true feelings and weaknesses. That night, I found out better. That night, I realized that no matter how good I became in the manipulation of symbols, I could never hope to move anyone without allowing myself to be moved, that I could reveal only slight truths unless I was willing to reveal the truths about myself. I did not enjoy the realization. For I was no fonder of self-revelation than my father, and though I knew I would love to do with written words what my father had done in speech, I was not sure I could pay the price. I was not sure I wanted to.

I do not know why my career as a writer did not end there. All I know is that, in fact, it began there. For out of that night came the only idea I have that could truly be called an aesthetic standard: expensiveness. When I ask myself, as all writers do, whether to write something this way or that way, whether to keep this bit, or throw it away, I ask myself, along with all the practical, technical, editorial questions, Does it cost? Is it possible that someone reading might discover something about me that I would rather not have him know? Is there something truly private here, something I would never admit face to face, unless, perhaps, I was drunk?

I would like to say that if the answer to those questions is No, I go back and dig down inside myself until I do find something it will cost me to say; the truth is I do not always do that. But I believe I should. And I believe that someday, when I am good enough, not as a manipulator of words and phrases but as a human being, I will. And I believe that each time I work, and make the effort, I get closer to that ideal.

I doubt that could be called a religious expression. That I act upon it is, however, a matter of faith. For I cannot prove that there is anything to be gained from writing with that sort of aesthetic in mind. I cannot show that my work will be read by more people, that my books will sell more copies, that I will make more money, get better reviews. I cannot truly say that the work is better—I believe it is, but I cannot prove it. Despite the fact that I cannot prove it, however, I believe this aesthetic of cost does make a difference in my writing and the reception of it. This belief is important. For without it I would not be able to pay the price of writing in the way that pleases me. I would write, but, by my standards, I would do it badly. Eventually I would give it up, or become a prostitute, in it only for the money. I need not fear this, because I do believe. The capacity for belief is something I acquired from being so much in contact with others who believed. This, perhaps, is the most important influence on me from the faith of my father.

PATRICIA HAMPL

Memory and Imagination

Patricia Hampl (1946–   ), poet and memoirist, was born in St. Paul, Minnesota, to parents of Czech and Irish descent. She has published two volumes of poetry, *Woman before an Aquarium* (1978) and *Resort and Other Poems* (1983), and a much-praised autobiography, *A Romantic Education*, winner of the Houghton Mifflin Literary Fellowship in 1981. "I suppose," she has said, "I write about all the things I had intended to leave behind, to grow out of, or deny: being a Midwesterner, a Catholic, a woman." In 1987, Hampl published *Spillville*, an imaginative re-creation of another Czech artist's experience in the Midwest—composer Antonín Dvořák's visit in a small Iowa town in 1893. Hampl teaches a correspondence course in autobiographical writing at the University of Minnesota. The following essay began a section of her textbook for the course and was later expanded especially for inclusion in *The Dolphin Reader* (1986). In it you will find her argument for the political importance of writing about our own pasts.

When I was seven, my father, who played the violin on Sundays   1
with a nicely tortured flair which we considered artistic, led me by the hand down a long, unlit corridor in St. Luke's School basement, a sort of tunnel that ended in a room full of pianos. There many little girls and a single sad boy were playing truly tortured scales and arpeggios in a mash of troubled sound. My father gave me over to Sister Olive Marie, who did look remarkably like an olive.

Her oily face gleamed as if it had just been rolled out of a can and   2
laid on the white plate of her broad, spotless wimple. She was a small, plump woman; her body and the small window of her face seemed to interpret the entire alphabet of olive: her face was a sallow green olive placed upon the jumbo ripe olive of her black habit. I trusted her instantly and smiled, glad to have my hand placed in the hand of a woman who made sense, who provided the

satisfaction of being what she was: an Olive who looked like an olive.

My father left me to discover the piano with Sister Olive Marie so   3
that one day I would join him in mutually tortured piano-violin duets for the edification of my mother and brother who sat at the table meditatively spooning in the last of their pineapple sherbet until their part was called for: they put down their spoons and clapped while we bowed, while the sweet ice in their bowls melted, while the music melted, and we all melted a little into each other for a moment.

But first Sister Olive must do her work. I was shown middle C,   4
which Sister seemed to think terribly important. I stared at middle C and then glanced away for a second. When my eye returned, middle C was gone, its slim finger lost in the complicated grasp of the keyboard. Sister Olive struck it again, finding it with laughable ease. She emphasized the importance of middle C, its central position, a sort of North Star of sound. I remember thinking, "Middle C is the belly button of the piano," an insight whose originality and accuracy stunned me with pride. For the first time in my life I was astonished by metaphor. I hesitated to tell the kindly Olive for some reason; apparently I understood a true metaphor is a risky business, revealing of the self. In fact, I have never, until this moment of writing it down, told my first metaphor to anyone.

Sunlight flooded the room; the pianos, all black, gleamed. Sister   5
Olive, dressed in the colors of the keyboard, gleamed; middle C shimmered with meaning and I resolved never—never—to forget its location: it was the center of the world.

Then Sister Olive, who had had to show me middle C twice but   6
who seemed to have drawn no bad conclusions about me anyway, got up and went to the windows on the opposite wall. She pulled the shades down, one after the other. The sun was too bright, she said. She sneezed as she stood at the windows with the sun shedding its glare over her. She sneezed and sneezed, crazy little convulsive sneezes, one after another, as helpless as if she had the hiccups.

"The sun makes me sneeze," she said when the fit was over and   7
she was back at the piano. This was odd, too odd to grasp in the mind. I associated sneezing with colds, and colds with rain, fog, snow and bad weather. The sun, however, had caused Sister Olive to sneeze in this wild way, Sister Olive who gleamed benignly and who was so certain of the location of the center of the world. The universe wobbled a bit and became unreliable. Things were not, after all, necessarily what they seemed. Appearance deceived: here was the sun acting totally out of character, hurling this woman into

sneezes, a woman so mild that she was named, so it seemed, for a bland object on a relish tray.

I was given a red book, the first Thompson book, and told to play 8 the first piece over and over at one of the black pianos where the other children were crashing away. This, I was told, was called practicing. It sounded alluringly adult, practicing. The piece itself consisted mainly of middle C, and I excelled, thrilled by my savvy at being able to locate that central note amidst the cunning camouflage of all the other white keys before me. Thrilled too by the shiny red book that gleamed, as the pianos did, as Sister Olive did, as my eager eyes probably did. I sat at the formidable machine of the piano and got to know middle C intimately, preparing to be as tortured as I could manage one day soon with my father's violin at my side.

But at the moment Mary Katherine Reilly was at my side, play- 9 ing something at least two or three lessons more sophisticated than my piece. I believe she even struck a chord. I glanced at her from the peasantry of single notes, shy, ready to pay homage. She turned toward me, stopped playing, and sized me up.

Sized me up and found a person ready to be dominated. Without 10 introduction she said, "My grandfather invented the collapsible opera hat."

I nodded, I acquiesced, I was hers. With that little stroke it was 11 decided between us—that she should be the leader, and I the side-kick. My job was admiration. Even when she added, "But he didn't make a penny from it. He didn't have a patent"—even then, I knew and she knew that this was not an admission of powerless-ness, but the easy candor of a master, of one who can afford a weakness or two.

With the clairvoyance of all fated relationships based on domi- 12 nance and submission, it was decided in advance: that when the time came for us to play duets, I should always play second piano, that I should spend my allowance to buy her the Twinkies she craved but was not allowed to have, that finally, I should let her copy from my test paper, and when confronted by our teacher, confess with convincing hysteria that it was I, I who had cheated, who had reached above myself to steal what clearly belonged to the rightful heir of the inventor of the collapsible opera hat. . . .

There must be a reason I remember that little story about my first 13 piano lesson. In fact, it isn't a story, just a moment, the beginning of what could perhaps become a story. For the memoirist, more than for the fiction writer, the story seems already *there*, already accomplished and fully achieved in history ("in reality," as we naively say). For the memoirist, the writing of the story is a matter of transcription.

That, anyway, is the myth. But no memoirist writes for long   14 without experiencing an unsettling disbelief about the reliability of memory, a hunch that memory is not, after all, *just* memory. I don't know why I remembered this fragment about my first piano lesson. I don't, for instance, have a single recollection of my first arithmetic lesson, the first time I studied Latin, the first time my grandmother tried to teach me to knit. Yet these things occurred too, and must have their stories.

It is the piano lesson that has trudged forward, clearing the haze   15 of forgetfulness, showing itself bright with detail more than thirty years after the event. I did not choose to remember the piano lesson. It was simply there, like a book that has always been on the shelf, whether I ever read it or not, the binding and title showing as I skim across the contents of my life. On the day I wrote this fragment I happened to take that memory, not some other, from the shelf and paged through it. I found more detail, more event, perhaps a little more entertainment than I had expected, but the memory itself was there from the start. Waiting for me.

Or was it? When I reread what I had written just after I finished   16 it, I realized that I had told a number of lies. I *think* it was my father who took me the first time for my piano lesson—but maybe he only took me to meet my teacher and there was no actual lesson that day. And did I even know then that he played the violin— didn't he take up his violin again much later, as a result of my piano playing, and not the reverse? And is it even remotely accurate to describe as "tortured" the musicianship of a man who began every day by belting out "Oh What a Beautiful Morning" as he shaved?

More: Sister Olive Marie did sneeze in the sun, but was her   17 name Olive? As for her skin tone—I would have sworn it was olive-like; I would have been willing to spend the better part of an afternoon trying to write the exact description of imported Italian or Greek olive her face suggested: I wanted to get it right. But now, were I to write that passage over, it is her intense black eyebrows I would see, for suddenly they seem the central fact of that face, some indicative mark of her serious and patient nature. But the truth is, I don't remember the woman at all. She's a sneeze in the sun and a finger touching middle C. That, at least, is steady and clear.

Worse: I didn't have the Thompson book as my piano text. I'm   18 sure of that because I remember envying children who did have this wonderful book with its pictures of children and animals printed on the pages of music.

As for Mary Katherine Reilly. She didn't even go to grade school with me (and her name isn't Mary Katherine Reilly—but I made that change on purpose). I met her in Girl Scouts and only went to school with her later, in high school. Our relationship was not really one of leader and follower; I played first piano most of the time in duets. She certainly never copied anything from a test paper of mine: she was a better student, and cheating just wasn't a possibility with her. Though her grandfather (or someone in her family) did invent the collapsible opera hat and I remember that she was proud of that fact, she didn't tell me this news as a deft move in a childish power play.

So, what was I doing in this brief memoir? Is it simply an example of the curious relation a fiction writer has to the material of her own life? Maybe. That may have some value in itself. But to tell the truth (if anyone still believes me capable of telling the truth), I wasn't writing fiction. I was writing memoir—or was trying to. My desire was to be accurate. I wished to embody the myth of memoir: to write as an act of dutiful transcription.

Yet clearly the work of writing narrative caused me to do something very different from transcription. I am forced to admit that memoir is not a matter of transcription, that memory itself is not a warehouse of finished stories, not a static gallery of framed pictures. I must admit that I invented. But why?

Two whys: why did I invent, and then, if a memoirist must inevitably invent rather than transcribe, why do I—why should anybody—write memoir at all?

I must respond to these impertinent questions because they, like the bumper sticker I saw the other day commanding all who read it to QUESTION AUTHORITY, challenge my authority as a memoirist and as a witness.

It still comes as a shock to realize that I don't write about what I know: I write in order to find out what I know. Is it possible to convey to a reader the enormous degree of blankness, confusion, hunch and uncertainty lurking in the act of writing? When I am the reader, not the writer, I too fall into the lovely illusion that the words before me (in a story by Mavis Gallant, an essay by Carol Bly, a memoir by M. F. K. Fisher), which *read* so inevitably, must also have been *written* exactly as they appear, rhythm and cadence, language and syntax, the powerful waves of the sentences laying themselves on the smooth beach of the page one after another faultlessly.

But here I sit before a yellow legal pad, and the long page of the preceding two paragraphs is a jumble of crossed-out lines, false starts, confused order. A mess. The mess of my mind trying to find out what it wants to say. This is a writer's frantic, grabby mind, not the poised mind of a reader ready to be edified or entertained.

I sometimes think of the reader as a cat, endlessly fastidious, 26 capable, by turns, of mordant indifference and riveted attention, luxurious, recumbent, and ever poised. Whereas the writer is absolutely a dog, panting and moping, too eager for an affectionate scratch behind the ears, lunging frantically after any old stick thrown in the distance.

The blankness of a new page never fails to intrigue and terrify 27 me. Sometimes, in fact, I think my habit of writing on long yellow sheets comes from an atavistic fear of the writer's stereotypic "blank white page." At least when I begin writing, my page isn't utterly blank; at least it has a wash of color on it, even if the absence of words must finally be faced on a yellow sheet as truly as on a blank white one. Well, we all have our ways of whistling in the dark.

If I approach writing from memory with the assumption that I 28 know what I wish to say, I assume that intentionality is running the show. Things are not that simple. Or perhaps writing is even more profoundly simple, more telegraphic and immediate in its choices than the grating wheels and chugging engine of logic and rational intention. The heart, the guardian of intuition with its secret, often fearful intentions, is the boss. Its commands are what a writer obeys—often without knowing it. Or, I do.

That's why I'm a strong adherent of the first draft. And why it's 29 worth pausing for a moment to consider what a first draft really is. By my lights, the piano lesson memoir is a first draft. That doesn't mean it exists here exactly as I first wrote it. I like to think I've cleaned it up from the first time I put it down on paper. I've cut some adjectives here, toned down the hyperbole there, smoothed a transition, cut a repetition—that sort of housekeeperly tidying-up. But the piece remains a first draft because I haven't yet gotten to know it, haven't given it a chance to tell me anything. For me, writing a first draft is a little like meeting someone for the first time. I come away with a wary acquaintanceship, but the real friendship (if any) and genuine intimacy—that's all down the road. Intimacy with a piece of writing, as with a person, comes from paying attention to the revelations it is capable of giving, not by imposing my own preconceived notions, no matter how well-intentioned they might be.

I try to let pretty much anything happen in a first draft. A careful 30 first draft is a failed first draft. That may be why there are so many inaccuracies in the piano lesson memoir: I didn't censor, I didn't judge. I kept moving. But I would not publish this piece as a memoir on its own in its present state. It isn't the "lies" in the piece that give me pause, though a reader has a right to expect a memoir to be as accurate as the writer's memory can make it. No, it isn't the lies themselves that makes the piano lesson memoir a first draft and therefore "unpublishable."

The real trouble: the piece hasn't yet found its subject; it isn't yet 31 about what it wants to be about. Note: what *it* wants, not what I want. The difference has to do with the relation a memoirist—any writer, in fact—has to unconscious or half-known intentions and impulses in composition.

Now that I have the fragment down on paper, I can read this 32 little piece as a mystery which drops clues to the riddle of my feelings, like a culprit who wishes to be apprehended. My narrative self (the culprit who has invented) wishes to be discovered by my reflective self, the self who wants to understand and make sense of a half-remembered story about a nun sneezing in the sun. . . .

We only store in memory images of value. The value may be lost 33 over the passage of time (I was baffled about why I remembered that sneezing nun, for example), but that's the implacable judgment of feeling: *this*, we say somewhere deep within us, is something I'm hanging on to. And of course, often we cleave to things because they possess heavy negative charges. Pain likes to be vivid.

Over time, the value (the feeling) and the stored memory (the 34 image) may become estranged. Memoir seeks a permanent home for feeling and image, a habitation where they can live together in harmony. Naturally, I've had a lot of experiences since I packed away that one from the basement of St. Luke's School; that piano lesson has been effaced by waves of feeling for other moments and episodes. I persist in believing the event has value—after all, I remember it—but in writing the memoir I did not simply relive the experience. Rather, I explored the mysterious relationship between all the images I could round up and the even more impacted feelings that caused me to store the images safely away in memory. Stalking the relationship, seeking the congruence between stored image and hidden emotion—that's the real job of memoir.

By writing about that first piano lesson, I've come to know 35 things I could not know otherwise. But I only know these things as a result of reading this first draft. While I was writing, I was following the images, letting the details fill the room of the page and use

the furniture as they wished. I was their dutiful servant—or
thought I was. In fact, I was the faithful retainer of my hidden
feelings which were giving the commands.

I really did feel, for instance, that Mary Katherine Reilly was far   36
superior to me. She was smarter, funnier, more wonderful in every
way—that's how I saw it. Our friendship (or she herself) did not
require that I become her vassal, yet perhaps in my heart that was
something I wanted; I wanted a way to express my feeling of
admiration. I suppose I waited until this memoir to begin to find
the way.

Just as, in the memoir, I finally possess that red Thompson book   37
with the barking dogs and bleating lambs and winsome children. I
couldn't (and still can't) remember what my own music book was,
so I grabbed the name and image of the one book I could remember. It was only in reviewing the piece after writing it that I saw my
inaccuracy. In pondering this "lie," I came to see what I was up to:
I was getting what I wanted. At last.

The truth of many circumstances and episodes in the past   38
emerges for the memoirist through details (the red music book, the
fascination with a nun's name and gleaming face), but these details
are not merely information, not flat facts. Such details are not
allowed to lounge. They must work. Their work is the creation of
symbol. But it's more accurate to call it the *recognition* of symbol.
For meaning is not "attached" to the detail by the memoirist;
meaning is revealed. That's why a first draft is important. Just as
the first meeting (good or bad) with someone who later becomes
the beloved is important and is often reviewed for signals, meanings, omens, and indications.

Now I can look at that music book and see it not only as "a   39
detail," but for what it is, how it *acts*. See it as the small red door
leading straight into the dark room of my childhood longing and
disappointment. That red book *becomes* the palpable evidence of
that longing. In other words, it becomes symbol. There is no symbol, no life-of-the-spirit in the general or the abstract. Yet a writer
wishes—indeed all of us wish—to speak about profound matters
that are, like it or not, general and abstract. We wish to talk to each
other about life and death, about love, despair, loss, and innocence.
We sense that in order to live together we must learn to speak of
peace, of history, of meaning and values. Those are a few.

We seek a means of exchange, a language which will renew   40
these ancient concerns and make them wholly and pulsingly ours.
Instinctively, we go to our store of private images and associations
for our authority to speak of these weighty issues. We find, in our
details and broken and obscured images, the language of symbol.

Here memory impulsively reaches out its arms and embraces imagination. That is the resort to invention. It isn't a lie, but an act of necessity, as the innate urge to locate personal truth always is.

All right. Invention is inevitable. But why write memoir? Why 41
not call it fiction and be done with all the hashing about, wondering where memory stops and imagination begins? And if memoir seeks to talk about "the big issues," about history and peace, death and love—why not leave these reflections to those with expert and scholarly knowledge? Why let the common or garden variety memoirist into the club? I'm thinking again of that bumper sticker: why Question Authority?

My answer, of course, is a memoirist's answer. Memoir must be 42
written because each of us must have a created version of the past. Created: that is, real, tangible, made of the stuff of a life lived in place and in history. And the down side of any created thing as well: we must live with a version that attaches us to our limitations, to the inevitable subjectivity of our points of view. We must acquiesce to our experience and our gift to transform experience into meaning and value. You tell me your story, I'll tell you my story.

If we refuse to do the work of creating this personal version of 43
the past, someone else will do it for us. That is a scary political fact. "The struggle of man against power," a character in Milan Kundera's novel *The Book of Laughter and Forgetting* says, "is the struggle of memory against forgetting." He refers to willful political forgetting, the habit of nations and those in power (Question Authority!) to deny the truth of memory in order to disarm moral and ethical power. It's an efficient way of controlling masses of people. It doesn't even require much bloodshed, as long as people are entirely willing to give over their personal memories. Whole histories can be rewritten. As Czeslaw Milosz said in his 1980 Nobel Prize lecture, the number of books published that seek to deny the existence of the Nazi death camps now exceeds one hundred.

What is remembered is what *becomes* reality. If we "forget" 44
Auschwitz,[1] if we "forget" My Lai,[2] what then do we remember? And what is the purpose of our remembering? If we think of memory naively, as a simple story, logged like a documentary in the archive of the mind, we miss its beauty but also its function.

1. Polish site in World War II of the concentration camp Auschwitz-Birkenau, where more than a million prisoners, most of them Jews, were exterminated.
2. Incident in 1968 during the Vietnam war, in which American troops massacred unarmed Vietnamese civilians, including women and children.

The beauty of memory rests in its talent for rendering detail, for paying homage to the senses, its capacity to love the particles of life, the richness and idiosyncrasy of our existence. The function of memory, on the other hand, is intensely personal and surprisingly political.

Our capacity to move forward as developing beings rests on a 45 healthy relation with the past. Psychotherapy, that widespread method of mental health, relies heavily on memory and on the ability to retrieve and organize images and events from the personal past. We carry our wounds and perhaps even worse, our capacity to wound, forward with us. If we learn not only to tell our stories but to listen to what our stories tell us—to write the first draft and then return for the second draft—we are doing the work of memoir.

Memoir is the intersection of narration and reflection, of story- 46 telling and essay-writing. It can present its story *and* reflect and consider the meaning of the story. It is a peculiarly open form, inviting broken and incomplete images, half-recollected fragments, all the mass (and mess) of detail. It offers to shape this confusion—and in shaping, of course it necessarily creates a work of art, not a legal document. But then, even legal documents are only valiant attempts to consign the truth, the whole truth and nothing but the truth to paper. Even they remain versions.

Locating touchstones—the red music book, the olive Olive, my 47 father's violin playing—is deeply satisfying. Who knows why? Perhaps we all sense that we can't grasp the whole truth and nothing but the truth of our experience. Just can't be done. What can be achieved, however, is a version of its swirling, changing wholeness. A memoirist must acquiesce to selectivity, like any artist. The version we dare to write is the only truth, the only relationship we can have with the past. Refuse to write your life and you have no life. At least, that is the stern view of the memoirist.

Personal history, logged in memory, is a sort of slide projector 48 flashing images on the wall of the mind. And there's precious little order to the slides in the rotating carousel. Beyond that confusion, who knows who is running the projector? A memoirist steps into this darkened room of flashing, unorganized images and stands blinking for a while. Maybe for a long while. But eventually, as with any attempt to tell a story, it is necessary to put something first, then something else. And so on, to the end. That's a first draft. Not necessarily the truth, not even *a* truth sometimes, but the first attempt to create a shape.

The first thing I usually notice at this stage of composition is the 49 appalling inaccuracy of the piece. Witness my first piano lesson draft. Invention is screamingly evident in what I intended to be transcription. But here's the further truth: I feel no shame. In fact, it's only now that my interest in the piece truly quickens. For I can see what isn't there, what is shyly hugging the walls, hoping not to be seen. I see the filmy shape of the next draft. I see a more acute version of the episode or—this is more likely—an entirely new piece rising from the ashes of the first attempt.

The next draft of the piece would have to be a true re-vision, a   50
new seeing of the materials of the first draft. Nothing merely cosmetic will do—no rouge buffing up the opening sentence, no glossy adjective to lift a sagging line, nothing to attempt covering a patch of gray writing. None of that. I can't say for sure, but my hunch is the revision would lead me to more writing about my father (why was I so impressed by that ancestral inventor of the collapsible opera hat? Did I feel I had nothing as remarkable in my own background? Did this make me feel inadequate?). I begin to think perhaps Sister Olive is less central to this business than she is in this draft. She is meant to be a moment, not a character.

And so I might proceed, if I were to undertake a new draft of the   51
memoir. I begin to feel a relationship developing between a former self and me.

And, even more compelling, a relationship between an old   52
world and me. Some people think of autobiographical writing as the precious occupation of a particularly self-absorbed person. Maybe, but I don't buy that. True memoir is written in an attempt to find not only a self but a world.

The self-absorption that seems to be the impetus and embarrass-   53
ment of autobiography turns into (or perhaps always was) a hunger for the world. Actually, it begins as hunger for *a* world, one gone or lost, effaced by time or a more sudden brutality. But in the act of remembering, the personal environment expands, resonates beyond itself, beyond its "subject," into the endless and tragic recollection that is history.

We look at old family photographs in which we stand next to   54
black, boxy Fords and are wearing period costumes, and we do not gaze fascinated because there we are young again, or there we are standing, as we never will again in life, next to our mother. We stare and drift because there we are . . . historical. It is the dress, the black car that dazzle us now and draw us beyond our mother's bright arms which once caught us. We reach into the attractive impersonality of something more significant than ourselves. We write memoir, in other words. We accept the humble position of writing a version rather than "the whole truth."

I suppose I write memoir because of the radiance of the past—it   55 draws me back and back to it. Not that the past is beautiful. In our communal memoir, in history, the death camps *are* back there. In intimate life too, the record is usually pretty mixed. "I could tell you stories . . ." people say and drift off, meaning terrible things have happened to them.

But the past is radiant. It has the light of lived life. A memoirist   56
wishes to touch it. No one owns the past, though typically the first act of new political regimes, whether of the left or the right, is to attempt to re-write history, to grab the past and make it over so the end comes out right. So their power looks inevitable.

No one owns the past, but it is a grave error (another age would   57
have said a grave sin) not to inhabit memory. Sometimes I think it is all we really have. But that may be a trifle melodramatic. At any rate, memory possesses authority for the fearful self in a world where it is necessary to have authority in order to Question Authority.

There may be no more pressing intellectual need in our culture   58
than for people to become sophisticated about the function of memory. The political implications of the loss of memory are obvious. The authority of memory is a personal confirmation of selfhood. To write one's life is to live it twice, and the second living is both spiritual and historical, for a memoir reaches deep within the personality as it seeks its narrative form and also grasps the life-of-the-times as no political treatise can.

Our most ancient metaphor says life is a journey. Memoir is   59
travel writing, then, notes taken along the way, telling how things looked and what thoughts occurred. But I cannot think of the memoirist as a tourist. This is the traveller who goes on foot, living the journey, taking on mountains, enduring deserts, marveling at the lush green places. Moving through it all faithfully, not so much a survivor with a harrowing tale to tell as a pilgrim, seeking, wondering.

SUSAN GLASPELL

Trifles

Susan Glaspell (1882–1948) was born in Davenport, Iowa, the daughter of a feed dealer and an immigrant Irishwoman. She took her B.A. from Drake University in 1899 and began her professional career by writing sentimental short stories for popu-

lar magazines. In 1915, she and her husband George Cram Cook
(a Harvard graduate from her hometown) joined Eugene O'Neill
in founding the Provincetown Players, one of the most influential
theater groups in U.S. history. Although she was from that point
on identified as part of the literary avant-garde, her work continued to show her admiration for the pioneers who had settled
the Midwest, and especially for strong, capable farm women.
Several of Glaspell's one-act plays were collected in *Plays* (1920).
Among her full-length plays are *The Inheritors* (1921), *The Comic
Artist* (1927), and *Alison's House* (1930), which won a Pulitzer
Prize. Her novels include *Fidelity* (1915) and *Judd Rankin's
Daughter* (1945). "Trifles," a one-act play produced by the Prov-
incetown Players in 1916, is still a favorite of little theater groups.

Characters

GEORGE HENDERSON, *County Attorney*	MRS. PETERS
HENRY PETERS, *Sheriff*	MRS. HALE
LEWIS HALE, *A Neighboring Farmer*	

SCENE

The kitchen in the now abandoned farmhouse of JOHN WRIGHT, *a
gloomy kitchen, and left without having been put in order—
unwashed pans under the sink, a loaf of bread outside the breadbox, a
dish towel on the table—other signs of incompleted work. At the rear
the outer door opens and the* SHERIFF *comes in followed by the* COUNTY
ATTORNEY *and* HALE. *The* SHERIFF *and* HALE *are men in middle life,
the* COUNTY ATTORNEY *is a young man; all are much bundled up and
go at once to the stove. They are followed by two women—the*
SHERIFF'*s wife first; she is a slight wiry woman, a thin nervous face.*
MRS. HALE *is larger and would ordinarily be called more comfortable
looking, but she is disturbed now and looks fearfully about as she
enters. The women have come in slowly, and stand close together near
the door.*

COUNTY ATTORNEY. [*Rubbing his hands.*] This feels good. Come up   1
to the fire, ladies.

MRS. PETERS. [*After taking a step forward.*] I'm not—cold.

SHERIFF. [*Unbuttoning his overcoat and stepping away from the stove as
if to mark the beginning of official business.*] Now, Mr. Hale, before
we move things about, you explain to Mr. Henderson just what
you saw when you came here yesterday morning.

COUNTY ATTORNEY. By the way, has anything been moved? Are
things just as you left them yesterday?

SHERIFF. [*Looking about.*] It's just the same. When it dropped below   5
zero last night I thought I'd better send Frank out this morning

to make a fire for us—no use getting pneumonia with a big case
on, but I told him not to touch anything except the stove—and
you know Frank.

COUNTY ATTORNEY. Somebody should have been left here
yesterday.

SHERIFF. Oh—yesterday. When I had to send Frank to Morris Center for that man who went crazy—I want you to know I had my
hands full yesterday, I knew you could get back from Omaha by
today and as long as I went over everything here myself—

COUNTY ATTORNEY. Well, Mr. Hale, tell just what happened when
you came here yesterday morning.

HALE. Harry and I had started to town with a load of potatoes. We
came along the road from my place and as I got here I said, "I'm
going to see if I can't get John Wright to go in with me on a
party telephone." I spoke to Wright about it once before and he
put me off, saying folks talked too much anyway, and all he
asked was peace and quiet—I guess you know about how much
he talked himself; but I thought maybe if I went to the house
and talked about it before his wife, though I said to Harry that I
didn't know as what his wife wanted made much difference to
John—

COUNTY ATTORNEY. Let's talk about that later, Mr. Hale. I do want   10
to talk about that, but tell now just what happened when you
got to the house.

HALE. I didn't hear or see anything; I knocked at the door, and still
it was all quiet inside. I knew they must be up, it was past eight
o'clock. So I knocked again, and I thought I heard somebody
say, "Come in." I wasn't sure, I'm not sure yet, but I opened the
door—this door [*Indicating the door by which the two women are
still standing*] and there in that rocker—[*Pointing to it.*] sat Mrs.
Wright. [*They all look at the rocker.*]

COUNTY ATTORNEY. What—was she doing?

HALE. She was rockin' back and forth. She had her apron in her
hand and was kind of—pleating it.

COUNTY ATTORNEY. And how did she—look?

HALE. Well, she looked queer.   15

COUNTY ATTORNEY. How do you mean—queer?

HALE. Well, as if she didn't know what she was going to do next.
And kind of done up.

COUNTY ATTORNEY. How did she seem to feel about your coming?

HALE. Why, I don't think she minded—one way or other. She
didn't pay much attention. I said, "How do, Mrs. Wright, it's
cold, ain't it?" And she said, "Is it?"—and went on kind of
pleating at her apron. Well, I was surprised; she didn't ask me to

come up to the stove, or to set down, but just sat there, not even looking at me, so I said, "I want to see John." And then she—laughed. I guess you would call it a laugh. I thought of Harry and the team outside, so I said a little sharp: "Can't I see John?" "No," she says, kind o' dull like. "Ain't he home?" says I. "Yes," says she, "he's home." "Then why can't I see him?" I asked her, out of patience. " 'Cause he's dead," says she. *"Dead?"* says I. She just nodded her head, not getting a bit excited, but rockin' back and forth. "Why—where is he?" says I, not knowing what to say. She just pointed upstairs—like that [*Himself pointing to the room above*]. I got up, with the idea of going up there. I walked from there to here—then I says, "Why, what did he die of?" "He died of a rope round his neck," says she, and just went on pleatin' at her apron. Well, I went out and called Harry. I thought I might—need help. We went upstairs and there he was lyin'—

COUNTY ATTORNEY. I think I'd rather have you go into that upstairs   20 where you can point it all out. Just go on now with the rest of the story.

HALE. Well, my first thought was to get that rope off. It looked . . . [*Stops, his face twitches.*] . . . but Harry, he went up to him, and he said, "No, he's dead all right, and we'd better not touch anything." So we went back down stairs. She was still sitting that same way. "Has anybody been notified?" I asked. "No," says she, unconcerned. "Who did this, Mrs. Wright?" said Harry. He said it businesslike—and she stopped pleatin' of her apron. "I don't know," she says. "You don't *know?"* says Harry. "No," says she. "Weren't you sleepin' in the bed with him?" says Harry. "Yes," says she, "but I was on the inside." "Somebody slipped a rope round his neck and strangled him and you didn't wake up?" says Harry. "I didn't wake up," she said after him. We must 'a looked as if we didn't see how that could be, for after a minute she said, "I sleep sound." Harry was going to ask her more questions but I said maybe we ought to let her tell her story first to the coroner, or the sheriff, so Harry went fast as he could to Rivers' place, where there's a telephone.

COUNTY ATTORNEY. And what did Mrs. Wright do when she knew that you had gone for the coroner?

HALE. She moved from that chair to this one over here [*Pointing to a small chair in the corner.*] and just sat there with her hands held together and looking down. I got a feeling that I ought to make some conversation, so I said I had come in to see if John wanted to put in a telephone, and at that she started to laugh, and then she stopped and looked at me—scared. [*The* COUNTY ATTORNEY, *who has had his notebook out, makes a note.*] I dunno, maybe it wasn't scared. I wouldn't like to say it was. Soon Harry got back, and then Dr. Lloyd came, and you, Mr. Peters, and so I guess that's all I know that you don't.

COUNTY ATTORNEY. [*Looking around.*] I guess we'll go upstairs first—and then out to the barn and around there. [*To the* SHERIFF] You're convinced that there was nothing important here—nothing that would point to any motive.

SHERIFF. Nothing here but kitchen things.   25

[*The* COUNTY ATTORNEY, *after again looking around the kitchen, opens the door of a cupboard closet. He gets up on a chair and looks on a shelf. Pulls his hand away, sticky.*]

COUNTY ATTORNEY. Here's a nice mess.

[*The women draw nearer.*]

MRS. PETERS. [*To the other woman.*] Oh, her fruit; it did freeze. [*To the* COUNTY ATTORNEY] She worried about that when it turned so cold. She said the fire'd go out and her jars would break.

SHERIFF. Well, can you beat the women! Held for murder and worryin' about her preserves.

COUNTY ATTORNEY. I guess before we're through she may have something more serious than preserves to worry about.

HALE. Well, women are used to worrying over trifles.   30

[*The two women move a little closer together.*]

COUNTY ATTORNEY. [*With the gallantry of a young politician.*] And yet, for all their worries, what would we do without the ladies? [*The women do not unbend. He goes to the sink, takes a dipperful of water from the pail and pouring it into a basin, washes his hands. Starts to wipe them on the roller towel, turns it for a cleaner place.*] Dirty towels! [*Kicks his foot against the pans under the sink.*] Not much of a housekeeper, would you say, ladies?

MRS. HALE. [*Stiffly.*] There's a great deal of work to be done on a farm.

COUNTY ATTORNEY. To be sure. And yet [*With a little bow to her*] I know there are some Dickson county farmhouses which do not have such roller towels.

[*He gives it a pull to expose its full length again.*]

MRS. HALE. Those towels get dirty awful quick. Men's hands aren't always as clean as they might be.

COUNTY ATTORNEY. Ah, loyal to your sex, I see. But you and Mrs.   35
Wright were neighbors. I suppose you were friends, too.

MRS. HALE. [*Shaking her head.*] I've not seen much of her of late years. I've not been in this house—it's more than a year.

COUNTY ATTORNEY. And why was that? You didn't like her?

MRS. HALE. I liked her all well enough. Farmers' wives have their hands full, Mr. Henderson. And then—

COUNTY ATTORNEY. Yes—?

MRS. HALE. [*Looking about.*] It never seemed a very cheerful place. ⁴⁰

COUNTY ATTORNEY. No—it's not cheerful. I shouldn't say she had the homemaking instinct.

MRS. HALE. Well, I don't know as Wright had, either.

COUNTY ATTORNEY. You mean that they didn't get on very well?

MRS. HALE. No, I don't mean anything. But I don't think a place'd be any cheerfuller for John Wright's being in it.

COUNTY ATTORNEY. I'd like to talk more of that a little later. I want ⁴⁵ to get the lay of things upstairs now.

[*He goes to the left, where three steps lead to a stair door.*]

SHERIFF. I suppose anything Mrs. Peters does'll be all right. She was to take in some clothes for her, you know, and a few little things. We left in such a hurry yesterday.

COUNTY ATTORNEY. Yes, but I would like to see what you take, Mrs. Peters, and keep an eye out for anything that might be of use to us.

MRS. PETERS. Yes, Mr. Henderson.

[*The women listen to the men's steps on the stairs, then look about the kitchen.*]

MRS. HALE. I'd hate to have men coming into my kitchen, snooping around and criticising.

[*She arranges the pans under sink which the* COUNTY ATTORNEY *had shoved out of place.*]

MRS. PETERS. Of course it's no more than their duty. ⁵⁰

MRS. HALE. Duty's all right, but I guess that deputy sheriff that came out to make the fire might have got a little of this on. [*Gives the roller towel a pull.*] Wish I'd thought of that sooner. Seems mean to talk about her for not having things slicked up when she had to come away in such a hurry.

MRS. PETERS. [*Who has gone to a small table in the left rear corner of the room, and lifted one end of a towel that covers a pan.*] She had bread set.

[*Stands still.*]

MRS. HALE. [*Eyes fixed on a loaf of bread beside the breadbox, which is on a low shelf at the other side of the room. Moves slowly toward it.*] She was going to put this in there. [*Picks up loaf, then abruptly drops it. In a manner of returning to familiar things.*] It's a shame about her fruit. I wonder if it's all gone. [*Gets up on the chair and looks.*] I think there's some here that's all right, Mrs. Peters. Yes—here; [*Holding it toward the window.*] this is cherries, too.

[*Looking again.*] I declare I believe that's the only one. [*Gets down, bottle in her hand. Goes to the sink and wipes it off on the outside.*] She'll feel awful bad after all her hard work in the hot weather. I remember the afternoon I put up my cherries last summer.

[*She puts the bottle on the big kitchen table, center of the room. With a sigh, is about to sit down in the rocking-chair. Before she is seated realizes what chair it is; with a slow look at it, steps back. The chair which she has touched rocks back and forth.*]

MRS. PETERS. Well, I must get those things from the front room closet. [*She goes to the door at the right, but after looking into the other room, steps back.*] You coming with me, Mrs. Hale? You could help me carry them.

[*They go in the other room; reappear,* MRS. PETERS *carrying a dress and skirt,* MRS. HALE *following with a pair of shoes.*]

MRS. PETERS. My, it's cold in there.   55

[*She puts the clothes on the big table, and hurries to the stove.*]

MRS. HALE. [*Examining her skirt.*] Wright was close. I think maybe that's why she kept so much to herself. She didn't even belong to the Ladies Aid. I suppose she felt she couldn't do her part, and then you don't enjoy things when you feel shabby. She used to wear pretty clothes and be lively, when she was Minnie Foster, one of the town girls singing in the choir. But that—oh, that was thirty years ago. This all you was to take in?

MRS. PETERS. She said she wanted an apron. Funny thing to want, for there isn't much to get you dirty in jail, goodness knows. But I suppose just to make her feel more natural. She said they was in the top drawer in this cupboard. Yes, here. And then her little shawl that always hung behind the door. [*Opens stair door and looks.*] Yes, here it is.

[*Quickly shuts door leading upstairs.*]

MRS. HALE. [*Abruptly moving toward her.*] Mrs. Peters?

MRS. PETERS. Yes, Mrs. Hale?

MRS. HALE. Do you think she did it?   60

MRS. PETERS. [*In a frightened voice.*] Oh, I don't know.

MRS. HALE. Well, I don't think she did. Asking for an apron and her little shawl. Worrying about her fruit.

MRS. PETERS. [*Starts to speak, glances up, where footsteps are heard in the room above. In a low voice.*] Mr. Peters says it looks bad for her. Mr. Henderson is awful sarcastic in a speech and he'll make fun of her sayin' she didn't wake up.

MRS. HALE. Well, I guess John Wright didn't wake when they was slipping that rope under his neck.

MRS. PETERS. No, it's strange. It must have been done awful crafty   65
and still. They say it was such a—funny way to kill a man,
rigging it all up like that.

MRS. HALE. That's just what Mr. Hale said. There was a gun in the
house. He says that's what he can't understand.

MRS. PETERS. Mr. Henderson said coming out that what was
needed for the case was a motive; something to show anger,
or—sudden feeling.

MRS. HALE. [*Who is standing by the table.*] Well, I don't see any signs
of anger around here. [*She puts her hand on the dish towel which
lies on the table, stands looking down at table, one half of which is
clean, the other half messy.*] It's wiped to here. [*Makes a move as if
to finish work, then turns and looks at loaf of bread outside the
breadbox. Drops towel. In that voice of coming back to familiar
things.*] Wonder how they are finding things upstairs. I hope she
had it a little more red-up up there. You know, it seems kind of
sneaking. Locking her up in town and then coming out here and
trying to get her own house to turn against her!

MRS. PETERS. But Mrs. Hale, the law is the law.

MRS. HALE. I s'pose 'tis. [*Unbuttoning her coat.*] Better loosen up   70
your things, Mrs. Peters. You won't feel them when you go out.
[MRS. PETERS *takes off her fur tippet, goes to hang it on hook at back of
room, stands looking at the under part of the small corner table.*]

MRS. PETERS. She was piecing a quilt.
[*She brings the large sewing basket and they look at the bright pieces.*]

MRS. HALE. It's log cabin pattern. Pretty, isn't it? I wonder if she
was goin' to quilt it or just knot it?
[*Footsteps have been heard coming down the stairs. The* SHERIFF
enters followed by HALE *and the* COUNTY ATTORNEY.]

SHERIFF. They wonder if she was going to quilt it or just knot it!
[*The men laugh; the women look abashed.*]

COUNTY ATTORNEY. [*Rubbing his hands over the stove.*] Frank's fire
didn't do much up there, did it? Well, let's go out to the barn
and get that cleared up.
[*The men go outside.*]

MRS. HALE. [*Resentfully.*] I don't know as there's anything so   75
strange, our takin' up our time with little things while we're
waiting for them to get the evidence. [*She sits down at the big table
smoothing out a block with decision.*] I don't see as it's anything to
laugh about.

MRS. PETERS. [*Apologetically.*] Of course they've got awful important things on their minds.
[*Pulls up a chair and joins* MRS. HALE *at the table.*]

MRS. HALE. [*Examining another block.*] Mrs. Peters, look at this one.
Here, this is the one she was working on, and look at the sewing! All the rest of it has been so nice and even. And look at this!
It's all over the place! Why, it looks as if she didn't know what
she was about!
[*After she has said this they look at each other, then start to glance
back at the door. After an instant* MRS. HALE *has pulled at a knot and
ripped the sewing.*]
MRS. PETERS. Oh, what are you doing, Mrs. Hale?
MRS. HALE. [*Mildly.*] Just pulling out a stitch or two that's not
sewed very good. [*Threading a needle.*] Bad sewing always made
me fidgety.
MRS. PETERS. [*Nervously.*] I don't think we ought to touch things.   80
MRS. HALE. I'll just finish up this end. [*Suddenly stopping and leaning
forward.*] Mrs. Peters?
MRS. PETERS. Yes, Mrs. Hale?
MRS. HALE. What do you suppose she was so nervous about?
MRS. PETERS. Oh—I don't know. I don't know as she was nervous.
I sometimes sew awful queer when I'm just tired. [MRS. HALE
starts to say something, looks at MRS. PETERS, *then goes on sewing.*]
Well, I must get these things wrapped up. They may be through
sooner than we think. [*Putting apron and other things together.*] I
wonder where I can find a piece of paper, and string.
MRS. HALE. In that cupboard, maybe.   85
MRS. PETERS. [*Looking in cupboard.*] Why, here's a birdcage. [*Holds it
up.*] Did she have a bird, Mrs. Hale?
MRS. HALE. Why, I don't know whether she did or not—I've not
been here for so long. There was a man around last year selling
canaries cheap, but I don't know as she took one; maybe she
did. She used to sing real pretty herself.
MRS. PETERS. [*Glancing around.*] Seems funny to think of a bird
here. But she must have had one, or why would she have a
cage? I wonder what happened to it.
MRS. HALE. I s'pose maybe the cat got it.
MRS. PETERS. No, she didn't have a cat. She's got that feeling some   90
people have about cats—being afraid of them. My cat got in her
room and she was real upset and asked me to take it out.
MRS. HALE. My sister Bessie was like that. Queer, ain't it?
MRS. PETERS. [*Examining the cage.*] Why, look at this door. It's
broke. One hinge is pulled apart.
MRS. HALE. [*Looking too.*] Looks as if someone must have been
rough with it.
MRS. PETERS. Why, yes.
[*She brings the cage forward and puts it on the table.*]

MRS. HALE. I wish if they're going to find any evidence they'd be   95
about it. I don't like this place.

MRS. PETERS. But I'm awful glad you came with me, Mrs. Hale. It
would be lonesome for me sitting here alone.

MRS. HALE. It would, wouldn't it? [*Dropping her sewing.*] But I tell
you what I do wish, Mrs. Peters. I wish I had come over sometimes when *she* was here. I—[*Looking around the room.*]—wish I
had.

MRS. PETERS. But of course you were awful busy, Mrs. Hale—your
house and your children.

MRS. HALE. I could've come. I stayed away because it weren't
cheerful—and that's why I ought to have come. I—I've never
liked this place. Maybe because it's down in a hollow and you
don't see the road. I dunno what it is but it's a lonesome place
and always was. I wish I had come over to see Minnie Foster
sometimes. I can see now—
[*Shakes her head.*]

MRS. PETERS. Well, you mustn't reproach yourself, Mrs. Hale.   100
Somehow we just don't see how it is with other folks until—
something comes up.

MRS. HALE. Not having children makes less work—but it makes a
quiet house, and Wright out to work all day, and no company
when he did come in. Did you know John Wright, Mrs. Peters?

MRS. PETERS. Not to know him; I've seen him in town. They say he
was a good man.

MRS. HALE. Yes—good; he didn't drink, and kept his word as well
as most, I guess, and paid his debts. But he was a hard man,
Mrs. Peters. Just to pass the time of day with him—[*Shivers.*]
Like a raw wind that gets to the bone. [*Pauses, her eye falling on
the cage.*] I should think she would 'a wanted a bird. But what
do you suppose went with it?

MRS. PETERS. I don't know, unless it got sick and died.
[*She reaches over and swings the broken door, swings it again. Both
women watch it.*]

MRS. HALE. You weren't raised round here, were you? [MRS. PETERS   105
shakes her head.] You didn't know—her?

MRS. PETERS. Not till they brought her yesterday.

MRS. HALE. She—come to think of it, she was kind of like a bird
herself—real sweet and pretty, but kind of timid and—fluttery.
How—she—did—change. [*Silence; then as if struck by a happy
thought and relieved to get back to every day things.*] Tell you what,
Mrs. Peters, why don't you take the quilt in with you? It might
take up her mind.

MRS. PETERS. Why, I think that's a real nice idea, Mrs. Hale. There couldn't possibly be any objection to it, could there? Now, just what would I take? I wonder if her patches are in here—and her things.

[*They look in the sewing basket.*]

MRS. HALE. Here's some red. I expect this has got sewing things in it. [*Brings out a fancy box.*] What a pretty box. Looks like something somebody would give you. Maybe her scissors are in here. [*Opens box. Suddenly puts her hand to her nose.*] Why—[MRS. PETERS *bends nearer, then turns her face away.*] There's something wrapped up in this piece of silk.

MRS. PETERS. Why, this isn't her scissors.   110

MRS. HALE. [*Lifting the silk.*] Oh, Mrs. Peters—it's—

[MRS. PETERS *bends closer.*]

MRS. PETERS. It's the bird.

MRS. HALE. [*Jumping up.*] But, Mrs. Peters—look at it! Its neck! Look at its neck! It's all—other side *to.*

MRS. PETERS. Somebody—wrung—its—neck.

[*Their eyes meet. A look of growing comprehension, of horror. Steps are heard outside.* MRS. HALE *slips box under quilt pieces, and sinks into her chair. Enter* SHERIFF *and* COUNTY ATTORNEY. MRS. PETERS *rises.*]

COUNTY ATTORNEY. [*As one turning from serious things to little pleas-*   115
antries.] Well, ladies, have you decided whether she was going to quilt it or knot it?

MRS. PETERS. We think she was going to—knot it.

COUNTY ATTORNEY. Well, that's interesting, I'm sure. [*Seeing the birdcage.*] Has the bird flown?

MRS. HALE. [*Putting more quilt pieces over the box.*] We think the—cat got it.

COUNTY ATTORNEY. [*Preoccupied.*] Is there a cat?

[MRS. HALE *glances in a quick covert way at* MRS. PETERS.]

MRS. PETERS. Well, not *now.* They're superstitious, you know. They   120
leave.

COUNTY ATTORNEY. [*To* SHERIFF PETERS, *continuing an interrupted con-versation.*] No sign at all of anyone having come from the out-side. Their own rope. Now let's go up again and go over it piece by piece. [*They start upstairs.*] It would have to have been some-one who knew just the—

[MRS. PETERS *sits down. The two women sit there not looking at one another, but as if peering into something and at the same time holding back. When they talk now it is in the manner of feeling their way over strange ground, as if afraid of what they are saying, but as if they can not help saying it.*]

MRS. HALE. She liked the bird. She was going to bury it in that pretty box.

MRS. PETERS. [*In a whisper.*] When I was a girl—my kitten—there was a boy took a hatchet, and before my eyes—and before I could get there—[*Covers her face an instant.*] If they hadn't held me back I would have—[*Catches herself, looks upstairs where steps are heard, falters weakly.*]—hurt him.

MRS. HALE. [*With a slow look around her.*] I wonder how it would seem never to have had any children around. [*Pause.*] No, Wright wouldn't like the bird—a thing that sang. She used to sing. He killed that, too.

MRS. PETERS. [*Moving uneasily.*] We don't know who killed the bird.   125

MRS. HALE. I knew John Wright.

MRS. PETERS. It was an awful thing was done in this house that night, Mrs. Hale. Killing a man while he slept, slipping a rope around his neck that choked the life out of him.

MRS. HALE. His neck. Choked the life out of him.

[*Her hand goes out and rests on the birdcage.*]

MRS. PETERS. [*With rising voice.*] We don't know who killed him. We don't *know*.

MRS. HALE. [*Her own feeling not interrupted.*] If there'd been years and years of nothing, then a bird to sing to you, it would be awful—still, after the bird was still.   130

MRS. PETERS. [*Something within her speaking.*] I know what stillness is. When we homesteaded in Dakota, and my first baby died—after he was two years old, and me with no other then—

MRS. HALE. [*Moving.*] How soon do you suppose they'll be through, looking for the evidence?

MRS. PETERS. I know what stillness is. [*Pulling herself back.*] The law has got to punish crime, Mrs. Hale.

MRS. HALE. [*Not as if answering that.*] I wish you'd seen Minnie Foster when she wore a white dress with blue ribbons and stood up there in the choir and sang. [*A look around the room.*] Oh, I *wish* I'd come over here once in a while! That was a crime! That was a crime! Who's going to punish that?

MRS. PETERS. [*Looking upstairs.*] We mustn't—take on.   135

MRS. HALE. I might have known she needed help! I know how things can be—for women. I tell you, it's queer, Mrs. Peters. We live close together and we live far apart. We all go through the same things—it's all just a different kind of the same thing. [*Brushes her eyes; noticing the bottle of fruit, reaches out for it.*] If I was you I wouldn't tell her her fruit was gone. Tell her it *ain't*.

Tell her it's all right. Take this in to prove it to her. She—she
may never know whether it was broke or not.

MRS. PETERS. [*Takes the bottle, looks about for something to wrap it in;
takes petticoat from the clothes brought from the other room, very
nervously begins winding this around the bottle. In a false voice.*] My,
it's a good thing the men couldn't hear us. Wouldn't they just
laugh! Getting all stirred up over a little thing like a—dead
canary. As if that could have anything to do with—with—
wouldn't they *laugh!*

[*The men are heard coming down stairs.*]

MRS. HALE. [*Under her breath.*] Maybe they would—maybe they
wouldn't.

COUNTY ATTORNEY. No, Peters, it's all perfectly clear except a reason
for doing it. But you know juries when it comes to women. If
there was some definite thing. Something to show—something
to make a story about—a thing that would connect up with this
strange way of doing it—

[*The women's eyes meet for an instant. Enter* HALE *from outer door.*]

HALE. Well, I've got the team around. Pretty cold out there.   140

COUNTY ATTORNEY. I'm going to stay here a while by myself. [*To the*
SHERIFF.] You can send Frank out for me, can't you? I want to go
over everything. I'm not satisfied that we can't do better.

SHERIFF. Do you want to see what Mrs. Peters is going to take in?

[*The* COUNTY ATTORNEY *goes to the table, picks up the apron,
laughs.*]

COUNTY ATTORNEY. Oh, I guess they're not very dangerous things
the ladies have picked out. [*Moves a few things about, disturbing
the quilt pieces which cover the box. Steps back.*] No, Mrs. Peters
doesn't need supervising. For that matter, a sheriff's wife is married to the law. Ever think of it that way, Mrs. Peters?

MRS. PETERS. Not—just that way.

SHERIFF. [*Chuckling.*] Married to the law. [*Moves toward the other*   145
room.] I just want you to come in here a minute, George. We
ought to take a look at these windows.

COUNTY ATTORNEY. [*Scoffingly.*] Oh, windows!

SHERIFF. We'll be right out, Mr. Hale.

[HALE *goes outside. The* SHERIFF *follows the* COUNTY ATTORNEY *into
the other room. Then* MRS. HALE *rises, hands tight together, looking
intensely at* MRS. PETERS, *whose eyes make a slow turn, finally meeting* MRS. HALE'*s. A moment* MRS. HALE *holds her, then her own eyes
point the way to where the box is concealed. Suddenly* MRS. PETERS
*throws back quilt pieces and tries to put the box in the bag she is
wearing. It is too big. She opens box, starts to take bird out, cannot
touch it, goes to pieces, stands there helpless. Sound of a knob turning*

in the other room. MRS. HALE *snatches the box and puts it in the pocket of her big coat. Enter* COUNTY ATTORNEY *and* SHERIFF.]
COUNTY ATTORNEY. [*Facetiously.*] Well, Henry, at least we found out that she was not going to quilt it. She was going to—what is it you call it, ladies?
MRS. HALE. [*Her hand against her pocket.*] We call it—knot it, Mr. Henderson.

CURTAIN

FLANNERY O'CONNOR

Revelation

(Mary) Flannery O'Connor (1925–1964), graduated from Georgia State College for Women (A.B.) and the University of Iowa (M.F.A.). A committed Catholic, O'Connor had deep family roots in rural Georgia, which she called "a real Bible Belt," but which she knew to be filled with as exotic a variety of lost souls as one could find anywhere. Her subject, she once said, was "the action of grace in territory held largely by the devil." O'Connor's stories combine religious themes, grotesque humor, and the realism of someone who has studied her neighbors carefully. Often, the moment of discovery in an O'Connor story comes when a character blinded by pride catches a glimpse of his or her life as God might see it. Such a moment of truth, as one critic has noted, can strike the character "with the force of a mugging." O'Connor's novels include *Wise Blood* (1952) and *The Violent Bear It Away* (1960). Collections of her short stories include *A Good Man is Hard to Find* (1955), *Everything that Rises Must Converge* (1965), and *The Complete Stories* (1971). *Mystery and Manners* (1969) collects several of O'Connor's lectures on the craft of fiction. "Revelation" was first published in *The Sewanee Review* in 1964.

The doctor's waiting room, which was very small, was almost full when the Turpins entered and Mrs. Turpin, who was very large, made it look even smaller by her presence. She stood looming at the head of the magazine table set in the center of it, a living demonstration that the room was inadequate and ridiculous. Her little bright black eyes took in all the patients as she sized up the seating situation. There was one vacant chair and a place on the sofa occupied by a blond child in a dirty blue romper who should have been told to move over and make room for the lady. He was 1

five or six, but Mrs. Turpin saw at once that no one was going to
tell him to move over. He was slumped down in the seat, his arms
idle at his sides and his eyes idle in his head; his nose ran
unchecked.

Mrs. Turpin put a firm hand on Claud's shoulder and said in a
voice that included everyone that wanted to listen, "Claud, you sit
in that chair there," and gave him a push down into the vacant
one. Claud was florid and bald and sturdy, somewhat shorter than
Mrs. Turpin, but he sat down as if he were accustomed to doing
what she told him to.

Mrs. Turpin remained standing. The only man in the room besides Claud was a lean stringy old fellow with a rusty hand spread
out on each knee, whose eyes were closed as if he were asleep or
dead or pretending to be so as not to get up and offer her his seat.
Her gaze settled agreeably on a well-dressed grey-haired lady
whose eyes met hers and whose expression said: if that child belonged to me, he would have some manners and move over—
there's plenty of room there for you and him too.

Claud looked up with a sigh and made as if to rise.

"Sit down," Mrs. Turpin said. "You know you're not supposed   5
to stand on that leg. He has an ulcer on his leg," she explained.

Claud lifted his foot onto the magazine table and rolled his
trouser leg up to reveal a purple swelling on a plump marble-white
calf.

"My!" the pleasant lady said. "How did you do that?"

"A cow kicked him," Mrs. Turpin said.

"Goodness!" said the lady.

Claud rolled his trouser leg down.   10

"Maybe the little boy would move over," the lady suggested, but
the child did not stir.

"Somebody will be leaving in a minute," Mrs. Turpin said. She
could not understand why a doctor—with as much money as they
made charging five dollars a day just to stick their head in the
hospital door and look at you—couldn't afford a decent-sized
waiting room. This one was hardly bigger than a garage. The table
was cluttered with limp-looking magazines and at one end of it
there was a big green glass ash tray full of cigaret butts and cotton
wads with little blood spots on them. If she had had anything to do
with the running of the place, that would have been emptied every
so often. There were no chairs against the wall at the head of the
room. It had a rectangular-shaped panel in it that permitted a view
of the office where the nurse came and went and the secretary
listened to the radio. A plastic fern in a gold pot sat in the opening

and trailed its fronds down almost to the floor. The radio was softly
playing gospel music.

Just then the inner door opened and a nurse with the highest
stack of yellow hair Mrs. Turpin had ever seen put her face in the
crack and called for the next patient. The woman sitting beside
Claud grasped the two arms of her chair and hoisted herself up; she
pulled her dress free from her legs and lumbered through the door
where the nurse had disappeared.

Mrs. Turpin eased into the vacant chair, which held her tight as a
corset. "I wish I could reduce," she said, and rolled her eyes and
gave a comic sigh.

"Oh, *you* aren't fat," the stylish lady said.   15

"Ooooo I am too," Mrs. Turpin said. "Claud he eats all he wants
to and never weighs over one hundred and seventy-five pounds,
but me I just look at something good to eat and I gain some
weight," and her stomach and shoulders shook with laughter.
"You can eat all you want to, can't you, Claud?" she asked turning
to him.

Claud only grinned.

"Well, as long as you have such a good disposition," the stylish
lady said, "I don't think it makes a bit of difference what size you
are. You just can't beat a good disposition."

Next to her was a fat girl of eighteen or nineteen, scowling into a
thick blue book which Mrs. Turpin saw was entitled *Human Development*. The girl raised her head and directed her scowl at Mrs.
Turpin as if she did not like her looks. She appeared annoyed that
anyone should speak while she tried to read. The poor girl's face
was blue with acne and Mrs. Turpin thought how pitiful it was to
have a face like that at that age. She gave the girl a friendly smile
but the girl only scowled the harder. Mrs. Turpin herself was fat but
she had always had good skin, and, though she was forty-seven
years old, there was not a wrinkle in her face except around her
eyes from laughing too much.

Next to the ugly girl was the child, still in exactly the same   20
position, and next to him was a thin leathery old woman in a
cotton print dress. She and Claud had three sacks of chicken feed in
their pump house that was in the same print. She had seen from
the first that the child belonged with the old woman. She could tell
by the way they sat—kind of vacant and white-trashy, as if they
would sit there until Doomsday if nobody called and told them to
get up. And at right angles but next to the well-dressed pleasant
lady was a lank-faced woman who was certainly the child's
mother. She had on a yellow sweat shirt and wine-colored slacks,

both gritty-looking, and the rims of her lips were stained with snuff. Her dirty yellow hair was tied behind with a piece of red paper ribbon. Worse than niggers any day, Mrs. Turpin thought.

The gospel hymn playing was, "When I looked up and He looked down," and Mrs. Turpin, who knew it, supplied the last line mentally, "And wona these days I know I'll we-eara crown."

Without appearing to, Mrs. Turpin always noticed people's feet. The well-dressed lady had on red and grey suede shoes to match her dress. Mrs. Turpin had on her good black patent leather pumps. The ugly girl had on Girl Scout shoes and heavy socks. The old woman had on tennis shoes and the white-trashy mother had on what appeared to be bedroom slippers, black straw with gold braid threaded through them—exactly what you would have expected her to have on.

Sometimes at night when she couldn't go to sleep, Mrs. Turpin would occupy herself with the question of who she would have chosen to be if she couldn't have been herself. If Jesus had said to her before he made her, "There's only two places available for you. You can either be a nigger or white-trash," what would she have said? "Please, Jesus, please," she would have said, "just let me wait until there's another place available," and he would have said, "No, you have to go right now and I have only those two places so make up your mind." She would have wiggled and squirmed and begged and pleaded but it would have been no use and finally she would have said, "All right, make me a nigger then—but that don't mean a trashy one." And he would have made her a neat clean respectable Negro woman, herself but black.

Next to the child's mother was a red-headed youngish woman, reading one of the magazines and working a piece of chewing gum, hell for leather, as Claud would say. Mrs. Turpin could not see the woman's feet. She was not white-trash, just common. Sometimes Mrs. Turpin occupied herself at night naming the classes of people. On the bottom of the heap were most colored people, not the kind she would have been if she had been one, but most of them; then next to them—not above, just away from—were the white-trash; then above them were the home-owners, and above them the home-and-land owners, to which she and Claud belonged. Above she and Claud were people with a lot of money and much bigger houses and much more land. But here the complexity of it would begin to bear in on her, for some of the people with a lot of money were common and ought to be below she and Claud and some of the people who had good blood had lost their money and had to rent and then there were colored people who owned their homes and land as well. There was a colored dentist in town who had two red Lincolns and a swimming pool and a farm with registered white-face cattle on it. Usually by the time she had fallen asleep all the classes of people were moiling and roiling around in her head, and she would dream they were all crammed in together in a box car, being ridden off to be put in a gas oven.

"That's a beautiful clock," she said and nodded to her right. It 25
was a big wall clock, the face encased in a brass sunburst.

"Yes, it's very pretty," the stylish lady said agreeably. "And right on the dot too," she added, glancing at her watch.

The ugly girl beside her cast an eye upward at the clock, smirked, then looked directly at Mrs. Turpin and smirked again. Then she returned her eyes to her book. She was obviously the lady's daughter because, although they didn't look anything alike as to disposition, they both had the same shape of face and same blue eyes. On the lady they sparkled pleasantly but in the girl's seared face they appeared alternately to smolder and to blaze.

What if Jesus had said, "All right, you can be white-trash or a nigger or ugly!"

Mrs. Turpin felt an awful pity for the girl, though she thought it was one thing to be ugly and another to act ugly.

The woman with the snuff-stained lips turned around in her 30
chair and looked up at the clock. Then she turned back and appeared to look a little to the side of Mrs. Turpin. There was a cast in one of her eyes. "You want to know wher you can get one of themther clocks?" she asked in a loud voice.

"No, I already have a nice clock," Mrs. Turpin said. Once somebody like her got a leg in the conversation, she would be all over it.

"You can get you one with green stamps," the woman said. "That's most likely wher he got hisn. Save you up enough, you can get you most anythang. I got me some joo'ry."

Ought to have got you a wash rag and some soap, Mrs. Turpin thought.

"I get contour sheets with mine," the pleasant lady said.

The daughter slammed her book shut. She looked straight in 35
front of her, directly through Mrs. Turpin and on through the yellow curtain and the plate glass window which made the wall behind her. The girl's eyes seemed lit all of a sudden with a peculiar light, an unnatural light like night road signs give. Mrs. Turpin turned her head to see if there was anything going on outside that she should see, but she could not see anything. Figures passing cast only a pale shadow through the curtain. There was no reason the girl should single her out for her ugly looks.

"Miss Finley," the nurse said, cracking the door. The gum-chewing woman got up and passed in front of her and Claud and went into the office. She had on red high-heeled shoes.

Directly across the table, the ugly girl's eyes were fixed on Mrs. Turpin as if she had some very special reason for disliking her.

"This is wonderful weather, isn't it?" the girl's mother said.

"It's good weather for cotton if you can get the niggers to pick it," Mrs. Turpin said, "but niggers don't want to pick cotton any more. You can't get the white folks to pick it and now you can't get the niggers—because they got to be right up there with the white folks."

"They gonna *try* anyways," the white-trash woman said, leaning   40
forward.

"Do you have one of those cotton-picking machines?" the pleasant lady asked.

"No," Mrs. Turpin said, "they leave half the cotton in the field. We don't have much cotton anyway. If you want to make it farming now, you have to have a little of everything. We got a couple of acres of cotton and a few hogs and chickens and just enough white-face that Claud can look after them himself."

"One thang I don't want," the white-trash woman said, wiping her mouth with the back of her hand. "Hogs. Nasty stinking things, a-gruntin and a-rootin all over the place."

Mrs. Turpin gave her the merest edge of her attention. "Our hogs are not dirty and they don't stink," she said. "They're cleaner than some children I've seen. Their feet never touch the ground. We have a pig-parlor—that's where you raise them on concrete," she explained to the pleasant lady, "and Claud scoots them down with the hose every afternoon and washes off the floor." Cleaner by far than that child right there, she thought. Poor nasty little thing. He had not moved except to put the thumb of his dirty hand into his mouth.

The woman turned her face away from Mrs. Turpin. "I know I   45
wouldn't scoot down no hog with no hose," she said to the wall.

You wouldn't have no hog to scoot down, Mrs. Turpin said to herself.

"A-gruntin and a-rootin and a-groanin," the woman muttered.

"We got a little of everything," Mrs. Turpin said to the pleasant lady. "It's no use in having more than you can handle yourself with help like it is. We found enough niggers to pick our cotton this year but Claud he has to go after them and take them home again in the evening. They can't walk that half a mile. No they can't. I tell you," she said and laughed merrily, "I sure am tired of buttering up niggers, but you got to love em if you want em to work for you.

When they come in the morning, I run out and I say, 'Hi yawl this morning?' and when Claud drives them off to the field I just wave to beat the band and they just wave back." And she waved her hand rapidly to illustrate.

"Like you read out of the same book," the lady said, showing she understood perfectly.

"Child, yes," Mrs. Turpin said. "And when they come in from the field, I run out with a bucket of icewater. That's the way it's going to be from now on," she said. "You may as well face it."

"One thang I know," the white-trash woman said. "Two thangs I ain't going to do: love no niggers or scoot down no hog with no hose." And she let out a bark of contempt.

The look that Mrs. Turpin and the pleasant lady exchanged indicated they both understood that you had to *have* certain things before you could *know* certain things. But every time Mrs. Turpin exchanged a look with the lady, she was aware that the ugly girl's peculiar eyes were still on her, and she had trouble bringing her attention back to the conversation.

"When you got something," she said, "you got to look after it." And when you ain't got a thing but breath and britches, she added to herself, you can afford to come to town every morning and just sit on the Court House coping and spit.

A grotesque revolving shadow passed across the curtain behind her and was thrown palely on the opposite wall. Then a bicycle clattered down against the outside of the building. The door opened and a colored boy glided in with a tray from the drug store. It had two large red and white paper cups on it with tops on them. He was a tall, very black boy in discolored white pants and a green nylon shirt. He was chewing gum slowly, as if to music. He set the tray down in the office opening next to the fern and stuck his head through to look for the secretary. She was not in there. He rested his arms on the ledge and waited, his narrow bottom stuck out, swaying slowly to the left and right. He raised a hand over his head and scratched the base of his skull.

"You see that button there, boy?" Mrs. Turpin said. "You can punch that and she'll come. She's probably in the back somewhere."

"Is thas right?" the boy said agreeably, as if he had never seen the button before. He leaned to the right and put his finger on it. "She sometime out," he said and twisted around to face his audience, his elbows behind him on the counter. The nurse appeared and he twisted back again. She handed him a dollar and he rooted in his pocket and made the change and counted it out to her. She gave him fifteen cents for a tip and he went out with the empty tray. The heavy door swung to slowly and closed at length with the sound of suction. For a moment no one spoke.

"They ought to send all them niggers back to Africa," the white-trash woman said. "That's wher they come from in the first place."

"Oh, I couldn't do without my good colored friends," the pleasant lady said.

"There's a heap of things worse than a nigger," Mrs. Turpin agreed. "It's all kinds of them just like it's all kinds of us."

"Yes, and it takes all kinds to make the world go round," the   60
lady said in her musical voice.

As she said it, the raw-complexioned girl snapped her teeth together. Her lower lip turned downwards and inside out, revealing the pale pink inside her mouth. After a second it rolled back up. It was the ugliest face Mrs. Turpin had ever seen anyone make and for a moment she was certain that the girl had made it at her. She was looking at her as if she had known and disliked her all her life—all of Mrs. Turpin's life, it seemed too, not just all the girl's life. Why, girl, I don't even know you, Mrs. Turpin said silently.

She forced her attention back to the discussion. "It wouldn't be practical to send them back to Africa," she said. "They wouldn't want to go. They got it too good here."

"Wouldn't be what they wanted—if I had anythang to do with it," the woman said.

"It wouldn't be a way in the world you could get all the niggers back over there," Mrs. Turpin said. "They'd be hiding out and lying down and turning sick on you and wailing and hollering and raring and pitching. It wouldn't be a way in the world to get them over there."

"They got over here," the trashy woman said. "Get back like   65
they got over."

"It wasn't so many of them then," Mrs. Turpin explained.

The woman looked at Mrs. Turpin as if here was an idiot indeed but Mrs. Turpin was not bothered by the look, considering where it came from.

"Nooo," she said, "they're going to stay here where they can go to New York and marry white folks and improve their color. That's what they all want to do, every one of them, improve their color."

"You know what comes of that, don't you?" Claud asked.

"No, Claud, what?" Mrs. Turpin said.   70

Claud's eyes twinkled. "White-faced niggers," he said with never a smile.

Everybody in the office laughed except the white-trash and the ugly girl. The girl gripped the book in her lap with white fingers. The trashy woman looked around her from face to face as if she thought they were all idiots. The old woman in the feed sack dress continued to gaze expressionless across the floor at the high-top shoes of the man opposite her, the one who had been pretending to be asleep when the Turpins came in. He was laughing heartily, his hands still spread out on his knees. The child had fallen to the side and was lying now almost face down in the old woman's lap.

While they recovered from their laughter, the nasal chorus on the radio kept the room from silence.

> *You go to blank blank*
> *And I'll go to mine*
> *But we'll all blank along*
> *To-geth-ther,*
> *And all along the blank*
> *We'll hep eachother out*
> *Smile-ling in any kind of*
> *Weath-ther!*

Mrs. Turpin didn't catch every word but she caught enough to agree with the spirit of the song and it turned her thoughts sober. To help anybody out that needed it was her philosophy of life. She never spared herself when she found somebody in need, whether they were white or black, trash or decent. And of all she had to be thankful for, she was most thankful that this was so. If Jesus had said, "You can be high society and have all the money you want and be thin and svelte-like, but you can't be a good woman with it," she would have had to say, "Well don't make me that then. Make me a good woman and it don't matter what else, how fat or how ugly or how poor!" Her heart rose. He had not made her a nigger or white-trash or ugly! He had made her herself and given her a little of everything. Jesus, thank you! she said. Thank you thank you thank you! Whenever she counted her blessings she felt as buoyant as if she weighed one hundred and twenty-five pounds instead of one hundred and eighty.

"What's wrong with your little boy?" the pleasant lady asked the white-trashy woman.

"He has a ulcer," the woman said proudly. "He ain't give me a minute's peace since he was born. Him and her are just alike," she said, nodding at the old woman, who was running her leathery fingers through the child's pale hair. "Look like I can't get nothing down them two but Co' Cola and candy."

That's all you try to get down em, Mrs. Turpin said to herself. Too lazy to light the fire. There was nothing you could tell her about people like them that she didn't know already. And it was not just that they didn't have anything. Because if you gave them everything, in two weeks it would all be broken or filthy or they would have chopped it up for lightwood. She knew all this from her own experience. Help them you must, but help them you couldn't.

All at once the ugly girl turned her lips inside out again. Her eyes were fixed like two drills on Mrs. Turpin. This time there was no mistaking that there was something urgent behind them.

Girl, Mrs. Turpin exclaimed silently, I haven't done a thing to you! The girl might be confusing her with somebody else. There was no need to sit by and let herself be intimidated. "You must be in college," she said boldly, looking directly at the girl. "I see you reading a book there."

The girl continued to stare and pointedly did not answer.

Her mother blushed at this rudeness. "The lady asked you a   80
question, Mary Grace," she said under her breath.

"I have ears," Mary Grace said.

The poor mother blushed again. "Mary Grace goes to Wellesley College," she explained. She twisted one of the buttons on her dress. "In Massachusetts," she added with a grimace. "And in the summer she just keeps right on studying. Just reads all the time, a real book worm. She's done real well at Wellesley; she's taking English and Math and History and Psychology and Social Studies," she rattled on, "and I think it's too much. I think she ought to get out and have fun."

The girl looked as if she would like to hurl them all through the plate glass window.

"Way up north," Mrs. Turpin murmured and thought, well, it hasn't done much for her manners.

"I'd almost rather to have him sick," the white-trash woman   85
said, wrenching the attention back to herself. "He's so mean when he ain't. Look like some children just take natural to meanness. It's some gets bad when they get sick but he was the opposite. Took sick and turned good. He don't give me no trouble now. It's me waitin to see the doctor," she said.

If I was going to send anybody back to Africa, Mrs. Turpin thought, it would be your kind, woman. "Yes, indeed," she said aloud, but looking up at the ceiling, "it's a heap of things worse than a nigger." And dirtier than a hog, she added to herself.

"I think people with bad dispositions are more to be pitied than anyone on earth," the pleasant lady said in a voice that was decidedly thin.

"I thank the Lord he has blessed me with a good one," Mrs. Turpin said. "The day has never dawned that I couldn't find something to laugh at."

"Not since she married me anyways," Claud said with a comical straight face.

Everybody laughed except the girl and the white-trash.   90

Mrs. Turpin's stomach shook. "He's such a caution," she said, "that I can't help but laugh at him."

The girl made a loud ugly noise through her teeth.

Her mother's mouth grew thin and tight. "I think the worst thing in the world," she said, "is an ungrateful person. To have everything and not appreciate it. I know a girl," she said, "who has parents who would give her anything, a little brother who loves her dearly, who is getting a good education, who wears the best clothes, but who can never say a kind word to anyone, who never smiles, who just criticizes and complains all day long."

"Is she too old to paddle?" Claud asked.

The girl's face was almost purple.   95

"Yes," the lady said, "I'm afraid there's nothing to do but leave her to her folly. Some day she'll wake up and it'll be too late."

"It never hurt anyone to smile," Mrs. Turpin said. "It just makes you feel better all over."

"Of course," the lady said sadly, "but there are just some people you can't tell anything to. They can't take criticism."

"If it's one thing I am," Mrs. Turpin said with feeling, "it's grateful. When I think who all I could have been besides myself and what all I got, a little of everything, and a good disposition besides, I just feel like shouting, 'Thank you, Jesus, for making everything the way it is!' It could have been different!" For one thing, somebody else could have got Claud. At the thought of this, she was flooded with gratitude and a terrible pang of joy ran through her. "Oh thank you, Jesus, Jesus, thank you!" she cried aloud.

The book struck her directly over her left eye. It struck almost at   100
the same instant that she realized the girl was about to hurl it. Before she could utter a sound, the raw face came crashing across the table toward her, howling. The girl's fingers sank like clamps into the soft flesh of her neck. She heard the mother cry out and Claud shout, "Whoa!" There was an instant when she was certain that she was about to be in an earthquake.

All at once her vision narrowed and she saw everything as if it were happening in a small room far away, or as if she were looking at it through the wrong end of a telescope. Claud's face crumpled and fell out of sight. The nurse ran in, then out, then in again. Then the gangling figure of the doctor rushed out of the inner door. Magazines flew this way and that as the table turned over. The girl fell with a thud and Mrs. Turpin's vision suddenly reversed itself and she saw everything large instead of small. The eyes of the white-trashy woman were staring hugely at the floor. There the girl, held down on one side by the nurse and on the other by her mother, was wrenching and turning in their grasp. The doctor was kneeling astride her, trying to hold her arm down. He managed after a second to sink a long needle into it.

Mrs. Turpin felt entirely hollow except for her heart which swung from side to side as if it were agitated in a great empty drum of flesh.

"Somebody that's not busy call for the ambulance," the doctor said in the off-hand voice young doctors adopt for terrible occasions.

Mrs. Turpin could not have moved a finger. The old man who had been sitting next to her skipped nimbly into the office and made the call, for the secretary still seemed to be gone.

"Claud!" Mrs. Turpin called.   105

He was not in his chair. She knew she must jump up and find him but she felt like some one trying to catch a train in a dream, when everything moves in slow motion and the faster you try to run the slower you go.

"Here I am," a suffocated voice, very unlike Claud's, said.

He was doubled up in the corner on the floor, pale as paper, holding his leg. She wanted to get up and go to him but she could not move. Instead, her gaze was drawn slowly downward to the churning face on the floor, which she could see over the doctor's shoulder.

The girl's eyes stopped rolling and focused on her. They seemed a much lighter blue than before, as if a door that had been tightly closed behind them was now open to admit light and air.

Mrs. Turpin's head cleared and her power of motion returned.   110
She leaned forward until she was looking directly into the fierce brilliant eyes. There was no doubt in her mind that the girl did know her, knew her in some intense and personal way, beyond time and place and condition. "What you got to say to me?" she asked hoarsely and held her breath, waiting, as for a revelation.

The girl raised her head. Her gaze locked with Mrs. Turpin's. "Go back to hell where you came from, you old wart hog," she whispered. Her voice was low but clear. Her eyes burned for a moment as if she saw with pleasure that her message had struck its target.

Mrs. Turpin sank back in her chair.

After a moment the girl's eyes closed and she turned her head wearily to the side.

The doctor rose and handed the nurse the empty syringe. He leaned over and put both hands for a moment on the mother's shoulders, which were shaking. She was sitting on the floor, her lips pressed together, holding Mary Grace's hand in her lap. The girl's fingers were gripped like a baby's around her thumb. "Go on to the hospital," he said. "I'll call and make the arrangements."

"Now let's see that neck," he said in a jovial voice to Mrs. Turpin. He began to inspect her neck with his two fingers. Two little moon-shaped lines like pink fish bones were indented over her windpipe. There was the beginning of an angry red swelling above her eye. His fingers passed over this also.

"Let me be," she said thickly and shook him off. "See about Claud. She kicked him."

"I'll see about him in a minute," he said and felt her pulse. He was a thin grey-haired man, given to pleasantries. "Go home and have yourself a vacation the rest of the day," he said and patted her on the shoulder.

Quit your pattin me, Mrs. Turpin growled to herself.

"And put an ice pack over that eye," he said. Then he went and squatted down beside Claud and looked at his leg. After a moment he pulled him up and Claud limped after him into the office.

Until the ambulance came, the only sounds in the room were the tremulous moans of the girl's mother, who continued to sit on the floor. The white-trash woman did not take her eyes off the girl. Mrs. Turpin looked straight ahead at nothing. Presently the ambulance drew up, a long dark shadow, behind the curtain. The attendants came in and set the stretcher down beside the girl and lifted her expertly onto it and carried her out. The nurse helped the mother gather up her things. The shadow of the ambulance moved silently away and the nurse came back in the office.

"That ther girl is going to be a lunatic, ain't she?" the white-trash woman asked the nurse, but the nurse kept on to the back and never answered her.

"Yes, she's going to be a lunatic," the white-trash woman said to the rest of them.

"Po' critter," the old woman murmured. The child's face was still in her lap. His eyes looked idly out over her knees. He had not moved during the disturbance except to draw one leg up under him.

"I thank Gawd," the white-trash woman said fervently, "I ain't a lunatic."

Claud came limping out and the Turpins went home.

As their pick-up truck turned into their own dirt road and made the crest of the hill, Mrs. Turpin gripped the window ledge and looked out suspiciously. The land sloped gracefully down through a field dotted with lavender weeds and at the start of the rise their small yellow frame house, with its little flower beds spread out around it like a fancy apron, sat primly in its accustomed place between two giant hickory trees. She would not have been startled to see a burnt wound between two blackened chimneys.

Neither of them felt like eating so they put on their house clothes and lowered the shade in the bedroom and lay down, Claud with his leg on a pillow and herself with a damp washcloth over her eye. The instant she was flat on her back, the image of a razor-backed hog with warts on its face and horns coming out behind its ears snorted into her head. She moaned, a low quiet moan.

"I am not," she said tearfully, "a wart hog. From hell." But the denial had no force. The girl's eyes and her words, even the tone of her voice, low but clear, directed only to her, brooked no repudiation. She had been singled out for the message, though there was trash in the room to whom it might justly have been applied. The full force of this fact struck her only now. There was a woman there who was neglecting her own child but she had been overlooked. The message had been given to Ruby Turpin, a respectable, hard-working, church-going woman. The tears dried. Her eyes began to burn instead with wrath.

She rose on her elbow and the washcloth fell into her hand. Claud was lying on his back, snoring. She wanted to tell him what the girl had said. At the same time, she did not wish to put the image of herself as a wart hog from hell into his mind.

"Hey, Claud," she muttered and pushed his shoulder.   130

Claud opened one pale baby blue eye.

She looked into it warily. He did not think about anything. He just went his way.

"Wha, whasit?" he said and closed the eye again.

"Nothing," she said. "Does your leg pain you?"

"Hurts like hell," Claud said.   135

"It'll quit terreckly," she said and lay back down. In a moment Claud was snoring again. For the rest of the afternoon they lay there. Claud slept. She scowled at the ceiling. Occasionally she raised her fist and made a small stabbing motion over her chest as if she was defending her innocence to invisible guests who were like the comforters of Job, reasonable-seeming but wrong.

About five-thirty Claud stirred. "Got to go after those niggers," he sighed, not moving.

She was looking straight up as if there were unintelligible handwriting on the ceiling. The protuberance over her eye had turned a greenish-blue. "Listen here," she said.

"What?"

"Kiss me."   140

Claud leaned over and kissed her loudly on the mouth. He

pinched her side and their hands interlocked. Her expression of ferocious concentration did not change. Claud got up, groaning and growling, and limped off. She continued to study the ceiling.

She did not get up until she heard the pick-up truck coming back with the Negroes. Then she rose and thrust her feet in her brown oxfords, which she did not bother to lace, and stumped out onto the back porch and got her red plastic bucket. She emptied a tray of ice cubes into it and filled it half full of water and went out into the back yard. Every afternoon after Claud brought the hands in, one of the boys helped him put out hay and the rest waited in the back of the truck until he was ready to take them home. The truck was parked in the shade under one of the hickory trees.

"Hi yawl this evening?" Mrs. Turpin asked grimly, appearing with the bucket and the dipper. There were three women and a boy in the truck.

"Us doin nicely," the oldest woman said. "Hi you doin?" and her gaze struck immediately on the dark lump on Mrs. Turpin's forehead. "You done fell down, ain't you?" she asked in a solicitous voice. The old woman was dark and almost toothless. She had on an old felt hat of Claud's set back on her head. The other two women were younger and lighter and they both had new bright green sun hats. One of them had hers on her head; the other had taken hers off and the boy was grinning beneath it.

Mrs. Turpin set the bucket down on the floor of the truck. "Yawl hep yourselves," she said. She looked around to make sure Claud had gone. "No. I didn't fall down," she said, folding her arms. "It was something worse than that." 145

"Ain't nothing bad happen to you!" the old woman said. She said it as if they all knew that Mrs. Turpin was protected in some special way by Divine Providence. "You just had you a little fall."

"We were in town at the doctor's office for where the cow kicked Mr. Turpin," Mrs. Turpin said in a flat tone that indicated they could leave off their foolishness. "And there was this girl there. A big fat girl with her face all broke out. I could look at that girl and tell she was peculiar but I couldn't tell how. And me and her mama were just talking and going along and all of a sudden WHAM! She throws this big book she was reading at me and . . ."

"Naw!" the old woman cried out.

"And then she jumps over the table and commences to choke me."

"Naw!" they all exclaimed, "naw!" 150

"Hi come she do that?" the old woman asked. "What ail her?"

Mrs. Turpin only glared in front of her.

"Somethin ail her," the old woman said.

"They carried her off in an ambulance," Mrs. Turpin continued, "but before she went she was rolling on the floor and they were trying to hold her down to give her a shot and she said something to me." She paused. "You know what she said to me?"

"What she say?" they asked.   155

"She said," Mrs. Turpin began, and stopped, her face very dark and heavy. The sun was getting whiter and whiter, blanching the sky overhead so that the leaves of the hickory tree were black in the face of it. She could not bring forth the words. "Something real ugly," she muttered.

"She sho shouldn't said nothin ugly to you," the old woman said. "You so sweet. You the sweetest lady I know."

"She pretty too," the one with the hat on said.

"And stout," the other one said. "I never knowed no sweeter white lady."

"That's the truth befo' Jesus," the old woman said. "Amen! You   160
jes as sweet and pretty as you can be."

Mrs. Turpin knew just exactly how much Negro flattery was worth and it added to her rage. "She said," she began again and finished this time with a fierce rush of breath, "that I was an old wart hog from hell."

There was an astounded silence.

"Where she at?" the youngest woman cried in a piercing voice. "Lemme see her. I'll kill her!"

"I'll kill her with you!" the other one cried.   165

"She b'long in the sylum," the old woman said emphatically. "You the sweetest white lady I know."

"She pretty too," the other two said. "Stout as she can be and sweet. Jesus satisfied with her!"

"Deed he is," the old woman declared.

Idiots! Mrs. Turpin growled to herself. You could never say anything intelligent to a nigger. You could talk at them but not with them. "Yawl ain't drunk your water," she said shortly. "Leave the bucket in the truck when you're finished with it. I got more to do than just stand around and pass the time of day," and she moved off and into the house.

She stood for a moment in the middle of the kitchen. The dark   170
protuberance over her eye looked like a miniature tornado cloud which might any moment sweep across the horizon of her brow. Her lower lip protruded dangerously. She squared her massive shoulders. Then she marched into the front of the house and out the side door and started down the road to the pig parlor. She had the look of a woman going single-handed, weaponless, into battle.

The sun was a deep yellow now like a harvest moon and was

rising westward very fast over the far tree line as if it meant to reach the hogs before she did. The road was rutted and she kicked several good-sized stones out of her path as she strode along. The pig parlor was on a little knoll at the end of a lane that ran off from the side of the barn. It was a square of concrete as large as a small room, with a board fence about four feet high around it. The concrete floor sloped slightly so that the hog wash could drain off into a trench where it was carried to the field for fertilizer. Claud was standing on the outside, on the edge of the concrete, hanging onto the top board, hosing down the floor inside. The hose was connected to the faucet of a water trough nearby.

Mrs. Turpin climbed up beside him and glowered down at the hogs inside. There were seven long-snouted bristly shoats in it— tan with liver-colored spots—and an old sow a few weeks off from farrowing. She was lying on her side grunting. The shoats were running about shaking themselves like idiot children, their little slit pig eyes searching the floor for anything left. She had read that pigs were the most intelligent animal. She doubted it. They were supposed to be smarter than dogs. There had even been a pig astronaut. He had performed his assignment perfectly but died of a heart attack afterwards because they left him in his electric suit, sitting upright throughout his examination when naturally a hog should be on all fours.

A-gruntin and a-rootin and a-groanin.

"Gimme that hose," she said, yanking it away from Claud. "Go on and carry them niggers home and then get off that leg."

"You look like you might have swallowed a mad dog," Claud observed, but he got down and limped off. He paid no attention to her humors. [175]

Until he was out of earshot, Mrs. Turpin stood on the side of the pen, holding the hose and pointing the stream of water at the hind quarters of any shoat that looked as if it might try to lie down. When he had had time to get over the hill, she turned her head slightly and her wrathful eyes scanned the path. He was nowhere in sight. She turned back again and seemed to gather herself up. Her shoulders rose and she drew in her breath.

"What do you send me a message like that for?" she said in a low fierce voice, barely above a whisper but with the force of a shout in its concentrated fury. "How am I a hog and me both? How am I saved and from hell too?" Her free fist was knotted and with the other she gripped the hose, blindly pointing the stream of water in and out of the eye of the old sow whose outraged squeal she did not hear.

The pig parlor commanded a view of the back pasture where

their twenty beef cows were gathered around the hay-bales Claud
and the boy had put out. The freshly cut pasture sloped down to
the highway. Across it was their cotton field and beyond that a
dark green dusty wood which they owned as well. The sun was
behind the wood, very red, looking over the paling of trees like a
farmer inspecting his own hogs.

"Why me?" she rumbled. "It's no trash around here, black or
white, that I haven't given to. And break my back to the bone
every day working. And do for the church."

She appeared to be the right size woman to command the arena   180
before her. "How am I a hog?" she demanded. "Exactly how am I
like them?" and she jabbed the stream of water at the shoats.
"There was plenty of trash there. It didn't have to be me."

"If you like trash better, go get yourself some trash then," she
railed. "You could have made me trash. Or a nigger. If trash is what
you wanted why didn't you make me trash?" She shook her fist
with the hose in it and a watery snake appeared momentarily in
the air. "I could quit working and take it easy and be filthy," she
growled. "Lounge about the sidewalks all day drinking root beer.
Dip snuff and spit in every puddle and have it all over my face. I
could be nasty.

"Or you could have made me a nigger. It's too late for me to be a
nigger," she said with deep sarcasm, "but I could act like one. Lay
down in the middle of the road and stop traffic. Roll on the
ground."

In the deepening light everything was taking on a mysterious
hue. The pasture was growing a peculiar glassy green and the
streak of highway had turned lavender. She braced herself for a
final assault and this time her voice rolled out over the pasture.
"Go on," she yelled, "call me a hog! Call me a hog again. From
hell. Call me a wart hog from hell. Put that bottom rail on top.
There'll still be a top and bottom!"

A garbled echo returned to her.

A final surge of fury shook her and she roared, "Who do you   185
think you are?"

The color of everything, field and crimson sky, burned for a
moment with a transparent intensity. The question carried over the
pasture and across the highway and the cotton field and returned
to her clearly like an answer from beyond the wood.

She opened her mouth but no sound came out of it.

A tiny truck, Claud's, appeared on the highway, heading rapidly
out of sight. Its gears scraped thinly. It looked like a child's toy. At
any moment a bigger truck might smash into it and scatter Claud's
and the niggers' brains all over the road.

Mrs. Turpin stood there, her gaze fixed on the highway, all her muscles rigid, until in five or six minutes the truck reappeared, returning. She waited until it had had time to turn into their own road. Then like a monumental statue coming to life, she bent her head slowly and gazed, as if through the very heart of mystery, down into the pig parlor at the hogs. They had settled all in one corner around the old sow who was grunting softly. A red glow suffused them. They appeared to pant with a secret life. Until the sun slipped finally behind the tree line, Mrs. Turpin 190 remained there with her gaze bent to them as if she were absorbing some abysmal life-giving knowledge. At last she lifted her head. There was only a purple streak in the sky, cutting through a field of crimson and leading, like an extension of the highway, into the descending dusk. She raised her hands from the side of the pen in a gesture hieratic and profound. A visionary light settled in her eyes. She saw the streak as a vast swinging bridge extending upward from the earth through a field of living fire. Upon it a vast horde of souls were rumbling toward heaven. There were whole companies of white-trash, clean for the first time in their lives, and bands of black niggers in white robes, and battalions of freaks and lunatics shouting and clapping and leaping like frogs. And bringing up the end of the procession was a tribe of people whom she recognized at once as those who, like herself and Claud, had always had a little of everything and the God-given wit to use it right. She leaned forward to observe them closer. They were marching behind the others with great dignity, accountable as they had always been for good order and common sense and respectable behavior. They alone were on key. Yet she could see by their shocked and altered faces that even their virtues were being burned away. She lowered her hands and gripped the rail of the hog pen, her eyes small but fixed unblinkingly on what lay ahead. In a moment the vision faded but she remained where she was, immobile.

At length she got down and turned off the faucet and made her slow way on the darkening path to the house. In the woods around her the invisible cricket choruses had struck up, but what she heard were the voices of the souls climbing upward into the starry field and shouting hallelujah.

NATURE AND CIVILIZATION

Nature and Civilization: Preview

wrapped it tighter in our fists. The pupa began to jerk violently, in heart-stopping knocks.

The first reason people kept a dog was to acquire an ally on the hunt, a friend at night. Then it was to maintain an avenue to animality, as our own nearness began to recede. But as we lose our awareness of all animals, dogs are becoming a bridge to nowhere.

Somebody was forever petting and stroking the plump little animals, crooning to them, as they were raised for strange, unstated reasons, but surely not to be castrated and slaughtered and skinned and eaten. They were, after all, friends.

You'd think they were rats or roaches, the way people began to talk. Get those goldfish out of that pond, I don't care how you do it. Dynamite, if necessary. But get rid of them.

I see a dog's track, or is it a coyote's? I get down on my hands and knees to sniff out a scent. What am I doing? I entertain expectations of myself as preposterous as when I landed in Tokyo—I felt so at home there that I thought I would break into fluent Japanese.

We evolved over millions of years in the wild, where survival depended on our awareness of the landscape, the weather, and the animals. We haven't been domesticated long enough to have lost those senses. . . . We can design a zoo that will make the hair stand up on the back of your neck.

Once I heard her come up very late, and as I thought I heard her singing softly, I opened my door and peeked out. When she passed my room, with the white bitch nestled in her arms, her face seemed to me surprisingly young and unblemished, even though it was dirty, and I saw a rip in her skirt. I went to bed terrified, knowing this was the end.

JOSEPH BRUCHAC III   Turtle Meat   228

"Turtle, I believe I got you and you got me," Homer said. He slipped a turn of rope around his left foot with his free arm. He kept pulling back as hard as he could to free his sleeve but the turtle had it. "I understand you, Turtle," he said, "you don't like to let go."

Overview and Ideas for Writing

Asking whether humans live in nature or in civilization is in some ways like asking whether they walk on their left feet or their right. Since Darwin's time, we have become accustomed to viewing ourselves as well-dressed apes, bundles of animal instincts over which civilization has cast a thin veneer. On the other hand, we realize what an enormous barrier of self-consciousness and acculturation this thin veneer becomes when we try to find the "natural" self beneath. As Brigid Brophy says, "there isn't and never was a natural man. We are a species that doesn't occur wild." The question is not whether we belong to nature or civilization but how we can deal with our dual citizenship.

This unit is filled with close observation. E. B. White, Loren Eiseley, Annie Dillard, Harry Crews, Lewis Thomas, and Gretel Ehrlich—different as they are in their styles and attitudes—all work from descriptions of what they have experienced with their five senses. Like them, you will have had some experiences that illustrate the relation of humans to nature: downtown, at the zoo, with pets, at the city's edge, in a small town or on a farm, in the wilderness. To write about such experiences in enough detail to allow your reader to understand them is a step toward turning sight into insight.

If you are interested in extending your vision with some research, Edward Hoagland's essay and Melissa Greene's may give you ideas. Hoagland is concerned about our dwindling experience with animals and our tendency to denature the few animals we continue to think about. Your own library research, interviews, or surveys might turn up some useful information on these points. Are the numbers of hunters, fishermen, backpackers, and canoeists increasing or decreasing? Are vacationers seeking out encounters with animals, or are they avoiding them? What daily contacts do ordinary people have with animals? Were the popular representations of animals fifty or a hundred years ago actually less anthropomorphic? Similar questions are raised by Melissa Greene, along with vexing ones about the elimination of entire species and habitats. Research into these ecological problems and what can be done about them is obviously important.

The essays by C. S. Lewis, Konrad Lorenz, and Brigid Brophy raise some controversial questions. Under what circumstances (if any) is vivisection justifiable? Is it true that no animal other than man has achieved true language? Is our civilization really in danger of "gravely underestimating the toughness of plants," as Brophy said a quarter century ago?

C. S. LEWIS

Vivisection

C(live) S(taples) Lewis (1898–1963) was born in Belfast, Ireland, and became one of the world's best-known scholars of medieval and Renaissance literature. Perhaps his most influential work is *The Allegory of Love* (1936), which made the case that Europeans who lived before "the slow evolution of the passion of romantic love" in the thirteenth century had a psychological make-up fundamentally different from that of their modern descendants. Perhaps because of his own transformation from an atheist to a defender of Christian faith, Lewis had a remarkable ability to understand psychologies and intellectual positions different from his own, and he used this ability not only in his scholarly work, but in a science fiction trilogy (*Out of the Silent Planet*, 1938; *Perelandra*, 1943; *That Hideous Strength*, 1945) and a series of children's books. Interest in working out an argument from an alien perspective is also evident in Lewis's many essays on moral, religious, and ethical questions. *The Screwtape Letters* (1942), for example, is written from the point of view of a devil, and *The Problem of Pain* (1943) raises the possibility that, from God's perspective, pain is a tool for instilling discipline. "Vivisection" was first published as a pamphlet in 1947.

It is the rarest thing in the world to hear a rational discussion of vivisection. Those who disapprove of it are commonly accused of 'sentimentality', and very often their arguments justify the accusation. They paint pictures of pretty little dogs on dissecting tables. But the other side lie open to exactly the same charge. They also often defend the practice by drawing pictures of suffering women and children whose pain can be relieved (we are assured) only by the fruits of vivisection. The one appeal, quite as clearly as the other, is addressed to emotion, to the particular emotion we call pity. And neither appeal proves anything. If the thing is right—and if right at all, it is a duty—then pity for the animal is one of the temptations we must resist in order to perform that duty. If the thing is wrong, then pity for human suffering is precisely the temptation which will most probably lure us into doing that wrong thing. But the real question—whether it is right or wrong—remains meanwhile just where it was.

A rational discussion of this subject begins by inquiring whether pain is, or is not, an evil. If it is not, then the case against vivisection falls. But then so does the case for vivisection. If it is not defended on the ground that it reduces human suffering, on what ground can it be defended? And if pain is not an evil, why should human suffering be reduced? We must therefore assume as a basis for the whole discussion that pain is an evil, otherwise there is nothing to be discussed.

Now if pain is an evil then the infliction of pain, considered in itself, must clearly be an evil act. But there are such things as necessary evils. Some acts which would be bad, simply in themselves, may be excusable and even laudable when they are necessary means to a greater good. In saying that the infliction of pain, simply in itself, is bad, we are not saying that pain ought never to be inflicted. Most of us think that it can rightly be inflicted for a good purpose—as in dentistry or just and reformatory punishment. The point is that it always requires justification. On the man whom we find inflicting pain rests the burden of showing why an act which in itself would be simply bad is, in those particular circumstances, good. If we find a man giving pleasure it is for us to prove (if we criticise him) that his action is wrong. But if we find a man inflicting pain it is for him to prove that his action is right. If he cannot, he is a wicked man. 3

Now vivisection can only be defended by showing it to be right that one species should suffer in order that another species should be happier. And here we come to the parting of the ways. The Christian defender and the ordinary 'scientific' (i.e. naturalistic) defender of vivisection, have to take quite different lines. 4

The Christian defender, especially in the Latin countries, is very apt to say that we are entitled to do anything we please to animals because they 'have no souls'. But what does this mean? If it means that animals have no consciousness, then how is this known? They certainly behave as if they had, or at least the higher animals do. I myself am inclined to think that far fewer animals than is supposed have what we should recognise as consciousness. But that is only an opinion. Unless we know on other grounds that vivisection is right we must not take the moral risk of tormenting them on a mere opinion. On the other hand, the statement that they 'have no souls' may mean that they have no moral responsibilities and are not immortal. But the absence of 'soul' in that sense makes the infliction of pain upon them not easier but harder to justify. For it means that animals cannot deserve pain, nor profit morally by the discipline of pain, nor be recompensed by happiness in another life for suffering in this. Thus all the factors which render pain more tolerable or make it less totally evil in the case of human beings will be lacking in the beasts. 'Soullessness', in so far as it is relevant to the question at all, is an argument against vivisection. 5

The only rational line for the Christian vivisectionist to take is to 6
say that the superiority of man over beast is a real objective fact,
guaranteed by Revelation, and that the propriety of sacrificing
beast to man is a logical consequence. We are 'worth more than
many sparrows',[1] and in saying this we are not merely expressing a
natural preference for our own species simply because it is our own
but conforming to a hierarchical order created by God and really
present in the universe whether any one acknowledges it or not.
The position may not be satisfactory. We may fail to see how a
benevolent Deity could wish us to draw such conclusions from the
hierarchical order He has created. We may find it difficult to formulate a human right of tormenting beasts in terms which would not
equally imply an angelic light of tormenting men. And we may feel
that though objective superiority is rightly claimed for man, yet
that very superiority ought partly to *consist in* not behaving like a
vivisector: that we ought to prove ourselves better than the beasts
precisely by the fact of acknowledging duties to them which they
do not acknowledge to us. But on all these questions different
opinions can be honestly held. If on grounds of our real, divinely
ordained, superiority a Christian pathologist thinks it right to
vivisect, and does so with scrupulous care to avoid the least dram
or scruple of unnecessary pain, in a trembling awe at the responsibility which he assumes, and with a vivid sense of the high mode in
which human life must be lived if it is to justify the sacrifices made
for it, then (whether we agree with him or not) we can respect his
point of view.

But of course the vast majority of vivisectors have no such 7
theological background. They are most of them naturalistic and
Darwinian. Now here, surely, we come up against a very alarming
fact. The very same people who will most contemptuously brush
aside any consideration of animal suffering if it stands in the way of
'research' will also, in another context, most vehemently deny that
there is any radical difference between man and the other animals.
On the naturalistic view the beasts are at bottom just the same
sort of thing as ourselves. Man is simply the cleverest of the an-
thropoids. All the grounds on which a Christian might defend
vivisection are thus cut from under our feet. We sacrifice other
species to our own not because our own has any objective
metaphysical privilege over others, but simply because it is ours. It
may be very natural to have this loyalty to our own species, but let
us hear no more from the naturalists about the 'sentimentality' of
anti-vivisectionists. If loyalty to our own species, preference for

1. Matthew x. 31. [author's note]

man simply because we are men, is not a sentiment, then what is? It may be a good sentiment or a bad one. But a sentiment it certainly is. Try to base it on logic and see what happens!

But the most sinister thing about modern vivisection is this. If a mere sentiment justifies cruelty, why stop at a sentiment for the whole human race? There is also a sentiment for the white man against the black, for a *Herrenvolk* against the non-Aryans, for 'civilized' or 'progressive' peoples against 'savage' or 'backward' peoples. Finally, for our own country, party, or class against others. Once the old Christian idea of a total difference in kind between man and beast has been abandoned, then no argument for experiments on animals can be found which is not also an argument for experiments on inferior men. If we cut up beasts simply because they cannot prevent us and because we are backing our own side in the struggle for existence, it is only logical to cut up imbeciles, criminals, enemies, or capitalists for the same reasons. Indeed, experiments on men have already begun. We all hear that Nazi scientists have done them. We all suspect that our own scientists may begin to do so, in secret, at any moment.

The alarming thing is that the vivisectors have won the first round. In the nineteenth and eighteenth century a man was not stamped as a 'crank' for protesting against vivisection. Lewis Carroll protested, if I remember his famous letter correctly, on the very same ground which I have just used.[2] Dr. Johnson—a man whose mind had as much *iron* in it as any man's—protested in a note on *Cymbeline* which is worth quoting in full. In Act I, scene v, the Queen explains to the Doctor that she wants poisons to experiment on 'such creatures as We count not worth the hanging,—but none human.'[3] The Doctor replies:

Your Highness
Shall from this practice but make hard your heart.[4]

Johnson comments: 'The thought would probably have been more amplified, had our author lived to be shocked with such experiments as have been published in later times, by a race of men that have practised tortures without pity, and related them without

2. 'Vivisection as a Sign of the Times', *The Works of Lewis Carroll*, ed. Roger Lancelyn Green (London, 1965), pp. 1089–92. See also 'Some Popular Fallacies about Vivisection', *ib.*, pp. 1092–1100. [author's note]
3. Shakespeare, *Cymbeline*, I, v, 25–26. [author's note]
4. Ibid., 23. [author's note]

shame, and are yet suffered to erect their heads among human beings.'[5]

The words are his, not mine, and in truth we hardly dare in these   10
days to use such calmly stern language. The reason why we do not
dare is that the other side has in fact won. And though cruelty even
to beasts is an important matter, their victory is symptomatic of
matters more important still. The victory of vivisection marks a
great advance in the triumph of ruthless, non-moral utilitarianism over the old world of ethical law; a triumph in which we, as
well as animals, are already the victims, and of which Dachau
and Hiroshima mark the more recent achievements. In justifying
cruelty to animals we put ourselves also on the animal level. We
choose the jungle and must abide by our choice.

You will notice I have spent no time in discussing what actually   11
goes on in the laboratories. We shall be told, of course, that there is
surprisingly little cruelty. That is a question with which, at present,
I have nothing to do. We must first decide what should be allowed:
after that it is for the police to discover what is already being done.

E. B. WHITE

Twins

E(lwyn) B(rooks) White (1899–1985), after failing as a newspaper reporter, became the principal writer of short comments for
"The Talk of the Town" section of *The New Yorker*. Harold Ross,
the magazine's founder and editor, insisted that these comments
be unsigned and employ the editorial "we," a practice which,
White complained, could make the writer sound like "a composite personality." White, however, kept his individual perspective:
"Once in a while we think of ourself as 'we,' but not often." His
voice is so distinctive that his admirers need not see a signature to
recognize his work. Originally published as an anonymous
"comment" in *The New Yorker* on June 12, 1948, "Twins" shows
E. B. White at the top of his form. As you read it, notice the way
White concentrates on description but implies by his style an
attitude toward the deer, the city, the other zoo-goers, and even
his shoes. Both the style and the attitude can be productively

5. *Johnson on Shakespeare: Essays and Notes Selected and Set Forth with an Introduction*
by Sir Walter Raleigh (London, 1908), p. 181. [author's note]

contrasted to that of Harry Crews ("Pages from the Life of a
Georgia Innocent") and Brigid Brophy ("The Menace of
Nature").

On a warm, miserable morning last week we went up to the   1
Bronx Zoo to see the moose calf and to break in a new pair of black
shoes. We encountered better luck than we had bargained for. The
cow moose and her young one were standing near the wall of the
deer park below the monkey house, and in order to get a better
view we strolled down to the lower end of the park, by the brook.
The path there is not much travelled. As we approached the corner
where the brook trickles under the wire fence, we noticed a red
deer getting to her feet. Beside her, on legs that were just learning
their business, was a spotted fawn, as small and perfect as a trinket
seen through a reducing glass. They stood there, mother and child,
under a gray beech whose trunk was engraved with dozens of
hearts and initials. Stretched on the ground was another fawn, and
we realized that the doe had just finished twinning. The second
fawn was still wet, still unrisen. Here was a scene of rare sylvan
splendor, in one of our five favorite boroughs, and we couldn't
have asked for more. Even our new shoes seemed to be working
out all right and weren't hurting much.
    The doe was only a couple of feet from the wire, and we sat   2
down on a rock at the edge of the footpath to see what sort of start
young fawns get in the deep fastnesses of Mittel Bronx. The
mother, mildly resentful of our presence and dazed from her labor,
raised one forefoot and stamped primly. Then she lowered her
head, picked up the afterbirth, and began dutifully to eat it, allowing it to swing crazily from her mouth, as though it were a bunch of
withered beet greens. From the monkey house came the loud,
insane hooting of some captious primate, filling the whole woodland with a wild hooroar. As we watched, the sun broke weakly
through, brightened the rich red of the fawns, and kindled their
white spots. Occasionally a sightseer would appear and wander
aimlessly by, but of all who passed none was aware that anything extraordinary had occurred. "Looka the kangaroos!" a child
cried. And he and his mother stared sullenly at the deer and then
walked on.
    In a few moments the second twin gathered all his legs and all   3
his ingenuity and arose, to stand for the first time sniffing the
mysteries of a park for captive deer. The doe, in recognition of his
achievement, quit her other work and began to dry him, running
her tongue against the grain and paying particular attention to the
key points. Meanwhile the first fawn tiptoed toward the shallow

brook, in little stops and goes, and started across. He paused mid-
stream to make a slight contribution, as a child does in bathing.
Then, while his mother watched, he continued across, gained the
other side, selected a hiding place, and lay down under a skunk-
cabbage leaf next to the fence, in perfect concealment, his legs
folded neatly under him. Without actually going out of sight, he
had managed to disappear completely in the shifting light and
shade. From somewhere a long way off a twelve-o'clock whistle
sounded. We hung around awhile, but he never budged. Before we
left, we crossed the brook ourself, just outside the fence, knelt,
reached through the wire, and tested the truth of what we had
once heard: that you can scratch a new fawn between the ears
without starting him. You can indeed.

KONRAD LORENZ

The Language of Animals

Konrad Lorenz (1903–1989) kept more than a few pets when he
was growing up in Austria. Encouraged by his parents, he raised
a menagerie of fish, birds, monkeys, dogs, cats, and rabbits, and
in the process acquired an interest in animals that eventually
made him a scientist of international importance and a recipient
of the Nobel Prize (1973). Lorenz was the founder of ethology,
the modern science of animal behavior. His work combined
scrupulous observation and experimentation with bold speculation about the consciousness of animals. Some scientists have
been uneasy with Lorenz's attributing to animals mental and
emotional states analogous to our own. Lorenz, however, argued
that such analogies are sometimes compelling. Observing that an
octopus' eye is structurally similar to our own, he once argued,
we naturally conclude that it is used for seeing; observing a pattern of jealous behavior in a dog that corresponds to the pattern
of our own jealous behavior, we naturally conclude that the dog
is experiencing similar emotions. "To call an animal jealous is
just as legitimate as to call an octopus' eye an eye or a lobster's leg
a leg."

Animals do not possess a language in the true sense of the word.   1
In the higher vertebrates, as also in insects, particularly in the
socially living species of both great groups, every individual has a
certain number of innate movements and sounds for expressing

feelings. It has also innate ways of reacting to these signals whenever it sees or hears them in a fellow-member of the species. The
highly social species of birds such as the jackdaw or the greylag
goose, have a complicated code of such signals which are uttered
and understood by every bird without any previous experience.
The perfect coordination of social behaviour which is brought
about by these actions and reactions conveys to the human observer the impression that the birds are talking and understanding a
language of their own. Of course, this purely innate signal code of
an animal species differs fundamentally from human language,
every word of which must be learned laboriously by the human
child. Moreover, being a genetically fixed character of the species—
just as much as any bodily character—this so-called language is,
for every individual animal species, ubiquitous in its distribution.
Obvious though this fact may seem, it was, nevertheless, with
something akin to naïve surprise that I heard the jackdaws in
northern Russia "talk" exactly the same, familiar "dialect" as my
birds at home in Altenberg. The superficial similarity between
these animal utterances and human languages diminishes further
as it becomes gradually clear to the observer that the animal, in all
these sounds and movements expressing its emotions, has in no
way the conscious intention of influencing a fellow-member of its
species. This is proved by the fact that even geese or jackdaws
reared and kept singly make all these signals as soon as the corresponding mood overtakes them. Under these circumstances the
automatic and even mechanical character of these signals becomes
strikingly apparent and reveals them as entirely different from human words.

In human behaviour, too, there are mimetic signs which auto-   2
matically transmit a certain mood and which escape one, without
or even contrary to one's intention of thereby influencing anybody
else: the commonest example of this is yawning. Now the mimetic
sign by which the yawning mood manifests itself is an easily perceived optical and acoustical stimulus whose effect is, therefore,
not particularly surprising. But, in general, such crude and patent
signals are not always necessary in order to transmit a mood. On
the contrary, it is characteristic of this particular effect that it is
often brought about by diminutive sign stimuli which are hardly
perceptible by conscious observation. The mysterious apparatus for
transmitting and receiving the sign stimuli which convey moods is
age-old, far older than mankind itself. In our own case, it has
doubtless degenerated as our word-language developed. Man has
no need of minute intention-displaying movements to announce
his momentary mood: he can say it in words. But jackdaws or dogs

are obliged to "read in each other's eyes" what they are about to do in the next moment. For this reason, in higher and social animals, the transmitting, as well as the receiving apparatus of "mood-convection" is much better developed and more highly specialized than in us humans. All expressions of animal emotions, for instance, the "Kia" and "Kiaw" note of the jackdaw, are therefore not comparable to our spoken language, but only to those expressions such as yawning, wrinkling the brow and smiling, which are expressed unconsciously as innate actions and also understood by a corresponding inborn mechanism. The "words" of the various animal "languages" are merely interjections.

Though man may also have numerous gradations of unconscious mimicry, no George Robey or Emil Jannings would be able, in this sense, to convey, by mere miming, as the greylag goose can, whether he was going to walk or fly, or to indicate whether he wanted to go home or to venture further afield, as a jackdaw can do quite easily. Just as the transmitting apparatus of animals is considerably more efficient than that of man, so also is their receiving apparatus. This is not only capable of distinguishing a large number of signals, but, to preserve the above simile, it responds to much slighter transmissions than does our own. It is incredible, what minimal signs, completely imperceptible to man, animals will receive and interpret rightly. Should one member of a jackdaw flock that is seeking for food on the ground fly upwards merely to seat itself on the nearest apple-tree and preen its feathers, then none of the others will cast so much as a glance in its direction; but, if the bird takes to wing with intent to cover a longer distance, then it will be joined, according to its authority as a member of the flock, by its spouse or also a larger group of jackdaws, in spite of the fact that it did not emit a single "Kia." 3

In this case, a man well versed in the ways and manners of jackdaws might also, by observing the minutest intention-displaying movements of the bird, be able to predict—if with less accuracy than a fellow-jackdaw—how far that particular bird was going to fly. There are instances in which a good observer can equal and even surpass an animal in its faculty of "understanding" and anticipating the intentions of its fellow, but in other cases he cannot hope to emulate it. The dog's "receiving set" far surpasses our own analogous apparatus. Everybody who understands dogs knows with what almost uncanny certitude a faithful dog recognizes in its master whether the latter is leaving the room for some reason uninteresting to his pet, or whether the longed-for daily walk is pending. Many dogs achieve even more in this respect. My Alsatian Tito, the great-great-great-great-great-grandmother of the 4 dog I now possess, knew, by "telepathy," exactly which people got on my nerves, and when. Nothing could prevent her from biting, gently but surely, all such people on their posteriors. It was particularly dangerous for authoritative old gentlemen to adopt towards me, in discussion, the well-known "you are, of course, too young" attitude. No sooner had the stranger thus expostulated, than his hand felt anxiously for the place in which Tito had punctiliously chastised him. I could never understand how it was that this reaction functioned just as reliably when the dog was lying under the table and was therefore precluded from seeing the faces and gestures of the people round it: how did she know who I was speaking to or arguing with?

This fine canine understanding of the prevailing mood of a master is not really telepathy. Many animals are capable of perceiving the smallest movements, withheld from the human eye. And a dog, whose whole powers of concentration are bent on serving his master and who literally "hangs on his every word" makes use of this faculty to the utmost. Horses too have achieved considerable feats in this field. So it will not be out of place to speak here of the tricks which have brought some measure of renown to certain animals. There have been "thinking" horses which could work out square roots, and a wonder-dog Rolf, an Airedale terrier, which went so far as to dictate its last will and testament to its mistress. All these "counting," "talking" and "thinking" animals "speak" by knocking or barking sounds, whose meaning is laid down after the fashion of a Morse code. At first sight, their performances are really astounding. You are invited to set the examination yourself and you are put opposite the horse, terrier or whatever animal it is. You ask, how much is twice two; the terrier scrutinizes you intently and barks four times. In a horse, the feat seems still more prodigious for he does not even look at you. In dogs, who watch the examiner closely, it is obvious that their attention is concentrated upon the latter and not, by any means, on the problem itself. But the horse has no need to turn his eyes towards the examiner since, even in a direction in which the animal is not directly focusing, it can see, by indirect vision, the minutest movement. And it is you yourself who betray, involuntarily to the "thinking" animal, the right solution. Should one not know the right answer oneself, the poor animal would knock or bark on desperately, waiting in vain for the sign which would tell him to stop. As a rule, this sign is forthcoming, since few people are capable, even with the utmost self-control, of withholding an unconscious and involuntary signal. That it is the human being who finds the solution and communicates it was once proved by one of my colleagues in the case of a dachshund which had become quite famous and which belonged to an elderly spinster. The method was perfidious: It consisted in suggesting a wrong solution of all the problems not to the "counting" dog, but to his mistress. To this end, my friend made cards on one side of which a simple problem was printed in fat letters. The cards, however, unknown to the dog's owner, were constructed of several layers of transparent paper on the last of which another problem was inscribed in such a manner as to be visible from behind, when the front side was presented to the animal. The unsuspecting lady, seeing, in looking-glass writing, what she imagined to be the problem to be solved, transmitted involuntarily to the dog a solution which did not correspond to that of the problem on the front of the card, and was intensely surprised when, for the first time in her experience, her pet continued to give wrong answers. Before ending the séance, my friend adopted different tactics and presented mistress and dog with a problem, which, for a change, the dog could answer and the lady could not: He put before the animal a rag impregnated with the smell of a bitch in season. The dog grew excited, wagged his tail and whined—he knew what he was smelling and a really knowledgeable dog owner might have known, too, from observing his behaviour. Not so the old lady. When the dog was asked what the rag smelled of, he promptly morsed *her* answer: "Cheese!"

The enormous sensitivity of many animals to certain minute movements of expression, as, for example, the above described capacity of the dog to perceive the friendly or hostile feelings which his master harbours for another person, is a wonderful thing. It is therefore not surprising that the naïve observer, seeking to assign to the animal human qualities, may believe that a being which can guess even such inward unspoken thoughts, must, still more, understand every word that the beloved master utters; now an intelligent dog does understand a considerable number of words, but, on the other hand, it must not be forgotten that the ability to understand the minutest expressional movements is thus acute in animals for the very reason that they lack true speech.

As I have already explained, all the innate expressions of emotion, such as the whole complicated "signal code" of the jackdaw, are far removed from human language. When your dog nuzzles you, whines, runs to the door and scratches it, or puts his paws on the wash basin under the tap, and looks at you imploringly, he does something that comes far nearer to human speech than anything that a jackdaw or goose can ever "say," no matter how clearly "intelligible" and appropriate to the occasion the finely differentiated expressional sounds of these birds may appear. The dog wants to make you open the door or turn on the tap, and what he does has the specific and purposeful motive of influencing you in a certain direction. He would never perform these movements if you were not present. But the jackdaw or goose merely gives unconscious expression to its inward mood and the "Kia" or "Kiaw," or the warning sound escapes the bird involuntarily; when in a certain mood, it must utter the corresponding sound, whether or not there is anybody there to hear it.

The intelligible actions of the dog described above are not innate   8 but are individually learned and governed by true insight. Every individual dog has different methods of making himself understood by his master and will adapt his behaviour according to the situation. My bitch Stasie, the great-grandmother of the dog I now possess, having once eaten something which disagreed with her, wanted to go out during the night. I was at that time overworked, and slept very soundly, so that she did not succeed in waking me and indicating her requirements, by her usual signs; to her whining and nosing I had evidently only responded by burying myself still deeper in my pillows. This desperate situation finally induced her to forget her normal obedience and to do a thing which was strictly forbidden her: she jumped on my bed and then proceeded literally to dig me out of the blankets and roll me on the floor. Such an adaptability to present needs is totally lacking in the "vocabulary" of birds: they never roll you out of bed.

Parrots and large corvines are endowed with "speech" in still   9 another sense: they can imitate human words. Here, an association of thought between the sounds and certain experiences is sometimes possible. This imitating is nothing other than the so-called mocking found in many song birds. Willow warblers, red-backed shrikes and many others are masters of this art. Mocking consists of sounds, learned by imitation, which are not innate and are uttered only while the bird is singing; they have no "meaning" and bear no relation whatsoever to the inborn "vocabulary" of the species. This also applies to starlings, magpies and jackdaws, who not only "mock" birds' voices but also successfully imitate human words. However, the talking of big corvines and parrots is a somewhat different matter. It still bears that character of playfulness and lack of purpose which is also inherent in the mocking of smaller birds and which is loosely akin to the play of more intelligent animals. But a corvine or a parrot will utter its human words independently of song and it is undeniable that these sounds may occasionally have a definite thought association.

Many grey parrots, as well as others, will say "good morning"   10 only once a day and at the appropriate time. My friend Professor

Otto Koehler possessed an ancient grey parrot which, being addicted to the vice of feather-plucking, was nearly bald. This bird answered to the name of "Geier" which in German means vulture. Geier was certainly no beauty but he redeemed himself by his speaking talents. He said "good morning" and "good evening" quite aptly and, when a visitor stood up to depart, he said, in a benevolent bass voice "Na, auf Wiedersehen." But he only said this if the guest really departed. Like a "thinking" dog, he was tuned in to the finest, involuntarily given signs; what these signs were, we never could find out and we never once succeeded in provoking the retort by staging a departure. But when the visitor really left, no matter how inconspicuously he took his leave, promptly and mockingly came the words "Na, auf Wiedersehen!"

The well-known Berlin ornithologist, Colonel von Lukanus, also 11 possessed a grey parrot which became famous through a feat of memory. Von Lukanus kept, among other birds, a tame hoopoe named "Höpfchen." The parrot, which could talk well, soon mastered this word. Hoopoes unfortunately do not live long in captivity, though grey parrots do; so, after a time, "Höpfchen" went the way of all flesh and the parrot appeared to have forgotten his name—at any rate, he did not say it any more. Nine years later, Colonel von Lukanus acquired another hoopoe and, as the parrot set eyes on him for the first time, he said at once, and then repeatedly, "Höpfchen" . . . "Höpfchen". . . .

In general, these birds are just as slow in learning something new 12 as they are tenacious in remembering what they have once learned. Everyone who has tried to drum a new word into the brain of a starling or a parrot knows with what patience one must apply oneself to this end, and how untiringly one must again and again repeat the word. Nevertheless, such birds can, in exceptional cases, learn to imitate a word which they have heard seldom, perhaps only once. However, this apparently only succeeds when a bird is in an exceptional state of excitement; I myself have seen only two such cases. My brother had, for years, a delightfully tame and lively blue-fronted Amazon parrot named Papagallo, which had an extraordinary talent for speech. As long as he lived with us in Altenberg, Papagallo flew just as freely around as most of my other birds. A talking parrot that flies from tree to tree and at the same time says human words, gives a much more comical effect than one that sits in a cage and does the same thing. When Papagallo, with loud cries of "Where's the Doc?" flew about the district, sometimes in a genuine search for his master, it was positively irresistible.

Still funnier, but also remarkable from a scientific point of 13 view, was the following performance of the bird; Papagallo feared nothing and nobody, with the exception of the chimney-sweep. Birds are very apt to fear things which are up above. And this tendency is associated with the innate dread of the bird of prey swooping down from the heights. So everything that appears against the sky, has for them something of the meaning of "bird of prey." As the black man, already sinister in his darkness, stood up on the chimney stack and became outlined against the sky, Papagallo fell into a panic of fear and flew, loudly screaming, so far away that we feared he might not come back. Months later, when the chimney-sweep came again, Papagallo was sitting on the weathercock, squabbling with the jackdaws who wanted to sit there too. All at once, I saw him grow long and thin and peer down anxiously into the village street; then he flew up and away, shrieking in raucous tones, again and again, "the chimney-sweep is coming, the chimney-sweep is coming." The next moment, the black man walked through the doorway of the yard!

Unfortunately, I was unable to find out how often Papagallo had seen the chimney-sweep before and how often he had heard the excited cry of our cook which heralded his approach. It was, without a doubt, the voice and intonation of this lady which the bird reproduced. But he had certainly not heard it more than three times at the most and, each time, only once and at an interval of months.

The second case known to me in which a talking bird learned human words after hearing them only once or very few times, concerns a hooded crow. Again it was a whole sentence which thus impressed itself on the bird's memory. "Hansl," as the bird was called, could compete in speaking talent with the most gifted parrot. The crow had been reared by a railwayman, in the next village, and it flew about freely and had grown into a well-proportioned, healthy fellow, a good advertisement for the rearing ability of its foster-father. Contrary to popular opinion, crows are not easy to rear and, under the inadequate care which they usually receive, mostly develop into those stunted, half-crippled specimens which are so often seen in captivity. One day, some village boys brought me a dirt-encrusted hooded crow whose wings and tail were clipped to small stumps. I was hardly able to recognize, in this pathetic being, the once beautiful Hansl. I bought the bird, as, on principle, I buy all unfortunate animals that the village boys bring me and this I do partly out of pity and partly because amongst these stray animals there might be one of real interest. And this one certainly was! I rang up Hansl's master who told me that the bird had actually been missing some days and begged me to adopt him till the next moult. So, accordingly, I put the crow in the pheasant pen and gave it concentrated food, so that, in the imminent new moult, it would grow good new wing and tail feathers. At this time, when the bird was, of necessity, a prisoner, I found out that Hansl had a surprising gift of the gab and he gave me the opportunity of hearing plenty! He had, of course, picked up just what you would expect a tame crow to hear that sits on a tree, in the village street, and listens to the "language" of the inhabitants.

I later had the pleasure of seeing this bird recover his full plumage and I freed him as soon as he was fully capable of flight. He returned forthwith to his former master, in Wordern, but continued, a welcome guest, to visit us from time to time. Once he was missing for several weeks and, when he returned, I noticed that he had, on one foot, a broken digit which had healed crooked. And this is the whole point of the history of Hansl, the hooded crow. For we know just how he came by this little defect. And from whom do we know it? Believe it or not, Hansl told us himself! When he suddenly reappeared, after his long absence, he knew a new sentence. With the accent of a true street urchin, he said, in lower Austrian dialect, a short sentence which, translated into broad Lancashire, would sound like "Got 'im in t'bloomin' trap!" There was no doubt about the truth of this statement. Just as in the case of Papagallo, a sentence which he had certainly not heard often, had stuck in Hansl's memory because he had heard it in a moment of great apprehension, that is, immediately after he had been caught. How he got away again, Hansl unfortunately did not tell us.

In such cases, the sentimental animal lover, crediting the creature with human intelligence, will take an oath on it that the bird understands what he says. This, of course, is quite incorrect. Not even the cleverest "talking" birds which, as we have seen, are certainly capable of connecting their sound-expressions with particular occurrences, learn to make practical use of their powers, to achieve purposefully even the simplest object. Professor Koehler, who can boast of the greatest successes in the science of training animals, and who succeeded in teaching pigeons to count up to six, tried to teach the above-mentioned, talented grey parrot "Geier" to say "food" when he was hungry and "water" when he was dry. This attempt did not succeed, nor, so far, has it been achieved by anybody else. In itself, the failure is remarkable. Since, as we have seen, the bird is able to connect his sound utterances with certain occurrences, we should expect him, first of all, to connect them with a purpose; but this, surprisingly, he is unable to do. In all other cases, where an animal learns a new type of behaviour, it does so to achieve some purpose. The most curious types of behaviour may be thus acquired, especially with the object of influencing the human keeper. A most grotesque habit of this kind was learned by a Blumenau's parakeet which belonged to Prof. Karl von Frisch. The scientist only let the bird fly freely when he had just watched it have an evacuation of the bowels, so that, for the next ten minutes, his well-kept furniture was not endangered. The parakeet learned very quickly to associate these facts and, as he was passionately fond of leaving his cage, he would force out a minute dropping with all his might, every time Prof. von Frisch came near the cage. He even squeezed desperately when it was impossible to produce anything, and really threatened to do himself an injury by the violence of his straining. You just had to let the poor thing out, every time you saw him!

Yet the clever "Geier," much cleverer than that little parakeet, 18 could not even learn to say "food" when he was hungry. The whole complicated apparatus of the bird's syrinx and brain that makes imitation and association of thought possible, appears to have no function in connection with the survival of the species. We ask ourselves vainly what it is there for!

I only know one bird that learned to use a human word when 19 he wanted a particular thing and who thus connected a sound-expression with a purpose, and it is certainly no coincidence that it was a bird of that species which I consider to have the highest mental development of all, namely the raven. Ravens have a certain innate call-note which corresponds to the "Kia" of the jackdaw and has the same meaning, that is, the invitation to others to fly with the bird that utters it. In the raven, this note is a sonorous, deep-throated, and, at the same time, sharply metallic "krackrackrack." Should the bird wish to persuade another of the same species which is sitting on the ground to fly with it, he executes the same kind of movements as described in the chapter on jackdaws: he flies, from behind, close above the other bird and, in passing it, wobbles with his closely folded tail, at the same time emitting a particularly sharp "krackrackrackrack" which sounds almost like a volley of small explosions.

My raven Roah, so named after the call-note of the young raven, 20 was, even as a mature bird, a close friend of mine and accompanied me, when he had nothing better to do, on long walks and even on skiing tours, or on motorboat excursions on the Danube. Particularly in his later years he was not only shy of strange people, but also had a strong aversion to places where he had once been frightened or had had any other unpleasant experience. Not only did he hesitate to come down from the air to join me in such places, but he could not bear to see me linger in what he considered to be a dangerous spot. And, just as my old jackdaws tried to make their truant children leave the ground and fly after them, so Roah bore down upon me from behind, and, flying close over my head, he wobbled with his tail and then swept upwards again, at the same time looking backwards over his shoulder to see if I was following. In accompaniment to this sequence of movements—which, to stress the fact again, is entirely innate—Roah, instead of uttering the above described call-note, said his own name, with human intonation. The most peculiar thing about this was that Roah used the human word for me only. When addressing one of his own species, he employed the normal innate call-note. To suspect that I had unconsciously trained him would obviously be wrong; for this could only have taken place if, by pure chance, I had walked up to Roah at the very moment when he happened to be calling his name, and, at the same time, to be wanting my company. Only if this rather unlikely coincidence of three factors had repeated itself on several occasions, could a corresponding association of thought have been formed by the bird, and that certainly was not the case. The old raven must, then, have possessed a sort of insight that "Roah" was my call-note! Solomon was not the only man who could speak to animals, but Roah is, so far as I know, the only animal that has ever spoken a human word to a man, in its right context—even if it was only a very ordinary call-note.

Translated by Marjorie Kerr Wilson

LOREN EISELEY

The Brown Wasps

Loren Eiseley (1907–1977) was one of those highly imaginative thinkers who cannot be neatly pigeonholed. He was a sociologist, anthropologist, historian of science, archeologist, and poet. Fascinated by evolution, he wrote such books as *Darwin's Century: Evolution and the Men Who Discovered It* (1958), *The Mind as Nature* (1962), and *Darwin and the Mysterious Mr. X: New Light on the Evolutionists* (1979). Eiseley spent a lifetime thinking about the long journey that began with the first living cell and has led to the diversity of life on earth. In his essays and poems, the present moment sometimes seems like a thin pane of glass through which he looks backward at an immense past: The evolutionary prehistory is always there, connecting the human jaw with the snake's jaw, the human hand with the bat's wing, human emotions with the emotions of our animal cousins. "The Brown Wasps" was originally published in *Gentry*, a small literary magazine, in 1957.

There is a corner in the waiting room of one of the great Eastern 1 stations where women never sit. It is always in the shadow and overhung by rows of lockers. It is, however, always frequented— not so much by genuine travelers as by the dying. It is here that a certain element of the abandoned poor seeks a refuge out of the weather, clinging for a few hours longer to the city that has fathered them. In a precisely similar manner I have seen, on a sunny day in midwinter, a few old brown wasps creep slowly over an abandoned wasp nest in a thicket. Numbed and forgetful and frost-blackened, the hum of the spring hive still resounded faintly in their sodden tissues. Then the temperature would fall and they would drop away into the white oblivion of the snow. Here in the station it is in no way different save that the city is busy in its snows. But the old ones cling to their seats as though these were symbolic and could not be given up. Now and then they sleep, their gray old heads resting with painful awkwardness on the backs of the benches.

Also they are not at rest. For an hour they may sleep in the 2 gasping exhaustion of the ill-nourished and aged who have to walk in the night. Then a policeman comes by on his round and nudges them upright.

"You can't sleep here," he growls. 3

A strange ritual then begins. An old man is difficult to waken. 4 After a muttered conversation the policeman presses a coin into his hand and passes fiercely along the benches prodding and gesturing toward the door. In his wake, like birds rising and settling behind the passage of a farmer through a cornfield, the men totter up, move a few paces and subside once more upon the benches.

One man, after a slight, apologetic lurch, does not move at all. 5 Tubercularly thin, he sleeps on steadily. The policeman does not look back. To him, too, this has become a ritual. He will not have to notice it again officially for another hour.

Once in a while one of the sleepers will not awake. Like the 6 brown wasps, he will have had his wish to die in the great droning center of the hive rather than in some lonely room. It is not so bad here with the shuffle of footsteps and the knowledge that there are others who share the bad luck of the world. There are also the whistles and the sounds of everyone, everyone in the world, start-

ing on journeys. Amidst so many journeys somebody is bound to
come out all right. Somebody.

Maybe it was on a like thought that the brown wasps fell away   7
from the old paper nest in the thicket. You hold till the last, even if
it is only to a public seat in a railroad station. You want your place
in the hive more than you want a room or a place where the aged
can be eased gently out of the way. It is the place that matters, the
place at the heart of things. It is life that you want, that bruises your
gray old head with the hard chairs; a man has a right to his place.

But sometimes the place is lost in the years behind us. Or some-   8
times it is a thing of air, a kind of vaporous distortion above a heap
of rubble. We cling to a time and place because without them man
is lost, not only man but life. This is why the voices, real or unreal,
which speak from the floating trumpets at spiritualist seances are so
unnerving. They are voices out of nowhere whose only reality lies
in their ability to stir the memory of a living person with some
fragment of the past. Before the medium's cabinet both the dead
and the living revolve endlessly about an episode, a place, an event
that has already been engulfed by time.

This feeling runs deep in life; it brings stray cats running over   9
endless miles, and birds homing from the ends of the earth. It is as
though all living creatures, and particularly the more intelligent,
can survive only by fixing or transforming a bit of time into space
or by securing a bit of space with its objects immortalized and made
permanent in time. For example, I once saw, on a flower pot in my
own living room, the efforts of a field mouse to build a remembered
field. I have lived to see this episode repeated in a thousand guises,
and since I have spent a large portion of my life in the shade of a
nonexistent tree, I think I am entitled to speak for the field mouse.

One day as I cut across the field which at that time extended on   10
one side of our suburban shopping center, I found a giant slug
feeding from a runnel of pink ice cream in an abandoned Dixie
cup. I could see his eyes telescope and protrude in a kind of dim,
uncertain ecstasy as his dark body bunched and elongated in the
curve of the cup. Then, as I stood there at the edge of the concrete,
contemplating the slug, I began to realize it was like standing on a
shore where a different type of life creeps up and fumbles tentatively among the rocks and sea wrack. It knows its place and will
only creep so far until something changes. Little by little as I stood
there I began to see more of this shore that surrounds the place of
man. I looked with sudden care and attention at things I had been
running over thoughtlessly for years. I even waded out a short
way into the grass and the wild-rose thickets to see more. A huge

black-belted bee went droning by and there were some indistinct
scurryings in the underbrush.

    Then I came to a sign which informed me that this field was to be   11
the site of a new Wanamaker suburban store. Thousands of obscure lives were about to perish, the spores of puffballs would go
smoking off to new fields, and the bodies of little white-footed mice
would be crunched under the inexorable wheels of the bulldozers.
Life disappears or modifies its appearances so fast that everything
takes on an aspect of illusion—a momentary fizzing and boiling
with smoke rings, like pouring dissident chemicals into a retort.
Here man was advancing, but in a few years his plaster and bricks
would be disappearing once more into the insatiable maw of the
clover. Being of an archaeological cast of mind, I thought of this
fact with an obscure sense of satisfaction and waded back through
the rose thickets to the concrete parking lot. As I did so, a mouse
scurried ahead of me, frightened of my steps if not of that ominous
Wanamaker sign. I saw him vanish in the general direction of my
apartment house, his little body quivering with fear in the great
open sun on the blazing concrete. Blinded and confused, he was
running straight away from his field. In another week scores would
follow him.

    I forgot the episode then and went home to the quiet of my living   12
room. It was not until a week later, letting myself into the apartment, that I realized I had a visitor. I am fond of plants and had
several ferns standing on the floor in pots to avoid the noon glare
by the south window.

    As I snapped on the light and glanced carelessly around the   13
room, I saw a little heap of earth on the carpet and a scrabble of
pebbles that had been kicked merrily over the edge of one of the
flower pots. To my astonishment I discovered a full-fledged burrow
delving downward among the fern roots. I waited silently. The
creature who had made the burrow did not appear. I remembered
the wild field then, and the flight of the mice. No house mouse, no
Mus domesticus, had kicked up this little heap of earth or sought
refuge under a fern root in a flower pot. I thought of the desperate little creature I had seen fleeing from the wild-rose thicket.
Through intricacies of pipes and attics, he, or one of his fellows,
had climbed to this high green solitary room. I could visualize what
had occurred. He had an image in his head, a world of seed pods
and quiet, of green sheltering leaves in the dim light among the
weed stems. It was the only world he knew and it was gone.

    Somehow in his flight he had found his way to this room with   14
drawn shades where no one would come till nightfall. And here he
had smelled green leaves and run quickly up the flower pot to

dabble his paws in common earth. He had even struggled half the afternoon to carry his burrow deeper and had failed. I examined the hole, but no whiskered twitching face appeared. He was gone. I gathered up the earth and refilled the burrow. I did not expect to find traces of him again.

Yet for three nights thereafter I came home to the darkened 15 room and my ferns to find the dirt kicked gaily about the rug and the burrow reopened, though I was never able to catch the field mouse within it. I dropped a little food about the mouth of the burrow, but it was never touched. I looked under beds or sat reading with one ear cocked for rustlings in the ferns. It was all in vain; I never saw him. Probably he ended in a trap in some other tenant's room.

But before he disappeared I had come to look hopefully for his 16 evening burrow. About my ferns there had begun to linger the insubstantial vapor of an autumn field, the distilled essence, as it were, of a mouse brain in exile from its home. It was a small dream, like our dreams, carried a long and weary journey along pipes and through spider webs, past holes over which loomed the shadows of waiting cats, and finally, desperately, into this room where he had played in the shuttered daylight for an hour among the green ferns on the floor. Every day these invisible dreams pass us on the street, or rise from beneath our feet, or look out upon us from beneath a bush.

Some years ago the old elevated railway in Philadelphia was torn 17 down and replaced by a subway system. This ancient El with its barnlike stations containing nut-vending machines and scattered food scraps had, for generations, been the favorite feeding ground of flocks of pigeons, generally one flock to a station along the route of the El. Hundreds of pigeons were dependent upon the system. They flapped in and out of its stanchions and steel work or gathered in watchful little audiences about the feet of anyone who rattled the peanut-vending machines. They even watched people who jingled change in their hands, and prospected for food under the feet of the crowds who gathered between trains. Probably very few among the waiting people who tossed a crumb to an eager pigeon realized that this El was like a food-bearing river, and that the life which haunted its banks was dependent upon the running of the trains with their human freight.

I saw the river stop. 18

The time came when the underground tubes were ready; the 19 traffic was transferred to a realm unreachable by pigeons. It was like a great river subsiding suddenly into desert sands. For a day, for two days, pigeons continued to circle over the El or stand close to the red vending machines. They were patient birds, and surely this great river which had flowed through the lives of unnumbered generations was merely suffering from some momentary drought.

They listened for the familiar vibrations that had always her-   20
alded an approaching train; they flapped hopefully about the head of an occasional workman walking along the steel runways. They passed from one empty station to another, all the while growing hungrier. Finally they flew away.

I thought I had seen the last of them about the El, but there was a   21
revival and it provided a curious instance of the memory of living things for a way of life or a locality that has long been cherished. Some weeks after the El was abandoned workmen began to tear it down. I went to work every morning by one particular station, and the time came when the demolition crews reached this spot. Acetylene torches showered passersby with sparks, pneumatic drills hammered at the base of the structure, and a blind man who, like the pigeons, had clung with his cup to a stairway leading to the change booth, was forced to give up his place.

It was then, strangely, momentarily, one morning that I wit-   22
nessed the return of a little band of the familiar pigeons. I even recognized one or two members of the flock that had lived around this particular station before they were dispersed into the streets. They flew bravely in and out among the sparks and the hammers and the shouting workmen. They had returned—and they had returned because the hubbub of the wreckers had convinced them that the river was about to flow once more. For several hours they flapped in and out through the empty windows, nodding their heads and watching the fall of girders with attentive little eyes. By the following morning the station was reduced to some burned-off stanchions in the street. My bird friends had gone. It was plain, however, that they retained a memory for an insubstantial struc-ture now compounded of air and time. Even the blind man clung to it. Someone had provided him with a chair, and he sat at the same corner staring sightlessly at an invisible stairway where, so far as he was concerned, the crowds were still ascending to the trains.

I have said my life has been passed in the shade of a nonexistent   23
tree, so that such sights do not offend me. Prematurely I am one of the brown wasps and I often sit with them in the great droning hive of the station, dreaming sometimes of a certain tree. It was planted sixty years ago by a boy with a bucket and a toy spade in a little Nebraska town. That boy was myself. It was a cottonwood sapling and the boy remembered it because of some words spoken by his father and because everyone died or moved away who was sup-posed to wait and grow old under its shade. The boy was passed

from hand to hand, but the tree for some intangible reason had taken root in his mind. It was under its branches that he sheltered; it was from this tree that his memories, which are my memories, led away into the world.

After sixty years the mood of the brown wasps grows heavier upon one. During a long inward struggle I thought it would do me good to go and look upon that actual tree. I found a rational excuse in which to clothe this madness. I purchased a ticket and at the end of two thousand miles I walked another mile to an address that was still the same. The house had not been altered. 24

I came close to the white picket fence and reluctantly, with great effort, looked down the long vista of the yard. There was nothing there to see. For sixty years that cottonwood had been growing in my mind. Season by season its seeds had been floating farther on the hot prairie winds. We had planted it lovingly there, my father and I, because he had a great hunger for soil and live things growing, and because none of these things had long been ours to protect. We had planted the little sapling and watered it faithfully, and I remembered that I had run out with my small bucket to drench its roots the day we moved away. And all the years since it had been growing in my mind, a huge tree that somehow stood for my father and the love I bore him. I took a grasp on the picket fence and forced myself to look again. 25

A boy with the hard bird eye of youth pedaled a tricycle slowly up beside me. 26

"What'cha lookin' at?" he asked curiously. 27

"A tree," I said. 28

"What for?" he said. 29

"It isn't there," I said, to myself mostly, and began to walk away at a pace just slow enough not to seem to be running. 30

"What isn't there?" the boy asked. I didn't answer. It was obvious I was attached by a thread to a thing that had never been there, or certainly not for long. Something that had to be held in the air, or sustained in the mind, because it was part of my orientation in the universe and I could not survive without it. There was more than an animal's attachment to a place. There was something else, the attachment of the spirit to a grouping of events in time; it was part of our morality. 31

So I had come home at last, driven by a memory in the brain as surely as the field mouse who had delved long ago into my flower pot or the pigeons flying forever amidst the rattle of nut-vending machines. These, the burrow under the greenery in my living room and the red-bellied bowls of peanuts now hovering in midair in the minds of pigeons, were all part of an elusive world that existed 32 nowhere and yet everywhere. I looked once at the real world about me while the persistent boy pedaled at my heels.

It was without meaning, though my feet took a remembered   33
path. In sixty years the house and street had rotted out of my mind. But the tree, the tree that no longer was, that had perished in its first season, bloomed on in my individual mind, unblemished as my father's words. "We'll plant a tree here, son, and we're not going to move any more. And when you're an old, old man you can sit under it and think how we planted it here, you and me, together."

I began to outpace the boy on the tricycle.   34

"Do you live here, Mister?" he shouted after me suspiciously. I   35
took a firm grasp on airy nothing—to be precise, on the bole of a great tree. "I do," I said. I spoke for myself, one field mouse, and several pigeons. We were all out of touch but somehow permanent. It was the world that had changed.

BRIGID BROPHY

The Menace of Nature

Brigid Brophy (1929–   ), after completing an undergraduate degree in classics at Oxford University, found work as a secretary first for a London camera firm and later for a distributor of pornographic books. By 1954, however, she had established herself as a prize-winning novelist. Since then she has produced several novels, scores of essays, a psychoanalytic study of civilization (*Black Ship to Hell*, 1962), a book on Mozart and another on the "decadent" artist Aubrey Beardsley. Perhaps the most characteristic of her titles, however, is *Fifty Works of English Literature We Could Do Without* (1968). Brophy is an iconoclast by nature: She challenges every complacent assumption she finds. "The Menace of Nature" (first published in London's *New Statesman* in 1965) attacks several beliefs most of us accept without a second thought: that the city is stressful and the country relaxing, that a rural landscape is more beautiful than a block of buildings, that when we get "back to the land" we are making contact with something basic to human nature. Not only does Brophy challenge beliefs some of us cherish, but she addresses us with more familiarity than we are accustomed to: she seems to pluck at our sleeves rather than address us from behind a lectern.

So? Are you just back? Or are you, perhaps, staying on there for   1
the extra week? By "there" I mean, of course, one of the few spots
left where the machine has not yet gained the upper hand; some
place as yet unstrangled by motorways and unfouled by concrete
mixers; a place where the human spirit can still—but for how
much longer?—steep itself in natural beauty and recuperate after
the nervous tension, the sheer stress, of modern living.

Well (I assume you're *enough* recuperated to stand this informa-   2
tion?): I think you've been piously subscribing to a heresy. It's a
heresy I incline offhand to trace, with an almost personally piqued
sense of vendetta, to the old heresiarch himself, the sometimes
great, often bathetic but never cogently thoughtful poet, William
Wordsworth. Since the day he let the seeds of heresy fall (on, no
doubt, the Braes of the Yarrow or the Banks of Nith), the thing has
spread and enlarged itself into one of the great parroted, meaningless (but slightly paranoid) untruths of our age.

I am not trying to abolish the countryside. (I *state* this because it is   3
true; I emphasise it because I don't want the lynch mob outside my
window.) I'm not such a pig as to want the country built on or
littered up with bottles and plastic bags merely because it doesn't
appeal to *me*. As it happens, my own taste for countryside, though
small, is existent. I've found the country very pleasant to be driven
through in a tolerably fast car by someone whose driving I trust
and whose company I like. But I admit that landscape as such
bores me—to the extent that I have noticed myself in picture galleries automatically pausing to look at "Landscape with Ruins" or
"Bandits in a Landscape" but walking straight past the pure landscapes at a speed which is obviously trying to simulate the effect of
being driven past in a car.

I'm not, however, out to dissuade *you* from spending your holi-   4
day as a sort of legalised bandit in the landscape. Neither am I anti-
holiday. Holidays have been sniped at lately as things everyone
feels an obligation to enjoy but no one really does. Yet I suspect
there would be fewer dissatisfied holiday-makers if social pressure
didn't try to limit our choice to "Landscape" or "Landscape with
Seascape." You can be made to feel quite guiltily antisocial in the
summer months if you are, like me, constitutionally unable either
to relax or to take a suntan. Indeed, relaxation is becoming this
decade's social *sine qua non*, like Bridge in the 'thirties. They'll
scarcely let you have a *baby* these days if you can't satisfy them
beforehand you're adept at relaxing. But on the in some ways more
private question of having a holiday, constitutional urbanites are
still free, if only they can resist being shamed onto the beaches, to

opt out of a rest and settle for the change which even the proverb allows to be as good as it. By simply exchanging their own for a foreign city, they are released from the routine of earning their daily bread and washing up after it, but don't suffer the disorientation, the uncorseted discomfort, which overtakes an urbanite cast up on a beach with no timetable to live by except the tides.

Still, it isn't in the holidays but during the rest of the year that the great rural heresy does its damage. How many, for example, of the middle-class parents who bring up their children in London do so with unease or even apology, with a feeling that they are selfishly depriving the children of some "natural heritage" and sullying their childhood with urban impurities? Some parents even let this guilt drive them out to the suburbs or further, where they believe they cancel the egocentricity of their own need or desire for the town by undergoing the martyrdom of commuting. This parental masochism may secure the child a rural heritage (though parents should enquire, before moving, whether their child has the rural temperament and *wants* the rural heritage) but it deprives him of the cultural one; he gains the tennis club but is condemned to the tennis club light-opera society's amateur production of *No, No, Nanette* because the trains don't run late enough to bring him home after Sadler's Wells.[1]

The notion that "nature" and "nature study" are somehow "nice" for children, regardless of the children's own temperament, is a sentimental piety—and often a hypocritical one, like the piety which thinks Sunday School nice for *them* though we don't go to church ourselves. (In fact, it is we middle-aged who may need fresh air and exercise; the young are cat-like enough to remain lithe without.) Historically, it is not inept to trace the supposed affinity between children and "nature" to Wordsworth's time. It was about that time that there settled on England, like a drizzle, the belief that sex is *not* "nice" for children. Children's sexual curiosity was diverted to "the birds and the bees" and gooseberry bushes; and birds, bees and bushes—in other words, "nature"—have remained "suitable" for children ever since.

If the romantic belief in children's innocence is now exploded, its numinous energy has only gone to strengthen the even more absurd romantic belief in the innocence of landscape's, as opposed to man-created, beauty. But I reject utterly the imputation that a brook is purer than Bach or a breeze more innocent than *As You Like It*. I warn you I shall be suspicious of this aesthetic faculty of

1. Theater in London, primarily used by visiting theatrical companies.

yours that renders you so susceptible to the beauty of Snowdon[2] if it leaves you unable to see anything in All Souls', Langham Place; and I shall be downright sceptical of it if (I am making allowance for your sensibility to run exclusively in that landscape groove which mine leaves out) you doat on the Constable country but feel it vaguely impure to take a 74 to the V.&A. to see a Constable.

You'll protest you feel no such impurity. Yet didn't you read the first paragraph of this article without taking so much as a raised eyebrow's worth of exception? Didn't you let the assumption pass that the city is corrupt? Weren't you prepared to accept from me, as you have from a hundred august authorities—sociologists, physicians, psychologists—that *idée reçue*[3] about the nervous tension and stress of modern urban life? But what in heaven's name is this stressful modern urban life being compared with? Life in a medieval hamlet? Will no one take into account the symptoms into which the stress of *that* erupted—the epidemics of dancing madness and flagellation frenzy? Or life in a neolithic cave—whose stress one can only imagine and flinch at? 8

The truth is that the city is a device for *reducing* stress—by giving humans a freer choice of escapes from the pressure (along with the weather) of their environment. The device doesn't always work perfectly: traffic jams *are* annoying; the motor car does maim and must be prevented from doing so: but the ambulance which arrives so mercifully quick is also powered by a motor. The city is one of the great indispensable devices of civilisation (itself only a device for centralising beauty and transmitting it as a heritage). It is one of the cardinal simple brilliant inventions, like currency. Like currency, it is a medium of exchange and thereby of choice—whereas the country is a place where one is under the thumb of chance, constrained to love one's neighbour not out of philanthropy but because there's no other company. 9

What's more, in the eighteenth century the city was suddenly upgraded from a device of civilisation to a manifestation of it. The city became an art form. (The form had been discovered, but not very consciously remarked, earlier. It was discovered, like many art forms, by accident—often, as at Venice and Bruges, an accident of water.) We are in dire danger now of clogging up our cities as 10

2. The references in the last sentence in the paragraph are: *Snowdon*, highest mountain in Wales, in a district noted for scenic beauty; *All Soul's, Langham Place*, church in London built 1822–25 by John Nash; *Constable country*, rural areas in southern Great Britain painted by the famous landscape painter John Constable (1776–1837); *a 74*, a bus; *the V.&A.*, the Victoria & Albert Museum in London, where a number of Constables are hung.
3. An idea generally accepted by everyone.

devices and at the same time despoiling them as works of art; and one of the biggest villains in this process is our rural heresy.

Most western European beings have to live in cities, and all but   11
the tiny portion of them who are temperamental rustics would do so contentedly, without wasting energy in guilt, and with an appreciative eye for the architecturescapes round them, had they not been told that liking the country is purer and more spiritual. Our cities run to squalor and our machines run amok because our citizens' minds are not on the job of mastering the machines and using them to make the cities efficient and beautiful. Their eyes are blind to the Chirico-esque[4] handsomeness of the M1, because their hearts are set on a rustic Never-Never Land. Rustic sentimentality makes us build our suburban villas to mimic cottages, and then pebble-dash their outside walls in pious memory of the holiday we spent sitting agonised on the shingle. The lovely terraced façades of London are being undermined, as by subsidence, by our yearning, our sickly nostalgia, for a communal country childhood that never existed. We neglect our towns for a fantasy of going "back" to the land, back to our "natural" state. But there isn't and never was a natural man. We are a species that doesn't occur wild. No pattern in his genes instructs man on what pattern to build his nest. Instead, if he's fortunate, the Muses whisper to him the ground-plan of an architectural folly. Even in his cave, he frescoed the walls. All that is infallibly natural to our species is to make things that are artificial. We are *homo artifex, homo faber, homo Fabergé*.[5] Yet we are so ignorant of our own human nature that our cities are falling into disrepair and all we worry about is their encroachment on "nature."

For, as I said at the start, the rural fantasy is paranoid. A glance   12
at history shews that it is human life which is frail, and civilisation which flickers in constant danger of being blown out. But the rural fantasy insists that every plant is a delicate plant. The true paranoid situation is on the other foot. I wouldn't wish to do (and if we live at sensibly high densities there's no need to do) either, but were I forced either to pull down a Nash terrace or to build over a meadow, I'd choose the latter. If you don't like what you've put up on the meadow, you can take it away again and the meadow will

---

4. The allusion is to Giorgio de Chirico, an early twentieth-century Italian painter whose mysterious, symbolic work influenced surrealist painters. The M1 is a major northbound highway out of London.
5. Very freely translatable either as "man the craftsman, man the builder, man the perfumed" or as "man the tool-user, man the engineer, man the jeweler." Fabergé is the name of both an international manufacturer of fragrances and a brilliant Russian goldsmith, known especially for his Imperial Easter eggs.

re-seed itself in a year or two; but human semen is lucky if it engenders an architectural genius a century. The whole Words-worthian fallacy consists in gravely underestimating the toughness of plants. In fact, no sooner does civilisation admit a crack—no sooner does a temple of Apollo lapse into disuse—than a weed forces its wiry stem through the crack and urges the blocks of stone further apart. During the last war, the bomber engines were hardly out of earshot before the loosestrife[6] leapt up on the bombed site. Whether we demolish our cities in a third world war or just let them tumble into decay, the seeds of the vegetable kingdom are no doubt waiting to seize on the rubble or sprout through the cracks. *Aux armes, citoyens.*[7] To your trowels and mortar. Man the concrete mixers. The deep mindless silence of the countryside is massing in the Green Belt, ready to move in.

ANNIE DILLARD

The Fixed

Annie Dillard (1945–   ), wrote her master's thesis on Henry David Thoreau's *Walden* in 1968. Like Thoreau, she combines a philosophical interest in nature with unusual abilities as a close observer and recorder of the world around her. The combination is so striking that it brought Dillard from obscurity to national prominence at one stroke with the publication of her Pulitzer Prize-winning *Pilgrim at Tinker Creek* (1974), from which "The Fixed" is excerpted. Since then she has published a steady stream of poetry and prose, including *Holy the Firm* (1978), *Tickets for a Prayer Wheel* (1982), *Teaching a Stone to Talk* (1982), and *An American Childhood* (1987). *Pilgrim at Tinker Creek* is a guidebook to the author's neighborhood: its most common gesture is a pointing finger and a plea for us to look at what we commonly overlook. If we follow her instructions, we discover once again that our neighborhood is the earth and that our relationship with our neighbors is troubling.

I have just learned to see praying mantis egg cases. Suddenly I   1
see them everywhere; a tan oval of light catches my eye, or I notice

6. A wild flowering plant.
7. "To arms, citizens"—a call to battle (the third line of the French national anthem, *La Marseillaise*, written at the time of the French Revolution, 1792).

a blob of thickness in a patch of slender weeds. As I write I can see the one I tied to the mock orange hedge outside my study window. It is over an inch long and shaped like a bell, or like the northern hemisphere of an egg cut through its equator. The full length of one of its long sides is affixed to a twig; the side that catches the light is perfectly flat. It has a dead straw, deadweed color, and a curious brittle texture, hard as varnish, but pitted minutely, like frozen foam. I carried it home this afternoon, holding it carefully by the twig, along with several others—they were light as air. I dropped one without missing it until I got home and made a count.

Within the week I've seen thirty or so of these egg cases in a   2
rose-grown field on Tinker Mountain, and another thirty in weeds along Carvin's Creek. One was on a twig of tiny dogwood on the mud lawn of a newly built house. I think the mail-order houses sell them to gardeners at a dollar apiece. It beats spraying, because each case contains between one hundred twenty-five to three hundred fifty eggs. If the eggs survive ants, woodpeckers, and mice—and most do—then you get the fun of seeing the new mantises hatch, and the smug feeling of knowing, all summer long, that they're out there in your garden devouring gruesome numbers of fellow insects all nice and organically. When a mantis has crunched up the last shred of its victim, it cleans its smooth green face like a cat.

In late summer I often see a winged adult stalking the insects   3
that swarm about my porch light. Its body is a clear, warm green; its naked, triangular head can revolve uncannily, so that I often see one twist its head to gaze at me as it were over its shoulder. When it strikes, it jerks so suddenly and with such a fearful clatter of raised wings, that even a hardened entomologist like J. Henri Fabre[1] confessed to being startled witless every time.

Adult mantises eat more or less everything that breathes and is   4
small enough to capture. They eat honeybees and butterflies, including monarch butterflies. People have actually seen them seize and devour garter snakes, mice, and even *hummingbirds*. Newly hatched mantises, on the other hand, eat small creatures like aphids and each other. When I was in elementary school, one of the teachers brought in a mantis egg case in a Mason jar. I watched the newly hatched mantises emerge and shed their skins; they were spidery and translucent, all over joints. They trailed from the egg case to the base of the Mason jar in a living bridge that looked like Arabic calligraphy, some baffling text from the Koran inscribed down the air by a fine hand. Over a period of several hours, during which time the teacher never summoned the nerve or the sense to

1. Noted French observer of the behavior of insects (1823–1915).

release them, they ate each other until only two were left. Tiny legs were still kicking from the mouths of both. The two survivors grappled and sawed in the Mason jar; finally both died of injuries. I felt as though I myself should swallow the corpses, shutting my eyes and washing them down like jagged pills, so all that life wouldn't be lost.

When mantises hatch in the wild, however, they straggle about prettily, dodging ants, till all are lost in the grass. So it was in hopes of seeing an eventual hatch that I pocketed my jackknife this afternoon before I set out to walk. Now that I can see the egg cases, I'm embarrassed to realize how many I must have missed all along. I walked east through the Adams' woods to the cornfield, cutting three undamaged egg cases I found at the edge of the field. It was a clear, picturesque day, a February day without clouds, without emotion or spirit, like a beautiful woman with an empty face. In my fingers I carried the thorny stems from which the egg cases hung like roses; I switched the bouquet from hand to hand, warming the free hand in a pocket. Passing the house again, deciding not to fetch gloves, I walked north to the hill by the place where the steers come to drink from Tinker Creek. There in the weeds on the hill I found another eight egg cases. I was stunned—I cross this hill several times a week, and I always look for egg cases here, because it was here that I had once seen a mantis laying her eggs.

It was several years ago that I witnessed this extraordinary procedure, but I remember, and confess, an inescapable feeling that I was watching something not real and present, but a horrible nature movie, a "secrets-of-nature" short, beautifully photographed in full color, that I had to sit through unable to look anywhere else but at the dimly lighted EXIT signs along the walls, and that behind the scenes some amateur moviemaker was congratulating himself on having stumbled across this little wonder, or even on having contrived so natural a setting, as though the whole scene had been shot very carefully in a terrarium in someone's greenhouse.

I was ambling across this hill that day when I noticed a speck of pure white. The hill is eroded; the slope is a rutted wreck of red clay broken by grassy hillocks and low wild roses whose roots clasp a pittance of topsoil. I leaned to examine the white thing and saw a mass of bubbles like spittle. Then I saw something dark like an engorged leech rummaging over the spittle, and then I saw the praying mantis.

She was upside-down, clinging to a horizontal stem of wild rose by her feet which pointed to heaven. Her head was deep in dried grass. Her abdomen was swollen like a smashed finger; it tapered to a fleshy tip out of which bubbled a wet, whipped froth. I couldn't believe my eyes. I lay on the hill this way and that, my knees in thorns and my cheeks in clay, trying to see as well as I could. I poked near the female's head with a grass; she was clearly undisturbed, so I settled my nose an inch from that pulsing abdomen. It puffed like a concertina, it throbbed like a bellows; it roved, pumping, over the glistening, clabbered surface of the egg case testing and patting, thrusting and smoothing. It seemed to act so independently that I forgot the panting brown stick at the other end. The bubble creature seemed to have two eyes, a frantic little brain, and two busy, soft hands. It looked like a hideous, harried mother slicking up a fat daughter for a beauty pageant, touching her up, slobbering over her, patting and hemming and brushing and stroking.

The male was nowhere in sight. The female had probably eaten   9
him. Fabre says that, at least in captivity, the female will mate with and devour up to seven males, whether she has laid her egg cases or not. The mating rites of mantises are well known: a chemical produced in the head of the male insect says, in effect, "No, don't go near her, you fool, she'll eat you alive." At the same time a chemical in his abdomen says, "Yes, by all means, now and forever yes."

While the male is making up what passes for his mind, the   10
female tips the balance in her favor by eating his head. He mounts her. Fabre describes the mating, which sometimes lasts six hours, as follows: "The male, absorbed in the performance of his vital functions, holds the female in a tight embrace. But the wretch has no head; he has no neck; he has hardly a body. The other, with her muzzle turned over her shoulder continues very placidly to gnaw what remains of the gentle swain. And, all the time, that masculine stump, holding on firmly, goes on with the business! . . . I have seen it done with my own eyes and have not yet recovered from my astonishment."

I watched the egg-laying for over an hour. When I returned the   11
next day, the mantis was gone. The white foam had hardened and browned to a dirty suds; then, and on subsequent days, I had trouble pinpointing the case, which was only an inch or so off the ground. I checked on it every week all winter long. In the spring the ants discovered it; every week I saw dozens of ants scrambling over the sides, unable to chew a way in. Later in the spring I climbed the hill every day, hoping to catch the hatch. The leaves of the trees had long since unfolded, the butterflies were out, and the robins' first broods were fledged; still the egg case hung silent and full on the stem. I read that I should wait for June, but still I visited

the case every day. One morning at the beginning of June everything was gone. I couldn't find the lower thorn in the clump of
three to which the egg case was fixed. I couldn't find the clump of
three. Tracks ridged the clay, and I saw the lopped stems: somehow
my neighbor had contrived to run a tractor-mower over that steep
clay hill on which there grew nothing to mow but a few stubby
thorns.

So. Today from this same hill I cut another three undamaged   12
cases and carried them home with the others by their twigs. I also
collected a suspiciously light cynthia moth cocoon. My fingers
were stiff and red with cold, and my nose ran. I had forgotten the
Law of the Wild, which is, "Carry Kleenex." At home I tied the
twigs with their egg cases to various sunny bushes and trees in
the yard. They're easy to find because I used white string; at any
rate, I'm unlikely to mow my own trees. I hope the woodpeckers
that come to the feeder don't find them, but I don't see how they'd
get a purchase on them if they did.

Night is rising in the valley; the creek has been extinguished for   13
an hour, and now only the naked tips of trees fire tapers into the
sky like trails of sparks. The scene that was in the back of my brain
all afternoon, obscurely, is beginning to rise from night's lagoon. It
really has nothing to do with praying mantises. But this afternoon I
threw tiny string lashings and hitches with frozen hands, gingerly,
fearing to touch the egg cases even for a minute because I remembered the Polyphemus moth.[2]

I have no intention of inflicting all my childhood memories on   14
anyone. Far less do I want to excoriate my old teachers who, in
their bungling, unforgettable way, exposed me to the natural
world, a world covered in chitin, where implacable realities hold
sway. The Polyphemus moth never made it to the past; it crawls in
that crowded, pellucid pool at the lip of the great waterfall. It is as
present as this blue desk and brazen lamp, as this blackened window before me in which I can no longer see even the white string
that binds the egg case to the hedge, but only my own pale, astonished face.

Once, when I was ten or eleven years old, my friend Judy   15
brought in a Polyphemus moth cocoon. It was January; there were
doily snowflakes taped to the schoolroom panes. The teacher kept
the cocoon in her desk all morning and brought it out when we

2. Polyphemus, in classical mythology, was a one-eyed giant (a Cyclops) whom the
hero Odysseus blinded. (*Odyssey*, Book 9). A Polyphemus moth has a large eyespot
on each hind wing.

were getting restless before recess. In a book we found what the adult moth would look like; it would be beautiful. With a wingspread of up to six inches, the Polyphemus is one of the few huge American silk moths, much larger than, say, a giant or tiger swallowtail butterfly. The moth's enormous wings are velveted in a rich, warm brown, and edged in bands of blue and pink delicate as a watercolor wash. A startling "eyespot," immense, and deep blue melding to an almost translucent yellow, luxuriates in the center of each hind wing. The effect is one of a masculine splendor foreign to the butterflies, a fragility unfurled to strength. The Polyphemus moth in the picture looked like a mighty wraith, a beating essence of the hardwood forest, alien-skinned and brown, with spread, blind eyes. This was the giant moth packed in the faded cocoon. We closed the book and turned to the cocoon. It was an oak leaf sewn into a plump oval bundle; Judy had found it loose in a pile of frozen leaves.

We passed the cocoon around; it was heavy. As we held it in our   16
hands, the creature within warmed and squirmed. We were delighted, and wrapped it tighter in our fists. The pupa began to jerk violently, in heart-stopping knocks. Who's there? I can still feel those thumps, urgent through a muffling of spun silk and leaf, urgent through the swaddling of many years, against the curve of my palm. We kept passing it around. When it came to me again it was hot as a bun; it jumped half out of my hand. The teacher intervened. She put it, still heaving and banging, in the ubiquitous Mason jar.

It was coming. There was no stopping it now, January or not.   17
One end of the cocoon dampened and gradually frayed in a furious battle. The whole cocoon twisted and slapped around in the bottom of the jar. The teacher fades, the classmates fade, I fade: I don't remember anything but that thing's struggle to be a moth or die trying. It emerged at last, a sodden crumple. It was a male; his long antennae were thickly plumed, as wide as his fat abdomen. His body was very thick, over an inch long, and deeply furred. A gray, furlike plush covered his head; a long, tan furlike hair hung from his wide thorax over his brown-furred, segmented abdomen. His multijointed legs, pale and powerful, were shaggy as a bear's. He stood still, but he breathed.

He couldn't spread his wings. There was no room. The chemical   18
that coated his wings like varnish, stiffening them permanently, dried, and hardened his wings as they were. He was a monster in a Mason jar. Those huge wings stuck on his back in a torture of random pleats and folds, wrinkled as a dirty tissue, rigid as leather.

They made a single nightmare clump still wracked with useless, frantic convulsions.

The next thing I remember, it was recess. The school was in   19
Shadyside, a busy residential part of Pittsburgh. Everyone was playing dodgeball in the fenced playground or racing around the concrete schoolyard by the swings. Next to the playground a long delivery drive sloped downhill to the sidewalk and street. Someone—it must have been the teacher—had let the moth out. I was standing in the driveway, alone, stock-still, but shivering. Someone had given the Polyphemus moth his freedom, and he was walking away.

He heaved himself down the asphalt driveway by infinite de-   20
grees, unwavering. His hideous crumpled wings lay glued and rucked on his back, perfectly still now, like a collapsed tent. The bell rang twice; I had to go. The moth was receding down the driveway, dragging on. I went; I ran inside. The Polyphemus moth is still crawling down the driveway, crawling down the driveway hunched, crawling down the driveway on six furred feet, forever.

EDWARD HOAGLAND

Dogs, and the Tug of Life

Edward Hoagland (1932–   ) has two homes: an apartment on the waterfront in his native New York City and an isolated house in northern Vermont, where he writes by kerosene lamp because the nearest electricity is two miles away. His recent works of fiction include a book of short stories (*City Tales*) and a novel (*Seven Rivers West*), both published in 1986. His recent collections of essays include *The Edward Hoagland Reader* (1979), *The Tugman's Passage* (1982), and *Heart's Desire: The Best of Edward Hoagland* (1988). Hoagland is an informal essayist, working in the tradition of E. B. White and Henry David Thoreau, both of whom he admires. One critic has observed that a Hoagland essay "announces a subject, broaches it, and at once collapses sideways with the author's delight and curiosity in things." But the collapse is actually carefully controlled, and eventually the reader realizes that Hoagland has brought the pieces together into one picture—too often, these days, a picture of "the holocaust that is steadily consuming the natural world." "Dogs, and the Tug of Life" was first published in *Harper's* in February 1975.

It used to be that you could tell just about how poor a family was   1
by how many dogs they had. If they had one, they were probably
doing all right. It was only American to keep a dog to represent the
family's interests in the intrigues of the back alley; not to have a
dog at all would be like not acknowledging one's poor relations.
Two dogs meant that the couple were dog lovers, with growing
children, but still might be members of the middle class. But if a
citizen kept three, you could begin to suspect he didn't own much
else. Four or five irrefutably marked the household as poor folk,
whose yard was also full of broken cars cannibalized for parts. The
father worked not much, fancied himself a hunter; the mother's
teeth were black. And an old bachelor living in a shack might
possibly have even more, but you knew that if one of them, chasing
a moth, didn't upset his oil lamp some night and burn him up, he'd
fetch up in the poorhouse soon, with the dogs shot. Nobody got
poor feeding a bunch of dogs, needless to say, because the more
dogs a man had, the less he fed them. Foraging as a pack, they led
an existence of their own, but served as evidence that life was
awfully lonesome for him and getting out of hand. If a dog really
becomes a man's best friend his situation is desperate.

That dogs, low-comedy confederates of small children and   2
ragged bachelors, should have turned into an emblem of having
made it to the middle class—like the hibachi, like golf clubs and a
second car—seems at the very least incongruous. Puppies which in
the country you would have to carry in a box to the church fair to
give away are bringing seventy-five dollars apiece in some of the
pet stores, although in fact dogs are in such oversupply that one
hundred and fifty thousand are running wild in New York City
alone.

There is another line of tradition about dogs, however. Show   3
dogs, toy dogs, foxhounds for formal hunts, Doberman guard dogs,
bulldogs as ugly as a queen's dwarf. An aristocratic Spanish lady
once informed me that when she visits her Andalusian estate each
fall the mastiffs rush out and fawn about her but would tear to
pieces any of the servants who have accompanied her from Madrid. In Mississippi it was illegal for a slave owner to permit his
slaves to have a dog, just as it was to teach them how to read. A
"negro dog" was a hound trained by a bounty hunter to ignore the
possums, raccoons, hogs and deer in the woods that other dogs
were supposed to chase, and trail and tree a runaway. The planters themselves, for whom hunting was a principal recreation,
whooped it up when a man unexpectedly became their quarry.
They caught each other's slaves and would often sit back and let
the dogs do the punishing. Bennet H. Barrow of West Feliciana

Parish in Louisiana, a rather moderate and representative plantation owner, recounted in his diary of the 1840s, among several
similar incidents, this for November 11, 1845: In "5 minutes had
him up & a going, And never in my life did I ever see as excited
beings as R & myself, ran ½ miles & caught him dogs soon tore
him naked, took him Home Before the other negro(es) at dark &
made the dogs give him another over hauling." Only recently in
Louisiana I heard what happened to two Negroes who happened to
be fishing in a bayou off the Blind River, where four white men
with a shotgun felt like fishing alone. One was forced to pretend to
be a scampering coon and shinny up a telephone pole and hang
there till he fell, while the other impersonated a baying, bounding
hound.

Such memories are not easy to shed, particularly since child-   4
hood, the time when people can best acquire a comradeship with
animals, is also when they are likely to pick up their parents' fears.
A friend of mine hunts quail by jeep in Texas with a millionaire
who brings along forty bird dogs, which he deploys in eight pla-
toons that spell each other off. Another friend though, will grow
apprehensive at a dinner party if the host lets a dog loose in the
room. The toothy, mysterious creature lies dreaming on the carpet, its paws pulsing, its eyelids open, the nictitating membranes
twitching; how can he be certain it won't suddenly jump up and
attack his legs under the table? Among Eastern European Jews,
possession of a dog was associated with the hard-drinking goyishe[1]
peasantry, traditional antagonists, or else with the gentry, and
many carried this dislike to the New World. An immigrant fleeing
a potato famine or the hunger of Calabria[2] might be no more
equipped with the familiar British-German partiality to dogs—a
failing which a few rugged decades in a great city's slums would
not necessarily mend. The city had urbanized plenty of native
farmers' sons as well, and so it came about that what to rural
America had been the humblest, most natural amenity—friendship with a dog—has been transmogrified into a piece of the jigsaw
of moving to the suburbs: there to cook outdoors, another bit of
absurdity to the old countryman, whose toilet was outdoors but
who was pleased to be able to cook and eat his meals inside the
house.

There are an estimated forty million dogs in the United States   5

1. Non-Jewish, i.e., Gentile.
2. Region in southern Italy, forming the toe of the peninsular "boot"; severe economic hardship and natural disasters forced large-scale emigration from Calabria in
the late nineteenth and early twentieth centuries.

(nearly two for every cat). Thirty-seven thousand of them are being destroyed in humane institutions every day, a figure which indicates that many more are in trouble. Dogs are hierarchal beasts, with several million years of submission to the structure of a wolf pack in their breeding. This explains why the Spanish lady's mastiffs can distinguish immediately between the mistress and her retainers, and why it is about as likely that one of the other guests at the dinner party will attack my friend's legs under the table as that the host's dog will, once it has accepted his presence in the room as proper. Dogs need leadership, however; they seek it, and when it's not forthcoming quickly fall into difficulties in a world where they can no longer provide their own.

"Dog" is "God" spelled backwards—one might say, way back-   6
wards. There's "a dog's life," "dog days," "dog-sick," "dog-tired," "dog-cheap," "dog-eared," "doghouse," and "dogs" meaning villains or feet. Whereas a wolf's stamina was measured in part by how long he could go without water, a dog's is becoming a matter of how long he can *hold* his water. He retrieves a rubber ball instead of coursing deer, chases a broom instead of hunting marmots. His is the lowest form of citizenship: that tug of life at the end of the leash is like the tug at the end of a fishing pole, and then one doesn't have to kill it. On stubby, amputated-looking feet he leads his life, which if we glance at it attentively is a kind of cutout of our own, all the more so for being riskier and shorter. Bam! A member of the family is dead on the highway, as we expected he would be, and we just cart him to the dump and look for a new pup.

Simply the notion that he lives on four legs instead of two has   7
come to seem astonishing—like a goat or cow wearing horns on its head. And of course to keep a dog is a way of attempting to bring nature back. The primitive hunter's intimacy, telepathy, with the animals he sought, surprising them at their meals and in their beds, then stripping them of their warm coats to expose a frame so like our own, is all but lost. Sport hunters, especially the older ones, retain a little of it still; and naturalists who have made up their minds not to kill wild animals nevertheless appear to empathize primarily with the predators at first, as a look at the tigers, bears, wolves, mountain lions on the project list of an organization such as the World Wildlife Fund will show. This is as it should be, these creatures having suffered from our brotherly envy before. But in order to really enjoy a dog, one doesn't merely try to train him to be semihuman. The point of it is to open oneself to the possibility of becoming partly a dog (after all, there are plenty of sub- or semi-human beings around whom we don't wish to adopt). One wants to rediscover the commonality of animal and man—to see an

animal eat and sleep that hasn't forgotten how to enjoy doing such things—and the directness of its loyalty.

The trouble with the current emphasis on preserving "endangered species" is that, however beneficial to wildlife the campaign works out to be, it makes all animals seem like museum pieces, worth saving for sentimental considerations and as figures of speech (to "shoot a sitting duck"), but as a practical matter already dead and gone. On the contrary, some animals are flourishing. In 1910 half a million deer lived in the United States, in 1960 seven million, in 1970 sixteen million. What has happened is that now that we don't eat them we have lost that close interest.

Wolf behavior prepared dogs remarkably for life with human beings. So complete and complicated was the potential that it was only a logical next step for them to quit their packs in favor of the heady, hopeless task of trying to keep pace with our own community development. The contortions of fawning and obeisance which render group adjustment possible among such otherwise forceful fighters—sometimes humping the inferior members into the shape of hyenas—are what squeezes them past our tantrums, too. Though battling within the pack is mostly accomplished with body checks that do no damage, a subordinate wolf bitch is likely to remain so in awe of the leader that she will cringe and sit on her tail in response to his amorous advances, until his female co-equal has had a chance to notice and dash over and redirect his attention. Altogether, he is kept so busy asserting his dominance that this top-ranked female may not be bred by him, finally, but by the male which occupies the second rung. Being breadwinners, dominant wolves feed first and best, just as we do, so that to eat our scraps and leavings strikes a dog as normal procedure. Nevertheless, a wolf puppy up to eight months old is favored at a kill, and when smaller can extract a meal from any pack member—uncles and aunts as well as parents—by nosing the lips of the adult until it regurgitates a share of what it's had. The care of the litter is so much a communal endeavor that the benign sort of role we expect dogs to play within our own families toward children not biologically theirs comes naturally to them.

For dogs and wolves the tail serves as a semaphore of mood and social code, but dogs carry their tails higher than wolves do, as a rule, which is appropriate, since the excess spirits that used to go into lengthy hunts now have no other outlet than backyard negotiating. In addition to an epistolary anal gland, whose message-carrying function has not yet been defined, the anus itself, or stool when sniffed, conveys how well the animal has been eating—in effect, its income bracket—although most dog foods are sorrily monotonous compared to the hundreds of tastes a wolf encounters, perhaps dozens within the carcass of a single moose. We can speculate on a dog's powers of taste because its olfactory area is proportionately fourteen times larger than a man's, its sense of smell at least a hundred times as keen.

The way in which a dog presents his anus and genitals for inspection indicates the hierarchal position that he aspires to, and other dogs who sniff his genitals are apprised of his sexual condition. From his urine they can undoubtedly distinguish age, build, state of sexual activity and general health, even hours after he's passed by. Male dogs dislike running out of urine, as though an element of potency were involved, and try to save a little; they prefer not to use a scent post again until another dog has urinated there, the first delight and duty of the ritual being to stake out a territory, so that when they are walked hurriedly in the city it is a disappointment to them. The search is also sexual, because bitches in heat post notices about. In the woods a dog will mark his drinking places, and watermark a rabbit's trail after chasing it, as if to notify the next predator that happens by exactly who it was that put such a whiff of fear into the rabbit's scent. Similarly, he squirts the tracks of bobcats and of skunks with an aloof air unlike his brisk and cheery manner of branding another dog's or fox's trail, and if he is in a position to do so, will defecate excitedly on a bear run, leaving behind his best effort, which no doubt he hopes will strike the bear as a bombshell. 11

The chief complaint people lodge against dogs is their extraordinary stress upon lifting the leg and moving the bowels. Scatology did take up some of the slack for them when they left behind the entertainments of the forest. The forms of territoriality replaced the substance. But apart from that, a special zest for life is characteristic of dogs and wolves—in hunting, eating, relieving themselves, in punctiliously maintaining a home territory, a pecking order and a love life, and educating the resulting pups. They grin and grimace and scrawl graffiti with their piss. A lot of inherent strategy goes into these activities: the way wolves spell each other off, both when hunting and in their governess duties around the den, and often "consult" as a pack with noses together and tails wagging before flying in to make a kill. (Tigers, leopards, house cats base their social relations instead upon what ethologists call "mutual avoidance.") The nose is a dog's main instrument of discovery, corresponding to our eyes, and so it is that he is seldom offended by organic smells, such as putrefaction, and sniffs intently for the details of illness, gum bleeding and diet in his master and his fel- 12 lows, and for the story told by scats, not closing off the avenue for any reason—just as we rarely shut our eyes against new information, even the tragic or unpleasant kind.

Though dogs don't see as sharply as they smell, trainers usually rely on hand signals to instruct them, and most firsthand communication in a wolf pack also seems to be visual—by the expressions of the face, by body english and the cant of the tail. A dominant wolf squares his mouth, stares at and "rides up" on an inferior, standing with his front legs on its back, or will pretend to stalk it, creeping along, taking its muzzle in his mouth, and performing nearly all of the other discriminatory pranks and practices familiar to anybody who has a dog. In fact, what's funny is to watch a homely mutt as tiny as a shoebox spin through the rigmarole which a whole series of observers in the wilderness have gone to great pains to document for wolves.

Dogs proffer their rear ends to each other in an intimidating fashion, but when they examine the region of the head it is a friendlier gesture, a snuffling between pals. One of them may come across a telltale bone fragment caught in the other's fur, together with a bit of mud to give away the location of bigger bones. On the same impulse, wolves and free-running dogs will sniff a wanderer's toes to find out where he has been roaming. They fondle and propitiate with their mouths also, and lovers groom each other's fur with tongues and teeth adept as hands. A bitch wolf's period in heat includes a week of preliminary behavior and maybe two weeks of receptivity—among animals, exceptionally long. Each actual copulative tie lasts twenty minutes or a half an hour, which again may help to instill affection. Wolves sometimes begin choosing a mate as early as the age of one, almost a year before they are ready to breed. Dogs mature sexually a good deal earlier, and arrive in heat twice a year instead of once—at any season instead of only in midwinter, like a wolf, whose pups' arrival must be scheduled unfailingly for spring. Dogs have not retained much responsibility for raising their young, and the summertime is just as perilous as winter for them because, apart from the whimsy of their owners, who put so many of them to sleep, their nemesis is the automobile. Like scatology, sex helps fill the gulf of what is gone.

The scientist David Mech has pointed out how like the posture of a wolf with a nosehold on a moose (as other wolves attack its hams) are the antics of a puppy playing tug-of-war at the end of a towel. Anybody watching a dog's exuberance as it samples bites of long grass beside a brook, or pounds into a meadow bristling with the odors of woodchucks, snowshoe rabbits, grouse, a doe and buck, field mice up on the seedheads of the weeds, kangaroo mice jumping, chipmunks whistling, weasels and shrews on the hunt, a plunging fox, a porcupine couched in a tree, perhaps can begin to imagine the variety of excitements under the sky that his ancestors relinquished in order to move indoors with us. He'll lie down with a lamb to please us, but as he sniffs its haunches, surely he must remember atavistically that this is where he'd start to munch.

There is poignancy in the predicament of a great many animals: 16 as in the simple observation which students of the California condor have made that this huge, most endangered bird prefers the carrion meat of its old standby, the deer, to all the dead cows, sheep, horses and other substitutes it sees from above, sprawled about. Animals are stylized characters in a kind of old saga— stylized because even the most acute of them have little leeway as they play out their parts. (*Rabbits*, for example, I find terribly affecting, imprisoned in their hop.) And as we drift away from any cognizance of them, we sacrifice some of the intricacy and grandeur of life. Having already lost so much, we are hardly aware of what remains, but to a primitive snatched forward from an earlier existence it might seem as if we had surrendered a richness comparable to all the tapestries of childhood. Since this is a matter of the imagination as well as of animal demographics, no Noah projects, no bionomic discoveries on the few sanctuaries that have been established are going to reverse the swing. The very specialists in the forefront of finding out how animals behave, when one meets them, appear to be no more intrigued than any ordinary Indian was.

But we continue to need—as aborigines did, as children do—a 17 parade of morality tales which are more concise than those that politics, for instance, later provides. So we've had Aesop's and medieval and modern fables about the grasshopper and the ant, the tiger and Little Black Sambo, the wolf and the three pigs, Br'er Rabbit and Br'er Bear, Goldilocks and her three bears, Pooh Bear, Babar and the rhinos, Walt Disney's animals, and assorted humbler scary bats, fat hippos, funny frogs, and eager beavers. Children have a passion for clean, universal definitions, and so it is that animals have gone with children's literature as Latin has with religion. Through them they first encountered death, birth, their own maternal feelings, the gap between beauty and cleverness, or speed and good intentions. The animal kingdom boasted the powerful lion, the mothering goose, the watchful owl, the tardy tortoise, Chicken Little, real-life dogs that treasure bones, and mink that grow posh pelts from eating crawfish and mussels.

In the cartoons of two or three decades ago, Mouse doesn't get 18 along with Cat because Cat must catch Mouse or miss his supper.

Dog, on the other hand, detests Cat for no such rational reason, only the capricious fact that dogs don't dote on cats. Animal stories are bounded, yet enhanced, by each creature's familiar lineaments, just as a parable about a prince and peasant, a duchess and a milkmaid, a blacksmith and a fisherman, would be. Typecasting, like the roll of a metered ode, adds resonance and dignity, summoning up all of the walruses and hedgehogs that went before: the shrewd image of Br'er Rabbit to assist his suburban relative Bugs Bunny behind the scenes. But now, in order to present a tale about the contest between two thieving crows and a scarecrow, the storyteller would need to start by explaining that once upon a time crows used to eat a farmer's corn if he didn't defend it with a mock man pinned together from old clothes. Crows are having a hard go of it and may soon receive game-bird protection.

One way childhood is changing, therefore, is that the nonhuman figures—"Wild Things" or puppet monsters—constructed by the best of the new artificers, like Maurice Sendak or the *Sesame Street* writers, are distinctly humanoid, ballooned out of faces, torsos met on the subway. The televised character Big Bird does not resemble a bird the way Bugs Bunny remained a rabbit—though already he was less so than Br'er or Peter Rabbit. Big Bird's personality, her confusion, haven't the faintest connection to an ostrich's. Lest she be confused with an ostrich, her voice has been slotted unmistakably toward the prosaic. Dr. Seuss did transitional composites of worldwide fauna, but these new shapes—a beanbag like the *Sesame Street* Grouch or Cookie Monster or Herry Monster, and the floral creations in books—have been conceived practically from scratch by the artist ("in the night kitchen," to use a Sendak phrase), and not transferred from the existing caricatures of nature. In their conversational conflicts they offer him a fresh start, which may be a valuable commodity, whereas if he were dealing with an alligator, it would, while giving him an old-fashioned boost in the traditional manner, at the same time box him in. A chap called Alligator, with that fat snout and tail, cannot squirm free of the solidity of actual alligators. Either it must stay a heavyweight or else play on the sternness of reality by swinging over to impersonate a cream puff and a Ferdinand.

Though animal programs on television are popular, what with the wave of nostalgia and "ecology" in the country, we can generally say about the animal kingdom, "The King is dead, long live the King." Certainly the talent has moved elsewhere. Those bulbous Wild Things and slant-mouthed beanbag puppets derived from the denizens of Broadway—an argumentative night news vendor, a lady on a traffic island—have grasped their own destinies, as

19

20

characters on the make are likely to. It was inevitable they would. There may be a shakedown to remove the elements that would be too bookish for children's literature in other hands, and another shakedown because these first innovators have been more city-oriented than suburban. New authors will shift the character sources away from Broadway and the subway and the ghetto, but the basic switch has already been accomplished—from the ancient juxtaposition of people, animals, and dreams blending the two, to people and monsters that grow solely out of people by way of dreams.

Which leaves us in the suburbs, with dogs as a last link. Cats are   21
too independent to care, but dogs are in an unenviable position, they hang so much upon our good opinion. We are coming to *have* no opinion; we don't pay enough attention to form an opinion. Though they admire us, are thrilled by us, heroize us, we regard them as a hobby or a status symbol, like a tennis racquet, and substitute leash laws for leadership—expect them not simply to learn English but to grow hands, because their beastly paws seem stranger to us every year. If they try to fondle us with their handy-jack mouths, we read it as a bite; and like used cars, they are disposed of when the family relocates, changes its "bag," or in the scurry of divorce. The first reason people kept a dog was to acquire an ally on the hunt, a friend at night. Then it was to maintain an avenue to animality, as our own nearness began to recede. But as we lose our awareness of all animals, dogs are becoming a bridge to nowhere. We can only pity their fate.

HARRY CREWS

Pages from the Life of a Georgia Innocent

Harry Crews (1935–   ) grew up in Bacon County, Georgia, part of a poor family living in one of the most impoverished regions of the rural South. He now teaches English at the University of Florida in Gainesville, is the author of several novels, including *The Knockout Artist* (1988), and frequently publishes essays in *Playboy* and other magazines. He has not, however, forgotten his heritage or sentimentalized it. "Pages from the Life of a Georgia Innocent" appeared in Crews's monthly column in *Esquire*, in July 1976. That Crews chose to call this column

"Grits" (a slang term for rough-edged Southerners) tells a great deal about where he is, quite literally, coming from. Crews is known for mixing pain, humor, and a deliberate roughness of style: One critic has said that reading his work is like undergoing major surgery under the influence of laughing gas. You can read more about Crews's difficult early years in Bacon County in his autobiography, *A Childhood* (1978).

1   Not very long ago I went with my twelve-year-old boy to a Disney movie, one of those things that show a farm family, poor but God knows honest, out there on the land building character through hunger and hard work. The hunger and hard work seemed to be a hell of a lot of fun. The deprivation was finally so rewarding you could hardly stand it. The farm was full of warm, fuzzy, furry, damp-nosed creatures: bawling calves and braying mules and dogs that were treated like people. There was a little pain here and there but just so much as would teach important lessons to all of us. It sometimes even brought a tear to the eye, but not a real tear because the tear only served to prove that a family out in the middle of nowhere scratching in the earth for survival didn't have it so bad after all. Somebody was forever petting and stroking the plump little animals, crooning to them, as they were raised for strange, unstated reasons, but surely not to be castrated and slaughtered and skinned and eaten. They were, after all, friends.

2   If somebody got sick, he'd just pop into an old, rattling but trustworthy pickup truck and go off to town, where a kindly doctor would receive him immediately into his office and effect an instant cure by looking down his throat and asking him to say Ah. No mention was made of payment.

3   As my boy and I came out of the movie, blinking in the sunlight, it occurred to me that Disney and others—the folks who bring you *The Waltons*, say, or *The Little House on the Prairie*—had managed to sell this strange vision of poverty and country life not only to suburbanites, while the suburbanites stuffed themselves with malt balls and popcorn, but also to people in little towns throughout the South who had proof in their daily lives to the contrary.

4   All fantasy. Now there is nothing wrong with fantasy. I love it, even live off it at times. But driving home, the reality behind the fantasy began to go bad on me. It seemed immoral and dangerous to show so many smiles without an occasional glimpse of the skull underneath.

5   As we were going down the driveway, my boy, Byron, said: "That was a great movie, huh, Dad?"

"Yeah," I said. "Great."   6
"I wish I could've lived in a place like that," he said.   7
"No, you don't," I said. "You just think you do."   8

My grandmother in Bacon County, Georgia, raised biddies: tiny   9
cheeping bits of fluff that city folk allow their children to squeeze to
death at Easter. But city children are not the only ones who love
biddies; hawks love them, too. Hawks like to swoop into the yard
and carry off one impaled on their curved talons. Perhaps my
grandmother, in her secret heart, knew that hawks even then were
approaching the time when they would be on the endangered-
species list. Whether she did or not, I'm sure she often felt she and
her kind were already on the list. It would not do.

I'll never forget the first time I saw her get rid of a hawk. Chick-   10
ens, as everybody knows, are cannibals. Let a biddy get a spot of
blood on it from a scrape or a raw place and the other biddies will
simply eat it alive. My grandmother penned up all the biddies
except the puniest one, already half pecked to death by the other
cute little bits of fluff, and she set it out in the open yard by itself.
First, though, she put arsenic on its head. I—about five years old
and sucking on a sugar-tit—saw the hawk come in low over the
fence, its red tail fanned, talons stretched, and nail the poisoned
biddy where it squatted in the dust. The biddy never made a sound
as it was carried away. My gentle grandmother watched it all with
satisfaction before she let her other biddies out of the pen.

Another moment from my childhood that comes instantly to   11
mind was about a chicken, too; a rooster. He was boss cock of the
whole farm, a magnificent bird nearly two feet tall. At the base of a
chicken's throat is its craw, a kind of pouch into which the bird
swallows food, as well as such things as grit, bits of rock and shell.
For reasons I don't understand they sometimes become craw-
bound. The stuff in the craw does not move; it remains in the craw
and swells and will ultimately cause death. That's what would
have happened to the rooster if the uncle who practically raised me
hadn't said one day: "Son, we got to fix him."

He tied the rooster's feet so we wouldn't be spurred and took out   12
his castrating knife, honed to a razor's edge, and sterilized it over a
little fire. He soaked a piece of fine fishing line and a needle in
alcohol. I held the rooster on its back, a wing in each hand. With
the knife my uncle split open the craw, cleaned it out, then sewed it
up with the fishing line. The rooster screamed and screamed. But it
lived to be cock of the walk again.

Country people never did anything worse to their stock than   13 they sometimes were forced to do to themselves. We had a man who farmed with us, a man from up north somewhere who had drifted down into Georgia with no money and a mouth full of bad teeth. Felix was his name and he was good with a plow and an ax, a hard worker. Most of the time you hardly knew he was on the place, he was so quiet and well-mannered. Except when his teeth began to bother him. And they bothered him more than a little. He lived in a shedlike little room off the side of the house. The room didn't have much in it: a ladder-back chair, a kerosene lamp, a piece of broken glass hanging on the wall over a pan of water where he shaved as often as once a week, a slat-board bed, and in one corner a chamber pot—which we called a slop jar—for use in the middle of the night when nature called. I slept in a room on the other side of the wall from him. I don't remember how old I was the night of his terrible toothache, but I do remember I was still young enough to wear a red cotton gown with five little pearl buttons down the front my grandmother had made for me.

When I heard him kick the slop jar, I knew it was his teeth. I just 14
didn't know how bad it was. When the ladder-back chair splintered, I knew it was a bad hurt, even for Felix. A few times that night I managed to slip off to sleep only to be jarred awake when he would run blindly into the thin wall separating us. He groaned and cursed, not loudly but steadily, sometimes for as long as half an hour. Ordinarily, my mother would have fixed a hot poultice for his jaw or at least tried to do *something*, but he was a proud man and when he was really dying from his teeth, he preferred to suffer, if not in silence, at least by himself. The whole house was kept awake most of the night by his thrashing and groaning, by the wash pan being knocked off the shelf, by his broken shaving mirror being broken again, and by his blind charges into the wall.

See, our kindly country dentist would not have gotten out of his 15
warm bed for anything less than money. And Felix didn't have any money. Besides, the dentist was in town ten miles away and we didn't have a rattling, trustworthy old truck. The only way we had to travel was two mules. And so there was nothing for Felix to do but what he was doing and it built practically no character at all. Looking back on it now, I can see that it wasn't even human. The sounds coming through the wall sure as hell weren't human anyway. On a Georgia dirt farm, pain reduced everything—man and beast alike—to the lowest common denominator. And it was pretty low and pretty common. Not something you'd want to watch while you ate malt balls and popcorn.

I was huddled under the quilts shaking with dread—my nerves 16

190

Harry Crews

were shot by the age of four and so they have remained—when I
heard Felix kick open the door to his room and thump down the
wooden steps in his heavy brogan work shoes, which he'd not
taken off all night. I couldn't imagine where he was going but I
knew I wanted to watch whatever was about to happen. The only
thing worse than my nerves is my curiosity, which has always been
untempered by pity or compassion, a serious character failing in
most societies but a sanity-saving virtue in Georgia when I was a
child.

It was February and I went out the front door barefoot onto the 17
frozen ground. I met Felix coming around the corner of the house.
In the dim light I could see the craziness in his eyes, the same
craziness you see in the eyes of a trapped fox when it has not quite
been able to chew through its own leg. Felix headed straight for the
well, with me behind him, shaking in my thin cotton gown. He
took the bucket from the nail on the rack built over the open wall
and sent it shooting down hard as he could to break the inch of ice
that was over the water. As he was drawing the bucket up on the
pulley, he seemed to see me for the first time.

"What the hell, boy! What the hell!" His voice was as mad as his 18
eyes and he either would not or could not say anything else. He
held the bucket and took a mouthful of the freezing water. He held
it a long time, spat it out, and filled his mouth again.

He turned the bucket loose and let it fall again into the well 19
instead of hanging it back on the nail where it belonged. With his
cheeks swelling with water he took something out of the back
pocket of his overalls. As soon as I saw what he had I knew beyond
all belief and good sense what he meant to do, and suddenly I was
no longer cold but stood on the frozen ground in a hot passion
waiting to see him do it, to see if he *could* do it.

He had a piece of croker sack about the size of a half-dollar in his 20
left hand and a pair of wire pliers in his right. He spat the water out
and reached way back in his rotten mouth and put the piece of sack
over the tooth. He braced his feet against the well and stuck the
pliers in over the sackcloth. He took the pliers in both hands and
immediately a forked vein leapt in his forehead. The vein in his
neck popped big as a pencil. He pulled and twisted and pulled and
never made a sound.

It took him a long time and finally as he fought with the pliers 21
and with himself his braced feet slipped so that he was flat on his
back when the blood broke from his mouth, followed by the pliers
holding a tooth with roots half an inch long. He got slowly to his
feet, sweat running off his face, and held the bloody tooth up
between us.

He looked at the tooth and said in his old, recognizable voice: 22
"Huh now, you sumbitch!"

LEWIS THOMAS

Ponds

Lewis Thomas (1913–   ) is a physician by vocation and a
naturalist by avocation. He became a writer almost by accident:
In 1970 he was asked to deliver the keynote address at a medical
symposium on inflammation. "This kind of conference," he later
observed, "tends to be rather heavy going and my talk was designed to lighten the proceedings at the outset by presenting a
rather skewed view of inflammation." The address was such a
success that Thomas was soon asked to become a regular columnist for the *New England Journal of Medicine*. The terms were
simple: no pay for Thomas, but an absolutely free hand to write
what he wished. "Ponds" was published in the *Journal* in 1978.
Like many of Thomas's essays, it presents a "rather skewed"
view of contemporary America's relationship with nature. It is
precisely the skewing that has given Thomas a wide audience
and led to the reprinting of his essays as a series of popular books:
The Lives of a Cell: Notes of a Biology Watcher (1974), *The Medusa
and the Snail: More Notes of a Biology Watcher* (1979), and *Late
Night Thoughts on Listening to Mahler's Ninth Symphony* (1983).

Large areas of Manhattan are afloat. I remember when the new   1
Bellevue Hospital was being built, fifteen years ago; the first stage
was the most spectacular and satisfying, an enormous square lake.
It was there for the two years, named Lake Bellevue, while the
disconsolate Budget Bureau went looking for cash to build the next
stage. It was fenced about and visible only from the upper windows
of the old hospital, but pretty to look at, cool and blue in midsummer, frozen gleaming as Vermont in January. The fence, like all city
fences, was always broken, and we could have gone down to the
lake and used it, but it was known to be an upwelling of the East
River. At Bellevue there were printed rules about the East River: if
anyone fell in, it was an emergency for the Infectious-Disease Service, and the first measures, after resuscitation, were massive doses
of whatever antibiotics the hospital pharmacy could provide.
   But if you cleaned the East River you could have ponds all over   2
town, up and down the East Side of Manhattan anyway. If you

lifted out the Empire State Building and the high structures nearby, you would have, instantly, an inland sea. A few holes bored in the right places would let water into the subways, and you'd have lovely underground canals all across to the Hudson, uptown to the Harlem River, downtown to the Battery, a Venice underground, without pigeons.

It wouldn't work, though, unless you could find a way to keep   3
out the fish. New Yorkers cannot put up with live fish out in the open. I cannot explain this, but it is so.

There is a new pond, much smaller than Lake Bellevue, on First   4
Avenue between Seventieth and Seventy-first, on the east side of the street. It emerged sometime last year, soon after a row of old flats had been torn down and the hole dug for a new apartment building. By now it is about average size for Manhattan, a city block long and about forty feet across, maybe eight feet deep at the center, more or less kidney-shaped, rather like an outsized suburban swimming pool except for the things floating, and now the goldfish.

With the goldfish, it is almost detestable. There are, clearly vis-   5
ible from the sidewalk, hundreds of them. The neighborhood people do not walk by and stare into it through the broken fence, as would be normal for any other Manhattan pond. They tend to cross the street, looking away.

Now there are complaints against the pond, really against the   6
goldfish. How could people do such a thing? Bad enough for pet dogs and cats to be abandoned, but who could be so unfeeling as to abandon goldfish? They must have come down late at night, carrying their bowls, and simply dumped them in. How could they?

The ASPCA[1] was called, and came one afternoon with a row-   7
boat. Nets were used, and fish taken away in new custodial bowls, some to Central Park, others to ASPCA headquarters, to the fish pound. But the goldfish have multiplied, or maybe those people with their bowls keep coming down late at night for their furtive, unfeeling dumping. Anyway, there are too many fish for the ASPCA, for which this seems to be a new kind of problem. An official stated for the press that the owners of the property would be asked to drain the pond by pumping, and then the ASPCA would come back with nets to catch them all.

You'd think they were rats or roaches, the way people began to   8
talk. Get those goldfish out of that pond, I don't care how you do it. Dynamite, if necessary. But get rid of them. Winter is coming,

1. American Society for the Prevention of Cruelty to Animals.

someone said, and it is deep enough so that they'll be swimming around underneath the ice. Get them out.

It is this knowledge of the East River, deep in the minds of all 9 Manhattan residents, more than the goldfish themselves, I think. Goldfish in a glass bowl are harmless to the human mind, maybe even helpful to minds casting about for something, anything, to think about. But goldfish let loose, propagating themselves, worst of all *surviving* in what has to be a sessile eddy of the East River, somehow threaten us all. We do not like to think that life is possible under some conditions, especially the conditions of a Manhattan pond. There are four abandoned tires, any number of broken beer bottles, fourteen shoes and a single sneaker, and a visible layer, all over the surface, of that grayish-green film that settles on all New York surfaces. The mud at the banks of the pond is not proper country mud but reconstituted Manhattan landfill, ancient garbage, fossilized coffee grounds and grapefruit rind, the defecation of a city. For goldfish to be swimming in such water, streaking back and forth mysteriously in small schools, feeding, obviously feeding, looking as healthy and well-off as goldfish in the costliest kind of window-box aquarium, means something is wrong with our standards. It is, in some deep sense beyond words, insulting.

I thought I noticed a peculiar sort of fin on the under-surface of 10 two of the fish. Perhaps, it occurs to me now in a rush of exultation, in such a pond as this, with all its chemical possibilities, there are contained some mutagens, and soon there will be schools of mutant goldfish. Give them just a little more time, I thought. And then, with the most typically Manhattan thought I've ever thought, I thought: The ASPCA will come again, next month, with their rowboat and their nets. The proprietor will begin pumping out the pond. The nets will flail, the rowboat will settle, and then the ASPCA officials will give a sudden shout of great dismay. And with a certain amount of splashing and grayish-greenish spray, at all the edges of the pond, up all the banks of ancient New York landfill mud, crawling on their new little feet, out onto the sidewalks, up and down and across the street, into doorways and up the fire escapes, some of them with little suckers on their little feet, up the sides of buildings and into open windows, looking for something, will come the goldfish.

It won't last, of course. Nothing like this ever does. The mayor 11 will come and condemn it in person. The Health Department will come and recommend the purchase of cats from out of town because of the constitutional boredom of city cats. The NIH will send up teams of professionals from Washington with a new kind of antifish spray, which will be recalled four days later because of toxicity to cats.

After a few weeks it will be finished anyway, like a lot of New 12
York events. The goldfish will dive deep and vanish, the pond will fill up with sneakers, workmen will come and pour concrete over everything, and by next year the new building will be up and occupied by people all unaware of their special environmental impact. But what a time it was.

GRETEL EHRLICH

Looking for a Lost Dog

Gretel Ehrlich (1946–   ) was raised in Santa Barbara, California, so close to the beach that on quiet nights she "could hear the seals barking on the channel islands." Educated at Bennington College and UCLA, she worked briefly in New York as a film editor, and it was to make a documentary film that she came to Wyoming in 1976. She quickly fell in love with what she saw there, and today is a rancher near Shell. She says that if she rode a horse north, it would take her three days to reach the nearest fence, and that in three directions she has an unobstructed horizon for a hundred miles. In addition to miscellaneous essays, Ehrlich has published two books of poetry, *Geode/Rock Body* (1970) and *To Touch the Water* (1981), and a collection of essays about her ranch life, *The Solace of Open Spaces* (1985). "Looking for a Lost Dog" first appeared in *New Age Journal*, June 1986. In 1988 she published her first novel, *Heart Mountain*, which involves the relationship of a young Caucasian rancher with Japanese-Americans forced into a concentration camp near his home during World War II.

The most valuable thoughts which I entertain are anything but what I thought. Nature abhors a vacuum, and if I can only walk with sufficient carelessness I am sure to be filled.

HENRY DAVID THOREAU

I started off this morning looking for my lost dog. He's a red 1
heeler, blotched brown and white, and I tell people he looks like a big saddle shoe. Born at Christmas on a thirty-below-zero night, he's tough, though his right front leg is crooked where it froze to the ground.

It's the old needle-in-the-haystack routine: small dog, huge   2
landscape, and rugged terrain. While moving cows once, he fell in
a hole and disappeared. We heard him whining but couldn't see
him. When we put our ears to the ground, we could hear the hole
that had swallowed him.

It's no wonder human beings are so narcissistic. The way our   3
ears are constructed, we can only hear what's right next to us or
else the internal monologue inside. I've taken to cupping my hands
behind my ears—mule-like—and pricking them all the way forward or back to hear what's happened or what's ahead.

"Life is polyphonic," a Hungarian friend in her eighties said. She   4
was a child prodigy from Budapest who had soloed on the violin in
Paris and Berlin by the time she was twelve. "Childishly, I once
thought hearing had mostly to do with music," she said. "Now that
I'm too old to play the fiddle, I know it has to do with the great
suspiration of life everywhere."

But back to the dog. I'm walking and looking and listening for   5
him, though there is no trail, no clue, no direction to the search.
Whimsically, I head north toward the falls. They're set in a deep
gorge where Pre-Cambrian rock piles up to ten thousand feet on
either side. A raven creaks overhead, flies into the cleft, glides
toward a panel of white water splashing over a ledge, and comes
out cawing.

To find what is lost is an art in some cultures. The Navajos   6
employ "hand tremblers," usually women, who go into a trance
and "see" where the lost article or person is located. When I asked
one such diviner what it was like when she was in trance, she said,
"Lots of noise, but noise that's hard to hear."

Near the falls the ground flattens into a high-altitude valley be-   7
fore the mountains rise vertically. The falls roar, but they're overgrown with spruce, pine, willow, and wild rose, and the closer I
get, the harder it is to see the water. Perhaps that is how it will be in
my search for the dog.

We're worried about Frenchy because last summer he was bitten   8
three times by rattlesnakes. After the first bite he walked toward
me, reeled dramatically, and collapsed. I could see the two holes in
his nose where the fangs went in, and I felt sure he was dying. I
drove him twenty miles to the vet; by the time we arrived, Frenchy
resembled a monster. His nose and neck had swollen as though a
football had been sewn under the skin.

I walk and walk. Past the falls, through a pass, toward a larger,   9
rowdier creek. The sky goes black. In the distance snow on the Owl
Creek Mountains glares. A blue ocean seems to stretch between,
and the black sky hangs over like a frown. A string of cottonwoods

whose new, tender leaves are the color of limes pulls me downstream. I come into the meadow with the abandoned apple orchard. The trees have leaves but have lost most of their blossoms. I
feel as if I had caught strangers undressed.

The sun comes back, and the wind. It brings no dog, but ducks   10
slide overhead. An Eskimo from Barrow, Alaska, told me the reason spring has such firece winds is so birds coming north will have
something to fly on.

To find what's lost; to lose what's found. Several times I've   11
thought I might be "losing my mind." Of course, minds aren't
literally misplaced—on the contrary, we live too much under
them. As with viewing the falls, we can lose sight of what is too
close. It is between the distant and close-up views that the struggle
between impulse and reason, logic and passion takes place.

The feet move; the mind wanders. In his journals Thoreau   12
wrote: "The saunterer, in the good sense, is no more vagrant than
the meandering river, which is all the while sedulously seeking the
shortest course to the sea."

Today I'm filled with longings—for what I'm not, for what is   13
impossible, for people I love who can't be in my life. Passions of all
sorts struggle soundlessly, or else, like the falls, they are all noise
but can't be seen. My hybrid anguish spends itself as recklessly and
purposefully as water.

Now I'm following a game trail up a sidehill. It's a mosaic of   14
tracks—elk, deer, rabbit, and bird. If city dwellers could leave im-
prints in cement, it would look this way: tracks would overlap, go
backward and forward like the peregrine saunterings of the mind.

I see a dog's track, or is it a coyote's? I get down on my hands   15
and knees to sniff out a scent. What am I doing? I entertain expectations of myself as preposterous as when I landed in Tokyo—I felt
so at home there that I thought I would break into fluent Japanese.
Now I sniff the ground and smell only dirt. If I spent ten years
sniffing, would I learn scents?

The tracks veer off the trail and disappear. Descending into a dry   16
wash whose elegant, tortured junipers and tumbled boulders resemble a Japanese garden, I trip on a sagebrush root. I look. Deep
in the center of the plant there is a bird's nest, but instead of eggs, a
locust stares up at me.

Some days I think this one place isn't enough. That's when   17
nothing is enough, when I want to live multiple lives and be allowed to love without limits. Those days, like today, I walk with a
purpose but no destination. Only then do I see, at least momentarily, that everything is here. To my left a towering cottonwood is
lunatic with birdsong. Under it I'm a listening post while its great

gray trunk—like a baton or the source of something—heaves its
green symphony into the air.

I walk and walk: from the falls, over Grouse Hill, to the dry   18
wash. Today it is enough to make a shadow.

MELISSA GREENE

No Rms, Jungle Vu

Melissa Greene (1952–   ) is a free-lance writer in Atlanta,
Georgia. A 1975 graduate of Oberlin College, she says she tends
to write to preserve the memory of things that are vanishing from
the world. She has written, for instance, about a practicing
"granny woman" (traditional midwife) in rural Georgia and is
presently at work on a book about an isolated community on the
coast of Georgia that seems largely unaffected by the passing of
the last few decades. Though Greene has no training in zoology,
she became interested in writing the essay below when an Atlanta newspaper carried a profile of Jon Coe. Not only was she
impressed by Coe's interest in preserving or re-creating fragments
of natural habitat, but she wanted to meet the man who said that
he could design a zoo that would make the zoo-goer's hair stand
on end. The essay originally appeared in a slightly longer form in
the *Atlantic Monthly* in December 1987.

"The Egyptians have been civilized for four thousand years . . .   1
my own ancestors probably a lot less," Jon Charles Coe says. "We
evolved over millions of years in the wild, where survival depended on our awareness of the landscape, the weather, and the
animals. We haven't been domesticated long enough to have lost
those senses. In my opinion, it is the business of the zoo to slice
right through that sophisticated veneer, to recall us to our origins. I
judge the effectiveness of a zoo exhibit in the pulse rate of the zoo-
goer. We can design a zoo that will make the hair stand up on the
back of your neck."

A revolution is under way in zoo design, which was estimated to   2
be a $20 million business last year. Jon Coe and Grant Jones are
the vanguard. Coe, forty-six, is a stocky man with a long, curly
beard. He is an associate professor of landscape architecture at the
University of Pennsylvania and a senior partner in the zoo-design

firm of Coe Lee Robinson Roesch, in Philadelphia. Grant Jones, a
senior partner in the architectural firm Jones & Jones, in Seattle, is
at forty-eight a trendsetter in the design of riverfront areas, botanical gardens, and historical parks, as well as zoos. Coe and Jones
were classmates at the Harvard School of Design, and Coe worked
for Jones & Jones until 1981.

Ten years ago in Seattle they created the Woodland Park gorilla   3
exhibit in collaboration with Dennis Paulson, a biologist, and with
David Hancocks, an architect and the director of the Woodland
Park Zoo. The exhibit is still praised by experts as the best ever
done. It has become an international standard for the replication of
wilderness in a zoo exhibit and for the art of including and engag-
ing the zoo-goer. Dian Fossey, the field scientist who lived for
fifteen years near the wild mountain gorillas of Rwanda before her
murder there, in December of 1985, flew to Seattle as a consultant
to the designers of Woodland Park. When the exhibit was completed, Johnpaul Jones, Grant Jones's partner (the two are not
related), sent photographs to her. She wrote back that she had
shown the photos to her colleagues at the field station and they had
believed them to be photos of wild gorillas in Rwanda. "Your firm,
under the guidance of [Mr.] Hancocks, has made a tremendously
important advancement toward the captivity conditions of gorillas," Fossey wrote. "Had such existed in the past, there would
undoubtedly be more gorillas living in captivity."

"Woodland Park has remained a model for the zoo world," says   4
Terry Maple, the new director of Zoo Atlanta, a professor of comparative psychology (a field that examines the common origins of
animal and human behavior) at the Georgia Institute of Technology, and the author of numerous texts and articles on primate
behavior. "Woodland Park changed the way we looked at the zoo
environment. Before Woodland Park, if the gorillas weren't in
cages, they were on beautiful mown lawns, surrounded by moats.
In good zoos they had playground equipment. In Woodland Park
the staff had to teach the public not to complain that the gorilla
exhibit looked unkempt."

"As far as gorilla habitats go," Maple says, "Cincinnati's is pretty   5
good; San Diego's is pretty good; Columbus's has a huge cage, so
aesthetically it loses a great deal, but socially it's terrific; San Francisco's is a more technical solution, naturalistic but surrounded by
walls. Woodland Park's is the best in the world."

In Woodland Park the zoo-goer must step off the broad paved   6
central boulevard onto a narrow path engulfed by vegetation to get
to the gorillas. Coe planted a big-leaf magnolia horizontally, into
the bank of a man-made hill, so that it would grow over the path.

("People forget that a landscape architect not only can do this," he said on a recent tour of the exhibit, indicating a pretty circle of peonies, "but can also do *this*"—he pointed to a shaggy, weed-covered little hill. "I *designed* that hill.")

The path leads to a wooden lean-to with a glass wall on one side   7 that looks into a rich, weedy, humid clearing. Half a dozen heavy-set, agile gorillas part the tall grasses, stroll leaning on their knuck-les, and sit nonchalantly among clumps of comfrey, gnawing celery stalks. The blue-black sheen of their faces and fur on a field of green is electrifying. The social organization of the gorillas is ex-pressed by their interaction around a couple of boulders in the foreground of the exhibit. All the gorillas enjoy climbing on the boulders, but the young ones yield to their elders and the adult females yield to the adult males, two silverback gorillas. The silver-backs drum their chests with their fists rapidly and perfunctorily while briefly rising on two feet—not at all like Tarzan. The fists make a rapid thudding noise, which seems to mean, "Here I come." Each silverback climbs to his rostrum, folds his arms, and glares at the other. As in nature, their relationship is by turns civil but not friendly, and contentious but not bullying.

The zoo-goers in the lean-to, observing all this, feel fortunate   8 that the troop of gorillas chooses to stay in view, when it appar-ently has acres and acres in which to romp. Moss-covered boulders overlap other boulders in the distance, a stream fringed with ferns wanders among them, birds roost in the forty-foot-high treetops, and caves and nests beyond the bend in the stream are available to the gorillas as a place of retreat. "Flight distance" is the zoological term for the distance an animal needs to retreat from an approach-ing creature in order to feel safe—the size of the cushion of empty space it wishes to maintain around itself. (Several years ago Jon Coe accepted an assignment to design a nursing home, a conven-tional job that was unusual for him. He designed the home with flight distance. Sitting rooms and visiting areas were spacious near the front door but grew smaller as one progressed down the hall toward the residents' rooms. A resident overwhelmed by too much bustle in the outer areas could retreat down the hall to quieter and quieter environments.)

In fact the gorillas in Woodland Park do not have so much space   9 to explore. The exhibit is 13,570 square feet (about a third of an acre), which is generous but not limitless. The arrangement of overlapping boulders and trees in the distance is meant to trick the eye. There are no fences or walls against which to calculate depth, and the visitor's peripheral vision is deliberately limited by the dimensions of the lean-to. Wider vision might allow a visitor to calculate his position within Woodland Park, or might give him an inappropriate glimpse—as happens in almost every other zoo in the world—of a snowshoe rabbit or an Amazon porcupine or a North American zoo-goer, over the heads of the West African gorillas. Coe measured and calculated the sight lines to ensure that the view was an uncorrupted one into the heart of the rain forest.

The boulders themselves contain a trick. Coe designed them to   10
contain heating coils, so that in the miserable, misty Seattle winter they give off a warm aura, like an electric blanket. The boulders serve two purposes: they help the tropical gorillas put up with the Seattle winter, and they attract the gorillas to within several feet of the lean-to and the zoo-goers. It is no coincidence that much of the drama of the gorillas' everyday life is enacted three feet away from the lean-to. The patch of land in front of the lean-to is shady and cool in summer. The gorillas freely choose where to spend their day, but the odds have been weighted heavily in favor of their spending it in front of the lean-to.

"Their old exhibit was a six-hundred-square-foot tile bath-   11
room," says Grant Jones, a tall, handsome, blue-eyed man. "The gorillas displayed a lot of very neurotic behavior. They were aggressive, sad, angry, lethargic. They had no flight distance. The people were behind the glass day and night, the people pounded on the glass, the gorillas were stressed out, totally, all the time. Their only way to deal with it was to sleep or to show intense anger. They'd pick up their own feces and smear it across the glass. They were not interacting with one another.

"My assumption was that when they left their cage to enter their   12
new outdoor park, that behavior would persist. On the first day, although they were frightened when they came into the new park, they were tranquil. They'd never felt the wind; they'd never seen a bird fly over; they'd never seen water flowing except for the drain in the bottom of their cubicle. Instantly they became quiet and curious. The male was afraid to enter into the environment and stood at the door for hours. His mate came and took him by the hand and led him. They only went about halfway. They stopped at a small stream. They sat and picked up some leaves and dipped them in the water and took a bite of the leaves. They leaned back and saw clouds moving over. It was spellbinding. I assumed they would never recover from the trauma of how they'd been kept. It turned out to be a matter of two or three days."

"Picture the typical zoo exhibit," Jon Coe says. "You stroll along   13
a sidewalk under evenly spaced spreading maples, beside colorful bedding plants. On your right is a polar-bear exhibit. There is a well-pruned hedge of boxwood with a graphic panel in it. The

panel describes interesting features of the species, including the fact that polar bears often are seen swimming far out to sea. In the exhibit a bear is splashing in a bathtub. Very little is required of the viewers and very little is gained by them. The visitor is bored for two reasons: first because the setting is too obvious, and second because of a feeling of security despite the close presence of a wild animal.

"When planning this exhibit, we learned that in the wild, goril- 14 las like to forage at the edge of a forest, in clearings created by tribal people who fell the trees, burn off the undergrowth, farm for a couple of years, then move on. After they move on, the forest moves back in and the gorillas forage there. We set about to re-create that scene. We got lots of charred stumps, and we took a huge dead tree from a power-line clearing a few miles from here. The story is plant succession, and how the gorillas exploit the early plants growing back over the abandoned farmland."

Coe relies on stagecraft and drama to break down the zoo-goer's 15 sense of security. When walking through a client zoo for the first time, long before he has prepared a master plan, he offers a few suggestions: Get rid of the tire swings in the chimp exhibit. Get rid of the signs saying NIMBA THE ELEPHANT and JOJO THE CHEETAH. Stop the publicized feeding of the animals, the baby elephant's birthday party, and any other element contributing to either an anthropomorphized view ("Do the elephants call each *other* Nimba and Bomba?") or a view of wild beasts as tame pets.

"How can we improve our ability to get and hold the attention 16 of the zoo-goer?" he asks. "We must create a situation that transcends the range of stimulation people are used to and enhances the visitor's perception of the animal. A zoo animal that *appears* to be unrestrained and dangerous should receive our full attention, possibly accompanied by an adrenal rush, until its potential for doing us harm is determined."

For ten years Coe and others have been experimenting with the 17 relative positions of zoo-goers and zoo animals. Coe now designs exhibits in which the animal terrain surrounds and is actually higher than the zoo paths, so that zoo-goers must look up to see the animals. The barriers between animals and people are camouflaged so effectively that zoo-goers may be uncertain whether an animal has access to them or not. In JungleWorld, the Bronx Zoo's recently opened $9.5 million indoor tropical forest nearly an acre in size, conceived by William Conway, the director of the zoo, a python lives inside a tree trunk that apparently has fallen across the zoo-goers' walkway. "We made the interior of the log brighter and tilted the glass away from the outside light to avoid all reflections," says Charles Beier, an associate curator. "It's an old jeweler's trick. When people glance overhead, there appears to be no barrier between them and the snake." The screams of horror provoked by the python are quite a different matter from the casual conversations that people engage in while strolling past rows of terrariums with snakes inside.

"We are trying to get people to be prepared to look for animals in 18 the forest, not have everything brightly lighted and on a platform in front of them," says John Gwynne, the deputy director for design of the New York Zoological Society, which operates the Bronx Zoo. "We have lots of dead trees and dead grass in here. It's actually very hard to train a gardener not to cut off the dead branches. We're trying to create a wilderness, not a garden—something that can catch people by surprise."

·   ·   ·

The profession of zoo design is a relatively new one. In the past, 19 when a zoo director said that a new lion house was required, the city council solicited bids and hired a popular local architect—the one who did the suburban hospital and the new high school—and paid him to fly around the country and get acquainted with lion houses. He visited four or five and learned design tips from each: how wide to space the bars, for example, and how thick to pour the cement. Then he flew home and drew a lion house.

"As recently as fifteen years ago there was no Jones & Jones or 20 Jon Coe," says William Conway, of the Bronx Zoo. "There were very few architects around then who had any concept of what animals were all about or who would go—as Jon Coe has gone—to Africa to see and sketch and try to understand, so that he knew what the biologist was talking about. The problem of the zoologist in the zoo was that, in the past, he was very often dealing with an architect who wanted to make a monument."

"The downfall of most zoos has been that they've hired architects," says Ace Torre, a designer in New Orleans, who holds 21 degrees in architecture and landscape architecture. "Some of the more unfortunate zoos hired six different architects. Each one made his own statement. As a result, the zoo is a patchwork of architectural tributes."

In 1975 the City of Seattle asked Grant Jones, whose firm had 22 restored the splendid Victorian copper-roofed pergolas and the elegant walkways and the granite statuary of the city's Pioneer Square Historic District, to design the Woodland Park Zoo gorilla house. The City of Seattle—specifically, David Hancocks, the zoo director—had made a novel choice. Jones was an anomaly in the world of architecture in that he prided himself on having never designed anything taller than three stories. Most of his buildings were made of wood, and they tended to be situated in national parks. Instead of making a grand tour of gorilla houses, Jones consulted field scientists and gorilla experts who had seen how gorillas lived in the wild.

"When they asked me to design a gorilla exhibit," Jones says, "I 23 naturally rephrased the problem in my own mind as designing a landscape with gorillas in it. In what sort of landscape would I want to behold gorillas? I would want to include mystery and discovery. I'd like to see the gorillas from a distance first, and then up close. I'd like to be able to intrude on them and see what's going on without their knowing I'm there. I'd want to give them flight distance, a place to back off and feel secure. And I would want an experience that would take me back to a primordial depth myself. How did I spend my day some millions of years ago, living in proximity to this animal?"

"We asked Dian Fossey to visit Seattle," David Hancocks says, 24 "and she became the most crucial member of the design team. We had so many people telling us we were being very foolish. A zoo director on the East Coast called to say he'd put a potted palm in a cage where a gorilla had lived for fifteen years. The gorilla pulled it out by the roots, ate it, and got sick."

"Driving in from the airport, we asked Fossey what the rain 25 forest looked like," Jon Coe says. "She kept turning this way and that way in her seat, saying, 'It looks like that! It looks just like that!' Of course, Seattle is in a belt of temperate rain forest. Fossey was in an alpine tropical rain forest. The plants are not identical, but they are very similar. We realized that we could stand back and let the native plants take over the exhibit and the overall effect would be very much the same.

"And there were trees, forty-foot-tall trees, in the area slated for 26 the gorillas. What to do about the trees? No zoo in the world had let gorillas have unlimited access to trees. We thought of the gorilla as a terrestrial animal. The wisdom at the time said that the trees had to come down. We brought George Schaller, probably the world's preeminent field scientist, to Seattle, and asked him about the trees. His response was, 'I don't know if they're going to fall out of them or not, but somebody has to do this.' "

"They didn't fall out of the trees," Jones says, "but Kiki [one of 27 the silverbacks] escaped. We'd brought in some rock-climbers to try to get out of the exhibit when it was finished, and we'd made a few modifications based on their suggestions. Jon figured out an elaborate jumping matrix: if a gorilla can jump this far on the horizontal, how far can he go on a downward slope, et cetera. The problem is, you can't program in motivation. At some point the motivation may be so great that you'll find yourself saying, 'Whoops, the tiger can jump thirteen feet, not twelve. Guess we should have made it wider.'

"We had planted some hawthorn trees about four to five inches 28 in diameter, ten feet high, and had hoped they were large enough that the gorillas would accept them. They accepted everything else, but these trees were standing too much alone, too conspicuous. Kiki pulled all the branches off of one, then ripped it out of the ground. It stood by itself; the roots were like a tripod. He played with that thing for a number of days.

"The keepers were aware of how we must never let them have a 29 big long stick because they might put it across the moat, walk across it, and get out. They saw that tree but it was clearly not long enough to bridge the moat. We all discussed it, and decided it wasn't a problem. During that same period Kiki began disappearing for three hours at a time, and we didn't know where he was. It's a large environment, and he could have been off behind some shrubbery. One of the keepers told us later that he'd seen Kiki sitting on the edge of the big dry moat at the back of the habitat. One day Kiki climbed down into the moat.

"I imagine he took his tree with him to the far corner, leaned it 30 up against the wall, and considered it. At some point he must have made a firm decision. He got a toehold on the roots, pressed his body to the wall, lifted himself up in one lunge, and hung from the top of the moat. Then he pulled himself up and landed in the rhododendrons. He was out, he was in the park."

"He was sitting in the bushes and some visitors saw him," Coe 31 says. "They raced to the director's office and reported it to Hancocks." His response was calm, according to Coe. Anxious visitors often reported that there were gorillas loose in the trees. "The gorilla's not out," said Hancocks. "The exhibit, you see, is called landscape immersion. It's intended to give you the *impression* that the gorillas are free."

The visitors thanked Hancocks and left. He overheard one re- 32 mark to the other, "Still, it just doesn't seem right having him sit there on the sidewalk like that."

"Sidewalk?" Hancocks said.   33

"We called the police," says Hancocks, "not to control the 34 gorilla but to stop people from coming into the zoo. Jim Foster, the vet, fed fruit to Kiki and calmed him down while we tried to figure out what to do. We put a ladder across the moat and Jim climbed on it to show Kiki how to cross. Kiki actually tried it, but the ladder

wobbled and fell, and he retreated. It was getting dark. We finally
had to tranquilize him and carry him back."

"It's been seven years since," Jones says, "and Kiki never has   35
tried again, although he clearly knows how to do it. He doesn't
want to leave. In fact I am frequently called in by zoos that are
having problems with escape. They always want to know, Should
we make the moats wider? The bars closer together? Should we
chain the animal? Yet escape is almost never a design problem. It is
a question of motivation. It is a social problem."

"One of the roles a silverback has in life," Coe says, "is to patrol   36
his territory. Kiki wasn't escaping *from* something. He was exploring outward from the center of his territory to define its edges."

"If Kiki had escaped from a conventional ape house, the city   37
would have panicked," Hancocks says. "But in the year or two the
exhibit had been open, Seattle had lost the hairy-monster-of-the-
ape-house image, and saw gorillas as quiet and gentle."

Shortly after, one of the local papers carried a cartoon of Kiki   38
roller-skating arm-in-arm with two buxom beauties through the
adjacent Greenlake Park, and another had a cartoon of him pole-
vaulting over the moat.

.   .   .

The current revolution in zoo design—the landscape revolu-   39
tion—is driven by three kinds of change that have occurred during
this century. First are great leaps in animal ecology, veterinary
medicine, landscape design, and exhibit technology, making possible unprecedented realism in zoo exhibits. Second, and perhaps
most important, is the progressive disappearance of wilderness—
the very subject of zoos—from the earth. Third is knowledge
derived from market research and from environmental psychology,
making possible a sophisticated focus on the zoo-goer.

Zoo-related sciences like animal ecology and veterinary medi-   40
cine for exotic animals barely existed fifty years ago and tremendous advances have been made in the last fifteen years. Zoo veterinarians now inoculate animals against diseases they once died
of. Until recently, keeping the animals alive required most of a
zoo's resources. A cage modeled after a scientific laboratory or an
operating room—tile-lined and antiseptic, with a drain in the
floor—was the best guarantee of continued physical health. In the
late 1960s and early 1970s zoo veterinarians and comparative psychologists began to realize that stress was as great a danger as
disease to the captive wild animals. Directors thus sought less
stressful forms of confinement than the frequently-hosed-down
sterile cell.

Field scientists also published findings about the complex social   41
relations among wild animals. Zoos began to understand that captive animals who refused to mate often were reacting to the improper social configurations in which they were confined. Gorillas,
for example, live in large groups in the wild. Zoos had put them in
pairs, and then only at breeding time—"believing them monogamous, as we'd like to think we are," Coe says. Interaction between
the male and the female gorilla was stilted, hostile, abnormal. Successful breeding among captive gorillas didn't begin until they were
housed in large family groups. Golden lion tamarins, in contrast,
refused to mate when they were caged in groups. Only very recently did researchers affiliated with the National Zoo discover that
these beautiful little monkeys *are* monogamous.

Science first affected the design of zoos in 1735, when Linnaeus   42
published his *Systema Naturae* and people fell in love with classification. The resultant primate house, carnivore house, and reptile
house allowed the public to grasp the contemporary scientific
understanding of the animal world. "At the turn of the century a
zoo was a place where you went to learn what kinds of animals
there were," Conway says. "The fact that they were in little cages
didn't matter. You could see this was an Arabian oryx, a scimitar-
horned oryx, a beisa oryx, and so on. It wasn't at that time so
important to have an idea of what they do, or the way they live,
or how they evolved." The taxonomic approach informed the
design of science museums, aquariums, botanical gardens, and ar-
boretums.

Today zoo directors and designers can draw on whole libraries of   43
information about animal behavior and habitat. Exhibit designers
can create entire forests of epoxy and fiber-glass trees, reinforced
concrete boulders, waterfalls, and artificial vines, with mist provided by cloud machines. A zoo director can oversee the creation
of astoundingly realistic habitats for the animals.

But zoo directors and designers cannot simply create magnificent   44
animal habitats and call them a zoo. That would be something
else—a wildlife preserve, a national park. A zoo director has to
think about bathrooms: zoos are for people, not animals. A zoo
director has to think about bond issues and the fact that the city
council, which also finances garbage collection, trims a little more
from his budget each year. He has to be aware that the zoo is
competing with a vast entertainment industry for the leisure hours
and dollars of the public.

"If you're not smiling at Disney World, you're fired the next   45
day," says Robert Yokel, the director of the Miami Metrozoo. He is
a laid-back, blue-jeaned, suntanned man with wild, scant hair.

"Happy, happy, happy, that's the whole concept. They are the premier operators. They taught the rest of the industry how a park should be run: keep it clean, make it convenient, make the ability to spend dollars very easy. They do everything top drawer. They drew over thirteen million people last year. It's an escape. It's a fantasy." Obviously, the director of the Miami zoo, more than most, has to worry about Disney World. He is surrounded, as well, by Monkey Jungle, the Miami Seaquarium, Busch Gardens, Parrot Jungle, Orchid Jungle, Flamingo Gardens, Lion Country Safari, and the beach. If Florida legalizes gambling, he may never see anyone again. But Yokel is not alone in the zoo world in appreciating what commercial entertainment parks offer the public.

The public today has more leisure time and disposable income   46
than ever before, more children than at any time since the 1950s, and more sophistication about animals—thanks to television, movies, and libraries—than at any time in history. Although a Greek in the age of Homer might not have been able to identify an anteater or a koala, many two-year-olds today can. However, there are other claims on people's time. Although, according to statistics, zoo-going is an entrenched habit with Americans, it is no longer likely that a station wagon packed with kids and heading down the highway on Sunday afternoon will turn in at the zoo. The family has been to Disney World, to Six Flags; they've been to theme parks where the hot-dog vendors wear period costumes and the concession stands look like log cabins; they've visited amusement parks where the whole environment, from the colorful banners to the trash cans, all sparkling clean and brightly painted, shrieks of fun. The local zoo, with its broad tree-lined avenues, pacing leopards, and sleeping bears, seems oddly antiquated and sobering by comparison. So zoo directors must ask, Are our visitors having a good time? Will they come back soon? Would they rather be at Disney World? What will really excite them?

Zoos used to be simpler. Once upon a time—in pharaonic Egypt,   47
in Imperial Rome, in the Austro-Hungarian Empire, in the traveling menageries and bear shows of Western Europe and Russia in the 1800s, even in the United States at the turn of the century—it was sufficient for the zoo to pluck an animal from the teeming wild populations in Asia and Africa and display it, as an exotic specimen, to an amazed populace. (And if the animal sickened in captivity, there was nothing to do but wait for it to die and send for another one. Not only had veterinary medicine not evolved adequately but there was no pressure by concerned wildlife groups for zoos to maintain and reproduce their own stock. The animals were out there.)

Already occupied with the welfare of their animals and the   48
amusement of their zoo-goers, zoo directors today must be responsible to the larger reality that the wilderness is disappearing and the
animals with it. Today the cement-block enclosure or quarter-acre
plot allotted by a zoo may be the last protected ground on earth for
an animal whose habitat is disappearing under farmland, villages,
or cities. The word *ark* is used with increasing frequency by zoo
professionals. In this country, zoos house members of half a dozen
species already extinct in the wild, and of hundreds more on the
verge of extinction. Zoo-goers are confronted by skull logos denot-
ing vanishing animals. The new designers like Coe and Jones, and
directors like Conway, Maple, Graham, Dolan, George Rabb, at
Chicago Brookfield, and Michael Robinson, at the National Zoo,
belong as no designers or directors ever before belonged to the
international community of zoologists and conservationists who
have as their goal the preservation of the wild.

"This is a desperate time," William Conway says. The New York   49
Zoological Society, under his leadership, also operates one of the
largest and oldest wildlife-conservation organizations in the world,
Wildlife Conservation International, which sponsors sixty-two
programs in thirty-two countries. Conway is a slender, distinguished, avuncular gentleman with a pencil-line moustache. For
him it seems quite a personal matter, a subject of intense private
distress, that the earth is losing its wildlife and he doesn't know
how many species are going, or what they are, or where they are,
or how to save them.

"We are certainly at the rate of losing a species a day now,   50
probably more," he says. "Who knows how many species there are
on earth? Suppose, for the sake of argument, there are ten million
species of animals out there. If we have one million in the year
2087 we will be doing very well. The human population is increasing at the rate of a hundred and fifty a minute. The tropical moist
forest is decreasing at the rate of fifty acres a minute. And there is
not a hope in the world of slowing this destruction and this population increase for quite some time. Most of the animals we hold
dear, the big, charismatic mega-vertebrates, almost all of them will
be endangered within the next twenty years. The people who are
going to do that have already been born.

"And the destruction is being effected by some poor guy and his   51
wife and their five children who are hacking out a few acres of
ground to try to eat. That's where most of the fifty acres a minute
are going: forty-eight that way and two to the bulldozers. In
Rwanda there is a mountain-gorilla preserve that supports two
hundred and forty gorillas. It recently was calculated that the park

could sustain two thousand human families, people with no other place to live, no land. Now, how can you justify saving the land for two hundred and forty gorillas when you could have two thousand human families? That's one side of the story. Here's the other: if you were to do that, to put those two thousand families in there, the mountain gorilla would disappear completely, and that would take care of Rwanda's population-expansion needs for slightly less than three months. It's a very discouraging picture."

Michael Robinson, the director of the National Zoo, is a rotund   52
and rosy-cheeked Englishman. "I have spent twenty years in the tropics, and it is difficult to talk about them in a detached, scientific manner," he says. "They are the richest ecosystem on earth. They have been here for millions of years. Perhaps eighty percent of all the animals in the world live there and have evolved relationships of breathtaking complexity. The northern hardwood forests have perhaps forty species of trees per hectare. The rain forest has closer to a hundred and fifty to two hundred species per hectare. Once the rain forest is cut down, it takes about a hundred years for the trees to grow back. We estimate that it would take at least six hundred years before the forest has returned to its original state, with all the plants and animals there."

"The American Association of Zoological Parks and Aquariums   53
Species Survival Plan has only thirty-seven endangered species," Conway says. "We should have at least a thousand. How are we going to do it? My God, there are only one thousand seven hundred and eighty-five spaces for big cats in the United States. One thousand seven hundred and eighty-five. How many races of tigers are out there? Five or six. Several races of lions. Several races of leopards, to say nothing of snow leopards, jaguars, fishing cats, cheetahs, and so on. And you have to maintain a minimum population of two to three hundred animals each to have a population that is genetically and demographically sound. What in bloody hell are we going to do?"

Zoos in America are doing two things to try to save the wild   54
animals. The front-line strategy is conservation biology and captive propagation, employing all the recent discoveries in human fertility, such as *in vitro* fertilization, embryo transplantation, and surrogate motherhood. Zoos around the world have hooked into a computerized data-base called ISIS, so that if a rare Indian rhino goes into heat in Los Angeles—or, for that matter, in the wilds of India—a healthy male rhino to donate sperm can be located.

The second-line strategy is to attempt to save the wilderness itself   55
through educating the public. Zoo directors and designers point out that there are 115 million American zoo-goers each year, and that

if even 10 percent of them were to join conservation organizations, to boycott goods produced from the bones, horns, organs, and hides of endangered species, to vote to assist poor nations that are attempting to preserve their forests (perhaps by allowing debt payments to be eased in proportion to the numbers of wild acres preserved), their strength would be felt. The point of the landscape-immersion exhibits is to give the public a taste of what is out there, what is being lost.

It is dawning on zoo professionals that they are, in part, respon-   56
sible for the American public's unfamiliarity with ecology and lack of awareness that half a dozen species a week are being driven into extinction, and that the precious tropical rain forest may vanish within our lifetime. "By itself, the sight of caged animals does not engender respect for animals," the environmental psychologist Robert Sommer wrote in 1972 in a pioneering essay titled "What Did We Learn at the Zoo?" "Despite excellent intentions, even the best zoos may be creating animal stereotypes that are not only incorrect but that actually work against the interests of wildlife preservation." Terry Maple says, "Zoos used to teach that animals are weird and they live alone."

In the past the only zoo people who paid much attention to zoo-   57
goers were the volunteers assigned to drum up new members. The question they usually asked about zoo-goers was, Can we attract ten thousand of them in August? rather than, How have we influenced their attitudes about wildlife? With the decline of the wild and the dedication of zoos to educating the public, zoo professionals have grown curious about zoo-goers. What do they think? What are they saying as they nudge each other and point? Why do they shoot gum balls at the hippos? What exactly *are* they learning at the zoo? In search of answers to such questions, behavioral scientists are strolling through zoos around the country. They clock the number of seconds zoo-goers look at an exhibit. They count how many zoo-goers read the educational placards. They record the casual utterances of passers-by. And they note the age and gender of the zoo-goers who carve their initials on the railings. (They excite the envy of their co-equals in the science-museum world. "Researchers [at zoos] can linger for inordinate amounts of time at exhibits under the guise of waiting for an animal to do something," Beverly Serrell wrote in *Museum News* in 1980. "Standing next to a skeleton doesn't afford such a convenient cover.")

A fairly sharply focused portrait of the average North American   58
zoo-goer has emerged. For example, data collected by the Smith-

sonian Institution at the National Zoo in 1979 revealed that zoo-goers arrive at the gates in any one of eighty-four "visitor constellations." One of the most common constellations is one parent accompanied by one or more children. On weekdays mothers predominate. On weekends fathers are sighted. In another study Professor Edward G. Ludwig, of State University College at Fredonia, New York, observed that the adult unaccompanied by children seemed to have "an aura of embarrassment." A survey published in 1976 found that zoo-goers tend to have more education and larger annual incomes than the population at large, and a 1979 survey found that zoo-goers are ignorant of basic ecological principles much more than are backpackers, birdwatchers, and members of wildlife organizations.

In a group of four zoo-goers, it's likely that only one or two will read an informational sign. Nearly all conversation will be confined to the friends and family members with whom the zoo-goer arrives. The most common form of conversation at the zoo is a declarative sentence following "Watch!" or "Look!" The second most common form is a question. Robert Yokel, in Miami, believes that the two questions asked most frequently by zoo-goers are "Where is the bathroom?" and "Where is the snack bar?" Zoo-goers typically look at exhibits for about ninety seconds. Some never stop walking. Ludwig found that most people will stop for animals that beg, animals that are feeding, baby animals, animals that make sounds, or animals that are mimicking human behavior. People express irritation or annoyance with animals that sleep, eliminate, or regurgitate.

Zoo visitors do not like to lose their way within a zoo, and they get disgruntled when they find themselves backtracking. "We do not enjoy walking in circles and we invariably do," said one of the 300 respondents to the Smithsonian study. "Then we get irritated with ourselves."

Jim Peterson, a senior partner in the natural-history exhibit design firm of Bios, in Seattle, has identified the "first-fish syndrome." Within twenty feet of the entrance to an aquarium, visitors need to see a fish or they become unhappy. They will rush past the finest backlighted high-tech hands-on exhibitry to find that first fish. Similarly, Peterson has noted that visitors in zoos can tolerate only fifty feet between animals. Any greater distance inspires them to plow through foliage and create their own viewing blind.

Most "noncompliant behavior," such as unauthorized feeding of animals or attempting to climb over barriers, comes from juveniles and teens in mixed-gender groupings and children accompanied by both parents. A 1984 study by Valerie D. Thompson suggested that two parents tend to be involved with each other, freeing the children to perform antisocial acts; and that among teenagers there is "a close tie between noncompliant behavior and attempting to impress a member of the opposite sex."

Ted Finlay, a graduate student working with Terry Maple at Zoo   63
Atlanta, wrote a master's thesis titled "The Influence of Zoo Environments on Perceptions of Animals," one of the first studies to focus on zoo design. Finlay majored in psychology and animal behavior with a minor in architecture, with the intention of becoming a zoo psychologist. For the research for his dissertation he prepared a slide show of animals in three environments: free, caged, and in various types of naturalistic zoo exhibits. Two hundred and sixty-seven volunteers viewed the slides and rated their feelings about the animals. The free animals were characterized as "free," "wild," and "active." Caged animals were seen as "restricted," "tame," and "passive." Animals in naturalistic settings were rated like the free animals if no barrier was visible. If the barrier *was* visible, they were rated like caged animals—that is to say, less favorably.

The zoo-goer who emerges from the research literature—be-   64
nighted and happy-go-lucky, chomping his hot dog, holding his nose in the elephant house and scratching under his arms in the monkey house to make his children laugh—is a walking anachronism. He is the creation of an outmoded institution—the conventional zoo—in which the primate house, carnivore house, and reptile house, all lined with tile, glow with an unreal greenish light as if the halls were subterranean, and in which giraffes, zebras, and llamas stand politely, and as if on tiptoe, on the neatly mown lawns of the moated exhibits.

Once it was education enough for the public to file past the   65
captive gorilla in its cage and simply absorb the details of its peculiar or frightening countenance. "One ape in a cage, shaking its steel bars," Terry Maple says, "was a freak show, a horror show, King Kong! You'd go there to be scared, to scream, to squeeze your girlfriend." Despite gilded, or dingy, surroundings, a tusked creature in eighteenth-century Versailles, or downtown Pittsburgh, had the aura of a savage, strange, flowered wilderness.

"Pee-you!" is the primal, universal response of schoolchildren   66
herded into an elephant house. Adults more discreetly crinkle their noses, turn their heads, and laugh. The unspoken impressions are that elephants are filthy, tread in their own feces, attract flies, require hosing down, eat mush, and no wonder they are housed in cinder-block garages. These are not the sort of impressions that

might inspire a zoo-goer to resist—much less protest—the marketing of souvenirs made of ivory.

Moated exhibits display animals in garden-like settings, with   67
bedding plants along cement walkways. A koala seated alone in
the branch of a single artificial tree above a bright-green lawn looks
as if he'd be at home in a Southern California back yard, next to the
patio. The visitors looking at such exhibits appreciate the animals
in them more and pronounce them "beautiful" or "interesting,"
but the subliminal message here is that animals are like gentle pets
and thrive nicely in captivity. The visitors are hard pressed to explain what the big deal is about the rain forest or why zoologists
talk about it, their voices cracking, the way twelfth-century Crusaders must have discussed the Holy Land.

. . .

One evening, just at dusk, Coe hurried alone through the Wood-   68
land Park Zoo. He'd worked late on some sketches, and the zoo
had closed. He would have to let himself out. The lions in the
Serengeti Plains exhibit galloped back and forth through their yellow grass, whipping their tails. They ran and ran and pulled up
short at the brink of their hidden moat, panting, their nostrils flaring. Coe just happened to be passing by. One of the dun-colored
male lions approached and crouched at the very edge of the moat,
and growled. Jon Coe froze.

Now, Coe had designed the exhibit. He knew that he was look-   69
ing up at the lion because he'd elevated its territory to instill fear
and respect in the zoo-goer. He knew that he seemed to be walking
beside the wild, dark African plains because he'd considered issues
like sight lines and cross-viewing. He knew that a concealed moat
lay between him and the lion, and that the width of the moat was
the standard width used by zoos all over the world. But he also
knew that you can't program in motivation. The lion looked at him
and crouched; he could hear it snorting. Then it growled again—
king of the darkness on the grassy plain. The hair stood up on the
back of Coe's neck.

JOSÉ DONOSO

Paseo

José Donoso (1924–   ) was born into a wealthy and eccentric
family in Santiago, Chile. There he attended an English school,

where he acquired a British accent and a lifelong distaste for regimentation. He left before graduating and traveled to Argentina, working for a time as a shepherd on the pampas and as a dockhand in Buenos Aires. After returning briefly to Santiago to complete his secondary education, he attended Princeton University from 1947 to 1951. In 1955 he published *Veraneo y otros uentos (Summertime and Other Stories)*, a book that Donoso and his friends sold on street corners in Santiago, as they did his first novel, *Coronación,* two years later. The novel won the William Faulkner Foundation Prize in 1962 and was translated into English in 1965. Donoso's fourth novel, *The Obscene Bird of Night* (1970, English translation 1973), achieved international fame and made him one of the leading practitioners of a style sometimes called "magical realism." "Paseo" ("The Walk") was first published in *Sur,* November-December 1959, and was translated into English in 1969.

I

This happened when I was very young, when my father and Aunt Mathilda, his maiden sister, and my uncles Gustav and Armand were still living. Now they are all dead. Or I should say, I prefer to think they are all dead: it is too late now for the questions they did not ask when the moment was right, because events seemed to freeze all of them into silence. Later they were able to construct a wall of forgetfulness or indifference to shut out everything, so that they would not have to harass themselves with impotent conjecture. But then, it may not have been that way at all. My imagination and my memory may be deceiving me. After all, I was only a child then, with whom they did not have to share the anguish of their inquiries, if they made any, nor the result of their discussions.

What was I to think? At times I used to hear them closeted in the library, speaking softly, slowly, as was their custom. But the massive door screened the meaning of their words, permitting me to hear only the grave and measured counterpoint of their voices. What was it they were saying? I used to hope that, inside there, abandoning the coldness which isolated each of them, they were at last speaking of what was truly important. But I had so little faith in this that, while I hung around the walls of the vestibule near the library door, my mind became filled with the certainty that they had chosen to forget, that they were meeting only to discuss, as always, some case in jurisprudence relating to their specialty in maritime law. Now I think that perhaps they were right in wanting to blot out everything. For why should one live with the terror of having to acknowledge that the streets of a city can swallow up a human being, leaving him without life and without death, suspended as it were, in a dimension more dangerous than any dimension with a name?

One day, months after, I came upon my father watching the street from the balcony of the drawing room on the second floor. The sky was close, dense, and the humid air weighed down the large, limp leaves of the ailanthus trees. I drew near my father, eager for an answer that would contain some explanation.

"What are you doing here, Papa?" I murmured.

When he answered, something closed over the despair on his   5
face, like the blow of a shutter closing on a shameful scene.

"Don't you see? I'm smoking . . ." he replied.

And he lit a cigarette.

It wasn't true. I knew why he was peering up and down the street, his eyes darkened, lifting his hand from time to time to stroke his smooth chestnut whiskers: it was in hope of seeing them reappear, returning under the trees of the sidewalk, the white bitch trotting at heel.

Little by little I began to realize that not only my father but all of them, hiding from one another and without confessing even to themselves what they were doing, haunted the windows of the house. If someone happened to look up from the sidewalk he would surely have seen the shadow of one or another of them posted beside a curtain, or faces aged with grief spying out from behind the window panes.

In those days the street was paved with quebracho wood, and   10
under the ailanthus trees a clangorous streetcar used to pass from time to time. The last time I was there neither the wooden pavements nor the streetcars existed any longer. But our house was still standing, narrow and vertical like a little book pressed between the bulky volumes of new buildings, with shops on the ground level and a crude sign advertising knitted undershirts covering the balconies of the second floor.

When we lived there all the houses were tall and slender like our own. The block was always happy with the games of children playing in the patches of sunshine on the sidewalks, and with the gossip of the servant girls on their way back from shopping. But our house was not happy. I say it that way, "it was not happy" instead of "it was sad," because that is exactly what I mean to say. The word "sad" would be wrong because it has too definite a connotation, a weight and a dimension of its own. What took place in our house was exactly the opposite: an absence, a lack, which because it was unacknowledged was irremediable, something that, if it weighed, weighed by not existing.

My mother died when I was only four years old, so the presence of a woman was deemed necessary for my care. As Aunt Mathilda was the only woman in the family and she lived with my uncles Armand and Gustav, the three of them came to live at our house, which was spacious and empty.

Aunt Mathilda discharged her duties towards me with that propriety which was characteristic of everything she did. I did not doubt that she loved me, but I could never feel it as a palpable experience uniting us. There was something rigid in her affections, as there was in those of the men of the family. With them, love existed confined inside each individual, never breaking its boundaries to express itself and bring them together. For them to show affection was to discharge their duties to each other perfectly, and above all not to inconvenience, never to inconvenience. Perhaps to express love in any other way was unnecessary for them now, since they had so long a history together, had shared so long a past. Perhaps the tenderness they felt in the past had been expressed to the point of satiation and found itself stylized now in the form of certain actions, useful symbols which did not require further elucidation. Respect was the only form of contact left between those four isolated individuals who walked the corridors of the house which, like a book, showed only its narrow spine to the street.

I, naturally, had no history in common with Aunt Mathilda. How could I, if I was no more than a child then who could not understand the gloomy motivations of his elders? I wished that their confined feeling might overflow and express itself in a fit of rage, for example, or with some bit of foolery. But she could not guess this desire of mine because her attention was not focused on me: I was a person peripheral to her life, never central. And I was not central because the entire center of her being was filled up with my father and my uncles. Aunt Mathilda was born the only woman, an ugly woman moreover, in a family of handsome men, and on realizing that for her marriage was unlikely, she dedicated herself to looking out for the comfort of those three men, by keeping house for them, by taking care of their clothes and providing their favorite dishes. She did these things without the least servility, proud of her role because she did not question her brothers' excellence. Furthermore, like all women, she possessed in the highest degree the faith that physical well-being is, if not principal, certainly primary, and that to be neither hungry nor cold nor uncomfortable is the basis for whatever else is good. Not that these defects caused her grief, but rather they made her impatient, and when she saw affliction about her she took immediate steps to remedy what, without doubt, were errors in a world that should be, that had to be, perfect. On another plane, she was intolerant of shirts which were not stupendously well-ironed, of meat that was not of the finest quality, of the humidity that owing to someone's carelessness had crept into the cigar-box.

After dinner, following what must have been an ancient ritual in the family, Aunt Mathilda went upstairs to the bedrooms, and in each of her brothers' rooms she prepared the beds for sleeping, parting the sheets with her bony hands. She spread a shawl at the foot of the bed for that one, who was subject to chills, and placed a feather pillow at the head of this one, for he usually read before going to sleep. Then, leaving the lamps lighted beside those enormous beds, she came downstairs to the billiard room to join the men for coffee and for a few rounds, before, as if bewitched by her, they retired to fill the empty effigies of the pajamas she had arranged so carefully upon the white, half-opened sheets.

But Aunt Mathilda never opened my bed. Each night, when I went up to my room, my heart thumped in the hope of finding my bed opened with the recognizable dexterity of her hands. But I had to adjust myself to the less pure style of the servant girl who was charged with doing it. Aunt Mathilda never granted me that mark of importance because I was not her brother. And not to be "one of my brothers" seemed to her a misfortune of which many people were victims, almost all in fact, including me, who after all was only the son of one of them.

Sometimes Aunt Mathilda asked me to visit her in her room where she sat sewing by the tall window, and she would talk to me. I listened attentively. She spoke to me about her brothers' integrity as lawyers in the intricate field of maritime law, and she extended to me her enthusiasm for their wealth and reputation, which I would carry forward. She described the embargo on a shipment of oranges, told of certain damages caused by miserable tugboats manned by drunkards, of the disastrous effects that arose from the demurrage of a ship sailing under an exotic flag. But when she talked to me of ships her words did not evoke the hoarse sounds of ships' sirens that I heard in the distance on summer nights when, kept awake by the heat, I climbed to the attic, and from an open window watched the far-off floating lights, and those blocks of darkness surrounding the city that lay forever out of reach for me because my life was, and would ever be, ordered perfectly. I realize now that Aunt Mathilda did not hint at this magic because she did not know of it. It had no place in her life, as it had no place in the life of anyone destined to die with dignity in order afterward to be installed in a comfortable heaven, a heaven identical to our house. Mute, I listened to her words, my gaze fastened on the white thread that, as she stretched it against her black blouse, seemed to capture all of the light from the window. I exulted at the world of security that her words projected for me, that magnificent straight road which leads to a death that is not dreaded since it is exactly like this life, without anything fortuitous or unexpected. Because death was not terrible. Death was the final incision, clean and definitive, nothing more. Hell existed, of course, but not for us. It was rather for chastising the other inhabitants of the city and those anonymous seamen who caused the damages that, when the cases were concluded, filled the family coffers.

Aunt Mathilda was so removed from the idea of fear that, since I now know that love and fear go hand in hand, I am tempted to think that in those days she did not love anyone. But I may be mistaken. In her rigid way she may have been attached to her brothers by a kind of love. At night, after supper, they gathered in the billiard room for a few games. I used to go in with them. Standing outside that circle of imprisoned affections, I watched for a sign that would show me the ties between them did exist, and did, in fact, bind. It is strange that my memory does not bring back anything but shades of indeterminate grays in remembering the house, but when I evoke that hour, the strident green of the table, the red and white of the balls and the little cube of blue chalk become inflamed in my memory, illumined by the low lamp whose shade banished everything else into dusk. In one of the family's many rituals, the voice of Aunt Mathilda rescued each of the brothers by turn from the darkness, so that they might make their plays.

"Now, Gustav . . ."

And when he leaned over the green table, cue in hand, Uncle   20
Gustav's face was lit up, brittle as paper, its nobility contradicted by his eyes, which were too small and spaced too close together. Finished playing, he returned to the shadow, where he lit a cigar whose smoke rose lazily until it was dissolved in the gloom of the ceiling. Then his sister said: "All right, Armand . . ."

And the soft, timid face of Uncle Armand, with his large sky-blue eyes concealed by gold-rimmed glasses, bent down underneath the light. His game was generally bad because he was "the baby," as Aunt Mathilda sometimes referred to him. After the comments aroused by his play he took refuge behind his newspaper and Aunt Mathilda said: "Pedro, your turn . . ."

I held my breath when I saw him lean over to play, held it even more tightly when I saw him succumb to his sister's command. I prayed, as he got up, that he would rebel against the order established by his sister's voice. I could not see that this order was in itself a kind of rebellion, constructed by them as a protection against chaos, so that they might not be touched by what can be neither explained nor resolved. My father, then, leaned over the green cloth, his practiced eye gauging the exact distance and positions of the billiards. He made his play, and making it, he exhaled in such a way that his mustache stirred about his half-opened mouth. Then he handed me his cue so I might chalk it with the blue cube. With this minimal role that he assigned to me, he let me touch the circle that united him with the others, without letting me take part in it more than tangentially.

Now it was Aunt Mathilda's turn. She was the best player. When I saw her face, composed as if from the defects of her brothers' faces, coming out of the shadow, I knew that she was going to win. And yet . . . had I not seen her small eyes light up that face so like a brutally clenched fist, when by chance one of them succeeded in beating her? That spark appeared because, although she might have wished it, she would never have permitted herself to let any of them win. That would be to introduce the mysterious element of love into a game that ought not to include it, because affection should remain in its place, without trespassing on the strict reality of a carom shot.

II

I never did like dogs. One may have frightened me when I was very young, I don't know, but they have always displeased me. As there were no dogs at home and I went out very little, few occasions presented themselves to make me uncomfortable. For my aunt and uncles and for my father, dogs, like all the rest of the animal kingdom, did not exist. Cows, of course, supplied the cream for the dessert that was served in a silver dish on Sundays. Then there were the birds that chirped quite agreeably at twilight in the branches of the elm tree, the only inhabitant of the small garden at the rear of the house. But animals for them existed only in the proportion in which they contributed to the pleasure of human beings. Which is to say that dogs, lazy as city dogs are, could not even dent their imagination with a possibility of their existence.

Sometimes, on Sunday, Aunt Mathilda and I used to go to Mass 25 early to take communion. It was rare that I succeeded in concentrating on the sacrament, because the idea that she was watching me without looking generally occupied the first place of my conscious mind. Even when her eyes were directed to the altar, or her head bowed before the Blessed Sacrament, my every movement drew her attention to it. And on leaving the church she told me with sly reproach that it was without doubt a flea trapped in the pews that prevented me from meditating, as she had suggested, that death is the good foreseen end, and from praying that it might not be painful, since that was the purpose of masses, novenas and communions.

This was such a morning. A fine drizzle was threatening to turn into a storm, and the quebracho pavements extended their shiny fans, notched with streetcar rails, from sidewalk to sidewalk. As I was cold and in a hurry to get home I stepped up the pace beside Aunt Mathilda, who was holding her black mushroom of an umbrella above our heads. There were not many people in the street since it was so early. A dark-complexioned gentleman saluted us without lifting his hat, because of the rain. My aunt was in the process of telling me how surprised she was that someone of mixed blood had bowed to her with so little show of attention, when suddenly, near where we were walking, a streetcar applied its brakes with a screech, making her interrupt her monologue. The conductor looked out through his window:

"Stupid dog!" he shouted.

We stopped to watch.

A small white bitch escaped from between the wheels of the streetcar and, limping painfully, with her tail between her legs, took refuge in a doorway as the streetcar moved on again.

"These dogs," protested Aunt Mathilda. "It's beyond me how   30 they are allowed to go around like that."

Continuing on our way, we passed by the bitch huddled in the corner of a doorway. It was small and white, with legs which were too short for its size and an ugly pointed snout that proclaimed an entire genealogy of misalliances: the sum of unevenly matched breeds which for generations had been scouring the city, searching for food in the garbage cans and among the refuse of the port. She was drenched, weak, trembling with cold or fever. When we passed in front of her I noticed that my aunt looked at the bitch, and the bitch's eyes returned her gaze.

We continued on our way home. Several steps further I was on the point of forgetting the dog when my aunt surprised me by abruptly turning around and crying out: "Psst! Go away!"

She had turned in such absolute certainty of finding the bitch following us that I trembled with the mute question which arose from my surprise: How did she know? She couldn't have heard her, since she was following us at an appreciable distance. But she did not doubt it. Perhaps the look that had passed between them of which I saw only the mechanics—the bitch's head raised slightly toward Aunt Mathilda, Aunt Mathilda's slightly inclined toward the bitch—contained some secret commitment? I do not know. In any case, turning to drive away the dog, her peremptory "psst" had the sound of something like a last effort to repel an encroaching destiny. It is possible that I am saying all this in the light of things that happened later, that my imagination is embellishing with significance what was only trivial. However, I can say with certainty that in that moment I felt a strangeness, almost a fear of my aunt's sudden loss of dignity in condescending to turn around and confer rank on a sick and filthy bitch.

We arrived home. We went up the stairs and the bitch stayed down below, looking up at us from the torrential rain that had just been unleashed. We went inside, and the delectable process of breakfast following communion removed the white bitch from my mind. I have never felt our house so protective as that morning, never rejoiced so much in the security derived from those old walls that marked off my world.

In one of my wanderings in and out of the empty sitting rooms, I pulled back the curtain of a window to see if the rain promised to let up. The storm continued. And, sitting at the foot of the stairs still scrutinizing the house, I saw the white bitch. I dropped the curtain so that I might not see her there, soaked through and looking like one spellbound. Then, from the dark outer rim of the room, Aunt Mathilda's low voice surprised me. Bent over to strike a match to the kindling wood already arranged in the fireplace, she asked: "Is it still there?"

"What?"

I knew what.

"The white bitch . . ."

I answered yes, that it was.

III

It must have been the last storm of the winter, because I remember quite clearly that the following days opened up and the nights began to grow warmer.

The white bitch stayed posted on our doorstep scrutinizing our windows. In the mornings, when I left for school, I tried to shoo her away, but barely had I boarded the bus when I would see her reappear around the corner or from behind the mailbox. The servant girls also tried to frighten her away, but their attempts were as fruitless as mine, because the bitch never failed to return.

Once, we were all saying goodnight at the foot of the stairs before going up to bed. Uncle Gustav had just turned off the lights, all except the one on the stairway, so that the large space of the vestibule had become peopled with the shadowy bodies of furniture. Aunt Mathilda, who was entreating Uncle Armand to open the window of his room so a little air could come in, suddenly stopped speaking, leaving her sentence unfinished, and the movements of all of us, who had started to go up, halted.

"What is the matter?" asked Father, stepping down one stair.

"Go on up," murmured Aunt Mathilda, turning around and gazing into the shadow of the vestibule.

But we did not go up.   45

The silence of the room was filled with the sweet voice of each object: a grain of dirt trickling down between the wallpaper and the wall, the creaking of polished woods, the quivering of some loose crystal. Someone, in addition to ourselves, was where we were. A small white form came out of the darkness near the service door. The bitch crossed the vestibule, limping slowly in the direction of Aunt Mathilda, and without even looking at her, threw herself down at her feet.

It was as though the immobility of the dog enabled us to move again. My father came down two stairs. Uncle Gustav turned on the light. Uncle Armand went upstairs and shut himself in his room.

"What is this?" asked my father.

Aunt Mathilda remained still.

"How could she have come in?" she asked aloud.   50

Her question seemed to acknowledge the heroism implicit in having either jumped walls in that lamentable condition, or come into the basement through a broken pane of glass, or fooled the servants' vigilance by creeping through a casually opened door.

"Mathilda, call one of the girls to take her away," said my father, and went upstairs followed by Uncle Gustav.

We were left alone looking at the bitch. She called a servant, telling the girl to give her something to eat and the next day to call a veterinarian.

"Is she going to stay in the house?" I asked.

"How can she walk in the street like that?" murmured Aunt   55
Mathilda. "She has to get better so we can throw her out. And she'd better get well soon because I don't want animals in the house."

Then she added: "Go upstairs to bed."

She followed the girl who was carrying the dog out.

I sensed that ancient drive of Aunt Mathilda's to have everything go well about her, that energy and dexterity which made her sovereign of immediate things. Is it possible that she was so secure within her limitations that for her the only necessity was to overcome imperfections, errors not of intention or motive, but of condition? If so, the white bitch was going to get well. She would see to it because the animal had entered the radius of her power. The veterinarian would bandage the broken leg under her watchful eye, and protected by rubber gloves and an apron, she herself would take charge of cleaning the bitch's pustules with disinfectant that would make her howl. But Aunt Mathilda would remain deaf to those howls, sure that whatever she was doing was for the best.

And so it was. The bitch stayed in the house. Not that I saw her, but I could feel the presence of any stranger there, even though confined to the lower reaches of the basement. Once or twice I saw Aunt Mathilda with the rubber gloves on her hands, carrying a vial full of red liquid. I found a plate with scraps of food in a passage of the basement where I went to look for the bicycle I had just been given. Weakly, buffered by walls and floors, at times the suspicion of a bark reached my ears.

One afternoon I went down to the kitchen. The bitch came in, painted like a clown with red disinfectant. The servants threw her out without paying her any mind. But I saw that she was not hobbling any longer, that her tail, limp before, was curled up like a feather, leaving her shameless bottom in plain view.

That afternoon I asked Aunt Mathilda: "When are you going to throw her out?"

"Who?" she asked.

She knew perfectly well.

"The white bitch."

"She's not well yet," she replied.

Later I thought of insisting, of telling her that surely there was nothing now to prevent her from climbing the garbage cans in search of food. I didn't do it because I believe it was the same night that Aunt Mathilda, after losing the first round of billiards, decided that she did not feel like playing another. Her brothers went on playing, and she, ensconced in the leather sofa, made a mistake in calling their names. There was a moment of confusion. Then the thread of order was quickly picked up again by the men, who knew how to ignore an accident if it was not favorable to them. But I had already seen.

It was as if Aunt Mathilda were not there at all. She was breathing at my side as she always did. The deep, silencing carpet yielded under her feet as usual and her tranquilly crossed hands weighed on her skirt. How is it possible to feel with the certainty I felt then the absence of a person whose heart is somewhere else? The following nights were equally troubled by the invisible slur of her absence. She seemed to have lost all interest in the game and left off calling her brothers by their names. They appeared not to notice it. But they must have, because their games became shorter and I noticed an infinitesimal increase in the deference with which they treated her.

One night, as we were going out of the dining room, the bitch appeared in the doorway and joined the family group. The men paused before they went into the library so that their sister might lead the way to the billiard room, followed this time by the white bitch. They made no comment, as if they had not seen her, beginning their game as they did every night.

The bitch sat down at Aunt Mathilda's feet. She was very quiet. Her lively eyes examined the room and followed the players' strategies as if all of that amused her greatly. She was fat now and had a shiny coat. Her whole body, from her quivering snout to her tail ready to waggle, was full of an abundant capacity for fun. How long had she stayed in the house? A month? Perhaps more. But in that month Aunt Mathilda had forced her to get well, caring for her not with displays of affection but with those hands of hers which could not refrain from mending what was broken. The leg was well. She had disinfected, fed and bathed her, and now the white bitch was whole.

In one of his plays Uncle Armand let the cube of blue chalk fall   70
to the floor. Immediately, obeying an instinct that seemed to surge up from her picaresque past, the bitch ran toward the chalk and snatched it with her mouth away from Uncle Armand, who had bent over to pick it up. Then followed something surprising: Aunt Mathilda, as if suddenly unwound, burst into a peal of laughter that agitated her whole body. We remained frozen. On hearing her laugh, the bitch dropped the chalk, ran towards her with tail waggling aloft, and jumped up onto her lap. Aunt Mathilda's laugh relented, but Uncle Armand left the room. Uncle Gustav and my father went on with the game: now it was more important than ever not to see, not to see anything at all, not to comment, not to consider onself alluded to by these events.

I did not find Aunt Mathilda's laugh amusing, because I may have felt the dark thing that had stirred it up. The bitch grew calm sitting on her lap. The cracking noises of the balls when they hit seemed to conduct Aunt Mathilda's hand first from its place on the edge of the sofa, to her skirt, and then to the curved back of the sleeping animal. On seeing that expressionless hand reposing there, I noticed that the tension which had kept my aunt's features clenched before, relented, and that a certain peace was now softening her face. I could not resist. I drew closer to her on the sofa, as if to a newly kindled fire. I hoped that she would reach out to me with a look or include me with a smile. But she did not.

IV

When I arrived from school in the afternoon, I used to go directly to the back of the house and, mounting my bicycle, take turn after turn around the narrow garden, circling the pair of cast-iron benches and the elm tree. Behind the wall, the chestnut trees were beginning to display their light spring down, but the seasons did not interest me, for I had too many serious things to think about. And since I knew that no one came down into the garden until the suffocation of midsummer made it imperative, it seemed to be the best place for meditating about what was going on inside the house.

One might have said that nothing was going on. But how could I remain calm in the face of the entwining relationship which had sprung up between my aunt and the white bitch? It was as if Aunt Mathilda, after having resigned herself to an odd life of service and duty, had found at last her equal. And as women-friends do, they carried on a life full of niceties and pleasing refinements. They ate bonbons that came in boxes wrapped frivolously with ribbons. My aunt arranged tangerines, pineapples and grapes in tall crystal bowls, while the bitch watched her as if on the point of criticizing her taste or offering a suggestion.

Often when I passed the door of her room, I heard a peal of laughter like the one which had overturned the order of her former life that night. Or I heard her engage in a dialogue with an inter-locutor whose voice I did not hear. It was a new life. The bitch, the guilty one, slept in a hamper near her bed, an elegant, feminine hamper, ridiculous to my way of thinking, and followed her every-where except into the dining room. Entrance there was forbidden her, but waiting for her friend to come out again, she followed her to the billiard room and sat at her side on the sofa or on her lap, exchanging with her from time to time complicitory glances.

How was it possible? I used to ask myself: why had she waited until now to go beyond herself and establish a dialogue? At times she appeared insecure about the bitch, fearful that, in the same way she had arrived one fine day, she might also go, leaving her with all this new abundance weighing on her hands. Or did she still fear for her health? These ideas, which now seem to clear, floated blurred in my imagination while I listened to the gravel of the path crunch-ing under the wheels of my bicycle. What was not blurred, how-ever, was my vehement desire to become gravely ill, to see if I might also succeed in harvesting some kind of relationship. Be-cause the bitch's illness had been the cause of everything. If it had not been for that, my aunt might have never joined in league with her. But I had a constitution of iron, and furthermore it was clear that Aunt Mathilda's heart did not have room for more than one love at a time.

My father and my uncles did not seem to notice any change. The bitch was very quiet and, abandoning her street ways, seemed to acquire manners more worthy of Aunt Mathilda. But still, she had somehow preserved all the sauciness of a female of the streets. It was clear that the hardships of her life had not been able to cloud either her good humor or her taste for adventure which, I felt, lay dangerously dormant inside her. For the men of the house it proved easier to accept her than to throw her out, since this would have forced them to revise their cannons of security.

One night, when the pitcher of lemonade had already made its appearance on the console table of the library, cooling that corner of the shadow, and the windows had been thrown open to the air, my father halted abruptly at the doorway of the billiard room.

"What is that?" he exclaimed, looking at the floor.

The three men stopped in consternation to look at a small, round pool on the waxed floor.

"Mathilda!" called Uncle Gustav.   80

She went to look and then reddened with shame. The bitch had taken refuge under the billiard table in the adjoining room. Walking over to the table my father saw her there, and changing direction sharply, he left the room, followed by his brothers.

Aunt Mathilda went upstairs. The bitch followed her. I stayed in the library with a glass of lemonade in my hand, and looked out at the summer sky, listening to some far-off siren from the sea, and to the murmur of the city stretched out under the stars. Soon I heard Aunt Mathilda coming down. She appeared with her hat on and with her keys chinking in her hand.

"Go up and go to bed," she said. "I'm going to take her for a walk on the street so that she can do her business."

Then she added something strange: "It's such a lovely night."

And she went out.   85

From that night on, instead of going up after dinner to open her brothers' beds, she went to her room, put her hat tightly on her head and came downstairs again, chinking her keys. She went out with the bitch without explaining anything to anyone. And my uncles and my father and I stayed behind in the billiard room, and later we sat on the benches of the garden, with all the murmuring of the elm tree and the clearness of the sky weighing down on us. These nocturnal walks of Aunt Mathilda's were never spoken of by her brothers. They never showed any awareness of the change that had occurred inside our house.

In the beginning Aunt Mathilda was gone at the most for twenty minutes or half an hour, returning to take whatever refreshment there was and to exchange some trivial commentary. Later, her sorties were inexplicably prolonged. We began to realize, or I did at least, that she was no longer a woman taking her dog out for hygienic reasons: outside there, in the streets of the city, something was drawing her. When waiting, my father furtively eyed his pocket watch, and if the delay was very great Uncle Gustav went up to the second floor pretending he had forgotten something there, to spy for her from the balcony. But still they did not speak. Once, when Aunt Mathilda stayed out too long, my father paced back and forth along the path that wound between the hydrangeas. Uncle Gustav threw away a cigar which he could not light to his satisfaction, then another, crushing it with the heel of his shoe. Uncle Armand spilled a cup of coffee. I watched them, hoping that at long last they would explode, that they would finally say something to fill the minutes that were passing by one after another, getting longer and longer and longer without the presence of Aunt Mathilda. It was twelve-thirty when she arrived.

"Why are you all waiting up for me?" she asked, smiling.

She was holding her hat in her hand, and her hair, ordinarily so well-groomed, was mussed. I saw that a streak of mud was soiling her shoes.

"What happened to you?" asked Uncle Armand.   90

"Nothing," came her reply, and with it she shut off any right of her brothers to meddle in those unknown hours that were now her life. I say they were her life because, during the minutes she stayed with us before going up to her room with the bitch, I perceived an animation in her eyes, an excited restlessness like that in the eyes of the animal: it was as though they had been washed in scenes to which even our imagination lacked access. Those two were accomplices. The night protected them. They belonged to the murmuring sound of the city, to the sirens of the ships which, crossing the dark or illuminated streets, the houses and factories and parks, reached my ears.

Her walks with the bitch continued for some time. Now we said good night immediately after dinner, and each one went up to shut himself in his room, my father, Uncle Gustav, Uncle Armand and I. But no one went to sleep before she came in, late, sometimes terribly late, when the light of dawn was already striking the top of our elm. Only after hearing her close the door of her bedroom did the pacing with which my father measured his room cease, or was the window in one of his brothers' rooms finally closed to exclude that fragment of the night which was no longer dangerous.

Once I heard her come up very late, and as I thought I heard her singing softly, I opened my door and peeked out. When she passed my room, with the white bitch nestled in her arms, her face seemed to me surprisingly young and unblemished, even though it was dirty, and I saw a rip in her skirt. I went to bed terrified, knowing this was the end.

I was not mistaken. Because one night, shortly after, Aunt Mathilda took the dog out for a walk after dinner, and did not return.

We stayed awake all night, each one in his room, and she did not   95
come back. No one said anything the next day. They went—I presume—to their office, and I went to school. She wasn't home when we came back and we sat silently at our meal that night. I wonder if they found out something definite that very first day. But I think not, because we all, without seeming to, haunted the windows of the house, peering into the street.

"Your aunt went on a trip," the cook answered me when I finally dared to ask, if only her.

But I knew it was not true.

Life continued in the house just as if Aunt Mathilda were still living there. It is true that they used to gather in the library for hours and hours, and closeted there they may have planned ways of retrieving her out of that night which had swallowed her. Several times a visitor came who was clearly not of our world, a plainclothesman perhaps, or the head of a stevedore's union come to pick up indemnification for some accident. Sometimes their voices rose a little, sometimes there was a deadened quiet, sometimes their voices became hard, sharp, as they fenced with the voice I did not know. But the library door was too thick, too heavy for me to hear what they were saying.

Translated by Lorraine O'Grady Freeman

JOSEPH BRUCHAC III

Turtle Meat

Joseph Bruchac III (1942–   ), a descendant of Abnaki Indians and Slovakian immigrants to the United States, has lived most of his life in upper New York state. Born in Saratoga Springs, he took his bachelor's degree at Cornell University, served three

years as a high school teacher in Ghana, West Africa, and returned to his native state to do graduate work at Syracuse University, SUNY-Albany, and Union Graduate School (Ph.D.,
1975). A prolific writer and translator of West African and Iro-
quois literature, he has contributed poems to over four hundred
periodicals and published several collections, including *Entering
Onondaga* (1978), *Translator's Son* (1981), and *Remembering the
Dawn* (1983). He is also the author of two novels, *The Dreams of
Jesse Brown* (1977) and *No Telephone to Heaven* (1984), and the
editor of anthologies of works by Native Americans, West Africans, and American prison inmates. Not a cloistered scholar,
Bruchac says he likes "to work outside, in the earthmother's soil,
with my hands." Bruchac's religion is animism—belief in an
indwelling soul in both animate beings and inanimate objects.
"Turtle Meat" appeared in *Earth Power Coming: Short Fiction in
Native American Literature* (1983).

"Old Man, come in. I need you!"   1

The old woman's cracked voice carried out to the woodshed
near the overgrown field. Once it had been planted with corn and
beans, the whole two acres. But now mustard rolled heads in the
wind and wild carrot bobbed among nettles and the blue flowers
of thistles. *A goat would like to eat those thistles,* Homer LaWare
thought. *Too bad I'm too old to keep a goat.* He put down the ax
handle he had been carving, cast one quick look at the old bamboo
fishing pole hanging over the door and then stood up.

"Coming over," he called out. With slow careful steps he crossed
the fifty yards between his shed and the single-story house with the
picture window and the gold-painted steps. He swung open the
screen door and stepped over the dishes full of dog food. *Always in
front of the door,* he thought.

"Where?" he called from the front room.

"Back here, I'm in the bathroom. I can't get up."   5

He walked as quickly as he could through the cluttered kitchen.
The breakfast dishes were still on the table. He pushed open the
bathroom door. Mollie was sitting on the toilet.

"Amalia Wind, what's wrong?" he said.

"My legs seem to of locked, Homer. Please just help me to get
up. I've been hearing the dogs yapping for me outside the door and
the poor dears couldn't even get to me. Just help me up."

He slipped his hand under her elbow and lifted her gently. He
could see that the pressure of his fingers on the white wrinkled
flesh of her arm was going to leave marks. She'd always been like
that. She always bruised easy. But it hadn't stopped her from coming for him . . . and getting him, all those years ago. It hadn't

stopped her from throwing Jake Wind out of her house and bringing Homer LaWare to her farm to be the hired man.

Her legs were unsteady for a few seconds but then she seemed to   10
be all right. He removed his arms from her.

"Just don't know how it happened, Homer. I ain't so old as that,
am I, Old Man?"

"No, Amalia. That must of was just a cramp. Nothing more than
that."

They were still standing in the bathroom. Her long grey dress
had fallen down to cover her legs but her underpants were still
around her ankles. He felt awkward. Even after all these years, he
felt awkward.

"Old Man, you just get out and do what you were doing. A
woman has to have her privacy. Get now."

"You sure?"   15

"Sure? My Lord! If I wasn't sure you think I'd have any truck
with men like you?" She poked him in the ribs. "You know what
you should do, Old Man? You should go down to the pond and do
that fishing you said you were going to."

He didn't want to leave her alone, but he didn't want to tell her
that. And there was something in him that urged him towards that
pond, the pond where the yellow perch had been biting for the last
few days according to Jack Crandall. Jack had told him that when
he brought his ax by to have Homer fit a new handle.

"I still got Jack's ax to fix, Amalia."

"And when did it ever take you more than a minute to fit a
handle into anything, *Old Man?*" There was a wicked gleam in her
eye. For a few seconds she looked forty years younger in the old
man's eyes.

He shook his head.   20

"Miss Wind, I swear those ladies were right when they said you
was going to hell." She made a playful threatening motion with
her hand and he backed out the door. "But I'm going."

It took him another hour to finish carving the handle to the right
size. It slid into the head like a hand going into a velvet glove. His
hands shook when he started the steel wedge that would hold it
tight, but it took only three strokes with the maul to put the wedge
in. He looked at his hands, remembering the things they'd done.
Holding the reins of the last horse they'd had on the farm—twenty
years ago. Or was it thirty? Lifting the sheets back from Mollie's
white body that first night. Swinging in tight fists at the face of Jake
Wind the night he came back, drunk and with a loaded .45 in his
hand. He'd gone down hard and Homer had emptied the shells out
of the gun and broken its barrel with his maul on his anvil. Though

Jake had babbled of the law that night, neither the law nor Jake ever came back to the Wind farm. It had been Amalia's all along. Her father'd owned it and Jake had married her for it. She'd never put the property in any man's name, never would. That was what she always said.

"I'm not asking, Amalia," that was what Homer had said to her after the first night they'd spent in the brass bed, just before he'd dressed and gone back to sleep the night away in his cot in the shed. He always slept there. All the years. "I'm not asking for any property, Amalia. It's the Indian in me that don't want to own no land."

That was Homer's favorite saying. Whenever there was something about him that seemed maybe different from what others expected he would say simply, "It's the Indian in me." Sometimes he thought of it not just as a part of him but as another man, a man with a name he didn't know but would recognize if he heard it.

His father had said that same phrase often. His father had come   25
down from Quebec and spoke French and, sometimes, to his first wife who had died when Homer was six, another language that Homer never heard again after her death. His father had been a quiet man who made baskets from the ash trees that grew on their farm. "But he never carried them into town," Homer said with pride. "He just stayed on the farm and let people come to him if they wanted to buy them."

The farm had gone to a younger brother who sold out and moved West. There had been two other children. None of them got a thing, except Homer who got his father's best horse. In those years Homer was working for Seneca Smith at his mill. Woods work, two-man saws and sledding the logs out in the snow. He had done it until his thirtieth year when Amalia had asked him to come and work her farm. Though people had talked, he had done it. When anyone asked why he let himself be run by a woman that way he said, in the same quiet voice his father had used, "It's the Indian in me."

The pond was looking glass smooth. Homer stood beside the boat. Jack Crandall had given him the key to it. He looked in the water. He saw his face, the skin lined and brown as an old map. Wattles of flesh hung below his chin like the comb of a rooster.

"Shit, you're a good-looking man, Homer LaWare," he said to his reflection. "Easy to see what a woman sees in you." He thought again of Mollie sitting in the rocker and looking out the picture window. As he left he heard her old voice calling the names of the small dogs she loved so much. *Those dogs were the only ones ever give back her love,* he thought, *not that no-good daughter. Last time she*

*come was Christmas in '68 to give her that pissy green shawl and try to
run me off again.*

Homer stepped into the boat. Ripples wiped his face from the
surface of the pond. He put his pole and the can of worms in front
of him and slipped the oars into the oarlocks, one at a time, breathing hard as he did so. He pulled the anchor rope into the boat and
looked out across the water. A brown stick projected above the
water in the middle of the pond. *Least it looks like a stick, but if it
moves it . . .* The stick moved . . . slid across the surface of the water
for a few feet and then disappeared. He watched with narrowed
eyes until it reappeared a hundred feet further out. It was a turtle, a
snapping turtle. Probably a big one.

"I see you out there, Turtle," Homer said. "Maybe you and me   30
are going to see more of each other."

He felt in his pocket for the familiar feel of his bone-handled
knife. He pushed the red handkerchief that held it deep in his
pocket more firmly into place. Then he began to row. He stopped in
the middle of the pond and began to fish. Within a few minutes he
began to pull in the fish, yellow-stomached perch with bulging
dark eyes. Most of them were a foot long. He stopped when he had
a dozen and began to clean them, leaving the baited line in the
water. He pulled out the bone-handled knife and opened it. The
blade was thin as the handle of a spoon from thirty years of sharp-
ening. It was like a razor. Homer always carried a sharp knife. He
made a careful slit from the ventral opening of the fish up to its gills
and spilled out the guts into the water, leaning over the side of the
boat as he did so. He talked as he cleaned the fish.

"Old Knife, you cut good," he said. He had cleaned nearly every
fish, hardly wasting a moment. Almost as fast as when he was a
boy. *Some things didn't go from you so . . .*

The jerking of his pole brought him back from his thoughts. It
was being dragged overboard. He dropped the knife on the seat and
grabbed the pole as it went over. He pulled up on it and it bent
almost double. *No fish pulls like that.* It was the turtle. He began
reeling the line in, slow and steady so it wouldn't break. Soon he
saw it, wagging its head back and forth, coming up from the green
depths of the pond where it had been gorging on the perch guts
and grabbed his worm.

"Come up and talk, Turtle," Homer said.

The turtle opened its mouth as if to say something and the hook   35
slipped out, the pole jerking back in Homer's hands. Its jaws were
too tough for the hook to stick in. But the turtle stayed there, just
under the water. It was big, thirty pounds at least. It was looking

for more food. Homer put another worm on the hook with trembling hands and dropped it in front of the turtle's mouth.

"Turtle, take this one too."

He could see the wrinkled skin under its throat as it turned its head. A leech of some kind was on the back of its head, another hanging onto its right leg. It was an old turtle. Its skin was rough, its shell green with algae. It grabbed the hook with a sideways turn of its head. As Homer pulled up to snag the hook it reached forward with its paws and grabbed the line like a man grabbing a rope. Its front claws were as long as the teeth of a bear.

Homer pulled. The turtle kept the hook in its mouth and rose to the surface. It was strong and the old man wondered if he could hold it up. Did he want turtle meat that much? But he didn't cut the line. The mouth was big enough to take off a finger, but he kept pulling in line. It was next to the boat and the hook was only holding because of the pressure on the line. A little slack and it would be gone. Homer slipped the pole under his leg and grabbed with his other hand for the anchor rope, began to fasten a noose in it as the turtle shook its head, moving the twelve-foot boat as it struggled. He could smell it now. The heavy musk of the turtle was everywhere. It wasn't a good smell or a bad smell. It was only the smell of the turtle.

Now the noose was done. He hung it over the side. It was time for the hard part now, the part that was easy for him when his arms were young and his chest wasn't caved in like a broken box. He reached down fast and grabbed the tail, pulling it so that the turtle came half out of the water. The boat almost tipped but Homer kept his balance. The turtle swung its head, mouth open and wide enough to swallow a softball. It hissed like a snake, ready to grab at anything within reach. With his other hand, gasping as he did it, feeling the turtle's rough tail tear the skin of his palm as it slipped from his other hand, Homer swung the noose around the turtle's head. Its own weight pulled the slip knot tight. The turtle's jaws clamped tight with a snap on Homer's sleeve.

"Turtle, I believe I got you and you got me," Homer said. He 40 slipped a turn of rope around his left foot with his free arm. He kept pulling back as hard as he could to free his sleeve but the turtle had it. "I understand you, Turtle," he said, "you don't like to let go." He breathed hard, closed his eyes for a moment. Then he took the knife in his left hand. He leaned over and slid it across the turtle's neck. Dark fluid blossomed out into the water. A hissing noise came from between the clenched jaws, but the turtle held onto the old man's sleeve. For a long time the blood came out but the turtle still held on. Finally Homer took the knife and cut the end of his sleeve off, leaving it in the turtle's mouth.

He sat up straight for the first time since he had hooked the turtle and looked around. It was dark. He could hardly see the shore. He had been fighting the turtle for longer than he thought.

By the time he had reached the shore and docked the boat the sounds of the turtle banging itself against the side of the boat had stopped. He couldn't tell if blood was still flowing from its cut throat because night had turned all of the water that same color. He could't find the fish in the bottom of the boat. It didn't matter. The raccoons could have them. He had his knife and his pole and the turtle. He dragged it back up to the old Ford truck. It was too heavy to carry.

There were cars parked in the driveway when he pulled in. He had to park near the small mounds beside his shed that were marked with wooden plaques and neatly lettered names. He could hear voices as he walked through the darkness.

"Old fool's finally come back," he heard a voice saying. The voice was rough as a rusted hinge. It was the voice of Amalia's daughter.

He pushed through the door. "Where's Amalia?" he said. Some-   45
one screamed. The room was full of faces and they were all looking at him.

"Old bastard looks like he scalped someone," a pock-faced man with grey crew-cut hair muttered.

Homer looked at himself. His arms and hands were covered with blood of the turtle. His tattered right sleeve barely reached his elbow. His trousers were muddy. His fly was half-way open. "Where's Amalia?" he demanded again.

"What the hell have you been up to, you old fart?" said the raspy voice of the daughter. He turned to stare into her loose-featured face. She was sitting in Amalia's rocker.

"I been fishin'."

The daughter stood up and walked toward him. She looked like   50
her father. Jake Wind was written all over her face, carved into her bones.

"You want to know where Moms is, huh? Wanta know where your old sweetheart's gone to? Well, I'll tell you. She's been sent off to a home that'll take care of her, even if she is cracked. Come in and find her sittin' talking to dogs been dead for years. Dishes full of dog food for ghosts. Maybe you better eat some of it because your meal ticket's been cancelled, you old bastard. This man is a doctor and he's decided my dear mother was mentally incompetent. The ambulance took her outta here half an hour ago."

She kept talking, saying things she had longed to say for years. Homer LaWare wasn't listening. His eyes took in the details of the room he had walked through every day for the last forty years, the furniture he had mended when it was broken, the picture window he had installed, the steps he had painted, the neatly stacked dishes he had eaten his food from three times each day for almost half a century. The daughter was still talking, talking as if this were a scene she had rehearsed for many years. But he wasn't listening. Her voice was getting louder. She was screaming. Homer hardly heard her. He closed his eyes, remembering how the turtle held onto his sleeve even after its throat was cut and its life was leaking out into the pond.

The screaming stopped. He opened his eyes and saw that the man with the grey crew-cut hair was holding the daughter's arms. She was holding a plate in her hands. Maybe she had been about to hit him with it. It didn't matter. He looked at her. He looked at the other people in the room. They seemed to be waiting for him to say something.

"I got a turtle to clean out," he said, knowing what it was in him that spoke. Then he turned and walked into the darkness.

PROGRESS

Progress: Preview

WENDELL BERRY   Against PCs   364

> That computers are expected to become as common as TV sets in "the future" does not impress me or matter to me. I do not own a TV set. I do not see that computers are bringing us one step nearer to anything that does matter to me.

NATHANIEL HAWTHORNE   The Birthmark   370

> "Georgiana, you have led me deeper than ever into the heart of science. I feel myself fully competent to render this dear cheek as faultless as its fellow; and then, most beloved, what will be my triumph when I shall have corrected what Nature left imperfect in her fairest work!"

Overview and Ideas for Writing

On June 30, 1858, three eminent statesmen burst out of a committee room in the British Houses of Parliament "in the greatest haste and confusion." Prime Minister Gladstone and Chancellor of the Exchequer Disraeli hurried along with handkerchiefs clapped to their noses; Sir James Graham, less restrained, "seemed to be attacked by a sudden fit of expectoration." The wind had shifted and was blowing off the Thames, which Disraeli described as "a stygian pool reeking with ineffable and intolerable horrors." The City of London, capital of the Industrial Revolution, had fouled its own nest. Cholera was rampant, and the smell of factory wastes and human excrement combined to make life miserable for those who couldn't escape to the less advanced countryside. Technological progress had, at any rate, been getting rather mixed reviews in the 1850s. Poets like Tennyson and Longfellow were looking resolutely backward at figures like King Arthur and Hiawatha. The great art critic John Ruskin was extolling the virtues of Gothic art and architecture. Henry David Thoreau was publishing *Walden*. The word *artificial*, which in the eighteenth century had had largely positive connotations, was now a term of condemnation.

The solution to London's "Great Stink" was not, however, to tear down the factories and send the people back to the country. Within two weeks of getting that famous noseful of London air, Disraeli had introduced legislation that would produce one of the great feats of modern engineering, Sir Joseph Bazalgette's drainage system: eighty-two miles of brick sewers, tunnelled under a heavily built-up city, capable of channeling away 420 million gallons of waste daily and making London habitable again. Though some "Great Stink" seems always near—in our time, for instance, the problem of disposal of nuclear waste—modern technology has until now always managed to find a Bazalgette to make life longer, safer, more prosperous, and more comfortable.

We often forget how revolutionary industrial society is. For most of the four million years before the "Great Stink," our ancestors lived in a world very different from ours: agriculture is only 10,000 years old; the first cities didn't appear until 5,000 years ago, the first coins until about 2,600 years ago. When Adam Smith wrote *The Wealth of Nations,* a tiny minority of the world's people worked at distinct jobs for fixed wages. Today working for wages is the rule, and people who sell what they make (or make what they sell) are unusual. The new world of cash economies, science, factories, mass consumption, and the expectation of constant progress is still an experiment however. Whether the experiment is succeeding is one of the questions on which the essays in this unit turn. The writers range from enthusiasts for progress (notably Adam Smith, Aldous Huxley, and Lewis Thomas) to skeptics who have chosen to live relatively simple lives in the face of advancing technology (notably Henry David Thoreau, Sue Hubbell, and Wendell Berry).

Whether you are inclined to align yourself with the enthusiasts or the skeptics, your own experience can provide you with some valuable insights. You could, for example, carefully observe a day, hour, or even a few minutes of your own life and then consider the role that recent technology has played. How much were you affected by products that did not exist a hundred years ago? Fifty? Twenty-five? In what ways were you a beneficiary of progress and in what ways a victim? You might also write interestingly about your experience with a state of technology higher or lower than that most of us are accustomed to.

If you want to do research, the history of technology provides an inexhaustible supply of topics. You might, for example, trace the evolution of one of the inventions that shape our lives, show how it came into general use, and evaluate its impact. Daniel Boorstin's essay will give you some ideas with which to work. You could analyze the process by which something is built or made: Adam Smith, Henry David Thoreau, Jomo Kenyatta, Sue Hubbell, and Mark Kramer give you a varied set of patterns for such analysis and a variety of ways to think about the connection between how people work and who they are.

ADAM SMITH

Division of Labor

Adam Smith (1723–1790) was born in the small Scottish fishing village of Kirkcaldy. At the age of four, according to his biographer John Rae, Smith was kidnapped by gypsies, but soon recaptured. Rae adds wryly that Smith would "have made a poor gypsy." A notoriously absent-minded professor at the University of Glasgow (he once fell into a pit while deep in conversation), he was fascinated by economics and the development of new manufacturing processes. He was a friend of James Watt, inventor of the steam engine, and an acute observer of the state of technology at the beginning of the Industrial Revolution. *The Wealth of Nations* (1776) is Smith's masterpiece. In it he argues that man's natural desire to trade leads logically to division of labor and that the "invisible hand" of a free marketplace adjusts production to meet the needs of society. In the following excerpt, Smith illustrates the benefits of division of labor by introducing the famous example of a pin factory.

The greatest improvement in the productive powers of labour, 1 and the greater part of the skill, dexterity, and judgment with which it is any where directed, or applied, seem to have been the effects of the division of labour.

The effects of the division of labour, in the general business of 2 society, will be more easily understood, by considering in what manner it operates in some particular manufactures. It is commonly supposed to be carried furthest in some very trifling ones; not perhaps that it really is carried further in them than in others of more importance: but in those trifling manufactures which are destined to supply the small wants of but a small number of people, the whole number of workmen must necessarily be small; and those employed in every different branch of the work can often be collected into the same workhouse, and placed at once under the view of the spectator. In those great manufactures, on the contrary, which are destined to supply the great wants of the great body of the people, every different branch of the work employs so great a number of workmen, that it is impossible to collect them all into the same workhouse. We can seldom see more, at one time, than those employed in one single branch. Though in such manufactures, therefore, the work may really be divided into a much greater number of parts, than in those of a more trifling nature, the division is not near so obvious, and has accordingly been much less observed.

To take an example, therefore, from a very trifling manufacture; but one in which the division of labour has been very often taken notice of, the trade of the pin-maker; a workman not educated to this business (which the division of labour has rendered a distinct trade), nor acquainted with the use of the machinery employed in it (to the invention of which the same division of labour has probably given occasion), could scarce, perhaps, with his utmost industry, make one pin in a day, and certainly could not make twenty. But in the way in which this business is now carried on, not only the whole work is a peculiar trade, but it is divided into a number of branches, of which the greater part are likewise peculiar trades. One man draws out the wire, another straights it, a third cuts it, a fourth points it, a fifth grinds it at the top for receiving the head; to make the head requires two or three distinct operations; to put it on, is a peculiar business, to whiten the pins is another; it is even a trade by itself to put them into the paper; and the important business of making a pin is, in this manner, divided into about eighteen distinct operations, which, in some manufactories, are all performed by distinct hands, though in others the same man will sometimes perform two or three of them. I have seen a small manufactory of this kind where ten men only were employed, and where some of them consequently performed two or three distinct operations. But though they were very poor, and therefore but indifferently accommodated with the necessary machinery, they could, when they exerted themselves, make among them about twelve pounds of pins in a day. There are in a pound upwards of four thousand pins of a middling size. Those ten persons, therefore, could make among them upwards of forty-eight thousand pins in a day. Each person, therefore, making a tenth part of forty-eight thousand pins, might be considered as making four thousand eight hundred pins in a day. But if they had all wrought separately and independently, and without any of them having been educated to this peculiar business, they certainly could not each of them have made twenty, perhaps not one pin in a day; that is, certainly, not the two hundred and fortieth, perhaps not the four thousand eight hundredth part of what they are at present capable of performing, in consequence of a proper division and combination of their different operations.

In every other art and manufacture, the effects of the division of labour are similar to what they are in this very trifling one; though, in many of them, the labour can neither be so much subdivided, nor reduced to so great a simplicity of operation. The division of labour, however, so far as it can be introduced, occasions, in every art, a proportionable increase of the productive powers of labour. The separation of different trades and employments from one another, seems to have taken place, in consequence of this advantage. This separation too is generally carried furthest in those countries which enjoy the highest degree of industry and improvement; what is the work of one man in a rude state of society, being generally that of several in an improved one. In every improved society, the farmer is generally nothing but a farmer; the manufacturer, nothing but a manufacturer. The labour too which is necessary to produce any one complete manufacture, is almost always divided among a great number of hands. How many different trades are employed in each branch of the linen and woollen manufactures, from the growers of the flax and the wool, to the bleachers and smoothers of the linen, or to the dyers and dressers of the cloth!

This great increase of the quantity of work, which, in conse-   5
quence of the division of labour, the same number of people are capable of performing, is owing to three different circumstances; first, to the increase of dexterity in every particular workman; secondly, to the saving of the time which is commonly lost in passing from one species of work to another; and lastly, to the invention of a great number of machines which facilitate and abridge labour, and enable one man to do the work of many.

First, the improvement of the dexterity of the workman neces-   6
sarily increases the quantity of the work he can perform; and the division of labour, by reducing every man's business to some one simple operation, and by making this operation the sole employment of his life, necessarily increases very much the dexterity of the workman. A common smith, who, though accustomed to handle the hammer, has never been used to make nails, if upon some particular occasion he is obliged to attempt it, will scarce, I am assured, be able to make above two or three hundred nails in a day, and those too very bad ones. A smith who has been accustomed to make nails, but whose sole or principal business has not been that of a nailer, can seldom with his utmost diligence make more than eight hundred or a thousand nails in a day. I have seen several boys under twenty years of age who had never exercised any other trade but that of making nails, and who, when they exerted themselves, could make, each of them, upwards of two thousand three hundred nails in a day. The making of a nail, however, is by no means one of the simplest operations. The same person blows the bellows, stirs or mends the fire as there is occasion, heats the iron, and

forges every part of the nail: In forging the head too he is obliged to change his tools. The different operations into which the making of a pin, or of a metal button, is subdivided, are all of them much more simple, and the dexterity of the person, of whose life it has been the sole business to perform them, is usually much greater. The rapidity with which some of the operations of those manufactures are performed, exceeds what the human hand could, by those who had never seen them, be supposed capable of acquiring.

Secondly, the advantage which is gained by saving the time commonly lost in passing from one sort of work to another, is much greater than we should at first view be apt to imagine it. It is impossible to pass very quickly from one kind of work to another, that is carried on in a different place, and with quite different tools. A country weaver, who cultivates a small farm, must lose a good deal of time in passing from his loom to the field, and from the field to his loom. When the two trades can be carried on in the same workhouse, the loss of time is no doubt much less. It is even in this case, however, very considerable. A man commonly saunters a little in turning his hand from one sort of employment to another. When he first begins the new work he is seldom very keen and hearty; his mind, as they say, does not go to it, and for some time he rather trifles than applies to good purpose. The habit of sauntering and of indolent careless application, which is naturally, or rather necessarily acquired by every country workman who is obliged to change his work and his tools every half hour, and to apply his hand in twenty different ways almost every day of his life; renders him almost always slothful and lazy, and incapable of any vigorous application even on the most pressing occasions. Independent, therefore, of his deficiency in point of dexterity, this cause alone must always reduce considerably the quantity of work which he is capable of performing. 7

Thirdly, and lastly, every body must be sensible how much labour is facilitated and abridged by the application of proper machinery. It is unnecessary to give any example. I shall only observe, therefore, that the invention of all those machines by which labour is so much facilitated and abridged, seems to have been originally owing to the division of labour. Men are much more likely to discover easier and readier methods of attaining any object, when the whole attention of their minds is directed towards that single object, than when it is dissipated among a great variety of things. But in consequence of the division of labour, the whole of every man's attention comes naturally to be directed towards some one very simple object. It is naturally to be expected, therefore, that some one or other of those who are employed in each particular 8 branch of labour should soon find out easier and readier methods of performing their own particular work, wherever the nature of it admits of such improvement. A great part of the machines made use of in those manufactures in which labour is most subdivided, were originally the inventions of common workmen, who, being each of them employed in some very simple operation, naturally turned their thoughts towards finding out easier and readier methods of performing it. Whoever has been much accustomed to visit such manufactures, must frequently have been shewn very pretty machines, which were the inventions of such workmen, in order to facilitate and quicken their own particular part of the work. In the first fire-engines, a boy was constantly employed to open and shut alternately the communication between the boiler and the cylinder, according as the piston either ascended or descended. One of those boys, who loved to play with his companions, observed that, by tying a string from the handle of the valve which opened this communication to another part of the machine, the valve would open and shut without his assistance, and leave him at liberty to divert himself with his play-fellows. One of the greatest improvements that has been made upon this machine, since it was first invented, was in this manner the discovery of a boy who wanted to save his own labour.

All the improvements in machinery, however, have by no means been the inventions of those who had occasion to use the machines. Many improvements have been made by the ingenuity of the makers of the machines, when to make them became the business of a peculiar trade; and some by that of those who are called philosophers or men of speculation, whose trade it is not to do any thing, but to observe every thing; and who, upon that account, are often capable of combining together the powers of the most distant and dissimilar objects. In the progress of society, philosophy or speculation becomes, like every other employment, the principal or sole trade and occupation of a particular class of citizens. Like every other employment too, it is subdivided into a great number of different branches, each of which affords occupation to a peculiar tribe or class of philosophers; and this subdivision of employment in philosophy, as well as in every other business, improves dexterity, and saves time. Each individual becomes more expert in his own peculiar branch, more work is done upon the whole, and the quantity of science is considerably increased by it. 9

It is the great multiplication of the productions of all the different arts, in consequence of the division of labour, which occasions, in a well-governed society, that universal opulence which extends itself to the lowest ranks of the people. Every workman has a great 10 quantity of his own work to dispose of beyond what he himself has occasion for; and every other workman being exactly in the same situation, he is enabled to exchange a great quantity of his own goods for a great quantity, or, what comes to the same thing, for the price of a great quantity of theirs. He supplies them abundantly with what they have occasion for, and they accommodate him as amply with what he has occasion for, and a general plenty diffuses itself through all the different ranks of the society.

Observe the accommodation of the most common artificer or day-labourer in a civilized and thriving country, and you will perceive that the number of people of whose industry a part, though but a small part, has been employed in procuring him this accommodation, exceeds all computation. The woollen coat, for example, which covers the day-labourer, as coarse and rough as it may appear, is the produce of the joint labour of a great multitude of workmen. The shepherd, the sorter of the wool, the wool-comber or carder, the dyer, the scribbler, the spinner, the weaver, the fuller, the dresser, with many others, must all join their different arts in order to complete even this homely production. How many merchants and carriers, besides, must have been employed in transporting the materials from some of those workmen to others who often live in a very distant part of the country! how much commerce and navigation in particular, how many ship-builders, sailors, sail-makers, rope-makers, must have been employed in order to bring together the different drugs made use of by the dyer, which often come from the remotest corners of the world! What a variety of labour too is necessary in order to produce the tools of the meanest of those workmen! To say nothing of such complicated machines as the ship of the sailor, the mill of the fuller, or even the loom of the weaver, let us consider only what a variety of labour is requisite in order to form that very simple machine, the shears with which the shepherd clips the wool. The miner, the builder of the furnace for smelting the ore, the feller of the timber, the burner of the charcoal to be made use of in the smelting-house, the brick-maker, the brick-layer, the workmen who attend the furnace, the mill-wright, the forger, the smith, must all of them join their different arts in order to produce them. Were we to examine, in the same manner, all the different parts of his dress and household furniture, the coarse linen shirt which he wears next his skin, the shoes which cover his feet, the bed which he lies on, and all the different parts which compose it, the kitchen-grate at which he prepares his victuals, the coals which he makes use of for that purpose, dug from the bowels of the earth, and brought to him perhaps by a long sea and a long land carriage, all the other utensils

11

of his kitchen, all the furniture of his table, the knives and forks, the earthen or pewter plates upon which he serves up and divides his victuals, the different hands employed in preparing his bread and his beer, the glass window which lets in the heat and the light, and keeps out the wind and the rain, with all the knowledge and art requisite for preparing that beautiful and happy invention, without which these northern parts of the world could scarce have afforded a very comfortable habitation, together with the tools of all the different workmen employed in producing those different conveniencies; if we examine, I say, all these things, and consider what a variety of labour is employed about each of them, we shall be sensible that without the assistance and co-operation of many thousands, the very meanest person in a civilized country could not be provided, even according to, what we very falsely imagine, the easy and simple manner in which he is commonly accommodated. Compared, indeed, with the more extravagant luxury of the great, his accommodation must no doubt appear extremely simple and easy; and yet it may be true, perhaps, that the accommodation of an European prince does not always so much exceed that of an industrious and frugal peasant, as the accommodation of the latter exceeds that of many an African king, the absolute master of the lives and liberties of ten thousand naked savages.

HENRY DAVID THOREAU

The Fitness in a Man's Building His Own House

Henry David Thoreau (1817–1862) was educated at Harvard College and returned to his native town of Concord, Massachusetts, where he worked sporadically as a schoolteacher and a surveyor. From July 4, 1845, to September 6, 1847, he lived in a cabin made with his own hands by the shore of Walden Pond, near Concord. There he wrote his first book, *A Week on the Concord and Merrimack Rivers* (published in 1849), and completed the first draft of *Walden, or Life in the Woods* (1854). Thoreau, more than any other writer in America, has become identified with a spirit of independence that resists all forms of centralization and specialization. American nationalism had no appeal for him: during his stay at Walden he was arrested for refusing to pay his poll tax to a government that tolerated slavery and fought an imperialistic war against Mexico. Similarly, he would not endorse an economic system that turned men into wage slaves, even if the system increased their supposed prosperity: "It is hard to have a southern overseer; it is worse to have a northern one; but worst of all when you are the slave-driver of yourself." The excerpt below is taken from *Walden*'s first chapter, "Economy," which responds to the theories of men like Adam Smith.

Near the end of March, 1845, I borrowed an axe and went down   1
to the woods by Walden Pond, nearest to where I intended to build my house, and began to cut down some tall, arrowy white pines, still in their youth, for timber. It is difficult to begin without borrowing, but perhaps it is the most generous course thus to permit your fellow-men to have an interest in your enterprise. The owner of the axe, as he released his hold on it, said that it was the apple of his eye; but I returned it sharper than I received it. It was a pleasant hillside where I worked, covered with pine woods, through which I looked out on the pond, and a small open field in the woods where pines and hickories were springing up. The ice in the pond was not yet dissolved, though there were some open spaces, and it was all dark-colored and saturated with water. There were some slight flurries of snow during the days that I worked there; but for the most part when I came out on to the railroad, on my way home, its yellow sand-heap stretched away gleaming in the hazy atmosphere, and the rails shone in the spring sun, and I heard the lark and pewee and other birds already come to commence another year with us. They were pleasant spring days, in which the winter of man's discontent was thawing as well as the earth, and the life that had lain torpid began to stretch itself. One day, when my axe had come off and I had cut a green hickory for a wedge, driving it with a stone, and had placed the whole to soak in a pond-hole in order to swell the wood, I saw a striped snake run into the water, and he lay on the bottom, apparently without inconvenience, as long as I stayed there, or more than a quarter of an hour; perhaps because he had not yet fairly come out of the torpid state. It appeared to me that for a like reason men remain in their present low and primitive condition; but if they should feel the influence of the spring of springs arousing them, they would of necessity rise to a higher and more ethereal life. I had previously seen the snakes in frosty mornings in my path with portions of their bodies still numb and inflexible, waiting for the sun to thaw them. On the 1st of April it rained and melted the ice, and in the early part of the day, which was very foggy, I heard a stray goose groping about over the pond and cackling as if lost, or like the spirit of the fog.

So I went on for some days cutting and hewing timber, and also   2

studs and rafters, all with my narrow axe, not having many com-
municable or scholar-like thoughts, singing to myself,—

> Men say they know many things;
> But lo! they have taken wings,—
> The arts and sciences,
> And a thousand appliances:
> The wind that blows
> Is all that anybody knows.

I hewed the main timbers six inches square, most of the studs on
two sides only, and the rafters and floor timbers on one side, leaving the rest of the bark on, so that they were just as straight and
much stronger than sawed ones. Each stick was carefully mortised
or tenoned by its stump, for I had borrowed other tools by this
time. My days in the woods were not very long ones; yet I usually
carried my dinner of bread and butter, and read the newspaper in
which it was wrapped, at noon, sitting amid the green pine boughs
which I had cut off, and to my bread was imparted some of their
fragrance, for my hands were covered with a thick coat of pitch.
Before I had done I was more the friend than the foe of the pine
tree, though I had cut down some of them, having become better
acquainted with it. Sometimes a rambler in the wood was attracted
by the sound of my axe, and we chatted pleasantly over the chips
which I had made.

By the middle of April, for I made no haste in my work, but
rather made the most of it, my house was framed and ready for the
raising. I had already bought the shanty of James Collins, an Irishman who worked on the Fitchburg Railroad, for boards. James
Collins' shanty was considered an uncommonly fine one. When I
called to see it he was not at home. I walked about the outside, at
first unobserved from within, the window was so deep and high. It
was of small dimensions, with a peaked cottage roof, and not much
else to be seen, the dirt being raised five feet all around as if it were
a compost heap. The roof was the soundest part, though a good
deal warped and made brittle by the sun. Doorsill there was none,
but a perennial passage for the hens under the door-board. Mrs. C.
came to the door and asked me to view it from the inside. The hens
were driven in by my approach. It was dark, and had a dirt floor for
the most part, dank, clammy, and aguish, only here a board and
there a board which would not bear removal. She lighted a lamp to
show me the inside of the roof and the walls, and also that the
board floor extended under the bed, warning me not to step into
the cellar, a sort of dust hole two feet deep. In her own words, they
were "good boards overhead, good boards all around, and a good

window,"—of two whole squares originally, only the cat had passed out that way lately. There was a stove, a bed, and a place to sit, an infant in the house where it was born, a silk parasol, gilt-framed looking-glass, and a patent new coffee-mill nailed to an oak sapling, all told. The bargain was soon concluded, for James had in the meanwhile returned. I to pay four dollars and twenty-five cents to-night, he to vacate at five to-morrow morning, selling to nobody else meanwhile: I to take possession at six. It were well, he said, to be there early, and anticipate certain indistinct but wholly unjust claims on the score of ground rent and fuel. This he assured me was the only encumbrance. At six I passed him and his family on the road. One large bundle held their all,—bed, coffee-mill, looking-glass, hens,—all but the cat; she took to the woods and became a wild cat, and, as I learned afterward, trod in a trap set for wood-chucks, and so became a dead cat at last.

I took down this dwelling the same morning, drawing the nails, and removed it to the pond-side by small cartloads, spreading the boards on the grass there to bleach and warp back again in the sun. One early thrush gave me a note or two as I drove along the woodland path. I was informed treacherously by a young Patrick that neighbor Seeley, an Irishman, in the intervals of the carting, transferred the still tolerable, straight, and drivable nails, staples, and spikes to his pocket, and then stood when I came back to pass the time of day, and look freshly up, unconcerned, with spring thoughts, at the devastation; there being a dearth of work, as he said. He was there to represent spectatordom, and help make this seemingly insignificant event one with the removal of the gods of Troy.[1]

I dug my cellar in the side of a hill sloping to the south, where a woodchuck had formerly dug his burrow, down through sumach and blackberry roots, and the lowest stain of vegetation, six feet square by seven deep, to a fine sand where potatoes would not freeze in any winter. The sides were left shelving, and not stoned; but the sun having never shone on them, the sand still keeps its place. It was but two hours' work. I took particular pleasure in this breaking of ground, for in almost all latitudes men dig into the earth for an equable temperature. Under the most splendid house in the city is still to be found the cellar where they store their roots as of old, and long after the superstructure has disappeared posterity remark its dent in the earth. The house is still but a sort of porch at the entrance of a burrow.

At length, in the beginning of May, with the help of some of my

4

5

6

---

1. Virgil's *Aeneid* begins with the hero's moving the household gods from the devastation of Troy.

acquaintances, rather to improve so good an occasion for neighborliness than from any necessity, I set up the frame of my house. No man was ever more honored in the character of his raisers than I. They are destined, I trust, to assist at the raising of loftier structures one day. I began to occupy my house on the 4th of July, as soon as it was boarded and roofed, for the boards were carefully feather-edged and lapped, so that it was perfectly impervious to rain, but before boarding I laid the foundation of a chimney at one end, bringing two cartloads of stones up the hill from the pond in my arms. I built the chimney after my hoeing in the fall, before a fire became necessary for warmth, doing my cooking in the meanwhile out of doors on the ground, early in the morning: which mode I still think is in some respects more convenient and agreeable than the usual one. When it stormed before my bread was baked, I fixed a few boards over the fire, and sat under them to watch my loaf, and passed some pleasant hours in that way. In those days, when my hands were much employed, I read but little, but the least scraps of paper which lay on the ground, my holder, or tablecloth, afforded me as much entertainment, in fact answered the same purpose as the *Iliad*.

It would be worth the while to build still more deliberately than I   7
did, considering, for instance, what foundation a door, a window, a cellar, a garret, have in the nature of man, and perchance never raising any superstructure until we found a better reason for it than our temporal necessities even. There is some of the same fitness in a man's building his own house that there is in a bird's building its own nest. Who knows but if men constructed their dwellings with their own hands, and provided food for themselves and families simply and honestly enough, the poetic faculty would be universally developed, as birds universally sing when they are so engaged? But alas! we do like cowbirds and cuckoos, which lay their eggs in nests which other birds have built, and cheer no traveller with their chattering and unmusical notes. Shall we forever resign the pleasure of construction to the carpenter? What does architecture amount to in the experience of the mass of men? I never in all my walks came across a man engaged in so simple and natural an occupation as building his house. We belong to the community. It is not the tailor alone who is the ninth part of a man;[2] it is as much the preacher, and the merchant, and the farmer. Where is this division of labor to end? and what object does it finally serve? No doubt another *may* also think for me; but it is not therefore desirable that he should do so to the exclusion of my thinking for myself.

2. "It takes nine tailors to make a man": a popular saying of the nineteenth century.

True, there are architects so called in this country, and I have   8
heard of one at least possessed with the idea of making architectural ornaments have a core of truth, a necessity, and hence a
beauty, as if it were a revelation to him. All very well perhaps from
his point of view, but only a little better than the common dilettan-
tism. A sentimental reformer in architecture, he began at the cornice, not at the foundation. It was only how to put a core of truth
within the ornaments, that every sugarplum, in fact, might have an
almond or caraway seed in it,—though I hold that almonds are
most wholesome without the sugar,—and not how the inhabitant,
the indweller, might build truly within and without, and let the
ornaments take care of themselves. What reasonable man ever
supposed that ornaments were something outward and in the skin
merely,—that the tortoise got his spotted shell, or the shell-fish its
mother-o'-pearl tints, by such a contract as the inhabitants of
Broadway their Trinity Church? But a man has no more to do with
the style of architecture of his house than a tortoise with that of its
shell: nor need the soldier be so idle as to try to paint the precise
color of his virtue on his standard. The enemy will find it out. He
may turn pale when the trial comes. This man seemed to me to
lean over the cornice, and timidly whisper his half truth to the rude
occupants who really knew it better than he. What of architectural
beauty I now see, I know has gradually grown from within outward, out of the necessities and character of the indweller, who is
the only builder,—out of some unconscious truthfulness, and no-
bleness, without ever a thought for the appearance and whatever
additional beauty of this kind is destined to be produced will be
preceded by a like unconscious beauty of life. The most interesting
dwellings in this country, as the painter knows, are the most un-
pretending, humble log huts and cottages of the poor commonly; it
is the life of the inhabitants whose shells they are, and not any
peculiarity in their surfaces merely, which makes them *picturesque;*
and equally interesting will be the citizen's suburban box, when his
life shall be as simple and as agreeable to the imagination, and
there is as little straining after effect in the style of his dwelling. A
great proportion of architectural ornaments are literally hollow,
and a September gale would strip them off, like borrowed plumes,
without injury to the substantials. They can do without *architecture*
who have no olives nor wines in the cellar. What if an equal ado
were made about the ornaments of style in literature, and the
architects of our Bibles spent as much time about their cornices as
the architects of our churches do? So are made the *belles-lettres* and
the *beaux-arts* and their professors. Much it concerns a man, forsooth, how a few sticks are slanted over him or under him, and

what colors are daubed upon his box. It would signify somewhat, if, in any earnest sense, *he* slanted them and daubed it; but the spirit having departed out of the tenant, it is of a piece with constructing his own coffin,—the architecture of the grave,—and "carpenter" is but another name for "coffin-maker." One man says, in his despair or indifference to life, take up a handful of the earth at your feet, and paint your house that color. Is he thinking of his last and narrow house? Toss up a copper for it as well. What an abundance of leisure he must have! Why do you take up a handful of dirt? Better paint your house your own complexion; let it turn pale or blush for you. An enterprise to improve the style of cottage architecture! When you have got my ornaments ready, I will wear them.

Before winter I built a chimney, and shingled the sides of my house, which were already impervious to rain, with imperfect and sappy shingles made of the first slice of the log, whose edges I was obliged to straighten with a plane. 9

I have thus a tight shingled and plastered house, ten feet wide by fifteen long, and eight-feet posts, with a garret and a closet, a large window on each side, two trap-doors, one door at the end, and a brick fireplace opposite. The exact cost of my house, paying the usual price for such materials as I used, but not counting the work, all of which was done by myself, was as follows; and I give the details because very few are able to tell exactly what their houses cost, and fewer still, if any, the separate cost of the various materials which compose them:— 10

Boards	$8 03½,	mostly shanty boards.
Refuse shingles for roof and sides	4 00	
Laths	1 25	
Two second-hand windows with glass	2 43	
One thousand old brick ...	4 00	
Two casks of lime	2 40	That was high.
Hair	0 31	More than I needed.
Mantle-tree iron	0 15	
Nails	3 90	
Hinges and screws	0 14	
Latch	0 10	
Chalk	0 01	
Transportation	1 40	{ I carried a good part on my back.
In all	$28 12½	

These are all the materials, excepting the timber, stones, and   11
sand, which I claimed by squatter's right. I have also a small
woodshed adjoining, made chiefly of the stuff which was left after
building the house.

I intend to build me a house which will surpass any on the main   12
street in Concord in grandeur and luxury, as soon as it pleases me
as much and will cost me no more than my present one.

I thus found that the student who wishes for a shelter can obtain   13
one for a lifetime at an expense not greater than the rent which he
now pays annually. If I seem to boast more than is becoming, my
excuse is that I brag for humanity rather than for myself; and
my shortcomings and inconsistencies do not affect the truth of
my statement. Notwithstanding much cant and hypocrisy,—chaff
which I find it difficult to separate from my wheat, but for which I
am as sorry as any man,—I will breathe freely and stretch myself in
this respect, it is such a relief to both the moral and physical system; and I am resolved that I will not through humility become the
devil's attorney. I will endeavor to speak a good word for the truth.
At Cambridge College the mere rent of a student's room, which is
only a little larger than my own, is thirty dollars each year, though
the corporation had the advantage of building thirty-two side by
side and under one roof, and the occupant suffers the inconvenience of many and noisy neighbors, and perhaps a residence in
the fourth story. I cannot but think that if we had more true wisdom in these respects, not only less education would be needed,
because, forsooth, more would already have been acquired, but the
pecuniary expense of getting an education would in a great measure vanish. Those conveniences which the student requires at
Cambridge or elsewhere cost him or somebody else ten times as
great a sacrifice of life as they would with proper management on
both sides. Those things for which the most money is demanded
are never the things which the student most wants. Tuition, for
instance, is an important item in the term bill, while for the far
more valuable education which he gets by associating with the
most cultivated of his contemporaries no charge is made. The mode
of founding a college is, commonly, to get up a subscription of
dollars and cents, and then, following blindly the principles of a
division of labor to its extreme,—a principle which should never be
followed but with circumspection,—to call in a contractor who
makes this a subject of speculation, and he employs Irishmen or
other operatives actually to lay the foundations, while the students
that are to be are said to be fitting themselves for it; and for these
oversights successive generations have to pay. I think that it would
be *better than this*, for the students, or those who desire to be

benefited by it, even to lay the foundation themselves. The student who secures his coveted leisure and retirement by systematically shirking any labor necessary to man obtains but an ignoble and unprofitable leisure, defrauding himself of the experience which alone can make leisure fruitful. "But," says one, "you do not mean that the students should go to work with their hands instead of their heads?" I do not mean that exactly, but I mean something which he might think a good deal like that; I mean that they should not *play* life, or *study* it merely, while the community supports them at this expensive game, but earnestly *live* it from beginning to end. How could youths better learn to live than by at once trying the experiment of living? Methinks this would exercise their minds as much as mathematics. If I wished a boy to know something about the arts and sciences, for instance, I would not pursue the common course, which is merely to send him into the neighborhood of some professor, where anything is professed and practised but the art of life;—to survey the world through a telescope or a microscope, and never with his natural eye; to study chemistry, and not learn how his bread is made, or mechanics, and not learn how it is earned; to discover new satellites to Neptune, and not detect the motes in his eyes, or to what vagabond he is a satellite himself; or to be devoured by the monsters that swarm all around him, while contemplating the monsters in a drop of vinegar. Which would have advanced the most at the end of a month,—the boy who had made his own jackknife from the ore which he had dug and smelted, reading as much as would be necessary for this—or the boy who had attended the lectures on metallurgy at the Institute in the meanwhile, and had received a Rodgers penknife from his father? Which would be most likely to cut his fingers? . . . To my astonishment I was informed on leaving college that I had studied navigation!—why, if I had taken one turn down the harbor I should have known more about it. Even the *poor* student studies and is taught only *political* economy, while that economy of living which is synonymous with philosophy is not even sincerely professed in our colleges. The consequence is, that while he is reading Adam Smith, Ricardo, and Say,[3] he runs his father in debt irretrievably.

As with our colleges, so with a hundred "modern improvements"; there is an illusion about them; there is not always a positive advance. The devil goes on exacting compound interest to the last for his early share and numerous succeeding investments in them. Our inventions are wont to be pretty toys, which distract our   14

3. Noted political economists.

attention from serious things. They are but improved means to an unimproved end, an end which it was already but too easy to arrive at; as railroads lead to Boston or New York. We are in great haste to construct a magnetic telegraph from Maine to Texas; but Maine and Texas, it may be, have nothing important to communicate. Either is in such a predicament as the man who was earnest to be introduced to a distinguished deaf woman, but when he was presented, and one end of her ear trumpet was put into his hand, had nothing to say. As if the main object were to talk fast and not to talk sensibly. We are eager to tunnel under the Atlantic and bring the Old World some weeks nearer to the New; but perchance the first news that will leak through into the broad, flapping American ear will be that the Princess Adelaide has the whooping cough. After all, the man whose horse trots a mile a minute does not carry the most important messages; he is not an evangelist, nor does he come round eating locusts and wild honey.[4] I doubt if Flying Childers ever carried a peck of corn to mill.[5]

One says to me, "I wonder that you do not lay up money; you   15
love to travel; you might take the cars and go to Fitchburg today and see the country." But I am wiser than that. I have learned that the swiftest traveller is he that goes afoot. I say to my friend, Suppose we try who will get there first. The distance is thirty miles; the fare ninety cents. That is almost a day's wages. I remember when wages were sixty cents a day for laborers on this very road. Well, I start now on foot, and get there before night; I have travelled at that rate by the week together. You will in the meanwhile have earned your fare, and arrive there sometime to-morrow, or possibly this evening, if you are lucky enough to get a job in season. Instead of going to Fitchburg, you will be working here the greater part of the day. And so, if the railroad reached round the world, I think that I should keep ahead of you; and as for seeing the country and getting experience of that kind, I should have to cut your acquaintance altogether.

Such is the universal law, which no man can ever outwit, and   16
with regard to the railroad even we may say it is as broad as it is long. To make a railroad round the world available to all mankind is equivalent to grading the whole surface of the planet. Men have an indistinct notion that if they keep up this activity of joint stocks and spades long enough all will at length ride somewhere, in next to no time, and for nothing; but though a crowd rushes to the depot, and the conductor shouts "All aboard!" when the smoke is

4. As John the Baptist did.
5. An undefeated English racehorse of the eighteenth century.

blown away and the vapor condensed, it will be perceived that a few are riding, but the rest are run over,—and it will be called, and will be, "A melancholy accident." No doubt they can ride at last who shall have earned their fare, that is, if they survive so long, but they will probably have lost their elasticity and desire to travel by that time. This spending of the best part of one's life earning money in order to enjoy a questionable liberty during the least valuable part of it reminds me of the Englishman who went to India to make a fortune first, in order that he might return to England and live the life of a poet. He should have gone up garret at once. "What!" exclaim a million Irishmen starting up from all the shanties in the land, "is not this railroad which we have built a good thing?" Yes, I answer, *comparatively* good, that is, you might have done worse; but I wish, as you are brothers of mine, that you could have spent your time better than digging in this dirt.

JOMO KENYATTA

Gikuyu Industries

Jomo Kenyatta (1894?–1978) was born in a small Kikuyu[1] agricultural village in Kenya, then part of British East Africa. When he was ten years old, he developed a serious infection and was taken for surgery to a Christian mission, where he met his first Europeans. Fascinated, he ran away from home and became a pupil at the mission. Later he moved to Nairobi and held various government posts, becoming active in organizations that promoted the rights of Kikuyu natives suffering under the domination of white settlers. In 1929 he moved to London to lobby for the rights of his people. There he met and studied with Bronislaw Malinowski, the renowned anthropologist, and completed an academic thesis that he revised for popular publication as *Facing Mount Kenya* (1938). As the following excerpt shows, this book describes Kikuyu customs that were beginning to decline in the face of European influences. After World War II, Kenyatta established himself as one of Africa's leading politicians. Jailed from 1952 to 1961 for alleged terrorist connections, Kenyatta was released in time to negotiate the terms of Kenya's independence and to become its first president in 1964. Kenyatta's speeches

1. *Kikuyu* and *Gikuyu* are alternate spellings for the name of Kenyatta's tribe. *Kikuyu* is more commonly used.

have been collected in two volumes, *Harambee!* (1964) and *Suffering without Bitterness* (1968).

IRONWORK

For centuries the Gikuyu people have developed the technique   1
of procuring iron ore from the sand, and so the use of iron tools has
been well established in the Gikuyu country from time immemorial. In Gikuyu legends and stories we are told how, in the beginning of things, the animals were divided into two sections for domestication purposes. The divider, Mogai, gave one section of the
animals to men and the other to women. At this time people did
not possess any iron tools; they used wooden knives and spears.
The women took to slaughtering their animals for food and other
purposes; they did this with wooden knives, and it took a long time
to kill and skin one animal. The legends go on to tell us that owing
to the pain inflicted on the animals through this slow process of
killing and skinning with blunt wooden knives, the animals could
not stand it much longer. One night, when the women were sleeping, the animals gathered together and decided to run away from
these cruel human beings. All the animals possessed by the women
ran away and scattered in the forests and plains; at the same time
they selected their own chiefs and leaders and defended themselves
from being captured by the human beings. The lion and leopard
were chosen as the defenders of jungles; the elephant, buffalo, and
rhinoceros as the defenders of the forests; the hippopotamus as the
defender of rivers and lakes, and so on. From this time the animals
which were possessed by the women became wild animals, and the
men's animals, which at that time were not used for killing, remained domesticated.

Women tried hard to get their animals back from the forests and   2
jungles, but they did not succeed; they pleaded with the Mogai to
help them get their animals back, but Mogai would not listen to
their petition, for he said that the women had treated their animals
cruelly and therefore he had given them freedom to roam freely in
the forests, plains, and jungles. When the men saw the crisis which
had befallen the women they held a conference and decided to
send a delegation to the Mogai and ask him what they should do
with their animals, which were increasing by leaps and bounds.
The delegates took with them a fine lamb which was fawn-coloured all over its body. They told Mogai that they wanted to
sacrifice the lamb to him, but they did not like to kill and skin it
with the blunt wooden knives for fear of losing their herds as had
happened to the women. To their request the Mogai replied: "You

are wise men, for you have remembered to seek my advice. I can see that you know that I have given you these animals and I have power to take them away from you. For your faith in me I will give you good advice about how to get better tools, not only for sacrifices, but also for your general use. I will make you the masters of your animals with new tools, but I command you to share these with your unfortunate womenfolk."

At this juncture Mogai directed the men to a site in a river-bed 3 and said to them: "Take sand from this site. Dry it in the sun; then make a fire and put the sand therein, and through this process you will get iron. I will give you wisdom to make better tools and you will not have to use blunt wooden tools any more." From this time the Gikuyu, following the advice of Mogai, entered into the phase of metal or iron culture.

Apart from these legends and stories which have been handed 4 down from generation to generation, we have no other records to show exactly when and how this evolution took place.

The fact that the Gikuyu have been well acquainted with the 5 technique and the development of ironwork can be proved by the number of iron implements and ornaments of purely Gikuyu origin which are to be found in all branches of activities in the Gikuyu community. The chief iron articles in the Gikuyu society are the following: spears, swords, digging- and clearing-knives of different sizes, ear- and finger-rings, arrow heads, bracelets of various shapes and sizes, axes and fine chains, hammers and tongs, tweezers, etc.

With these preliminary remarks we will proceed to describe how 6 the work of procuring iron is done. The iron is obtained from ore. The method adopted by the Gikuyu for this purpose of collecting iron ore is that of washing sand which is secured from certain districts and in a particular river. The sand is carefully washed in a river by experienced men; the black substances that contain ore are put together and are handed over to the women and children, who help to spread the ore in the sun to dry. It is worth noting that the whole family of a smith takes part in the work, and the work is divided among the group. When a man is busy in the river washing the sand, his wife or wives and children are busy spreading the iron ore in the sun to dry. This method of working may seem primitive in the eyes of the machine-man of the Western world, but nevertheless the system fulfilled the needs of the community. In the olden days there was only one great demand for iron—namely, during the time of initiation, when the young warriors needed new equipment for war or protection. The chief demand in this direction was for spears and swords. This did not necessarily mean that a new supply of iron was to follow, for there was always a bit of iron in every homestead left over from worn-out tools or those which had broken and could not be mended. These bits of iron were collected and put away to be used in the future for supplying a spear or a sword to the son of the homestead. For this reason the iron production, as mentioned above, was not everyday work. Some smiths had never participated in the work of iron production; they lived on repairs and renewing or joining up together the old bits of iron to produce a new tool or weapon.

After the sand containing iron ore is dried it is carried to the   7
smithy. There it is put in a fire made of a special mixture of charcoals. Some of these are made from a particular tree and others from a special banana plant. The two kinds of charcoals are mixed. The banana charcoal is said to have particular value in smelting iron. Its substances help to put the pure iron together and to separate it from impure matters.

Before the process of smelting is actually started, a short ritual is   8
performed by the smith and his assistants. The ritual consists of sprinkling a little Gikuyu beer over the furnace, accompanied by a few ceremonial words directed to Mogai and the ancestral spirits. In the absence of beer a little water fulfils the ritual duty. After the ceremony of invoking the spirits of ancestors and appealing to Mogai for guidance and protection in the enterprise, the work of smelting iron is proceeded with. Two bellows are employed simultaneously to keep the fire burning. They are worked by assistants, who learn the profession by means of watching the smith doing the work. In other words, they learn by example. The bellows are put in motion, the charcoals are carefully laid, and then the sand is slowly sprinkled over the burning fire by the trained hands of the smith. The heat is kept at a regulated temperature by adding the required amount of charcoals in the furnace. At the same time the blowing of the bellows is kept in check. Sometimes the heat is intensified, and at other times it is slowed down. In this way the temperature is kept at the required degree, which reduces the ore to metallic iron, which is technically called "blooms" (*gekama*).

The smith, with his assistants, continues to work from morning   9
till the evening, especially when they have plenty of sand containing ore to melt. In the evening the melted iron is left in the furnace to cool. Early the next morning the smith, followed by his assistants, takes a small quantity of beer made of sugar-cane or honey. On his arrival at the smithy he performs a short ceremony of greeting the ancestral spirits who have guarded the work during the night. The ceremony consists of sprinkling the beer over and round the furnace and again over the working tools. The communion

between the smith and the ancestor spirits in this respect is considered to be of great importance, for the spirits of ancestors are said to be very closely connected with ironwork, and especially male spirits. It is believed that unless these are appeased they can render the ironwork unsuccessful by causing the tools or weapons which are made of the iron to break, and thus reduce the popularity of the smith. This belief is founded on the ground that the male ancestors have had their bitter experiences as warriors and some of them had met their deaths in battle-fields in which the iron weapons were used. And even those who had not met their deaths in this way have suffered pain in one way or another, by being wounded either in battle or in the general activities of a warrior's life.

When the ritual of communing with the ancestral spirits is completed, the iron "blooms," which have run together into small lumps, are taken out from the furnace. These are joined into a big heap by a mass of slag which has flowed during the melting. After the big pile of slag is taken out, the "blooms" are knocked out and collected together. The next step that follows is to heat the "blooms" and hammer a few of them together, according to the quantity required, to make a spear or sword or other iron articles. The irons thus beaten in heaps are known as *mondwa*, and they are sold according to sizes.

If a man wants a spear he will not buy a ready-made spear but the *mondwa*, and then pay the smith for making the spear. Sometimes the same smith fulfils both tasks of selling the *mondwa* and of making the spear. But there are others who do not make iron, and their duty is merely to make articles with material supplied by their customers.

The smith clan holds an important position in the community; members of that clan are respected and feared. In the first place they command respect because of their skill in ironwork, without which the community would have difficulty in obtaining the necessary implements for various activities, for iron implements play an important part in the economic, religious, social, and political life of the Gikuyu. In the second place the smiths are feared for the fact that strong curses rest with the smith clan. If a smith should curse a man or family there is no form of purification that could cleanse the cursed individual or the group. The curse consists of cutting a piece of red-hot iron on an anvil and at the same time uttering spells, e.g. *Ng'ania wa Ng'ania arutwika ta kiriha geeke. Mahori maake marohehenjeka, ngoro yake erotweka ta kiriha geeke.* This means: "May So and-so (proper name given) be cut like this iron. Let his lungs be smashed to smithereens. Let his heart be cut off like this iron."

HUT-BUILDING

It is a common ambition of every Gikuyu young man to own a   13
hut or huts, which means implicitly to have a wife or wives. The
establishment of a homestead gives a man special status in the
community; he is referred to as *muthuri* (an elder), and is considered capable of holding a responsible position in tribal affairs. Thus,
it is the desire of every Gikuyu man to work hard and accumulate
property which will enable him to build a homestead of his own.
There is a proverb in Gikuyu which says: *"Wega uumaga na mocie,"*
that is, the quality of a man is judged by his homestead. With these
few remarks we will proceed to describe how a hut is built.

Gikuyu huts are of the round type, with wooden walls and grass   14
thatched roofs. The actual building of a hut takes only one day; and
as soon as it is completed, a new fire is drilled from sacred fire-
sticks, *"githegethi na Geka kia Igongona."* But in case of rebuilding,
the fire from the old hut is preserved to be transferred to the new
hut. The fire is ritually lit in the new hut, and after a short ceremony of communing with the ancestral spirits the owner moves
into the new homestead. Sometimes two or more huts are built
simultaneously, as in the case of a man having more than one wife
or a large family which could not be housed in one hut. But general
custom requires that even a man with one wife should have two
huts, one for his wife's private use and one for himself for general
use. The woman's hut is called *nyomba*. Here it is taboo for a mere
stranger to enter, because *nyomba* is considered as the traditional
sacred abode of the family and the proper place to hold communion with their ancestral spirits. All aspects of religious and magical ceremonies and sacrifices which concern the family are centered around the *nyomba*. It is for fear of defilement and ill-luck
that strangers are not allowed to cross this sacred threshold. The
man's hut is called *thingira;* in this, friends and casual visitors
are entertained.

Nowadays the system of having two huts for a man with only   15
one wife is dying out, owing to the heavy burden of hut taxes
imposed on the people by the British Government. The result has
been congestion, whole families being crowded in one hut, for
many such families can hardly maintain their livelihood and at the
same time afford to find money for hut taxation.

We have mentioned that a hut is built and occupied in the same   16
day; this statement may puzzle those who are not acquainted with
the Gikuyu method of building. To avoid this, let us at once explain
how the work that expedites the putting up of a hut is organised.
Most important of all is the Gikuyu collective method of working.
A few days before the erection of a hut or huts the building materi-

als are collected. In doing this the division of labour according to sex plays an important role. The work of cutting wood necessary for building falls on men; women take the responsibility of providing thatching grass and other materials.

When a family is engaged in the work of building a hut or huts the help of neighbours and friends is necessary in order to expedite the work. A man goes round asking his friends to help him, and at the same time telling them what kind of building materials he would like them to supply him with. In the same manner the wife visits her women friends, requesting them to help in various ways. Those who cannot take part in collecting building materials are asked to help in providing food and drink for the builders' feast, which is called *"iruga ria mwako."* On the day appointed many of these friends will turn up, bringing with them the required materials for building. The man and his wife or wives receive their helpers joyfully and bid them to sit down and rest. After all have arrived a feast is provided, consisting of a variety of food and drink. During the feasting this group of men and women entertain themselves with traditional songs relating to teamwork. Before they part, a day is appointed when the actual building of a hut or huts will take place. 17

It is obvious that without this sytem of team-work it would take a man a long time to complete the work, especially in a community where the system of paid labour is traditionally unknown. In its place, mutual help guided by the rules of give and take plays a significant part. In every branch of work reciprocity is the fundamental principle governing the relationship between a man and his neighbours, and also between various groups or clans and the tribe. If a man, after having been asked to give his service, absents himself without a good reason, especially when his neighbour has urgent work, such as building a hut or a cattle kraal, which has to be completed in one day (for it is feared that should a hut or a kraal be left unfinished and unoccupied, evil spirits might dwell therein and, therefore, cause constant misfortune to the future occupants and their herd), the result will be that the defaulter will find himself socially boycotted for his individualistic attitude. When a man has thus been ostracised, *"kohingwo,"* he will have to pay a fine of one sheep or a he-goat to his neighbours for his bad behaviour. When the fine is paid, the animal is slaughtered for a feast, and then, after a short ceremony of reunion, the man's status as a good and helpful neighbour is re-acknowledged. 18

After the building materials have been collected, the head of the family selects a plot where he wishes to establish his new homestead. In selecting the plot care is taken to see that the land is not 19 associated with any ancestral curse or taboo. The plot must also be one that has been lawfully acquired. The homestead must not be built on or near a graveyard, or on a place where a fierce battle has taken place, resulting in loss of lives. Such places are considered as the resting homes for the departed spirits, and to disturb them would mean to invoke their anger.

When these preliminary arrangements have been made, the man prepares sugar-cane or honey beer for the foundation ceremony. Early in the morning, on the day of building a hut or huts, a small quantity of the beer is taken to the selected plot and, in communion with the ancestral spirits, it is sprinkled on the ground where the new home is to be built. Sometimes milk or uncooked gruel, *"gethambio,"* is preferred for this ceremony, according to the custom of the clan to which the individual belongs. After the ancestral spirits have been summoned to join in the work of building, the friends who have gathered to help their neighbour start to clear and to level the ground. Then the foundation is marked according to the size of the hut which a man wants. To make a good circle a kind of string compass is employed. A stick is put in the centre of the circle and a string tied to it, then a man holds one end of the string and, after measuring the required paces, he holds the string tight and then goes round, marking the ground until the circle lines meet. This is called *"gokurura kiea."* When this is done the builders start digging holes in the ground for the outer wall. The holes are about one foot deep and about six inches in diameter. After this the inner circle is marked, which divides the hut into several apartments. Immediately the wall is erected and the roof put on. This completes the men's work in building, leaving the thatching to the womenfolk.

While the women are engaged in thatching, the men retire to a feast which has been awaiting them. During the feasting the men sing songs relating to the art of building; those who are clever and hard workers are highly praised in these songs; at the same time contemptuous phrases are uttered for laziness. In some of the phrases men call on the women in teasing tones, saying: "Look on those lazy-bones who are working like chameleons, the sun is going down, do you want us to make torches for you? Do hurry up and join us in feasting, and let us utter blessings for the homestead before the sun is completely gone down." To this the women answer in chorus, saying: "You men, you lack the most important art in building, namely, thatching. A wall and an empty roof cannot protect you from heavy rain, nor from burning sun. It is our careful thatching that makes a hut worth living in. We are not chameleons, but we do thatch our huts like *'nyoni ya nyagathanga'* (this is the name of a small bird in Gikuyu which is well known by its sweet songs and the neatness of its nest)." In many of the Gikuyu cradle stories and legends *nyoni y nyagathanga* and its work is highly praised. This acts as an encouragement to both boys and girls to become industrious in their future activities in life. It is characteristic of the Gikuyu people to sing inspiring songs while performing a task, for it is said: "to work in a happy mood is to make the task easier, and to relieve the heart from fatigue." (*"Koruta wera na ngoro theru ni kohothia wera na konyihia minoga."*)

When the women have finally finished thatching they join the   22 men in feasting. Before the party comes to a close the owner of the homestead brings the remainder of the beer or the milk which has been sprinkled on the foundation; he hands it to a ceremonial elder, who after pouring the liquid into a ritual horn, calls upon those present to stand up. Then the ceremonial elder, with his hands raised holding the horn, turns towards Kere-Nyaga (Mount Kenya). In this position he chants a prayer, calling for a blessing for the homestead and its future prosperity. The following is the form of the prayer used for such an occasion:

> *"Wee Githuri oikaraga Kere-Nyaga; kerathimo geaku nikeo getomaga mecie ethegee. Namo marakara maku, nemo mahukagia mecie. Togogo-thaitha tweturaneire ohamwe na ngoma cia aciari aito. Togokoria ate orinderere mocie oyo na otome wethegee. Reke atumia ona mahio mathathare. Thaaai, thathayai Ngai, thaaaai."*

The following is the translation of the above prayer: "You, the   23 Great Elder, who dwells on the Kere-Nyaga, your blessing allows homesteads to spread. Your anger destroys homesteads. We beseech You, and in this we are in harmony with the spirits of our ancestors: we ask You to guard this homestead and let it spread. Let the women, herd, and flock be prolific. (Chorus) Peace, praise, or beseech ye, Ngai (God), peace be with us."

After this the homestead is declared open. The next thing is to   24 light the fire which we have mentioned in our earlier description. Two children, male and female, are selected for this ritual; they are looked upon as a symbol of peace and prosperity for the homestead. The ceremonial elder hands the fire to the children and instructs them how to light it; at the same time he gives them the ritual words to be used in this connection. The children enter the hut, with the elder following behind them, to see that the ritual is correctly carried out. Behind this small procession the owner of the homestead and his wife follow carrying firewood to kindle the fire, for it is considered as a bad omen for such a fire to go out. After the fire has been properly lit, things are moved in without any further ceremony.

Let us glance inside a woman's hut. It may be some six paces   25
from the entrance to the fire-place in the centre. The roof is supported at the outside by the wall, in the inside by a series of poles
equidistant from the centre. The poles fulfil a twofold purpose;
besides supporting the roof, they are the mainstays of partitions
which divide the hut into apartments. These apartments depend
upon the needs of the occupant—her bedroom is essential, and no
less so is the store-room next door to it. Should a daughter live
with her mother, her room will be next to the store-room, and
should the woman keep one or two animals (sheep or goats) for
fattening, they will have their compartment farther round the wall,
just inside the door, on the right as you enter. These rooms will
occupy the whole of the right inside of the hut, leaving free only
the space between the fire-place and the inner circle of poles. Each
apartment communicates immediately with this space.

To the left of a person entering the hut is a long partition, ex-   26
tending almost from the door to the woman's bedroom. Between
this and the outer wall the animals sleep at night. The scheme is
thus simple; first the fire-place, then the circle in which people may
sit, then the outer apartments. The accompanying diagram will
make this clear. A woman's hut is considered as the cradle of the
family tradition; it has many taboos which, for the harmony and
the prosperity of the family, must be strictly observed. Among
other things, fire must be lit in the hut every evening, and there
must be someone to sleep in it every night. The wife is debarred by
custom from having sexual intercourse anywhere else but inside

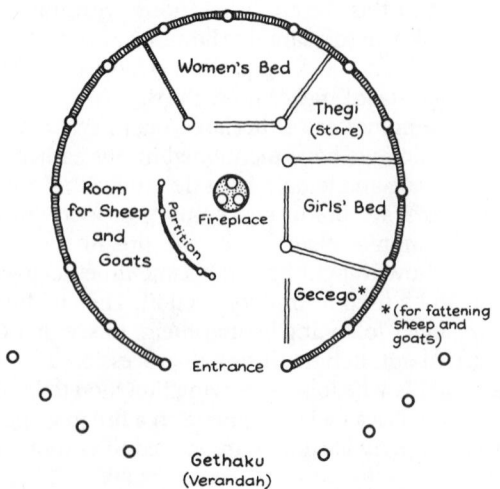

the hut. Sexual intercourse must not take place in the day-time, even with her husband, neither must it be performed whilst food is being cooked, or the food will have to be thrown away, for an act of this nature renders the food unclean and unfit for human consumption. Anyone eating such food will have *thahu* (defilement), and will have to be cleansed by a *mondo mogo* (witch-doctor), for it is feared that unless this is done, disaster will befall such a man.

The man's hut, unlike that of the woman, is very simple; it has only one partition, and sometimes none at all. When there is one, it is used to divide the bedstead from the fire-place. The rest of the hut is left open; this is to provide a large sitting-place for the family and their visitors. For the man's hut is used for general purposes, whereas the woman's hut is strictly used for her private purposes and family matters. 27

A well-built hut generally lasts for about ten or more years; occasionally the roof has to be re-thatched, especially in the interval between the heavy and the short rains. The wall has also to be repaired every now and again; holes between the wood are filled with cow or sheep dung. This method serves two purposes; in the first place it keeps draughts out, and in the second it preserves the wood and prevents it being eaten by the ants. The wood preserved in this way becomes useful in the future building of new huts, especially when old ones are pulled down. Some building materials have been with a family for a considerable number of years, and they are looked upon as sacred relics. 28

E. B. WHITE

Progress and Change

E. B. White (1899–1985) established his reputation writing short comments for *The New Yorker* (see "Twins," p. 147). In 1929 he collaborated with James Thurber on *Is Sex Necessary?*, a spoof of contemporary marriage manuals. The book sold so well that it allowed White to marry and eventually to buy a small farm in Maine. In 1938, White and his wife moved to the farm and he gave up weekly comments in *The New Yorker* in favor of one longer monthly essay for *Harper's Magazine*. "Progress and Change," one of the *Harper's* essays, was published in July 1939 and reprinted in *One Man's Meat* (1942). Like *The New Yorker* comments, White's informal essays for *Harper's* are widely cited as among the best of their kind ever produced in America. One of the keys to their success is the way they blend a weighty thesis with a light tone. Another is White's remarkable sense of the language, which allowed him to surprise the reader with words that are both unexpected and exact.

1 My friends in the city tell me that the Sixth Avenue El is coming down, but that's a hard thing for anyone to believe who once lived in its fleeting and audible shadow. The El was the most distinguished and outstanding vein on the town's neck, a varicosity tempting to the modern surgeon. One wonders whether New York can survive this sort of beauty operation, performed in the name of civic splendor and rapid transit.

2 A resident of the city grew accustomed to the heavenly railroad which swung implausibly in air, cutting off his sun by day, wandering in and out of his bedchamber by night. The presence of the structure and the passing of the trains were by all odds the most pervasive of New York's influences. Here was a sound which, if it ever got in the conch of your ear, was ineradicable—forever singing, like the sea. It punctuated the morning with brisk tidings of repetitious adventure, and it accompanied the night with sad but reassuring sounds of life-going-on—the sort of threnody which cricket and katydid render for suburban people sitting on screened porches, the sort of lullaby which the whippoorwill sends up to the Kentucky farm wife on a summer evening.

3 I spent a lot of time, once, doing nothing in the vicinity of Sixth Avenue. Naturally I know something of the El's fitful charm. It was, among other things, the sort of railroad you would occasionally ride just for the hell of it, a higher existence into which you would escape unconsciously and without destination. Let's say you had just emerged from the Child's on the west side of Sixth Avenue between 14th and 15th Streets, where you had had a bowl of vegetable soup and a stack of wheat cakes. The syrup still was a cloying taste on your tongue. You intended to go back to the apartment and iron a paragraph, or wash a sock. But miraculously, at the corner of 14th, there rose suddenly in front of you a flight of stairs all wrapt in celestial light, with treads of shining steel, and risers richly carved with the names of the great, and a canopy overhead where danced the dust in the shafts of golden sunshine. As in a trance, you mounted steadily to the pavilion above, where there was an iron stove and a man's hand visible through a mousehole. And the first thing you knew you were in South Ferry, with another of life's inestimable journeys behind you—and before you the dull, throbbing necessity of getting uptown again.

4 For a number of years I went to work every morning on the

uptown trains of the Sixth Avenue El. I had it soft, because my journey wasn't at the rush hour and I often had the platform of the car to myself. It was a good way to get where you wanted to go, looking down on life at just the right speed, and peeking in people's windows, where the sketchy pantomime of potted plant and half-buttoned undershirt and dusty loft provided a curtain raiser to the day. The railroad was tolerant and allowed its passengers to loll outdoors if they wished; and on mornings when the air was heady that was the place to be—with the sudden whiff of the candy factory telling you that your ride was half over, and the quick eastward glance through 24th Street to check your time with the clock in the Metropolitan Tower, visible for the tenth part of a second.

The El always seemed to me to possess exactly the right degree of substantiality: it seemed reasonably strong and able to carry its load, and competent with that easy slovenly competence of an old drudge; yet it was perceptibly a creature of the clouds, the whole structure vibrating ever so slightly following the final grasping success of the applied brake. The El had giddy spells, too—days when a local train would shake off its patient, plodding manner and soar away in a flight of sheer whimsy, skipping stations in a drunken fashion and scaring the pants off everybody. To go roaring past a scheduled stop, hell bent for 53rd Street and the plunge into space, was an experience which befell every El rider more than once. On this line a man didn't have to be a locomotophobe to suffer from visions of a motorman's lifeless form slumped over an open throttle. And if the suspense got too great and you walked nervously to the front of the train the little window in the booth gave only the most tantalizing view of the driver—three inert fingers of a gloved hand, or a *Daily News* wedged in some vital cranny.

One thing I always admired about the El was the way it tormented its inexperienced customers. Veterans like myself, approaching a station stop, knew to a fraction of an inch how close it was advisable to stand to the little iron gates on the open type cars. But visitors to town had no such information. When the train halted and the guard, pulling his two levers, allowed the gates to swing in and take the unwary full in the stomach, there was always a dim pleasure in it for the rest of us. Life has little enough in the way of reward; these small moments of superiority are not to be despised.

The El turned the Avenue into an arcade. That, in a way, was its chief contribution. It made Sixth Avenue as distinct from Fifth as Fifth is from Jones Street. Its pillars, straddling the car tracks in the long channel of the night, provided the late cruising taxicab with the supreme challenge, and afforded the homing pedestrian, his wine too much with him, forest sanctuary and the friendly accommodation of a tree.

Of course I have read about the great days of the El, when it was the railroad of the élite and when financial giants rode elegantly home from Wall Street in its nicely appointed coaches. But I'm just as glad I didn't meet the El until after it had lost its money. Its lazy crescendos, breaking into one's dreams, will always stick in the mind—and the soiled hands of the guards on the bellcords, and the brusque, husky-throated bells that had long ago lost their voices, cuing each other along the whole length of the train. Yes, at this distance it's hard to realize that the Sixth Avenue El is just a problem in demolition. I can't for the life of me imagine what New York will have to offer in its place. It will have to be something a good deal racier, a good deal more open and aboveboard, than a new subway line. [8]

I suppose a man can't ask railroads to stand still. For twenty or thirty years the railroads of America stood about as still as was consistent with swift transportation. The gas mantles were removed and electric lights installed, but outside of that the cars remained pretty much the same. It's only in the past couple of years that the railroads, fretting over the competition from busses and planes, have set about transforming their interiors into cocktail lounges, ballrooms, and modern apartments. [9]

In my isolated position here in the country, I have plenty of time to study Pullman trends—which are readily accessible in full-page color ads in the popular magazines. I note that the Pullman Company, although emphasizing the high safety factor implicit in Pullman travel, is advertising a new type of accommodation called, somewhat ominously, "S.O.S." This is the Single Occupancy Section. It is for the dollar-wise and the travel-wise, the ads point out. From the illustration, the single occupancy section appears to have a dead body in it, hooded in a sheet, bound and gagged. There is also a live occupant—a girl in a pink dressing gown, apparently in the best of spirits. More careful examination of the photograph reveals that the dead body is nothing more nor less than the bed itself, which has reared up on its hind end and been lashed to the bulkhead, while the occupant (who is single, of course) stands erect and goes through the motions of dressing in comfort. [10]

I feel that the Pullman Company, in introducing the note of *comfort* into its adventurous calling, is perhaps slipping outside the particular field in which it has made such an enviable reputation. This being able to stand erect in an ordinary single berth and dress in something like ease—isn't it likely to destroy the special flavor of Pullman travel? I don't take a night journey on a railroad for the sake of duplicating the experiences and conveniences of my own [11] home: when I travel I like to get into some new kind of difficulty, not just the same old trouble I put up with around the house.

Travelers, I will admit, differ temperamentally, differ in their wants and needs; but for me the Pullman Company will never improve on its classic design of upper and lower berth. In my eyes it is a perfect thing, perfect in conception and execution, this small green hole in the dark moving night, this soft warren in a hard world. In it I have always found the peace of spirit which accompanies grotesque bodily situations, peace and a wonderful sense of participation in cosmic rhythms and designs. I have experienced these even on cold nights when I all but died from exposure, under blankets of virgin gossamer. 12

In a Pullman berth, a man can truly be alone with himself. (The nearest approach to this condition is to be found in a hotel bedroom, but a hotel room can be mighty depressing sometimes, it stands so still.) Now if a modern Pullman proposes to provide headroom for everyone it will have to answer for whatever modification this may cause in human character. The old act of drawing one's pants on and off while in a horizontal position did much to keep Man in a mood of decent humility. It gave him a picture of himself at a moment of wild comic contortion. To tuck in the tails of a shirt while supine demanded a certain persistence, a certain virtuosity, wholly healthful and character-building. 13

The new single occupancy section, besides changing all this and permitting a man to stand erect as though he had no ape in his family background, has another rather alarming feature. The bed not only is capable of being cocked up by the occupant, to resemble a cadaver, but it can be hoisted by a separate control from the aisle by the dark, notional hand of the porter as he glides Puckishly through the car. It does not sound conducive to calm. 14

In resenting progress and change, a man lays himself open to censure. I suppose the explanation of anyone's defending anything as rudimentary and cramped as a Pullman berth is that such things are associated with an earlier period in one's life and that this period in retrospect seems a happy one. People who favor progress and improvements are apt to be people who have had a tough enough time without any extra inconvenience. Reactionaries who pout at innovations are apt to be well-heeled sentimentalists who had the breaks. Yet for all that, there is always a subtle danger in life's refinements, a dim degeneracy in progress. I have just been refining the room in which I sit, yet I sometimes doubt that a writer should refine or improve his workroom by so much as a dictionary: one thing leads to another and the first thing you know he has a stuffed chair and is fast asleep in it. Half a man's life is devoted to 15 what he calls improvements, yet the original had some quality which is lost in the process. There was a fine natural spring of water on this place when I bought it. Our drinking water had to be lugged in a pail, from a wet glade of alder and tamarack. I visited the spring often in those first years and had friends there—a frog, a woodcock, and an eel which had churned its way all the way up through the pasture creek to enjoy the luxury of pure water. In the normal course of development, the spring was rocked up, fitted with a concrete curb, a copper pipe, and an electric pump. I have visited it only once or twice since. This year my only gesture was the purely perfunctory one of sending a sample to the state bureau of health for analysis. I felt cheap, as though I were smelling an old friend's breath.

Another phase of life here which has lost something through refinement is the game of croquet. We used to have an old croquet set whose wooden balls, having been chewed by dogs, were no rounder than eggs. Paint had faded, wickets were askew. The course had been laid out haphazardly and eagerly by a child, and we all used to go out there on summer nights and play good-naturedly, with the dogs romping on the lawn in the beautiful light, and the mosquitoes sniping at us, and everyone in good spirits, racing after balls and making split shots for the sheer love of battle. Last spring we decided the croquet set was beyond use, and invested in a rather fancy new one with hoops set in small wooden sockets, and mallets with rubber faces. The course is now exactly seventy-two feet long and we lined the wickets up with a string; but the little boy is less fond of it now, for we make him keep still while we are shooting. A dog isn't even allowed to cast his shadow across the line of play. There are frequent quarrels of a minor nature, and it seems to me we return from the field of honor tense and out of sorts.

16

ALDOUS HUXLEY

Hyperion to a Satyr[1]

Aldous Huxley (1894–1963) was planning a career as a physician when, at the age of sixteen, he contracted an eye disease that

---

1. In Shakespeare's *Hamlet*, the prince compares his dead father to his stepfather: "So excellent a king, that was, to this / Hyperion to a Satyr."

left him temporarily blind and changed his plans. His scientific interests, however, shaped his literary career. Huxley was a prolific novelist, essayist, and poet. His early work, including the novels *Chrome Yellow* (1921) and *Antic Hay* (1923) are full of cynical social comment, as is his most famous novel *Brave New World* (1932). In general, his later novels and essays replace cynicism with mysticism. *The Perennial Philosophy* (1945) explores oriental religion, and *The Doors of Perception* (1954) and *Heaven and Hell* (1956) report on Huxley's experiences with hallucinogenic drugs. "Hyperion to a Satyr" (from *Tomorrow and Tomorrow and Tomorrow*, 1956) shows that even in Huxley's mystical years, his interest in science and technology was strong. In this essay, in fact, he argues that technicians may be doing more than mystics to bring about the ideal of human benevolence.

A few months before the outbreak of the Second World War I took a walk with Thomas Mann on a beach some fifteen or twenty miles southwest of Los Angeles. Between the breakers and the highway stretched a broad belt of sand, smooth, gently sloping and (blissful surprise!) void of all life but that of the pelicans and godwits. Gone was the congestion of Santa Monica and Venice. Hardly a house was to be seen; there were no children, no promenading loincloths and brassières, not a single sun-bather was practicing his strange obsessive cult. Miraculously, we were alone. Talking of Shakespeare and the musical glasses, the great man and I strolled ahead. The ladies followed. It was they, more observant than their all too literary spouses, who first remarked the truly astounding phenomenon. "Wait," they called, "wait!" And when they had come up with us, they silently pointed. At our feet, and as far as the eye could reach in all directions, the sand was covered with small whitish objects, like dead caterpillars. Recognition dawned. The dead caterpillars were made of rubber and had once been contraceptives of the kind so eloquently characterized by Mantegazza as *"una tela di ragno contro l'infezione, una corazza contro il piacere."*[2]

> *Continuous as the stars that shine*
> *And twinkle in the milky way,*
> *They stretched in never-ending line*
> *Along the margin of a bay:*
> *Ten thousand saw I at a glance . . .*[3]

2. "A cobweb against infection, a breastplate against pleasure": Paolo Mantegazza (1831–1910) was an Italian physiologist and anthropologist known for his popular works on medicine.
3. The lines are from William Wordsworth's "I Wandered Lonely as a Cloud." They describe daffodils.

Ten thousand? But we were in California, not the Lake District.
The scale was American, the figures astronomical. Ten million saw
I at a glance. Ten million emblems and mementoes of Modern
Love.

> *O bitter barren woman! what's the name,*
> *The name, the name, the new name thou hast won?*

And the old name, the name of the bitter fertile woman—what
was that? These are questions that can only be asked and talked
about, never answered in any but the most broadly misleading
way. Generalizing about Woman is like indicting a Nation—an
amusing pastime, but very unlikely to be productive either of truth
or utility.

Meanwhile, there was another, a simpler and more concrete   2
question: How on earth had these objects got here, and why in
such orgiastic profusion? Still speculating, we resumed our walk. A
moment later our noses gave us the unpleasant answer. Offshore
from this noble beach was the outfall through which Los Angeles
discharged, raw and untreated, the contents of its sewers. The emblems of modern love and the other things had come in with the
spring tide. Hence that miraculous solitude. We turned and made
all speed towards the parked car.

Since that memorable walk was taken, fifteen years have passed.   3
Inland from the beach, three or four large cities have leapt into
existence. The bean fields and Japanese truck gardens of those
ancient days are now covered with houses, drugstores, supermar-
kets, drive-in theaters, junior colleges, jet-plane factories, laun-
dromats, six-lane highways. But instead of being, as one would
expect, even more thickly constellated with Malthusian flotsam
and unspeakable jetsam, the sands are now clean, the quarantine
has been lifted. Children dig, well-basted sun-bathers slowly
brown, there is splashing and shouting in the surf. A happy consummation—but one has seen this sort of thing before. The novelty
lies, not in the pleasantly commonplace end—people enjoying
themselves—but in the fantastically ingenious means whereby that
end has been brought about.

Forty feet above the beach, in a seventy-five-acre oasis scooped   4
out of the sand dunes, stands one of the marvels of modern technology, the Hyperion Activated Sludge Plant. But before we start to
discuss the merits of activated sludge, let us take a little time to
consider sludge in its unactivated state, as plain, old-fashioned dirt.

Dirt, with all its concomitant odors and insects, was once ac-   5
cepted as an unalterable element in the divinely established Order
of Things. In his youth, before he went into power politics as

Innocent III, Lotario de' Conti found time to write a book on the *Wretchedness of Man's Condition.* "How filthy the father," he mused, "how low the mother, how repulsive the sister!" And no wonder! For "dead, human beings give birth to flies and worms; alive, they generate worms and lice." Moreover, "consider the plants, consider the trees. They bring forth flowers and leaves and fruits. But what do *you* bring forth? Nits, lice, vermin. Trees and plants exude oil, wine, balm—and *you,* spittle, snot, urine, ordure. *They* diffuse the sweetness of all fragrance—*you,* the most abominable stink." In the Age of Faith, Homo sapiens was also Homo pediculosus, also Homo immundus—a little lower than the angels, but dirty by definition, lousy, not *per accidens,*[4] but in his very essence. And as for man's helpmate—*si nec extremis digitis flegma vel stercus tangere patimur, quomodo ipsum stercoris saccum amplecti desideramus?* "We who shrink from touching, even with the tips of our fingers, a gob of phlegm or a lump of dung, how is it that we crave for the embraces of this mere bag of night-soil?" But men's eyes are not, as Odo of Cluny wished they were, "like those of the lynxes of Boeotia"; they cannot see through the smooth and milky surfaces into the palpitating sewage within. That is why

> There swims no goose so grey but soon or late
> Some honest gander takes her for his mate.

That is why (to translate the notion into the language of medieval orthodoxy), every muck-bag ends by getting herself embraced—with the result that yet another stinker-with-a-soul finds himself embarked on a sea of misery, bound for a port which, since few indeed can hope for salvation, is practically certain to be Hell. The embryo of this future reprobate is composed of "foulest seed," combined with "blood made putrid by the heat of lust." And as though to make it quite clear what He thinks of the whole proceeding, God has decreed that "the mother shall conceive in stink and nastiness."

That there might be a remedy for stink and nastiness—namely soap and water—was a notion almost unthinkable in the thirteenth century. In the first place, there was hardly any soap. The substance was known to Pliny, as an import from Gaul and Germany. But more than a thousand years later, when Lotario de' Conti wrote his book, the burgesses of Marseilles were only just beginning to consider the possibility of manufacturing the stuff in bulk. In England no soap was made commercially until halfway through the fourteenth century. Moreover, even if soap had been

6

4. "By accident."

abundant, its use for mitigating the "stink and nastiness," then inseparable from love, would have seemed, to every right-thinking theologian, an entirely illegitimate, because merely physical, solution to a problem in ontology and morals—an escape, by means of the most vulgarly materialistic trick, from a situation which God Himself had intended, from all eternity, to be as squalid as it was sinful. A conception without stink and nastiness would have the appearance—what a blasphemy!—of being Immaculate. And finally there was the virtue of modesty. Modesty, in that age of codes and pigeonholes, had its Queensberry Rules—no washing below the belt. Sinful in itself, such an offense against modesty in the present was fraught with all kinds of perils for modesty in the future. Havelock Ellis observed, when he was practicing obstetrics in the London slums, that modesty was due, in large measure, to a fear of being disgusting. When his patients realized that "I found nothing disgusting in whatever was proper and necessary to be done under the circumstances, it almost invariably happened that every sign of modesty at once disappeared." Abolish "stink and nastiness," and you abolish one of the most important sources of feminine modesty, along with one of the most richly rewarding themes of pulpit eloquence.

A contemporary poet has urged his readers not to make love to   7
those who wash too much. There is, of course, no accounting for tastes; but there *is* an accounting for philosophical opinions. Among many other things, the greatly gifted Mr. Auden is a belated representative of the school which held that sex, being metaphysically tainted, ought also to be physically unclean.

Dirt, then, seemed natural and proper, and dirt in fact was ev-   8
erywhere. But, strangely enough, this all-pervading squalor never generated its own psychological antidote—the complete indifference of habit. Everybody stank, everybody was verminous; and yet, in each successive generation, there were many who never got used to these familiar facts. What has changed in the course of history is not the disgusted reaction to filth, but the moral to be drawn from that reaction. "Filth," say the men of the twentieth century, "is disgusting. Therefore let us quickly do something to get rid of filth." For many of our ancestors, filth was as abhorrent as it seems to almost all of us. But how different was the moral they chose to draw! "Filth is disgusting," they said. "Therefore the human beings who produce the filth are disgusting, and the world they inhabit is a vale, not merely of tears, but of excrement. This state of things has been divinely ordained, and all we can do is cheerfully to bear our vermin, loathe our nauseating carcasses and hope (without much reason, since we shall probably be damned) for an early translation

to a better place. Meanwhile it is an observable fact that villeins are filthier even than lords. It follows, therefore, that they should be treated as badly as they smell." This loathing for the poor on account of the squalor in which they were condemned to live outlasted the Middle Ages and has persisted to the present day. The politics of Shakespeare's aristocratic heroes and heroines are the politics of disgust. "Footboys" and other members of the lower orders are contemptible because they are lousy—not in the metaphorical sense in which that word is now used, but literally; for the louse, in Sir Hugh Evans' words, "is a familiar beast to man, and signifies love." And the lousy were also the smelly. Their clothes were old and unclean, their bodies sweaty, their mouths horrible with decay. It made no difference that, in the words of a great Victorian reformer, "by no prudence on their part can the poor avoid the dreadful evil of their surroundings." They were disgusting and that, for the aristocratic politician, was enough. To canvass the common people's suffrages was merely to "beg their stinking breath." Candidates for elective office were men who "stand upon the breath of garlic eaters." When the citizens of Rome voted against him, Coriolanus told them that they were creatures,[5]

> whose breath I hate
> As reek o' th' rotten fens, whose loves I prize
> As the dead carcasses of unburied men
> That do corrupt my air.

And, addressing these same citizens, "You are they," says [9] Menenius,

> You are they
> That made the air unwholesome when you cast
> Your stinking greasy caps in hooting at
> Coriolanus' exile.

Again, when Caesar was offered the crown, "the rabblement [10] shouted and clapped their chopped hands, and threw up their sweaty night-caps, and uttered such a deal of stinking breath, because Caesar had refused the crown, that it had almost choked Caesar; for he swounded and fell down at it; and for mine own part," adds Casca, "I durst not laugh for fear of opening my lips and receiving the bad air." The same "mechanic slaves, with greasy aprons" haunted Cleopatra's imagination in her last hours.

---

5. The three indented quotations that follow are from Shakespeare's plays *Coriolanus*, *Julius Caesar*, and *Antony and Cleopatra*.

In their thick breaths,
Rank of gross diet, shall we be enclouded,
And forced to drink their vapours.

In the course of evolution man is supposed to have sacrificed the   11
greater part of his olfactory center to his cortex, his sense of smell to
his intelligence. Nevertheless, it remains a fact that in politics, no
less than in love and social relations, smell judgments continue to
play a major role. In the passages cited above, as in all the analogous passages penned or uttered since the days of Shakespeare,
there is the implication of an argument, which can be formulated
in some such terms as these. "Physical stink is a symbol, almost a
symptom, of intellectual and moral inferiority. All the members of
a certain group stink physically. Therefore, they are intellectually and morally vile, inferior and, as such, unfit to be treated as
equals."

Tolstoy, who was sufficiently clear-sighted to recognize the un-   12
desirable political consequences of cleanliness in high places and
dirt among the poor, was also sufficiently courageous to advocate,
as a remedy, a general retreat from the bath. Bathing, he saw, was a
badge of class distinction, a prime cause of aristocratic exclusiveness. For those who, in Mr. Auden's words, "wash too much,"
find it exceedingly distasteful to associate with those who wash too
little. In a society where, let us say, only one in five can afford the
luxury of being clean and sweet-smelling, Christian brotherhood
will be all but impossible. Therefore, Tolstoy argued, the bathers
should join the unwashed majority. Only where there is equality in
dirt can there be a genuine and unforced fraternity.

Mahatma Gandhi, who was a good deal more realistic than his   13
Russian mentor, chose a different solution to the problem of differential cleanliness. Instead of urging the bathers to stop washing,
he worked indefatigably to help the non-bathers to keep clean.
Brotherhood was to be achieved, not by universalizing dirt, vermin
and bad smells, but by building privies and scrubbing floors.

Spengler, Sorokin, Toynbee—all the philosophical historians   14
and sociologists of our time have insisted that a stable civilization
cannot be built except on the foundations of religion. But if man
cannot live by bread alone, neither can he live exclusively on meta-
physics and worship. The gulf between theory and practice, between the ideal and the real, cannot be bridged by religion alone.
In Christendom, for example, the doctrines of God's fatherhood
and the brotherhood of man have never been self-implementing.
Monotheism has proved to be powerless against the divisive forces
first of feudalism and then of nationalistic idolatry. And within

these mutually antagonistic groups, the injunction to love one's neighbor as oneself has proved to be as ineffective, century after century, as the commandment to worship one God.

A century ago the prophets who formulated the theories of the 15 Manchester School were convinced that commerce, industrialization and improved communications were destined to be the means whereby the age-old doctrines of monotheism and human brotherhood would at last be implemented. Alas, they were mistaken. Instead of abolishing national rivalries, industrialization greatly intensified them. With the march of technological progress, wars became bloodier and incomparably more ruinous. Instead of uniting nation with nation, improved communications merely extended the range of collective hatreds and military operations. That human beings will, in the near future, voluntarily give up their nationalistic idolatry, seems, in these middle years of the twentieth century, exceedingly unlikely. Nor can one see, from this present vantage point, any technological development capable, by the mere fact of being in existence, of serving as an instrument for realizing those religious ideals, which hitherto mankind has only talked about. Our best consolation lies in Mr. Micawber's hope that, sooner or later, "Something will Turn Up."[6]

In regard to brotherly love within the mutually antagonistic 16 groups, something *has* turned up. That something is the development, in many different fields, of techniques for keeping clean at a cost so low that practically everybody can afford the luxury of not being disgusting.

For creatures which, like most of the carnivores, make their 17 home in a den or burrow, there is a biological advantage in elementary cleanliness. To relieve nature in one's bed is apt, in the long run, to be unwholesome. Unlike the carnivores, the primates are under no evolutionary compulsion to practice the discipline of the sphincters. For these free-roaming nomads of the woods, one tree is as good as another and every moment is equally propitious. It is easy to house-train a cat or a dog, all but impossible to teach the same desirable habits to a monkey. By blood we are a good deal closer to poor Jocko than to Puss or Tray. Man's instincts were developed in the forest; but ever since the dawn of civilization, his life has been lived in the more elaborate equivalent of a rabbit warren. His notions of sanitation were not, like those of the cat, inborn, but had to be painfully acquired. In a sense the older theologians were quite right in regarding dirt as natural to man—an essential element in the divinely appointed order of his existence.

6. Micawber is a luckless optimist in Charles Dickens' *David Copperfield.*

But in spite of its unnaturalness, the art of living together with-   18
out turning the city into a dunghill has been repeatedly discovered.
Mohenjo-daro, at the beginning of the third millennium B.C., had a
water-borne sewage system; so, several centuries before the siege
of Troy, did Cnossos; so did many of the cities of ancient Egypt,
albeit only for the rich. The poor were left to demonstrate their
intrinsic inferiority by stinking, in their slums, to high heaven. A
thousand years later Rome drained her swamps and conveyed her
filth to the contaminated Tiber by means of the Cloaca Maxima.
But these solutions to the problem of what we may politely call
"unactivated sludge" were exceptional. The Hindus preferred to
condemn a tithe of their population to untouchability and the daily
chore of carrying slops. In China the thrifty householder tanked the
family sludge and sold it, when mature, to the highest bidder.
There was a smell, but it paid, and the fields recovered some of the
phosphorus and nitrogen of which the harvesters had robbed
them. In medieval Europe every alley was a public lavatory, every
window a sink and garbage chute. Droves of pigs were dedicated to
St. Anthony and, with bells round their necks, roamed the streets,
battening on the muck. (When operating at night, burglars and
assassins often wore bells. Their victims heard the reassuring tinkle,
turned over in their beds and went to sleep again—it was only the
blessed pigs.) And meanwhile there were cesspools (like the black
hole into which that patriotic Franciscan, Brother Salimbene,[7] de-
liberatcly dropped his relic of St. Dominic), there was portable
plumbing, there were members of the lower orders, whose duty it
was to pick up the unactivated sludge and deposit it outside the city
limits. But always the sludge accumulated faster than it could be
removed. The filth was chronic and, in the slummier quarters,
appalling. It remained appalling until well into the nineteenth century. As late as the early years of Queen Victoria's reign sanitation
in the East End of London consisted in dumping everything into
the stagnant pools that still stood between the jerry-built houses.
From the peak of their superior (but still very imperfect) cleanliness
the middle and upper classes looked down with unmitigated horror at the Great Unwashed. "The Poor" were written and spoken
about as though they were creatures of an entirely different species.

---

7. Huxley slightly misremembers a story of monastic rivalry in the *Chronicle* of the
thirteenth century monk. He assumes that it was the Franciscan Salimbene who
visited a Dominican monastery, begged for a relic of St. Dominic, "put it to the vilest
uses, and cast it at last into the cesspool. Then he cried aloud, saying, 'Alas! help me,
brothers, for I seek the relic of your saint which I have lost among the filth.'" The
outline of the story is accurate, but Huxley has confused the characters.

And no wonder! Nineteenth-century England was loud with Non-
Conformist and Tractarian piety; but in a society most of whose
members stank and were unclean the practice of brotherly love was
out of the question.

The first modern sewage systems, like those of Egypt before   19
them, were reserved for the rich and had the effect of widening still
further the gulf between rulers and ruled. But endemic typhus and
several dangerous outbreaks of Asiatic cholera lent weight to the
warnings and denunciations of the sanitary reformers. In self-
defense the rich had to do something about the filth in which their
less fortunate neighbors were condemned to live. Sewage systems
were extended to cover entire metropolitan areas. The result was
merely to transfer the sludge problem from one place to another.
"The Thames," reported a Select Committee of 1836, "receives the
excrementitious matter from nearly a million and a half of human
beings; the washing of their foul linen; the filth and refuse of many
hundred manufactories; the offal and decomposing vegetable substances from the markets; the foul and gory liquid from the slaugh-
ter-houses; and the purulent abominations from hospitals and
dissecting rooms, too disgusting to detail. Thus that most noble
river, which has been given us by Providence for our health, recreation and beneficial use, is converted into the Common sewer of
London, and the sickening mixture it contains is daily pumped up
into the water for the inhabitants of the most civilized capital of
Europe."

In England the heroes of the long campaign for sanitation were a   20
strangely assorted band. There was a bishop, Blomfield of London;
there was the radical Edwin Chadwick, a disciple of Jeremy
Bentham; there was a physician, Dr. Southwood Smith; there was
a low-church man of letters, Charles Kingsley; and there was the
seventh Earl of Shaftesbury, an aristocrat who had troubled to
acquaint himself with the facts of working-class life. Against them
were marshaled the confederate forces of superstition, vested interest, and brute inertia. It was a hard fight; but the cholera was a
staunch ally, and by the end of the century the worst of the mess
had been cleared up, even in the slums. Writing in 1896, Lecky[8]
called it "the greatest achievement of our age." In the historian's
estimation, the sanitary reformers had done more for general
happiness and the alleviation of human misery than all the more
spectacular figures of the long reign put together. Their labors,
moreover, were destined to bear momentous fruit. When Lecky
wrote, upper-class noses could still find plenty of occasions for

8. British intellectual and social historian.

passing olfactory judgments on the majority. But not nearly so many as in the past. The stage was already set for the drama which is being played today—the drama whose theme is the transformation of the English caste system into an equalitarian society. Without Chadwick and his sewers, there might have been violent revolution, never that leveling by democratic process, that gradual abolition of untouchability, which are in fact taking place.

Hyperion—what joy the place would have brought to those passionately prosaic lovers of humanity, Chadwick and Bentham! And the association of the hallowed name with sewage, of sludge with the great god of light and beauty—what romantic furies it would have evoked in Keats and Blake! And Lotario de' Conti—how thunderously, in the name of religion, he would have denounced this presumptuous demonstration that Homo immundus can effectively modify the abjection of his predestined condition! And Dean Swift,[9] above all—how deeply the spectacle would have disturbed him! For, if Celia could relieve nature without turning her lover's bowels, if Yahoos, footmen and even ladies of quality did not *have* to stink, then, obviously, his occupation was gone and his neurosis would be compelled to express itself in some other, some less satisfactory, because less excruciating, way.   21

An underground river rushes into Hyperion. Its purity of 99.7 per cent exceeds that of Ivory Soap. But two hundred million gallons are a lot of water; and the three thousandth part of that daily quota represents a formidable quantity of muck. But happily the ratio between muck and muckrakers remains constant. As the faecal tonnage rises, so does the population of aerobic and anaerobic bacteria. Busier than bees and infinitely more numerous, they work unceasingly on our behalf. First to attack the problem are the aerobes. The chemical revolution begins in a series of huge shallow pools, whose surface is perpetually foamy with the suds of Surf, Tide, Dreft and all the other monosyllables that have come to take the place of soap. For the sanitary engineers, these new detergents are a major problem. Soap turns very easily into something else; but the monosyllables remain intractably themselves, frothing so violently that it has become necessary to spray the surface of the aerobes' pools with overhead sprinklers. Only in this way can the suds be prevented from rising like the foam on a mug of beer and being blown about the countryside. And this is not the only price that must be paid for easier dishwashing. The detergents are greedy for oxygen. Mechanically and chemically, they prevent the aerobes   22

9. Jonathan Swift, represented in *The Dolphin Reader* by "A Modest Proposal," page 747.

from getting all the air they require. Enormous compressors must be kept working night and day to supply the needs of the suffocating bacteria. A cubic foot of compressed air to every cubic foot of sludgy liquid. What will happen when Zoom, Bang, and Whiz come to replace the relatively mild monosyllables of today, nobody, in the sanitation business, cares to speculate.

When, with the assistance of the compressors, the aerobes have 23 done all they are capable of doing, the sludge, now thickly concentrated, is pumped into the Digestion System. To the superficial glance, the Digestion System looks remarkably like eighteen very large Etruscan mausoleums. In fact it consists of a battery of cylindrical tanks, each more than a hundred feet in diameter and sunk fifty feet into the ground. Within these huge cylinders steam pipes maintain a cherishing heat of ninety-five degrees—the temperature at which the anaerobes are able to do their work with maximum efficiency. From something hideous and pestilential the sludge is gradually transformed by these most faithful of allies into sweetness and light—light in the form of methane, which fuels nine supercharged Diesel engines, each of seventeen hundred horsepower, and sweetness in the form of an odorless solid which, when dried, pelleted, and sacked, sells to farmers at ten dollars a ton. The exhaust of the Diesels raises the steam which heats the Digestion System, and their power is geared either to electric generators or centrifugal blowers. The electricity works the pumps and the machinery of the fertilizer plant, the blowers supply the aerobes with oxygen. Nothing is wasted. Even the emblems of modern love contribute their quota of hydrocarbons to the finished products, gaseous and solid. And meanwhile another torrent, this time about 99.95 per cent pure, rushes down through the submarine outfall and mingles, a mile offshore, with the Pacific. The problem of keeping a great city clean without polluting a river or fouling the beaches, and without robbing the soil of its fertility, has been triumphantly solved.

But untouchability depends on other things besides the bad sani- 24 tation of slums. We live not merely in our houses, but even more continuously in our garments. And we live not exclusively in health, but very often in sickness. Where sickness rages unchecked and where people cannot afford to buy new clothes or keep their old ones clean, the occasions for being disgusting are innumerable.

Thersites, in *Troilus and Cressida*, lists a few of the commoner 25 ailments of Shakespeare's time: "the rotten diseases of the south, the guts-griping, ruptures, catarrhs, loads o' gravel i' the back, lethargies, cold palsies, raw eyes, dirt-rotten livers, wheezing lungs, bladders full of imposthume, sciaticas, lime-kilns i' the palm, incurable bone-ache, and the rivelled fee-simple of the tetter." And there were scores of others even more repulsive. Crawling, flying, hopping, the insect carriers of infection swarmed uncontrollably. Malaria was endemic, typhus never absent, bubonic plague a regular visitor, dysentery, without benefit of plumbing, a commonplace. And meanwhile, in an environment that was uniformly septic, everything that *could* suppurate *did* suppurate. The Cook, in Chaucer's "Prologue," had a "mormal," or gangrenous sore, on his shin. The Summoner's face was covered with the "whelkes" and "knobbes" of a skin disease that would not yield to any known remedy. Every cancer was inoperable, and gnawed its way, through a hideous chaos of cellular proliferation and breakdown, to its foregone conclusion. The unmitigated horror surrounding illness explains the admiration felt, throughout the Middle Ages and early modern times, for those heroes and heroines of charity who voluntarily undertook the care of the sick. It explains, too, certain actions of the saints—actions which, in the context of modern life, seem utterly incomprehensible. In their filth and wretchedness, the sick were unspeakably repulsive. This dreadful fact was a challenge to which those who took their Christianity seriously responded by such exploits as the embracing of lepers, the kissing of sores, the swallowing of pus. The modern response to this challenge is soap and water, with complete asepsis as the ultimate ideal. The great gulf of disgust which used to separate the sick and the chronically ailing from their healthier fellows, has been, not indeed completely abolished, but narrowed everywhere and, in many places, effectively bridged. Thanks to hygiene, many who, because of their afflictions, used to be beyond the pale of love or even pity, have been re-admitted into the human fellowship. An ancient religious ideal has been implemented, at least in part, by the development of merely material techniques for dealing with problems previously soluble (and then how very inadequately, so far as the sick themselves were concerned!) only by saints.

"The essential act of thought is symbolization." Our minds ²⁶ transform experiences into signs. If these signs adequately represent the experiences to which they refer, and if we are careful to manipulate them according to the rules of a many-valued logic, we can deepen our understanding of experience and thereby achieve some control of the world and our own destiny. But these conditions are rarely fulfilled. In all too many of the affairs of life we combine ill-chosen signs in all kinds of irrational ways, and are thus led to unrealistic conclusions and inappropriate acts.

There is nothing in experience which cannot be transformed by ²⁷ the mind into a symbol—nothing which cannot be made to signify something else. We have seen, for example, that bad smells may be made to stand for social inferiority, dirt for a low IQ, vermin for immorality, sickness for a status beneath the human. No less important than these purely physiological symbols are the signs derived, not from the body itself, but from its coverings. A man's clothes are his most immediately perceptible attribute. Stinking rags or clean linen, liveries, uniforms, canonicals, the latest fashions—these are the symbols in terms of which men and women have thought about the relations of class with class, of person with person. In the *Institutions of Athens*, written by an anonymous author of the fifth century B.C., we read that it was illegal in Athens to assault a slave even when he refused to make way for you in the street. "The reason why this is the local custom shall be explained. If it were legal for the slave to be struck by the free citizen, your Athenian citizen himself would always be getting assaulted through being mistaken for a slave. Members of the free proletariat of Athens are no better dressed than slaves or aliens and no more respectable in appearance." But Athens—a democratic city state with a majority of "poor whites"—was exceptional. In almost every other society the wearing of cheap and dirty clothes has been regarded (such is the power of symbols) as the equivalent of a moral lapse—a lapse for which the wearers deserved to be ostracized by all decent people. In *Les Précieuses Ridicules*[10] the high-flown heroines take two footmen, dressed up in their masters' clothes, for marquises. The comedy comes to its climax when the pretenders are stripped of their symbolic finery and the girls discover the ghastly truth. *Et eripitur persona, manet res*[11]—or, to be more precise, *manet altera persona*. The mask is torn off and there remains—what? Another mask—the footman's.

In eighteenth-century England the producers of woolens were able to secure legislation prohibiting the import of cotton prints from the Orient and imposing an excise duty, not repealed until 1832, on the domestic product. But in spite of this systematic discouragement, the new industry prospered—inevitably; for it met a need, it supplied a vast and growing demand. Wool could not be cleaned, cotton was washable. For the first time in the history of Western Europe it began to be possible for all but the poorest women to look clean. The revolution then begun is still in progress. Garments of cotton and the new synthetic fibers have largely abolished the ragged and greasy symbols of earlier class distinctions. And meanwhile, for such fabrics as cannot be washed, the chemi-

28

10. *The Affected Young Women*, a play by Molière.
11. "And snatch away the mask, the thing remains."

cal industry has invented a host of new detergents and solvents. In the past, grease spots were a problem for which there was no solution. Proletarian garments were darkly shiny with accumulated fats and oils, and even the merchant's broadcloth, even the velvets and satins of lords and ladies displayed the ineradicable traces of last year's candle droppings, of yesterday's gravy. Dry cleaning is a modern art, a little younger than railway travel, a little older than the first Atlantic cable.

In recent years, and above all in America, the revolution in   29
clothing has entered a new phase. As well as cleanliness, elegance is being placed within the reach of practically everyone. Cheap clothes are mass-produced from patterns created by the most expensive designers. Unfashionableness was once a stigma hardly less damning, as a symbol of inferiority, than dirt. Fifty years ago a girl who wore cheap clothes proclaimed herself, by their obvious dowdiness, to be a person whom it was all but out of the question, if one were well off, to marry. Misalliance is still deplored; but, thanks to Sears and Ohrbach, it seems appreciably less dreadful than it did to our fathers.

Sewage systems and dry cleaning, hygiene and washable fabrics,   30
DDT and penicillin—the catalogue represents a series of technological victories over two great enemies: dirt and that system of untouchability, that unbrotherly contempt, to which, in the past, dirt has given rise.

It is, alas, hardly necessary to add that these victories are in no   31
sense definitive or secure. All we can say is that, in certain highly industrialized countries, technological advances have led to the disappearance of some of the immemorial symbols of class distinction. But this does not guarantee us against the creation of new symbols no less compulsive in their anti-democratic tendencies than the old. A man may be clean; but if, in a dictatorial state, he lacks a party card, he figuratively stinks and must be treated as an inferior at the best and, at the worst, an untouchable.

In the nominally Christian past two irreconcilable sets of sym-   32
bols bedeviled the Western mind—the symbols, inside the churches, of God's fatherhood and the brotherhood of man; and the symbols, outside, of class distinction, mammon worship and dynastic, provincial or national idolatry. In the totalitarian future— and if we go on fighting wars, the future of the West is bound to be totalitarian—the time-hallowed symbols of monotheism and brotherhood will doubtless be preserved. God will be One and men will all be His children, but in a strictly Pickwickian sense. Actually there will be slaves and masters, and the slaves will be taught to worship a parochial Trinity of Nation, Party, and Political Boss.

Samuel Butler's Musical Banks[12] will be even more musical than
they are today, and the currency in which they deal will have even
less social and psychological purchasing power than the homilies
of the Age of Faith.

Symbols are necessary—for we could not think without them.   33
But they are also fatal—for the thinking they make possible is just
as often unrealistic as it is to the point. In this consists the essentially tragic nature of the human situation. There is no way out,
except for those who have learned how to go beyond all symbols to
a direct experience of the basic fact of the divine immanence. *Tat
tvam asi*—thou art That. When this is perceived, the rest will be
added. In the meantime we must be content with such real but
limited goods as Hyperion, and such essentially precarious and
mutable sources of good as are provided by the more realistic of our
religious symbols.

RANDALL JARRELL

A Sad Heart at the Supermarket

Randall Jarrell (1914–1965) is primarily known as a poet and a
critic of poetry. His best-known early poems, collected in such
books as *Little Friend, Little Friend* (1945) and *Losses* (1948), were
reactions to the horrors of World War II. By the time he published his National Book Award–winning *The Woman at the
Washington Zoo* (1960), Jarrell had become very concerned about
America's preoccupation with material "progress," which
seemed at odds with older and weightier aspects of human nature. He became interested in psychoanalysis, dreams, myths,
and folk tales, all of which seemed to lead back to something
more significant than the world of television and household appliances. While Jarrell was in some ways a scholarly man—he
translated Chekhov from Russian and Goethe from German—his
words are plain, direct, and sharply opinionated. The passage
below is excerpted from an essay published in *Daedalus*, Spring,
1960.

Advertising men, businessmen speak continually of *media* or *the*   1
media or *the mass media*. One of their trade journals is named,

---

12. In Butler's *Erewhon* (1872), English institutions are ironically reflected in an
imaginary land. Equivalent to the English churches are the Erewhonian Musical
Banks, the money in which "had no direct commercial value in the outside world."

simply, *Media*. It is an impressive word: one imagines Mephistopheles offering Faust[1] *media that no man has ever known;* one feels, while the word is in one's ear, that abstract, overmastering powers, of a scale and intensity unimagined yesterday, are being offered one by the technicians who discovered and control them—offered, and at a price. The word has the clear fatal ring of that new world whose space we occupy so luxuriously and precariously; the world that produces mink stoles, rockabilly records, and tactical nuclear weapons by the million; the world that Attila, Galileo, Hansel and Gretel never knew.

And yet, it's only the plural of *medium*. "*Medium*," says the 2
dictionary, "that which lies in the middle; hence, middle condition or degree . . . A substance through which a force acts or an effect is transmitted . . . That through or by which anything is accomplished; as, an advertising *medium* . . . *Biol.* A nutritive mixture or substance, as broth, gelatin, agar, for cultivating bacteria, fungi, etc."

Let us name *our* trade journal *The Medium*. For all these media— 3
television, radio, movies, newspapers, magazines, and the rest—are a single medium, in whose depths we are all being cultivated. This Medium is of middle condition or degree, mediocre; it lies in the middle of everything, between a man and his neighbor, his wife, his child, his self; it, more than anything else, is the substance through which the forces of our society act upon us, and make us into what our society needs.

And what does it need? For us to need. 4

Oh, it needs for us to do or be many things: workers, technicians, 5
executives, soldiers, housewives. But first of all, last of all, it needs for us to be buyers; consumers; beings who want much and will want more—who want consistently and insatiably. Find some spell to make us turn away from the stoles, the records, and the weapons, and our world will change into something to us unimaginable. Find some spell to make us see that the product or service that yesterday was an unthinkable luxury today is an inexorable necessity, and our world will go on. It is the Medium which casts this spell—which is this spell. As we look at the television set, listen to the radio, read the magazines, the frontier of necessity is always being pushed forward. The Medium shows us what our new needs are—how often, without it, we should not have

1. According to legend, Mephistopheles (the personification of the devil) offered the learned doctor Faust youth, knowledge, and magic—in exchange for his soul. In the German dramatist Goethe's (1749–1832) *Faust*, Mephistopheles tells Faust, "I am giving you things that no man has ever known."

known!—and it shows us how they can be satisfied by buying something. The act of buying something is at the root of our world; if anyone wishes to paint the genesis of things in our society, he will paint a picture of God holding out to Adam a check-book or credit card or Charge-A-Plate.

But how quickly our poor naked Adam is turned into a con- 6 sumer, is linked to others by the great chain of buying!

> *No outcast he, bewildered and depressed:*
> *Along his infant veins are interfused*
> *The gravitation and the filial bond*
> *Of nature that connect him with the world.*[2]

Children of three or four can ask for a brand of cereal, sing some soap's commercial; by the time that they are twelve or thirteen they are not children but teen-age consumers, interviewed, graphed, analyzed. They are well on their way to becoming that ideal figure of our culture, the knowledgeable consumer. Let me define him: the knowledgeable consumer is someone who, when he comes to Weimar,[3] knows how to buy a Weimaraner.

Daisy's voice sounded like money[4]; everything about the knowl- 7 edgeable consumer looks like or sounds like or feels like money, and informed money at that. To live is to consume, to understand life is to know what to consume: he has learned to understand this, so that his life is a series of choices—correct ones—among the products and services of the world. He is able to choose to consume something, of course, only because sometime, somewhere, he or someone else produced something—but just when or where or what no longer seems to us of as much interest. We may still go to Methodist or Baptist or Presbyterian churches on Sunday, but the Protestant ethic of frugal industry, of production for its own sake, is gone.

Production has come to seem to our society not much more than 8 a condition prior to consumption. "The challenge of today," an advertising agency writes, "is to make the consumer raise his level of demand." This challenge has been met: the Medium has found it easy to make its people feel the continually increasing lacks, the many specialized dissatisfactions (merging into one great dissatisfaction, temporarily assuaged by new purchases) that it needs for them to feel. When in some magazine we see the Medium at its

2. Wordsworth, *The Prelude*, 2: 241–44.
3. Weimar is a German city rich with historical and cultural associations; a Weimaraner is a breed of dog.
4. Daisy Buchanan, in F. Scott Fitzgerald's *The Great Gatsby*.

most nearly perfect, we hardly know which half is entertaining and distracting us, which half making us buy: some advertisement may be more ingeniously entertaining than the text beside it, but it is the text which has made us long for a product more passionately. When one finishes *Holiday* or *Harper's Bazaar* or *House and Garden* or *The New Yorker* or *High Fidelity* or *Road and Track* or—but make your own list—buying something, going somewhere seems a necessary completion to the act of reading the magazine.

Reader, isn't buying or fantasy-buying an important part of your   9 and my emotional life? (If you reply, *No,* I'll think of you with bitter envy as more than merely human; as deeply un-American.) It is a standard joke that when a woman is bored or sad she buys something, to cheer herself up; but in this respect we are all women together, and can hear complacently the reminder of how feminine this consumer-world of ours has become. One imagines as a characteristic dialogue of our time an interview in which someone is asking of a vague gracious figure, a kind of Mrs. America: "But while you waited for the intercontinental ballistic missiles what did you *do?*" She answers: "I bought things."

She reminds one of the sentinel at Pompeii[5]—a space among   10 ashes, now, but at his post: she too did what she was supposed to do. Our society has delivered us—most of us—from the bonds of necessity, so that we no longer struggle to find food to keep from starving, clothing and shelter to keep from freezing; yet if the ends for which we work and of which we dream are only clothes and restaurants and houses, possessions, consumption, how have we escaped?—we have exchanged man's old bondage for a new voluntary one. It is more than a figure of speech to say that the consumer is trained for his job of consuming as the factory-worker is trained for his job of producing; and the first can be a longer, more complicated training, since it is easier to teach a man to handle a tool, to read a dial, than it is to teach him to ask, always, for a name-brand aspirin—to want, someday, a stand-by generator.

What is that? You don't know? I used not to know, but the   11 readers of *House Beautiful* all know, so that now I know. It is the electrical generator that stands in the basement of the suburban houseowner, shining, silent, till at last one night the lights go out, the furnace stops, the freezer's food begins to—

Ah, but it's frozen for good, the lights are on forever; the owner   12 has switched on the stand-by generator.

5. The ancient Italian city of Pompeii was buried by an eruption of Mount Vesuvius in A.D. 79: the cinders and ashes remarkably preserved the city's ruins, including human beings who died on the spot.

But you don't see that he really needs the generator, you'd 13
rather have seen him buy a second car? He has two. A second
bathroom? He has four. When the People of the Medium doubled
everything, he doubled everything; and now that he's gone twice
round he will have to wait three years, or four, till both are obsoles-
cent—but while he waits there are so many new needs that he can
satisfy, so many things a man can buy. "Man wants but little here
below/ Nor wants that little long," said the poet;[6] what a lie! Man
wants almost unlimited quantities of almost everything, and he
wants it till the day he dies.

Sometimes in *Life* or *Look* we see a double-page photograph of 14
some family standing on the lawn among its possessions: station-
wagon, swimming-pool, power-cruiser, sports-car, tape-recorder,
television sets, radios, cameras, power lawn-mower, garden tractor, lathe, barbecue-set, sporting equipment, domestic appliances—all the gleaming, grotesquely imaginative paraphernalia of
its existence. It was hard to get everything on two pages, soon it
will need four. It is like a dream, a child's dream before Christmas;
yet if the members of the family doubt that they are awake, they
have only to reach out and pinch something. The family seems pale
and small, a negligible appendage, beside its possessions; only a
human being would need to ask: "Which owns which?" We are
fond of saying that something is not just something but "a way of
life"; this too is a way of life—our way, the way.

Emerson, in his spare stony New England, a few miles from 15
Walden, could write: "Things are in the saddle/ And ride mankind."[7] He could say more now: that they are in the theater and
studio, and entertain mankind; are in the pulpit and preach to
mankind. The values of business, in a business society like our
own, are reflected in every sphere: values which agree with them
are reinforced, values which disagree are cancelled out or have lip
service paid to them. In business what sells is good, and that's the
end of it—that is what *good* means; if the world doesn't beat a path
to your door, your mouse-trap wasn't better. The values of the
Medium—which is both a popular business itself and the cause of
popularity in other businesses—are business values: money, success, celebrity. If we are representative members of our society, the
Medium's values are ours; and even if we are unrepresentative,
non-conforming, our hands are—too often—subdued to the ele-

6. English poet Oliver Goldsmith (1728–1774).
7. American poet and philosopher Ralph Waldo Emerson (1803–1882), a friend of
Henry David Thoreau (see excerpt from Thoreau's *Walden*, page 249 in *The Dolphin
Reader*).

ment they work in, and our unconscious expectations are all that
we consciously reject. Darwin said that he always immediately
wrote down evidence against a theory because otherwise, he'd
noticed, he would forget it; in the same way, we keep forgetting the
existence of those poor and unknown failures whom we might
rebelliously love and admire.

If you're so smart why aren't you rich? is the ground-bass of our   16
society, a grumbling and quite unanswerable criticism, since the
society's non-monetary values *are* directly convertible into money.
Celebrity turns into testimonials, lectures, directorships, presiden-
cies, the capital gains of an autobiography *Told To* some professional ghost who photographs the man's life as Bachrach[8] photographs his body. I read in the newspapers a lyric and perhaps
exaggerated instance of this direct conversion of celebrity into
money: his son accompanied Adlai Stevenson[9] on a trip to Russia,
took snapshots of his father, and sold them (to accompany his
father's account of the trip) to *Look* for $20,000. When Liberace
said that his critics' unfavorable reviews hurt him so much that he
cried all the way to the bank, one had to admire the correctness
and penetration of his press-agent's wit—in another age, what
might not such a man have become!

DANIEL J. BOORSTIN

Technology and Democracy

Daniel J. Boorstin (1914–   ), a summa cum laude graduate of
Harvard and a Rhodes Scholar with two degrees from Oxford
University, is a lawyer by training. He has, however, become one
of America's best-known historians, largely because of his interest in topics that historians with more formal training have
tended to ignore, including the effects of mass media on the lives
of ordinary citizens. Among his many books, perhaps the best
known are *The Decline of Radicalism: Reflections of America Today*
(1969), *The Americans: The Democratic Experience* (Pulitzer Prize,
1974), and *The Republic of Technology* (1978). In all these works,
there is an optimism about the effects of technology and prosperity that some critics have labeled as "boosterism" and even

8. Well-known American photography studio.
9. American statesman (1900–1965).

"vulgarity." When Boorstin talks about the drawbacks of technological progress, as he did in this 1972 lecture delivered at the
University of Michigan, he deserves special attention because he
is examining the limitations of his own pet thesis.

One of the most interesting and characteristic features of democ-   1
racy is, of course, the difficulty of defining it. And this difficulty has
been compounded in the United States, where we have been giving
new meanings to almost everything. It is, therefore, especially easy
for anyone to say that democracy in America has failed.

"Democracy," according to political scientists, usually describes   2
a form of government by the people, either directly or through their
elected representatives. But I prefer to describe a democratic society
as one which is governed by a spirit of equality and dominated by
the desire to equalize, to give everything to everybody. In the
United States the characteristic wealth and skills and know-how
and optimism of our country have dominated this quest.

My first and overshadowing proposition is that our problems   3
arise not so much from our failures as from our successes. Of course
no success is complete; only death is final. But we have probably
come closer to attaining our professed objectives than any other
society of comparable size and extent, and it is from this that our
peculiarly American problems arise.

The use of technology to democratize our daily life has given a   4
quite new shape to our hopes. In this final chapter I will explore
some of the consequences of democracy, not for government but
for experience. What are the consequences for everybody every day
of this effort to democratize life in America? And especially the
consequences of our fantastic success in industry and technology
and in invention?

There have been at least four of these consequences. I begin with   5
what I call *attenuation,* which means the thinning out or the flattening of experience. We might call this the democratizing of experience. It might otherwise be described as the decline of poignancy.
One of the consequences of our success in technology, of our
wealth, of our energy and our imagination, has been the removal
of distinctions, not just between people but between everything
and everything else, between every place and every other place,
between every time and every other time. For example, television
removes the distinction between being here and being there. And
the same kind of process, of thinning out, of removing distinctions,
has appeared in one area after another of our lives.

For instance, in the seasons. One of the great unheralded ⁶
achievements of American civilization was the rise of transportation and refrigeration, the development of techniques of canning
and preserving meat, vegetables, and fruits in such a way that it
became possible to enjoy strawberries in winter, to enjoy fresh
meat at seasons when the meat was not slaughtered, to thin out the
difference between the diet of winter and the diet of summer. There
are many unsung heroic stories in this effort.

One of them, for example, was the saga of Gustavus Swift in ⁷
Chicago. In order to make fresh meat available at a relatively low
price to people all over the country, it was necessary to be able to
transport it from the West, where the cattle were raised, to the
Eastern markets and the cities where population was concentrated.
Gustavus Swift found the railroad companies unwilling to manufacture refrigerator cars. They were afraid that, if refrigeration was
developed, the cattle would be butchered in the West and then
transported in a more concentrated form than when the cattle had
to be carried live. The obvious consequence, they believed, would
be to reduce the amount of freight. So they refused to develop the
refrigerator car. Gustavus Swift went ahead and developed it, only
to find that he had more cars than he had use for. The price of fresh
meat went down in the Eastern cities, and Gustavus Swift had
refrigerator cars on his hands. He then sent agents to the South and
to other parts of the country, and tried to encourage people to raise
produce which had to be carried in refrigerator cars. One of the
consequences of this was the development of certain strains of fruit
and vegetables, especially of fruit, which would travel well. And
Georgia became famous for the peaches which were grown partly
as a result of Swift's efforts to encourage people to raise something
that he could carry in his refrigerator cars.

There were other elements in this story which we may easily ⁸
forget—for example, how central heating and air conditioning
have affected our attitude toward the seasons, toward one time of
year or another. Nowadays visitors from abroad note that wherever
they are in our country, it is not unusual to find that in winter it is
often too warm indoors, and in summer, often too cool.

But the development of central heating during the latter part of ⁹
the nineteenth century had other, less obvious consequences. For
example, as people built high-rise apartments in the cities they
found it impossible to have a fireplace in every room. You could
not construct a high building with hundreds of apartments and
have enough room for all the chimneys. So central heating was
developed and this became a characteristic of city life. As central
heating was developed it was necessary to have a place to put the

machinery, and the machinery went in the cellar. But formerly people, even in the cities, had used their cellars to store fruit and vegetables over the winter. When the basement was heated by a furnace, of course it was no longer possible to store potatoes or other vegetables or fruit there. This increased the market for fresh fruits and vegetables that were brought in from truck farms just outside the cities or by refrigerator cars from greater distances. And this was another way of accelerating the tendency toward equalizing the seasons and equalizing the diet of people all over the country.

Also important in attenuating experience was the development 10 of what I would call homogenized space, especially the development of vertical space as a place to live in. There is a great deal less difference between living on the thirty-fifth floor and living on the fortieth floor of an apartment building than there is between living in a house in the middle of a block and living on the corner. The view is pretty much the same as you go up in the air. Vertical space is much more homogenized, and as we live in vertical space more and more, we live in places where "where we are" makes much less difference than it used to.

An important element in this which has been a product of 11 American technology is, of course, glass. We forget that the innovations in the production of glass resulting in large sheets which you could look through was an achievement largely of American technology in the nineteenth century. Of course, one by-product was the development of the technology of bottling, which is related to some of the levelings-out of the seasons which I mentioned before in relation to food. But we forget that when we admire those old leaded-glass windows which we see in medieval or early modern buildings, what we are admiring is the inability of people to produce plate glass.

When a large plate of glass became technologically possible, this 12 affected daily life in the United States. It affected merchandising, for example, because the "show window" became possible in which you could, with a relatively unobstructed view, display garments and other large objects in a way to make them appealing to people who passed by. But glass was also important in producing one of the main characteristics of modern American architecture— an architecture in which there is relatively less difference between the indoors and the outdoors than elsewhere. And that is one of the great functions of glass in modern architecture.

Along with the attenuation of places and time comes the attenu- 13 ation of occasions and events. One of the more neglected aspects of modern technology is what I have called the rise of "repeatable experience." It used to be thought that one of the characteristics of life, one of the things that distinguished being alive from being dead, was the uniqueness of the individual moment. Something happened which could never happen again. If you missed it then, you were out of luck. But the growth of popular photography, which we can trace from about 1888 when Kodak #1 went on the market, began to allow everybody to make his own experience repeatable. If you had not seen this baby when he was so cute, you could still see him that way right now if you were so unlucky as to be in the living room with the parents who wanted to show you. Kodak #1 was a great achievement and was the beginning of our taking for granted that there was such a thing as a repeatable experience.

The phonograph, of course, beginning about 1877, created new   14 opportunities to repeat audible experience. If you want to hear the voice of Franklin Delano Roosevelt now, you can hear him on a record. At the opening of the Woodrow Wilson Center for International Scholars at the Smithsonian Institution in 1971, part of the dedicating ceremony was the playing of a record with the voice of Woodrow Wilson. It was not a very warm voice, but it was identifiable and distinctive. The growth of the phonograph, then, has accustomed us to the fact that experience is not a one-time thing.

When we watch the Winter Olympics in our living room and see   15 the ski jumper in the seventy-meter jump who makes a mistake or who performs very well, we can see the same performance just a minute later with all the failures and successes pointed out. Is instant replay the last stage in the technology of repeatable experience?

In the attenuating of events there is another element which I call   16 the "pseudo-event." As more and more of the events which have public notice are planned in advance, as the accounts of them are made available before they happen, then it becomes the responsibility of the event to live up to its reputation. In this way the spontaneity of experience, the unpredictableness of experience, dissolves and disappears. The difference between the present and the future becomes less and less.

Another aspect of this is what I have called the "neutralization   17 of risks," a result of the rise of insurance. For insurance, too, is a way of reducing the difference between the future and the present. You reduce risks by assuring yourself that if your house burns down, at least you will have the money so you can rebuild it. In this sense, insurance, and especially casualty insurance, provides a way of thinning out the difference between present and future, removing the suspense and the risk of experience.

What have been the everyday consequences of the democratiz- 18 ing of property for our experience of property? In his classic defense of property in his essay *On Civil Government* (1690), John Locke argued that because property is the product of the mixing of a person's labor with an object, no government has the right to take it without his consent. This simplistic conception of property has dominated a great deal of political and economic thinking. It was prominent in the thinking of the authors of the Declaration of Independence and of the Founding Fathers of the Constitution. It was based on a simpler society where there was something poignant and characteristic about the experience of ownership. Owning meant the right to exclude people. You had the pleasure of possession.

But what has happened to property in our society? Of course, 19 the most important new form of property in modern American life is corporate property: shares of stock in a corporation. And the diffusion of the ownership of shares is one of the most prominent features of American life. There are companies like AT&T, for example, which have as many as a million stockholders. What does it mean to be a stockholder? You are a lucky person. You own property and you have some shares. So what? One doesn't need to be rich or even middle-class in this country to own shares of stock. But very few of my friends who own shares of stock know precisely what it means or what their legal powers are as stockholders. They are solicited to send in their proxies—by somebody who has a special interest in getting them to vote for something or other. They feel very little pleasure of control; they don't have the sense of wreaking themselves on any object. Yet this—a share of stock—is the characteristic and most important form of property in modern times. This property, too, is attenuated.

Other developments in American life concerning property have 20 had a similar effect. For example, installment and credit buying. This phenomenon first grew in connection with the wide marketing of the sewing machine and then in relation to the cash register, but its efflorescence has come with the automobile. When it became necessary to sell millions of automobiles—and necessary in order to keep the machinery of our society going to sell them to people who could not afford to lay out the full cost of an automobile—it was necessary to find ways of financing their purchases. Installment and credit buying was developed. One of the results was that people became increasingly puzzled over whether they did or did not (and if so in what sense) own their automobile. Of course, it is not uncommon for people to divest themselves of their physical control of an object like an automobile or a color television set before they have really acquired full ownership—and then to enter on another ambiguous venture of part ownership.

Another aspect of this is the rise of franchising: the development 21 of what I would call the "semi-independent businessman." In the United States today, between 35 percent and 50 percent of all retail merchandising is done through franchised outlets. Well, of course, we all know what a franchised outlet is; a typical example would be a McDonald's hamburger stand or any other outlet in which the person who is in control of the shop has been authorized to use a nationally advertised name like Midas Mufflers or Colonel Sanders' Kentucky Fried Chicken. He is then instructed in the conduct of his business. He must meet certain standards in order to be allowed to continue to advertise as a Holiday Inn or Howard Johnson or whatever. And he is in business "for himself." Now, what does that mean? If you go into a franchised outlet and you find the hamburger unsatisfactory, what can you do? Whom would you complain to? The man who runs the shop has received his instructions and his materials from the people who have franchised him. It is not his fault. And, of course, it's not the fault of the people at the center who franchised him, because the shop is probably badly run by the franchisee.

This phenomenon grew out of the needs of the automobile be- 22 cause in order to sell Fords or any other makes, it was necessary to have an outlet which would take continuous responsibility for stocking parts. Then the purchaser could replace that part at the outlet where he had purchased the car. After automobile franchising came the franchising of filling stations. People wanted some assurance about the quality of the fuel they put in their cars; they were given this by the identification of what they purchased with some nationally advertised brand in which they had confidence.

Now, perhaps the most important example of attenuation, of the 23 decline of poignancy in our experience in relation to property, is so obvious and so universal that it has hardly been discussed. That is packaging. Until relatively recently if you went into a store to buy coffee, you would have to bring a container to the grocery store, and the grocer would ladle out the coffee to you.

Packaging began to develop in this country after the Civil War. 24 In a sense it was a by-product of the Civil War because the necessities of the war (especially the need to package flour) produced certain innovations which were important. And later there were decisive, although what seem to us rather trivial, innovations. For example, the invention of the folding box was important. Until there was a way to make boxes which could be transported and stored compactly, it was impossible or impractical to use them for industrial purposes. The folding box and certain improvements in the paper bag, such as the paper bag that had a square bottom so that it could stand up, and on the side of which you could print an advertisement—these were American inventions.

If we will risk seeming pompous or pedantic, we can say that the most important consequences of packaging have been epistemological. They have had to do with the nature of knowledge and they have especially had the effect of confusing us about what knowledge is, and what's real, about what's form and what's substance. When you think about a Winston cigarette, you don't think about the tobacco inside the cigarette. You think about the package. And in one area after another of American life, the form and the content become confused, and the form becomes that which dominates our consciousness. One area perhaps in which this has ceased to be true, happily or otherwise, is the area which I have always thought of as an aspect of packaging—namely, clothing. In the United States we have developed ready-made clothing, too, in such a way as to obscure the differences of social class and even of sex. 25

All around us we see attenuation—as our technology has succeeded, as we have tried to make everything available to everybody. The very techniques we use in preparing our food, in transporting our food, in controlling the climate and temperature of the rooms we live in, the shapes of the buildings in which we do business and reside, the ways we look at past experience—in all these ways our experience becomes attenuated. As we democratize experience, the poignancy of the moment, of the season, of the control of the object, of the spontaneous event, declines. 26

Now to a second consequence of the success of our technology for our daily experience. This is what I would call the *decline of congregation*. Or it might be called a new segregation. This is the consequence of increasingly organized and centralized sources of anything and everything. Example: Rebecca at the well.[1] When I wrote an article for the issue of *Life* magazine which was intended to celebrate the twenty-fifth anniversary of the introduction of television in this country, I entitled the article at first "Rebecca at the TV Set." But my friends at *Life* said, "Rebecca who?" Deferring to 27

1. The wife of Isaac and mother of Jacob and Esau, Genesis 24.

their greater, wider knowledge of American life and of the literariness of the American people, instead we called it simply "The New Segregation."

When Rebecca lived in her village and needed to get water for   28
the household, she went to the well. At the well she met the other
women of the village; she heard the gossip; she met her fiancé
there, as a matter of fact. And then what happened? With the
progress of democracy and technology, running water was introduced; and Rebecca stayed in the kitchenette of her eighth-floor
apartment. She turned the faucet on and got the water out of the
faucet; she didn't have to go to the well any more. She had only the
telephone to help her collect gossip and she would have to find
other ways to meet her fiancé. This is a parable of the problem of
centralizing sources of everything.

The growth of centralized plumbing was itself, of course, a nec-   29
essary by-product of the development of the skyscraper and the
concentration of population in high buildings. You had to have
effective sanitary facilities. But we forget other features of this development. Even those of us who have never made much use of
the old "privy" know that the privy characteristically had more
than one hole in it. Why was this? The plural facility was not
peculiar simply to the privy; it was also found in the sanitary
arrangements of many older buildings, including some of the
grandest remaining medieval structures. The development of centralized plumbing led to privatizing; "privy" was the wrong word
for the old facility. The privatizing of the bodily functions made
them less sociable. People engaged in them in private.

The most dramatic example today of the privatizing of experi-   30
ence by centralizing a facility is, of course, television. We could
start with the newspaper, for that matter. The town crier com-
municated the news to people in their presence. If you wanted to
hear it you had to be there, or talk to somebody else who was there
when he brought the news. But as the newspaper developed, with
inexpensive printing, the messages were brought to you and you
could look at them privately as you sat by yourself at breakfast.
Television is perhaps one of the most extreme examples of the
decline of congregation. Until the development of television, if you
wanted to see a play you had to go out to a theater; if you wanted
to hear a concert you had to go to a concert hall. These performances were relatively rare. They were special events. But with the
coming of television, everybody acquired his private theater. Rebecca had her theater in her kitchen. She no longer needed to go
out for entertainment.

The centralized source, the centralizing of the source, then, led to   31 the isolating of the consumer. Of course, much was gained by this. But one of the prices paid was the decline of congregation—congregation being the drawing together of people where they could enjoy and react to and respond to the reactions and feelings of their fellows.

There is a third consequence of our technological success in democratic America, which I would call the new determinism, or *the rising sense of momentum*. Technology has had a deep and pervasive effect on our attitude toward history, and especially on the citizen's attitude toward his control over the future. In the seventeenth century the Puritans spoke about Providence; that was their characteristic way of describing the kind of control that God exercised over futurity. In the nineteenth century, when people became more scientifically minded, they still retained some notion of divine foresight in the form of the concept of destiny or mission or purpose. But in our time in this country we have developed a different kind of approach toward futurity; and this is what I would call the sense of momentum.

Momentum in physics is the product of a body's mass and its linear velocity. Increasing scale and speed of operation increase the momentum. One of the characteristics of our technology and especially of our most spectacular successes has been to increase this sense of momentum. I will mention three obvious examples. It happens that each of these developments came, too, as a result of overwhelming international pressure. When such pressures added to the forces at work inside the nation, in each case they produced a phenomenon of great mass and velocity which became very difficult to stop.

The first example is, of course, atomic research. The large-scale concerted efforts in this country to build an atomic bomb began and were accelerated at the time of World War II because of rumors that the Nazis were about to succeed in nuclear fission. When this information became available, national resources were massed and organized in an unprecedented fashion; futurity was scheduled and groups were set to work in all parts of the continent exploring different possible ways of finding the right form of uranium or of some other element. And the search for the first atomic chain reaction, which was accomplished at my University of Chicago, went on.

One of the more touching human aspects of this story is the account, now well chronicled by several historians, of the frantic efforts of the atomic scientists, the people who had been most instrumental in getting this process started (Albert Einstein, Leo Szilard, and James Franck, among others), when they saw that the atomic bomb was about to become possible, to persuade the President of the United States either not to use the bomb or to use it only in a demonstration in the uninhabited mid-Pacific. Such a use, they urged, would so impress the enemy with the horrors of the bomb that he would surrender, eliminating the need for us to use the bomb against a live target. They pursued this purpose—trying to put the brakes on military use of the bomb—with a desperation that even exceeded the energy they had shown in developing the bomb. But, of course, they had no success.

They could develop the bomb, but they couldn't stop it. Why?   36
There were many reasons, including President Truman's reasonable belief that use of the bomb could in the long run save the hundreds of thousands of Japanese and American lives that would have been lost in an invasion, and also would shorten the war. But surely one reason was that there had already been too much investment in the bomb. Billions of dollars had gone into the making of it. People were organized all over the country in various ways. It was impossible to stop.

Another example of this kind of momentum is the phenomenon   37
of space exploration. I happen to be an enthusiast for space exploration, so by describing this momentum I do not mean to suggest that I think the space enterprise itself has not been a good thing. Nevertheless, as a historian I am increasingly impressed by the pervasive phenomenon of momentum in our time. Billions of dollars have been spent in developing the machinery for going off to the moon or going then to Mars or elsewhere. The mass of the operation has been enormous. The velocity of it is enormous, and it becomes virtually impossible to stop. The recent problem with the SST is a good example. For when any enterprise in our society has reached a certain scale, the consequences in unemployment and in dislocation of the economy are such that it becomes every year more difficult to cease doing what we are already doing.

A third example, more in the area of institutions, is foreign aid: 38
the international pressures to give foreign aid to one country or another. We have an enormous mass of wealth being invested, a great velocity with lots of people going off all over the world and performing this operation of giving aid, and it becomes almost impossible to stop it. The other countries resent the decline of aid and consider it a hostile act, even though they might not have felt that way if we hadn't started the aid in the first place. Foreign aid is, I think, the most characteristic innovation in foreign policy in this century.

Each of these three enterprises illustrates the attitude of the   39
American citizen in the later twentieth century toward his control

over experience. Increasingly, the citizen comes to feel that events are moving, and moving so fast with such velocity and in such mass that he has very little control. The sense of momentum itself becomes possible only because of our success in achieving these large purposes which no other democratic society, no other society before us, had even imagined.

Now, what does this bring us to? Before I come to my fourth and concluding point on the ways in which the successes of democracy have affected our experience, I would like briefly to recall some of the remedies that have been suggested for the ills of democracy and the problems of democracy in the past. Al Smith once said, "All the ills of democracy can be cured by more democracy." I must confess, though I admire Al Smith for some of his enterprises, the Empire State Building for example, I think he was on the wrong track here. In fact, I would take an almost contrary position. Even at the risk of seeming flip, I might sum up the democratic paradoxes that I have been describing: "Getting there is *all* the fun." 40

Is there a law of democratic impoverishment? Is it possible that while *democratizing* enriches experience, *democracy* dilutes experience? 41

Example: photography. Before the invention of photography, it was a remarkable experience to see an exact likeness of the Sphinx or of Notre Dame or of some exotic animal or to see a portrait of an ancestor. Then, as photography was publicized in the 1880's and thoroughly popularized in this century, it opened up a fantastic new range of experience for everybody. Suddenly people were able to see things they had never been able to see before. And then what happened? Everyone had a camera, or two or three cameras; and everywhere he went he took pictures and when he came home he had to find a victim, somebody to show the pictures to. And this became more and more difficult. 42

While photography was being introduced, it was life-enriching and vista-opening; but once it was achieved, once everybody had a camera, the people were looking in their cameras instead of looking at the sight they had gone to see. It had an attenuating effect. A picture came to mean less and less, simply because people saw pictures everywhere. And the experience of being there also somehow meant less because the main thing people saw everywhere was the inside of their viewfinders, and their concern over their lens cap and finding the proper exposure made it hard for them to notice what was going on around them at the moment. 43

Another example is, of course, the phonograph. Has the phono- 44

graph—in its universal late-twentieth-century uses—necessarily
made people more appreciative of music? In the 1920's when I was
raised in Tulsa, Oklahoma, I had never heard an opera, nor had I
really heard any classical music properly performed by an or-
chestra. But in our living room we had a wind-up Victrola, and I
heard Galli-Curci singing arias from *Rigoletto*, and I heard Caruso,
and I heard some symphonies, and it was fantastic. And then hi-fi
came and everybody had a phonograph, a hi-fi machine or a little
transistor radio which you could carry with you and hear music
any time.

Today when I walk into the elevator in an office building, it is   45
not impossible that I will hear Beethoven or Verdi. Sitting in the
airplane I hear Mozart coming out of the public-address system.
Wherever we go we hear music whether we want to hear it or not,
whether we are in the mood for it or not. It becomes an everywhere, all-the-time thing. The experience is attenuated.

And one of the most serious consequences of all this, finally, is   46
the attenuation of community itself. What holds people together?
What has held people together in the past? For the most part it has
been their sense of humanity, their pleasure in the presence of one
another, their feeling for another person's expression, the sound of
a voice, the look on his or her face. But the kind of community I
describe increasingly becomes attenuated. People are trying to enjoy the community all by themselves.

We are led to certain desperate quests in American life. These,   47
the by-products of our success, are clues to the vitality and energy
of our country, to the quest for novelty to keep life interesting and
vistas open, to the quest for community and the quest for auton-
omy. Can we inoculate ourselves against these perils of our technological success? Samuel Butler once said, "If I die prematurely, at
any rate I shall be saved from being bored by my own success."
Our problem, too, is partly that.

And now a fourth characteristic of the relation of technology   48
to democracy in our time: *the belief in solutions.* One of the most
dangerous popular fallacies—nourished by American history and
by some of our most eloquent and voluble patriots—is the notion
that democracy is attainable. There is a subtle difference between
American democratic society and many earlier societies in the extent to which their ideals could be attained. The objectives of other
societies have for the most part been definable and attainable. Aristocracy and monarchy do present attainable ideals. Even totalitarianism presents objectives which can be attained in the sense in
which the objectives of democracy never can be.

This nation has been a place of renewal, of new beginnings for   49 nations and for man. Vagueness has been a national resource: the vagueness of the continent, the mystery of our resources, the vagueness of our social classes, the misty miasma of our hopes.

Our society has been most distinctively a way of reaching for 50 rather than of finding. American democracy, properly speaking, has been a process and not a product, a quest and not a discovery. But a great danger which has been nourished by our success in technology has been the belief in solutions. For technological problems there *are* solutions. It is possible to set yourself the task of developing an economic and workable internal-combustion engine, a prefabricated house, or a way of reaching the moon. Technological problems are capable of solutions.

We are inclined, then, using the technological problem as our 51 prototype, to believe that somehow democracy itself is a solution, a dissolving of the human condition. But we should have learned, and even the history of technology—especially the history of technology in our democratic society—should have taught us otherwise.

In human history in the long run there are no solutions, only 52 problems. This is what I have suggested in my description of "self-liquidating" ideals. And the examples are all around us—in our effort to create a pluralistic society by assimilating and Americanizing people, in our effort to give everybody an uncrowded wilderness vacation, in our effort to find an exciting new model each year.

Every seeming solution is a new problem. When you democ- 53 ratize the speedy automobile and give everybody an automobile, the result is a traffic jam; and this is the sense in which the "solution" of technological problems presents us with obstacles to the fulfillment of what is human in our society. When we think about American democratic society, then, we must learn not to think about a condition, but about a process; not about democracy, but about the quest for democracy, which we might call "democratizing."

The most distinctive feature of our system is not a system, but a 54 quest, not a neat arrangement of men and institutions, but a flux. What other society has ever committed itself to so tantalizing, so fulfilling, so frustrating a community enterprise?

To prepare ourselves for this view of American democracy there 55 are two sides to our personal need. One is on the side of prudence and wisdom; the other on the side of poetry and imagination.

On the side of prudence, there is a need for a sense of history. 56 Only by realizing the boundaries that we have been given can we discover how to reach beyond them. Only so can we have the wisdom not to mistake passing fads for great movements, not to mistake the fanaticisms of a few for the deep beliefs of the many, not to mistake fashion for revolution. This wisdom is necessary if we are to secure sensibly the benefits of a free society for those who have for whatever reason been deprived of its benefits. We were not born yesterday, nor was the nation. And between the day before yesterday and yesterday, crucial events have happened. We can discover these and come to terms with them only through history. As Pascal said, "It is only by knowing our condition that we can transcend it." Our technology brings us the omnipresent present. It dulls our sense of history, and if we are not careful it can destroy it.

We in the U.S.A. are always living in an age of transition. Yet we   57
have tended to believe that our present is always the climax of history, even though American history shows that the climax is always in the future. By keeping suspense alive, we can prepare ourselves for the shocks of change.

And finally, on the side of poetry and imagination, how do we   58
keep alive the spirit of adventure, what I would call the exploring spirit? This should be the easiest because it is the most traditional of our achievements and efforts. We must remember that we live in a new world. We must keep alive the exploring spirit. We must not sacrifice the infinite promise of the unknown, of man's unfulfilled possibilities in the universe's untouched mysteries, for the cozy satisfactions of predictable, statistical benefits. Space exploration is a symbol.

Recently I had the pleasure of talking with Thor Heyerdahl, the   59
Kon Tiki man, whose latest venture was the Ra expedition, in which he explored the possibilities of men having come from Egypt or elsewhere in the Mediterranean to this continent long ago in boats made of reeds. He and his crew, to test their hypothesis, actually crossed the Atlantic in a reed boat. And as I talked to Thor Heyerdahl about the Ra expedition, I said that it must have been a terrible feeling of risk when you suddenly left the sight of land and got out into the open sea. It seemed to me that the fear and perils of the open sea would be the greatest. Thor Heyerdahl said not at all: the great dangers, the dangers of shoals and rocks, existed along the shore. The wonderful sense of relief, he observed, came when he went out on the ocean where there was openness all around, although also high waves and strong currents. The promise of American democracy, I suggest, depends on our ability to stay at sea, to work together in community while we all reach to the open horizon.

JERRY MANDER

The Walling of Awareness

Jerry Mander (1936–   ), educated at the University of Pennsylvania and Columbia University, moved west to become a successful advertising man in San Francisco during the economic
boom of the 1960s and early 1970s. In 1967 he and two friends
published a best-seller, *The Great International Paper Airplane
Book*, a tongue-in-cheek account of a pseudocontest invented by
the authors and sponsored by *Scientific American*. By 1970, Mander's great success in marketing products of dubious value began
to alarm him, and he became an increasingly radical critic of the
role of business and advertising in American society. He was for a
time a member of Public Service Communication, a media team
that used its skills to promote causes instead of products. In 1978
he published *Four Arguments for the Abolition of Television*, a negatively reviewed but widely discussed attack on the reshaping of
human consciousness by market-oriented media. "The Walling
of Awareness" is the opening chapter of this controversial book.

During a six-month period on 1973, *The New York Times* re-   1
ported the following scientific findings:

A major research institute spent more than $50,000 to discover   2
that the best bait for mice is cheese.

Another study found that mother's milk was better balanced   3
nutritionally for infants than commercial formulas. That study also
proved that mother's milk was better for human infants than cow's
milk or goat's milk.

A third study established that a walk is considerably healthier for   4
the human respiratory and circulatory systems, in fact for overall
health and vitality, than a ride in a car. Bicycling was also found to
be beneficial.

A fourth project demonstrated that the juice of fresh oranges has   5
more nutritional value than either canned or frozen orange juice.

A fifth study proved conclusively that infants who are touched a   6
lot frequently grow into adults with greater self-confidence and
have a more integrated relationship with the world than those who
are not touched. This study found that touching, not merely sexual
touching, but *any* touching of one person by another, seemed to aid
general health and even mental development among adults as well
as children.

The remarkable thing about these five studies, of course, is that   7 anyone should have found it necessary to undertake them. That some people did find them necessary can only mean that they felt there was some uncertainty about how the answers would turn out.

And yet, anyone who has seen a mouse eating cheese or who   8
has been touched by the hand of another person already knows a great deal about these things, assuming he or she gives credence to personal observation.

Similarly, anyone who has ever considered the question of   9
artificial milk versus human milk is unlikely to assume that Nestle's or Similac will improve on a feeding arrangement that accounted for the growth of every human infant before modern times.

That any people retain doubts on these questions is symptomatic   10
of two unfortunate conditions of modern existence: Human beings no longer trust personal observation, even of the self-evident, until it is confirmed by scientific or technological institutions; human beings have lost insight into natural processes—how the world works, the human role as one of many interlocking parts of the worldwide ecosystem—because natural processes are now exceedingly difficult to observe.

These two conditions combine to limit our knowledge and   11
understanding to what we are told. They also leave us unable to judge the reliability or unreliability of the information we go by.

The problem begins with the physical environment in which we   12
live.

MEDIATED ENVIRONMENTS

When he was about five years old, my son Kai asked me,   13
"Daddy, who built Mt. Tamalpais?"

Kai's question shocked me. I said, "Nobody built Mt. Tamalpais;   14
it grew up out of the Earth thousands of years ago. No person could build a mountain."

I don't think this satisfied him, but it did start me on a new train   15
of thought.

I think that was the first moment that I really looked around at   16
the urban world in which he and I and the rest of our family and the majority of the people in this country live. I wanted to know how he could have gotten the notion that human beings are responsible for the construction of mountains. I soon realized that his mistaken impression was easy to understand; it was one that we all share on a deeper level.

Most Americans spend their lives within environments created   17
by human beings. This is less the case if you live in Montana than if

you live in Manhattan, but it is true to some extent all over the country. Natural environments have largely given way to human-created environments.

What we see, hear, touch, taste, smell, feel, and understand   18
about the world has been processed for us. Our experiences of the world can no longer be called direct, or primary. They are secondary, mediated experiences.

When we are walking in a forest, we can see and feel what the   19
planet produces directly. Forests grow on their own without human intervention. When we see a forest, or experience it in other ways, we can count on the experience being directly between us and the planet. It is not mediated, interpreted, or altered.

On the other hand, when we live in cities, no experience is   20
directly between us and the planet. Virtually all experience is mediated in some way. Concrete covers whatever would grow from the ground. Buildings block the natural vistas. The water we drink comes from a faucet, not from a stream or the sky. All foliage has been confined by human considerations and redesigned according to human tastes. There are no wild animals, there are no rocky terrains, there is no cycle of bloom and decline. There is not even night and day. No food grows anywhere.

Most of us give little importance to this change in human experi-   21
ence of the world, if we notice it at all. We are so surrounded by a reconstructed world that it is difficult to grasp how astonishingly different it is from the world of only one hundred years ago, and that it bears virtually no resemblance to the world in which human beings lived for four million years before that. That this might affect the way we think, including our understanding of how our lives are connected to any nonhuman system, is rarely considered.

In fact, most of us assume that human understanding is now   22
more thorough than before, that we know more than we ever did. This is because we have such faith in our rational, intellectual processes and the institutions we have created that we fail to observe their limits.

I have heard small children ask whether apples and oranges   23
grow in stores. "Of course not," we tell them. "Fruit grows from the ground somewhere out in the countryside, and then it's put into trucks and brought to the stores."

But is this true? Have you seen that? Do you have a sense that   24
what you are eating was once alive, growing on its own?

We learn in schools that fruit grows from the ground. We see   25
pictures of fruit growing. But when we live in cities, confined to the walls and floors of our concrete environments, we don't actually

see the slow process of a blossom appearing on a tree, then becoming a bud that grows into an apple. We learn this, but we can't really "know" what it means, or that a whole cycle is operating: sky to ground to root through tree to bud ripening into fruit that we can eat. Nor do we see particular value in this knowledge. It remains an idea to us, an abstraction that is difficult to integrate into our consciousness without direct experience of the process. Therefore we don't develop a feeling about it, a caring. In the end how can our children or we really grasp that fruit growing from trees has anything to do with humans growing from eating the fruit?

We have learned that water does not really originate in the pipes   26
where we get it. We are educated to understand that it comes from sky (we have seen that, it is true!), lands in some faraway mountains, flows into rivers, which flow into little reservoirs, and then somehow it all goes through pipes into the sinks in our homes and then back out to—where? The ocean.

We learn there is something called evaporation that takes the   27
water we don't need up to the sky. But is this true? Is there a pattern to it? How does it collect in the sky? Is it okay to rearrange the cycle with cloud seeding? Is it okay to collect the water in dams? Does anyone else need water? Do plants drink it? How do they get it? Does water go into the ground? In cities it rolls around on concrete and then pours into sewers. Since we are unable to observe most of the cycle, we learn about it in knowledge museums: schools, textbooks. We study to know. What we know is what we have studied. We know what the books say. What the books say is what the authors of the books learned from "experts" who, from time to time, turn out to be wrong.

Everyone knows about night and day. Half the time it's dark,   28
half the time it's light.

However, it doesn't work that way in our homes or outside in   29
the streets. There is always light, and it is always the same, controlled by an automatic switch downtown. The stars are obscured by the city glow. The moon is washed out by a filter of light. It becomes a semimoon and our awareness of it inevitably dims.

We say it is night, but darkness moods and feelings lie dormant   30
in us. Faced with *real* darkness, we become frightened, overreact, like a child whose parents have always left the light on. In three generations since Edison, we have become creatures of light alone.

One evening during 1975, I went with my family to a small park   31
in the middle of San Francisco to watch a partial eclipse of the moon. We saw it rise above the buildings, but it had little power. Hundreds of street lamps, flashing signs, and lighted buildings in-

truded. The street lamps, those new mercury-vapor arcs that give off a harsh pinkish-white light, were the worst problem. It was difficult to feel anything for the moon seen through this pinkish filter. The children became bored. We went for an ice cream.

Later that same evening, I went alone to a different park on a high hill. I imagined the city lights gone dark. I turned them off in my mind. Without the buildings diverting me, I gained the briefest feeling for how the moon must have been experienced by human beings of earlier centuries, why whole cultures and religions were based upon it, how they could know every nuance of its cycle and those of the stars, and how they could understand its connection with planting times, tides, and human fertility.   32

Only recently has our own culture produced new studies confirming the moon's effect on our bodies and minds, as well as its effect on plants. Earlier cultures, living without filters, did not need to rediscover the effects. People remained personally sensitive to their connections with the natural world. For most of us, this sensitivity and knowledge, or science, of older cultures is gone. If there are such connections, we have little awareness of them. Our environment has intervened.   33

Not long ago after the eclipse I just described, my wife, Anica, was told by her ninety-year-old grandmother that we should not permit our children to sleep where the moonlight could bathe them. Born in preindustrial Yugoslavia and having spent most of her life without technology, the old woman said the moon had too much power. One night, our oldest son, Yari, who was eight at the time, spent an evening at a friend's house, high on a hill, sleeping near a curtainless south-facing window. He called us in the morning to tell us of a disturbing thing that had happened to him during the night. He had awakened to find himself standing flush against the window, facing the full moon. He had gotten out of bed while still asleep, walked over to the window, and stood facing the moon. Only then did he wake up. He was frightened, he said, more by the oddness of the experience than any sense of real danger. Actually, he thought it rather special but didn't like having an experience different from what is expected and accepted, which is *not* to experience the power of the moon. He had been taught that what he had just been through couldn't happen; he wished it hadn't and it hasn't since.   34

Yari, like most of the rest of us, does not wish to accept the validity of his personal experience. The people who define the moon are now the scientists, astronomers, and geologists who tell us which interactions with the world are possible and which are   35 not, ridiculing any evidence to the contrary. The moon's cycle affects the oceans, they say, but it doesn't affect the body. Does that sound right to you? It doesn't to me. And yet, removed from any personal awareness of the moon, unable even to see it very well, let alone experience it, how are we to know what is right and what is wrong? Most of us cannot say if, this very evening, the moon will be out at all.

Perhaps you are a jogger. I am not, but friends have told me how 36 that experience has broken them out of technologically created notions of time and distance. I have one friend in San Francisco who runs from his Russian Hill apartment to Ocean Beach and then back again, every morning. This is a distance of about eight miles. There was a time, he told me, when the idea of walking, or bicycling that distance seemed impossible to him. Now the distance seems manageable, even easy. Near, not far. He has recovered a personal sense of distance.

I have made similar discoveries myself. Some years ago I decided 37 to walk to work every day instead of driving. It changed getting to work into a pleasurable experience—no traffic jams or parking hassles—and I would stop now and then for coffee and a chat with a friend. More important, it changed my conception of distance. My office was twenty blocks from my home, about a thirty-minute walk. I noticed that walking that distance was extremely easy. I hadn't known that my previous conception of twenty blocks was one which technology had created. My knowledge was car-knowledge. I had become mentally and physically a car-person. Now I was connecting distance and range to my body, making the conception personal rather than mechanical, outside myself.

On another occasion, while away on a camping trip with my two 38 children, I learned something about internal versus institutional-technological rhythm.

The three of us were suffering an awful boredom at first. My 39 children complained that there was nothing to *do*. We were all so attuned to events coming along at urban speed in large, prominent packages, that our bodies and minds could not attune to the smaller, more subtle events of a forest.

By the second day, however, the children began to throw rocks 40 into a stream and I found myself hearing things that I hadn't heard the day before: wind, the crunch of leaves under foot. The air was somehow clearer and fresher than it seemed to have been the day before. I began to wander around, aimlessly but interestedly.

On the third day, the children began to notice tiny creatures. 41 They watched them closely and learned more about their habits in that one day than I know even now. They were soon imitating squirrels, birds, snakes, and they began to invent some animals.

By the fourth day, our urban-rhythm memory had given way to   42
the natural rhythms of the forest. We started to take in all kinds of things that a few days before we hadn't noticed were there. It was as if our awareness was a dried-out root system that had to be fed.

Returning to the city a few days later, we could feel the speedup   43
take place. It was like running to catch up with a train.

SENSORY-DEPRIVATION ENVIRONMENTS

The modern office building is the archetypal example of the   44
mediated environment. It contains nothing that did not first exist as a design plan in a human mind. The spaces are square, flat, and small, eliminating a sense of height, depth, and irregularity. The decor is rigidly controlled to a bland uniformity from room to room and floor to floor. The effect is to dampen all interest in the space one inhabits.

Most modern office buildings have hermetically sealed windows.   45
The air is processed, the temperature regulated. It is always the same. The body's largest sense organ, the skin, feels no wind, no changes in temperature, and is dulled.

Muzak homogenizes the sound environment. Some buildings   46
even use "white noise," a deliberate mix of electronic sounds that merge into a hum. Seemingly innocuous, it fills the ears with an even background tone, obscuring random noises or passing conversation which might arouse interest or create a diversion.

The light remains constant from morning through night, from   47
room to room until our awareness of light is as dulled as our awareness of temperature, and we are not aware of the passage of time. We are told that a constant level of light is good for our eyes, that it relieves strain. Is this true? What about the loss of a range of focus and the many changes in direction and intensity of light that our flexible eyes are designed to accommodate?

Those who build artificial environments view the senses as sin-   48
gle, monolithic things, rather than abilities that have a range of capacity for a reason. We know, for example, that our eyes can see from the extremely dark to the extremely bright, from far to near, from distinct to indistinct, from obvious to subtle. They perceive objects moving quickly and those that are still. The eye is a wonderfully flexible organ, able to adjust instantly to a dazzling array of information, constantly changing, multileveled, perceiving objects far and near moving at different speeds simultaneously. A fully functioning visual capacity is equal to everything the natural envi-

ronment offers as visual information. This would have to be so, since the interaction between the senses and the natural environment *created* the ranges of abilities that we needed to have. Sight did not just arrive one day, like Adam's rib; it coevolved with the ingredients around it which it was designed to see. When our eyes are continually exercised, when flexibility and dynamism are encouraged, then they *are* equal to the variety of stimuli that night and day have to offer. It is probably not wise always to have "good light" or to be for very long at fixed distances from anything. The result will be lack of exercise and eventual atrophy of the eyes' abilities.

When we reduce an aspect of environment from varied and   49
multidimensional to fixed, we also change the human being who lives within it. Humans give up the capacity to adjust, just as the person who only walks cannot so easily handle the experience of running. The lungs, the heart, and other muscles have not been exercised. The human being then becomes a creature with a narrower range of abilities and fewer feelings about the loss. We become grosser, simpler, less varied, like the environment.

The common response to this is that if we lose wide-spectrum   50
sensory experience, we gain a deeper mental experience. This is not true. We only have less nonmental experience so the mental life seems richer by comparison. In fact, mental life is more enriched by a fully functioning sensory life.

In recent years, researchers have discovered some amazing   51
things about the connections between mental and physical life by doing sensory-deprivation experiments. In such experiments, a human subject is cut off from as much sensory information as possible. This can be accomplished, for example, by a totally blank environment—white walls, no furniture, no sounds, constant temperature, constant light, no food and no windows. A more thorough method is to put the blindfolded subject inside a temperature-controlled suit floating in a water tank with only tubes to provide air and water, which are also at body temperature. This sensory-deprivation tank eliminates the tactile sense as well as an awareness of up and down.

Researchers have found that when sensory stimuli are sup-   52
pressed this way, the subject at first lives a mental life because mental images are the only stimulation. But after a while, these images become disoriented and can be frightening. Disconnected from the world outside the mind, the subject is rootless and ungrounded.

If the experience goes on long enough, a kind of madness devel-   53
ops which can be allayed only by reintroducing sensory stimuli, direct contact with the world outside the subject's mind.

Before total disorientation occurs, a second effect takes place. 54
That is a dramatic increase in focus on any stimulus at all that is
introduced. In such a deprived environment, one single stimulus
acquires extraordinary power and importance. In the most literal
sense, the subject loses perspective and cannot put the stimulus in
context. Such experiments have proven to be effective in halting
heavy smoking habits, for example, when the experimenter speaks
instructions to stop smoking or describes to the subject through a
microphone the harmful, unpleasant aspects of smoking.

These experiments have shown that volunteers can be pro- 55
grammed to believe and do things they would not have done in a
fully functional condition. The technique could be called brain-
washing.

It would be going too far to call our modern offices sen- 56
sory-deprivation chambers, but they are most certainly sensory-
reduction chambers. They may not brainwash, but the elimination
of sensory stimuli definitely increases focus on the task at hand, the
work to be done, to the exclusion of all else. Modern offices were
designed for that very purpose by people who knew what they
were doing.

If people's senses were stimulated to experience anything ap- 57
proaching their potential range, it would be highly unlikely that
people would sit for eight long hours at desks, reading memoranda,
typing documents, studying columns of figures or pondering sales
strategies. If birds were flying through the room, and wind were
blowing the papers about, if the sun were shining in there, or
people were lolling about on chaise lounges or taking baths while
listening to various musical presentations, this would certainly divert the office worker from the mental work he or she is there to
do. In fact, if offices were so arranged, little business would get
done. This is why they are not so arranged. Any awareness of the
senses, aside from their singular uses in reading and sometimes
talking and listening, would be disastrous for office environments
that require people to stay focused within narrow and specific
functional modes.

Feeling is also discouraged by these environments. Reducing 58
sensual variations is one good way of reducing feeling since the one
stimulates the other. But there is also a hierarchy of values which
further the process. Objectivity is the highest value that can be
exhibited by an executive in an office. Orderliness is the highest
value for a subordinate office worker. Both of these are most easily
achieved if the human is effectively disconnected from the distractions of her or his senses, feelings, and intuitions.

With the field of experience so drastically reduced for office 59 workers, the stimuli which remain—paper work, mental work, business—loom larger and obtain an importance they would not have in a wider, more varied, more stimulating environment. The worker gets interested in them largely because that is what is available to get interested in.

Curiously, however, while eschewing feeling and intuition, 60
business people often cannot resist using them. They come out as aberrations—fierce competitive drive, rage at small inconveniences, decisions that do not fit the models of objectivity. Such behavior in business sometimes makes me think of blades of grass growing upward through the pavement.

A more poignant example, perhaps, is that modern offices have 61
proved to be such hot sexual environments. Aside from the occasional potted plant, the only creatures in offices with which it is possible to experience anything are other humans. With all other organic life absent and with the senses deprived of most possibilities for human experience, the occasional body which passes the desk becomes an especially potent sensual event, the only way out of the condition of suspended experience, and the only way to experience oneself as alive. In fact, the confinement of human beings within artificial environments may be a partial explanation of our new culture-wide obsession with and focus on sex.

I have been speaking mainly of cities. This has only been because 62
their effects are most obvious. I don't want to create the impression that suburbs, retirement communities, recreational communities, and the like offer any greater access to a wider range of experience.

Those places do have large trees, for example, and more small 63
animals. The sky is more visible, without giant buildings to alter the view. But in most ways, suburban-type environments reveal less of natural processes than cities do. Cities, at least, offer a critical ingredient of the natural world, diversity, albeit a diversity that is confined to only human life forms. It does not nearly approach the complexity of any acre of an ordinary forest.

In suburbs the totality of experience is plotted in advance 64
and then marketed on the basis of the plan. "We will have everything to serve the recreational needs of your family: playgrounds, ball fields, golf course, tennis courts, bowling alleys, and picnic grounds." This, plus a front lawn, a back lawn, two large trees, and an attentive police force makes up the total package. Human beings then live inside that package.

Places formerly as diverse as forest, desert, marsh, plain, and 65
mountain have been unified into suburban tracts. The human senses, seeking outward for knowledge and stimulation, find only what has been prearranged by other humans.

In many ways the same can be said of rural environments. Land   66
which once supported hundreds of varieties of plant and animal
life has been transformed by agribusinesses. Insect life has been
largely eliminated by massive spraying. For hundreds of square
miles, the only living things are artichokes or tomatoes laid out in
straight rows. The child seeking to know how nature works finds
only spray planes, automated threshers, and miles of rows of a
single crop.

ROOMS INSIDE ROOMS

There are differences of opinion about what the critical moments   67
were that led human beings away from the primary forms of experience—between person and planet—into secondary, mediated
environments. Some go back as far as the control of fire, the domestication of animals, the invention of agriculture, or the imposition of monotheism and patriarchy.

In my opinion, however, the most significant recent moment   68
came with the control of electricity for power, about four generations ago. This made it possible to begin moving nearly all human
functions indoors, and made the outdoors more like indoors.

In less than four generations out of an estimated one hundred   69
thousand, we have fundamentally changed the nature of our interaction with the planet.

Our environment no longer grows on its own, by its own design,   70
in its own time. The environment in which *we* live has been totally
reconstructed solely by human intention and creation.

We find ourselves living inside a kind of nationwide room. We   71
look around it and see only our own creations.

We go through life believing we are experiencing the world   72
when actually our experiences are confined within entirely human
conceptions. Our world has been thought up.

Our environment itself is the manifestation of the mental proc-   73
esses of other humans. Of all the species of the planet, and all the
cultures of the human species, we twentieth-century Americans
have become the first in history to live predominantly inside pro-
jections of our own minds.

We live in a kind of maelstrom, going ever deeper into our own   74
thought processes, into subterranean caverns, where nonhuman
reality is up, up, away somewhere. We are within a system of ever
smaller, ever deeper concentric circles, and we consider each new
depth that we reach greater progress and greater knowledge.

Our environment itself becomes an editor, filter, and medium   75
between ourselves and an alternative nonhuman, unedited, organic planetary reality.

We ask the child to understand nature and care about it, to know   76 the difference between what humans create and what the planet does, but how can the child know these things? The child lives with us in a room inside a room inside another room. The child sees an apple in a store and assumes that the apple and the store are organically connected. The child sees streets, buildings, and a mountain and assumes it was all put there by humans. How can the child assume otherwise? That is the obvious conclusion in a world in which all reality *is* created by humans.

As adults, we assume we are not so vulnerable to this mistake,   77
that we are educated and our minds can save us. We "know" the difference between natural and artificial. And yet, we have no greater contact with the wider world than the child has.

Most people still give little importance to any of this. Those who   78
take note of these changes usually speak of them in esoteric, aesthetic, or philosophical terms. It makes good discussion at parties and in philosophy classes.

As we go, however, I hope it will become apparent that the most   79
compelling outcome of these sudden changes in the way we experience life is the inevitable political one.

Living within artificial, reconstructed, arbitrary environments   80
that are strictly the products of human conception, we have no way to be sure that we know what is true and what is not. We have lost context and perspective. What we know is what other humans tell us.

Therefore, whoever controls the processes of re-creation effec-   81
tively redefines reality for everyone else, and creates the entire world of human experience, our field of knowledge. We become subject to them. The confinement of our experience becomes the basis of their control of us.

The role of the media in all this is to confirm the validity of the   82
arbitrary world in which we live. The role of television is to project that world, via images, into our heads, all of us at the same time.

MARK KRAMER

The Ruination of the Tomato

Mark Kramer (1944–   ) abandoned his graduate program at Indiana University in 1968 and became a farmer in western Massachusetts in 1969, supplementing his income by teaching at the University of Massachusetts. He soon began to write about farming, publishing *Mother Walker and the Pig Tragedy* in 1972, writing and codirecting *Crisis in Yankee Agriculture*, for which he won a blue ribbon from the American Film Festival in 1979, and publishing *Three Farms: Making Milk, Meat, and Money from the American Soil* in 1980. *Three Farms* required Kramer to make repeated visits over several years to his subject farms: a small dairy operation in Massachusetts, a larger hog farm in Iowa, and a huge corporate farm in California. In 1983, Kramer published another in-depth study of a field of work affected by mechanization and specialization, *Invasive Procedures: A Year in the World of Two Surgeons.* He is now at work on another book "about people whose lives are tangled up with changing technology and new businesses." "The Ruination of the Tomato" was first published in *The Atlantic* in January 1980.

Sagebrush and lizards rattle and whisper behind me. I stand in   1
the moonlight, the hot desert at my back. It's tomato harvest time, 3 A.M. The moon is almost full and near to setting. Before me stretches the first lush tomato field to be taken this morning. The field is farmed by a company called Tejon Agricultural Partners, and lies three hours northeast of Los Angeles in the middle of the bleak, silvery drylands of California's San Joaquin Valley. Seven hundred sixty-six acres, more than a mile square of tomatoes— a shaggy, vegetable-green rug dappled with murky red dots, 105,708,000 ripe tomatoes lurking in the night. The field is large and absolutely level. It would take an hour and a half to walk around it. Yet, when I raise my eyes past the field to the much vaster valley floor, and to the mountains that loom farther out, the enormous crop is lost in a big flat world.

This harvest happens nearly without people. A hundred million   2
tomatoes grown, irrigated, fed, sprayed, now taken, soon to be cooled, squashed, boiled, barreled, and held at the ready, then canned, shipped, sold, bought, and after being sold and bought a few more times, uncanned and dumped on pizza. And such is the magnitude of the vista, and the dearth of human presence, that it is easy to look elsewhere and put this routine thing out of mind. But that quality—of blandness overlaying a wondrous integration of technology, finances, personnel, and business systems—seems to be what the "future" has in store.

Three large tractors steam up the road toward me, headlights   3
glaring, towing three thin-latticed towers which support floodlights. The tractors drag the towers into place around an assembly field, then hydraulic arms raise them to vertical. They illuminate a large, sandy work yard where equipment is gathering—fuel trucks, repair trucks, concession trucks, harvesters, tractor-trailers towing

big open hoppers. Now small crews of Mexicans, their sunburns tinted light blue in the glare of the three searchlights, climb aboard the harvesters; shadowy drivers mount tractors and trucks. The night fills with the scent of diesel fumes and with the sound of large engines running evenly.

The six harvesting machines drift across the gray-green tomato-leaf sea. After a time, the distant ones come to look like steamboats afloat across a wide bay. The engine sounds are dispersed. A company foreman dashes past, tally sheets in hand. He stops nearby only long enough to deliver a one-liner. "We're knocking them out like Johnny-be-good," he says, punching the air slowly with his right fist. Then he runs off, laughing. 4

The nearest harvester draws steadily closer, moving in at about the speed of a slow amble, roaring as it comes. Up close, it looks like the aftermath of a collision between a grandstand and a San Francisco tram car. It's two stories high, rolls on wheels that don't seem large enough, astraddle a wide row of jumbled and unstaked tomato vines. It is not streamlined. Gangways, catwalks, gates, conveyors, roofs, and ladders are fastened all over the lumbering rig. As it closes in, its front end snuffles up whole tomato plants as surely as a hungry pig loose in a farmer's garden. Its hind end excretes a steady stream of stems and rejects. Between the ingestion and the elimination, fourteen laborers face each other on long benches. They sit on either side of a conveyor that moves the new harvest rapidly past them. Their hands dart out and back as they sort through the red stream in front of them. 5

Watching them is like peering into the dining car of a passing train. The folks aboard, though, are not dining but working hard for low wages, culling what is not quite fit for pizza sauce—the "greens," "molds," "mechanicals," and the odd tomato-sized clod of dirt which has gotten past the shakers and screens that tug tomato from vine and dump the harvest onto the conveyor. 6

The absorbing nature of the work is according to plan. The workers aboard this tiny outpost of a tomato sauce factory are attempting to accomplish a chore at which they cannot possibly succeed, one designed in the near past by some anonymous practitioner of the new craft of *management*. As per cannery contract, each truckload of tomatoes must contain no more than 4 percent green tomatoes, 3 percent tomatoes suffering mechanical damage from the harvester, 1 percent tomatoes that have begun to mold, and .5 percent clods of dirt. 7

"The whole idea of this thing," a farm executive had explained earlier in the day, "is to get as many tons as you can per hour. Now, the people culling on the machines strive to sort everything 8 that's defective. But to us, that's as bad as them picking out too little. We're getting $40 to $47 a ton for tomatoes—a bad price this year—and each truckload is 50,000 pounds, 25 tons, 1100 bucks a load. If we're allowed 7 or 8 percent defective tomatoes in the load and we don't have 7 or 8 percent defective tomatoes in the load, we're giving away money. And what's worse, we're paying these guys to make the load too good. It's a double loss. Still, you can't say to your guys, 'Hey, leave 4 percent greens and 1 percent molds when you sort the tomatoes on that belt.' It's impossible. On most jobs you strive for perfection. They do. But you want to stop them just the right amount short of perfection—because the cannery will penalize you if your load goes over spec. So what you do is run the belt too fast, and sample the percentages in the output from each machine. If the load is too poor, we add another worker. If it's too good, we send someone home.''

The workers converse as they ride the machine toward the edge   9
of the desert. Their lips move in an exaggerated manner, but they don't shout. The few workers still needed at harvest time have learned not to fight the machine. They speak under, rather than over, the din of the harvest. They chat, and their hands stay constantly in fast motion.

Until a few years ago, it took a crowd of perhaps 600 laborers to   10
harvest a crop this size. The six machines want about a hundred workers tonight—a hundred workers for 100 million tomatoes, a million tomatoes per worker in the course of the month it will take to clear the field. The trucks come and go. The harvesters sweep back and forth across the field slowly. Now one stands still in midfield. A big service truck of the sort that tends jet planes drives across the field toward it, dome light flashing. It seems that whatever breaks can be fixed here.

After the first survey, there is nothing new to see. It will be this   11
way for the entire month. Like so many scenes in the new agriculture, the essence of this technological miracle is its productivity, and that is reflected in the very uneventfulness of the event. The miracle is permeated with the air of everyday-ness. Each detail must have persons behind it—the inventions and techniques signal insights into systems, corporate decisions, labor meetings, contracts, phone calls, handshakes, hidden skills, management guidelines. Yet the operation is smooth-skinned. Almost nothing anyone does here requires manual skills or craft beyond the ability to drive and follow orders. And everyone—top to bottom—has his orders.

The workday mood leaves the gentleman standing next to me in   12
good humor. We'll call him Johnny Riley, and at this harvest time

he is still a well placed official at this farm. He is fiftyish and has a
neatly trimmed black beard. His eyebrows and eyelashes match the
beard, and his whole face, round, ruddy, and boyish, beams behind
heavy, black-framed glasses. He's a glad-hander, a toucher, with
double-knit everything, a winning smile that demands acknowl-
edgement, and praise to give out. It is enjoyable to talk with him.

"There are too many people out here on the job with their   13
meters running. We can't afford trouble with tomato prices so low.
If something hasn't been planned right, and it costs us extra money
to get it straightened out, it's my ass," he says.

The tomato harvester that has been closing for some time, bear-   14
ing down on our outpost by the edge of the field, is now dangerously near. Behind the monster stretches a mile-and-a-quarter-
long row of uprooted stubble, shredded leaves, piles of dirt, and
smashed tomatoes. Still Johnny Riley holds his ground. He has to
raise his voice to make himself heard.

"I don't like to blow my own horn," he shouts, "but there are   15
secrets to agriculture you just have to find out for yourself. Here's
one case in point. It may seem small to you at first, but profits come
from doing the small things right. And one of the things I've found
over the years is that a long row is better. Here's why. When you
get to the end of a row, the machine here . . ." Riley gestures up at
the harvester, notices our plight, and obligingly leads me to one
side. He continues, ". . . the machine here has to turn around
before it can go back the other way. And that's when people get off
and smoke. Long rows keep them on the job more minutes per
hour. You've got less turns with long rows, and the people don't
notice this. Especially at night, with lights on, row length is an
important tool for people management. Three fourths of the growers don't realize that. I shouldn't tell you so—it sounds like I'm
patting myself on the back—but they don't."

And sure enough, as the harvester climbs off the edge of the   16
tomato field and commences its turn on the sandy work road, the
crew members descend from the catwalk, scramble to the ground,
and light up cigarettes. Johnny Riley nods knowingly to me, then
nods again as a young fellow in a John Deere cap drives out of the
darkness in a yellow pickup to join us in the circle of light the
harvester has brought with it. It's as if he arrived to meet
the harvester—which, it turns out, is what he did do. He is introduced as Buck Klein. Riley seems avuncular and proud as he talks
about him.

"He's the field supervisor. Just a few years ago he was delivering   17
material for a fertilizer company. Soon he was their dispatcher,
then took orders. He organized the job. He came here to do pes-

ticides, and we've been moving him up." Buck Klein keeps a neutral face for the length of this history, for which I admire him. He is of average height, sturdily built, sports a brush moustache that matches his short, dark blond hair. He wears a western shirt, a belt with a huge buckle that says "Cotton" on it, and cowboy boots. He has come on business.

"We just got a truck back," he says, "all the way from the 18 cannery at Fullerton—three hundred miles of travel and it's back with an unacceptable load. It's got 12 percent mechanical damages, so something's beating on the tomatoes. And this is the machine that's been doing it."

Johnny Riley appears to think for a moment. "We had three 19 loads like that today. Seven percent, 11 percent, and 17 percent mechanicals. You got to take the truck back, get some workers to take out the center of the load and put in some real good tomatoes before you send it back. It ties up workers, and it ties up a truck."

Buck and I join the crew for one lap of harvesting. Then, while 20 the crew members smoke, Buck and a staff mechanic go at the machine with wrenches and screwdrivers. Finally, it is fixed. As we drive off in his truck, Buck talks about the nature of corporate farming. "We have budget sheets for every crop. It's what the management spends their time worrying about, instead of how to make the crops better. It's all high finance. It makes sense, if you think about what they have in it. But I'll tell you something. It's expensive to farm here."

Buck points across the darkness, to the lights of the assembly 21 yard. "Just beyond those lights there's a guy owns a piece—a section of land, and he grows tomatoes there, too. A guy who works with the harvesters here, he knows tomatoes pretty well. And he says that guy has a break-even of about 18 tons—18 tons of $40 tomatoes pay his costs, and he's watching every row, growing better than 30 tons to the acre. Our break-even is 24 tons. Why? Because we're so much bigger. They give me more acres than I feel I can watch that closely. The partnership charges 35 bucks an acre management fee, good prices for this and that in the budget. And there is a stack of management people here, where that guy drives his own tractor while he thinks about what to do next. You can't beat him. This is not simple enough here.

"Here, they're so big, and yet they are always looking for a way 22 to cut a dollar out of your budget. Trying to get more and more efficient. It's the workers who they see as the big expense here. They say, okay, management is us, but maybe we can cut out some of those people on the harvesting machines. We can rent these machines from the custom harvester company for $6 a ton bare.

We got to pay the workers by the hour even when we're holding up the picking. Twenty workers to a machine some nights and $2.90 a worker is 58 bucks for an hour of down time. You keep moving or send people home.

"Of course this will all be a thing of the past soon. There's a new   23
machine out—Blackwelder makes it—and it's not an experimental model. I mean, it's on the job, at $104,000 and up a shot, and it still pays. It does the same work, only better, with only two workers on it. It's faster, and there's no labor bill. It's an electronic sort. It has a blue belt and little fingers and electric eyes, and when it spots a tomato that isn't right, the little fingers push it out of the way. You just set the amount of greens you want left alone, and it does that, too. We're going to have two of them running later in the harvest, soon as they finish another job."

"What about the workers who have always followed the tomato   24
harvest?" I ask.

"They're in trouble," says Buck, shaking his head. "They'll still   25
be needed, but only toward the end of the harvest. At the beginning, most of what these cullers take away is greens. The electric eye can do that. But at the end of the harvest, most of what they take away is spoiled reds, stuff that gets overripe before we pick it, and they say the machines don't do that as well. That leaves a lot of workers on welfare, or whatever they can get, hanging around waiting for the little bit we need them. They get upset about being sent away. This one guy trying to get his sister on a machine, he's been coming up to me all evening saying things about the other workers. I just ignore it, though. It's all part of the job, I guess."

The trouble in which California farm labor finds itself is old   26
trouble. And yet, just a few years ago, when harvesting of cannery tomatoes was still done by hand, ten times the labor was required on the same acreage to handle a harvest that yielded only a third of what Tejon Agricultural Partners and other growers expect these days. The transformation of the tomato industry has happened in the course of about twenty years.

Much has been written recently about this phenomenon, and   27
with good reason. The change has been dramatic, and is extreme. Tomatoes we remember from the past tasted rich, delicate, and juicy. Tomatoes hauled home in today's grocery bag taste bland, tough, and dry. The new taste is the taste of modern agriculture.

The ruination of the tomato was a complex procedure. It re-   28
quired cooperation from financial, engineering, marketing, scientific, and agricultural parties that used to go their separate ways more and cross paths with less intention. Now larger institutions

control the money that consumers spend on tomatoes. It is no more possible to isolate a "cause" for this shift than it is possible to claim that it's the spark plugs that cause a car to run. However, we can at least peer at the intricate machinery that has taken away our tasty tomatoes and given us pale, scientific fruit.

Let us start then, somewhat arbitrarily, with processors of 29 tomatoes, especially with the four canners—Del Monte, Heinz, Campbell, and Libby, McNeill & Libby—that sell 72 percent of the nation's tomato sauce. What has happened to the quality of tomatoes in general follows from developments in the cannery tomato trade.

The increasingly integrated processors have consolidated, 30 shifted, and "reconceptualized" their plants. In the fast world of marketing processed tomatoes, the last thing executives want is to be caught with too many cans of pizza sauce, fancy grade, when the marketplace is starved for commercial catsup. What processors do nowadays is capture the tomatoes and process them until they are clean and dead, but still near enough to the head of the assembly line so they have not yet gone past the squeezer that issues tomato juice or the sluice gate leading to the spaghetti sauce vat, the paste vat, the aspic tank, or the cauldrons of anything in particular. The mashed stuff of tomato products is stored until demand is clear. Then it's processed the rest of the way. The new manufacturing concept is known in the trade as aseptic barreling, and it leads to success by means of procrastination.

The growers supplying the raw materials for these tightly con- 31 trolled processors have contracted in advance of planting season for the sale of their crops. It's the only way to get in. At the same time, perhaps stimulated by this new guaranteed marketplace—or perhaps stimulating it—these surviving growers of tomatoes have greatly expanded the size of their planting. The interaction of large growers and large processors has thus crowded many smaller growers out of the marketplace, not because they can't grow tomatoes as cheaply as the big growers (they can) but because they can't provide large enough units of production to attract favorable contracts with any of the few canners in their area.

In turn, the increasing size of tomato-growing operations has 32 encouraged and been encouraged by a number of developments in technology. Harvesters (which may have been the "cause" precipitating the other changes in the system) have in large part replaced persons in the fields. But the new machines became practical only after the development of other technological components—especially new varieties of tomato bred for machine harvesting, and new chemicals that make machine harvesting economical.

What is remarkable about the tomato from the grower's point of   33
view is its rapid increase in popularity. In 1920, each American ate
18.1 pounds of tomato. These days we each eat 50.5 pounds of
tomato. Half a million acres of cropland grow tomatoes, yielding
nearly 9 million tons, worth over $900 million on the market.
Today's California tomato acre yields 24 tons, while the same acre
in 1960 yielded 17 tons and in 1940, 8 tons.

The increased consumption of tomatoes reflects changing eating   34
habits in general. Most food we eat nowadays is prepared, at least
in part, somewhere other than in the home kitchen, and most of
the increased demand for tomatoes is for processed products—
catsup, sauce, juice, canned tomatoes, and paste for "homemade"
sauce. In the 1920s, tomatoes were grown and canned commercially from coast to coast. Small canneries persisted into the 1950s.

Tomatoes were then a labor-intensive crop, requiring planting,   35
transplanting, staking, pruning. And, important in the tale of
changing tomato technology, because tomatoes used to ripen a few
at a time, each field required three or four forays by harvesting
crews to recover successively ripening fruits. The forces that have
changed the very nature of tomato-related genetics, farming practices, labor requirements, business configurations, and buying patterns started with the necessity, built so deeply into the structure of
our economic system, for the constant perfection of capital utili-
zation.

Some critics sometimes seem to imply that the new mechaniza-   36
tion is a conspiracy fostered by fat cats up top to make their own
lives softer. But though there are, surely, greedy conspirators
mixed in with the regular folks running tomato farms and tomato
factories and tomato research facilities, the impulse for change at
each stage of the tomato transformation—from the points of view
of those effecting the change—is "the system." The system always
pressures participants to *meet the competition.*

Even in the 1920s, more tomatoes were grown commercially for   37
processing than for fresh consumption, by a ratio of about two to
one. Today the ratio has increased to about seven to one. Fifty
years ago California accounted for about an eighth of all tomatoes
grown in America. Today, California grows about 85 percent of
tomatoes. Yet as recently as fifteen years ago, California grew only
about half the tomato crop. And fifteen years ago, the mechanical
harvester first began to show up in the fields of the larger farms.

Before the harvester came, the average California planting was   38
about 45 acres. Today, plantings exceed 350 acres. Tomato production in California used to be centered in family farms around
Merced. It has now shifted to the corporate farms of Kern County,

where Tejon Agricultural Partners operates. Of the state's 4000 or so growers harvesting canning tomatoes in the late sixties, 85 percent have left the business since the mechanical harvester came around. Estimates of the number of part-time picking jobs lost go as high as 35,000.

The introduction of the harvester brought about other changes 39 too. Processors thought that tomatoes ought to have more solid material, ought to be less acid, ought to be smaller. Engineers called for tomatoes that had tougher skins and were oblong so they wouldn't roll back down tilted conveyor belts. Larger growers, more able to substitute capital for labor, wanted more tonnage per acre, resistance to cracking from sudden growth spurts that follow irrigation, leaf shade for the fruit to prevent scalding by the hot sun, determinate plant varieties that grow only so high to keep those vines in rows, out of the flood irrigation ditches.

As geneticists selectively bred for these characteristics, they lost 40 control of others. They bred for thickwalledness, less acidity, more uniform ripening, oblongness, leafiness, and high yield—and they could not also select for flavor. And while the geneticists worked on tomato characteristics, chemists were perfecting an aid of their own. Called ethylene, it is in fact also manufactured by tomato plants themselves. All in good time, it promotes reddening. Sprayed on a field of tomatoes that has reached a certain stage of maturity (about 15 percent of the field's tomatoes must have started to "jell"), the substance causes the plants to start the enzyme activity that induces redness. About half of the time a tomato spends between blossom and ripeness is spent at full size, merely growing red. (Tomatoes in the various stages of this ripening are called, in the trade, immature greens, mature greens, breakers, turnings, pinks, light reds, and reds.) Ethylene cuts this reddening time by a week or more and clears the field for its next use. It recovers investment sooner. Still more important, it complements the genetic work, producing plants with a determined and common ripening time so machines can harvest in a single pass. It guarantees precision for the growers. The large-scale manufacturing system that buys the partnership's tomatoes requires predictable results. On schedule, eight or ten or fourteen days after planes spray, the crop will be red and ready. The gas complements the work of the engineers, too, loosening the heretofore stubborn attachment of fruit and stem. It makes it easier for the new machines to shake the tomatoes free of the vines.

The result of this integrated system of tomato seed and tomato 41 chemicals and tomato hardware and tomato know-how has been, of course, the reformation of tomato business.

According to a publication of the California Agrarian Action 42
Project, a reform-oriented research group located at Davis (some of
whose findings are reflected in this article), the effects of an emerging "low-grade oligopoly" in tomato processing are discoverable.
Because of labor savings and increased efficiency of machine harvesting, the retail price of canned tomatoes should have dropped in
the five years after the machines came into the field. Instead, it
climbed 111 percent, and it did so in a period that saw the overall
price of processed fruits and vegetables climb only 76 percent.

There are "social costs" to the reorganization of the tomato proc- 43
essing industry as well. The concentration of plants concentrates
work opportunities formerly not only more plentiful but more dispersed in rural areas. It concentrates problems of herbicide, pes-
ticide, and salinity pollution.

As the new age of cannery tomato production has overpowered 44
earlier systems of production, a kind of flexibility in tomato growing, which once worked strongly to the consumer's advantage, has
been lost. The new high-technology tomato system involves substantial investment "up front" for seed, herbicides and pesticides,
machinery, water, labor, and for the "management" of growing,
marketing, and financing the crop.

In order to reduce the enormous risks that might, in the old 45
system, have fallen to single parties, today's tomato business calls
for "jointing" of the tomatoes. Growers nowadays share the burden of planting, raising, harvesting, and marketing—"farming"
together with a "joint contractor." The tomatoes grown by Johnny
Riley and Buck Klein on land held by Tejon Agricultural Partners
were grown under a joint contract with Basic Vegetable Products, Inc., of Vacaville, California. TAP's president at the time,
Jack Morgan, was previously executive vice president of Basic
Vegetable.

"Jointing" deals are expensive both to set up and to administer. 46
The tomato-growing business situation is becoming so Byzantine
that the "per unit cost of production," the cost to a grower of
producing a pound of tomatoes, is no longer the sole determinant
of who gets to grow America's tomatoes. Once, whoever could sell
the most cheaply won the competitive race to market. Today, the
cost of doing all business supersedes, for large-scale operations,
simple notions such as growing tomatoes inexpensively. Market
muscle, tax advantages, clout with financiers, control of supply, all
affect the competitive position of TAP as much as does the expense
of growing tomatoes.

The consequence of joint contracting for the consumer is a 47
higher-priced tomato. Risks that until recently were undertaken by
growers and processors and distributors separately, because they

were adversaries, are passed on to consumers now by participants that have allied. Growers are more certain they will recover the cost of production.

Howard Leach, who was president of TAP's parent company, 48 Tejon Ranch, at the time of the tomato harvest, understood very well the economic implications for consumers of joint contracting.

"Productivity lessens," Leach explained to me. "Risk to the pro- 49 ducer lessens, which is why we do it. The consumer gets more cost because the processor who puts money in will try to lower supply until it matches the anticipated demand. If you're Hunt-Wesson, you gear up to supply what you forecast that sales will be. You want an assured crop, so you contract for an agreed price. You're locked in, and so is the farming organization. But they are locked into a price they are assured of, and they are big enough to affect the supply."

Under this sort of business condition, the marketplace is fully 50 occupied by giants. It is no place for the little guy with a truckload or two of tomatoes—even if his price is right. Farmers who once planted twenty or thirty acres of cannery tomatoes as a speculative complement to other farming endeavors are for the most part out of the picture, with no place to market their crops and no place to finance their operating expenses. As John Wood, a family farmer turned corporate manager, who currently runs TAP, puts it, "The key thing today is the ability to muscle into the marketplace. These days, it's a vicious fight to do so." And Ray Peterson, the economist and former vice president of Tejon Ranch, sums up the importance of the business side of farming now that the new technology has increased the risk and scale of each venture. "Today," he says, "vegetable farming is more marketing than farming."

The "jointing" of vegetable crops integrates the farming opera- 51 tion with the marketing, processing, and vending operations so closely that it takes teams of lawyers to describe just where one leaves off and another begins. And joint contracting is only one of several sorts of financial and managerial integration with suppliers and marketers that occur in the new tomato scene. Today chemical companies consult as technical experts with farming organizations. Equipment companies consult with farming organizations about what machines will do the jobs that need doing. Operations lease equipment from leasing companies run by banks that also lend them funds to operate. Financial organizations that lend growers vast sums of capital for both development and operations receive in return not merely interest but negotiated rights to oversee some decision-making processes. Agricultural academics sit on agribusiness corporate boards.

Today the cannery tomato farmer has all but ceased to exist as a 52 discrete and identifiable being. The organizations and structures that do what farmers once did operate as part and parcel of an economy functioning at a nearly incomprehensible level of integration. So much for the tasty tomato.

LEWIS THOMAS

House Calls: Medicine Before 1937

Lewis Thomas (1913–   ) achieved sudden literary fame with the publication in 1974 of *The Lives of a Cell: Notes of a Biology Watcher*, a slim volume of essays originally published in the *New England Journal of Medicine*. He has since published two more volumes of essays from the *Journal*: *The Medusa and the Snail: More Notes of a Biology Watcher* (1979) and *Late Night Thoughts While Listening to Mahler's Ninth Symphony* (1983). Thomas's literary success should not obscure the fact that his lifework has been that of a physician and medical researcher. His volume of professional publications—about two hundred articles in scientific and medical journals—dwarfs his literary output. Thomas is a specialist in pathology and has been the dean of the medical schools at New York University and Yale. He is currently President and Chief Executive Officer at Sloan-Kettering Cancer Center in New York City. As you will see from the following excerpt from *The Youngest Science: Notes of a Medicine-Watcher* (1983), the period of Thomas's medical career corresponds almost exactly to the period in which truly modern medicine evolved.

My father took me along on house calls whenever I was around   1
the house, all through my childhood. He liked company, and I
liked watching him and listening to him. This must have started
when I was five years old, for I remember riding in the front seat
from one house to another, and back and forth from the hospital,
when my father and many of the people on the streets were wearing gauze masks; it was the 1918 influenza epidemic.

One of the frequent calls which I found fascinating was at a big   2
house on Sanford Avenue; he never parked the car in front of this
house, but usually left it, and me, a block away around the corner.
Later, he explained that the patient was a prominent Christian
Scientist, a pillar of that church. He could perfectly well have
parked in front if there had been a clearer understanding all around
of what he was up to, for it was, in its way, faith healing.

I took the greatest interest in his doctor's bag, a miniature black   3
suitcase, fitted inside to hold his stethoscope and various glass
bottles and ampules, syringes and needles, and a small metal case
for instruments. It smelled of Lysol and ether. All he had in the bag
was a handful of things. Morphine was the most important, and
the only really indispensable drug in the whole pharmacopoeia.
Digitalis was next in value. Insulin had arrived by the time he had
been practicing for twenty years, and he had it. Adrenalin was
there, in small glass ampules, in case he ran into a case of anaphylactic shock; he never did. As he drove his rounds, he talked about
the patients he was seeing.

I'm quite sure my father always hoped I would want to become a   4
doctor, and that must have been part of the reason for taking me
along on his visits. But the general drift of his conversation was
intended to make clear to me, early on, the aspect of medicine that
troubled him most all through his professional life; there were so
many people needing help, and so little that he could do for any of
them. It was necessary for him to be available, and to make all
these calls at their homes, but I was not to have the idea that he
could do anything much to change the course of their illnesses. It
was important to my father that I understand this; it was a central
feature of the profession, and a doctor should not only be prepared
for it but be even more prepared to be honest with himself about it.

It was not always easy to be honest, he said. One of his first   5
patients, who had come to see him in his new office when he was
an unknown in town, was a man complaining of grossly bloody
urine. My father examined him at length, took a sample of the
flawed urine, did a few other tests, and found himself without a
diagnosis. To buy time enough to read up on the matter, he gave
the patient a bottle of Blaud's pills, a popular iron remedy for
anemia at the time, and told him to come back to the office in four
days. The patient returned on the appointed day jubilant, carrying
a flask of crystal-clear urine, totally cured. In the following months
my father discovered that his reputation had been made by this
therapeutic triumph. The word was out, all over town, that that
new doctor, Thomas, had gifts beyond his own knowledge—this
last because of my father's outraged protests that his Blaud's pills
could have had nothing whatever to do with recovery from bloody
urine. The man had probably passed a silent kidney stone and that
was all there was to it, said my father. But he had already gained
the reputation of a healer, and it grew through all the years of his
practice, and there was nothing he could do about it.

Even now, twenty-five years after his death, I meet people from   6
time to time who lived once in Flushing, or whose parents lived

there, and I hear the same anecdotes about his abilities: children with meningitis or rheumatic fever whose lives had been saved by him, patients with pneumonia who had recovered under his care, even people with incurable endocarditis, overwhelming typhoid fever, peritonitis, whatall.

But the same stories are told about any good, hardworking 7 general practitioner of that day. Patients do get better, some of them anyway, from even the worst diseases; there are very few illnesses, like rabies, that kill all comers. Most of them tend to kill some patients and spare others, and if you are one of the lucky ones and have also had at hand a steady, knowledgeable doctor, you become convinced that the doctor saved you. My father's early instructions to me, sitting in the front of his car on his rounds, were that I should be careful not to believe this of myself if I became a doctor.

Nevertheless, despite his skepticism, he carried his prescription 8 pad everywhere and wrote voluminous prescriptions for all his patients. These were fantastic formulations, containing five or six different vegetable ingredients, each one requiring careful measuring and weighing by the druggist, who pounded the powder, dissolved it in alcohol, and bottled it with a label giving only the patient's name, the date, and the instructions about dosage. The contents were a deep mystery, and intended to be a mystery. The prescriptions were always written in Latin, to heighten the mystery. The purpose of this kind of therapy was essentially reassurance. A skilled, experienced physician might have dozens of different formulations in his memory, ready for writing out in flawless detail at a moment's notice, but all he could have predicted about them with any certainty were the variations in the degree of bitterness of taste, the color, the smell, and the likely effects of the concentrations of alcohol used as solvent. They were placebos, and they had been the principal mainstay of medicine, the sole technology, for so long a time—millennia—that they had the incantatory power of religious ritual. My father had little faith in the effectiveness of any of them, but he used them daily in his practice. They were expected by his patients; a doctor who did not provide such prescriptions would soon have no practice at all; they did no harm, so far as he could see; if nothing else, they gave the patient something to do while the illness, whatever, was working its way through its appointed course.

The United States Pharmacopoeia, an enormous book, big as the 9 family Bible, stood on a bookshelf in my father's office, along with scores of textbooks and monographs on medicine and surgery. The ingredients that went into the prescriptions, and the recipes for their compounding and administration, were contained in the

Pharmacopoeia. There was no mistaking the earnestness of that volume; it was a thousand pages of true belief: this set of ingredients was useful in pulmonary tuberculosis, that one in "acute indigestion" (the term then used for what later turned out to be coronary thrombosis), another in neurasthenia (weak nerves; almost all patients had weak nerves, one time or another), and so on, down through the known catalogue of human ailments. There was a different prescription for every circumstance, often three or four. The most popular and widely used ones were the "tonics," good for bucking up the spirits; these contained the headiest concentrations of alcohol. Opium had been the prime ingredient in the prescriptions of the nineteenth century, edited out when it was realized that great numbers of elderly people, especially "nervous" women, were sitting in their rocking chairs, addicted beyond recall.

The tradition still held when I was a medical student at Harvard. In the outpatient department of the Boston City Hospital, through which hundreds of patients filed each day for renewal of their medications, each doctor's desk had a drawerful of prescriptions already printed out to save time, needing only the doctor's signature. The most popular one, used for patients with chronic, obscure complaints, was *Elixir of I, Q, and S,* iron, quinine, and strychnine, each ingredient present in tiny amounts, dissolved in the equivalent of bourbon.

Medicine was subject to recurrent fads in therapy throughout my father's career. Long before his time, homeopathy emerged and still had many devout practitioners during his early years; this complex theory, involving what was believed to be the therapeutic value of "like versus like," and the administration of minuscule quantities of drugs that imitated the symptoms of the illness in question, took hold in the mid-nineteenth century in reaction against the powerfully toxic drugs then in common use—mercury, arsenic, bismuth, strychnine, aconite, and the like. Patients given the homeopathic drugs felt better and had a better chance of surviving, about the same as they would have had without treatment, and the theory swept the field for many decades.

A new theory, attributing all human disease to the absorption of toxins from the lower intestinal tract, achieved high fashion in the first decade of this century. "Autointoxication" became the fundamental disorder to be overcome by treatment, and the strongest measures were introduced to empty the large bowel and keep it empty. Cathartics, ingenious variations of the enema, and other devices for stimulating peristalsis took over medical therapy. My father, under persuasion by a detail man from one of the medical supply houses, purchased one of these in 1912, a round lead object the size of a bowling ball, encased in leather. This was to be loaned to the patient, who was instructed to lie flat in bed several times daily and roll it clockwise around the abdomen, following the course of the colon. My father tried it for a short while on a few patients, with discouraging results, and one day placed it atop a cigar box which he had equipped with wheels and a long string, and presented it to my eldest sister, who tugged it with pleasure around the corner to a neighbor's house. That was the last he saw of the ball until twelve years later, when the local newspaper announced in banner headlines that a Revolutionary War cannon ball had been discovered in the excavated garden behind our neighbor's yard. The ball was displayed for public view on the neighbor's mantel, to the mystification of visiting historians, who were unable to figure out the trajectory from any of the known engagements of the British or American forces; several learned papers were written on the problem. My father claimed privately to his family, swearing us to secrecy, that he had, in an indirect sense anyway, made medical history.

So far as I know, he was never caught up again by medical   13
theory. He did not believe in focal infections when this notion appeared in the 1920s, and must have lost a lucrative practice by not removing normal tonsils, appendixes, and gallbladders. When the time for psychosomatic disease arrived, he remained a skeptic. He indulged my mother by endorsing her administration of cod-liver oil to the whole family, excepting himself, and even allowed her to give us something for our nerves called Eskay's Neurophosphates, which arrived as samples from one of the pharmaceutical houses. But he never convinced himself about the value of medicine.

His long disenchantment with medical therapy was gradually   14
replaced by an interest in surgery, for which he found himself endowed with a special talent. At last, when he was in his early fifties, he decided to give up general practice and concentrate exclusively on surgery. He was very good at it, and his innate skepticism made him uniquely successful as a surgical consultant. Years later, after his death, I was told by some of his younger colleagues that his opinion was especially valued, and widely sought throughout the county, because of his known reluctance to operate on a patient until he was entirely convinced that the operation was absolutely necessary. His income must have suffered because of this, but his reputation was solidly established.

.   .   .

My father went to P & S in 1901, the College of Physicians and   15
Surgeons of Columbia University, two years after he was graduated

from Princeton. The education he received was already being influenced by the school of therapeutic nihilism for which Sir William Osler and his colleagues at Johns Hopkins had been chiefly
responsible. This was in reaction to the kind of medicine taught
and practiced in the early part of the nineteenth century, when
anything that happened to pop into the doctor's mind was tried out
for the treatment of illness. The medical literature of those years
makes horrifying reading today: paper after learned paper recounts
the benefits of bleeding, cupping, violent purging, the raising of
blisters by vesicant ointments, the immersion of the body in either
ice water or intolerably hot water, endless lists of botanical extracts
cooked up and mixed together under the influence of nothing
more than pure whim, and all these things were drilled into the
heads of medical students—most of whom learned their trade as
apprentices in the offices of older, established doctors. Osler and his
colleagues introduced a revolution in medicine. They pointed out
that most of the remedies in common use were more likely to do
harm than good, that there were only a small number of genuine
therapeutic drugs—digitalis and morphine the best of all, and they
laid out a new, highly conservative curriculum for training medical
students. By the time my father reached P & S, the principal concern of the faculty of medicine was the teaching of diagnosis. The
recognition of specific illnesses, based on what had been learned
about the natural history of disease and about the pathologic
changes in each illness, was the real task of the doctor. If he could
make an accurate diagnosis, he could forecast from this information what the likely outcome was to be for each of his patients'
illnesses.

But medical students of those decades had other hard things to   16
learn about. Prescriptions were an expected ritual, laid on as a kind
of background music for the real work of the sixteen-hour day.
First of all, the physician was expected to walk in and take over; he
became responsible for the outcome whether he could affect it or
not. Second, it was assumed that he would *stand by*, on call, until it
was over. Third, and this was probably the most important of his
duties, he would explain what had happened and what was likely
to happen. All three duties required experience to be done well.
The first two needed a mixture of intense curiosity about people in
general and an inborn capacity for affection, hard to come by but
indispensable for a good doctor. The third, the art of prediction,
needed education, and was the sole contribution of the medical
school; good medical schools produced doctors who could make
an accurate diagnosis and knew enough of the details of the natural
history of disease to be able to make a reliable prognosis. This was

all there was to science in medicine, and the store of information which made diagnosis and prognosis possible for my father's generation was something quite new in the early part of the twentieth century.

The teaching hospitals of that time were organized in much the same way as now, although they existed on a much smaller scale than in today's huge medical centers. The medical school was responsible for appointing all the physicians and surgeons who worked on the wards, and these people held academic titles on the medical school faculty. The professor and head of the Department of Medicine in P & S was also the chief of the internal medicine service in Roosevelt Hospital, the professor of surgery ran the surgical service, the pediatrics professor was in charge of all the children's wards, and so forth. The medical students were assigned in rotation to each of the clinical services during the last two years of medical school. Interns were selected from applicants who were graduates of all of the country's medical schools, and the competition for appointments in the teaching hospitals was as intense then as it is today. To be posted as intern on one of the teaching services at Roosevelt Hospital was regarded as a sure ticket for a successful career as a practitioner in the New York City area. The P & S faculty included some of the city's leading physicians and surgeons, who made ward rounds each day with an entourage of students and interns, and taught their juniors everything they knew about medicine. Through this mechanism, the interns also had opportunities to observe, at first hand, some of the imperfections of medicine.

When my father was an intern, one of the attending physicians on the P & S medical service of Roosevelt Hospital was an elderly, highly successful pomposity of New York medicine, typical of the generation trained long before the influence of Sir William Osler. This physician enjoyed the reputation of a diagnostician, with a particular skill in diagnosing typhoid fever, then the commonest disease on the wards of New York's hospitals. He placed particular reliance on the appearance of the tongue, which was universal in the medicine of that day (now entirely inexplicable, long forgotten). He believed that he could detect significant differences by palpating that organ. The ward rounds conducted by this man were, essentially, tongue rounds; each patient would stick out his tongue while the eminence took it between thumb and forefinger, feeling its texture and irregularities, then moving from bed to bed, diagnosing typhoid in its earliest stages over and over again, and turning out a week or so later to have been right, to everyone's amazement. He was a more productive carrier, using only his hands, than Typhoid Mary.

.   .   .

My medical education was, in principle, much like that of my father. The details had changed a lot since his time, especially in the fields of medical science relating to disease mechanisms; physiology and biochemistry had become far more complex and also more illuminating; microbiology and immunology had already, by the early 1930s, transformed our understanding of the causation of the major infectious diseases. But the *purpose* of the curriculum was, if anything, even more conservative than thirty years earlier. It was to teach the recognition of disease entities, their classification, their signs, symptoms, and laboratory manifestations, and how to make an accurate diagnosis. The treatment of disease was the most minor part of the curriculum, almost left out altogether. There was, to be sure, a course in pharmacology in the second year, mostly concerned with the mode of action of a handful of everyday drugs: aspirin, morphine, various cathartics, bromides, barbiturates, digitalis, a few others. Vitamin B was coming into fashion as a treatment for delirium tremens, later given up. We were provided with a thin, pocket-size book called *Useful Drugs*, one hundred pages or so, and we carried this around in our white coats when we entered the teaching wards and clinics in the third year, but I cannot recall any of our instructors ever referring to this volume. Nor do I remember much talk about treating disease at any time in the four years of medical school except by the surgeons, and most of their discussions dealt with the management of injuries, the drainage or removal of infected organs and tissues, and, to a very limited extent, the excision of cancers.

The medicine we were trained to practice was, essentially, Osler's medicine. Our task for the future was to be diagnosis and explanation. Explanation was the real business of medicine. What the ill patient and his family wanted most was to know the name of the illness, and then, if possible, what had caused it, and finally, most important of all, how it was likely to turn out.

The successes possible in diagnosis and prognosis were regarded as the triumph of medical science, and so they were. It had taken long decades of careful, painstaking observation of many patients; the publication of countless papers describing the detailed aspects of one clinical syndrome after another; more science, in the correlation of the clinical features of disease with the gross and microscopic abnormalities, contributed by several generations of pathologists. By the 1930s we thought we knew as much as could ever be known about the dominant clinical problems of the time: syphilis, tuberculosis, lobar pneumonia, typhoid, rheumatic fever, erysipelas, poliomyelitis. Most of the known varieties of cancer had been meticulously classified, and estimates of the duration of life could be made with some accuracy. The electrocardiogram had arrived, adding to the fair precision already possible in the diagnosis of heart disease. Neurology possessed methods for the localization of disease processes anywhere in the nervous system. When we had learned all that, we were ready for our M.D. degrees, and it was expected that we would find out about the actual day-to-day management of illness during our internship and residency years.

During the third and fourth years of school we also began to 22 learn something that worried us all, although it was not much talked about. On the wards of the great Boston teaching hospitals—the Peter Bent Brigham, the Massachusetts General, the Boston City Hospital, and Beth Israel—it gradually dawned on us that we didn't know much that was really useful, that we could do nothing to change the course of the great majority of the diseases we were so busy analyzing, that medicine, for all its façade as a learned profession, was in real life a profoundly ignorant occupation.

Some of this we were actually taught by our clinical professors, 23 much more we learned from each other in late-night discussions. When I am asked, as happens occasionally, which member of the Harvard faculty had the greatest influence on my education in medicine, I no longer grope for a name on that distinguished roster. What I remember now, from this distance, is the influence of my classmates. We taught each other; we may even have set careers for each other without realizing at the time that so fundamental an educational process was even going on. I am not so troubled as I used to be by the need to reform the medical school curriculum. What worries me these days is that the curriculum, whatever its sequential arrangement, has become so crowded with lectures and seminars, with such masses of data to be learned, that the students may not be having enough time to instruct each other in what may lie ahead.

The most important period for discovering what medicine would 24 be like was a three-month ward clerkship in internal medicine that was a required part of the fourth year of medical school. I applied for the clerkship at the Beth Israel Hospital, partly because of the reputation of Professor Hermann Blumgart and partly because several of my best friends were also going there. Ward rounds with Dr. Blumgart were an intellectual pleasure, also good for the soul. I

became considerably less anxious about the scale of medical ignorance as we followed him from bed to bed around the open circular
wards of the B.I. I've seen his match only three or four times since
then. He was a tall, thin, quick-moving man, with a look of high
intelligence, austerity, and warmth all at the same time. He had the
special gift of perceiving, almost instantaneously, while still approaching the bedside of a new patient, whether the problem was a
serious one or not. He seemed to do this by something like intuition; at times when there were no particular reasons for alarm that
could be sensed by others in the retinue, Blumgart would become
extremely alert and attentive, requiring the resident to present
every last detail of the history, and then moving closer to the bedside, asking his own questions of the patient, finally performing his
physical examination. To watch a master of physical diagnosis in
the execution of a complete physical examination is something of
an aesthetic experience, rather like observing a great ballet dancer
or a concert cellist. Blumgart did all this swiftly, then asked a few
more questions, then drew us away to the corridor outside the
ward for his discussion, and then his diagnosis, sometimes a death
sentence. Then back to the bedside for a brief private talk with the
patient, inaudible to the rest of us, obviously reassuring to the
patient, and on to the next bed. So far as I know, from that three
months of close contact with Blumgart for three hours every morning, he was never wrong, not once. But I can recall only three or
four patients for whom the diagnosis resulted in the possibility of
doing something to change the course of the illness, and each of
these involved calling in the surgeons to do the something—
removal of a thyroid nodule, a gallbladder, an adrenal tumor. For
the majority, the disease had to be left to run its own course, for
better or worse.

There were other masters of medicine, each as unique in his way   25
as Blumgart, surrounded every day by interns and medical students
on the wards of the other Boston hospitals.

The Boston City Hospital, the city's largest, committed to the   26
care of indigent Bostonians, was divided into five separate clinical
services, two staffed by Harvard Medical School (officially designated as the Second and Fourth services), two by Tufts, and one by
Boston University. The most spectacular chiefs on the Harvard faculty were aggregated on the City Hospital wards, drawn there in
the 1920s by the creation of the Thorndike Memorial Laboratories,
a separate research institute on the hospital grounds, directly attached by a series of ramps and tunnels to the buildings containing
the teaching wards. The Thorndike was founded by Dr. Francis
Weld Peabody, still remembered in Boston as perhaps the best of

Harvard physicians. Peabody was convinced that the study of human disease should not be conducted solely by bedside observations, as had been largely the case for the research done by physicians up to that time, nor by pure bench research in the university laboratories; he believed that the installation of a fully equipped research institute, containing laboratories for investigations of any promising line of inquiry, directly in communication with the hospital wards, offered the best opportunity for moving the field forward.

Peabody was also responsible for the initial staffing of the Thorn-   27
dike. By the time I arrived, in 1937, the array of talent was formidable: George Minot (who had already received his Nobel prize for the discovery of liver extract as a cure for pernicious anemia), William Castle (who discovered the underlying deficiency in pernicious anemia), Chester Keefer, Soma Weiss, Maxwell Finland, John Dingle, Eugene Stead—each of them running a laboratory, teaching on the wards, and providing research training for young doctors who came for two- or three-year fellowship stints from teaching hospitals across the country. The Thorndike was a marvelous experiment, a model for what were to become the major departments of medicine in other medical schools, matched at the time only by the hospital of the Rockefeller Institute in New York.

Max Finland built and then ran the infectious disease service. He   28
and his associates had done most of the definitive work on antipneumococcal sera in the treatment of lobar pneumonia, testing each new preparation of rabbit antiserum as it arrived from the Lederle Laboratories. Later, Finland's laboratories were to become a national center for the clinical evaluation of penicillin, streptomycin, chloromycetin, and all the other antibiotics which followed during the 1950s and 1960s. As early as 1937, medicine was changing into a technology based on genuine science. The signs of change were there, hard to see because of the overwhelming numbers of patients for whom we could do nothing but stand by, but unmistakably there all the same. Syphilis could be treated in its early stages, and eventually cured, by Paul Ehrlich's arsphenamine; the treatment took a long time, many months, sometimes several years. If arsphenamine was started in the late stages of the disease, when the greatest damage was under way—in the central nervous system and the major arteries—the results were rarely satisfactory—but in the earliest stages, the chancre and then the rash of secondary syphilis, the spirochete could be killed off and the Wassermann reaction reversed. The treatment was difficult and hazardous, the side effects of the arsenical drugs were appalling, sometimes fatal (I cannot imagine such a therapy being introduced

and accepted by any of today's FDA or other regulatory agencies), but it did work in many cases, and it carried a powerful message for the future: it was possible to destroy an invading microorganism, intimately embedded within the cells and tissues, without destroying the cells themselves. Chemotherapy for infectious disease in general lay somewhere ahead, and we should have known this.

Immunology was beginning to become an applied science. 29 Thanks to the basic research launched twenty years earlier by Avery, Heidelberger, and Goebbel, it was known that pneumococci possessed specific carbohydrates in their capsules which gave rise to highly specific antibodies. By the mid-1930s, rabbit antipneumococcal sera were available for the treatment of the commonest forms of lobar pneumonia. The sera were difficult and expensive to prepare, and sometimes caused overwhelming anaphylactic reactions in patients already moribund from their infection, but they produced outright cures in many patients. Pernicious anemia, a uniformly fatal disease, was spectacularly reversed by liver extract (much later found to be due to the presence of vitamin B_{12} in the extracts). Diabetes mellitus could be treated—at least to the extent of reducing the elevated blood sugar and correcting the acidosis that otherwise led to diabetic coma and death—by the insulin preparation isolated by Banting and Best. Pellagra, a common cause of death among the impoverished rural populations in the South, had become curable with Goldberger's discovery of the vitamin B complex and the subsequent identification of nicotinic acid. Diphtheria could be prevented by immunization against the toxin of diphtheria bacilli and, when it occurred, treated more or less effectively with diphtheria antitoxin.

All these things were known at the time of my internship at the 30 Boston City Hospital, but they seemed small advances indeed. The major diseases, which filled the wards to overflowing during the long winter months, were infections for which there was no treatment at all.

The two great hazards to life were tuberculosis and tertiary 31 syphilis. These were feared by everyone, in the same way that cancer is feared today. There was nothing to be done for tuberculosis except to wait it out, hoping that the body's own defense mechanisms would eventually hold the tubercle bacillus in check. Some patients were helped by collapsing the affected lung (by injecting air into the pleural space, or by removing the ribs overlying the lung), and any number of fads were introduced for therapy—mountain resorts, fresh air, sunshine, nutritious diets—but for most patients tuberculosis simply ran its own long debilitating course despite all efforts. Tertiary syphilis was even worse. The wards of insane asylums were filled with psychotic patients permanently incapacitated by this disease—"general paresis of the insane"; some benefit was claimed for fever therapy; but there were few real cures. Rheumatic fever, the commonest cause of fatal heart disease in children, was shown by Coburn to be the result of infection by hemolytic streptococci; aspirin, the only treatment available, relieved the painful arthritis in this disease but had no effect on the heart lesions. For most of the infectious diseases on the wards of the Boston City Hospital in 1937, there was nothing to be done beyond bed rest and good nursing care.

Then came the explosive news of sulfanilamide, and the start of the real revolution in medicine.   32

I remember the astonishment when the first cases of pneumococcal and streptococcal septicemia were treated in Boston in 1937. The phenomenon was almost beyond belief. Here were moribund patients, who would surely have died without treatment, improving in their appearance within a matter of hours of being given the medicine and feeling entirely well within the next day or so.   33

The professionals most deeply affected by these extraordinary events were, I think, the interns. The older physicians were equally surprised, but took the news in stride. For an intern, it was the opening of a whole new world. We had been raised to be ready for one kind of profession, and we sensed that the profession itself had changed at the moment of our entry. We knew that other molecular variations of sulfanilamide were on their way from industry, and we heard about the possibility of penicillin and other antibiotics; we became convinced, overnight, that nothing lay beyond reach for the future. Medicine was off and running.   34

ALICE BLOOM

On a Greek Holiday

Alice Bloom (1935–   ) took both her B.A. and her M.A. in English at Washington University in St. Louis. She teaches at the University of Maine in Farmington and lives at the end of a snowplow route in a house so isolated that the sound of an automobile will bring both dogs and people to the window. After living much of her adult life in Midwestern suburbs, she has recently learned how to fish for smelt and make maple syrup. Bloom has published essays in several journals, including *The Hudson Review*, where a version of "On a Greek Holiday" ap-

peared in August 1983. The following excerpt picks up after she
has set the scene, an isolated strip of bare sand to which tourists
are ferried so that they can take off as many of their clothes as
they dare and lie exposed to a burning sun that the local Greeks
avoid. Most of the women are bare-breasted. The men "lie on
their beach mats, clothed in their tiny suits," reading the latest
best-sellers or "adjusting the knobs on multiwave radios."

. . . Two women are walking toward us, at noon, across the   1
nearly deserted rocks. Most of the other swimmers and sunbathers
are up in the cafe, eating lunch under the fig trees, the grapevine.
These two women are not together, they walk several feet apart,
and they do not look at each other. One is tall and blond, dressed in
a flowered bikini and clogs, a tourist, English or American or Scandinavian or German. The other woman, a Greek, is carrying a
basket, walking quickly, and gives the impression of being on a
neighborhood errand. She is probably from one of the small old
farms—sheep, olive trees, hens, gardens, goats—that border this
stretch of sea and climb a little way into the pine and cypress
woods.

Both are smoking and both walk upright. Beyond that, there is   2
so little similarity they could belong to different planets, eras,
species, sexes. The tourist looks young, the Greek looks old; actually, she looks as old as a village well and the blonde looks like a
drawn-out infant, but there could be as little as five or ten years
difference between them.

The Greek woman is short and heavy, waistless, and is wearing a   3
black dress, a black scarf pulled low around her eyes, a black
sweater, thick black stockings, black shoes. She is stupendously
there, black but for the walnut of her face, in the white sun, against
the white space. She looks, at once, as if she could do everything
she's ever done, anything needed, and also at once, she gives off an
emanation of humor, powers, secrets, determinations, acts. She is
moving straight ahead, like a moving church, a black peaked roof,
a hot black hat, a dark tent, like a doom, a government, a force for
good and evil, an ultimatum, a determined animal. She probably
can't read, or write; she may never in her life have left this island;
but she is beautiful, she could crush you, love you, mend you,
deliver you of child or calf or lamb or illusion, bleed a pig, spear a
fish, wring a supper's neck, till a field, coax an egg into life. Her sex
is like a votive lamp flickering in a black, airless room. As she
comes closer, she begins to crochet—that's what's in her basket,
balls of cotton string and thick white lace coming off the hook and
her brown fingers.

The blond tourist, struggling along the hot pebbles in her clogs, is   4
coming back to her beach mat and friends. She looks as though she
couldn't dress a doll without having a fit of sulks and throwing it
down in a tantrum. It may not be the case, of course. She is on
holiday, on this Greek island, which fact means both money and
time. She is no doubt capable, well meaning, and by the standards
and expectations of most of the world's people, well educated and
very rich and very comfortable. She can undoubtedly read and
write, most blond people can, and has, wherever she comes from, a
vote, a voice, a degree of some kind, a job, a career perhaps, money
certainly, opinions, friends, health, talents, habits, central heating,
living relatives, personalized checks, a return ticket, a summer
wardrobe, the usual bits and clamor we all, tourists, have. But
presence, she has not. Nor authority, nor immediacy, nor joy for
the eye, nor a look of adding to the world, not of strength nor
humor nor excitement. Nearly naked, pretty, without discernible
blemish, blond, tall, tan, firm, the product of red meat and whole
milk, vitamins, orange juice, women's suffrage, freedom of religion, child labor laws, compulsory education, the anxious, dancing, lifelong attendance of uncounted numbers of furrow-browed
adults, parents, teachers, pediatricians, orthodontists, counselors,
hairdressers, diet and health and career and exercise and fashion
consultants, still, she is not much to look at. She looks wonderful,
but your eye, your heart, all in you that wants to look out on the
substance of the people of the day, doesn't care, isn't interested
long, is, in fact, diminished a little.

She could be anything—a professor of Romance languages at a   5
major university, a clerk in a Jermyn Street shop, a flight attendant,
a Stockholm lawyer, but nothing shows of that life or luck or work
or history, not world, not pain or freedom or sufficiency. What you
think of, what her person walking toward you in the fierce noon
light forces you to think of, after the momentary, automatic envy
of her perfections, is that she looks as though she's never had
enough—goods or rights or attention or half-decent days. Whether
she is or not, she looks unutterably dissatisfied and peevish. And
yet, in order to be here on this blue-white beach on this July day,
unless you are chasing your own stray goat across the rocks, requires a position of luxury, mobility, and privilege common to us
but beyond any imagining of the Greek woman who walks here
too with a basket of string and her hot, rusty clothes but who,
however, and not at all paradoxically, exudes a deep, sustained
bass note of slumbering, solid contentment.

Insofar as ignorance always makes a space, romance rushes in to   6
people it. With so little fact at hand about either of these lives, fact

that might make things plain and profound as only fact can do, there is little but romance, theories, guesswork, and yet, it seems, this accidental conjunction of women in the sun, considered, says it is not a matter of the one, the blonde, being discontent in spite of much and the other, the farm woman in black, being smugly, perhaps ignorantly content with little. That theory is too much the stuff of individual virtue, and of fairy tales: grateful peasant, happy with scraps and rags, and querulous, bitchy princess, untried, suffering every pea, pursued by frogs, awaiting a magic deliverance. Because in literal, daily fact, the Greek woman has more than the tourist, and the tourist, wherever she comes from and despite her list of equipment and privileges, is also, in literal daily fact, deprived. To see this as a possible deciphering of this scene means to stop thinking of the good life strictly in terms of goods, services, and various rights, and think instead, insofar as we can, of other, almost muted because so nearly lost to us, needs of life.

Beyond seeing that she has two arms, two good legs, a tanned   7
skin, blond hair, and friends, I know nothing about this particular tourist. Beyond knowing that she has two arms, two good legs, a face that could stop or move an army, a black dress, and can crochet lace, I know nothing about this particular peasant woman. I don't even know, it's only a clumsy guess, that "peasant" should be the qualifying adjective. I can only talk about these women as they appeared, almost a mirage in the shimmer of beach heat, almost icons, for a moment and walked past; and as they are on an island where I, too, have spent a notch of time. Whatever the Greek woman, and her kind, have enjoyed or missed, have suffered or lost in war, under dictatorship, under occupation, from men, in poverty or plenty, I don't know. The other woman, I won't further describe, won't guess at, for she is familiar to us; she is us.

I don't know in what order of importance, should that order   8
exist or be articulable, the Greek woman would place what occurs on the visible street of her life. For that is all I do see, all that we can see, and it wrings the heart, that visible street. For one thing, in most places, the street is not yet given over to the demands of the motor. The Greek is still a citizen and a large part of this day is given to whatever life goes on in public, and that life takes place on the street. Much of what we do in private, in isolation, in small personally chosen groups—eating, drinking, talking, staring into space—is, in Greece, done on the impersonal, random street. This habit of daily gathering, which is done for no particular reason, that is, there is no special occasion, lends to every day and night the feel of mild, but lively festival.

Second, among the other visible things that "underdeveloped"   9 means, it means that—due either to a generous wisdom that has survived or else to funding that is not yet available—there is not enough money for the fit to invent shelters for the unfit. For whatever reasons, the Greek woman still lives in a culture where this has not yet happened. That is, not only are the streets used by and for people, but all sorts of people are on them, still privileged to their piece of the sun, the common bread, the work, the gossip, the ongoing parade. Our children are pitying and amazed. After several days on these streets they assume that in Greece there are more fat and slow and old, more crippled and maimed, more feeble of mind and body, more blind and begging, more, in general, outcast folks than we, Americans, have. They are especially amazed at how *old* people get to be in Greece. Being young and American, and not living in New York, the only city we have that approximates the fullness and variety of a village, they assume this is evidence of extreme longevity on the one hand, and evidence of extreme bad health on the other. It was as hard to explain about American nursing homes and other asylums and institutions as it was to explain about public nudity, how archeologists find hidden ruins, and other questions that came up on the trip.

A "developed" country is seldom mysterious but always mystifying. Where do things come from and where do they go? Life can be looked at, but not often comprehended in any of its ordinary particulars: food, shelter, work, money, producing and buying and selling. The Greek woman on the beach, again for many reasons, does still live in a world that, in those particulars—food, shelter, work, product, etc.—is comprehensible. Outside the few urban, industrial areas in Greece, it is still possible to build and conduct life without the benefit of technicians, specialists, explainers, bureaucrats, middlemen, and other modern experts. This means that there is possible an understanding of, a connection with, and a lack of technological mystification to many of the elements, objects, and products commonly lived with in any day. A typical Greek house is so simple and cunning that it could be built, or destroyed, by almost anyone. This may mean less convenience, but it also means more comprehension. For the ordinary person, there is relatively little of the multiform, continual, hardly-much-thought-about incomprehensibility of daily things—where does this lamb chop come from? where does this wash water go?—that most people in developed countries live with, or manage to ignore, every day. Therefore, for this Greek woman on the beach and her kind, there is another mind possible, one that sees, and understands, and in most instances can control many details; and a mind in which, therefore, many mysteries can grow a deeper root.

Food, to take another example, is eaten in season and most of it   11
is locally grown, harvested or butchered, processed, sold, and consumed. There is no particular moral virtue in this fact, but this fact
does signify the possibility of a sharper, more acute (it sees, it has to
see and comprehend more details), and more satisfied intelligence.
Having money means being able to buy the end product; therefore,
money replaces the need for intricate knowledge of processes;
therefore, money replaces knowledge. The understanding of a glass
of water or wine, a melon, an onion, or a fried fish, from inception
to end, does mean living with a different kind of mind than the one
that results from having merely bought and consumed the wine or
fish or onion at the end. In that sense, therefore, it is possible that
the unhappy peevishness and dissatisfaction on the face of the
pretty tourist comes in part from a life of being left out of knowledge of the intricate details of the complete cycle of any single thing
she is able to consume.

Including the country of Greece.   12

There is a new world everywhere now that money will buy. It is   13
a world without a nation, though it exists as an overlay of life,
something on the order of the computer, in almost any country of
the globe. It is an international accommodation, and wherever
it exists—whether in Madrid, London, Istanbul, Athens, Cleveland—it resembles a large airport lounge. In this way, the new
world specially constructed everywhere for tourists is something
like the thousands of Greek churches, as alike as eggs, and no
matter what their size all modeled on the single great discovered
design of Constantine's Hagia Sophia.

Inside this international accommodation is allowed only so   14
much of any specific country as lends itself as background, decor,
and trinkets. In this sense, the travel posters are an accurate portrayal of exactly how little can happen on a well-engineered trip:
scenery and "gifts." Because most of the world is still what would
be termed "poor," the more money you can spend, nearly any-
place, the more you are removed from the rich, complex life of that
place. It is possible to buy everything that puts an average American life—taps that mix hot and cold, flush toilets, heating and
cooling systems, menus in English—on top of any other existing
world. It is possible to pay for every familiar security and comfort
and, as the posters show, still have been *there* having it. At the end
of the trip, you can say that you were there.

However, the extent to which one buys familiarity, in most of   15
the world today, is also the extent to which one will not see, smell,
taste, feel, or in any way be subjected to, enlightened by, or entered

by that piece of the world and its people. The world's people are
not blind to this fear of the unfamiliar and uncomfortable, nor
insensitive to the dollars that will be paid to ward it off. In the
winter months, when life returns to normal, the friendly Greek
"waiters" resume their lives as masons, carpenters, builders, mechanics, schoolteachers, and so forth, a fact unknown to or overlooked by many tourists who assume, for example, that many
unfinished buildings, seen languishing in the summer season, are
due to neglect, laziness, disinterest, or what have you.

We all assume, and usually safely, that the more money you   16
have the more you can buy. In travel, however, the opposite is
true. The less money you spend, the less money you have to spend,
perhaps, the more your chances of getting a whiff, now and then,
of what another place is like. There are the ideals: walking a country, living there, learning its language. Short of that, those conditions which most of us cannot meet, one can try spending as little
as possible: class-D hotels, public transportation, street meals. And
then one must try to be as brave and patient and good-humored
and healthy as possible because, without a doubt, the less money
you spend the closer you come to partaking of very annoying,
confusing, exhausting, foreign, debilitating, sometimes outrageous
discomfort.

For instance, the two things one would most want to avoid in   17
Greece in the summer are the intense heat and the unworldly,
unimaginable, unforeseeable amount of din. Pandemonium is, after all, a Greek idea, but in actual life, it is hardly confined to the
hour of noon. Silence is a vacuum into which, like proverbial
nature, a single Greek will rush with a pure love of noise. Two
Greeks together produce more noise than 200 of any other Western
nation. Greeks love above all else the human voice, raised in any
emotion; next to that they love their actions with objects. One
Greek with any object—a string of beads, a two-cylinder engine,
preferably one on the eternal blink, a rug to beat, a single child to
mind, a chair to be moved—will fill all time and space with his
operation; it will be the Platonic scrape of metal chair leg on stone
street; it will be the one explanation to last for all eternity why the
child should not torture the cat in the garden. A generalization:
Greeks love horns, bells, animal cries, arguments, dented fenders,
lengthy explanations, soccer games, small motors, pots and pans,
cases of empty bottles, vehicles without mufflers, cups against
saucers, fireworks, political songs, metal awnings, loudspeakers,
musical instruments, grandmothers, the Orthodox liturgy, traffic
jams, the sound of breaking glass, and Mercedes taxicabs that too-
tle "Mary Had a Little Lamb."

A further generalization: the above generalization is one that   18
only *not* spending money will buy. That is, you have to be in a
class-F room, in a hotel on the harbor, one flight above a taverna
frequented by fishermen, 120 degrees in the room, no screens,
mosquito coils burning in the unmoving air through the night, and
through the night—a donkey in heat tethered in the walled garden
below your shuttered, only shuttered, window. In other words, it's
quiet and cool, at the Hilton; and there are, God and international
capitalism be thanked, no donkeys.

SUE HUBBELL

Beekeeper

Sue Hubbell (1935–   ) was born in Kalamazoo, Michigan,
and educated at Swarthmore, the University of Michigan, the
University of Southern California, and Drexel Institute. From
1960 to 1972 she worked steadily as a bookstore manager or as a
librarian. In 1973, however, she became a beekeeper in southern
Missouri, earning a living by selling the honey produced by 18
million honeybees. In 1986, after making some modest contributions to newspapers and magazines, she published *A Country
Year: Living the Questions,* a book that immediately captured a
national audience. Like Thoreau's *Walden,* the book is built on
the cycle of the seasons, beginning with spring and ending, significantly, with a second spring. The following excerpts take us
through three seasons and give a sense of a life more independent
of contemporary technology than most of us will ever lead.

Anyone who has kept bees is a pushover for a swarm of them.   1
We always drop whatever we are doing and go off to pick one up
when asked to do so. It doesn't make sense, because from a standpoint of serious beekeeping and honey production a swarm isn't
much good. Swarms are headed up by old queens with not much
vitality or egg-laying potential left, and so a beekeeper should replace her with a new queen from a queen breeder. He will probably
have to feed and coddle the swarm through its first year; it will
seldom produce any extra honey the first season. And yet we always hive them.

There is something really odd about swarms, and I notice that   2
beekeepers don't talk about it much, probably because it is the sort

of thing we don't feel comfortable about trying to put into words, something the other side of rationality.

The second year I kept bees, I picked up my first swarm. I was in the middle of the spring beework, putting in ten to twelve hours a day, and very attuned to what the bees were doing out there in their hives. That day had begun with a heavy rainstorm, and so rather than working out in the beeyards, I was in the honey house making new equipment. By afternoon the rain had stopped, but the air was warm and heavy, charged and expectant. I began to feel odd, tense and anticipatory, and when the back of my neck began to prickle I decided to take a walk out to the new hives I had started. Near them, hanging pendulously from the branch of an apple tree, was a swarm of bees. Individual bees were still flying in from all directions, adding their numbers to those clinging around their queen.

In the springtime some colonies of bees, for reasons not well understood, obey an impulse to split in two and thus multiply by swarming. The worker bees thoughtfully raise a new queen bee for the parent colony, and then a portion of the bees gather with the old queen, gorge themselves with honey and fly out of the hive, never to return, leaving all memory of their old home behind. They cluster somewhere temporarily, such as on the branch of my apple tree. If a beekeeper doesn't hive them, scout bees fly from the cluster and investigate nearby holes and spaces, and report back to the cluster on the suitability of new quarters.

We know about two forms of honeybee communication. One is chemical: information about food sources and the wellbeing of the queen and colony is exchanged as bees continually feed one another with droplets of nectar which they have begun to process and chemically tag. The other form of communication is tactile: bees tell other bees about good things such as food or the location of a new home by patterned motions. These elaborate movements, which amount to a highly stylized map of landmarks, direction and the sun's position, are called the bee dance.

Different scout bees may find different locations for the swarm and return to dance about their finds. Eventually, sometimes after several days, an agreement is reached, rather like the arrival of the Sense of the Meeting among Quakers, and all the bees in the cluster fly off to their new home.

I watched the bees on my apple tree for a while with delight and pleasure, and then returned to the barn to gather up enough equipment to hive them. As I did so, I glanced up at the sky. It was still dark from the receding thunderstorm, but a perfect and dazzling rainbow arched shimmering against the deep blue sky, its curve making a stunning and pleasing contrast with the sharp inverted V of the barn roof. I returned to the apple tree and shook the bees into the new beehive, noticing that I was singing snatches of one of Handel's coronation anthems. It seemed as appropriate music to hive a swarm by as any I knew.

Since then, I have learned to pay attention in the springtime when the air feels electric and full of excitement. It was just so one day last week. I had been working quietly along the row of twelve hives in an outyard when the hair on the back of my neck began to stand on end. I looked up to see the air thick with bees flying in toward me from the north. The swarm was not from any of my hives, but for some reason bees often cluster near existing hives while they scout a new location. I closed up the hive I was working on and stood back to watch. I was near a slender post oak sapling, and the bees began to light on one of its lower limbs right next to my elbow. They came flying in, swirling as they descended, spiraling around me and the post oak until I was enveloped by the swarm, the air moving gently from the beat of their wings. I am not sure how long I stood there. I lost all sense of time and felt only elation, a kind of human emotional counterpart of the springlike, optimistic, burgeoning, state that the bees were in. I stood quietly; I was nothing more to the bees than an object to be encircled on their way to the spot where they had decided, in a way I could not know, to cluster. In another sense I was not remote from them at all, but was receiving all sorts of meaningful messages in the strongest way imaginable outside of human mental process and language. My skin was tingling as the bees brushed past and I felt almost a part of the swarm.

Eventually the bees settled down in the cluster. Regaining a more suitable sense of my human condition and responsibilities, I went over to my pickup and got the empty hive that I always carry with me during swarming season. I propped it up so that its entrance was just under the swarm. A frame of comb from another hive was inside and the bees in the cluster could smell it, so they began to walk up into the entrance. I watched, looking for the queen, for without her the swarm would die. It took perhaps twenty minutes for all of them to file in, and the queen, a long, elegant bee, was one of the last to enter.

I screened up the entrance and put the hive in the back of the pickup. After I was finished with my work with the other hives in the beeyard, I drove back home with my new swarm.

I should have ordered a new queen bee, killed the old one and replaced her, but in doing that I would have destroyed the identity of the swarm. Every colony of bees takes its essence, character and personality from the queen who is mother to all its members. As a commercial beekeeper, it was certainly my business to kill the old queen and replace her with a vigorous new one so that the colony would become a good honey producer.

But I did not.   12

.   .   .

This week I have started cutting my firewood. It should be cut   13
months ahead of time to let it dry and cure, so that it will burn hot in the winter. It is June now, and almost too late to be cutting firewood, but during the spring I was working with the bees from sunup until sundown and didn't have time. By midday it is stifling back in the woods, so I go out at sunrise and cut wood for a few hours, load it into the pickup and bring it back to stack below the barn.

I like being out there early. The spiders have spun webs to catch   14
night-flying insects, and as the rising sun slants through the trees, the dewdrops that line the webs are turned into exquisite, delicate jewels. The woodlot smells of shade, leaf mold and damp soil. Wild turkey have left fresh bare spots where they scratched away the leaves looking for beetles and grubs. My dogs like being there too, and today snuffled excitedly in a hollow at the base of a tree. The beagle shrieked into it, his baying muffled. The squirrel who may have denned in the tree last night temporarily escaped their notice and sat on a low limb eying the two dogs suspiciously, tail twitching. A sunbeam lit up a tall thistle topped with a luxuriant purple blossom from which one butterfly and one honeybee sipped nectar. Red-eyed vireos sang high in the treetops where I could not see them.

For me their song ended when I started the chain saw. It makes a   15
terrible racket, but I am fond of it. It is one of the first tools I learned to master on my own, and it is also important to me. My woodstove, a simple black cast-iron-and-sheet-metal affair, is the only source of heat for my cabin in the winter, and if I do not have firewood to burn in it, the dogs, cat, the houseplants, the water in my pipes and I will all freeze. It is wonderfully simple and direct: cut wood or die.

When Paul was here he cut the firewood and I, like all Ozark   16
wives, carried the cut wood to the pickup. When he left, he left his chain saw, but it was a heavy, vibrating, ill-tempered thing. I weigh a hundred and five pounds, and although I could lift it, once I had it running it shook my hands so much that it became impossibly dangerous to use. One year I hired a man to cut my wood, but I was not pleased with the job he did, and so the next year, although

I could not afford it, I bought the finest, lightest, best-made chain saw money could buy. It is a brand that many woodcutters use, and has an antivibration device built into even its smaller models.

The best chain saws are formidable and dangerous tools. My brother nearly cut off his arm with one. A neighbor who earns his living in timber just managed to kill the engine on his when he was cutting overhead and a branch snapped the saw back toward him. The chain did not stop running until it had cut through the beak of his cap. He was very solemn when I told him that I had bought my own chain saw, and he gave me a good piece of advice. "The time to worry about a chain saw," he said, "is when you stop being afraid of it." 17

I am cautious. I spend a lot of time sizing up a tree before I fell it. Once it is down, I clear away the surrounding brush before I start cutting it into lengths. That way I will not trip and lose my balance with the saw running. A dull chain and a poorly running saw are dangerous, so I've learned to keep mine in good shape and I sharpen the chain each time I use it. 18

This morning I finished sawing up a tree from the place where I had been cutting for the past week. In the process I lost, in the fallen leaves somewhere, my scrench—part screwdriver, part wrench—that I use to make adjustments on the saw. I shouldn't have been carrying it in my pocket, but the chain on the saw's bar had been loose; I had tightened it and had not walked back to the pickup to put it away. Scolding myself for being so careless, I began looking for another tree to cut, but stopped to watch a fawn that I had frightened from his night's sleeping place. He was young and his coat was still spotted, but he ran so quickly and silently that the two dogs, still sniffing after the squirrel, never saw him. 19

I like to cut the dead trees from my woodlot, leaving the ones still alive to flourish, and I noticed a big one that had recently died. This one was bigger than I feel comfortable about felling. I've been cutting my own firewood for six years now, but I am still awed by the size and weight of a tree as it crashes to the ground, and I have to nerve myself to cut the really big ones. 20

I wanted this tree to fall on a stretch of open ground that was free of other trees and brush, so I cut a wedge-shaped notch on that side of it. The theory is that the tree, thus weakened, will fall slowly in the direction of the notch when the serious cut, slightly above the notch on the other side, is made. The trouble is that trees, particularly dead ones that may have rot on the inside, do not know the theory and may fall in an unexpected direction. That is the way accidents happen. I was aware of this, and scared, besides, to be cutting down such a big tree; as a result, perhaps I cut too timid a 21 wedge. I started sawing through on the other side, keeping an eye on the tree top to detect the characteristic tremble that signals a fall. I did not have time to jam the plastic wedge in my back pocket into the cut to hold it open because the tree began to fall in my direction, exactly opposite where I had intended. I killed the engine on the saw and jumped out of the way.

There was no danger, however. Directly in back of where I had been standing were a number of other trees, which was why I had wanted to have the sawed one fall in the opposite direction; as my big tree started to topple, its upper branches snagged in another one, and it fell no further. I had sawed completely through the tree, but now the butt end had trapped my saw against the stump. I had cut what is descriptively called a "widow maker." If I had been cutting with someone else, we could have used a second saw to cut out mine and perhaps brought down the tree, but this is dangerous and I don't like to do it. I could not even free my saw by taking it apart, for I had lost my scrench, so I drove back to the barn and gathered up the tools I needed; a socket wrench, chains and a portable winch known as come-along. A come-along is a cheery, sensible tool for a woman. It has a big hook at one end and another hook connected to a steel cable at the other. The cable is wound around a ratchet gear operated by a long handle to give leverage. It divides a heavy job up into small manageable bits that require no more than female strength, and I have used it many times to pull my pickup free from mud and snow.

The day was warming up and I was sweating by the time I got back to the woods, but I was determined to repair the botch I had made of the morning's woodcutting. Using the socket wrench, I removed the bar and chain from the saw's body and set it aside. The weight of the saw gone, I worked free the bar and chain pinched under the butt of the tree. Then I sat down on the ground, drank ice water from my thermos and figured out how I was going to pull down the tree.

Looking at the widow maker, I decided that if I could wind one of the chains around the butt of it, and another chain around a nearby standing tree, then connect the two with the come-along, I might be able to winch the tree to the ground. I attached the chains and come-along appropriately and began. Slowly, with each pump of the handle against the ratchet gear, the tree sank to the ground.

The sun was high in the sky, the heat oppressive and my shirt and jeans were soaked with sweat, so I decided to leave the job of cutting up the tree until tomorrow. I gathered my tools together, and in the process found the scrench, almost hidden in the leaf mold. Then I threw all the tools into the back of the pickup, and sat on the tailgate to finish off the rest of the ice water and listen to the red-eyed vireo singing.

It is satisfying, of course, to build up a supply of winter warmth, 26 free except for the labor. But there is also something heady about becoming a part of the forest process. It sounds straightforward enough to say that when I cut firewood I cull and thin my woods, but that puts me in the business of deciding which trees should be encouraged and which should be taken.

I like my great tall black walnut, so I have cut the trees around it 27 to give it the space and light it needs to grow generously. Dog-woods don't care. They frost the woods with white blossoms in the spring, and grow extravagantly in close company. If I clear a patch, within a year or two pine seedlings move in, grow up exuberantly, compete and thin themselves to tolerable spacing. If I don't cut a diseased tree, its neighbors may sicken and die. If I cut away one half of a forked white oak, the remaining trunk will grow straight and sturdy. Sap gone, a standing dead tree like the one I cut today will make good firewood, and so invites cutting. But if I leave it, it will make a home for woodpeckers, and later for flying squirrels and screech owls. Where I leave a brush pile of top branches, rabbits make a home. If I leave a fallen tree, others will benefit: ants, spiders, beetles and wood roaches will use it for shelter and food, and lovely delicate fungi will grow out of it before it mixes with leaf mold to become a part of a new layer of soil.

One person with a chain saw makes a difference in the woods, 28 and by making a difference becomes part of the woodland cycle, a part of the abstraction that is the forest community.

.   .   .

I keep twenty hives of bees here in my home beeyard, but most 29 of my hives are scattered in outyards across the Ozarks, where I can find the thickest stands of wild blackberries and other good things for bees. I always have a waiting list of farmers who would like the bees on their land, for the clover in their pastures is more abundant when the bees are there to pollinate it.

One of the farmers, a third-generation Ozarker and a dairyman 30 with a lively interest in bees, came over today for a look at what my neighbors call my honey factory. My honey house contains a shiny array of stainless-steel tanks with clear plastic tubing connecting them, a power uncapper for slicing open honeycomb, an extractor for spinning honey out of the comb, and a lot of machinery and equipment that whirs, thumps, hums and looks very special. The dairyman, shrewd in mountain ways, looked it all over carefully and then observed, "Well . . . ll . . . ll, wouldn't say for sure now, but it looks like a still to me."

There have been droughty years and cold wet ones when flowers 31 refused to bloom and I would have been better off with a still back up here on my mountain top, but the weather this past year was perfect from a bee's standpoint, and this August I ran 33,000 pounds of honey through my factory. This was nearly twice the normal crop, and everything was overloaded, starting with me. Neither I nor my equipment is set up to handle this sort of harvest, even with extra help.

I always need to hire someone, a strong young man who is not 32 afraid of being stung, to help me harvest the honey from the hives.

The honey I take is the surplus that the bees will not need for the 33 winter; they store it above their hives in wooden boxes called supers. To take it from them, I stand behind each hive with a gasoline-powered machine called a beeblower and blow the bees out of the supers with a jet of air. Meanwhile, the strong young man carries the supers, which weigh about sixty pounds each, and stacks them on pallets in the truck. There may be thirty to fifty supers in every outyard, and we have only about half an hour to get them off the hives, stacked and covered before the bees get really cross about what we are doing. The season to take the honey in this part of the country is summer's end, when the temperature is often above ninety-five degrees. The nature of the work and the temper of the bees require that we wear protective clothing while doing the job: a full set of coveralls, a zippered bee veil and leather gloves. Even a very strong young man works up a considerable sweat wrapped in a bee suit in hot weather hustling sixty-pound supers—being harassed by angry bees at the same time.

This year my helper has been Ky, my nephew, who wanted to 34 learn something about bees and beekeeping. He is a sweet, gentle, cooperative giant of a young man who, because of a series of physical problems, lacks confidence in his own ability to get on in the world.

As soon as he arrived, I set about to desensitize him to bee stings. 35 The first day, I put a piece of ice on his arm to numb it; then, holding the bee carefully by her head, I placed her abdomen on the numbed spot and let her sting him there. A bee's stinger is barbed and stays in the flesh, pulling loose from her body as she struggles to free herself. Lacking her stinger, the bee will live only a short time. The bulbous poison sac at the top of the stinger continues to pulsate after the bee has left, its muscles pumping the venom and forcing the barbed stinger deeper into the flesh.

I wanted Ky to have only a partial dose of venom that first day, 36
so after a minute I scraped the stinger out with my fingernail and
watched his reaction closely. A few people—about one percent of
the population—are seriously sensitive to bee venom. Each sting
they receive can cause a more severe reaction than the one before,
reactions ranging from hives, difficulty in breathing and accelerated
heartbeat, to choking, anaphylactic shock and death. Ky had been
stung a few times in his life and didn't think he was seriously
allergic, but I wanted to make sure.

The spot where the stinger went in grew red and began to swell. 37
This was a normal reaction, and so was the itchiness that Ky felt
the next day. That time I let a bee sting him again, repeating the
procedure, but leaving the stinger in his arm a full ten minutes,
until the venom sac was emptied. Again the spot was red, swollen
and itchy, but had disappeared the next day. Thereafter Ky decided
that he didn't need the ice cube any more, and began holding the
bee himself to administer his own stings. I kept him at one sting a
day until he had no redness or swelling from the full sting, and
then had him increase to two stings daily. Again the greater
amount of venom caused redness and swelling, but soon his body
could tolerate them without an allergic reaction. I gradually had
him build up to ten full stings a day with no reaction.

To encourage Ky, I had told him that what he was doing might 38
help protect him from the arthritis that runs in our family.
Beekeepers generally believe that getting stung by bees is a healthy
thing, and that bee venom alleviates the symptoms of arthritis.
When I first began keeping bees, I supposed this to be just another
one of the old wives' tales that make beekeeping such an entertaining occupation, but after my hands were stung the pain in my
fingers disappeared and I too became a believer. Ky was polite,
amused and skeptical of what I told him, but he welcomed my
taking a few companionable stings on my knuckles along with him.

In desensitizing Ky to bee venom, I had simply been interested in 39
building up his tolerance to stings so that he could be an effective
helper when we took the honey from the hives, for I knew that he
would be stung frequently. But I discovered that there had been a
secondary effect on Ky that was more important: he was enormously pleased with himself for having passed through what he
evidently regarded as a rite of initiation. He was proud and delighted in telling other people about the whole process. He was
now one tough guy.

I hoped he was prepared well enough for our first day of work. I 40
have had enough strong young men work for me to know what
would happen the first day: he would be stung royally.

Some beekeepers insist that bees know their keeper—that they   41
won't sting that person, but *will* sting a stranger. This is nonsense,
for summertime bees live only six weeks and I often open a particular hive less frequently than that, so I am usually a stranger to my
bees; yet I am seldom stung. Others say that bees can sense fear or
nervousness. I don't know if this is true or not, but I do know that
bees' eyes are constructed in such a way that they can detect dis-
continuities and movement very well and stationary objects less
well. This means that a person near their hives who moves with
rapid, jerky motions attracts their attention and will more often be
blamed by the bees when their hives are being meddled with than
will the person whose motions are calm and easy. It has been my
experience that the strong young man I hire for the honey harvest
is always stung unmercifully for the first few days while he is new
to the process and a bit tense. Then he learns to become easier with
the bees and settles down to his job. As he gains confidence and
assurance, the bees calm down too, and by the end of the harvest
he usually is only stung a few times a day.

I knew that Ky very much wanted to do a good job with me that   42
initial day working in the outyards. I had explained the procedures
we would follow in taking the honey from the hives, but of course
they were new to him and he was anxious. The bees from the first
hive I opened flung themselves on him. Most of the stingers could
not penetrate his bee suit, but in the act of stinging a bee leaves a
chemical trace that marks the person stung as an enemy, a chemical sign other bees can read easily. This sign was read by the bees in
each new hive I opened, and soon Ky's bee suit began to look like a
pincushion, bristling with stingers. In addition, the temperature
was starting to climb and Ky was sweating. Honey oozing from
combs broken between the supers was running down the front of
his bee suit when he carried them to the truck. Honey and sweat
made the suit cling to him, so that the stingers of angry bees could
penetrate the suit and he could feel the prick of each one as it
entered his skin. Hundreds of bees were assaulting him and finally
drove him out of the beeyard, chasing him several hundred yards
before they gave up the attack. There was little I could do to help
him but try to complete the job quickly, so I took the supers off the
next few hives myself, carried them to the truck and loaded them.
Bravely, Ky returned to finish the last few hives. We tied down the
load and drove away. His face was red with exertion when he
unzipped his bee veil. He didn't have much to say as we drove to
the next yard, but sat beside me gulping down ice water from the
thermos bottle.

At the second yard the bees didn't bother Ky as we set up the   43 equipment. I hoped that much of the chemical marker the bees had left on him had evaporated, but as soon as I began to open the hives they were after him again. Soon a cloud of angry bees enveloped him, accompanying him to the truck and back. Because of the terrain, the truck had to be parked at an odd angle and Ky had to bend from the hips as he loaded it, stretching the fabric of the bee suit taut across the entire length of his back and rear, allowing the bees to sting through it easily. We couldn't talk over the noise of the beeblower's engine, but I was worried about how he was taking hundreds more stings. I was removing the bees from the supers as quickly as I could, but the yard was a good one and there were a lot of supers there.

In about an hour's time Ky carried and stacked what we later   44
weighed in as a load of 2,500 pounds. The temperature must have been nearly a hundred degrees. After he had stacked the last super, I drove the truck away from the hives and we tied down the load. Ky's long hair was plastered to his face and I couldn't see the expression on it, but I knew he had been pushed to his limits and I was concerned about him. He tried to brush some of the stingers out of the seat of his bee suit before he sat down next to me in the truck in an uncommonly gingerly way. Unzipping his bee veil, he tossed it aside, pushed the hair back from his sweaty face, reached for the thermos bottle, gave me a sunny and triumphant grin and said, "If I ever get arthritis of the ass, I'll know all that stuff you've been telling me is a lot of baloney."

                              ·   ·   ·

My farm lies north of town. After the first two miles, the black   45
top gives way to a five-mile stretch of rocky road that shakes apart the pickups my neighbors and I drive. My mailbox is at the junction of this road and a mile-and-a-half gravel lane that meanders between it and the cabin, skirting the cliffs of the river that runs fast and clear below. Lichens, ferns and mosses grow there, and wind and rain have eroded caves and root holds for scrubby, twisted trees on the cliff faces. The thin soil at the top sustains a richer growth, and in the springtime the cliff top is abloom, first with serviceberry, then redbud and dogwood. In the summer, oaks shade the lane, grass grows in the middle of it, and black-eyed Susans grow beside it. In the winter, winds howl up out of the river gorge, driving snow across the lane in drifts so deep that sometimes I am marooned for a week or more.

I returned yesterday from a honey-selling trip and was grateful,   46
as I always am, to turn at the mailbox and head down my lane. I drive a big three-quarter ton white truck on these trips, one fitted

out to carry a 5,000-pound load, a truck new enough to be repaired if it should break down in Hackensack without hours of poking around in a salvage yard, the source of parts for "Press on Regardless."

The white truck is commodious and dependable, and I am fond   47
of it. It is a part of my life. One night I dropped off to sleep after reading about the nature of the soul. I dreamed about my own soul, and found that it is a female white truck, buoyant, impatient, one that speeds along, almost too fast in an exhilarating way, skimming slightly above the road, not quite keeping to the pathway. I rather enjoy having a soul of that sort.

Like many of my neighbors, I am poor. I live on an income well   48
below the poverty line—although it does not seem like poverty when the redbud and dogwood are in bloom together—and when I travel I have to be careful about expenses. I eat in restaurants as little as possible, and I sleep in the truck: I pull into a truck stop, unroll my sleeping bag on the front seat and sleep there, as warm and comfortable as can be. In the morning I brush my teeth in the truck-stop restroom, and have my morning coffee in the restaurant. When I travel, people seldom notice or talk to me. I am unnoticeable in my ordinariness. If I were young and pretty, I might attract attention. But I am too old to be pretty, and rumpled besides, so I am invisible. This delights me, for I can sit in a booth at the truck stop, drink my coffee and watch without being watched.

One morning I was having coffee at 5:30 A.M., snugged up in a   49
booth in a truck stop in New Mexico. The truckers were eating their breakfasts, straddling the stools at the horseshoe-shaped counter. A three-sided projection screen hung from the ceiling, showing slides that changed every minute or so. The truckers watched, absorbed, as the slides alternated between the animate and the inanimate. A supertruck, dazzling in the sunshine, every tailpipe and chrome strip gleaming, was followed by a D-cup woman, pouring out of her teeny dress, provocatively pumping gasoline into a truck. The next slide was a low shot of a truck grille; this was followed by a scene with a plump blonde in a cute cop outfit, showing rather more breast and crotch than one would think regulation, arresting a naughty trucker.

I watched the truckers as they watched the screen, chewing   50
away on the leathery eggs-over-easy, their eyes glassy, as intent on chrome as on flesh. I finished my coffee and drove on unnoticed.

The trip I returned from yesterday was to Dallas, and as sales   51
trips go, it was a good one. Its maze of freeways make it easy to get around, and I was grateful to the food buyers, who placed Texas-sized orders.

On the way to Dallas I stopped for lunch at an Oklahoma restau- 52
rant which had big windows facing the parking lot. Seeing the
signs on my truck proclaiming my business and home town, the
man at the cash register gave me a big grin when I walked inside
and asked, "You the sweetest thing in Missouri?"

If there is one skill I have learned from living in the Ozarks, it is 53
how to talk Good Old Boy, so I quickly replied, "Shore am," and
took my seat at a table to order a bowl of soup. As I paid the tab,
my new friend inquired about the honey business; when he found
out that my truck was loaded with honey for sale in Dallas, he
bought a case for the restaurant gift shop and asked to be put on my
mailing list. "Now that's Joe Ben Ponder, you hear? Joe *Ben*," he
said in his soft southern Oklahoma drawl.

It seemed like an auspicious beginning for a sales trip, and I 54
badly needed a good one. I had just returned from Boston and New
York, where sales had been poor, although the trip was good in
some ways. In Boston I stayed with Liddy and Brian, and one
evening they took me to the Harvard chapel, where Gustav
Leonhardt played a program of baroque music on the chapel organ.
It was beautiful and I enjoyed it; I also enjoyed seeing other friends
and relatives whom I love and see too seldom, but I did not make
any money. In New York there are stores on every corner that sell
French bread, marvelous cheeses, imported salmon, exquisite del-
icacies and honey, some of it made by my honeybees. But then
there is another such store in the middle of the block. The customers are spread thin, and many places where I have sold honey for
years have fired their managers and hired new ones, groping for a
formula that will bring in the dollars once again. Macy's and
Zabar's were having a war, and their buyers had no time for me.
Sales elsewhere were poor, too, for it cut no French mustard with
new managers that honey from my bees had been selling in the
store for ten years. I drove up to Westchester and southern Connecticut to set up new accounts in the suburbs.

In my worn jeans and steel-toed work boots, one of which has a 55
hole in it from the time I dripped battery acid on it, I wandered
through those fashionable towns peddling honey, towns filled with
women out buying things to drape on themselves, and things to
put in their houses, and things to take care of the things hanging on
themselves and the things in their houses.

Twenty or twenty-five years ago I lived on the edge of lives like 56
these. In those days the women used to drive station wagons, and
today they drive sleek little cars, but the look of strain on their faces
is the same today as it was back then. I was glad to escape that life
then and at the end of the sales day I was glad to escape in my

white truck and head westward onto the Interstates with their
green signs and truck stops, toward Missouri, toward my wild
mountain top, toward home.

WENDELL BERRY

Against PCs

Wendell Berry (1934–   ) is a poet, novelist, and essayist with
an increasingly wide readership. Born in rural Kentucky, Berry
took a B.A. and M.A. from the University of Kentucky and
taught briefly at New York University before returning to his
native state to farm and teach. Among his books of poetry are *The
Broken Ground* (1964), *Openings* (1968), *Farming: A Handbook*
(1970), and *Collected Poems* (1985). Many of his short stories and
novels are set in the fictional Kentucky town of Port William and
involve the tensions created caring for land and exploiting it. His
essays are collected in such volumes as *The Unsettling of America:
Culture and Agriculture* (1977) and *Standing by Words* (1983).
Berry lives on and continues to work a hundred-acre farm whose
soil had been ruined by unsound practices aimed at increasing
the previous owners' short-term profits. He lives near farmland
that has been destroyed by strip mining. A good deal of his labor,
physical and literary, goes into undoing the damage he sees
around him. "Against PCs" initially appeared as "Why I Will Not
Buy a Computer" in *New England Review and Bread Loaf Quarterly*
(Autumn 1987), but was soon reprinted in *Harper's Magazine*.
Following Berry's essay, you will find responses from a number
of *Harper's* readers and a rejoinder by the author.

Like almost everybody else, I am hooked to the energy corpora-   1
tions, which I do not admire. I hope to become less hooked to
them. In my work, I try to be as little hooked to them as possible.
As a farmer, I do almost all of my work with horses. As a writer, I
work with a pencil or a pen and a piece of paper.

My wife types my work on a Royal standard typewriter bought   2
new in 1956, and as good now as it was then. As she types, she
sees things that are wrong, and marks them with small checks in
the margins. She is my best critic because she is the one most
familiar with my habitual errors and weaknesses. She also understands, sometimes better than I do, what *ought* to be said. We have,

I think, a literary cottage industry that works well and pleasantly. I do not see anything wrong with it.

A number of people, by now, have told me that I could greatly improve things by buying a computer. My answer is that I am not going to do it. I have several reasons, and they are good ones.

The first is the one I mentioned at the beginning. I would hate to think that my work as a writer could not be done without a direct dependence on strip-mined coal. How could I write conscientiously against the rape of nature if I were, in the act of writing, implicated in the rape? For the same reason, it matters to me that my writing is done in the daytime, without electric light.

I do not admire the computer manufacturers a great deal more than I admire the energy industries. I have seen their advertisements, attempting to seduce struggling or failing farmers into the belief that they can solve their problems by buying yet another piece of expensive equipment. I am familiar with their propaganda campaigns that have put computers into public schools in need of books. That computers are expected to become as common as TV sets in "the future" does not impress me or matter to me. I do not own a TV set. I do not see that computers are bringing us one step nearer to anything that does matter to me: peace, economic justice, ecological health, political honesty, family and community stability, good work.

What would a computer cost me? More money, for one thing, than I can afford, and more than I wish to pay to people whom I do not admire. But the cost would not be just monetary. It is well understood that technological innovation always requires the discarding of the "old model"—the "old model" in this case being not just our old Royal standard, but my wife, my critic, my closest reader, my fellow worker. Thus (and I think this is typical of present day technological innovation), what would be superseded would be not only some thing, but some body. In order to be technologically up-to-date as a writer, I would have to sacrifice an association that I am dependent upon and that I treasure.

My final and perhaps my best reason for not owning a computer is that I do not wish to fool myself. I disbelieve, and therefore strongly resent, the assertion that I or anybody else could write better or more easily with a computer than with a pencil. I do not see why I should not be as scientific about this as the next fellow: When somebody has used a computer to write work that is demonstrably better than Dante's, and when this better is demonstrably attributable to the use of a computer, then I will speak of computers with a more respectful tone of voice, though I still will not buy one.

To make myself as plain as I can, I should give my standards for   8
technological innovation in my own work. They are as follows:

1. The new tool should be cheaper than the one it replaces.

2. It should be at least as small in scale as the one it replaces.

3. It should do work that is clearly and demonstrably better than
the one it replaces.

4. It should use less energy than the one it replaces.

5. If possible, it should use some form of solar energy, such as that
of the body.

6. It should be repairable by a person of ordinary intelligence,
provided that he or she has the necessary tools.

7. It should be purchasable and repairable as near to home as
possible.

8. It should come from a small, privately-owned shop or store that
will take it back for maintenance and repair.

9. It should not replace or disrupt anything good that already exists, and this includes family and community relationships.

LETTERS OF RESPONSE

Wendell Berry ["Against PCs," Readings, September] pro-   9
vides writers enslaved by the computer with a handy alternative: Wife—a low-tech energy-saving device. Drop a pile of
handwritten notes on Wife and you get back a finished manuscript, edited while it was typed. What computer can do that?
Wife meets all of Berry's uncompromising standards for technological innovation: she's cheap, repairable near home, and
good for the family structure. Best of all, Wife is politically
correct because she breaks a writer's "direct dependence on
strip-mined coal."

History teaches us that Wife can also be used to beat rugs
and wash clothes by hand, thus eliminating the need for the
vacuum cleaner and washing machine, two more nasty machines that threaten the act of writing.

Gordon Inkeles
Miranda, Calif.

I have no quarrel with Berry because he prefers to write   10
with pencil and paper; that is his choice. But he implies that I
and others are somehow impure because we choose to write
on a computer. I do not admire the energy corporations, either. Their shortcoming is not that they produce electricity but

how they go about it. They are poorly managed because they are blind to long-term consequences. To solve this problem, wouldn't it make more sense to correct the precise error they are making rather than simply ignore their product? I would be happy to join Berry in a protest against strip mining, but I intend to keep plugging this computer into the wall with a clear conscience.

James Rhoads
Battle Creek, Mich.

I enjoyed reading Berry's declaration of intent never to buy   11
a personal computer in the same way that I enjoy reading about the belief systems of unfamiliar tribal cultures. I tried to imagine a tool that would meet Berry's criteria for superiority to his old manual typewriter. The clear winner is the quill pen. It is cheaper, smaller, more energy-efficient, humanpowered, easily repaired, and nondisruptive of existing relationships.

Berry also requires that this tool must be "clearly and de-monstrably better" than the one it replaces. But surely we all recognize by now that "better" is in the mind of the beholder. To the quill pen aficionado, the benefits obtained from elegant calligraphy might well outweigh all others.

I have no particular desire to see Berry use a word proc-   12
essor; if he doesn't like computers, that's fine with me. How-ever, I do object to his portrayal of this reluctance as a moral virtue. Many of us have found that computers can be an in-valuable tool in the fight to protect our environment. In addi-tion to helping me write, my personal computer gives me access to up-to-the-minute reports on the workings of the EPA and the nuclear industry. I participate in electronic bulle-tin boards on which environmental activists discuss strategy and warn each other about urgent legislative issues. Perhaps Berry feels that the Sierra Club should eschew modern print-ing technology, which is highly wasteful of energy, in favor of having its members hand-copy the club's magazines and other mailings each month?

Nathaniel S. Borenstein
Pittsburgh, Pa.

The value of a computer to a writer is that it is a tool not for   13
generating ideas but for typing and editing words. It is cheaper than a secretary (or a wife!) and arguably more fuel-efficient.

And it enables spouses who are not inclined to provide free labor more time to concentrate on *their* own work.

We should support alternatives both to coal-generated electricity and to IBM-style technocracy. But I am reluctant to entertain alternatives that presuppose the traditional subservience of one class to another. Let the PCs come and the wives and servants go seek more meaningful work.

Toby Koosman
Knoxville, Tenn.

Berry asks how he could write conscientiously against the   14
rape of nature if in the act of writing on a computer he was implicated in the rape. I find it ironic that a writer who sees the underlying connectedness of things would allow his diatribe against computers to be published in a magazine that carries ads for the National Rural Electric Cooperative Association, Marlboro, Phillips Petroleum, McDonnell Douglas, and, yes, even Smith-Corona. If Berry rests comfortably at night, he must be using sleeping pills.

Bradley C. Johnson
Grand Forks, N.D.

WENDELL BERRY REPLIES:

The foregoing letters surprised me with the intensity of the feel-   15
ings they expressed. According to the writers' testimony, there is nothing wrong with their computers; they are utterly satisfied with them and all that they stand for. My correspondents are certain that I am wrong and that I am, moreover, on the losing side, a side already relegated to the dustbin of history. And yet they grow huffy and condescending over my tiny dissent. What are they so anxious about?

I can only conclude that I have scratched the skin of a technolog-   16
ical fundamentalism that, like other fundamentalisms, wishes to monopolize a whole society and, therefore, cannot tolerate the smallest difference of opinion. At the slightest hint of a threat to their complacency, they repeat, like a chorus of toads, the notes sounded by their leaders in industry. The past was gloomy, drudgery-ridden, servile, meaningless, and slow. The present, thanks only to purchasable products, is meaningful, bright, lively, centralized, and fast. The future, thanks only to more purchasable

products, is going to be even better. Thus consumers become sales-
men, and the world is made safer for corporations.

I am also surprised by the meanness with which two of these   17
writers refer to my wife. In order to imply that I am a tyrant, they
suggest by both direct statement and innuendo that she is subservient, characterless, and stupid—a mere "device" easily forced to
provide meaningless "free labor." I understand that it is impossible
to make an adequate public defense of one's private life, and so I
will only point out that there are a number of kinder possibilities
that my critics have disdained to imagine: that my wife may do this
work because she wants to and likes to; that she may find some use
and some meaning in it; that she may not work for nothing. These
gentlemen obviously think themselves feminists of the most correct
and principled sort, and yet they do not hesitate to stereotype and
insult, on the basis of one fact, a woman they do not know. They
are audacious and irresponsible gossips.

In his letter, Bradley C. Johnson rushes past the possibility of   18
sense in what I said in my essay by implying that I am or ought to
be a fanatic. That I am a person of this century and am implicated
in many practices that I regret is fully acknowledged at the beginning of my essay. I did not say that I proposed to end forthwith all
my involvement in harmful technology, for I do not know how to
do that. I said merely that I want to limit such involvement, and to
a certain extent I do know how to do that. If some technology does
damage to the world—as two of the above letters seem to agree
that it does—then why is it not reasonable, and indeed moral, to
try to limit one's use of that technology? *Of course*, I think that I am
right to do this.

I would not think so, obviously, if I agreed with Nathaniel S.   19
Borenstein that " 'better' is in the mind of the beholder." But if he
truly believes this, I do not see why he bothers with his personal
computer's "up-to-the-minute reports on the workings of the EPA
and the nuclear industry" or why he wishes to be warned about
"urgent legislative issues." According to his system, the "better" in
a bureaucratic, industrial, or legislative mind is as good as the
"better" in his. His mind apparently is being subverted by an objective standard of some sort, and he had better look out.

Borenstein does not say what he does after his computer has   20
drummed him awake. I assume from his letter that he must send
donations to conservation organizations and letters to officials. Like
James Rhoads, at any rate, he has a clear conscience. But this is
what is wrong with the conservation movement. It has a clear
conscience. The guilty are always other people, and the wrong is
always somewhere else. That is why Borenstein finds his "elec-

tronic bulletin board" so handy. To the conservation movement, it is only production that causes environmental degradation; the consumption that supports the production is rarely acknowledged to be at fault. The ideal of the run-of-the-mill conservationist is to impose restraints upon production without limiting consumption or burdening the consciences of consumers.

But virtually all of our consumption now is extravagant, and 21
virtually all of it consumes the world. It is not beside the point that most electrical power comes from strip-mined coal. The history of the exploitation of the Appalachian coal fields is long, and it is available to readers. I do not see how anyone can read it and plug in any appliance with a clear conscience. If Rhoads can do so, that does not mean that his conscience is clear; it means that his conscience is not working.

To the extent that we consume, in our present circumstances, we 22
are guilty. To the extent that we guilty consumers are conservationists, we are absurd. But what can we do? Must we go on writing letters to politicians and donating to conservation organizations until the majority of our fellow citizens agree with us? Or can we do something directly to solve our share of the problem?

I am a conservationist. I believe wholeheartedly in putting pressure on the politicians and in maintaining the conservation organizations. But I wrote my little essay partly in distrust of centralization. I don't think that the government and the conservation organizations alone will ever make us a conserving society. Why do I need a centralized computer system to alert me to environmental crises? That I live every hour of every day in an environmental crisis I know from all my senses. Why then is not my first duty to reduce, so far as I can, my own consumption?

Finally, it seems to me that none of my correspondents recog- 23
nizes the innovativeness of my essay. If the use of a computer is a new idea, then a newer idea is not to use one.

NATHANIEL HAWTHORNE

The Birthmark

Nathaniel Hawthorne (1804–1864) was descended from Puritan settlers of New England, and his fiction concentrates on themes that would have been familiar to his ancestors: the striving for moral perfection, the consequences of sin, and the role of

America as a country where humanity had a chance to make a better world. Hawthorne's views on these subjects were more complex than any doctrine, however. In such novels as *The Scarlet Letter* (1850) and *The House of the Seven Gables* (1851), he suggested that overt sin may lead to salvation and that the truly endangered soul may be the one striving most proudly for purity. The danger of seeking a supernatural perfection is a common theme in Hawthorne's stories, whether the seeker is a Christian ("Young Goodman Brown"), the mythological king Midas ("The Golden Touch"), or a scientist ("Rappaccini's Daughter"). "The Birthmark" was published in Hawthorne's best-known collection of short stories, *Mosses from an Old Manse* (1846).

In the latter part of the last century there lived a man of science,   1
an eminent proficient in every branch of natural philosophy, who not long before our story opens had made experience of a spiritual affinity more attractive than any chemical one. He had left his laboratory to the care of an assistant, cleared his fine countenance from the furnace smoke, washed the stain of acids from his fingers, and persuaded a beautiful woman to become his wife. In those days, when the comparatively recent discovery of electricity and other kindred mysteries of Nature seemed to open paths into the region of miracle, it was not unusual for the love of science to rival the love of woman in its depth and absorbing energy. The higher intellect, the imagination, the spirit, and even the heart might all find their congenial aliment in pursuits which, as some of their ardent votaries believed, would ascend from one step of powerful intelligence to another, until the philosopher should lay his hand on the secret of creative force and perhaps make new worlds for himself. We know not whether Aylmer possessed this degree of faith in man's ultimate control over Nature. He had devoted himself, however, too unreservedly to scientific studies ever to be weaned from them by any second passion. His love for his young wife might prove the stronger of the two; but it could only be by intertwining itself with his love of science and uniting the strength of the latter to his own.

Such a union accordingly took place, and was attended with truly remarkable consequences and a deeply impressive moral. One day, very soon after their marriage, Aylmer sat gazing at his wife with a trouble in his countenance that grew stronger until he spoke.

"Georgiana," said he, "has it never occurred to you that the mark upon your cheek might be removed?"

"No, indeed," said she, smiling; but, perceiving the seriousness

of his manner, she blushed deeply. "To tell you the truth, it has
been so often called a charm that I was simple enough to imagine it
might be so."

"Ah, upon another face perhaps it might," replied her husband;   5
"but never on yours. No, dearest Georgiana, you came so nearly
perfect from the hand of Nature that this slightest possible defect,
which we hesitate whether to term a defect or a beauty, shocks me,
as being the visible mark of earthly imperfection."

"Shocks you, my husband!" cried Georgiana, deeply hurt; at
first reddening with momentary anger, but then bursting into tears.
"Then why did you take me from my mother's side? You cannot
love what shocks you!"

To explain this conversation, it must be mentioned that in the
centre of Georgiana's left cheek there was a singular mark, deeply
interwoven, as it were, with the texture and substance of her face.
In the usual state of her complexion—a healthy though delicate
bloom—the mark wore a tint of deeper crimson, which imperfectly
defined its shape amid the surrounding rosiness. When she blushed
it gradually became more indistinct, and finally vanished amid the
triumphant rush of blood that bathed the whole cheek with its
brilliant glow. But if any shifting motion caused her to turn pale
there was the mark again, a crimson stain upon the snow, in what
Aylmer sometimes deemed an almost fearful distinctness. Its shape
bore not a little similarity to the human hand, though of the smallest pygmy size. Georgiana's lovers were wont to say that some fairy
at her birth hour had laid her tiny hand upon the infant's cheek,
and left this impress there in token of the magic endowments that
were to give her such sway over all hearts. Many a desperate swain
would have risked life for the privilege of pressing his lips to the
mysterious hand. It must not be concealed, however, that the impression wrought by this fairy sign manual varied exceedingly according to the difference of temperament in the beholders. Some
fastidious persons—but they were exclusively of her own sex—
affirmed that the bloody hand, as they chose to call it, quite destroyed the effect of Georgiana's beauty and rendered her countenance even hideous. But it would be as reasonable to say that one
of those small blue stains which sometimes occur in the purest
statuary marble would convert the Eve of Powers[1] to a monster.
Masculine observers, if the birthmark did not heighten their admiration, contented themselves with wishing it away, that the world
might possess one living specimen of ideal loveliness without the
semblance of a flaw. After his marriage,—for he thought little or

1. Hiram Powers was a leading American sculptor of the nineteenth century.

nothing of the matter before,—Aylmer discovered that this was the case with himself.

Had she been less beautiful,—if Envy's self could have found aught else to sneer at,—he might have felt his affection heightened by the prettiness of this mimic hand, now vaguely portrayed, now lost, now stealing forth again and glimmering to and fro with every pulse of emotion that throbbed within her heart; but, seeing her otherwise so perfect, he found this one defect grow more and more intolerable with every moment of their united lives. It was the fatal flaw of humanity which Nature, in one shape or another, stamps ineffaceably on all her productions, either to imply that they are temporary and finite, or that their perfection must be wrought by toil and pain. The crimson hand expressed the ineludible gripe in which mortality clutches the highest and purest of earthly mould, degrading them into kindred with the lowest, and even with the very brutes, like whom their visible frames return to dust. In this manner, selecting it as the symbol of his wife's liability to sin, sorrow, decay, and death, Aylmer's sombre imagination was not long in rendering the birthmark a frightful object, causing him more trouble and horror than ever Georgiana's beauty, whether of soul or sense, had given him delight.

At all the seasons which should have been their happiest he invariably, and without intending it, nay, in spite of a purpose to the contrary, reverted to this one disastrous topic. Trifling as it at first appeared, it so connected itself with innumerable trains of thought and modes of feeling that it became the central point of all. With the morning twilight Aylmer opened his eyes upon his wife's face and recognized the symbol of imperfection; and when they sat together at the evening hearth his eyes wandered stealthily to her cheek, and beheld, flickering with the blaze of the wood fire, the spectral hand that wrote mortality where he would fain have worshipped. Georgiana soon learned to shudder at his gaze. It needed but a glance with the peculiar expression that his face often wore to change the roses of her cheek into a deathlike paleness, amid which the crimson hand was brought strongly out, like a bas-relief of ruby on the whitest marble.

Late one night, when the lights were growing dim so as hardly to   10
betray the stain on the poor wife's cheek, she herself, for the first time, voluntarily took up the subject.

"Do you remember, my dear Aylmer," said she, with a feeble attempt at a smile, "have you any recollection, of a dream last night about this odious hand?"

"None! none whatever!" replied Aylmer, starting; but then he added, in a dry, cold tone, affected for the sake of concealing the real depth of his emotion, "I might well dream of it; for, before I fell asleep, it had taken a pretty firm hold of my fancy."

"And you did dream of it?" continued Georgiana, hastily; for she dreaded lest a gush of tears should interrupt what she had to say. "A terrible dream! I wonder that you can forget it. Is it possible to forget this one expression?—'It is in her heart now; we must have it out!' Reflect, my husband; for by all means I would have you recall that dream."

The mind is in a sad state when Sleep, the all-involving, cannot confine her spectres within the dim region of her sway, but suffers them to break forth, affrighting this actual life with secrets that perchance belong to a deeper one. Aylmer now remembered his dream. He had fancied himself with his servant Aminadab, attempting an operation for the removal of the birthmark; but the deeper went the knife, the deeper sank the hand, until at length its tiny grasp appeared to have caught hold of Georgiana's heart; whence, however, her husband was inexorably resolved to cut or wrench it away.

When the dream had shaped itself perfectly in his memory Aylmer sat in his wife's presence with a guilty feeling. Truth often finds its way to the mind close muffled in robes of sleep, and then speaks with uncompromising directness of matters in regard to which we practise an unconscious self-deception during our waking moments. Until now he had not been aware of the tyrannizing influence acquired by one idea over his mind, and of the lengths which he might find in his heart to go for the sake of giving himself peace.

"Aylmer," resumed Georgiana, solemnly, "I know not what may be the cost to both of us to rid me of this fatal birthmark. Perhaps its removal may cause cureless deformity; or it may be the stain goes as deep as life itself. Again: do we know that there is a possibility, on any terms, of unclasping the firm gripe of this little hand which was laid upon me before I came into the world?"

"Dearest Georgiana, I have spent much thought upon the subject," hastily interrupted Aylmer. "I am convinced of the perfect practicability of its removal."

"If there be the remotest possibility of it," continued Georgiana, "let the attempt be made, at whatever risk. Danger is nothing to me; for life, while this hateful mark makes me the object of your horror and disgust,—life is a burden which I would fling down with joy. Either remove this dreadful hand, or take my wretched life! You have deep science. All the world bears witness of it. You have achieved great wonders. Cannot you remove this little, little mark, which I cover with the tips of two small fingers? Is this beyond your power, for the sake of your own peace, and to save your poor wife from madness?"

"Noblest, dearest, tenderest wife," cried Aylmer, rapturously, "doubt not my power. I have already given this matter the deepest thought—thought which might almost have enlightened me to create a being less perfect than yourself. Georgiana, you have led me deeper than ever into the heart of science. I feel myself fully competent to render this dear cheek as faultless as its fellow; and then, most beloved, what will be my triumph when I shall have corrected what Nature left imperfect in her fairest work! Even Pygmalion, when his sculptured woman assumed life, felt not greater ecstasy than mine will be."

"It is resolved, then," said Georgiana, faintly smiling. "And, 20 Aylmer, spare me not, though you should find the birthmark take refuge in my heart at last."

Her husband tenderly kissed her cheek—her right cheek—not that which bore the impress of the crimson hand.

The next day Aylmer apprised his wife of a plan that he had formed whereby he might have opportunity for the intense thought and constant watchfulness which the proposed operation would require; while Georgiana, likewise, would enjoy the perfect repose essential to its success. They were to seclude themselves in the extensive apartments occupied by Aylmer as a laboratory, and where, during his toilsome youth, he had made discoveries in the elemental powers of Nature that had roused the admiration of all the learned societies in Europe. Seated calmly in this laboratory, the pale philosopher had investigated the secrets of the highest cloud region and of the profoundest mines; he had satisfied himself of the causes that kindled and kept alive the fires of the volcano; and had explained the mystery of the fountains, and how it is that they gush forth, some so bright and pure, and others with such rich medicinal virtues, from the dark bosom of the earth. Here, too, at an earlier period, he had studied the wonders of the human frame, and attempted to fathom the very process by which Nature assimilates all her precious influences from earth and air, and from the spiritual world, to create and foster man, her masterpiece. The latter pursuit, however, Aylmer had long laid aside in unwilling recognition of the truth—against which all seekers sooner or later stumble—that our great creative Mother, while she amuses us with apparently working in the broadest sunshine, is yet severely careful to keep her own secrets, and, in spite of her pretended openness, shows us nothing but results. She permits us, indeed, to mar, but seldom to mend, and, like a jealous patentee, on no account to make. Now, however, Aylmer resumed these half-forgotten inves-

tigations; not, of course, with such hopes or wishes as first suggested them; but because they involved much physiological truth
and lay in the path of his proposed scheme for the treatment of
Georgiana.

As he led her over the threshold of the laboratory, Georgiana
was cold and tremulous. Aylmer looked cheerfully into her face,
with intent to reassure her, but was so startled with the intense
glow of the birthmark upon the whiteness of her cheek that he
could not restrain a strong convulsive shudder. His wife fainted.

"Aminadab! Aminadab!" shouted Aylmer, stamping violently
on the floor.

Forthwith there issued from an inner apartment a man of low   25
stature, but bulky frame, with shaggy hair hanging about his vis-
age, which was grimed with the vapors of the furnace. This person-
age had been Aylmer's underworker during his whole scientific
career, and was admirably fitted for that office by his great mechanical readiness, and the skill with which, while incapable of com-
prehending a single principle, he executed all the details of his
master's experiments. With his vast strength, his shaggy hair, his
smoky aspect, and the indescribable earthiness that incrusted him,
he seemed to represent man's physical nature; while Aylmer's
slender figure, and pale, intellectual face, were no less apt a type of
the spiritual element.

"Throw open the door of the boudoir, Aminadab," said Aylmer,
"and burn a pastil."

"Yes, master," answered Aminadab, looking intently at the
lifeless form of Georgiana; and then he muttered to himself, "If she
were my wife, I'd never part with that birthmark."

When Georgiana recovered consciousness she found herself
breathing an atmosphere of penetrating fragrance, the gentle potency of which had recalled her from her deathlike faintness. The
scene around her looked like enchantment. Aylmer had converted
those smoky, dingy, sombre rooms, where he had spent his brightest years in recondite pursuits, into a series of beautiful apartments
not unfit to be the secluded abode of a lovely woman. The walls
were hung with gorgeous curtains, which imparted the combination of grandeur and grace that no other species of adornment can
achieve; and, as they fell from the ceiling to the floor, their rich and
ponderous folds, concealing all angles and straight lines, appeared
to shut in the scene from infinite space. For aught Georgiana knew,
it might be a pavilion among the clouds. And Aylmer, excluding
the sunshine, which would have interfered with his chemical processes, had supplied its place with perfumed lamps, emitting flames
of various hue, but all uniting in a soft, impurpled radiance. He

now knelt by his wife's side, watching her earnestly, but without alarm; for he was confident in his science, and felt that he could draw a magic circle round her within which no evil might intrude.

"Where am I? Ah, I remember," said Georgiana, faintly; and she placed her hand over her cheek to hide the terrible mark from her husband's eyes.

"Fear not, dearest!" exclaimed he. "Do not shrink from me! 30 Believe me, Georgiana, I even rejoice in this single imperfection, since it will be such a rapture to remove it."

"O, spare me!" sadly replied his wife. "Pray do not look at it again. I never can forget that convulsive shudder."

In order to soothe Georgiana, and, as it were, to release her mind from the burden of actual things, Aylmer now put in practice some of the light and playful secrets which science had taught him among its profounder lore. Airy figures, absolutely bodiless ideas, and forms of unsubstantial beauty came and danced before her, imprinting their momentary footsteps on beams of light. Though she had some indistinct idea of the method of these optical phenomena, still the illusion was almost perfect enough to warrant the belief that her husband possessed sway over the spiritual world. Then again, when she felt a wish to look forth from her seclusion, immediately, as if her thoughts were answered, the procession of external existence flitted across a screen. The scenery and the figures of actual life were perfectly represented, but with that bewitching yet indescribable difference which always makes a picture, an image, or a shadow so much more attractive than the original. When wearied of this, Aylmer bade her cast her eyes upon a vessel containing a quantity of earth. She did so, with little interest at first; but was soon startled to perceive the germ of a plant shooting upward from the soil. Then came the slender stalk; the leaves gradually unfolded themselves; and amid them was a perfect and lovely flower.

"It is magical!" cried Georgiana. "I dare not touch it."

"Nay, pluck it," answered Aylmer,—"pluck it, and inhale its brief perfume while you may. The flower will wither in a few moments and leave nothing save its brown seed vessels; but thence may be perpetuated a race as ephemeral as itself."

But Georgiana had no sooner touched the flower than the whole 35 plant suffered a blight, its leaves turning coal-black as if by the agency of fire.

"There was too powerful a stimulus," said Aylmer, thoughtfully.

To make up for this abortive experiment, he proposed to take her portrait by a scientific process of his own invention. It was to be effected by rays of light striking upon a polished plate of metal.

Georgiana assented; but, on looking at the result, was affrighted to find the features of the portrait blurred and indefinable; while the minute figure of a hand appeared where the cheek should have been. Aylmer snatched the metallic plate and threw it into a jar of corrosive acid.

Soon, however, he forgot these mortifying failures. In the intervals of study and chemical experiment he came to her flushed and exhausted, but seemed invigorated by her presence, and spoke in glowing language of the resources of his art. He gave a history of the long dynasty of the alchemists, who spent so many ages in quest of the universal solvent by which the golden principle might be elicited from all things vile and base. Aylmer appeared to believe that, by the plainest scientific logic, it was altogether within the limits of possibility to discover this long-sought medium; "but," he added, "a philosopher who should go deep enough to acquire the power would attain too lofty a wisdom to stoop to the exercise of it." Not less singular were his opinions in regard to the elixir vitae. He more than intimated that it was at his option to concoct a liquid that should prolong life for years, perhaps interminably; but that it would produce a discord in Nature which all the world, and chiefly the quaffer of the immortal nostrum, would find cause to curse.

"Aylmer, are you in earnest?" asked Georgiana, looking at him with amazement and fear. "It is terrible to possess such power, or even to dream of possessing it."

"O, do not tremble, my love," said her husband. "I would not wrong either you or myself by working such inharmonious effects upon our lives; but I would have you consider how trifling, in comparison, is the skill requisite to remove this little hand." 40

At the mention of the birthmark, Georgiana, as usual, shrank as if a red-hot iron had touched her cheek.

Again Aylmer applied himself to his labors. She could hear his voice in the distant furnace room giving directions to Aminadab, whose harsh, uncouth, misshapen tones were audible in response, more like the grunt or growl of a brute than human speech. After hours of absence, Aylmer reappeared and proposed that she should now examine his cabinet of chemical products and natural treasures of the earth. Among the former he showed her a small vial, in which, he remarked, was contained a gentle yet most powerful fragrance, capable of impregnating all the breezes that blow across a kingdom. They were of inestimable value, the contents of that little vial; and, as he said so, he threw some of the perfume into the air and filled the room with piercing and invigorating delight.

"And what is this?" asked Georgiana, pointing to a small crystal globe containing a gold-colored liquid. "It is so beautiful to the eye that I could imagine it the elixir of life."

"In one sense it is," replied Aylmer; "or rather, the elixir of immortality. It is the most precious poison that ever was concocted in this world. By its aid I could apportion the lifetime of any mortal at whom you might point your finger. The strength of the dose would determine whether he were to linger out years, or drop dead in the midst of a breath. No king on his guarded throne could keep his life if I, in my private station, should deem that the welfare of millions justified me in depriving him of it."

"Why do you keep such a terrific drug?" inquired Georgiana   45
in horror.

"Do not mistrust me, dearest," said her husband, smiling; "its virtuous potency is yet greater than its harmful one. But see! here is a powerful cosmetic. With a few drops of this in a vase of water, freckles may be washed away as easily as the hands are cleansed. A stronger infusion would take the blood out of the cheek, and leave the rosiest beauty a pale ghost."

"Is it with this lotion that you intend to bathe my cheek?" asked Georgiana, anxiously.

"O, no," hastily replied her husband; "this is merely superficial. Your case demands a remedy that shall go deeper."

In his interviews with Georgiana, Aylmer generally made minute inquiries as to her sensations, and whether the confinement of the rooms and the temperature of the atmosphere agreed with her. These questions had such a particular drift that Georgiana began to conjecture that she was already subjected to certain physical influences, either breathed in with the fragrant air or taken with her food. She fancied likewise, but it might be altogether fancy, that there was a stirring up of her system—a strange, indefinite sensation creeping through her veins, and tingling, half painfully, half pleasurably, at her heart. Still, whenever she dared to look into the mirror, there she beheld herself pale as a white rose and with the crimson birthmark stamped upon her cheek. Not even Aylmer now hated it so much as she.

To dispel the tedium of the hours which her husband found it   50
necessary to devote to the processes of combination and analysis, Georgiana turned over the volumes of his scientific library. In many dark old tomes she met with chapters full of romance and poetry. They were the works of the philosophers of the middle ages, such as Albertus Magnus, Cornelius Agrippa, Paracelsus, and the famous friar who created the prophetic Brazen Head. All these antique naturalists stood in advance of their centuries, yet were imbued with some of their credulity, and therefore were believed,

and perhaps imagined themselves to have acquired from the investigation of Nature a power above Nature, and from physics a sway over the spiritual world. Hardly less curious and imaginative were the early volumes of the Transactions of the Royal Society, in which the members, knowing little of the limits of natural possibility, were continually recording wonders or proposing methods whereby wonders might be wrought.

But to Georgiana, the most engrossing volume was a large folio from her husband's own hand, in which he had recorded every experiment of his scientific career, its original aim, the methods adopted for its development, and its final success or failure, with the circumstances to which either event was attributable. The book, in truth, was both the history and emblem of his ardent, ambitious, imaginative, yet practical and laborious life. He handled physical details as if there were nothing beyond them; yet spiritualized them all and redeemed himself from materialism by his strong and eager aspiration towards the infinite. In his grasp the veriest clod of earth assumed a soul. Georgiana, as she read, reverenced Aylmer and loved him more profoundly than ever, but with a less entire dependence on his judgment than heretofore. Much as he had accomplished, she could not but observe that his most splendid successes were almost invariably failures, if compared with the ideal at which he aimed. His brightest diamonds were the merest pebbles, and felt to be so by himself, in comparison with the inestimable gems which lay hidden beyond his reach. The volume, rich with achievements that had won renown for its author, was yet as melancholy a record as ever mortal hand had penned. It was the sad confession and continual exemplification of the shortcomings of the composite man, the spirit burdened with clay and working in matter, and of the despair that assails the higher nature at finding itself so miserably thwarted by the earthly part. Perhaps every man of genius, in whatever sphere, might recognize the image of his own experience in Aylmer's journal.

So deeply did these reflections affect Georgiana that she laid her face upon the open volume and burst into tears. In this situation she was found by her husband.

"It is dangerous to read in a sorcerer's books," said he with a smile, though his countenance was uneasy and displeased. "Georgiana, there are pages in that volume which I can scarcely glance over and keep my senses. Take heed lest it prove detrimental to you."

"It has made me worship you more than ever," said she.

"Ah, wait for this one success," rejoined he, "then worship me if 55 you will. I shall deem myself hardly unworthy of it. But come, I have sought you for the luxury of your voice. Sing to me, dearest."

So she poured out the liquid music of her voice to quench the thirst of his spirit. He then took his leave with a boyish exuberance of gayety, assuring her that her seclusion would endure but a little longer, and that the result was already certain. Scarcely had he departed when Georgiana felt irresistibly impelled to follow him. She had forgotten to inform Aylmer of a symptom which for two or three hours past had begun to excite her attention. It was a sensation in the fatal birthmark, not painful, but which induced a restlessness throughout her system. Hastening after her husband, she intruded for the first time into the laboratory.

The first thing that struck her eye was the furnace, that hot and feverish worker, with the intense glow of its fire, which by the quantities of soot clustered above it seemed to have been burning for ages. There was a distilling apparatus in full operation. Around the room were retorts, tubes, cylinders, crucibles, and other apparatus of chemical research. An electrical machine stood ready for immediate use. The atmosphere felt oppressively close, and was tainted with gaseous odors which had been tormented forth by the processes of science. The severe and homely simplicity of the apartment, with its naked walls and brick pavement, looked strange, accustomed as Georgiana had become to the fantastic elegance of her boudoir. But what chiefly, indeed almost solely, drew her attention, was the aspect of Aylmer himself.

He was pale as death, anxious and absorbed, and hung over the furnace as if it depended upon his utmost watchfulness whether the liquid which it was distilling should be the draught of immortal happiness or misery. How different from the sanguine and joyous mien that he had assumed for Georgiana's encouragement!

"Carefully now, Aminadab; carefully, thou human machine; carefully, thou man of clay," muttered Aylmer, more to himself than his assistant. "Now, if there be a thought too much or too little, it is all over."

"Ho! ho!" mumbled Aminadab. "Look, master! look!"   60

Aylmer raised his eyes hastily, and at first reddened, then grew paler than ever, on beholding Georgiana. He rushed towards her and seized her arm with a gripe that left the print of his fingers upon it.

"Why do you come hither? Have you no trust in your husband?" cried he, impetuously. "Would you throw the blight of that fatal birthmark over my labors? It is not well done. Go, prying woman! go!"

"Nay, Aylmer," said Georgiana with the firmness of which she possessed no stinted endowment, "it is not you that have a right to complain. You mistrust your wife; you have concealed the anxiety with which you watch the development of this experiment. Think

382 *Nathaniel Hawthorne*

not so unworthily of me, my husband. Tell me all the risk we run, and fear not that I shall shrink; for my share in it is far less than your own."

"No, no, Georgiana!" said Aylmer, impatiently; "it must not be."

"I submit," replied she, calmly. "And, Aylmer, I shall quaff whatever draught you bring me; but it will be on the same principle that would induce me to take a dose of poison if offered by your hand."

"My noble wife," said Aylmer, deeply moved, "I knew not the height and depth of your nature until now. Nothing shall be concealed. Know, then, that this crimson hand, superficial as it seems, has clutched its grasp into your being with a strength of which I had no previous conception. I have already administered agents powerful enough to do aught except to change your entire physical system. Only one thing remains to be tried. If that fail us we are ruined."

"Why did you hesitate to tell me this?" asked she.

"Because, Georgiana," said Aylmer, in a low voice, "there is danger."

"Danger? There is but one danger—that this horrible stigma shall be left upon my cheek!" cried Georgiana. "Remove it, remove it, whatever be the cost, or we shall both go mad!"

"Heaven knows your words are too true," said Aylmer, sadly. "And now, dearest, return to your boudoir. In a little while all will be tested."

He conducted her back and took leave of her with a solemn tenderness which spoke far more than his words how much was now at stake. After his departure Georgiana became rapt in musings. She considered the character of Aylmer and did it completer justice than at any previous moment. Her heart exulted, while it trembled, at his honorable love—so pure and lofty that it would accept nothing less than perfection nor miserably make itself contented with an earthlier nature than he had dreamed of. She felt how much more precious was such a sentiment than that meaner kind which would have borne with the imperfection for her sake, and have been guilty of treason to holy love by degrading its perfect idea to the level of the actual; and with her whole spirit she prayed that, for a single moment, she might satisfy his highest and deepest conception. Longer than one moment she well knew it could not be; for his spirit was ever on the march, ever ascending, and each instant required something that was beyond the scope of the instant before.

The sound of her husband's footsteps aroused her. He bore a

crystal goblet containing a liquor colorless as water, but bright enough to be the draught of immortality. Aylmer was pale; but it seemed rather the consequence of a highly-wrought state of mind and tension of spirit than of fear or doubt.

"The concoction of the draught has been perfect," said he, in answer to Georgiana's look. "Unless all my science have deceived me, it cannot fail."

"Save on your account, my dearest Aylmer," observed his wife, "I might wish to put off this birthmark of mortality by relinquishing mortality itself in preference to any other mode. Life is but a sad possession to those who have attained precisely the degree of moral advancement at which I stand. Were I weaker and blinder, it might be happiness. Were I stronger, it might be endured hopefully. But, being what I find myself, methinks I am of all mortals the most fit to die."

"You are fit for heaven without tasting death!" replied her husband. "But why do we speak of dying? The draught cannot fail. Behold its effect upon this plant."

On the window seat there stood a geranium diseased with yellow blotches which had overspread all its leaves. Aylmer poured a small quantity of the liquid upon the soil in which it grew. In a little time, when the roots of the plant had taken up the moisture, the unsightly blotches began to be extinguished in a living verdure.   75

"There needed no proof," said Georgiana, quietly. "Give me the goblet. I joyfully stake all upon your word."

"Drink, then, thou lofty creature!" exclaimed Aylmer, with fervid admiration. "There is no taint of imperfection on thy spirit. Thy sensible frame, too, shall soon be all perfect."

She quaffed the liquid and returned the goblet to his hand.

"It is grateful," said she, with a placid smile. "Methinks it is like water from a heavenly fountain; for it contains I know not what of unobtrusive fragrance and deliciousness. It allays a feverish thirst that had parched me for many days. Now, dearest, let me sleep. My earthly senses are closing over my spirit like the leaves around the heart of a rose at sunset."

She spoke the last words with a gentle reluctance, as if it required almost more energy than she could command to pronounce   80
the faint and lingering syllables. Scarcely had they loitered through her lips ere she was lost in slumber. Aylmer sat by her side, watching her aspect with the emotions proper to a man the whole value of whose existence was involved in the process now to be tested. Mingled with this mood, however, was the philosophic investigation characteristic of the man of science. Not the minutest symptom escaped him. A heightened flush of the cheek, a slight irregularity

of breath, a quiver of the eyelid, a hardly perceptible tremor through the frame,—such were the details which, as the moments passed, he wrote down in his folio volume. Intense thought had set its stamp upon every previous page of that volume; but the thoughts of years were all concentrated upon the last.

While thus employed, he failed not to gaze often at the fatal hand, and not without a shudder. Yet once, by a strange and unaccountable impulse, he pressed it with his lips. His spirit recoiled, however, in the very act; and Georgiana, out of the midst of her deep sleep, moved uneasily and murmured as if in remonstrance. Again Aylmer resumed his watch. Nor was it without avail. The crimson hand, which at first had been strongly visible upon the marble paleness of Georgiana's cheek, now grew more faintly outlined. She remained not less pale than ever; but the birthmark, with every breath that came and went lost somewhat of its former distinctness. Its presence had been awful; its departure was more awful still. Watch the stain of the rainbow fading out of the sky, and you will know how that mysterious symbol passed away.

"By Heaven! it is well nigh gone!" said Aylmer to himself, in almost irrepressible ecstasy. "I can scarcely trace it now. Success! success! And now it is like the faintest rose color. The lightest flush of blood across her cheek would overcome it. But she is so pale!"

He drew aside the window curtain and suffered the light of natural day to fall into the room and rest upon her cheek. At the same time he heard a gross, hoarse chuckle, which he had long known as his servant Aminadab's expression of delight.

"Ah, clod! ah, earthly mass!" cried Aylmer, laughing in a sort of frenzy, "you have served me well! Matter and spirit—earth and heaven—have both done their part in this! Laugh, thing of the senses! You have earned the right to laugh."

These exclamations broke Georgiana's sleep. She slowly unclosed her eyes and gazed into the mirror which her husband had arranged for that purpose. A faint smile flitted over her lips when she recognized how barely perceptible was now that crimson hand which had once blazed forth with such disastrous brilliancy as to scare away all their happiness. But then her eyes sought Aylmer's face with a trouble and anxiety that he could by no means account for. 85

"My poor Aylmer!" murmured she.

"Poor? Nay, richest, happiest, most favored!" exclaimed he. "My peerless bride, it is successful! You are perfect!"

"My poor Aylmer," she repeated, with a more than human tenderness, "you have aimed loftily; you have done nobly. Do not repent that, with so high and pure a feeling, you have rejected the best the earth could offer. Aylmer, dearest Aylmer, I am dying!"

Alas! it was too true! The fatal hand had grappled with the mystery of life, and was the bond by which an angelic spirit kept itself in union with a mortal frame. As the last crimson tint of the birthmark—that sole token of human imperfection—faded from her cheek, the parting breath of the now perfect woman passed into the atmosphere, and her soul, lingering a moment near her husband, took its heavenward flight. Then a hoarse, chuckling laugh was heard again! Thus ever does the gross fatality of earth exult in its invariable triumph over the immortal essence which, in this dim sphere of half development, demands the completeness of a higher state. Yet, had Aylmer reached a profounder wisdom, he need not thus have flung away the happiness which would have woven his mortal life of the selfsame texture with the celestial. The momentary circumstance was too strong for him; he failed to look beyond the shadowy scope of time, and, living once for all in eternity, to find the perfect future in the present.

AGGRESSION

Aggression: Preview

I saw stars, and fell backwards from the speeding car into the dust of the road, my feet becoming entangled in the steel spokes of my bicycle. The white men piled out and stood over me.

"Nigger, ain' yuh learned no better sense'n tha' yet?" asked the man who hit me. "Ain' yuh learned t' say *sir* t' a white man yet?"

The absence of women, I would argue, is not a mere "result" of patriarchy or a "consequence" of sexism; it is intrinsic to the psychology of the warrior, just as war itself—and the endless preparations and celebrations it demands—may be intrinsic to the perpetuation of patriarchy.

As for me, I could not reconcile the romanticized view of war that runs like a red streak through our literature—and the glowing aura of selfless patriotism that had led us to put our lives at forfeit—with the wet, green hell from which I had barely escaped.

Almost every culture has its own version of an ideal warrior's code. . . . It has often been honored in the breach, especially in the nation-states of the epoch we call civilization. Still it remains an ideal to be realized, a guide to living that might prove useful in today's complex and vexing world.

. . . for educated men to emphasize their superiority over other people . . . by dressing differently, or by adding titles before, or letters after their names are acts that rouse competition and jealousy—emotions which, as we need scarcely draw upon biography to prove, nor ask psychology to show, have their share in encouraging a disposition towards war.

So that is what I feel about force and violence. It is, alas! the ultimate reality on this earth, but it does not always get to the front. Some people call its absences "decadence"; I call them "civilisation" and find in such interludes the chief justification for the human experiment.

If, one hundred years from now, there are still human beings capable of
thinking about the past, and if they turn their sights on our own time,
what they will see through the cross hairs of memory will be a place
very like the Arsenal, a fenced wilderness devoted to the building and
harboring of the instruments of death.

Why should we want to shoot him? What had he done to us? Weren't
we chums (the word lingers painfully in my memory)? Weren't we?
Didn't we understand him and didn't he understand us? Did either of us
imagine for an instant that he'd shoot us for all the so-and-so brigadiers
in the so-and-so British Army?

Overview and Ideas for Writing

"The war against war is going to be no holiday excursion or
camping party"—so begins William James's famous essay "The
Moral Equivalent of War" (1910). Though James wrote the essay
for the Association for International Cooperation, he did not see
humans as a particularly cooperative species: "Our ancestors have
bred pugnacity into our bone and marrow, and thousands of years
of peace won't breed it out of us." The daily newspaper often seems
to support James's view. On the front page are reports of wars,
murders, battles between rival groups; inside are stories of rapes
and domestic batterings. But whether such violence is an inevitable
outgrowth of human nature remains an unsettled question.

The first four essays in this unit approach from different perspectives the question of our supposed genetic disposition to aggression: we have the observations of an anthropologist, two students
of animal behavior, and a feminist opponent of those who market
"the premise that man is the most aggressive and bloodthirsty
creature on the face of the earth." The next three essays concern
socially sponsored violence in a warlike South American tribe, in a
group of obedient citizens from Connecticut, and in Southern racists from America's not-too-distant past. The remaining seven
selections deal with the causes and effects of warfare among modern nations. They include combat narratives, words of praise for
good soldiers, critiques of the social conditions that promote
militarism, reflections on the role of force in human affairs, and a

memoir of a childhood on one of America's largest military arsenals.

Your own writing may contribute to any of these sets of essays. As Elaine Morgan points out, the data on the biological basis of human aggression is so ambiguous that it creates "the kind of rumpus where anybody can join in." You could join by doing research that will allow you to evaluate the arguments of Morgan, Margaret Mead, and Konrad Lorenz. Has Morgan misrepresented the views of her opponents? How valid and how pertinent are Mead's examples of peaceful cultures? What criticisms can you make of Lorenz's argument that warfare has a phylogenetic basis? You might explore the various interpretations that can be placed on the behavior of Jane Goodall's chimpanzees, or you might consider the likelihood that the aggressive human behavior described in the unit's later essays is directly related to the chimps' behavior.

Your first reaction to the essays by Napoleon Chagnon, Stanley Milgram, and Richard Wright may be to ask, "How can people do such things?" This is not only a natural reaction, but a good starting point for an essay. Are there common factors that allow or encourage the violence we see in these three essays? Do the same factors help explain the violence we see in the unit's other essays? Personal experience, too, may help you understand and explain the ways societies encourage or direct aggression; you may never have been involved in the kind of violence these three essays report, but you have probably had experience with more subtle forms of confrontation and conflict.

The essays by Barbara Ehrenreich, William Manchester, George Leonard, and Virginia Woolf and the story by Frank O'Connor all focus on the ethics and psychology of the soldier. As George Leonard points out "the very idea of the 'good' warrior" seems a contradiction in terms, and yet "only the most fevered idealist would dispense entirely with soldiers and policemen." Your own writing might help you sort through some of the difficulties this quandary creates. If government-sponsored violence is ever acceptable, where do we draw the line between legitimate and illegitimate uses of it? What attitudes toward the military should we instill in our children? And what, to raise the question Virginia Woolf discusses, can private individuals without military or political power do to make warfare less likely?

Perhaps you will want to squeeze these questions into one larger, more personal question as E. M. Forster and Scott Russell Sanders do: How do you live in a world where there are "explosives above our heads as well as beneath our feet"?

KONRAD LORENZ

The Biological Basis of Human Aggression

Konrad Lorenz (1903–1989) is the founder of ethology, the
scientific study of patterns in animal behavior, and received the
Nobel Prize for Physiology or Medicine in 1973. Lorenz was
confident from an early stage in his career that many of the
behavior patterns he saw in dogs, geese, and other animals were
"phylogenetic"—that is, a part of the common genetic heritage
of species derived from a common ancestor. His investigations
were interrupted by World War II, in which he served the German army as a physician on the Eastern front; he was captured
by the Russians and held prisoner from 1944 to 1948. Not surprisingly, he became interested in the biological basis for warfare
and in 1963 published *Das sogenannte Böse*, translated into English three years later as *On Aggression*. "The Biological Basis of
Human Aggression" is excerpted from this influential book. As
you read, bear in mind that some of Lorenz's most remarkable
scientific discoveries had to do with "imprinting," the forging of
a close psychological link between, for example, mother and
child in a variety of species. What Lorenz calls "the militant
enthusiasm" stems from a combination of biologically based aggression and a kind of imprinting.

Let us imagine that an absolutely unbiased investigator on an-   1
other planet, perhaps on Mars, is examining human behavior on
earth, with the aid of a telescope whose magnification is too small
to enable him to discern individuals and follow their separate behavior, but large enough for him to observe occurrences such as
migrations of peoples, wars, and similar great historical events. He
would never gain the impression that human behavior was dictated by intelligence, still less by responsible morality. If we suppose our extraneous observer to be a being of pure reason, devoid
of instincts himself and unaware of the way in which all instincts in
general and aggression in particular can miscarry, he would be at a
complete loss how to explain history at all. The ever-recurrent
phenomena of history do not have reasonable causes. It is a mere
commonplace to say that they are caused by what common parlance so aptly terms "human nature." Unreasoning and unreasonable human nature causes two nations to compete, though no
economic necessity compels them to do so; it induces two political
parties or religions with amazingly similar programs of salvation to
fight each other bitterly, and it impels an Alexander or a Napoleon

to sacrifice millions of lives in his attempt to unite the world under his scepter. We have been taught to regard some of the persons who have committed these and similar absurdities with respect, even as "great" men, we are wont to yield to the political wisdom of those in charge, and we are all so accustomed to these phenomena that most of us fail to realize how abjectly stupid and undesirable the historical mass behavior of humanity actually is.

Having realized this, however, we cannot escape the question   2
why reasonable beings do behave so unreasonably. Undeniably, there must be superlatively strong factors which are able to overcome the commands of individual reason so completely and which are so obviously impervious to experience and learning. As Hegel[1] said, "What experience and history teach us is this—that people and governments never have learned anything from history, or acted on principles deduced from it."

All these amazing paradoxes, however, find an unconstrained   3
explanation, falling into place like the pieces of a jigsaw puzzle, if one assumes that human behavior, and particularly human social behavior, far from being determined by reason and cultural tradition alone, is still subject to all the laws prevailing in all phylogenetically adapted instinctive behavior.[2] Of these laws we possess a fair amount of knowledge from studying the instincts of animals. Indeed, if our extra-mundane observer were a knowledgeable ethologist, he would unavoidably draw the conclusion that man's social organization is very similar to that of rats, which, like humans, are social and peaceful beings within their clans, but veritable devils toward all fellow members of their species not belonging to their own community. If, furthermore, our Martian naturalist knew of the explosive rise in human populations, the ever-increasing destructiveness of weapons, and the division of mankind into a few political camps, he would not expect the future of humanity to be more rosy than that of several hostile clans of rats on a ship almost devoid of food. And this prognosis would even be optimistic, for in the case of rats, reproduction stops automatically when a certain state of overcrowding is reached while man as yet has no workable system for preventing the so-called population explosion. Furthermore, in the case of the rats it is likely that after the wholesale slaughter enough individuals would be left over to propagate the species. In the case of man, this would not be so certain after the use of the hydrogen bomb.

It is a curious paradox that the greatest gifts of man, the unique   4
faculties of conceptual thought and verbal speech which have

1. Georg Wilhelm Friedrich Hegel (1770–1831), eminent German philosopher.
2. All behavior that is part of our genetic inheritance from our prehuman ancestors.

raised him to a level high above all other creatures and given him mastery over the globe, are not altogether blessings, or at least are blessings that have to be paid for very dearly indeed. All the great dangers threatening humanity with extinction are direct consequences of conceptual thought and verbal speech. They drove man out of the paradise in which he could follow his instincts with impunity and do or not do whatever he pleased. There is much truth in the parable of the tree of knowledge and its fruit, though I want to make an addition to it to make it fit into my own picture of Adam: that apple was thoroughly unripe! Knowledge springing from conceptual thought robbed man of the security provided by his well-adapted instincts long, long before it was sufficient to provide him with an equally safe adaptation. Man is, as Arnold Gehlen has so truly said, by nature a jeopardized creature.

Conceptual thought and speech changed all man's evolution by achieving something which is equivalent to the inheritance of acquired characters. We have forgotten that the verb "inherit" had a juridic connotation long before it acquired a biological one. When a man invents, let us say, bow and arrow, not only his progeny but his entire community will inherit the knowledge and the use of these tools and possess them just as surely as organs grown on the body. Nor is their loss any more likely than the rudimentation of an organ of equal survival value. Thus, within one or two generations a process of ecological adaptation can be achieved which, in normal phylogeny and without the interference of conceptual thought, would have taken a time of an altogether different, much greater order of magnitude. Small wonder, indeed, if the evolution of social instincts and, what is even more important, social inhibitions could not keep pace with the rapid development forced on human society by the growth of traditional culture, particularly material culture. 5

Obviously, instinctive behavior mechanisms failed to cope with the new circumstances which culture unavoidably produced even at its very dawn. There is evidence that the first inventors of pebble tools, the African Australopithecines, promptly used their new weapon to kill not only game, but fellow members of their species as well. Peking Man, the Prometheus who learned to preserve fire, used it to roast his brothers: beside the first traces of the regular use of fire lie the mutilated and roasted bones of Sinanthropus pekinensis himself. 6

·   ·   ·

Not that our prehuman ancestor, even at a stage as yet devoid of moral responsibility, was a fiend incarnate; he was by no means poorer in social instincts and inhibitions than a chimpanzee, 7 which, after all, is—his irascibility not withstanding—a social and friendly creature. But whatever his innate norms of social behavior may have been, they were bound to be thrown out of gear by the invention of weapons. If humanity survived, as, after all, it did, it never achieved security from the danger of self-destruction. If moral responsibility and unwillingness to kill have indubitably increased, the ease and emotional impunity of killing have increased at the same rate. The distance at which all shooting weapons take effect screens the killer against the stimulus situation which would otherwise activate his killing inhibitions. The deep, emotional layers of our personality simply do not register the fact that the crooking of the forefinger to release a shot tears the entrails of another man. No sane man would even go rabbit hunting for pleasure if the necessity of killing his prey with his natural weapons brought home to him the full, emotional realization of what he is actually doing.

The same principle applies, to an even greater degree, to the use 8 of modern remote-control weapons. The man who presses the releasing button is so completely screened against seeing, hearing, or otherwise emotionally realizing the consequences of his action, that he can commit it with impunity—even if he is burdened with the power of imagination. Only thus can it be explained that perfectly good-natured men, who would not even smack a naughty child, proved to be perfectly able to release rockets or to lay carpets of incendiary bombs on sleeping cities, thereby committing hundreds and thousands of children to a horrible death in the flames. The fact that it is good, normal men who did this, is as eerie as any fiendish atrocity of war!

As an indirect consequence, the invention of artificial weapons 9 has brought about a most undesirable predominance of intraspecific selection within mankind. In the third chapter, in which I discussed the survival value of aggression, and also in the tenth, dealing with the structure of society in rats, I have already spoken of the manner in which competition between the fellow members of one species can produce unadaptive results when it exerts a selection pressure totally unrelated to extra-specific environment.[3]

When man, by virtue of his weapons and other tools, of his 10 clothing and of fire, had more or less mastered the inimical forces

3. In chapter three, Lorenz argues that once humans had achieved primitive technology, the natural environment no longer shaped the direction of evolution. Instead, "natural" selection came to mean selection of those who could compete most successfully with members of their own species. Thus, the evolutionary process can develop an increasingly violent or antisocial humanity.

of his extra-specific environment, a state of affairs must have prevailed in which the counter-pressures of the hostile neighboring hordes had become the chief selecting factor determining the next steps of human evolution. Small wonder indeed if it produced a dangerous excess of what has been termed the "warrior virtues" of man.

. . .

In reality, militant enthusiasm is a specialized form of communal 11 aggression, clearly distinct from and yet functionally related to the more primitive forms of petty individual aggression. Every man of normally strong emotions knows, from his own experience, the subjective phenomena that go hand in hand with the response of militant enthusiasm. A shiver runs down the back and, as more exact observation shows, along the outside of both arms. One soars elated, above all the ties of everyday life, one is ready to abandon all for the call of what, in the moment of this specific emotion, seems to be a sacred duty. All obstacles in its path become unimportant; the instinctive inhibitions against hurting or killing one's fellows lose, unfortunately, much of their power. Rational considerations, criticism, and all reasonable arguments against the behavior dictated by militant enthusiasm are silenced by an amazing reversal of all values, making them appear not only untenable but base and dishonorable. Men may enjoy the feeling of absolute righteousness even while they commit atrocities. Conceptual thought and moral responsibility are at their lowest ebb. As a Ukrainian proverb says: "When the banner is unfurled, all reason is in the trumpet."

The subjective experiences just described are correlated with the 12 following, objectively demonstrable phenomena. The tone of the entire striated musculature is raised, the carriage is stiffened, the arms are raised from the sides and slightly rotated inward so that the elbows point outward. The head is proudly raised, the chin stuck out, and the facial muscles mime the "hero face," familiar from the films. On the back and along the outer surface of the arms the hair stands on end. This is the objectively observed aspect of the shiver!

Anybody who has ever seen the corresponding behavior of the 13 male chimpanzee defending his band or family with self-sacrificing courage will doubt the purely spiritual character of human enthusiasm. The chimp, too, sticks out his chin, stiffens his body, and raises his elbows; his hair stands on end, producing a terrifying magnification of his body contours as seen from the front. The inward rotation of his arms obviously has the purpose of turning the longest-haired side outward to enhance the effect. The whole combination of body attitude and hair-raising constitutes a bluff. This is also seen when a cat humps its back, and is calculated to make the animal appear bigger and more dangerous than it really is. Our shiver, which in German poetry is called a *"heiliger Schauer,"* a "holy" shiver, turns out to be the vestige of a prehuman vegetative response of making a fur bristle which we no longer have.

To the humble seeker of biological truth there cannot be the slightest doubt that human militant enthusiasm evolved out of a communal defense response of our prehuman ancestors. The unthinking single-mindedness of the response must have been of high survival value even in a tribe of fully evolved human beings. It was necessary for the individual male to forget all his other allegiances in order to be able to dedicate himself, body and soul, to the cause of the communal battle. *"Was schert mich Weib, was schert mich Kind"*—"What do I care for wife or child," says the Napoleonic soldier in a famous poem by Heinrich Heine, and it is highly characteristic of the reaction that this poet, otherwise a caustic critic of emotional romanticism, was so unreservedly enraptured by his enthusiasm for the "great" conqueror as to find this supremely apt expression.   14

The object which militant enthusiasm tends to defend has changed with cultural development. Originally it was certainly the community of concrete, individually known members of a group, held together by the bond of personal love and friendship. With the growth of the social unit, the social norms and rites held in common by all its members became the main factor holding it together as an entity, and therewith they became automatically the symbol of the unit. By a process of true Pavlovian conditioning plus a certain amount of irreversible imprinting[4] these rather abstract values have in every human culture been substituted for the primal, concrete object of the communal defense reaction.   15

This traditionally conditioned substitution of object has important consequences for the function of militant enthusiasm. On the one hand, the abstract nature of its object can give it a definitely inhuman aspect and make it positively dangerous—what do I care for wife or child; on the other hand it makes it possible to recruit militant enthusiasm in the service of really ethical values. Without   16

---

4. The most famous example of Pavlovian conditioning is one in which dogs come to associate the ringing of a bell with the appearance of food: eventually the sound causes them to salivate. The classical instance of imprinting involves baby birds who, during a crucial stage of their development, will fix all their attention on the object nearest them and will forever after respond to that object as they would to their mother.

the concentrated dedication of militant enthusiasm neither art, nor science, nor indeed any of the great endeavors of humanity would ever have come into being. Whether enthusiasm is made to serve these endeavors, or whether man's most powerfully motivating instinct makes him go to war in some abjectly silly cause, depends almost entirely on the conditioning and/or imprinting he has undergone during certain susceptible periods of his life. There is reasonable hope that our moral responsibility may gain control over the primeval drive, but our only hope of its ever doing so rests on the humble recognition of the fact that militant enthusiasm is an instinctive response with a phylogenetically determined releasing mechanism and that the only point at which intelligent and responsible supervision can get control is in the conditioning of the response to an object which proves to be a genuine value under the scrutiny of the categorical question.[5]

Like the triumph ceremony of the greylag goose, militant enthusiasm in man is a true autonomous instinct: it has its own appetitive behavior, its own releasing mechanisms, and, like the sexual urge or any other strong instinct, it engenders a specific feeling of intense satisfaction. The strength of its seductive lure explains why intelligent men may behave as irrationally and immorally in their political as in their sexual lives. Like the triumph ceremony, it has an essential influence on the social structure of the species. Humanity is not enthusiastically combative because it is split into political parties, but it is divided into opposing camps because this is the adequate stimulus situation to arouse militant enthusiasm in a satisfying manner. "If ever a doctrine of universal salvation should gain ascendancy over the whole earth to the exclusion of all others," writes Erich von Holst, "it would at once divide into two strongly opposing factions (one's own true one and the other heretical one) and hostility and war would thrive as before, mankind being—unfortunately—what it is!" 17

The first prerequisite for rational control of an instinctive behavior pattern is the knowledge of the stimulus situation which releases it. Militant enthusiasm can be elicited with the predictability of a reflex when the following environmental situations arise. First of all, a social unit with which the subject identifies himself must appear to be threatened by some danger from outside. That which is threatened may be a concrete group of people, the family or a little community of close friends, or else it may be a larger social unit held together and symbolized by its own specific social norms and rites. As the latter assume the character of autonomous values 18

5. The categorical question ("What if everyone behaved this way?") was used as an ethical standard by Immanuel Kant (1724–1804).

... they can, quite by themselves, represent the object in whose defense militant enthusiasm can be elicited. From all this it follows that this response can be brought into play in the service of extremely different objects, ranging from the sports club to the nation, or from the most obsolete mannerisms or ceremonials to the ideal of scientific truth or of the incorruptibility of justice.

A second key stimulus which contributes enormously to the releasing of intense militant enthusiasm is the presence of a hated enemy from whom the threat to the above "values" emanates. This enemy, too, can be of a concrete or of an abstract nature. It can be "the" Jews, Huns, Boches, tyrants, etc., or abstract concepts like world capitalism, Bolshevism, fascism, and any other kind of ism; it can be heresy, dogmatism, scientific fallacy, or what not. Just as in the case of the object to be defended, the enemy against whom to defend it is extremely variable, and demagogues are well versed in the dangerous art of producing supranormal dummies to release a very dangerous form of militant enthusiasm. 19

A third factor contributing to the environmental situation eliciting the response is an inspiring leader figure. Even the most emphatically antifascistic ideologies apparently cannot do without it, as the giant pictures of leaders displayed by all kinds of political parties prove clearly enough. Again the unselectivity of the phylogenetically programmed response allows for a wide variation in the conditioning to a leader figure. Napoleon, about whom so critical a man as Heinrich Heine became so enthusiastic, does not inspire me in the least; Charles Darwin does. 20

A fourth, and perhaps the most important, prerequisite for the full eliciting of militant enthusiasm is the presence of many other individuals, all agitated by the same emotion. Their absolute number has a certain influence on the quality of the response. Smaller numbers at issue with a large majority tend to obstinate defense with the emotional value of "making a last stand," while very large numbers inspired by the same enthusiasm feel the urge to conquer the whole world in the name of their sacred cause. Here the laws of mass enthusiasm are strictly analogous to those of flock formation described in Chapter Eight;[6] here, too, the excitation grows in proportion, perhaps even in geometrical progression, with the increasing number of individuals. This is exactly what makes militant mass enthusiasm so dangerous. 21

---

6. In chapter eight, Lorenz shows that, particularly in the presence of an enemy, a wide variety of species show a nearly irresistible tendency to crowd together, surrendering the value of free movement in order to secure the safety of not being singled out as prey.

I have tried to describe, with as little emotional bias as possible, the human response of enthusiasm, its phylogenetic origin, its instinctive as well as its traditionally handed-down components and prerequisites. I hope I have made the reader realize, without actually saying so, what a jumble our philosophy of values is. What is a culture? A system of historically developed social norms and rites which are passed on from generation to generation because emotionally they are felt to be values. What is a value? Obviously, normal and healthy people are able to appreciate something as a high value for which to live and, if necessary, to die, for no other reason than that it was evolved in cultural ritualization and handed down to them by a revered elder. Is, then, a value only defined as the object on which our instinctive urge to preserve and defend traditional social norms has become fixated? Primarily and in the early stages of cultural development this indubitably was the case. The obvious advantages of loyal adherence to tradition must have exerted a considerable selection pressure. However, the greatest loyalty and obedience to culturally ritualized norms of behavior must not be mistaken for responsible morality. Even at their best, they are only functionally analogous to behavior controlled by rational responsibility. In this respect, they are no whit different from the instinctive patterns of social behavior. . . . Also they are just as prone to miscarry under circumstances for which they have not been "programmed" by the great constructor, natural selection.

In other words, the need to control, by wise rational responsibility, all our emotional allegiances to cultural values is as great as, if not greater than, the necessity to keep in check our other instincts. None of them can ever have such devastating effects as unbridled militant enthusiasm when it infects great masses and overrides all other considerations by its single-mindedness and its specious nobility. It is not enthusiasm in itself that is in any way noble, but humanity's great goals which it can be called upon to defend. That indeed is the Janus[7] head of man: The only being capable of dedicating himself to the very highest moral and ethical values requires for this purpose a phylogenetically adapted mechanism of behavior whose animal properties bring with them the danger that he will kill his brother, convinced that he is doing so in the interests of these very same high values. *Ecce homo!*[8]

22

23

---

7. A two-headed Roman god, associated with doorways and with the beginnings and ends of things.
8. "Behold the man!," the words of Pontius Pilate as he surrendered Jesus to the mob (John 19:5).

JANE GOODALL

The Hierarchy

Jane Goodall (1934–   ) was determined from the age of eight to live with and study African animals. She had the good fortune, soon after completing her secondary schooling in England, to be hired as a secretary by Dr. Louis S. B. Leakey, an eminent anthropologist and the director of the National Museum of Natural History in Nairobi, Kenya. Leakey was so impressed by Goodall's intelligent interest in animals that he chose her as chief researcher in a chimpanzee-observation project in a remote section of Kenya. Goodall proved to be a superb researcher: she was the first European to discover that chimpanzees sometimes hunt and eat meat and that they make primitive tools. After five years on the project, Goodall had enough data to produce a doctoral thesis that was accepted by Cambridge University: she thus became the eighth person in history to receive a Ph.D. from Cambridge without having earned a bachelor's degree. "The Hierarchy" is excerpted from Goodall's *In the Shadow of Man* (1971), a book that became popular partly because of her clear, direct style, partly because of the interest we naturally take in the species biologists believe to be our nearest nonhuman relative.

Mike's rise to the number one or top-ranking position in the   1
chimpanzee community was both interesting and spectacular. In 1963 Mike had ranked almost bottom in the adult male dominance hierarchy. He had been the last to gain access to bananas, and had been threatened and actually attacked by almost every other adult male. At one time he even had appeared almost bald from losing so many handfuls of hair during aggressive incidents with his fellow apes.

When Hugo[1] and I had left the Gombe Stream at the end of that   2
year preparatory to getting married, Mike's position had not changed; yet when we returned four months later we found a very different Mike. Kris and Dominic told us the beginning of his story—how he had started to use empty four-gallon kerosene cans more and more often during his charging displays. We did not have to wait many days before we witnessed Mike's techniques for ourselves.

There was one incident I remember particularly vividly. A group   3
of five adult males, including top-ranking Goliath, David Gray-

_____
1. Baron Hugo von Lawick, Jane Goodall's husband.

beard, and the huge Rodolf, were grooming[2] each other. The session had been going on for some twenty minutes. Mike was sitting about thirty yards apart from them, frequently staring toward the group, occasionally idly grooming himself.

All at once Mike calmly walked over to our tent and took hold of   4
an empty kerosene can by the handle. Then he picked up a second can and, walking upright, returned to the place where he had been sitting. Armed with his two cans Mike continued to stare toward the other males. After a few minutes he began to rock from side to side. At first the movement was almost imperceptible, but Hugo and I were watching him closely. Gradually he rocked more vigorously, his hair slowly began to stand erect, and then, softly at first, he started a series of pant-hoots. As he called, Mike got to his feet and suddenly he was off, charging toward the group of males, hitting the two cans ahead of him. The cans, together with Mike's crescendo of hooting, made the most appalling racket: no wonder the erstwhile peaceful males rushed out of the way. Mike and his cans vanished down a track, and after a few moments there was silence. Some of the males reassembled and resumed their interrupted grooming session, but the others stood around somewhat apprehensively.

After a short interval that low-pitched hooting began again, fol-   5
lowed almost immediately by the appearance of the two rackety cans with Mike close behind them. Straight for the other males he charged, and once more they fled. This time, even before the group could reassemble, Mike set off again; but he made straight for Goliath—and even he hastened out of his way like all the others. Then Mike stopped and sat, all his hair on end, breathing hard. His eyes glared ahead and his lower lip was hanging slightly down so that the pink inside showed brightly and gave him a wild appearance.

Rodolf was the first of the males to approach Mike, uttering soft   6
pant-grunts of submission, crouching low and pressing his lips to Mike's thigh. Next he began to groom Mike, and two other males approached, pant-grunting, and also began to groom him. Finally David Graybeard went over to Mike, laid one hand on his groin, and joined in the grooming. Only Goliath kept away, sitting alone and staring toward Mike. It was obvious that Mike constituted a serious threat to Goliath's hitherto unchallenged supremacy.

Mike's deliberate use of man-made objects was probably an indi-   7
cation of superior intelligence. Many of the adult males had at

---

2. Grooming among chimpanzees involves cleaning and smoothing the hair and removing parasites; the behavior is significant socially as well as hygienically.

some time or another dragged a kerosene can to enhance their charging displays in place of the more normal branches or rocks; but only Mike apparently had been able to profit from the chance experience and learn to seek out the cans deliberately to his own advantage. The cans, of course, made several times more noise than a branch when dragged along the ground at speed, and eventually Mike was able to keep three cans ahead of him at once for about sixty yards as he ran flat-out across the camp clearing. No wonder that males previously his superiors rushed out of Mike's way.

Charging displays usually occur at a time of emotional excite-   8 ment—when a chimpanzee arrives at a food source, joins up with another group, or when he is frustrated. But it seemed that Mike actually *planned* his charging displays; almost, one might say, in cold blood. Often when he got up to fetch his cans he showed no visible signs of frustration or excitement; that came afterward when, armed with his display props, he began to rock from side to side, raise his hair, and hoot.

Eventually Mike's use of kerosene cans became dangerous—he   9 learned to hurl them ahead of him at the close of a charge. Once he got me on the back of my head, and once he hit Hugo's precious movie camera. We decided to remove all the cans, and went through a nightmare period while Mike tried to drag about all manner of other objects. Once he got hold of Hugo's tripod— luckily when the camera was not mounted—and once he managed to grab and pull down the large cupboard in which we kept a good deal of food and all our crockery and cutlery. The noise and the trail of destruction were unbelievable. Finally, however, we managed to dig things into the ground or hide them away, and like his companions Mike had to resort to branches and rocks.

By that time, however, his top-ranking status was assured, al-   10 though it was fully another year before Mike himself seemed to feel quite secure in his position. He continued to display very frequently and vigorously, and the lower-ranking chimps had increasing reason to fear him, since often he would attack a female or youngster viciously at the slightest provocation. In particular, as might be expected, a tense relation prevailed between Mike and the formerly dominant male, Goliath.

Goliath did not relinquish his position without a struggle. His   11 displays also increased in frequency and vigor and he too became more aggressive. There was a time, toward the start of this battle for dominance, when Hugo and I feared for Goliath's sanity. After attacking a couple of youngsters and charging back and forth dragging huge branches, he would sit, with hair on end, his sides heaving from exertion, a froth of saliva glistening at his half-open mouth, and a glint in his eyes that to us looked not far from madness. We actually had a soldered-mesh iron cage built in Kigoma[3] and, when this had been set up in camp, we retreated inside when Goliath's temper was at its worst.

One day when Mike was sitting in camp, a series of distinctive, rather melodious pant-hoots with characteristic quavers at the close announced the return of Goliath, who for two weeks had been somewhere down in the southern part of the reserve. Mike responded immediately, hooting in turn and charging across the clearing. Then he climbed a tree and sat staring over the valley, every hair on end.

12

A few minutes later Goliath appeared, and as he reached the outskirts of the camp clearing he commenced one of his spectacular displays. He must have seen Mike, because he headed straight for him, dragging a huge branch. He leaped into a tree near Mike's and was motionless. For a moment Mike stared toward him and then he too began to display, swaying the branches of his tree, swinging to the ground, hurling a few rocks, and, finally, leaping up into Goliath's tree and swaying the branches there. When he stopped, Goliath immediately reciprocated, swinging about in the tree and rocking the branches. Presently, as one of his wild leaps took him quite close to Mike, Mike also displayed, and for a few unbelievable moments both of the splendid male chimpanzees were swaying branches within a few feet of each other until I thought the whole tree must crash to the ground. An instant later both chimps were on the ground displaying in the undergrowth. Eventually they both stopped and sat staring at each other. It was Goliath who moved next, standing upright as he rocked a sapling; when he paused Mike charged past him, hurling a rock and drumming with his feet on the trunk of a tree.

13

This went on for nearly half an hour: first one male and then the other displayed, and each performance seemed to be more vigorous, more spectacular than the one preceding it. Yet during all that time, apart from occasionally hitting one another with the ends of the branches they swayed, neither chimpanzee actually attacked the other. Unexpectedly, after an extra long pause, it looked as if Goliath's nerve had broken. He rushed up to Mike, crouched beside him with loud, nervous pant-grunts, and began to groom him with feverish intensity. For a few moments Mike ignored Goliath completely. Suddenly he turned and, with a vigor almost matching

14

3. A small town in western Tanzania.

Goliath's, began to groom his vanquished rival. There they sat, grooming each other without pause for over an hour.

That was the last real duel between the two males. From then on 15 it seemed that Goliath accepted Mike's superiority, and a strangely intense relationship grew up between the two. They often greeted one another with much display of emotion, embracing or patting one another, kissing each other in the neck; afterward they usually started grooming each other. During these grooming sessions it appeared that the tension between them was eased, soothed by the close, friendly physical contact. Afterward they sometimes fed or rested quite close to each other, looking peaceful and relaxed as though the bitter rivalry of the past had never been.

ELAINE MORGAN

Primate Politics

Elaine Morgan (1920–   ) is a British writer of plays and tele-vision scripts, including two prize-winning serials ("A Pin to See the Peepshow" and "How Green Was My Valley") and two prize-winning documentaries ("Joey" and "Marie Curie"). She is best known in the United States for *The Descent of Woman* (1972), a bold plunge into the complexities of human evolution-ary theory by a writer who admits that she is only an amateur in the field. The book irritated some professional anthropologists, but others found it full of stimulating ideas. Among the most interesting of these is the suggestion that in interpreting both the fossil record and evidence gathered from animal behavior, the world's anthropologists have created a masculine myth of human evolution: one that exaggerates the importance of aggression and domination. Morgan suggests that Homo sapiens evolved from a line of cooperators rather than a line of competitors.

We are now entering the realm of primate politics. This, like sex, 1 is an area where the protagonists are apt to lose their cool. Purely abstract concepts, such as the nature of aggression, and heredity versus environment, are likely to be debated with an air of tightly leashed politeness, and with suppressed mutterings of 'Anarchist!' 'Fascist!' 'Marxist!' clearly audible between the lines. I am as little likely as any of them to attain a godlike objectivity, but I assume this is the kind of rumpus where anybody can join in—and any-

way 'Feminist!' will make a refreshingly new epithet for ethologists
to hiss.

When you begin reading about primate social behaviour and its   2
relevance to human evolution, the first thing you will notice is that
everybody seems to be talking about baboons and macaques—
especially about baboons.

At first this seems a little odd, because biologically we are not   3
very closely related to these animals. They aren't even apes—they
are only monkeys. Yet on these two species exclusively most popular discussion of human social inheritance has centred. The index
to Robert Ardrey's *Social Contract* gives thirty-eight lines of references to baboons and macaques, whereas no other primate—ape,
monkey, or prosimian—has more than four. Lionel Tiger's chapter
in *Men in Groups* on primate male bonding concentrates wholly on
these species except for a brief discussion on langurs. He spends no
time at all on the apes.

Now, why should this be? Admittedly the baboon is a popular   4
and successful species, and since he is largely a ground-dweller he
is easier to study than some others. But chimpanzees and gorillas,
being much more closely related to homo sapiens, have attracted
the concentrated attention of many observers recently, and we
have learned a great deal about their behaviour. It is puzzling that
the popularizers have so little to say about our nearest kith and kin.

It seems to me they have taken a look at our kith and kin and   5
rapidly concluded that the way chimps and gorillas behave doesn't
explain anything. It all depends, you see, on what you are setting
out to explain. If you are starting out with the premise that man is
the most aggressive and bloodthirsty creature on the face of the
earth, then these cousins of ours will be nothing but an embarrassment to you. A few quotations will be enough to make this plain.

First, the gorilla. He is, says Ardrey, a 'gentle, inoffensive, sub-   6
missive creature for whom a minimum of tyranny yields a maximum of results.' Irven de Vore calls him a 'mild-mannered vegetarian who likes to mind his own business' and lives 'in a state of
mild and amiable serenity. . . . His dominance over the group is
absolute, but normally genial. . . . The leaders are usually quite
approachable. Females nestle against them and infants crawl happily over their huge bodies. Amity reigns. When a band of gorillas
is at rest, the young play, the mothers tend their infants, and the
other adults lie at peace and soak up the sun.' You can see that's
not the kind of stuff that sells newspapers.

And the chimpanzee is just as frustrating for the blood-and-   7
thunder boys. Ardrey: 'The amiable chimpanzee seems to found
his society on nothing very much but his own good nature. There is

an order of dominance but it is not at all severe. When band meets band in the forest or on the savannah, there is enormous excitement but no antagonism, and all may wind up feeding in the same trees. The chimpanzee has demonstrated, I presume, that we must reckon on some degree of innate amity in the primate potential. . . . The chimp is the only primate who has achieved that arcadian existence of primal innocence which we once believed was the paradise that man had somehow left. . . .'

De Vore: 'Chimpanzees are the most compliant of the apes. They 8 revel in applause; they love attention. . . . They learn to control their emotions. In the wild, a young chimpanzee learns as it matures not to irritate the adults. As a juvenile, it learns to control its natural exuberance in play with infants of the group so as to avoid injuring them. . . .'

These two, I repeat, are our closest evolutionary relatives. You 9 might reasonably expect to be able to go into a library and find three or four books explaining that this is why *homo sapiens*, by and large, is also a mild-mannered and unassuming species. You should be so lucky!

No, no—the baboon is the one you are invited to contemplate. 10 Ardrey hurries the chimp offstage with a parting sneer to the effect that it's all very well to be amiable but see where it's leading him, he's an 'evolutionary failure' (as though only amiable creatures became extinct). Then he settles down to the interesting part:

'The student of man may find the baboon the most instructive of 11 species. Among primates his aggressiveness is second [*sic*] only to man's. He is a born bully, a born criminal, a born candidate for the hangman's noose. He is submissive as a truck, as inoffensive as a bulldozer, as gentle as a power-driven lawn-mower. He has predatory inclinations and enjoys nothing better than killing and devouring the newborn fawns of the delicate gazelle. And he will steal anything. . . .' And so on. While his male reader avidly polishes his spectacles and thinks: 'Yeah, that's me all right. Tell me more about the bulldozer and how I ravaged that delicate gazelle.'

He reads on and learns how the male baboon is twice the size of 12 the female. He keeps a herd of them in terrified subjection; he is fiercely jealous of them when they are in oestrus; if one of them strays he will punish her severely and fight any intruding male; if he is strong enough he will hog all the best food and impose his will brutally on weaker males. He demands instant and unquestioning obedience, and when danger threatens he will marshal his troops and stand up and fight like a hero, shoulder to shoulder with his loyal comrades.

He is not really very much like the man who is reading the book. 13

But the man who is reading the book (to say nothing of the man who is writing it) gets no end of a kick out of thinking that all that power and passion and brutal virility is seething within him, just below the skin, only barely held in leash by the conscious control of his intellect. He used to like reading about gorillas when we judged them by their faces and their roaring, but the more he learns about them the more he begins to suspect they're a little bit wishy-washy; so he averts his eyes from the primate family tree, forgets that he descended from apes, and identifies with the baboon even if it means making a monkey of himself.

A few general facts about the structure of anthropoid societies 14 will help to put the picture into perspective. We will omit the very rare species, like the gibbon, whose society consists only of the nuclear family, and concern ourselves with the vast majority which form into larger bands or troops.

They fall into two major categories—according to whether their 15 societies are acentric or centripetal. I have taken these terms from a detailed study of primate societies by Michael Chance and Clifford Jolly. An acentric society is individualistic and loosely structured. (If you favour it you can call it democratic; if you disapprove you can call it anarchic.) A centripetal society is highly structured and organized around one or more alpha-male leaders. (If you favour it you can call it a society of law and order; if you disapprove you can call it tyranny.)

A favourite example of the acentric type is the patas monkey, 16 and a favourite example of the centripetal is the baboon.

The factor that splits them right down the middle is how they 17 react to danger. If you are a patas monkey and you venture out into the open you remain all the while keenly alert. Even while you advance, your eyes are darting around, checking on everything in your environment, making sure the way is open for you to retreat the way you came, searching for an even quicker way up into the branches if one should be available. At the swish of a tail or the sound of voices you can be off like a shot, and all your equally alert companions will do the same. The whole band of you will scatter like the sparks of an exploding firework and you'll all end up high in the branches, and safe.

But if you are a baboon you will take a diametrically opposite 18 view. You pay comparatively little attention to your environment. You may be in the middle of a plain where the environment is pretty featureless. You may feel that it's a long way between trees, and a hungry leopard or an angry farmer could easily bring you down in your tracks before you reached one. If you scatter you only make it easier for a predator to pick you off. Much the best bet is for everyone to stick together, and the safest place to retreat to is the vicinity of whichever of your comrades has the sharpest teeth and the most courage. So when *your* eyes are darting, what they are checking up on is where you are in relation to the alpha male or males. If he moves on, you can't afford to be left behind; and if he signals some danger you haven't been aware of, you'd better believe he knows best, and close ranks, and do what you're told.

Clearly the position of males in these two societies will differ   19
radically. If a patas troop scents danger the first thing that happens is that the single male gets as far away as possible from the female assembly and while they scatter he puts up a display of bouncing around to divert the attacker's attention before running away himself. They don't have to obey him—they simply have to disperse. Scattering is their answer to everything. Patas monkeys have no submission gestures because if they are threatened they simply run; but they are pretty non-aggressive anyway, and the high-level threats of baboon society are unknown.

Roughly speaking, this is the sort of behaviour displayed by the   20
'bandarlog', the monkeys who drove Rudyard Kipling[1] wild with irritation and contempt, because Kipling was a pukka sahib and the bandarlog were an undisciplined mob who couldn't even co-operate or concentrate, or (as he portrayed them) even finish a sentence:

> *Now we are going to—never mind!*
> *Brother, thy tail hangs down behind!*

Among baboons, on the other hand, the males have to be bul-   21
lies. The troop has to rally to them. And since not even baboons are *born* disciplined, discipline has to be inculcated. Females, juveniles, and subordinates have to be taught their place, and frequently reminded of their place, by threats and punishments and bites on the neck. Usually they learn fast, and a display of fangs or the flash of an alpha's eyelids is enough to keep everyone in line. As long as they remain in line the alpha's rule is benevolent and administered with rough justice and old-fashioned chivalry. Mothers with infants are always flanked by protecting male outriders when the troop is on the move, and in disputes between subordinates the leader sides with the weaker of the two. (Perhaps chivalry isn't quite the word—if the dispute is between a female and a subordinate male he'll usually back the male.)

·   ·   ·

1. Rudyard Kipling (1865–1936), British writer closely identified with the British era of colonial power.

The next big question, since homo sapiens relates most closely to   22
the apes, is: how do we classify the gorilla and the chimpanzee?
Are they acentric like the patas, or centripetal like the baboon? In
fact they don't behave very much like either; but two of the criteria
for identifying the basis of their social structure are (a) is there a
leading male, or signs of a ranking order among males?; and (b)
when there is danger, do they scatter or do they clump together?

The answer on both counts suggests that, like the baboons, apes   23
form centripetal societies. The signs of this are not so clear and
unequivocal as among the baboons—except for the very obvious
dominance of the alpha gorilla—but if you keep a close watch
on the attention structure you will be left in no doubt; they are
centripetal.

We are now confronted with two major questions: Are our own   24
social instincts analogous to theirs, and how do they manage to
make a centripetal society work without all the slashing and snarling and bullying and cowering that is such a feature of baboon
social interactions?

The difficulty in comparing human society with any other ani-   25
mal's is that the cultural components in it are so powerful that they
tend to blur any inherited instincts that may exist. If you are examining an English public school, or a Nazi S.S. troop, each of them in
its different style would convince you that our instincts are those of
the baboon. If you consider the aggregations of human beings at
Woodstock[2] or the hippie colony at Haight Ashbury, or the reactions of people in an earthquake, you would feel tolerably certain
that our instincts are those of a comparatively amorphous troop,
like the patas.

Fortunately, however, it is quite easy to find social groups of   26
human beings which behave in exactly the same way all over the
world and in every type of culture. I am referring, of course, to our
juvenile clusters—unsupervised groups of children up to the age of
about six.

Adriaan Kortland gives a vivid account of chimpanzee response   27
to a potential threat, which he elicited by placing a stuffed leopard in a strategic situation and observing the chimps' reactions.
If you have ever watched (or in your childhood participated in) a
group of small children reacting to an unfamiliar, slightly alarming animal—say a large grass snake—you will be struck by the
resemblance.

---

2. Nearly 500,000 young people gathered near Woodstock, New York, in 1969 for a
haphazardly organized three-day rock concert that became the symbol of America's
antiwar counterculture.

'Following a moment of dead silence on catching sight of the   28
leopard, there was a burst of yelling and barking, accompanied by
every member of the group charging about in different directions.
A few fled, but returned soon afterwards to join the majority, who
began leaping up and down and charging the leopard, brandishing
big sticks or broken-off trees. . . . Some of the blood-curdling
barking was loud enough to wake a human neighbour 600 yards
away. . . . Interspersed with these communal or individual charges
were periods of seeking and giving reassurance by holding out the
hands, touching their neighbours. . . . Voiding of diarrhoea and
enormous amounts of intense body scratching took place. The attacks on the leopard were more or less rhythmical, and followed by
brief increases in fear symptoms and the seeking of reassurance and
longer periods of sitting down watching the leopard. The aggressive
aspects gradually waned after an hour, being replaced by intense
inquisitiveness. . . . One chimpanzee poked it with its fist, another
smelled it, and finally the leopard's head was detached from the
body and rolled about. Another chimpanzee seized the tail and
they all rushed off into the bush with the body.'

This is not at all like the baboon, and not at all like the patas   29
monkey, but it seems to me to be more like unprocessed humanity
than either of them.

As to how the apes' centripetal society works, the essential key   30
to being high in a primate ranking order is the ability to command
the attention of other members of the troop. There are two ways of
doing this, as has emerged from the work of H. B. Virgo and M. J.
Waterhouse, and V. Reynolds and G. Luscombe.

The two methods are classified by Michael Chance as the agonic   31
mode and the hedonic mode. The baboon aspiring to dominance
commands attention by biting and threat displays with his huge
canine teeth. This is the agonic mode, and is a pretty reliable one. If
someone slashed your lip open yesterday you are at least going to
be acutely aware of him next time you pass him in the street,
especially if he pulls his knife again and snarls.

Robert Ardrey is rapt with admiration for the primate society   32
constructed on this principle and uses it for pointing a moral to
misguided liberals: 'It is as if, buried in the baboon subconscious,
the truth, like one's shadow, can never be far away. . . . The secret
of his success would lie in that undistinguished, unwashable brain.
The baboon will never persuade himself that aggressiveness is a
product of frustration. The young will never blame their failures on
lack of parental love in infancy. Should the proposition that competition is somehow wrong come baboon way, small brains would
be dumbfounded; should some mutant baboon idealist insist upon

it, he would be greeted with the lifted eyebrows not of human surprise but of monkey threat. . . .'

That's one in the eye for permissiveness. There is, however, a 33 drawback to the baboon's agonic organization. The brain is undistinguished and unwashable, all right; no subversive heresies will ever penetrate it. But it is so totally unwashable that it is unlikely ever to become any more distinguished. The structure is so rigid that true communication is at a minimum—it is limited to the ritual posturings of swaggering arrogance on one side and cringing submission on the other.

The typical encounter between superior and inferior is brief and 34 leads to flight, or withdrawal to a respectful distance. This immediately ends the interaction. The whole complex system depends on everyone's performing his or her stereotyped role, and any new behaviour pattern which might disturb this, however adaptive it might prove if generally followed, would never get off the ground. What Ardrey calls the baboon's 'thunderous evolutionary success' has been achieved by the same means, and at the same cost, as the thunderous evolutionary success of the termite colony. They do their own thing to perfection, but they have left no options open. It is unlikely that they will ever go on to do anything else.

The hedonic mode favoured by the apes is quite different. Here 35 again, a high place in the ranking order is attained by an outstanding ability to command the attention of one's fellows. But the apes are more advanced than the monkeys, and they have made a discovery which perhaps more than anything else made possible our own dramatic mental forward leap. They learned that you don't necessarily have to bite someone in order to make him take notice of you. Among gorillas and chimpanzees this type of physical aggression is extremely rare.

So how do they do it? Primatologists call it 'display': to put it in 36 the simplest possible terms, they do it by showing off. They seek for ways of making themselves conspicuous: they bounce around and shake the branches. They find interesting objects, and their companions cluster around to see what they've got and what they're going to do with it. The dominant gorilla, the alpha silverback, of whom much is expected, has been seen to mount the most stupendous show-stopping performances in this line.

First he starts by hooting. He gives anything up to forty hoots at 37 an increasing tempo. He picks a leaf and puts it in his mouth. He stands up on his hind legs, grabbing a handful of vegetation and throwing it into the air. Then he beats his chest up to twenty times with his hands, using them alternately, and slightly cupped. Sometimes for good measure he kicks one leg into the air while he is doing it. Immediately after the chest beating he starts a curious sideways run, first a few steps bipedally and then charging sideways like a gigantic crab, sweeping one arm through the vegetation, slapping at the undergrowth, shaking branches, breaking off or tearing up whole trees. Finally he thumps the ground, usually with one palm but sometimes with two, as who should say 'Follow that, buster!' Of course no one can, though even infant gorillas of six months old have been known to rise shakily on to their hind legs and slap at their puny chests, watched by their mothers as fondly as if they were aspiring Hollywood tots at their first audition.

You can see it's no accident that the chimp in captivity willingly   38
learns new tricks and loves applause. You could waste a lifetime trying to teach a baboon to ride a bicycle, or even perform some simpler trick more within his capacity. He just doesn't see what's in it for him. But for the chimpanzee it is his method of acquiring dominance. To extend his repertoire improves his ability to attract attention, and as long as fascinated eyes are focused on his efforts, even though they are human eyes, he has a rewarding belief that he has added to his status. And he's right, isn't he?

Two major advantages accrue to the hedonic mode. Firstly,   39
while dominance by threat stultifies social interaction, dominance by display promotes it. Threats cut individuals off from one another, but display brings them closer, to watch and investigate and congratulate. As Michael Chance comments: 'Display behaviour, responded to by greeting, stimulates and enhances the tendency of individuals to develop many forms of contact behaviour or behaviour at close quarters. Manipulation, not only by grooming, but also by holding and investigation, is jointly engaged in. . . . Their attention may also switch to the environment or to other objects and give rise to manipulation of objects as tools. . . . In the hedonic mode, display leads to outgoing but flexible social relations which can act as the medium for the dissemination of information within the society.'

The second major advantage is the incentive given to be-   40
havioural innovations which may prove advantageous to the species. The baboon's neck-biting is a good trick as far as it goes, but a bite is a bite is a bite; whereas the young ape, competing for attention with other young apes, is daily stimulated to search for something new by the troop's constant unspoken challenge: *'Etonne-moi!'*[3]

Which mode was the hominid's society cast in? It seems glar-   41

3. "Astonish me!"

ingly obvious that only the hedonic mode could have led us to where we are today. But if you want confirmation, I urge you again to consult the largest available pool of virtually uninhibited human social interaction. Most males, through no fault of their own, have not had the ethological advantage of spending up to ten years of their lives in the constant company of the young of their own species, but they are still free to stroll along to the nearest nursery school or infants' playground and observe what happens when children first begin to construct a social framework for themselves. For every encounter which takes the form of two small boys hitting each other, there will be fifteen or twenty which are causing the whole yard to ring with cries of 'Look at me!' 'Hey, watch this!' 'Look—can you do this?' 'Look at me, I'm a cowboy!' 'Look what I've done!' 'Look what I've found!' 'Look at my new doll!' 'Come and see Johnnie, he can stand on his head!'—while the unstable Johnnie is gasping 'Everybody look at me—quick!'

You don't have to be outstanding in size or courage or aggression   42
to make your mark in such a society. If you're double-jointed, or can wiggle your ears, or draw better pictures, or turn better cartwheels than anyone else, then you've got status. It doesn't matter what it is as long as it ensures that when you raise the cry of 'Look!' somebody will look.

So, with all due respect to the baboon and his admirers, I submit   43
that *homo sapiens* as a social being is modelled ineradicably on the hedonic mode of dominance by display, and that basically our relations with our fellows resemble more than anything else those of the chimpanzee, with all that implies of amiability, flexibility, curiosity, and exhibitionism, as well as the tendency to react to sudden peril with a slackening of the bowels and a desire to hold somebody's hand—or even sometimes dive for cover without waiting to warn the whole troop, a piece of turpitude no baboon would ever be guilty of.

MARGARET MEAD

Warfare Is Only an Invention – Not a Biological Necessity

Margaret Mead (1901–1978) is notable for her studies of both primitive peoples and complex contemporary cultures. Her graduate work in anthropology led to her first major work, *Coming of*

Age in Samoa (1928), an investigation of the ways Samoan culture conditions sexual behavior and the individual's image of
herself or himself. This influential book was followed by *Growing
Up in New Guinea* (1930) and *Sex and Temperament in Three Primitive Societies* (1935). Mead's studies greatly enhanced our awareness that nature allows a wide range of cultures and that our own
culture is neither inevitable nor perfect. In 1964, Mead became
curator of ethnology for the American Museum of Natural History, and in 1972 she was elected president of the American
Association for the Advancement of Science. In the second half
of her life, Mead applied her anthropological perspective to a
number of America's social and political problems, including
racism, sexual biases, and violence. "Warfare Is Only an Invention" first appeared in the journal *Asia* in August 1940.

Is war a biological necessity, a sociological inevitability or just a   1
bad invention? Those who argue for the first view endow man with
such pugnacious instincts that some outlet in aggressive behavior is
necessary if man is to reach full human stature. It was this point of
view which lay back of William James's famous essay, "The Moral
Equivalent of War," in which he tried to retain the warlike virtues
and channel them in new directions. A similar point of view has
lain back of the Soviet Union's attempt to make competition between groups rather than between individuals. A basic, competitive, aggressive, warring human nature is assumed, and those who
wish to outlaw war or outlaw competitiveness merely try to find
new and less socially destructive ways in which these biologically
given aspects of man's nature can find expression. Then there are
those who take the second view: warfare is the inevitable concomitant of the development of the state, the struggle for land and
natural resources of class societies springing, not from the nature of
man, but from the nature of history. War is nevertheless inevitable
unless we change our social system and outlaw classes, the struggle
for power, and possessions; and in the event of our success warfare
would disappear, as a symptom vanishes when the disease is cured.

One may hold a sort of compromise position between these two   2
extremes; one may claim that all aggression springs from the frustration of man's biologically determined drives and that, since all
forms of culture are frustrating, it is certain each new generation
will be aggressive and the aggression will find its natural and inevitable expression in race war, class war, nationalistic war, and so
on. All three of these positions are very popular today among those
who think seriously about the problems of war and its possible
prevention, but I wish to urge another point of view, less defeatist
perhaps than the first and third, and more accurate than the sec-

ond: that is, that warfare, by which I mean recognized conflict between two groups *as groups,* in which each group puts an army (even if the army is only fifteen pygmies) into the field to fight and kill, if possible, some of the members of the army of the other group—that warfare of this sort is an invention like any other of the inventions in terms of which we order our lives, such as writing, marriage, cooking our food instead of eating it raw, trial by jury or burial of the dead, and so on. Some of this list any one will grant are inventions: trial by jury is confined to very limited portions of the globe; we know that there are tribes that do not bury their dead but instead expose or cremate them; and we know that only part of the human race has had the knowledge of writing as its cultural inheritance. But, whenever a way of doing things is found universally, such as the use of fire or the practice of some form of marriage, we tend to think at once that it is not an invention at all but an attribute of humanity itself. And yet even such universals as marriage and the use of fire are inventions like the rest, very basic ones, inventions which were perhaps necessary if human history was to take the turn that it has taken, but nevertheless inventions. At some point in his social development man was undoubtedly without the institution of marriage or the knowledge of the use of fire.

The case for warfare is much clearer because there are peoples even today who have no warfare. Of these the Eskimo are perhaps the most conspicuous examples, but the Lepchas of Sikkim described by Geoffrey Gorer in *Himalayan Village* are as good. Neither of these peoples understands war, not even defensive warfare. The idea of warfare is lacking, and this idea is as essential to really carrying on war as an alphabet or a syllabary is to writing. But whereas the Lepchas are a gentle, unquarrelsome people, and the advocates of other points of view might argue that they are not full human beings or that they had never been frustrated and so had no aggression to expand in warfare, the Eskimo case gives no such possibility of interpretation. The Eskimo are not a mild and meek people; many of them are turbulent and troublesome. Fights, theft of wives, murder, cannibalism, occur among them—all outbursts of passionate men goaded by desire or intolerable circumstance. Here are men faced with hunger, men faced with loss of their wives, men faced with the threat of extermination by other men, and here are orphan children, growing up miserably with no one to care for them, mocked and neglected by those about them. The personality necessary for war, the circumstances necessary to goad men to desperation are present, but there is no war. When a traveling Eskimo entered a settlement he might have to fight the strongest man in the settlement to establish his position among them, but this was a test of strength and bravery, not war. The idea of warfare, of one *group* organizing against another *group* to maim and wound and kill them was absent. And without that idea passions might rage but there was no war.

But, it may be argued, isn't this because the Eskimo have such a   4
low and undeveloped form of social organization? They own no land, they move from place to place, camping, it is true, season after season on the same site, but this is not something to fight for as the modern nations of the world fight for land and raw materials. They have no permanent possessions that can be looted, no towns that can be burned. They have no social classes to produce stress and strains within the society which might force it to go to war outside. Doesn't the absence of war among the Eskimo, while disproving the biological necessity of war, just go to confirm the point that it is the state of development of the society which accounts for war, and nothing else?

We find the answer among the pygmy peoples of the Andaman   5
Islands in the Bay of Bengal. The Andamans also represent an exceedingly low level of society; they are a hunting and food-gathering people; they live in tiny hordes without any class stratification; their houses are simpler than the snow houses of the Eskimo. But they knew about warfare. The army might contain only fifteen determined pygmies marching in a straight line, but it was the real thing none the less. Tiny army met tiny army in open battle, blows were exchanged, casualties suffered, and the state of warfare could only be concluded by a peacemaking ceremony.

Similarly, among the Australian aborigines, who built no per-   6
manent dwellings but wandered from water hole to water hole over their almost desert country, warfare—and rules of "international law"—were highly developed. The student of social evolution will seek in vain for his obvious causes of war, struggle for lands, struggle for power of one group over another, expansion of population, need to divert the minds of a populace restive under tyranny, or even the ambition of a successful leader to enhance his own prestige. All are absent, but warfare as a practice remained, and men engaged in it and killed one another in the course of a war because killing is what is done in wars.

From instances like these it becomes apparent that an inquiry   7
into the causes of war misses the fundamental point as completely as does an insistence upon the biological necessity of war. If a people have an idea of going to war and the idea that war is the way in which certain situations, defined within their society, are to be handled, they will sometimes go to war. If they are a mild and

unaggressive people, like the Pueblo Indians, they may limit themselves to defensive warfare; but they will be forced to think in terms of war because there are peoples near them who have warfare as a pattern, and offensive, raiding, pillaging warfare at that. When the pattern of warfare is known, people like the Pueblo Indians will defend themselves, taking advantage of their natural defenses, the *mesa* village site, and people like the Lepchas, having no natural defenses and no idea of warfare, will merely submit to the invader. But the essential point remains the same. There is a way of behaving which is known to a given people and labeled as an appropriate form of behavior; a bold and warlike people like the Sioux or the Maori may label warfare as desirable as well as possible; a mild people like the Pueblo Indians may label warfare as undesirable; but to the minds of both peoples the possibility of warfare is present. Their thoughts, their hopes, their plans are oriented about this idea, that warfare may be selected as the way to meet some situation.

So simple peoples and civilized peoples, mild peoples and violent, assertive peoples, will all go to war if they have the invention, just as those· peoples who have the custom of dueling will have duels and peoples who have the pattern of vendetta will indulge in vendetta. And, conversely, peoples who do not know of dueling will not fight duels, even though their wives are seduced and their daughters ravished; they may on occasion commit murder but they will not fight duels. Cultures which lack the idea of the vendetta will not meet every quarrel in this way. A people can use only the forms it has. So the Balinese have their special way of dealing with a quarrel between two individuals: if the two feel that the causes of quarrel are heavy they may go and register their quarrel in the temple before the gods, and, making offerings, they may swear never to have anything to do with each other again. Today they register such mutual "not-speaking" with the Dutch government officials. But in other societies, although individuals might feel as full of animosity and as unwilling to have any further contact as do the Balinese, they cannot register their quarrel with the gods and go on quietly about their business because registering quarrels with the gods is not an invention of which they know. 8

Yet, if it be granted that warfare is after all an invention, it may nevertheless be an invention that lends itself to certain types of personality, to the exigent needs of autocrats, to the expansionist desires of crowded peoples, to the desire for plunder and rape and loot which is engendered by a dull and frustrating life. What, then, can we say of this congruence between warfare and its uses? If it is a form which fits so well, is not this congruence the essential point? 9

But even here the primitive material causes us to wonder, because there are tribes who go to war merely for glory, having no quarrel with the enemy, suffering from no tyrant within their boundaries, anxious neither for land nor loot nor women, but merely anxious to win prestige which within that tribe has been declared obtainable only by war and without which no young man can hope to win his sweetheart's smile of approval. But if, as was the case with the Bush Negroes of Dutch Guiana, it is artistic ability which is necessary to win a girl's approval, the same young man would have to be carving rather than going out on a war party.

In many parts of the world, war is a game in which the individ- 10 ual can win counters—counters which bring him prestige in the eyes of his own sex or of the opposite sex; he plays for these counters as he might, in our society, strive for a tennis championship. Warfare is a frame for such prestige-seeking merely because it calls for the display of certain skills and certain virtues; all of these skills—riding straight, shooting straight, dodging the missiles of the enemy, and sending one's own straight to the mark—can be equally well exercised in some other framework, and, equally, the virtues—endurance, bravery, loyalty, steadfastness—can be displayed in other contexts. The tie-up between proving oneself a man and proving this by a success in organized killing is due to a definition which many societies have made of manliness. And often, even in those societies which counted success in warfare a proof of human worth, strange turns were given to the idea, as when the plains Indians gave their highest awards to the man who touched a live enemy rather than to the man who brought in a scalp—from a dead enemy—because the latter was less risky. Warfare is just an invention known to the majority of human societies by which they permit their young men either to accumulate prestige or avenge their honor or acquire loot or wives or slaves or sago lands or cattle or appease the blood lust of their gods or the restless souls of the recently dead. It is just an invention, older and more widespread than the jury system, but none the less an invention.

But, once we have said this, have we said anything at all? De- 11 spite a few instances, dear to the hearts of controversialists, of the loss of the useful arts, once an invention is made which proves congruent with human needs or social forms, it tends to persist. Grant that war is an invention, that it is not a biological necessity nor the outcome of certain special types of social forms, still, once the invention is made, what are we to do about it? The Indian who had been subsisting on the buffalo for generations because with his primitive weapons he could slaughter only a limited number of buffalo did not return to his primitive weapons when he saw that the white man's more efficient weapons were exterminating the buffalo. A desire for the white man's cloth may mortgage the South Sea Islander to the white man's plantation, but he does not return to making bark cloth, which would have left him free. Once an invention is known and accepted, men do not easily relinquish it. The skilled workers may smash the first steam looms which they feel are to be their undoing, but they accept them in the end, and no movement which has insisted upon the mere abandonment of usable inventions has ever had much success. Warfare is here, as part of our thought; the deeds of warriors are immortalized in the words of our poets; the toys of our children are modeled upon the weapons of the soldier; the frame of reference within which our statesmen and our diplomats work always contains war. If we know that it is not inevitable, that it is due to historical accident that warfare is one of the ways in which we think of behaving, are we given any hope by that? What hope is there of persuading nations to abandon war, nations so thoroughly imbued with the idea that resort to war is, if not actually desirable and noble, at least inevitable whenever certain defined circumstances arise?

In answer to this question I think we might turn to the history of other social inventions, and inventions which must once have seemed as firmly entrenched as warfare. Take the methods of trial which preceded the jury system: ordeal and trial by combat. Unfair, capricious, alien as they are to our feeling today, they were once the only methods open to individuals accused of some offense. The invention of trial by jury gradually replaced these methods until only witches, and finally not even witches, had to resort to the ordeal. And for a long time the jury system seemed the one best and finest method of settling legal disputes, but today new inventions, trial before judges only or before commissions, are replacing the jury system. In each case the old method was replaced by a new social invention; the ordeal did not go out because people thought it unjust or wrong, it went out because a method more congruent with the institutions and feelings of the period was invented. And, if we despair over the way in which war seems such an ingrained habit of most of the human race, we can take comfort from the fact that a poor invention will usually give place to a better invention. 12

For this, two conditions at least are necessary. The people must recognize the defects of the old invention, and someone must make a new one. Propaganda against warfare, documentation of its terrible cost in human suffering and social waste, these prepare the ground by teaching people to feel that warfare is a defective social institution. There is further needed a belief that social invention is possible and the invention of new methods which will render war- 13 fare as out-of-date as the tractor is making the plow, or the motor car the horse and buggy. A form of behavior becomes out-of-date only when something else takes its place, and in order to invent forms of behavior which will make war obsolete, it is a first requirement to believe that an invention is possible.

NAPOLEON A. CHAGNON

Yanomamö: The Fierce People

Napoleon A. Chagnon (1938–   ), an anthropologist trained at the University of Michigan, has become one of the world's experts on the demographic, political, economic, and social aspects of tribal warfare, particularly among the Indians of South America. In addition to publishing numerous articles about the Yanomamö in popular and scientific journals, he has written and produced more than twenty documentary films about them, winning in the process such film prizes as the Grand Prize of the Brussels' Film Festival (1970) and two blue ribbons from the American Film Festival (1972, 1974). Chagnon's best-known books are *Yanomamö: The Fierce People* (1968) and *Studying the Yanomamö* (1974), but a few dog owners will recognize him as the coauthor of *Toward a Ph.D. for Dogs* (1975), an obedience-training manual. The following article first appeared in *Natural History* in 1967.

The Yanomamö Indians are a tribe in Venezuela and Brazil who   1
practice a slash-and-burn way of horticultural life. Traditionally, they have been an inland "foot" tribe, avoiding larger rivers and settling deep in the tropical jungle. Until about 1950 they had no sustained contact with other peoples except, to a minor extent, with another tribe, the Carib-speaking Makiritaris to the northeast.

I recently lived with the Yanomamö for more than a year, doing   2
research sponsored by the U.S. Public Health Service, with the cooperation of the Venezuela Institute for Scientific Research. My purpose was to study Yanomamö social organization, language, sex practices, and forms of violence, ranging from treacherous raids to chest-pounding duels.

Those Yanomamö who have been encouraged to live on the   3
larger rivers (Orinoco, Mavaca, Ocamo, and Padamo) are slowly beginning to realize that they are not the only people in the world;

there is also a place called Caraca-tedi (Caracas), from whence come foreigners of an entirely new order. These foreigners speak an incomprehensible language, probably a degenerate form of Yanomamö. They bring malaria pills, machetes, axes, cooking pots, and *copetas* ("guns"), have curious ideas about indecency, and speak of a new "spirit."

However, the Yanomamö remain a people relatively unadul- 4
terated by outside contacts. They are also fairly numerous. Their population is roughly 10,000, the larger portion of them distributed throughout southern Venezuela. Here, in basins of the upper Orinoco and all its tributaries, they dwell in some 75 scattered villages, each of which contains from 40 to 300 individuals.

The largest, most all-embracing human reality to these people is 5
humanity itself; Yanomamö means true human beings. Their conception of themselves as the only true "domestic" beings (those that dwell in houses) is demonstrated by the contempt with which they treat non-Yanomamö, who, in their language, are "wild." For instance, when referring to themselves, they use an honorific pronoun otherwise reserved for important spirits and headmen; when discussing *nabäs* ("non-Yanomamö"), an ordinary pronoun is enough. Again, in one of the myths about their origin, the first people to be created were the Yanomamö. All others developed by a process of degeneration and are, therefore, not quite on a par with the Yanomamö.

In addition to meaning "people," Yanomamö also refers to the 6
language. Their tribal name does not designate a politically organized entity but is more or less equivalent to our concept of humanity. (This, of course, makes their most outstanding characteristic— chronic warfare, of which I shall speak in detail—seem rather an anomaly.) Sub-Yanomamö groupings are based on language differences, historical separation, and geographical location.

For instance, two distinguishable groups, Waika (from *waikaö*— 7
"to kill off") and Shamatari, speak nearly identical dialects; they are differentiated mostly on the basis of a specific event that led to their separation. The Shamatari, the group I know best, occupy the area south of the Orinoco to, and including portions of, northern Brazil. Their differentiation from the Waika probably occurred in the past 75 years.

According to the Indians, there was a large village on a northern 8
tributary of the upper Orinoco River, close to its headwaters. The village had several factions, one of which was led by a man called Kayabawä (big tree). A notably corpulent man, he also had the name Shamatari, derived from *shama*, the "tapir," a robust ungulate found throughout tropical South America. As the story goes,

Shamatari's faction got into a fight with the rest of the village over the possession of a woman, and the community split into two warring halves. Gradually the fighting involved more villages, and Shamatari led his faction south, crossed the Orinoco, and settled there. He was followed by members of other villages that had taken his part in the fight.

Those who moved to the south side of the Orinoco came to be   9 called Shamataris by those living on the north side, and the term is now applied to any village in this area, whether or not it can trace its origin to the first supporters of Shamatari.

For the Yanomamö, the village is the maximum political unit   10 and the maximum sovereign body, and it is linked to other villages by ephemeral alliances, visiting and trade relationships, and inter-marriages. In essence, the village is a building—a continuous, open-roofed lean-to built on a circular plan and surrounded by a protective palisade of split palm logs. The roof starts at or near ground level, ascends at an angle of about 45 degrees, and reaches a height of some 20 to 25 feet. Individual segments under the continuous roof are not partitioned; from a hammock hung any-where beneath it one can see (and hear, thanks to the band shell nature of the structure) all that goes on within the village.

The palisade, about three to six feet behind the base of the roof,   11 is some ten feet high and is usually in various stages of disrepair, depending on the current warfare situation. The limited number of entrances are covered with dry palm leaves in the evening; if these are moved even slightly, the sound precipitates the barking of a horde of ill-tempered, underfed dogs, whose bad manners preadapt the stranger to what lies beyond the entrance.

A typical "house" (a segment under the continuous roof) shel-   12 ters a man, his wife or wives, their children, perhaps one or both of the man's parents, and, farther down, the man's brothers and their families. The roof is alive with cockroaches, scorpions, and spiders, and the ground is littered with the debris of numerous repasts— bird, fish, and animal bones; bits of fur; skulls of monkeys and other animals; banana and plantain peelings; feathers; and the seeds of palm fruits. Bows and arrows stand against housepoles all over the village, baskets hang from roof rafters, and firewood is stacked under the lower part of the roof where it slopes to the ground. Some men will be whittling arrow points with agouti[1]-tooth knives or tying feathers to arrow shafts. Some women will be spinning cotton, weaving baskets, or making hammocks or cotton

---

1. The agouti is a rodent about the size of a rabbit.

waistbands. The children, gathered in the center of the village clearing, frequently tie a string to a lizard and entertain themselves by shooting the animal full of tiny arrows. And, of course, many people will be outside the compound, working in their gardens, fishing, or collecting palm fruits in the jungle.

If it is a typical late afternoon, most of the older men are gathered in one part of the village, blowing one of their hallucinatory drugs (*ebene*) up each other's nostrils by means of a hollow tube and chanting to the forest demons (*hekuras*) as the drug takes effect. Other men may be curing a sick person by sucking, massaging, and exhorting the evil spirit from him. Everybody in the village is swatting vigorously at the voracious biting gnats, and here and there groups of people delouse each other's heads and eat the vermin.

In composition, the village consists of one or more groups of patrilineally related kinsmen (*mashis*), but it also contains other categories, including people who have come from other villages seeking spouses. All villages try to increase their size and consider it desirable for both the young men and young women to remain at home after marriage. Since one must marry out of his *mashi*, villages with only one patrilineage frequently lose their young men to other villages; they must go to another village to *siohamou* (to "son-in-law") if they want wives. The parents of the bride-to-be, of course, want the young man to remain in their village to help support them in their old age, particularly if they have few or no sons. They will frequently promise a young man one or more of the sisters of his wife in order to make his stay more attractive.

He, on the other hand, would rather return to his home village to be with his own kinsmen, and the tendency is for postmarital residence to be patrilocal (with the father of the groom). If a village is rich in axes and machetes, it can and does coerce its poorer · trading partners into permitting their young women to live permanently with the richer village. The latter thus obtains more women, while the poorer village gains some security in the trading network. The poor village then coerces other villages even poorer, or they raid them and steal their women.

The patrilineages that maintain the composition of the villages, rich or poor, include a man and his brothers and sisters, his children and his brothers' children, and the children of his sons and brothers' sons. The ideal marriage pattern is for a group of brothers to exchange sisters with another group of brothers. Furthermore, it is both permissible and desirable for a man to marry his mother's brother's daughter (his matrilateral cross-cousin) and/or his father's sister's daughter (his patrilateral cross-cousin) and, as we have seen earlier, to remain in his parents' village. Hence, the "ideal" village would have at least two patrilineages that exchanged marriageable people.

There is a considerable amount of adherence to these rules, and [17] both brother-sister exchange and cross-cousin marriage are common. However, there are also a substantial number of people in each village who are not related in these ways. For the most part they are women and their children who have been stolen from other villages, segments of lineages that have fled from their own village because of fights, and individuals—mostly young men— who have moved in and attached themselves to the household of one of the lineage (*mashi*) leaders.

Even if the sex ratio is balanced, there is a chronic shortage of [18] women. A pregnant woman or one who is still nursing her children must not have sexual relationships. This means that for as many as three years, even allowing for violations of the taboos, a woman is asexual as far as the men are concerned. Hence, men with pregnant wives, and bachelors too, are potentially disruptive in every village because they constantly seek liaisons with the wives of other men. Eventually such relationships are discovered and violence ensues.

The woman, even if merely suspected of having affairs with [19] other men, is beaten with a club; burned with a glowing brand; shot with a barbed arrow in a non-vital area, such as the buttocks, so that removal of the barb is both difficult and painful; or chopped on the arms or legs with a machete or ax. Most women over thirty carry numerous scars inflicted on them by their enraged husbands. My study of genealogies also indicates that not a few women have been killed outright by their husbands. The woman's punishment for infidelity depends on the number of brothers she has in the village, for if her husband is too brutal, her brothers may club him or take her away and give her to someone else.

The guilty man, on the other hand, is challenged to a fight with [20] clubs. This duel is rarely confined to the two parties involved, for their brothers and supporters join the battle. If nobody is seriously injured, the matter may be forgotten. But if the incidents are frequent, the two patrilineages may decide to split while they are still on relatively "peaceable" terms with each other and form two independent villages. They will still be able to reunite when threatened by raid from a larger village.

This is only one aspect of the chronic warfare of the Yano- [21] mamö—warfare that has a basic effect on settlement pattern and demography, intervillage political relationships, leadership, and social organization. The collective aggressive behavior is caused by the desire to accent "sovereignty"—the capacity to initiate fighting and to demonstrate this capacity to others.

Although the Yanomamö are habitually armed with lethal bows   22
and arrows, they have a graded system of violence within which they can express their *waiteri,* or "fierceness." The form of violence is determined by the nature of the affront or wrong to be challenged. The most benign form is a duel between two groups, in which an individual from each group stands (or kneels) with his chest stuck out, head up in the air, and arms held back and receives a hard blow to the chest. His opponent literally winds up and delivers a closed-fist blow from the ground, striking the man on the left pectoral muscle just above the heart. The impact frequently drops the man to his knees, and participants may cough up blood for several days after such a contest. After receiving several such blows, the man then has his turn to strike his opponent, while the respective supporters of each antagonist gather around and frenziedly urge their champion on.

All men in the two villages are obliged to participate as village   23
representatives, and on one occasion I saw some individuals take as many as three or four turns of four blows each. Duels of this type usually result from minor wrongs, such as a village being guilty of spreading bad rumors about another village, questioning its generosity or fierceness, or accusing it of gluttony at a feast. A variant of this form of duel is side slapping, in which an open-handed blow is delivered across the flank just above the pelvis.

More serious are the club fights. Although these almost invari-   24
ably result from cases in which a wife has been caught in an affair with another man, some fights follow the theft of food within the village. The usual procedure calls for a representative from each belligerent group. One man holds a ten-foot club upright, braces himself by leaning on the club and spreading his feet, then holds his head out for his opponent to strike. Following this comes his turn to do likewise to his adversary. These duels, more often than not, end in a free-for-all in which everybody clubs everybody else on whatever spot he can hit. Such brawls occasionally result in fatalities. However, since headmen of the respective groups stand by with bows drawn, no one dares deliver an intentionally killing blow, for if he does, he will be shot. The scalps of the older men are almost incredible to behold, covered as they are by as many as a dozen ugly welts. Yet, most of them proudly shave the top of their heads to display their scars.

Also precipitated by feuds over women are spear fights, which   25
are even more serious than club fights. Members of a village will

warn those of the offending village that they are coming to fight
with spears. They specify that they are not planning to shoot arrows unless the others shoot first. On the day of the fight, the
attackers enter the other village, armed with five or six sharpened
clubs or slender shafts some eight feet long and attempt to drive the
defenders out. If successful, the invaders steal all the valuable possessions—hammocks, cooking pots, and machetes—and retreat. In
the spear fight that occurred while I was studying the tribe, the
attackers were successful, but they wounded several individuals so
badly that one of them died. The fighting then escalated to a raid,
the penultimate form of violence.

Such raids may be precipitated by woman stealing or the killing   26
of a visitor (visitors are sometimes slain because they are suspected
of having practiced harmful magic that has led to a death in the
host's village). Raids also occur if a man kills his wife in a fit of
anger; her natal village is then obliged to avenge the death. Most
raids, however, are in revenge for deaths that occurred in previous
raids, and once the vendetta gets started, it is not likely to end for a
long time. Something else may trigger a raid. Occasionally an ambitious headman wearies of peaceful times—a rarity, certainly—
and deliberately creates a situation that will demonstrate his
leadership.

A revenge raid is preceded by a feast in which the ground bones   27
of the person to be avenged are mixed in a soup of boiled, ripe
plantains (the mainstay of Yanomamö diet) and swallowed.
Yanomamö are endocannibals, which means they consume the
remains of members of their own group. This ceremony puts the
raiders in the appropriate state of frenzy for the business of warfare.
A mock raid—rather like a dress rehearsal—is conducted in their
own village on the afternoon before the day of the raid, and a life-
size effigy of an enemy, constructed of leaves or a log, is slain. That
evening all the participants march, one at a time, to the center of
the village clearing, while clacking their bows and arrows and
screaming their versions of the calls of carnivorous birds, mam-
mals, and even insects.

When all have lined up facing the direction of the enemy village, 28
they sing their war song, "I am a meat-hungry buzzard," and shout
several times in unison until they hear the echo return from the
jungle. They then disperse to their individual sections of the village
to vomit the symbolic rotten flesh of the enemy that they, as symbolic carnivorous vultures and wasps, partook of in the lineup. The
same thing, with the exception of the song, is repeated at dawn the
following morning. Then the raiders, covered with black paint

made of chewed charcoal, march out of the village in single file and collect the hammocks and plantains that their women have previously set outside the village for them. On each night they spend en route to the enemy they fire arrows at a dummy in a mock raid. They approach the enemy village itself under cover of darkness, ambush the first person they catch, and retreat as rapidly as possible. If they catch a man and his family, they will shoot the man and steal the woman and her children. At a safe distance from her village, each of the raiders rapes the woman, and when they reach their own village, every man in the village may, if he wishes, do likewise before she is given to one of the men as a wife. Ordinarily she attempts to escape, but if caught, she may be killed. So constant is the threat of raids that every woman leaves her village in the knowledge that she may be stolen.

The supreme form of violence is the *nomohoni*—the "trick." During the dry season, the Yanomamö do a great deal of visiting. An entire village will go to another village for a ceremony that involves feasting, dancing, chanting, curing, trading, and just plain gossiping. Shortly after arrival, the visitors are invited to recline in the hammocks of the hosts. By custom they lie motionless to display their fine decorations while the hosts prepare food for them. But now suppose that a village has a grudge to settle with another, such as deaths to avenge. It enlists the support of a third village to act as accomplice. This third village, which must be on friendly terms with the intended victims, will invite them to a feast. While the guests recline defenseless in the hammocks, the hosts descend on them with axes and sharpened poles, treacherously killing as many as they can. Those that manage to escape the slaughter inside the village are shot outside the palisade by the village that instigated the *nomohoni*. The women and children will be shared between the two accomplices.

Throughout all this ferocity there are two organizational aspects of violence. One concerns leadership: A man must be able to demonstrate his fierceness if he is to be a true leader. It is equally important, however, that he have a large natural following—that is, he must have many male kinsmen to support his position and a quantity of daughters and sisters to distribute to other men. Lineage leaders cannot accurately be described as unilateral initiators of activities; rather, they are the vehicles through which the group's will is expressed. For example, when a certain palm fruit is ripe and is particularly abundant in an area some distance from the village, everybody knows that the whole village will pack its belongings and erect a temporary camp at that spot to collect the fruit. The headman does little more than set the date. When his kinsmen see him packing, they know that the time has come to leave for the collecting trip. True, the headman does have some initiative in raiding, but not even this is completely independent of the attitudes of his followers, which dictate that a death must be avenged. However, when the purpose of a raid is to steal women, the headman does have some freedom to act on his own initiative.

As a general rule, the smaller his natural following, the more   31
he is obliged to demonstrate his personal qualities of fierceness and leadership. Padudiwä, the headman of one of the lineages in Bisaasi-tedi, took pains to demonstrate his personal qualities whenever he could; he had only two living brothers and four living sisters in his group. Most of his demonstrations of ferocity were cruel beatings he administered to his four wives, none of whom had brothers in the village to take their part. Several young men who attached themselves to his household admired him for this.

Padudiwä was also responsible for organizing several raids while   32
I lived with the villagers of Bisaasi-tedi. Every one of them was against Patanowä-tedi, a village that was being raided regularly by some seven or eight other villages, so that the danger of being raided in return was correspondingly reduced. On one occasion, when three young men from Patanowä-tedi arrived as emissaries of peace, Padudiwä wanted to kill them, although he had lived with them at one time and they were fairly close relatives. The murder was prevented by the headman of the other—and larger—lineage in the village, who warned that if an attempt were made on the lives of the visitors he himself would kill Padudiwä.

Obviously then, Padudiwä's reputation was built largely on cal-   33
culated acts of fierceness, which carefully reduced the possibility of personal danger to himself and his followers, and on cunning and cruelty. To some extent he was obliged by the smallness of his gathering to behave in such a way, but he was certainly a man to treat with caution.

Despite their extreme aggressiveness, the Yanomamö have at   34
least two qualities I admired. They are kind and indulgent with children and can quickly forget personal angers. (A few even treated me almost as an equal—in their culture this was a considerable concession.) But to portray them as "noble savages" would be misleading. Many of them are delightful and charming people when confronted alone and on a personal basis, but the greater number of them are much like Padudiwä—or strive to be that way. As they frequently told me, *Yanomamö täbä waiteri!*—"Yanomamö are fierce!"

STANLEY MILGRAM

The Perils of Obedience

Stanley Milgram (1933–1984) was a leading social psychologist who worked in such areas as the effect of group pressure on the individual, the psychology of city life, and the effects of television. An ingenious experimenter, Milgram was able to get objective data on questions most of us see as matters of speculation or personal impression. To measure the influence of group pressure on individual judgment, for example, he developed an experiment in which the subject was asked to choose the longer of two lines; the experiment was so arranged that several other "judges" would pick the wrong answer before the subject had a chance to choose. Many subjects then chose the wrong answer, despite the evidence of their own senses. In the experiment reported in "The Perils of Obedience" (*Harper's Magazine*, December 1973), Milgram set out to learn how much aggressive behavior could be forced (or released) in ordinary people by authoritative commands. The results, as Milgram points out, shed new light on the causes of wartime atrocities.

Obedience is as basic an element in the structure of social life as one can point to. Some system of authority is a requirement of all communal living, and it is only the person dwelling in isolation who is not forced to respond, with defiance or submission, to the commands of others. For many people, obedience is a deeply ingrained behavior tendency, indeed a potent impulse overriding training in ethics, sympathy, and moral conduct.

The dilemma inherent in submission to authority is ancient, as old as the story of Abraham,[1] and the question of whether one should obey when commands conflict with conscience has been argued by Plato, dramatized in *Antigone*,[2] and treated to philosophic analysis in almost every historical epoch. Conservative philosophers argue that the very fabric of society is threatened by disobedience, while humanists stress the primacy of the individual conscience.

The legal and philosophic aspects of obedience are of enormous import, but they say very little about how most people behave in concrete situations. I set up a simple experiment at Yale University to test how much pain an ordinary citizen would inflict on another

1. Genesis 22.
2. Tragedy by Sophocles (ca. 496–406 B.C.), the Greek playwright.

person simply because he was ordered to by an experimental scientist. Stark authority was pitted against the subjects' strongest moral imperatives against hurting others, and, with the subjects' ears ringing with the screams of the victims, authority won more often than not. The extreme willingness of adults to go to almost any lengths on the command of an authority constitutes the chief finding of the study and the fact most urgently demanding explanation.

In the basic experimental design, two people come to a psychology laboratory to take part in a study of memory and learning. One of them is designated as a "teacher" and the other a "learner." The experimenter explains that the study is concerned with the effects of punishment on learning. The learner is conducted into a room, seated in a kind of miniature electric chair; his arms are strapped to prevent excessive movement, and an electrode is attached to his wrist. He is told that he will be read lists of simple word pairs, and that he will then be tested on his ability to remember the second word of a pair when he hears the first one again. Whenever he makes an error, he will receive electric shocks of increasing intensity.

The real focus of the experiment is the teacher. After watching the learner being strapped into place, he is seated before an impressive shock generator. The instrument panel consists of thirty lever switches set in a horizontal line. Each switch is clearly labeled with a voltage designation ranging from 15 to 450 volts. The following designations are clearly indicated for groups of four switches, going from left to right: Slight Shock, Moderate Shock, Strong Shock, Very Strong Shock, Intense Shock, Extreme Intensity Shock, Danger: Severe Shock. (Two switches after this last designation are simply marked XXX.)

When a switch is depressed, a pilot light corresponding to each switch is illuminated in bright red; an electric buzzing is heard; a blue light, labeled "voltage energizer," flashes; the dial on the voltage meter swings to the right; and various relay clicks sound off.

The upper left-hand corner of the generator is labeled SHOCK GENERATOR, TYPE ZLB, DYSON INSTRUMENT COMPANY, WALTHAM, MASS. OUTPUT 15 VOLTS—450 VOLTS.

Each subject is given a sample 45-volt shock from the generator before his run as teacher, and the jolt strengthens his belief in the authenticity of the machine.

The teacher is a genuinely naïve subject who has come to the laboratory for the experiment. The learner, or victim, is actually an actor who receives no shock at all. The point of the experiment is to see how far a person will proceed in a concrete and measurable situation in which he is ordered to inflict increasing pain on a protesting victim.

Conflict arises when the man receiving the shock begins to show   10
that he is experiencing discomfort. At 75 volts, he grunts; at 120 volts, he complains loudly; at 150, he demands to be released from the experiment. As the voltage increases, his protests become more vehement and emotional. At 285 volts, his response can be described only as an agonized scream. Soon thereafter, he makes no sound at all.

For the teacher, the situation quickly becomes one of gripping   11
tension. It is not a game for him; conflict is intense and obvious. The manifest suffering of the learner presses him to quit; but each time he hesitates to administer a shock, the experimenter orders him to continue. To extricate himself from this plight, the subject must make a clear break with authority.[3]

The subject, Gretchen Brandt,[4] is an attractive thirty-one-year-   12
old medical technician who works at the Yale Medical School. She had emigrated from Germany five years before.

On several occasions when the learner complains, she turns to   13
the experimenter coolly and inquires, "Shall I continue?" She promptly returns to her task when the experimenter asks her to do so. At the administration of 210 volts, she turns to the experimenter, remarking firmly, "Well, I'm sorry, I don't think we should continue."

EXPERIMENTER: The experiment requires that you go on until he has   14
learned all the word pairs correctly.

BRANDT: He has a heart condition, I'm sorry. He told you that   15
before.

EXPERIMENTER: The shocks may be painful but they are not   16
dangerous.

BRANDT: Well, I'm sorry, I think when shocks continue like this,   17
they *are* dangerous. You ask him if he wants to get out. It's his free will.

EXPERIMENTER: It is absolutely essential that we continue. . . .   18

BRANDT: I'd like you to ask him. We came here of our free will. If he   19
wants to continue I'll go ahead. He told you he had a heart condition. I'm sorry. I don't want to be responsible for anything happening to him. I wouldn't like it for me either.

EXPERIMENTER: You have no other choice.   20

3. The ethical problems of carrying out an experiment of this sort are too complex to be dealt with here, but they receive extended treatment in the book from which this article is adapted. [author's note]
4. Names of subjects described in this piece have been changed. [author's note]

BRANDT: I think we are here on our own free will. I don't want to   21
be responsible if anything happens to him. Please understand that.
She refuses to go further and the experiment is terminated.   22
The woman is firm and resolute throughout. She indicates in the   23
interview that she was in no way tense or nervous, and this corresponds to her controlled appearance during the experiment. She
feels that the last shock she administered to the learner was extremely painful and reiterates that she "did not want to be responsible for any harm to him."
The woman's straightforward, courteous behavior in the experi-   24
ment, lack of tension, and total control of her own action seem to
make disobedience a simple and rational deed. Her behavior is the
very embodiment of what I envisioned would be true for almost all
subjects.

Before the experiments, I sought predictions about the outcome   25
from various kinds of people—psychiatrists, college sophomores,
middle-class adults, graduate students and faculty in the behavioral
sciences. With remarkable similarity, they predicted that virtually
all subjects would refuse to obey the experimenter. The psychiatrists, specifically, predicted that most subjects would not go beyond 150 volts, when the victim makes his first explicit demand to
be free. They expected that only 4 percent would reach 300 volts,
and that only a pathological fringe of about one in a thousand
would administer the highest shock on the board.
These predictions were unequivocally wrong. Of the forty sub-   26
jects in the first experiment, twenty-five obeyed the orders of the
experimenter to the end, punishing the victim until they reached
the most potent shock available on the generator. After 450 volts
were administered three times, the experimenter called a halt to
the session. Many obedient subjects then heaved sighs of relief,
mopped their brows, rubbed their fingers over their eyes, or nervously fumbled cigarettes. Others displayed only minimal signs of
tension from beginning to end.
When the very first experiments were carried out, Yale under-   27
graduates were used as subjects, and about 60 percent of them
were fully obedient. A colleague of mine immediately dismissed
these findings as having no relevance to "ordinary" people, asserting that Yale undergraduates are a highly aggressive, competitive
bunch who step on each other's necks on the slightest provocation.
He assured me that when "ordinary" people were tested, the results would be quite different. As we moved from the pilot studies
to the regular experimental series, people drawn from every
stratum of New Haven life came to be employed in the experiment:

professionals, white-collar workers, unemployed persons, and industrial workers. *The experimental outcome was the same as we had observed among the students.*

Moreover, when the experiments were repeated in Princeton, Munich, Rome, South Africa, and Australia, the level of obedience was invariably somewhat *higher* than found in the investigation reported in this article. Thus one scientist in Munich found 85 percent of his subjects obedient.

Fred Prozi's reactions, if more dramatic than most, illuminate the conflicts experienced by others in less visible form. About fifty years old and unemployed at the time of the experiment, he has a good-natured, if slightly dissolute, appearance, and he strikes people as a rather ordinary fellow. He begins the session calmly but becomes tense as it proceeds. After delivering the 180-volt shock, he pivots around in his chair and, shaking his head, addresses the experimenter in agitated tones:

PROZI: I can't stand it. I'm not going to kill that man in there. You hear him hollering?

EXPERIMENTER: As I told you before, the shocks may be painful, but . . .

PROZI: But he's hollering. He can't stand it. What's going to happen to him?

EXPERIMENTER (his voice is patient, matter-of-fact): The experiment requires that you continue, Teacher.

PROZI: Aaah, but, unh, I'm not going to get that man sick in there— know what I mean?

EXPERIMENTER: Whether the learner likes it or not, we must go on, through all the word pairs.

PROZI: I refuse to take the responsibility. He's in there hollering!

EXPERIMENTER: It's absolutely essential that you continue, Prozi.

PROZI (indicating the unused questions): There's too many left here, I mean, Jeez, if he gets them wrong, there's too many of them left. I mean, who's going to take the responsibility if anything happens to that gentleman?

EXPERIMENTER: I'm responsible for anything that happens to him. Continue, please.

PROZI: All right. (Consults list of words.) The next one's "Slow— walk, truck, dance, music." Answer, please. (A buzzing sound indicates the learner has signaled his answer.) Wrong. A hundred and ninety-five volts. "Dance." (Zzumph!)

LEARNER (yelling): Let me out of here! My heart's bothering me! (Teacher looks at experimenter.)

EXPERIMENTER: Continue, please.

LEARNER (screaming): Let me out of here! You have no right to   43
keep me here! Let me out of here, my heart's bothering me, let me
out!

PROZI (shakes head, pats the table nervously): You see, he's holler-   44
ing. Hear that? Gee, I don't know.

EXPERIMENTER: The experiment requires . . .   45

PROZI (interrupting): I know it does, sir, but I mean—hunh! He   46
don't know what he's getting in for. He's up to 195 volts! (Experiment continues, through 210 volts, 225 volts, 240 volts, 255 volts,
270 volts, at which point Prozi, with evident relief, runs out of
word-pair questions.)

EXPERIMENTER: You'll have to go back to the beginning of that page   47
and go through them again until he's learned them all correctly.

PROZI: Aw, no. I'm not going to kill that man. You mean I've got to   48
keep going up with the scale? No, sir. He's hollering in there. I'm
not going to give him 450 volts.

EXPERIMENTER: The experiment requires that you go on.   49

LEARNER: Ohhh. I absolutely refuse to answer anymore. (Shouting   50
urgently now.) Let me out of here! You can't hold me here! Get me
out. Get-me-out-of-here!

EXPERIMENTER: Continue. The next word is "Green," please.   51

PROZI: "Green—grass, hat, ink, apple." (Nothing happens. No an-   52
swering buzz. Just gloomy silence.)

PROZI: I don't think he is going to answer.   53

EXPERIMENTER: If the learner doesn't answer in a reasonable time,   54
about four or five seconds, consider the answer wrong. And follow
the same procedures you have been doing for wrong answers. Say,
"Wrong," tell him the number of volts, give him the punishment,
read him the correct answer. Continue, please.

PROZI: "Green—grass, hat, ink, apple." Answer, please. (More si-   55
lence. Subject just sits there.)

EXPERIMENTER: Go on with the procedure, please.   56

PROZI: Three hundred and fifteen volts. The answer is "ink."   57
(Zzumph!)

LEARNER: Ohh. Ooohh.   58

PROZI (relieved to hear response): Next one . . .   59

LEARNER: I absolutely refuse to answer.   60

PROZI: You got to. You get a shock if you don't answer. (Experi-   61
ment continues with learner refusing to answer, and, finally, failing
even to grunt or groan. At 375 volts, the subject stands up.)

PROZI: I think something's happened to that fellow in there. I don't   62
get no answer. He was hollering at less voltage. Can't you check in
and see if he's all right, please?

EXPERIMENTER (with same detached calm): Not once we've started.   63
Please continue, Teacher.
PROZI (sits down, sighs deeply): "Cool—day, shade, water, paint."   64
Answer, please. Are you all right in there? Are you all right?
EXPERIMENTER: Please continue, Teacher. Continue, please. (Subject   65
pushes lever. Zzumph!)
PROZI (swiveling around in his chair): Something's happened to   66
that man in there. (Swiveling back.) Next one. "Low—dollar,
necklace, moon, paint." (Turning around again.) Something's hap-
pened to that man in there. You better check in on him, sir. He
won't answer or nothing.
EXPERIMENTER: Continue. Go on, please.   67
PROZI: You accept all responsibility?   68
EXPERIMENTER: The responsibility is mine. Correct. Please go on.   69
(Subject returns to his list, starts running through words as rapidly
as he can read them, works through to 450 volts.)
PROZI: That's that.   70
EXPERIMENTER: Continue using the 450 switch for each wrong an-   71
swer. Continue, please.
PROZI: But I don't get anything!   72
EXPERIMENTER: Please continue. The next word is "white."   73
PROZI: Don't you think you should look in on him, please?   74
EXPERIMENTER: Not once we've started the experiment.   75
PROZI: What if he's dead in there? (Gestures toward the room with   76
the electric chair.) I mean, he told me he can't stand the shock, sir. I
don't mean to be rude, but I think you should look in on him. All
you have to do is look in on him. All you have to do is look in the
door. I don't get no answer, no noise. Something might have happened to the gentleman in there, sir.
EXPERIMENTER: We must continue. Go on, please.   77
PROZI: You mean keep giving him what? Four-hundred-fifty volts,   78
what he's got now?
EXPERIMENTER: That's correct. Continue. The next word is "white."   79
PROZI (now at a furious pace): "White—cloud, horse, rock,   80
house." Answer, please. The answer is "horse." Four hundred and
fifty volts. (Zzumph!) Next word, "Bag—paint, music, clown,
girl." The answer is "paint." Four hundred and fifty volts.
(Zzumph!) Next word is "Short—sentence, movie . . ."
EXPERIMENTER: Excuse me, Teacher. We'll have to discontinue the   81
experiment.

Morris Braverman, another subject, is a thirty-nine-year-old so-   82
cial worker. He looks older than his years because of his bald head

and serious demeanor. His brow is furrowed, as if all the world's burdens were carried on his face. He appears intelligent and concerned.

When the learner refuses to answer and the experimenter instructs Braverman to treat the absence of an answer as equivalent to a wrong answer, he takes his instruction to heart. Before administering 300 volts he asserts officiously to the victim, "Mr. Wallace, your silence has to be considered as a wrong answer." Then he administers the shock. He offers halfheartedly to change places with the learner, then asks the experimenter, "Do I have to follow these instructions literally?" He is satisfied with the experimenter's answer that he does. His very refined and authoritative manner of speaking is increasingly broken up by wheezing laughter.

The experimenter's notes on Mr. Braverman at the last few shocks are:

Almost breaking up now each time gives shock. Rubbing face to hide laughter.

Squinting, trying to hide face with hand, still laughing.

Cannot control his laughter at this point no matter what he does.

Clenching fist, pushing it onto table.

In an interview after the session, Mr. Braverman summarizes the experiment with impressive fluency and intelligence. He feels the experiment may have been designed also to "test the effects on the teacher of being in an essentially sadistic role, as well as the reactions of a student to a learning situation that was authoritative and punitive."

When asked how painful the last few shocks administered to the learner were, he indicates that the most extreme category on the scale is not adequate (it read EXTREMELY PAINFUL) and places his mark at the edge of the scale with an arrow carrying it beyond the scale.

It is almost impossible to convey the greatly relaxed, sedate quality of his conversation in the interview. In the most relaxed terms, he speaks about his severe inner tension.

EXPERIMENTER: At what point were you most tense or nervous?

MR. BRAVERMAN: Well, when he first began to cry out in pain, and I realized this was hurting him. This got worse when he just blocked and refused to answer. There was I. I'm a nice person, I think, hurting somebody, and caught up in what seemed a mad situation . . . and in the interest of science, one goes through with it.

When the interviewer pursues the general question of tension, Mr. Braverman spontaneously mentions his laughter.

"My reactions were awfully peculiar. I don't know if you were watching me, but my reactions were giggly, and trying to stifle laughter. This isn't the way I usually am. This was a sheer reaction to a totally impossible situation. And my reaction was to the situation of having to hurt somebody. And being totally helpless and caught up in a set of circumstances where I just couldn't deviate and I couldn't try to help. This is what got me."

Mr. Braverman, like all subjects, was told the actual nature and   96
purpose of the experiment, and a year later he affirmed in a questionnaire that he had learned something of personal importance: "What appalled me was that I could possess this capacity for obedience and compliance to a central idea, i.e., the value of a memory experiment, even after it became clear that continued adherence to this value was at the expense of violation of another value, i.e., don't hurt someone who is helpless and not hurting you. As my wife said, 'You can call yourself Eichmann.'[5] I hope I deal more effectively with any future conflicts of values I encounter."

One theoretical interpretation of this behavior holds that all peo-   97
ple harbor deeply aggressive instincts continually pressing for expression, and that the experiment provides institutional justification for the release of these impulses. According to this view, if a person is placed in a situation in which he has complete power over another individual, whom he may punish as much as he likes, all that is sadistic and bestial in man comes to the fore. The impulse to shock the victim is seen to flow from the potent aggressive tendencies, which are part of the motivational life of the individual, and the experiment, because it provides social legitimacy, simply opens the door to their expression.

It becomes vital, therefore, to compare the subject's performance   98
when he is under orders and when he is allowed to choose the shock level.

The procedure was identical to our standard experiment, except   99
that the teacher was told that he was free to select any shock level on any of the trials. (The experimenter took pains to point out that the teacher could use the highest levels on the generator, the lowest, any in between, or any combination of levels.) Each subject proceeded for thirty critical trials. The learner's protests were coordinated to standard shock levels, his first grunt coming at 75 volts, his first vehement protest at 150 volts.

The average shock used during the thirty critical trials was less   100
than 60 volts—lower than the point at which the victim showed the first signs of discomfort. Three of the forty subjects did not go

5. Adolf Eichmann (1906–1962), chief executioner in the Nazi extermination campaign against European Jews.

beyond the very lowest level on the board, twenty-eight went no higher than 75 volts, and thirty-eight did not go beyond the first loud protest at 150 volts. Two subjects provided the exception, administering up to 325 and 450 volts, but the overall result was that the great majority of people delivered very low, usually painless, shocks when the choice was explicitly up to them.

This condition of the experiment undermines another com-   101
monly offered explanation of the subjects' behavior—that those who shocked the victim at the most severe levels came only from the sadistic fringe of society. If one considers that almost two-thirds of the participants fall into the category of "obedient" subjects, and that they represented ordinary people drawn from working, mana-gerial, and professional classes, the argument becomes very shaky. Indeed, it is highly reminiscent of the issue that arose in connection with Hannah Arendt's 1963 book, *Eichmann in Jerusalem*. Arendt contended that the prosecution's effort to depict Eichmann as a sadistic monster was fundamentally wrong, that he came closer to being an uninspired bureaucrat who simply sat at his desk and did his job. For asserting her views, Arendt became the object of con-siderable scorn, even calumny. Somehow, it was felt that the mon-strous deeds carried out by Eichmann required a brutal, twisted personality, evil incarnate. After witnessing hundreds of ordinary persons submit to the authority in our own experiments, I must conclude that Arendt's conception of the banality of evil comes closer to the truth than one might dare imagine. The ordinary person who shocked the victim did so out of a sense of obligation—an impression of his duties as a subject—and not from any pecu-liarly aggressive tendencies.

This is, perhaps, the most fundamental lesson of our study: ordi-   102
nary people, simply doing their jobs, and without any particular hostility on their part, can become agents in a terrible destructive process. Moreover, even when the destructive effects of their work become patently clear, and they are asked to carry out actions incompatible with fundamental standards of morality, relatively few people have the resources needed to resist authority.

Many of the people were in some sense against what they did to   103
the learner, and many protested even while they obeyed. Some were totally convinced of the wrongness of their actions but could not bring themselves to make an open break with authority. They often derived satisfaction from their thoughts and felt that—within themselves, at least—they had been on the side of the angels. They tried to reduce strain by obeying the experimenter but "only slightly," encouraging the learner, touching the generator switches

gingerly. When interviewed, such a subject would stress that he had "asserted my humanity" by administering the briefest shock possible. Handling the conflict in this manner was easier than defiance.

The situation is constructed so that there is no way the subject   104
can stop shocking the learner without violating the experimenter's definitions of his own competence. The subject fears that he will appear arrogant, untoward, and rude if he breaks off. Although these inhibiting emotions appear small in scope alongside the violence being done to the learner, they suffuse the mind and feelings of the subject, who is miserable at the prospect of having to repudiate the authority to his face. (When the experiment was altered so that the experimenter gave his instructions by telephone instead of in person, only a third as many people were fully obedient through 450 volts.) It is a curious thing that a measure of compassion on the part of the subject—an unwillingness to "hurt" the experimenter's feelings—is part of those binding forces inhibiting his disobedience. The withdrawal of such deference may be as painful to the subject as to the authority he defies.

The subjects do not derive satisfaction from inflicting pain, but   105
they often like the feeling they get from pleasing the experimenter. They are proud of doing a good job, obeying the experimenter under difficult circumstances. While the subjects administered only mild shocks on their own initiative, one experimental variation showed that, under orders, 30 percent of them were willing to deliver 450 volts even when they had to forcibly push the learner's hand down on the electrode.

Bruno Batta is a thirty-seven-year-old welder who took part in   106
the variation requiring the use of force. He was born in New Haven, his parents in Italy. He has a rough-hewn face that conveys a conspicuous lack of alertness. He has some difficulty in mastering the experimental procedure and needs to be corrected by the experimenter several times. He shows appreciation for the help and willingness to do what is required. After the 150-volt level, Batta has to force the learner's hand down on the shock plate, since the learner himself refuses to touch it.

When the learner first complains, Mr. Batta pays no attention to   107
him. His face remains impassive, as if to dissociate himself from the learner's disruptive behavior. When the experimenter instructs him to force the learner's hand down, he adopts a rigid, mechanical procedure. He tests the generator switch. When it fails to function, he immediately forces the learner's hand onto the shock plate. All

the while he maintains the same rigid mask. The learner, seated alongside him, begs him to stop, but with robotic impassivity he continues the procedure.

What is extraordinary is his apparent total indifference to the learner; he hardly takes cognizance of him as a human being. Meanwhile, he relates to the experimenter in a submissive and courteous fashion. 108

At the 330-volt level, the learner refuses not only to touch the shock plate but also to provide any answers. Annoyed, Batta turns to him, and chastises him: "You better answer and get it over with. We can't stay here all night." These are the only words he directs to the learner in the course of an hour. Never again does he speak to him. The scene is brutal and depressing, his hard, impassive face showing total indifference as he subdues the screaming learner and gives him shocks. He seems to derive no pleasure from the act itself, only quiet satisfaction at doing his job properly. 109

When he administers 450 volts, he turns to the experimenter and asks, "Where do we go from here, Professor?" His tone is deferential and expresses his willingness to be a cooperative subject, in contrast to the learner's obstinacy. 110

At the end of the session he tells the experimenter how honored he has been to help him, and in a moment of contrition, remarks, "Sir, sorry it couldn't have been a full experiment." 111

He has done his honest best. It is only the deficient behavior of the learner that has denied the experimenter full satisfaction. 112

The essence of obedience is that a person comes to view himself as the instrument for carrying out another person's wishes, and he therefore no longer regards himself as responsible for his actions. Once this critical shift of viewpoint has occurred, all of the essential features of obedience follow. The most far-reaching consequence is that the person feels responsible *to* the authority directing him but feels no responsibility *for* the content of the actions that the authority prescribes. Morality does not disappear—it acquires a radically different focus: the subordinate person feels shame or pride depending on how adequately he has performed the actions called for by authority. 113

Language provides numerous terms to pinpoint this type of morality: *loyalty, duty, discipline* all are terms heavily saturated with moral meaning and refer to the degree to which a person fulfills his obligations to authority. They refer not to the "goodness" of the person per se but to the adequacy with which a subordinate fulfills his socially defined role. The most frequent defense of the individual who has performed a heinous act under command of authority 114 is that he has simply done his duty. In asserting this defense, the individual is not introducing an alibi concocted for the moment but is reporting honestly on the psychological attitude induced by submission to authority.

For a person to feel responsible for his actions, he must sense   115
that the behavior has flowed from "the self." In the situation we have studied, subjects have precisely the opposite view of their actions—namely, they see them as originating in the motives of some other person. Subjects in the experiment frequently said, "If it were up to me, I would not have administered shocks to the learner."

Once authority has been isolated as the cause of the subject's   116
behavior, it is legitimate to inquire into the necessary elements of authority and how it must be perceived in order to gain his compliance. We conducted some investigations into the kinds of changes that would cause the experimenter to lose his power and to be disobeyed by the subject. Some of the variations revealed that:

• *The experimenter's physical presence has a marked impact on his*   117
authority. As cited earlier, obedience dropped off sharply when orders were given by telephone. The experimenter could often induce a disobedient subject to go on by returning to the laboratory.

• *Conflicting authority severely paralyzes action.* When two experi-   118
menters of equal status, both seated at the command desk, gave incompatible orders, no shocks were delivered past the point of their disagreement.

• *The rebellious action of others severely undermines authority.* In one   119
variation, three teachers (two actors and a real subject) administered a test and shocks. When the two actors disobeyed the experimenter and refused to go beyond a certain shock level, thirty-six of forty subjects joined their disobedient peers and refused as well.

Although the experimenter's authority was fragile in some re-   120
spects, it is also true that he had almost none of the tools used in ordinary command structures. For example, the experimenter did not threaten the subjects with punishment—such as loss of income, community ostracism, or jail—for failure to obey. Neither could he offer incentives. Indeed, we should expect the experimenter's authority to be much less than that of someone like a general, since the experimenter has no power to enforce his imperatives, and since participation in a psychological experiment scarcely evokes the sense of urgency and dedication found in warfare. Despite these limitations, he still managed to command a dismaying degree of obedience.

I will cite one final variation of the experiment that depicts a   121
dilemma that is more common in everyday life. The subject was

not ordered to pull the lever that shocked the victim, but merely to perform a subsidiary task (administering the word-pair test) while another person administered the shock. In this situation, thirty-seven of forty adults continued to the highest level on the shock generator. Predictably, they excused their behavior by saying that the responsibility belonged to the man who actually pulled the switch. This may illustrate a dangerously typical arrangement in a complex society: it is easy to ignore responsibility when one is only an intermediate link in a chain of action.

The problem of obedience is not wholly psychological. The form   122
and shape of society and the way it is developing have much to do with it. There was a time, perhaps, when people were able to give a fully human response to any situation because they were fully absorbed in it as human beings. But as soon as there was a division of labor things changed. Beyond a certain point, the breaking up of society into people carrying out narrow and very special jobs takes away from the human quality of work and life. A person does not get to see the whole situation but only a small part of it, and is thus unable to act without some kind of overall direction. He yields to authority but in doing so is alienated from his own actions.

Even Eichmann was sickened when he toured the concentration   123
camps, but he had only to sit at a desk and shuffle papers. At the same time the man in the camp who actually dropped Cyclon-b into the gas chambers was able to justify *his* behavior on the ground that he was only following orders from above. Thus there is a fragmentation of the total human act; no one is confronted with the consequences of his decision to carry out the evil act. The person who assumes responsibility has evaporated. Perhaps this is the most common characteristic of socially organized evil in modern society.

RICHARD WRIGHT

The Ethics of Living Jim Crow: An Autobiographical Sketch

Richard Wright (1908–1960) was born near Natchez, Mississippi, the son of a millworker and a schoolteacher. His education was interrupted by his family's frequent moves from town to town, and he left school at fifteen. Thereafter, he took his education into his own hands, forging a note that allowed him to get books from the segregated public library in Memphis, Tennessee: "Dear Madam: Will you please let this nigger boy have some books on H. L. Mencken." Wright lived through some of the worst years of legalized segregation and systematic violence against American blacks. In *Uncle Tom's Children* (1938) and *Native Son* (1940) he produced starkly realistic fiction that showed how the oppression of blacks could drive them to political radicalism or reduce them to brutality. In 1945 Wright published his autobiography, *Black Boy*, perhaps his most important work. Soon after, he moved to France, where he continued to produce fiction and nonfiction and was politically active in encouraging independence movements in Africa. "The Ethics of Living Jim Crow" was first published as part of a Federal Writers' Project anthology in 1937, then as the introduction to *Uncle Tom's Children*.

My first lesson in how to live as a Negro came when I was quite small. We were living in Arkansas. Our house stood behind the railroad tracks. Its skimpy yard was paved with black cinders. Nothing green ever grew in that yard. The only touch of green we could see was far away, beyond the tracks, over where the white folks lived. But cinders were good enough for me and I never missed the green growing things. And anyhow cinders were fine weapons. You could always have a nice hot war with huge black cinders. All you had to do was crouch behind the brick pillars of a house with your hands full of gritty ammunition. And the first woolly black head you saw pop out from behind another row of pillars was your target. You tried your very best to knock it off. It was great fun.

I never fully realized the appalling disadvantages of a cinder environment till one day the gang to which I belonged found itself engaged in a war with the white boys who lived beyond the tracks. As usual we laid down our cinder barrage, thinking that this would wipe the white boys out. But they replied with a steady bombardment of broken bottles. We doubled our cinder barrage, but they hid behind trees, hedges, and the sloping embankments of their lawns. Having no such fortifications, we retreated to the brick pillars of our homes. During the retreat a broken milk bottle caught me behind the ear, opening a deep gash which bled profusely. The sight of blood pouring over my face completely demoralized our ranks. My fellow-combatants left me standing paralyzed in the center of the yard, and scurried for their homes. A kind neighbor saw me and rushed me to a doctor, who took three stitches in my neck.

I sat brooding on my front steps, nursing my wound and waiting   3
for my mother to come from work. I felt that a grave injustice had
been done me. It was all right to throw cinders. The greatest harm a
cinder could do was leave a bruise. But broken bottles were
dangerous; they left you cut, bleeding, and helpless.

When night fell, my mother came from the white folks' kitchen.   4
I raced down the street to meet her. I could just feel in my bones
that she would understand. I knew she would tell me exactly what
to do next time. I grabbed her hand and babbled out the whole
story. She examined my wound, then slapped me.

"How come yuh didn't hide?" she asked me. "How come yuh   5
awways fightin'?"

I was outraged, and bawled. Between sobs I told her that I didn't   6
have any trees or hedges to hide behind. There wasn't a thing I
could have used as a trench. And you couldn't throw very far
when you were hiding behind the brick pillars of a house. She
grabbed a barrel stave, dragged me home, stripped me naked, and
beat me till I had a fever of one hundred and two. She would
smack my rump with the stave, and while the skin was still smarting, impart to me gems of Jim Crow wisdom. I was never to throw
cinders any more. I was never to fight any more wars. I was never,
never, under any conditions, to fight *white* folks again. And they
were absolutely right in clouting me with the broken milk bottle.
Didn't I know she was working hard every day in the hot kitchens
of the white folks to make money to take care of me? When was I
ever going to learn to be a good boy? She couldn't be bothered
with my fights. She finished by telling me that I ought to be thankful to God as long as I lived that they didn't kill me.

All that night I was delirious and could not sleep. Each time I   7
closed my eyes I saw monstrous white faces suspended from the
ceiling, leering at me.

From that time on, the charm of my cinder yard was gone. The   8
green trees, the trimmed hedges, the cropped lawns grew very
meaningful, became a symbol. Even today when I think of white
folks, the hard, sharp outlines of white houses surrounded by trees,
lawns, and hedges are present somewhere in the background of my
mind. Through the years they grew into an overreaching symbol
of fear.

It was a long time before I came in close contact with white folks   9
again. We moved from Arkansas to Mississippi. Here we had the
good fortune not to live behind the railroad tracks, or close to white
neighborhoods. We lived in the very heart of the local Black Belt.
There were black churches and black preachers; there were black
schools and black teachers; black groceries and black clerks. In fact,

everything was so solidly black that for a long time I did not even think of white folks, save in remote and vague terms. But this could not last forever. As one grows older one eats more. One's clothing costs more. When I finished grammar school I had to go to work. My mother could no longer feed and clothe me on her cooking job.

There is but one place where a black boy who knows no trade 10 can get a job, and that's where the houses and faces are white, where the trees, lawns, and hedges are green. My first job was with an optical company in Jackson, Mississippi. The morning I applied I stood straight and neat before the boss, answering all his questions with sharp yessirs and nosirs. I was very careful to pronounce my *sirs* distinctly, in order that he might know that I was polite, that I knew where I was, and that I knew he was a *white* man. I wanted that job badly.

He looked me over as though he were examining a prize poodle. 11 He questioned me closely about my schooling, being particularly insistent about how much mathematics I had had. He seemed very pleased when I told him I had had two years of algebra.

"Boy, how would you like to learn something around here?" he 12 asked me.

"I'd like it fine, sir," I said, happy. I had visions of "working my 13 way up." Even Negroes have those visions.

"All right," he said. "Come on." 14

I followed him to the small factory. 15

"Pease," he said to a white man of about thirty-five, "this is 16 Richard. He's going to work for us."

Pease looked at me and nodded. 17

I was then taken to a white boy of about seventeen. 18

"Morrie, this is Richard, who's going to work for us." 19

"Whut yuh sayin' there, boy!" Morrie boomed at me. 20

"Fine!" I answered. 21

The boss instructed these two to help me, teach me, give me jobs 22 to do, and let me learn what I could in my spare time.

My wages were five dollars a week. 23

I worked hard, trying to please. For the first month I got along 24 O.K. Both Pease and Morrie seemed to like me. But one thing was missing. And I kept thinking about it. I was not learning anything and nobody was volunteering to help me. Thinking they had forgotten that I was to learn something about the mechanics of grinding lenses, I asked Morrie one day to tell me about the work. He grew red.

"Whut yuh tryin' t' do, nigger, get smart?" he asked. 25

"Naw; I ain' tryin' t' git smart," I said. 26

"Well, don't, if yuh know whut's good for yuh!" 27

I was puzzled. Maybe he just doesn't want to help me, I thought. ²⁸
I went to Pease.

"Say, are yuh crazy, you black bastard?" Pease asked me, his ²⁹
gray eyes growing hard.

I spoke out, reminding him that the boss had said I was to be ³⁰
given a chance to learn something.

"Nigger, you think you're *white,* don't you?" ³¹

"Naw, sir!" ³²

"Well, you're acting mighty like it!" ³³

"But, Mr. Pease, the boss said . . ." ³⁴

Pease shook his fist in my face. ³⁵

"This is a *white* man's work around here, and you better watch ³⁶
yourself!"

From then on they changed toward me. They said good-morning ³⁷
no more. When I was a bit slow performing some duty, I was called
a lazy black son-of-a-bitch.

Once I thought of reporting all this to the boss. But the mere idea ³⁸
of what would happen to me if Pease and Morrie should learn that
I had "snitched" stopped me. And after all the boss was a white
man, too. What was the use?

The climax came at noon one summer day. Pease called me to ³⁹
his work-bench. To get to him I had to go between two narrow
benches and stand with my back against a wall.

"Yes, sir," I said. ⁴⁰

"Richard, I want to ask you something," Pease began pleasantly, ⁴¹
not looking up from his work.

"Yes, sir," I said again. ⁴²

Morrie came over, blocking the narrow passage between the ⁴³
benches. He folded his arms, staring at me solemnly.

I looked from one to the other, sensing that something was ⁴⁴
coming.

"Yes, sir," I said for the third time. ⁴⁵

Pease looked up and spoke very slowly. ⁴⁶

"Richard, *Mr.* Morrie here tells me you called me *Pease.*" ⁴⁷

I stiffened. A void seemed to open up in me. I knew this was the ⁴⁸
show-down.

He meant that I had failed to call him Mr. Pease. I looked at ⁴⁹
Morrie. He was gripping a steel bar in his hands. I opened my
mouth to speak, to protest, to assure Pease that I had never called
him simply *Pease,* and that I had never had any intentions of doing
so, when Morrie grabbed me by the collar, ramming my head
against the wall.

"Now, be careful, nigger!" snarled Morrie, baring his teeth. "*I* ⁵⁰
heard yuh call 'im *Pease!* 'N' if you say yuh didn't, yuh're callin' me
a *lie,* see?" He waved the steel bar threateningly.

If I had said: No, sir, Mr. Pease, I never called you *Pease*, I would   51
have been automatically calling Morrie a liar. And if I had said:
Yes, sir, Mr. Pease, I called you *Pease*, I would have been pleading
guilty to having uttered the worst insult that a Negro can utter to a
southern white man. I stood hesitating, trying to frame a neutral
reply.

"Richard, I asked you a question!" said Pease. Anger was creep-   52
ing into his voice.

"I don't remember calling you *Pease*, Mr. Pease," I said cau-   53
tiously. "And if I did, I sure didn't mean . . ."

"You black son-of-a-bitch! You called me *Pease*, then!" he spat,   54
slapping me till I bent sideways over a bench. Morrie was on top of
me, demanding:

"Didn't yuh call 'im *Pease?* If yuh say yuh didn't I'll rip yo' gut   55
string loose with this bar, yuh black granny dodger! Yuh can't call a
white man a lie 'n' git erway with it, you black son-of-a-bitch!"

I wilted. I begged them not to bother me. I knew what they   56
wanted. They wanted me to leave.

"I'll leave," I promised. "I'll leave right *now*."   57

They gave me a minute to get out of the factory. I was warned   58
not to show up again, or tell the boss.

I went.   59

When I told the folks at home what had happened, they called   60
me a fool. They told me that I must never again attempt to exceed
my boundaries. When you are working for white folks, they said,
you got to "stay in your place" if you want to keep working.

2

My Jim Crow education continued on my next job, which was   61
portering in a clothing store. One morning, while polishing brass
out front, the boss and his twenty-year-old son got out of their car
and half dragged and half kicked a Negro woman into the store. A
policeman standing at the corner looked on, twirling his night-
stick. I watched out of the corner of my eye, never slackening the
strokes of my chamois upon the brass. After a few minutes, I heard
shrill screams coming from the rear of the store. Later the woman
stumbled out, bleeding, crying, and holding her stomach. When
she reached the end of the block, the policeman grabbed her and
accused her of being drunk. Silently, I watched him throw her into
a patrol wagon.

When I went to the rear of the store, the boss and his son were   62
washing their hands in the sink. They were chuckling. The floor
was bloody and strewn with wisps of hair and clothing. No doubt I
must have appeared pretty shocked, for the boss slapped me reas-
suringly on the back.

"Boy, that's what we do to niggers when they don't want to pay   63
their bills," he said, laughing.

His son looked at me and grinned.   64

"Here, hava cigarette," he said.   65

Not knowing what to do, I took it. He lit his and held the match 66
for me. This was a gesture of kindness, indicating that even if they
had beaten the poor old woman, they would not beat me if I knew
enough to keep my mouth shut.

"Yes, sir," I said, and asked no questions.   67

After they had gone, I sat on the edge of a packing box and   68
stared at the bloody floor till the cigarette went out.

That day at noon, while eating in a hamburger joint, I told my   69
fellow Negro porters what had happened. No one seemed surprised. One fellow, after swallowing a huge bite, turned to me
and asked:

"Huh! Is tha' all they did t' her?"   70

"Yeah. Wasn't tha' enough?" I asked.   71

"Shucks! Man, she's a lucky bitch!" he said, burying his lips   72
deep into a juicy hamburger. "Hell, it's a wonder they didn't lay
her when they got through."

3

I was learning fast, but not quite fast enough. One day, while I 73
was delivering packages in the suburbs, my bicycle tire was punc-
tured. I walked along the hot, dusty road, sweating and leading my
bicycle by the handle-bars.

A car slowed at my side.   74

"What's the matter, boy?" a white man called.   75

I told him my bicycle was broken and I was walking back to   76
town.

"That's too bad," he said. "Hop on the running board."   77

He stopped the car. I clutched hard at my bicycle with one hand   78
and clung to the side of the car with the other.

"All set?"   79

"Yes, sir," I answered. The car started.   80

It was full of young white men. They were drinking. I watched   81
the flask pass from mouth to mouth.

"Wanna drink, boy?" one asked.   82

I laughed as the wind whipped my face. Instinctively obeying the 83
freshly planted precepts of my mother, I said:

"Oh, no!"   84

The words were hardly out of my mouth before I felt something   85
hard and cold smash me between the eyes. It was an empty whisky
bottle. I saw stars, and fell backwards from the speeding car into

the dust of the road, my feet becoming entangled in the steel spokes of my bicycle. The white men piled out and stood over me.

"Nigger, ain' yuh learned no better sense'n tha' yet?" asked the 86
man who hit me. "Ain' yuh learned t' say *sir* t' a white man yet?"

Dazed, I pulled to my feet. My elbows and legs were bleeding. 87
Fists doubled, the white man advanced, kicking my bicycle out of the way.

"Aw, leave the bastard alone. He's got enough," said one. 88

They stood looking at me. I rubbed my shins, trying to stop the 89
flow of blood. No doubt they felt a sort of contemptuous pity, for one asked:

"Yuh wanna ride t' town now, nigger? Yuh reckon yuh know 90
enough t' ride now?"

"I wanna walk," I said, simply. 91

Maybe it sounded funny. They laughed. 92

"Well, walk, yuh black son-of-a-bitch!" 93

When they left they comforted me with: 94

"Nigger, yuh sho better be damn glad it wuz us yuh talked t' tha' 95
way. Yuh're a lucky bastard, 'cause if yuh'd said tha' t' somebody else, yuh might've been a dead nigger now."

4

Negroes who have lived South know the dread of being caught 96
alone upon the streets in white neighborhoods after the sun has set. In such a simple situation as this the plight of the Negro in America is graphically symbolized. While white strangers may be in these neighborhoods trying to get home, they can pass unmolested. But the color of a Negro's skin makes him easily recognizable, makes him suspect, converts him into a defenseless target.

Late one Saturday night I made some deliveries in a white neigh- 97
borhood. I was pedaling my bicycle back to the store as fast as I could, when a police car, swerving toward me, jammed me into the curbing.

"Get down and put up your hands!" the policemen ordered. 98

I did. They climbed out of the car, guns drawn, faces set, and 99
advanced slowly.

"Keep still!" they ordered. 100

I reached my hands higher. They searched my pockets and pack- 101
ages. They seemed dissatisfied when they could find nothing incriminating. Finally, one of them said:

"Boy, tell your boss not to send you out in white neighborhoods 102
after sundown."

As usual, I said: 103

"Yes, sir." 104

5

My next job was a hall-boy in a hotel. Here my Jim Crow educa-   105
tion broadened and deepened. When the bell-boys were busy, I
was often called to assist them. As many of the rooms in the hotel
were occupied by prostitutes, I was constantly called to carry them
liquor and cigarettes. These women were nude most of the time.
They did not bother about clothing, even for bell-boys. When you
went into their rooms, you were supposed to take their nakedness
for granted, as though it startled you no more than a blue vase or a
red rug. Your presence awoke in them no sense of shame, for you
were not regarded as human. If they were alone, you could steal
sidelong glimpses at them. But if they were receiving men, not a
flicker of your eyelids could show. I remember one incident vividly.
A new woman, a huge, snowy-skinned blonde, took a room on
my floor. I was sent to wait upon her. She was in bed with a thick-
set man; both were nude and uncovered. She said she wanted
some liquor and slid out of bed and waddled across the floor to get
her money from a dresser drawer. I watched her.

"Nigger, what in hell are you looking at?" the white man asked   106
me, raising himself upon his elbows.

"Nothing," I answered, looking miles deep into the blank wall of   107
the room.

"Keep your eyes where they belong, if you want to be healthy!"   108
he said.

"Yes, sir."   109

6

One of the bell-boys I knew in this hotel was keeping steady   110
company with one of the Negro maids. Out of a clear sky the police
descended upon his home and arrested him, accusing him of bas-
tardy. The poor boy swore he had had no intimate relations with
the girl. Nevertheless, they forced him to marry her. When the
child arrived, it was found to be much lighter in complexion than
either of the two supposedly legal parents. The white men around
the hotel made a great joke of it. They spread the rumor that some
white cow must have scared the poor girl while she was carrying
the baby. If you were in their presence when this explanation was
offered, you were supposed to laugh.

7

One of the bell-boys was caught in bed with a white prostitute.   111
He was castrated and run out of town. Immediately after this all the
bell-boys and hall-boys were called together and warned. We were

given to understand that the boy who had been castrated was a "mighty, mighty lucky bastard." We were impressed with the fact that next time the management of the hotel would not be responsible for the lives of "trouble-makin' niggers." We were silent.

8

One night just as I was about to go home, I met one of the Negro maids. She lived in my direction, and we fell in to walk part of the way home together. As we passed the white night-watchman, he slapped the maid on her buttock. I turned around, amazed. The watchman looked at me with a long, hard, fixed-under stare. Suddenly he pulled his gun and asked: [112]

"Nigger, don't yuh like it?" [113]

I hesitated. [114]

"I asked yuh don't yuh like it?" he asked again, stepping forward. [115]

"Yes, sir," I mumbled. [116]

"Talk like it, then!" [117]

"Oh, yes, sir!" I said with as much heartiness as I could muster. [118]

Outside, I walked ahead of the girl, ashamed to face her. She caught up with me and said: [119]

"Don't be a fool! Yuh couldn't help it!" [120]

This watchman boasted of having killed two Negroes in self-defense. [121]

Yet, in spite of all this, the life of the hotel ran with an amazing smoothness. It would have been impossible for a stranger to detect anything. The maids, the hall-boys, and the bell-boys were all smiles. They had to be. [122]

9

I had learned my Jim Crow lessons so thoroughly that I kept the hotel job till I left Jackson for Memphis. It so happened that while in Memphis I applied for a job at a branch of the optical company. I was hired. And for some reason, as long as I worked there, they never brought my past against me. [123]

Here my Jim Crow education assumed quite a different form. It was no longer brutally cruel, but subtly cruel. Here I learned to lie, steal, to dissemble. I learned to play that dual role which every Negro must play if he wants to eat and live. [124]

For example, it was almost impossible to get a book to read. It was assumed that after a Negro had imbibed what scanty schooling the state furnished he had no further need for books. I was always borrowing books from men on the job. One day I mustered enough courage to ask one of the men to let me get books from the library [125]

in his name. Surprisingly, he consented. I cannot help but think
that he consented because he was a Roman Catholic and felt a
vague sympathy for Negroes, being himself an object of hatred.
Armed with a library card, I obtained books in the following manner: I would write a note to the librarian, saying: "Please let this
nigger boy have the following books." I would then sign it with the
white man's name.

When I went to the library, I would stand at the desk, hat in   126
hand, looking as unbookish as possible. When I received the books
desired I would take them home. If the books listed in the note
happened to be out, I would sneak into the lobby and forge a new
one. I never took any chances guessing with the white librarian
about what the fictitious white man would want to read. No doubt
if any of the white patrons had suspected that some of the volumes
they enjoyed had been in the home of a Negro, they would not
have tolerated it for an instant.

The factory force of the optical company in Memphis was much   127
larger than that in Jackson, and more urbanized. At least they liked
to talk, and would engage the Negro help in conversation whenever possible. By this means I found that many subjects were taboo
from the white man's point of view. Among the topics they did not
like to discuss with Negroes were the following: American white
women; the Ku Klux Klan; France, and how Negro soldiers fared
while there; French women; Jack Johnson[1]; the entire northern
part of the United States; the Civil War; Abraham Lincoln; U.S.
Grant; General Sherman; Catholics; the Pope; Jews; the Republican Party; slavery; social equality; Communism; Socialism; the
13th and 14th Amendments to the Constitution; or any topic calling for positive knowledge or manly self-assertion on the part of
the Negro. The most accepted topics were sex and religion.

There were many times when I had to exercise a great deal of   128
ingenuity to keep out of trouble. It is a southern custom that all
men must take off their hats when they enter an elevator. And
especially did this apply to us blacks with rigid force. One day I
stepped into an elevator with my arms full of packages. I was
forced to ride with my hat on. Two white men stared at me coldly.
Then one of them very kindly lifted my hat and placed it upon my
armful of packages. Now the most accepted response for a Negro to
make under such circumstances is to look at the white man out of
the corner of his eye and grin. To have said: "Thank you!" would
have made the white man *think* that you *thought* you were receiv-

1. Jack Johnson (1878–1946), a black American, was heavyweight boxing champion of the world from 1908 to 1915.

ing from him a personal service. For such an act I have seen Negroes take a blow in the mouth. Finding the first alternative distasteful, and the second dangerous, I hit upon an acceptable course
of action which fell safely between these two poles. I immediately—no sooner than my hat was lifted—pretended that my
packages were about to spill, and appeared deeply distressed with
keeping them in my arms. In this fashion I evaded having to acknowledge his service, and, in spite of adverse circumstances, salvaged a slender shred of personal pride.

How do Negroes feel about the way they have to live? How do   129
they discuss it when alone among themselves? I think this question
can be answered in a single sentence. A friend of mine who ran an
elevator once told me:

"Lawd, man! Ef it wuzn't fer them polices 'n' them ol' lynch-   130
mobs, there wouldn't be nothin' but uproar down here!"

BARBARA EHRENREICH

Oliver North and the Warrior Caste

Barbara Ehrenreich (1941–   ) took her Ph.D. in health sciences from Rockefeller University in 1968 and quickly set to
work (with her husband John) on a scathing critique of health
care in the United States: *The American Health Empire* (1970). She
then joined Deirdre English in a series of three books about male
domination of health care for women, including *For Her Own
Good* (1978). Thereafter, she published two feminist critiques of
changing sex roles in the United States: *The Hearts of Men* (1983)
and *Re-making Love* (with Elizabeth Hess and Gloria Jacobs,
1986). A prolific writer on a wide range of subjects, Ehrenreich
has been since 1981 a contributing editor for *MS. Magazine.*
"Oliver North and the Warrior Caste" appeared in *MS.* in May
1987 when the controversy over the "Iran-Contra affair" was at
its height. North, who was involved in covert plans to supply
arms to the Nicaraguan Contras, was convicted on three felony
counts on May 4, 1989.

When I first saw Oliver North on television, testifying—or   1
rather, declining to testify before the House Committee on Foreign
Affairs—I was so taken by the expression on his face that I almost
missed the main point. The expression was one of exaggerated

attentiveness: eyebrows drawn up high into the center of his forehead, the corners of his mouth tucked down ceremoniously toward
his chin. It was the kind of face you might wear for a solemn
occasion where it would be tactless, if not incriminating, to break
out into a grin.

The main point, however, is not that Oliver North may have   2
enjoyed his role in Iranscam, or been amused by the feeble institution of Congress. The main point—the only real message of his
silent testimony—was the uniform. This prince of Reagan's secret
government had chosen to confront the public in a costume that
proclaimed his license to kill—not just impersonally as a President
may by pressing a button—but, if necessary, messily and by hand.
A civilian official in a civilian government, he had chosen to come
as a warrior.

I think that this may be one of the more useful ways to think of   3
North and his cabal of collaborators: as members of the oldest male
elite there is, the Warrior Caste. Not that, in the crafting of Iranscam, ideology was unimportant—or profiteering, or personal
neurosis, or sheer hell-raising adventurism. But the same mixed
motives have inspired the warrior elite throughout history, from
the sacking of Troy to the raids of Genghis Khan and the Crusades
against the Muslim world. What defines the Warrior Caste, and
sets it apart from the mass of average military men, is a love of war
that knows no bounds, accepts no peace, and always seeks, in the
ashes of the last battle, the sparks that might ignite the next. For
North and many of his key collaborators, the sequence was Vietnam, then Nicaragua, with detours into war-torn Angola and pre-
revolutionary Iran. The end of one war demanded the creation of
the next.

I have been thinking about the Warrior Caste ever since a re-   4
markable book, Klaus Theweleit's *Male Fantasies* (the English edition was just published by the University of Minnesota Press), introduced me to a group of men who might be considered the
psychological prototype of the modern warrior elite, the German
Freikorpsmen. These were officers who refused to disarm after
World War I, but instead returned to Germany and organized private armies to battle the rebellious working class of their own
nation. They went on, in the thirties, to become the core of Hitler's
SA[1] and, in some cases, key functionaries in the Third Reich. Thus
for them, the period between 1914 and 1945 was continuous,
almost uninterrupted, war, in no small part because they made it

1. *Sturmabteilungen* or Storm Troopers, the strong-arm squads of the Nazi party.

so. Historian Robert Waite quotes a Freikorpsman who had en-
listed in the German army at the age of 16: "People told us that the
War [World War I] was over. That made us laugh. We ourselves
are the War. Its flame burns strongly in us. It envelops our whole
being and fascinates us with the enticing urge to destroy. We
obeyed . . . and marched onto the battlefields of the postwar world
just as we had gone into battle on the Western Front: singing,
reckless and filled with the joy of adventure . . . silent, deadly,
remorseless in battle."

We are a long way, of course, from the trenches of the Western   5
Front and the street battles of postwar Berlin, but some of the same
"joy" and "enticing urge" seem to have driven Oliver North. The
son of an army colonel and brother of two officers, North had been
in such a hurry to get to Vietnam in 1968 that he skipped a summer
leave. According to the Washington *Post*, friends said he didn't
want to miss the war. In Vietnam, he was a hero, or, depending on
your point of view, a maniac. "He burned inside," a Marine Corps
buddy has said, unconsciously echoing the Freikorpsman quoted
above. "He was a zealot."

Back from Vietnam in 1969, North poured his energies into his   6
job as a Marine instructor. Other instructors seem to have thought
him a bit mad, coming to class in camouflage paint, bush hat,
bandoliers across his chest, with four guns and three knives tucked
about his person. "He was pumped up after Vietnam," a friend
explained to the press, and dashed back to that unhappy country at
his first chance—to testify in 1970 on behalf of a fellow Marine
charged with murdering 16 Vietnamese women and children at
Son Thang. While the trial dragged on, he passed the time by
volunteering for "killer teams" on nighttime patrol. Even hardened
Marines thought this was going a little far, "hiding behind trees
and slitting throats on his own time."

North could take anything, except, apparently, the stress of   7
peace. Assigned to a routine Marine Corps job in 1974, he experienced a psychotic episode. His superior officer reportedly found
him in his quarters, "babbling incoherently and running around
naked, waving a .45 pistol." He had nothing to live for, he explained, and he may have meant nothing to kill for.

That problem—the horror of peace—would be solved once he   8
reached the dark inner core of Reagan's secret government. North
had spent the rest of the 1970s in the Marines and then headed for
the Naval War college, where he impressed enough higher-ups to
get a White House appointment in 1981. From his post in the
National Security Council, he designed the invasion of Grenada,

abetted the South Africa–supported guerrillas in Angola, engineered the hijacking of the *Achille Lauro*[2] hijackers, and seems to have almost single-handedly managed the covert war against Nicaragua. He no longer had to wait for wars or worry about getting to a war too late. He could make his own.

It matters, of course, that North has a specific ideology to defend.   9
No doubt he sees himself as a steadfast crusader against Communism, and not as a macho thrill-seeker. But the thrill is there, and even temporary warriors, soldiers who gladly return to the routines of peacetime, often describe combat as the peak event of their lives. "I had the most tremendous experiences of all of life: of fear, of jubilance, of misery, of hope, of comradeship, and of the endless excitement, the theatrics of it," a World War II veteran told Studs Terkel in his book *The Good War.* After an experience like that, "everything," to quote another of Terkel's vets, "is anticlimactic."

I will admit that this is alien territory to me, the psychology of   10
the warrior. In part, this is because his anticlimactic "everything" is all that I, and probably you the reader, have ever known or experienced: work, love, children, family, friends, and the peaceful struggles we wage in the name of love and children. As feminists, we may honor myths and tales of women warriors, but, overwhelmingly and throughout history, women have inhabited a world that warriors happily leave behind, or arrive at—only to destroy.

There is another reason for our ignorance of the warrior mental-   11
ity. In our generation of feminist scholars, the history of war and warriors has taken second place to "social history"—the attempt to reconstruct how ordinary people have gone about their lives, producing what they need and reproducing themselves. We rejected the conventional history of "king and battles" for what Sheila Rowbotham has called the "hidden history" of everyday life, almost to the point of forgetting how much of everyday life has, for millennia, been shaped by battles and dominated by warrior elites.

But I do not think we will ever understand either history or   12
women's place in it without a *feminist* understanding of the Warrior Caste: history, because so much of it is made by warriors; women, because our very absence from the warriors' ranks must be understood, finally, as a profound clue to the mystery of male power and gender itself. The absence of women, I would argue, is not a mere "result" of patriarchy or a "consequence" of sexism; it is intrinsic to the psychology of the warrior, just as war itself—and

2. The *Achille Lauro,* an Italian passenger ship, was hijacked on October 7, 1985. The Palestine Liberation Organization was held responsible.

the endless preparations and celebrations it demands—may be intrinsic to the perpetuation of patriarchy.

In his brilliant psychoanalytical study of the Freikorpsmen, 13
Theweleit offers one of the links between militarism and patriarchy: war, to those permanent warriors, was a condition of life *because* it was an escape from women and all things female. The Freikorpsmen, whose letters and diaries Theweleit analyzes, did not just hate women; in a way they did not even *see* women, including their own wives—except as intruders, threats, yawning "swamps" in which a man could be engulfed. Nor was this a matter of "repressed homosexuality" or sexuality of any kind. For these prototypical warriors, the only resolution of the horror of women was the murder of women (as well as men), an act they describe not only with relish, but with relief.

Now, quite aside from Theweleit's thesis, I would argue that any 14
prestigious, socially pervasive, all-male institution serves to perpetuate patriarchy, whether it is the men's longhouse of a tribal society or the executive class of an industrial society. The reason is simple: as long as the male career trajectory is a movement from a world centered on women (mothers) to a world in which there are no women, "growing up" for men will always mean growing away from women. And for the men who "grow up," women will always be reminders of their own vulnerability and helpless infancy. Women will be feared, contemned, or perhaps merely patronized as incomplete and childish versions of men.

Some feminist theorists have suggested that the earliest such 15
institution of patriarchy was the male hunting band. But for most of recorded history, and in most of the world, the premier institution of male power has probably been the military, and especially the warrior elite. Not all societies hunt, and not all societies organize their religions around male-only hierarchies, but almost all societies that can make any claim to being "civilized" have cultivated the Warrior Caste. I think, for example, of the remarkable parallels, even in their style of warfare and codes of honor, between the samurai of feudal Japan and the knights of feudal Europe: as if their Warrior Caste had a kind of historical inevitability, transcending physical distance, language, and everything we know as "culture."

My guess is that the historical "success" of the Warrior Caste 16
rests on the fact that it is, in more than one sense, self-propagating. First, in a geographical sense: the existence of a warrior elite in City-State 1 called forth its creation in City-State 2—otherwise the latter was likely to be reduced to rubble and the memories of

slaves. Natural selection, as it has operated in human history, favors not only the clever but the murderous.

Second, and quite apart from ordinary biology, the Warrior   17
Caste has the ability to reproduce itself from one generation to the next. Only women can produce children, of course; but—more to the point—only wars can produce *warriors*. One war leads to the next, in part because each war incubates the warriors who will fight the next, or, I should say, *create*, the next. The First World War engendered the warrior elite that ushered in the Third Reich, and hence the Second World War. And Vietnam created men like Oliver North, who, through subterfuge and stealth, nourished the fledgling war in Central America.

But to return to North: the real point, it occurs to me, may not   18
have been the uniform, after all. For the key characteristic of the Warrior Caste in its modern form is that it does *not* dress up in battle costume or indulge in recreational throat-slitting. The men of the true warrior elite in the United States today (and no doubt in the Soviet Union as well) wear tailored suits, kiss their wives good-bye in the morning, and spend their days at desks, plotting covert actions, megadeaths, and "low-intensity" interventions. They are peaceable, even genial, fellows, like the President himself. But still I would say, to the extent that they hoard the resources of the nation for the purposes of destruction, they live for war.

The real lesson of Iranscam, with its winding trail of blood and   19
money, guns and drugs, may be to remind us that we have not evolved so far at all from the most primitive barbarism of the Warrior Caste. That caste has institutionalized itself in the bureaucracy of the "national security" state—the CIA, the National Security Council, the Pentagon. But insofar as their business is still murder (and there can be no other name, I think, for the business of the contras and their American supporters), our modern, gray-flannel warriors are blood brothers to the mercenaries and thugs who made up North's "secret team"—and are spiritual descendants of that Freikorps officer who could say, in exultation, "We are the war."

Our task—we who cherish "daily life" and life itself—is to end   20
the millennia-old reign of the Warrior Caste. There are two parts to this task. One is to uproot the woman-hating, patriarchal consciousness that leads some men to find transcendence and even joy in war, and only war. That will take time, though we have made a decent start. The other part is to remember that war itself is the crucible in which new warriors are created. If we cannot stop the warriors' fevered obsessions, and bring these men back into the human fold, we can at least try to stop their wars.

WILLIAM MANCHESTER

Okinawa: The Bloodiest Battle of All

William Manchester (1922–   ) served in the Marine Corps in
the South Pacific during World War II and returned to take degrees from Massachusetts State College and the University of
Missouri while working as a journalist. In 1947 he became a
reporter for the Baltimore *Sun* and in 1951 published his first
book, *Disturber of the Peace: The Life of H. L. Mencken.* Thereafter,
Manchester enjoyed modest success as a novelist and launched a
career writing extensively researched books on the history of his
own times, including *A Rockefeller Family Portrait* (1959), *The
Death of a President* (1967), *The Arms of Krupp* (1968), *American
Caesar: Douglas MacArthur, 1880–1964* (1968), *The Glory and the
Dream: A Narrative History of America, 1932–1972* (1974), and *The
Last Lion, Winston Spencer Churchill* (volume 1, 1983; volume 2,
1988). Manchester's tendency to blend personal experience and
subjective impressions with data gathered from research has
alarmed some historians, but few denied the effectiveness of the
technique when he used it in *Good-bye, Darkness* (1980), his
memoir/history of war in the South Pacific. Few have written so
effectively about the experience of twentieth-century warfare.
"Okinawa: The Bloodiest Battle of All" appeared in the *New York
Times Magazine* on June 14, 1987.

On Okinawa today, Flag Day will be observed with an extraordi-   1
nary ceremony: two groups of elderly men, one Japanese, the
other American, will gather for a solemn rite.

They could scarcely have less in common. Their motives are   2
mirror images; each group honors the memory of men who tried to
slay the men honored by those opposite them. But theirs is a common grief. After forty-two years the ache is still there. They are
really united by death, the one great victor in modern war.

They have come to Okinawa to dedicate a lovely monument in   3
remembrance of the Americans, Japanese and Okinawans killed
there in the last and bloodiest battle of the Pacific war. More than
200,000 perished in the 82-day struggle—twice the number of
Japanese lost at Hiroshima and more American blood than had
been shed at Gettysburg. My own regiment—I was a sergeant in
the 29th Marines—lost more than 80 percent of the men who had
landed on April 1, 1945. Before the battle was over, both the
Japanese and American commanding generals lay in shallow
graves.

Okinawa lies 330 miles southwest of the southernmost Japanese 4
island of Kyushu; before the war, it was Japanese soil. Had there
been no atom bombs—and at that time the most powerful Americans, in Washington and at the Pentagon, doubted that the device
would work—the invasion of the Nipponese homeland would
have been staged from Okinawa, beginning with a landing on
Kyushu to take place November 1. The six Marine divisions, storm-
ing ashore abreast, would lead the way. President Truman asked
General Douglas MacArthur, whose estimates of casualties on the
eve of battles had proved uncannily accurate, about Kyushu. The
general predicted a million Americans would die in that first phase.

Given the assumption that nuclear weapons would contribute 5
nothing to victory, the battle of Okinawa had to be fought. No one
doubted the need to bring Japan to its knees. But some Americans
came to hate the things we had to do, even when convinced that
doing them was absolutely necessary; they had never understood
the bestial, monstrous and vile means required to reach the objective—an unconditional Japanese surrender. As for me, I could not
reconcile the romanticized view of war that runs like a red streak
through our literature—and the glowing aura of selfless patriotism
that had led us to put our lives at forfeit—with the wet, green hell
from which I had barely escaped. Today, I understand. I was there,
and was twice wounded. This is the story of what I knew and when
I knew it.

To our astonishment, the Marine landing on April 1 was uncon- 6
tested. The enemy had set a trap. Japanese strategy called first for
kamikazes to destroy our fleet, cutting us off from supply ships;
then Japanese troops would methodically annihilate the men
stranded ashore using the trench-warfare tactics of World War I—
cutting the Americans down as they charged heavily fortified positions. One hundred and ten thousand Japanese troops were waiting on the southern tip of the island. Intricate entrenchments,
connected by tunnels, formed the enemy's defense line, which ran
across the waist of Okinawa from the Pacific Ocean to the East
China Sea.

By May 8, after more than five weeks of fighting, it became clear 7
that the anchor of this line was a knoll of coral and volcanic ash,
which the Marines christened Sugar Loaf Hill. My role in mastering
it—the crest changed hands more than eleven times—was the central experience of my youth, and of all the military bric-a-brac that
I put away after the war, I cherish most the Commendation from
General Lemuel C. Shepherd, Jr., U.S.M.C., our splendid division
commander, citing me for "gallantry in action and extraordinary
achievement," adding, "Your courage was a constant source of

inspiration . . . and your conduct throughout was in keeping with the highest tradition of the United States Naval Service."

The struggle for Sugar Loaf lasted ten days; we fought under the 8 worst possible conditions—a driving rain that never seemed to slacken, day or night. (I remember wondering, in an idiotic moment—no man in combat is really sane—whether the battle could be called off, or at least postponed, because of bad weather.)

Newsweek called Sugar Loaf "the most critical local battle of the 9 war." *Time* described a company of Marines—270 men—assaulting the hill. They failed; fewer than 30 returned. Fletcher Pratt, the military historian, wrote that the battle was unmatched in the Pacific war for "closeness and desperation." Casualties were almost unbelievable. In the 22d and 29th Marine regiments, two out of every three men fell. The struggle for the dominance of Sugar Loaf was probably the costliest engagement in the history of the Marine Corps. But by early evening on May 18, as night thickened over the embattled armies, the 29th Marines had taken Sugar Loaf, this time for keeps.

On Okinawa today, the ceremony will be dignified, solemn, 10 seemly. It will also be anachronistic. If the Japanese dead of 1945 were resurrected to witness it, they would be appalled by the acceptance of defeat, the humiliation of their emperor—the very idea of burying Japanese near the barbarians from across the sea and then mourning them together. Americans, meanwhile, risen from their graves, would ponder the evolution of their own society, and might wonder, What ever happened to patriotism?

When I was a child, a bracket was screwed to the sill of a front 11 attic window; its sole purpose was to hold the family flag. At first light, on all legal holidays—including Election Day, July 4, Memorial Day and, of course, Flag Day—I would scamper up to show it. The holidays remain, but mostly they mean long weekends.

In the late 1920s, during my childhood, the whole town of At- 12 tleboro, Massachusetts, would turn out to cheer the procession on Memorial Day. The policemen always came first, wearing their number-one uniforms and keeping perfect step. Behind them was a two-man vanguard—the mayor and, at his side, my father, hero of the 5th Marines and Belleau Wood, wearing his immaculate dress blues and looking like a poster of a Marine, with one magnificent flaw: the right sleeve of his uniform was empty. He had lost the arm in the Argonne. I now think that, as I watched him pass by, my own military future was already determined.

The main body of the parade was led by five or six survivors of 13 the Civil War, too old to march but sitting upright in open Pierce-

Arrows and Packards, wearing their blue uniforms and broad-brimmed hats. Then, in perfect step, came a contingent of men in their fifties, with their blanket rolls sloping diagonally from shoulder to hip—the Spanish-American War veterans. After these—and anticipated by a great roar from the crowd—came the dough-boys of World War I, some still in their late twenties. They were acclaimed in part because theirs had been the most recent conflict, but also because they had fought in the war that—we then thought—had ended all wars.

Americans still march in Memorial Day parades, but attendance   14
is light. One war has led to another and another and yet another, and the cruel fact is that few men, however they die, are remembered beyond the lifetimes of their closest relatives and friends. In the early 1940s, one of the forces that kept us on the line, under heavy enemy fire, was the conviction that this battle was of immense historical import, and that those of us who survived it would be forever cherished in the hearts of Americans. It was rather diminishing to return in 1945 and discover that your own parents couldn't even pronounce the names of the islands you had conquered.

But what of those who *do* remain faithful to patriotic holidays?   15
What are they commemorating? Very rarely are they honoring what actually happened, because only a handful know, and it's not their favorite topic of conversation. In World War II, 16 million Americans entered the armed forces. Of these, fewer than a million saw action. Logistically, it took nineteen men to back up one man in combat. All who wore uniforms are called veterans, but more than 90 percent of them are as uninformed about the killing zones as those on the home front.

If all Americans understood the nature of battle, they might be   16
vulnerable to truth. But the myths of warfare are embedded deep in our ancestral memories. By the time children have reached the age of awareness, they regard uniforms, decorations and Sousa marches as exalted, and those who argue otherwise are regarded as unpatriotic.

General MacArthur, quoting Plato, said: "Only the dead have   17
seen the end of war." One hopes he was wrong, for war, as it had existed for over four thousand years, is now obsolete. As late as the spring of 1945, it was possible for one man, with a rifle, to make a difference, however infinitesimal, in the struggle to defeat an enemy who had attacked us and threatened our West Coast. The bomb dropped on Hiroshima made the man ludicrous, even pitiful. Soldiering has been relegated to Sartre's[1] theater of the absurd. The

1. Jean Paul Sartre (1905–1980), existentialist philosopher, dramatist, and novelist.

image of the man as protector and defender of the home has been destroyed (and I suggest that that seed of thought eventually led women to re-examine their own role in society).

Until nuclear weapons arrived, the glorifying of militarism was 18 the nation's hidden asset. Without it, we would almost certainly have been defeated by the Japanese, probably by 1943. In 1941 American youth was isolationist and pacifist. Then war planes from Imperial Japan destroyed our fleet at Pearl Harbor on December 7, and on December 8 recruiting stations were packed. Some of us later found fighting rather different from what had been advertised. Yet in combat these men risked their lives—and often lost them—in hope of winning medals. There is an old soldier's saying: "A man won't sell you his life, but he'll give it to you for a piece of colored ribbon."

Most of the men who hit the beaches came to scorn eloquence. 19 They preferred the 130-year-old "Word of Cambronne." As dusk darkened the Waterloo battlefield, with the French in full retreat, the British sent word to General Pierre Cambronne, commander of the Old Guard. His position, they pointed out, was hopeless, and they suggested he capitulate. Every French textbook reports his reply as "The Old Guard dies but never surrenders." What he actually said was *"Merde."*[2]

If you mention this incident to members of the U.S. 101st Air- 20 borne Division, they will immediately understand. "Nuts" was not Brigadier General Anthony C. McAuliffe's answer to the Nazi demand that he hoist a white flag over Bastogne. Instead, he quoted Cambronne.

The character of combat has always been determined by the 21 weapons available to men when their battles were fought. In the beginning they were limited to hand weapons—clubs, rocks, swords, lances. At the Battle of Camlann in 539, England's Arthur—a great warrior, not a king—led a charge that slew 930 Saxons, including their leader.

It is important to grasp the fact that those 930 men were not 22 killed by snipers, grenades or shells. The dead were bludgeoned or stabbed to death, and we have a pretty good idea how this was done. One of the facts withheld from civilians during World War II was that Kabar fighting knives, with seven-inch blades honed to such precision that you could shave with them, were issued to Marines and that we were taught to use them. You never cut downward. You drove the point of your blade into a man's lower belly and ripped upward. In the process, you yourself became

2. Shit.

soaked in the other man's gore. After that charge at Camlann, Arthur must have been half drowned in blood.

The Battle of Agincourt,[3] fought nearly one thousand years later, represented a slight technical advance: crossbows and long bows had appeared. All the same, Arthur would have recognized the battle. Like all engagements of the time, this one was short. Killing by hand is hard work, and hot work. It is so exhausting that even men in peak condition collapse once the issue of triumph or defeat is settled. And Henry V's spear carriers and archers were drawn from social classes that had been undernourished for as long as anyone could remember. The duration of medieval battles could have been measured in hours, even minutes.

The Battle of Waterloo, fought exactly four hundred years later, is another matter. By 1815, the Industrial Revolution had begun cranking out appliances of death, primitive by today's standards, but revolutionary for infantrymen of that time. And Napoleon had formed mass armies, pressing every available man into service. It was a long step toward total war, and its impact was immense. Infantrymen on both sides fought with single-missile weapons— muskets or rifles—and were supported by (and were the target of) artillery firing cannonballs.

The fighting at Waterloo continued for three days; for a given regiment, however, it usually lasted one full day, much longer than medieval warfare. A half century later, Gettysburg lasted three days and cost 43,497 men. Then came the marathon slaughters of 1914–1918, lasting as long as ten months (Verdun) and producing hundreds of thousands of corpses lying, as F. Scott Fitzgerald wrote afterward, "like a million bloody rugs." Winston Churchill, who had been a dashing young cavalry officer when Victoria was queen, said of the new combat: "War, which was cruel and magnificent, has become cruel and squalid."

It may be said that the history of war is one of men packed together, getting closer and closer to the ground and then deeper and deeper into it. In the densest combat of World War I, battalion frontage—the length of the line into which the 1,000-odd men were squeezed—had been 800 yards. On Okinawa, on the Japanese fortified line, it was less than 600 yards—about 18 inches per man. We were there and deadlocked for more than a week in the relentless rain. During those weeks we lost nearly 4,000 men.

23

24

25

26

---

3. A famous battle (1415 A.D.) in which English archers decimated the French cavalry.

And now it is time to set down what this modern battlefield was   27
like.

All greenery had vanished; as far as one could see, heavy   28
shellfire had denuded the scene of shrubbery. What was left resembled a cratered moonscape. But the craters were vanishing,
because the rain had transformed the earth into a thin porridge—
too thin even to dig foxholes. At night you lay on a poncho as a
precaution against drowning during the barrages. All night, every
night, shells erupted close enough to shake the mud beneath you at
the rate of five or six a minute. You could hear the cries of the dying
but could do nothing. Japanese infiltration was always imminent,
so the order was to stay put. Any man who stood up was cut in half
by machine guns manned by fellow Marines.

By day, the mud was hip deep; no vehicles could reach us. As   29
you moved up the slope of the hill, artillery and mortar shells were
bursting all around you, and, if you were fortunate enough to
reach the top, you encountered the Japanese defenders, almost face
to face, a few feet away. To me, they looked like badly wrapped
brown paper parcels someone had soaked in a tub. Their eyes
seemed glazed. So, I suppose, did ours.

Japanese bayonets were fixed; ours weren't. We used the knives,   30
or, in my case, a .45 revolver and M1 carbine. The mud beneath
our feet was deeply veined with blood. It was slippery. Blood is
very slippery. So you skidded around, in deep shock, fighting as
best you could until one side outnumbered the other. The outnumbered side would withdraw for reinforcements and then counterat-
tack.

During those ten days I ate half a candy bar. I couldn't keep   31
anything down. Everyone had dysentery, and this brings up an
aspect of war even Robert Graves, Siegfried Sassoon, Edmund
Blunden and Ernest Hemingway avoided. If you put more than a
quarter million men in a line for three weeks, with no facilities for
the disposal of human waste, you are going to confront a disgusting
problem. We were fighting and sleeping in one vast cesspool.
Mingled with that stench was another—the corrupt and corrupting
odor of rotting human flesh.

My luck ran out on June 5, more than two weeks after we had   32
taken Sugar Loaf Hill and killed the seven thousand Japanese soldiers defending it. I had suffered a slight gunshot wound above the
right knee on June 2, and had rejoined my regiment to make an
amphibious landing on Oroku Peninsula behind enemy lines. The
next morning several of us were standing in a stone enclosure
outside some Okinawan tombs when a six-inch rocket mortar shell
landed among us.

The best man in my section was blown to pieces, and the slime of 33
his viscera enveloped me. His body had cushioned the blow, saving
my life; I still carry a piece of his shinbone in my chest. But I
collapsed, and was left for dead. Hours later corpsmen found me
still breathing, though blind and deaf, with my back and chest a
junkyard of iron fragments—including, besides the piece of shinbone, four pieces of shrapnel too close to the heart to be removed.
(They were not dangerous, a Navy surgeon assured me, but they
still set off the metal detector at the Buffalo airport.)

Between June and November I underwent four major operations 34
and was discharged as 100 percent disabled. But the young have
strong recuperative powers. The blindness was caused by shock,
and my vision returned. I grew new eardrums. In three years I was
physically fit. The invisible wounds remain.

Most of those who were closest to me in the early 1940s had left 35
New England campuses to join the Marines, knowing it was the
most dangerous branch of the service. I remember them as bright,
physically strong and inspired by an idealism and love of country
they would have been too embarrassed to acknowledge. All of us
despised the pompousness and pretentiousness of senior officers. It
helped that, almost without exception, we admired and respected
our commander in chief. But despite our enormous pride in being
Marines, we saw through the scam that had lured so many of us to
recruiting stations.

Once we polled a rifle company, asking each man why he had 36
joined the Marines. A majority cited *To the Shores of Tripoli,* a
marshmallow of a movie starring John Payne, Randolph Scott and
Maureen O'Hara. Throughout the film the uniform of the day was
dress blues; requests for liberty were always granted. The implication was that combat would be a lark, and when you returned,
spangled with decorations, a Navy nurse like Maureen O'Hara
would be waiting in your sack. It was peacetime again when John
Wayne appeared on the silver screen as Sergeant Stryker in *Sands of
Iwo Jima,* but that film underscores the point; I went to see it with
another ex-Marine, and we were asked to leave the theater because
we couldn't stop laughing.

After my evacuation from Okinawa, I had the enormous plea- 37
sure of seeing Wayne humiliated in person at Aiea Heights Naval
Hospital in Hawaii. Only the most gravely wounded, the litter
cases, were sent there. The hospital was packed, the halls lined
with beds. Between Iwo Jima and Okinawa, the Marine Corps was
being bled white.

Each evening, Navy corpsmen would carry litters down to the 38 hospital theater so the men could watch a movie. One night they had a surprise for us. Before the film the curtains parted and out stepped John Wayne, wearing a cowboy outfit—ten-gallon hat, bandanna, checkered shirt, two pistols, chaps, boots and spurs. He grinned his aw-shucks grin, passed a hand over his face and said, "Hi ya, guys!" He was greeted by a stony silence. Then somebody booed. Suddenly everyone was booing.

This man was a symbol of the fake machismo we had come to   39
hate, and we weren't going to listen to him. He tried and tried to make himself heard, but we drowned him out, and eventually he quit and left. If you liked *Sands of Iwo Jima*, I suggest you be careful. Don't tell it to the Marines.

And so we weren't macho. Yet we never doubted the justice of   40
our cause. If we had failed—if we had lost Guadalcanal, and the Navy's pilots had lost the Battle of Midway—the Japanese would have invaded Australia and Hawaii, and California would have been in grave danger. In 1942 the possibility of an Axis victory was very real. It is possible for me to loathe war—and with reason—yet still honor the brave men, many of them boys, really, who fought with me and died beside me. I have been haunted by their loss these forty-two years, and I shall mourn them until my own death releases me. It does not seem too much to ask that they be remembered on one day each year. After all, they sacrificed their futures that you might have yours.

Yet I will not be on Okinawa for the dedication today. I would   41
enjoy being with Marines; the ceremony will be moving, and we would be solemn, remembering our youth and the beloved friends who died there.

Few, if any, of the Japanese survivors agreed to attend the cere-   42
mony. However, Edward L. Fox, chairman of the Okinawa Memorial Shrine Committee, capped almost six years' campaigning for a monument when he heard about a former Japanese naval officer, Yoshio Yazaki—a meteorologist who had belonged to a four-thousand-man force led by Rear Admiral Minoru Ota—and persuaded him to attend.

On March 31, 1945, Yazaki-san had been recalled to Tokyo, and   43
thus missed the battle of Okinawa. Ten weeks later—exactly forty-two years ago today—Admiral Ota and his men committed seppuku, killing themselves rather than face surrender. Ever since then Yazaki has been tormented by the thought that his comrades have joined their ancestors and he is here, not there.

Finding Yazaki was a great stroke of luck for Fox, for whom an   44
Okinawa memorial had become an obsession. His own division

commander tried to discourage him. The Japanese could hardly be expected to back a memorial on the site of their last great military defeat. But Yazaki made a solution possible.

If Yazaki can attend, why can't I? I played a role in the early   45
stages of Buzz Fox's campaign and helped write the tribute to the Marines that is engraved on the monument. But when I learned that Japanese were also participating, I quietly withdrew. There are too many graves between us, too much gore, too many memories of too many atrocities.

In 1978, revisiting Guadalcanal, I encountered a Japanese busi-   46
nessman who had volunteered to become a kamikaze pilot in 1945 and was turned down at the last minute. Mutual friends suggested that we meet. I had expected no difficulty; neither, I think, did he. But when we confronted each other, we froze.

I trembled, suppressing the sudden, startling surge of primitive   47
rage within. And I could see, from his expression, that this was difficult for him, too. Nations may make peace. It is harder for fighting men. On simultaneous impulse we both turned and walked away.

I set this down in neither pride nor shame. The fact is that some   48
wounds never heal. Yazaki, unlike Fox, is dreading the ceremony. He does not expect to be shriven of his guilt. He knows he must be there but can't say why. Men are irrational, he explains, and adds that he feels very sad.

So do I, Yazaki-san, so do I.   49

GEORGE LEONARD

The Warrior

George B. Leonard (1923–   ) was a combat pilot in the Southwest Pacific during World War II. He received the Air Medal and three battle stars, served in Japan during the U.S. occupation, and eventually rose to the rank of captain. Returning to the United States, he completed his undergraduate degree at the University of North Carolina. He soon went to work for *Look* magazine, becoming a senior editor by the time he was thirty. Leonard has been an eager pursuer of excellence in peace as well as war. His award-winning 1968 book, *Education and Ecstasy*, is a visionary look at the potential of schools to liberate the minds and souls of students. *The Ultimate Athlete* (1975) presents sports as a path toward self-mastery and self-realization. *The End of Sex* (1983) decries the sexual revolution because it has encouraged self-indulgence instead of the disciplined tenderness of "high monogamy." "The Warrior" appeared in *Esquire* in July 1986.

America has discovered a new hero, the latest in a lineage that goes back to Davy Crockett and Daniel Boone, to the Lone Ranger and the western marshal with the fast draw. This new hero, like his predecessors, is always on the side of Right, but not necessarily on the side of the Establishment. Unlike the World War II team player, he is a lone fighter, a common man who through strenuous self-discipline and rigorous training has developed extraordinary skills, which he puts to use with devastating results. He is an elite-forces man with the muscles of a Western body builder and the mind-set of an Eastern martial artist. He is Chuck Norris *Missing in Action* and *The Delta Force*, Arnold Schwarzenegger in *Commando*, and Fred Ward in *Remo Williams: The Adventure Begins*. Above all, he is Sylvester Stallone in *Rambo: First Blood Part II*.

This is the new American warrior, a man who, lacking the gritty camaraderie of a John Wayne or the urbane wit of a James Bond, slaughters commies and other enemies of the state by the score, cutting through bureaucratic inertia with a stream of machine-gun bullets. This is the warrior as an American revenge fantasy, a vivid dream image of single-minded, unrestrained action that would somehow erase the frustrations of Vietnam, Iran, and Lebanon, and set things right in one miraculous catharsis of blood and gore.

The picture of Rambo running barechested through the Vietnamese jungle wielding a huge knife and shooting explosive arrows is a lurid exaggeration, an example of the Freudian notion that whatever is repressed (as we repressed all sympathy for the fighting man during the Vietnam era) is likely to return to consciousness, perhaps in a grotesque form. But it is more than that. For it challenges us with a fundamental question, one that is particularly difficult in a free and democratic society:

If not Rambo, who?

It is a question that tends to paralyze our mental processes. For many of us who are dedicated to peace, the very idea of the "good" warrior seems a contradiction. We are haunted by images of armed soldiers in a city square, of innocent people kidnapped, tortured, or made to "disappear." The word "military" can conjure up the word "dictatorship." The word "police" joins all too easily with "state."

Still, in this violent and dangerous world, only the most fevered idealist would dispense entirely with soldiers and policemen. So the question remains: If not Rambo, who? If we're going to have people to whom we give the job of risking their own lives and, if necessary, taking the lives of others, how are we to deal with them? How are we to *think* about them? And, beyond that, is there some way that the warrior spirit at its best and highest can contribute to a lasting peace and to the quality of our individual lives during the time of peace?

I approach these questions not as a distant, dispassionate observer, but as one who served as a combat pilot in the southwest Pacific in World War II and as an air-intelligence officer during the Korean War. More recently, I've spent fifteen years studying and practicing a martial art called aikido, one dedicated to harmony, but a martial art nonetheless, with roots that go back to the medieval Japanese samurai. Through my association with this art, I've developed training programs and simulation games designed to produce the warrior spirit in men and women who never plan to go to war.   7

Among the people drawn to these programs, one in particular stands out as having dedicated himself wholeheartedly to the warrior's path. He is Jack Cirie, a highly decorated Marine veteran with two tours of duty in Vietnam. Cirie is a thoughtful man who has spent twenty-two years studying the way of the warrior. He is now in charge of an experimental training program for Army Special Forces troops. He is devoted to world peace. Cirie and I have spent countless hours exploring the mysterious paradoxes that keep cropping up around the subject of warriorship: the remorseless interplay of creation and destruction, the ageless relationship between violent action and noble character.   8

Jack Cirie went to Yale in the early 1960s. He was an All-Ivy League football defensive back and Yale's Most Valuable Player in his junior year. He majored in Latin-American studies, and considered joining the Peace Corps. Most of his friends were going to law school or into their fathers' businesses. Cirie was interviewed by Colgate-Palmolive, and that was the end of his job interviews. "I decided that what I wanted was a military experience, and for me that meant going to war. I wanted to be in a position where everything was at risk, where you get a chance to see inside yourself."   9

Cirie got what he asked for. Early in 1965, after six months of Marine officers school, he arrived at a place called Phu Bai, near Hue. It was just one day after the first contingent of U.S. Marines landed. "I got off the airplane, got in a jeep, and drove over to where the battalion was setting up their base. I was met by my company executive officer, who greeted me as a newly arrived platoon commander. He handed me a map, some gear for my pack, and pointed out toward the horizon. 'Your platoon's out there,' he said, 'and you've got an hour to get there before it gets dark.' "   10

His first major test as a leader came just before the summer   11
monsoon season: It was cloudy and cooler than usual, and very,
very dark. They got to the Vietnamese graveyard at midnight, exactly as planned. The graveyard overlooked a road that the Vietcong used when getting rice from a nearby village. It was a perfect
spot for an ambush, and as Cirie positioned the twenty-four men
he had brought on the mission so that they were in a line parallel to
the road, he said to himself that everything was going like clockwork; nothing could go wrong.

Now the men were sitting or squatting, their weapons trained on   12
the killing zone along the road. Cirie started working his way from
one end of the line to the other, moving as quietly as he could in
the pitch darkness, putting his hand on each Marine's shoulder in
turn, making sure that weapons were pointed in the right direction,
whispering words of encouragement. He was just three feet from
the last man in the line, a machine gunner, just making out the
man's dark outline, just reaching out to touch his shoulder, when
the inexplicable happened. The machine gunner jumped to his feet
in terror, and, almost at the same instant, Cirie found himself looking straight into the bright-orange muzzle flashes of AK-47 automatic rifles, less than six feet away.

They figured it all out later and realized the odds for its happen-   13
ing that way were about a million to one. A group of Vietcong had
picked the same spot for an ambush, and had moved in only minutes after the Marines. The first VC, in fact, had probably bumped
into the machine gunner in the darkness, then had raised his gun
and fired. At that instant, without thought, Cirie dropped to the
ground and started firing his pistol in the direction of the muzzle
flashes. His men also began firing, but most of them, not knowing
what had happened, were aiming at the road, not at the Vietcong.
The machine gunner lay dying a few feet away. Bullets were flying
everywhere.

For Cirie, it was a moment outside of time. Lying there on the   14
ground firing at the VC in a void of darkness lit only by muzzle
flashes, he was briefly tempted to do nothing more, to indulge in
the luxury of incomprehension. But he rose to his feet, amazed at
how calm he felt. His overriding sensation was one of relief; at last
he was getting a chance to do what he as a leader was supposed to
do. He began moving among his men, telling them to stop firing, to
watch the flanks, to stay calm. He ordered flares shot up to light the
scene. And all the time he was doing this, he was strangely, marvelously detached, almost as if he were out of his body. The
Marines stayed there until it started getting light, then returned to
their base camp. The Vietcong had withdrawn, leaving a trail of
blood, but none of their dead or wounded.

The episode in the graveyard—one more variation in an age-old   15
story—sealed Cirie's unspoken compact with his men. What they
had learned to expect from a leader had been fulfilled.

Four years later, Cirie returned to Vietnam as a captain, a U.S.   16
adviser to a South Vietnamese battalion. And there were more of
those moments outside ordinary time, more days of tedium and
hours of terror, more than enough opportunities to look inside
yourself in the presence of death. And, for whatever it was worth,
there was the validation that comes with decorations and words
about valor above and beyond the call of duty.

Is this, then, what it is to be a warrior—to test yourself under fire   17
and pass the test? For Jack Cirie, that was only the beginning.
"After my second tour," he said, "I realized it was not in the cards
for me to die a quick and glorious death. I was going to live. So
what was I going to do about that? How was I going to face and
deal with living? That was stage two in the warrior game. I was
going to live, and I wanted to live as a warrior. So I figured I'd
better start planning to live a good life."

"Being a warrior without a war has its problems," said Colonel   18
Bull Meechum in *The Great Santini*. "A man with outward courage
dares to die, a man with inward courage dares to live," wrote the
Chinese sage Lao-tzu. But where in today's world do you find
guidance for living a good life, much less living it as a warrior?
Sometimes in unexpected places. Just at the time—the late 1960s
and early 1970s—when America's privileged young people were
disparaging the warriors who fought in Vietnam, those same people were avidly reading the books of Carlos Castaneda. And if there
is any one theme that runs through these books, it is that life is best
lived, every instant of it, as a warrior.

In 1963, Castaneda, an anthropology student, became the ap-   19
prentice of a Yaqui Indian shaman named Don Juan Matus, who
lived in the northern Mexican desert. His books, which include *The
Teachings of Don Juan, A Separate Reality,* and *Tales of Power,* describe the adventures and ordeals of his apprenticeship.

To become a "man of knowledge," Don Juan tells Castaneda, it   20
is necessary to be a warrior. A warrior is not one who goes to war
or kills people, but rather one who exhibits integrity in his actions
and control over his life. The warrior's courage is unassailable, but
even more important are his will and patience. He lives every moment in full awareness of his own death, and, in light of this
awareness, all complaints, regrets, and moods of sadness or melancholy are seen as foolish indulgences.

Don Juan's warrior pursues power and acts strategically in order   21 to achieve self-mastery. "The spirit of a warrior is not geared to indulging and complaining, nor is it geared to winning or losing. The spirit of a warrior is geared only to struggle. . . . Thus the outcome matters very little to him." The warrior aims to follow his heart, to choose consciously the items that make up his world, to be exquisitely aware of everything around him, to attain total control, then act with total abandon. He seeks, in short, to live an impeccable life.

Castaneda's notion of the warrior resonates with ancient echoes. Almost every culture has had its own version of an ideal warrior's code. It exists in its purest form, unwritten, among peoples we call primitive—American Indians, African tribesmen. It has often been honored in the breach, especially in the nation-states of the epoch we call civilization. Still, it remains an ideal to be realized, a guide to living that might prove useful in today's complex and vexing world. 22

The warrior's code achieved a particularly vivid realization in Japan between 1603 and 1867. It was then, during the largely peaceful Tokugawa shogunate, that *bushido*, "the way of the warrior," came into full flower. Under bushido, the Japanese samurai spent long hours in the mastery of his martial skills, but also was expected to practice such things as tea ceremony, *sumi* painting, and the composition of poetry; lifelong training and self-development was a central element, as it is in other warrior codes. In matters of loyalty, honor, veracity, and justice or rectitude, the code was demanding and undeviating. Courage for the samurai meant an integration of physical and moral bravery, based on serenity in moments of danger. Martial ferocity was tempered by an exquisite sense of courtesy, which led to harmony of mind and body, and benevolence, which was seen as a composite of magnanimity, affection, love, and compassion. 23

In bushido, as in Don Juan's teachings, the warrior's life was shaped by his awareness of death. "The idea most vital and essential to the warrior," wrote Daido-ji Yusan in the seventeenth-century *Primer of Bushido*, "is that of death, which he ought to have before his mind day and night, night and day, from the dawn of the first day of the year until the last minute of the last day of it. . . . Think of what a frail thing life is, especially that of a warrior. This being so, you will come to consider every day of your life your last and dedicate it to the fulfillment of your obligations." 24

He might not strike you at first as a warrior. He is a man of medium height, frame, and age. He wears glasses and has a moustache, and the graciously tweedy look about him might make you 25 guess that he is a university professor. Donald Levine is, in fact, a professor of sociology and dean of the College at the University of Chicago. He is also a dedicated martial artist. I had wanted to meet him ever since reading a short version of his article "The Liberal Arts and the Martial Arts" in *The New York Times,* and the complete article in the journal *Liberal Education.*

Levine's article, I thought, went a long way toward clarifying the   26
role of the warrior in a free society. In it, he defines the liberal arts as including all education that is undertaken for self-development, all learning that exists essentially for its own sake rather than for some utilitarian purpose. Liberal education, according to Levine, first emerged in two unique cultures, those of classical Greece and China. In both of those cultures, such education was considered the highest human activity. And, though it might seem strange in light of today's academic climate, it included the cultivation of combat skills as well as intellectual skills. In both the East and the West, in other words, the martial arts and the liberal arts arose together, and were equally revered.

In the centuries that followed, this ideal was often lost. Both the   27
arts of combat and the education of the intellect were at times corrupted and put to narrow and exploitative uses. But during certain creative moments in history—for example, when the Buddhist monk Bodhidharma introduced Ch'an (Zen) Buddhism and the forerunner of Shaolin temple boxing to China in the sixth century A.D.—the liberal education of both body and mind has flourished.

After reading his article, I arranged a meeting with Levine. We   28
talked for an hour or so at my house, then drove to the *dojo* (martial-arts school) and changed into our training uniforms. As I stepped on the mat, I felt free from the web of words that so often entangles people in pretense and misunderstanding. It is not that the mat is less rigorous than the world of verbal discourse, but rather that it is absolutely rigorous. The mat is the world under a magnifying glass, where every action creates its unarguable consequence, and pretense is simply out of the question.

Levine and I took turns attacking and throwing, and in a matter   29
of minutes knew more about each other, at a deeper level, than we had known in an hour of talk. For my part, I was struck by Levine's powerful determination, by an unbendable will that was not readily apparent in conversation. After class, still flushed from an hour and a half of vigorous training, we went to dinner and continued our discussion of his ideas, but with an ease and camaraderie that hadn't been there before.

What about now? I asked him. Do the martial arts have anything   30
significant to offer late-twentieth-century America?

"Yes, I can see this as a time when the body and mind are being   31
reunified, a time when the liberal arts can learn a great deal from
the martial arts. This is true, of course, only when the martial arts
are practiced primarily for mastery of their intrinsically beautiful
forms and for self-development rather than primarily for self-
defense or for the brutal sensationalism you see in the movies. And
arts like aikido, which tie ethical vision right into daily practice, are
just what this country needs. Remember what the founder said: the
point of aikido training is to create persons who evince 'a spirit of
loving protection for all beings, who bind the world together in
peace and unity.' "

The heart of this way of life is practice itself, the regular, system-   32
atic, unremitting practice of the dedicated martial artist. And then
there is a progression of learning common to the martial arts that
leads to the transcendence of mere technique. "One begins by self-
consciously practicing a certain technique," Levine had written in
his article. "One proceeds slowly, deliberately, reflectively; but one
keeps on practicing, until the technique becomes internalized and
one is no longer self-conscious when executing it. After a set of
techniques has been thoroughly internalized, one begins to grasp
the principles behind them. And finally, when one has understood
and internalized the basic principles, one no longer responds mechanically to a given attack, but begins to use the art creatively and
in a manner whereby one's individual style and insights can find
expression." A fine way of learning for the scholar—and for the
warrior.

"Do you consider yourself a warrior?" I asked.   33

He paused. It was a tough question. "More and more," Levine   34
said. "More and more. It means being ready to die on a moment's
notice. And not worry about encumbrances, such as academic
honors or worldly ambitions. I couldn't have survived, let alone
done as well as I have in this job, without my martial-arts practice.
It's the kind of job that can grind you to a pulp. My predecessors
had a hard time finishing their terms. It's a man-killing job. Two
months after I became dean, I had to go to the hospital, suffering
from stress. At that point, I said to myself, 'Look, you're not going
to let this happen to you.' So I took control of my life. I was a chain
pipe smoker. I threw all my pipes away. I began practicing more
regularly. I began treating my job in an aikido way. I realized that
my whole life was *randori* [under attack simultaneously by several
people], so I handled it like randori. I stayed centered and calm
under pressure. I kept my integrity. I remembered that, for both
Plato and Aristotle, the list of most important virtues starts with
courage and ends with philosophic wisdom, with prudence and

justice in between. I guess you could say that, as best I could, I've lived as a warrior. And it has worked for me."

To go from Rambo to the dean of a prestigious college in search   35
of the warrior ideal might seem to be stretching things. But late last
year, I had the opportunity to spend two days with twenty-four
real-life Rambos, and discovered that the stretch was not as great as
might be imagined.

They were Green Berets, members of the U.S. Army Special   36
Forces, who had volunteered for an experimental six-month
course in advanced mind-body training run by a Seattle-based organization called SportsMind. Most of them had gone through
Army Ranger training. All were skilled in hand-to-hand combat
and the use of various weapons, parachuting, scuba diving, rock
climbing, skiing, escape and evasion, and other specialized military
skills, some of them classified. The experimental training program,
designed to add a psychophysical component to an already rigorous schedule of military training, included daily aikido training
aimed at integrating the physical and the mental.

Jack Cirie, who had recently retired from the Marines as a   37
lieutenant colonel, led the training. Richard Heckler, who is a
Ph.D. in psychology as well as a gifted aikidoist, was engaged for
both his psychology and martial-arts skills. I was one of several
consultants called in during the six months of the program; my job
was to serve as a guest aikido instructor, and to lecture on challenge and change as expressed in two of my books, which were on
the trainees' reading list.

I met the Special Forces men at a small, unused base theater that   38
had been converted to a dojo. They were dressed in white martial-
arts uniforms; the only concession to military dress was the presence of olive-drab name patches sewn to the uniforms above the
left breast. The men ranged in age from twenty-two to forty-one,
and in rank from buck sergeant to captain. But age and rank held
little significance as they kneeled at the edge of the mat. As is
customary in aikido training, I knelt in front of them, facing a
photograph of the master who founded the art. I bowed, straightened up, and then clapped twice sharply, a traditional gesture sig-
naling readiness. My new students clapped along with me, and I
could sense their power and decisiveness.

I started with warm-up exercises, followed by some gentle   39
stretching, then demonstrated the first martial-arts technique. As
the men paired off and took turns attacking each other, I moved
from one to the other, making suggestions, providing individual
demonstrations.

It was quickly apparent that these elite troopers were expert   40 learners. This should have come as no surprise. The peacetime military is primarily a gigantic educational institution, and most military men today spend most of their time learning new skills and honing those they already know. I could spot a certain amount of kidding around, and anything that wasn't fully understood was quickly challenged. But these were students any teacher would love to teach. They were fiercely attentive. They worked hard. They were willing to try anything. They were exceptionally eager to master each technique.

At the same time, these soldiers exhibited a sense of courtesy 41 and respect in their relationship with me that seemed neither forced nor pro forma. And, though I knew they were superb fighting men, I saw in them none of the gratuitous brutality that marks the cinematic version of the Special Forces trooper. At one point during my lecture, I asked how many of them felt that Rambo accurately represented the Special Forces soldier. Only one man—the group jokester—raised his hand. Then I asked how many had enjoyed the movie. Most raised their hands. They had liked the action. But one man told Jack Cirie that unless Rambo started carrying his "ruck," he wasn't going to see any more of his movies. The ruck, or rucksack, is the symbolic and literal mark of the real Green Beret. Unless you've paid your dues by humping a hundred or so kilometers with eighty or ninety pounds in your ruck, you're just a Hollywood warrior.

How did they define the ideal warrior? It was a subject I kept 42 bringing up during informal talks, a subject that also had been discussed in previous classroom sessions. It appeared that these men's definition was not far removed from that of the perennial warrior's code. They cited loyalty, patience, intensity, calmness, compassion, and will. They agreed that the true warrior knows himself, knows his limitations. "It's not that you don't have holes," Cirie said, "it's that you're aware of the holes."

Self-mastery, according to the Special Forces men, is a warrior's 43 central motivation. He is always practicing, always seeking to hone his skills, so as to become the best possible instrument for accomplishing his mission. The warrior takes calculated risks and tests himself repeatedly. He works well within a group but also is a self-starter. He believes in something greater than himself: a religion, a cause. He does not worship violence but is at home with it. He is human, not a robot. He may snivel (their word for complain), but he is not a victim. One top sergeant, who had been in Vietnam, said, "We're all acolyte warriors until we've been tested in combat." But others felt that the warrior could exist even outside of the military.

What most struck me was the importance these elite soldiers 44

placed on service and protection. Again and again this subject
came up in our conversations, not only as a warrior ideal, but also
as a compelling justification for their way of life itself. "These
guys," Heckler said to me in a crowded restaurant, "genuinely feel
they're protecting everybody in this room."

A stocky redhead told me of leaving the service after his first   45
tour, and getting a job in St. Louis. "I was driving to work one
morning on the expressway and I heard on my car radio about the
Marines getting killed in Beirut. I can clearly remember seeing the
rising sun, real red in my rear-view mirror. When I got to my exit, I
just kept driving, and I went and signed up for another tour. I was
making $30,000 as an electrician, and I could have made more.
But I didn't want money. I wanted to serve." At the time of the
Mexican earthquake, when volunteers were needed for rescue
work, this man was among the first to suggest going. "Why don't
they just send us on down there?" he kept saying. "We could do
the job."

Do these men love war? No question they want to be where the   46
action is. But that's not the whole story. On one occasion, members of the training group were waiting at a ski lift. Dressed in
combat camouflage, they attracted considerable attention from the
civilians also waiting there. A small group of curious ten- to
twelve-year-olds struck up a conversation.

"I bet you've got a doll that looks just like us," a trooper said.   47
One of the boys smiled and nodded.

"Do you like war?" another boy asked.   48

"Do you like cancer?" the trooper responded.   49

There was subdued applause among the civilian onlookers.   50

It would be just as much a mistake to glorify as to denigrate the   51
serviceman, or the warrior ideal. But in a culture where million-
dollar lottery winners are accorded headline glory, where putting
together an essentially destructive stock deal is considered a heroic
act, where the Good Life is tied in with getting a corner office and
driving a certain make of German car, and where "the one who
dies with the most toys wins" is offered as gospel truth rather than
as a sick joke, I found it refreshing to have met people who hold
alternative views and live by different precepts.

If not Rambo, who?   52

We've learned that military and police forces possess great   53
power to oppress as well as protect, and it's clear that, for a free
society to survive, they must be thoroughly depoliticized and
placed firmly under civilian authority and review. It's also clear
that armed forces can become so overarmed and eager for action

that they can provoke conflict rather than promote peace. To beat swords into plowshares, especially in a nuclear age, remains one of the highest human endeavors. Meanwhile, it seems obvious that as long as wars of any sort exist, it's better to have good soldiers than bad ones. Rambo won't do. He's too sullen, headstrong, self-centered, delinquent, and—face it—unreal; he doesn't carry his ruck. Nor do we need the generally two-dimensional, brutish, bullet-spraying locoes of other action films, or the real-life fantasists who buy exotic weapons and try to cover their inadequacies with camouflage cloth. We need military men and women who are effective, who are professional, who live by a spoken or unspoken warrior's code, and who are dedicated to keeping the peace. Such men and women do exist. They don't deserve to be represented as distorted superheroes. They do deserve to be acknowledged and appreciated for what they are.

And what about war itself? In his seminal book *The Warriors*, 54 philosopher J. Glenn Gray, a World War II combat veteran, writes, "No human power could atone for the injustice, suffering, and degradation of spirit of a single day of warfare." At the same time, he reminds us of war's terrible and enduring appeal: the opportunity to yield to destructive impulses, to sacrifice for others, to live vividly in the moment. The appeal of war is not a popular subject, but until we deal with it openly and undogmatically we may never find a warrior's path toward peace.

One friend of mine—a peace-loving man who served as a medic 55 with General George S. Patton's forces as they fought their way across Germany—has told me that the early-morning smell of a cup of coffee in a snow-covered German forest is more real, even now, forty years later, than anything in his present surroundings. And the unbelieving, strangely amused look on the pilot's face in the plane next to me as his windscreen was shattered by ground fire just north of Manila remains as marvelously crystal-clear today as it was then. "We do not know," Gray writes, "whether a peaceful society can be made attractive enough to wean men away from the appeals of battle. Today we are seeking to make war so horrible that men will be frightened away from it. But this is hardly likely to be more fruitful in the future than it has been in the past. More productive will certainly be our efforts to eliminate the social, economic, and political injustices that are always the immediate occasion of hostilities. Even then, we shall be confronted with the spiritual emptiness and inner hunger that impel many men toward combat. Our society has not begun to wrestle with this problem of how to provide fulfillment to human life, to which war is so often an illusory path."

I've come to believe that Gray is right. The problem is not that   56
war is so often vivid, but that peace is so often drab. Looking at this
same problem back in 1910, the psychologist William James argued that we need "a moral equivalent of war," a way of living
that would provide the challenges of combat without its horrors.
James's argument, it seems to me, becomes more compelling with
the development of each new weapons system. In this light, peace
advocates are indeed doing important work in opposing war
through public statements, petitions, and demonstrations. But the
end of war—can we imagine it?—might require something more
fundamental: the creation of a peace that is not only just, but also
vivid.

The work of creating a more vivid peace must address the prob-   57
lem of our spiritual emptiness and inner hunger. It might well
require that we relinquish some of our currently fashionable cynicism and give more energy, as Gray suggests, to values that could
be called moral and spiritual. But there's something else: We need
passion. We need challenge and risk. We need to be pushed to our
limits. And I believe this is just what happens when we accept a
warrior's code, when we try to live each moment as a warrior,
whether in education, job, marriage, child rearing, or recreation.
The truth is that we don't have to go to combat to go to war. Life is
fired at us like a bullet, and there is no escaping it short of death.
All escape attempts—drugs, aimless travel, the distractions of the
media, empty material pursuits—are sure to fail in the long run, as
more and more of us are beginning to learn.

Could it be that the current popularity of Rambo and the other   58
warrior films goes beyond neopatriotism and revenge fantasies?
Let's at least consider the possibility that the warrior rage also
signifies something we haven't yet put into words: that there are
many potential warriors among us, that each of us, at some level,
wants to meet life head-on, to risk everything for what he believes
in, to develop himself to the fullest, and to serve others.

When the samurai Kikushi was ordained a *bodhisattva* (one de-   59
voted to lifelong service), his master told him, "You must concentrate upon and consecrate yourself wholly to each day, as though a
fire were raging in your hair." On those frequent occasions when
statements like this sound hopelessly overblown and quite impossible to achieve in real life, I recall something Jack Cirie said during
one of our conversations: "Believing you can be perfect is the fatal
imperfection. Believing you're invulnerable is the ultimate vulnerability. Being a warrior doesn't mean winning or even succeeding. But it does mean putting your life on the line. It means risking
and failing and risking again, as long as you live."

VIRGINIA WOOLF

The Society of Outsiders and the Prevention of War

Virginia Woolf (1882–1941) was educated at home by her father, Sir Leslie Stephen, an eminent biographer and critic. After his death, Woolf became one of the central figures in the Blooms-bury group of London intellectuals, which included E. M. For-ster, Lytton Strachey, and John Maynard Keynes. A prolific writer, Woolf developed new forms for the novel in *Mrs. Dallo-way* (1925), *To the Lighthouse* (1927), and *The Waves* (1931). Woolf's essays generally defy conventional forms as well, seem-ing to follow no fixed plan, but returning with added force to Woolf's fundamental themes, many of which we would today call feminist. *A Room of One's Own* (1929) describes the dif-ficulties of women, particularly women writers, in an essen-tially patriarchal society. *Three Guineas* (1938), from which "The Society of Outsiders and the Prevention of War" is excerpted, addresses the question of what "an educated man's daughter" can do to help prevent war. It was written while England was on the brink of war with Germany and London was preparing itself for German bombing.

War, as the result of impersonal forces, is you will agree beyond the grasp of the untrained mind. But war as the result of human nature is another thing. Had you not believed that human nature, the reasons, the emotions of the ordinary man and woman, lead to war, you would not have written asking for our help. You must have argued, men and women, here and now, are able to exert their wills; they are not pawns and puppets dancing on a string held by invisible hands. They can act, and think for themselves. Perhaps even they can influence other people's thoughts and ac-tions. Some such reasoning must have led you to apply to us; and with justification. For happily there is one branch of education which comes under the heading "unpaid-for education"—that understanding of human beings and their motives which, if the word is rid of its scientific associations, might be called psychology. Marriage, the one great profession open to our class since the dawn of time until the year 1919;[1] marriage, the art of choosing the

---

1. The Sex Disqualification [Removal] Act of 1919 allowed women to "exercise any public function" available to men.

human being with whom to live life successfully, should have taught us some skill in that. But here again another difficulty confronts us. For though many instincts are held more or less in common by both sexes, to fight has always been the man's habit, not the woman's. Law and practice have developed that difference, whether innate or accidental. Scarcely a human being in the course of history has fallen to a woman's rifle; the vast majority of birds and beasts have been killed by you, not by us; it is difficult to judge what we do not share.

How then are we to understand your problem, and if we cannot,   2
how can we answer your question, how to prevent war? The answer based upon our experience and our psychology—Why fight?—is not an answer of any value. Obviously there is for you some glory, some necessity, some satisfaction in fighting which we have never felt or enjoyed. Complete understanding could only be achieved by blood transfusion and memory transfusion—a miracle still beyond the reach of science. But we who live now have a substitute for blood transfusion and memory transfusion which must serve at a pinch. There is that marvellous, perpetually renewed, and as yet largely untapped aid to the understanding of human motives which is provided in our age by biography and autobiography. Also there is the daily paper, history in the raw. There is thus no longer any reason to be confined to the minute span of actual experience which is still, for us, so narrow, so circumscribed. We can supplement it by looking at the picture of the lives of others. It is of course only a picture at present, but as such it must serve. It is to biography then that we will turn first, quickly and briefly, in order to attempt to understand what war means to you. Let us extract a few sentences from a biography.

First, this from a soldier's life: 3

> "I have had the happiest possible life, and have always been working for war, and have now got into the biggest in the prime of life for a soldier. . . . Thank God, we are off in an hour. Such a magnificent regiment! Such men, such horses! Within ten days I hope Francis and I will be riding side by side straight at the Germans."[2]

To which the biographer adds: 4

> "From the first hour he had been supremely happy, for he had found his true calling."

To that let us add this from an airman's life: 5

> "We talked of the League of Nations and the prospects of peace and disarmament. On this subject he was not so much militarist as martial.

---

2. *Francis and Riversdale Grenfell*, by John Buchan, pp. 189, 205. [author's note]

The difficulty to which he could find no answer was that if permanent peace were ever achieved, and armies and navies ceased to exist, there would be no outlet for the manly qualities which fighting developed, and that human physique and human character would deteriorate."[3]

Here, immediately, are three reasons which lead your sex to fight; war is a profession; a source of happiness and excitement; and it is also an outlet for manly qualities, without which men would deteriorate. But that these feelings and opinions are by no means universally held by your sex is proved by the following extract from another biography, the life of a poet who was killed in the European war: Wilfred Owen. 6

> "Already I have comprehended a light which never will filter into the dogma of any national church: namely, that one of Christ's essential commands was: Passivity at any price! Suffer dishonour and disgrace, but never resort to arms. Be bullied, be outraged, be killed; but do not kill. . . . Thus you see how pure Christianity will not fit in with pure patriotism."

And among some notes for poems that he did not live to write are these: 7

> "The unnaturalness of weapons. . . . Inhumanity of war. . . . The insupportability of war. . . . Horrible beastliness of war. . . . Foolishness of war."[4]

From these quotations it is obvious that the same sex holds very different opinions about the same thing. But also it is obvious, from today's newspaper, that however many dissentients there are, the great majority of your sex are today in favour of war. The Scarborough Conference of educated men, the Bournemouth Conference of working men are both agreed that to spend £300,000,000 annually upon arms is a necessity. They are of opinion that Wilfred Owen was wrong; that it is better to kill than to be killed. Yet since biography shows that differences of opinion are many, it is plain that there must be some one reason which prevails in order to bring about this overpowering unanimity. Shall we call it, for the sake of brevity, "patriotism"? What then, we must ask next, is this "patriotism" which leads you to go to war? Let the Lord Chief Justice of England interpret it for us: 8

> "Englishmen are proud of England. For those who have been trained in English schools and universities, and who have done the work of their lives in England, there are few loves stronger than the love we have for our country. When we consider other nations, when

3. *Antony (Viscount Knebworth)*, by the Earl of Lytton, p. 355. [author's note]
4. *The Poems of Wilfred Owen*, edited by Edmund Blunden, pp. 25, 41. [author's note]

we judge the merits of the policy of this country or of that, it is the standard of our own country that we apply. . . . Liberty has made her abode in England. England is the home of democratic institutions. . . . It is true that in our midst there are many enemies of liberty—some of them, perhaps, in rather unexpected quarters. But we are standing firm. It has been said that an Englishman's Home is his Castle. The home of Liberty is in England. And it is a castle indeed—a castle that will be defended to the last. . . . Yes, we are greatly blessed, we Englishmen."[5]

That is a fair general statement of what patriotism means to an 9 educated man and what duties it imposes upon him. But the educated man's sister—what does "patriotism" mean to her? Has she the same reasons for being proud of England, for loving England, for defending England? Has she been "greatly blessed" in England? History and biography when questioned would seem to show that her position in the home of freedom has been different from her brother's; and psychology would seem to hint that history is not without its effect upon mind and body. Therefore her interpretation of the word "patriotism" may well differ from his. And that difference may make it extremely difficult for her to understand his definition of patriotism and the duties it imposes. If then our answer to your question, "How in your opinion are we to prevent war?" depends upon understanding the reasons, the emotions, the loyalties which lead men to go to war, this letter had better be torn across and thrown into the waste-paper basket. For it seems plain that we cannot understand each other because of these differences. It seems plain that we think differently according as we are born differently; there is a Grenfell point of view; a Knebworth point of view; a Wilfred Owen point of view; a Lord Chief Justice's point of view and the point of view of an educated man's daughter.

.   .   .

The educated man's daughter has now at her disposal an in- 10 fluence which is different from any influence that she has possessed before. It is not the influence which the great lady, the Siren, possesses; nor is it the influence which the educated man's daughter possessed when she had no vote; nor is it the influence which she possessed when she had a vote but was debarred from the right to earn her living. It differs, because it is an influence from which the charm element has been removed; it is an influence from which the money element has been removed. She need no longer use her

5. Lord Heward, proposing the toast of "England" at the banquet of the Society of St. George at Cardiff. [author's note]

charm to procure money from her father or brother. Since it is beyond the power of her family to punish her financially she can express her own opinions. In place of the admirations and antipathies which were often unconsciously dictated by the need of money she can declare her genuine likes and dislikes. In short, she need not acquiesce; she can criticize. At last she is in possession of an influence that is disinterested.

Such in rough and rapid outlines is the nature of our new weapon, the influence which the educated man's daughter can exert now that she is able to earn her own living. The question that has next to be discussed, therefore, is how can she use this new weapon to help you to prevent war? And it is immediately plain that if there is no difference between men who earn their livings in the professions and women who earn their livings, then this letter can end; for if our point of view is the same as yours then we must add our six-pence to your guinea;[6] follow your methods and repeat your words. But, whether fortunately or unfortunately, that is not true. The two classes still differ enormously. And to prove this, we need not have recourse to the dangerous and uncertain theories of psychologists and biologists; we can appeal to facts. Take the fact of education. Your class has been educated at public schools and universities for five or six hundred years, ours for sixty. Take the fact of property. Your class possesses in its own right and not through marriage practically all the capital, all the land, all the valuables, and all the patronage in England. Our class possesses in its own right and not through marriage practically none of the capital, none of the land, none of the valuables, and none of the patronage in England. That such differences make for very considerable differences in mind and body, no psychologist or biologist would deny. It would seem to follow then as an indisputable fact that "we"—meaning by "we" a whole made up of body, brain, and spirit, influenced by memory and tradition—must still differ in some essential respects from "you," whose body, brain, and spirit have been so differently trained and are so differently influenced by memory and tradition. Though we see the same world, we see it through different eyes. Any help we can give you must be different from that you can give yourselves, and perhaps the value of that help may lie in the fact of that difference. Therefore before we agree to sign your manifesto or join your society, it might be well to discover where the difference lies, because then we may discover where the help lies also. Let us then by way of a very elementary beginning lay before you a photograph—a crudely coloured photo-

11

6. In Woolf's time, there were 252 pence to a guinea.

graph—of your world as it appears to us who see it from the threshold of the private house; through the shadow of the veil that St. Paul still lays upon our eyes;[7] from the bridge which connects the private house with the world of public life.

Your world, then, the world of professional, of public life, seen from this angle undoubtedly looks queer. At first sight it is enormously impressive. Within quite a small space are crowded together St. Paul's, the Bank of England, the Mansion House, the massive if funereal battlements of the Law Courts; and on the other side, Westminster Abbey and the Houses of Parliament.[8] There, we say to ourselves, pausing, in this moment of transition on the bridge, our fathers and brothers have spent their lives. All these hundreds of years they have been mounting those steps, passing in and out of those doors, ascending those pulpits, preaching, money-making, administering justice. It is from this world that the private house (somewhere, roughly speaking, in the West End) has derived its creeds, its laws, its clothes and carpets, its beef and mutton. And then, as is now permissible, cautiously pushing aside the swing doors of one of these temples, we enter on tiptoe and survey the scene in greater detail. The first sensation of colossal size, of majestic masonry is broken up into a myriad points of amazement mixed with interrogation. Your clothes in the first place make us gape with astonishment. How many, how splendid, how extremely ornate they are—the clothes worn by the educated man in his public capacity! Now you dress in violet; a jewelled crucifix swings on your breast; now your shoulders are covered with lace; now furred with ermine; now slung with many linked chains set with precious stones. Now you wear wigs on your heads; rows of graduated curls descend to your necks. Now your hats are boat-shaped, or cocked; now they mount in cones of black fur; now they are made of brass and scuttle-shaped; now plumes of red, now of blue hair surmount them. Sometimes gowns cover your legs; sometimes gaiters. Tabards embroidered with lions and unicorns swing from your shoulders; metal objects cut in star shapes or in circles glitter and twinkle upon your breasts. Ribbons of all colours—blue, purple, crimson—cross from shoulder to shoulder. After the comparative simplicity of your dress at home, the splendour of your public attire is dazzling.

But far stranger are two other facts that gradually reveal them-

7. See 1 Corinthians II: 3–10.
8. These buildings are associated with the concentrated power of the British church and state, and—in the case of Westminster Abbey—with eminence in learning and art as well.

selves when our eyes have recovered from their first amazement. Not only are whole bodies of men dressed alike summer and winter—a strange characteristic to a sex which changes its clothes according to the season, and for reasons of private taste and comfort—but every button, rosette, and stripe seems to have some symbolical meaning. Some have the right to wear plain buttons only; others rosettes; some may wear a single stripe; others three, four, or five. And each curl or stripe is sewn on at precisely the right distance apart—it may be one inch for one man, one inch and a quarter for another. Rules again regulate the gold wire on the shoulders, the braid on the trousers, the cockades on the hats—but no single pair of eyes can observe all these distinctions, let alone account for them accurately.

Even stranger, however, than the symbolic splendour of your clothes are the ceremonies that take place when you wear them. Here you kneel; there you bow; here you advance in procession behind a man carrying a silver poker; here you mount a carved chair; here you appear to do homage to a piece of painted wood; here you abase yourselves before tables covered with richly worked tapestry. And whatever these ceremonies may mean, you perform them always together, always in step, always in the uniform proper to the man and the occasion.   14

Apart from the ceremonies, such decorative apparel appears to us at first sight strange in the extreme. For dress, as we use it, is comparatively simple. Besides the prime function of covering the body, it has two other offices—that it creates beauty for the eye, and that it attracts the admiration of your sex. Since marriage until the year 1919—less than twenty years ago—was the only profession open to us, the enormous importance of dress to a woman can hardly be exaggerated. It was to her what clients are to you—dress was her chief, perhaps her only, method of becoming Lord Chancellor.[9] But your dress in its immense elaboration has obviously another function. It not only covers nakedness, gratifies vanity, and creates pleasure for the eye, but it serves to advertise the social, professional, or intellectual standing of the wearer. If you will excuse the humble illustration, your dress fulfils the same function as the tickets in a grocer's shop. But, here, instead of saying, "This is margarine; this pure butter; this is the finest butter in the market," it says, "This man is a clever man—he is Master of Arts; this man is a very clever man—he is Doctor of Letters; this man is a most clever man—he is a Member of the Order of Merit." It is this   15

9. President of the House of Lords; in the British peerage, the Lord Chancellor ranks just below the Archbishop of Canterbury.

function—the advertisement function—of your dress that seems to us most singular. In the opinion of St. Paul, such advertisement, at any rate for our sex, was unbecoming and immodest; until a very few years ago we were denied the use of it. And still the tradition, or belief, lingers among us that to express worth of any kind, whether intellectual or moral, by wearing pieces of metal, or ribbon, coloured hoods or gowns, is a barbarity which deserves the ridicule which we bestow upon the rites of savages. A woman who advertised her motherhood by a tuft of horsehair on the left shoulder would scarcely, you will agree, be a venerable object.

But what light does our difference here throw upon the problem   16 before us? What connection is there between the sartorial splendours of the educated man and the photograph of ruined houses and dead bodies?[10] Obviously the connection between dress and war is not far to seek; your finest clothes are those that you wear as soldiers. Since the red and the gold, the brass and the feathers are discarded upon active service, it is plain that their expensive and not, one might suppose, hygienic splendour is invented partly in order to impress the beholder with the majesty of the military office, partly in order through their vanity to induce young men to become soldiers. Here, then, our influence and our difference might have some effect; we, who are forbidden to wear such clothes ourselves, can express the opinion that the wearer is not to us a pleasing or an impressive spectacle. He is on the contrary a ridiculous, a barbarous, a displeasing spectacle. But as the daughters of educated men we can use our influence more effectively in another direction, upon our own class—the class of educated men. For there, in courts and universities, we find the same love of dress. There, too, are velvet and silk, fur and ermine. We can say that for educated men to emphasize their superiority over other people, either in birth or intellect, by dressing differently, or by adding titles before, or letters after their names are acts that rouse competition and jealousy—emotions which, as we need scarcely draw upon biography to prove, nor ask psychology to show, have their share in encouraging a disposition towards war. If then we express the opinion that such distinctions make those who possess them ridiculous and learning contemptible, we should do something, indirectly, to discourage the feelings that lead to war. Happily we can now do more than express an opinion; we can refuse all such

10. Earlier in the essay, Woolf has introduced into evidence a photograph of a house bombed to splinters in the Spanish Civil War, then at its height. The photograph shows dead children and an adult body "so mutilated that it might . . . be the body of a pig."

distinctions and all such uniforms for ourselves. This would be a slight but definite contribution to the problem before us—how to prevent war; and one that a different training and a different tradition puts more easily within our reach than within yours.

.   .   .

That request then for a guinea answered, and the cheque signed, only one further request of yours remains to be considered—it is that we should fill up a form and become members of your society. On the face of it that seems a simple request, easily granted. For what can be simpler than to join the society to which this guinea has just been contributed? On the face of it, how easy, how simple; but in the depths, how difficult, how complicated. . . . What possible doubts, what possible hesitations can those dots stand for? What reason or what emotion can make us hesitate to become members of a society whose aims we approve, to whose funds we have contributed? It may be neither reason nor emotion, but something more profound and fundamental than either. It may be difference. Different we are, as facts have proved, both in sex and in education. And it is from that difference, as we have already said, that our help can come, if help we can, to protect liberty, to prevent war. But if we sign this form which implies a promise to become active members of your society, it would seem that we must lose that difference and therefore sacrifice that help. To explain why this is so is not easy, even though the gift of a guinea has made it possible (so we have boasted) to speak freely without fear or flattery. Let us then keep the form unsigned on the table before us while we discuss, so far as we are able, the reasons and the emotions which make us hesitate to sign it. For those reasons and emotions have their origin deep in the darkness of ancestral memory; they have grown together in some confusion; it is very difficult to untwist them in the light.

To begin with an elementary distinction: a society is a conglomeration of people joined together for certain aims; while you, who write in your own person with your own hand are single. You the individual are a man whom we have reason to respect; a man of the brotherhood, to which, as biography proves, many brothers have belonged. Thus Anne Clough,[11] describing her brother, says: "Arthur is my best friend and adviser. . . . Arthur is the comfort

17

18

---

11. Anne Clough (1820–1892), English educator and founder of the first residential house for women at Cambridge University. Sister of the poet Arthur Clough (1819–1861).

and joy of my life; it is for him, and from him, that I am incited to
seek after all that is lovely and of good report." To which William
Wordsworth,[12] speaking of his sister but answering the other as if
one nightingale called to another in the forests of the past, replies:

> *"The Blessing of my later years*
> *Was with me when a Boy:*
> *She gave me eyes, she gave me ears;*
> *And humble cares, and delicate fears;*
> *A heart, the fountain of sweet tears;*
> *And love, and thought, and joy."*[13]

Such was, such perhaps still is, the relationship of many brothers   19
and sisters in private, as individuals. They respect each other and
help each other and have aims in common. Why then, if such can
be their private relationship, as biography and poetry prove, should
their public relationship, as law and history prove, be so very different? And here, since you are a lawyer, with a lawyer's memory, it
is not necessary to remind you of certain decrees of English law
from its first records to the year 1919 by way of proving that the
public, the society relationship of brother and sister has been very
different from the private. The very word "society" sets tolling in
memory the dismal bells of a harsh music: shall not, shall not, shall
not. You shall not learn; you shall not earn; you shall not own; you
shall not—such was the society relationship of brother to sister for
many centuries. And though it is possible, and to the optimistic
credible, that in time a new society may ring a carillon of splendid
harmony, and your letter heralds it, that day is far distant. Inevitably we ask ourselves, is there not something in the conglomeration
of people into societies that releases what is most selfish and violent, least rational and humane in the individuals themselves? Inevitably we look upon society, so kind to you, so harsh to us, as an
ill-fitting form that distorts the truth; deforms the mind; fetters the
will. Inevitably we look upon societies as conspiracies that sink the
private brother, whom many of us have reason to respect, and
inflate in his stead a monstrous male, loud of voice, hard of fist,
childishly intent upon scoring the floor of the earth with chalk
marks, within whose mystic boundaries human beings are penned,
rigidly, separately, artificially; where, daubed red and gold, decorated like a savage with feathers he goes through mystic rites and

12. British Romantic poet (1770–1850).
13. *Memoir of Anne J. Clough,* by B. A. Clough, pp. 38, 67. "The Sparrow's Nest," by
William Wordsworth. [author's note]

enjoys the dubious pleasures of power and dominion while we, "his" women, are locked in the private house without share in the many societies of which his society is composed. For such reasons compact as they are of many memories and emotions—for who shall analyse the complexity of a mind that holds so deep a reservoir of time past within it?—it seems both wrong for us rationally and impossible for us emotionally to fill up your form and join your society. For by so doing we should merge our identity in yours; follow and repeat and score still deeper the old worn ruts in which society, like a gramophone whose needle has stuck, is grinding out with intolerable unanimity "Three hundred millions spent upon arms." We should not give effect to a view which our own experience of "society" should have helped us to envisage. Thus, Sir, while we respect you as a private person and prove it by giving you a guinea to spend as you choose, we believe that we can help you most effectively by refusing to join your society; by working for our common ends—justice and equality and liberty for all men and women—outside your society, not within.

But this, you will say, if it means anything, can only mean that you, the daughters of educated men, who have promised us your positive help, refuse to join our society in order that you may make another of your own. And what sort of society do you propose to found outside ours, but in co-operation with it, so that we may both work together for our common ends? That is a question which you have every right to ask, and which we must try to answer in order to justify our refusal to sign the form you send. Let us then draw rapidly in outline the kind of society which the daughters of educated men might found and join outside your society but in co-operation with its ends. In the first place, this new society, you will be relieved to learn, would have no honorary treasurer, for it would need no funds. It would have no office, no committee, no secretary; it would call no meetings; it would hold no conferences. If name it must have, it could be called the Outsiders' Society. That is not a resonant name, but it has the advantage that it squares with facts—the facts of history, of law, of biography; even, it may be, with the still hidden facts of our still unknown psychology. It would consist of educated men's daughters working in their own class—how indeed can they work in any other?—and by their own methods for liberty, equality, and peace. Their first duty, to which they would bind themselves not by oath, for oaths and ceremonies have no part in a society which must be anonymous and elastic before everything, would be not to fight with arms. This is easy for them to observe, for in fact, as the papers

20

inform us, "the Army Council have no intention of opening re-cruiting for any women's corps."[14] The country ensures it. Next they would refuse in the event of war to make munitions or nurse the wounded. Since in the last war both these activities were mainly discharged by the daughters of working men, the pressure upon them here too would be slight, though probably disagreeable. On the other hand the next duty to which they would pledge themselves is one of considerable difficulty, and calls not only for courage and initiative, but for the special knowledge of the ed-ucated man's daughter. It is, briefly, not to incite their brothers to fight, or to dissuade them, but to maintain an attitude of complete indifference. But the attitude expressed by the word "indifference" is so complex and of such importance that it needs even here further definition. Indifference in the first place must be given a firm footing upon fact. As it is a fact that she cannot understand what instinct compels him, what glory, what interest, what manly satisfaction fighting provides for him—"without war there would be no outlet for the manly qualities which fighting develops"—as fighting thus is a sex characteristic which she cannot share, the counterpart some claim of the maternal instinct which he cannot share, so is it an instinct which she cannot judge. The outsider therefore must leave him free to deal with this instinct by himself, because liberty of opinion must be respected, especially when it is based upon an instinct which is as foreign to her as centuries of tradition and education can make it. This is a fundamental and instinctive distinction upon which indifference may be based. But the outsider will make it her duty not merely to base her indiffer-ence upon instinct, but upon reason. When he says, as history proves that he has said, and may say again, "I'm fighting to protect our country" and thus seeks to rouse her patriotic emotion, she will ask herself, "What does 'our country' mean to me an out-sider?" To decide this she will analyse the meaning of patriotism in her own case. She will inform herself of the position of her sex and her class in the past. She will inform herself of the amount of land, wealth, and property in the possession of her own sex and class in the present—how much of "England" in fact belongs to her. From the same sources she will inform herself of the legal protection which the law has given her in the past and now gives her. And if he adds that he is fighting to protect her body, she will reflect upon

14. "It was stated yesterday at the War Office that the Army Council have no intention of opening recruiting for any women's corps" (*The Times*, October 22nd, 1937). This marks a prime distinction between the sexes. Pacifism is enforced upon women. Men are still allowed liberty of choice. [author's note]

the degree of physical protection that she now enjoys when the words "Air Raid Precaution" are written on blank walls. And if he says that he is fighting to protect England from foreign rule, she will reflect that for her there are no "foreigners," since by law she becomes a foreigner if she marries a foreigner. And she will do her best to make this a fact, not by forced fraternity, but by human sympathy. All these facts will convince her reason (to put it in a nutshell) that her sex and class has very little to thank England for in the past; not much to thank England for in the present; while the security of her person in the future is highly dubious. But probably she will have imbibed, even from the governess, some romantic notion that Englishmen, those fathers and grandfathers whom she sees marching in the picture of history, are "superior" to the men of other countries. This she will consider it her duty to check by comparing French historians with English; German with French; the testimony of the ruled—the Indians or the Irish, say—with the claims made by their rulers. Still some "patriotic" emotion, some ingrained belief in the intellectual superiority of her own country over other countries may remain. Then she will compare English painting with French painting; English music with German music; English literature with Greek literature, for translations abound. When all these comparisons have been faithfully made by the use of reason, the outsider will find herself in possession of very good reasons for her indifference. She will find that she has no good reason to ask her brother to fight on her behalf to protect "our" country. " 'Our country,' " she will say, "throughout the greater part of its history has treated me as a slave; it has denied me education or any share in its possessions. 'Our' country still ceases to be mine if I marry a foreigner. 'Our' country denies me the means of protecting myself, forces me to pay others a very large sum annually to protect me, and is so little able, even so, to protect me that Air Raid precautions are written on the wall. Therefore if you insist upon fighting to protect me, or 'our' country, let it be understood, soberly and rationally between us, that you are fighting to gratify a sex instinct which I cannot share; to procure benefits which I have not shared and probably will not share; but not to gratify my instincts, or to protect myself or my country. For," the outsider will say, "in fact, as a woman, I have no country. As a woman I want no country. As a woman my country is the whole world." And if, when reason has said its say, still some obstinate emotion remains, some love of England dropped into a child's ears by the cawing of rooks in an elm tree, by the splash of waves on a beach, or by English voices murmuring nursery rhymes, this drop of pure, if irrational, emotion she will make serve her to give to

England first what she desires of peace and freedom for the whole world.

Such then will be the nature of her "indifference" and from this 21 indifference certain actions must follow. She will bind herself to take no share in patriotic demonstrations; to assent to no form of national self-praise; to make no part of any claque or audience that encourages war; to absent herself from military displays, tournaments, tattoos, prize-givings, and all such ceremonies as encourage the desire to impose "our" civilization of "our" dominion upon other people. The psychology of private life, moreover, warrants the belief that this use of indifference by the daughters of educated men would help materially to prevent war. For psychology would seem to show that it is far harder for human beings to take action when other people are indifferent and allow them complete freedom of action, than when their actions are made the centre of excited emotion. The small boy struts and trumpets outside the window: implore him to stop; he goes on; say nothing; he stops. That the daughters of educated men then should give their brothers neither the white feather of cowardice nor the red feather of courage, but no feather at all; that they should shut the bright eyes that rain influence, or let those eyes look elsewhere when war is discussed—that is the duty to which outsiders will train themselves in peace before the threat of death inevitably makes reason powerless.

·   ·   ·

The outsiders then would bind themselves not only to earn their 22 own livings, but to earn them so expertly that their refusal to earn them would be a matter of concern to the work master. They would bind themselves to obtain full knowledge of professional practices, and to reveal any instance of tyranny or abuse in their professions. And they would bind themselves not to continue to make money in any profession, but to cease all competition and to practise their profession experimentally, in the interests of research and for love of the work itself, when they had earned enough to live upon. Also they would bind themselves to remain outside any profession hostile to freedom, such as the making or the improvement of the weapons of war. And they would bind themselves to refuse to take office or honour from any society which, while professing to respect liberty, restricts it, like the universities of Oxford and Cambridge. And they would consider it their duty to investigate the claims of all public societies to which, like the Church and the universities, they are forced to contribute as taxpayers as carefully and fearlessly as they would investigate the claims of private societies to which they contribute voluntarily. They would make it their business to scrutinize the endowments of the schools and universities and the objects upon which that money is spent. As with the educational, so with the religious profession. By reading the New Testament in the first place and next those divines and historians whose works are all easily accessible to the daughters of educated men, they would make it their business to have some knowledge of the Christian religion and its history. Further they would inform themselves of the practice of that religion by attending Church services, by analysing the spiritual and intellectual value of sermons; by criticizing the opinions of men whose profession is religion as freely as they would criticize the opinions of any other body of men. Thus they would be creative in their activities, not merely critical. By criticizing education they would help to create a civilized society which protects culture and intellectual liberty. By criticizing religion they would attempt to free the religious spirit from its present servitude and would help, if need be, to create a new religion based, it might well be, upon the New Testament, but, it might well be, very different from the religion now erected upon that basis. And in all this, and in much more than we have time to particularize, they would be helped, you will agree, by their position as outsiders, that freedom from unreal loyalties, that freedom from interested motives which are at present assured them by the State.

It would be easy to define in greater number and more exactly 23 the duties of those who belong to the Society of Outsiders, but not profitable. Elasticity is essential; and some degree of secrecy, as will be shown later, is at present even more essential. But the description thus loosely and imperfectly given is enough to show you, Sir, that the Society of Outsiders has the same ends as your society— freedom, equality, peace; but that it seeks to achieve them by the means that a different sex, a different tradition, a different education, and the different values which result from those differences have placed within our reach. Broadly speaking, the main distinction between us who are outside society and you who are inside society must be that whereas you will make use of the means provided by your position—leagues, conferences, campaigns, great names, and all such public measures as your wealth and political influence place within your reach—we, remaining outside, will experiment not with public means in public but with private means in private.

E. M. FORSTER

What I Believe

E(dward) M(organ) Forster (1879–1970) was born in London and took degrees in classics and history from Cambridge University in 1901, after which for two decades he lived alternately in England and abroad—in Greece, Italy, India, and Egypt. By then he had four novels to his credit, including two now recognized as classics, *A Room with a View* (1908) and *Howards End* (1910). *A Passage to India*, arguably his masterpiece, appeared in 1924. Thereafter, he published no novel during his lifetime: love in its various forms had been the theme of Forster's novels, and he was hampered by his inability to reveal to the British public the homosexual love expressed in the stories he continued to write. Though he stopped publishing fiction, Forster continued to publish essays, many of them collected in *Abinger Harvest* (1936) and *Two Cheers for Democracy* (1951). The essays are part of a brilliant battle fought by a liberal humanist against what he saw as a rising tide of bigotry, greed, and militarism. "What I Believe" was written in 1939, on the brink of World War II.

I do not believe in Belief. But this is an age of faith, and there are 1 so many militant creeds that, in self-defence, one has to formulate a creed of one's own. Tolerance, good temper and sympathy are no longer enough in a world which is rent by religious and racial persecution, in a world where ignorance rules, and science, who ought to have ruled, plays the subservient pimp. Tolerance, good temper and sympathy—they are what matter really, and if the human race is not to collapse they must come to the front before long. But for the moment they are not enough, their action is no stronger than a flower, battered beneath a military jackboot. They want stiffening, even if the process coarsens them. Faith, to my mind, is a stiffening process, a sort of mental starch, which ought to be applied as sparingly as possible. I dislike the stuff. I do not believe in it, for its own sake, at all. Herein I probably differ from most people, who believe in Belief, and are only sorry they cannot swallow even more than they do. My law-givers are Erasmus and Montaigne, not Moses and St. Paul. My temple stands not upon Mount Moriah but in that Elysian Field where even the immoral are admitted. My motto is: "Lord, I disbelieve—help thou my unbelief."[1]

1. *Erasmus/Montaigne:* humanists, not religious figures, as were *Moses* and *Paul; Mt. Moriah:* Biblical site where Abraham was to sacrifice his son Isaac; *Elysian Fields:* in

I have, however, to live in an Age of Faith—the sort of epoch I   2
used to hear praised when I was a boy. It is extremely unpleasant
really. It is bloody in every sense of the word. And I have to keep
my end up in it. Where do I start?

With personal relationships. Here is something comparatively   3
solid in a world full of violence and cruelty. Not absolutely solid,
for Psychology has split and shattered the idea of a "Person," and
has shown that there is something incalculable in each of us, which
may at any moment rise to the surface and destroy our normal
balance. We don't know what we are like. We can't know what
other people are like. How, then, can we put any trust in personal
relationships, or cling to them in the gathering political storm? In
theory we cannot. But in practice we can and do. Though A is not
unchangeably A or B unchangeably B, there can still be love and
loyalty between the two. For the purpose of living one has to
assume that the personality is solid, and the "self" is an entity, and
to ignore all contrary evidence. And since to ignore evidence is one
of the characteristics of faith, I certainly can proclaim that I believe
in personal relationships.

Starting from them, I get a little order into the contemporary   4
chaos. One must be fond of people and trust them if one is not to
make a mess of life, and it is therefore essential that they should not
let one down. They often do. The moral of which is that I must,
myself, be as reliable as possible, and this I try to be. But reliability
is not a matter of contract—that is the main difference between the
world of personal relationships and the world of business relationships. It is a matter for the heart, which signs no documents.
In other words, reliability is impossible unless there is a natural
warmth. Most men possess this warmth, though they often have
bad luck and get chilled. Most of them, even when they are politicians, *want* to keep faith. And one can, at all events, show one's
own little light here, one's own poor little trembling flame, with
the knowledge that it is not the only light that is shining in the
darkness, and not the only one which the darkness does not comprehend. Personal relations are despised today. They are regarded
as bourgeois luxuries, as products of a time of fair weather which is
now past, and we are urged to get rid of them, and to dedicate
ourselves to some movement or cause instead. I hate the idea of
causes, and if I had to choose between betraying my country and
betraying my friend, I hope I should have the guts to betray my
country. Such a choice may scandalise the modern reader, and he

---

Greek mythology, Paradise, a happy land; *Lord, I disbelieve:* Forster's adaptation of
the words of a man witnessing Jesus' performance of a miracle in healing his son—
"Lord, I believe . . ." (Mark 9:24).

may stretch out his patriotic hand to the telephone at once and ring up the police. It would not have shocked Dante, though. Dante places Brutus and Cassius in the lowest circle of Hell[2] because they had chosen to betray their friend Julius Caesar rather than their country Rome. Probably one will not be asked to make such an agonising choice. Still, there lies at the back of every creed something terrible and hard for which the worshipper may one day be required to suffer, and there is even a terror and a hardness in this creed of personal relationships, urbane and mild though it sounds. Love and loyalty to an individual can run counter to the claims of the State. When they do—down with the State, say I, which means that the State would down me.

This brings me along to Democracy, "even Love, the Beloved   5
Republic, which feeds upon Freedom and lives." Democracy is not a Beloved Republic really, and never will be. But it is less hateful than other contemporary forms of government, and to that extent it deserves our support. It does start from the assumption that the individual is important, and that all types are needed to make a civilisation. It does not divide its citizens into the bossers and the bossed—as an efficiency-regime tends to do. The people I admire most are those who are sensitive and want to create something or discover something, and do not see life in terms of power, and such people get more of a chance under a democracy than elsewhere. They found religions, great or small, or they produce literature and art, or they do disinterested scientific research, or they may be what is called "ordinary people," who are creative in their private lives, bring up their children decently, for instance, or help their neighbours. All these people need to express themselves; they cannot do so unless society allows them liberty to do so, and the society which allows them most liberty is a democracy.

Democracy has another merit. It allows criticism, and if there is   6
not public criticism there are bound to be hushed-up scandals. That is why I believe in the Press, despite all its lies and vulgarity, and why I believe in Parliament. Parliament is often sneered at because it is a Talking Shop. I believe in it *because* it is a talking shop. I believe in the Private Member who makes himself a nuisance. He gets snubbed and is told that he is cranky or ill-informed, but he does expose abuses which would otherwise never have been mentioned, and very often an abuse gets put right just by being mentioned. Occasionally, too, a well-meaning public official starts losing his head in the cause of efficiency, and thinks himself God Almighty. Such officials are particularly frequent in the Home

2. In *The Divine Comedy*, masterpiece of Italian poet Dante Alighieri (1265–1321).

Office. Well, there will be questions about them in Parliament sooner or later, and then they will have to mind their steps. Whether Parliament is either a representative body or an efficient one is questionable, but I value it because it criticises and talks, and because its chatter gets widely reported.

So Two Cheers for Democracy: one because it admits variety and   7
two because it permits criticism. Two cheers are quite enough: there is no occasion to give three. Only Love the Beloved Republic deserves that.

What about Force, though? While we are trying to be sensitive   8
and advanced and affectionate and tolerant, an unpleasant question pops up: does not all society rest upon force? If a government cannot count upon the police and the army, how can it hope to rule? And if an individual gets knocked on the head or sent to a labour camp, of what significance are his opinions?

This dilemma does not worry me as much as it does some. I   9
realise that all society rests upon force. But all the great creative actions, all the decent human relations, occur during the intervals when force has not managed to come to the front. These intervals are what matter. I want them to be as frequent and as lengthy as possible, and I call them "civilisation." Some people idealise force and pull it into the foreground and worship it, instead of keeping it in the background as long as possible. I think they make a mistake, and I think that their opposites, the mystics, err even more when they declare that force does not exist. I believe that it exists, and that one of our jobs is to prevent it from getting out of its box. It gets out sooner or later, and then it destroys us and all the lovely things which we have made. But it is not out all the time, for the fortunate reason that the strong are so stupid. Consider their conduct for a moment in the Niebelung's Ring.[3] The giants there have the guns, or in other words the gold; but they do nothing with it, they do not realise that they are all-powerful, with the result that the catastrophe is delayed and the castle of Walhalla, insecure but glorious, fronts the storms. Fafnir, coiled round his hoard, grumbles and grunts; we can hear him under Europe today; the leaves of the wood already tremble, and the Bird calls its warnings uselessly. Fafnir will destroy us, but by a blessed dispensation he is stupid and slow, and creation goes on just outside the poisonous blast of his breath. The Nietzschean would hurry the monster up, the mystic

3. *Der Ring des Nibelungen* (first performance 1876), opera in four parts by German composer Richard Wagner, based on medieval Scandinavian legends. Forster, writing on the eve of World War II, sees in the story certain lessons for his contemporaries.

would say he did not exist, but Wotan, wiser than either, hastens to create warriors before doom declares itself. The Valkyries are symbols not only of courage but of intelligence; they represent the human spirit snatching its opportunity while the going is good, and one of them even finds time to love. Brünnhilde's last song hymns the recurrence of love, and since it is the privilege of art to exaggerate, she goes even further, and proclaims the love which is eternally triumphant and feeds upon freedom, and lives.

So that is what I feel about force and violence. It is, alas! the ultimate reality on this earth, but it does not always get to the front. Some people call its absences "decadence"; I call them "civilisation" and find in such interludes the chief justification for the human experiment. I look the other way until fate strikes me. Whether this is due to courage or to cowardice in my own case I cannot be sure. But I know that if men had not looked the other way in the past, nothing of any value would survive. The people I respect most behave as if they were immortal and as if society was eternal. Both assumptions are false: both of them must be accepted as true if we are to go on eating and working and loving, and are to keep open a few breathing holes for the human spirit. No millennium seems likely to descend upon humanity; no better and stronger League of Nations will be instituted; no form of Christianity and no alternative to Christianity will bring peace to the world or integrity to the individual; no "change of heart" will occur. And yet we need not despair, indeed, we cannot despair; the evidence of history shows us that men have always insisted on behaving creatively under the shadow of the sword; that they have done their artistic and scientific and domestic stuff for the sake of doing it, and that we had better follow their example under the shadow of the aeroplanes. Others, with more vision or courage than myself, see the salvation of humanity ahead, and will dismiss my conception of civilisation as paltry, a sort of tip-and-run game. Certainly it is presumptuous to say that we *cannot* improve, and that Man, who has only been in power for a few thousand years, will never learn to make use of his power. All I mean is that, if people continue to kill one another as they do, the world cannot get better than it is, and that since there are more people than formerly, and their means for destroying one another superior, the world may well get worse. What is good in people—and consequently in the world— is their insistence on creation, their belief in friendship and loyalty for their own sakes; and though Violence remains and is, indeed, the major partner in this muddled establishment, I believe that creativeness remains too, and will always assume direction when violence sleeps. So, though I am not an optimist, I cannot agree

10

with Sophocles that it were better never to have been born. And although, like Horace, I see no evidence that each batch of births is superior to the last, I leave the field open for the more complacent view. This is such a difficult moment to live in, one cannot help getting gloomy and also a bit rattled, and perhaps short-sighted.

In search of a refuge, we may perhaps turn to hero-worship. But here we shall get no help, in my opinion. Hero-worship is a dangerous vice, and one of the minor merits of a democracy is that it does not encourage it, or produce that unmanageable type of citizen known as the Great Man. It produces instead different kinds of small men—a much finer achievement. But people who cannot get interested in the variety of life, and cannot make up their own minds, get discontented over this, and they long for a hero to bow down before and to follow blindly. It is significant that a hero is an integral part of the authoritarian stock-in-trade today. An efficiency-regime cannot be run without a few heroes stuck about it to carry off the dullness—much as plums have to be put into a bad pudding to make it palatable. One hero at the top and a smaller one each side of him is a favourite arrangement, and the timid and the bored are comforted by the trinity, and, bowing down, feel exalted and strengthened.

No, I distrust Great Men. They produce a desert of uniformity around them and often a pool of blood too, and I always feel a little man's pleasure when they come a cropper. Every now and then one reads in the newspapers some such statement as: "The coup d'état appears to have failed, and Admiral Toma's whereabouts is at present unknown." Admiral Toma had probably every qualification for being a Great Man—an iron will; personal magnetism, dash, flair, sexlessness—but fate was against him, so he retires to unknown whereabouts instead of parading history with his peers. He fails with a completeness which no artist and no lover can experience, because with them the process of creation is itself an achievement, whereas with him the only possible achievement is success.

I believe in aristocracy, though—if that is the right word, and if a democrat may use it. Not an aristocracy of power, based upon rank and influence, but an aristocracy of the sensitive, the considerate and the plucky. Its members are to be found in all nations and classes, and all through the ages, and there is a secret understanding between them when they meet. They represent the true human tradition, the one permanent victory of our queer race over cruelty and chaos. Thousands of them perish in obscurity, a few are great names. They are sensitive for others as well as for themselves, they are considerate without being fussy, their pluck is not swankiness but the power to endure, and they can take a joke. I give no examples—it is risky to do that—but the reader may as well consider whether this is the type of person he would like to meet and to be, and whether (going farther with me) he would prefer that this type should *not* be an ascetic one. I am against asceticism myself. I am with the old Scotsman who wanted less chastity and more delicacy. I do not feel that my aristocrats are a real aristocracy if they thwart their bodies, since bodies are the instruments through which we register and enjoy the world. Still, I do not insist. This is not a major point. It is clearly possible to be sensitive, considerate and plucky and yet be an ascetic too. If anyone possesses the first three qualities, I will let him in! On they go—an invincible army, yet not a victorious one. The aristocrats, the elect, the chosen, the Best People—all the words that describe them are false, and all attempts to organise them fail. Again and again Authority, seeing their value, has tried to net them and to utilise them as the Egyptian Priesthood or the Christian Church or the Chinese Civil Service or the Group Movement, or some other worthy stunt. But they slip through the net and are gone; when the door is shut, they are no longer in the room; their temple, as one of them remarked, is the Holiness of the Heart's Affection,[4] and their kingdom, though they never possess it, is the wide-open world.

With this type of person knocking about, and constantly crossing one's path if one has eyes to see or hands to feel, the experiment of earthly life cannot be dismissed as a failure. But it may well be hailed as a tragedy, the tragedy being that no device has been found by which these private decencies can be transmitted to public affairs. As soon as people have power they go crooked and sometimes dotty as well, because the possession of power lifts them into a region where normal honesty never pays. For instance, the man who is selling newspapers outside the Houses of Parliament can safely leave his papers to go for a drink and his cap beside them: anyone who takes a paper is sure to drop a copper into the cap. But the men who are inside the Houses of Parliament—they cannot trust one another like that, still less can the Government they compose trust other governments. No caps upon the pavement here, but suspicion, treachery and armaments. The more highly public life is organised the lower does its morality sink; the nations of today behave to each other worse than they ever did in the past, they cheat, rob, bully and bluff, make war without notice,

14

4. English poet John Keats (1795–1821) wrote "I am certain of nothing but the holiness of the Heart's affection and the truth of Imagination."

and kill as many women and children as possible; whereas primitive tribes were at all events restrained by taboos. It is a humiliating outlook—though the greater the darkness, the brighter shine the little lights, reassuring one another, signalling: "Well, at all events, I'm still here. I don't like it very much, but how are you?" Unquenchable lights of my aristocracy! Signals of the invincible army! "Come along—anyway, let's have a good time while we can." I think they signal that too.

The Saviour of the future—if ever he comes—will not preach a   15
new Gospel. He will merely utilise my aristocracy, he will make effective the good will and the good temper which are already existing. In other words, he will introduce a new technique. In economics, we are told that if there was a new technique of distribution, there need be no poverty, and people would not starve in one place while crops were being ploughed under in another. A similar change is needed in the sphere of morals and politics. The desire for it is by no means new; it was expressed, for example, in theological terms by Jacopone da Todi over six hundred years ago. "Ordina questo amore, O tu che m'ami," he said; "O thou who lovest me—set this love in order." His prayer was not granted, and I do not myself believe that it ever will be, but here, and not through a change of heart, is our probable route. Not by becoming better, but by ordering and distributing his native goodness, will Man shut up Force into its box, and so gain time to explore the universe and to set his mark upon it worthily. At present he only explores it at odd moments, when Force is looking the other way, and his divine creativeness appears as a trivial byproduct, to be scrapped as soon as the drums beat and the bombers hum.

Such a change, claim the orthodox, can only be made by Chris-   16
tianity, and will be made by it in God's good time: man always has failed and always will fail to organise his own goodness, and it is presumptuous of him to try. This claim—solemn as it is—leaves me cold. I cannot believe that Christianity will ever cope with the present world-wide mess, and I think that such influence as it retains in modern society is due to the money behind it, rather than to its spiritual appeal. It was a spiritual force once, but the indwelling spirit will have to be restated if it is to calm the waters again, and probably restated in a non-Christian form. Naturally a lot of people, and people who are not only good but able and intelligent, will disagree here; they will vehemently deny that Christianity has failed, or they will argue that its failure proceeds from the wickedness of men, and really proves its ultimate success. They have Faith, with a large F. My faith has a very small one, and I only

intrude it because these are strenuous and serious days, and one likes to say what one thinks while speech is comparatively free: it may not be free much longer.

The above are the reflections of an individualist and a liberal   17 who has found liberalism crumbling beneath him and at first felt ashamed. Then, looking around, he decided there was no special reason for shame, since other people, whatever they felt, were equally insecure. And as for individualism—there seems no way of getting off this, even if one wanted to. The dictator-hero can grind down his citizens till they are all alike, but he cannot melt them into a single man. That is beyond his power. He can order them to merge, he can incite them to mass-antics, but they are obliged to be born separately, and to die separately, and, owing to these unavoidable termini, will always be running off the totalitarian rails. The memory of birth and the expectation of death always lurk within the human being, making him separate from his fellows and consequently capable of intercourse with them. Naked I came into the world, naked I shall go out of it! And a very good thing too, for it reminds me that I am naked under my shirt, whatever its colour.

SCOTT RUSSELL SANDERS

At Play in the Paradise of Bombs

Scott Russell Sanders (1945–   ), a native of Tennessee, took his Ph.D. at Cambridge University and is now a professor of English at Indiana University. He has always been interested in science as well as the arts and has written in a variety of genres, including science fiction, realistic fiction, folktales, children's stories, and historical novels. He writes, he says, "to understand our place in nature, trace the sources of our violence, and speculate about the future evolution of our species." Among his works are *Wilderness Plots: Tales about the Settlement of the American Land* (1983), *Fetching the Dead: Stories* (1984), *Wonders Hidden: Audubon's Early Years* (1984), *Terrarium* (1985), and *The Engineer of Beasts* (1988). "At Play in the Paradise of Bombs" is the first chapter of *The Paradise of Bombs* (1987), a collection of personal narratives about the culture of violence in America.

Twice a man's height and topped by strands of barbed wire, a   1 chain-link fence stretched for miles along the highway leading up to the main gate of the Arsenal. Beside the gate were tanks, hulking dinosaurs of steel, one on each side, their long muzzles slanting down to catch trespassers in a cross-fire. A soldier emerged from the gatehouse, gun on hip, silvered sunglasses blanking his eyes.

My father stopped our car. He leaned out the window and handed the guard some papers which my mother had been nervously clutching.

"With that license plate, I had you pegged for visitors," said the guard. "But I see you've come to stay."

His flat voice ricocheted against the rolled-up windows of the back seat where I huddled beside my sister. I hid my face in the upholstery, to erase the barbed wire and tanks and mirror-eyed soldier, and tried to wind myself into a ball as tight as the fist of fear in my stomach. By and by, our car eased forward into the Arsenal, the paradise of bombs.

This was in April of 1951, in Ohio. We had driven north from Tennessee, where spring had already burst the buds of trees and cracked the flowers open. Up here on the hem of Lake Erie the earth was bleak with snow. I had been told about northern winters, but in the red clay country south of Memphis I had seen only occasional flurries, harmless as confetti, never this smothering quilt of white. My mother had been crying since Kentucky. Sight of the Arsenal's fences and guard shacks looming out of the snow brought her misery to the boil. "It's like a concentration camp," she whispered to my father. I had no idea what she meant. I was not quite six, born two months after the gutting of Hiroshima and Nagasaki. My birth sign was the mushroom cloud. "It looks exactly like those pictures of the German camps," she lamented. Back in Tennessee, the strangers who had bought our farm were clipping bouquets from her garden. Those strangers had inherited everything—the barn and jittery cow, the billy goat fond of cornsilks, the crops of beans and potatoes already planted, the creek bottom cleared of locust trees, the drawling voices of neighbors, the smell of cotton dust.

My father had worked through the Second World War at a munitions plant near his hometown in Mississippi. Now his company, hired by the Pentagon to run this Ohio Arsenal, was moving him north to supervise the production lines where artillery shells and land mines and bombs were loaded with explosives. Later I would hear stories about those loadlines. The concrete floors were so saturated with TNT that any chance spark would set off a quake. The workers used tools of brass to guard against sparks, but every now and again a careless chump would drop a pocket knife or shell casing, and lose a leg. Once a forklift dumped a pallet of barrels and blew out an entire factory wall, along with three munitions loaders.

In 1951 I was too young to realize that what had brought on all this bustle in our lives was the war in Korea; too green to notice which way the political winds were blowing. Asia was absorbing bullets and bombs as quickly as the Arsenal could ship them. At successive news conferences, President Truman meditated aloud on whether or not to spill *the* Bomb—the sip of planetary hemlock—over China. Senator McCarthy[1] was denouncing Reds from every available podium, pinning a single handy label on all the bugbears of the nation. Congress had recently passed bills designed to hamstring unions and slam the doors of America in the faces of immigrants. The Soviet Union had detonated its own atomic weapons, and the search was on for the culprits who had sold our secret. How else but through treachery could such a benighted nation ever have built such a clever bomb? In the very month of our move to the Arsenal, Julius and Ethel Rosenberg were sentenced to death.[2] Too late, J. Robert Oppenheimer was voicing second thoughts about the weapon he had helped build. In an effort to preserve our lead in the race toward oblivion, our scientists were perfecting the hydrogen bomb.

We rolled to our new home in the Arsenal over the impossible snow, between parking lots filled with armored troop carriers, jeeps, strafing helicopters, wheeled howitzers, bulldozers, Sherman tanks, all the brawny machines of war. On the front porch of our Memphis home I had read GI Joe comic books, and so I knew the names and shapes of these death-dealing engines. In the gaudy cartoons the soldiers had seemed like two-legged chunks of pure glory, muttering speeches between bursts on their machine guns, clenching the pins of grenades between their dazzling teeth. Their weapons had seemed like tackle worthy of gods. But as we drove between those parking lots crowded with real tanks, past guard houses manned by actual soldiers, a needle of dread pierced my brain.

Thirty years later the needle is still there, and is festering. I realize now that in moving from a scrape-dirt farm in Tennessee to a munitions factory in Ohio I had leaped overnight from the nineteenth century into the heart of the twentieth. I had landed in a place that concentrates the truth about our condition more po-

7

8

9

---

1. Joseph McCarthy (1908–1957), U.S. senator from Wisconsin who rose to prominence by accusing (often falsely) hundreds of Americans of having Communist ties.
2. Julius (1918–1953) and Ethel (1916–1953) Rosenberg were executed as members of a Communist spy ring.

tently than any metropolis or suburb. If, one hundred years from now, there are still human beings capable of thinking about the past, and if they turn their sights on our own time, what they will see through the cross hairs of memory will be a place very like the Arsenal, a fenced wilderness devoted to the building and harboring of the instruments of death.

Our house was one of twenty white frame boxes arrayed in a   10 circle about a swatch of lawn. Originally built for the high-ranking military brass, some of these government quarters now also held civilians—the doctors assigned to the base hospital, the engineers who carried slide-rules dangling from their belts, the accountants and supervisors, the managerial honchos. In our children's argot, this hoop of houses became the Circle, the beginning and ending point of all our journeys. Like campers drawn up around a fire, like wagons wound into a fearful ring, the houses faced inward on the Circle, as if to reassure the occupants, for immediately outside that tamed hoop the forest began, a tangled, beast-haunted woods stretching for miles in every direction.

Through our front door I looked out on mowed grass, flower   11 boxes, parked cars, the curves of concrete, the wink of windows. From the back door I saw only trees, bare dark bones thrust up from the snow in that first April, snarled green shadows in all the following summers. Not many nights after we had settled in, I glimpsed a white-tailed deer lurking along the edge of that woods out back, the first of thousands I would see over the years. The Arsenal was a sanctuary for deer, I soon learned, and also for beaver, fox, turkey, geese, every manner of beast smaller than wolves and bears. Protected by that chain-link fence, which kept out hunters and woodcutters as well as spies, the animals had multiplied to very nearly their ancient numbers, and the trees grew thick and old until they died with their roots on. So throughout my childhood I had a choice of where to play—inside the charmed Circle or outside in the wild thickets.

Viewed on a map against Ohio's bulldozed land, the Arsenal   12 was only a tiny patch of green, about thirty square miles; some of it had been pasture as recently as ten years earlier, when the government bought the land. It was broken up by airstrips and bunkers and munitions depots; guards cruised its perimeter and bored through its heart twenty-four hours a day. But to my young eyes it seemed like an unbounded wilderness. The biggest parcel of land for the Arsenal had belonged to a U.S. senator, who—in the selfless tradition of public servants—grew stinking rich from the sale. The rest was purchased from farmers, some of them descendants of the hardbitten New England folks who had settled that corner of Ohio, most of them reluctant to move. One of the old-timers refused to budge from his house until the wrecking crew arrived, and then he slung himself from a noose tied to a rafter in his barn. By the time I came along to investigate, all that remained of his place was the crumbling silo; but I found it easy to imagine him strung up there, roped to his roof-beam, riding his ship as it went down. Every other year or so, the older children would string a scarecrow from a rafter in one of the few surviving barns, and then lead the younger children in for a grisly look. I only fell for the trick once, but the image of that dangling husk is burned into my mind.

Rambling through the Arsenal's twenty-one thousand acres, at 13 first in the safe back seats of our parents' cars, then on bicycles over the gravel roads, and later on foot through the backcountry, we children searched out the ruins of those abandoned farms. Usually the buildings had been torn down and carted away, and all that remained were the cellar holes half-filled with rubble, the skewed limestone foundations, the stubborn flowers. What used to be lawns were grown up in sumac, maple, blackberry. The rare concrete walks and driveways were shattered, sown to ferns. Moss grew in the chiseled names of the dead on headstones in backyard cemeteries. We could spy a house site in the spring by the blaze of jonquils, the blue fountain of lilacs, the forsythia and starry columbine; in the summer by roses; in the fall by the glow of mums and zinnias. Asparagus and rhubarb kept pushing up through the meadows. The blasted orchards kept squeezing out plums and knotty apples and bee-thick pears. From the cellar holes wild grapevines twisted up to ensnarl the shade trees. In the ruins we discovered marbles, bottles, the bone handles of knives, the rusty heads of hammers, and the tips of plows. And we dug up keys by the fistful, keys of brass and black iron, skeleton keys to ghostly doors. We gathered the fruits of other people's planting, staggering home with armfuls of flowers, sprays of pussywillow and bittersweet, baskets of berries, our faces sticky with juice.

Even where the army's poisons had been dumped, nature did 14 not give up. In a remote corner of the Arsenal, on land which had been used as a Boy Scout camp before the war, the ground was so filthy with the discarded makings of bombs that not even guards would go there. But we children went, lured on by the scarlet warning signs. DANGER. RESTRICTED AREA. The skull-and-cross-bones aroused in us dreams of pirates. We found the log huts overgrown with vines, the swimming lake a bog of algae and cattails, the stone walls scattered by the heave of frost. The only scrap of metal we discovered was a bell, its clapper rusted solid to the rim. In my bone marrow I carry traces of the poison from that graveyard of bombs, as we all carry a smidgen of radioactivity from every atomic blast. Perhaps at this very moment one of those alien molecules, like a grain of sand in an oyster, is irritating some cell in my body, or in your body, to fashion a pearl of cancer.

Poking about in the ruins of camp and farms, I felt a wrestle of emotions, half sick with loss, half exultant over the return of forest. It was terrifying and at the same time comforting to see how quickly the green wave lapped over the human remains, scouring away the bold marks of occupation. The displaced farmers, gone only a decade, had left scarcely more trace than the ancient Indians who had heaped up burial mounds in this territory. We hunted for Indian treasure, too, digging in every suspicious hillock until our arms ached. We turned up shards of pottery, iridescent shells, fiery bits of flint; but never any bones. The best arrow points and ax-heads we invariably discovered not by looking, but by chance, when jumping over a creek or scratching in the dirt with a bare incurious toe. This was my first lesson in the Zen of seeing, seeing by not-looking. 15

With or without looking, we constantly stumbled across the more common variety of mound in the Arsenal, the hump-backed bunkers where munitions were stored. Implausibly enough, they were called igloos. There were rows and rows of them, strung out along rail beds like lethal beads. Over the concrete vaults grass had been planted, so that from the air, glimpsed by enemy bombers, they would look like undulating hills. Sheep kept them mowed. The signs surrounding the igloos were larger and more strident than those warning us to keep away from the waste dumps. These we respected, for we feared that even a heavy footfall on the grassy roof of a bunker might set it off. Three or four had blown up over the years, from clumsy handling or the quirk of chemicals. Once a jet trainer crashed into a field of them and skidded far enough to trigger a pair. These numbers multiplied in our minds, until we imagined the igloos popping like corn. No, no, they were set far enough apart to avoid a chain reaction if one should explode, my father assured me. But in my reckoning the munitions bunkers were vaults of annihilation. I stubbornly believed that one day they all would blow, touched off by lightning, maybe, or by an enemy agent. Whenever I stole past those fields of bunkers or whenever they drifted like a flotilla of green humpbacked whales through my dreams, I imagined fire leaping from one to another, the spark flying outward to consume the whole creation. This poison I also carry in my bones, this conviction that we build our lives in mine 16 fields. Long before I learned what new sort of bombs had devoured Hiroshima and Nagasaki, I knew from creeping among those igloos full of old-fashioned explosives that, on any given day, someone else's reckless step might consume us all.

Of course we played constantly at war. How could we avoid it?   17
At the five-and-dime we bought plastic soldiers, their fists molded permanently around machine guns and grenades, their faces frozen into expressions of bravery or bloodlust. They were all men, all except the weaponless nurse who stood with uplifted lantern to inspect the wounded; and those of us who toyed at this mayhem were all boys. In the unused garden plot out back of the Circle, we excavated trenches and foxholes, embedded cannons inside rings of pebbles, heaped dirt into mounds to simulate ammo bunkers. Our miniature tanks left treadmarks in the dust exactly like those cut into the blacktop roads by real tanks. Running miniature trucks, our throats caught the exact groan of the diesel convoys that hauled army reservists past our door every summer weekend. When we grew tired of our Lilliputian battles, we took up weapons in our own hands. Any stick would do for a gun, any rock for a bomb. At the drugstore we bought war comics and on wet after-noons we studied war movies on television to instruct us in the plots for our games. No one ever chose to play the roles of Japs or Nazis or Commies, and so the hateful labels were hung on the smallest or shabbiest kids. For the better part of my first three years in the Arsenal I was a villain, consigned to the Yellow Peril or the Red Plague. Like many of the runts, even wearing the guise of a bad guy I refused to go down, protesting every lethal shot from the good guys. If all the kids eligible to serve as enemies quit the game, the Americans just blasted away at invisible foes, GI's against the universe.

Whenever we cared to we could glance up from our play in the   18
garden battlefield and see the dish of a radar antenna spinning silently beyond the next ridge. We knew it scoured the sky for enemy bombers and, later, missiles. The air was filled with elec-tronic threats. Every mile or so along the roads there were spiky transmitters, like six-foot-tall models of the Empire State Building, to magnify and boom along radio messages between security head-quarters and the cruising guards. Imagining dire secrets whispered in code, I keened my ears to catch these broadcasts, as if by one particular resonance of brain cells I might snare the voices inside my skull. What I eventually heard, over a shortwave radio owned by one of the older boys, were guards jawing about lunch, mutter-

ing about the weather, about wives or bills or bowling, swearing aimlessly, or counting deer.

Our favorite family outing on the long summer evenings, after supper, after the washing of dishes, was to drive the gravel roads of the Arsenal and count deer. We would surprise them in clearings, a pair or a dozen, grass drooping from their narrow muzzles, jaws working. They would lift their delicate heads and gaze at us with slick dark eyes, some of the bucks hefting intricate antlers, the fresh does thick-uddered, the fawns still dappled. If the herd was large enough to make counting tricky, my father would stop the car. And if we kept very still, the deer, after studying us awhile, would go back to their grazing. But any slight twitch, a throat cleared or the squeak of a window crank, would startle them. First one white tail would jerk up, then another and another, the tawny bodies wheeling, legs flashing, and the deer would vanish like smoke. Some nights we counted over three hundred.

There were so many deer that in bad winters the managers of the Arsenal ordered the dumping of hay on the snow to keep the herds from starving. When my father had charge of this chore, I rode atop the truckload of bales, watching the tire slices trail away behind us in the frozen crust. Still the weak went hungry. Sledding, we would find their withered carcasses beside the gnawed stems of elderberry bushes. A few generations earlier, wolves and mountain lions would have helped out the snow, culling the slow-of-foot. But since the only predators left were two-legged ones, men took on the task of thinning the herds, and naturally they culled out the strongest, the heavy-antlered bucks, the meaty does. Early each winter the game officials would guess how many deer ought to be killed, and would sell that many hunting tags. Most of the licenses went to men who worked on the Arsenal, the carpenters and munitions loaders and firemen. But a quantity would always be reserved for visiting military brass.

They rolled into the Arsenal in chauffeured sedans or swooped down in star-spangled planes, these generals and colonels. Their hunting clothes smelled of moth balls. Their shotguns glistened with oil. Jeeps driven by orderlies delivered them to the brushwood blinds, where they slouched on canvas chairs and slugged whiskey to keep warm, waiting for the deer to run by. The deer always ran obligingly by, because men and boys hired from nearby towns would have been out since dawn beating the bushes, scaring up a herd and driving it down the ravine past the hidden generals, who pumped lead into the torrent of flesh.

Each deer season of my childhood I heard about this hunt. It swelled in my imagination to the scale of myth, outstripped in glory the remote battles of the last war, seemed more grand even than the bloody feuds between frontiersmen and Indians. I itched to go along, cradling my own shotgun, but my father said no, not until the winter after my thirteenth birthday. If I can't carry a gun, I begged, let me watch the hunt with empty hands. And so, the year I turned eleven he let me join the beaters, who would be herding deer for a party of shooters from the Pentagon.

A freezing rain the night before had turned the world to glass.   23
As we fanned out over the brittle snow, our bootsteps sounded like the shattering of windows. We soon found our deer, lurking where they had to be, in the frozen field where hay had been dumped. Casting about them our net of bodies, we left open only the path that led to the ravine where the officers waited. With a clap of hands we set them scurrying, the white tails like an avalanche, black hoofs punching the snow, lank hams kicking skyward. Not long after, we heard the crackle of shotguns. When the shooting was safely over, I hurried up to inspect the kills. The deer lay with legs crumpled beneath their bellies or jutting stiffly out, heads askew, tongues dangling like handles of leather. The wounded ones had stumbled away, trailing behind them ropes of blood; my father and the other seasoned hunters had run after to finish them off. The generals were tramping about in the red snow, noisily claiming their trophies, pinning tags on the ear of each downed beast. The local men gutted the deer. They heaped the steaming entrails on the snow and tied ropes through the tendons of each hind leg and dragged them to the waiting jeeps. I watched it all to the end that once, rubbed my face in it, and never again asked to work as a beater, or to watch the grown men shoot, or to hunt.

With the money I was paid for herding deer, I bought the fixings   24
for rocket fuel. That was the next stage in our playing at war, the launching of miniature missiles. We started by wrapping tinfoil around the heads of kitchen matches, graduated to aluminum pipes crammed with gunpowder, and then to machined tubes that burned zinc or magnesium. On the walls of our bedrooms we tacked photos of real rockets, the V-2 and Viking; the homely Snark, Hound Dog, Bullpup, Honest John, Little John, Mighty Mouse, Davy Crockett; and the beauties with godly names—Atlas, Titan, Jupiter, Juno, Nike-Hercules—the pantheon of power. By then I knew what rode in the nose cones, I knew what sort of bombs had exploded in Japan two months before my birth, I even knew, from reading physics books, how we had snared those fierce bits of sun. But I grasped these awesome facts in the same numb

way I grasped the definition of infinity. I carried the knowledge in me like an ungerminated seed.

There was a rumor among the children that atomic bombs were 25 stored in the Arsenal. The adults denied it, as they denied our belief that ghosts of Indians haunted the burial mounds or that shades of strung-up farmers paced in the haylofts of barns, as they dismissed all our bogies. We went searching anyway. Wasting no time among the igloos, which were too obvious, too vulnerable, we searched instead in the boondocks for secret vaults that we felt certain would be surrounded by deadly electronics and would be perfect in their camouflage. Traipsing along railway spurs, following every set of wheeltracks, we eventually came to a fenced compound that satisfied all our suspicions. Through the gridwork of wire and above the earthen ramparts we could see the gray concrete skulls of bunkers. We felt certain that the eggs of annihilation had been laid in those vaults, but none of us dared climb the fence to investigate. It was as if, having sought out the lair of a god, we could not bring ourselves to approach the throne.

In our searches for the Bomb we happened across a good many 26 other spots we were not supposed to see—dumps and man-made deserts, ponds once used for hatching fish and now smothered in oil, machine guns rusting in weeds, clicking signal boxes. But the most alluring discovery of all was the graveyard of bombers. This was a field crammed with the ratty hulks of World War II Flying Fortresses, their crumpled green skins painted with enigmatic numbers and symbols, their wings twisted, propellers shattered, cockpits open to the rain. In one of them we found a pair of mannequins rigged up in flight gear, complete with helmets, wires running from every joint in their artificial bodies. What tests they had been used for in these crashed planes we had no way of guessing; we borrowed their gear and propped them in back to serve as navigators and bombardiers. Most of the instruments had been salvaged, but enough remained for us to climb into the cockpits and fly imaginary bombing runs. Sitting where actual pilots had sat, clutching the butterfly wings of a steering wheel, gazing out through a cracked windshield, we rained fire and fury on the cities of the world. Not even the sight of the deer's guts steaming on the red snow had yet given me an inkling of how real streets would look beneath our storm of bombs. I was drunk on the fancied splendor of riding those metal leviathans, making them dance by a touch of my fingers. At the age when Samuel Clemens[3] sat on the bank of the Mississippi River smitten by the power of steamboats, I

3. Mark Twain (1835–1910).

watched rockets sputter on their firing stand, I sat in the gutted cockpits of old bombers, hungry to pilot sky ships.

The sky over the Arsenal was sliced by plenty of routine ships,   27 the screaming fighters, droning trainers, groaning transports, percussive helicopters; but what caught the attention of the children were the rare, rumored visitations of flying saucers. To judge by reports in the newspaper and on television, UFOs were sniffing about here and there all over the earth. We studied the night sky hopefully, fearfully, but every promising light we spied turned into a commonplace aircraft. I was beginning to think the aliens had declared the Arsenal off-limits. But then a neighbor woman, who sometimes looked after my sister and me in the afternoons, told us she had ridden more than once in a flying saucer that used to come fetch her in the wee hours from the parking lot behind the Bachelor Officers' Quarters. Mrs. K. was about fifty when we knew her, a stunted woman who gave the impression of being too large for her body, as if at birth she had been wrapped in invisible cords which were beginning to give way; she had a pinched face and watery eyes, a mousy bookkeeper for a husband, and no children. She was fastidious about her house, where the oak floors gleamed with wax, bathrooms glittered like jeweled chambers, and fragile knickknacks balanced on shelves of glass. When my mother dropped us by her place for an afternoon's stay, we crept about in terror of sullying or breaking something. In all her house there was nothing for children to play with except, stashed away in the bottom drawer of her desk, a dogeared pack of cards, a pair of dice, and a miniature roulette wheel. Soon tiring of these toys, my sister and I sat on the waxed floor and wheedled her into talking. At first she would maunder on about the life she had led on military bases around the world, the bridge parties and sewing circles; but eventually her eyes would begin to water and her teeth to chatter and she would launch into the history of her abduction by the aliens.

"They're not at all like devils," she insisted, "but more like   28 angels, with translucent skin that glows almost as if there were lights inside their bodies." And their ship bore no resemblance to saucers, she claimed. It was more like a diamond as large as a house, all the colors of the rainbow streaming through the facets. The angelic creatures stopped her in the parking lot during one of her stargazing walks, spoke gentle English inside her head, took her on board their craft, and put her to sleep. When she awoke she was lying naked, surrounded by a ring of princely aliens, and the landscape visible through the diamond walls of the ship was the vague purple of wisteria blossoms. "They weren't the least bit crude or nasty," she said, the words coming so fast they were jamming together in her throat, "no, no, they examined me like the most polite of doctors, because all they wanted was to save us from destroying ourselves, you see, and in order to do that, first they had to understand our anatomy, and that's why they had chosen me, don't you see, they had singled me out to teach them about our species," she insisted, touching her throat, "and to give me the secret of our salvation, me of all people, you see, *me*."

My sister had the good sense to keep mum about our babysitter's   29 stories, but I was so razzled by hopes of meeting with these aliens and learning their world-saving secrets that I blabbed about the possibility to my mother, who quickly wormed the entire chronicle from me. We never visited Mrs. K. again, but often we would see her vacuuming the lawn in front of her house. "Utterly crazy," my mother declared.

Mrs. K. was not alone in her lunacy. Every year or so one of the   30 career soldiers, having stared too long into the muzzle of his own gun, would go berserk or break down weeping. A guard began shooting deer from his jeep and leaving the carcasses in heaps on the roads. A janitor poured muriatic acid into the swimming pool and then down his own throat. One Christmastime, the lieutenant colonel who played Santa Claus started raving at the annual gift-giving and terrified the expectant children out of their wits. It took five fathers to muscle him down and make him quit heaving presents from his bag of gewgaws. To this day I cannot see Santa's white beard and red suit without flinching. Life on military reservations had also crazed many of the army wives, who turned to drink and drugs. Now and again an ambulance would purr into the Circle and cart one of them away for therapy. When at home, they usually kept hidden, stewing in bedrooms, their children grown and gone or off to school or buried in toys. Outside, with faces cracked like the leather of old purses, loaded up with consoling chemicals, the crazed women teetered carefully down the sidewalk, as if down a tightrope over an abyss.

The Arsenal fed on war and the rumors of war. When the Penta-   31 gon's budget was fat, the Arsenal's economy prospered. We could tell how good or bad the times were by reading our fathers' faces, or by counting the pickup trucks in the parking lots. The folks who lived just outside the chain-link fence in trailers and tarpaper shacks did poorly in the slow spells, but did just fine whenever an outbreak of Red Scare swept through Congress. In the lulls between wars, the men used to scan the headlines looking for omens of strife in the way farmers would scan the horizon for promises of rain.

In 1957, when the Arsenal was in the doldrums and parents   32
were bickering across the dinner table, one October afternoon between innings of a softball game somebody read aloud the news
about the launching of Sputnik. The mothers clucked their tongues
and the fathers groaned; but soon the wise heads among them
gloated, for they knew this Russian feat would set the load-lines
humming, and it did.

Our model rocketeering took on a new cast. It occurred to us   33
that any launcher capable of parking a satellite in orbit could plant
an H-bomb in the Circle. If one of those bitter pills ever landed, we
realized from our reading, there would be no Circle, no dallying
deer, no forests, no Arsenal. Suddenly there were explosives above
our heads as well as beneath our feet. The cracks in the faces of the
crazed ladies deepened. Guards no longer joked with us as we
passed through the gates to school. We children forgot how to
sleep. For hours after darkness we squirmed on our beds, staring
skyward. "Why don't you eat?" our mothers scolded. Aged thirteen or fourteen, I stood one day gripping the edge of the marble-
topped table in our living room, staring through a glass bell at the
spinning golden balls of an anniversary clock, and cried, "I don't
ever want to be a soldier, not ever, ever!"

Each weekend in summer the soldiers still played war. They   34
liked to scare up herds of deer with their tanks and pin them
against a corner of the fence. Snooping along afterward, we discovered tufts of hair and clots of flesh caught in the barbed wire from
the bucks that had leapt over. Once, after a weekend soldier's
cigarette had set off a brushfire, we found the charred bodies of a
dozen deer jammed against a fence. We filled ourselves with that
sight, and knew what it meant. There we lay, every child in the
Arsenal, every adult, every soul within reach of the bombs—
twisted black lumps trapped against a fence of steel. I have
dreamed of those charred deer ever since. During the war in Vietnam, every time I read or heard about napalm, my head filled with
visions of those blackened lumps.

To a child, it seemed the only salvation was in running away.   35
Parents and the family roof were no protection from this terror. My
notebooks filled with designs for orbiting worlds that we could
build from scratch and for rocket ships that would carry us to fresh,
unpoisoned planets. But I soon realized that no more than a handful of us could escape to the stars; and there was too much on
earth—the blue fountains of lilacs, the red streak of a fox across
snow, the faces of friends—that I could never abandon. I took
longer and longer walks through the backwoods of the Arsenal,
soaking in the green juices; but as I grew older, the forest seemed to

shrink, the fences drew in, the munitions bunkers and the desolate chemical dumps seemed to spread like a rash, until I could not walk far in any direction without stumbling into a reminder of our preparations for doom.

Because the foundations of old farms were vanishing beneath 36 the tangle of barriers and saplings, for most of my childhood I had allowed myself to believe that nature would undo whatever mess we made. But the scars from these new chemicals resisted the return of life. The discolored dirt remained bare for years and years. Tank trucks spraying herbicides to save the cost of mowing stripped the roads and meadows of wildflowers. Fish floated belly-up in the scum of ponds. The shells of bird eggs, laced with molecules of our invention, were too flimsy to hold new chicks. The threads of the world were beginning to unravel.

In a single winter a hired trapper cleared out the beavers, which 37 had been snarling the waterways, and the foxes, which had troubled the family dogs. Our own collie, brought as a puppy from Memphis, began to chase deer with a pack of dogs. At night he would slink back home with bloody snout and the smell of venison on his laboring breath. The guards warned us to keep him in, but he broke every rope. Once I saw the pack of them, wolves again, running deer across a field. Our collie was in the lead, gaining on a doe, and as I watched he bounded up and seized her by the ear and dragged her down, and the other dogs clamped on at the belly and throat. I preferred this wild killing to the shooting-gallery slaughter of the hunting season. If our own dogs could revert to wildness, perhaps there was still hope for the earth. But one day the guards shot the whole wolfish pack. Nature, in the largest sense of natural laws, would outlast us; but no particular scrap of it, no dog or pond or two-legged beast was guaranteed to survive.

There was comfort in the tales forever circulating among the 38 children of marvelous deer glimpsed at dusk or dawn, bucks with white legs, a doe with pale fur in the shape of a saddle on her back, and, one year, a pair of ghostly albinos. Several of the children had seen the all-white deer. In 1962 I spent most of the summer sunsets looking for them, needing to find them, hungering for these tokens of nature's prodigal energies. By September I had still seen neither hide nor hair of them. That October was the showdown over the placement of Soviet missiles in Cuba; Kennedy and Khrushchev squared off at the opposite ends of a nuclear street, hands hovering near the butts of their guns. For two weeks, while these desperadoes brooded over whether to start the final shooting, I quit going to school and passed all the hours of daylight outdoors, looking for those albino deer. Once, on the edge of a thicket, on the edge of darkness, I thought I glimpsed them, milky spirits, wisps of fog. But I could not be sure. Eventually the leaders of the superpowers lifted their hands a few inches away from their guns; the missiles did not fly. I returned to my studies, but gazed stupidly at every page through a meshwork of fear. In December the existence of the albino deer was proven beyond a doubt, for one afternoon in hunting season an Army doctor and his wife drove into the Circle with the pair of ghostly bodies tied onto the hood of their car.

The following year—the year when John Kennedy was killed and I registered for the draft and the tide of U.S. soldiers began to lap against the shores of Asia—my family moved from the Arsenal. "You'll sleep better now," my mother assured me. "You'll fatten up in no time." During the twelve years of our stay inside the chain-link fences, almost every night at suppertime outdated bombs would be detonated at the ammo dump. The concussion rattled the milkglass and willowware in the corner cupboard, rattled the forks against our plates, the cups against our teeth. It was like the muttering of local gods, a reminder of who ruled our neighborhood. From the moment I understood what those explosions meant, what small sparks they were of the engulfing fire, I lost my appetite. But even outside the Arsenal, a mile or an ocean away, every night at suppertime my fork still stuttered against the plate, my teeth still chattered from the remembered explosions. They still do. Everywhere now there are bunkers beneath the humped green hills; electronic challenges and threats needle through the air we breathe; the last wild beasts fling themselves against our steel boundaries. The fences of the Arsenal have stretched outward until they circle the entire planet. I feel, now, I can never move outside. 39

FRANK O'CONNOR

Guests of the Nation

Frank O'Connor was the pseudonym of Michael O'Donovan (1903–1966). The son of poor parents from Ireland's County Cork, O'Connor joined the Irish Republican army as a teen-ager and fought in the civil war that gained independence from Great Britain for Ireland's twenty-six southern counties. After the new Irish Free State made peace with Britain, O'Connor continued to fight in the IRA's futile war to end British control of the six counties of Northern Ireland. Arrested and imprisoned for his

IRA activities, O'Connor used his time in captivity to continue his self-education. Released in 1923, he pursued a career as a librarian, translator of Gaelic literature, director of the Abbey Theatre, and writer of short stories and literary criticism. In Ireland, he is known for his role in the Irish Literary Revival, especially for his translations of centuries-old Gaelic texts and for his association with such figures as William Butler Yeats, Lady Gregory, and Sean O'Casey. Internationally, he is known for his short fiction: "Storytelling . . . ," he wrote, "doesn't deal with problems; it doesn't have any solutions to offer; it just states the human condition." "Guests of the Nation" appeared in *The Atlantic Monthly* in January 1931.

At dusk the big Englishman Belcher would shift his long legs out   1
of the ashes and ask, "Well, chums, what about it?" and Noble or me would say, "As you please, chum" (for we had picked up some of their curious expressions), and the little Englishman 'Awkins would light the lamp and produce the cards. Sometimes Jeremiah Donovan would come up of an evening and supervise the play, and grow excited over 'Awkins's cards (which he always played badly), and shout at him as if he was one of our own, "Ach, you divil you, why didn't you play the tray?" But, ordinarily, Jeremiah was a sober and contented poor devil like the big Englishman Belcher, and was looked up to at all only because he was a fair hand at documents, though slow enough at these, I vow. He wore a small cloth hat and big gaiters over his long pants, and seldom did I perceive his hands outside the pockets of that pants. He reddened when you talked to him, tilting from toe to heel and back and looking down all the while at his big farmer's feet. His uncommon broad accent was a great source of jest to me, I being from the town as you may recognize.

I couldn't at the time see the point of me and Noble being with   2
Belcher and 'Awkins at all, for it was and is my fixed belief you could have planted that pair in any untended spot from this to Claregalway and they'd have stayed put and flourished like a native weed. I never seen in my short experience two men that took to the country as they did.

They were handed on to us by the Second Battalion to keep   3
when the search for them became too hot, and Noble and myself, being young, took charge with a natural feeling of responsibility. But little 'Awkins made us look right fools when he displayed he knew the countryside as well as we did and something more. "You're the bloke they calls Bonaparte?" he said to me. "Well, Bonaparte, Mary Brigid Ho'Connell was arskin abaout you and

said 'ow you'd a pair of socks belonging to 'er young brother." For it seemed, as they explained it, that the Second used to have little evenings of their own, and some of the girls of the neighborhood would turn in, and seeing they were such decent fellows, our lads couldn't well ignore the two Englishmen, but invited them in and were hail-fellow-well-met with them. 'Awkins told me he learned to dance "The Walls of Limerick" and "The Siege of Ennis" and "The Waves of Tory" in a night or two, though naturally he could not return the compliment, because our lads at that time did not dance foreign dances on principle.

So whatever privileges and favors Belcher and 'Awkins had with   4
the Second they duly took with us, and after the first evening we gave up all pretense of keeping a close eye on their behavior. Not that they could have got far, for they had a notable accent and wore khaki tunics and overcoats with civilian pants and boots. But it's my belief they never had an idea of escaping and were quite contented with their lot.

Now, it was a treat to see how Belcher got off with the old   5
woman of the house we were staying in. She was a great warrant to scold, and crotchety even with us, but before ever she had a chance of giving our guests, as I may call them, a lick of her tongue, Belcher had made her his friend for life. She was breaking sticks at the time, and Belcher, who hadn't been in the house for more than ten minutes, jumped up out of his seat and went across to her.

"Allow me, madam," he says, smiling his queer little smile;   6
"please allow me," and takes the hatchet from her hand. She was struck too parlatic[1] to speak, and ever after Belcher would be at her heels carrying a bucket, or basket, or load of turf, as the case might be. As Noble wittily remarked, he got into looking before she leapt, and hot water or any little thing she wanted Belcher would have it ready for her. For such a huge man (and though I am five foot ten myself I had to look up to him) he had an uncommon shortness— or should I say lack—of speech. It took us some time to get used to him walking in and out like a ghost, without a syllable out of him. Especially because 'Awkins talked enough for a platoon, it was strange to hear big Belcher with his toes in the ashes come out with a solitary "Excuse me, chum," or "That's right, chum." His one and only abiding passion was cards, and I will say for him he was a good card player. He could have fleeced me and Noble many a time; only if we lost to him, 'Awkins lost to us, and 'Awkins played with the money Belcher gave him.

'Awkins lost to us because he talked too much, and I think now   7

1. Paralytic.

we lost to Belcher for the same reason. 'Awkins and Noble would spit at one another about religion into the early hours of the morning; the little Englishman as you could see worrying the soul out of young Noble (whose brother was a priest) with a string of questions that would puzzle a cardinal. And to make it worse, even in treating of these holy subjects, 'Awkins had a deplorable tongue; I never in all my career struck across a man who could mix such a variety of cursing and bad language into the simplest topic. Oh, a terrible man was little 'Awkins, and a fright to argue! He never did a stroke of work, and when he had no one else to talk to he fixed his claws into the old woman.

I am glad to say that in her he met his match, for one day when ⁸ he tried to get her to complain profanely of the drought she gave him a great comedown by blaming the drought upon Jupiter Pluvius (a deity neither 'Awkins nor I had ever even heard of, though Noble said among the pagans he was held to have something to do with rain). And another day the same 'Awkins was swearing at the capitalists for starting the German war, when the old dame laid down her iron, puckered up her little crab's mouth, and said, "Mr. 'Awkins, you can say what you please about the war, thinking to deceive me because I'm an ignorant old woman, but I know well what started the war. It was that Italian count that stole the heathen divinity out of the temple in Japan, for believe me, Mr. 'Awkins, nothing but sorrow and want follows them that disturbs the hidden powers!" Oh, a queer old dame, as you remark!

So one evening we had our tea together, and 'Awkins lit the ⁹ lamp and we all sat in to cards. Jeremiah Donovan came in too, and sat down and watched us for a while. Though he was a shy man and didn't speak much, it was easy to see he had no great love for the two Englishmen, and I was surprised it hadn't struck me so clearly before. Well, like that in the story, a terrible dispute blew up late in the evening between 'Awkins and Noble, about capitalists and priests and love for your own country.

"The capitalists," says 'Awkins, with an angry gulp, "the capi- ¹⁰ talists pays the priests to tell you all abaout the next world, so's you won't notice what they do in this!"

"Nonsense, man," says Noble, losing his temper, "before ever a ¹¹ capitalist was thought of people believed in the next world."

'Awkins stood up as if he was preaching a sermon. "Oh, they ¹² did, did they?" he says with a sneer. "They believed all the things you believe, that's what you mean? And you believe that God created Hadam and Hadam created Shem and Shem created Jehosophat? You believe all the silly hold fairytale abaout Heve and Heden and the happle? Well, listen to me, chum. If you're entitled to 'old to a silly belief like that, I'm entitled to 'old to my own silly belief—which is, that the fust thing your God created was a bleedin' capitalist with mirality and Rolls-Royce complete. Am I right, chum?" he says then to Belcher.

"You're right, chum," says Belcher, with his queer smile, and 13 gets up from the table to stretch his long legs into the fire and stroke his mustache. So, seeing that Jeremiah Donovan was going, and there was no knowing when the conversation about religion would be over, I took my hat and went out with him. We strolled down towards the village together, and then he suddenly stopped, and blushing and mumbling, and shifting, as his way was, from toe to heel, he said I ought to be behind keeping guard on the prisoners. And I, having it put to me so suddenly, asked him what the hell he wanted a guard on the prisoners at all for, and said that so far as Noble and me were concerned we had talked it over and would rather be out with a column. "What use is that pair to us?" I asked him.

He looked at me for a spell and said, "I thought you knew we 14 were keeping them as hostages." "Hostages—?" says I, not quite understanding. "The enemy," he says in his heavy way, "have prisoners belong' to us, and now they talk of shooting them. If they shoot our prisoners we'll shoot theirs, and serve them right." "Shoot them?" said I, the possibility just beginning to dawn on me. "Shoot them exactly," said he. "Now," said I, "wasn't it very unforeseen of you not to tell me and Noble that?" "How so?" he asks. "Seeing that we were acting as guards upon them, of course." "And hadn't you reason enough to guess that much?" "We had not, Jeremiah Donovan, we had not. How were we to know when the men were on our hands so long?" "And what difference does it make? The enemy have our prisoners as long or longer, haven't they?" "It makes a great difference," said I. "How so?" said he sharply; but I couldn't tell him the difference it made, for I was struck too silly to speak. "And when may we expect to be released from this anyway?" said I. "You may expect it tonight," says he. "Or tomorrow or the next day at latest. So if it's hanging round here that worries you, you'll be free soon enough."

I cannot explain it even now, how sad I felt, but I went back to 15 the cottage, a miserable man. When I arrived the discussion was still on, 'Awkins holding forth to all and sundry that there was no next world at all and Noble answering in his best canonical style that there was. But I saw 'Awkins was after having the best of it. "Do you know what, chum?" he was saying, with his saucy smile.

"I think you're jest as big a bleedin' hunbeliever as I am. You say you believe in the next world and you know jest as much abaout the next world as I do, which is sweet damn-all. What's 'Eaven? You dunno. Where's 'Eaven? You dunno. Who's in 'Eaven? You dunno. You know sweet damn-all! I arsk you again, do they wear wings?"

"Very well then," says Noble, "they do; is that enough for you? They do wear wings." "Where do they get them then? Who makes them? 'Ave they a fact'ry for wings? 'Ave they a sort of store where you 'ands in your chit and tikes your bleedin' wings? Answer me that."   16

"Oh, you're an impossible man to argue with," says Noble. "Now listen to me—" And off the pair of them went again.   17

It was long after midnight when we locked up the Englishmen and went to bed ourselves. As I blew out the candle I told Noble what Jeremiah Donovan had told me. Noble took it very quietly. After we had been in bed about an hour he asked me did I think we ought to tell the Englishmen. I having thought of the same thing myself (among many others) said no, because it was more than likely the English wouldn't shoot our men, and anyhow it wasn't to be supposed the Brigade who were always up and down with the Second Battalion and knew the Englishmen well would be likely to want them bumped off. "I think so," says Noble. "It would be sort of cruelty to put the wind up them now." "It was very unforeseen of Jeremiah Donovan anyhow," says I, and by Noble's silence I realized he took my meaning.   18

So I lay there half the night, and thought and thought, and picturing myself and young Noble trying to prevent the Brigade from shooting 'Awkins and Belcher sent a cold sweat out through me. Because there were men on the Brigade you daren't let nor hinder without a gun in your hand, and at any rate, in those days disunion between brothers seemed to me an awful crime. I knew better after.   19

It was next morning we found it so hard to face Belcher and 'Awkins with a smile. We went about the house all day scarcely saying a word. Belcher didn't mind us much; he was stretched into the ashes as usual with his usual look of waiting in quietness for something unforeseen to happen, but little 'Awkins gave us a bad time with his audacious gibing and questioning. He was disgusted at Noble's not answering him back. "Why can't you tike your beating like a man, chum?" he says. "You with your Hadam and Heve! I'm a Communist—or an Anarchist. An Anarchist, that's what I am." And for hours after he went round the house, mumbling when the fit took him "Hadam and Heve! Hadam and Heve!"   20

I don't know clearly how we got over that day, but get over it we 21
did, and a great relief it was when the tea things were cleared away
and Belcher said in his peaceable manner, "Well, chums, what
about it?" So we all sat round the table and 'Awkins produced the
cards, and at that moment I heard Jeremiah Donovan's footsteps
up the path, and a dark presentiment crossed my mind. I rose
quietly from the table and laid my hand on him before he reached
the door. "What do you want?" I asked him. "I want those two
soldier friends of yours," he says reddening. "Is that the way it is,
Jeremiah Donovan?" I ask. "That's the way. There were four of
our lads went west this morning, one of them a boy of sixteen."
"That's bad, Jeremiah," says I.

At that moment Noble came out, and we walked down the path 22
together talking in whispers. Feeney, the local intelligence officer,
was standing by the gate. "What are you going to do about it?" I
asked Jeremiah Donovan. "I want you and Noble to bring them
out: you can tell them they're being shifted again; that'll be the
quietest way." "Leave me out of that," says Noble suddenly.
Jeremiah Donovan looked at him hard for a minute or two. "All
right so," he said peaceably. "You and Feeney collect a few tools
from the shed and dig a hole by the far end of the bog. Bonaparte
and I'll be after you in about twenty minutes. But whatever else
you do, don't let anyone see you with the tools. No one must know
but the four of ourselves."

We saw Feeney and Noble go round to the houseen where the 23
tools were kept, and sidled in. Everything if I can so express myself
was tottering before my eyes, and I left Jeremiah Donovan to do
the explaining as best he could, while I took a seat and said nothing. He told them they were to go back to the Second. 'Awkins let a
mouthful of curses out of him at that, and it was plain that Belcher,
though he said nothing, was duly perturbed. The old woman was
for having them stay in spite of us, and she did not shut her mouth
until Jeremiah Donovan lost his temper and said some nasty things
to her. Within the house by this time it was pitch dark, but no one
thought of lighting the lamp, and in the darkness the two Englishmen fetched their khaki topcoats and said good-bye to the
woman of the house. "Just as a man mikes a 'ome of a bleedin'
place," mumbles 'Awkins, shaking her by the hand, "some bastard
at Headquarters thinks you're too cushy and shunts you off." Belcher shakes her hand very hearty. "A thousand thanks, madam,"
he says, "a thousand thanks for everything . . ." as though he'd
made it all up.

We go round to the back of the house and down towards the 24
fatal bog. Then Jeremiah Donovan comes out with what is in his

mind. "There were four of our lads shot by your fellows this morning so now you're to be bumped off." "Cut that stuff out," says 'Awkins, flaring up. "It's bad enough to be mucked about such as we are without you plying at soldiers." "It's true," says Jeremiah Donovan, "I'm sorry, 'Awkins, but 'tis true," and comes out with the usual rigmarole about doing our duty and obeying our superiors. "Cut it out," says 'Awkins irritably. "Cut it out!"

Then, when Donovan sees he is not being believed he turns to 25 me, "Ask Bonaparte here," he says. "I don't need to arsk Bonaparte. Me and Bonaparte are chums." "Isn't it true, Bonaparte?" says Jeremiah Donovan solemnly to me. "It is," I say sadly, "it is." 'Awkins stops. "Now, for Christ's sike. . . ." "I mean it, chum," I say. "You daon't saound as if you mean it. You knaow well you don't mean it." "Well, if he don't I do," says Jeremiah Donovan. "Why the 'ell sh'd you want to shoot me, Jeremiah Donovan?" "Why the hell should your people take out four prisoners and shoot them in cold blood upon a barrack square?" I perceive Jeremiah Donovan is trying to encourage himself with hot words.

Anyway, he took little 'Awkins by the arm and dragged him on, 26 but it was impossible to make him understand that we were in earnest. From which you will perceive how difficult it was for me, as I kept feeling my Smith and Wesson and thinking what I would do if they happened to put up a fight or ran for it, and wishing in my heart they would. I knew if only they ran I would never fire on them. "Was Noble in this?" 'Awkins wanted to know, and we said yes. He laughed. But why should Noble want to shoot him? Why should we want to shoot him? What had he done to us? Weren't we chums (the word lingers painfully in my memory)? Weren't we? Didn't we understand him and didn't he understand us? Did either of us imagine for an instant that he'd shoot us for all the so-and-so brigadiers in the so-and-so British Army? By this time I began to perceive in the dusk the desolate edges of the bog that was to be their last earthly bed, and, so great a sadness overtook my mind, I could not answer him. We walked along the edge of it in the darkness, and every now and then 'Awkins would call a halt and begin again, just as if he was wound up, about us being chums, and I was in despair that nothing but the cold and open grave made ready for his presence would convince him that we meant it all. But all the same, if you can understand, I didn't want him to be bumped off.

At last we saw the unsteady glint of a lantern in the distance and 27 made towards it. Noble was carrying it, and Feeney stood somewhere in the darkness behind, and somehow the picture of the two of them so silent in the boglands was like the pain of death in my heart. Belcher, on recognizing Noble, said "'Allo, chum" in his usual peaceable way, but 'Awkins flew at the poor boy immediately, and the dispute began all over again, only that Noble hadn't a word to say for himself, and stood there with the swaying lantern between his gaitered legs.

It was Jeremiah Donovan who did the answering. 'Awkins   28
asked for the twentieth time (for it seemed to haunt his mind) if anybody thought he'd shoot Noble. "You would," says Jeremiah Donovan shortly. "I wouldn't, damn you!" "You would if you knew you'd be shot for not doing it." "I wouldn't, not if I was to be shot twenty times over; he's my chum. And Belcher wouldn't—isn't that right, Belcher?" "That's right, chum," says Belcher peaceably. "Damned if I would. Anyway, who says Noble'd be shot if I wasn't bumped off? What d'you think I'd do if I was in Noble's place and we were out in the middle of a blasted bog?" "What would you do?" "I'd go with him wherever he was going. I'd share my last bob with him and stick by 'im through thick and thin."

"We've had enough of this," says Jeremiah Donovan, cocking   29
his revolver. "Is there any message you want to send before I fire?" "No, there isn't, but . . ." "Do you want to say your prayers?" 'Awkins came out with a cold-blooded remark that shocked even me and turned to Noble again. "Listen to me, Noble," he said. "You and me are chums. You won't come over to my side, so I'll come over to your side. Is that fair? Just you give me a rifle and I'll go with you wherever you want."

Nobody answered him.   30

"Do you understand?" he said. "I'm through with it all. I'm a   31
deserter or anything else you like, but from this on I'm one of you. Does that prove to you that I mean what I say?" Noble raised his head, but as Donovan began to speak he lowered it again without answering. "For the last time have you any messages to send?" says Donovan in a cold and excited voice.

"Ah, shut up, you, Donovan; you don't understand me, but   32
these fellows do. They're my chums; they stand by me and I stand by them. We're not the capitalist tools you seem to think us."

I alone of the crowd saw Donovan raise his Webley to the back   33
of 'Awkins's neck, and as he did so I shut my eyes and tried to say a prayer. 'Awkins had begun to say something else when Donovan let fly, and, as I opened my eyes at the bang, I saw him stagger at the knees and lie out flat at Noble's feet, slowly, and as quiet as a child, with the lantern light falling sadly upon his lean legs and bright farmer's boots. We all stood very still for a while watching him settle out in the last agony.

Then Belcher quietly takes out a handkerchief, and begins to tie   34
it about his own eyes (for in our excitement we had forgotten to
offer the same to 'Awkins), and, seeing it is not big enough, turns
and asks for a loan of mine. I give it to him and as he knots the two
together he points with his foot at 'Awkins. "'E's not quite dead,"
he says, "better give 'im another." Sure enough 'Awkins's left knee
as we see it under the lantern is rising again. I bend down and put
my gun to his ear; then, recollecting myself and the company of
Belcher, I stand up again with a few hasty words. Belcher understands what is in my mind. "Give 'im 'is first," he says. "I don't
mind. Poor bastard, we dunno what's 'appening to 'im now." As
by this time I am beyond all feeling I kneel down again and skill-
fully give 'Awkins the last shot so as to put him forever out of pain.

Belcher who is fumbling a bit awkwardly with the handkerchiefs   35
comes out with a laugh when he hears the shot. It is the first time I
have heard him laugh, and it sends a shiver down my spine, coming as it does so inappropriately upon the tragic death of his old
friend. "Poor blighter," he says quietly, "and last night he was so
curious abaout it all. It's very queer, chums, I always think. Naow,
'e knows as much abaout it as they'll ever let 'im know, and last
night 'e was all in the dark."

Donovan helps him to tie the handkerchiefs about his eyes.   36
"Thanks, chum," he says. Donovan asks him if there are any messages he would like to send. "Naow, chum," he says, "none for
me. If any of you likes to write to 'Awkins's mother you'll find a
letter from 'er in 'is pocket. But my missus left me eight years ago.
Went away with another fellow and took the kid with her. I likes
the feelin' of a 'ome (as you may 'ave noticed) but I couldn't start
again after that."

We stand around like fools now that he can no longer see us.   37
Donovan looks at Noble and Noble shakes his head. Then Donovan
raises his Webley again and just at that moment Belcher laughs his
queer nervous laugh again. He must think we are talking of him;
anyway, Donovan lowers his gun. "'Scuse me, chums," says Belcher, "I feel I'm talking the 'ell of a lot . . . and so silly . . . abaout
me being so 'andy abaout a 'ouse. But this thing come on me so
sudden. You'll forgive me, I'm sure." "You don't want to say a
prayer?" asks Jeremiah Donovan. "No, chum," he replies, "I don't
think that'd 'elp. I'm ready if you want to get it over." "You understand," says Jeremiah Donovan, "it's not so much our doing. It's
our duty, so to speak." Belcher's head is raised like a real blind
man's, so that you can only see his nose and chin in the lamplight.
"I never could make out what duty was myself," he said, "but I
think you're all good lads, if that's what you mean. I'm not complaining." Noble, with a look of desperation, signals to Donovan,

and in a flash Donovan raises his gun and fires. The big man goes over like a sack of meal, and this time there is no need of a second shot.

I don't remember much about the burying, but that it was worse   38
than all the rest, because we had to carry the warm corpses a few yards before we sunk them in the windy bog. It was all mad lonely, with only a bit of lantern between ourselves and the pitch black-ness, and birds hooting and screeching all round disturbed by the guns. Noble had to search 'Awkins first to get the letter from his mother. Then having smoothed all signs of the grave away, Noble and I collected our tools, said good-bye to the others, and went back along the desolate edge of the treacherous bog without a word. We put the tools in the houseen and went into the house. The kitchen was pitch black and cold, just as we left it, and the old woman was sitting over the hearth telling her beads. We walked past her into the room, and Noble struck a match to light the lamp. Just then she rose quietly and came to the doorway, being not at all so bold or crabbed as usual.

"What did ye do with them?" she says in a sort of whisper, and   39
Noble took such a mortal start the match quenched in his trembling hand. "What's that?" he asks without turning round. "I heard ye," she said. "What did you hear?" asks Noble, but sure he wouldn't deceive a child the way he said it. "I heard ye. Do you think I wasn't listening to ye putting the things back in the houseen?" Noble struck another match and this time the lamp lit for him. "Was that what ye did with them?" she said, and Noble said noth-ing—after all what could he say?

So then, by God, she fell on her two knees by the door, and   40
began telling her beads, and after a minute or two Noble went on his knees by the fireplace, so I pushed my way out past her, and stood at the door, watching the stars and listening to the damned shrieking of the birds. It is so strange what you feel at such mo-ments, and not to be written afterwards. Noble says he felt he seen everything ten times as big, perceiving nothing around him but the little patch of black bog with the two Englishmen stiffening into it; but with me it was the other way, as though the patch of bog where the two Englishmen were was a thousand miles away from me, and even Noble mumbling just behind me and the old woman and the birds and the bloody stars were all far away, and I was some-how very small and very lonely. And anything that ever happened [to] me after I never felt the same about again.

FEMININITY
AND
MASCULINITY

Femininity and Masculinity: Preview

JOHN STEINBECK   The Chrysanthemums   608

> She was thirty-five. Her face was lean and strong and her eyes were as clear as water. Her figure looked blocked and heavy in her gardening costume, a man's black hat pulled low down over her eyes, clodhopper shoes, a figured print dress almost completely covered by a big corduroy apron with four big pockets.

Overview and Ideas for Writing

Until this century, sex roles in European and American cultures were delineated so precisely that anatomy seemed to be destiny. There were, to be sure, some manly women and some womanly men, but they served as exceptions to prove the rule. For example, when Shakespeare's Lady Macbeth decides to indulge in the masculine businesses of ambition and murder, she calls on the spirits to "unsex" her. About 250 years later, in 1854, Coventry Patmore wrote "The Angel in the House," a poem that separates the genders much the way Shakespeare had: Woman was a sweet civilizing influence that made "brutes men and men divine!"

The notion that men are destined to succeed or fail as competitors and women to succeed or fail as angels has not vanished from our culture, but feminism and social science have forced a reexamination. Virginia Woolf, whose "Professions for Women" (1930) has become a feminist classic, needed to look no further than the society around her to find that the forces defining the role of women were more political and economic than anatomical. Looking further abroad, Margaret Mead reported in *Sex and Temperament in Three Primitive Societies* (1935) her discovery of three New Guinea tribes that defined sex roles very differently from each other: in one both men and women had the mild disposition our culture attributes to women; in the second both men and women were fiercely aggressive; in the third the men wore curls, did the shopping, and said catty things about each other and the plainly dressed women were energetic and managerial.

Living three or four generations into the era of reexamination created by pioneers like Woolf and Mead, most of us understand intellectually the lessons they taught us, and our society has officially adjusted to them. "All right," Brigid Brophy wrote in 1963, "nobody's disputing it. Women are free. At least, they *look* free."

But the freedom to redefine sex roles continues to create tension and confusion, tragedy and comedy.

If you have a historical bent, you could contribute to the discussion by examining the change that has occurred during this century. How different are the relations between men and women in the novels of Virginia Woolf or Dorothy Sayers or other writers of their time from what they are today? How does the portrayal of the sexes in magazine articles and advertisements in the mid-1950s (when the fighter pilots of "The Right Stuff" went through flight training and Jan Morris climbed Everest in a "thoroughly masculine" expedition) differ from their portrayal in magazines today?

If controversy appeals to you, you should be able to find a subject by reading Perri Klass's "Are Women Better Doctors?" and the letters responding to it. If you wish to write from personal experience, you could, like Alice Walker and Susan Brownmiller, begin an essay with experiences that shaped your childhood view of masculinity and femininity and end, like them, with an evaluation of the implications of that view. Or you might, like Noel Perrin, Michael Norman, Dave Barry, or Leonard Riskin, write about the sometimes painful, sometimes humorous process of identifying the social ideal of masculinity or femininity and then defining your relation to it.

VIRGINIA WOOLF

Professions for Women

Virginia Woolf (1882–1941) by now has such an enormous reputation as a writer that we can hardly imagine the difficulties with which she started. Virginia Stephen was born at the height of the Victorian period into a high social class in which women did no serious work. Her mother died when she was three, and her father when she was twenty-two; she had virtually no formal education. And yet she had the strength of character to leave the respectable neighborhood of Kensington and join her sister and her two brothers in establishing a home in Bloomsbury, then thought shabby and disreputable. There she led a thoroughly bohemian life, talking late into the night, unchaperoned, with a brilliant circle of men, one of whom, Leonard Woolf, she married in 1912. By 1915 she had published her first novel, *The Voyage Out*, and by 1925 had published enough essays in periodicals to collect into *The Common Reader*. In an age when women were just beginning to enter the public world, Woolf had become a figure of some importance. She was frequently asked to address women's groups: "Professions for Women" was a talk delivered to the Women's Service League about 1930.

When your secretary invited me to come here, she told me that your Society is concerned with the employment of women and she suggested that I might tell you something about my own professional experiences. It is true I am a woman; it is true I am employed; but what professional experiences have I had? It is difficult to say. My profession is literature; and in that profession there are fewer experiences for women than in any other, with the exception of the stage—fewer, I mean, that are peculiar to women. For the road was cut many years ago—by Fanny Burney, by Aphra Behn, by Harriet Martineau, by Jane Austen, by George Eliot—many famous women, and many more unknown and forgotten, have been before me, making the path smooth, and regulating my steps. Thus, when I came to write, there were very few material obstacles in my way. Writing was a reputable and harmless occupation. The family peace was not broken by the scratching of a pen. No demand was made upon the family purse. For ten and sixpence one can buy paper enough to write all the plays of Shakespeare—if one has a mind that way. Pianos and models, Paris, Vienna and Berlin, masters and mistresses, are not needed by a writer. The cheapness of writing paper is, of course, the reason why women have succeeded as writers before they have succeeded in the other professions.

But to tell you my story—it is a simple one. You have only got to figure to yourselves a girl in a bedroom with a pen in her hand. She had only to move that pen from left to right—from ten o'clock to one. Then it occurred to her to do what is simple and cheap enough after all—to slip a few of those pages into an envelope, fix a penny stamp in the corner, and drop the envelope into the red box at the corner. It was thus that I became a journalist; and my effort was rewarded on the first day of the following month—a very glorious day it was for me—by a letter from an editor containing a cheque for one pound ten shillings and sixpence. But to show you how little I deserve to be called a professional woman, how little I know of the struggles and difficulties of such lives, I have to admit that instead of spending that sum upon bread and butter, rent, shoes and stockings, or butcher's bills, I went out and bought a cat—a beautiful cat, a Persian cat, which very soon involved me in bitter disputes with my neighbours.

What could be easier than to write articles and to buy Persian ₃
cats with the profits? But wait a moment. Articles have to be about
something. Mine, I seem to remember, was about a novel by a
famous man. And while I was writing this review, I discovered that
if I were going to review books I should need to do battle with a
certain phantom. And the phantom was a woman, and when I
came to know her better I called her after the heroine of a famous
poem, The Angel in the House. It was she who used to come
between me and my paper when I was writing reviews. It was she
who bothered me and wasted my time and so tormented me that at
last I killed her. You who come of a younger and happier generation may not have heard of her—you may not know what I mean
by the Angel in the House. I will describe her as shortly as I can.
She was intensely sympathetic. She was immensely charming. She
was utterly unselfish. She excelled in the difficult arts of family life.
She sacrificed herself daily. If there was a chicken, she took the leg;
if there was a draught she sat in it—in short she was so constituted
that she never had a mind or a wish of her own, but preferred to
sympathize always with the minds and wishes of others. Above
all—I need not say it—she was pure. Her purity was supposed to
be her chief beauty—her blushes, her great grace. In those days—
the last of Queen Victoria—every house had its Angel. And when I
came to write I encountered her with the very first words. The
shadow of her wings fell on my page; I heard the rustling of her
skirts in the room. Directly, that is to say, I took my pen in hand to
review that novel by a famous man, she slipped behind me and
whispered: "My dear, you are a young woman. You are writing
about a book that has been written by a man. Be sympathetic; be
tender; flatter; deceive; use all the arts and wiles of our sex. Never
let anybody guess that you have a mind of your own. Above all, be
pure." And she made as if to guide my pen. I now record the one
act for which I take some credit to myself, though the credit rightly
belongs to some excellent ancestors of mine who left me a certain
sum of money—shall we say five hundred pounds a year?—so that
it was not necessary for me to depend solely on charm for my
living. I turned upon her and caught her by the throat. I did my
best to kill her. My excuse, if I were to be had up in a court of law,
would be that I acted in self-defence. Had I not killed her she
would have killed me. She would have plucked the heart out of my
writing. For, as I found, directly I put pen to paper, you cannot
review even a novel without having a mind of your own, without
expressing what you think to be the truth about human relations,
morality, sex. And all these questions, according to the Angel in
the House, cannot be dealt with freely and openly by women; they

must charm, they must conciliate, they must—to put it bluntly—
tell lies if they are to succeed. Thus, whenever I felt the shadow of
her wing or the radiance of her halo upon my page, I took up the
inkpot and flung it at her. She died hard. Her fictitious nature was
of great assistance to her. It is far harder to kill a phantom than a
reality. She was always creeping back when I thought I had des-
patched her. Though I flatter myself that I killed her in the end, the
struggle was severe; it took much time that had better have been
spent upon learning Greek grammar; or in roaming the world in
search of adventures. But it was a real experience; it was an experience that was bound to befall all women writers at that time.
Killing the Angel in the House was part of the occupation of a
woman writer.

But to continue my story. The Angel was dead; what then re-   4
mained? You may say that what remained was a simple and common object—a young woman in a bedroom with an inkpot. In
other words, now that she had rid herself of falsehood, that young
woman had only to be herself. Ah, but what is "herself"? I mean,
what is a woman? I assure you, I do not know. I do not believe that
you know. I do not believe that anybody can know until she has
expressed herself in all the arts and professions open to human
skill. That indeed is one of the reasons why I have come here—out
of respect for you, who are in process of showing us by your
experiments what a woman is, who are in process of providing us,
by your failures and successes, with that extremely important piece
of information.

But to continue the story of my professional experiences. I made   5
one pound ten and six by my first review; and I bought a Persian
cat with the proceeds. Then I grew ambitious. A Persian cat is all
very well, I said; but a Persian cat is not enough. I must have a
motor car. And it was thus that I became a novelist—for it is a very
strange thing that people will give you a motor car if you will tell
them a story. It is a still stranger thing that there is nothing so
delightful in the world as telling stories. It is far pleasanter than
writing reviews of famous novels. And yet, if I am to obey your
secretary and tell you my professional experiences as a novelist, I
must tell you about a very strange experience that befell me as a
novelist. And to understand it you must try first to imagine a
novelist's state of mind. I hope I am not giving away professional
secrets if I say that a novelist's chief desire is to be as unconscious as
possible. He has to induce in himself a state of perpetual lethargy.
He wants life to proceed with the utmost quiet and regularity. He
wants to see the same faces, to read the same books, to do the same
things day after day, month after month, while he is writing, so

that nothing may break the illusion in which he is living—so that nothing may disturb or disquiet the mysterious nosings about, feelings round, darts, dashes and sudden discoveries of that very shy and illusive spirit, the imagination. I suspect that this state is the same both for men and women. Be that as it may, I want you to imagine me writing a novel in a state of trance. I want you to figure to yourselves a girl sitting with a pen in her hand, which for minutes, and indeed for hours, she never dips into the inkpot. The image that comes to my mind when I think of this girl is the image of a fisherman lying sunk in dreams on the verge of a deep lake with a rod held out over the water. She was letting her imagination sweep unchecked round every rock and cranny of the world that lies submerged in the depths of our unconscious being. Now came the experience, the experience that I believe to be far commoner with women writers than with men. The line raced through the girl's fingers. Her imagination had rushed away. It had sought the pools, the depths, the dark places where the largest fish slumber. And then there was a smash. There was an explosion. There was foam and confusion. The imagination had dashed itself against something hard. The girl was roused from her dream. She was indeed in a state of the most acute and difficult distress. To speak without figure she had thought of something, something about the body, about the passions which it was unfitting for her as a woman to say. Men, her reason told her, would be shocked. The consciousness of what men will say of a woman who speaks the truth about her passions had roused her from her artist's state of unconsciousness. She could write no more. The trance was over. Her imagination could work no longer. This I believe to be a very common experience with women writers—they are impeded by the extreme conventionality of the other sex. For though men sensibly allow themselves great freedom in these respects, I doubt that they realize or can control the extreme severity with which they condemn such freedom in women.

These then were two very genuine experiences of my own. 6 These were two of the adventures of my professional life. The first—killing the Angel in the House—I think I solved. She died. But the second, telling the truth about my own experiences as a body, I do not think I solved. I doubt that any woman has solved it yet. The obstacles against her are still immensely powerful—and yet they are very difficult to define. Outwardly, what is simpler than to write books? Outwardly, what obstacles are there for a woman rather than for a man? Inwardly, I think, the case is very different; she has still many ghosts to fight, many prejudices to overcome. Indeed it will be a long time still, I think, before a woman can sit down to write a book without finding a phantom to be slain, a rock to be dashed against. And if this is so in literature, the freest of all professions for women, how is it in the new professions which you are now for the first time entering? Those are the questions that I should like, had I time, to ask you. And indeed, if I have laid stress upon these professional experiences of mine, it is because I believe that they are, though in different forms, yours also. Even when the path is nominally open—when there is nothing to prevent a woman from being a doctor, a lawyer, a civil servant—there are many phantoms and obstacles, as I believe, looming in her way. To discuss and define them is I think of great value and importance; for thus only can the labour be shared, the difficulties be solved. But besides this, it is necessary also to discuss the ends and the aims for which we are fighting, for which we are doing battle with these formidable obstacles. Those aims cannot be taken for granted; they must be perpetually questioned and examined. The whole position, as I see it—here in this hall surrounded by women practising for the first time in history I know not how many different professions—is one of extraordinary interest and importance. You have won rooms of your own in the house hitherto exclusively owned by men. You are able, though not without great labour and effort, to pay the rent. You are earning your five hundred pounds a year. But this freedom is only a beginning; the room is your own, but it is still bare. It has to be furnished; it has to be decorated; it has to be shared. How are you going to furnish it, how are you going to decorate it? With whom are you going to share it, and upon what terms? These, I think, are questions of the utmost importance and interest. For the first time in history you are able to ask them; for the first time you are able to decide for yourselves what the answers should be. Willingly would I stay and discuss those questions and answers—but not tonight. My time is up; and I must cease.

7

DOROTHY SAYERS

Are Women Human?

Dorothy Sayers (1893–1957), unlike Virginia Woolf, had the benefits of a formal education. She was among the first women to enter Oxford University, where she made herself conspicuous by

wearing outrageous clothes and smoking cigars. Her scholarship
was stunning: she collaborated with her tutor on a translation of
the medieval French *Song of Roland*, passed her baccalaureate
examinations with first-class honors, and in 1920, when women
were first allowed to take degrees, collected three at once. She left
Oxford a poet and worked for a time as a teacher and editor to
support her writing. In the early 1920s, however, she decided
that she needed more income and turned to detective fiction and
advertising, for both of which she had great talent. Eventually the
success of Sayers's detective novels, featuring the aristocratic
amateur sleuth Lord Peter Wimsey, made her a comfortable living and allowed her to write full-time. Among her many collections of essays, *Unpopular Opinions* (1946) is perhaps the most
interesting. "Are Women Human?" is an address delivered to a
women's society in 1938.

When I was asked to come and speak to you, your Secretary   1
made the suggestion that she thought I must be interested in the
feminist movement. I replied—a little irritably, I am afraid—that I
was not sure I wanted to "identify myself," as the phrase goes, with
feminism, and that the time for "feminism," in the old-fashioned
sense of the word, had gone past. In fact, I think I went so far as to
say that, under present conditions, an aggressive feminism might
do more harm than good. As a result I was, perhaps not unnatu-
rally, invited to explain myself.

I do not know that it is very easy to explain, without offence or   2
risk of misunderstanding, exactly what I do mean, but I will try.

The question of "sex-equality" is, like all questions affecting   3
human relationships, delicate and complicated. It cannot be settled
by loud slogans or hard-and-fast assertions like "a woman is as
good as a man"—or "woman's place is the home"—or "women
ought not to take men's jobs." The minute one makes such assertions, one finds one has to qualify them. "A woman is as good as a
man" is as meaningless as to say, "a Kaffir is as good as a Frenchman" or "a poet is as good as an engineer" or "an elephant is as
good as a racehorse"—it means nothing whatever until you add:
"at doing what?" In a religious sense, no doubt, the Kaffir is as
valuable in the eyes of God as a Frenchman—but the average
Kaffir is probably less skilled in literary criticism than the average
Frenchman, and the average Frenchman less skilled than the average Kaffir in tracing the spoor of big game. There might be exceptions on either side: it is largely a matter of heredity and education.
When we balance the poet against the engineer, we are faced with
a fundamental difference of temperament—so that here our question is complicated by the enormous social problem whether

poetry or engineering is "better" for the State, or for humanity in general. There may be people who would like a world that was all engineers or all poets—but most of us would like to have a certain number of each; though here again, we should all differ about the desirable proportion of engineering to poetry. The only proviso we should make is that people with dreaming and poetical temperaments should not entangle themselves in engines, and that mechanically-minded persons should not issue booklets of bad verse. When we come to the elephant and the racehorse, we come down to bedrock physical differences—the elephant would make a poor showing in the Derby, and the unbeaten Eclipse himself would be speedily eclipsed by an elephant when it came to hauling logs.

That is so obvious that it hardly seems worth saying. But it is the mark of all movements, however well-intentioned, that their pioneers tend, by much lashing of themselves into excitement, to lose sight of the obvious. In reaction against the age-old slogan, "woman is the weaker vessel," or the still more offensive, "woman is a divine creature," we have, I think, allowed ourselves to drift into asserting that "a woman is as good as a man," without always pausing to think what exactly we mean by that. What, I feel, we ought to mean is something so obvious that it is apt to escape attention altogether, viz: not that every woman is, in virtue of her sex, as strong, clever, artistic, level-headed, industrious, and so forth as any man that can be mentioned; but, that a woman is just as much an ordinary human being as a man, with the same individual preferences, and with just as much right to the tastes and preferences of an individual. What is repugnant to every human being is to be reckoned always as a member of a class and not as an individual person. A certain amount of classification is, of course, necessary for practical purposes: there is no harm in saying that women, as a class, have smaller bones than men, wear lighter clothing, have more hair on their heads and less on their faces, go more pertinaciously to church or the cinema, or have more patience with small and noisy babies. In the same way, we may say that stout people of both sexes are commonly better-tempered than thin ones, or that university dons of both sexes are more pedantic in their speech than agricultural labourers, or that Communists of both sexes are more ferocious than Fascists—or the other way round. What is unreasonable and irritating is to assume that *all* one's tastes and preferences have to be conditioned by the class to which one belongs. That has been the very common error into which men have frequently fallen about women—and it is the error into which feminist women are, perhaps, a little inclined to fall into about themselves.

Take, for example, the very usual reproach that women nowa- 5
days always want to "copy what men do." In that reproach there is
a great deal of truth and a great deal of sheer, unmitigated, and
indeed quite wicked nonsense. There are a number of jobs and
pleasures which men have in times past cornered for themselves.
At one time, for instance, men had a monopoly of classical education. When the pioneers of university training for women demanded that women should be admitted to the universities, the cry
went up at once: "Why should women want to know about Aristotle?" The answer is NOT that *all* women would be the better for
knowing about Aristotle—still less, as Lord Tennyson seemed to
think, that they would be more companionable wives for their
husbands if they did know about Aristotle—but simply: "What
women want as a class is irrelevant. *I* want to know about Aristotle. It is true that most women care nothing about him, and a
great many male undergraduates turn pale and faint at the thought
of him—but I, eccentric individual that I am, do want to know
about Aristotle, and I submit that there is nothing in my shape or
bodily functions which need prevent my knowing about him."

That battle was won, and rightly won, for women. But there is a 6
sillier side to the university education of women. I have noticed
lately, and with regret, a tendency on the part of the women's
colleges to "copy the men" on the side of their failings and absurdities, and this is not so good. Because the constitution of the men's
colleges is autocratic, old-fashioned, and in many respects ineffi-
cient, the women are rather inclined to try and cramp their own
collegiate constitutions—which were mapped out on freer democratic lines—into the mediaeval mould of the men's—and that is
unsound. It contributes nothing to the university and it loses what
might have been a very good thing. The women students, too, have
a foolish trick of imitating and outdoing the absurdities of male
undergraduates. To climb in drunk after hours and get gated is silly
and harmless if done out of pure high spirits; if it is done "because
the men do it," it is worse than silly, because it is not spontaneous
and not even amusing.

Let me give one simple illustration of the difference between the 7
right and the wrong kind of feminism. Let us take this terrible
business—so distressing to the minds of bishops—of the women
who go about in trousers. We are asked: "Why do you want to go
about in trousers? They are extremely unbecoming to most of you.
You only do it to copy the men." To this we may very properly
reply: "It is true that they are unbecoming. Even on men they are
remarkably unattractive. But, as you men have discovered for
yourselves, they are comfortable, they do not get in the way of

one's activities like skirts and they protect the wearer from draughts about the ankles. As a human being, I like comfort, and dislike draughts. If the trousers do not attract you, so much the worse; for the moment I do not want to attract you. I want to enjoy myself as a human being, and why not? As for copying you, certainly you thought of trousers first and to that extent we must copy you. But we are not such abandoned copy-cats as to attach these useful garments to our bodies with braces. There we draw the line. These machines of leather and elastic are unnecessary and unsuited to the female form. They are, moreover, hideous beyond description. And as for indecency—of which you sometimes accuse the trousers—we at least can take our coats off without becoming the half-undressed bedroom spectacle that a man presents in his shirt and braces."

So that when we hear that women have once more laid hands   8
upon something which was previously a man's sole privilege, I think we have to ask ourselves: is this trousers or is it braces? Is it something useful, convenient, and suitable to a human being as such? Or is it merely something unnecessary to us, ugly, and adopted merely for the sake of collaring the other fellow's property? These jobs and professions, now. It is ridiculous to take on a man's job just in order to be able to say that "a woman has done it—yah!" The only decent reason for tackling any job is that it is *your* job and *you* want to do it.

At this point, somebody is likely to say: "Yes, that is all very   9
well. But it *is* the woman who is always trying to ape the man. She *is* the inferior being. You don't as a rule find the men trying to take the women's jobs away from them. They don't force their way into the household and turn women out of their rightful occupations."

Of course they do not. They have done it already.   10

Let us accept the idea that women should stick to their own   11
jobs—the jobs they did so well in the good old days before they started talking about votes and women's rights. Let us return to the Middle Ages and ask what we should get then in return for certain political and educational privileges which we should have to abandon.

It is a formidable list of jobs: the whole of the spinning industry,   12
the whole of the dyeing industry, the whole of the weaving industry. The whole catering industry and—which would not please Lady Astor,[1] perhaps—the whole of the nation's brewing and distilling. All the preserving, pickling, and bottling industry, all the

1. Lady Nancy Astor, first woman to sit in the British House of Commons, a champion of women's rights, public education, and temperance.

bacon-curing. And (since in those days a man was often absent from home for months together on war or business) a very large share in the management of landed estates. Here are the women's jobs—and what has become of them? They are all being handled by men. It is all very well to say that woman's place is the home—but modern civilisation has taken all these pleasant and profitable activities out of the home, where the women looked after them, and handed them over to big industry, to be directed and organised by men at the head of large factories. Even the dairy-maid in her simple bonnet has gone, to be replaced by a male mechanic in charge of a mechanical milking plant.

Now, it is very likely that men in big industries do these jobs   13
better than the women did them at home. The fact remains that the home contains much less of interesting activity than it used to contain. What is more, the home has so shrunk to the size of a small flat that—even if we restrict woman's job to the bearing and rearing of families—there is no room for her to do even that. It is useless to urge the modern woman to have twelve children, like her grandmother. Where is she to put them when she has got them? And what modern man wants to be bothered with them? It is perfectly idiotic to take away women's traditional occupations and then complain because she looks for new ones. Every woman is a human being—one cannot repeat that too often—and a human being *must* have occupation, if he or she is not to become a nuisance to the world.

I am not complaining that the brewing and baking were taken   14
over by the men. If they can brew and bake as well as women or better, then by all means let them do it. But they cannot have it both ways. If they are going to adopt the very sound principle that the job should be done by the person who does it best, then that rule must be applied universally. If the women make better office-workers than men, they must have the office work. If any individual woman is able to make a first-class lawyer, doctor, architect, or engineer, then she must be allowed to try her hand at it. Once lay down the rule that the job comes first and you throw that job open to every individual, man or woman, fat or thin, tall or short, ugly or beautiful, who is able to do that job better than the rest of the world.

Now, it is frequently asserted that, with women, the job does not   15
come first. What (people cry) are women doing with this liberty of theirs? What woman really prefers a job to a home and family? Very few, I admit. It is unfortunate that they should so often have to make the choice. A man does not, as a rule, have to choose. He gets both. In fact, if he wants the home and family, he usually has

to take the job as well, if he can get it. Nevertheless, there have been women, such as Queen Elizabeth and Florence Nightingale, who had the choice, and chose the job and made a success of it. And there have been and are many men who have sacrificed their careers for women—sometimes, like Antony or Parnell,[2] very disastrously. When it comes to a *choice*, then every man or woman has to choose as an individual human being, and, like a human being, take the consequences.

As human beings! I am always entertained—and also irritated— 16 by the newsmongers who inform us, with a bright air of discovery, that they have questioned a number of female workers and been told by one and all that they are "sick of the office and would love to get out of it." In the name of God, what human being is *not*, from time to time, heartily sick of the office and would *not* love to get out of it? The time of female officeworkers is daily wasted in sympathising with disgruntled male colleagues who yearn to get out of the office. No human being likes work—not day in and day out. Work is notoriously a curse—and if women *liked* everlasting work they would not be human beings at all. *Being* human beings, they like work just as much and just as little as anybody else. They dislike perpetual washing and cooking just as much as perpetual typing and standing behind shop counters. Some of them prefer typing to scrubbing—but that does not mean that they are not, as human beings, entitled to damn and blast the typewriter when they feel that way. The number of men who daily damn and blast typewriters is incalculable; but that does not mean that they would be happier doing a little plain sewing. Nor would the women.

I have admitted that there are very few women who would put 17 their job before every earthly consideration. I will go further and assert that there are very few men who would do it either. In fact, there is perhaps only one human being in a thousand who is passionately interested in his job for the job's sake. The difference is that if that one person in a thousand is a man, we say, simply, that he is passionately keen on his job; if she is a woman, we say she is a freak. It is extraordinarily entertaining to watch the historians of the past, for instance, entangling themselves in what they were pleased to call the "problem" of Queen Elizabeth. They invented the most complicated and astonishing reasons both for her success

2. Marc Antony allied himself with his lover Cleopatra and—perhaps as a result— lost to Augustus Caesar in the struggle for control of the Roman Empire. Charles Stewart Parnell's affair with "Kitty" O'Shea, wife of a political rival, resulted in a divorce scandal and a fall from power in 1890. Before the divorce, Parnell was a hero in Ireland's struggle for Home Rule.

as a sovereign and for her tortuous matrimonial policy. She was the
tool of Burleigh, she was the tool of Leicester, she was the fool of
Essex; she was diseased, she was deformed, she was a man in
disguise. She was a mystery, and must have some extraordinary
solution. Only recently has it occurred to a few enlightened people
that the solution might be quite simple after all. She might be one
of the rare people who were born into the right job and put that job
first. Whereupon a whole series of riddles cleared themselves up by
magic. She was in love with Leicester—why didn't she marry him?
Well, for the very same reason that numberless kings have not
married their lovers—because it would have thrown a spanner into
the wheels of the State machine. Why was she so blood-thirsty and
unfeminine as to sign the death-warrant of Mary Queen of Scots?
For much the same reasons that induced King George V to say that
if the House of Lords did not pass the Parliament Bill he would
create enough new peers to force it through—because she was, in
the measure of her time, a constitutional sovereign, and knew that
there was a point beyond which a sovereign could not defy Parliament. Being a rare human being with her eye to the job, she did
what was necessary; being an ordinary human being, she hesitated
a good deal before embarking on unsavoury measures—but as to
feminine mystery, there is no such thing about it, and nobody, had
she been a man, would have thought either her statesmanship or
her humanity in any way mysterious. Remarkable they were—but
she was a very remarkable person. Among her most remarkable
achievements was that of showing that sovereignty was one of the
jobs for which the right kind of woman was particularly well fitted.

  Which brings us back to this question of what jobs, if any, are   18
women's jobs. Few people would go so far as to say that all women
are well fitted for all men's jobs. When people do say this, it is
particularly exasperating. It is stupid to insist that there are as many
female musicians and mathematicians as male—the facts are otherwise, and the most we can ask is that if a Dame Ethel Smyth or
a Mary Somerville[3] turns up, she shall be allowed to do her work
without having aspersions cast either on her sex or her ability.
What we ask is to be human individuals, however peculiar and
unexpected. It is no good saying: "You are a little girl and therefore
you ought to like dolls"; if the answer is, "But I don't," there is no
more to be said. Few women happen to be natural born mechanics; but if there is one, it is useless to try and argue her into being
something different. What we must *not* do is to argue that the

3. Smyth (1858–1944), a prolific composer of symphonies, operas, choral works,
instrumental pieces, and songs, was also a militant suffragist. Somerville was a
nineteenth-century writer of works on celestial mechanics and physics.

occasional appearance of a female mechanical genius proves that all women would be mechanical geniuses if they were educated. They would not.

Where, I think, a great deal of confusion has arisen is in a failure to distinguish between special *knowledge* and special *ability*. There are certain questions on which what is called "the woman's point of view" is valuable, because they involve special *knowledge*. Women should be consulted about such things as housing and domestic architecture because, under present circumstances, they have still to wrestle a good deal with houses and kitchen sinks and can bring special knowledge to the problem. Similarly, some of them (though not all) know more about children than the majority of men, and their opinion, *as women*, is of value. In the same way, the opinion of colliers is of value about coal-mining, and the opinion of doctors is valuable about disease. But there are other questions—as for example, about literature or finance—on which the "woman's point of view" has no value at all. In fact, it does not exist. No special knowledge is involved, and a woman's opinion on literature or finance is valuable only as the judgment of an individual. I am occasionally desired by congenital imbeciles and the editors of magazines to say something about the writing of detective fiction "from the woman's point of view." To such demands, one can only say, "Go away and don't be silly. You might as well ask what is the female angle on an equilateral triangle."

In the old days it used to be said that women were unsuited to sit in Parliament, because they "would not be able to think imperially." That, if it meant anything, meant that their views would be cramped and domestic—in short, "the woman's point of view." Now that they *are* in Parliament, people complain that they are a disappointment: they vote like other people with their party and have contributed nothing to speak of from "the woman's point of view"—except on a few purely domestic questions, and even then they are not all agreed. It looks as though somebody was trying to have things both ways at once. Even critics must remember that women are human beings and obliged to think and behave as such. I can imagine a "woman's point of view" about town-planning, or the education of children, or divorce, or the employment of female shop-assistants, for here they have some special knowledge. But what in thunder is the "woman's point of view" about the devaluation of the franc or the abolition of the Danzig Corridor?[4] Even where women have special knowledge, they may disagree among

4. At the end of World War I, the allies promised Poland a "corridor" through Danzig to the sea. Because Danzig's population was overwhelmingly German, it became a focus of Nazi expansionism.

themselves like other specialists. Do doctors never quarrel or scientists disagree? Are women really *not human*, that they should be expected to toddle along all in a flock like sheep? I think that people should be allowed to drink as much wine and beer as they can afford and is good for them; Lady Astor thinks nobody should be allowed to drink anything of the sort. Where is the "woman's point of view"? Or is one or the other of us unsexed? If the unsexed one is myself, then I am unsexed in very good company. But I prefer to think that women are human and differ in opinion like other human beings. This does not mean that their opinions, as individual opinions, are valueless; on the contrary, the more able they are the more violently their opinions will be likely to differ. It only means that you cannot ask for "the woman's point of view," but only for the woman's special knowledge—and this, like all special knowledge, is valuable, though it is no guarantee of agreement.

"What," men have asked distractedly from the beginning of   21
time, "what on earth do women want?" I do not know that women, *as* women, want anything in particular, but as human beings they want, my good men, exactly what you want yourselves: interesting occupation, reasonable freedom for their pleasures, and a sufficient emotional outlet. What form the occupation, the pleasures, and the emotion may take, depends entirely upon the individual. You know that this is so with yourselves—why will you not believe that it is so with us. The late D. H. Lawrence, who certainly cannot be accused of underrating the importance of sex and talked a good deal of nonsense upon the subject, was yet occasionally visited with shattering glimpses of the obvious. He said in one of his *Assorted Articles*:

> "Man is willing to accept woman as an equal, as a man in skirts, as an angel, a devil, a baby-face, a machine, an instrument, a bosom, a womb, a pair of legs, a servant, an encyclopaedia, an ideal or an obscenity; the one thing he won't accept her as is a human being, a real human being of the feminine sex."

"Accepted as a human being!"—yes; not as an inferior class and   22
not, I beg and pray all feminists, as a superior class—not, in fact, as a class at all, except in a useful context. We are much too much inclined in these days to divide people into permanent categories, forgetting that a category only exists for its special purpose and must be forgotten as soon as that purpose is served. There is a fundamental difference between men and women, but it is not the only fundamental difference in the world. There is a sense in which my charwoman and I have more in common than either of us has

with, say, Mr. Bernard Shaw; on the other hand, in a discussion about art and literature, Mr. Shaw and I should probably find we had more fundamental interests in common than either of us had with my charwoman. I grant that, even so, he and I should disagree ferociously about the eating of meat—but that is not a difference between the sexes—on that point, that late Mr. G. K. Chesterton would have sided with me against the representative of his own sex. Then there are points on which I, and many of my own generation of both sexes, should find ourselves heartily in agreement; but on which the rising generation of young men and women would find us too incomprehensibly stupid for words. A difference of age is as fundamental as a difference of sex; and so is a difference of nationality. *All* categories, if they are insisted upon beyond the immediate purpose which they serve, breed class antagonism and disruption in the state, and that is why they are dangerous.

The other day, in the "Heart-to-Heart" column of one of our 23 popular newspapers, there appeared a letter from a pathetic gentleman about a little disruption threatening his married state. He wrote:

> "I have been married eleven years and think a great deal of the wedding anniversary. I remind my wife a month in advance and plan to make the evening a success. But she does not share my keenness, and, if I did not remind her, would let the day go by without a thought of its significance. I thought a wedding anniversary meant a lot to a woman. Can you explain this indifference?"

Poor little married gentleman, nourished upon generalisations— 24 and convinced that if his wife does not fit into the category of "a woman" there must be something wrong! Perhaps she resents being dumped into the same category as all the typical women of the comic stories. If so, she has my sympathy. "A" woman—not an individual person, disliking perhaps to be reminded of the remorseless flowing-by of the years and the advance of old age— but "a" woman, displaying the conventional sentimentalities attributed to her unfortunate and ridiculous sex.

A man once asked me—it is true that it was at the end of a very 25 good dinner, and the compliment conveyed may have been due to that circumstance—how I managed in my books to write such natural conversation between men when they were by themselves. Was I, by any chance, a member of a large, mixed family with a lot of male friends? I replied that, on the contrary, I was an only child and had practically never seen or spoken to any men of my own age till I was about twenty-five. "Well," said the man, "I shouldn't have expected a woman [meaning me] to have been able to make it so convincing." I replied that I had coped with this difficult problem by making my men talk, as far as possible, like ordinary human beings. This aspect of the matter seemed to surprise the other speaker; he said no more, but took it away to chew it over. One of these days it may quite likely occur to him that women, as well as men, when left to themselves, talk very much like human beings also.

Indeed, it is my experience that both men and women are funda- 26 mentally human, and that there is very little mystery about either sex, except the exasperating mysteriousness of human beings in general. And though for certain purposes it may still be necessary, as it undoubtedly was in the immediate past, for women to band themselves together, as women, to secure recognition of their requirements as a sex, I am sure that the time has now come to insist more strongly on each woman's—and indeed each man's—requirements as an individual person. It used to be said that women had no *esprit de corps*; we have proved that we have—do not let us run into the opposite error of insisting that there is an aggressively feminist "point of view" about everything. To oppose one class perpetually to another—young against old, manual labour against brain-worker, rich against poor, woman against man—is to split the foundations of the State; and if the cleavage runs too deep, there remains no remedy but force and dictatorship. If you wish to preserve a free democracy, you must base it—not on classes and categories, for this will land you in the totalitarian State, where no one may act or think except as the member of a category. You must base it upon the individual Tom, Dick, and Harry, on the individual Jack and Jill—in fact, upon you and me.

BRIGID BROPHY

Women

Brigid Brophy (1929–   ), prolific writer of fiction and essays, has an original mind full of surprises. She takes a very unsentimental view of nature (see "The Menace of Nature," p. 116), but is on principle a vegetarian and an advocate of animal rights. She has long been married to art historian Michael Levey, but is an advocate of sexual freedom and a denouncer of the hypocrisies of marriage. So successfully does she resist stereotyping and social

controls that her interest in "invisible cages" would seem to be
that of an escape artist rather than that of a prisoner. Though she
has a notoriously quick wit, Ms. Brophy's tough, lucid prose does
not come easily: "when I am writing, I don't sleep at night and I
don't wash my hair. If I have to go to a dinner party, I simply
write madly in my head while I eat. I'm like a medieval hermit."
"Women" was first published in *The Saturday Evening Post*, November 2, 1963.

All right, nobody's disputing it. Women are free. At least, they   1
look free. They even feel free. But in reality women in the western,
industrialised world today are like the animals in a modern zoo.
There are no bars. It appears that cages have been abolished. Yet in
practice women are still kept in their place just as firmly as the
animals are kept in their enclosures. The barriers which keep them
in now are invisible.

It is about forty years since the pioneer feminists, several of   2
whom were men, raised such a rumpus by rattling the cage bars—
or created such a conspicuous nuisance by chaining themselves to
them—that society was at last obliged to pay attention. The result
was that the bars were uprooted, the cage thrown open: where-
upon the majority of the women who had been held captive decided they would rather stay inside anyway.

To be more precise, they *thought* they decided; and society,   3
which can with perfect truth point out "Look, no bars," *thought* it
was giving them the choice. There are no laws and very little discrimination to prevent western, industrialised women from voting,
being voted for or entering the professions. If there are still comparatively few women lawyers and engineers, let alone women presidents of the United States, what are women to conclude except that
this is the result either of their own free choice or of something
inherent in female nature?

Many of them do draw just this conclusion. They have come   4
back to the old argument of the anti-feminists, many of whom
were women, that women are unfit by nature for life outside the
cage. And in letting this old wheel come full cycle women have
fallen victim to one of the most insidious and ingenious confidence
tricks ever perpetrated.

In point of fact, neither female nature nor women's individual   5
free choice has been put to the test. As American Negroes have
discovered, to be officially free is by no means the same as being
actually and psychologically free. A society as adept as ours has become at propaganda—whether political or commercial—should
know that "persuasion," which means the art of launching myths

and artificially inducing inhibitions, is every bit as effective as force of law. No doubt the reason society eventually agreed to abolish its anti-women laws was that it had become confident of commanding a battery of hidden dissuaders which would do the job just as well. Cage bars are clumsy methods of control, which excite the more rebellious personalities inside to rattle them. Modern society, like the modern zoo, has contrived to get rid of the bars without altering the fact of imprisonment. All the zoo architect needs to do is run a zone of hot or cold air, whichever the animal concerned cannot tolerate, round the cage where the bars used to be. Human animals are not less sensitive to social climate.

The ingenious point about the new-model zoo is that it deceives 6 both sides of the invisible barrier. Not only can the animal not see how it is imprisoned; the visitor's conscience is relieved of the unkindness of keeping animals shut up. He can say "Look, no bars round the animals," just as society can say "Look, no laws restricting women" even while it keeps women rigidly in place by zones of fierce social pressure.

There is, however, one great difference. A woman, being a 7 thinking animal, may actually be more distressed because the bars of her cage cannot be seen. What relieves society's conscience may afflict hers. Unable to perceive what is holding her back, she may accuse herself and her whole sex of craven timidity because women have not jumped at what has the appearance of an offer of freedom. Evidently quite a lot of women have succumbed to guilt of this sort, since in recent years quite an industry has arisen to assuage it. Comforting voices make the air as thick and reassuring as cotton wool while they explain that there is nothing shameful in not wanting a career, that to be intellectually unadventurous is no sin, that taking care of home and family may be personally "fulfilling" and socially valuable.

This is an argument without a flaw: except that it is addressed 8 exclusively to women. Address it to both sexes and instantly it becomes progressive and humane. As it stands, it is merely anti-woman prejudice revamped.

That many women would be happier not pursuing careers or 9 intellectual adventures is only part of the truth. The whole truth is that many *people* would be. If society had the clear sight to assure men as well as women that there is no shame in preferring to stay non-competitively and non-aggressively at home, many masculine neuroses and ulcers would be avoided, and many children would enjoy the benefit of being brought up by a father with a talent for the job instead of by a mother with no talent for it but a sense of guilt about the lack.

But society does nothing so sensible. Blindly it goes on insisting 10 on the tradition that men are the ones who go out to work and adventure—an arrangement which simply throws talent away. All the home-making talent which happens to be born inside male bodies is wasted; and our businesses and governments are staffed quite largely by people whose aptitude for the work consists solely of their being what is, by tradition, the right sex for it.

The pressures society exerts to drive men out of the house are 11 very nearly as irrational and unjust as those by which it keeps women in. The mistake of the early reformers was to assume that men were emancipated already and that therefore reform need ask only for the emancipation of women. What we ought to do now is go right back to scratch and demand the emancipation of both sexes. It is only because men are not free themselves that they have found it necessary to cheat women by the deception which makes them appear free when they are not.

The zones of hot and cold air which society uses to perpetuate its 12 uneconomic and unreasonable state of affairs are the simplest and most effective conceivable. Society is playing on our sexual vanity. Just as the sexual regions are the most vulnerable part of the body, sexuality is the most vulnerable part of the Ego. Tell a man that he is not a real man, or a woman that she is not one hundred per cent woman, and you are threatening both with not being attractive to the opposite sex. No one can bear not to be attractive to the opposite sex. That is the climate which the human animal cannot tolerate.

So society has us all at its mercy. It has only to murmur to the 13 man that staying at home is a feminine characteristic, and he will be out of the house like a bullet. It has only to suggest to the woman that logic and reason are the province of the masculine mind, whereas "intuition" and "feeling" are the female *forte*, and she will throw her physics textbooks out of the window, barricade herself into the house, and give herself up to having wishy-washy poetical feelings while she arranges the flowers.

She will, incidentally, take care that her feelings *are* wishy- 14 washy. She has been persuaded that to have cogent feelings, of the kind which really do go into great poems (most of which are by men), would make her an unfeminine woman, a woman who imitates men. In point of fact, she would not be imitating men as such, most of whom have never written a line of great poetry, but poets, most of whom so far happen to be men. But the bad logic passes muster with her because part of the mythology she has swallowed ingeniously informs her that logic is not her *forte*.

Should a woman's talent or intelligence be so irrepressible that 15 she insists on producing cogent works of art or watertight meshes of argument, she will be said to have "a mind like a man's." This is simply current idiom; translated, it means "a good mind." The use of the idiom contributes to an apparently watertight proof that all good minds are masculine, since whenever they occur in women they are described as "like a man's."

What is more, this habit of thought actually contributes to per-   16
petuating a state of affairs where most good minds really do belong to men. It is difficult for a woman to *want* to be intelligent when she has been told that to be so will make her like a man. She inclines to think an intelligence would be as unbecoming to her as a moustache; and many women have tried in furtive privacy to disembarrass themselves of intellect as though it were facial hair.

Discouraged from growing "a mind like a man's," women are   17
encouraged to have thoughts and feelings of a specifically feminine tone. For society is cunning enough not to place its whole reliance on threatening women with blasts of icy air. It also flatters them with a zone of hot air. The most deceptive and cynical of its blandishments is the notion that women have some specifically feminine contribution to make to culture. Unfortunately, as culture had already been shaped and largely built up by men before the invitation was issued, this leaves women little to do. Culture consists of reasoned thought and works of art composed of cogent feeling and imagination. There is only one way to be reasonable, and that is to reason correctly; and the only kind of art which is any good is good art. If women are to eschew reason and artistic imagination in favour of "intuition" and "feeling," it is pretty clear what is meant. "Intuition" is just a polite name for bad reasoning, and "feeling" for bad art.

In reality, the whole idea of a specifically feminine—or, for the   18
matter of that, masculine—contribution to culture is a contradiction of culture. A contribution to culture is not something which could not have been made by the other sex—it is something which could not have been made by any other *person*. Equally, the notion that anyone, of either sex, can create good art out of simple feeling, untempered by discipline, is a philistine one. The arts are a sphere where women seem to have done well; but really they have done *too* well—too well for the good of the arts. Instead of women sharing the esteem which ought to belong to artists, art is becoming smeared with femininity. We are approaching a philistine state of affairs where the arts are something which it is nice for women to take up in their spare time—men having slammed out of the house to get on with society's "serious" business, like making money, administering the country and running the professions.

In that "serious" sphere it is still rare to encounter a woman. A   19
man sentenced to prison would probably feel his punishment was
redoubled by indignity if he were to be sentenced by a woman
judge under a law drafted by a woman legislator—and if, on admission, he were to be examined by a woman prison doctor. If
such a thing happened every day, it would be no indignity but the
natural course of events. It has never been given the chance to
become the natural course of events and never will be so long
as women remain persuaded it would be unnatural of them to
want it.

So brilliantly has society contrived to terrorise women with this   20
threat that certain behaviour is unnatural and unwomanly that it
has left them no time to consider—or even sheerly observe—what
womanly nature really is. For centuries arrant superstitions were
accepted as natural law. The physiological fact that only women can
secrete milk for feeding babies was extended into the pure myth
that it was women's business to cook for and wait on the entire
family. The kitchen became woman's "natural" place because, for
the first few months of her baby's life, the nursery really was. To
this day a woman may suspect that she is unfeminine if she can
discover in herself no aptitude or liking for cooking. Fright has
thrown her into such a muddle that she confuses having no taste
for cookery with having no breasts, and conversely assumes that
nature has endowed the human female with a special handiness
with frying pans.

Even psycho-analysis, which in general has been the greatest   21
benefactor of civilisation since the wheel, has unwittingly reinforced the terrorisation campaign. The trouble was that it brought
with it from its origin in medical therapy a criterion of normality
instead of rationality. On sheer statistics every pioneer, genius and
social reformer, including the first woman who demanded to be let
out of the kitchen and into the polling both, is abnormal, along
with every lunatic and eccentric. What distinguishes the genius
from the lunatic is that the genius's abnormality is justifiable by
reason or aesthetics. If a woman who is irked by confinement to
the kitchen merely looks round to see what other women are doing
and finds they are accepting their kitchens, she may well conclude
that she is abnormal and had better enlist her psycho-analyst's help
towards "living with" her kitchen. What she ought to ask is
whether it is rational for women to be kept to the kitchen, and
whether nature really does insist on that in the way it insists
women have breasts. And in a far-reaching sense to ask that question is much more normal and natural than learning to "live with"
the handicap of women's inferior social status. The normal and

natural thing for human beings is not to tolerate handicaps but to reform society and to circumvent or supplement nature. We don't learn to live minus a leg; we devise an artificial limb.

That, indeed, is the crux of the matter. Not only are the distinc- 22 tions we draw between male nature and female nature largely arbitrary and often pure superstition: they are completely beside the point. They ignore the essence of *human* nature. The important question is not whether women are or are not less logical by nature than men, but whether education, effort and the abolition of our illogical social pressures can improve on nature and make them (and, incidentally, men as well) *more* logical. What distinguishes human from any other animal nature is its ability to be unnatural. Logic and art are not natural or instinctive activities; but our nature includes a propensity to acquire them. It is not natural for the human body to orbit the earth; but the human mind has a natural adventurousness which enables it to invent machines whereby the body can do so. There is, in sober fact, no such creature as a natural man. Go as far back as they will, the archaeologists cannot come on a wild man in his natural habitat. At his most primitive, he has already constructed himself an artificial habitat, and decorated it not by a standardised instinctual method, as birds build nests, but by individualised—that is, abnormal—works of art or magic. And in doing so he is not limited by the fingers nature gave him; he has extended their versatility by making tools.

Civilisation consists not necessarily in defying nature but in 23 making it possible for us to do so if we judge it desirable. The higher we can lift our noses from the grindstone of nature, the wider the area we have of choice; and the more choices we have freely made, the more individualised we are. We are at our most civilised when nature does not dictate to us, as it does to animals and peasants, but when we can opt to fall in with it or better it. If modern civilisation has invented methods of education which make it possible for men to feed babies and for women to think logically, we are betraying civilisation itself if we do not set both sexes free to make a free choice.

JAN MORRIS

To Everest

Jan Morris (1926–   ) was born James Humphrey Morris. He
served in the British army from 1943 to 1947 rising to the rank of
second lieutenant, after which he became a reporter and editor
for *The Times* of London. In 1953 he accompanied Sir Edmund
Hillary on the expedition to Mount Everest, climbing to the
22,000-foot level in order to be the first to report the news of the
successful assault on the summit. Thereafter he became an expert
foreign correspondent, reporting on wars and rebellions and
writing history and travel books, including *The Road to Hud-
dersfield: A Journey to Five Continents* (1963). Despite all his success and despite being the father of five children, he was not
comfortable in his masculine identity. "I was 3 or perhaps 4 years
old when I realized that I had been born into the wrong body,
and should really be a girl," Morris wrote in *Conundrum*, an
autobiography published in 1974. In 1964 he began to take hormones that would make him more feminine, a transformation
completed by surgery in 1972, when Morris became completely a
woman and changed the name James for the name Jan. As Jan,
Morris has continued to publish essays and books on travel, the
most recent being *Hongkong: Xianggong* (1988). "To Everest" is
the ninth chapter of *Conundrum*; it gives us a picture of the type of
masculinity Morris felt compelled to escape.

Though I resented my body, I did not dislike it. I rather admired   1
it, as it happened. It might not be the body beautiful, but it was lean
and sinewy, never ran to fat, and worked like a machine of quality,
responding exuberantly to a touch of the throttle or a long haul
home. Women, I think, never have quite this feeling about their
bodies, and I shall never have it again. It is a male prerogative, and
contributes no doubt to the male arrogance. In those days, though
for that very reason I did not want it, still I recognized the merits of
my physique, and had pleasure from its exercise.

I first felt its full power, as one might realize for the first time the   2
potential of a run-in car, in 1953, when I was assigned by *The Times*
to join the British expedition shortly to make the first ascent of
Mount Everest. This was essentially a physical undertaking. The
paper had exclusive rights to dispatches from the mountain, and I
was to be the only correspondent with the team, my job being
partly to see that dispatches from the expedition's leader got safely
home to London, but chiefly to write dispatches of my own. The

competition would be intense and very likely violent, communications were primitive to a degree, and the only way to do the job was to climb fairly high up the mountain myself and periodically, to put a complex operation simply, run down it again with the news. It was not particularly to my credit that I was given the assignment—at an agile twenty-six I was patently better suited for it than most of my colleagues at Printing House Square. I took exercise daily (as I still do), did not smoke (and still don't), and though excessively fond of wine, seldom drank spirits, not much liking the taste of them.

3   I was also, being some years out of the 9th Lancers, furiously keen.[1] There is something about the newspaper life, however specious its values and ridiculous its antics, that brings out the zest in its practitioners. It may be nonsense, but it is undeniably fun. I was not especially anxious to achieve fame in the trade, for I already felt instinctively that it would not be my life's occupation, but even so I would have stooped to almost any skulduggery to achieve what was, self-consciously even then, quaintly called a scoop. The news from Everest was to be mine, and anyone who tried to steal it from me should look out for trouble.

4   In such a mood, at such an age, at the peak of a young man's physical condition, I found myself in May, 1953, high on the flank of the world's greatest mountain.

5   Let me try to describe the sensation for my readers, as it seems to me today—and especially for my women readers, who are unlikely I now see to have experienced such a conjunction of energies.

6   Imagine first the setting. This is theatrically changeable. In the morning it is like living, reduced to minuscule proportions, in a bowl of broken ice cubes in a sunny garden. Somewhere over the rim, one assumes, there are green trees, fields, and flowers; within the bowl everything is a brilliant white and blue. It is silent in there. The mountain walls deaden everything and cushion the hours in a disciplinary hush. The only noise is a drip of water sometimes, the howl of a falling boulder or the rumble of a distant avalanche. The sky above is a savage blue, the sun glares mercilessly off the snow and ice, blistering one's lips, dazzling one's eyes, and filling that mountain declivity with its substance.

7   In the afternoon everything changes. Then the sky scowls down, high snow-clouds billow in from Tibet, a restless cruel wind blows

---

1. Morris soldiered with this British regiment from 1943–1947, rising to the rank of second lieutenant. Among these highly professional soldiers, shows of enthusiasm, or "keenness," were considered bad form.

up, and before long the snow is falling in slanted parallel across the landscape, blotting out sky, ridges, and all, and making you feel that your ice-bowl has been put back into the refrigerator. It is terribly cold. The afternoon is filled with sounds, the rush of wind, the flapping of tent-canvas, the squeak and creak of guy-ropes; and as the evening draws on the snow piles up around your tent, half burying it infinitesimally in the hulk of Everest, as though you have been prematurely incarcerated, or perhaps trapped in a sunken submarine—for you can see the line of snow slowly rising through the nylon walls of the tent, like water rising to submerge you.

But imagine now the young man's condition. First, he is con- 8 stant against this inconstant background. His body is running not in gusts and squalls, but at a steady high speed. He actually tingles with strength and energy, as though sparks might fly from his skin in the dark. Nothing sags in him. His body has no spare weight upon it, only muscles made supple by exercise. When, in the bright Himalayan morning, he emerges from his tent to make the long trek down the mountain to the Khumbu glacier below, it is as though he could leap down there in gigantic strides, singing as he goes. And when, the same evening perhaps, he labors up again through the driving snow, it is not a misery but a challenge to him, something to be outfaced, something actually to be enjoyed, as the deep snow drags at his feet, the water trickles down the back of his neck, and his face thickens with cold, ice, and wind.

There is no hardship to it, for it is not imposed upon him. He is 9 the master. He feels that anything is possible to him, and that his relative position to events will always remain the same. He does not have to wonder what his form will be tomorrow, for it will be the same as it is today. His mind, like his body, is tuned to the job, and will not splutter or falter. It is this feeling of unfluctuating control, I think, that women cannot share, and it springs of course not from the intellect or the personality, nor even so much from upbringing, but specifically from the body. The male body may be ungenerous, even uncreative in the deepest kind, but when it is working properly it is a marvelous thing to inhabit. I admit it in retrospect more than I did at the time, and I look back to those moments of supreme male fitness as one remembers champagne or a morning swim. Nothing could beat me, I knew for sure; and nothing did.

I think for sheer exuberance the best day of my life was my last 10 on Everest. The mountain had been climbed, and I had already begun my race down the glacier towards Katmandu, leaving the expedition to pack its gear behind me. By a combination of cunning and ingenuity I had already sent a coded message through an

Indian Army radio transmitter at Namche Bazar, twenty miles south of Everest, its operators being unaware of its meaning; but I did not know if it had reached London safely, so I was myself hastening back to Katmandu and the cable office with my own final dispatch. How brilliant I felt, as with a couple of Sherpa porters I bounded down the glacial moraine towards the green below! I was brilliant with the success of my friends on the mountain, I was brilliant with my knowledge of the event, brilliant with muscular tautness, brilliant with conceit, brilliant with awareness of the subterfuge, amounting very nearly to dishonesty, by which I hoped to have deceived my competitors and scooped the world. All those weeks at high altitude had suited me, too, and had given me a kind of heightened fervor, as though my brain had been quickened by drugs to keep pace with my body. I laughed and sang all the way down the glacier, and when next morning I heard from the radio that my news had reached London providentially on the eve of Queen Elizabeth's coronation, I felt as though I had been crowned myself.

I never mind the swagger of young men. It is their right to 11 swank, and I know the sensation!

Once more on Everest I was the outsider—formally this time, as 12 well as tacitly. None of the climbers would have guessed, I am sure, how irrevocably distinct I felt from them; but they were aware that I was not a climber, and had been attached to the expedition only to watch. At first I was supposed to provide my own victuals and equipment, but it seemed rather silly to maintain such segregation twenty thousand feet above nowhere, so I soon pooled my resources with theirs, and pitched my tent among them.

On Everest, nevertheless, I realized more explicitly some truths 13 about myself. Though I was as fit as most of those men, I responded to different drives. I would have suffered almost anything to get those dispatches safely back to London, but I did not share the mountaineers' burning urge to see that mountain climbed. Perhaps it was too abstract an objective for me—certainly I was not animated by any respect for inviolate nature, which I have always disliked, preferring like George Leigh-Mallory a blend of tame and wild. I was pleased when they did climb Everest, but chiefly for a less than elevated reason—patriotic pride, which I knew to be unworthy of their efforts, but which I could not suppress.

I well understood the masochistic relish of challenge which im- 14 pelled them, and which stimulated me too, but the blankness of the achievement depressed me. One of the older Everesters, H. W. Tilman, once quoted G. K. Chesterton to illustrate the urge of alpinism: "I think the immense act has something about it human and excusable; and when I endeavor to analyze the reason of this feeling I find it to lie, not in the fact that the thing was big or bold or successful, but in the fact that the thing was perfectly useless to everybody, including the person who did it." Leigh-Mallory presumably meant much the same, when he talked of climbing Everest simply "because it was there." But this elusive prize, this snatching at air, this nothingness, left me dissatisfied, as I think it would leave most women. Nothing had been discovered, nothing made, nothing improved.

I have always discounted the beauty of clouds, because their airy   15
impermanence seems to me to disqualify them from the truest beauty, just as I have never responded to kinetic art, and love the shifting light of nature only because it reveals new shapes and meaning in the solids down below. Nor do I like sea views, unless there is land to be seen beyond them. A similar distrust of the ephemeral or the un-finite weakened my response to the triumph of Everest in 1953. It was a grand adventure, I knew, and my part in relaying its excitements to the world was to transform my professional life, and dog me ever after; yet even now I dislike that emptiness at its climax, that perfect uselessness, and feel in a slightly ashamed and ungrateful way that it was really all rather absurd.

For it was almost like a military expedition—the colonel in com-   16
mand, not so long from Montgomery's staff, the little army of porters who wound their way bent-back with their loads over the hills from Katmandu, the meticulously packed and listed stores, the briefings, the air of ordered determination. It was a superbly successful expedition—nobody killed, nobody disgraced—and looking back upon it now I see its cohesion as a specifically male accomplishment. Again constancy was the key. Men more than women respond to the team spirit, and this is partly because, if they are of an age, of a kind, and in a similar condition, they work together far more like a mechanism. Elations and despondencies are not so likely to distract them. Since their pace is more regular, all can more easily keep to it. They are distinctly more rhythm than melody.

In 1953 the rhythm was steadier than it might be now, for it   17
was conscious then as well as constitutional. Stiff upper lip and fair play were integral to the British masculine ethos, and shame was a powerful impulse towards achievement. Social empathy, too, strongly reinforced the sense of maleness. The functional efficiency of class I had already discovered in the Army, and it was the same on Everest. Hunt's climbers were men of the officer class, as they would then have been called, and they were bound by common

tastes and values. They spoke the same language, shared the same kind of past, enjoyed the same pleasures. Three of them had been to the same school. In a social sense they formed a kind of club; in an imperial sense, and this was almost the last of the imperial adventures, they were a company of sahibs attended by their multitudinous servants.

One could not, I think, apply these categories to women of equal   18 intelligence in similar circumstances, and less and less can one now apply them to men. Class has lost its binding function; patriotism has lost its elevating force; young men are no longer ashamed of weaknesses; the stiff upper lip is no longer an ideal, only a music hall sally. The barrier between the genders is flimsier now, and no expedition will ever again go to the Himalayas so thoroughly masculine as Hunt's. It embarrasses me rather to have to admit that from that day to this, none has gone there more successfully.

I need not belabor my sense of alienation from this formidable   19 team. I liked most of its members very much, and have remained friends with some to this day, but my sense of detachment was extreme, and though I shamelessly accepted their help throughout the adventure, still I was always at pains to cherish my separateness. I hated to think of myself as one of them, and when in England we were asked to sign menus, maps, or autograph books, I used carefully to sign myself James Morris of *The Times*—until the climbers, fancying I fear altogether different motives in me, asked me not to. At the same time a wayward self-consciousness—for I was a child of the age, too—compelled me to keep up male appearances, perhaps as much for my own persuasion as for anyone else's. I even overdid it rather. I grew a beard, and when at the end of the expedition I walked into the communications room at the British Embassy in Katmandu with my tin mug jangling from the belt of my trousers, the wireless operator asked acidly if I *had* to look so jungly. He did not know how cruelly the jibe hurt, for in a few words it cut this way and that through several skins of self-protection.

Everest taught me new meanings of maleness, and emphasized   20 once more my own inner dichotomy. Yet paradoxically my most evocative memory of the experience haunts me with a truth of an altogether different kind. Often when there was a lull on the mountain I would go down the glacier and wander among the moraines. Sometimes I went south, towards the distant Buddhist temple at Thyangboehe where the deodars shaded the green turf, and the bells, gongs, and trumpets of the monks sounded from their shambled refectory. Sometimes I clambered into the snows of the north, towards the great wall of the Lho La, over whose ominous white ridge stood the peaks of Tibet. I vaguely hoped to catch a glimpse of an abominable snowman, and I was looking too for traces of the lemurs and mountain hares which sometimes, I had been told, penetrated those high deserts.

I saw no animals ever. What I found instead was a man. I saw   21
him first in the extreme distance, across an absolutely blank snowfield at about nineteen thousand feet, to which I had climbed from the glacier below for the sake of the view. At first I was frightened, for I could not make out what he was—only a small black swaying speck, indescribably alone in the desolation. As he came closer I saw that he could only be human, so I plunged through the loose snow to meet him, and presently, there near the top of the world, thousands of feet and many miles above the trees, the streams, or human habitation, we met face to face. It was the strangest encounter of my life.

He was a holy man, wandering in the mountains, I suppose, for   22
wandering's sake. His brown, crinkled, squashed-up face looked back at me expressionless from beneath a yellow hood, and found it seemed nothing strange in my presence there. He wore a long yellow cloak and hide boots, and from his waist there hung a spoon and a cloth satchel. He carried nothing else, and he wore no gloves. I greeted him as best I could, but he did not answer, only smiling at me distantly and without surprise. Perhaps he was in a trance. I offered him a piece of chocolate, but he did not take it, simply standing there before me, slightly smiling, almost as though he were made of ice himself. Presently we parted, and without a word he continued on his unfaltering journey, apparently making for Tibet without visible means of survival, and moving with a proud, gliding, and effortless motion that seemed inexorable. He did not appear to move fast, but when I looked around he had almost disappeared, and was no more than that small black speck again, inexplicably moving over the snows.

I envied him his insouciant speed, and wondered if he too felt   23
that tingling of the body, that sense of mastery, which had so deepened my sense of duality upon the slopes of Everest. But the more I thought about it, the more clearly I realized that he had no body at all.

ALICE WALKER

Brothers and Sisters

Alice Walker (1944–   ) was born in Eatonton, Georgia, the youngest of eight children. Her father, who she says was "wonderful at math" but "a terrible farmer," earned only about $300 a year as a sharecropper. The example of her mother, a determined woman who helped in the fields and worked as a maid, helped make Walker a "womanist," a term she invented to mean "a black feminist or woman of color." Both her parents were storytellers: Walker's career as a short story writer began when she was eight and started to write their stories down. After graduating at the top of her high school class, Walker attended Spelman College, then graduated from Sarah Lawrence College in 1965. Best known for her third novel *The Color Purple* (1982), which won the American Book Award and the Pulitzer Prize, Walker is also an accomplished poet and essayist. Her essays are collected in *In Search of Our Mothers' Gardens: Womanist Prose* (1983) and *Living by the Word* (1988). "Brothers and Sisters" was published under the pseudonym White Pine in *Ms. Magazine*, October 1975.

We lived on a farm in the South in the fifties, and my brothers,   1
the four of them I knew (the fifth had left home when I was three years old), were allowed to watch animals being mated. This was not unusual; nor was it considered unusual that my oldest sister and I were frowned upon if we even asked, innocently, what was going on. One of my brothers explained the mating one day, using words my father had given him: "The bull is getting a little something on his stick," he said. And he laughed. "What stick?" I wanted to know. "Where did he get it? How did he pick it up? Where did he put it?" All my brothers laughed.

I believe my mother's theory about raising a large family of five   2
boys and three girls was that the father should teach the boys and the mother teach the girls the facts, as one says, of life. So my father went around talking about bulls getting something on their sticks and she went around saying girls did not need to know about such things. They were "womanish" (a very bad way to be in those days) if they asked.

The thing was, watching the matings filled my brothers with an   3
aimless sort of lust, as dangerous as it was unintentional. They knew enough to know that cows, months after mating, produced calves, but they were not bright enough to make the same connection between women and their offspring.

Sometimes, when I think of my childhood, it seems to me a 4
particularly hard one. But in reality, everything awful that happened to me didn't seem to happen to *me* at all, but to my older
sister. Through some incredible power to negate my presence
around people I did not like, which produced invisibility (as well as
an ability to appear mentally vacant when I was nothing of the
kind), I was spared the humiliation she was subjected to, though at
the same time, I felt every bit of it. It was as if she suffered for my
benefit, and I vowed early in my life that none of things that made
existence so miserable for her would happen to me.

The fact that she was not allowed at official matings did not 5
mean she never saw any. While my brothers followed my father to
the mating pens on the other side of the road near the barn, she
stationed herself near the pigpen, or followed our many dogs until
they were in a mating mood, or, failing to witness something there,
she watched the chickens. On a farm it is impossible *not* to be
conscious of sex, to wonder about it, to dream . . . but to whom was
she to speak of her feelings? Not to my father, who thought all
young women perverse. Not to my mother, who pretended all her
children grew out of stumps she magically found in the forest. Not
to me, who never found anything wrong with this lie.

When my sister menstruated she wore a thick packet of clean 6
rags between her legs. It stuck out in front like a penis. The boys
laughed at her as she served them at the table. Not knowing any
better, and because our parents did not dream of actually *discussing*
what was going on, she would giggle nervously at herself. I hated
her for giggling, and it was at those times I would think of her as
dim-witted. She never complained, but she began to have strange
fainting fits whenever she had her period. Her head felt as if it were
splitting, she said, and everything she ate came up again. And her
cramps were so severe she could not stand. She was forced to
spend several days of each month in bed.

My father expected all of his sons to have sex with women. 7
"Like bulls," he said, "a man *needs* to get a little something on his
stick." And so, on Saturday nights, into town they went, chasing
the girls. My sister was rarely allowed into town alone, and if the
dress she wore fit too snugly at the waist, or if her cleavage dipped
too far below her collarbone, she was made to stay home.

"But why can't I go too," she would cry, her face screwed up 8
with the effort not to wail.

"They're boys, your brothers, *that's* why they can go." 9

Naturally, when she got the chance, she responded eagerly to 10
boys. But when this was discovered she was whipped and locked
up in her room.

I would go in to visit her.   11

"Straight Pine,"[1] she would say, "you don't know what it *feels*   12
like to want to be loved by a man."

"And if this is what you get for feeling like it I never will," I said,   13
with—I hoped—the right combination of sympathy and disgust.

"Men smell so good," she would whisper ecstatically. "And   14
when they look into your eyes, you just melt."

Since they were so hard to catch, naturally she thought almost   15
any of them terrific.

"Oh, that Alfred!" she would moon over some mediocre,   16
square-headed boy, "he's so *sweet!*" And she would take his ugly
picture out of her bosom and kiss it.

My father was always warning her not to come home if she ever   17
found herself pregnant. My mother constantly reminded her that
abortion was a sin. Later, although she never became pregnant, her
period would not come for months at a time. The painful symptoms, however, never varied or ceased. She fell for the first man
who loved her enough to beat her for looking at someone else, and
when I was still in high school, she married him.

My fifth brother, the one I never knew, was said to be different   18
from the rest. He had not liked matings. He would not watch them.
He thought the cows should be given a choice. My father had
disliked him because he was soft. My mother took up for him.
"Jason is just tender-hearted," she would say in a way that made
me know he was her favorite; "he takes after me." It was true that
my mother cried about almost anything.

Who was this oldest brother? I wondered.   19

"Well," said my mother, "he was someone who always loved   20
you. Of course he was a great big boy when you were born and out
working on his own. He worked on a road gang building roads.
Every morning before he left he would come in the room where
you were and pick you up and give you the biggest kisses. He used
to look at you and just smile. It's a pity you don't remember him."

I agreed.   21

At my father's funeral I finally "met" my oldest brother. He is   22
tall and black with thick gray hair above a young-looking face. I
watched my sister cry over my father until she blacked out from
grief. I saw my brothers sobbing, reminding each other of what a
great father he had been. My oldest brother and I did not shed a
tear between us. When I left my father's grave he came up and
introduced himself. "You don't ever have to walk alone," he said,
and put his arms around me.

---

1. A pseudonym. [author's note]

One out of five ain't *too* bad, I thought, snuggling up.   23

But I didn't discover until recently his true uniqueness: He is the   24
only one of my brothers who assumes responsibility for all his
children. The other four all fathered children during those Satur-
day-night chases of twenty years ago. Children—my nieces and
nephews whom I will probably never know—they neither acknowledge as their own, provide for, or even see.

It was not until I became a student of women's liberation ideol-   25
ogy that I could understand and forgive my father. I needed an
ideology that would define his behavior in context. The black
movement had given me an ideology that helped explain his color-
ism (he *did* fall in love with my mother partly because she was so
light; he never denied it). Feminism helped explain his sexism.
I was relieved to know his sexist behavior was not something
uniquely his own, but, rather, an imitation of the behavior of the
society around us.

All partisan movements add to the fullness of our understanding   26
of society as a whole. They never detract; or, in any case, one must
not allow them to do so. Experience adds to experience. "The more
things the better," as O'Connor and Welty both have said, speaking, one of marriage, the other of Catholicism.

I desperately needed my father and brothers to give me male   27
models I could respect, because white men (for example; being
particularly handy in this sort of comparison)—whether in films or
in person—offered man as dominator, as killer, and always as
hypocrite.

My father failed because he copied the hypocrisy. And my   28
brothers—except for one—never understood they must represent
half the world to me, as I must represent the other half to them.[2]

TOM WOLFE

The Right Stuff

Tom Wolfe (1931–   ) has a Ph.D. in American Studies from
Yale University, but only occasionally does he write like an academic. He is a leading practitioner of the "New Journalism,"

2. Since this essay was written, my brothers have offered their name, acknowledg-
ment, and some support to all their children. [author's note]

which he defines as "the use by people writing nonfiction of techniques which heretofore had been thought of as confined to the novel or short story, to create in one form both the objective reality of journalism and the kind of subjective reality that people have always gone to the novel for." The new journalism uses dialogue extensively, changes points of view, constructs scenes, and includes detailed descriptions of settings. It reveals, so far as possible, not only what human beings do, but what they essentially are. Wolfe's treatment of the Project Mercury astronauts in *The Right Stuff* (1979) is a particularly interesting study of seven men who share a common concept of the masculine ideal. Other notable recent works by Wolfe are *From Bauhaus to Our House* (1981), a study of modern architects, and *The Bonfire of the Vanities* (1987), a novel.

A young man might go into military flight training believing that 1 he was entering some sort of technical school in which he was simply going to acquire a certain set of skills. Instead, he found himself all at once enclosed in a fraternity. And in this fraternity, even though it was military, men were not rated by their outward rank as ensigns, lieutenants, commanders, or whatever. No, herein the world was divided into those who had it and those who did not. This quality, this *it*, was never named, however, nor was it talked about in any way.

As to just what this ineffable quality was . . . well, it obviously 2 involved bravery. But it was not bravery in the simple sense of being willing to risk your life. The idea seemed to be that any fool could do that, if that was all that was required, just as any fool could throw away his life in the process. No, the idea here (in the all-enclosing fraternity) seemed to be that a man should have the ability to go up in a hurtling piece of machinery and put his hide on the line and then have the moxie, the reflexes, the experience, the coolness, to pull it back in the last yawning moment—and then to go up again *the next day*, and the next day, and every next day, even if the series should prove infinite—and, ultimately, in its best expression, do so in a cause that means something to thousands, to a people, a nation, to humanity, to God. Nor was there *a test* to show whether or not a pilot had this righteous quality. There was, instead, a seemingly infinite series of tests. A career in flying was like climbing one of those ancient Babylonian pyramids made up of a dizzy progression of steps and ledges, a ziggurat, a pyramid extraordinarily high and steep; and the idea was to prove at every foot of the way up that pyramid that you were one of the elected and anointed ones who had *the right stuff* and could move higher and higher and even—ultimately, God willing, one day—that you might be able to join that special few at the very top, that elite who had the capacity to bring tears to men's eyes, the very Brotherhood of the Right Stuff itself.

None of this was to be mentioned, and yet it was acted out in a   3
way that a young man could not fail to understand. When a new flight (i.e., a class) of trainees arrived at Pensacola, they were brought into an auditorium for a little lecture. An officer would tell them: "Take a look at the man on either side of you." Quite a few actually swiveled their heads this way and that, in the interest of appearing diligent. Then the officer would say: "One of the three of you is not going to make it!"—meaning, not get his wings. That was the opening theme, the *motif* of primary training. We already know that one-third of you do not have the right stuff—it only remains to find out who.

Furthermore, that was the way it turned out. At every level in   4
one's progress up that staggeringly high pyramid, the world was once more divided into those men who had the right stuff to continue the climb and those who had to be *left behind* in the most obvious way. Some were eliminated in the course of the opening classroom work, as either not smart enough or not hardworking enough, and were left behind. Then came the basic flight instruction, in single-engine, propeller-driven trainers, and a few more— even though the military tried to make this stage easy—were washed out and left behind. Then came more demanding levels, one after the other, formation flying, instrument flying, jet training, all-weather flying, gunnery, and at each level more were washed out and left behind. By this point easily a third of the original candidates had been, indeed, eliminated . . . from the ranks of those who might prove to have the right stuff.

In the Navy, in addition to the stages that Air Force trainees   5
went through, the neophyte always had waiting for him, out in the ocean, a certain grim gray slab; namely, the deck of an aircraft carrier; and with it perhaps the most difficult routine in military flying, carrier landings. He was shown films about it, he heard lectures about it, and he knew that carrier landings were hazardous. He first practiced touching down on the shape of a flight deck painted on an airfield. He was instructed to touch down and gun right off. This was safe enough—the shape didn't move, at least— but it could do terrible things to, let us say, the gyroscope of the soul. *That shape!—it's so damned small!* And more candidates were washed out and left behind. Then came the day, without warning, when those who remained were sent out over the ocean for the

first of many days of reckoning with the slab. The first day was always a clear day with little wind and a calm sea. The carrier was so steady that it seemed, from up there in the air, to be resting on pilings, and the candidate usually made his first carrier landing successfully, with relief and even *élan*. Many young candidates looked like terrific aviators up to that very point—and it was not until they were actually standing on the carrier deck that they first began to wonder if they had the proper stuff, after all. In the training film the flight deck was a grand piece of gray geometry, perilous, to be sure, but an amazing abstract shape as one looks down upon it on the screen. And yet once the newcomer's two feet were on it . . . *Geometry*—my God, man, this is a . . . skillet! It *heaved*, it moved up and down underneath his feet, it pitched up, it pitched down, it rolled to port (this great beast *rolled!*) and it rolled to starboard, as the ship moved into the wind and, therefore, into the waves, and the wind kept sweeping across, sixty feet up in the air out in the open sea, and there were no railings whatsoever. This was a *skillet!*—a frying pan!—a short-order grill!—not gray but black, smeared with skid marks from one end to the other and glistening with pools of hydraulic fluid and the occasional jet-fuel slick, all of it still hot, sticky, greasy, runny, virulent from God knows what traumas—still ablaze!—consumed in detonations, explosions, flames, combustion, roars, shrieks, whines, blasts, horrible shudders, fracturing impacts, as little men in screaming red and yellow and purple and green shirts with black Mickey Mouse helmets over their ears skittered about on the surface as if for their very lives (you've said it now!), hooking fighter planes onto the catapult shuttles so that they can explode their afterburners and be slung off the deck in a red-mad fury with a *kaboom!* that pounds through the entire deck—a procedure that seems absolutely controlled, orderly, sublime, however, compared to what he is about to watch as aircraft return to the ship for what is known in the engineering stoicisms of the military as "recovery and arrest." To say that an F–4 was coming back onto this heaving barbecue from out of the sky at a speed of 135 knots . . . that might have been the truth in the training lecture, but it did not begin to get across the idea of what the newcomer saw from the deck itself, because it created the notion that perhaps the plane was gliding in. On the deck one knew differently! As the aircraft came closer and the carrier heaved on into the waves and the plane's speed did not diminish and the deck did not grow steady—indeed, it pitched up and down five or ten feet per greasy heave—one experienced a neural alarm that no lecture could have prepared him for: This is not an *airplane* coming toward me, it is a brick with some poor sonofabitch riding it (*someone much like myself!*), and it is not *gliding*, it is *falling*, a thirty-thousand-pound brick, headed not for a stripe on the deck but for *me*—and with a horrible *smash!* it hits the skillet, and with a blur of momentum as big as a freight train's it hurtles toward the far end of the deck—another blinding storm!—another roar as the pilot pushes the throttle up to full military power and another smear of rubber screams out over the skillet—and this is nominal!—quite okay!—for a wire stretched across the deck has grabbed the hook on the end of the plane as it hit the deck tail down, and the smash was the rest of the fifteen-ton brute slamming onto the deck, as it tripped up, so that it is now straining against the wire at full throttle, in case it hadn't held and the plane had "boltered" off the end of the deck and had to struggle up into the air again. And already the Mickey Mouse helmets are running toward the fiery monster . . . .

And the candidate, looking on, begins to *feel* that great heaving sun-blazing deathboard of a deck wallowing in his own vestibular system—and suddenly he finds himself backed up against his own limits. He ends up going to the flight surgeon with so-called conversion symptoms. Overnight he develops blurred vision or numbness in his hands and feet or sinusitis so severe that he cannot tolerate changes in altitude. On one level the symptom is real. He really cannot see too well or use his fingers or stand the pain. But somewhere in his subconscious he knows it is a plea and a beg-off; he shows not the slightest concern (the flight surgeon notes) that the condition might be permanent and affect him in whatever life awaits him outside the arena of the right stuff. 6

Those who remained, those who qualified for carrier duty—and even more so those who later on qualified for *night* carrier duty—began to feel a bit like Gideon's warriors. *So many have been left behind!* The young warriors were now treated to a deathly sweet and quite unmentionable sight. They could gaze at length upon the crushed and wilted pariahs who had washed out. They could inspect those who did not have that righteous stuff. 7

The military did not have very merciful instincts. Rather than packing up these poor souls and sending them home, the Navy, like the Air Force and the Marines, would try to make use of them in some other role, such as flight controller. So the washout has to keep taking classes with the rest of his group, even though he can no longer touch an airplane. He sits there in the classes staring at sheets of paper with cataracts of sheer human mortification over his eyes while the rest steal looks at him . . . this man reduced to an ant, this untouchable, this poor sonofabitch. And in what test had he been found wanting? Why, it seemed to be nothing less than 8 *manhood* itself. Naturally, this was never mentioned, either. Yet there it was. *Manliness, manhood, manly courage . . .* there was something ancient, primordial, irresistible about the challenge of this stuff, no matter what a sophisticated and rational age one might think he lived in.

Perhaps because it could not be talked about, the subject began   9 to take on superstitious and even mystical outlines. A man either had it or he didn't! There was no such thing as having *most* of it. Moreover, it could blow at any seam. One day a man would be ascending the pyramid at a terrific clip, and the next—bingo!—he would reach his own limits in the most unexpected way. Conrad and Schirra met an Air Force pilot who had had a great pal at Tyndall Air Force Base in Florida. This man had been the budding ace of the training class; he had flown the hottest fighter-style trainer, the T–38, like a dream; and then he began the routine step of being checked out in the T–33. The T–33 was not nearly as hot an aircraft as the T–38; it was essentially the old P–80 jet fighter. It had an exceedingly small cockpit. The pilot could barely move his shoulders. It was the sort of airplane of which everybody said, "You don't get into it, you *wear* it." Once inside a T–33 cockpit this man, this budding ace, developed claustrophobia of the most paralyzing sort. He tried everything to overcome it. He even went to a psychiatrist, which was a serious mistake for a military officer if his superiors learned of it. But nothing worked. He was shifted over to flying jet transports, such as the C–135. Very demanding and necessary aircraft they were, too, and he was still spoken of as an excellent pilot. But as everyone knew—and, again, it was never explained in so many words—only those who were assigned to fighter squadrons, the "fighter jocks," as they called each other with a self-satisfied irony, remained in the true fraternity. Those assigned to transports were not humiliated like washouts— *somebody* had to fly those planes—nevertheless, they, too, had been *left behind* for lack of the right stuff.

Or a man could go for a routine physical one fine day, feeling   10 like a million dollars, and be grounded for *fallen arches*. It happened!—just like that! (And try raising them.) Or for breaking his wrist and losing only *part* of its mobility. Or for a minor deterioration of eyesight, or for any of hundreds of reasons that would make no difference to a man in an ordinary occupation. As a result all fighter jocks began looking upon doctors as their natural enemies. Going to see a flight surgeon was a no-gain proposition; a pilot could only hold his own or lose in the doctor's office. To be grounded for a medical reason was no humiliation, looked at objectively. But it was a humiliation, nonetheless!—for it meant you no longer had that indefinable, unutterable, integral stuff. (It could blow at *any* seam.)

All the hot young fighter jocks began trying to test the limits 11 themselves in a superstitious way. They were like believing Presbyterians of a century before who used to probe their own experience to see if they were truly among *the elect*. When a fighter pilot was in training, whether in the Navy or the Air Force, his superiors were continually spelling out strict rules for him, about the use of the aircraft and conduct in the sky. They repeatedly forbade so-called hot-dog stunts, such as outside loops, buzzing, flat-hatting, hedge-hopping and flying under bridges. But somehow one got the message that the man who truly *had* it could ignore those rules—not that he should make a point of it, but that he *could*—and that after all there was only one way to find out—and that in some strange unofficial way, peeking through his fingers, his instructor halfway expected him to challenge all the limits. They would give a lecture about how a pilot should never fly without a good solid breakfast—eggs, bacon, toast, and so forth—because if he tried to fly with his blood-sugar level too low, it could impair his alertness. Naturally, the next day every hot dog in the unit would get up and have a breakfast consisting of one cup of black coffee and take off and go up into a vertical climb until the weight of the ship exactly canceled out the upward thrust of the engine and his air speed was zero, and he would hang there for one thick adrenal instant—and then fall like a rock, until one of three things happened: he keeled over nose first and regained his aerodynamics and all was well, he went into a spin and fought his way out of it, or he went into a spin and had to eject or crunch it, which was always supremely possible.

Likewise, "hassling"—mock dogfighting—was strictly forbid- 12 den, and so naturally young fighter jocks could hardly wait to go up in, say, a pair of F–100s and start the duel by making a pass at each other at 800 miles an hour, the winner being the pilot who could slip in behind the other one and get locked in on his tail ("wax his tail"), and it was not uncommon for some eager jock to try too tight an outside turn and have his engine flame out, where-upon, unable to restart it, he has to eject . . . and he shakes his fist at the victor as he floats down by parachute and his million-dollar aircraft goes *kaboom!* on the palmetto grass or the desert floor, and he starts thinking about how he can get together with the other guy back at the base in time for the two of them to get their stories straight before the investigation: "I don't know what happened, sir. I was pulling up after a target run, and it just flamed out on me." Hassling was forbidden, and hassling that led to the destruction of an aircraft was a serious court-martial offense, and the man's superiors knew that the engine hadn't *just flamed out*, but every unofficial impulse on the base seemed to be saying: "Hell, we wouldn't give you a nickel for a pilot who hasn't done some crazy rat-racing like that. It's all part of the right stuff."

The other side of this impulse showed up in the reluctance of the   13
young jocks to admit it when they had maneuvered themselves into a bad corner they couldn't get out of. There were two reasons why a fighter pilot hated to declare an emergency. First, it triggered a complex and very public chain of events at the field: all other incoming flights were held up, including many of one's comrades who were probably low on fuel; the fire trucks came trundling out to the runway like yellow toys (as seen from way up there), the better to illustrate one's hapless state; and the bureaucracy began to crank up the paper monster for the investigation that always followed. And second, to declare an emergency, one first had to reach that conclusion in his own mind, which to the young pilot was the same as saying: "A minute ago I still *had* it—now I need your help!" To have a bunch of young fighter pilots up in the air thinking this way used to drive flight controllers crazy. They would see a ship beginning to drift off the radar, and they couldn't rouse the pilot on the microphone for anything other than a few mean-ingless mumbles, and they would know he was probably out there with engine failure at a low altitude, trying to reignite by lowering his auxiliary generator rig, which had a little propeller that was supposed to spin in the slipstream like a child's pinwheel.

"Whiskey Kilo Two Eight, do you want to declare an emer-   14
gency?"

This would rouse him!—to say: "Negative, negative, Whiskey   15
Kilo Two Eight is not declaring an emergency."

Kaboom. Believers in the right stuff would rather crash and   16
burn.

One fine day, after he had joined a fighter squadron, it would   17
dawn on the young pilot exactly how the losers in the great frater-nal competition were now being left behind. Which is to say, not by instructors or other superiors or by failures at prescribed levels of competence, but by death. At this point the essence of the enter-prise would begin to dawn on him. Slowly, step by step, the ante had been raised until he was now involved in what was surely the grimmest and grandest gamble of manhood. Being a fighter pilot—for that matter, simply taking off in a single-engine jet fighter of the Century series, such as an F–102, or any of the military's other marvelous bricks with fins on them—presented a man, on a per-fectly sunny day, with more ways to get himself killed than his wife

and children could imagine in their wildest fears. If he was barreling down the runway at two hundred miles an hour, completing the takeoff run, and the board started lighting up red, should he (a) abort the takeoff (and try to wrestle with the monster, which was gorged with jet fuel, out in the sand beyond the end of the runway) or (b) eject (and hope that the goddamned human cannonball trick works at zero altitude and he doesn't shatter an elbow or a kneecap on the way out) or (c) continue the takeoff and deal with the problem aloft (knowing full well that the ship may be on fire and therefore seconds away from exploding)? He would have one second to sort out the options and act, and this kind of little workaday decision came up all the time. Occasionally a man would look coldly at the binary problem he was now confronting every day— Right Stuff/Death—and decide it wasn't worth it and voluntarily shift over to transports or reconnaissance or whatever. And his comrades would wonder, for a day or so, what evil virus had invaded his soul . . . as they left him behind. More often, however, the reverse would happen. Some college graduate would enter Navy aviation through the Reserves, simply as an alternative to the Army draft, fully intending to return to civilian life, to some waiting profession or family business; would become involved in the obsessive business of ascending the ziggurat pyramid of flying; and, at the end of his enlistment, would astound everyone back home and very likely himself as well by signing up for another one. What on earth got into him? He couldn't explain it. After all, the very words for it had been amputated. A Navy study showed that two-thirds of the fighter pilots who were rated in the top rungs of their groups—i.e., the hottest young pilots—reenlisted when the time came, and practically all were college graduates. By this point, a young fighter jock was like the preacher in *Moby Dick* who climbs up into the pulpit on a rope ladder and then pulls the ladder up behind him; except the pilot could not use the words necessary to express the vital lessons. Civilian life, and even home and hearth, now seemed not only far away but far *below*, back down many levels of the pyramid of the right stuff.

A fighter pilot soon found he wanted to associate only with other fighter pilots. Who else could understand the nature of the little proposition (right stuff/death) they were all dealing with? And what other subject could compare with it? It was riveting! To talk about it in so many words was forbidden, of course. The very words *death, danger, bravery, fear* were not to be uttered except in the occasional specific instance or for ironic effect. Nevertheless, the subject could be adumbrated in *code* or *by example*. Hence the endless evenings of pilots huddled together talking about flying. On these long and drunken evenings (the bane of their family life) certain theorems would be propounded and demonstrated—and all by *code* and *example*. One theorem was: There are no *accidents* and no fatal flaws in the machines; there are only pilots with the wrong stuff. (i.e., blind Fate can't kill me.) When Bud Jennings crashed and burned in the swamps at Jacksonville, the other pilots in Pete Conrad's squadron said: *How could he have been so stupid?* It turned out that Jennings had gone up in the SNJ with his cockpit canopy opened in a way that was expressly forbidden in the manual, and carbon monoxide had been sucked in from the exhaust, and he passed out and crashed. All agreed that Bud Jennings was a good guy and a good pilot, but his epitaph on the ziggurat was: *How could he have been so stupid?* This seemed shocking at first, but by the time Conrad had reached the end of that bad string at Pax River,[1] he was capable of his own corollary to the theorem: viz., no single factor ever killed a pilot; there was always a chain of mistakes. But what about Ted Whelan, who fell like a rock from 8,100 feet when his parachute failed? Well, the parachute was merely part of the chain: first, someone should have caught the structural defect that resulted in the hydraulic leak that triggered the emergency; second, Whelan did not check out his seat-parachute rig, and the drogue failed to separate the main parachute from the seat; but even after those two mistakes, Whelan had fifteen or twenty seconds, as he fell, to disengage himself from the seat and open the parachute manually. Why just stare at the scenery coming up to smack you in the face! And everyone nodded. (He failed—but I wouldn't have!) Once the theorem and the corollary were understood, the Navy's statistics about one in every four Navy aviators dying meant nothing. The figures were averages, and averages applied to those with average stuff.

A riveting subject, especially if it were one's own hide that was on the line. Every evening at bases all over America, there were military pilots huddled in officers clubs eagerly cutting the right stuff up in coded slices so they could talk about it. What more compelling topic of conversation was there in the world? In the Air Force there were even pilots who would ask the tower for priority landing clearance so that they could make the beer call on time, at 4 P.M. sharp, at the Officers Club. They would come right out and state the reason. The drunken rambles began at four and sometimes went on for ten or twelve hours. Such conversations! They diced that righteous stuff up into little bits, bowed ironically to it,

1. During the "bad string" in 1955, ten of Charles "Pete" Conrad's close friends had been killed in accidents.

stumbled blindfolded around it, groped, lurched, belched, staggered, bawled, sang, roared, and feinted at it with self-deprecating humor. Nevertheless!—they never mentioned it by name. No, they used the approved codes, such as: "Like a jerk I got myself into a hell of a corner today." They told of how they "lucked out of it." To get across the extreme peril of his exploit, one would use certain oblique cues. He would say, "I looked over at Robinson"—who would be known to the listeners as a non-com who sometimes rode backseat to read radar—"and he wasn't talking any more, he was just staring at the radar, like this, giving it that *zombie* look. Then I *knew* I was in trouble!" Beautiful! Just right! For it would also be known to the listeners that the non-coms advised one another: "*Never* fly with a lieutenant. *Avoid* captains and majors. Hell, man, do yourself a favor: don't fly with anybody below colonel." Which in turn said: "Those young bucks shoot dice with death!" And yet once in the air the non-com had his own standards. He was determined to remain as outwardly cool as the pilot, so that when the pilot did something that truly petrified him, he would say nothing; instead, he would turn silent, catatonic, like a zombie. Perfect! *Zombie.* There you had it, compressed into a single word, all of the foregoing. I'm a hell of a pilot! I shoot dice with death! And now all you fellows know it! And I haven't spoken of that unspoken stuff even once!

The talking and drinking began at the beer call, and then the boys would break for dinner and come back afterward and get more wasted and more garrulous or else more quietly fried, drinking good cheap PX booze until 2 A.M. The night was young! Why not get the cars and go out for a little proficiency run? It seemed that every fighter jock thought himself an ace driver, and he would do anything to obtain a hot car, especially a sports car, and the drunker he was, the more convinced he would be about his driving skills, as if the right stuff, being indivisible, carried over into any enterprise whatsoever, under any conditions. A little proficiency run, boys! (There's only one way to find out!) And they would roar off in close formation from, say, Nellis Air Force Base, down Route 15, into Las Vegas, barreling down the highway, rat-racing, sometimes four abreast, jockeying for position, piling into the most listless curve in the desert flats as if they were trying to root each other out of the groove at the Rebel 500—and then bursting into downtown Las Vegas with a rude fraternal roar like the Hell's Angels—and the natives chalked it up to youth and drink and the bad element that the Air Force attracted. They knew nothing about the right stuff, of course.

Femininity

Susan Brownmiller (1935–   ) was an actress in New York
from 1955 to 1959, then worked as an editor, researcher, and
staff writer for various magazines and news organizations. She
also helped organize Women Against Pornography and New
York Radical Feminists. In 1975, after four years of research, she
published *Against Our Will,* a study in which she argued that
"rape is nothing more or less than a conscious process of intimidation by which *all men* keep *all women* in a state of fear." Books
with such radical theses rarely achieve great popularity, but
Brownmiller's became a Book-of-the-Month Club selection and
was serialized in four magazines. In 1984 she published *Femininity,* a book that explores in detail the social ideal of femininity
and the limitations that ideal imposes on women. Since 1984
Brownmiller has published a number of essays and reviews on
gardening and a novel, *Waverly Place* (1989). "Femininity" is
taken from *Femininity.*

We had a game in our house called "setting the table" and I was   1
Mother's helper. Forks to the left of the plate, knives and spoons to
the right. Placing the cutlery neatly, as I recall, was one of my first
duties, and the event was alive with meaning. When a knife or a
fork dropped on the floor, that meant a man was unexpectedly
coming to dinner. A falling spoon announced the surprise arrival
of a female guest. No matter that these visitors never arrived on
cue, I had learned a rule of gender identification. Men were
straight-edged, sharply pronged and formidable, women were
softly curved and held the food in a rounded well. It made perfect
sense, like the division of pink and blue that I saw in babies, an
orderly way of viewing the world. Daddy, who was gone all day at
work and who loved to putter at home with his pipe, tobacco and
tool chest, was knife and fork. Mommy and Grandma, with their
ample proportions and pots and pans, were grownup soup spoons,
large and capacious. And I was a teaspoon, small and slender, easy
to hold and just right for pudding, my favorite dessert.

Being good at what was expected of me was one of my earliest   2
projects, for not only was I rewarded, as most children are, for
doing things right, but excellence gave pride and stability to my
childhood existence. Girls were different from boys, and the expression of that difference seemed mine to make clear. Did my
loving, anxious mother, who dressed me in white organdy pina-

fores and Mary Janes and who cried hot tears when I got them dirty, give me my first instruction? Of course. Did my doting aunts and uncles with their gifts of pretty dolls and miniature tea sets add to my education? Of course. But even without the appropriate toys and clothes, lessons in the art of being feminine lay all around me and I absorbed them all: the fairy tales that were read to me at night, the brightly colored advertisements I pored over in magazines before I learned to decipher the words, the movies I saw, the comic books I hoarded, the radio soap operas I happily followed whenever I had to stay in bed with a cold. I loved being a little girl, or rather I loved being a fairy princess, for that was who I thought I was.

As I passed through a stormy adolescence to a stormy maturity,   3
femininity increasingly became an exasperation, a brilliant, subtle esthetic that was bafflingly inconsistent at the same time that it was minutely, demandingly concrete, a rigid code of appearance and behavior defined by do's and don't-do's that went against my rebellious grain. Femininity was a challenge thrown down to the female sex, a challenge no proud, self-respecting young woman could afford to ignore, particularly one with enormous ambition that she nursed in secret, alternately feeding or starving its inchoate life in tremendous confusion.

"Don't lose your femininity" and "Isn't it remarkable how she   4
manages to retain her femininity?" had terrifying implications. They spoke of a bottom-line failure so irreversible that nothing else mattered. The pinball machine has registered "tilt," the game had been called. Disqualification was marked on the forehead of a woman whose femininity was lost. No records would be entered in her name, for she had destroyed her birthright in her wretched, ungainly effort to imitate a man. She walked in limbo, this hapless creature, and it occurred to me that one day I might see her when I looked in the mirror. If the danger was so palpable that warning notices were freely posted, wasn't it possible that the small bundle of resentments I carried around in secret might spill out and place the mark on my own forehead? Whatever quarrels with femininity I had I kept to myself; whatever handicaps femininity imposed, they were mine to deal with alone, for there was no women's movement to ask the tough questions, or to brazenly disregard the rules.

Femininity, in essence, is a romantic sentiment, a nostalgic tradi-   5
tion of imposed limitations. Even as it hurries forward in the 1980s, putting on lipstick and high heels to appear well dressed, it trips on the ruffled petticoats and hoopskirts of an era gone by. Invariably and necessarily, femininity is something that women had more of

in the past, not only in the historic past of prior generations, but in each woman's personal past as well—in the virginal innocence that is replaced by knowledge, in the dewy cheek that is coarsened by age, in the "inherent nature" that a woman seems to misplace so forgetfully whenever she steps out of bounds. Why should this be so? The XX chromosomal message has not been scrambled, the estrogen-dominated hormonal balance is generally as biology intended, the reproductive organs, whatever use one has made of them, are usually in place, the breasts of whatever size are most often where they should be. But clearly, biological femaleness is not enough.

Femininity always demands more. It must constantly reassure its   6
audience by a willing demonstration of difference, even when one does not exist in nature, or it must seize and embrace a natural variation and compose a rhapsodic symphony upon the notes. Suppose one doesn't care to, has other things on her mind, is clumsy or tone-deaf despite the best instruction and training? To fail at the feminine difference is to appear not to care about men, and to risk the loss of their attention and approval. To be insufficiently feminine is viewed as a failure in core sexual identity, or as a failure to care sufficiently about oneself, for a woman found wanting will be appraised (and will appraise herself) as mannish or neutered or simply unattractive, as men have defined these terms.

We are talking, admittedly, about an exquisite esthetic. Enor-   7
mous pleasure can be extracted from feminine pursuits as a creative outlet or purely as relaxation; indeed, indulgence for the sake of fun, or art, or attention, is among femininity's great joys. But the chief attraction (and the central paradox, as well) is the competitive edge that femininity seems to promise in the unending struggle to survive, and perhaps to triumph. The world smiles favorably on the feminine woman: it extends little courtesies and minor privilege. Yet the nature of this competitive edge is ironic, at best, for one works at femininity by accepting restrictions, by limiting one's sights, by choosing an indirect route, by scattering concentration and not giving one's all as a man would to his own, certifiably masculine, interests. It does not require a great leap of imagination for a woman to understand the feminine principle as a grand collection of compromises, large and small, that she simply must make in order to render herself a successful woman. If she has difficulty in satisfying femininity's demands, if its illusions go against her grain, or if she is criticized for her shortcomings and imperfections, the more she will see femininity as a desperate strategy of appeasement, a strategy she may not have the wish or the courage to abandon, for failure looms in either direction.

It is fashionable in some quarters to describe the feminine and 8
masculine principles as polar ends of the human continuum, and to
sagely profess that both polarities exist in all people. Sun and
moon, yin and yang, soft and hard, active and passive, etcetera,
may indeed be opposites, but a linear continuum does not illuminate the problem. (Femininity, in all its contrivances, is a very
active endeavor.) What, then, is the basic distinction? The masculine principle is better understood as a driving ethos of superiority designed to inspire straightforward, confident success, while the
feminine principle is composed of vulnerability, the need for protection, the formalities of compliance and the avoidance of conflict—in short, an appeal of dependence and good will that gives
the masculine principle its romantic validity and its admiring applause.

Femininity pleases men because it makes them appear more 9
masculine by contrast; and, in truth, conferring an extra portion of
unearned gender distinction on men, an unchallenged space in
which to breathe freely and feel stronger, wiser, more competent, is
femininity's special gift. One could say that masculinity is often an
effort to please women, but masculinity is known to please by
displays of mastery and competence while femininity pleases by
suggesting that these concerns, except in small matters, are beyond
its intent. Whimsy, unpredictability and patterns of thinking and
behavior that are dominated by emotion, such as tearful expressions of sentiment and fear, are thought to be feminine precisely
because they lie outside the established route to success.

If in the beginnings of history the feminine woman was defined 10
by her physical dependency, her inability for reasons of reproductive biology to triumph over the forces of nature that were the tests
of masculine strength and power, today she reflects both an economic and emotional dependency that is still considered "natural,"
romantic and attractive. After an unsettling fifteen years in which
many basic assumptions about the sexes were challenged, the economic disparity did not disappear. Large numbers of women—
those with small children, those left high and dry after a mid-life
divorce—need financial support. But even those who earn their
own living share a universal need for connectedness (call it love, if
you wish). As unprecedented numbers of men abandon their sexual interest in women, others, sensing opportunity, choose to demonstrate their interest through variety and a change in partners. A
sociological fact of the 1980s is that female competition for two
scarce resources—men and jobs—is especially fierce.

So it is not surprising that we are currently witnessing a renewed 11
interest in femininity and an unabashed indulgence in feminine

pursuits. Femininity serves to reassure men that women need them and care about them enormously. By incorporating the decorative and the frivolous into its definition of style, femininity functions as an effective antidote to the unrelieved seriousness, the pressure of making one's way in a harsh, difficult world. In its mandate to avoid direct confrontation and to smooth over the fissures of conflict, femininity operates as a value system of niceness, a code of thoughtfulness and sensitivity that in modern society is sadly in short supply.

There is no reason to deny that indulgence in the art of feminine   12
illusion can be reassuring to a woman, if she happens to be good at
it. As sexuality undergoes some dizzying revisions, evidence that
one is a woman "at heart" (the inquisitor's question) is not without worth. Since an answer of sorts may be furnished by piling on additional documentation, affirmation can arise from such identifiable but trivial feminine activities as buying a new eyeliner, experimenting with the latest shade of nail color, or bursting into tears at the outcome of a popular romance novel. Is there anything destructive in this? Time and cost factors, a deflection of energy and an absorption in fakery spring quickly to mind, and they need to be balanced, as in a ledger book, against the affirming advantage.

NOEL PERRIN

The Androgynous Man

Noel Perrin (1927–   ) teaches English at Dartmouth College,
farms, and writes essays, collected in *A Passport Secretly Green*
(1961), *First Person Rural* (1978), *Second Person Rural* (1980), and
Third Person Rural (1983). He also takes a lively interest in literature that lies somewhat off the beaten path. His *Dr. Bowlder's Legacy* (1970) is a history of expurgated books, and *A Reader's Delight* (1988) contains essays on meritorious works so unfamiliar that many of them are out of print. "The Androgynous Man" appeared in the "About Men" column of the *New York Times Magazine* on February 5, 1984.

The summer I was 16, I took a train from New York to Steam-   1
boat Springs, Colo., where I was going to be assistant horse wrangler at a camp. The trip took three days, and since I was much too

shy to talk to strangers, I had quite a lot of time for reading. I read all of *Gone With the Wind.* I read all the interesting articles in a couple of magazines I had, and then I went back and read all the dull stuff. I also took all the quizzes, a thing of which magazines were even fuller then than now.

The one that held my undivided attention was called "How   2
Masculine/Feminine Are You?" It consisted of a large number of inkblots. The reader was supposed to decide which of four objects each blot most resembled. The choices might be a cloud, a steam engine, a caterpillar and a sofa.

When I finished the test, I was shocked to find that I was barely   3
masculine at all. On a scale of 1 to 10, I was about 1.2. Me, the horse wrangler? (And not just wrangler, either. That summer, I had to skin a couple of horses that died—the camp owner wanted the hides.)

The results of that test were so terrifying to me that for the first   4
time in my life I did a piece of original analysis. Having unlimited time on the train, I looked at the "masculine" answers over and over, trying to find what it was that distinguished real men from people like me—and eventually I discovered two very simple patterns. It was "masculine" to think the blots looked like man-made objects, and "feminine" to think they looked like natural objects. It was masculine to think they looked like things capable of causing harm, and feminine to think of innocent things.

Even at 16, I had the sense to see that the compilers of the test   5
were using rather limited criteria—maleness and femaleness are both more complicated that *that*—and I breathed a huge sigh of relief. I wasn't necessarily a wimp, after all.

That the test did reveal something other than the superficiality of   6
its makers I realized only many years later. What it revealed was that there is a large class of men and women both, to which I belong, who are essentially androgynous. That doesn't mean we're gay, or low in the appropriate hormones, or uncomfortable performing the jobs traditionally assigned our sexes. (A few years after that summer, I was leading troops in combat and, unfashionable as it now is to admit this, having a very good time. War is exciting. What a pity the 20th century went and spoiled it with high-tech weapons.)

What it does mean to be spiritually androgynous is a kind of   7
freedom. Men who are all-male, or he-man, or 100 percent red-blooded Americans, have a little biological set that causes them to be attracted to physical power, and probably also to dominance. Maybe even to watching football. I don't say this to criticize them. Completely masculine men are quite often wonderful people: good

husbands, good (though sometimes overwhelming) fathers, good members of society. Furthermore, they are often so unself-consciously at ease in the world that other men seek to imitate them. They just aren't as free as us androgynes. They pretty nearly have to be what they are; we have a range of choices open.

The sad part is that many of us never discover that. Men who are not 100 percent red-blooded Americans—say, those who are only 75 percent red-blooded—often fail to notice their freedom. They are too busy trying to copy the he-men ever to realize that men, like women, come in a wide variety of acceptable types. Why this frantic imitation? My answer is mere speculation, but not casual. I have speculated on this for a long time.   8

Partly they're just envious of the he-man's unconscious ease. Mostly they're terrified of finding that there may be something wrong with them deep down, some weakness at the heart. To avoid discovering that, they spend their lives acting out the role that the he-man naturally lives. Sad.   9

One thing that men owe to the women's movement is that this kind of failure is less common than it used to be. In releasing themselves from the single ideal of the dependent woman, women have more or less incidentally released a lot of men from the single ideal of the dominant male. The one mistake the feminists have made, I think, is in supposing that *all* men need this release, or that the world would be a better place if all men achieved it. It wouldn't. It would just be duller.   10

So far I have been pretty vague about just what the freedom of the androgynous man is. Obviously it varies with the case. In the case I know best, my own, I can be quite specific. It has freed me most as a parent. I am, among other things, a fairly good natural mother. I like the nurturing role. It makes me feel good to see a child eat—and it turns me to mush to see a 4-year-old holding a glass with both small hands, in order to drink. I even enjoyed sewing patches on the knees of my daughter Amy's Dr. Dentons when she was at the crawling stage. All that pleasure I would have lost if I had made myself stick to the notion of the paternal role that I started with.   11

Or take a smaller and rather ridiculous example. I feel free to kiss cats. Until recently it never occurred to me that I would want to, though my daughters have been doing it all their lives. But my elder daughter is now 22, and in London. Of course, I get to look after her cat while she is gone. He's a big, handsome farm cat named Petrushka, very unsentimental, though used from kitten-hood to being kissed on the top of the head by Elizabeth. I've   12 gotten very fond of him (he's the adventurous kind of cat who likes to climb hills with you), and one night I simply felt like kissing him on the top of the head, and did. Why did no one tell me sooner how silky cat fur is?

Then there's my relation to cars. I am completely unembarrassed 13 by my inability to diagnose even minor problems in whatever object I happen to be driving, and don't have to make some insider's remark to mechanics to try to establish that I, too, am a "Man With His Machine."

The same ease extends to household maintenance. I do it, of 14 course. Service people are expensive. But for the last decade my house has functioned better than it used to because I've had the aid of a volume called "Home Repairs Any Woman Can Do," which is pitched just right for people at my technical level. As a youth, I'd as soon have touched such a book as I would have become a transvestite. Even though common sense says there is really nothing sexual whatsoever about fixing sinks.

Or take public emotion. All my life I have easily been moved by 15 certain kinds of voices. The actress Siobhan McKenna's, to take a notable case. Give her an emotional scene in a play, and within 10 words my eyes are full of tears. In boyhood, my great dread was that someone might notice. I struggled manfully, you might say, to suppress this weakness. Now, of course, I don't see it as a weakness at all, but as a kind of fulfillment. I even suspect that the true he-men feel the same way, or one kind of them does, at least, and it's only the poor imitators who have to struggle to repress themselves.

Let me come back to the inkblots, with their assumption that 16 masculine equates with machinery and science, and feminine with art and nature. I have no idea whether the right pronoun for God is He, She, or It. But this I'm pretty sure of. If God could somehow be induced to take that test, God would not come out macho, and not feminismo, either, but right in the middle. Fellow androgynes, it's a nice thought.

MICHAEL NORMAN

Standing His Ground

Michael Norman (1947–   ), an ex-Marine and a veteran of the Vietnam War, has been on the metropolitan staff of the *New*

York Times and has done considerable free-lance writing, much of it published in the *New York Times Magazine*. He has also worked as a reporter-producer for public television and is the coauthor (with Beth Scott) of *Haunted Wisconsin* (1980) and *Haunted Heartland* (1985), collections of spooky tales from the Midwest. *These Good Men* (1990), his book about the comradeship of soldiers, grows directly from his experience in Vietnam. "Standing His Ground" appeared in the "About Men" column of the *New York Times Magazine* on April 4, 1984.

I have bruised a knuckle and bloodied another man's nose, but I   1
am not, by most measures, a fighter. The last time I broke the peace
was more than a decade ago in a small restaurant on the west slope
of the Rocky Mountains in Colorado. My stepfather had encountered an old nemesis. Words were exchanged and the distance
between the two narrowed. I stepped in to play the peacemaker
and ended up throwing the first punch. For the record, my target, a
towering 230-pound horseman, easily absorbed the blow and then
dispatched the gnat in front of him.

The years since have been filled with discretion—I preach it,   2
embrace it and hide behind it. I am now the careful watchman who
keeps his eye on the red line and reroutes pressure before it has a
chance to blow. Sometimes, I backslide and turn a domestic misde-
meanor into a capital case or toss the cat out of the house without
bothering to see where he lands. But I do not punch holes in the
plaster or call my antagonists to the woodshed. The Furies may
gather, but the storm always stays safely out to sea. And yet, lately,
I have been struggling with this forced equanimity. The messenger
of reason, the advocate of accord, once again has the urge to throw
the first punch—in spirit at least.

All of this began rather quietly, a deep stirring that would come   3
and go and never take form, an old instinct, perhaps trying to
reassert itself. I was angry, restless, combative, but I could not say
why. It was a mystery of sorts. I was what I was expected to be, the
very model of a modern man, a partner instead of a husband, a
proponent of peace over action, thin-skinned rather than thick, a
willow instead of a stone. And yet there was something about this
posture that did not fit my frame. Then, an acquaintance, a gentle
man who spent his Peace Corps days among the villagers of Nepal,
suddenly acted out of character. He got into an argument with a
local brute in a neighborhood tavern and instead of walking away
from trouble, stood his ground. It was, he said, a senseless confrontation, but he had no regrets, and it made me think of Joey.

Joey, the bully of the sixth grade, used to roam the hallways   4
picking victims at random and slugging them on the arm. When he

rounded a corner, we scattered or practiced a crude form of mysticism and tried to think ourselves invisible in the face of the beast. Since I was slow and an inept mystic, my mother kept on hand an adequate supply of Ben Gay to ease the bruises and swelling.

One day, a boy named Tony told the marauder that he had had   5
enough and an epic duel was scheduled in the playground after school. Tony had been taking boxing lessons on the sly. He had developed a stinging left jab and when the appointed hour arrived, he delivered it in the name of every bruised shoulder in the school.

The meek pack of which Tony was once a part took courage   6
from his example and several weeks later when a boy at my bus stop sent me sprawling, I returned the favor.

There were only a few challenges after that. On the way up, a   7
Joey would occasionally round the corner. But in the circles I traveled, he was the exception rather than the rule. In the Marine Corps in Vietnam, we were consumed by a much larger kind of warfare. In college, faculty infighting and bullying aside, violence was considered anti-intellectual. And in the newsrooms where I have practiced my trade, reporters generally have been satisfied with pounding a keyboard instead of their editors.

And then came Colorado and the battle of the west slope. For   8
years, I was embarrassed by the affair. I could have walked away and dragged my stepfather with me. As it was, we almost ended up in jail. I had provoked a common brawl, a pointless, self-destructive exercise. The rationalist had committed the most irrational of acts. It was not a matter of family or honor, hollow excuses. I had simply succumbed to instinct, and I deeply regretted it. But not any longer. Now I see virtue in that vulgar display of macho. It disqualifies me from the most popular male club—the brotherhood of nurturers, fraternity sensitivus.

From analyst's couch to tavern booth, their message is the same: 9
The male animus is out of fashion. The man of the hour is supposed to be gentle, thoughtful, endearing and compassionate, a wife to his woman, a mother to his son, an androgynous figure with the self-knowledge of a hermaphrodite. He takes his lumps on the psyche, not the chin, and bleeds with emotion. Yes, in the morning, he still puts on a three-piece suit, but his foulard, the finishing touch, is a crying towel.

He is so ridden with guilt, so pained about the sexist sins of his   10
kind, he bites at his own flanks. Not only does he say that he dislikes being a man, but broadly proclaims that the whole idea of manhood in America is pitiful.

He wants to free himself from the social conditioning of the past,   11
to cast off the yoke of traditional male roles and rise above the

banality of rituals learned at boot camp or on the practice field. If science could provide it, he would swallow an antidote of testosterone, something to stop all this antediluvian thumping and bashing.

And he has gone too far. Yes, the male code needs reform. Our 12 rules and our proscriptions have trapped us in a kind of perpetual adolescence. Why else would a full-grown rationalist think he could get even with Joey by taking a poke at another bully 25 years later in a bar in Colorado? No doubt there is something pitiful about that.

But the fashion for reform, the drive to emasculate macho, has 13 produced a kind of numbing androgyny and has so blurred the lines of gender that I often find myself wanting to emulate some of the women I know—bold, aggressive, vigorous role models.

It sometimes seems that the only exclusively male trait left is the 14 impulse to throw a punch, the last male watermark, so to speak, that is clear and readable. Perhaps that is why the former Peace Corps volunteer jumped into a brawl and why I suspect that the new man—the model of sensitivity, the nurturer—goes quietly through the day with a clenched fist behind his back.

DAVE BARRY

Lost in the Kitchen

Dave Barry (1947–   ) is a nationally syndicated columnist for *The Miami Herald* and the 1988 winner of the Pulitzer Prize for Commentary. After taking his B.A. in English from Haverford College, Barry worked as a small-town newspaper reporter in Pennsylvania, then as a consultant of effective writing for various businesses. In 1983 humor became his full-time job. Besides his weekly column, he is the author of nine books, including *Taming the Screw: Several Million Homeowners' Problems* (1983), *Babies and Other Hazards of Sex* (1984), *Stay Fit Until You're Dead* (1985), and *Claw Your Way to the Top* (1987). "Lost in the Kitchen" appeared in *The Miami Herald* and other newspapers in May 1986.

Men are still basically scum when it comes to helping out in the 1 kitchen. This is one of two insights I had last Thanksgiving, the other one being that Thanksgiving night must be the slowest night of the year in terms of human sexual activity. Nobody wants to engage in human sexual activity with somebody who smells vaguely like yams and is covered with a thin layer of turkey grease, which describes pretty much everybody in the United States on Thanksgiving except the Detroit Lions, who traditionally play football that day and would therefore be too tired.

But that, as far as I can tell, is not my point. My point is that despite all that has been said in the past 20 years or so about sexual equality, most men make themselves as useful around the kitchen as ill-trained Labrador retrievers. This is not just my opinion: It is a scientific finding based on an exhaustive study of what happened last Thanksgiving when my family had dinner at the home of friends named Arlene and Gene. 2

Picture a typical Thanksgiving scene: On the floor, three small children and a dog who long ago had her brain eaten by fleas are running as fast as they can directly into things, trying to injure themselves. On the television, the Detroit Lions are doing pretty much the same thing. 3

In the kitchen, Arlene, a prosecuting attorney responsible for a large staff, is doing something with those repulsive organs that are placed in little surprise packets inside turkeys, apparently as a joke. Surrounding Arlene are thousands of steaming cooking containers. I would no more enter that kitchen than I would attempt to park a nuclear aircraft carrier, but my wife, who runs her own business, glides in very casually and picks up EXACTLY the right kitchen implement and starts doing EXACTLY the right thing without receiving any instructions whatsoever. She quickly becomes enshrouded in steam. 4

So Gene and I, feeling like the scum we are, finally bumble over and ask what we can do to help, and from behind the steam comes Arlene's patient voice asking us to please keep an eye on the children. Which we try to do. 5

But there is a famous law of physics that goes: "You cannot watch small children and the Detroit Lions at the same time, and let's face it, the Detroit Lions are more interesting." So we would start out watching the children, and then one of us would sneak a peek at the TV and say, "Hey! Look at this tackle!" And then we'd have to watch for a while to see the replay and find out whether the tackled person was dead or just permanently disabled. By then the children would have succeeded in injuring themselves or the dog, and this voice from behind the kitchen steam would call, VERY patiently, "Gene, PLEASE watch the children." 6

I realize this is awful. I realize this sounds just like Ozzie and Harriet. I also realize that there are some males out there, with 7 hyphenated last names, who have advanced much farther than Gene and I have, who are not afraid to stay home full time and get coated with baby vomit while their wives work as test pilots, and who go into the kitchen on a daily basis to prepare food for other people, as opposed to going in there to get a beer and maybe some peanut butter on a spoon. But I think Gene and I are fairly typical. I think most males rarely prepare food for others, and when they do, they have their one specialty dish (spaghetti, in my case) that they prepare maybe twice a year in a very elaborate production, for which they expect to be praised as if they had developed, right there in the kitchen, a cure for heart disease.

In defense of men, let me say this: Women do not make it easy to   8
learn. Let's say a woman is in the kitchen, working away after having been at her job all day, and the man, feeling guilty, finally shuffles in and offers to help. So the woman says something like: "Well, you can cut up the turnips." Now to the WOMAN, who had all this sexist Home Economics training back in the pre-feminism era, this is a very simple instruction. It is the absolute simplest thing she can think of.

I asked my wife to read this and tell me what she thought. This is   9
what she said: She said before Women's Liberation, men took care of the cars and women took care of the kitchen, whereas now that we have Women's Liberation, men no longer feel obligated to take care of the cars. This seemed pretty accurate to me, so I thought I'd just tack it on to the end here, while she makes waffles.

PERRI KLASS

Are Women Better Doctors?

Perri Klass (1958–   ) graduated from Harvard Medical School in 1986, the year after her novel *Recombinations* was published. Throughout her years as a medical student and resident, Klass has contributed articles and reviews to the *New York Times*. She has also published a collection of short stories, *I Am Having an Adventure* (1986), and *A Not Entirely Benign Procedure* (1987), the story of her four years as a medical student. "Are Women Better Doctors?" appeared in the *New York Times Magazine* on April 10, 1988, and created a controversy reflected in the letters to the editor that appeared on May 8.

There was a conundrum that used to turn up now and then, 1
when I was in high school, designed to test your level of consciousness. A father and son go fishing, and on the way home they're in
an auto accident. The father is killed instantly. The boy is rushed to
the hospital, where the surgeon takes one look at him and screams,
"Oh, my God, it's my son!" What is the relationship between the
surgeon and the child?

Obviously, the surgeon is the child's mother; surely no one had 2
to think twice about that. Well, 15 years ago, lots of people would
ponder the puzzle, making up complex stepfather/grandfather link-
ages, trying to explain how a child could have no father, yet still
have a parent who was a doctor.

In 1969, 9 percent of the first-year medical students in America 3
were women; in 1987, it was 37 percent. In 1970, women accounted for 8 percent of all the physicians in America and 11
percent of all residents. In 1985, they made up 15 percent of all
physicians and 26 percent of all residents.

I did not go to medical school during the pioneering age. When I 4
started at Harvard Medical School, in 1982, 53 of the 165 students
in my class were women. Moreover, I chose to go into pediatrics,
the medical specialty with the highest percentage of female residents—50 percent nationwide. I have never had the experience of
being the only woman in the lecture hall, the only female resident
in the hospital. During my own medical training, so far at least, I
have not had reason to feel like a scholarship student from an alien
tribe.

When I set out to write about women in medicine, I wanted to 5
bypass the tone of patronizing surprise that so often attends
women in male-dominated professions ("She uses a scalpel! She
has curly blond hair and a white coat all covered with blood!"). I
also wanted to avoid some of the classic topics that apply a kind of
prurience to the situation of the female doctor. (So what's it like
when you have to do a physical exam on a man?) With the increase in women doctors, it's time to look more specifically at what
kinds of doctors we are choosing to be, both in terms of specialty
and in terms of style.

According to the Association of American Medical Colleges, 6
men and women applying to medical school have comparable acceptance rates. Of applicants for the fall of 1987, 61 percent of the
men and 60 percent of the women were accepted by at least one
school. After medical school, however, men and women follow
somewhat different paths. According to statistics compiled for
1986, 50 percent of pediatric residents were women, only 12 per-

cent of surgical residents were women, and just 1.4 percent of
vascular surgery residents were women. Women were heavily concentrated in psychiatry (40 percent of the residents were women),
and in dermatology (44 percent), preventive medicine (36 percent), pathology (38 percent), and obstetrics and gynecology (45
percent). The frontier for women in medicine, then, is really not in
medical school, but in certain of the medical specialties, where they
are almost as rare as ever. Women are choosing some of the fields
that provide regular working hours and no night call (dermatology,
pathology), but ob-gyn and pediatrics can both require long hours
and night duty. In surgery, where the disparity between male and
female doctors is greatest, part of the problem for women may be
the need to delay starting a family for five to seven years of infa-
mously arduous training.

It seems to be pretty well agreed that back when there were   7
fewer women in medicine, medical school and residency were often fraught with unpleasantness and loneliness. Many women
have written about the sexual innuendoes and the sense of exclusion. On the other hand, the more recent medical school graduates
I interviewed could remember a few rotten professors and bad
moments, but none felt she had been the victim of any real discrimination.

I spoke with male and female colleagues, teachers and friends of   8
friends in the vast and complex Boston teaching-hospital system. I
also spent time in Kansas City and spoke to doctors in other parts of
the country. Boston is hardly a typical place to learn or practice
medicine. Affectionately and not-so-affectionately referred to as
"Mecca," Boston has a reputation as the most heavily academic
city for medicine in the country, possibly the world. The female
experience in medicine there can never be considered typical.
Some will swear that women have it easy in Boston because the
medicine is dynamic, young, on the cutting edge, and others will
insist that nowhere is the old-boy network stronger.

Are women doctors different? With a few exceptions, I got ver-   9
sions of the same response from all the women doctors I interviewed, young or old, avowedly feminist or not. First you get the
disclaimer : I've known some wonderful male doctors, I've known
some awful female doctors, generalizations are impossible. (I make
that disclaimer myself; I've known wonderful, brilliant, sensitive
male doctors. Fellow residents. Teachers. My son's pediatrician.
Why, some of my best friends. . . .) And then, hesitantly, even
apologetically, or else frankly and with a smile, comes the generalization: Yes, women are different as doctors—they're better.

Kansas City announces proudly in the courtesy magazine found 10
in hotel rooms: "When Procter & Gamble wants to know if people
like its toothpaste, it turns to Kansas City. Market researchers call
Kansas City a 'typically American' market. . . ." In Kansas City, I
interviewed a wide range of female residents, doctors, academic
physicians, and specialists.

Linda L. Dorzab started medical school at the University of Mis- 11
souri, Kansas City, at the age of 33, after spending 11 years teaching grade school and working with emotionally disturbed children.
Last June, she finished her internal-medicine residency and began
a private practice as an internist affiliated with Menorah Medical
Center. For the first month or so, there were few patients, maybe
only one a day, but by February it was as high as nine a day. Dr.
Dorzab is proud to make a visitor welcome in her newly arranged
office, a welcoming, plant-filled place with a large mahogany desk
and, nearby, a small table designed for less-threatening doctor-
patient conversations. An ebullient, friendly, informal woman, Dr.
Dorzab says that ever since entering medical school, she had
dreamed of an office in which she could make her patients comfortable.

Given her experience with disturbed children, Dr. Dorzab had 12
originally considered going into psychiatry, "but they gave me a
stethoscope, and it was all so interesting." She was older than most
of the other students and had a comparatively weak science background, but the art of medicine, she thinks, came more easily to her
than to some of the younger students. Still, she had trouble performing on rounds, the high-pressure on-the-spot situations that
are often the traditional hazing occasions for medical students. "I
still have the same personality as when I was a teacher, I tend to
show my vulnerability—which is O.K. with my patients." She has
had to develop a more businesslike manner with colleagues.

I ask her about mentors. She names two women, saying of both 13
of them that "they maintained femininity and class, and always
looked confident." One is Dr. Marjorie S. Sirridge, an assistant
dean at Dr. Dorzab's alma mater, the University of Missouri at
Kansas City. Dr. Sirridge, who graduated from medical school in
1944—one of very few women in her class—insists she never felt
overt discrimination. Oh, sure, her college advisers told her she'd
never get to medical school, but that only made her more determined to go. "I was first in my class from grade one through high
school; that gives confidence."

Dr. Sirridge graduated from medical school first in her class, too. 14
But during residency, she got pregnant and was informed that

"pregnant residents were not acceptable." She dropped out of medicine for several years, then found her way back by working for no pay and no training credit. She went into private practice as a hematologist, pursued research on her own and eventually found her way into academic medicine.

Dr. Sirridge's office is decorated with pictures of her grandchildren, and a poster of Marie Curie. She is extremely cordial, but speaks with the authority of someone who is accustomed to giving her opinions publicly. It is clear that she feels protective about the medical students she watches over, and that she is proud of Dr. Dorzab, now striking out on her own. 15

Dr. Sirridge worries that female medical students don't pursue leadership roles as readily as their male colleagues. On the other hand, she thinks women do much better when it comes to human interaction. "For the women, relationships with patients are very important, a very positive thing," she says. "Many men also have this quality, but men in positions of power in medical education and government by and large do not." 16

The craving for female role models is very strong among women beginning medical school. (The numbers here are not so encouraging; in 1987, two American medical schools out of 127 had female deans, and 73 academic departments out of approximately 2,000 had female chairs.) Role models are important for a very basic reason: in the first year of medical school, you learn biochemistry, physiology, pathology, in traditional classroom settings. For the remaining two years, you serve a kind of apprenticeship in a hospital, consolidating that knowledge and absorbing institutional logic and medical routine. It is during this latter period that you also learn how to be a doctor. 17

Many of the traditional techniques used by male doctors don't work as well for women. Most obviously, we have more trouble assuming the mantle of all-knowing, paternal medical authority. As a result, many female doctors have found themselves searching for new ways to interact with patients, with nurses, and with fellow doctors. And it isn't just vague inspiration we're talking about here, it's who you're emulating as you prepare to walk into that room to talk to a couple about their dying baby. Whose example do you follow in acknowledging their grief and the failure of medicine to help, while retaining the authority you need as a doctor? And how much authority do you need as a doctor, anyway? 18

Dr. Nevada H. Mitchell practices internal medicine, with a subspecialty in geriatrics. She was born in Kansas City, went to Vassar, then came home, married, and started teaching. She had thought about medical school, but didn't feel she had what it would take. 19

She decided to become a doctor after reading in the Vassar alumni magazine about classmates who had gone to medical school. Dr. Mitchell has no doubt at all about the difference between male and female doctors: "There's a world of difference. The women I come into contact with are less aggressive, more likely to have one-on-one relationships with patients, less likely to go for a high volume of patients, but also less likely to be out here in private practice." Dr. Mitchell returns several times to the issue of being "out here," explaining that many women take jobs with health maintenance organizations, or HMO's, for the security of a regular salary and the convenience of limited working hours. "You need a certain aggressiveness to choose private practice," she says, with some satisfaction.

Dr. Mitchell cannot think of a female doctor she wanted to be 20
like—"I didn't have that many examples. I developed my own style and image." But she tells me I ought to talk to a female gynecologic surgeon who operated on her. She says she felt that in earlier discussions with a male doctor, he had placed less emphasis on maintaining the option of future pregnancy. Dr. Mitchell, who is 40 and has a 16-year-old daughter, wanted to keep her options open. She felt that Dr. Marilyn R. Richardson, the surgeon she eventually chose, had taken her wishes more seriously.

Ironically, Dr. Richardson, a 39-year-old obstetrician-gynecolo- 21
gist specializing in reproductive endocrinology, thinks that's nonsense. She is highly professional, authoritative, and decided in her opinions. Patients who come looking for a female gynecologist, she says, bring along "a misconception that has evolved with consumer awareness, an erroneous belief that women doctors are more compassionate, more understanding."

When I repeat Dr. Mitchell's account of her surgery, Dr. Richard- 22
son says she doubts that being female has anything to do with her mode of doctoring. "It was a male mentor who taught me sensitivity toward the preservation of fertility," she says. She describes her style as a composite of this mentor and of her father, also in ob-gyn—and of techniques she developed on her own.

I mention that one of the places I always feel a very sharp differ- 23
ence between male and female doctors is in the operating room. Yes, she agrees, the way that women run an operating room is different: "Men are often arbitrary, demanding, and disrespectful, and the level of efficiency suffers. Women don't usually command quite as fiercely . . . you get camaraderie with the other staff members."

Dr. Susan Love agrees. One of the first female surgical residents 24
at a major Boston teaching hospital, Dr. Love, 40, finished her

training in 1980. She went into private practice in general surgery, though she initially had trouble getting a position on the staff of the hospital where she had just been chief surgical resident.

In her practice, Dr. Love found she was encountering many   25
women with breast disease who preferred to see a woman doctor, and eventually she decided to specialize in the field. She now has a partner—another woman surgeon—and they are looking for a third surgeon. For an appointment with Dr. Love in a nonemergency situation, the wait is now five months.

Dr. Love says she had to suppress many of her basic values in   26
order to get through her surgical residency: "Most women have problems, unless they can block out their previous socialization. Surgeons don't really like having women, and don't make it comfortable for them. Things that women like—talking to patients—aren't important. It's how many operations you've done, how many hours you've been up, how many notches on your belt. If you get through your five or six years of training, you can regain your values, but it's a real 'if.' Most men never get them back."

She runs an operating room by "treating the nurses like intelli-   27
gent people, talking to them, teaching them. I'm not the big ruler." Are men always so different? "Surgery is a lot of ritual and a little science," she says. "The boys need high mass, incense, and altarboys. They need more boosting up. The women are much lower church."

Dr. Love offers an example of something she does differently,   28
something no one taught her: before a patient is put to sleep, she makes it a practice to hold that person's hand. "I'm usually the only person in the room they really know, and it's the scariest time," she says. "The boys scrub, then come in when the patient's asleep. I got razzed for it, but they're used to it now."

Female doctors behave differently with their patients than male   29
doctors, Dr. Love says: "I spend more time in empathy, talking, explaining, teaching, and it's a much more equal power relationship." She tells the story of a recent patient, an 84-year-old woman with breast cancer who was asked by a male surgeon,"Are you vain?" Embarrassed, the woman said she wasn't. The surgeon advised her, in that case, to have a mastectomy rather than a more limited procedure. "But then her niece pointed out, 'You bought a new bra to come to the doctor, and you combed your hair over your hearing aid.' " The doctor had simply assumed that an elderly woman would have no desire to preserve her breast.

Dr. Love's anecdotes are often sharp. She describes a male sur-   30
geon who explained to a patient that a particular implant used in breast reconstruction felt just like a normal breast. He meant, of

course, that to someone *touching* the breast, the texture would be close to natural, not that the woman would have normal feeling in the implant.

I heard over and over from women doctors that women are   31 better at talking to people and better at listening. Dr. Carol B. Lindsley, a pediatric rheumatologist at the University of Kansas Medical Center, says the female medical students are "more sensitive to patient and family needs, more patient, pay more attention to detail." Dr. Dorzab says, "My patients say women listen better and are better at acknowledging it when something is bothering the patient." Some doctors said female patients were particularly grateful for this extra consideration; others felt that male patients welcomed it also.

But Dr. Deborah A. Stanford, a resident in internal medicine at   32 the University of Alabama in Birmingham, sees no difference between the male and female interns she supervises: "Capabilities, compassion, endurance—no difference."

Dr. John J. Skillman, chief of vascular surgery and director of the   33 surgical-residency program at Beth Israel Hospital in Boston, says, "We're trying to train the absolutely best people we can." He acknowledges that surgery remains a male-dominated specialty, with women facing "unofficial prejudice," but feels that the residency program he supervises makes women welcome: "We expect women, like all residents, to develop their teaching skills and their command of the team—I don't see that there's much difference there."

Dr. Michelle Harrison, who wrote "A Woman in Residence," in   34 1982, about her experiences during an ob-gyn residency, comments: "As outsiders, we experience ourselves as different, but are we all that different in how we see patients? I don't see any major revolution."

Certainly, there are differences in the way male and female doc-   35 tors approach relationships at work, and the increase of women doctors has shaken up traditional habits. Though the notion that nurses resent female doctors is much exaggerated, women doctors are, of course, often mistaken for nurses; many patients assume that a woman with a stethoscope is by definition a nurse. Some women doctors mind this, others take it in stride. "You have to have a sense of humor," says Dr. Lois J. McKinley, an internist in Kansas City. "I took care of one patient for weeks, and when he was getting ready to leave, he was still saying, 'Oh nurse, would you prop up my pillows?' Nursing people are good people; being mistaken for a nurse is not the worst thing that could happen."

Dr. Mitchell agrees: "If I walk into a room and someone asks me   36 for a bedpan, I just go ahead and put 'em on it!'' She is laughing. "But when they call my office and ask, 'Dr. Mitchell—when will he be in?' I tell them, '*He* will never be in!''

It is generally assumed among women doctors that we have to   37 be more polite and more careful with nurses than our male colleagues do; a fairer way of putting this would probably be that nurses have had to put up with a lot of rudeness from doctors over the years, and that though they make some of the traditional female allowances for traditional male patterns of behavior, they are unwilling to accept these same patterns from other women. Or, as Dr. Richardson says, "When you make a big mess in the operating room, there's something different in your mind when you walk out and leave it for another woman to clean up.''

What would be taken as normal behavior in men (especially   38 surgeons, who maintain the most traditional doctor-nurse power structure) is considered aggressive and obnoxious in women. Dr. Lore Nelson, who is to become chief resident in pediatrics at the University of Kansas Medical Center later this year, complains, half-seriously, "A male surgeon can walk in to do some procedure and everything will be all ready, but if I go to draw blood, nothing's set up for me, and I have to go ask a nurse, 'Can you please help me?' ''

Shaking up the patterns doesn't appear to be an entirely bad   39 thing. The traditional doctor-nurse relationship, like the traditional male-female relationship it parodied, left a lot to be desired. Surely, a good doctor is part caretaker, and surely a good nurse's observations should be a part of any decisions being made. I suspect the more polite, more politic behavior demanded of female doctors may be closer to good manners, but also to good medicine, than the supposed norm.

A study of medical school faculty members with M.D.'s who   40 were given their first appointments in 1976 found that by 1987 17 percent of the men were tenured, compared with 12 percent of the women. Twelve percent of the men had attained the rank of full professor, compared with 3 percent of the women. Either women are encountering prejudice and resistance as they try to make their way in the world of academic medicine and research, or, as is often suggested, they are diluting their ambition, going more slowly— usually in order to give time to family.

Dr. Harrison, the former ob-gyn resident and now a family phy-   41 sician and psychiatrist (she specializes in the treatment of premenstrual syndrome), thinks there are different standards for men and women. "Personality factors enter into the promotion of women,'' she says, "while arrogant and obnoxious men are promoted without that being an issue." But she also thinks that women "have tremendous problems around issues of power." And, she adds, "There's the problem of how to combine a family with a medical career, which tends to relegate women to salaried positions with less possibility for advancement."

But women doctors are in demand in some specialties. Dr. Stanley E. Sagov, who practices family medicine in Cambridge, Mass., is specifically interested in finding a female associate. He is disturbed by the imbalance of a practice in which the doctors are male and the support personnel are female. Further, he says, "It's a marketing issue. People, especially ob-gyn patients, are looking for female providers." 42

It is very difficult to pin down whether there are salary discrepancies between male and female doctors. According to the American Medical Association's 1985–86 data, women doctors earn 62 cents for every dollar earned by male doctors—but this does not take into account the differential distribution in higher- and lower-paying specialties or the fact that more women are recent graduates. 43

Will the remaining all-male fields ever integrate? Janet Bickel, senior staff associate and director for women's studies at the Association of American Medical Colleges, wonders whether we will end up with a medical establishment in which certain lower-paid, less prestigious jobs will be filled largely by women. 44

I had my baby in my second year of medical school. It was not an extremely common thing to do, but neither was it unheard of. Certainly, I didn't feel any pressure to drop out, to take time off, to get my belly out of sight. I didn't feel it would be held against me that I had a baby along the way. 45

Several women in my residency program are pregnant. On the other hand, that's pediatrics again, a field with lots of women, in which even the biggest wheels have to be committed to the idea that babies are important. Most residents work nights and come home rarely and in poor condition. Few residency programs provide coverage in case of sickness; there's a macho ideology that gives points for working when you're sick. Taking a day off to stay home with a sick child is really against the rules and ends up loading more work on your already overworked fellow residents, which in turn creates animosity toward people with children. 46

Nevada Mitchell started medical school when her daughter was 3, and residency when she was 7. A single mother, she chose her residency program because she could live in the same building as 47 her brother and sister-in-law. She requested Friday night call because she wouldn't have to take her daughter to school the next day. When her daughter got sick and she decided to stay home for a day, the attending physician commented, "Interns don't stay home unless they're hospitalized or dead."

These difficulties are not, of course, unique to women. Although 48 men are somewhat more likely to have spouses who delay their own careers, I have heard complaints about male colleagues who are too eager to get home to their families. The fact is that, at least for now, certain intensities of career are essentially incompatible with any kind of parenthood. You don't have very much to do with your child if your ideal is to spend every waking moment in the hospital, whether you are the father or mother. The influx of women into medicine, we can hope, will help us to design medical careers that will enable all doctors to lead more integrated lives.

Women are an increasing presence in American medicine, and 49 with that change comes a certain amount of freedom. Many of the women doctors I talked to feel strongly that they have not simply adopted the mannerisms and techniques of the male prototype. If this is more than just a convenient prejudice, then the effect of women on the medical profession may be both interesting and profound in the years to come.

Recently, I told my 4-year-old son he was due for his annual 50 checkup with his pediatrician. He looked distinctly nervous (rumors about shots had obviously been making their way around the day-care center), and asked me anxiously, "Is she a nice doctor?" I thought about the doctors my son knows best—me and my close friends, most of them female. I picked my words carefully. It was clearly one of those critical moments requiring all a mother's wisdom and tact. "Benjamin, I have to tell you somthing," I said. "Boys can be doctors too, if they want to. If they go to school and learn how, boys can be very good doctors, really."

LETTERS OF RESPONSE

Since our daughter Victoria was born in March 1987, with major heart defects, we have had ample opportunity to observe both male and female doctors ("Are Women Better Doctors?" by Perri Klass, April 10). We were overwhelmingly impressed by the quality of her medical care—by women and men doctors. However, we were struck by the differences in attitudes of male and female doctors at her hospital of primary care.

After having undergone numerous tests last summer, she arrived for open-heart surgery in January. But because of a respiratory infection, she was not admitted then. The admitting anesthesiologist, the woman responsible for rejecting the admission, took at least a half hour to speak with us, to review her reasons for not admitting Victoria and to give suggestions for rescheduling her admission.

Victoria was admitted for surgery one month later, in February, and again had a female anesthesiologist. The morning of her operation, that doctor took the time to play with Victoria for several minutes, to insure that our baby was happy being borne off by someone who was, therefore, not entirely a stranger. That was our last memory of her, being carried, happy, down a hall, as she did not survive the surgery.

In the midst of our subsequent sorrow, we have no quarrel with the quality of care Victoria received from medical personnel, male and female. All of her care-givers were superb. However, it was the women who made her, and us, feel a human part of the entire process.

Deborah Curtis Donovan
Portland, Me.

Perri Klass asks if women are better doctors. The question is sexist and irrelevant. A female physician is no less able to perform open-heart surgery than a male doctor is able to tell patients, caringly, that they have cancer. Sensitivity, empathy, and sincerity are not female qualities; they are human ones. "Better" doctors possess them, and they come in all colors and sexes.

The reasons for the schism in patient-physician relations are many. Contemporary medical practice emphasizes dependence on high technology and laboratory medicine over the "hands-on" approach to patients. Medical schools' admissions departments look for high grades and test scores over personal qualities in their applicants. A litigious society puts doctors on the defensive. In order to make a living, doctors rarely find adequate time to talk with their patients.

David M. Lans, D.O.
New York, N.Y.

Perri Klass mentions the scarcity of women in leadership positions in medicine. Working at a university has given me the opportunity to observe this phenomenon, and to think about it.

One reason for the small number of women in leadership positions is, of course, that women have entered medicine in significant numbers only recently, and thus have not yet had a chance to work their way to the top. However, other forces have conspired to keep these numbers low. Some residual prejudice against giving women power still exists, but, more importantly, most women physicians I know are not as unambivalent in seeking power as men are, and have not acquired the habit of using power comfortably. Effective use of power to organize the work of others is an almost athletic skill that requires first a decision on whether the situation calls for maximum force or optimal control. Knowing how much force to use requires practice, from a fairly young age, to develop skill and the expectation of success. I have watched accomplished women physicians err in each direction.

In my generation, it was still a major achievement for a woman to become a doctor, and fewer of us aspired to become the leaders in the field. Younger women have acquired the expectation of authority earlier in their lives and wasted less energy proving their right to be in medicine. I think they have a better shot at using power gracefully, and I consider this progress.

Ruth Kahan Kaminer, M.D.
White Plains

As a medical student in Boston, soon to begin a residency in obstetrics and gynecology, I read Perri Klass's article with interest.

I'm not sure, however, that Dr. Klass proves her central thesis—that women make better doctors. Each patient has his own image of the ideal physician. It would be difficult to be the best for everyone. The correct conclusion, I think, is that good *people* make better doctors. Let us hope that medical schools and teaching hospitals continue to develop training programs that allow young physicians, male and female, to grow as persons as well as clinicians.

Jeff Ecker
(Harvard Medical School, Class of '88)
Brookline, Mass.

LEONARD L. RISKIN

Unsportsmanlike Conduct

Leonard L. Riskin (1942–   ) is a law professor at the University of Missouri, where he trains lawyers and others in techniques for resolving conflicts without doing legal battle. He is the co-author of *Dispute Resolution and Lawyers* (1987) and has lately begun writing for the sheer pleasure of it. "Unsportsmanlike Conduct" appeared in the "About Men" column of the *New York Times Magazine* on Super Bowl Sunday, January 22, 1989.

As our 9-year-old son stretched to turn off the television during the halftime show of the football game, my wife stopped him. "That's the only part Daddy likes," she said. We all laughed at the role turnabout in our household: My wife, an otherwise appealing woman, loves to watch football on television, and I do not. But the laughter covered a malady that has afflicted me since age 17. For almost 30 years, I have not followed sports, and I have not tried very hard to hide it.

I never read the sports pages. I am not sure which cities have major league baseball teams, or which teams are in which divisions. I could not tell you who was in the World Series in 1984, or even 1987. By noon tomorrow, I probably will have forgotten who played in today's Super Bowl. And I do not care. Except for one problem: This personality distortion has truncated my relations with men.

I was quite normal as a boy, sportswise, an avid fan, an adequate athlete. I knew, without even trying, the batting average of every major leaguer. Some of the early Milwaukee Braves lived nearby; I saw Del Crandall and Billy Bruton and Hank Aaron working in their front yards. To me they glittered, on and off the field.

I knew I would join them, someday. Maybe I could not be a pro in one of the major sports; competition was too keen. But there were so many sports, probably some I had not yet heard about. Surely I could excel in one. But except for winning the Steuben Junior High School doubles Ping-Pong tournament, I never did.

This dreadful reality did not sink in until I was almost out of high school. And gradually I began to watch sports less; something else —reading, studying, seeing a movie, almost anything—was always more important, more interesting. Why should I care whether a team from Cleveland, with players drawn from across the country, beat a team from Pittsburgh—similarly constituted—especially when both teams might be owned by people who live in Texas.

To me, it was all hype, designed to make money for the owners 6 by exploiting the athletes and lending a false sense of meaning and community to people whose lives were otherwise lacking. (Final proof came when the Braves moved to Atlanta in 1965.) I felt bored during games, untouched by the drama and passion. And when I occasionally allowed myself to become involved, to care, my team always seemed to lose.

This has not been an easy path. By being myself, I have re- 7 peatedly disappointed other men. Monday and Tuesday mornings in a Washington office building held some of the worse moments for me. "What did you think of Calvin Hill?" a colleague would ask. Without reflection, I would not know the sport of the season, and even with reflection, and though he was the star running back of the Washington Redskins at the time, I did not know who Calvin Hill was or what he did. I had let my colleague down. He had considered me a regular guy, and I was not.

I often disappointed fellow passengers on airplanes who would 8 want to talk about prominent local athletes or coaches. I smiled and sighed; sometimes I nodded knowingly; but other times I admitted "I don't follow sports," a quick way to end the conversation and send my companion back to the in-flight magazine.

The most painful evening came as part of a job interview, when 9 my hosts took my wife, Casey, and me to a professional basketball game. We both studied for it. Even under these conditions, I could not make myself concentrate on the game, and Casey had to protect me by joining vigorously in the game-time kibitzing. My hosts' assumption that I was normal was so powerful that I got the job. Not until after I was tenured did I confess.

I will never forget the puzzled and hurt look on my father's face 10 on one of my visits home in the early 1970s. He mentioned the Milwaukee Brewers, and I asked whether the minor-league team of my early childhood had returned. (I had no idea that the Brewers were a major-league team that had moved to Milwaukee several years earlier after a short incarnation as the Seattle Pilots.) He first asked if I was kidding and then wondered aloud, with only a hint of a smile, "Where did I go wrong?" He began to worry about how I would survive in the world.

And not without cause. Although my condition has never inter- 11 fered with close friendships, I often feel excluded, odd, during the casual conversations about sports that seem to provide a kind of glue to a group of men, or—like the weather—at least something to talk about until you could get to more important matters. For men, talking sports affirms not only their masculinity, but also their equality; no one assumes the C.E.O. is necessarily a better Monday morning quarterback than the janitor. I missed out on this kind of connection, and often I could not find a substitute.

Sometimes I see hope. I occasionally tell another man about my attitude and he will claim to feel the same way. Almost always my hopes are dashed. Later he will qualify his detachment: He doesn't watch *professional* football or he doesn't go to *college* basketball games because the crowd is obnoxious—but he does listen on the radio. Worse, yet, I feel betrayed when I hear him talking sports with other men. 12

In the last few years, things have started to change for me for two reasons. First, we moved to a small college town, so I see the players and coaches on the street. Now I see how sports can ennoble and how the team's record affects the lives, spirits and finances of so many members of this community. I see how sports matter. 13

Second, and much more important, was that our son, Andrew, developed a passionate interest in sports several years ago. Entering the world of sports with him has given me as much joy as anything in my family life. Watching him play tennis or soccer, taking him to a basketball game, lying on the floor watching Monday Night Football—each of these events we enjoy together, not only as father and son, but also as two men. Together we can admire the athletes' grace, courage and skill. Andrew dreams of playing professional tennis, or baseball, or soccer, and I am glad. 14

So although I now pay some attention to the University of Missouri teams, you could not call me a sports fan. I still find most football games insufferably boring and some of the fans unforgivably nasty, and I do not know the name of that new quarterback. But I have reaped some additional benefits from my new knowledge. I initiate, and enjoy, conversations about the games with men I do not know—in the gas station, the liquor store, the university corridors. I often can respond now when my colleagues ask me questions. But I still feel like a bit of a fraud; I do not *really* care, and I think if they understood me, they would comprehend that. Yet at another level, I realize that they do not want to know, because they want to assume I am normal, just like them. 15

While I typed this, the peace in my study was shattered by Andrew and Casey's screams. The Chicago Bears must have scored a touchdown. I think they were playing the Colts. Yes, the Baltimore Colts. 16

JOHN STEINBECK

The Chrysanthemums

John (Ernst) Steinbeck (1902–1968) was born in the Salinas
Valley of California, the setting for many of his novels and stories.
Rugged and athletic in his youth, Steinbeck spent the summers of
his high school years working as a hired hand on the Valley
ranches. He attended Stanford University for five years but did
not take a degree and for the next several years worked as a
laborer and occasionally as a reporter. He published the first of
his eighteen novels in 1929. His most enduring works—those
which earned him the Nobel Prize in 1962—were written during
the Great Depression: *Tortilla Flat* (1935), *In Dubious Battle*
(1936), *Of Mice and Men* (1937), *The Long Valley* (1938), and his
Pulitzer Prize–winner *The Grapes of Wrath* (1939). Steinbeck's
work during this period repeatedly protests the oppression of
migrant laborers and small farmers who have been pushed off
their land by commercial interests. His view of the human condition has been called optimistic because his characters embrace
life so eagerly, but it has also been called pessimistic because they
are often crushed by economic and social forces. "The Chrysanthemums" is from *The Long Valley*.

The high grey-flannel fog of winter closed off the Salinas Valley   1
from the sky and from all the rest of the world. On every side it sat
like a lid on the mountains and made of the great valley a closed
pot. On the broad, level land floor the gang plows bit deep and left
the black earth shining like metal where the shares had cut. On the
foothill ranches across the Salinas River, the yellow stubble fields
seemed to be bathed in pale cold sunshine, but there was no sunshine in the valley now in December. The thick willow scrub along
the river flamed with sharp and positive yellow leaves.

It was a time of quiet and of waiting. The air was cold and
tender. A light wind blew up from the southwest so that the farmers were mildly hopeful of a good rain before long; but fog and rain
do not go together.

Across the river, on Henry Allen's foothill ranch there was little
work to be done, for the hay was cut and stored and the orchards
were plowed up to receive the rain deeply when it should come.
The cattle on the higher slopes were becoming shaggy and rough-
coated.

Elisa Allen, working in her flower garden, looked down across
the yard and saw Henry, her husband, talking to two men in busi-

ness suits. The three of them stood by the tractor shed, each man with one foot on the side of the little Fordson. They smoked cigarettes and studied the machine as they talked.

Elisa watched them for a moment and then went back to her 5 work. She was thirty-five. Her face was lean and strong and her eyes were as clear as water. Her figure looked blocked and heavy in her gardening costume, a man's black hat pulled low down over her eyes, clodhopper shoes, a figured print dress almost completely covered by a big corduroy apron with four big pockets to hold the snips, the trowel and scratcher, the seeds and the knife she worked with. She wore heavy leather gloves to protect her hands while she worked.

She was cutting down the old year's chrysanthemum stalks with a pair of short and powerful scissors. She looked down toward the men by the tractor shed now and then. Her face was eager and mature and handsome; even her work with the scissors was over-eager, over-powerful. The chrysanthemum stems seemed too small and easy for her energy.

She brushed a cloud of hair out of her eyes with the back of her glove, and left a smudge of earth on the cheek in doing it. Behind her stood the neat white farm house with red geraniums close-banked around it as high as the windows. It was a hard-swept looking little house, with hard-polished windows, and a clean mud-mat on the front steps.

Elisa cast another glance toward the tractor shed. The strangers were getting into their Ford coupe. She took off a glove and put her strong fingers down into the forest of new green chrysanthemum sprouts that were growing around the old roots. She spread the leaves and looked down among the close-growing stems. No aphids were there, no sowbugs or snails or cutworms. Her terrier fingers destroyed such pests before they could get started.

Elisa started at the sound of her husband's voice. He had come near quietly, and he leaned over the wire fence that protected her flower garden from cattle and dogs and chickens.

"At it again," he said. "You've got a strong new crop coming." 10

Elisa straightened her back and pulled on the gardening glove again. "Yes. They'll be strong this coming year." In her tone and on her face there was a little smugness.

"You've got a gift with things," Henry observed. "Some of those yellow chrysanthemums you had this year were ten inches across. I wish you'd work out in the orchard and raise some apples that big."

Her eyes sharpened. "Maybe I could do it, too. I've a gift with things, all right. My mother had it. She could stick anything in the

ground and make it grow. She said it was having planters' hands
that knew how to do it."

"Well, it sure works with flowers," he said.

"Henry, who were those men you were talking to?"   15

"Why, sure, that's what I came to tell you. They were from the
Western Meat Company. I sold those thirty head of three-year-old
steers. Got nearly my own price, too."

"Good," she said. "Good for you."

"And I thought," he continued, "I thought how it's Saturday
afternoon, and we might go into Salinas for dinner at a restaurant,
and then to a picture show—to celebrate, you see."

"Good," she repeated. "Oh, yes. That will be good."

Henry put on his joking tone. "There's fights tonight. How'd you   20
like to go to the fights?"

"Oh, no," she said breathlessly. "No, I wouldn't like fights."

"Just fooling, Elisa. We'll go to a movie. Let's see. It's two now.
I'm going to take Scotty and bring down those steers from the hill.
It'll take us maybe two hours. We'll go in town about five and have
dinner at the Cominos Hotel. Like that?"

"Of course I'll like it. It's good to eat away from home."

"All right, then. I'll go get up a couple of horses."

She said, "I'll have plenty of time to transplant some of these   25
sets, I guess."

She heard her husband calling Scotty down by the barn. And a
little later she saw the two men ride up the pale yellow hillside in
search of the steers.

There was a little square sandy bed kept for rooting the chrysanthemums. With her trowel she turned the soil over and over, and
smoothed it and patted it firm. Then she dug ten parallel trenches
to receive the sets. Back at the chrysanthemum bed she pulled out
the little crisp shoots, trimmed off the leaves of each one with her
scissors and laid it on a small orderly pile.

A squeak of wheels and plod of hoofs came from the road. Elisa
looked up. The country road ran along the dense bank of willows
and cottonwoods that bordered the river, and up this road came a
curious vehicle, curiously drawn. It was an old spring-wagon, with
a round canvas top on it like the cover of a prairie schooner. It was
drawn by an old bay horse and a little grey-and-white burro. A big
stubble-bearded man sat between the cover flaps and drove the
crawling team. Underneath the wagon, between the hind wheels, a
lean and rangy mongrel dog walked sedately. Words were painted
on the canvas in clumsy, crooked letters. "Pots, pans, knives,
sisors, lawn mores. Fixed." Two rows of articles and the trium-

phantly definitive "Fixed" below. The black paint had run down in little sharp points beneath each letter.

Elisa, squatting on the ground, watched to see the crazy, loose-jointed wagon pass by. But it didn't pass. It turned into the farm road in front of her house, crooked old wheels skirling and squeaking. The rangy dog darted from between the wheels and ran ahead. Instantly the two ranch shepherds flew out at him. Then all three stopped, and with stiff and quivering tails, with taut straight legs, with ambassadorial dignity, they slowly circled, sniffing daintily. The caravan pulled up to Elisa's wire fence and stopped. Now the newcomer dog, feeling out-numbered, lowered his tail and retired under the wagon with raised hackles and bared teeth.

The man on the wagon seat called out. "That's a bad dog in a fight when he gets started." 30

Elisa laughed. "I see he is. How soon does he generally get started?"

The man caught up her laughter and echoed it heartily. "Sometimes not for weeks and weeks," he said. He climbed stiffly down, over the wheel. The horse and the donkey drooped like unwatered flowers.

Elisa saw that he was a very big man. Although his hair and beard were greying, he did not look old. His worn black suit was wrinkled and spotted with grease. The laughter had disappeared from his face and eyes the moment his laughing voice ceased. His eyes were dark, and they were full of the brooding that gets in the eyes of teamsters and of sailors. The calloused hands he rested on the wire fence were cracked, and every crack was a black line. He took off his battered hat.

"I'm off my general road, ma'am," he said. "Does this dirt road cut over across the river to the Los Angeles highway?"

Elisa stood up and shoved the thick scissors in her apron pocket. 35 "Well, yes, it does, but it winds around and then fords the river. I don't think your team could pull through the sand."

He replied with some asperity. "It might surprise you what them beasts can pull through."

"When they get started?" she asked.

He smiled for a second. "Yes. When they get started."

"Well," said Elisa, "I think you'll save time if you go back to the Salinas road and pick up the highway there."

He drew a big finger down the chicken wire and made it sing. "I 40 ain't in any hurry, ma'am. I go from Seattle to San Diego and back every year. Takes all my time. About six months each way. I aim to follow nice weather."

Elisa took off her gloves and stuffed them in the apron pocket with the scissors. She touched the under edge of her man's hat, searching for fugitive hairs. "That sounds like a nice kind of a way to live," she said.

He leaned confidently over the fence. "Maybe you noticed the writing on my wagon. I mend pots and sharpen knives and scissors. You got any of them things to do?"

"Oh, no," she said quickly. "Nothing like that." Her eyes hardened with resistance.

"Scissors is the worst thing," he explained. "Most people just ruin scissors trying to sharpen 'em but I know how. I got a special tool. It's a little bobbit kind of thing, and patented. But it sure does the trick."

"No. My scissors are all sharp."   45

"All right, then. Take a pot," he continued earnestly, "a bent pot, or a pot with a hole. I can make it like new so you don't have to buy no new ones. That's a saving for you."

"No," she said shortly. "I tell you I have nothing like that for you to do."

His face fell to an exaggerated sadness. His voice took on a whining undertone. "I ain't had a thing to do today. Maybe I won't have no supper tonight. You see I'm off my regular road. I know folks on the highway clear from Seattle to San Diego. They save their things for me to sharpen up because they know I do it so good and save them money."

"I'm sorry," Elisa said irritably. "I haven't anything for you to do."

His eyes left her face and fell to searching the ground. They   50
roamed about until they came to the chrysanthemum bed where she had been working. "What's them plants, ma'am?"

The irritation and resistance melted from Elisa's face. "Oh, those are chrysanthemums, giant whites and yellows. I raise them every year, bigger than anybody around here."

"Kind of a long-stemmed flower? Looks like a quick puff of colored smoke?" he asked.

"That's it. What a nice way to describe them."

"They smell kind of nasty till you get used to them," he said.

"It's a good bitter smell," she retorted, "not nasty at all."   55

He changed his tone quickly. "I like the smell myself."

"I had ten-inch blooms this year," she said.

The man leaned farther over the fence. "Look. I know a lady down the road a piece, has got the nicest garden you ever seen. Got nearly every kind of flower but no chrysanthemums. Last time I was mending a copper-bottom washtub for her (that's a hard job but I do it good), she said to me, 'If you ever run acrost some nice chrysanthemums I wish you'd try to get me a few seeds.' That's what she told me."

Elisa's eyes grew alert and eager. "She couldn't have known much about chrysanthemums. You can raise them from seed, but it's much easier to root the little sprouts you see there."

"Oh," he said. "I s'pose I can't take none to her, then."   60

"Why yes you can," Elisa cried. "I can put some in damp sand, and you can carry them right along with you. They'll take root in the pot if you keep them damp. And then she can transplant them."

"She'd sure like to have some, ma'am. You say they're nice ones?"

"Beautiful," she said. "Oh, beautiful." Her eyes shone. She tore off the battered hat and shook out her dark pretty hair. "I'll put them in a flower pot, and you can take them right with you. Come into the yard."

While the man came through the picket gate Elisa ran excitedly along the geranium-bordered path to the back of the house. And she returned carrying a big red flower pot. The gloves were forgotten now. She kneeled on the ground by the starting bed and dug up the sandy soil with her fingers and scooped it into the bright new flower pot. Then she picked up the little pile of shoots she had prepared. With her strong fingers she pressed them into the sand and tamped around them with her knuckles. The man stood over her. "I'll tell you what to do," she said. "You remember so you can tell the lady."

"Yes, I'll try to remember."   65

"Well, look. These will take root in about a month. Then she must set them out, about a foot apart in good rich earth like this, see?" She lifted a handful of dark soil for him to look at. "They'll grow fast and tall. Now remember this. In July tell her to cut them down, about eight inches from the ground."

"Before they bloom?" he asked.

"Yes, before they bloom." Her face was tight with eagerness. "They'll come right up again. About the last of September the buds will start."

She stopped and seemed perplexed. "It's the budding that takes the most care," she said hesitantly. "I don't know how to tell you." She looked deep into his eyes, searchingly. Her mouth opened a little, and she seemed to be listening. "I'll try to tell you," she said. "Did you ever hear of planting hands?"

"Can't say I have, ma'am."   70

"Well, I can only tell you what it feels like. It's when you're picking off the buds you don't want. Everything goes right down into your fingertips. You watch your fingers work. They do it themselves. You can feel how it is. They pick and pick the buds. They never make a mistake. They're with the plant. Do you see? Your fingers and the plant. You can feel that, right up your arm. They know. They never make a mistake. You can feel it. When you're like that you can't do anything wrong. Do you see that? Can you understand that?"

She was kneeling on the ground looking up at him. Her breast swelled passionately.

The man's eyes narrowed. He looked away, self-consciously. "Maybe I know," he said. "Sometimes in the night in the wagon there—"

Elisa's voice grew husky. She broke in on him. "I've never lived as you do but I know what you mean. When the night is dark— why, the stars are sharp-pointed, and there's quiet. Why, you rise up and up! Every pointed star gets driven into your body. It's like that. Hot and sharp and—lovely."

Kneeling there, her hand went out toward his legs in the greasy 75 black trousers. Her hesitant fingers almost touched the cloth. Then her hand dropped to the ground. She crouched low like a fawning dog.

He said, "It's nice, just like you say. Only when you don't have no dinner, it ain't."

She stood up then, very straight, and her face was ashamed. She held the flower pot out to him and placed it gently in his arms. "Here. Put it in your wagon, on the seat, where you can watch it. Maybe I can find something for you to do."

At the back of the house she dug in the can pile and found two old and battered aluminum saucepans. She carried them back and gave them to him. "Here, maybe you can fix these."

His manner changed. He became professional. "Good as new I can fix them." At the back of his wagon he set a little anvil, and out of an oily tool box dug a small machine hammer. Elisa came through the gate to watch him while he pounded out the dents in the kettles. His mouth grew sure and knowing. At a difficult part of the work he sucked his under-lip.

"You sleep right in the wagon?" Elisa asked.   80

"Right in the wagon, ma'am. Rain or shine I'm dry as a cow in there."

"It must be nice," she said. "It must be very nice. I wish women could do such things."

"It ain't the right kind of a life for a woman."

Her upper lip raised a little, showing her teeth. "How do you know? How can you tell?" she said.

"I don't know ma'am," he protested. "Of course I don't know. 85 Now here's your kettles, done. You don't have to buy no new ones."

"How much?"

"Oh, fifty cents'll do. I keep my prices down and my work good. That's why I have all them satisfied customers up and down the highway."

Elisa brought him a fifty-cent piece from the house and dropped it in his hand. "You might be surprised to have a rival some time. I can sharpen scissors, too. And I can beat the dents out of little pots. I could show you what a woman might do."

He put his hammer back in the oily box and shoved the little anvil out of sight. "It would be a lonely life for a woman, ma'am, and a scarey life, too, with animals creeping under the wagon all night." He climbed over the singletree, steadying himself with a hand on the burro's white rump. He settled himself in the seat, picked up the lines. "Thank you kindly, ma'am," he said. "I'll do like you told me; I'll go back and catch the Salinas road."

"Mind," she called, "if you're long in getting there, keep the 90 sand damp."

"Sand, ma'am? . . . Sand? Oh, sure. You mean round the chrysanthemums. Sure I will." He clucked his tongue. The beasts leaned luxuriously into their collars. The mongrel dog took his place between the back wheels. The wagon turned and crawled out the entrance road and back the way it had come, along the river.

Elisa stood in front of her wire fence watching the slow progress of the caravan. Her shoulders were straight, her head thrown back, her eyes half-closed, so that the scene came vaguely into them. Her lips moved silently, forming the words "Good-bye—good-bye." Then she whispered. "That's a bright direction. There's a glowing there." The sound of her whisper startled her. She shook herself free and looked about to see whether anyone had been listening. Only the dogs had heard. They lifted their heads toward her from their sleeping in the dust, and then stretched out their chins and settled asleep again. Elisa turned and ran hurriedly into the house.

In the kitchen she reached behind the stove and felt the water tank. It was full of hot water from the noonday cooking. In the bathroom she tore off her soiled clothes and flung them into the corner. And then she scrubbed herself with a little block of pumice, legs and thighs, loins and chest and arms, until her skin was scratched and red. When she had dried herself she stood in front of a mirror in her bedroom and looked at her body. She tightened her stomach and threw out her chest. She turned and looked over her shoulder at her back.

After a while she began to dress, slowly. She put on her newest underclothing and her nicest stockings and the dress which was the symbol of her prettiness. She worked carefully on her hair, pencilled her eyebrows and rouged her lips.

Before she was finished she heard the little thunder of hoofs and   95
the shouts of Henry and his helper as they drove the red steers into the corral. She heard the gate bang shut and set herself for Henry's arrival.

His step sounded on the porch. He entered the house calling "Elisa, where are you?"

"In my room, dressing. I'm not ready. There's hot water for your bath. Hurry up. It's getting late."

When she heard him splashing in the tub, Elisa laid his dark suit on the bed, and shirt and socks and tie beside it. She stood his polished shoes on the floor beside the bed. Then she went to the porch and sat primly and stiffly down. She looked toward the river road where the willow-line was still yellow with frosted leaves so that under the high grey fog they seemed a thin band of sunshine. This was the only color in the grey afternoon. She sat unmoving for a long time. Her eyes blinked rarely.

Henry came banging out of the door, shoving his tie inside his vest as he came. Elisa stiffened and her face grew tight. Henry stopped short and looked at her. "Why—why, Elisa. You look so nice!"

"Nice? You think I look nice? What do you mean by 'nice'?"   100
Henry blundered on. "I don't know. I mean you look different, strong and happy."

"I am strong? Yes, strong. What do you mean 'strong'?"

He looked bewildered. "You're playing some kind of a game," he said helplessly. "It's a kind of a play. You look strong enough to break a calf over your knee, happy enough to eat it like a watermelon."

For a second she lost her rigidity. "Henry! Don't talk like that. You didn't know what you said." She grew complete again. "I'm strong," she boasted. "I never knew before how strong."

Henry looked down toward the tractor shed, and when he   105
brought his eyes back to her, they were his own again. "I'll get out the car. You can put on your coat while I'm starting."

Elisa went into the house. She heard him drive to the gate and idle down his motor, and then she took a long time to put on her hat. She pulled it here and pressed it there. When Henry turned the motor off she slipped into her coat and went out.

The little roadster bounced along on the dirt road by the river, raising the birds and driving the rabbits into the brush. Two cranes flapped heavily over the willow-line and dropped into the riverbed. Far ahead on the road Elisa saw a dark speck. She knew.

She tried not to look as they passed it, but her eyes would not obey. She whispered to herself sadly. "He might have thrown them off the road. That wouldn't have been much trouble, not very much. But he kept the pot," she explained. "He had to keep the pot. That's why he couldn't get them off the road."

The roadster turned a bend and she saw the caravan ahead. She   110
swung full around toward her husband so she could not see the little covered wagon and the mismatched team as the car passed them.

In a moment they had left behind them the man who had not known or needed to know what she said, the bargainer. She did not look back.

To Henry, she said loudly, to be heard above the motor, "It will be good, to-night, a good dinner."

"Now you're changed again," Henry complained. He took one hand from the wheel and patted her knee. "I ought to take you in to dinner oftener. It would be good for both of us. We get so heavy out on the ranch."

"Henry," she asked, "could we have wine at dinner?"

"Sure. Say! That will be fine."   115

She was silent for a while; then she said, "Henry, at those prize fights do the men hurt each other very much?"

"Sometimes a little, not often. Why?"

"Well, I've read how they break noses, and blood runs down their chests. I've read how the fighting gloves get heavy and soggy with blood."

He looked around at her. "What's the matter, Elisa? I didn't know you read things like that." He brought the car to a stop, then turned to the right over the Salinas River bridge.

"Do any women ever go to the fights?" she asked.   120

"Oh, sure, some. What's the matter, Elisa? Do you want to go? I don't think you'd like it, but I'll take you if you really want to go."

She relaxed limply in the seat. "Oh, no. I don't want to go. I'm sure I don't." Her face was turned away from him. "It will be enough if we can have wine. It will be plenty." She turned up her coat collar so he could not see that she was crying weakly—like an old woman.

INSIDERS AND
OUTSIDERS

Insiders and Outsiders: Preview

NADINE GORDIMER Which New Era Would That Be? 727

He had never met her before but he knew the type well—had seen it over and over again at meetings of the Congress of Democrats, and other organizations where progressive whites met progressive blacks. These were the white women who, Jake knew, persisted in regarding themselves as your equal.

Overview and Ideas for Writing

"Having been a Gentile at my first preparatory school and a Jew at my second, I know what I am talking about. I know how the poison works, and I know that if the average man is anyone in particular he is a preparatory school boy," says E. M. Forster in "Jew-Consciousness." The statement contains two implications you may want to consider as you plan your own essays. First, it suggests that most of us can speak with some authority about discrimination because the schools we attended were miniature societies filled with prejudices. As someone familiar with the politics of schools and neighborhoods, you could, like Cynthia Ozick, Richard Rodriguez, and Roger Wilkins, write about your experience of being excluded from a group you wanted to join. Or you could write about your experience as an insider consciously or unconsciously excluding others from your circle. If you decide to examine your life in a world of discriminators, you can compare your observations with the generalizations Virginia Woolf and C. S. Lewis have drawn about the psychology of exclusion.

But Forster's statement raises questions that go beyond individual discrimination. Even if there is in all of us individually some innate desire to hold ourselves above others, social forces define which groups are systematically suppressed. Forster points to the Fascist propaganda machine as one of the forces behind anti-Semitism in England in 1939; he does not discuss the forces that have shaped his generation's attitude toward other groups, including women. "If the average *man* is anyone in particular he is a preparatory school *boy*." Though Forster personally liked and admired several women and created memorable female characters in his novels, he was a member of a generation unaccustomed to thinking of women as having a role in public life. Women his age had not attended preparatory schools because they were not allowed to take degrees from British universities. Nor could they vote, in England or the United States, until after World War I, when Forster was entering middle age. In this and several other ways, they were so effectively excluded from public life that writers were untroubled by the use of *man* as the equivalent of *human*.

If you want to write a research essay, you might examine the social forces that have created, and continue to create, prejudices against entire groups of people. How can we account for the hostility millions of Americans felt toward N. Scott Momaday's Kiowa ancestors or toward the blacks Martin Luther King led in protests three decades ago? You might look for answers not only in the writing of historians but in primary sources: Examine for yourself the books, magazines, and newspapers people read then; see what you can learn from autobiographical writing and fiction. You might also examine the ways that these or other groups that have historically been victims of discrimination are treated in the media today. Is our society freer of irrational biases than it was fifty years ago, or is the level of prejudice about the same, with some change in targets and methods?

VIRGINIA WOOLF

The Patriarchy

Virginia Woolf (1882–1941), the daughter of a distinguished
Victorian biographer, was denied formal education because
women could not take degrees from British universities until
1920. Nonetheless, she became one of the first women in British
history to be a literary professional, supporting herself by writing
and by operating (with her husband Leonard) a successful publishing firm, the Hogarth Press. The disadvantages under which
she labored were considerable (see "Professions for Women," p.
536) and showed her that English women, however they might
be pampered and honored, were a political underclass. Out of
this awareness grew *A Room of One's Own* (1929), a book based
on addresses given to women's societies in 1928. "The Patriarchy," the book's second chapter, re-creates Woolf's train of
thought as she attempts to write a talk on Women and Fiction.

The scene, if I may ask you to follow me, was now changed. The
leaves were still falling, but in London now, not Oxbridge;[1] and I
must ask you to imagine a room, like many thousands, with a
window looking across people's hats and vans and motor-cars to
other windows, and on the table inside the room a blank sheet of
paper on which was written in large letters WOMEN AND FICTION,
but no more. The inevitable sequel to lunching and dining at Oxbridge seemed, unfortunately, to be a visit to the British Museum.
One must strain off what was personal and accidental in all these
impressions and so reach the pure fluid, the essential oil of truth.
For that visit to Oxbridge and the luncheon and the dinner had
started a swarm of questions. Why did men drink wine and women
water? Why was one sex so prosperous and the other so poor?
What effect has poverty on fiction? What conditions are necessary
for the creation of works of art?—a thousand questions at once
suggested themselves. But one needed answers, not questions; and
an answer was only to be had by consulting the learned and the
unprejudiced, who have removed themselves above the strife of
tongue and the confusion of body and issued the result of their
reasoning and research in books which are to be found in the
British Museum. If truth is not to be found on the shelves of the

1. A portmanteau word for the universities of Oxford and Cambridge, the scene of
the first chapter.

British Museum, where I asked myself, picking up a notebook and a pencil, is truth?

Thus provided, thus confident and enquiring, I set out in the pursuit of truth. The day, though not actually wet, was dismal, and the streets in the neighborhood of the Museum were full of open coal-holes, down which sacks were showering; four-wheeled cabs were drawing up and depositing on the pavement corded boxes containing, presumably, the entire wardrobe of some Swiss or Italian family seeking fortune or refuge or some other desirable commodity which is to be found in the boarding-houses of Bloomsbury in the winter. The usual hoarse-voiced men paraded the streets with plants on barrows. Some shouted; others sang. London was like a workshop. London was like a machine. We were all being shot backwards and forwards on this plain foundation to make some pattern. The British Museum was another department of the factory. The swing-doors swung open; and there one stood under the vast dome, as if one were a thought in the huge bald forehead which is so splendidly encircled by a band of famous names. One went to the counter; one took a slip of paper; one opened a volume of the catalogue, and . . . . . the five dots here indicate five separate minutes of stupefaction, wonder, and bewilderment. Have you any notion how many books are written about women in the course of one year? Have you any notion how many are written by men? Are you aware that you are, perhaps, the most discussed animal in the universe? Here had I come with a notebook and a pencil proposing to spend a morning reading, supposing that at the end of the morning I should have transferred the truth to my notebook. But I should need to be a herd of elephants, I thought, and a wilderness of spiders, desperately referring to the animals that are reputed longest lived and most multitudinously eyed, to cope with all this. I should need claws of steel and beak of brass even to penetrate the husk. How shall I ever find the grains of truth embedded in all this mass of paper, I asked myself, and in despair began running my eye up and down the long list of titles. Even the names of the books gave me food for thought. Sex and its nature might well attract doctors and biologists; but what was surprising and difficult of explanation was the fact that sex—woman, that is to say—also attracts agreeable essayists, light-fingered novelists, young men who have taken the M.A. degree; men who have taken no degree; men who have no apparent qualification save that they are not women. Some of these books were, on the face of it, frivolous and facetious; but many, on the other hand, were serious and prophetic, moral and hortatory. Merely to read the titles suggested innumerable schoolmasters, innumerable clergymen mounting their platforms and pulpits and holding forth with a loquacity which far exceeded the hour usually allotted to such discourse on this one subject. It was a most strange phenomenon; and apparently—here I consulted the letter M—one confined to male sex. Women do not write books about men—a fact that I could not help welcoming with relief, for if I had first to read all that men have written about women, then all that women have written about men, the aloe that flowers once in a hundred years would flower twice before I could set pen to paper. So, making a perfectly arbitrary choice of a dozen volumes or so, I sent my slips of paper to lie in the wire tray, and waited in my stall, among the other seekers for the essential oil of truth.

What could be the reason, then, of this curious disparity, I wondered, drawing cartwheels on the slips of paper provided by the British taxpayer for other purposes. Why are women, judging from this catalogue, so much more interesting to men than men to women? A very curious fact it seemed, and my mind wandered to picture the lives of men who spend their time writing books about women; whether they were old or young, married or unmarried, red-nosed or hump-backed—anyhow, it was flattering, vaguely, to feel oneself the object of such attention, provided that it was not entirely bestowed by the crippled and the infirm—so I pondered until all such frivolous thoughts were ended by an avalanche of books sliding down on to the desk in front of me. Now the trouble began. The student who has been trained in research at Oxbridge has no doubt some method of shepherding his question past all distractions till it runs into its answer as a sheep runs into its pen. The student by my side, for instance, who was copying assiduously from a scientific manual was, I felt sure, extracting pure nuggets of the essential ore every ten minutes or so. His little grunts of satisfaction indicated so much. But if, unfortunately, one has had no training in a university, the question far from being shepherded to its pen flies like a frightened flock hither and thither, helter-skelter, pursued by a whole pack of hounds. Professors, schoolmasters, sociologists, clergymen, novelists, essayists, journalists, men who had no qualification save that they were not women, chased my simple and single question—Why are women poor?—until it became fifty questions; until the fifty questions leapt frantically into mid-stream and were carried away. Every page in my notebook was scribbled over with notes. To show the state of mind I was in, I will read you a few of them, explaining that the page was headed quite simply, WOMEN AND POVERTY, in block letters; but what followed was something like this:

Condition in Middle Ages of,
Habits in the Fiji Islands of,
Worshipped as goddesses by,
Weaker in moral sense than,
Idealism of,
Greater conscientiousness of,
South Sea Islanders, age of puberty among,
Attractiveness of,
Offered as sacrifice to,
Small size of brain of,
Profounder sub-consciousness of,
Less hair on the body of,
Mental, moral and physical inferiority of,
Love of children of,
Greater length of life of,
Weaker muscles of,
Strength of affections of,
Vanity of,
Higher education of,
Shakespeare's opinion of,
Lord Birkenhead's opinion of,
Dean Inge's opinion of,
La Bruyère's opinion of,
Dr. Johnson's opinion of,
Mr. Oscar Browning's opinion of, . . .

Here I drew breath and added, indeed, in the margin, Why does
Samuel Butler[2] say, "Wise men never say what they think of
women"? Wise men never say anything else apparently. But, I
continued, leaning back in my chair and looking at the vast dome
in which I was a single but by now somewhat harassed thought,
what is so unfortunate is that wise men never think the same thing
about women. Here is Pope[3]:

Most women have no character at all.

And here is La Bruyère[4]:

Les femmes sont extrêmes; elles sont meilleures ou pires que
les hommes—[5]

---

2. Samuel Butler (1835–1902), English novelist.
3. Alexander Pope (1688–1744), English poet.
4. Jean de La Bruyère (1645–1696), French essayist.
5. "Women are extreme; they are better or worse than men."

a direct contradiction by keen observers who were contemporary. Are they capable of education or incapable? Napoleon thought them incapable. Dr. Johnson[6] thought the opposite. Have they souls or have they not souls? Some savages say they have none. Others, on the contrary, maintain that women are half divine and worship them on that account. Some sages hold that they are shallower in the brain; others that they are deeper in the consciousness. Goethe honoured them; Mussolini despises them. Wherever one looked men thought about women and thought differently. It was impossible to make head or tail of it all, I decided, glancing with envy at the reader next door who was making the neatest abstracts, headed often with an A or a B or a C, while my own notebook rioted with the wildest scribble of contradictory jottings. It was distressing, it was bewildering, it was humiliating. Truth had run through my fingers. Every drop had escaped.

I could not possibly go home, I reflected, and add as a serious   4 contribution to the study of women and fiction that women have less hair on their bodies than men, or that the age of puberty among the South Sea Islanders is nine—or is it ninety?—even the handwriting had become in its distraction indecipherable. It was disgraceful to have nothing more weighty or respectable to show after a whole morning's work. And if I could not grasp the truth about W. (as for brevity's sake I had come to call her) in the past, why bother about W. in the future? It seemed pure waste of time to consult all those gentlemen who specialise in women and her effect on whatever it may be—politics, children, wages, morality— numerous and learned as they are. One might as well leave their books unopened.

But while I pondered I had unconsciously, in my listlessness, in   5 my desperation, been drawing a picture where I should, like my neighbour, have been writing a conclusion. I had been drawing a face, a figure. It was the face and figure of Professor von X. engaged in writing his monumental work entitled *The Mental, Moral, and Physical Inferiority of the Female Sex*. He was not in my picture a man attractive to women. He was heavily built; he had a great jowl; to balance that he had very small eyes; he was very red in the face. His expression suggested that he was labouring under some emotion that made him jab his pen on the paper as if he were killing some noxious insect as he wrote, but even when he had killed it that did not satisfy him; he must go on killing it; and even so, some cause for anger and irritation remained. Could it be his wife, I asked, looking at my picture. Was she in love with a cavalry officer? Was

6. Samuel Johnson (1709–1784), English essayist and lexicographer.

the cavalry officer slim and elegant and dressed in astrachan? Had
he been laughed at, to adopt the Freudian theory, in his cradle by a
pretty girl? For even in his cradle the professor, I thought, could
not have been an attractive child. Whatever the reason, the professor was made to look very angry and very ugly in my sketch, as he
wrote his great book upon the mental, moral, and physical inferiority of women. Drawing pictures was an idle way of finishing an
unprofitable morning's work. Yet it is in our idleness, in our
dreams, that the submerged truth sometimes comes to the top. A
very elementary exercise in psychology, not to be dignified by the
name of psycho-analysis, showed me, on looking at my notebook,
that the sketch of the angry professor had been made in anger.
Anger had snatched my pencil while I dreamt. But what was anger
doing there? Interest, confusion, amusement, boredom—all these
emotions I could trace and name as they succeeded each other
throughout the morning. Had anger, the black snake, been lurking
among them? Yes, said the sketch, anger had. It referred me unmistakably to the one book, to the one phrase, which had roused the
demon; it was the professor's statement about the mental, moral,
and physical inferiority of women. My heart had leapt. My cheeks
had burnt. I had flushed with anger. There was nothing specially
remarkable, however foolish, in that. One does not like to be told
that one is naturally the inferior of a little man—I looked at the
student next me—who breathes hard, wears a ready-made tie, and
has not shaved this fortnight. One has certain foolish vanities. It is
only human nature, I reflected, and began drawing cartwheels and
circles over the angry professor's face till he looked like a burning
bush or a flaming comet—anyhow, an apparition without human
semblance or significance. The professor was nothing now but a
faggot burning on the top of Hampstead Heath. Soon my own
anger was explained and done with; but curiosity remained. How
explain the anger of the professors? Why were they angry? For
when it came to analysing the impression left by these books there
was always an element of heat. This heat took many forms; it
showed itself in satire, in sentiment, in curiosity, in reprobation.
But there was another element which was often present and could
not immediately be identified. Anger, I called it. But it was anger
that had gone underground and mixed itself with all kinds of other
emotions. To judge from its odd effects, it was anger disguised and
complex, not anger simple and open.

 Whatever the reason, all these books, I thought, surveying the   6
pile on the desk, are worthless for my purposes. They were worthless scientifically, that is to say, though humanly they were full of
instruction, interest, boredom, and very queer facts about the

habits of the Fiji Islanders. They had been written in the red light of emotion and not in the white light of truth. Therefore they must be returned to the central desk and restored each to his own cell in the enormous honeycomb. All that I had retrieved from that morning's work had been the one fact of anger. The professors—I lumped them together thus—were angry. But why, I asked myself, having returned the books, why, I repeated, standing under the colonnade among the pigeons and the prehistoric canoes, why are they angry? And, asking myself this question, I strolled off to find a place for luncheon. What is the real nature of what I call for the moment their anger? I asked. Here was a puzzle that would last all the time that it takes to be served with food in a small restaurant somewhere near the British Museum. Some previous luncher had left the lunch edition of the evening paper on a chair, and, waiting to be served, I began idly reading the headlines. A ribbon of very large letters ran across the page. Somebody had made a big score in South Africa. Lesser ribbons announced that Sir Austen Chamberlain was at Geneva. A meat axe with human hair on it had been found in a cellar, Mr. Justice —— commented in the Divorce Courts upon the Shamelessness of Women. Sprinkled about the paper were other pieces of news. A film actress had been lowered from a peak in California and hung suspended in mid-air. The weather was going to be foggy. The most transient visitor to this planet, I thought, who picked up this paper could not fail to be aware, even from this scattered testimony, that England is under the rule of a patriarchy. Nobody in their senses could fail to detect the dominance of the professor. His was the power and the money and the influence. He was the proprietor of the paper and its editor and sub-editor. He was the Foreign Secretary and the Judge. He was the cricketer; he owned the racehorses and the yachts. He was the director of the company that pays two hundred per cent to its shareholders. He left millions to charities and colleges that were ruled by himself. He suspended the film actress in mid-air. He will decide if the hair on the meat axe is human; he it is who will acquit or convict the murderer, and hang him, or let him go free. With the exception of the fog he seemed to control everything. Yet he was angry. I knew that he was angry by this token. When I read what he wrote about women I thought, not of what he was saying, but of himself. When an arguer argues dispassionately he thinks only of the argument; and the reader cannot help thinking of the argument too. If he had written dispassionately about women, had used indisputable proofs to establish his argument and had shown no trace of wishing that the result should be one thing rather than another, one would not have been angry either. One would have accepted the fact, as one accepts the fact that a pea is green or a canary yellow. So be it, I should have said. But I had been angry because he was angry. Yet it seemed absurd, I thought, turning over the evening paper, that a man with all this power should be angry. Or is anger, I wondered, somehow, the familiar, the attendant sprite on power? Rich people, for example, are often angry because they suspect that the poor want to seize their wealth. The professors, or patriarchs, as it might be more accurate to call them, might be angry for that reason partly, but partly for one that lies a little less obviously on the surface. Possibly they were not "angry" at all; often, indeed, they were admiring, devoted, exemplary in the relations of private life. Possibly when the professor insisted a little too emphatically upon the inferiority of women, he was concerned not with their inferiority, but with his own superiority. That was what he was protecting rather hot-headedly and with too much emphasis, because it was a jewel to him of the rarest price. Life for both sexes— and I looked at them, shouldering their way along the pavement— is arduous, difficult, a perpetual struggle. It calls for gigantic courage and strength. More than anything, perhaps, creatures of illusion as we are, it calls for confidence in oneself. Without self-confidence we are as babes in the cradle. And how can we generate this imponderable quality, which is yet so invaluable, most quickly? By thinking that other people are inferior to oneself. By feeling that one has some innate superiority—it may be wealth, or rank, a straight nose, or the portrait of a grandfather by Romney[7]— for there is no end to the pathetic devices of the human imagina-tion—over other people. Hence the enormous importance to a patriarch who has to conquer, who has to rule, of feeling that great numbers of people, half the human race indeed, are by nature inferior to himself. It must indeed be one of the chief sources of his power. But let me turn the light of this observation on to real life, I thought. Does it help to explain some of those psychological puz-zles that one notes in the margin of daily life? Does it explain my astonishment the other day when Z, most humane, most mod-est of men, taking up some book by Rebecca West[8] and reading a passage in it, exclaimed, "The arrant feminist! She says that men are snobs!" The exclamation, to me so surprising—for why was Miss West an arrant feminist for making a possibly true if uncom-plimentary statement about the other sex?—was not merely the cry of wounded vanity; it was a protest against some infringement of his power to believe in himself. Woman have served all these

---

7. George Romney (1734–1802), English painter of portraits and landscapes.
8. Rebecca West (1892–1983), English journalist and novelist.

centuries as looking-glasses possessing the magic and delicious power of reflecting the figure of man at twice its natural size. Without that power probably the earth would still be swamp and jungle. The glories of all our wars would be unknown. We should still be scratching the outlines of deer on the remains of mutton bones and bartering flints for sheepskins or whatever simple ornament took our unsophisticated taste. Supermen and Fingers of Destiny would never have existed. The Czar and the Kaiser would never have worn their crowns or lost them. Whatever may be their use in civilised societies, mirrors are essential to all violent and heroic action. That is why Napoleon and Mussolini both insist so emphatically upon the inferiority of women, for if they were not inferior, they would cease to enlarge. That serves to explain in part the necessity that women so often are to men. And it serves to explain how restless they are under her criticism; how impossible it is for her to say to them this book is bad, this picture is feeble, or whatever it may be, without giving far more pain and rousing far more anger than a man would do who gave the same criticism. For if she begins to tell the truth, the figure in the looking-glass shrinks; his fitness for life is diminished. How is he to go on giving judgement, civilising natives, making laws, writing books, dressing up, and speechifying at banquets, unless he can see himself at breakfast and at dinner at least twice the size he really is? So I reflected, crumbling my bread and stirring my coffee and now and again looking at the people in the street. The looking-glass vision is of supreme importance because it charges the vitality; it stimulates the nervous system. Take it away and man may die, like the drug fiend deprived of his cocaine. Under the spell of that illusion, I thought, looking out of the window, half the people on the pavement are striding to work. They put on their hats and coats in the morning under its agreeable rays. They start the day confident, braced, believing themselves desired at Miss Smith's tea party; they say to themselves as they go into the room, I am the superior of half the people here, and it is thus that they speak with that self-confidence, that self-assurance, which have had such profound consequences in public life and lead to such curious notes in the margin of the private mind.

But these contributions to the dangerous and fascinating subject of the psychology of the other sex—it is one, I hope, that you will investigate when you have five hundred a year of your own—were interrupted by the necessity of paying the bill. It came to five shillings and ninepence. I gave the waiter a ten-shilling note and he went to bring me change. There was another ten-shilling note in my purse; I noticed it, because it is a fact that still takes my breath

away—the power of my purse to breed ten-shilling notes automatically. I open it and there they are. Society gives me chicken and
coffee, bed and lodging, in return for a certain number of pieces of
paper which were left me by an aunt, for no other reason than that
I share her name.

My aunt, Mary Beton, I must tell you, died by a fall from her   8
horse when she was riding out to take the air in Bombay. The news
of my legacy reached me one night about the same time that the act
was passed that gave votes to women. A solicitor's letter fell into
the post-box and when I opened it I found that she had left me five
hundred pounds a year for ever. Of the two—the vote and the
money—the money, I own, seemed infinitely the more important.
Before that I had made my living by cadging odd jobs from newspapers, by reporting a donkey show here or a wedding there; I had
earned a few pounds by addressing envelopes, reading to old
ladies, making artificial flowers, teaching the alphabet to small
children in a kindergarten. Such were the chief occupations that
were open to women before 1918. I need not, I am afraid, describe
in any detail the hardness of the work, for you know perhaps
women who have done it; nor the difficulty of living on the money
when it was earned, for you may have tried. But what still remains
with me as a worse infliction than either was the poison of fear and
bitterness which those days bred in me. To begin with, always to be
doing work that one did not wish to do, and to do it like a slave,
flattering and fawning, not always necessarily perhaps, but it
seemed necessary and the stakes were too great to run risks; and
then the thought of that one gift which it was death to hide—a
small one but dear to the possessor—perishing and with it myself,
my soul—all this became like a rust eating away the bloom of the
spring, destroying the tree at its heart. However, as I say, my aunt
died; and whenever I change a ten-shilling note a little of that
rust and corrosion is rubbed off; fear and bitterness go. Indeed, I
thought, slipping the silver into my purse, it is remarkable, remembering the bitterness of those days, what a change of temper a fixed
income will bring about. No force in the world can take from me
my five hundred pounds. Food, house, and clothing are mine for
ever. Therefore not merely do effort and labour cease, but also
hatred and bitterness. I need not hate any man; he cannot hurt me.
I need not flatter any man; he has nothing to give me. So imperceptibly I found myself adopting a new attitude towards the other
half of the human race. It was absurd to blame any class or any sex,
as a whole. Great bodies of people are never responsible for what
they do. They are driven by instincts which are not within their
control. They too, the patriarchs, the professors, had endless

difficulties, terrible drawbacks to contend with. Their education had been in some ways as faulty as my own. It had bred in them defects as great. True, they had money and power, but only at the cost of harbouring in their breasts an eagle, a vulture, for ever tearing the liver out and plucking at the lungs—the instinct for possession, the rage for acquisition which drives them to desire other people's fields and goods perpetually; to make frontiers and flags; battleships and poison gas; to offer up their own lives and their children's lives. Walk through the Admiralty Arch (I had reached that monument), or any other avenue given up to trophies and cannon, and reflect upon the kind of glory celebrated there. Or watch in the spring sunshine the stockbroker and the great barrister going indoors to make money and more money and more money when it is a fact that five hundred pounds a year will keep one alive in the sunshine. These are unpleasant instincts to harbour, I reflected. They are bred of the conditions of life; of the lack of civilisation, I thought, looking at the statue of the Duke of Cambridge, and in particular at the feathers in his cocked hat, with a fixity that they have scarcely ever received before. And, as I realised these drawbacks, by degrees fear and bitterness modified themselves into pity and toleration; and then in a year or two, pity and toleration went, and the greatest release of all came, which is freedom to think of things in themselves. That building, for example, do I like it or not? Is that picture beautiful or not? Is that in my opinion a good book or a bad? Indeed my aunt's legacy unveiled the sky to me, and substituted for the large and imposing figure of a gentleman, which Milton recommended for my perpetual adoration, a view of the open sky.

So thinking, so speculating, I found my way back to my house 9
by the river. Lamps were being lit and an indescribable change had come over London since the morning hour. It was as if the great machine after labouring all day had made with our help a few yards of something very exciting and beautiful—a fiery fabric flashing with red eyes, a tawny monster roaring with hot breath. Even the wind seemed flung like a flag as it lashed the houses and rattled the hoardings.

In my little street, however, domesticity prevailed. The house 10
painter was descending his ladder; the nursemaid was wheeling the perambulator carefully in and out back to nursery tea; the coalheaver was folding his empty sacks on top of each other; the woman who keeps the green-grocer's shop was adding up the day's takings with her hands in red mittens. But so engrossed was I with the problem you have laid upon my shoulders that I could not see even these usual sights without referring them to one centre. I

thought how much harder it is now than it must have been even a century ago to say which of these employments is the higher, the more necessary. Is it better to be a coal-heaver or a nursemaid; is the charwoman who has brought up eight children of less value to the world than the barrister who has made a hundred thousand pounds? It is useless to ask such questions; for nobody can answer them. Not only do the comparative values of the charwomen and lawyers rise and fall from decade to decade, but we have no rods with which to measure them even as they are at the moment. I had been foolish to ask my professor to furnish me with "indisputable proofs" of this or that in his argument about women. Even if one could state the value of any one gift at the moment, those values will change; in a century's time very possibly they will have changed completely. Moreover, in a hundred years, I thought, reaching my own doorstep, women will have ceased to be the protected sex. Logically they will take part in all the activities and exertions that were once denied them. The nursemaid will heave coal. The shop-woman will drive an engine. All assumptions founded on the facts observed when women were the protected sex will have disappeared—as, for example (here a squad of soldiers marched down the street), that women and clergymen and gardeners live longer than other people. Remove that protection, expose them to the same exertions and activities, make them soldiers and sailors and engine-drivers and dock labourers, and will not women die off so much younger, so much quicker, than men that one will say, "I saw a woman today," as one used to say, "I saw an aeroplane." Anything may happen when womanhood has ceased to be a protected occupation, I thought, opening the door. But what bearing has all this upon the subject of my paper, Women and Fiction? I asked, going indoors.

E. M. FORSTER

Jew-Consciousness

E. M. Forster (1879–1970) was one of the great novelists of his time and one of its finest essayists. Although he stopped publishing novels after 1924, the rise of fascism led him to produce some of his best nonfiction in the 1930s, including several essays collected in *Two Cheers for Democracy* (1951). Always sympathetic to the individual, however idiosyncratic, Forster raised in opposition to the fascist aristocracy of power the idea of "an aristocracy

of the sensitive, the considerate, and the plucky." His ideal aristocrats, he said, "are sensitive for others as well as for themselves,
they are considerate without being fussy, their pluck is not
swankiness but the power to endure, and they can take a joke."
In "Jew-Consciousness," originally published in *New Statesman
and Nation* on January 7, 1939, Forster gives a humanist response
to the tide of anti-Semitism that was sweeping not only Germany
but England and, as he put it, "assailing the human mind at its
source."

Long, long ago, while Queen Victoria[1] reigned, I attended two
preparatory schools. At the first of these, it was held to be a disgrace to have a sister. Any little boy who possessed one was liable
to get teased. The word would go round: "Oh, you men, have you
seen the Picktoes' sister?" The men would then reel about with
sideway motions, uttering cries of "sucks" and pretending to faint
with horror, while the Picktoes, who had hitherto held their own
socially in spite of their name, found themselves banished into the
wilderness, where they mourned, Major with Minor, in common
shame. Naturally anyone who had a sister hid her as far as possible,
and forbade her to sit with him at a Prizegiving or to speak to him
except in passing and in a very formal manner. Public opinion was
not bitter on the point, but it was quite definite. Sisters were disgraceful. I got through all right myself, because my conscience was
clear, and though charges were brought against me from time to
time they always fell through.

It was a very different story at my second school. Here, sisters
were negligible, but it was a disgrace to have a mother. Crabbe's
mother, Gob's mother, eeugh! No words were too strong, no
sounds too shrill. And since mothers at that time of life are commoner than sisters, and also less biddable, the atmosphere of this
school was less pleasant, and the sense of guilt stronger. Nearly
every little boy had a mother in a cupboard, and dreadful revelations occurred. A boy would fall ill and a mother would swoop and
drive him away in a cab. A parcel would arrive with "From
Mummy for her darling" branded upon it. Many tried to divert
suspicion by being aggressive and fastening female parents upon
the weak. One or two, who were good at games and had a large
popularity-surplus, took up a really heroic line, acknowledged
their mother brazenly, and would even be seen walking with her
across the playing-field, like King Carol with Madame Lupescu.[2]

1. Queen of England from 1837 to 1901. Forster was at preparatory school during
the last years of her reign.
2. Carol II (1893–1953) King of Rumania, and his mistress, with whom he lived
after being forced to renounce his right of succession to the throne in 1925.

We admired such boys and envied them, but durst not imitate them. The margin of safety was too narrow. The convention was established that a mother spelt disgrace, and no individual triumph could reverse this.

Those preparatory schools prepared me for life better than I ₃ realised, for having passed through two imbecile societies, a sister-conscious and a mother-conscious, I am now invited to enter a third. I am asked to consider whether the people I meet and talk about are or are not Jews, and to form an opinion on them until this fundamental point has been settled. What revolting tosh! Neither science nor religion nor common sense has one word to say in its favour. All the same, Jew-consciousness is in the air, and it remains to be seen how far it will succeed in poisoning it. I don't think we shall ever reintroduce ghettos into England; I wouldn't say for certain, since no one knows what wickedness may not develop in his country or in himself if circumstances change. I don't think we shall go savage. But I do think we shall go silly. Many people have gone so already. Today, the average man suspects the people he dislikes of being Jews, and is surprised when the people he likes are Jews. Having been a Gentile at my first preparatory school and a Jew at my second, I know what I am talking about. I know how the poison works, and I know that if the average man is anyone in particular he is a preparatory school boy. On the surface, things do not look too bad. Labour and Liberalism behave with their expected decency and denounce persecution, and respectability generally follows suit. But beneath the surface things are not so good and anyone who keeps his ears open in railway carriages or pubs or country lanes can hear a very different story. A nasty side of our nation's character has been scratched up—the sniggering side. People who would not ill-treat Jews themselves, or even be rude to them, enjoy tittering over their misfortunes; they giggle when pogroms[3] are instituted by someone else and synagogues defiled vicariously. "Serve them right really, Jews." This makes unpleasant reading, but anyone who cares to move out of his own enlightened little corner will discover that it is true. The grand Nordic argument, "He's a bloody capitalist so he must be a Jew, and as he's a Jew he must be a Red," has already taken root in our filling-stations and farms. Men employ it more frequently than women, and young men more frequently than old ones. The best way of confuting it is to say sneeringly, "That's propaganda." When "That's propaganda" has been repeated several times, the sniggering stops, for no goose likes to think that he

3. Organized massacres, particularly of Jews.

has been got at. There is another reply which is more intellectual but which requires more courage. It is to say, "Are you sure you're not a Jew yourself? Do you know who your eight great-grandparents were? Can you swear that all the eight are Aryan?" Cool reasonableness would be best of all, of course, but it does not work in the world of today any better than in my preparatory schools. The only effective check to silliness is silliness of a cleverer type.

Jew-mania was the one evil which no one foretold at the close of the last war. All sorts of troubles were discerned and discernible—nationalism, class-warfare, the split between the haves and the have-nots, the general lowering of cultural values. But no prophet, so far as I know, had foreseen this anti-Jew horror, whereas today no one can see the end of it. There had been warnings, of course, but they seemed no more ominous than a poem by Hilaire Belloc.[4] Back in India, in 1921, a Colonel lent me the Protocols of the Elders of Zion,[5] and it was such an obvious fake that I did not worry. I had forgotten my preparatory schools, and did not see that they were about to come into their own. To me, anti-Semitism is now the most shocking of all things. It is destroying much more than the Jews; it is assailing the human mind at its source, and inviting it to create false categories before exercising judgment. I am sure we shall win through. But it will take a long time. Perhaps a hundred years must pass before men can think back to the mentality of 1918, or can say with the Prophet Malachi, "Have we not all one father? Hath not one God created us?"[6] For the moment, all that we can do is to dig in our heels, and prevent silliness from sliding into insanity.

C. S. LEWIS

The Inner Ring

C. S. Lewis (1898–1963), professor of medieval and Renaissance English at Cambridge University, was also a novelist, a writer of children's books, and a popular speaker on moral and religious

4. English writer (1870–1953) of essays and children's verse.
5. A fake document purporting to give the proceedings of a conference of Jews in the late nineteenth century, at which they proposed to overthrow Christianity and control the world.
6. Malachi 2:10.

issues. In the early 1940s, he delivered a series of radio talks on the BBC that were later collected in *Mere Christianity* (1952), a book still very popular among Christians of all denominations. In 1942 he published his best-known book, *The Screwtape Letters,* in which he impersonated a veteran devil in hell who writes letters encouraging the efforts of a novice devil hard at work on earth. Lewis's witty, intelligent defenses of traditional morality and religion led him to challenge many of the secular orthodoxies of the twentieth century. "The Inner Ring" was the Memorial Lecture at King's College, University of London, in 1944. In it you will find a challenge to Sigmund Freud's assumption that sex is the strongest of all human drives.

May I read you a few lines from Tolstoi's *War and Peace*?   1

> When Boris entered the room, Prince Andrey was listening to an old general, wearing his decorations, who was reporting something to Prince Andrey, with an expression of soldierly servility on his purple face. "Alright. Please wait!" he said to the general, speaking in Russian with the French accent which he used when he spoke with contempt. The moment he noticed Boris he stopped listening to the general who trotted imploringly after him and begged to be heard, while Prince Andrey turned to Boris with a cheerful smile and a nod of the head. Boris now clearly understood—what he had already guessed—that side by side with the system of discipline and subordination which were laid down in the Army Regulations, there existed a different and a more real system—the system which compelled a tightly laced general with a purple face to wait respectfully for his turn while a mere captain like Prince Andrey chatted with a mere second lieutenant like Boris. Boris decided at once that he would be guided not by the official system but by this other unwritten system.[1]

When you invite a middle-aged moralist to address you, I sup-   2
pose I must conclude, however unlikely the conclusion seems, that you have a taste for middle-aged moralising. I shall do my best to gratify it. I shall in fact give you advice about the world in which you are going to live. I do not mean by this that I am going to attempt to talk on what are called current affairs. You probably know quite as much about them as I do. I am not going to tell you—except in a form so general that you will hardly recognise it—what part you ought to play in post-war reconstruction. It is not, in fact, very likely that any of you will be able, in the next ten years, to make any direct contribution to the peace or prosperity of Europe. You will be busy finding jobs, getting married, acquiring

---

1. Part III, chapter 9. [author's note]

facts. I am going to do something more old-fashioned than you perhaps expected. I am going to give advice. I am going to issue warnings. Advice and warnings about things which are so perennial that no one calls them "current affairs."

And of course everyone knows what a middle-aged moralist of   3 my type warns his juniors against. He warns them against the World, the Flesh, and the Devil. But one of this trio will be enough to deal with today. The Devil, I shall leave strictly alone. The association between him and me in the public mind has already gone quite as deep as I wish: in some quarters it has already reached the level of confusion, if not of identification. I begin to realise the truth of the old proverb that he who sups with that formidable host needs a long spoon. As for the Flesh, you must be very abnormal young people if you do not know quite as much about it as I do. But on the World I think I have something to say.

In the passage I have just read from Tolstoi, the young second   4 lieutenant Boris Dubretskoi discovers that there exist in the army two different systems or hierarchies. The one is printed in some little red book and anyone can easily read it up. It also remains constant. A general is always superior to a colonel and a colonel to a captain. The other is not printed anywhere. Nor is it even a formally organised secret society with officers and rules which you would be told after you had been admitted. You are never formally and explicitly admitted by anyone. You discover gradually, in almost indefinable ways, that it exists and that you are outside it; and then later, perhaps, that you are inside it. There are what correspond to passwords, but they too are spontaneous and informal. A particular slang, the use of particular nicknames, an allusive manner of conversation, are the marks. But it is not constant. It is not easy, even at a given moment, to say who is inside and who is outside. Some people are obviously in and some are obviously out, but there are always several on the border-line. And if you come back to the same Divisional Headquarters, or Brigade Headquarters, or the same regiment or even the same company, after six weeks' absence, you may find this second hierarchy quite altered. There are no formal admissions or expulsions. People think they are in it after they have in fact been pushed out of it, or before they have been allowed in: this provides great amusement for those who are really inside. It has no fixed name. The only certain rule is that the insiders and outsiders call it by different names. From inside it may be designated, in simple cases, by mere enumeration: it may be called "You and Tony and me." When it is very secure and comparatively stable in membership it calls itself "we." When it has to be suddenly expanded to meet a particular emergency it

calls itself "All the sensible people at this place." From outside, if
you have despaired of getting into it, you call it "That gang" or
"They" or "So-and-so and his set" or "the Caucus" or "the Inner
Ring." If you are a candidate for admission you probably don't call
it anything. To discuss it with the other outsiders would make you
feel outside yourself. And to mention it in talking to the man who
is inside, and who may help you if this present conversation goes
well, would be madness.

Badly as I may have described it, I hope you will all have recog-   5
nised the thing I am describing. Not, of course, that you have been
in the Russian Army or perhaps in any army. But you have met the
phenomenon of an Inner Ring. You discovered one in your house
at school before the end of the first term. And when you had
climbed up to somewhere near it by the end of your second year,
perhaps you discovered that within the Ring there was a Ring yet
more inner, which in its turn was the fringe of the great school
Ring to which the house Rings were only satellites. It is even possible that the School Ring was almost in touch with a Masters' Ring.
You were beginning, in fact, to pierce through the skins of the
onion. And here, too, at your university—shall I be wrong in
assuming that at this very moment, invisible to me, there are several rings—independent systems or concentric rings—present in
this room? And I can assure you that in whatever hospital, inn of
court, diocese, school, business, or college you arrive after going
down, you will find the Rings—what Tolstoi calls the second or
unwritten systems.

All this is rather obvious. I wonder whether you will say the   6
same of my next step, which is this. I believe that in all men's lives
at certain periods, and in many men's lives at all periods between
infancy and extreme old age, one of the most dominant elements is
the desire to be inside the local Ring and the terror of being left
outside. This desire, in one of its forms, has indeed had ample
justice done to it in literature. I mean, in the form of snobbery.
Victorian fiction is full of characters who are hag-ridden by the
desire to get inside that particular Ring which is, or was, called
Society. But it must be clearly understood that "Society," in that
sense of the word, is merely one of a hundred Rings and snobbery
therefore only one form of the longing to be inside. People who
believe themselves to be free, and indeed are free, from snobbery,
and who read satires on snobbery with tranquil superiority, may be
devoured by the desire in another form. It may be the very intensity
of their desire to enter some quite different Ring which renders
them immune from the allurements of high life. An invitation from

a duchess would be very cold comfort to a man smarting under the sense of exclusion from some artistic or communist côterie. Poor man—it is not large, lighted rooms, or champagne, or even scandals about peers and Cabinet Ministers that he wants: it is the sacred little attic or studio, the heads bent together, the fog of tobacco smoke, and the delicious knowledge that we—we four or five all huddled beside this stove—are the people who *know*. Often the desire conceals itself so well that we hardly recognise the pleasures of fruition. Men tell not only their wives but themselves that it is a hardship to stay late at the office or the school on some bit of important extra work which they have been let in for because they and So-and-so and the two others are the only people left in the place who really know how things are run. But it is not quite true. It is a terrible bore, of course, when old Fatty Smithson draws you aside and whispers "Look here, we've got to get you in on this examination somehow" or "Charles and I saw at once that you've got to be on this committee." A terrible bore . . . ah, but how much more terrible if you were left out! It is tiring and unhealthy to lose your Saturday afternoons: but to have them free because you don't matter, that is much worse.

Freud would say, no doubt, that the whole thing is a subterfuge 7 of the sexual impulse. I wonder whether the shoe is not sometimes on the other foot, I wonder whether, in ages of promiscuity, many a virginity has not been lost less in obedience to Venus than in obedience to the lure of the caucus. For of course, when promiscuity is the fashion, the chaste are outsiders. They are ignorant of something that other people know. They are uninitiated. And as for lighter matters, the number who first smoked or first got drunk for a similar reason is probably very large.

I must now make a distinction. I am not going to say that the 8 existence of Inner Rings is an evil. It is certainly unavoidable. There must be confidential discussions: and it is not only not a bad thing, it is (in itself) a good thing, that personal friendship should grow up between those who work together. And it is perhaps impossible that the official hierarchy of any organisation should quite coincide with its actual workings. If the wisest and most energetic people invariably held the highest posts, it might coincide; since they often do not, there must be people in high positions who are really deadweights and people in lower positions who are more important than their rank and seniority would lead you to suppose. In that way the second, unwritten system is bound to grow up. It is necessary; and perhaps it is not a necessary evil. But the desire which draws us into Inner Rings is another matter. A thing may be morally neutral and yet the desire for that thing may be dangerous. As Byron has said:

> Sweet is a legacy, and passing sweet
> The unexpected death of some old lady.

The painless death of a pious relative at an advanced age is not an evil. But an earnest desire for her death on the part of her heirs is not reckoned a proper feeling, and the law frowns on even the gentlest attempt to expedite her departure. Let Inner Rings be an unavoidable and even an innocent feature of life, though certainly not a beautiful one: but what of our longing to enter them, our anguish when we are excluded, and the kind of pleasure we feel when we get in?

I have no right to make assumptions about the degree to which   9
any of you may already be compromised. I must not assume that you have ever first neglected, and finally shaken off, friends whom you really loved and who might have lasted you a lifetime, in order to court the friendship of those who appeared to you more important, more esoteric. I must not ask whether you have ever derived actual pleasure from the loneliness and humiliation of the outsiders after you yourself were in: whether you have talked to fellow members of the Ring in the presence of outsiders simply in order that the outsiders might envy; whether the means whereby, in your days of probation, you propitiated the Inner Ring, were always wholly admirable. I will ask only one question—and it is, of course, a rhetorical question which expects no answer. In the whole of your life as you now remember it, has the desire to be on the right side of that invisible line ever prompted you to any act or word on which, in the cold small hours of a wakeful night, you can look back with satisfaction? If so, your case is more fortunate than most.

But I said I was going to give advice, and advice should deal with   10
the future, not the past. I have hinted at the past only to awake you to what I believe to be the real nature of human life. I don't believe that the economic motive and the erotic motive account for everything that goes on in what we moralists call the World. Even if you add Ambition I think the picture is still incomplete. The lust for the esoteric, the longing to be inside, take many forms which are not easily recognisable as Ambition. We hope, no doubt, for tangible profits from every Inner Ring we penetrate: power, money, liberty to break rules, avoidance of routine duties, evasion of discipline. But all these would not satisfy us if we did not get in addition the delicious sense of secret intimacy. It is no doubt a great convenience to know that we need fear no official reprimands from our

official senior because he is old Percy, a fellow-member of our Ring. But we don't value the intimacy only for the sake of convenience; quite equally we value the convenience as a proof of the intimacy.

My main purpose in this address is simply to convince you that this desire is one of the great permanent mainsprings of human action. It is one of the factors which go to make up the world as we know it—this whole pell-mell of struggle, competition, confusion, graft, disappointment, and advertisement, and if it is one of the permanent mainsprings then you may be quite sure of this. Unless you take measures to prevent it, this desire is going to be one of the chief motives of your life, from the first day on which you enter your profession until the day when you are too old to care. That will be the natural thing—the life that will come to you of its own accord. Any other kind of life, if you lead it, will be the result of conscious and continuous effort. If you do nothing about it, if you drift with the stream, you will in fact be an "inner ringer." I don't say you'll be a successful one; that's as may be. But whether by pining and moping outside Rings that you can never enter, or by passing triumphantly further and further in—one way or the other you will be that kind of man.

I have already made it fairly clear that I think it better for you not to be that kind of man. But you may have an open mind on the question. I will therefore suggest two reasons for thinking as I do.

It would be polite and charitable, and in view of your age reasonable too, to suppose that none of you is yet a scoundrel. On the other hand, by the mere law of averages (I am saying nothing against free will) it is almost certain that at least two or three of you before you die will have become something very like scoundrels. There must be in this room the makings of at least that number of unscrupulous, treacherous, ruthless egotists. The choice is still before you: and I hope you will not take my hard words about your possible future characters as a token of disrespect to your present characters. And the prophecy I make is this. To nine out of ten of you the choice which could lead to scoundrelism will come, when it does come, in no very dramatic colours. Obviously bad men, obviously threatening or bribing, will almost certainly not appear. Over a drink or a cup of coffee, disguised as a triviality and sandwiched between two jokes, from the lips of a man, or woman, whom you have recently been getting to know rather better and whom you hope to know better still—just at the moment when you are most anxious not to appear crude, or naïf, or a prig—the hint will come. It will be the hint of something which is not quite in accordance with the technical rules of fair play: something which the public, the ignorant, romantic public, would never understand: something which even the outsiders in your own profession are apt to make a fuss about: but something, says your new friend, which "we"—and at the word "we" you try not to blush for mere plea- sure—something "we always do." And you will be drawn in, if you are drawn in, not by desire for gain or ease, but simply because at that moment, when the cup was so near your lips, you cannot bear to be thrust back again into the cold outer world. It would be so terrible to see the other man's face—that genial, confidential, delightfully sophisticated face—turn suddenly cold and contemp- tuous, to know that you had been tried for the Inner Ring and rejected. And then, if you are drawn in, next week it will be some- thing a little further from the rules, and next year something fur- ther still, but all in the jolliest, friendliest spirit. It may end in a crash, a scandal, and penal servitude: it may end in millions, a peerage and giving the prizes at your old school. But you will be a scoundrel.

That is my first reason. Of all the passions the passion for the 14
Inner Ring is most skilful in making a man who is not yet a very bad man do very bad things.

My second reason is this. The torture allotted to the Danaids in 15
the classical underworld, that of attempting to fill sieves with water, is the symbol not of one vice but of all vices. It is the very mark of a perverse desire that it seeks what is not to be had. The desire to be inside the invisible line illustrates this rule. As long as you are governed by that desire you will never get what you want. You are trying to peel an onion: if you succeed there will be noth- ing left. Until you conquer the fear of being an outsider, an outsider you will remain.

This is surely very clear when you come to think of it. If you 16
want to be made free of a certain circle for some wholesome rea- son—if, say, you want to join a musical society because you really like music—then there is a possibility of satisfaction. You may find yourself playing in a quartet and you may enjoy it. But if all you want is to be in the know, your pleasure will be short-lived. The circle cannot have from within the charm it had from outside. By the very act of admitting you it has lost its magic. Once the first novelty is worn off the members of this circle will be no more interesting than your old friends. Why should they be? You were not looking for virtue or kindness or loyalty or humour or learning or wit or any of the things that can be really enjoyed. You merely wanted to be "in." And that is a pleasure that cannot last. As soon as your new associates have been staled to you by custom, you will be looking for another Ring. The rainbow's end will still be ahead

of you. The old Ring will now be only the drab background for your endeavour to enter the new one.

And you will always find them hard to enter, for a reason you 17 very well know. You yourself, once you are in, want to make it hard for the next entrant, just as those who are already in made it hard for you. Naturally. In any wholesome group of people which holds together for a good purpose, the exclusions are in a sense accidental. Three or four people who are together for the sake of some piece of work exclude others because there is work only for so many or because the others can't in fact do it. Your little musical group limits its numbers because the rooms they meet in are only so big. But your genuine Inner Ring exists for exclusion. There'd be no fun if there were no outsiders. The invisible line would have no meaning unless most people were on the wrong side of it. Exclusion is no accident: it is the essence.

The quest of the Inner Ring will break your hearts unless you 18 break it. But if you break it, a surprising result will follow. If in your working hours you make the work your end, you will presently find yourself all unawares inside the only circle in your profession that really matters. You will be one of the sound craftsmen, and other sound craftsmen will know it. This group of craftsmen will by no means coincide with the Inner Ring or the Important People or the People in the Know. It will not shape that professional policy or work up that professional influence which fights for the profession as a whole against the public: nor will it lead to those periodic scandals and crises which the Inner Ring produces. But it will do those things which that profession exists to do and will in the long run be responsible for all the respect which that profession in fact enjoys and which the speeches and advertisements cannot maintain. And if in your spare time you consort simply with the people you like, you will again find that you have come unawares to a real inside: that you are indeed snug and safe at the centre of something which, seen from without, would look exactly like an Inner Ring. But the difference is that its secrecy is accidental, and its exclusiveness a by-product, and no one was led thither by the lure of the esoteric: for it is only four or five people who like one another meeting to do things that they like. This is friendship. Aristotle placed it among the virtues. It causes perhaps half of all the happiness in the world, and no Inner Ring can ever have it.

We are told in Scripture that those who ask get. That is true, in 19 senses I can't now explore. But in another sense there is much truth in the schoolboy's principle "them as asks shan't have." To a young person, just entering on adult life, the world seems full of "insides," full of delightful intimacies and confidentialities, and he desires to enter them. But if he follows that desire he will reach no "inside" that is worth reaching. The true road lies in quite another direction. It is like the house in *Alice Through the Looking Glass.*[2]

HARRY GOLDEN

The Vertical Negro Plan

Harry (Lewis) Golden (1902–1981), born in New York City of immigrant parents, was originally named Harry Goldhurst. He attended City College for three years but left without a degree. Goldhurst worked at various low-paying jobs, eventually became a stockbroker, and in 1929 pled guilty to a charge of mail fraud. Released after four years in jail, he changed his name to Harry Golden. The experience, as Adlai Stevenson remarked, "deepened Harry Golden's understanding, lengthened his vision, and enlarged his heart." In 1938 Golden moved South to work for the Charlotte (North Carolina) *Observer*. In 1941, he founded the *Carolina Israelite*, circulation 800. As a Jew and a Northerner, Golden faced enormous odds in putting out a one-man liberal newspaper, but he soon picked up readers from around the nation, including Harry Truman, William Faulkner, and Carl Sandburg. By 1958, Golden had 10,000 subscribers. That year his first collection of essays from the *Israelite, Only in America,* became a best-seller. "The Vertical Negro Plan" appeared in the *Israelite* in 1956, when the South was in the throes of the desegregation crisis created by *Brown* v. *Board of Education.*

Those who love North Carolina will jump at the chance to share   1
in the great responsibility confronting our Governor and the State Legislature. A special session of the Legislature (July 25–28, 1956) passed a series of amendments to the State Constitution. These proposals submitted by the Governor and his Advisory Education Committee included the following:

> (A) The elimination of the compulsory attendance law, "to prevent any child from being forced to attend a school with a child of another race."
>
> (B) The establishment of "Education Expense Grants" for education in a private school, "in the case of a child assigned to a public school attended by a child of another race."

2. Lewis Carroll's Alice imagines that the mirror over her mantel is actually a window through which she sees another room in another house.

(C) A "uniform system of local option" whereby a majority of the folks in a school district may suspend or close a school if the situation becomes "intolerable."

But suppose a Negro child applies for this "Education Expense Grant" and says he wants to go to a private school too? There are fourteen Supreme Court decisions involving the use of public funds; there are only two "decisions" involving the elimination of racial discrimination in the public schools.   2

The Governor has said that critics of these proposals have not offered any constructive advice or alternatives. Permit me, therefore, to offer an idea for the consideration of the members of the regular sessions. A careful study of my plan, I believe, will show that it will save millions of dollars in tax funds and eliminate forever the danger to our public education system. Before I outline my plan, I would like to give you a little background.   3

One of the factors involved in our tremendous industrial growth and economic prosperity is the fact that the South, voluntarily, has all but eliminated VERTICAL SEGREGATION. The tremendous buying power of the twelve million Negroes in the South has been based wholly on the absence of racial segregation. The white and Negro stand at the same grocery and supermarket counters; deposit money at the same bank teller's window; pay phone and light bills to the same clerk; walk through the same dime and department stores, and stand at the same drugstore counters.   4

It is only when the Negro "sets" that the fur begins to fly.   5

Now, since we are not even thinking about restoring VERTICAL SEGREGATION, I think my plan would not only comply with the Supreme Court decisions, but would maintain "sitting-down" segregation. Now here is the GOLDEN VERTICAL NEGRO PLAN. Instead of all those complicated proposals, all the next session needs to do is pass one small amendment which would provide only desks in all the public schools of our state—no seats.   6

The desks should be those standing-up jobs, like the old-fashioned bookkeeping desk. Since no one in the South pays the slightest attention to a VERTICAL NEGRO, this will completely solve our problem. And it is not such a terrible inconvenience for young people to stand up during their classroom studies. In fact, this may be a blessing in disguise. They are not learning to read sitting down, anyway; maybe standing up will help. This will save more millions of dollars in the cost of our remedial English course when the kids enter college. In whatever direction you look with the GOLDEN VERTICAL NEGRO PLAN, you save millions of dollars, to say nothing of eliminating forever any danger to our public education system upon which rests the destiny, hopes, and happiness of this society.   7

My WHITE BABY PLAN offers another possible solution to the   8
segregation problem—this time in a field other than education.

Here is an actual case history of the "White Baby Plan to End   9
Racial Segregation":

Some months ago there was a revival of the Laurence Olivier   10
movie, *Hamlet*, and several Negro schoolteachers were eager to see
it. One Saturday afternoon they asked some white friends to lend
them two of their little children, a three-year-old girl and a six-
year-old boy, and, holding these white children by the hands, they
obtained tickets from the movie-house cashier without a moment's
hesitation. They were in like Flynn.

This would also solve the baby-sitting problem for thousands   11
and thousands of white working mothers. There can be a mutual
exchange of references, then the people can sort of pool their children at a central point in each neighborhood, and every time a
Negro wants to go to the movies all she needs to do is pick up a
white child—and go.

Eventually the Negro community can set up a factory and manu-   12
facture white babies made of plastic, and when they want to go to
the opera or to a concert, all they need do is carry that plastic doll in
their arms. The dolls, of course, should all have blond curls and
blue eyes, which would go even further; it would give the Negro
woman and her husband priority over the whites for the very best
seats in the house.

While I still have faith in the WHITE BABY PLAN, my final proposal   13
may prove to be the most practical of all.

Only after a successful test was I ready to announce formally the   14
GOLDEN "OUT-OF-ORDER" PLAN.

I tried my plan in a city of North Carolina, where the Negroes   15
represent 39 per cent of the population.

I prevailed upon the manager of a department store to shut the   16
water off in his "white" water fountain and put up a sign, "Out-of-
Order." For the first day or two the whites were hesitant, but little
by little they began to drink out of the water fountain belonging to
the "coloreds"—and by the end of the third week everybody was
drinking the "segregated" water; with not a single solitary complaint to date.

I believe the test is of such sociological significance that the   17
Governor should appoint a special committee of two members of
the House and two Senators to investigate the GOLDEN "OUT-OF-
ORDER" PLAN. We kept daily reports on the use of the unsegregated
water fountain which should be of great value to this committee.
This may be the answer to the necessary uplifting of the white
morale. It is possible that the whites may accept desegregation if

they are assured that the facilities are still "separate," albeit "Out-of-Order."

As I see it now, the key to my Plan is to keep the "Out-of-Order" 18
sign up for at least two years. We must do this thing gradually.

MARTIN LUTHER KING, JR.

Letter from Birmingham Jail

Martin Luther King, Jr. (1929–1968), was the dominant leader
of the American civil rights movement from 1955 until his assas-
sination. A gifted student and the son and grandson of eloquent
Baptist ministers, he received his B.A. from Morehouse College
when he was nineteen years old. At Crozer Theological Seminary
(where he studied until 1951), he became acquainted with the
ideas of Mohandas Gandhi, the great Indian advocate of nonviolent protest. After taking his Ph.D. from Boston University in
1955, he became pastor of a church in Montgomery, Alabama,
where he led the famous bus boycott that initiated more than a
decade of civil rights protests. Soon King organized the Southern
Christian Leadership Conference, a network of civil rights leaders
extending throughout the South. Arrested in 1963 during desegregation demonstrations in Birmingham, Alabama, King
wrote his "Letter from Birmingham Jail" in response to a public
letter from a group of eight clergymen who opposed the demonstrations. His letter received national attention when it was re-
published in *The Christian Century* and *The Atlantic Monthly*. The
following version is from King's *Why We Can't Wait* (1964).

April 16, 1963[1]

MY DEAR FELLOW CLERGYMEN:

While confined here in the Birmingham city jail, I came across   1
your recent statement calling my present activities "unwise and

1. This response to a published statement by eight fellow clergymen from Alabama
(Bishop C. C. J. Carpenter, Bishop Joseph A. Durick, Rabbi Hilton L. Grafman,
Bishop Paul Hardin, Bishop Holan B. Harmon, the Reverend George M. Murray, The
Reverend Edward V. Ramage and the Reverend Earl Stallings) was composed under
somewhat constricting circumstances. Begun on the margins of the newspaper in
which the statement appeared while I was in jail, the letter was continued on scraps
of writing paper supplied by a friendly Negro trusty, and concluded on a pad my
attorneys were eventually permitted to leave me. Although the text remains in
substance unaltered, I have indulged in the author's prerogative of polishing it for
publication. [author's note]

untimely." Seldom do I pause to answer criticism of my work and ideas. If I sought to answer all the criticisms that cross my desk, my secretaries would have little time for anything other than such correspondence in the course of the day, and I would have no time for constructive work. But since I feel that you are men of genuine good will and that your criticisms are sincerely set forth, I want to try to answer your statement in what I hope will be patient and reasonable terms.

I think I should indicate why I am here in Birmingham, since 2 you have been influenced by the view which argues against "outsiders coming in." I have the honor of serving as president of the Southern Christian Leadership Conference, an organization operating in every southern state, with headquarters in Atlanta, Georgia. We have some eighty-five affiliated organizations across the South, and one of them is the Alabama Christian Movement for Human Rights. Frequently we share staff, educational, and financial resources with our affiliates. Several months ago the affiliate here in Birmingham asked us to be on call to engage in a nonviolent direct-action program if such were deemed necessary. We readily consented, and when the hour came we lived up to our promise. So I, along with several members of my staff, am here because I was invited here. I am here because I have organizational ties here.

But more basically, I am in Birmingham because injustice is 3 here. Just as the prophets of the eighth century B.C. left their villages and carried their "thus saith the Lord" far beyond the boundaries of their home towns, and just as the Apostle Paul left his village of Tarsus and carried the gospel of Jesus Christ to the far corners of the Greco-Roman world, so am I compelled to carry the gospel of freedom beyond my own home town. Like Paul, I must constantly respond to the Macedonian call for aid.

Moreover, I am cognizant of the interrelatedness of all com- 4 munities and states. I cannot sit idly by in Atlanta and not be concerned about what happens in Birmingham. Injustice anywhere is a threat to justice everywhere. We are caught in an inescapable network of mutuality, tied in a single garment of destiny. Whatever affects one directly, affects all indirectly. Never again can we afford to live with the narrow, provincial "outside agitator" idea. Anyone who lives inside the United States can never be considered an outsider anywhere within its bounds.

You deplore the demonstrations taking place in Birmingham. 5 But your statement, I am sorry to say, fails to express a similar concern for the conditions that brought about the demonstrations. I am sure that none of you would want to rest content with the superficial kind of social analysis that deals merely with effects and does not grapple with underlying causes. It is unfortunate that demonstrations are taking place in Birmingham, but it is even more unfortunate that the city's white power structure left the Negro community with no alternative.

In any nonviolent campaign there are four basic steps: collection 6 of the facts to determine whether injustices exist; negotiation; self-purification; and direct action. We have gone through all these steps in Birmingham. There can be no gainsaying the fact that racial injustice engulfs this community. Birmingham is probably the most thoroughly segregated city in the United States. Its ugly record of brutality is widely known. Negroes have experienced grossly unjust treatment in the courts. There have been more unsolved bombings of Negro homes and churches in Birmingham than in any other city in the nation. These are the hard, brutal facts of the case. On the basis of these conditions, Negro leaders sought to negotiate with the city fathers. But the latter consistently refused to engage in good-faith negotiation.

Then, last September, came the opportunity to talk with leaders 7 of Birmingham's economic community. In the course of the negotiations, certain promises were made by the merchants—for example, to remove the stores' humiliating racial signs. On the basis of these promises, the Reverend Fred Shuttlesworth and the leaders of the Alabama Christian Movement for Human Rights agreed to a moratorium on all demonstrations. As the weeks and months went by, we realized that we were the victims of a broken promise. A few signs, briefly removed, returned; the others remained.

As in so many past experiences, our hopes had been blasted, and 8 the shadow of deep disappointment settled upon us. We had no alternative except to prepare for direct action, whereby we would present our very bodies as a means of laying our case before the conscience of the local and the national community. Mindful of the difficulties involved, we decided to undertake a process of self-purification. We began a series of workshops on nonviolence, and we repeatedly asked ourselves: "Are you able to accept blows without retaliating?" "Are you able to endure the ordeal of jail?" We decided to schedule our direct-action program for the Easter season, realizing that except for Christmas, this is the main shopping period of the year. Knowing that a strong economic-withdrawal program would be the by-product of direct action, we felt that this would be the best time to bring pressure to bear on the merchants for the needed change.

Then it occurred to us that Birmingham's mayoral election was 9 coming up in March, and we speedily decided to postpone action until after election day. When we discovered that the Commis-

sioner of Public Safety, Eugene "Bull" Connor, had piled up
enough votes to be in the runoff, we decided again to postpone
action until the day after the run-off so that the demonstrations
could not be used to cloud the issues. Like many others, we waited
to see Mr. Connor defeated, and to this end we endured postponement after postponement. Having aided in this community need,
we felt that our direct-action program could be delayed no longer.

You may well ask: "Why direct action? Why sit-ins, marches,   10
and so forth? Isn't negotiation a better path?" You are quite right in
calling for negotiation. Indeed, this is the very purpose of direct
action. Nonviolent direct action seeks to create such a crisis and
foster such a tension that a community which has constantly refused to negotiate is forced to confront the issue. It seeks so to
dramatize the issue that it can no longer be ignored. My citing the
creation of tension as part of the work of the nonviolent-resister
may sound rather shocking. But I must confess that I am not afraid
of the word "tension." I have earnestly opposed violent tension,
but there is a type of constructive, nonviolent tension which is
necessary for growth. Just as Socrates felt that it was necessary to
create a tension in the mind so that individuals could rise from the
bondage of myths and half-truths to the unfettered realm of creative analysis and objective appraisal, so must we see the need for
nonviolent gadflies to create the kind of tension in society that will
help men rise from the dark depths of prejudice and racism to the
majestic heights of understanding and brotherhood.

The purpose of our direct-action program is to create a situation   11
so crisis-packed that it will inevitably open the door to negotiation.
I therefore concur with you in your call for negotiation. Too long
has our beloved Southland been bogged down in a tragic effort to
live in monologue rather than dialogue.

One of the basic points in your statement is that the action that I   12
and my associates have taken in Birmingham is untimely. Some
have asked: "Why didn't you give the new city administration time
to act?" The only answer that I can give to this query is that the
new Birmingham administration must be prodded about as much
as the outgoing one, before it will act. We are sadly mistaken if we
feel that the election of Albert Boutwell as mayor will bring the
millennium to Birmingham. While Mr. Boutwell is a much more
gentle person than Mr. Connor, they are both segregationists, dedicated to maintenance of the status quo. I have hope that Mr. Boutwell will be reasonable enough to see the futility of massive resistance to desegregation. But he will not see this without pressure
from devotees of civil rights. My friends, I must say to you that we
have not made a single gain in civil rights without determined legal

and nonviolent pressure. Lamentably, it is an historical fact that privileged groups seldom give up their privileges voluntarily. Individuals may see the moral light and voluntarily give up their unjust posture; but, as Reinhold Niebuhr has reminded us, groups tend to be more immoral than individuals.

We know through painful experience that freedom is never 13 voluntarily given by the oppressor; it must be demanded by the oppressed. Frankly, I have yet to engage in a direct-action campaign that was "well timed" in the view of those who have not suffered unduly from the disease of segregation. For years now I have heard the word "Wait!" It rings in the ear of every Negro with piercing familiarity. This "Wait" has almost always meant "Never." We must come to see, with one of our distinguished jurists, that "justice too long delayed is justice denied."

We have waited for more than 340 years for our constitutional 14 and God-given rights. The nations of Asia and Africa are moving with jetlike speed toward gaining political independence, but we still creep at horse-and-buggy pace toward gaining a cup of coffee at a lunch counter. Perhaps it is easy for those who have never felt the stinging darts of segregation to say, "Wait." But when you have seen vicious mobs lynch your mothers and fathers at will and drown your sisters and brothers at whim; when you have seen hate-filled policemen curse, kick, and even kill your black brothers and sisters; when you see the vast majority of your twenty million Negro brothers smothering in an airtight cage of poverty in the midst of an affluent society; when you suddenly find your tongue twisted and your speech stammering as you seek to explain to your six-year-old daughter why she can't go to the public amusement park that has just been advertised on television, and see tears welling up in her eyes when she is told that Funtown is closed to colored children, and see ominous clouds of inferiority beginning to form in her little mental sky, and see her beginning to distort her personality by developing an unconscious bitterness toward white people; when you have to concoct an answer for a five-year-old son who is asking: "Daddy, why do white people treat colored people so mean?"; when you take a cross-country drive and find it necessary to sleep night after night in the uncomfortable corners of your automobile because no motel will accept you; when you are humiliated day in and day out by nagging signs reading "white" and "colored"; when your first name becomes "nigger," your middle name becomes "boy" (however old you are) and your last name becomes "John," and your wife and mother are never given the respected title "Mrs."; when you are harried by day and haunted by night by the fact that you are a Negro, living constantly at tiptoe stance, never quite knowing what to expect next, and are plagued with inner fears and outer resentments; when you are forever fighting a degenerating sense of "nobodiness"—then you will understand why we find it difficult to wait. There comes a time when the cup of endurance runs over, and men are no longer willing to be plunged into the abyss of despair. I hope, sirs, you can understand our legitimate and unavoidable impatience.

You express a great deal of anxiety over our willingness to break 15 laws. This is certainly a legitimate concern. Since we so diligently urge people to obey the Supreme Court's decision of 1954 outlawing segregation in the public schools, at first glance it may seem rather paradoxical for us consciously to break laws. One may well ask: "How can you advocate breaking some laws and obeying others?" The answer lies in the fact that there are two types of laws: just and unjust. I would be the first to advocate obeying just laws. One has not only a legal but a moral responsibility to obey just laws. Conversely, one has a moral responsibility to disobey unjust laws. I would agree with St. Augustine that "an unjust law is no law at all."

Now, what is the difference between the two? How does one 16 determine whether a law is just or unjust? A just law is a man-made code that squares with the moral law or the law of God. An unjust law is a code that is out of harmony with the moral law. To put it in the terms of St. Thomas Aquinas: An unjust law is a human law that is not rooted in eternal law and natural law. Any law that uplifts human personality is just. Any law that degrades human personality is unjust. All segregation statutes are unjust because segregation distorts the soul and damages the personality. It gives the segregator a false sense of superiority and the segregated a false sense of inferiority. Segregation, to use the terminology of the Jewish philosopher Martin Buber, substitutes an "I–it" relationship for an "I–thou" relationship and ends up relegating persons to the status of things. Hence segregation is not only politically, economically, and sociologically unsound, it is morally wrong and sinful. Paul Tillich has said that sin is separation. Is not segregation an existential expression of man's tragic separation, his awful estrangement, his terrible sinfulness? Thus it is that I can urge men to obey the 1954 decision of the Supreme Court, for it is morally right; and I can urge them to disobey segregation ordinances, for they are morally wrong.

Let us consider a more concrete example of just and unjust laws. 17 An unjust law is a code that a numerical or power majority group compels a minority group to obey but does not make binding on itself. This is *difference* made legal. By the same token, a just law is a code that a majority compels a minority to follow and that it is willing to follow itself. This is *sameness* made legal.

Let me give another explanation. A law is unjust if it is inflicted [18] on a minority that, as a result of being denied the right to vote, had no part in enacting or devising the law. Who can say that the legislature of Alabama which set up that state's segregation laws was democratically elected? Throughout Alabama all sorts of devious methods are used to prevent Negroes from becoming registered voters, and there are some counties in which, even though Negroes constitute a majority of the population, not a single Negro is registered. Can any law enacted under such circumstances be considered democratically structured?

Sometimes a law is just on its face and unjust in its application. [19] For instance, I have been arrested on a charge of parading without a permit. Now, there is nothing wrong in having an ordinance which requires a permit for a parade. But such an ordinance becomes unjust when it is used to maintain segregation and to deny citizens the First-Amendment privilege of peaceful assembly and protest.

I hope you are able to see the distinction I am trying to point out. [20] In no sense do I advocate evading or defying the law, as would the rabid segregationist. That would lead to anarchy. One who breaks an unjust law must do so openly, lovingly, and with a willingness to accept the penalty. I submit that an individual who breaks a law that conscience tells him is unjust, and who willingly accepts the penalty of imprisonment in order to arouse the conscience of the community over its injustice, is in reality expressing the highest respect for law.

Of course, there is nothing new about this kind of civil disobedi- [21] ence. It was evidenced sublimely in the refusal of Shadrach, Meshach, and Abednego to obey the laws of Nebuchadnezzar,[2] on the ground that a higher moral law was at stake. It was practiced superbly by the early Christians, who were willing to face hungry lions and the excruciating pain of chopping blocks rather than submit to certain unjust laws of the Roman Empire. To a degree, academic freedom is a reality today because Socrates practiced civil disobedience. In our own nation, the Boston Tea Party represented a massive act of civil disobedience.

We should never forget that everything Adolf Hitler did in Ger- [22] many was "legal" and everything the Hungarian freedom fighters did in Hungary was "illegal." It was "illegal" to aid and comfort a Jew in Hitler's Germany. Even so, I am sure that, had I lived in

---

2. King refers to the Biblical story recorded in Daniel, chapter 3.

Germany at the time, I would have aided and comforted my Jewish brothers. If today I lived in a Communist country where certain principles dear to the Christian faith are suppressed, I would openly advocate disobeying that country's antireligious laws.

I must make two honest confessions to you, my Christian and Jewish brothers. First, I must confess that over the past few years I have been gravely disappointed with the white moderate. I have almost reached the regrettable conclusion that the Negro's great stumbling block in his stride toward freedom is not the White Citizen's Counciler or the Ku Klux Klanner, but the white moderate, who is more devoted to "order" than to justice; who prefers a negative peace which is the absence of tension to a positive peace which is the presence of justice; who constantly says: "I agree with you in the goal you seek, but I cannot agree with your methods of direct action"; who paternalistically believes he can set the timetable for another man's freedom; who lives by a mythical concept of time and who constantly advises the Negro to wait for a "more convenient season." Shallow understanding from people of good will is more frustrating than absolute misunderstanding from people of ill will. Lukewarm acceptance is much more bewildering than outright rejection. 23

I had hoped that the white moderate would understand that law and order exist for the purpose of establishing justice and that when they fail in this purpose they become the dangerously structured dams that block the flow of social progress. I had hoped that the white moderate would understand that the present tension in the South is a necessary phase of the transition from an obnoxious negative peace, in which the Negro passively accepted his unjust plight, to a substantive and positive peace, in which all men will respect the dignity and worth of human personality. Actually, we who engage in nonviolent direct action are not the creators of tension. We merely bring to the surface the hidden tension that is already alive. We bring it out in the open, where it can be seen and dealt with. Like a boil that can never be cured so long as it is covered up but must be opened with all its ugliness to the natural medicines of air and light, injustice must be exposed, with all the tension its exposure creates, to the light of human conscience and the air of national opinion before it can be cured. 24

In your statement you assert that our actions, even though peaceful, must be condemned because they precipitate violence. But is this a logical assertion? Isn't this like condemning a robbed man because his possession of money precipitated the evil act of robbery? Isn't this like condemning Socrates because his unswerving commitment to truth and his philosophical inquiries precip- 25 itated the act by the misguided populace in which they made him drink hemlock? Isn't this like condemning Jesus because his unique God-consciousness and never-ceasing devotion to God's will precipitated the evil act of crucifixion? We must come to see that, as the federal courts have consistently affirmed, it is wrong to urge an individual to cease his efforts to gain his basic constitutional rights because the quest may precipitate violence. Society must protect the robbed and punish the robber.

I had also hoped that the white moderate would reject the myth 26 concerning time in relation to the struggle for freedom. I have just received a letter from a white brother in Texas. He writes: "All Christians know that the colored people will receive equal rights eventually, but it is possible that you are in too great a religious hurry. It has taken Christianity almost two thousand years to accomplish what it has. The teachings of Christ take time to come to earth." Such an attitude stems from a tragic misconception of time, from the strangely irrational notion that there is something in the very flow of time that will inevitably cure all ills. Actually, time itself is neutral; it can be used either destructively or constructively. More and more I feel that the people of ill will have used time much more effectively than have the people of good will. We will have to repent in this generation not merely for the hateful words and actions of the bad people but for the appalling silence of the good people. Human progress never rolls in on wheels of inevitability; it comes through the tireless efforts of men willing to be co-workers with God, and without this hard work, time itself becomes an ally of the forces of social stagnation. We must use time creatively, in the knowledge that the time is always ripe to do right. Now is the time to make real the promise of democracy and transform our pending national elegy into a creative psalm of brotherhood. Now is the time to lift our national policy from the quicksand of racial injustice to the solid rock of human dignity.

You speak of our activity in Birmingham as extreme. At first I 27 was rather disappointed that fellow clergymen would see my nonviolent efforts as those of an extremist. I began thinking about the fact that I stand in the middle of two opposing forces in the Negro community. One is a force of complacency, made up in part of Negroes who, as a result of long years of oppression, are so drained of self-respect and a sense of "somebodiness" that they have adjusted to segregation; and in part of a few middle-class Negroes who, because of a degree of academic and economic security and because in some ways they profit by segregation, have become insensitive to the problems of the masses. The other force is one of bitterness and hatred, and it comes perilously close to advocating violence. It is expressed in the various black nationalist groups that are springing up across the nation, the largest and best-known being Elijah Muhammad's Muslim movement. Nourished by the Negro's frustration over the continued existence of racial discrimination, this movement is made up of people who have lost faith in America, who have absolutely repudiated Christianity, and who have concluded that the white man is an incorrigible "devil."

I have tried to stand between these two forces, saying that we 28
need emulate neither the "do-nothingism" of the complacent nor the hatred and despair of the black nationalist. For there is the more excellent way of love and nonviolent protest. I am grateful to God that, through the influence of the Negro church, the way of nonviolence became an integral part of our struggle.

If this philosophy had not emerged, by now many streets of the 29
South would, I am convinced, be flowing with blood. And I am further convinced that if our white brothers dismiss as "rabble-rousers" and "outside agitators" those of us who employ nonviolent direct action, and if they refuse to support our nonviolent efforts, millions of Negroes will, out of frustration and despair, seek solace and security in black-nationalist ideologies—a development that would inevitably lead to a frightening racial nightmare.

Oppressed people cannot remain oppressed forever. The yearn- 30
ing for freedom eventually manifests itself, and that is what has happened to the American Negro. Something within has reminded him of his birthright of freedom, and something without has reminded him that it can be gained. Consciously or unconsciously, he has been caught up by the *Zeitgeist*,[3] and with his black brothers of Africa and his brown and yellow brothers of Asia, South America and the Caribbean, the United States Negro is moving with a sense of great urgency toward the promised land of racial justice. If one recognizes this vital urge that has engulfed the Negro community, one should readily understand why public demonstrations are taking place. The Negro has many pent-up resentments and latent frustrations, and he must release them. So let him march; let him make prayer pilgrimages to the city hall; let him go on freedom rides—and try to understand why he must do so. If his repressed emotions are not released in nonviolent ways, they will seek expression through violence; this is not a threat but a fact of history. So I have not said to my people: "Get rid of your discontent." Rather, I have tried to say that this normal and healthy discontent can be channeled into the creative outlet of nonviolent direct action. And now this approach is being termed extremist.

3. The spirit of the age.

But though I was initially disappointed at being categorized as   31
an extremist, as I continued to think about the matter I gradually
gained a measure of satisfaction from the label. Was not Jesus an
extremist for love: "Love your enemies, bless them that curse you,
do good to them that hate you, and pray for them which despite-
fully use you, and persecute you." Was not Amos an extremist for
justice: "Let justice roll down like waters and righteousness like an
ever-flowing stream." Was not Paul an extremist for the Christian
gospel: "I bear in my body the marks of the Lord Jesus." Was not
Martin Luther an extremist: "Here I stand; I cannot do otherwise,
so help me God." And John Bunyan: "I will stay in jail to the end
of my days before I make a butchery of my conscience." And
Abraham Lincoln: "This nation cannot survive half slave and half
free." And Thomas Jefferson: "We hold these truths to be self-
evident, that all men are created equal . . ." So the question is not
whether we will be extremists, but what kind of extremists we will
be. Will we be extremists for hate or for love? Will we be extremists
for the preservation of injustice or for the extension of justice? In
that dramatic scene on Calvary's hill three men were crucified. We
must never forget that all three were crucified for the same crime—
the crime of extremism. Two were extremists for immorality, and
thus fell below their environment. The other, Jesus Christ, was an
extremist for love, truth, and goodness, and thereby rose above his
environment. Perhaps the South, the nation, and the world are in
dire need of creative extremists.

I had hoped that the white moderate would see this need. Per-   32
haps I was too optimistic; perhaps I expected too much. I suppose I
should have realized that few members of the oppressor race can
understand the deep groans and passionate yearnings of the oppressed race, and still fewer have the vision to see that injustice
must be rooted out by strong, persistent, and determined action. I
am thankful, however, that some of our white brothers in the
South have grasped the meaning of this social revolution and committed themselves to it. They are still all too few in quantity, but
they are big in quality. Some—such as Ralph McGill, Lillian Smith,
Harry Golden, James McBride Dabbs, Ann Braden, and Sarah Patton Boyle—have written about our struggle in eloquent and prophetic terms. Others have marched with us down nameless streets
of the South. They have languished in filthy, roach-infested jails,
suffering the abuse and brutality of policemen who view them as
"dirty nigger-lovers." Unlike so many of their moderate brothers
and sisters, they have recognized the urgency of the moment and
sensed the need for powerful "action" antidotes to combat the
disease of segregation.

Let me take note of my other major disappointment. I have been   33
so greatly disappointed with the white church and its leadership.
Of course, there are some notable exceptions. I am not unmindful
of the fact that each of you has taken some significant stands on
this issue. I commend you, Reverend Stallings, for your Christian
stand on this past Sunday, in welcoming Negroes to your worship
service on a nonsegregated basis. I commend the Catholic leaders
of this state for integrating Spring Hill College several years ago.

But despite these notable exceptions, I must honestly reiterate   34
that I have been disappointed with the church. I do not say this as
one of those negative critics who can always find something wrong
with the church. I say this as a minister of the gospel, who loves the
church; who was nurtured in its bosom; who has been sustained
by its spiritual blessings and who will remain true to it as long as
the cord of life shall lengthen.

When I was suddenly catapulted into the leadership of the bus   35
protest in Montgomery, Alabama, a few years ago, I felt we would
be supported by the white church. I felt that the white ministers,
priests, and rabbis of the South would be among our strongest
allies. Instead, some have been outright opponents, refusing to
understand the freedom movement and misrepresenting its leaders; all too many others have been more cautious than courageous
and have remained silent behind the anesthetizing security of
stained-glass windows.

In spite of my shattered dreams, I came to Birmingham with the   36
hope that the white religious leadership of this community would
see the justice of our cause and, with deep moral concern, would
serve as the channel through which our just grievances could reach
the power structure. I had hoped that each of you would understand. But again I have been disappointed.

I have heard numerous southern religious leaders admonish   37
their worshipers to comply with a desegregation decision because it
is the law, but I have longed to hear white ministers declare: "Follow this decree because integration is morally right and because the
Negro is your brother." In the midst of blatant injustices inflicted
upon the Negro, I have watched white churchmen stand on the
sideline and mouth pious irrelevancies and sanctimonious trivi-
alities. In the midst of a mighty struggle to rid our nation of racial
and economic injustice, I have heard many ministers say: "Those
are social issues, with which the gospel has no real concern." And I
have watched many churches commit themselves to a completely
otherworldly religion which makes a strange, un-Biblical distinction between body and soul, between the sacred and the secular.

I have traveled the length and breadth of Alabama, Mississippi,   38 and all the other southern states. On sweltering summer days and crisp autumn mornings I have looked at the South's beautiful churches with their lofty spires pointing heavenward. I have beheld the impressive outlines of her massive religious-education buildings. Over and over I have found myself asking: "What kind of people worship here? Who is their God? Where were their voices when the lips of Governor Barnett[4] dripped with words of interposition and nullification? Where were they when Governor Wallace[5] gave a clarion call for defiance and hatred? Where were their voices of support when bruised and weary Negro men and women decided to rise from the dark dungeons of complacency to the bright hills of creative protest?"

Yes, these questions are still in my mind. In deep disappointment   39
I have wept over the laxity of the church. But be assured that my tears have been tears of love. There can be no deep disappointment where there is not deep love. Yes, I love the church. How could I do otherwise? I am in the rather unique position of being the son, the grandson and the great-grandson of preachers. Yes, I see the church as the body of Christ. But, oh! How we have blemished and scarred that body through social neglect and through fear of being nonconformists.

There was a time when the church was very powerful—in the   40
time when the early Christians rejoiced at being deemed worthy to suffer for what they believed. In those days the church was not merely a thermometer that recorded the ideas and principles of popular opinion; it was a thermostat that transformed the mores of society. Whenever the early Christians entered a town, the people in power became disturbed and immediately sought to convict the Christians for being "disturbers of the peace" and "outside agitators." But the Christians pressed on, in the conviction that they were "a colony of heaven," called to obey God rather than man. Small in number, they were big in commitment. They were too God-intoxicated to be "astronomically intimidated." By their effort and example they brought an end to such ancient evils as infanticide and gladiatorial contests.

Things are different now. So often the contemporary church is a   41
weak, ineffectual voice with an uncertain sound. So often it is an archdefender of the status quo. Far from being disturbed by the presence of the church, the power structure of the average commu-

4. Ross Barnett, governor of Mississippi, in 1962 ordered resistance to the registration of a black student, James Meredith, at the University of Mississippi.
5. George Wallace, governor of Alabama, stood in a doorway of the University of Alabama in a symbolic effort to block the registration of two black students in 1963.

nity is consoled by the church's silent—and often even vocal—
sanction of things as they are.

But the judgment of God is upon the church as never before. If   42
today's church does not recapture the sacrificial spirit of the early
church, it will lose its authenticity, forfeit the loyalty of millions,
and be dismissed as an irrelevant social club with no meaning for
the twentieth century. Every day I meet young people whose disappointment with the church has turned into outright disgust.

Perhaps I have once again been too optimistic. Is organized reli-   43
gion too inextricably bound to the status quo to save our nation
and the world? Perhaps I must turn my faith to the inner spiritual
church, the church within the church, as the true *ekklesia*[6] and the
hope of the world. But again I am thankful to God that some noble
souls from the ranks of organized religion have broken loose from
the paralyzing chains of conformity and joined us as active partners
in the struggle for freedom. They have left their secure congrega-
tions and walked the streets of Albany, Georgia, with us. They
have gone down the highways of the South on tortuous rides for
freedom. Yes, they have gone to jail with us. Some have been
dismissed from their churches, have lost the support of their
bishops and fellow ministers. But they have acted in the faith that
right defeated is stronger than evil triumphant. Their witness has
been the spiritual salt that has preserved the true meaning of the
gospel in these troubled times. They have carved a tunnel of hope
through the dark mountain of disappointment.

I hope the church as a whole will meet the challenge of this   44
decisive hour. But even if the church does not come to the aid of
justice, I have no despair about the future. I have no fear about the
outcome of our struggle in Birmingham, even if our motives are at
present misunderstood. We will reach the goal of freedom in Birmingham and all over the nation, because the goal of America is
freedom. Abused and scorned though we may be, our destiny is
tied up with America's destiny. Before the pilgrims landed at Plym-
outh, we were here. Before the pen of Jefferson etched the majestic
words of the Declaration of Independence across the pages of history, we were here. For more than two centuries our forebears
labored in this country without wages; they made cotton king;
they built the homes of their masters while suffering gross injustice
and shameful humiliation—and yet out of a bottomless vitality
they continued to thrive and develop. If the inexpressible cruelties
of slavery could not stop us, the opposition we now face will surely
fail. We will win our freedom because the sacred heritage of our

6. Literally, "assembly of the people."

nation and the eternal will of God are embodied in our echoing demands.

Before closing I feel impelled to mention one other point in your statement that has troubled me profoundly. You warmly commended the Birmingham police force for keeping "order" and "preventing violence." I doubt that you would have so warmly commended the police force if you had seen its dogs sinking their teeth into unarmed, nonviolent Negroes. I doubt that you would so quickly commend the policemen if you were to observe their ugly and inhumane treatment of Negroes here in the city jail; if you were to watch them push and curse old Negro women and young Negro girls; if you were to see them slap and kick old Negro men and young boys; if you were to observe them, as they did on two occasions, refuse to give us food because we wanted to sing our grace together. I cannot join you in your praise of the Birmingham police department. 45

It is true that the police have exercised a degree of discipline in handling the demonstrators. In this sense they have conducted themselves rather "nonviolently" in public. But for what purpose? To preserve the evil system of segregation. Over the past few years I have consistently preached that nonviolence demands that the means we use must be as pure as the ends we seek. I have tried to make clear that it is wrong to use immoral means to attain moral ends. But now I must affirm that it is just as wrong, or perhaps even more so, to use moral means to preserve immoral ends. Perhaps Mr. Connor and his policemen have been rather nonviolent in public, as was Chief Pritchett in Albany, Georgia, but they have used the moral means of nonviolence to maintain the immoral end of racial injustice. As T. S. Eliot has said: "The last temptation is the greatest treason: To do the right deed for the wrong reason." 46

I wish you had commended the Negro sit-inners and demonstrators of Birmingham for their sublime courage, their willingness to suffer, and their amazing discipline in the midst of great provocation. One day the South will recognize its real heroes. They will be the James Merediths, with the noble sense of purpose that enables them to face jeering and hostile mobs, and with the agonizing loneliness that characterizes the life of the pioneer. They will be old, oppressed, battered Negro women, symbolized in a seventy-two-year-old woman in Montgomery, Alabama, who rose up with a sense of dignity and with her people decided not to ride segregated buses, and who responded with ungrammatical profundity to one who inquired about her weariness: "My feets is tired, but my soul is at rest." They will be the young high school and college students, the young ministers of the gospel and a host of their 47 elders, courageously and nonviolently sitting in at lunch counters and willingly going to jail for conscience' sake. One day the South will know that when these disinherited children of God sat down at lunch counters, they were in reality standing up for what is best in the American dream and for the most sacred values in our Judaeo-Christian heritage, thereby bringing our nation back to those great wells of democracy which were dug deep by the founding fathers in their formulation of the Constitution and the Declaration of Independence.

Never before have I written so long a letter. I'm afraid it is much too long to take your precious time. I can assure you that it would have been much shorter if I had been writing from a comfortable desk, but what else can one do when he is alone in a narrow jail cell, other than write long letters, think long thoughts, and pray long prayers? 48

If I have said anything in this letter that overstates the truth and indicates an unreasonable impatience, I beg you to forgive me. If I have said anything that understates the truth and indicates my having a patience that allows me to settle for anything less than brotherhood, I beg God to forgive me. 49

I hope this letter finds you strong in the faith. I also hope that circumstances will soon make it possible for me to meet each of you, not as an integrationist or a civil-rights leader but as a fellow clergyman and a Christian brother. Let us all hope that the dark clouds of racial prejudice will soon pass away and the deep fog of misunderstanding will be lifted from our fear-drenched communities, and in some not too distant tomorrow the radiant stars of love and brotherhood will shine over our great nation with all their scintillating beauty. 50

> Yours for the cause of Peace and Brotherhood,
> MARTIN LUTHER KING, JR.

N. SCOTT MOMADAY

The Way to Rainy Mountain

N(avarre) Scott Momaday (1934–   ) is the son of a Kiowa father and a mother of mixed white and Cherokee ancestry. He spent his earliest years among Kiowas on a family farm in Oklahoma. Later he moved with his parents to New Mexico, where they taught in reservation schools. Momaday took a B.A. in English from the University of New Mexico and an M.A. and

Ph.D. from Stanford University. Like his father, he is an accomplished artist, and like his mother, he is a skilled writer. Among his best-known works are *House Made of Dawn* (1968), a Pulitzer Prize–winning novel; *The Gourd Dancer* (1976), a book of poems he also illustrated; and *The Way to Rainy Mountain* (1969), a collection of traditional Kiowa stories. Many of the stories in *Rainy Mountain* were told to Momaday by his father (who illustrated the book), his grandmother, and several of his grandmother's friends "who were in close touch with the oral tradition of the tribe." Its introduction, first published as a separate essay in *The Reporter* (1967), gives a sense of what Momaday values in his Kiowa heritage and what he sees threatened by the dominance of white civilization.

A single knoll rises out of the plain in Oklahoma, north and west 1
of the Wichita Range. For my people, the Kiowas, it is an old landmark, and they gave it the name Rainy Mountain. The hardest weather in the world is there. Winter brings blizzards, hot tornadic winds arise in the spring, and in the summer the prairie is an anvil's edge. The grass turns brittle and brown, and it cracks beneath your feet. There are green belts along the rivers and creeks, linear groves of hickory and pecan, willow, and witch hazel. At a distance in July or August the steaming foliage seems almost to writhe in fire. Great green-and-yellow grasshoppers are everywhere in the tall grass, popping up like corn to sting the flesh, and tortoises crawl about on the red earth, going nowhere in the plenty of time. Loneliness is an aspect of the land. All things in the plain are isolate; there is no confusion of objects in the eye, but *one* hill or *one* tree or *one* man. To look upon that landscape in the early morning, with the sun at your back, is to lose the sense of proportion. Your imagination comes to life, and this, you think, is where Creation was begun.

I returned to Rainy Mountain in July. My grandmother had died 2
in the spring, and I wanted to be at her grave. She had lived to be very old and at last infirm. Her only living daughter was with her when she died, and I was told that in death her face was that of a child.

I like to think of her as a child. When she was born, the Kiowas 3
were living that last great moment of their history. For more than a hundred years they had controlled the open range from the Smoky Hill River to the Red, from the headwaters of the Canadian to the fork of the Arkansas and Cimarron. In alliance with the Comanches, they had ruled the whole of the southern Plains. War was their sacred business, and they were among the finest horsemen the world has ever known. But warfare for the Kiowas was preeminently a matter of disposition rather than of survival, and

they never understood the grim, unrelenting advance of the U.S. Cavalry. When at last, divided and ill-provisioned, they were driven onto the Staked Plains in the cold rains of autumn, they fell into panic. In Palo Duro Canyon they abandoned their crucial stores to pillage and had nothing then but their lives. In order to save themselves, they surrendered to the soldiers at Fort Sill and were imprisoned in the old stone corral that now stands as a military museum. My grandmother was spared the humiliation of those high gray walls by eight or ten years, but she must have known from birth the affliction of defeat, the dark brooding of old warriors.

Her name was Aho, and she belonged to the last culture to   4
evolve in North America. Her forebears came down from the high country in western Montana nearly three centuries ago. They were a mountain people, a mysterious tribe of hunters whose language has never been positively classified in any major group. In the late seventeenth century they began a long migration to the south and east. It was a long journey toward the dawn, and it led to a golden age. Along the way the Kiowas were befriended by the Crows, who gave them the culture and religion of the Plains. They acquired horses, and their ancient nomadic spirit was suddenly free of the ground. They acquired Tai-me, the sacred Sun Dance doll, from that moment the object and symbol of their worship, and so shared in the divinity of the sun. Not least, they acquired the sense of destiny, therefore courage and pride. When they entered upon the southern Plains, they had been transformed. No longer were they slaves to the simple necessity of survival; they were a lordly and dangerous society of fighters and thieves, hunters and priests of the sun. According to their origin myth, they entered the world through a hollow log. From one point of view, their migration was the fruit of an old prophecy, for indeed they emerged from a sunless world.

Although my grandmother lived out her long life in the shadow   5
of Rainy Mountain, the immense landscape of the continental interior lay like memory in her blood. She could tell of the Crows, whom she had never seen, and of the Black Hills, where she had never been. I wanted to see in reality what she had seen more perfectly in the mind's eye, and traveled fifteen hundred miles to begin my pilgrimage.

Yellowstone, it seemed to me, was the top of the world, a region   6
of deep lakes and dark timber, canyons and waterfalls. But, beautiful as it is, one might have the sense of confinement there. The skyline in all directions is close at hand, the high wall of the woods and deep cleavages of shade. There is a perfect freedom in the moun-

tains, but it belongs to the eagle and the elk, the badger and the bear. The Kiowas reckoned their stature by the distance they could see, and they were bent and blind in the wilderness.

Descending eastward, the highland meadows are a stairway to the plain. In July the inland slope of the Rockies is luxuriant with flax and buckwheat, stonecrop and larkspur. The earth unfolds and the limit of the land recedes. Clusters of trees and animals grazing far in the distance cause the vision to reach away and wonder to build upon the mind. The sun follows a longer course in the day, and the sky is immense beyond all comparison. The great billowing clouds that sail upon it are shadows that move upon the grain like water, dividing light. Farther down, in the land of the Crows and Blackfeet, the plain is yellow. Sweet clover takes hold of the hills and bends upon itself to cover and seal the soil. There the Kiowas paused on their way; they had come to the place where they must change their lives. The sun is at home on the plains. Precisely there does it have the certain character of a god. When the Kiowas came to the land of the Crows, they could see the dark lees of the hill at dawn across the Bighorn River, the profusion of light on the grain shelves, the oldest deity ranging after the solstices. Not yet would they veer southward to the caldron of the land that lay below; they must wean their blood from the northern winter and hold the mountains a while longer in their view. They bore Tai-me in procession to the east. 7

A dark mist lay over the Black Hills, and the land was like iron. At the top of a ridge I caught sight of Devil's Tower upthrust against the gray sky as if in the birth of time the core of the earth had broken through its crust and the motion of the world was begun. There are things in nature that engender an awful quiet in the heart of man; Devil's Tower is one of them. Two centuries ago, because they could not do otherwise, the Kiowas made a legend at the base of the rock. My grandmother said: 8

> "Eight children were there at play, seven sisters and their brother. Suddenly the boy was struck dumb; he trembled and began to run upon his hands and feet. His fingers became claws, and his body was covered with fur. Directly there was a bear where the boy had been. The sisters were terrified; they ran, and the bear after them. They came to the stump of a great tree, and the tree spoke to them. It bade them climb upon it and as they did so, it began to rise into the air. The bear came to kill them, but they were just beyond its reach. It reared against the tree and scored the bark all around with its claws. The seven sisters were borne into the sky, and they became the stars of the Big Dipper."

From that moment, and so long as the legend lives, the Kiowas have kinsmen in the night sky. Whatever they were in the mountains, they could be no more. However tenuous their well-being, however much they had suffered and would suffer again, they had found a way out of the wilderness.

My grandmother had a reverence for the sun, a holy regard that   9
now is all but gone out of mankind. There was a wariness in her and an ancient awe. She was a Christian in her later years, but she had come a long way about, and she never forgot her birthright. As a child she had been to the Sun Dances; she had taken part in those annual rites, and by them she had learned the restoration of her people in the presence of Tai-me. She was about seven when the last Kiowa Sun Dance was held in 1887 on the Washita River above Rainy Mountain Creek. The buffalo were gone. In order to consummate the ancient sacrifice—to impale the head of a buffalo bull upon the medicine tree—a delegation of old men journeyed into Texas, there to beg and barter for an animal from the Goodnight herd. She was ten when the Kiowas came together for the last time as a living Sun Dance culture. They could find no buffalo; they had to hang an old hide from the sacred tree. Before the dance could begin, a company of soldiers rode out from Fort Sill under orders to disperse the tribe. Forbidden without cause the essential act of their faith, having seen the wild herds slaughtered and left to rot upon the ground, the Kiowas backed away forever from the medicine tree. That was July 20, 1890, at the great bend of the Washita. My grandmother was there. Without bitterness, and for as long as she lived, she bore a vision of deicide.

Now that I can have her only in memory, I see my grandmother   10
in the several postures that were peculiar to her: standing at the wood stove on a winter morning and turning meat in a great iron skillet; sitting at the south window, bent above her beadwork, and afterwards, when her vision had failed, looking down for a long time into the fold of her hands; going out upon a cane, very slowly as she did when the weight of age came upon her; praying. I remember her most often at prayer. She made long, rambling prayers out of suffering and hope, having seen many things. I was never sure that I had the right to hear, so exclusive were they of all mere custom and company. The last time I saw her she prayed standing by the side of her bed at night, naked to the waist, the light of a kerosene lamp moving upon her dark skin. Her long, black hair, always drawn and braided in the day, lay upon her shoulders and against her breasts like a shawl. I do not speak Kiowa, and I never understood her prayers, but there was something inherently sad in the sound, some merest hesitation upon the syllables of sorrow. She began in a high and descending pitch, exhausting her breath to silence; then again and again—and always the same intensity of effort, of something that is, and is not, like urgency in the human

voice. Transported so in the dancing light among the shadows of her room, she seemed beyond the reach of time. But that was illusion; I think I knew then that I should not see her again.

Houses are like sentinels in the plain, old keepers of the weather watch. There, in a very little while, wood takes on the appearance of great age. All colors wear soon away in the wind and rain, and then the wood is burned gray and the grain appears and the nails turn red with rust. The windowpanes are black and opaque; you imagine there is nothing within, and indeed there are many ghosts, bones given up to the land. They stand here and there against the sky, and you approach them for a longer time than you expect. They belong in the distance; it is their domain. 11

Once there was a lot of sound in my grandmother's house, a lot of coming and going, feasting and talk. The summers there were full of excitement and reunion. The Kiowas are a summer people; they abide the cold and keep to themselves; but when the season turns and the land becomes warm and vital, they cannot hold still; an old love of going returns upon them. The aged visitors who came to my grandmother's house when I was a child were made of lean and leather, and they bore themselves upright. They wore great black hats and bright ample shirts that shook in the wind. They rubbed fat upon their hair and wound their braids with strips of colored cloth. Some of them painted their faces and carried the scars of old and cherished enmities. They were an old council of warlords, come to remind and be reminded of who they were. Their wives and daughters served them well. The women might indulge themselves; gossip was at once the mark and compensation of their servitude. They made loud and elaborate talk among themselves, full of jest and gesture, fright and false alarm. They went abroad in fringed and flowered shawls, bright beadwork, and German silver. They were at home in the kitchen, and they prepared meals that were banquets. 12

There were frequent prayer meetings, and great nocturnal feasts. When I was a child, I played with my cousins outside, where the lamplight fell upon the ground and the singing of the old people rose up around us and carried away into the darkness. There were a lot of good things to eat, a lot of laughter and surprise. And afterwards, when the quiet returned, I lay down with my grandmother and could hear the frogs away by the river and feel the motion of the air. 13

Now there is a funeral silence in the rooms, the endless wake of some final word. The walls have closed in upon my grandmother's house. When I returned to it in mourning, I saw for the first time in my life how small it was. It was late at night, and there was a white moon, nearly full. I sat for a long time on the stone steps by the 14

kitchen door. From there I could see out across the land; I could see
the long row of trees by the creek, the low light upon the rolling
plains, and the stars of the Big Dipper. Once I looked at the moon
and caught sight of a strange thing. A cricket had perched upon the
handrail, only a few inches away from me. My line of vision was
such that the creature filled the moon like a fossil. It had gone
there, I thought, to live and die, for there of all places, was its small
definition made whole and eternal. A warm wind rose up and
purled like the longing within me.

The next morning I awoke at dawn and went out on the dirt   15
road to Rainy Mountain. It was already hot, and the grasshoppers
began to fill the air. Still, it was early in the morning, and the birds
sang out of the shadows. The long yellow grass on the mountain
shone in the bright light, and a scissortail hied above the land.
There, where it ought to be, at the end of a long and legendary
way, was my grandmother's grave. Here and there on the dark
stones were ancestral names. Looking back once, I saw the mountain and came away.

CYNTHIA OZICK

We Are the Crazy Lady
and Other Feisty Feminist Fables

Cynthia Ozick (1928–   ) was born in New York City into a
family of storytellers. She remembers her grandmother's tales of
growing up in a Russian village and her parents' accounts of the
lives of their neighbors, who sounded—she later realized—like
characters from a novel by Jane Austen or Anthony Trollope.
Ozick took her B.A. in English from New York University in
1949 and her M.A. from Ohio State University the next year; she
is also a student of Hebrew language and Jewish literature.
Among her works of fiction are *Trust* (1966), *The Pagan Rabbi
and Other Stories* (1971), *Bloodshed and Three Novellas* (1976), and
The Messiah of Stockholm (1987). Her essays have been collected in
Art and Ardor (1983) and *Metaphor and Memory* (1988). Ozick
describes herself as a "classical feminist"—one who objects to
the segregation of men's and women's intellectual, social, and
political lives. Lately, she has complained that those who present
women's literature as a separate realm "instigate and inflame the
old prejudices *in the name* of feminism." "We are the Crazy Lady"
was first published in *Ms. Magazine* in the spring of 1973.

I. THE CRAZY LADY DOUBLE

A long, long time ago, in another century—1951, in fact—when   1
you, dear younger readers, were most likely still in your nuclear-
family playpen (where, if female, you cuddled a rag-baby to your
potential titties, or, if male, let down virile drool over your plastic
bulldozer), The Famous Critic[1] told me never, never to use a parenthesis in the very first sentence. This was in a graduate English
seminar at Columbia University. To get into this seminar, you had
to submit to a grilling wherein you renounced all former allegiance
to the then-current literary religion, New Criticism, which considered that only the text existed, not the world. I passed the interview
by lying—cunningly, and against my real convictions. I said that
probably the world *did* exist—and walked triumphantly into the
seminar room.

There were four big tables arranged in a square, with everyone's   2
feet sticking out into the open middle of the square. You could tell
who was nervous, and how much, by watching the pairs of feet
twist around each other. The Great Man presided awesomely from
the high bar of the square. His head was a majestic granite-gray,
like a centurion in command; he *looked* famous. His clean shoes
twitched only slightly, and only when he was angry.

It turned out he was angry at me a lot of the time. He was angry   3
because he thought me a disrupter, a rioter, a provocateur, and a
fool; also crazy. And this was twenty years ago, before these things
were *de rigueur*[2] in the universities. Everything was very quiet in
those days: there were only the Cold War and Korea and Joe
McCarthy and the Old Old Nixon, and the only revolutionaries
around were in Henry James's *The Princess Casamassima.*

Habit governed the seminar. Where you sat the first day was   4
where you settled forever. So, to avoid the stigmatization of the
ghetto, I was careful not to sit next to the other woman in the class:
the Crazy Lady.

At first the Crazy Lady appeared to be remarkably intelligent.   5
She was older than the rest of us, somewhere in her thirties (which
was why we thought of her as a Lady), with wild tan hair, a
noticeably breathing bosom, eccentric gold-rimmed old-pensioner
glasses, and a tooth-crowded wild mouth that seemed to get wilder
the more she talked. She talked like a motorcycle, fast and urgent.
Everything she said was almost brilliant, only not actually on
point, and frenetic with hostility. She was tough and negative. She

---

1. Lionel Trilling, influential literary critic and writer (1905–1975).
2. "Indispensable," required; in this instance Ozick means "a matter of course,
usual."

volunteered a lot and she stood up and wobbled with rage, pulling at her hair and mouth. She fought the Great Man point for point, piecemeal and wholesale, mixing up queerly-angled literary insights with all sorts of private and public fury. After the first meetings he was fed up with her. The rest of us accepted that she probably wasn't all there, but in a room where everyone was on the make for recognition—you talked to save your life, and the only way to save your life was to be the smartest one that day—she was a nuisance, a distraction, a pain in the ass. The class became a bunch of Good Germans, determinedly indifferent onlookers to a vindictive match between the Critic and the Crazy Lady, until finally he subdued her by shutting his eyes, and, when that didn't always work, by cutting her dead and lecturing right across the sound of her strong, strange voice.

All this was before R. D. Laing[3] had invented the superiority of   6
madness, of course, and, cowards all, no one liked the thought of being tarred with the Crazy Lady's brush. Ignored by the boss, in the middle of everything she would suddenly begin to mutter to herself. She mentioned certain institutions she'd been in, and said we all belonged there. The people who sat on either side of her shifted chairs. If the Great Man ostracized the Crazy Lady, we had to do it too. But one day the Crazy Lady came in late and sat down in the seat next to mine, and stayed there the rest of the semester.

Then an odd thing happened. There, right next to me, was the   7
noisy Crazy Lady, tall, with that sticking-out sighing chest of hers, orangey curls dripping over her nose, snuffling furiously for attention. And there was I, a brownish runt, a dozen years younger and flatter and shyer than the Crazy Lady, in no way her twin, physically or psychologically. In those days I was bone-skinny, small, sallow and myopic, and so scared I could trigger diarrhea at one glance from the Great Man. All this stress on looks is important: the Crazy Lady and I had our separate bodies, our separate brains. We handed in our separate papers.

But the Great Man never turned toward me, never at all, and if   8
ambition broke feverishly through shyness so that I dared to push an idea audibly out of me, he shut his eyes when I put up my hand. This went on for a long time. I never got to speak, and I began to have the depressing feeling that he hated me. It was no small thing to be hated by the man who had written the most impressive criticism of the century. What in hell was going on? I was in trouble; like everyone else in that demented contest, I wanted to

---

3. Scottish psychiatrist (b. 1927) whose lifework has been devoted to the study of insanity, especially schizophrenia.

excel. Then, one slow afternoon, wearily, the Great Man let his eyes fall on me. He called me by name, but it was not my name—it was the Crazy Lady's. The next week the papers came back—and there, right at the top of mine, in the Great Man's own handwriting, was a rebuke to the Crazy Lady for starting an essay with a parenthesis in the first sentence, a habit he took to be a continuing sign of that unruly and unfocused mentality so often exhibited in class. And then a Singular Revelation crept coldly through me: because the Crazy Lady and I sat side by side, because we were a connected blur of Woman, the Famous Critic, master of ultimate distinctions, couldn't tell us apart. The Crazy Lady and I! He couldn't tell us apart! It didn't matter that the Crazy Lady was crazy! *He couldn't tell us apart!*

Moral 1: All cats are gray at night,
              all darkies look alike.   9

Moral 2: Even among intellectual humanists, every woman has   10
a *Doppelgänger*[4]—every other woman.

II. THE LECTURE, 1

I was invited by a women's group to be guest speaker at a Book-   11
Author Luncheon. The women themselves had not really chosen me: the speaker had been selected by a male leader and imposed on them. The plan was that I would autograph copies of my book, eat a good meal, and then lecture. The woman in charge of the programming telephoned to ask me what my topic would be. This was a matter of some concern, since they had never had a woman author before, and no one knew how the idea would be received. I offered as my subject "The Contemporary Poem."

When the day came, everything went as scheduled—the auto-   12
graphing, the food, the welcoming addresses. Then it was time to go to the lectern. I aimed at the microphone and began to speak of poetry. A peculiar rustling sound flew up from the audience. All the women were lifting their programs to the light, like hundreds of wings. Confused murmurs ran along the walls. Something was awry; I began to feel very uncomfortable. Then I too took up the program. It read: "Topic: The Contemporary Home."

Moral: Even our ears practice the caste system.   13

III. THE LECTURE, 2

I was in another country, the only woman at a philosophical   14
seminar lasting three days. On the third day, I was to read a paper. I had accepted the invitation with a certain foreknowledge. I knew,

4. German for "double-goer": a ghostly double.

for instance, that I could not dare to be the equal of any other speaker. To be an equal would be to be less. I understood that mine had to be the most original and powerful paper of all. I had no choice; I had to toil beyond my most extreme possibilities. This was not ambition, but only fear of disgrace.

For the first two days, I was invisible. When I spoke, people 15 tapped impatiently, waiting for the interruption to end. No one took either my presence or my words seriously. At meals, I sat with my colleagues' wives.

The third day arrived, and I read my paper. It was successful 16 beyond my remotest imaginings. I was interviewed, and my remarks appeared in newspapers in a language I could not understand. The Foreign Minister invited me to his home. I hobnobbed with famous poets.

Now my colleagues noticed me. But they did not notice me as a 17 colleague. They teased and kissed me. I had become their mascot.

Moral: There is no route out of caste which does not instantly 18 lead back into it.

IV. PROPAGANDA

For many years I had noticed that no book of poetry by a woman 19 was ever reviewed without reference to the poet's sex. The curious thing was that, in the two decades of my scrutiny, there were *no* exceptions whatever. It did not matter whether the reviewer was a man or woman: in every case the question of the "feminine sensibility" of the poet was at the center of the reviewer's response. The maleness of the male poets, on the other hand, hardly ever seemed to matter.

Determined to ridicule this convention, I wrote a tract, a piece of 20 purely tendentious mockery, in the form of a short story. I called it "Virility."

The plot was, briefly, as follows: A very bad poet, lustful for 21 fame, is despised for his pitiful lucubrations and remains unpublished. But luckily, he comes into possession of a cache of letters written by his elderly spinster aunt, who lives an obscure and secluded working-class life in a remote corner of England. The letters contain a large number of remarkable poems; the aunt, it turns out, is a genius. The bad poet publishes his find under his own name, and instantly attains world-wide adulation. Under the title *Virility*, the poems become immediate classics. They are translated into dozens of languages and are praised and revered for their unmistakably masculine qualities: their strength, passion, wisdom, energy, boldness, brutality, worldliness, robustness, authenticity, sensuality, compassion. A big, handsome, sweating man, the poet swaggers from country to country, courted everywhere, pursued by admirers, yet respected by the most demanding critics.

Meanwhile, the old aunt dies. The supply of genius runs out. 22 Bravely and contritely the poor poet confesses his ruse, and, in a burst of honesty, publishes the last batch under the real poet's name; the book is entitled *Flowers from Liverpool*. But the poems are at once found negligible and dismissed: "Thin feminine art," say the reviews, "a lovely girlish voice." And: "Limited one-dimensional vision." "Choked with female inwardness." "The fine womanly intuition of a competent poetess." The poems are utterly forgotten.

I included this fable in a collection of short stories. In every 23 review the salvo went unnoticed. Not one reviewer recognized that the story was a sly tract. Not one reviewer saw the smirk or the point. There was one delicious comment, though. "I have some reservations," a man in Washington, D.C., wrote, "about the credibility of some of her male characters when they are chosen as narrators."

Moral: In saying what is obvious, never choose cunning. Yelling 24 works better.

V. HORMONES

During a certain period of my life, I was reading all the time, and 25 fairly obsessively. Sometimes, though, sunk in a book of criticism or philosophy, I would be brought up short. Consider: here is a paragraph that excites the intellect; inwardly, one assents passionately to its premises; the writer's idea is an exact diagram of one's own deepest psychology or conviction; one feels oneself seized as for a portrait. Then the disclaimer, the excluding shove: "It is, however, otherwise with the female sex. . . ." A rebuke from the World of Thinking: *I didn't mean you, lady*. In the instant one is in possession of one's humanity most intensely, it is ripped away.

These moments I discounted. What is wrong—intrinsically, psy- 26 chologically, culturally, morally—can be dismissed.

But to dismiss in this manner is to falsify one's most genuine 27 actuality. A Jew reading of the aesthetic glories of European civilization without taking notice of his victimization during, say, the era of the building of the great cathedrals, is self-forgetful in the most dangerous way. So would be a black who read of King Cotton[5] with an economist's objectivity.

---

5. The reference is to the importance of cotton in the economy of the American South in the first half of the nineteenth century—a condition heavily dependent on the labor of black slaves.

I am not offering any strict analogy between the situation of   28
women and the history of Jews or colonialized blacks, as many
politically radical women do (though the analogy with blacks is
much the more frequent one). It seems to me to be abusive of
language in the extreme when some women speak, in the generation after Auschwitz, of the "oppression" of women. Language
makes culture, and we make a rotten culture when we abuse
words. We raise up rotten heroines. I use "rotten" with particular
attention to its precise meaning: foul, putrid, tainted, stinking. I am
thinking now especially of a radical women's publication, *Off Our
Backs*, which not long ago presented Leila Khaled, terrorist and
foiled murderer, as a model for the political conduct of women.

But if I would not support the extreme analogy (and am never   29
surprised when black women, who have a more historical comprehension of actual, not figurative, oppression, refuse to support the
analogy), it is anyhow curious to see what happens to the general
culture when any enforced class in any historical or social condition is compelled to doubt its own self-understanding—when
identity is externally defined, when individual humanity is called
into question as being different from "standard" humanity. What
happens is that the general culture, along with the object of its
debasement, is also debased. If you laugh at women, you play
Beethoven in vain.

If you laugh at women, your laboratory will lie.   30

We can read in Charlotte Perkins Gilman's[6] 1912 essay, "Are   31
Women Human Beings?", an account of an opinion current sixty
years ago. Women, said one scientist, are not only "not the human
race—they are not even half the human race, but a sub-species set
apart for purposes of reproduction merely."

A physician said: "No doctor can ever lose sight of the fact that 32
the mind of woman is always threatened with danger from the
reverberations of her physiological emergencies." He concluded
this entirely on the basis of his invalid patients.

Though we are accustomed to the idea of "progress" in science   33
and medicine, if not in civilization generally, the fact is that more
information has led to something very like regression.

I talked with an intelligent physician, the Commissioner of   34
Health of a middle-sized city in Connecticut, a man who sees
medicine not discretely but as part of the social complex—was
treated to a long list of all the objective differences between men
and women, including particularly an account of current endo-
crinal studies relating to female hormones. Aren't all of these facts?

6. An American feminist writer (1860–1935).

he asked. How can you distrust facts? Very good, I said, I'm willing to take your medically-educated word for it. I'm not afraid of facts, I welcome facts—*but a congeries of facts is not equivalent to an idea.* This is the essential fallacy of the so-called "scientific" mind. People who mistake facts for ideas are incomplete thinkers; they are gossips.

You tell me, I said, that my sense of my own humanity as being 35 "standard" humanity—which is, after all, a subjective idea—is refuted by hormonal research. My psychology, you tell me, which in your view is the source of my ideas, is the result of my physiology: it is not I who express myself, it is my hormones which express me. A part is equal to the whole, you say. Worse yet, the whole is simply the issue of the part: my "I" is a flash of chemicals. You are willing to define all my humanity by hormonal investigation under a microscope: this you call "objective irrefutable fact," as if tissue-culture were equivalent to culture. But each scientist can assemble his own (subjective) constellation of "objective irrefutable fact," just as each social thinker can assemble his own (subjective) selection of traits to define "humanity" by. Who can prove what is "standard" humanity, and which sex, class, or race is to be exempted from whole participation in it? On what basis do you regard female hormones as causing a modification from normative humanity? And what better right do you have to define normative humanity by what males have traditionally apperceived than by what females have traditionally apperceived—assuming (as I, lacking presumptuousness, do not) that their apperceptions have not been the same? Only Tiresias—that mythological character who was both man and woman[7]—is in a position to make the comparison and present the proof. And then not even Tiresias, because to be a hermaphrodite is to be a monster, and not human.

"Why are you so emotional about all this?" said the Commis- 36 sioner of Health. "You see how it is? Those are your female hormones working on you right now."

Moral: Defamation is only applied research. 37

VI. AMBITION

After thirteen years, I at last finished a novel. The first seven 38 years were spent in a kind of apprenticeship—the book that came out of that time was abandoned without much regret. A second

---

7. In Greek mythology, Tiresias the seer, after being transformed for a time into a woman, was asked by the gods to settle an argument as to whether men or women enjoyed love more. Having seen it from both sides, he voted in favor of women.

one was finished in six weeks and buried. It took six years to write the third novel, and this one was finally published.

How I lived through those years is impossible to recount in a   39
short space. I was a recluse, a priest of Art. I read seas of books. I believed in the idea of masterpieces. I was scornful of the world of journalism, jobs, everydayness. I did not live like any woman I knew, although it never occurred to me to reflect on this of my own volition. I lived like some men I had read about—Flaubert, or Proust, or James: the subjects of those literary biographies I endlessly drank in. I did not think of them as men but as writers. I read the diaries of Virginia Woolf, and biographies of George Eliot, but I did not think of them as women. I thought of them as writers. I thought of myself as a writer. I went on reading and writing.

It goes without saying that all this time my relatives regarded me   40
as abnormal. I accepted this. It seemed to me, from what I had read, that most writers were abnormal. Yet on the surface I could easily have passed for normal. The husband goes to work, the wife stays home—that is what is normal. Well, I was married. My husband went to his job every day. His job paid the rent and bought the groceries. I stayed home, reading and writing, and felt myself to be an economic parasite. To cover guilt, I joked that I had been given a grant from a very private, very poor, foundation; I meant my husband.

But my relatives never thought of me as a parasite. The very   41
thing I was doubtful about—my economic dependence—they considered my due as a woman. They saw me not as a failed writer without an income, but as a childless housewife, a failed woman. They did not think me abnormal because I was a writer, but because I was not properly living my life as a woman. In one respect we were in agreement utterly—my life was failing terribly, terribly. For me it was because, already deep into my thirties, I had not yet published a book. For them, it was because I had not yet borne a child.

I was a pariah,[8] not only because I was a deviant, but because I   42
was not recognized as the kind of deviant I meant to be. A failed woman is not the same as a failed writer. Even as a pariah I was the wrong kind of pariah.

Still, relations are only relations, and what I aspired to, what I   43
was in thrall to, was Art; was Literature; not familial contentment. I knew how to distinguish the trivial from the sublime. In Literature and in Art, I saw, my notions were not pariah notions: *there*, I inhabited the mainstream. So I went on reading and writing; I

8. A social outcast.

went on believing in Art, and my intention was to write a master-piece. Not a saucer of well-polished craft (the sort of thing "women writers" are always accused of being accomplished at), but something huge, contemplative, Tolstoyan. My ambition was a craw.

I called the book *Trust*. I began it in the summer of 1957 and finished it in November of 1963, on the day President John Kennedy was assassinated. In manuscript it was 801 pages divided into four parts: "America," "Europe," "Birth," "Death." The title was meant to be ironic. In reality, it was about distrust. It seemed to me I had touched on distrust in every order or form of civilization. It seemed to me I had left nothing out. It was (though I did not know this then) a very hating book. What it hated above all was the whole—the whole!—of Western Civilization. It told how America had withered into another Europe; it dreamed dark and murderous pagan dreams, and hated what it dreamed.

In style, the book was what has come to be called "mandarin": a difficult, aristocratic, unrelenting virtuoso prose. It was, in short, unreadable. I think I knew this; I was sardonic enough to say, echoing Joyce about *Finnegans Wake*,[9] "I expect you to spend your life at this." In any case, I had spent a decade-and-a-half of my own life at it, and though I did not imagine the world would fall asunder at its appearance, I thought—at the very least—the ambition, the all-swallowingness, the wild insatiability of the writer would be plain to everyone who read it. I had, after all, taken History for my subject: not merely History as an aggregate of events, but History as a judgment on events. No one could say my theme was flighty. Of all the novelists I read—and in those days I read them all, broiling in the envy of the unpublished, which is like no envy on earth—who else had dared so vastly?

During that period, Françoise Sagan's[10] first novel was published. I held the thin little thing and laughed. Women's pulp!

My own novel, I believed, contained everything—the whole world.

But there was one element I had consciously left out, though on principle I did not like to characterize it or think about it much. The truth is I was thinking about it all the time. It was only a fiction-technicality, but I was considerably afraid of it. It was the question of the narrator's "sensibility." The narrator, as it happened, was a young woman; I had chosen her to be the eye—and the "I"—of the novel because all the other characters in some way focused on

44

45

46

47

48

9. Notoriously difficult novel by Irish novelist James Joyce (1882–1941).
10. French novelist (b. 1935). Her first work, *Bonjour Tristesse* ("Hello, Sadness"), is the story of an adolescent's tragic attempt to prevent her father's remarriage.

her, and she was the one most useful to my scheme. Nevertheless I
wanted her not to live. Everything I was reading in reviews of other
people's books made me fearful: I would have to be very, very
cautious, I would have to drain my narrator of emotive value of
any kind. I was afraid to be pegged as having written a "women's"
novel, and nothing was more certain to lead to that than a point-
of-view seemingly lodged in a woman; no one takes a woman's
novel seriously. I was in terror, above all, of sentiment and feeling,
those telltale taints. I kept the fury and the passion for other, safer,
characters.

So what I left out of my narrator entirely, sweepingly, with   49
exquisite consciousness of what exactly I *was* leaving out, was any
shred of "sensibility." I stripped her of everything, even a name. I
crafted and carpentered her; she was for me a bloodless device,
fulcrum or pivot, a recording voice, a language-machine. She confronted moment or event, took it in, gave it out. And what to me
was all the more wonderful about this nameless fiction-machine I
had invented was that the machine itself, though never alive, was a
character in the story, without ever influencing the story. My
machine-narrator was there for efficiency only, for flexibility, for
craftiness, for subtlety, but never, never, as a "woman." I wiped
the "woman" out of her. And I did it out of fear, out of vicarious
vindictive critical imagination, out of the terror of my ambition, out
of, maybe, paranoia. I meant my novel to be taken for what it really
was. I meant to make it impossible for it to be mistaken for something else.

Publication.   50

Review in *The New York Times* Sunday Book Review.   51

Review is accompanied by a picture of a naked woman seen   52
from the back. Her bottom is covered by some sort of drapery.

Title of review: "Daughter's Reprieve."   53

Excerpts from review: "These events, interesting in themselves,   54
exist to reveal the sensibility of the narrator." "She longs to play
some easy feminine role." "She has been unable to define herself
as a woman." "Thus the daughter, at the age of twenty-two, is
eager for the prerequisites that should have been hers as a woman,
but is floundering badly in their pursuit." "Her protagonist insists
on coming to terms with the recalcitrant sexual elements in her
life." "The main body of the novel, then, is a revelation of the
narrator's inner, turbulent, psychic dream."

O rabid rotten Western Civilization, where are you? O judging   55
History, O foul Trust and fouler Distrust, where?

O Soap Opera, where did you come from?   56

(Meanwhile the review in *Time* was calling me a "housewife.")   57

Pause.   58

All right, let us take up the rebuttals one by one.   59

Q. Maybe you *did* write a soap opera without knowing it. Maybe   60
you only *thought* you were writing about Western Civilization
when you were really only rewriting Stella Dallas.[11]

A. A writer may be unsure of everything—trust the tale not the   61
teller is a good rule—but not of his obsessions; of these he is
certain. If I were rewriting Stella Dallas, I would turn her into the
Second Crusade and demobilize her.

Q. Maybe you're like the blind Jew who wants to be a pilot, and   62
when they won't give him the job he says they're anti-Semitic.
Look, the book was lousy, you deserved a lousy review.

A. You mistake me, I never said it was a bad review. It was in   63
fact an extremely favorable review, full of gratifying adjectives.

Q. But your novel languished anyhow?   64

A. Perished, is dead and buried. I sometimes see it exhumed on   65
the shelf in the public library. It's always there. No one ever bor-
rows it.

Q. Dummy! You should've written a soap opera. Women are   66
good at that.

A. Thank you. You almost remind me of another Moral: In   67
conceptual life, junk prevails. Even if you do not produce junk, it
will be taken for junk.

Q. What does that have to do with women?   68

A. The products of women are frequently taken for junk.   69

Q. And if a woman *does* produce junk . . .?   70

A. Glory—they will treat her almost like a man who produces   71
junk. They will say her name on television.

Q. Bitter, bitter!   72

A. Not at all. Again you misunderstand. You see, I have come   73
round to thinking (I learned it from television commercials, as a
matter of fact) that there *is* a Women's Culture—a sort of tribal,
separatist, ghettoized thing. And I propose that we cultivate it.

Q. You mean *really* writing Women's Novels? On purpose?   74

A. Nothing like that. The novel was invented by men. It isn't   75
ours, you see, and to us it is to *assimilate*. I see now where I went
wrong! So I propose that we return to our pristine cultural origins,
earn the respect of the male race, and regain our self-esteem.

---

11. *Stella Dallas* (1923) was originally a magazine serial by Olive Higgins Prouty. The
story was taken up by almost every conceivable genre (novel, film, play) and finally
became a long-running soap opera, which is what its name connotes today.

Q. All that? Really? How?   76
A. *We will revive the Quilting Bee!*   77
Q. Oh, splendid, splendid! What a genius you are!   78
A. I always knew it.   79

RICHARD RODRIGUEZ

Going Home Again: The New American Scholarship Boy

Richard Rodriguez (1944–   ) was born in San Francisco of
Mexican-American immigrant parents. When he entered public
school in Sacramento, he spoke little English, but he became an
excellent student, taking a B.A. from Stanford University and an
M.A. from Columbia University. He seemed destined to become
a college professor, but while studying English Renaissance literature in London in 1973, he abruptly gave up academic life. In
1982 he published *Hunger of Memory: The Education of Richard
Rodriguez*, an autobiographical work that created political controversy because it opposed affirmative action and bilingual education. In this book and in several essays, Rodriguez has revealed
the difficulties of being a double outsider, alienated from academic culture by his ethnic background and separated from his
family by his education. "Going Home Again" appeared in *The
American Scholar* in 1974.

At each step, with every graduation from one level of education   1
to the next, the refrain from bystanders was strangely the same:
"Your parents must be so proud of you." I suppose that my parents
were proud, although I suspect, too, that they felt more than pride
alone as they watched me advance through my education. They
seemed to know that my education was separating us from one
another, making it difficult to resume familiar intimacies. Mixed
with the instincts of parental pride, a certain hurt also communi-
cated itself—too private ever to be adequately expressed in words,
but real nonetheless.

The autobiographical facts pertinent to this essay are simply   2
stated in two sentences, though they exist in somewhat awkward
juxtaposition to each other. I am the son of Mexican-American
parents, who speak a blend of Spanish and English, but who read
neither language easily. I am about to receive a Ph.D. in English

Renaissance literature. What sort of life—what tensions, feelings, conflicts—connects these two sentences? I look back and remember my life from the time I was seven or eight years old as one of constant movement away from a Spanish-speaking folk culture toward the world of the English-language classroom. As the years passed, I felt myself becoming less like my parents and less comfortable with the assumption of visiting relatives that I was still the Spanish-speaking child they remembered. By the time I began college, visits home became suffused with silent embarrassment: there seemed so little to share, however strong the ties of our affection. My parents would tell me what happened in their lives or in the lives of relatives; I would respond with news of my own. Polite questions would follow. Our conversations came to seem more like interviews.

A few months ago, my dissertation nearly complete, I came 3 upon my father looking through my bookcase. He quietly fingered the volumes of Milton's tracts and Augustine's theology with that combination of reverence and distrust those who are not literate sometimes show for the written word. Silently, I watched him from the door of the room. However much he would have insisted that he was "proud" of his son for being able to master the texts, I knew, if pressed further, he would have admitted to complicated feelings about my success. When he looked across the room and suddenly saw me, his body tightened slightly with surprise, then we both smiled.

For many years I kept my uneasiness about becoming a success 4 in education to myself. I did so in part because I wanted to avoid vague feelings that, if considered carefully, I would have no way of dealing with; and in part because I felt that no one else shared my reaction to the opportunity provided by education. When I began to rehearse my story of cultural dislocation publicly, however, I found many listeners willing to admit to similar feelings from their own pasts. Equally impressive was the fact that many among those I spoke with were *not* from nonwhite racial groups, which made me realize that one can grow up to enter the culture of the academy and find it a "foreign" culture for a variety of reasons, ranging from economic status to religious heritage. But why, I next wondered, was it that, though there were so many of us who came from childhood cultures alien to the academy's, we voiced our uneasiness to one another and to ourselves so infrequently? Why did it take *me* so long to acknowledge publicly the cultural costs I had paid to earn a Ph.D. in Renaissance English literature? Why, more precisely, am I writing these words only now when my connection to my past barely survives except as nostalgic memory?

Looking back, a person risks losing hold of the present while   5
being confounded by the past. For the child who moves to an
academic culture from a culture that dramatically lacks academic
traditions, looking back can jeopardize the certainty he has about
the desirability of this new academic culture. Richard Hoggart's
description, in *The Uses of Literacy*, of the cultural pressures on such
a student, whom Hoggart calls the "scholarship boy," helps make
the point. The scholarship boy must give nearly unquestioning
allegiance to academic culture, Hoggart argues, if he is to succeed at
all, so different is the milieu of the classroom from the culture he
leaves behind. For a time, the scholarship boy may try to balance
his loyalty between his concretely experienced family life and
the more abstract mental life of the classroom. In the end, though,
he must choose between the two worlds: if he intends to succeed
as a student, he must, literally and figuratively, separate himself
from his family, with its gregarious life, and find a quiet place to be
alone with his thoughts.

After a while, the kind of allegiance the young student might   6
once have given his parents is transferred to the teacher, the new
parent. Now without the support of the old ties and certainties of
the family, he almost mechanically acquires the assumptions, practices, and style of the classroom milieu. For the loss he might
otherwise feel, the scholarship boy substitutes an enormous enthusiasm for nearly everything having to do with school.

How readily I read my own past into the portrait of Hoggart's   7
scholarship boy. Coming from a home in which mostly Spanish
was spoken, for example, I had to decide to forget Spanish when I
began my education. To succeed in the classroom, I needed psychologically to sever my ties with Spanish. Spanish represented an
alternate culture as well as another language—and the basis of my
deepest sense of relationship to my family. Although I recently
taught myself to read Spanish, the language that I see on the
printed page is not quite the language I heard in my youth. That
other Spanish, the spoken Spanish of my family, I remember with
nostalgia and guilt: guilt because I cannot explain to aunts and
uncles why I do not answer their questions any longer in their own
idiomatic language. Nor was I able to explain to teachers in graduate school, who regularly expected me to read and speak Spanish
with ease, why my very ability to reach graduate school as a student of English literature in the first place required me to loosen my
attachments to a language I spoke years earlier. Yet, having lost the
ability to speak Spanish, I never forgot it so totally that I could not
understand it. Hearing Spanish spoken on the street reminded me
of the community I once felt a part of, and still cared deeply about.

I never forgot Spanish so thoroughly, in other words, as to move outside the range of its nostalgic pull.

Such moments of guilt and nostalgia were, however, just that— momentary. They punctuated the history of my otherwise successful progress from *barrio*[1] to classroom. Perhaps they even encouraged it. Whenever I felt my determination to succeed wavering, I tightened my hold on the conventions of academic life.

Spanish was one aspect of the problem, my parents another. They could raise deeper, more persistent doubts. They offered encouragement to my brothers and me in our work, but they also spoke, only half jokingly, about the way education was putting "big ideas" into our heads. When we would come home, for example, and challenge assumptions we earlier believed, they would be forced to defend their beliefs (which, given our new verbal skills, they did increasingly less well) or, more frequently, to submit to our logic with the disclaimer, "It's what we were taught in our time to believe. . . ." More important, after we began to leave home for college, they voiced regret about how "changed" we had become, how much further away from one another we had grown. They partly yearned for a return to the time before education assumed their children's primary loyalty. This yearning was renewed each time they saw their nieces and nephews (none of whom continued their education beyond high school, all of whom continued to speak fluent Spanish) living according to the conventions and assumptions of their parents' culture. If I was already troubled by the time I graduated from high school by that refrain of congratulations ("Your parents must be so proud. . . ."), I realize now how much more difficult and complicated was my progress into academic life for my parents, as they saw the cultural foundation of their family erode, than it was for me.

Yet my parents were willing to pay the price of alienation and continued to encourage me to become a scholarship boy because they perceived, as others of the lower classes had before them, the relation between education and social mobility. Lacking the former themselves made them acutely aware of its necessity as prerequisite for the latter. They sent their children off to school in the hopes of their acquiring something "better" beyond education. Notice the assumption here that education is something of a tool or license—a means to an end, which has been the traditional way the lower or working classes have viewed the value of education in the past. That education might alter children in more basic ways than providing them with skills, certificates of proficiency, and even up-

1. The Hispanic neighborhood within a city.

ward mobility, may come as a surprise for some, but the financial
cost is usually tolerated.

Complicating my own status as a scholarship boy in the last ten   11
years was the rise, in the mid-1960s, of what was then called "the
Third World Student Movement." Racial minority groups, led
chiefly by black intellectuals, began to press for greater access to
higher education. The assumption behind their criticism, like the
assumption of white working-class families, was that educational
opportunity was useful for economic and social advancement. The
racial minority leaders went one step further, however, and it was
this step that was probably most revolutionary. Minority students
came to the campus feeling that they were representative of larger
groups of people—that, indeed, they were advancing the condition
of entire societies by their matriculation. Actually, this assumption
was not altogether new to me. Years before, educational success
was something my parents urged me to strive for precisely because
it would reflect favorably on *all* Mexican-Americans—specifically,
my intellectual achievement would help deflate the stereotype of
the "dumb Pancho." This early goal was only given greater currency by the rhetoric of the Third World spokesmen. But it was the
fact that I felt myself suddenly much more a "public" Mexican-
American, a representative of sorts, that was to prove so crucial for
me during these years.

One college admissions officer assured me one day that he recog-   12
nized my importance to his school precisely as deriving from the
fact that, after graduation, I would surely be "going back to [my]
community." More recently, teachers have urged me not to trouble
over the fact that I am not "representative" of my culture, assuring
me that I can serve as a "model" for those still in the *barrio* working toward academic careers. This is the line that I hear, too,
when being interviewed for a faculty position. The interviewer
almost invariably assumes that, because I am racially a Mexican-
American, I can serve as a special counselor to minority students.
The expectation is that I still retain the capacity for intimacy with
"my people."

This new way of thinking about the possible uses of education is   13
what has made the entrance of minority students into higher education so dramatic. When the minority group student was accepted
into the academy, he came—in everyone's mind—as part of a
"group." When I began college, I barely attracted attention except
perhaps as a slightly exotic ("Are you from India?") brown-
skinned student; by the time I graduated, my presence was annually noted by, among others, the college public relations office as
"one of the fifty-two students with Spanish surnames enrolled this

year." By having his presence announced to the campus in this way the minority group student was unlike any other scholarship boy the campus had seen before. The minority group student now dramatized more publicly, if also in new ways, the issues of cultural dislocation that education forces, issues that are not solely racial in origin. When Richard Rodriguez *became* a Chicano, the dilemmas he earlier had as a scholarship boy were complicated but not decisively altered by the fact that he had assumed a group identity.

The assurance I heard that, somehow, I was being useful to my   14
community by being a student was gratefully believed, because it gave me a way of dealing with the guilt and cynicism that each year came my way along with the scholarships, grants, and, lately, job offers from schools which a few years earlier would have refused me admission as a student. Each year, in fact, it became harder to believe that my success had anything to do with my intellectual performance, and harder to resist the conclusion that it was due to my minority group status. When I drove to the airport, on my way to London as a Fulbright Fellow[2] last year, leaving behind cousins of my age who were already hopelessly burdened by financial insecurity and dead-end jobs, momentary guilt could be relieved by the thought that somehow my trip was beneficial to persons other than myself. But, of course, if the thought was a way of dealing with the guilt, it was also the reason for the guilt. Sitting in a university library, I would notice a janitor of my own race and grow uneasy; I was, I knew, in a rough way a beneficiary of his condition. Guilt was accompanied by cynicism. The most dazzlingly talented minority students I know today refuse to believe that their success is wholly based on their own talent, or even that when they speak in a classroom anyone hears them as anything but *the* voice of their minority group. It is scarcely surprising, then, though initially it probably seemed puzzling, that so many of the angriest voices on the campus against the injustices of racism came from those not visibly its primary victims.

It became necessary to believe the rhetoric about the value of   15
one's presence on campus simply as a way of living with one's "success." Among ourselves, however, minority group students often admitted to a shattering sense of loss—the feeling that, somehow, something was happening to us. Especially from students who had not yet become accustomed, as by that time I had, to the campus, I remember hearing confessions of extreme discomfort and isolation. Our close associations, the separate dining-room

2. The Fulbright Act (1946) provides an exchange program for American students and teachers and those of many other countries.

tables, and the special dormitories helped to relieve some of the pain, but only some of it.

Significant here was the development of the ethnic studies concept—black studies, Chicano studies, et cetera—and the related assumption held by minority group students in a number of departments that they could keep in touch with their old cultures by making these cultures the subject of their study. Here again one notices how different the minority student was from other comparable students: other scholarship boys—poor Jews and the sons of various immigrant cultures—came to the academy singly, much more inclined to accept the courses and material they found. The ethnic studies concept was an indication that, for a multitude of reasons, the new racial minority group students were not willing to give up so easily their ties with their old cultures. 16

The importance of these new ethnic studies was that they introduced the academy to subject matter that generally deserved to be studied, and at the same time offered a staggering critique of the academy's tendency toward parochialism. Most minority group intellectuals never noted this tendency toward academic parochialism. They more often saw the reason for, say, the absence of a course on black literature in an English department as a case of simple racism. That it might instead be an instance of the fact that academic culture can lose track of human societies and whole areas of human experience was rarely raised. Never asking such a question, the minority group students never seemed to wonder either if as teachers their own courses might suffer the same cultural limitations other seminars and classes suffered. Consequently, in a peculiar way the new minority group critics of higher education came to justify the academy's assumptions. The possibility that academic culture could encourage one to grow out of touch with cultures beyond its conceptual horizon was never seriously considered. 17

Too often in the last ten years one heard minority group students repeat the joke, never very funny in the first place, about the racial minority academic who ended up sounding more "white" than white academics. Behind the scorn for such a figure was the belief that the new generation of minority group students would be able to avoid having to make similar kinds of cultural concessions. The pressures that might have led to such conformity went unexamined. 18

For the last few years my annoyance at hearing such jokes was doubtless related to the fact that I was increasingly beginning to sense that I was the "bleached" academic the minority group students found so laughable. I suppose I had always sensed that my cultural allegiance was undergoing subtle alterations as I was being 19 educated. Only when I finished my course work in graduate school and went off to England for my dissertation year did I grasp how far I had traveled from my cultural origins. My year in England was actually my first opportunity to write and reflect upon the kind of material that I would spend my life producing. It was my first chance, too, to be free simultaneously of the distractions of course-work and of the insecurities of trying to find my niche in academic life. Sitting in the reading room of the British Museum, I no longer doubted that I had joined academic society. Ironically, this feeling of having finally arrived allowed me to look back to the community whence I came. That I was geographically farther away from my home than I had ever been lent a metaphorical resonance to the cultural distance I suddenly felt.

But that feeling was not pleasing. The reward of feeling a part of the world of the British Museum was an odd one. Each morning I would arrive at the reading room and grow increasingly depressed by the silence and what the silence implied—that my life as a scholar would require self-absorption. Who, I wondered, would find my work helpful enough to want to read it? Was not my dissertation—whose title alone would puzzle my relatives—only my grandest exercise thus far in self-enclosure? The sight of the heads around me bent over their texts and papers, many so thoroughly engrossed that they wouldn't look up at the silent clock overhead for hours at a stretch, made me recall the remarkable noises of life in my family home. The tedious prose I was writing, a prose constantly qualified by footnotes, reminded me of the capacity for passionate statement those of the culture I was born into commanded—and which, could it be, I had now lost.   20

As I remembered it during those gray English afternoons, the past rushed forward to define more precisely my present condition. Remembering my youth, a time when I was not restricted to a chair but ran barefoot under a summer sun that tightened my skin with its white heat, made the fact that it was only my mind that "moved" each hour in the library painfully obvious.   21

I did need to figure out where I had lost touch with my past. I started to become alien to my family culture the day I became a scholarship boy. In the British Museum the realization seemed obvious. But later, returning to America, I returned to minority group students who were still speaking of their cultural ties to their past. How was I to tell them what I had learned about myself in England?   22

A short while ago, a group of enthusiastic Chicano under-graduates came to my office to ask me to teach a course to high school students in the *barrio* on the Chicano novel. This new litera-   23 ture, they assured me, has an important role to play in helping to shape the consciousness of a people currently without adequate representation in literature. Listening to them I was struck immediately with the cultural problems raised by their assumption. I told them that the novel is not capable of dealing with Chicano experience adequately, simply because most Chicanos are not literate, or are at least not yet comfortably so. This is not something Chicanos need to apologize for (though, I suppose, remembering my own childhood ambition to combat stereotypes of the Chicano as mental menial, it is not something easily admitted). Rather the genius and value of those Chicanos who do not read seem to me to be largely that their reliance on voice, the spoken word, has given them the capacity for intimate conversation that I, as someone who now relies heavily on the written word, can only envy. The second problem, I went on, is more in the nature of a technical one: the novel, in my opinion, is not a form capable of being true to the basic sense of communal life that typifies Chicano culture. What the novel as a literary form is best capable of representing is solitary existence set against a large social background. Chicano novelists, not coincidentally, nearly always fail to capture the breathtakingly rich family life of most Chicanos, and instead often describe only the individual Chicano in transit between Mexican and American cultures.

I said all of this to the Chicano students in my office, and could   24
see that little of it made an impression. They seemed only frustrated by what they probably took to be a slick, academic justification for evading social responsibility. After a time, they left me, sitting alone. . . .

There is a danger of being misunderstood here. I am not suggest-   25
ing that an academic cannot reestablish ties of any kind with his old culture. Indeed, he can have an impact on the culture of his childhood. But as an academic, one exists by definition in a culture separate from one's nonacademic roots and, therefore, any future ties one has with those who remain "behind" are complicated by one's new cultural perspective.

Paradoxically, the distance separating the academic from his   26
nonacademic past can make his past seem, if not closer, then clearer. It is possible for the academic to understand the culture from which he came "better" than those who still live within it. In my own experience, it has only been as I have come to appraise my past through categories and notions derived from the social sciences that I have been able to think of Chicano life in cultural terms at all. Characteristics I took for granted or noticed only in passing—

the spontaneity, the passionate speech, the trust in concrete experience, the willingness to think communally rather than individually—these are all significant phenomena to me now as aspects of a
total culture. (My parents have neither the time nor the inclination
to think about their culture as a culture.) Able to conceptualize a
sense of Chicano culture, I am now also more attracted to that
culture than I was before. The temptation now is to try to preserve
those traits of my old culture that have not yet, in effect, atrophied.

The racial self-consciousness of minority group students during   27
the last few years evident in the ethnic costumes, the stylized gestures, and the idiomatic though often evasive devices for insisting
on one's continuing membership in the community of the past, are
also indications that the minority group student has gained a new
appreciation of the culture of his origin precisely because of his
earlier alienation from it. As a result, Chicano students sometimes
become more Chicano than most Chicanos. I remember, for example, my father's surprise when, walking across my college campus one afternoon, we came upon two Chicano academics wearing
serapes. He and my mother were also surprised—indeed offended—when they earlier heard student activists use the word
"Chicano." For them the term was a private one, primarily descriptive of persons they knew. It suggested intimacy. Hearing the word
shouted into a microphone by a stranger left them bewildered.
What they could not understand was that the student activist finds
it easier than they to use "Chicano" in a more public way, for his
distance from their culture and his membership in academic culture permits a wider and more abstract view.

The Mexican-Americans who begin to call themselves Chicanos   28
in this new way are actually forming a new version of what it
means to be a Chicano. The culture that didn't see itself as a culture
is suddenly prized and identified for being one. The price one pays
for this new self-consciousness is the knowledge of just that—it is
new—and this knowledge is not available to those who remain at
home. So it is knowledge that separates as well as unites people.
Wanting more desperately than ever to assert his ties with the
newly visible culture, the minority group student is tempted to
exploit those characteristics of that culture that might yet survive in
him. But the self-consciousness never allows one to feel completely
at ease with the old culture. Worse, the knowledge of the culture of
the past often leaves one feeling strangely solitary. At home, I hear
relatives speak and find myself analyzing too much of what they
say. It is embarrassing being a cultural anthropologist in one's own
family kitchen. I keep feeling myself little more than a cultural
voyeur. I often come away from family gatherings suspecting, in

fact, that what conceptions of my culture I carry with me are no more than illusions. Because they were never there before, because no one back home shares them, I grow less and less to trust their reliability: too often they seem no more than mental bubbles floating before an academic's eye.

Many who have taught minority group students in the last decade testify to sensing characteristics of a childhood culture still very much alive in these students. Should the teacher make these students aware of these characteristics? Initially, most of us would probably answer negatively. Better to trust the unconscious survival of the past than the always problematical, sometimes even clownish, re-creations of it. But the cultural past cannot be assured of survival; perhaps many of its characteristics are lost simply because the student is never encouraged to look for them. Even those that do survive do so tenuously. As a teacher, one can only hope that the best qualities in his minority group students' cultural legacy aren't altogether snuffed out by academic education.   29

More easy to live with and distinguishable from self-conscious awareness of the past are the ways the past unconsciously survives—perhaps even yet survives in me. As it turns out, the issue becomes less acute with time. With each year, the chance that the student is unaware of his cultural legacy is diminished as the habit of academic reflectiveness grows stronger. Although the culture of the academy makes innocence about one's cultural past less likely, this same culture, and the conceptual tools it provides, increases the desire to want to write and speak about the past. The paradox persists.   30

Awaiting the scholarship boy who finally acknowledges the fact that his perceptions of reality have changed is the dilemma of action. The sentimental reaction to this knowledge entails merely a refusal to renew contact with one's nonacademic culture lest one contaminate it. The problem, however, with this sentimental solution is that it overlooks the way academic culture renders one capable of dealing with the transactions of mass society. Academic culture, with its habits of conceptualization and abstraction, allows those of us from other cultures to deal with each other in a mass society. In this sense academic culture does have a profound political impact. Although people intent upon social mobility think of education as a means to an end, education does become an end: its culture allows one to exist more easily in a society increasingly anonymous and impersonal. The truth is, the academic's distance from his own experience brings the capacity for communicating with bureaucracies and understanding one's position in society—a prerequisite for political action.   31

If the sentimental reaction to nonacademic culture is to fear 32
changing it, the political response, typical especially of working-
class and lately minority group leaders, is to see higher education
solely in terms of its political and social possibilities. Its cultural
consequences, in this view, are disregarded. At this time when we
are so keenly aware of social and economic inequality, it might
seem beside the point to warn those who are working to bring
about equality that education alters culture as well as economic
status. And yet, if there is one main criticism that I, as a minority
group student, must make of minority group leaders in their past
attacks on the "racism" of the academy, it is that they never distinguished between my right to higher education and the desirability
of my actually entering the academy—which is another way of
saying again that they never recognized that there were things I
could lose by becoming a scholarship boy.

Certainly, the academy changes those from alien cultures more 33
than it is changed by them. While minority groups had an impact
on higher education, largely because of their advantage in coming
as a group, within the last few years students such as myself, who
finally ended up certified as academics, also ended up sounding
very much like the academics we found when we came to the
campus. I do not enjoy making such admissions. But perhaps now
the time has come when questions about the cultural costs of education ought to be delayed no longer. Those of us who have been
scholarship boys know in our bones that our education has exacted
a large price in exchange for the large benefits it has conferred
upon us. And what is sadder to consider, after we have paid that
price, we go home and casually change the cultures that nurtured
us. My parents today understand how they are "Chicanos" in a
large and impersonal sense. The gains from such knowledge are
clear. But so, too, are the reasons for regret.

ROGER WILKINS

Confessions of a Blue-Chip Black

Roger Wilkins (1932–   ) was born in Kansas City and grew
up there, in Harlem, and in Grand Rapids, Michigan. He received
his undergraduate and legal education at the University of Michigan. After serving briefly as a welfare worker in Cleveland and as
a private attorney in New York, Wilkins went to Washington,
D.C. to serve in various administrative posts. He was assistant

attorney general from 1966 to 1969, a post he left to serve as director of the Ford Foundation's domestic programs. This position gave him "daily association with blackness," since he helped develop projects intended to aid the urban black underclass. But as Wilkins realized with increasing discomfort, the Foundation itself was part of a white power structure safely isolated from the reality of urban poverty. In 1972 he resigned and began to write articles and editorials for the *New York Times*. "Confessions of a Blue-Chip Black," which first appeared in *Harper's Magazine* in April 1982, is from Wilkins's autobiography, *A Man's Life* (1982).

Early in the spring of 1932—six months after Earl's brother, 1
Roy, left Kansas City to go to New York to join the national staff of the National Association for the Advancement of Colored People, and eight months before Franklin Roosevelt was elected president for the first time—Earl and Helen Wilkins had the first and only child to be born of their union. I was born in a little segregated hospital in Kansas City called Phillis Wheatley.[1] The first time my mother saw me, she cried. My head was too long and my color, she thought, was blue.

My parents never talked about slavery or my ancestors. Images 2
of Africa were images of backwardness and savagery. Once, when I was a little boy, I said to my mother after a friend of my parents left the house: "Mr. Bledsoe is black, isn't he, mama."

"Oh," she exclaimed. "Never say anybody is black. That's a 3
terrible thing to say."

Next time Mr. Bledsoe came to the house, I commented, 4
"Mama, Mr. Bledsoe is navy blue."

When I was two years old and my father was in the tuberculosis 5
sanitarium, he wrote me a letter, which I obviously couldn't read, but which tells a lot about how he planned to raise his Negro son.

Friday, March 22, 1934

Dear Roger—
Let me congratulate you upon having reached your second birthday. Your infancy is now past and it is now that you should begin to turn your thoughts upon those achievements which are expected of a brilliant young gentleman well on his way to manhood.

During the next year, you should learn the alphabet; you should learn certain French and English idioms which are a part of every

1. Black American poet, 1753?–1784.

cultivated person's vocabulary: you should gain complete control of those natural functions which, uncontrolled, are a source of worry and embarrassment to even the best of grandmothers: you should learn how to handle table silver so that you will be able to eat gracefully and conventionally: and you should learn the fundamental rules of social living—politeness, courtesy, consideration for others, and the rest.

This should not be difficult for you. You have the best and most patient of mothers in your sterling grandmother and your excellent mother. Great things are expected of you. Never, never forget that.

Love,
Your Father

We lived in a neat little stucco house on a hill in a small Negro 6
section called Roundtop. I had no sense of being poor or of any anxiety about money. At our house, not only was there food and furniture and all the rest, there was even a baby grand piano that my mother would play sometimes. And there was a cleaning lady, Mrs. Turner, who came every week.

When it was time for me to go to school, the board of education 7
provided us with a big yellow bus, which carried us past four or five perfectly fine schools down to the middle of the large Negro community, to a very old school called Crispus Attucks.[2] I have no memories of those bus rides except for my resentment of the selfishness of the whites who wouldn't let us share those newer-looking schools near to home.

My father came home when I was four and died when I was 8
almost nine. He exuded authority. He thought the women hadn't been sufficiently firm with me, so he instituted a spanking program with that same hard hairbrush that my grandmother had used so much to try to insure that I didn't have "nigger-looking" hair.

After my father's death, the family moved to New York. Our 9
apartment was in that legendary uptown area called Sugar Hill, where blacks who had it made were said to live the sweet life. I lived with my mother, my grandmother, and my mother's younger sister, Zelma. My Uncle Roy and his wife, Minnie, a New York social worker, lived on the same floor. My Aunt Marvel and her husband, Cecil, lived one floor down.

As life in New York settled into a routine, my life came to be 10
dominated by four women: my mother, her sisters, and her

---

2. American mulatto, 1723?–1770; led mob in "Boston Massacre" and was killed by British troops.

mother. Nobody else had any children, so everybody concentrated on me.

Sometime early in 1943 my mother's work with the YMCA took   11
her to Grand Rapids, Michigan, where she made a speech and met
a forty-four-year-old bachelor doctor who looked like a white
man. He had light skin, green eyes, and "good hair"—that is, hair
that was as straight and as flat as white people's hair. He looked so
like a white person that he could have passed for white. There was
much talk about people who had passed. They were generally
deemed to be bad people, for they were not simply selfish, but also
cruel to those whom they left behind. On the other hand, people
who could pass, but did not, were respected.

My mother remarried in October 1943, and soon I was once   12
more on a train with my grandmother, heading toward Grand
Rapids and my new home. This train also took me, at the age of
twelve, beyond the last point in my life when I would feel totally at
peace with my blackness.

My new home was in the north end of Grand Rapids, a com-   13
pletely white neighborhood. This would be the place I would
henceforth think of as home. And it would be the place where I
would become more Midwestern than Harlemite, more American
than black, and more complex than was comfortable or necessary for the middle-class conformity that my mother had in mind
for me.

Grand Rapids was pretty single-family houses and green spaces.   14
The houses looked like those in *Look* magazine or in *Life*. You could
believe, and I did, that there was happiness inside. To me, back
then, the people seemed to belong to the houses as the houses
belonged to the land, and all of it had to do with being white. They
moved and walked and talked as if the place, the country, and the
houses were theirs, and I envied them.

I spent the first few weeks exploring Grand Rapids on a new bike   15
my stepfather had bought for me. The people I passed would look
back at me with intense and sometimes puzzled looks on their faces
as I pedaled by. Nobody waved or even smiled. They just stopped
what they were doing to stand and look. As soon as I saw them
looking, I would look forward and keep on riding.

One day I rode for miles, down and up and down again. I was   16
past Grand Rapids' squatty little downtown, and farther south until
I began to see some Negro people. There were black men and
women and some girls, but it was the boys I was looking for. Then I
saw a group: four of them. They were about my age, and they were
dark. Though their clothes were not as sharp as the boys' in the

Harlem Valley, they were old, and I took the look of poverty and the deep darkness of their faces to mean that they were like the hard boys of Harlem.

One of them spotted me riding toward them and pointed. "Hey, lookit that bigole skinny bike," he said. Then they all looked at my bike and at me. I couldn't see expressions on their faces; only the blackness and the coarseness of their clothes. Before any of the rest of them had a chance to say anything, I stood up on the pedals and wheeled the bike in a U-turn and headed back on up toward the north end of town. It took miles for the terror to finally subside. 17

Farther on toward home, there was a large athletic field. As I neared the field, I could see some large boys in shorts moving determinedly around a football. When I got to the top of the hill that overlooked the field, I stopped and stood, one foot on the ground and one leg hanging over the crossbar, staring down at them. All the boys were white and big and old—sixteen to eighteen. I had never seen a football workout before, and I was fascinated. I completely forgot everything about color, theirs or mine. 18

Then one of them saw me. He pointed and said, "Look, there's the little coon watchin us." 19

I wanted to be invisible. I was horrified. My heart pounded, and my arms and legs shook, but I managed to get back on my bike and ride home. 20

The first white friend I made was named Jerry Schild. On the second day of our acquaintance, he took me to his house, above a store run by his parents. I met his three younger siblings, including a very little one toddling around in bare feet and a soiled diaper. 21

While Jerry changed the baby, I looked around the place. It was cheap, all chintz and linoleum. The two soft pieces of furniture, a couch and an overstuffed chair, had gaping holes and were hemorrhaging their fillings. And there were an awful lot of empty brown beer bottles sitting around, both in the kitchen and out on the back porch. While the place was not dirty, it made me very sad. Jerry and his family were poor in a way I had never seen people be poor before, in Kansas City or even in Harlem. 22

Jerry's father wasn't there that day and Jerry didn't mention him. But later in the week, when I went to call for Jerry, I saw him. I yelled for Jerry from downstairs in the back and his father came to the railing of the porch on the second floor. He was a skinny man in overalls with the bib hanging down crookedly because it was fastened only on the shoulder. His face was narrow and wrinkled and his eyes were set deep in dark hollows. He had a beer bottle in his hand and he looked down at me. "Jerry ain't here," he said. He turned away and went back inside. 23

One day our front doorbell rang and I could hear my mother's   24
troubled exclamation. "Jerry! What's wrong?" Jerry was crying so
hard he could hardly talk. "My father says I can't play with you
anymore because you're not good enough for us."

Creston High School, which served all the children from the   25
north end of Grand Rapids, was all white and middle-class. Nobody talked to me that first day, but I was noticed. When I left
school at the end of the day I found my bike leaning up against the
fence where I had left it, with a huge glob of slimy spit on my
shaggy saddle cover. People passed by on their way home and
looked at me and spit. I felt a hollowness behind my eyes, but I
didn't cry. I just got on the bike, stood up on the pedals, and rode it
home without sitting down. And it went that way for about the
first two weeks. After the third day, I got rid of the saddle cover
because the plain leather was a lot easier to clean.

But the glacier began to thaw. One day in class, the freckle-faced   26
kid with the crewcut sitting next to me was asking everybody for a
pencil. And then he looked at me and said, "Maybe you can lend
me one." Those were the best words I had heard since I first met
Jerry. This kid had included me in the human race in front of
everybody. His name was Jack Waltz.

And after a while when the spitters had subsided and I could   27
ride home sitting down, I began to notice that little kids my size
were playing pickup games in the end zones of the football field. It
looked interesting, but I didn't know anybody and didn't know
how they would respond to me. So I just rode on by for a couple of
weeks, slowing down each day, trying to screw up my courage to
go in.

But then one day, I saw Jack Waltz there. I stood around the   28
edges of the group watching. It seemed that they played forever
without even noticing me, but finally someone had to go home and
the sides were unbalanced. Somebody said, "Let's ask him."

As we lined up for our first huddle, I heard somebody on the   29
other side say, "I hope he doesn't have a knife." One of the guys on
my side asked me, "Can you run the ball?" I said yes, so they gave
me the ball and I ran three quarters of the length of the field for a
touchdown. And I made other touchdowns and other long runs
before the game was over. When I thought about it later that night,
I became certain that part of my success was due to the imaginary
knife that was running interference for me. But no matter. By the
end of the game, I had a group of friends. Boys named Andy and
Don and Bill and Gene and Rich. We left the field together and
some of them waved and yelled, "See ya tomorra, Rog."

And Don De Young, a pleasant round-faced boy, even lived   30 quite near me. So, after parting from everybody else, he and I went on together down to the corner of Coit and Knapp. As we parted, he suggested that we meet to go to school together the next day. I had longed for that but I hadn't suggested it for fear of a rebuff for overstepping the limits of my race. I had already learned one of the great tenets of Negro survival in America: to live the reactive life. It was like the old Negro comedian who once said, "When the man asks how the weather is, I know nuff to look keerful at his face 'fore even I look out the window." So, I waited for him to suggest it, and my patience was rewarded. I was overjoyed and grateful.

I didn't spend all my time in the north end. Soon after I moved to 31
Grand Rapids, Pop introduced me to some patients he had with a son my age. The boy's name was Lloyd Brown, and his father was a bellman downtown at the Pantlind Hotel. Lloyd and I often rode bikes and played basketball in his backyard. After a while, my mother asked me why I never had Lloyd come out to visit me. It was a question I dreaded, but she pressed on. "After all," she said, "you've had a lot of meals at his house and it's rude not to invite him back." I knew she was right and I also hated the whole idea of it.

With my friends in the north, race was never mentioned. Ever. I 32
carried my race around with me like an open basket of rotten eggs. I knew I could drop one at any moment and it would explode with a stench over everything. This was in the days when the movies either had no blacks at all or featured rank stereotypes like Stepin Fetchit,[3] and the popular magazines like *Life, Look,* the *Saturday Evening Post,* and *Colliers* carried no stories about Negroes, had no ads depicting Negroes, and generally gave the impression that we did not exist in this society. I knew that my white friends, being well brought up, were just too polite to mention this disability that I had. And I was grateful to them, but terrified, just the same, that maybe someday one of them would have the bad taste to notice what I was.

It seemed to me that my tenuous purchase in this larger white 33
world depended on the maintenance between me and my friends in the north end of our unspoken bargain to ignore my difference, my shame, and their embarrassment. If none of us had to deal with it, I thought, we could all handle it. My white friends behaved as if they perceived the bargain exactly as I did. It was a delicate equation, and I was terrified that Lloyd's presence in the North End would rip apart the balance.

I am so ashamed of that shame now that I cringe when I write it. 34

3. A lazy black character in the film *Hearts in Dixie* (1929).

But I understand that boy now as he could not understand himself then. I was an American boy, though I did not fully comprehend that either. I was fully shaped and formed by America, where white people had all the power in sight, and they owned everything in sight except our house. Their beauty was the real beauty; there wasn't any other beauty. A real human being had straight hair, a white face, and thin lips. Other people, who looked different, were lesser beings.

No wonder, then, that most black men desired the forbidden   35
fruit of white loins. No wonder, too, that we thought that the most beautiful and worthy Negro people were those who looked most white. We blacks used to have a saying: "If you're white, you're all right. If you're brown, stick around. If you're black, stand back." I was brown.

It was not that we in my family were direct victims of racism. On   36
the contrary, my stepfather clearly had a higher income than the parents of most students in my high school. Unlike those of most of my contemporaries, black and white, my parents had college degrees. Within Grand Rapids' tiny Negro community, they were among the elite. The others were the lawyer, the dentist, the undertaker, and the other doctor.

But that is what made race such exquisite agony. I did have a   37
sense that it was unfair for poor Negroes to be relegated to bad jobs—if they had jobs at all—and to bad or miserable housing, but I didn't feel any great sense of identity with them. After all, the poor blacks in New York had also been the hard ones: the ones who tried to take my money, to beat me up, and to keep me perpetually intimidated. Besides, I had heard it intimated around my house that their behavior, sexual or otherwise, left a good deal to be desired.

So I thought that maybe they just weren't ready for this society,   38
but that I was. And it was dreadfully unfair for white people to just look at my face and lips and hair and decide that I was inferior. By being a model student and leader, I thought I was demonstrating how well Negroes could perform if only the handicaps were removed and they were given a chance. But deep down I guess I was also trying to demonstrate that I was not like those other people; that I was different. My message was quite clear: I was *not nigger*. But the world didn't seem quite ready to make such fine distinctions, and it was precisely that fact—though at the time I could scarcely even have admitted it to myself—that was the nub of the race issue for me.

I would sometimes lie on my back and stare up at passing clouds   39
and wonder why God had played a dirty trick by making me a

Negro. It all seemed so random. So unfair to me. To *me!* But in school I was gaining more friends, and the teachers respected me. It got so that I could go for days not thinking very much about being Negro, until something made the problem unavoidable.

One day in history class, for instance, the teacher asked each of us to stand and tell in turn where our families had originated. Many of the kids in the class were Dutch with names like Vander Jagt, De Young, and Ripstra. My pal Andy was Scots-Irish. When it came my turn, I stood up and burned with shame and when I would speak, I lied. And then I was even more ashamed because I exposed a deeper shame. "Some of my family was English," I said—Wilkins is an English name—"and the rest of it came from . . . Egypt." Egypt!

One Saturday evening after one of our sandlot games, I went over to Lloyd's. Hearing my stories, Lloyd said mildly that he'd like to come up and play some Saturday. I kept on talking, but all the time my mind was repeating: "Lloyd wants to play. He wants to come up to the North End on Saturday. Next Saturday. Next Saturday." I was trapped.

So, after the final story about the final lunge, when I couldn't put it off any longer, I said. "Sure. Why not?" But, later in the evening, after I had had some time to think, I got Lloyd alone. "Say, look," I said. "Those teams are kinda close, ya know. I mean, we don't switch around. From team to team. Or new guys, ya know?"

Lloyd nodded, but he was getting a funny look on his face . . . part unbelieving and part hurt. So I quickly interjected before he could say anything, "Naw, man. Naw. Not like you shouldn't come and play. Just that we gotta have some good reason for you to play on our team, you dig?"

"Yeah," Lloyd said, his face still puzzled, but no longer hurt.

"Hey, I know," I said. "I got it. We'll say you're my cousin. If you're my cousin, see, then you gotta play. Nobody can say you can't be on my team, because you're family, right?"

"Oh, right. Okay," Lloyd said, his face brightening. "Sure, we'll say we're cousins. Solid."

I felt relieved as well. I could have a Negro cousin. It wasn't voluntary. It wouldn't be as if I had gone out and made a Negro friend deliberately. A person couldn't help who his cousins were.

There began to be a cultural difference between me and other blacks my age too. Black street language had evolved since my Harlem days, and I had not kept pace. Customs, attitudes, and the other common social currencies of everyday black life had evolved away from me. I didn't know how to talk, to banter, to move my body. If I was tentative and responsive in the North End, where I lived, I was tense, stiff, and awkward when I was with my black contemporaries. One day I was standing outside the church trying, probably at my mother's urging, to make contact. Conversational sallies flew around me while I stood there stiff and mute, unable to participate. Because the language was so foreign to me, I understood little of what was being said, but I did know that the word used for a white was *paddy*. Then a boy named Nickerson, the one whom my mother particularly wanted me to be friends with, inclined his head slightly toward me and said, to whoops of laughter, "technicolor paddy." My feet felt rooted in stone, and my head was aflame. I never forgot that phrase.

I have rarely felt so alone as I did that day riding home from 49 church. Already partly excluded by my white friends, I was now almost completely alienated from my own people as well. But I felt less uncomfortable and less vulnerable in the white part of town. It was familiar enough to enable me to ward off most unpleasantness.

And then there was the problem of girls. They were everywhere, 50 the girls. They all had budding bosoms, they all smelled pink, they all brushed against the boys in the hall, they were all white, and, in 1947–49, they were all inaccessible.

There were some things you knew without ever knowing how 51 you knew them. You knew that Mississippi was evil and dangerous, that New York was east, and the Pacific ocean was west. And in the same way you knew that white women were the most desirable and dangerous objects in the world. Blacks were lynched in Mississippi and such places sometimes just for looking with the wrong expression at white women. Blacks of a very young age knew that white women of any quality went with the power and style that went with the governance of America—though, God knows, we had so much self-hate that when a white woman went with a Negro man, we promptly decided she was trash, and we also figured that if she would go with him she would go with any Negro.

Nevertheless, as my groin throbbed at fifteen and sixteen and 52 seventeen, *they* were often the only ones there. One of them would be in the hallway opening her locker next to mine. Her blue sweater sleeve would be pushed up to just below the elbow, and as she would reach high on a shelf to stash away a book, I would see the tender dark hair against the white skin of her forearm. And I would ache and want to touch that arm and follow that body hair to its source.

Some of my friends, of course, did touch some of those girls. My 53 friends and I would talk about athletics and school and their loves. But they wouldn't say a word about the dances and the hayrides they went to.

I perceived they liked me and accepted me as long as I moved   54
aside when life's currents took them to where I wasn't supposed to
be. I fit into their ways when they talked about girls, even their
personal girls. And, indeed, I fit into the girls' lives when they were
talking about boys, most particularly their own personal boys. Because I was a boy, I had insight. But I was also Negro, and therefore
a neuter. So a girl who was alive and sensuous night after night in
my fantasies would come to me earnestly in the day and talk about
Rich or Gene or Andy. She would ask what he thought about her,
whether he liked to dance, whether, if she invited him to her house
for a party, he would come. She would tell me her fears and her
yearnings, never dreaming for an instant that I had yearnings too
and that she was their object.

There may be few more powerful obsessions than a teenage   55
boy's fixation on a love object. In my case it came down to a thin
brunette named Marge McDowell. She was half a grade behind
me, and she lived in a small house on a hill. I found excuses to
drive by it all the time. I knew her schedule at school, so I could
manage to be in most of the hallways she had to use going from
class to class. We knew each other, and she had once confided a
strong but fleeting yearning for my friend Rich Kippen. I thought
about her constantly.

Finally, late one afternoon after school, I came upon her alone in   56
a hallway. "Marge," I blurted, "can I ask you something?"

She stopped and smiled and said, "Sure, Roger, what?"   57

"Well I was wondering," I said. "I mean. Well, would you go to   58
the hayride next week with me."

Her jaw dropped and her eyes got huge. Then she uttered a small   59
shriek and turned, hugging her books to her bosom the way girls
do, and fled. I writhed with mortification in my bed that night and
for many nights after.

In my senior year, I was elected president of the Creston High   60
School student council. It was a breakthrough of sorts.

ANNIE DILLARD

Singing with the Fundamentalists

Annie Dillard (1945–   ) first came into prominence as a
writer with the publication of her Pulitzer Prize–winning *Pilgrim
at Tinker Creek* (1974), and many readers continue to think of her
as a solitary, mystical nature writer in the tradition of Henry
David Thoreau. In recent years, however, Dillard has put her

powers of observation to other uses. In 1987 she published *An American Childhood,* an account of her early years that re-creates "a child's interior life—vivid, superstitious, and timeless—and a child's growing awareness of the world." She has also published essays that examine the people around her with the same intensity that she examined nature in *Pilgrim at Tinker Creek.* "Singing with the Fundamentalists" (from *Yale Review,* January 1985), describing her experiences with a group often ostracized on college campuses, is one of these. Like many of her best essays it combines minute observation with curiosity about large questions of the value and meaning of human life.

It is early spring. I have a temporary office at a state university on   1
the West Coast. The office is on the third floor. It looks down on the Square, the enormous open courtyard at the center of campus. From my desk I see hundreds of people moving between classes. There is a large circular fountain in the Square's center.

Early one morning, on the first day of spring quarter, I hear   2
singing. A pack of students has gathered at the fountain. They are singing something which, at this distance, and through the heavy window, sounds good.

I know who these singing students are: they are the Fundamen-   3
talists. This campus has a lot of them. Mornings they sing on the Square; it is their only perceptible activity. What are they singing? Whatever it is, I want to join them, for I like to sing; whatever it is, I want to take my stand with them, for I am drawn to their very absurdity, their innocent indifference to what people think. My colleagues and students here, and my friends everywhere, dislike and fear Christian fundamentalists. You may never have met such people, but you've heard what they do: they pile up money, vote in blocs, and elect right-wing crazies; they censor books; they carry handguns; they fight fluoride in the drinking water and evolution in the schools; probably they would lynch people if they could get away with it. I'm not sure my friends are correct. I close my pen and join the singers on the Square.

There is a clapping song in progress. I have to concentrate to   4
follow it:

> *Come on, rejoice,*
> *And let your heart sing,*
> *Come on, rejoice,*
> *Give praise to the king.*
> *Singing alleluia—*
> *He is the king of kings;*
> *Singing alleluia—*
> *He is the king of kings.*

Two song leaders are standing on the broad rim of the fountain; the water is splashing just behind them. The boy is short, hard-faced, with a moustache. He bangs his guitar with the backs of his fingers. The blonde girl, who leads the clapping, is bouncy; she wears a bit of make-up. Both are wearing blue jeans.

The students beside me are wearing blue jeans too—and athletic 5 jerseys, parkas, football jackets, turtlenecks, and hiking shoes or jogging shoes. They all have canvas or nylon book bags. They look like any random batch of seventy or eighty students at this university. They are grubby or scrubbed, mostly scrubbed; they are tall, fair, or red-headed in large proportions. Their parents are white-collar workers, blue-collar workers, farmers, loggers, orchardists, merchants, fishermen; their names are, I'll bet, Olsen, Jensen, Seversen, Hansen, Klokker, Sigurdsen.

Despite the vigor of the clapping song, no one seems to be giving 6 it much effort. And no one looks at anyone else; there are no sentimental glances and smiles, no glances even of recognition. These kids don't seem to know each other. We stand at the fountain's side, out on the broad, bricked Square in front of the science building, and sing the clapping song through three times.

It is quarter to nine in the morning. Hundreds of people are 7 crossing the Square. These passersby—faculty, staff, students—pay very little attention to us; this morning singing has gone on for years. Most of them look at us directly, then ignore us, for there is nothing to see: no animal sacrifices, no lynchings, no collection plate for Jesse Helms,[1] no seizures, snake handling, healing, or glossolalia. There is barely anything to hear. I suspect the people glance at us to learn if we are really singing: how could so many people make so little sound? My fellow singers, who ignore each other, certainly ignore passersby as well. Within a week, most of them will have their eyes closed anyway.

We move directly to another song, a slower one. 8

> He is my peace
> Who has broken down every wall;
> He is my peace,
> He is my peace.

> Cast all your cares on him,
> For he careth for you—oo—oo
> He is my peace,
> He is my peace.

I am paying strict attention to the song leaders, for I am singing 9 at the top of my lungs and I've never heard any of these songs

1. Jesse Helms (1921–   ), an ultraconservative U.S. Senator from North Carolina.

before. They are not the old American low-church Protestant hymns; they are not the old European high-church Protestant hymns. These hymns seem to have been written just yesterday, apparently by the same people who put out lyrical Christian greeting cards and bookmarks.

"Where do these songs come from?" I ask a girl standing next to   10
me. She seems appalled to be addressed at all, and startled by the question. "They're from the praise albums!" she explains, and moves away.

The songs' melodies run dominant, subdominant, dominant,   11
tonic, dominant. The pace is slow, about the pace of "Tell Laura I Love Her," and with that song's quavering, long notes. The lyrics are simple and repetitive; there are very few of them to which a devout Jew or Mohammedan could not give whole-hearted assent. These songs are similar to the things Catholics sing in church these days. I don't know if any studies have been done to correlate the introduction of contemporary songs into Catholic churches with those churches' decline in membership, or with the phenomenon of Catholic converts' applying to enter cloistered monasteries directly, without passing through parish churches.

> *I'm set free to worship,*
> *I'm set free to praise him,*
> *I'm set free to dance before the Lord . . .*

At nine o'clock sharp we quit and scatter. I hear a few quiet "see   12
you"s. Mostly the students leave quickly, as if they didn't want to be seen. The Square empties.

The next day we show up again, at twenty to nine. The same two   13
leaders stand on the fountain's rim; the fountain is pouring down behind them.

After the first song, the boy with the moustache hollers, "Move   14
on up! Some of you guys aren't paying attention back there! You're talking to each other. I want you to concentrate!" The students laugh, embarrassed for him. He sounds like a teacher. No one moves. The girl breaks into the next song, which we join at once:

> *In my life, Lord,*
> *Be glorified, be glorified, be glorified;*
> *In my life, Lord,*
> *Be glorified, be glorified, today.*

At the end of this singularly monotonous verse, which is straining my tolerance for singing virtually anything, the boy with the moustache startles me by shouting, "Classes!"

At once, without skipping a beat, we sing, "In my classes, Lord,   15 be glorified, be glorified . . ." I give fleet thought to the class I'm teaching this afternoon. We're reading a little "Talk of the Town"[2] piece called "Eggbag," about a cat in a magic store on Eighth Avenue. "Relationships!" the boy calls. The students seem to sing "In my relationships, Lord," more easily than they sang "classes." They seemed embarrassed by "classes." In fact, to my fascination, they seem embarrassed by almost everything. Why are they here? I will sing with the Fundamentalists every weekday morning all spring; I will decide, tentatively, that they come pretty much for the same reasons I do: each has a private relationship with "the Lord" and will put up with a lot of junk for it.

I have taught some Fundamentalist students here, and know a   16
bit of what they think. They are college students above all, worried about their love lives, their grades, and finding jobs. Some support moderate Democrats; some support moderate Republicans. Like their classmates, most support nuclear freeze, ERA, and an end to the draft. I believe they are divided on abortion and busing. They are not particularly political. They read *Christianity Today* and *Campus Life* and *Eternity*—moderate, sensible magazines, I think; they read a lot of C. S. Lewis. (One such student, who seemed perfectly tolerant of me and my shoddy Christianity, introduced me to C. S. Lewis's critical book on Charles Williams.) They read the Bible. I think they all "believe in" organic evolution. The main thing about them is this: there isn't any "them." Their views vary. They don't know each other.

Their common Christianity puts them, if anywhere, to the left of   17
their classmates. I believe they also tend to be more able than their classmates to think well in the abstract, and also to recognize the complexity of moral issues. But I may be wrong.

In 1980, the media were certainly wrong about television   18
evangelists. Printed estimates of Jerry Falwell's television audience ranged from 18 million to 30 million people. In fact, according to Arbitron's actual counts, fewer than 1.5 million people were watching Falwell. And, according to an Emory University study, those who did watch television evangelists didn't necessarily vote with them. Emory University sociologist G. Melton Mobley reports, "When that message turns political, they cut it off." Analysis of the 1982 off-year election turned up no Fundamentalist bloc voting. The media were wrong, but no one printed retractions.

The media were wrong, too, in a tendency to identify all fun-   19

2. "The Talk of the Town" is a regular feature of *The New Yorker*, consisting of short, unsigned essays.

damentalist Christians with Falwell and his ilk, and to attribute to them, across the board, conservative views.

Someone has sent me two recent issues of *Eternity: The Evangel-*   20
ical Monthly. One lead article criticizes a television preacher for saying that the United States had never used military might to take land from another nation. The same article censures Newspeak, saying that government rhetoric would have us believe in a "clean bomb," would have us believe that we "defend" America by invading foreign soil, and would have us believe that the dictatorships we support are "democracies." "When the President of the United States says that one reason to support defense spending is because it creates jobs," this lead article says, "a little bit of *1984* begins to surface." Another article criticizes a "heavy-handed" opinion of Jerry Falwell Ministries—in this case a broadside attack on artificial insemination, surrogate motherhood, and lesbian motherhood. Browsing through *Eternity*, I find a double crostic.[3] I find an intelligent, analytical, and enthusiastic review of the new London Philharmonic recording of Mahler's second symphony—a review which stresses the "glorious truth" of the Jewish composer's magnificent work, and cites its recent performance in Jerusalem to celebrate the recapture of the Western Wall following the Six Day War. Surely, the evangelical Christians who read this magazine are not book-burners. If by chance they vote with the magazine's editors, then it looks to me as if they vote with the American Civil Liberties Union and Americans for Democratic Action.

Every few years some bold and sincere Christian student at this   21
university disagrees with a professor in class—usually about the professor's out-of-hand dismissal of Christianity. Members of the faculty, outraged, repeat the stories of these rare and uneven encounters for years on end, as if to prove that the crazies are everywhere, and gaining ground. The notion is, apparently, that these kids can't think for themselves. Or they wouldn't disagree.

Now again the moustached leader asks us to move up. There is   22
no harangue, so we move up. (This will be a theme all spring. The leaders want us closer together. Our instinct is to stand alone.) From behind the tall fountain comes a wind; on several gusts we get sprayed. No one seems to notice.

We have time for one more song. The leader, perhaps sensing   23
that no one likes him, blunders on. "I want you to pray this one through," he says. "We have a lot of people here from a lot of

3. A double-crostic is a difficult word puzzle that requires the solver to re-create a long quotation.

different fellowships, but we're all one body. Amen?" They don't like it. He gets a few polite Amens. We sing:

> Bind us together, Lord,
> With a bond that can't be broken;
> Bind us together, Lord,
> With love.

Everyone seems to be in a remarkably foul mood today. We don't like this song. There is no one here under seventeen, and, I think, no one here who believes that love is a bond that can't be broken. We sing the song through three times; then it is time to go.

The leader calls after our retreating backs, "Hey, have a good 24
day! Praise Him all day!" The kids around me roll up their eyes privately. Some groan; all flee.

The next morning is very cold. I am here early. Two girls are 25
talking on the fountain's rim; one is part Indian. She says, "I've got all the Old Testament, but I can't get the New. I screw up the New." She takes a breath and rattles off a long list, ending with "Jonah, Micah, Nahum, Habakkuk, Zephaniah, Haggai, Zechariah, Malachi." The other girl produces a slow, sarcastic applause. I ask one of the girls to help me with the words to a song. She is agreeable, but says, "I'm sorry, I can't. I just became a Christian this year, so I don't know all the words yet."

The others are coming; we stand and separate. The boy with the 26
moustache is gone, replaced by a big, serious fellow in a green down jacket. The bouncy girl is back with her guitar; she's wearing a skirt and wool knee socks. We begin, without any preamble, by singing a song that has so few words that we actually stretch one syllable over eleven separate notes. Then we sing a song in which the men sing one phrase and the women echo it. Everyone seems to know just what to do. In the context of our vapid songs, the lyrics of this one are extraordinary:

> I was nothing before you found me.
> Heartache! Broken people! Ruined lives
> Is why you died on Calvary.

The last line rises in a regular series of half-notes. Now at last some people are actually singing; they throw some breath into the business. There is a seriousness and urgency to it: "Heartache! Broken people! Ruined lives . . . I was nothing."

We don't look like nothing. We look like a bunch of students of 27
every stripe, ill-shaven or well-shaven, dressed up or down, but dressed warmly against the cold: jeans and parkas, jeans and heavy

sweaters, jeans and scarves and blow-dried hair. We look ordinary. But I think, quite on my own, that we are here because we know this business of nothingness, brokenness, and ruination. We sing this song over and over.

Something catches my eye. Behind us, up in the science build-   28
ing, professors are standing alone at opened windows.

The long brick science building has three upper floors of faculty   29
offices, thirty-two windows. At one window stands a bearded man, about forty; his opening his window is what caught my eye. He stands full in the open window, his hands on his hips, his head cocked down toward the fountain. He is drawn to look, as I was drawn to come. Up on the building's top floor, at the far right window, there is another: an Asian-American professor, wearing a white shirt, is sitting with one hip on his desk, looking out and down. In the middle of the row of windows, another one, an old professor in a checked shirt, stands sideways to the opened win-dow, stands stock-still, his long, old ear to the air. Now another window cranks open, another professor—or maybe a graduate student—leans out, his hands on the sill.

We are all singing, and I am watching these five still men, my   30
colleagues, whose office doors are surely shut—for that is the cus-tom here: five of them alone in their offices in the science building who have opened their windows on this very cold morning, who motionless hear the Fundamentalists sing, utterly unknown to each other.

We sing another four songs, including the clapping song, and   31
one which repeats, "This is the day which the Lord hath made; rejoice and be glad in it." All the professors but one stay by their opened windows, figures in a frieze. When after ten minutes we break off and scatter, each cranks his window shut. Maybe they have nine o'clock classes too.

I miss a few sessions. One morning of the following week, I   32
rejoin the Fundamentalists on the Square. The wind is blowing from the north; it is sunny and cold. There are several new de-velopments.

Someone has blown up rubber gloves and floated them in the   33
fountain. I saw them yesterday afternoon from my high office win-dow, and couldn't quite make them out: I seemed to see hands in the fountain waving from side to side, like those hands wagging on springs which people stick in the back windows of their cars. I saw these many years ago in Quito and Guayaquil, where they were a great fad long before they showed up here. The cardboard hands

said, on their palms, HOLA GENTE, hello people. Some of them just said HOLA, hello, with a little wave to the universe at large, in case anybody happened to be looking. It is like our sending radio signals to planets in other galaxies: HOLA, if anyone is listening. Jolly folk, these Ecuadorians, I thought.

Now, waiting by the fountain for the singing, I see that these 34 particular hands are long surgical gloves, yellow and white, ten of them, tied off at the cuff. They float upright and they wave, *hola, hola, hola;* they mill around like a crowd, bobbing under the fountain's spray and back again to the pool's rim, *hola.* It is a good prank. It is far too cold for the university's maintenance crew to retrieve them without turning off the fountain and putting on rubber boots.

From all around the Square, people are gathering for the singing. 35 There is no way I can guess which kids, from among the masses crossing the Square, will veer off to the fountain. When they get here, I never recognize anybody except the leaders.

The singing begins without ado as usual, but there is something 36 different about it. The students are growing prayerful, and they show it this morning with a peculiar gesture. I'm glad they weren't like this when I first joined them, or I never would have stayed.

Last night there was an educational television special, part of 37 "Middletown."[4] It was a segment called "Community of Praise," and I watched it because it was about Fundamentalists. It showed a Jesus-loving family in the Midwest; the treatment was good and complex. This family attended the prayer meetings, healing sessions, and church services of an unnamed sect—a very low-church sect, whose doctrine and culture were much more low-church than those of the kids I sing with. When the members of this sect prayed, they held their arms over their heads and raised their palms, as if to feel or receive a blessing or energy from above.

Now today on the Square there is a new serious mood. The 38 leaders are singing with their eyes shut. I am impressed that they can bang their guitars, keep their balance, and not fall into the pool. It is the same bouncy girl and earnest boy. Their eyeballs are rolled back a bit. I look around and see that almost everyone in this crowd of eighty or so has his eyes shut and is apparently praying the words of this song or praying some other prayer.

Now as the chorus rises, as it gets louder and higher and simpler 39 in melody—

4. A 1983 PBS series that updated a book published in 1929, *Middletown: A Study in Contemporary American Culture,* by Robert and Helen Merrell Lynd.

I exalt thee,
I exalt thee,
I exalt thee,
Thou art the Lord—

then, at this moment, hands start rising. All around me, hands are
going up—that tall girl, that blond boy with his head back, the red-
headed boy up front, the girl with the McDonald's jacket. Their
arms rise as if pulled on strings. Some few of them have raised their
arms very high over their heads and are tilting back their palms.
Many, many more of them, as inconspicuously as possible, have
raised their hands to the level of their chins.

What is going on? Why are these students today raising their   40
palms in this gesture, when nobody did it last week? Is it because
the leaders have set a prayerful tone this morning? Is it because this
gesture always accompanies this song, just as clapping accompanies other songs? Or is it, as I suspect, that these kids watched
the widely publicized documentary last night just as I did, and are
adopting, or trying out, the gesture?

It is a sunny morning, and the sun is rising behind the leaders   41
and the fountain, so those students have their heads tilted, eyes
closed, and palms upraised toward the sun. I glance up at the
science building and think my own prayer: thank God no one is
watching this.

The leaders cannot move around much on the fountain's rim.   42
The girl has her eyes shut; the boy opens his eyes from time to time,
glances at the neck of his guitar, and closes his eyes again.

When the song is over, the hands go down, and there is some   43
desultory chatting in the crowd, as usual: can I borrow your library
card? And, as usual, nobody looks at anybody.

All our songs today are serious. There is a feudal theme to them,   44
or a feudal analogue:

I will eat from abundance of your household.
I will dream beside your streams of righteousness.

You are my king.

Enter his gates
with thanksgiving in your heart;
come before his courts with praise.

He is the king of kings.

Thou art the Lord.

All around me, eyes are closed and hands are raised. There is no   45
social pressure to do this, or anything else. I've never known any

group to be less cohesive, imposing fewer controls. Since no one looks at anyone, and since passersby no longer look, everyone out here is inconspicuous and free. Perhaps the palm-raising has begun because the kids realize by now that they are not on display; they're praying in their closets, right out here on the Square. Over the course of the next weeks, I will learn that the palm-raising is here to stay.

The sun is rising higher. We are singing our last song. We are 46 praying. We are alone together.

> He is my peace
> Who has broken down every wall . . .

When the song is over, the hands go down. The heads lower, the 47 eyes open and blink. We stay still a second before we break up. We have been standing in a broad current; now we have stepped aside. We have dismantled the radar cups; we have closed the telescope's vault. Students gather their book bags and go. The two leaders step down from the fountain's rim and pack away their guitars. Everyone scatters. I am in no hurry, so I stay after everyone is gone. It is after nine o'clock, and the Square is deserted. The fountain is playing to an empty house. In the pool the cheerful hands are waving over the water, bobbing under the fountain's veil and out again in the current, *hola*.

PERRI KLASS

Learning the Language

Perri Klass (1958–   ) graduated from Harvard Medical School in 1986. During her years as a medical student, she not only published a novel and gave birth to a son but contributed essays to *Mademoiselle, Discover, Massachusetts Medicine,* and the *New York Times.* These essays gave a fresh and sometimes discomforting picture of medical-school education; several were later collected in *A Not Entirely Benign Procedure: Four Years as a Medical Student* (1987). Klass says that writing about medical school while going through it changed the nature of the experience: "I have found that in order to write about my training so that people outside the medical profession can understand what I am talking about I have had to preserve a certain level of naïveté for myself." In "Learning the Language," first published in the

"Hers" column of the *New York Times* in 1984, Klass's naïveté
allows her to see some hidden functions of medical jargon.

"Mrs. Tolstoy is your basic LOL in NAD, admitted for a soft rule- 1
out MI," the intern announces. I scribble that on my patient list. In
other words, Mrs. Tolstoy is a Little Old Lady in No Apparent
Distress who is in the hospital to make sure she hasn't had a heart
attack (rule out a Myocardial Infarction). And we think it's unlikely that she has had a heart attack (a *soft* rule-out).

If I learned nothing else during my first three months of working 2
in the hospital as a medical student, I learned endless jargon and
abbreviations. I started out in a state of primeval innocence, in
which I didn't even know that "s̄ CP, SOB, N/V" meant "without
chest pain, shortness of breath, or nausea and vomiting." By the
end I took the abbreviations so much for granted that I would
complain to my mother the English professor, "And can you believe I had to put down *three* NG tubes last night?"

"You'll have to tell me what an NG tube is if you want me to 3
sympathize properly," my mother said. NG, nasogastric—isn't it
obvious?

I picked up not only the specific expressions but also the patterns 4
of speech and the grammatical conventions; for example, you
never say that a patient's blood pressure fell or that his cardiac
enzymes rose. Instead, the patient is always the subject of the verb:
"He dropped his pressure." "He bumped his enzymes." This sort of
construction probably reflects the profound irritation of the intern
when the nurses come in the middle of the night to say that Mr.
Dickinson has disturbingly low blood pressure. "Oh, he's gonna
hurt me bad tonight," the intern might say, inevitably angry at Mr.
Dickinson for dropping his pressure and creating a problem.

When chemotherapy fails to cure Mrs. Bacon's cancer, what we 5
say is, "Mrs. Bacon failed chemotherapy."

"Well, we've already had one hit today, and we're up next, but 6
at least we've got mostly stable players on our team." This means
that our team (group of doctors and medical students) has already
gotten one new admission today, and it is our turn again, so we'll
get whoever is admitted next in emergency, but at least most of the
patients we already have are fairly stable, that is, unlikely to drop
their pressures or in any other way get suddenly sicker and hurt us
bad. Baseball metaphor is pervasive. A no-hitter is a night without
any new admissions. A player is always a patient—a nitrate player
is a patient on nitrates, a unit player is a patient in the intensive
care unit, and so on, until you reach the terminal player.

It is interesting to consider what it means to be winning, or doing   7
well, in this perennial baseball game. When the intern hangs up
the phone and announces, "I got a hit," that is not cause for
congratulations. The team is not scoring points; rather, it is getting
hit, being bombarded with new patients. The object of the game
from the point of view of the doctors, considering the players for
whom they are already responsible, is to get as few new hits as
possible.

This special language contributes to a sense of closeness and   8
professional spirit among people who are under a great deal of
stress. As a medical student, I found it exciting to discover that I'd
finally cracked the code, that I could understand what doctors said
and wrote, and could use the same formulations myself. Some
people seem to become enamored of the jargon for its own sake,
perhaps because they are so deeply thrilled with the idea of
medicine, with the idea of themselves as doctors.

I knew a medical student who was referred to by the interns on   9
the team as Mr. Eponym because he was so infatuated with epony-
mous terminology, the more obscure the better. He never said
"capillary pulsations" if he could say "Quincke's pulses." He
would lovingly tell over the multinamed syndromes—Wolff-
Parkinson-White, Lown-Ganong-Levine, Schönlein-Henoch—
until the temptation to suggest Schleswig-Holstein or Stevenson-
Kefauver or Baskin-Robbins became irresistible to his less reverent
colleagues.

And there is the jargon that you don't ever want to hear yourself   10
using. You know that your training is changing you, but there are
certain changes you think would be going a little too far.

The resident was describing a man with devastating terminal   11
pancreatic cancer. "Basically he's CTD," the resident concluded. I
reminded myself that I had resolved not to be shy about asking
when I didn't understand things. "CTD?" I asked timidly.

The resident smirked at me. "Circling The Drain."   12

The images are vivid and terrible. "What happened to Mrs. Mel-   13
ville?"

"Oh, she boxed last night." To box is to die, of course.   14

Then there are the more pompous locutions that can make the   15
beginning medical student nervous about the effects of medical
training. A friend of mine was told by his resident, "A pregnant
woman with sickle-cell represents a failure of genetic counseling."

Mr. Eponym, who tried hard to talk like the doctors, once ex-   16
plained to me, "An infant is basically a brainstem preparation."
The term "brainstem preparation," as used in neurological research, refers to an animal whose higher brain functions have been

destroyed so that only the most primitive reflexes remain, like the sucking reflex, the startle reflex, and the rooting reflex.

And yet at other times the harshness dissipates into a strangely elusive euphemism. "As you know, this is a not entirely benign procedure," some doctor will say, and that will be understood to imply agony, risk of complications, and maybe even a significant mortality rate. 17

The more extreme forms aside, one most important function of medical jargon is to help doctors maintain some distance from their patients. By reformulating a patient's pain and problems into a language that the patient doesn't even speak, I suppose we are in some sense taking those pains and problems under our jurisdiction and also reducing their emotional impact. This linguistic separation between doctors and patients allows conversations to go on at the bedside that are unintelligible to the patient. "Naturally, we're worried about adeno-CA," the intern can say to the medical student, and lung cancer need never be mentioned. 18

I learned a new language this past summer. At times it thrills me to hear myself using it. It enables me to understand my colleagues, to communicate effectively in the hospital. Yet I am uncomfortably aware that I will never again notice the peculiarities and even atrocities of medical language as keenly as I did this summer. There may be specific expressions I manage to avoid, but even as I remark them, promising myself I will never use them, I find that this language is becoming my professional speech. It no longer sounds strange in my ears—or coming from my mouth. And I am afraid that as with any new language, to use it properly you must absorb not only the vocabulary but also the structure, the logic, the attitudes. At first you may notice these new and alien assumptions every time you put together a sentence, but with time and increased fluency you stop being aware of them at all. And as you lose that awareness, for better or for worse, you move closer and closer to being a doctor instead of just talking like one. 19

LESLIE MARMON SILKO

Lullaby

Leslie Marmon Silko (1948–   ) was born and raised on the Laguna Pueblo Indian reservation in New Mexico. Her experience there provided the background for *Ceremony* (1977), the first novel published by a Native American woman. The novel tells the story of a Pueblo soldier's return to the reservation after World War II. Deranged by the killing of Japanese soldiers who look like his own relatives and unable to find help either in white society or in the arts of the reservation's dispirited medicine men, he meets a mixed-blood outcast who teaches him traditional ritual, folklore, and myth and prepares him to be cured. The tensions here are typical of those in Silko's other works: the dominant white culture, with its military and economic might, is juxtaposed with a Native American culture that lives in memory, story, song, and attachment to the landscape. Other books by Silko include *Laguna Woman: Poems* (1974) and *Storyteller* (1981), a collection of anecdotes, photographs, folk tales, and short stories. "Lullaby" is from *Storyteller*.

The sun had gone down but the snow in the wind gave off its 1 own light. It came in thick tufts like new wool—washed before the weaver spins it. Ayah reached out for it like her own babies had, and she smiled when she remembered how she had laughed at them. She was an old woman now, and her life had become memories. She sat down with her back against the wide cotton-wood tree, feeling the rough bark on her back bones; she faced east and listened to the wind and snow sing a high-pitched Yeibechei song. Out of the wind she felt warmer, and she could watch the wide fluffy snow fill in her tracks, steadily, until the direction she had come from was gone. By the light of the snow she could see the dark outline of the big arroyo a few feet away. She was sitting on the edge of Cebolleta Creek, where in the springtime the thin cows would graze on grass already chewed flat to the ground. In the wide deep creek bed where only a trickle of water flowed in the summer, the skinny cows would wander, looking for new grass along winding paths splashed with manure.

Ayah pulled the old Army blanket over her head like a shawl. 2 Jimmie's blanket—the one he had sent to her. That was a long time ago and the green wool was faded, and it was unraveling on the edges. She did not want to think about Jimmie. So she thought about the weaving and the way her mother had done it. On the tall wooden loom set into the sand under a tamarack tree for shade. She could see it clearly. She had been only a little girl when her grandma gave her the wooden combs to pull the twigs and burrs from the raw, freshly washed wool. And while she combed the wool, her grandma sat beside her, spinning a silvery strand of yarn around the smooth cedar spindle. Her mother worked at the loom with yarns dyed bright yellow and red and gold. She watched them dye the yarn in boiling black pots full of beeweed petals, juniper berries, and sage. The blankets her mother made were soft and woven so tight that rain rolled off them like birds' feathers. Ayah remembered sleeping warm on cold windy nights, wrapped in her mother's blankets on the hogan's sandy floor.

The snow drifted now, with the northwest wind hurling it in gusts. It drifted up around her black overshoes—old ones with little metal buckles. She smiled at the snow which was trying to cover her little by little. She could remember when they had no black rubber overshoes; only the high buckskin leggings that they wrapped over their elkhide moccasins. If the snow was dry or frozen, a person could walk all day and not get wet; and in the evenings the beams of the ceiling would hang with lengths of pale buckskin leggings, drying out slowly. 3

She felt peaceful remembering. She didn't feel cold any more. Jimmie's blanket seemed warmer than it had ever been. And she could remember the morning he was born. She could remember whispering to her mother, who was sleeping on the other side of the hogan, to tell her it was time now. She did not want to wake the others. The second time she called to her, her mother stood up and pulled on her shoes; she knew. They walked to the old stone hogan together, Ayah walking a step behind her mother. She waited alone, learning the rhythms of the pains while her mother went to call the old woman to help them. The morning was already warm even before dawn and Ayah smelled the bee flowers blooming and the young willow growing at the springs. She could remember that so clearly, but his birth merged into the births of the other children and to her it became all the same birth. They named him for the summer morning and in English they called him Jimmie. 4

It wasn't like Jimmie died. He just never came back, and one day a dark blue sedan with white writing on its doors pulled up in front of the boxcar shack where the rancher let the Indians live. A man in a khaki uniform trimmed in gold gave them a yellow piece of paper and told them that Jimmie was dead. He said the Army would try to get the body back and then it would be shipped to them; but it wasn't likely because the helicopter had burned after it crashed. All of this was told to Chato because he could understand English. She stood inside the doorway holding the baby while Chato listened. Chato spoke English like a white man and he spoke Spanish too. He was taller than the white man and he stood straighter too. Chato didn't explain why; he just told the military man they could keep the body if they found it. The white man looked bewildered; he nodded his head and he left. Then Chato 5 looked at her and shook his head, and then he told her, "Jimmie isn't coming home anymore," and when he spoke, he used the words to speak of the dead. She didn't cry then, but she hurt inside with anger. And she mourned him as the years passed, when a horse fell with Chato and broke his leg, and the white rancher told them he wouldn't pay Chato until he could work again. She mourned Jimmie because he would have worked for his father then; he would have saddled the big bag horse and ridden the fence lines each day, with wire cutters and heavy gloves, fixing the breaks in the barbed wire and putting the stray cattle back inside again.

She mourned him after the white doctors came to take Danny and Ella away. She was at the shack alone that day they came. It was back in the days before they hired Navajo women to go with them as interpreters. She recognized one of the doctors. She had seen him at the children's clinic at Cañoncito about a month ago. They were wearing khaki uniforms and they waved papers at her and a black ball-point pen, trying to make her understand their English words. She was frightened by the way they looked at the children, like the lizard watches the fly. Danny was swinging on the tire swing on the elm tree behind the rancher's house, and Ella was toddling around the front door, dragging the broomstick horse Chato made for her. Ayah could see they wanted her to sign the papers, and Chato had taught her to sign her name. It was something she was proud of. She only wanted them to go, and to take their eyes away from her children.

She took the pen from the man without looking at his face and she signed the papers in three different places he pointed to. She stared at the ground by their feet and waited for them to leave. But they stood there and began to point and gesture at the children. Danny stopped swinging. Ayah could see his fear. She moved suddenly and grabbed Ella into her arms; the child squirmed, trying to get back to her toys. Ayah ran with the baby toward Danny; she screamed for him to run and then she grabbed him around his chest and carried him too. She ran south into the foothills of juniper trees and black lava rock. Behind her she heard the doctors running, but they had been taken by surprise, and as the hills became steeper and the cholla cactus were thicker, they stopped. When she reached the top of the hill, she stopped to listen in case they were circling around her. But in a few minutes she heard a car engine start and they drove away. The children had been too surprised to cry while she ran with them. Danny was shaking and Ella's little fingers were gripping Ayah's blouse.

She stayed up in the hills for the rest of the day, sitting on a black lava boulder in the sunshine where she could see for miles all around her. The sky was light blue and cloudless, and it was warm for late April. The sun warmth relaxed her and took the fear and anger away. She lay back on the rock and watched the sky. It seemed to her that she could walk into the sky, stepping through clouds endlessly. Danny played with little pebbles and stones, pretending they were birds eggs and then little rabbits. Ella sat at her feet and dropped fistfuls of dirt into the breeze, watching the dust and particles of sand intently. Ayah watched a hawk soar high above them, dark wings gliding; hunting or only watching, she did not know. The hawk was patient and he circled all afternoon before he disappeared around the high volcanic peak the Mexicans called Guadalupe.

Late in the afternoon, Ayah looked down at the gray boxcar   9
shack with the paint all peeled from the wood; the stove pipe on the roof was rusted and crooked. The fire she had built that morning in the oil drum stove had burned out. Ella was asleep in her lap now and Danny sat close to her, complaining that he was hungry; he asked when they would go to the house. "We will stay up here until your father comes," she told him, "because those white men were chasing us." The boy remembered then and he nodded at her silently.

If Jimmie had been there he could have read those papers and   10
explained to her what they said. Ayah would have known then, never to sign them. The doctors came back the next day and they brought a BIA[1] policeman with them. They told Chato they had her signature and that was all they needed. Except for the kids. She listened to Chato sullenly; she hated him when he told her it was the old woman who died in the winter, spitting blood; it was her old grandma who had given the children this disease. "They don't spit blood," she said coldly. "The whites lie." She held Ella and Danny close to her, ready to run to the hills again. "I want a medicine man first," she said to Chato, not looking at him. He shook his head. "It's too late now. The policeman is with them. You signed the paper." His voice was gentle.

It was worse than if they had died: to lose the children and to   11
know that somewhere, in a place called Colorado, in a place full of sick and dying strangers, her children were without her. There had been babies that died soon after they were born, and one that died before he could walk. She had carried them herself, up to the boulders and great pieces of the cliff that long ago crashed down from Long Mesa; she laid them in the crevices of sandstone and

1. Bureau of Indian Affairs.

buried them in fine brown sand with round quartz pebbles that washed down the hills in the rain. She had endured it because they had been with her. But she could not bear this pain. She did not sleep for a long time after they took her children. She stayed on the hill where they had fled the first time, and she slept rolled up in the blanket Jimmie had sent her. She carried the pain in her belly and it was fed by everything she saw: the blue sky of their last day together and the dust and pebbles they played with; the swing in the elm tree and broomstick horse choked life from her. The pain filled her stomach and there was no room for food or for her lungs to fill with air. The air and the food would have been theirs.

She hated Chato, not because he let the policeman and doctors 12 put the screaming children in the government car, but because he had taught her to sign her name. Because it was like the old ones always told her about learning their language or any of their ways: it endangered you. She slept alone on the hill until the middle of November when the first snows came. Then she made a bed for herself where the children had slept. She did not lie down beside Chato again until many years later, when he was sick and shivering and only her body could keep him warm. The illness came after the white rancher told Chato he was too old to work for him anymore, and Chato and his old woman should be out of the shack by the next afternoon because the rancher had hired new people to work there. That had satisfied her. To see how the white man repaid Chato's years of loyalty and work. All of Chato's fine-sounding English talk didn't change things.

It snowed steadily and the luminous light from the snow gradu- 13 ally diminished into the darkness. Somewhere in Cebolleta a dog barked and other village dogs joined with it. Ayah looked in the direction she had come, from the bar where Chato was buying the wine. Sometimes he told her to go on ahead and wait; and then he never came. And when she finally went back looking for him, she would find him passed out at the bottom of the wooden steps to Azzie's Bar. All the wine would be gone and most of the money too, from the pale blue check that came to them once a month in a government envelope. It was then that she would look at his face and his hands, scarred by ropes and the barbed wire of all those years, and she would think, this man is a stranger; for forty years she had smiled at him and cooked his food, but he remained a stranger. She stood up again, with the snow almost to her knees, and she walked back to find Chato.

It was hard to walk in the deep snow and she felt the air burn in 14 her lungs. She stopped a short distance from the bar to rest and readjust the blanket. But this time he wasn't waiting for her on the bottom step with his old Stetson hat pulled down and his shoulders hunched up in his long wool overcoat.

She was careful not to slip on the wooden steps. When she   15
pushed the door open, warm air and cigarette smoke hit her face. She looked around slowly and deliberately, in every corner, in every dark place that the old man might find to sleep. The bar owner didn't like Indians in there, especially Navajos, but he let Chato come in because he could talk Spanish like he was one of them. The men at the bar stared at her, and the bartender saw that she left the door open wide. Snowflakes were flying inside like moths and melting into a puddle on the oiled wood floor. He motioned to her to close the door, but she did not see him. She held herself straight and walked across the room slowly, searching the room with every step. The snow in her hair melted and she could feel it on her forehead. At the far corner of the room, she saw red flames at the mica window of the old stove door; she looked behind the stove just to make sure. The bar got quiet except for the Spanish polka music playing on the jukebox. She stood by the stove and shook the snow from her blanket and held it near the stove to dry. The wet wool smell reminded her of new-born goats in early March, brought inside to warm near the fire. She felt calm.

In past years they would have told her to get out. But her hair   16
was white now and her face was wrinkled. They looked at her like she was a spider crawling slowly across the room. They were afraid; she could feel the fear. She looked at their faces steadily. They reminded her of the first time the white people brought her children back to her that winter. Danny had been shy and hid behind the thin white woman who brought them. And the baby had not known her until Ayah took her into her arms, and then Ella had nuzzled close to her as she had when she was nursing. The blonde woman was nervous and kept looking at a dainty gold watch on her wrist. She sat on the bench near the small window and watched the dark snow clouds gather around the mountains; she was worrying about the unpaved road. She was frightened by what she saw inside too: the strips of venison drying on a rope across the ceiling and the children jabbering excitedly in a language she did not know. So they stayed for only a few hours. Ayah watched the government car disappear down the road and she knew they were already being weaned from these lava hills and from this sky. The last time they came was in early June, and Ella stared at her the way the men in the bar were now staring. Ayah did not try to pick her up; she smiled at her instead and spoke

cheerfully to Danny. When he tried to answer her, he could not seem to remember and he spoke English words with the Navajo. But he gave her a scrap of paper that he had found somewhere and carried in his pocket; it was folded in half, and he shyly looked up at her and said it was a bird. She asked Chato if they were home for good this time. He spoke to the white woman and she shook her head. "How much longer?" he asked, and she said she didn't know; but Chato saw how she stared at the boxcar shack. Ayah turned away then. She did not say good-bye.

She felt satisfied that the men in the bar feared her. Maybe it was   17 her face and the way she held her mouth with teeth clenched tight, like there was nothing anyone could do to her now. She walked north down the road, searching for the old man. She did this because she had the blanket, and there would be no place for him except with her and the blanket in the old adobe barn near the arroyo. They always slept there when they came to Cebolleta. If the money and the wine were gone, she would be relieved because then they could go home again; back to the old hogan with a dirt roof and rock walls where she herself had been born. And the next day the old man could go back to the few sheep they still had, to follow along behind them, guiding them, into dry sandy arroyos where sparse grass grew. She knew he did not like walking behind old ewes when for so many years he rode big quarter horses and worked with cattle. But she wasn't sorry for him; he should have known all along what would happen.

There had not been enough rain for their garden in five years;   18 and that was when Chato finally hitched a ride into the town and brought back brown boxes of rice and sugar and big tin cans of welfare peaches. After that, at the first of the month they went to Cebolleta to ask the postmaster for the check; and then Chato would go to the bar and cash it. They did this as they planted the garden every May, not because anything would survive the summer dust, but because it was time to do this. The journey passed the days that smelled silent and dry like the caves above the canyon with yellow painted buffaloes on their walls.

He was walking along the pavement when she found him. He   19 did not stop or turn around when he heard her behind him. She walked beside him and she noticed how slowly he moved now. He smelled strong of woodsmoke and urine. Lately he had been forgetting. Sometimes he called her by his sister's name and she had been gone for a long time. Once she had found him wandering on the road to the white man's ranch, and she asked him why he was going that way; he laughed at her and said, "You know they can't run that ranch without me," and he walked on determined, limping on the leg that had been crushed many years before. Now he looked at her curiously, as if for the first time, but he kept shuffling along, moving slowly along the side of the highway. His gray hair had grown long and spread out on the shoulders of the long overcoat. He wore the old felt hat pulled down over his ears. His boots were worn out at the toes and he had stuffed pieces of an old red shirt in the holes. The rags made his feet look like little animals up to their ears in snow. She laughed at his feet; the snow muffled the sound of her laugh. He stopped and looked at her again. The wind had quit blowing and the snow was falling straight down; the southeast sky was beginning to clear and Ayah could see a star.

"Let's rest awhile," she said to him. They walked away from the 20 road and up the slope to the giant boulders that had tumbled down from the red sandrock mesa throughout the centuries of rainstorms and earth tremors. In a place where the boulders shut out the wind, they sat down with their backs against the rock. She offered half of the blanket to him and they sat wrapped together.

The storm passed swiftly. The clouds moved east. They were 21 massive and full, crowding together across the sky. She watched them with the feeling of horses—steely blue-gray horses startled across the sky. The powerful haunches pushed into the distances and the tail hairs streamed white mist behind them. The sky cleared. Ayah saw that there was nothing between her and the stars. The light was crystalline. There was no shimmer, no distortion through earth haze. She breathed the clarity of the night sky; she smelled the purity of the half moon and the stars. He was lying on his side with his knees pulled up near his belly for warmth. His eyes were closed now, and in the light from the stars and the moon, he looked young again.

She could see it descend out of the night sky: an icy stillness from 22 the edge of the thin moon. She recognized the freezing. It came gradually, sinking snowflake by snowflake until the crust was heavy and deep. It had the strength of the stars in Orion, and its journey was endless. Ayah knew that with the wine he would sleep. He would not feel it. She tucked the blanket around him, remembering how it was when Ella had been with her; and she felt the rush so big inside her heart for the babies. And she sang the only song she knew to sing for babies. She could not remember if she had ever sung it to her children, but she knew that her grandmother had sung it and her mother had sung it:

The earth is your mother,
  she holds you.
The sky is your father,
  he protects you.
Sleep,
sleep.
Rainbow is your sister,
  she loves you.
The winds are your brothers,
  they sing to you.
Sleep,
sleep.
We are together always
We are together always
There never was a time
when this
was not so.

NADINE GORDIMER

Which New Era Would That Be?

Nadine Gordimer (1923–   ) began to write when she was nine and published her first story when she was fifteen. A white South African whose short stories and novels have won her a wide readership in the United States as well as her native country, she is such an outspoken critic of apartheid that the South African government has banned three of her books. As early as 1959, when the power of whites in her country seemed unshakable, Gordimer was predicting a day when the white minority would be reduced to a few "foreign experts, employed at the Government's expense." Her 1987 novel, *A Sport of Nature*, is set in a future when majority rule has become a reality: the white protagonist works for the African National Congress, adopts an African name and style of dress, and marries a black politician. Most of Gordimer's fiction, however, does not concern itself with a visionary future but with a realistic present. Like E. M. Forster, her favorite writer, she has been widely praised for her ability to create credible characters of various races and political persuasions. This talent shows clearly in "Which New Era Would That Be?" from *Six Feet of the Country* (1956).

Jake Alexander, a big, fat coloured[1] man, half Scottish, half   1
African, was shaking a large pan of frying bacon on the gas stove in
the back room of his Johannesburg printing shop when he became
aware that someone was knocking on the door at the front of the
shop. The sizzling fat and the voices of the five men in the back
room with him almost blocked sounds from without, and the
knocking was of the steady kind that might have been going on for
quite a few minutes. He lifted the pan off the flame with one hand
and with the other made an impatient silencing gesture, directed at
the bacon as well as the voices. Interpreting the movement as one
of caution, the men hurriedly picked up the tumblers and cups in
which they had been taking their end-of-the-day brandy at their
ease, and tossed the last of it down. Little yellow Klaas, whose hair
was like ginger-coloured wire wool, stacked the cups and glasses
swiftly and hid them behind the dirty curtain that covered a row of
shelves.

"Who's that?" yelled Jake, wiping his greasy hands down his   2
pants.

There was a sharp and playful tattoo, followed by an English   3
voice: "Me—Alister. For heaven's sake, Jake!"

The fat man put the pan back on the flame and tramped through   4
the dark shop, past the idle presses, to the door, and flung it open.
"Mr Halford!" he said. "Well, good to see you. Come in, man. In
the back there, you can't hear a thing." A young Englishman with
gentle eyes, a stern mouth, and flat, colourless hair which grew in
an untidy, confused spiral from a double crown, stepped back to
allow a young woman to enter ahead of him. Before he could
introduce her, she held out her hand to Jake, smiling, and shook
his firmly. "Good evening. Jennifer Tetzel," she said.

"Jennifer, this is Jake Alexander," the young man managed to   5
get in, over her shoulder.

The two had entered the building from the street through an   6
archway lettered NEW ERA BUILDING. "Which new era would that
be?" the young woman had wondered aloud, brightly, while they
were waiting in the dim hallway for the door to be opened, and
Alister Halford had not known whether the reference was to the
discovery of deep-level gold mining that had saved Johannesburg
from the ephemeral fate of a mining camp in the 'nineties, or to the
optimism after the settlement of labour troubles in the 'twenties, or
to the recovery after the world went off the gold standard in the
'thirties—really, one had no idea of the age of these buildings in
this run-down end of the town. Now, coming in out of the deserted

---

1. In South Africa, *coloured* means of mixed white and black ancestry.

hallway gloom, which smelled of dust and rotting wood—the smell of waiting—they were met by the live, cold tang of ink and the homely, lazy odour of bacon fat—the smell of acceptance. There was not much light in the deserted workshop. The host blundered to the wall and switched on a bright naked bulb, up in the ceiling. The three stood blinking at one another for a moment: a coloured man with the fat of the man-of-the-world upon him, grossly dressed—not out of poverty but obviously because he liked it that way—in a rayon sports shirt that gaped and showed two hairy stomach rolls hiding his navel in a lipless grin, the pants of a good suit misbuttoned and held up round the waist by a tie instead of a belt, and a pair of expensive sports shoes, worn without socks; a young Englishman in a worn greenish tweed suit with a neo-Edwardian cut to the waistcoat that labelled it a leftover from undergraduate days; a handsome white woman who, as the light fell upon her, was immediately recognizable to Jake Alexander.

He had never met her before but he knew the type well—had seen it over and over again at meetings of the Congress of Democrats, and other organizations where progressive whites met progressive blacks. These were the white women who, Jake knew, persisted in regarding themselves as your equal. That was even worse, he thought, than the parsons who persisted in regarding *you* as *their* equal. The parsons had had ten years at school and seven years at a university and theological school; you had carried sacks of vegetables from the market to white people's cars from the time you were eight years old until you were apprenticed to a printer, and your first woman, like your mother, had been a servant, whom you had visited in a backyard room, and your first gulp of whisky, like many of your other pleasures, had been stolen while a white man was not looking. Yet the good parson insisted that your picture of life was exactly the same as his own: *you* felt as *he* did. But these women—oh, Christ!—these women felt as *you* did. They were sure of it. They thought they understood the humiliation of the black man walking the streets only by the permission of a pass written out by a white person, and the guilt and swagger of the coloured man light-faced enough to slink, fugitive from his own skin, into the preserves—the cinemas, bars, libraries—marked "EUROPEANS ONLY." Yes, breathless with stout sensitivity, they insisted on walking the whole teeter-totter of the colour line. There was no escaping their understanding. They even insisted on feeling the resentment *you* must feel at their identifying themselves with your feelings . . .

Here was the black hair of a determined woman (last year they wore it pulled tightly back into an oddly perched knot; this year it was cropped and curly as a lap dog's), the round, bony brow unpowdered in order to show off the tan, the red mouth, the unrouged cheeks, the big, lively, handsome eyes, dramatically painted, that would look into yours with such intelligent, eager honesty—eager to mirror what Jake Alexander, a big, fat coloured man interested in women, money, brandy, and boxing, was feeling. Who the hell wants a woman to look at you honestly, anyway? What has all this to do with a *woman*—with what men and women have for each other in their eyes? She was wearing a wide black skirt, a white cotton blouse baring a good deal of her breasts, and ear-rings that seemed to have been made by a blacksmith out of bits of scrap iron. On her feet she had sandals whose narrow thongs wound between her toes, and the nails of the toes were painted plum colour. By contrast, her hands were neglected-looking—sallow, unmanicured—and on one thin finger there swivelled a huge gold seal-ring. She was good-looking, he supposed with disgust.

He stood there, fat, greasy, and grinning at the two visitors so lingeringly that his grin looked insolent. Finally he asked, "What brings you this end of town, Mr Halford? Sight-seeing with the lady?" 9

The young Englishman gave Jake's arm a squeeze, where the short sleeve of the rayon shirt ended. "Just thought I'd look you up, Jake," he said, jolly. 10

"Come on in, come on in," said Jake on a rising note, shambling ahead of them into the company of the back room. "Here, what about a chair for the lady?" He swept a pile of handbills from the seat of a kitchen chair onto the dusty concrete floor, picked up the chair, and planked it down again in the middle of the group of men who had risen awkwardly at the visitors' entrance. "You know Maxie Ndube? And Temba?" Jake said, nodding at two of the men who surrounded him. 11

Alister Halford murmured with polite warmth his recognition of Maxie, a small, dainty-faced African in neat, businessman's dress, then said inquiringly and hesitantly to Temba, "Have we? When?" 12

Temba was a coloured man—a mixture of the bloods of black slaves and white masters, blended long ago, in the days when the Cape of Good Hope was a port of refreshment for the Dutch East India Company. He was tall and pale, with a large Adam's apple, enormous black eyes, and the look of a musician in a jazz band; you could picture a trumpet lifted to the ceiling in those long yellow hands, that curved spine hunched forward to shield a low note. "In Durban last year, Mr Halford, you remember?" he said eagerly. "I'm sure we met—or perhaps I only saw you there." 13

"Oh, at the Congress? Of course I remember you!" Halford 14
apologized. "You were in a delegation from the Cape?"

"Miss—?" Jake Alexander waved a hand between the young 15
woman, Maxie, and Temba.

"Jennifer. Jennifer Tetzel," she said again clearly, thrusting out 16
her hand. There was a confused moment when both men reached
for it at once and then hesitated, each giving way to the other.
Finally the handshaking was accomplished, and the young woman
seated herself confidently on the chair.

Jake continued, offhand, "Oh, and of course Billy Boy—" Alis- 17
ter signalled briefly to a black man with sad, blood-shot eyes, who
stood awkwardly, back a few steps, against some rolls of paper—
"and Klaas and Albert." Klaas and Albert had in their mixed blood
some strain of the Bushman, which gave them a batrachian yel-
lowness and toughness, like one of those toads that (prehistoric as
the Bushman is) are mythically believed to have survived into
modern times (hardly more fantastically than the Bushman himself
has survived) by spending centuries shut up in an air bubble in a
rock. Like Billy Boy, Klaas and Albert had backed away, and, as if
abasement against the rolls of paper, the wall, or the window were
a greeting in itself, the two little coloured men and the big African
only stared back at the masculine nods of Alister and the bright
smile of the young woman.

"You up from the Cape for anything special now?" Alister said 18
to Temba as he made a place for himself on a corner of a table that
was littered with photographic blocks, bits of type, poster proofs, a
bottle of souring milk, a bow-tie, a pair of red braces, and a number
of empty Coca-Cola bottles.

"I've been living in Durban for a year. Just got the chance of a lift 19
to Jo'burg," said the gangling Temba.

Jake had set himself up easily, leaning against the front of the 20
stove and facing Miss Jennifer Tetzel on her chair. He jerked his
head towards Temba and said, "Real banana boy." Young white
men brought up in the strong Anglo-Saxon tradition of the province of Natal are often referred to, and refer to themselves, as
"banana boys," even though fewer and fewer of them have any
connection with the dwindling number of vast banana estates that
once made their owners rich. Jake's broad face, where the bright-
pink cheeks of a Highland complexion—inherited, along with his
name, from his Scottish father—showed oddly through his coarse,
beige skin, creased up in appreciation of his own joke. And Temba
threw back his head and laughed, his Adam's apple bobbing, at the
idea of himself as a cricket-playing white public-school boy.

"There's nothing like Cape Town, is there?" said the young 21

woman to him, her head charmingly on one side, as if this conviction were something she and he shared.

"Miss Tetzel's up here to look us over. She's from Cape Town,"   22
Alister explained.

She turned to Temba with her beauty, her strong provoca-   23
tiveness, full on, as it were. "So we're neighbours?"

Jake rolled one foot comfortably over the other and a spluttering   24
laugh pursed out the pink inner membrane of his lips.

"Where did you live?" she went on, to Temba.   25

"Cape Flats," he said. Cape Flats is a desolate coloured slum in   26
the bush outside Cape Town.

"Me, too," said the girl, casually.   27

Temba said politely, "You're kidding," and then looked down   28
uncomfortably at his hands, as if they had been guilty of some
clumsy movement. He had not meant to sound so familiar; the
words were not the right ones.

"I've been there nearly ten months," she said.   29

"Well, some people've got queer tastes," Jake remarked, laugh-   30
ing, to no one in particular, as if she were not there.

"How's that?" Temba was asking her shyly, respectfully.   31

She mentioned the name of a social rehabilitation scheme that   32
was in operation in the slum. "I'm assistant director of the thing at
the moment. It's connected with the sort of work I do at the university, you see, so they've given me fifteen months' leave from my
usual job."

Maxie noticed with amusement the way she used the word   33
"job," as if she were a plumber's mate; he and his educated African friends—journalists and schoolteachers—were careful to
talk only of their "professions." "Good works," he said, smiling
quietly.

She planted her feet comfortably before her, wriggling on the   34
hard chair, and said to Temba with mannish frankness, "It's a
ghastly place. How in God's name did you survive living there? I
don't think I can last out more than another few months, and I've
always got my flat in Cape Town to escape to on Sundays, and
so on."

While Temba smiled, turning his protruding eyes aside slowly,   35
Jake looked straight at her and said, "Then why do you, lady, why
do you?"

"Oh, I don't know. Because I don't see why anyone else—any   36
one of the people who live there—should have to, I suppose." She
laughed before anyone else could at the feebleness, the philan-
thropic uselessness of what she was saying, "Guilt, what-have-
you . . ."

Maxie shrugged, as if at the mention of some expensive illness   37
he had never been able to afford and whose symptoms he could
not imagine.

There was a moment of silence; the two coloured men and the   38
big black man standing back against the wall watched anxiously, as
if some sort of signal might be expected, possibly from Jake Alexander, their boss, the man who, like themselves, was not white, yet
who owned his own business and had a car and money and
strange friends—sometimes even white people, such as these. The
three of them were dressed in the ill-matched cast-off clothing that
all humble workpeople who are not white wear in Johannesburg,
and they had not lost the ability of rural people to stare, unembarrassed and unembarrassing.

Jake winked at Alister; it was one of his mannerisms—a   39
bookie's wink, a stage comedian's wink. "Well, how's it going,
boy, how's it going?" he said. His turn of phrase was bar-room
bonhomie; with luck, he *could* get into a bar, too. With a hat to
cover his hair and his coat collar well up, and only a bit of greasy
pink cheek showing, he had slipped into the bars of the shabbier
Johannesburg hotels with Alister many times and got away with it.
Alister, on the other hand, had got away with the same sort of
thing narrowly several times, too, when he had accompanied Jake
to a shebeen[2] in a coloured location, where it was illegal for a white
man to be, as well as illegal for anyone at all to have a drink; twice
Alister had escaped a raid by jumping out of a window. Alister had
been in South Africa only eighteen months, as correspondent for a
newspaper in England, and because he was only two or three years
away from undergraduate escapades such incidents seemed to give
him a kind of nostalgic pleasure; he found them funny. Jake, for
his part, had decided long ago (with the great help of the money he
had made) that he would take the whole business of the colour bar
as humorous. The combination of these two attitudes, stemming
from such immeasurably different circumstances, had the effect of
making their friendship less self-conscious than is usual between a
white man and a coloured one.

"They tell me it's going to be a good thing on Saturday night?"   40
said Alister, in the tone of questioning someone in the know. He
was referring to a boxing match between two coloured heavy-
weights, one of whom was a protégé of Jake.

Jake grinned deprecatingly, like a fond mother. "Well, Pikkie's a   41
good boy," he said. "I tell you, it'll be something to see." He
danced about a little on his clumsy toes in pantomime of the way a

2. Unlicensed bar.

boxer nimbles himself, and collapsed against the stove, his belly shaking with laughter at his breathlessness.

"Too much smoking, too many brandies, Jake," said Alister.   42

"With me, it's too many women, boy."   43

"We were just congratulating Jake," said Maxie in his soft, pre-   44
cise voice, the indulgent, tongue-in-cheek tone of the protégé who
is superior to his patron, for Maxie was one of Jake's boys, too—of
a different kind. Though Jake had decided that for him being on
the wrong side of a colour bar was ludicrous, he was as indulgent
to those who took it seriously and politically, the way Maxie did, as
he was to any up-and-coming youngster who, say, showed talent
in the ring or wanted to go to America and become a singer. They
could all make themselves free of Jake's pocket, and his printing
shop, and his room in the lower end of the town, where the building had fallen below the standard of white people but was far
superior to the kind of thing most coloureds and blacks were accustomed to.

"Congratulations on what?" the young white woman asked.   45
She had a way of looking up around her, questioningly, from face
to face, that came of long familiarity with being the centre of attention at parties.

"Yes, you can shake my hand, boy," said Jake to Alister. "I   46
didn't see it, but these fellows tell me that my divorce went
through. It's in the papers today."

"Is that so? But from what I hear, you won't be a free man   47
long," Alister said teasingly.

Jake giggled, and pressed at one gold-filled tooth with a strong   48
fingernail. "You heard about the little parcel I'm expecting from
Zululand?" he asked.

"Zululand?" said Alister. "I thought your Lila came from Stel-   49
lenbosch."

Maxie and Temba laughed.   50

"Lila? *What* Lila?" said Jake with exaggerated innocence.   51

"You're behind the times," said Maxie to Alister.   52

"You know I like them—well, sort of round," said Jake. "Don't   53
care for the thin kind, in the long run."

"But Lila had red hair!" Alister goaded him. He remembered the   54
incongruously dyed, straightened hair on a fine coloured girl
whose nostrils dilated in the manner of certain fleshy water-plants
seeking prey.

Jennifer Tetzel got up and turned the gas off on the stove, behind   55
Jake. "That bacon'll be like charred string," she said.

Jake did not move—merely looked at her lazily. "This is not the   56
way to talk with a lady around." He grinned, unapologetic.

She smiled at him and sat down, shaking her ear-rings. "Oh, I'm   57

divorced myself. Are we keeping you people from your supper? Do
go ahead and eat. Don't bother about us."

Jake turned around, gave the shrunken rashers a mild shake,   58
and put the pan aside. "Hell, no," he said. "Any time. But—"
turning to Alister—"won't you have something to eat?" He
looked about, helpless and unconcerned, as if to indicate an
absence of plates and a general careless lack of equipment
such as white women would be accustomed to use when they
ate. Alister said quickly, no, he had promised to take Jennifer to
Moorjee's.

Of course, Jake should have known; a woman like that would   59
want to be taken to eat at an Indian place in Vrededorp, even
though she was white, and free to eat at the best hotel in town. He
felt suddenly, after all, the old gulf opening between himself and
Alister: what did *they* see in such women—bristling, sharp, all-
seeing, knowing women, who talked like men, who wanted to
show all the time that, apart from sex, they were exactly the same
as men? He looked at Jennifer and her clothes, and thought of the
way a white woman could look: one of those big, soft, European
women with curly yellow hair, with very high-heeled shoes that
made them shake softly when they walked, with a strong scent,
like hot flowers, coming up, it seemed, from their jutting breasts
under the lace and pink and blue and all the other pretty things
they wore—women with nothing resistant about them except,
buried in white, boneless fingers, those red, pointed nails that
scratched faintly at your palms.

"You should have been along with me at lunch today," said   60
Maxie to no one in particular. Or perhaps the soft voice, a vocal
tiptoe, was aimed at Alister, who was familiar with Maxie's work
as an organizer of African trade unions. The group in the room
gave him their attention (Temba with the little encouraging grunt
of one who has already heard the story), but Maxie paused a
moment, smiling ruefully at what he was about to tell. Then he
said, "You know George Elson?" Alister nodded. The man was a
white lawyer who had been arrested twice for his participation in
anti-colour-bar movements.

"Oh, George? I've worked with George often in Cape Town,"   61
put in Jennifer.

"Well," continued Maxie, "George Elson and I went out to one   62
of the industrial towns on the East Rand. We were interviewing the
bosses, you see, not the men, and at the beginning it was all right,
though, once or twice the girls in the offices thought I was George's
driver—'Your boy can wait outside.' " He laughed, showing small,
perfect teeth; everything about him was finely made—his straight-
fingered dark hands, the curved African nostrils of his small nose,

his little ears, which grew close to the sides of his delicate head. The others were silent, but the young woman laughed, too.

"We even got tea in one place," Maxie went on. "One of the   63
girls came in with two cups and a tin mug. But old George took the mug."

Jennifer Tetzel laughed again, knowingly.   64

"Then, just about lunch time, we came to this place I wanted to   65
tell you about. Nice chap, the manager. Never blinked an eye at me, called me Mister. And after we'd talked, he said to George, 'Why not come home with me for lunch?' So of course George said, 'Thanks, but I'm with my friend here.' 'Oh, that's O.K.,' said the chap. 'Bring him along.' Well, we go along to this house, and the chap disappears into the kitchen, and then he comes back and we sit in the lounge and have a beer, and then the servant comes along and says lunch is ready. Just as we're walking into the dining room, the chap takes me by the arm and says, 'I've had *your* lunch laid on a table on the stoep. You'll find it's all perfectly clean and nice, just what we're having ourselves.' "

"Fantastic," murmured Alister.   66

Maxie smiled and shrugged, looking around at them all. "It's   67
true."

"After he'd asked you, and he'd sat having a drink with you?"   68
Jennifer said closely, biting in her lower lip, as if this were a problem to be solved psychologically.

"Of course," said Maxie.   69

Jake was shaking with laughter, like some obscene Silenus.   70
There was no sound out of him, but saliva gleamed on his lips, and his belly, at the level of Jennifer Tetzel's eyes, was convulsed.

Temba said soberly, in the tone of one whose good will makes it   71
difficult for him to believe in the unease of his situation, "I certainly find it worse here than at the Cape. I can't remember, y'know, about buses. I keep getting put off European buses."

Maxie pointed to Jake's heaving belly. "Oh, I'll tell you a better   72
one than that," he said. "Something that happened in the office one day. Now, the trouble with me is, apparently, I don't talk like a native." This time everyone laughed, except Maxie himself, who, with the instinct of a good raconteur, kept a polite, modest, straight face.

"You know that's true," interrupted the young white woman.   73
"You have none of the usual softening of the vowels of most Africans. And you haven't got an Afrikaans[3] accent, as some Africans have, even if they get rid of the African thing."

3. One of the languages of South Africa, developed from the Dutch of seventeenth-century settlers.

"Anyway, I'd had to phone a certain firm several times," Maxie   74
went on, "and I'd got to know the voice of the girl at the other end,
and she'd got to know mine. As a matter of fact, she must have
liked the sound of me, because she was getting very friendly. We
fooled about a bit, exchanged first names, like a couple of kids—
hers was Peggy—and she said, eventually, 'Aren't you ever going
to come to the office yourself?' " Maxie paused a moment, and his
tongue flicked at the side of his mouth in a brief, nervous gesture.
When he spoke again, his voice was flat, like the voice of a man
who is telling a joke and suddenly thinks that perhaps it is not such
a good one after all. "So I told her I'd be in next day, about four.
I walked in, sure enough, just as I said I would. She was a pretty
girl, blonde, you know, with very tidy hair—I guessed she'd just
combed it to be ready for me. She looked up and said 'Yes?' holding out her hand for the messenger's book or parcel she thought I'd
brought. I took her hand and shook it and said, 'Well, here I am, on
time—I'm Maxie—Maxie Ndube.' "
"What'd she do?" asked Temba eagerly.   75
The interruption seemed to restore Maxie's confidence in his   76
story. He shrugged gaily. "She almost dropped my hand, and then
she pumped it like a mad thing, and her neck and ears went so red I
thought she'd burn up. Honestly, her ears were absolutely shining.
She tried to pretend she'd known all along, but I could see she was
terrified someone would come from the inner office and see her
shaking hands with a native. So I took pity on her and went away.
Didn't even stay for my appointment with her boss. When I went
back to keep the postponed appointment the next week, we pretended we'd never met."
Temba was slapping his knee. "God, I'd have loved to see her   77
face!" he said.
Jake wiped away a tear from his fat cheek—his eyes were light   78
blue, and produced tears easily when he laughed—and said,
"That'll teach you not to talk swanky, man. Why can't you talk like
the rest of us?"
"Oh, I'll watch out on the 'Missus' and 'Baas' stuff in future," 79
said Maxie.
Jennifer Tetzel cut into their laughter with her cool, practical 80
voice. "Poor little girl, she probably liked you awfully, Maxie, and
was really disappointed. You mustn't be too harsh on her. It's hard
to be punished for not being black."
The moment was one of astonishment rather than irritation.   81
Even Jake, who had been sure that there could be no possible
situation between white and black he could not find amusing, only
looked quickly from the young woman to Maxie, in a hiatus between anger, which he had given up long ago, and laughter, which

suddenly failed him. On this face was admiration more than anything else—sheer, grudging admiration. This one was the best one
yet. This one was the coolest ever.

"Is it?" said Maxie to Jennifer, pulling in the corners of his   82
mouth and regarding her from under slightly raised eyebrows. Jake
watched. Oh, she'd have a hard time with Maxie. Maxie wouldn't
give up his suffering-tempered blackness so easily. You hadn't
much hope of knowing what Maxie was feeling at any given moment, because Maxie not only never let you know but made you
guess wrong. But this one was the best yet.

She looked back at Maxie, opening her eyes very wide, twisting   83
her sandalled foot on the swivel of its ankle, smiling, "Really, I
assure you it is."

Maxie bowed to her politely, giving way with a falling gesture of 84
his hand.

Alister had slid from his perch on the crowded table, and now,   85
prodding Jake playfully in the paunch, he said, "We have to get
along."

Jake scratched his ear and said again, "Sure you won't have   86
something to eat?"

Alister shook his head. "We had hoped you'd offer us a drink,   87
but—"

Jake wheezed with laughter, but this time was sincerely con-   88
cerned. "Well, to tell you the truth, when we heard the knocking,
we just swallowed the last of the bottle off, in case it was someone
it shouldn't be. I haven't a drop in the place till tomorrow. Sorry,
chappie. Must apologize to you, lady, but we black men've got to
drink in secret. If we'd've known it was you two . . ."

Maxie and Temba had risen. The two wizened coloured men,   89
Klaas and Albert, and the sombre black Billy Boy shuffled helplessly, hanging about.

Alister said, "Next time, Jake, next time. We'll give you fair   90
warning and you can lay it on."

Jennifer shook hands with Temba and Maxie, called "Goodbye!   91
Goodbye!" to the others, as if they were somehow out of earshot in
that small room. From the door, she suddenly said to Maxie, "I feel
I must tell you. About that other story—your first one, about the
lunch. I don't believe it. I'm sorry, but I honestly don't. It's too
illogical to hold water."

It was the final self-immolation by honest understanding. There   92
was absolutely no limit to which that understanding would not go.
Even if she could not believe Maxie, she must keep her determined
good faith with him by confessing her disbelief. She would go to
the length of calling him a liar to show by frankness how much she

respected him—to insinuate, perhaps, that she was *with him*, even in the need to invent something about a white man that she, because she herself was white, could not believe. It was her last bid for Maxie.

The small, perfectly-made man crossed his arms and smiled, watching her go. Maxie had no price. 93

Jake saw his guests out of the shop, and switched off the light after he had closed the door behind them. As he walked back through the dark, where his presses smelled metallic and cool, he heard, for a few moments, the clear voice of the white woman and the low, noncommittal English murmur of Alister, his friend, as they went out through the archway into the street. 94

He blinked a little as he came back to the light and the faces that confronted him in the back room. Klaas had taken the dirty glasses from behind the curtain and was holding them one by one under the tap in the sink. Billy Boy and Albert had come closer out of the shadows and were leaning their elbows on a roll of paper. Temba was sitting on the table, swinging his foot. Maxie had not moved, and stood just as he had, with his arms folded. No one spoke. 95

Jake began to whistle softly through the spaces between his front teeth, and he picked up the pan of bacon, looked at the twisted curls of meat, jellied now in cold white fat, and put it down again absently. He stood a moment, heavily, regarding them all, but no one responded. His eye encountered the chair that he had cleared for Jennifer Tetzel to sit on. Suddenly he kicked it, hard, so that it went flying on to its side. Then, rubbing his big hands together and bursting into loud whistling to accompany an impromptu series of dance steps, he said "Now, boys!" and as they stirred, he planked the pan down on the ring and turned the gas up till it roared beneath it. 96

HAVING AND
HAVING NOT

Having and Having Not: Preview

Overview and Ideas for Writing

"There was a rich man, who was clothed in purple and fine linen
and who feasted sumptuously every day. And at his gate lay a poor
man named Lazarus, full of sores, who desired to be fed with what
fell from the rich man's table; moreover the dogs came and licked
his sores. The poor man died and was carried by the angels to
Abraham's bosom. The rich man also died and was buried; and in
Hades, being in torment, he lifted up his eyes and saw Abraham far
off and Lazarus in his bosom." The parable of the rich man and the
beggar from Luke's gospel is so ingrained in our society that it
troubles the conscience of Christians and non-Christians alike. In
the end the rich man, who has five prosperous and selfish brothers,
begs Abraham to raise Lazarus from the dead and send him back to
earth "so that he may warn them, lest they also come into this
place of torment." But Abraham refuses: "If they do not hear
Moses and the prophets, neither will they be convinced if some one
should rise from the dead." The story reminds most of us of beggars
we have passed in the streets and letters from charities we have
thrown away in irritation. Very few of us can look Lazarus squarely
in the eye.

The essays and the story in this unit present the relation between
the rich and the poor from a variety of perspectives. We have
representatives of the political right (Garrett Hardin, Charles Murray, and Myron Magnet) and the left (Clarence Darrow, E. M.
Forster, John Kenneth Galbraith). We also have one of the world's
great satirists (Jonathan Swift) and one of today's most brilliant
presenters of the point of view of the poor (Toni Cade Bambara).

Because this unit is rich in argumentative writing, it invites you to make arguments of your own. You could use one of the essays in the unit as the springboard for a type of essay frequently written by scholars and professionals: a fair summary of an argument you disagree with, followed by careful demonstration that some of the reasoning is questionable or some of the evidence is shaky. Argumentative essays rarely succeed without research, but bear in mind that research can take many forms. Darrow depends on his knowledge of history and of some statistics compiled by criminologists; Hardin relies heavily on "a little-known pamphlet" published in 1833; Magnet quotes a series of contemporary experts; Murray, a man known for his heavy reliance on statistics, abandons them here in favor of a "thought experiment" based partly on his experience as a Peace Corps worker. You may find your own research leading you to the local unemployment office or shelter for the homeless.

Strong as the unit's argumentative essays are, however, other options are open to you. Political questions lend themselves to irony and satire, as Swift and Galbraith show, and you may want to try your hand at the ironic essay. Or, like Forster and Bambara, you may want to write a narrative that shows us what it means to be a Have or a Have Not.

JONATHAN SWIFT

A Modest Proposal

FOR PREVENTING THE CHILDREN OF IRELAND
FROM
BEING A BURDEN TO THEIR PARENTS
OR
COUNTRY;
AND
FOR MAKING THEM BENEFICIAL TO THE
PUBLICK

Jonathan Swift (1667–1745) completed a bachelor's degree and
began a master's at Trinity College in his native city of Dublin. In
1688, when Irishmen rebelled in support of James II, the deposed
King of England, Swift sailed to England to avoid the troubles
and found a place as secretary to a cultured Englishman. After
becoming an Anglican priest and writing some largely forgotten
poetry, Swift began to publish satirical prose that won him powerful friends and enemies. In 1713 his friends secured him the
post of Dean of St. Patrick's Cathedral, Dublin. The next year,
Swift's Tory party fell from power and the Whigs—whom we
might associate with today's advocates of free-market capitalism—came to power. Swift withdrew to Ireland and devoted
much of his writing to discussions of Irish social and economic
affairs, including scathing attacks on the effects of Whig policies.
It was also in Ireland that he composed his great satirical novel,
Gulliver's Travels (1726). "A Modest Proposal" was published as
a pamphlet in 1729.

It is a melancholly Object to those, who walk through this great 1
Town or travel in the Country; when they see the Streets, the
Roads, and Cabbin-doors crowded with Beggars of the Female Sex,
followed by three, four, or six Children, all in Rags, and importun-
ing every Passenger for an Alms. These Mothers, instead of being
able to work for their honest Livelyhood, are forced to employ all
their Time in stroling to beg Sustenance for their helpless Infants;
who, as they grow up, either turn Thieves for want of Work; or
leave their dear Native Country, to fight for the Pretender in Spain,
or sell themselves to the Barbadoes.

I think it is agreed by all Parties, that this prodigious number of 2
Children in the Arms, or on the Backs, or at the Heels of their
Mothers, and frequently of their Fathers, is in the present deplor-

able state of the Kingdom, a very great additional Grievance; and therefore, whoever could find out a fair, cheap, and easy Method of making these Children sound and useful Members of the Commonwealth, would deserve so well of the Publick, as to have his Statue set up for a Preserver of the Nation.

But my Intention is very far from being confined to provide only   3
for the Children of professed Beggars: It is of a much greater Extent, and shall take in the whole Number of Infants at a certain Age, who are born of Parents in effect as little able to support them, as those who demand our Charity in the Streets.

As to my own Part, having turned my Thoughts, for many Years,   4
upon this important Subject, and maturely weighed the several Schemes of other Projectors, I have always found them grossly mistaken in their Computation. It is true, a Child, just dropt from its Dam, may be supported by her Milk, for a Solar Year with little other Nourishment; at most not above the Value of two Shillings; which the Mother may certainly get, or the Value in Scraps, by her lawful Occupation of Begging: and it is exactly at one Year old that I propose to provide for them in such a manner, as, instead of being a Charge upon their Parents or the Parish, or wanting Food and Raiment for the rest of their Lives; they shall, on the contrary, contribute to the Feeding and partly to the Cloathing, of many Thousands.

There is likewise another great Advantage in my Scheme, that it   5
will prevent those voluntary Abortions, and that horrid practice of Women murdering their Bastard Children, alas! too frequent among us; Sacrificing the poor innocent Babes, I doubt, more to avoid the Expence than the Shame; which would move Tears and Pity in the most Savage and inhuman breast.

The number of Souls in Ireland being usually reckoned one Million and a half; of these I calculate there may be about Two hundred Thousand Couple whose Wives are Breeders; from which number I subtract thirty Thousand Couples, who are able to maintain their own Children, although I apprehend there cannot be so many under the present Distresses of the Kingdom; but this being granted, there will remain an Hundred and Seventy Thousand Breeders. I again Subtract Fifty Thousand, for those Women who miscarry, or whose Children die by Accident, or Disease, within the Year. There only remain an Hundred and Twenty Thousand Children of poor Parents, annually born: The Question therefore is, How this Number shall be reared, and provided for? Which, as I have already said, under the present Situation of Affairs, is utterly impossible, by all the Methods hitherto proposed: For we can neither employ them in Handicraft or Agriculture; we neither build

Houses, (I mean in the Country) nor cultivate Land: They can very seldom pick up a Livelyhood by Stealing until they arrive at six Years old; except where they are of towardly Parts; although, I confess, they learn the Rudiments much earlier; during which Time, they can, however be properly looked upon only as Probationers; as I have been informed by a principal Gentleman in the County of Cavan, who protested to me, that he never knew above one or two Instances under the Age of six, even in a part of the Kingdom so renowned for the quickest Proficiency in that Art.

I am assured by our Merchants, that a Boy or a Girl before twelve   7
Years old, is no saleable Commodity; and even when they come to this Age, they will not yield above Three Pounds, or Three Pounds and half a Crown at most, on the Exchange; which cannot turn to Account either to the Parents or the Kingdom; the Charge of Nutriment and Rags, having been at least four Times that Value.

I shall now therefore humbly propose my own Thoughts; which   8
I hope will not be liable to the least Objection.

I have been assured by a very knowing American of my Ac-   9
quaintance in London, that a young healthy Child, well nursed is, at a Year old, a most delicious, nourishing and wholesome Food, whether Stewed, Roasted, Baked, or Boiled; and I make no doubt that it will equally serve in a Fricasie, or Ragoust.

I do therefore humbly offer it to publick Consideration, that of   10
the Hundred and Twenty Thousand Children, already computed, Twenty thousand may be reserved for Breed; whereof only one Fourth Part to be Males; which is more than we allow to Sheep, black Cattle, or Swine; and my Reason is, that these Children are seldom the Fruits of Marriage, a Circumstance not much regarded by our Savages; therefore, one Male will be sufficient to serve four Females. That the remaining Hundred thousand, may, at a Year old be offered in Sale to the Persons of Quality and Fortune, through the Kingdom; always advising the Mother to let them suck plentifully in the last Month, so as to render them plump, and fat for a good Table. A Child will make two Dishes at an Entertainment for Friends; and when the Family dines alone, the fore or hind Quarter will make a reasonable Dish; and seasoned with a little Pepper or Salt, will be very good Boiled on the fourth Day, especially in Winter.

I have reckoned upon a Medium, that a Child just born will   11
weigh Twelve Pounds; and in a Solar Year, if tolerably nursed, increaseth to 28 Pounds.

I grant this Food will be somewhat dear, and therefore very   12
proper for Landlords; who, as they have already devoured most of the Parents, seem to have the best Title to the Children.

Infant's Flesh will be in Season throughout the Year; but more   13
plentiful in March, and a little before and after; for we are told by a
grave Author an eminent French Physician, that Fish being a
prolifick Dyet, there are more Children born in Roman Catholick
Countries about Nine Months after Lent, than at any other Season:
Therefore reckoning a Year after Lent, the Markets will be more
glutted than usual; because the Number of Popish Infants, is, at
least, three to one in this Kingdom; and therefore it will have one
other Collateral advantage; by lessening the Number of Papists
among us.

I have already computed the Charge of nursing a Beggar's Child   14
(in which List I reckon all Cottagers, Labourers, and Four fifths of
the Farmers) to be about two Shillings per Annum, Rags included;
and I believe no Gentleman would repine to give Ten Shillings for
the Carcase of a good fat Child; which, as I have said, will make
four Dishes of excellent nutritive meat, when he hath only some
particular Friend, or his own Family, to dine with him. Thus the
Squire will learn to be a good Landlord, and grow popular among
his Tenants; the Mother will have Eight Shillings net Profit, and be
fit for Work till she produceth another Child.

Those who are more thrifty (as I must confess the Times require)   15
may flay the Carcase; the Skin of which artificially dressed, will
make admirable Gloves for Ladies, and Summer Boots for fine
Gentlemen.

As to our City of Dublin; Shambles[1] may be appointed for this   16
Purpose, in the most convenient Parts of it, and Butchers we may
be assured will not be wanting; although I rather recommend buying the Children alive, and dressing them hot from the Knife, as we
do roasting Pigs.

A very worthy Person, a true Lover of his Country, and whose   17
Virtues I highly esteem, was lately pleased, in discoursing on this
Matter, to offer a Refinement upon my Scheme. He said, that many
Gentlemen of this Kingdom, having of late destroyed their Deer; he
conceived that the Want of Venison might be well supplied by the
Bodies of young Lads and Maidens, not exceeding fourteen Years
of Age, nor under twelve; so great a Number of both Sexes in every
County being ready to Starve, for want of Work and Service: And
these to be disposed of by their Parents, if alive, or otherwise by
their nearest Relations. But with due Deference to so excellent a
Friend, and so deserving a Patriot, I cannot be altogether in his
Sentiments. For as to the Males, my American Acquaintance assured me from frequent Experience, that their Flesh was generally

---

1. Slaughterhouses.

tough and lean, like that of our School-boys, by continual Exercise, and their Taste disagreeable; and to fatten them would not answer the Charge. Then, as to the Females, it would, I think, with humble Submission, be a Loss to the Publick, because they soon would become Breeders themselves: And besides it is not improbable, that some scrupulous[2] People might be apt to censure such a Practice, (although indeed very unjustly) as a little bordering upon Cruelty; which, I confess, hath always been with me the strongest Objection against any Project, how well soever intended.

But in order to justify my Friend; he confessed, that this Expedient was put into his Head by the famous Salmanaazor, a Native of the Island Formosa, who came from thence to London, above twenty Years ago, and in Conversation told my Friend, that in his Country, when any young Person happened to be put to Death, the executioner sold the Carcase to Persons of Quality, as a prime Dainty, and that, in his Time, the Body of a plump Girl of fifteen, who was crucified for an Attempt to poison the Emperor, was sold to his Imperial Majesty's prime Minister of State, and other great Mandarins of the Court, in Joints from the Gibbet, at Four hundred Crowns. Neither indeed can I deny, that if the same Use were made of several plump young girls in this Town, who, without one single Groat to their Fortunes, cannot stir Abroad without a Chair, and appear at the Play-house, and Assemblies in foreign fineries, which they never will pay for; the Kingdom would not be the worse.

Some Persons of a desponding Spirit are in great Concern about the vast Number of poor People, who are Aged, Diseased, or Maimed; and I have been desired to imploy my Thoughts what Course may be taken, to ease the Nation of so grievous an Incumbrance. But I am not in the least Pain upon that Matter; because it is very well known, that they are every Day dying, and rotting, by Cold and Famine, and Filth, and Vermin, as fast as can be reasonably expected. And as to the younger Labourers, they are now in almost as hopeful a Condition: They cannot get Work, and consequently pine away for Want of Nourishment, to a Degree, that if at any Time they are accidentally hired to common Labour, they have not Strength to perform it; and thus the Country, and themselves, are in a fair Way of being delivered from the Evils to come.

I have too long digressed; and therefore shall return to my Subject. I think the Advantages by the Proposal which I have made are obvious, and many, as well as of the highest Importance.

For First, as I have already observed, it would greatly lessen the

2. "Over-nice or meticulous in matters of right and wrong" (*Oxford English Dictionary*).

Number of Papists, with whom we are Yearly overrun; being the principal Breeders of the Nation, as well as our most dangerous Enemies; and who stay at home on Purpose, with a Design to deliver the Kingdom to the Pretender;[3] hoping to take their Advantage by the Absence of so many good Protestants, who have chosen rather to leave their Country, than stay at home, and pay Tithes against their Conscience, to an idolatrous Episcopal Curate.[4]

Secondly, The poorer Tenants will have something valuable of their own, which, by Law, may be made liable to Distress,[5] and help to pay their Landlord's Rent; their Corn and Cattle being already seized, and Money a Thing unknown. 22

Thirdly, Whereas the Maintenance of an Hundred Thousand Children, from two Years old, and upwards, cannot be computed at less than ten Shillings a Piece per Annum, the Nation's Stock will be thereby encreased Fifty Thousand Pounds per Annum; besides the Profit of a new Dish, introduced to the Tables of all Gentlemen of Fortune in the Kingdom, who have any Refinement in Taste; and the Money will circulate among ourselves, the Goods being entirely of our own Growth and Manufacture. 23

Fourthly, The constant Breeders, besides the Gain of Eight Shillings Sterling per Annum, by the Sale of their Children, will be rid of the Charge of maintaining them after the first Year. 24

Fifthly, This Food would likewise bring great Custom[6] to Taverns, where the Vintners will certainly be so prudent, as to procure the best Receipts[7] for dressing it to Perfection; and consequently, have their Houses frequented by all the fine Gentlemen, who justly value themselves upon their Knowledge in good Eating; and a skilful Cook, who understands how to oblige his Guests, will contrive to make it as expensive as they please. 25

Sixthly, This would be a great Inducement to Marriage, which all wise Nations have either encouraged by Rewards, or enforced by Laws and Penalties. It would encrease the Care and Tenderness of Mothers towards their Children, when they were sure of a Settlement for Life, to the poor Babes, provided in some Sort by the Publick, to their annual Profit instead of Expence. We should soon see an honest Emulation among the married Women, which of them could bring the fattest Child to the Market. Men would be- 26

3. James Francis Edward Stuart claimed ("pretended to") the British throne by right of succession from his father, James II. He attempted to win it by force of arms in 1715.
4. To a minister of the Church of England.
5. Impoundment for debt.
6. Business.
7. Recipes.

come as fond of their Wives, during the Time of their Pregnancy, as they are now of their Mares in Foal, their Cows in Calf, or Sows when they are ready to farrow; nor offer to beat or kick them, (as is too frequent a Practice) for fear of a Miscarriage.

Many other Advantages might be enumerated. For instance, the 27 Addition of some Thousand Carcases in our Exportation of barrel'd Beef: The Propagation of Swine's Flesh, and Improvement in the Art of making good Bacon; so much wanted among us by the great Destruction of Pigs, too frequent at our Tables, and are no way comparable in Taste, or Magnificence, to a well-grown, fat yearling Child; which, roasted whole, will make a considerable Figure at a Lord Mayor's Feast, or any other publick Entertainment. But this, and many others, I omit; being studious of Brevity.

Supposing that one Thousand Families in this City, would be 28 constant Customers for Infants Flesh, besides others who might have it at merry Meetings, particularly Weddings and Christenings; I compute that Dublin would take off, annually, about Twenty Thousand Carcasses; and the rest of the Kingdom (where probably they will be sold somewhat cheaper) the remaining Eighty Thousand.

I can think of no one Objection, that will possibly be raised 29 against this Proposal; unless it should be urged, that the Number of People will be thereby much lessened in the Kingdom. This I freely own; and it was indeed one principal Design in offering it to the World. I desire the Reader will observe, that I calculate my Remedy for this one individual Kingdom of Ireland, and for no other that ever was, is, or, I think, ever can be upon Earth. Therefore, let no man talk to me of other Expedients: Of taxing our Absentees[8] at five Shillings a Pound: Of using neither Cloaths, nor Household Furniture, except what is of our own Growth and Manufacture: Of utterly rejecting the Materials and Instruments that promote foreign Luxury: Of curing the Expensiveness of Pride, Vanity, Idleness, and Gaming in our Women: Of introducing a Vein of Parsimony, Prudence and Temperance: Of learning to love our Country, wherein we differ even from Laplanders, and the Inhabitants of Topinamboo: Of quitting our Animosities, and Factions; nor act any longer like the Jews, who were murdering one another at the very Moment their City was taken: Of being a little cautious not to sell our Country and Consciences for nothing: Of teaching Landlords to have, at least, one Degree of Mercy towards their Tenants. Lastly, of Putting a Spirit of Honesty, Industry, and Skill

8. Absentee landlords; that is, those who owned estates in Ireland but lived in England.

into our Shopkeepers; who, if a Resolution could now be taken to buy only our native Goods, would immediately unite to cheat and exact upon us in the Price, the Measure, and the Goodness; nor could ever yet be brought to make one fair Proposal of just Dealing, though often and earnestly invited to it.

Therefore I repeat, let no Man talk to me of these and the like [30] Expedients; till he hath, at least, a Glimpse of Hope, that there will ever be some hearty and sincere Attempt to put them in Practice.

But, as to my self; having been wearied out for many Years with [31] offering vain, idle, visionary Thoughts; and at length utterly despairing of Success, I fortunately fell upon this Proposal; which, as it is wholly new, so it hath something solid and real, of no Expence and little Trouble, full in our own Power; and whereby we can incur no Danger in disobliging England: For this Kind of Commodity will not bear Exportation; the Flesh being of too tender a Consistence, to admit a long Continuance in Salt; although, perhaps, I could name a Country, which would be glad to eat up our whole Nation without it.

After all, I am not so violently bent upon my own Opinion, as to [32] reject any Offer, proposed by wise Men, which shall be found equally innocent, cheap, easy, and effectual. But before something of that Kind shall be advanced in Contradiction to my Scheme, and offering a better; I desire the Author, or Authors, will be pleased maturely to consider two Points. First, As Things now stand, how they will be able to find Food and Raiment, for a Hundred Thousand useless Mouths and Backs? And Secondly, There being a round Million of Creatures in human Figure, throughout this Kingdom; whose whole Subsistence, put into a common Stock, would leave them in Debt two Million Pounds Sterling; adding those, who are Beggars by Profession, to the Bulk of Farmers, Cottagers and Labourers, with their Wives and Children, who are Beggars in Effect; I desire those Politicians, who dislike my Overture, and may perhaps be so bold to attempt an Answer, that they will first ask the Parents of these Mortals, Whether they would not at this Day think it a great Happiness to have been sold for Food at a Year old, in the Manner I prescribe; and thereby have avoided such a perpetual Scene of Misfortunes, as they have since gone through; by the Oppression of Landlords; the Impossibility of paying Rent, without Money or Trade; the Want of common Sustenance, with neither House nor Cloaths, to cover them from the Inclemencies of the Weather; and the most inevitable Prospect of intailing the like, or greater Miseries upon their Breed for ever.

I profess, in the Sincerity of my Heart, that I have not the least [33] personal Interest, in endeavouring to promote this necessary Work, having no other Motive than the publick Good of my Country, by advancing our Trade, providing for Infants, relieving the Poor, and giving some Pleasure to the Rich. I have no Children, by which I can propose to get a single Penny; the youngest being nine Years Old and my Wife past Child-bearing.

CLARENCE DARROW

Address to the Prisoners
in the Cook County Jail

Clarence Darrow (1857–1938) was perhaps this century's most famous defense lawyer. After nine years of legal practice in Ohio, Darrow moved to Chicago, where he became a successful corporate lawyer, eventually the attorney for the Chicago and Northwestern Railway. In 1894 he quit this lucrative post to defend (without fee) Eugene V. Debs, leader of a strike against the railway. For seventeen years thereafter, Darrow was labor's most able advocate, winning a crucial trial that established unions' right to strike and exposing inhumane management practices in court and before Congress. In 1911, however, he fell from favor with labor when he entered a guilty plea on behalf of labor clients accused of bombing the offices of a Los Angeles newspaper. Thereafter, Darrow turned to criminal law, defending (among many others) John T. Scopes, accused of violating Tennessee law by teaching the theory of evolution in public school. Darrow's published works include *Crime: Its Causes and Treatment* (1922) and *The Story of My Life* (1932). The following speech was delivered to the prisoners in the Cook County, Illinois, jail in 1902.

If I looked at jails and crimes and prisoners in the way the   1
ordinary person does, I should not speak on this subject to you. The reason I talk to you on the question of crime, its cause and cure, is that I really do not in the least believe in crime. There is no such thing as a crime as the word is generally understood. I do not believe there is any sort of distinction between the real moral conditions of the people in and out of jail. One is just as good as the other. The people here can no more help being here than the people outside can avoid being outside. I do not believe that people are in jail because they deserve to be. They are in jail simply because they cannot avoid it on account of circumstances which are

entirely beyond their control and for which they are in no way responsible.

I suppose a great many people on the outside would say I was 2 doing you harm if they should hear what I say to you this afternoon, but you cannot be hurt a great deal anyway, so it will not matter. Good people outside would say that I was really teaching you things that were calculated to injure society, but it's worth while now and then to hear something different from what you ordinarily get from preachers and the like. These will tell you that you should be good and then you will get rich and be happy. Of course we know that people do not get rich by being good, and that is the reason why so many of you people try to get rich some other way, only you do not understand how to do it quite as well as the fellow outside.

There are people who think that everything in this world is an 3 accident. But really there is no such thing as an accident. A great many folks admit that many of the people in jail ought to be there, and many who are outside ought to be in. I think none of them ought to be here. There ought to be no jails; and if it were not for the fact that people on the outside are so grasping and heartless in their dealings with the people on the inside, there would be no such institution as jails.

I do not want you to believe that I think all you people here are 4 angels. I do not think that. You are people of all kinds, all of you doing the best you can—and that is evidently not very well. You are people of all kinds and conditions and under all circumstances. In one sense everybody is equally good and equally bad. We all do the best we can under the circumstances. But as to the exact things for which you are sent here, some of you are guilty and did the particular act because you needed the money. Some of you did it because you are in the habit of doing it, and some of you because you are born to it, and it comes to be as natural as it does, for instance, for me to be good.

Most of you probably have nothing against me, and most of you 5 would treat me the same way as any other person would, probably better than some of the people on the outside would treat me, because you think I believe in you and they know I do not believe in them. While you would not have the least thing against me in the world, you might pick my pockets. I do not think all of you would, but I think some of you would. You would not have anything against me, but that's your profession, a few of you. Some of the rest of you, if my doors were unlocked, might come in if you saw anything you wanted—not out of any malice to me, but because that is your trade. There is no doubt there are quite a number of people in this jail who would pick my pockets. And still I know this—that when I get outside pretty nearly everybody picks my pocket. There may be some of you who would hold up a man on the street, if you did not happen to have something else to do, and needed the money; but when I want to light my house or my office the gas company holds me up. They charge me one dollar for something that is worth twenty-five cents. Still all these people are good people; they are pillars of society and support the churches, and they are respectable.

When I ride on the streetcars I am held up—I pay five cents for a ride that is worth two and a half cents, simply because a body of men have bribed the city council and the legislature, so that all the rest of us have to pay tribute to them. 6

If I do not want to fall into the clutches of the gas trust and choose to burn oil instead of gas, then good Mr. Rockefeller holds me up, and he uses a certain portion of his money to build universities and support churches which are engaged in telling us how to be good. 7

Some of you are here for obtaining property under false pretenses—yet I pick up a great Sunday paper and read the advertisements of a merchant prince—"Shirtwaists for 39 cents, marked down from $3.00." 8

When I read the advertisement in the paper I see they are all lies. When I want to get out and find a place to stand anywhere on the face of the earth, I find that it has all been taken up long ago before I came here, and before you came here, and somebody says, "Get off, swim into the lake, fly into the air; go anywhere, but get off." That is because these people have the police and they have the jails and the judges and the lawyers and the soldiers and all the rest of them to take care of the earth and drive everybody off that comes in their way. 9

A great many people will tell you that all this is true, but that it does not excuse you. These facts do not excuse some fellow who reaches into my pocket and takes out a five-dollar bill. The fact that the gas company bribes the members of the legislature from year to year, and fixes the law, so that all you people are compelled to be "fleeced" whenever you deal with them; the fact that the streetcar companies and the gas companies have control of the streets; and the fact that the landlords own all the earth—this, they say, has nothing to do with you. 10

Let us see whether there is any connection between the crimes of the respectable classes and your presence in the jail. Many of you people are in jail because you have really committed burglary; many of you, because you have stolen something. In the meaning 11

of the law, you have taken some other person's property. Some of
you have entered a store and carried off a pair of shoes because you
did not have the price. Possibly some of you have committed murder. I cannot tell what all of you did. There are a great many people
here who have done some of these things who really do not know
themselves why they did them. I think I know why you did them—
every one of you; you did these things because you were bound to
do them. It looked to you at the time as if you had a chance to do
them or not, as you saw fit; but still, after all, you had no choice.
There may be people here who had some money in their pockets
and who still went out and got some more money in a way society
forbids. Now, you may not yourselves see exactly why it was you
did this thing, but if you look at the question deeply enough and
carefully enough you will see that there were circumstances that
drove you to do exactly the thing which you did. You could not
help it any more than we outside can help taking the positions that
we take. The reformers who tell you to be good and you will be
happy, and the people on the outside who have property to protect—they think that the only way to do it is by building jails and
locking you up in cells on weekdays and praying for you Sundays.

I think that all of this has nothing whatever to do with right   12
conduct. I think it is very easily seen what has to do with right
conduct. Some so-called criminals—and I will use this word because it is handy, it means nothing to me—I speak of the criminals
who get caught as distinguished from the criminals who catch
them—some of these so-called criminals are in jail for their first
offenses, but nine tenths of you are in jail because you did not have
a good lawyer and, of course, you did not have a good lawyer
because you did not have enough money to pay a good lawyer.
There is no very great danger of a rich man going to jail.

Some of you may be here for the first time. If we would open the   13
doors and let you out, and leave the laws as they are today, some of
you would be back tomorrow. This is about as good a place as you
can get anyway. There are many people here who are so in the
habit of coming that they would not know where else to go. There
are people who are born with the tendency to break into jail every
chance they get, and they cannot avoid it. You cannot figure out
your life and see why it was, but still there is a reason for it; and if
we were all wise and knew all the facts, we could figure it out.

In the first place, there are a good many more people who go to   14
jail in the wintertime than in the summer. Why is this? Is it because
people are more wicked in winter? No, it is because the coal trust
begins to get in its grip in the winter. A few gentlemen take possession of the coal, and unless the people will pay seven or eight

dollars a ton for something that is worth three dollars, they will have to freeze. Then there is nothing to do but to break into jail, and so there are many more in jail in the winter than in summer. It costs more for gas in the winter because the nights are longer, and people go to jail to save gas bills. The jails are electric-lighted. You may not know it, but these economic laws are working all the time, whether we know it or do not know it.

There are more people who go to jail in hard times than in good times—few people, comparatively, go to jail except when they are hard up. They go to jail because they have no other place to go. They may not know why, but it is true all the same. People are not more wicked in hard times. That is not the reason. The fact is true all over the world that in hard times more people go to jail than in good times, and in winter more people go to jail than in summer. Of course it is pretty hard times for people who go to jail at any time. The people who go to jail are almost always poor people— people who have no other place to live, first and last. When times are hard, then you find large numbers of people who go to jail who would not otherwise be in jail.

Long ago, Mr. Buckle, who was a great philosopher and historian, collected facts, and he showed that the number of people who are arrested increased just as the price of food increased. When they put up the price of gas ten cents a thousand, I do not know who will go to jail, but I do know that a certain number of people will go. When the meat combine raises the price of beef, I do not know who is going to jail, but I know that a large number of people are bound to go. Whenever the Standard Oil Company raises the price of oil, I know that a certain number of girls who are seamstresses, and who work night after night long hours for somebody else, will be compelled to go out on the streets and ply another trade, and I know that Mr. Rockefeller and his associates are responsible and not the poor girls in the jails.

First and last, people are sent to jail because they are poor. Sometimes, as I say, you may not need money at the particular time, but you wish to have thrifty forehanded habits, and do not always wait until you are in absolute want. Some of you people are perhaps plying the trade, the profession, which is called burglary. No man in his right senses will go into a strange house in the dead of night and prowl around with a dark lantern through unfamiliar rooms and take chances of his life, if he has plenty of the good things of the world in his own home. You would not take any such chances as that. If a man had clothes in his clothes-press and beefsteak in his pantry and money in the bank, he would not navigate around nights in houses where he knows nothing about the prem-

15

16

17

ises whatever. It always requires experience and education for this profession, and people who fit themselves for it are no more to blame than I am for being a lawyer. A man would not hold up another man on the street if he had plenty of money in his own pocket. He might do it if he had one dollar or two dollars, but he wouldn't if he had as much money as Mr. Rockefeller has. Mr. Rockefeller has a great deal better hold-up game than that.

The more that is taken from the poor by the rich, who have the chance to take it, the more poor people there are who are compelled to resort to these means for a livelihood. They may not understand it, they may not think so at once, but after all they are driven into that line of employment. 18

There is a bill before the legislature of this state to punish kidnaping children with death. We have wise members of the legislature. They know the gas trust when they see it and they always see it— they can furnish light enough to be seen; and this legislature thinks it is going to stop kidnaping children by making a law punishing kidnapers of children with death. I don't believe in kidnaping children, but the legislature is all wrong. Kidnaping children is not a crime, it is a profession. It has been developed with the times. It has been developed with our modern industrial conditions. There are many ways of making money—many new ways that our ancestors knew nothing about. Our ancestors knew nothing about a billion-dollar trust; and here comes some poor fellow who has no other trade and he discovers the profession of kidnaping children. 19

This crime is born, not because people are bad; people don't kidnap other people's children because they want the children or because they are devilish, but because they see a chance to get some money out of it. You cannot cure this crime by passing a law punishing by death kidnapers of children. There is one way to cure it. There is one way to cure all these offenses, and that is to give the people a chance to live. There is no other way, and there never was any other way since the world began; and the world is so blind and stupid that it will not see. If every man and woman and child in the world had a chance to make a decent, fair, honest living, there would be no jails and no lawyers and no courts. There might be some persons here or there with some peculiar formation of their brain, like Rockefeller, who would do these things simply to be doing them; but they would be very, very few, and those should be sent to a hospital and treated, and not sent to jail; and they would entirely disappear in the second generation, or at least in the third generation. 20

I am not talking pure theory. I will just give you two or three illustrations. 21

The English people once punished criminals by sending them away. They would load them on a ship and export them to Australia. England was owned by lords and nobles and rich people. They owned the whole earth over there, and the other people had to stay in the streets. They could not get a decent living. They used to take their criminals and send them to Australia—I mean the class of criminals who got caught. When these criminals got over there, and nobody else had come, they had the whole continent to run over, and so they could raise sheep and furnish their own meat, which is easier than stealing it. These criminals then became decent, respectable people because they had a chance to live. They did not commit any crimes. They were just like the English people who sent them there, only better. And in the second generation the descendants of those criminals were as good and respectable a class of people as there were on the face of the earth, and then they began building churches and jails themselves.

A portion of this country was settled in the same way, landing prisoners down on the southern coast; but when they got here and had a whole continent to run over and plenty of chances to make a living, they became respectable citizens, making their own living just like any other citizen in the world. But finally the descendants of the English aristocracy who sent the people over to Australia found out they were getting rich, and so they went over to get possession of the earth as they always do, and they organized land syndicates and got control of the land and ores, and then they had just as many criminals in Australia as they did in England. It was not because the world had grown bad; it was because the earth had been taken away from the people.

Some of you people have lived in the country. It's prettier than it is here. And if you have ever lived on a farm you understand that if you put a lot of cattle in a field, when the pasture is short they will jump over the fence; but put them in a good field where there is plenty of pasture, and they will be law-abiding cattle to the end of time. The human animal is just like the rest of the animals, only a little more so. The same thing that governs in the one governs in the other.

Everybody makes his living along the lines of least resistance. A wise man who comes into a country early sees a great undeveloped land. For instance, our rich men twenty-five years ago saw that Chicago was small and knew a lot of people would come here and settle, and they readily saw that if they had all the land around here it would be worth a good deal, so they grabbed the land. You cannot be a landlord because somebody has got it all. You must find some other calling. In England and Ireland and Scotland less than five per cent own all the land there is, and the people are bound to stay there on any kind of terms the landlords give. They must live the best they can, so they develop all these various professions—burglary, picking pockets, and the like.

Again, people find all sorts of ways of getting rich. These are 26 diseases like everything else. You look at people getting rich, organizing trusts and making a million dollars, and somebody gets the disease and he starts out. He catches it just as a man catches the mumps or the measles; he is not to blame, it is in the air. You will find men speculating beyond their means, because the mania of money-getting is taking possession of them. It is simply a disease— nothing more, nothing less. You cannot avoid catching it; but the fellows who have control of the earth have the advantage of you. See what the law is: when these men get control of things, they make the laws. They do not make the laws to protect anybody; courts are not instruments of justice. When your case gets into court it will make little difference whether you are guilty or innocent, but it's better if you have a smart lawyer. And you cannot have a smart lawyer unless you have money. First and last it's a question of money. Those men who own the earth make the laws to protect what they have. They fix up a sort of fence or pen around what they have, and they fix the law so the fellow on the outside cannot get in. The laws are really organized for the protection of the men who rule the world. They were never organized or enforced to do justice. We have no system for doing justice, not the slightest in the world.

Let me illustrate: Take the poorest person in this room. If the 27 community had provided a system of doing justice, the poorest person in this room would have as good a lawyer as the richest, would he not? When you went into court you would have just as long a trial and just as fair a trial as the richest person in Chicago. Your case would not be tried in fifteen or twenty minutes, whereas it would take fifteen days to get through with a rich man's case.

Then if you were rich and were beaten, your case would be 28 taken to the Appellate Court. A poor man cannot take his case to the Appellate Court; he has not the price. And then to the Supreme Court. And if he were beaten there he might perhaps go to the United States Supreme Court. And he might die of old age before he got into jail. If you are poor, it's a quick job. You are almost known to be guilty, else you would not be there. Why should anyone be in the criminal court if he were not guilty? He would not be there if he could be anywhere else. The officials have no time to look after all these cases. The people who are on the outside, who are running banks and building churches and making jails, they have no time to examine 600 or 700 prisoners each year to see whether they are guilty or innocent. If the courts were organized to promote justice the people would elect somebody to defend all these criminals, somebody as smart as the prosecutor—and give him as many detectives and as many assistants to help, and pay as much money to defend you as to prosecute you. We have a very able man for state's attorney, and he has many assistants, detectives, and policemen without end, and judges to hear the cases—everything handy.

Most all of our criminal code consists in offenses against prop-   29
erty. People are sent to jail because they have committed a crime against property. It is of very little consequence whether one hundred people more or less go to jail who ought not to go—you must protect property, because in this world property is of more importance than anything else.

How is it done? These people who have property fix it so they   30
can protect what they have. When somebody commits a crime it does not follow that he has done something that is morally wrong. The man on the outside who has committed no crime may have done something. For instance: to take all the coal in the United States and raise the price two dollars or three dollars when there is no need of it, and thus kill thousands of babies and send thousands of people to the poorhouse and tens of thousands to jail, as is done every year in the United States—this is a greater crime than all the people in our jails ever committed; but the law does not punish it. Why? Because the fellows who control the earth make the laws. If you and I had the making of the laws, the first thing we would do would be to punish the fellow who gets control of the earth. Nature put this coal in the ground for me as well as for them and nature made the prairies up here to raise wheat for me as well as for them, and then the great railroad companies came along and fenced it up.

Most all of the crimes for which we are punished are property   31
crimes. There are a few personal crimes, like murder—but they are very few. The crimes committed are mostly those against property. If this punishment is right the criminals must have a lot of property. How much money is there in this crowd? And yet you are all here for crimes against property. The people up and down the Lake Shore have not committed crime; still they have so much property they don't know what to do with it. It is perfectly plain why these people have not committed crimes against property; they make the laws and therefore do not need to break them. And in order for you to get some property you are obliged to break the rules of the game. I don't know but what some of you may have had a very nice chance to get rich by carrying a hod for one dollar a day,

twelve hours. Instead of taking that nice, easy profession, you are a burglar. If you had been given a chance to be a banker you would rather follow that. Some of you may have had a chance to work as a switchman on a railroad where you know, according to statistics, that you cannot live and keep all your limbs more than seven years, and you can get fifty dollars or seventy-five dollars a month for taking your lives in your hands; and instead of taking that lucrative position you chose to be a sneak thief, or something like that. Some of you made that sort of choice. I don't know which I would take if I was reduced to this choice. I have an easier choice.

I will guarantee to take from this jail, or any jail in the world, five   32
hundred men who have been the worst criminals and lawbreakers who ever got into jail, and I will go down to our lowest streets and take five hundred of the most abandoned prostitutes, and go out somewhere where there is plenty of land, and will give them a chance to make a living, and they will be as good people as the average in the community.

There is one remedy for the sort of condition we see here. The   33
world never finds it out, or when it does find it out it does not enforce it. You may pass a law punishing every person with death for burglary, and it will make no difference. Men will commit it just the same. In England there was a time when one hundred different offenses were punishable with death, and it made no difference. The English people strangely found out that so fast as they repealed the severe penalties and so fast as they did away with punishing men by death, crime decreased instead of increased; that the smaller the penalty the fewer the crimes.

Hanging men in our county jails does not prevent murder. It   34
makes murderers.

And this has been the history of the world. It's easy to see how to   35
do away with what we call crime. It is not so easy to do it. I will tell you how to do it. It can be done by giving the people a chance to live—by destroying special privileges. So long as big criminals can get the coal fields, so long as the big criminals have control of the city council and get the public streets for streetcars and gas rights—this is bound to send thousands of poor people to jail. So long as men are allowed to monopolize all the earth, and compel others to live on such terms as these men see fit to make, then you are bound to get into jail.

The only way in the world to abolish crime and criminals is to   36
abolish the big ones and the little ones together. Make fair conditions of life. Give men a chance to live. Abolish the right of private ownership of land, abolish monopoly, make the world partners in production, partners in the good things of life. Nobody would steal

if he could get something of his own some easier way. Nobody will commit burglary when he has a house full. No girl will go out on the streets when she has a comfortable place at home. The man who owns a sweatshop or a department store may not be to blame himself for the condition of his girls, but when he pays them five dollars, three dollars, and two dollars a week, I wonder where he thinks they will get the rest of their money to live. The only way to cure these conditions is by equality. There should be no jails. They do not accomplish what they pretend to accomplish. If you would wipe them out there would be no more criminals than now. They terrorize nobody. They are a blot upon any civilization, and a jail is an evidence of the lack of charity of the people on the outside who make the jails and fill them with the victims of their greed.

E. M. FORSTER

My Wood

E(dward) M(organ) Forster (1879–1970), the great English novelist and essayist, was allowed to pursue his career as a writer because of wealth inherited from a great aunt. The bequest troubled him because it made him a wealthy man in a world where so many were poor. In *Howards End* (1910), a novel concerned with the problems of wealth and poverty, Forster's protagonist argues that the right thing for a person who has inherited a million pounds to do is to give it to the poor. "Whatever you've got, I order you to give as many poor men as you can three hundred a year each," Margaret Schlegel says, specifying a sum that would in Forster's time have allowed the poor men an adequate income. If Forster was unwilling to make this sacrifice himself, he was equally unwilling to excuse himself for his selfishness. Though he was not an orthodox Christian, he was never able to get out of his mind the New Testament passages that are interspersed through "My Wood." The essay, originally published in 1926, was reprinted in *Abinger Harvest* (1936).

A few years ago I wrote a book which dealt in part with the   1
difficulties of the English in India. Feeling that they would have had no difficulties in India themselves, the Americans read the book freely. The more they read it the better it made them feel, and a cheque to the author was the result. I bought a wood with the cheque. It is not a large wood—it contains scarcely any trees, and it

is intersected, blast it, by a public footpath. Still, it is the first property that I have owned, so it is right that other people should participate in my shame, and should ask themselves, in accents that will vary in horror, this very important question: What is the effect of property upon the character? Don't let's touch economics; the effect of private ownership upon the community as a whole is another question—a more important question, perhaps, but another one. Let's keep to psychology. If you own things, what's their effect on you? What's the effect on me of my wood?

In the first place, it makes me feel heavy. Property does have this   2
effect. Property produces men of weight, and it was a man of weight who failed to get into the Kingdom of Heaven.[1] He was not wicked, that unfortunate millionaire in the parable, he was only stout; he stuck out in front, not to mention behind, and as he wedged himself this way and that in the crystalline entrance and bruised his well-fed flanks, he saw beneath him a comparatively slim camel passing through the eye of a needle and being woven into the robe of God. The Gospels all through couple stoutness and slowness. They point out what is perfectly obvious, yet seldom realized: that if you have a lot of things you cannot move about a lot, that furniture requires dusting, dusters require servants, servants require insurance stamps, and the whole tangle of them makes you think twice before you accept an invitation to dinner or go for a bathe in the Jordan. Sometimes the Gospels proceed further and say with Tolstoy that property is sinful; they approach the difficult ground of asceticism here, where I cannot follow them. But as to the immediate effects of property on people, they just show straightforward logic. It produces men of weight. Men of weight cannot, by definition, move like the lightning from the East unto the West, and the ascent of a fourteen-stone[2] bishop into a pulpit is thus the exact antithesis of the coming of the Son of Man. My wood makes me feel heavy.

In the second place, it makes me feel it ought to be larger.   3

The other day I heard a twig snap in it. I was annoyed at first, for   4
I thought that someone was blackberrying, and depreciating the value of the undergrowth. On coming nearer, I saw it was not a man who had trodden on the twig and snapped it, but a bird, and I felt pleased. My bird. The bird was not equally pleased. Ignoring the relation between us, it took fright as soon as it saw the shape of my face, and flew straight over the boundary hedge into a field, the property of Mrs. Henessy, where it sat down with a loud squawk. It

1. Luke 18: 18–25.
2. 196-pound.

had become Mrs. Henessy's bird. Something seemed grossly amiss here, something that would not have occurred had the wood been larger. I could not afford to buy Mrs. Henessy out, I dared not murder her, and limitations of this sort beset me on every side. Ahab did not want that vineyard[3]—he only needed it to round off his property, preparatory to plotting a new curve—and all the land around my wood has become necessary to me in order to round off the wood. A boundary protects. But—poor little thing—the boundary ought in its turn to be protected. Noises on the edge of it. Children throw stones. A little more, and then a little more, until we reach the sea. Happy Canute![4] Happier Alexander![5] And after all, why should even the world be the limit of possession? A rocket containing a Union Jack, will, it is hoped, be shortly fired at the moon. Mars. Sirius. Beyond which . . . But these immensities ended by saddening me. I could not suppose that my wood was the destined nucleus of universal dominion—it is so very small and contains no mineral wealth beyond the blackberries. Nor was I comforted when Mrs. Henessy's bird took alarm for the second time and flew clean away from us all, under the belief that it belonged to itself.

In the third place, property makes its owner feel that he ought to do something to it. Yet he isn't sure what. A restlessness comes over him, a vague sense that he has a personality to express—the same sense which, without any vagueness, leads the artist to an act of creation. Sometimes I think I will cut down such trees as remain in the wood, at other times I want to fill up the gaps between them with new trees. Both impulses are pretentious and empty. They are not honest movements towards money-making or beauty. They spring from a foolish desire to express myself and from an inability to enjoy what I have got. Creation, property, enjoyment form a sinister trinity in the human mind. Creation and enjoyment are both very very good, yet they are often unattainable without a material basis, and at such moments property pushes itself in as a substitute, saying, "Accept me instead—I'm good enough for all three." It is not enough. It is, as Shakespeare said of lust, "The expense of spirit in a waste of shame": it is "Before, a joy proposed; behind, a dream." Yet we don't know how to shun it. It is forced on us by our economic system as the alternative to starvation. It is also forced on us by an internal defect in the soul, by the feeling that in property may lie the germs of self-development and of

3. 1 Kings 21.
4. Also spelled Cnute (994–1035), king of the English, Danes, and Norwegians.
5. Alexander the Great (356 B.C.–323 B.C.), King of Macedonia and conqueror of some of the richest countries of the Mideast.

exquisite or heroic deeds. Our life on earth is, and ought to be, material and carnal. But we have not yet learned to manage our materialism and carnality properly; they are still entangled with the desire for ownership, where (in the words of Dante) "Possession is one with loss."

And this brings us to our fourth and final point: the blackberries. 6

Blackberries are not plentiful in this meagre grove, but they are 7 easily seen from the public footpath which traverses it, and all too easily gathered. Foxgloves, too—people will pull up the foxgloves, and ladies of an educational tendency even grub for toadstools to show them on the Monday in class. Other ladies, less educated, roll down the bracken in the arms of their gentlemen friends. There is paper, there are tins. Pray, does my wood belong to me or doesn't it? And, if it does, should I not own it best by allowing no one else to walk there? There is a wood near Lyme Regis, also cursed by a public footpath, where the owner has not hesitated on this point. He has built high stone walls each side of the path, and has spanned it by bridges, so that the public circulate like termites while he gorges on the blackberries unseen. He really does own his wood, this able chap. Dives in Hell did pretty well, but the gulf dividing him from Lazarus could be traversed by vision,[6] and nothing traverses it here. And perhaps I shall come to this in time. I shall wall in and fence out until I really taste the sweets of property. Enormously stout, endlessly avaricious, pseudo-creative, intensely selfish, I shall weave upon my forehead the quadruple crown of possession until those nasty Bolshies come and take it off again and thrust me aside into the outer darkness.

GARRETT HARDIN

The Tragedy of the Commons

Garrett Hardin (1915–   ), scientist, lecturer, and writer, is a professor emeritus of biology at the University of California, Santa Barbara, and a contributor of more than 200 scholarly articles to various periodicals. Hardin's clear head and plain language brought his textbook *Biology: Its Principles and Implications* (1949) into wide use. Since that time his writings have taken on a more controversial tone, and he has repeatedly forced his read-

6. Luke 16: 19–31.

ers to face the unhappy ethical implications of our present
ecological crisis in such books as *Exploring New Ethics for Survival*
(1972), *The Limits of Altruism* (1977), and *Filter Against Folly:
How to Survive Despite Economists, Ecologists, and the Merely Eloquent* (1985). Although Hardin never took a course in economics, "The Tragedy of the Commons" (first published in *Science* in
1968) has become a minor classic among economics texts.

At the end of a thoughtful article on the future of nuclear war,   1
Wiesner and York concluded that: "Both sides in the arms race are
. . . confronted by the dilemma of steadily increasing military
power and steadily decreasing national security. *It is our considered
professional judgment that this dilemma has no technical solution.* If the
great powers continue to look for solutions in the area of science
and technology only, the result will be to worsen the situation."

I would like to focus your attention not on the subject of the   2
article (national security in a nuclear world) but on the kind of
conclusion they reached, namely that there is no technical solution
to the problem. An implicit and almost universal assumption of
discussions published in professional and semipopular scientific
journals is that the problem under discussion has a technical solution. A technical solution may be defined as one that requires a
change only in the techniques of the natural sciences, demanding
little or nothing in the way of change in human values or ideas of
morality.

In our day (though not in earlier times) technical solutions are   3
always welcome. Because of previous failures in prophecy, it takes
courage to assert that a desired technical solution is not possible.
Wiesner and York exhibited this courage; publishing in a science
journal, they insisted that the solution to the problem was not to be
found in the natural sciences. They cautiously qualified their statement with the phrase, "It is our considered professional judgment. . . ." Whether they were right or not is not the concern of the
present article. Rather, the concern here is with the important concept of a class of human problems which can be called "no technical solution problems," and, more specifically, with the identification and discussion of one of these.

It is easy to show that the class is not a null class. Recall the game   4
of tick-tack-toe. Consider the problem, "How can I win the game
of tick-tack-toe?" It is well known that I cannot, if I assume (in
keeping with the conventions of game theory) that my opponent
understands the game perfectly. Put another way, there is no
"technical solution" to the problem. I can win only by giving a
radical meaning to the word "win." I can hit my opponent over the

head; or I can drug him; or I can falsify the records. Every way in which I "win" involves, in some sense, an abandonment of the game, as we intuitively understand it. (I can also, of course, openly abandon the game—refuse to play it. This is what most adults do.)

The class of "No technical solution problems" has members. My thesis is that the "population problem," as conventionally conceived, is a member of this class. How it is conventionally conceived needs some comment. It is fair to say that most people who anguish over the population problem are trying to find a way to avoid the evils of overpopulation without relinquishing any of the privileges they now enjoy. They think that farming the seas or developing new strains of wheat will solve the problem—technologically. I try to show here that the solution they seek cannot be found. The population problem cannot be solved in a technical way, any more than can the problem of winning the game of tick-tack-toe.

WHAT SHALL WE MAXIMIZE?

Population, as Malthus[1] said, naturally tends to grow "geometrically," or, as we would now say, exponentially. In a finite world this means that the per capita share of the world's goods must steadily decrease. Is ours a finite world?

A fair defense can be put forward for the view that the world is infinite; or that we do not know that it is not. But, in terms of the practical problems that we must face in the next few generations with the foreseeable technology, it is clear that we will greatly increase human misery if we do not, during the immediate future, assume that the world available to the terrestrial human population is finite. "Space" is no escape.

A finite world can support only a finite population; therefore, population growth must eventually equal zero. (The case of perpetual wide fluctuations above and below zero is a trivial variant that need not be discussed.) When this condition is met, what will be the situation of mankind? Specifically, can Bentham's[2] goal of "the greatest good for the greatest number" be realized?

No—for two reasons, each sufficient by itself. The first is a theoretical one. It is not mathematically possible to maximize for two (or more) variables at the same time. This was clearly stated by von Neumann and Morgenstern, but the principle is implicit in the theory of partial differential equations, dating back at least to D'Alembert (1717–1783).

1. English economist Thomas Malthus (1766–1834).
2. English philosopher Jeremy Bentham (1748–1832).

The second reason springs directly from biological facts. To live, 10
any organism must have a source of energy (for example, food).
This energy is utilized for two purposes: mere maintenance and
work. For man, maintenance of life requires about 1600 kilo-
calories a day ("maintenance calories"). Anything that he does
over and above merely staying alive will be defined as work, and is
supported by "work calories" which he takes in. Work calories are
used not only for what we call work in common speech; they are
also required for all forms of enjoyment, from swimming and automobile racing to playing music and writing poetry. If our goal is to
maximize population it is obvious what we must do: We must
make the work calories per person approach as close to zero as
possible. No gourmet meals, no vacations, no sports, no music, no
literature, no art. . . . I think that everyone will grant, without
argument or proof, that maximizing population does not maximize
goods. Bentham's goal is impossible.

In reaching this conclusion I have made the usual assumption 11
that it is the acquisition of energy that is the problem. The appearance of atomic energy has led some to question this assumption.
However, given an infinite source of energy, population growth
still produces an inescapable problem. The problem of the acquisition of energy is replaced by the problem of its dissipation, as J. H.
Fremlin has so wittily shown. The arithmetic signs in the analysis
are, as it were, reversed; but Bentham's goal is still unobtainable.

The optimum population is, then, less than the maximum. The 12
difficulty of defining the optimum is enormous; so far as I know,
no one has seriously tackled this problem. Reaching an acceptable
and stable solution will surely require more than one generation of
hard analytical work—and much persuasion.

We want the maximum good per person; but what is good? To 13
one person it is wilderness, to another it is ski lodges for thousands.
To one it is estuaries to nourish ducks for hunters to shoot; to
another it is factory land. Comparing one good with another is, we
usually say, impossible because goods are incommensurable. Incommensurables cannot be compared.

Theoretically this may be true; but in real life incommensurables 14
are commensurable. Only a criterion of judgment and a system of
weighting are needed. In nature the criterion is survival. Is it better
for a species to be small and hideable, or large and powerful?
Natural selection commensurates the incommensurables. The compromise achieved depends on a natural weighting of the values of
the variables.

Man must imitate this process. There is no doubt that in fact he 15
already does, but unconsciously. It is when the hidden decisions

are made explicit that the arguments begin. The problem for the years ahead is to work out an acceptable theory of weighting. Synergistic effects, nonlinear variation, and difficulties in discounting the future make the intellectual problem difficult, but not (in principle) insoluble.

Has any cultural group solved this practical problem at the present time, even on an intuitive level? One simple fact proves that none has: there is no prosperous population in the world today that has, and has had for some time, a growth rate of zero. Any people that has intuitively identified its optimum point will soon reach it, after which its growth rate becomes and remains zero.   16

Of course, a positive growth rate might be taken as evidence that a population is below its optimum. However, by any reasonable standards, the most rapidly growing populations on earth today are (in general) the most miserable. This association (which need not be invariable) casts doubt on the optimistic assumption that the positive growth rate of a population is evidence that it has yet to reach its optimum.   17

We can make little progress in working toward optimum population size until we explicitly exorcize the spirit of Adam Smith in the field of practical demography. In economic affairs, *The Wealth of Nations* (1776) popularized the "invisible hand," the idea that an individual who "intends only his own gain," is, as it were, "led by an invisible hand to promote . . . the public interest." Adam Smith did not assert that this was invariably true, and perhaps neither did any of his followers. But he contributed to a dominant tendency of thought that has ever since interfered with positive action based on rational analysis, namely, the tendency to assume that decisions reached individually will, in fact, be the best decisions for an entire society. If this assumption is correct it justifies the continuance of our present policy of laissez-faire in reproduction. If it is correct we can assume that men will control their individual fecundity so as to produce the optimum population. If the assumption is not correct, we need to reexamine our individual freedoms to see which ones are defensible.   18

TRAGEDY OF FREEDOM IN A COMMONS

The rebuttal to the invisible hand in population control is to be found in a scenario first sketched in a little-known pamphlet in 1833 by a mathematical amateur named William Forster Lloyd (1794–1852). We may well call it "the tragedy of the commons," using the word "tragedy" as the philosopher Whitehead used it: "The essence of dramatic tragedy is not unhappiness. It resides in the solemnity of the remorseless working of things." He then goes   19 on to say, "This inevitableness of destiny can only be illustrated in terms of human life by incidents which in fact involve unhappiness. For it is only by them that the futility of escape can be made evident in the drama."

The tragedy of the commons develops in this way. Picture a pasture open to all. It is to be expected that each herdsman will try to keep as many cattle as possible on the commons. Such an arrangement may work reasonably satisfactorily for centuries because tribal wars, poaching, and disease keep the numbers of both man and beast well below the carrying capacity of the land. Finally, however, comes the day of reckoning, that is, the day when the long-desired goal of social stability becomes a reality. At this point, the inherent logic of the commons remorselessly generates tragedy. 20

As a rational being, each herdsman seeks to maximize his gain. Explicitly or implicitly, more or less consciously, he asks, "What is the utility *to me* of adding one more animal to my herd?" This utility has one negative and one positive component. 21

1. The positive component is a function of the increment of one animal. Since the herdsman receives all the proceeds from the sale of the additional animal, the positive utility is nearly $+1$. 22

2. The negative component is a function of the additional overgrazing created by one more animal. Since, however, the effects of overgrazing are shared by all the herdsmen, the negative utility for any particular decision-making herdsman is only a fraction of -1. 23

Adding together the component partial utilities, the rational herdsman concludes that the only sensible course for him to pursue is to add another animal to his herd. And another; and another. . . . But this is the conclusion reached by each and every rational herdsman sharing a commons. Therein is the tragedy. Each man is locked into a system that compels him to increase his herd without limit—in a world that is limited. Ruin is the destination toward which all men rush, each pursuing his own best interest in a society that believes in the freedom of the commons. Freedom in a commons brings ruin to all. 24

Some would say that this is a platitude. Would that it were! In a sense, it was learned thousands of years ago, but natural selection favors the forces of psychological denial. The individual benefits as an individual from his ability to deny the truth even though society as a whole, of which he is a part, suffers. Education can counteract the natural tendency to do the wrong thing, but the inexorable succession of generations requires that the basis for this knowledge be constantly refreshed. 25

A simple incident that occurred a few years ago in Leominster, Massachusetts, shows how perishable the knowledge is. During 26 the Christmas shopping season the parking meters downtown were covered with plastic bags that bore tags reading: "Do not open until after Christmas. Free parking courtesy of the mayor and city council." In other words, facing the prospect of an increased demand for already scarce space, the city fathers reinstituted the system of the commons. (Cynically, we suspect that they gained more votes than they lost by this retrogressive act.)

In an approximate way, the logic of the commons has been 27 understood for a long time, perhaps since the discovery of agriculture or the invention of private property in real estate. But it is understood mostly only in special cases which are not sufficiently generalized. Even at this late date, cattlemen leasing national land on the western ranges demonstrate no more than an ambivalent understanding, in constantly pressuring federal authorities to increase the head count to the point where overgrazing produces erosion and weed-dominance. Likewise, the oceans of the world continue to suffer from the survival of the philosophy of the commons. Maritime nations still respond automatically to the shibboleth of the "freedom of the seas." Professing to believe in the "inexhaustible resources of the ocean," they bring species after species of fish and whales closer to extinction.

The national parks present another instance of the working out 28 of the tragedy of the commons. At present, they are open to all, without limit. The parks themselves are limited in extent—there is only one Yosemite Valley—whereas population seems to grow without limit. The values that visitors seek in the parks are steadily eroded. Plainly, we must soon cease to treat the parks as commons or they will be of no value to anyone.

What shall we do? We have several options. We might sell them 29 off as private property. We might keep them as public property, but allocate the right to enter them. The allocation might be on the basis of wealth, by the use of an auction system. It might be on the basis of merit, as defined by some agreed-upon standards. It might be by lottery. Or it might be on a first-come, first-served basis, administered to long queues. These, I think, are all the reasonable possibilities. They are all objectionable. But we must choose—or acquiesce in the destruction of the commons that we call our national parks.

POLLUTION

In a reverse way, the tragedy of the commons reappears in problems of pollution. Here it is not a question of taking something out of the commons, but of putting something in—sewage, or chemical, radioactive, and heat wastes into water; noxious and dangerous fumes into the air; and distracting and unpleasant advertising signs into the line of sight. The calculations of utility are much the same as before. The rational man finds that his share of the cost of the wastes he discharges into the commons is less than the cost of purifying his wastes before releasing them. Since this is true for everyone, we are locked into a system of "fouling our own nest," so long as we behave only as independent, rational, free-enterprisers.

The tragedy of the commons as a food basket is averted by pri-   31
vate property, or something formally like it. But the air and waters surrounding us cannot readily be fenced, and so the tragedy of the commons as a cesspool must be prevented by different means, by coercive laws or taxing devices that make it cheaper for the polluter to treat his pollutants than to discharge them untreated. We have not progressed as far with the solution of this problem as we have with the first. Indeed, our particular concept of private property, which deters us from exhausting the positive resources of the earth, favors pollution. The owner of a factory on the bank of a stream—whose property extends to the middle of the stream—often has difficulty seeing why it is not his natural right to muddy the waters flowing past his door. The law, always behind the times, requires elaborate stitching and fitting to adapt it to this newly perceived aspect of the commons.

The pollution problem is a consequence of population. It did not   32
much matter how a lonely American frontiersman disposed of his waste. "Flowing water purifies itself every ten miles," my grand-father used to say, and the myth was near enough to the truth when he was a boy, for there were not too many people. But as population became denser, the natural chemical and biological re-cycling processes became overloaded, calling for a redefinition of property rights.

HOW TO LEGISLATE TEMPERANCE?

Analysis of the pollution problem as a function of population   33
density uncovers a not generally recognized principle of morality, namely: *the morality of an act is a function of the state of the system at the time it is performed.* Using the commons as a cesspool does not harm the general public under frontier conditions, because there is no public; the same behavior in a metropolis is unbearable. A hundred and fifty years ago a plainsman could kill an American bison, cut out only the tongue for his dinner, and discard the rest of the animal. He was not in any important sense being wasteful. Today, with only a few thousand bison left, we would be appalled at such behavior.

In passing, it is worth noting that the morality of an act cannot   34
be determined from a photograph. One does not know whether a
man killing an elephant or setting fire to the grassland is harming
others until one knows the total system in which his act appears.
"One picture is worth a thousand words," said an ancient Chinese;
but it may take 10,000 words to validate it. It is as tempting to
ecologists as it is to reformers in general to try to persuade others
by way of the photographic shortcut. But the essence of an argument cannot be photographed: it must be presented rationally—in
words.

That morality is system-sensitive escaped the attention of most   35
codifiers of ethics in the past. "Thou shalt not . . ." is the form of
traditional ethical directives which make no allowance for particular circumstances. The laws of our society follow the pattern of
ancient ethics, and therefore are poorly suited to governing a complex, crowded, changeable world. Our epicyclic solution is to augment statutory law with administrative law. Since it is practically
impossible to spell out all the conditions under which it is safe to
burn trash in the back yard or to run an automobile without smog-
control, by law we delegate the details to bureaus. The result is
administrative law, which is rightly feared for an ancient reason—
Quis custodiet ipsos custodes?—"Who shall watch the watchers themselves?" John Adams said that we must have "a government of
laws and not men." Bureau administrators, trying to evaluate the
morality of acts in the total system, are singularly liable to corrup-
tion, producing a government by men, not laws.

Prohibition is easy to legislate (though not necessarily to en-   36
force); but how do we legislate temperance? Experience indicates
that it can be accomplished best through the mediation of administrative law. We limit possibilities unnecessarily if we suppose that
the sentiment of *Quis custodiet* denies us the use of administrative
law. We should rather retain the phrase as a perpetual reminder of
fearful dangers we cannot avoid. The great challenge facing us now
is to invent the corrective feedbacks that are needed to keep custodians honest. We must find ways to legitimate the needed authority of both the custodians and the corrective feedbacks.

FREEDOM TO BREED IS INTOLERABLE

The tragedy of the commons is involved in population problems   37
in another way. In a world governed solely by the principle of "dog
eat dog"—if indeed there ever was such a world—how many children a family had would not be a matter of public concern. Parents
who bred too exuberantly would leave fewer descendants, not
more, because they would be unable to care adequately for their

children. David Lack and others have found that such a negative feedback demonstrably controls the fecundity of birds. But men are not birds, and have not acted like them for millenniums, at least.

If each human family were dependent only on its own resources; *if* the children of improvident parents starved to death; *if*, thus, overbreeding brought its own "punishment" to the germ line— *then* there would be no public interest in controlling the breeding of families. But our society is deeply committed to the welfare state, and hence is confronted with another aspect of the tragedy of the commons. 38

In a welfare state, how shall we deal with the family, the religion, the race, or the class (or indeed any distinguishable and cohesive group) that adopts overbreeding as a policy to secure its own aggrandizement? To couple the concept of freedom to breed with the belief that everyone born has an equal right to the commons is to lock the world into a tragic course of action. 39

Unfortunately this is just the course of action that is being pursued by the United Nations. In late 1967, some thirty nations agreed to the following: 40

> The Universal Declaration of Human Rights describes the family as the natural and fundamental unit of society. It follows that any choice and decision with regard to the size of the family must irrevocably rest with the family itself, and cannot be made by anyone else.

It is painful to have to deny categorically the validity of this right; denying it, one feels as uncomfortable as a resident of Salem, Massachusetts, who denied the reality of witches in the seventeenth century. At the present time, in liberal quarters, something like a taboo acts to inhibit criticism of the United Nations. There is a feeling that the United Nations is "our last and best hope," that we shouldn't find fault with it; we shouldn't play into the hands of the archconservatives. However, let us not forget what Robert Louis Stevenson said: "The truth that is suppressed by friends is the readiest weapon of the enemy." If we love the truth we must openly deny the validity of the Universal Declaration of Human Rights, even though it is promoted by the United Nations. We should also join with Kingsley Davis in attempting to get Planned Parenthood-World Population to see the error of its ways in embracing the same tragic ideal. 41

CONSCIENCE IS SELF-ELIMINATING

It is a mistake to think that we can control the breeding of mankind in the long run by an appeal to conscience. Charles Galton Darwin made this point when he spoke on the centennial of 42 the publication of his grandfather's great book. The argument is straight-forward and Darwinian.

People vary. Confronted with appeals to limit breeding, some   43 people will undoubtedly respond to the plea more than others. Those who have more children will produce a larger fraction of the next generation than those with more susceptible consciences. The difference will be accentuated, generation by generation.

In C. G. Darwin's words: "It may well be that it would take   44 hundreds of generations for the progenitive instinct to develop in this way, but if it should do so, nature would have taken her revenge, and the variety *Homo contracipiens* would become extinct and would be replaced by the variety *Homo progenitivus*."[3]

The argument assumes that conscience or the desire for children   45 (no matter which) is hereditary—but hereditary only in the most general formal sense. The result will be the same whether the attitude is transmitted through germ cells, or exosomatically, to use A. J. Lotka's term. (If one denies the latter possibility as well as the former, then what's the point of education?) The argument has here been stated in the context of the population problem, but it applies equally well to any instance in which society appeals to an individual exploiting a commons to restrain himself for the general good—by means of his conscience. To make such an appeal is to set up a selective system that works toward the elimination of conscience from the race.

PATHOGENIC EFFECTS OF CONSCIENCE

The long-term disadvantage of an appeal to conscience should   46 be enough to condemn it; but has serious short-term disadvantages as well. If we ask a man who is exploiting a commons to desist "in the name of conscience," what are we saying to him? What does he hear?—not only at the moment but also in the wee small hours of the night when, half asleep, he remembers not merely the words we used but also the nonverbal communication cues we gave him unawares? Sooner or later, consciously or subconsciously, he senses that he has received two communications, and that they are contradictory: (i) (intended communication) "If you don't do as we ask, we will openly condemn you for not acting like a responsible citizen"; (ii) (the unintended communication) "If you *do* behave as we ask, we will secretly condemn you for a simpleton who

---

3. Roughly, man the contraceptionist (preventer of birth) . . . man the founder (of a family).

can be shamed into standing aside while the rest of us exploit the commons."

Every man then is caught in what Bateson has called a "double bind." Bateson and his coworkers have made a plausible case for viewing the double bind as an important causative factor in the genesis of schizophrenia. The double bind may not always be so damaging, but it always endangers the mental health of anyone to whom it is applied. "A bad conscience," said Nietzsche, "is a kind of illness." 47

To conjure up a conscience in others is tempting to anyone who wishes to extend his control beyond the legal limits. Leaders at the highest level succumb to this temptation. Has any president during the past generation failed to call on labor unions to moderate voluntarily their demands for higher wages, or to steel companies to honor voluntary guidelines on prices? I can recall none. The rhetoric used on such occasions is designed to produce feelings of guilt in noncooperators. 48

For centuries it was assumed without proof that guilt was a valuable, perhaps even an indispensable, ingredient of the civilized life. Now, in this post-Freudian world, we doubt it. 49

Paul Goodman speaks from the modern point of view when he says: "No good has ever come from feeling guilty, neither intelligence, policy, nor compassion. The guilty do not pay attention to the object but only to themselves, and not even to their own interests, which might make sense, but to their anxieties." 50

One does not have to be a professional psychiatrist to see the consequences of anxiety. We in the Western world are just emerging from a dreadful two-centuries-long Dark Ages of Eros that was sustained partly by prohibition laws, but perhaps more effectively by the anxiety-generating mechanism of education. Alex Comfort has told the story well in *The Anxiety Makers*; it is not a pretty one. 51

Since proof is difficult, we may even concede that the results of anxiety may sometimes, from certain points of view, be desirable. The larger question we should ask is whether, as a matter of policy, we should ever encourage the use of a technique the tendency (if not the intention) of which is psychologically pathogenic. We hear much talk these days of responsible parenthood; the coupled words are incorporated into the titles of some organizations devoted to birth control. Some people have proposed massive propaganda campaigns to instill responsibility into the nation's (or the world's) breeders. But what is the meaning of the word responsibility in this context? Is it not merely a synonym for the word conscience? When we use the word responsibility in the absence of 52 substantial sanctions are we not trying to browbeat a free man in a commons into acting against his own interest? Responsibility is a verbal counterfeit for a substantial *quid pro quo*.[4] It is an attempt to get something for nothing.

If the word responsibility is to be used at all, I suggest that it be in   53
the sense Charles Frankel uses it. "Responsibility," says this philosopher, "is the product of definite social arrangements." Notice that Frankel calls for social arrangements—not propaganda.

MUTUAL COERCION MUTUALLY AGREED UPON

The social arrangements that produce responsibility are arrange-   54
ments that create coercion, of some sort. Consider bank-robbing. The man who takes money from a bank acts as if the bank were a commons. How do we prevent such action? Certainly not by trying to control his behavior solely by a verbal appeal to his sense of responsibility. Rather than rely on propaganda we follow Frankel's lead and insist that a bank is not a commons; we seek the definite social arrangements that will keep it from becoming a commons. That we thereby infringe on the freedom of would-be robbers we neither deny nor regret.

The morality of bank-robbing is particularly easy to understand   55
because we accept complete prohibition of this activity. We are willing to say "Thou shalt not rob banks," without providing for exceptions. But temperance also can be created by coercion. Taxing is a good coercive device. To keep downtown shoppers temperate in their use of parking space we introduce parking meters for short periods, and traffic fines for longer ones. We need not actually forbid a citizen to park as long as he wants to; we need merely make it increasingly expensive for him to do so. Not prohibition, but carefully biased options are what we offer him. A Madison Avenue man might call this persuasion; I prefer the greater candor of the word coercion.

Coercion is a dirty word to most liberals now, but it need not   56
forever be so. As with the four-letter words, its dirtiness can be cleansed away by exposure to the light, by saying it over and over without apology or embarrassment. To many, the word coercion implies arbitrary decisions of distant and irresponsible bureaucrats; but this is not a necessary part of its meaning. The only kind of coercion I recommend is mutual coercion, mutually agreed upon by the majority of the people affected.

To say that we mutually agree to coercion is not to say that we   57

4. An equal exchange.

are required to enjoy it, or even to pretend we enjoy it. Who enjoys taxes? We all grumble about them. But we accept compulsory taxes because we recognize that voluntary taxes would favor the conscienceless. We institute and (grumblingly) support taxes and other coercive devices to escape the horror of the commons.

An alternative to the commons need not be perfectly just to be preferable. With real estate and other material goods, the alternative we have chosen is the institution of private property coupled with legal inheritance. Is this system perfectly just? As a genetically trained biologist I deny that it is. It seems to me that, if there are to be differences in individual inheritance, legal possession should be perfectly correlated with biological inheritance—that those who are biologically more fit to be the custodians of property and power should legally inherit more. But genetic recombination continually makes a mockery of the doctrine of "like father, like son," implicit in our laws of legal inheritance. An idiot can inherit millions, and a trust fund can keep his estate intact. We must admit that our legal system of private property plus inheritance is unjust—but we put up with it because we are not convinced, at the moment, that anyone has invented a better system. The alternative of the commons is too horrifying to contemplate. Injustice is preferable to total ruin.

It is one of the peculiarities of the warfare between reform and the status quo that it is thoughtlessly governed by a double standard. Whenever a reform measure is proposed it is often defeated when its opponents triumphantly discover a flaw in it. As Kingsley Davis has pointed out, worshippers of the status quo sometimes imply that no reform is possible without unanimous agreement, an implication contrary to historical fact. As nearly as I can make out, automatic rejection of proposed reforms is based on one of two unconscious assumptions: (i) that the status quo is perfect; or (ii) that the choice we face is between reform and no action; if the proposed reform is imperfect, we presumably should take no action at all, while we wait for a perfect proposal.

But we can never do nothing. That which we have done for thousands of years is also action. It also produces evils. Once we are aware that the status quo is action, we can then compare its discoverable advantages and disadvantages with the predicted advantages and disadvantages of the proposed reform, discounting as best we can for our lack of experience. On the basis of such a comparison, we can make a rational decision which will not involve the unworkable assumption that only perfect systems are tolerable.

RECOGNITION OF NECESSITY

Perhaps the simplest summary of this analysis of man's popula-   61
tion problems is this: the commons, if justifiable at all, is justifiable
only under conditions of low-population density. As the human
population has increased, the commons has had to be abandoned
in one aspect after another.

First we abandoned the commons in food gathering, enclosing   62
farm land and restricting pastures and hunting and fishing areas.
These restrictions are still not complete throughout the world.

Somewhat later we saw that the commons as a place for waste   63
disposal would also have to be abandoned. Restrictions on the
disposal of domestic sewage are widely accepted in the Western
world; we are still struggling to close the commons to pollution by
automobiles, factories, insecticide sprayers, fertilizing operations,
and atomic energy installations.

In a still more embryonic state is our recognition of the evils of   64
the commons in matters of pleasure. There is almost no restriction
on the propagation of sound waves in the public medium. The
shopping public is assaulted with mindless music, without its consent. Our government is paying out billions of dollars to create
supersonic transport which will disturb 50,000 people for every
one person who is whisked from coast to coast three hours faster.
Advertisers muddy the airwaves of radio and television and pollute
the view of travelers. We are a long way from outlawing the commons in matters of pleasure. Is this because our Puritan inheritance
makes us view pleasure as something of a sin, and pain (that is, the
pollution of advertising) as the sign of virtue?

Every new enclosure of the commons involves the infringement   65
of somebody's personal liberty. Infringements made in the distant
past are accepted because no contemporary complains of a loss. It
is the newly proposed infringements that we vigorously oppose;
cries of "rights" and "freedom" fill the air. But what does "freedom" mean? When men mutually agreed to pass laws against
robbing, mankind became more free, not less so. Individuals locked
into the logic of the commons are free only to bring on universal
ruin; once they see the necessity of mutual coercion, they become
free to pursue other goals. I believe it was Hegel who said, "Freedom is the recognition of necessity."

The most important aspect of necessity that we must now recog-   66
nize, is the necessity of abandoning the commons in breeding. No
technical solution can rescue us from the misery of overpopulation.
Freedom to breed will bring ruin to all. At the moment, to avoid
hard decisions many of us are tempted to propagandize for con-

science and responsible parenthood. The temptation must be resisted, because an appeal to independently acting consciences selects for the disappearance of all conscience in the long run, and an increase in anxiety in the short.

The only way we can preserve and nurture other and more 67
precious freedoms is by relinquishing the freedom to breed, and that very soon. "Freedom is the recognition of necessity"—and it is the role of education to reveal to all the necessity of abandoning the freedom to breed. Only so, can we put an end to this aspect of the tragedy of the commons.

JOHN KENNETH GALBRAITH

How to Get the Poor Off Our Conscience

John Kenneth Galbraith (1908–   ), born in Ontario and educated at the University of Toronto, the University of California (Ph.D., 1934), and Cambridge University, is one of the leading economists of our century. Among his many books the most influential are *The Affluent Society* (1958) and *The New Industrial State* (1967), in both of which he attacks the "conventional wisdom" that our economy is driven by the free choice of consumers. Instead, he argues, modern business "uses its political influence to persuade the government to maintain full employment and total demand for all output of all firms." Galbraith believes the economy is a kind of treadmill, designed by business interests to keep people working and consuming, regardless of what they might want if they were left to their own devices. Given this vision of the artificiality of "affluence" in Western societies, he is naturally distressed by the existence of what he sees as equally artificial poverty. As an adviser to Presidents Kennedy and Johnson, Galbraith is associated with the social programs Charles Murray finds objectionable. "How to Get the Poor Off Our Conscience" was published in *Harper's Magazine* in November 1985.

I would like to reflect on one of the oldest of human exercises, 1
the process by which over the years, and indeed over the centuries, we have undertaken to get the poor off our conscience.

Rich and poor have lived together, always uncomfortably and 2

sometimes perilously, since the beginning of time. Plutarch[1] was
led to say: "An imbalance between the rich and poor is the oldest
and most fatal ailment of republics." And the problems that arise
from the continuing co-existence of affluence and poverty—and
particularly the process by which good fortune is justified in the
presence of the ill fortune of others—have been an intellectual
preoccupation for centuries. They continue to be so in our own
time.

One begins with the solution proposed in the Bible: the poor   3
suffer in this world but are wonderfully rewarded in the next. Their
poverty is a temporary misfortune; if they are poor and also meek,
they eventually will inherit the earth. This is, in some ways, an
admirable solution. It allows the rich to enjoy their wealth while
envying the poor their future fortune.

Much, much later, in the twenty or thirty years following the   4
publication in 1776 of *The Wealth of Nations*—the late dawn of the
Industrial Revolution in Britain—the problem and its solution began to take on their modern form. Jeremy Bentham, a near contemporary of Adam Smith, came up with the formula that for
perhaps fifty years was extraordinarily influential in British and, to
some degree, American thought. This was utilitarianism. "By the
principle of utility," Bentham said in 1789, "is meant the principle
which approves or disapproves of every action whatsoever according to the tendency which it appears to have to augment or diminish the happiness of the party whose interest is in question." Virtue
is, indeed must be, self-centered. While there were people with
great good fortune and many more with great ill fortune, the social
problem was solved as long as, again in Bentham's words, there
was "the greatest good for the greatest number." Society did its
best for the largest possible number of people; one accepted that
the result might be sadly unpleasant for the many whose happiness
was not served.

In the 1830s a new formula, influential in no slight degree to this   5
day, became available for getting the poor off the public conscience. This is associated with the names of David Ricardo, a
stockbroker, and Thomas Robert Malthus, a divine. The essentials
are familiar: the poverty of the poor was the fault of the poor. And
it was so because it was a product of their excessive fecundity: their
grievously uncontrolled lust caused them to breed up to the full
limits of the available subsistence.

This was Malthusianism. Poverty being caused in the bed meant   6
that the rich were not responsible for either its creation or its

amelioration. However, Malthus was himself not without a certain feeling of responsibility: he urged that the marriage ceremony contain a warning against undue and irresponsible sexual intercourse—a warning, it is fair to say, that has not been accepted as a fully effective method of birth control. In more recent times, Ronald Reagan has said that the best form of population control emerges from the market. (Couples in love should repair to R. H. Macy's, not their bedrooms.) Malthus, it must be said, was at least as relevant.

By the middle of the nineteenth century, a new form of denial achieved great influence, especially in the United States. The new doctrine, associated with the name of Herbert Spencer, was Social Darwinism. In economic life, as in biological development, the overriding rule was survival of the fittest. That phrase—"survival of the fittest"—came, in fact, not from Charles Darwin but from Spencer, and expressed his view of economic life. The elimination of the poor is nature's way of improving the race. The weak and unfortunate being extruded, the quality of the human family is thus strengthened. 7

One of the most notable American spokespersons of Social Darwinism was John D. Rockefeller—the first Rockefeller—who said in a famous speech: "The American Beauty rose can be produced in the splendor and fragrance which bring cheer to its beholder only by sacrificing the early buds which grow up around it. And so it is in economic life. It is merely the working out of a law of nature and a law of God." 8

In the course of the present century, however, Social Darwinism came to be considered a bit too cruel. It declined in popularity, and references to it acquired a condemnatory tone. We passed on to the more amorphous denial of poverty associated with Calvin Coolidge and Herbert Hoover. They held that public assistance to the poor interfered with the effective operation of the economic system— that such assistance was inconsistent with the economic design that had come to serve most people very well. The notion that there is something economically damaging about helping the poor remains with us to this day as one of the ways by which we get them off our conscience. 9

With the Roosevelt revolution (as previously with that of Lloyd George in Britain), a specific responsibility was assumed by the government for the least fortunate people in the republic. Roosevelt and the presidents who followed him accepted a substantial measure of responsibility for the old through Social Security, for the unemployed through unemployment insurance, for the unemployable and the handicapped through direct relief, and for the sick 10 through Medicare and Medicaid. This was a truly great change, and for a time, the age-old tendency to avoid thinking about the poor gave way to the feeling that we didn't need to try—that we were, indeed, doing something about them.

In recent years, however, it has become clear that the search for 11 a way of getting the poor off our conscience was not at an end; it was only suspended. And so we are now again engaged in this search in a highly energetic way. It has again become a major philosophical, literary, and rhetorical preoccupation, and an economically not unrewarding enterprise.

Of the four, maybe five, current designs we have to get the poor 12 off our conscience, the first proceeds from the inescapable fact that most of the things that must be done on behalf of the poor must be done in one way or another by the government. It is then argued that the government is inherently incompetent, except as regards weapons design and procurement and the overall management of the Pentagon. Being incompetent and ineffective, it must not be asked to succor the poor; it will only louse things up or make things worse.

The allegation of government incompetence is associated in our 13 time with the general condemnation of the bureaucrat—again excluding those concerned with national defense. The only form of discrimination that is still permissible—that is, still officially encouraged in the United States today—is discrimination against people who work for the federal government, especially on social welfare activities. We have great corporate bureaucracies replete with corporate bureaucrats, but they are good; only public bureaucracy and government servants are bad. In fact, we have in the United States an extraordinarily good public service—one made up of talented and dedicated people who are overwhelmingly honest and only rarely given to overpaying for monkey wrenches, flashlights, coffee makers, and toilet seats. (When these aberrations have occurred, they have, oddly enough, all been in the Pentagon.) We have nearly abolished poverty among the old, greatly democratized health care, assured minorities of their civil rights, and vastly enhanced educational opportunity. All this would seem a considerable achievement for incompetent and otherwise ineffective people. We must recognize that the present condemnation of government and government administration is really part of the continuing design for avoiding responsibility for the poor.

The second design in this great centuries-old tradition is to argue 14 that any form of public help to the poor only hurts the poor. It destroys morale. It seduces people away from gainful employment. It breaks up marriages, since women can seek welfare for themselves and their children once they are without their husbands.

There is no proof of this—none, certainly, that compares that   15
damage with the damage that would be inflicted by the loss of
public assistance. Still, the case is made—and believed—that there
is something gravely damaging about aid to the unfortunate. This is
perhaps our most highly influential piece of fiction.

The third, and closely related, design for relieving ourselves of   16
responsibility for the poor is the argument that public-assistance
measures have an adverse effect on incentive. They transfer income
from the diligent to the idle and feckless, thus reducing the effort of
the diligent and encouraging the idleness of the idle. The modern
manifestation of this is supply-side economics. Supply-side economics holds that the rich in the United States have not been
working because they have too little income. So, by taking money
from the poor and giving it to the rich, we increase effort and
stimulate the economy. Can we really believe that any considerable
number of the poor prefer welfare to a good job? Or that business
people—corporate executives, the key figures in our time—are
idling away their hours because of the insufficiency of their pay?
This is a scandalous charge against the American businessperson,
notably a hard worker. Belief can be the servant of truth—but even
more of convenience.

The fourth design for getting the poor off our conscience is to   17
point to the presumed adverse effect on freedom of taking responsibility for them. Freedom consists of the right to spend a maximum
of one's money by one's own choice, and to see a minimum taken
and spent by the government. (Again, expenditure on national
defense is excepted.) In the enduring words of Professor Milton
Friedman, people must be "free to choose."

This is possibly the most transparent of all of the designs; no   18
mention is ordinarily made of the relation of income to the freedom
of the poor. (Professor Friedman is here an exception; through the
negative income tax, he would assure everyone a basic income.)
There is, we can surely agree, no form of oppression that is quite so
great, no construction on thought and effort quite so comprehen-
sive, as that which comes from having no money at all. Though we
hear much about the limitation on the freedom of the affluent
when their income is reduced through taxes, we hear nothing of
the extraordinary enhancement of the freedom of the poor from
having some money of their own to spend. Yet the loss of freedom
from taxation to the rich is a small thing as compared with the gain
in freedom from providing some income to the impoverished. Freedom we rightly cherish. Cherishing it, we should not use it as a
cover for denying freedom to those in need.

Finally, when all else fails, we resort to simple psychological de-   19
nial. This is a psychic tendency that in various manifestations is

common to us all. It causes us to avoid thinking about death. It
causes a great many people to avoid thought of the arms race and
the consequent rush toward a highly probable extinction. By the
same process of psychological denial, we decline to think of the
poor. Whether they be in Ethiopia, the South Bronx, or even in
such an Elysium as Los Angeles, we resolve to keep them off our
minds. Think, we are often advised, of something pleasant.

These are the modern designs by which we escape concern for   20
the poor. All, save perhaps the last, are in great inventive descent
from Bentham, Malthus, and Spencer. Ronald Reagan and his colleagues are clearly in a notable tradition—at the end of a long
history of effort to escape responsibility for one's fellow beings.
So are the philosophers now celebrated in Washington: George
Gilder, a greatly favored figure of the recent past, who tells to
much applause that the poor must have the cruel spur of their
own suffering to ensure effort; Charles Murray, who, to greater
cheers, contemplates "scrapping the entire federal welfare and
income-support structure for working and aged persons, including A.F.D.C., Medicaid, food stamps, unemployment insurance,
Workers' Compensation, subsidized housing, disability insurance,
and," he adds, "the rest. Cut the knot, for there is no way to untie
it." By a triage, the worthy would be selected to survive; the loss of
the rest is the penalty we should pay. Murray is the voice of
Spencer in our time; he is enjoying, as indicated, unparalleled
popularity in high Washington circles.

Compassion, along with the associated public effort, is the least   21
comfortable, the least convenient, course of behavior and action in
our time. But it remains the only one that is consistent with a
totally civilized life. Also, it is, in the end, the most truly conservative course. There is no paradox here. Civil discontent and its consequences do not come from contented people—an obvious point.
To the extent that we can make contentment as nearly universal as
possible, we will preserve and enlarge the social and political tran-
quillity for which conservatives, above all, should yearn.

CHARLES MURRAY

What's So Bad about Being Poor?

Charles Murray (1943–   ), born in Newton, Iowa, took his
bachelor's degree in history from Harvard in 1965 and im-

mediately joined the Peace Corps. He served for five years as a volunteer in rural Thailand and stayed for a sixth to do research on economic development. Returning to the United States, he completed his Ph.D. in political science at the Massachusetts Institute of Technology in 1974. Since then he has written extensively on crime and poverty and become one of the nation's most influential conservative thinkers. His 1982 monograph, *Safety Nets and the Truly Needy*, in which he argued that President Johnson's massive welfare spending had helped the poor no more than President Eisenhower's laissez-faire policies, so impressed the Manhattan Institute for Policy Research that it offered Murray an annual stipend of $35,000 to expand it into book form. The result, *Losing Ground: American Social Policy, 1950–1980* (1983), became one of the cornerstones of President Reagan's domestic policy. "What's So Bad about Being Poor?" (published in *National Review*, October 28, 1988) is based on Murray's 1988 book, *In Pursuit: Of Happiness and Good Government*.

One of the great barriers to a discussion of poverty and social   1
policy in the 1980s is that so few people who talk about poverty have ever been poor. The diminishing supply of the formerly poor in policy-making and policy-influencing positions is a side effect of progress. The number of poor households dropped dramatically from the beginning of World War II through the end of the 1960s. Despite this happy cause, however, it is a troubling phenomenon. From the beginning of American history through at least the 1950s, the new generation moving into positions of influence in politics, business, journalism, and academia was bound to include a large admixture of people who had grown up dirt-poor. People who had grown up in more privileged surroundings did not have to speculate about what being poor was like; someone sitting beside them, or at the head of the table, was likely to be able to tell them. It was easy to acknowledge then, as it is not now, that there is nothing so terrible about poverty *per se*. Poverty is not equivalent to destitution. Being poor does not necessarily mean being malnourished or ill-clothed. It does not automatically mean joylessness or despair. To be poor is not necessarily to be without dignity; it is not necessarily to be unhappy. When large numbers of people who were running the country had once been poor themselves, poverty could be kept in perspective.

Today, how many graduates of the Kennedy School of Govern-   2
ment or of the Harvard Business School have ever been really poor? How many have ever had close friends who were? How many even have parents who were once poor? For those who have never been poor and never even known any people who were once

poor, it is difficult to treat poverty as something other than a mystery. It is even more difficult to be detached about the importance of poverty, because to do so smacks of a "let them eat cake" mentality. By the same token, however, it is important that we who have never been poor be able to think about the relationship of poverty to social policy in a much more straightforward way than the nation's intellectuals and policy-makers have done for the past few decades. To that end, I propose a thought experiment based on the premise that tomorrow you had to be poor. I do not mean "low-income" by Western standards of affluence, but functioning near the subsistence level, as a very large proportion of the world's population still does.

In constructing this thought experiment, the first requirement is   3
to divorce yourself from certain reflexive assumptions. Do not think what it would be like to be poor while living in a community of rich people. I do not (yet) want to commingle the notions of absolute poverty and relative poverty, so you should imagine a community in which everyone else is as poor as you are, indeed, a world in which the existence of wealth is so far removed from daily life that is not real.

The second requirement is to avoid constructing an imaginary   4
person. The point is not to try to imagine yourself in the shoes of "a poor person" but to imagine what *you*, with your particular personality, experiences, strengths, and limitations (including your middle-class upbringing and values), would do if you were suddenly thrust into this position.

To do all this in the American context is difficult. Any scenario is   5
filled with extraneous factors. So let me suggest one that I used as a way of passing the time when I was a researcher driving on the back roads of rural Thailand many years ago. What if, I would muse, I had to live for the rest of my life in the next village I came to (perhaps a nuclear war would have broken out, thereby keeping me indefinitely in Thailand; any rationalization would do)?

In some ways, the prospect was grim. I had never been charmed   6
by sleeping under mosquito netting nor by bathing with a few buckets of cloudy well water. When circumstances permitted, I liked to end a day's work in a village by driving back to an air-conditioned hotel and a cold beer. But if I had no choice . . .

As it happens, Thailand has an attractive peasant culture. Sur-   7
vival itself is not a problem. The weather is always warm, so the requirements for clothes, fuel, and shelter are minimal. Village food is ample, if monotonous. But I would nonetheless be extremely poor, with an effective purchasing power of a few hundred dollars a year. The house I would live in would probably consist of a porch

and one or two small, unlit, unfurnished rooms. The walls might be of wood, more probably of woven bamboo or leaf mats. I would have (in those years) no electricity and no running water. Perhaps I would have a bicycle or a transistor radio. Probably the nearest physician would be many kilometers away. In sum: If the criterion for measuring poverty is material goods, it would be difficult to find a community in deepest Appalachia or a neighborhood in the most depressed parts of South Chicago that even approaches the absolute material poverty of the average Thai village in which I would have to make my life.

On the other hand, as I thought about spending the next fifty   8 years in a Thai village, I found myself wondering precisely what I would lack (compared to my present life) that would cause me great pain. The more I thought about the question, the less likely it seemed that I would be unhappy.

Since I lacked any useful trade, maybe I could swap the Jeep for   9 a few *rai* of land and become a farmer. Learning how to farm well enough to survive would occupy my time and attention for several years. After that, I might try to become an affluent farmer. One of the assets I would bring from my Western upbringing and schooling would be a haphazardly acquired understanding of cash crops, markets, and entrepreneurial possibilities, and perhaps I could parlay that, along with hard work, into some income and more land. It also was clear to me that I probably would enjoy this "career." I am not saying I would *choose* it, but rather that I could find satisfaction in learning how to be a competent rice farmer, even though it was not for me the most desired of all possible careers.

What about my personal life? Thais are among the world's most   10 handsome and charming people, and it was easy to imagine falling in love with a woman from the village, marrying her, and having a family with her. I could also anticipate the pleasure of watching my children grow up, probably at closer hand than I would in the United States. The children would not get the same education they would in the States, but I would have it within my power to see that they would be educated. A grade school is near every village. The priests in the local *wat* could teach them Buddhism. I could also become teacher to my children. A few basic textbooks in mathematics, science, and history; Plato and Shakespeare and the Bible; a dozen other well-chosen classics—all these could be acquired even in up-country Thailand. My children could reach adulthood literate, thoughtful, and civilized.

My children would do well in other ways too. They would grow   11 up in a "positive peer culture," as the experts say. Their Thai friends in the village would all be raised by their parents to be considerate, hard-working, pious, and honest—that's the way Thai villagers raise their children. My children would face few of the corrupting influences to be found in an American city.

Other personal pleasures? I knew I would find it easy to make   12
friends, and that some would become close. I would have other good times, too—celebrations on special occasions, but more often informal gatherings and jokes and conversation. If I read less, I would also read better. I would have great personal freedom as long as my behavior did not actively interfere with the lives of my neighbors (the tolerance for eccentric behavior in a Thai village is remarkably high). What about the physical condition of poverty? After a few months, I suspect that I would hardly notice.

You may conclude that this thought experiment is a transparent   13
setup. First I ask what it would be like to be poor, then I proceed to outline a near-idyllic environment in which to be poor. I assume that I have a legacy of education experiences that would help me spend my time getting steadily less poor. And then I announce that poverty isn't so bad after all. But the point of the thought experiment is not to suggest that all kinds of poverty are tolerable, and even less that all peasant societies are pleasant places to live. When poverty means the inability to get enough food or shelter, it is every bit as bad as usually portrayed. When poverty means being forced to remain in that condition, with no way of improving one's situation, it is as bad as portrayed. When poverty is conjoined with oppression, be it a caste system or a hacienda system or a people's republic, it is as bad as portrayed. *My thought experiment is not a paean to peasant life, but a paean to communities of free people.* If poverty is defined in terms of money, everybody in the Thai village is poor. If poverty is defined as being unable to live a modest but decent existence, hardly anyone there is poor.

Does this thought experiment fail when it is transported to the   14
United States? Imagine the same Thai village set down intact on the outskirts of Los Angeles. Surely its inhabitants must be miserable, living in their huts and watching the rest of the world live in splendor.

At this point in the argument, however, we need no longer think   15
in terms of thought experiments. This situation is one that has been faced by hundreds of thousands of immigrants to the United States, whether they came from Europe at the end of World War II or from Vietnam in the mid 1970s. Lawyers found themselves working as janitors, professors found themselves working on assembly lines. Sometimes they worked their way up and out, but many had to

remain janitors and factory workers, because they came here too late in life to retool their foreign-trained skills. But their children did not have to remain so, and they have not. A reading of their histories, in literature or in the oral testimony of their children, corroborates this pattern. Was a Latvian attorney forced to flee his country "happy" to have to work as a janitor? No. Was he prevented by his situation—specifically, by his poverty—from successfully pursuing happiness? Emphatically, no.

Let us continue the thought experiment nonetheless, with a 16 slightly different twist. This time, you are given a choice. One choice is to be poor in rural Thailand, as I have described it, with just enough food and shelter and a few hundred dollars a year in cash: a little beyond bare subsistence, but not much. Or you may live in the United States, receive a free apartment, free food, free medical care, and a cash grant, the package coming to a total that puts you well above the poverty line. There is, however, a catch: you are *required* to live in a particular apartment, and this apartment is located in a public-housing project in one of the burned-out areas of the South Bronx. A condition of receiving the rest of the package is that you continue to live, and raise your children, in the South Bronx (you do not have the option of spending all of your waking hours in Manhattan, just as the village thought experiment did not give you the option of taking vacations in Bangkok). You still have all the assets you took to the Thai village—once again, it is essential that you imagine not what it is like for an Alabama sharecropper to be transplanted to the South Bronx, but what it would be like *for you*.

In some ways, you would have much more access to distrac- 17 tions. Unlike the situation in the Thai village, you would have television you could watch all day, taking you vicariously into other worlds. And, for that matter, it would be much easier to get books than in a Thai village, and you would have much more money with which to buy them. You could, over time, fix up your apartment so that within its walls you would have an environment that looked and felt very like an apartment you could have elsewhere.

There is only one problem: You would have a terrible time once 18 you opened your door to the outside world. How, for example, are you going to raise your children in the South Bronx so that they grow up to be the adults you want them to be? (No, you don't have the option of sending them to live elsewhere.) How are you going to take a walk in the park in the evening? There are many good people in the South Bronx with whom you could become friends, just as in the village. But how are you to find them? And once they are found, how are you to create a functioning, mutually reinforcing community?

I suggest that as you think of answers to those questions, you   19
will find that, if you are to have much chance to be happy, the South Bronx needs to be changed in a way that the village did not—that, unlike the village as it stood, the South Bronx as it stands does not "work" as an environment for pursuing happiness. Let us ignore for the moment how these changes in environment could be brought about, by what combination of government's doing things and refraining from doing things. The fact is that hardly any of those changes involve greater income for you personally, but rather changes in the surrounding environment. There is a question that crystallizes the roles of personal *v.* environmental poverty in this situation: How much money would it take to persuade you to move self and family to this public-housing project in the South Bronx?

The purpose of the first two versions of the thought experiment   20
was to suggest a different perspective on one's own priorities regarding the pursuit of happiness, and by extension to suggest that perhaps public policy ought to reflect a different set of priorities as well. It is easy in this case, however, to assume that what one wants for oneself is not applicable to others. Thus, for example, it could be said that the only reason the thought experiments work (if you grant even that much) is that the central character starts out with enormous advantages of knowledge and values—which in themselves reflect the advantages of having grown up with plenty of material resources.

To explore that possibility, I ask you to bear with me for one   21
more thought experiment on this general topic, one I have found to be a touchstone. This time, the question is not what kinds of material resources you (with your fully developed set of advantages) need for your pursuit of happiness, but what a small child, without any developed assets at all, needs for his pursuit of happiness—specifically, what your own child needs.

Imagine that you are the parent of a small child, living in con-   22
temporary America, and in some way you are able to know that tomorrow you and your spouse will die and your child will be made an orphan. You do not have the option of sending the child to live with a friend or relative. You must select from among other and far-from-perfect choices. The choices, I assure you, are not veiled representations of anything else; the experiment is set up not to be realistic, but to evoke something about how you think.

Suppose first this choice: You may put your child with an ex-   23
tremely poor couple according to the official definition of "poor"—
which is to say, poverty that is measured exclusively in money.
This couple has so little money that your child's clothes will often be secondhand and there will be not even small luxuries to
brighten his life. Life will be a struggle, often a painful one. But you
also know that the parents work hard, will make sure your child
goes to school and studies, and will teach your child that integrity
and responsibility are primary values. Or you may put your child
with parents who will be as affectionate to your child as the first
couple but who have never worked, are indifferent to your child's
education, think that integrity and responsibility (when they think
of them at all) are meaningless words—but who have and will
always have plenty of food and good clothes and amenities, provided by others.

Which couple do you choose? The answer is obvious to me and I   24
imagine to most readers: the first couple, of course. But if you are
among those who choose the first couple, stop and consider what
the answer means. This is *your own child* you are talking about,
whom you would never let go hungry even if providing for your
child meant going hungry yourself. And yet you are choosing years
of privation for that same child. Why?

Perhaps I set up the thought experiment too starkly. Let us re-   25
peat it, adding some ambiguity. This time, the first choice is again
the poor-but-virtuous couple. But the second couple is rich. They
are, we shall say, the heirs to a great fortune. They will not beat
your child or in any other way maltreat him. We may even assume
affection on their part, as we will with the other couples. But, once
again, they have never worked and never will, are indifferent to
your child's education, and think that integrity and responsibility
(when they think of them at all) are meaningless words. They do,
however, possess millions of dollars, more than enough to last for
the life of your child and of your child's children. Now, in whose
care do you place your child? The poor couple or the rich one?

This time, it seems likely that some people will choose the rich   26
couple—or more accurately, it is possible to think of ways in which
the decision might be tipped in that direction. For example, a
wealthy person who is indifferent to a child's education might
nonetheless ship the child off to an expensive boarding school at
the earliest possible age. In that case, it is conceivable that the
wealthy ne'er-do-wells are preferable to the poor-but-virtuous
couple, *if* they end up providing the values of the poor family
through the surrogate parenting of the boarding school—dubious,
but conceivable. One may imagine other ways in which the money

might be used to compensate for the inadequacies of the parents. But failing those very chancy possibilities, I suggest that a great many parents on all sides of political fences would knowingly choose hunger and rags for their child rather than wealth.

Again, the question is: Why? What catastrophes are going to   27
befall the child placed in the wealthy home? What is the awful fate? Would it be so terrible if he grew up to be thoughtlessly rich? The child will live a life of luxury and have enough money to buy himself out of almost any problem that might arise. Why not leave it at that? Or let me put the question positively: In deciding where to send the child, what is one trying to achieve by these calculations and predictions and hunches? What is the good that one is trying to achieve? What is the criterion of success?

One may attach a variety of descriptors to the answer. Perhaps   28
you want the child to become a reflective, responsible adult. To value honesty and integrity. To be able to identify sources of lasting satisfaction. Ultimately, if I keep pushing the question (Why is honesty good? Why is being reflective good?), you will give the answer that permits no follow-up: You want your child to be happy. You are trying to choose the guardians who will best enable your child to pursue happiness. And, forced to a choice, material resources come very low on your list of priorities.

So far, I have limited the discussion to a narrow point: in decid- 29
ing how to enhance the ability of people to pursue happiness, solutions that increase material resources beyond subsistence *independently of other considerations* are bound to fail. Money *per se* is not very important. It quickly becomes trivial. Depending on other non-monetary conditions, poor people can have a rich assortment of ways of pursuing happiness, or affluent people can have very few.

The thought experiments were stratagems intended not to con-   30
vince you of any particular policy implications, but rather to induce you to entertain this possibility: When a policy trade-off involves (for example) imposing material hardship in return for some other policy good, *it is possible* (I ask no more than that for the time being) that imposing the material hardship is the right choice. For example, regarding the "orphaned child" scenario: *If* a policy leads to a society in which there are more of the first kind of parents and fewer of the second, the sacrifices in material resources available to the children involved might conceivably be worth it.

The discussion, with its steady use of the concept of "near-   31
subsistence" as "enough material resources to pursue happiness,"

has also been intended to point up how little our concept of poverty has to do with subsistence. Thus, for example, if one simply looks at the end result of how people live, a natural observation concerning contemporary America might be that we have large numbers of people who are living at a subsistence or subsubsistence level. But I have been using "subsistence" in its original sense: enough food to be adequately nourished, plus the most basic shelter and clothing. The traditional Salvation Army shelter provides subsistence, for example. In Western countries, and perhaps especially the United States, two problems tend to confuse the issue. One is that we have forgotten what subsistence means, so that an apartment with cockroaches, broken windows, and graffiti on the walls may be thought of as barely "subsistence level," even if it also has running water, electricity, heat, a television, and a pile of discarded fast-food cartons in the corner. It might be an awful place to live (for the reasons that the South Bronx can be an awful place to live), but it bears very little resemblance to what "subsistence" means to most of the world. Secondly, we tend to confuse the way in which some poor people *use* their resources (which indeed can often leave them in a near-subsistence state) with the raw purchasing power of the resources at their disposal. Take, for example, the apartment I just described and move a middle-class person with middle-class habits and knowledge into it, given exactly the same resources. Within days it would be still shabby but a different place. All of which is precisely the point of the thought experiments about Thailand and the South Bronx: money has very little to do with living a poverty-stricken life. Similarly, "a subsistence income" has very little to do with what Americans think of as poverty.

That being the case, I am arguing that the job of designing good 32 public policy must be reconstrued. We do not have the option of saying, "First we will provide for the material base, then worry about the other necessary conditions for pursuing happiness." These conditions interact. The ways in which people go about achieving safety, self-respect, and self-fulfillment in their lives are inextricably bound up with each other and with the way in which people go about providing for their material well-being. We do not have the option of doing one good thing at a time.

In discussing the conditions for pursuing happiness I have put 33 material resources first only because that is where they have stood in the political debate. I am suggesting that properly they should be put last.

MYRON MAGNET

The Rich and the Poor

Myron Magnet (1944–   ) studied English at Columbia University in the 1960s, taking a Ph.D. in Victorian literature and
becoming a professor in the English department. Magnet sees
literature as a tool for exploring the lives of ordinary people
and their relationship to the society around them. His book,
Dickens and the Social Order (1985), for example, concerns itself largely with the social problems created by poverty in nineteenth-century London. Eventually, Magnet's desire to write
about social and economic conditions led him away from the
study of Victorian literature and into the direct study of our own
times. He has written several articles on business, industry, and
poverty in the United States, most of them published in *Fortune*
magazine, where he is now a member of the editorial board.
"The Rich and the Poor" appeared in *Fortune* on June 6, 1988.
Magnet is currently at work on a book that expands on the ideas
presented here.

No novelist would dare put into a book the most extreme of the   1
dizzying contrasts of wealth and poverty that make up the ordinary
texture of life in today's American cities. The details are too outlandish to seem credible. Directly under the windows of the $6
million apartments that loom over Fifth Avenue, for instance,
where grandees like Jacqueline Onassis or Laurence Rockefeller
sleep, sleep the homeless, one and sometimes two on each park
bench, huddled among bundles turned dead gray by dirt and wear.
Across town last Christmas the line of fur-coated holiday makers
waiting outside a fashionable delicatessen to buy caviar at only
$259.95 a pound literally adjoined the ragged line of paupers wait-
ing for the soup kitchen to open at the church around the corner.
In the shiny atriums of the urban skyscrapers where 40-year-old
investment bankers make seven figures restructuring the industrial
landscape, derelicts with no place to go kill time. And every train
or bus commuter knows that his way home to suburban comfort
lies through a dreary gauntlet of homelessness and beggary.

Like Death stalking into the terror-struck banquet, the poverty   2
that inescapably intrudes into America's cities fills the prosperous
with disquiet. What's wrong with the country, they worry, that
these pathetic souls are everywhere? Does the same system that
enriches me degrade them? Am I responsible for their poverty—or

for getting them out of it? Says historian Gertrude Himmelfarb, author of *The Idea of Poverty*: "We're beginning to feel they're permanent, and they demoralize the whole society."

What really is the relation of the Haves to the Have-Nots—to the 3 homeless and underclass—in the America of the late Eighties? When the Haves think about this question, they generally reach for outmoded images: A reformed Scrooge gives meek Bob Cratchit a raise and a dose of paternalism, so that Tiny Tim doesn't die; good King Wenceslas carries a feast through the snow to his needy subject. But today's abject poor are nobody's exploited employees, nor are they bound to the Haves in anything like the organic hierarchy that was only a memory even when "Good King Wenceslas" was written 135 years ago.

Deeper thinkers analyze the problem in more sophisticated but 4 not much more accurate terms. According to a popular theory, the same Reagan Administration mind-set that unfettered the rich, helping to create the Wall Street baby tycoons, simultaneously immiserated the poor by unraveling the social safety net. The rich got a tax break, leaving less revenue to go to the poor.

One trouble with this theory that the rich have robbed the 5 poor—"economic violence," as candidate Jesse Jackson calls it—is that, while some programs of dubious efficacy indeed were cut, overall means-tested social spending has *risen* about 5% in real terms in the Eighties. More to the point, the Eighties boom that has enriched the tycoons has so far created an astonishing 14 million new jobs, close to a third of them unskilled, offering a way out of poverty to almost any poor person with no more than the willingness and discipline to work. Pointing up the tendentiousness of the "economic violence" argument, Hoover Institution economist Thomas Sowell refers to a centimillionaire landlord and a highly publicized homeless woman: "In other words, Donald Trump is making his millions off of Joyce Brown?"

Another argument blames large changes in the U.S. economy for 6 the persistence of poverty. These changes have in fact caused upheavals in the labor market, but they do not account for the specific plight of the underclass and the vast majority of the homeless. In this explanation, the same global economic forces that benefit the Haves by creating richly rewarded high-skill jobs impoverish the Have-Nots by sending low-skill jobs abroad or abolishing them altogether. If the poor had the necessary skills, there would be no problem. But, says William Woodside, chairman of Primerica's executive committee, "We're creating a two-tier society. The educa-

tional requirement for jobs is going up rapidly, and we're not giving the poor the kind of education required to handle the jobs that
are around today."

True, well-paid jobs requiring more than basic skills have mush-   7
roomed in the Eighties and will go on proliferating in the Nineties.
But unskilled and low-skill jobs—expanding at a slower rate but
from a much higher base—grew more in absolute numbers and
will do so for the rest of the century. Just look at the Help Wanted
signs in McDonald's windows and at the several million illegal
aliens working in restaurant kitchens and the like across the U.S.
These facts suggest no shortage of opportunity to enter the labor
market and, with ambition and energy enough to get training, to
advance up the ladder.

But this gets to the heart of the matter: The problem afflicting   8
today's poorest Americans is that they chronically do not work—
for a variety of reasons—and are radically disconnected from the
larger society. Says New York University political scientist Lawrence Mead, whose *Beyond Entitlement* is one of the key statements
in the current welfare reform debate: "Many jobs exist. You can't
say there's no work. The mystery is why people who are poor—
particularly welfare mothers and single men—don't go to work,
because work gets you above poverty. You can't really see poverty
any longer as something that's just visited on people."

The key to the mystery of why the poorest poor don't work in   9
the face of opportunity is that their poverty is less an economic
matter than a cultural one. Their upbringing has in many cases
deprived them of the inner resources to seize their chance, and they
pass on to their children a self-defeating set of values and attitudes,
along with an impoverished intellectual and emotional development that generally imprisons them in failure as well. Now in their
third generation, these poor are locked in the familiar pathology
that, even more than poverty, defines the underclass: leaving
school, out-of-wedlock teen pregnancy, nonwork, drug and alcohol abuse, welfare dependency, and crime.

The prosperous are indeed implicated in the poverty of the poor. 10
They are implicated even though they don't extract their BMWs
from the hides of the underclass, the way mine owners extracted
profits from the children who pulled the pit carts in the early days
of the Industrial Revolution, when "economic violence" was more
than a catch phrase. Instead, over the past 25 years the Haves have
created a culture—a set of values, attitudes, expectations, and social policies—that accords respect to behavior that, when poor
people practice it, keeps them in poverty. Worse, the culture of the
Haves withdrew respect from the behavior and attitudes that have

traditionally boosted people up the economic ladder—deferral of gratification, sobriety, thrift, dogged industry, and so on through the whole catalogue of antique-sounding virtues. Says Irving Kristol, co-editor of *The Public Interest* magazine: "It's hard to rise above poverty if society keeps deriding the human qualities that allow you to escape from it."

Nowadays it's easy to dismiss the idea that the values and beliefs that make up culture can determine the kind of lives people lead by shaping behavior and institutions. Formerly only Marxists scoffed at that idea. What's really real, they argued, are economic relations. Beliefs and values just float above, like insubstantial froth on the waves. Change the economic relations and you change the beliefs and values that passively reflect them. University of Chicago sociologist William Julius Wilson, in his influential book, *The Truly Disadvantaged*, advances an argument that is an up-to-the-minute case in point: Underclass women have babies out of wedlock because underclass men, unable to find jobs, aren't "marriageable" from an economic point of view. If you want to change that custom, he asserts, the *only* way to do it is to change the economic circumstances and give the men jobs. 11

But the relationship between culture and economic circumstances works the other way too. Says economist Walter E. Williams of George Mason University: "Cultural values such as being neat, paying attention to details, or showing up on time may explain economic mobility, rather than economic mobility occurring in the first place and then people acquiring those cultural characteristics." The main theme of Thomas Sowell's *Ethnic America* is that cultural differences account in large measure for the differing kinds, degrees, and rates of success among the various ethnic groups that have peopled America. The spectacular flourishing of America's Asian immigrants—including many who arrived destitute—is the most recent illustration of that truth. 12

Minorities make up a substantial majority of the underclass; blacks account for over half (though these are a small proportion of the U.S. black population). The new culture created by the Haves has been cruel to these minorities, especially poor blacks. In the Sixties, just when the successes of the civil rights movement were removing racial barriers to mainstream opportunities, the mainstream values that many poor blacks needed to seize those chances—values such as hard work and self-denial—came under sharp attack. Moreover, poor blacks needed all the support and encouragement to make their own fates that mainstream culture could give them. But mainstream culture—transformed from within by an adversarial "counterculture"—let them down. Issu- 13 ing the opposite of a call to responsibility and self-reliance, the larger culture told blacks that they were victims and that society, not they themselves, was responsible for their present and future condition.

Except for America's original settlers, all ethnic groups have   14
found their passage into mainstream middle-class culture difficult and sometimes painful. But even more than Irishmen fleeing fam-ine and political oppression or Jews fleeing pogroms, blacks have faced particular disadvantages in making that transition. Their his-torical experience in America includes plenty of possible causes: a slave system that intentionally kept slaves in deep ignorance, espe-cially of self-reliance; a sharecropping system that perpetuated de-pendency and that helped form, says journalist Nicholas Lemann in the *Atlantic*, the forebears of the underclass in Chicago's ghettos; generations of poverty, which, social psychologists have found, fosters the belief that one is the passive plaything of chance; and long-simmering resentments engendered by racism. Other, more advantageous legacies permitted many blacks to flow out of the ghettos and into the middle class in the Sixties and Seventies. But as a residue of a painful history, black culture preserved tendencies potentially unhelpful to some blacks in mastering opportunities that called for initiative, perseverance, and a tradition of education.

In the face of all of this, when it behooved mainstream culture to   15
assert traditional mainstream values with conviction, the Haves lost confidence even in the most fundamental of those values: the worth of the respectable working life, however humble. When it is pointed out that jobs are widely available to the low skilled, many Haves contemptuously ask, almost by reflex, why anyone would or should be willing to flip hamburgers for not much more than the minimum wage. Even so insightful an observer as Lazard Frères[1] partner Felix Rohatyn can sometimes strike this note. He speaks, for instance, of "the man and the wife slogging away in menial jobs that are dead-end jobs, with three kids, trying to deal with an environment that is very depressing" as "people who are living dead-end lives."

Think about that judgment. Suppose that the man spends his   16
working life as a short-order cook or janitor while his wife makes beds at the motel or cleans up at the nursing home. If both earned only the minimum wage, they could together support their family of five just above the poverty line. But in fact a big-city short-order cook would make two to three times the minimum wage and an urban nursing-home cleaner perhaps 50% more than it. From a

1. A major investment firm on Wall Street.

material point of view, their lives would be threadbare but tolerable. While it would be nice for everyone to make millions doing deals, even the world's richest society isn't that rich.

But you do not judge people's lives only from the material point 17 of view. Suppose that these two have brought up their children to respect the parents' hard work, to be curious about the world, to study in school, to take pleasure in family and community life, to consider themselves worthwhile people, to work hard and think about the future, to become skilled tradesmen or even professionals as adults, and to bring grandchildren to visit. If this is a dead end rather than a human accomplishment worthy of honor and admiration, then it's hard to know what life is about. And what makes it not a dead end is the cultural tissue of beliefs, values, and relationships that make family life meaningful and sustaining and that permit the rise of the next generation. Change that dimension, without changing the economic circumstances, and you've changed everything.

To say that young people are right to choose not to work rather 18 than to take "dead-end" jobs flipping hamburgers is an equally destructive devaluation of the work ethic that lifts people out of poverty. Says Wharton professor Herbert Northrup: "Dead-end jobs get people into the system. Fast-food outlets teach people how to go to work, to dress clean, to deal with people. Those who can go forward, do." Adds Harvard psychologist Jerome Kagan: "That's the American story—you start by flipping hamburgers."

How radically the great American Cultural Revolution changed 19 values, assumptions, and institutions is a familiar story that needs only brief retelling. It happened in the Sixties and Seventies, though it was foreshadowed a century ago, when writers and artists first started thinking of themselves as an avant-garde dedicated to dumbfounding the bourgeoisie and dancing upon its straitlaced values. A generation ago, ten years before the Summer of Love, a young and promising Norman Mailer proclaimed in an essay, "The White Negro," a new kind of man. He was the hipster, who knew from the atom bomb and the concentration camps that societies and states were murderous, and that under the shadow of mass annihilation one should learn what ghetto blacks already knew. One should learn from ghetto culture, Mailer said, to give up "the sophisticated inhibitions of civilization," to live in the moment, to follow the body and not the mind, "to divorce oneself from society" and "follow the rebellious imperative of the self," to forget "the single mate, the solid family, and the respectable love life," to choose a life of "Saturday night kicks," especially orgasm and marijuana. For 1957, this was prophetic: It contained in a nutshell much of the cultural program of the Sixties. Says political scientist Lawrence Mead: "It's precisely the more anarchic aspects of black culture that became popularized as white culture in the Sixties."

Yes, the Sixties were 20 years ago and more, and yes, belaboring 20
them now might seem like flogging a dead horse. But large, ingrained, intergenerational social pathologies such as homelessness and underclass culture don't spring up overnight from trivial causes. They are the mature harvest of seed sown by the Haves and rooted years ago. You can't hope to cure them without knowing what caused and furthered them.

What's more, while culture does evolve by gradual steps, the 21
really important shifts often occur in wholesale leaps that change the entire game rather than only a rule or two. In important cultural respects, America is still living under the sign of Aquarius, however worn and faded after the eras of hyperinflation and Reagan.

You doubt it? Then take a walk through the encampments of the 22
homeless in America's western cities—in Phoenix, say, or Santa Barbara—and look at the crowds of young men, mostly white, in their 20s, dressed like refugees from the Summer of Love: calico headbands, shoulder-length hair, torn jeans, black T-shirts emblazoned with Harley-Davidson or Grateful Dead logos.

Many of them are homeless because they are enslaved by the 23
specious liberation whose troops have worn that uniform for the past two decades. When middle-class college kids began their fling with "protest," drugs, sexual experimentation, and dropping out in the Sixties, they had a margin of safety because of their class. Working-class kids who today enlist under that washed-out banner, now *démodé*,[2] run a bigger risk. Once they drop out, some may never get back in, like these young men in the homeless encampments, devoid of skills, discipline, or direction, and most of them—along with one-third of the homeless nationwide—dependent on drugs, alcohol, or both.

Many have apparently been neglected or abused by families 24
whose disturbance or breakup is part of the general cultural unraveling. Deprived of family support and guidance, these young people feel they have little to turn to in the larger culture beyond the "freedom" that has landed them here, with petulantly angry looks understandably on their faces. Says Northwestern University sociologist Christopher Jencks: "One way to read the Sixties is to

2. Old-fashioned, antiquated.

say it was a failed experiment whose price was paid by the Have-Nots. The rest of us landed on our feet."

Leave the poor of these sunny, open-air encampments for the   25
ghetto underclass and you come upon a nightmare parody of
liberated Sixties culture. Sexual liberation? In urban ghettos like
New York's central Harlem, around 80% of all babies are born out
of wedlock, many to women still in their teens. Calvin Watkins, 31,
liberated with a vengeance, boasts to reporters that he has 19 children by four women, two of whom live with him in a Brooklyn
welfare hotel with nine of the kids: a tax-supported commune.

Drugs? Just when college kids started turning on with mari-   26
juana, the heroin epidemic overwhelmed the ghetto: Harlem and
Newark after 1966, Detroit after 1970. Now with crack cheap and
pervasive, the drug epidemic and the criminality that attends it are
even more nightmarish: 13-year-old pushers walk the streets, one
pocket crammed with a pistol they don't hesitate to use, the other
with twenties, fifties, hundreds. And crack is one of the main roads
to big-city homeless shelters, the subbasement of underclass life,
where you find pathology much more often than mere misfortune.
As for dropping out, 40% to 60% of inner city high school kids
don't graduate; as adults, a large but unknown proportion do not
work.

What made the Sixties so decisive a cultural break was that   27
protesting students won over many professors to their adversarial
stance. Once established in such central culture-disseminating institutions as the universities, the Sixties liberation mentality went
on to change the characters of other important American institutions—the law and the welfare system, for instance—through
which it reached out to affect the lives of the poor in concrete ways.

Shot through with racism, elitism, repression, capitalist exploita-   28
tion, and militarism—shouted the students—the existing social order had no legitimacy, and had even less by the early Seventies,
when radical feminists added sexism to the indictment. What relevance, students demanded, had a traditional college education to
all this injustice? In response, professors jettisoned *Paradise Lost*,
Plato, and Machiavelli in favor of *One Flew Over the Cuckoo's Nest*
and an array of now-forgotten contemporary leftist ideologues.

Soon professors decided that the Western cultural inheritance   29
they were entrusted to transmit was really part of the problem.
Plato, Milton, and their ilk were themselves elitists, sexists, racists.
For that reason, the values such writers embodied, however seemingly worthwhile, were fatally flawed and without authority. Men
like this couldn't really know what is true and good. The study

of literature and history became a study of how Western society and culture had victimized women, blacks, workers, the exploited poor. Don't think this is ancient history: The much-publicized dropping of some core classics from Stanford University's Western Culture program in favor of works by or about women, blacks, and non-Westerners is a new example. Utterly lost is the understanding that Western culture and society in general—and American society in particular, despite Vietnam and Watergate—are stupendous human achievements.

Inevitably these attitudes have filtered down into public schools.   30
There the children of the underclass, who get so little acculturation into the mainstream at home, no longer find a value-laden curriculum of myths and imagination-stirring tales of the Pilgrims and Squanto, say, or of the life of Marie Curie, that are the way a culture transmits its values and beliefs to children. Instead they find a curriculum so dedicated to escape being racist, sexist, and the rest that it has become virtually content-free.

Laws embody a culture's most strongly held values. But the   31
confusion about values that has pervaded the less tangible areas of American culture has also seeped into the legal system. In criminal law the results have been devastating, above all to the poor. Says Walter Williams: "The Sixties and Seventies accepted the whole philosophy of victimization—the criminal is viewed as the victim of society." Because of unjust economic deprivation, racism, or inequality, society rather than the criminal is responsible for his crime; he was driven to it, and society only compounds the injury by arresting and punishing him. At least partly in this spirit, the federal courts vastly expanded the procedural rights of criminal suspects.

Exactly when they were doing it, crime soared. Between 1963   32
and 1980 the robbery and rape rates almost quadrupled, the burglary and assault rates tripled, the murder rate more than doubled. And in the Sixties, while the overall crime rate was doubling, the prison population fell. In the mid-Seventies the average Chicago youthful offender was arrested more than 13 times before being sent to reform school. Today, if you're *convicted* of a serious crime in the U.S., the odds are better than 2 to 1 that you will not go to jail.

By reducing the risk that crime will bring punishment and by   33
asserting that a lawbreaker is not fully responsible for the evil he does, the culture of the Haves has affected the Have-Nots by making it easier for them to become criminals. And the poor who don't choose crime? The culture of the Haves devalues their achievement and the tremendous effort their respectability has cost them by not

holding the wrongdoers responsible. That's one less incentive to struggle.

The poor who do right suffer from the law's flaccidity in starker 34 ways. Says lawyer Edward Hayes, a former Bronx prosecutor and the model for the defense lawyer in Tom Wolfe's *The Bonfire of the Vanities*: "Most victims of crime are honest working people who happen to live in neighborhoods that have the underclass. In urban areas the hardest physical jobs are held by people who have to kill themselves to stay one step ahead of the underclass—and then they go home and the underclass is jumping on their backs."

Even more than the law, the welfare system is the institution 35 that the culture of the Haves reshaped in the Sixties to give the supposedly victimized poor little incentive to struggle out of their poverty. Since the mid-Sixties, a combination of Aid to Families with Dependent Children (the main welfare program), food stamps, Medicaid, and other benefits has provided welfare mothers with enough money to allow them to support their babies. In big, urban states, the financial package provides even more purchasing power than they could earn from a minimum-wage job. Becoming pregnant without a husband—something for which ample incentives already exist—is hardly a worry if one consequence is an income on which you can get by. Because welfare fosters passivity and a sense of worthlessness, it is especially hard to break out of the system and stop having illegitimate babies once you've started. Instead of helping the poor succeed, welfare gives them "incentives to fail," says political scientist Charles Murray, whose pioneering book *Losing Ground* showed how welfare helps perpetuate the underclass way of life.

One of the Sixties clichés was that society was like a mental 36 institution in which the gentle inhabitants were sane and the sadistic officials were crazy. That's the theme of *One Flew Over the Cuckoo's Nest*, and counterculture psychiatrists of the time presented madness as a rational response to an insane social order, an "alternate life-style" that didn't justify locking people up. These notions were part of a climate of opinion that utterly transformed the nation's mental health system, starting in 1963. The result: 100,000 to 150,000 severely mentally ill people, who in a more rational state of society would be under psychiatric care, now wander the streets homeless—one-third of America's homeless population, and the most visible and disturbing fraction of it.

Patients dumped from state hospitals into a virtually nonexistent 37 care system stopped taking their medicine, got crazier, and formed the first wave of the homeless. The current wave of the mentally ill homeless are younger people who were never institutionalized or medicated and who often make themselves sicker by using dope or alcohol to try to quiet the voices they hear.

When the Haves ask what responsibility they bear for the plight   38
of the poor, they ask because they want to help. It would debase their lives, they feel, to be implicated in degradation they didn't try to relieve. What more, they wonder, should they be doing? Says Charles Murray: "The emotional problem for the middle class is very real—but unrelated to the actual problem."

The bitter paradox is that much of what the Haves have done to   39
help the poor—out of decent and generous motives—is part of the problem. Like a driver pumping the gas into a flooded engine, the more help they bestow, the less able do the poor become to help themselves. The first thing the Haves should do is to stop pouring on more of what doesn't work. Says Thomas Sowell: "If people could just stop making things worse, it would be an enormously greater contribution than they're likely to make any other way."

Several signs hint that the culture might be turning in the direc-   40
tion Sowell indicates. Citizens are assessing the full menace of crack and its consequences, of an underclass that not only commits crimes but creates an atmosphere of pervasive threat in urban public spaces, of an untreated mentally ill population that not only erupts in brutal murders but also regularly yells threats at luckless passers-by, grabs or shoves them, and terrorizes children. Longtime liberal journalist Pete Hamill recently wrote a lead article in *Esquire* saying that after 25 years of enormous racial progress in America, it is no longer possible to blame white racism when trying to explain why so many black Americans fall into the underclass. Tom Wolfe's *The Bonfire of the Vanities*, a novel that emphatically does not depict the poor as victims, has been a best-seller for months.

The welfare reform movement is the most visible trend in the   41
right direction. The best workfare systems that welfare reform has produced aim at establishing a new norm: People are responsible for working for a living. Says Lawrence Mead: "That's the thing that's lacking in their lives—the sense of being responsible for anything at all."

What remains to do? It is often said that U.S. poverty is espe-   42
cially cruel because ever larger numbers of those below the poverty line are children. But how could it be otherwise, when the qualification for getting on welfare is having a child? The really iniquitous feature of the welfare system is that it offers incentives for the least

competent women to become the mothers of the next generation, perpetuating the underclass.

Welfare reform will come to grips with the underclass problem only if it removes every incentive to have an illegitimate child that the state will have to support—for instance by requiring girls under 18, at least, to live either with their parents or in state-run, supervised group homes to receive welfare benefits. Reformers will also need to include these women in workfare programs, most of which now miss them by exempting women with children under 6.

Chances for the most dramatic improvement are not with welfare mothers but with their children. Why wait until they are welfare mothers themselves to rescue them? Helping them requires child care and child development courses for the mothers and an expanded Head Start program for the kids. After that, schools must pass on values and aspirations that make children citizens rather than dependents.

The most useful contribution America's mainstream can make to the poor is to carve a new channel toward such values. They form a familiar destination, for these are the old American norms: that everyone is responsible for his fate; that we believe in freedom under the rule of law; that the public, communal life is a boon and not an oppression; that with energy, ingenuity, and skill you can make your own fate; that poverty should not so disable a child that he can't grow up to be President. If America ever really declines, it will not be because of military obligations that outstrip its economic capacity, as Paul Kennedy's best-selling *The Rise and Fall of the Great Powers* argues. It will be because it has lost confidence in its own most basic beliefs.

TONI CADE BAMBARA

The Lesson

Toni Cade Bambara (1939–   ) was born in New York City and educated at Queens College and City College, New York, with additional study of theater, mime, dance, film, and linguistics at eight other institutions in Europe and America. Prodigiously talented and politically committed, she has been a welfare investigator, a community organizer, a literacy instructor, a college professor, and a director of plays and films. As a writer, she works to "lift up a few useable truths" in a "racist, hard-headed, heedless society." But she also says that writing is a way for her to "hear myself, check myself," a discipline that makes her more honest and clear-headed. In a story like "The Lesson" (from *Gorilla, My Love,* 1972), both of Bambara's motives for writing seem to be at work. In a way, the story is a parable, plotted with a lesson in mind, but the parable comes to life because Bambara is writing about people and streets she knows. Bambara has published a second book of short stories, *The Sea Birds Are Still Alive* (1977), and two novels, *The Salt Eaters* (1980), and *If Blessing Comes* (1987).

Back in the days when everyone was old and stupid or young and foolish and me and Sugar were the only ones just right, this lady moved on our block with nappy hair and proper speech and no makeup. And quite naturally we laughed at her, laughed the way we did at the junk man who went about his business like he was some big-time president and his sorry-ass horse his secretary. And we kinda hated her too, hated the way we did the winos who cluttered up our parks and pissed on our handball walls and stank up our hallways and stairs so you couldn't halfway play hide-and-seek without a goddamn gas mask. Miss Moore was her name. The only woman on the block with no first name. And she was black as hell, cept for her feet, which were fish-white and spooky. And she was always planning these boring-ass things for us to do, us being my cousin, mostly, who lived on the block cause we all moved North the same time and to the same apartment then spread out gradual to breathe. And our parents would yank our heads into some kinda shape and crisp up our clothes so we'd be presentable for travel with Miss Moore, who always looked like she was going to church, though she never did. Which is just one of the things the grownups talked about when they talked behind her back like a dog. But when she came calling with some sachet she'd sewed up or some gingerbread she'd made or some book, why then they'd all be too embarrassed to turn her down and we'd get handed over all spruced up. She'd been to college and said it was only right that she should take responsibility for the young ones' education, and she not even related by marriage or blood. So they'd go for it. Specially Aunt Gretchen. She was the main gofer in the family. You got some ole dumb shit foolishness you want somebody to go for, you send for Aunt Gretchen. She been screwed into the go-along for so long, it's a blood-deep natural thing with her. Which is how she got saddled with me and Sugar and Junior in the first place while our mothers were in a la-de-da apartment up the block having a good ole time.

So this one day Miss Moore rounds us all up at the mailbox and   2
it's puredee hot and she's knockin herself out about arithmetic.
And school suppose to let up in summer I heard, but she don't
never let up. And the starch in my pinafore scratching the shit
outta me and I'm really hating this nappy-head bitch and her goddamn college degree. I'd much rather go to the pool or to the show
where it's cool. So me and Sugar leaning on the mailbox being
surly, which is a Miss Moore word. And Flyboy checking out what
everybody brought for lunch. And Fat Butt already wasting his
peanut-butter-and-jelly sandwich like the pig he is. And Junebug
punchin on Q.T.'s arm for potato chips. And Rosie Giraffe shifting
from one hip to the other waiting for somebody to step on her foot
or ask her if she from Georgia so she can kick ass, preferably
Mercedes'. And Miss Moore asking us do we know what money is,
like we a bunch of retards. I mean real money, she say, like it's only
poker chips or monopoly papers we lay on the grocer. So right
away I'm tired of this and say so. And would much rather snatch
Sugar and go to the Sunset and terrorize the West Indian kids and
take their hair ribbons and their money too. And Miss Moore files
that remark away for next week's lesson on brotherhood, I can tell.
And finally I say we oughta get to the subway cause it's cooler and
besides we might meet some cute boys. Sugar done swiped her
mama's lipstick, so we ready.

So we heading down the street and she's boring us silly about   3
what things cost and what our parents make and how much goes
for rent and how money ain't divided up right in this country. And
then she gets to the part about we all poor and live in the slums,
which I don't feature. And I'm ready to speak on that, but she steps
out in the street and hails two cabs just like that. Then she hustles
half the crew in with her and hands me a five-dollar bill and tells
me to calculate 10 percent tip for the driver. And we're off. Me and
Sugar and Junebug and Flyboy hangin out the window and hollering to everybody, putting lipstick on each other cause Flyboy a
faggot anyway, and making farts with our sweaty armpits. But I'm
mostly trying to figure how to spend this money. But they all
fascinated with the meter ticking and Junebug starts laying bets as
to how much it'll read when Flyboy can't hold his breath no more.
Then Sugar lays bets as to how much it'll be when we get there. So
I'm stuck. Don't nobody want to go for my plan, which is to jump
out at the next light and run off to the first bar-b-que we can find.
Then the driver tells us to get the hell out cause we there already.
And the meter reads eighty-five cents. And I'm stalling to figure
out the tip and Sugar say give him a dime. And I decide he don't
need it bad as I do, so later for him. But then he tries to take off

with Junebug foot still in the door so we talk about his mama something ferocious. Then we check out that we on Fifth Avenue and everybody dressed up in stockings. One lady in a fur coat, hot as it is. White folks crazy.

"This is the place," Miss Moore say, presenting it to us in the voice she uses at the museum. "Let's look in the windows before we go in."   4

"Can we steal?" Sugar asks very serious like she's getting the ground rules squared away before she plays. "I beg your pardon," say Miss Moore, and we fall out. So she leads us around the windows of the toy store and me and Sugar screamin, "This is mine, that's mine, I gotta have that, that was made for me, I was born for that," till Big Butt drowns us out.   5

"Hey, I'm goin to buy that there."   6
"That there? You don't even know what it is, stupid."   7
"I do so," he say punchin on Rosie Giraffe. "It's a microscope."   8
"Whatcha gonna do with a microscope, fool?"   9
"Look at things."   10
"Like what, Ronald?" ask Miss Moore. And Big Butt ain't got   11
the first notion. So here go Miss Moore gabbing about the thousands of bacteria in a drop of water and the somethinorother in a speck of blood and the million and one living things in the air around us is invisible to the naked eye. And what she say that for? Junebug go to town on that "naked" and we rolling. Then Miss Moore ask what it cost. So we all jam into the window smudgin it up and the price tag say $300. So then she ask how long'd take for Big Butt and Junebug to save up their allowances. "Too long," I say. "Yeh," adds Sugar, "outgrown it by that time." And Miss Moore say no, you never outgrow learning instruments. "Why, even medical students and interns and," blah, blah, blah. And we ready to choke Big Butt for bringing it up in the first damn place.

"This here costs four hundred eighty dollars," say Rosie Giraffe.   12
So we pile up all over her to see what she pointin out. My eyes tell me it's a chunk of glass cracked with something heavy, and different-color inks dripped into the splits, then the whole thing put into a oven or something. But for $480 it don't make sense.

"That's a paperweight made of semi-precious stones fused together under tremendous pressure," she explains slowly, with her hands doing the mining and all the factory work.   13

"So what's a paperweight?" asks Rosie Giraffe.   14

"To weigh paper with, dumbbell," say Flyboy, the wise man   15
from the East.

"Not exactly," say Miss Moore, which is what she say when you   16
warm or way off too. "It's to weigh paper down so it won't scatter

and make your desk untidy." So right away me and Sugar curtsy to each other and then to Mercedes who is more the tidy type.

"We don't keep paper on top of the desk in my class," say 17 Junebug, figuring Miss Moore crazy or lyin one.

"At home, then," she say. "Don't you have a calendar and a 18 pencil case and a blotter and a letter-opener on your desk at home where you do your homework?" And she know damn well what our homes look like cause she nosys around in them every chance she gets.

"I don't even have a desk," say Junebug. "Do we?" 19

"No. And I don't get no homework neither," says Big Butt. 20

"And I don't even have a home," say Flyboy like he do at school 21 to keep the white folks off his back and sorry for him. Send this poor kid to camp posters, is his specialty.

"I do," says Mercedes. "I have a box of stationery on my desk 22 and a picture of my cat. My godmother bought the stationery and the desk. There's a big rose on each sheet and the envelopes smell like roses."

"Who wants to know about your smelly-ass stationery," say 23 Rosie Giraffe fore I can get my two cents in.

"It's important to have a work area all your own so that . . ." 24

"Will you look at this sailboat, please," say Flyboy, cuttin her off 25 and pointin to the thing like it was his. So once again we tumble all over each other to gaze at this magnificent thing in the toy store which is just big enough to maybe sail two kittens across the pond if you strap them to the posts tight. We all start reciting the price tag like we in assembly. "Hand-crafted sailboat of fiberglass at one thousand one hundred ninety-five dollars."

"Unbelievable," I hear myself say and am really stunned. I read 26 it again for myself just in case the group recitation put me in a trance. Same thing. For some reason this pisses me off. We look at Miss Moore and she lookin at us, waiting for I dunno what.

"Who'd pay all that when you can buy a sailboat set for a quar- 27 ter at Pop's, a tube of glue for a dime, and a ball of string for eight cents? It must have a motor and a whole lot else besides," I say. "My sailboat cost me about fifty cents."

"But will it take water?" say Mercedes with her smart ass. 28

"Took mine to Alley Pond Park once," say Flyboy. "String 29 broke. Lost it. Pity."

"Sailed mine in Central Park and it keeled over and sank. Had to 30 ask my father for another dollar."

"And you got the strap," laugh Big Butt. "The jerk didn't even 31 have a string on it. My old man wailed on his behind."

Little Q.T. was staring hard at the sailboat and you could see he 32

wanted it bad. But he too little and somebody'd just take it from
him. So what the hell. "This boat for kids, Miss Moore?"

"Parents silly to buy something like that just to get all broke up,"   33
say Rosie Giraffe.

"That much money it should last forever," I figure.   34

"My father'd buy it for me if I wanted it."   35

"Your father, my ass," say Rosie Giraffe getting a chance to   36
finally push Mercedes.

"Must be rich people shop here," say Q.T.   37

"You are a very bright boy," say Flyboy. "What was your first   38
clue?" And he rap him on the head with the back of his knuckles,
since Q.T. the only one he could get away with. Though Q.T. liable
to come up behind you years later and get his licks in when you
half expect it.

"What I want to know is," I says to Miss Moore though I never   39
talk to her, I wouldn't give the bitch that satisfaction, "is how
much a real boat costs? I figure a thousand'd get you a yacht any
day."

"Why don't you check that out," she says, "and report back to   40
the group?" Which really pains my ass. If you gonna mess up a
perfectly good swim day least you could do is have some answers.
"Let's go in," she say like she got something up her sleeve. Only
she don't lead the way. So me and Sugar turn the corner to where
the entrance is, but when we get there I kinda hang back. Not that
I'm scared, what's there to be afraid of, just a toy store. But I feel
funny, shame. But what I got to be shamed about? Got as much
right to go in as anybody. But somehow I can't seem to get hold of
the door, so I step away from Sugar to lead. But she hangs back
too. And I look at her and she looks at me and this is ridiculous. I
mean, damn, I have never ever been shy about doing nothing or
going nowhere. But then Mercedes steps up and then Rosie Giraffe
and Big Butt crowd in behind and shove, and next thing we all
stuffed into the doorway with only Mercedes squeezing past us,
smoothing out her jumper and walking right down the aisle. Then
the rest of us tumble in like a glued-together jigsaw done all wrong.
And people lookin at us. And it's like the time me and Sugar
crashed into the Catholic church on a dare. But once we got in
there and everything so hushed and holy and the candles and the
bowin and the handkerchiefs on all the drooping heads, I just
couldn't go through with the plan. Which was for me to run up to
the altar and do a tap dance while Sugar played the nose flute and
messed around in the holy water. And Sugar kept givin me the
elbow. Then later teased me so bad I tied her up in the shower and
turned it on and locked her in. And she'd be there till this day if

Aunt Gretchen hadn't finally figured I was lyin about the boarder takin a shower.

Same thing in the store. We all walkin on tiptoe and hardly   41
touchin the games and puzzles and things. And I watched Miss Moore who is steady watchin us like she waitin for a sign. Like Mama Drewery watches the sky and sniffs the air and takes note of just how much slant is in the bird formation. Then me and Sugar bump smack into each other, so busy gazing at the toys, 'specially the sailboat. But we don't laugh and go into our fat-lady bump-stomach routine. We just stare at that price tag. Then Sugar run a finger over the whole boat. And I'm jealous and want to hit her. Maybe not her, but I sure want to punch somebody in the mouth.

"Watcha bring us here for, Miss Moore?"   42

"You sound angry, Sylvia. Are you mad about something?"   43
Givin me one of them grins like she tellin a grown-up joke that never turns out to be funny. And she's lookin very closely at me like maybe she plannin to do my portrait from memory. I'm mad, but I won't give her that satisfaction. So I slouch around the store bein very bored and say, "Let's go."

Me and Sugar at the back of the train watchin the tracks whizzin   44
by large then small then gettin gobbled up in the dark. I'm thinkin about this tricky toy I saw in the store. A clown that somersaults on a bar then does chin-ups just cause you yank lightly at his leg. Cost $35. I could see me askin my mother for a $35 birthday clown. "You wanna who that costs what?" she'd say, cocking her head to the side to get a better view of the hole in my head. Thirty-five dollars could buy new bunk beds for Junior and Gretchen's boy. Thirty-five dollars and the whole household could go visit Grand-daddy Nelson in the country. Thirty-five dollars would pay for the rent and the piano bill too. Who are these people that spend that much for performing clowns and $1000 for toy sailboats? What kinda work they do and how they live and how come we ain't in on it? Where we are is who we are, Miss Moore always pointin out. But it don't necessarily have to be that way, she always adds then waits for somebody to say that poor people have to wake up and demand their share of the pie and don't none of us know what kind of pie she talking about in the first damn place. But she ain't so smart cause I still got her four dollars from the taxi and she sure ain't gettin it. Messin up my day with this shit. Sugar nudges me in my pocket and winks.

Miss Moore lines us up in front of the mailbox where we started   45
from, seem like years ago, and I got a headache for thinkin so hard. And we lean all over each other so we can hold up under the draggy ass lecture she always finishes us off with at the end before

we thank her for borin us to tears. But she just looks at us like she readin tea leaves. Finally she say, "Well, what did you think of F.A.O. Schwarz?"

Rosie Giraffe mumbles, "White folks crazy."   46

"I'd like to go there again when I get my birthday money," says   47 Mercedes, and we shove her out the pack so she has to lean on the mailbox by herself.

"I'd like a shower. Tiring day," say Flyboy.   48

Then Sugar surprises me by sayin, "You know, Miss Moore, I   49 don't think all of us here put together eat in a year what that sailboat costs." And Miss Moore lights up like somebody goosed her. "And?" she say, urging Sugar on. Only I'm standin on her foot so she don't continue.

"Imagine for a minute what kind of society it is in which some   50 people can spend on a toy what it would cost to feed a family of six or seven. What do you think?"

"I think," say Sugar pushing me off her feet like she never done   51 before, cause I whip her ass in a minute, "that this is not much of a democracy if you ask me. Equal chance to pursue happiness means an equal crack at the dough, don't it?" Miss Moore is besides herself and I am disgusted with Sugar's treachery. So I stand on her foot one more time to see if she'll shove me. She shuts up, and Miss Moore looks at me, sorrowfully I'm thinkin. And somethin weird is goin on, I can feel it in my chest.

"Anybody else learn anything today?" lookin dead at me. I walk   52 away and Sugar has to run to catch up and don't even seem to notice when I shrug her arm off my shoulder.

"Well, we got four dollars anyway," she says.   53

"Uh hunh."   54

"We could go to Hascombs and get half a chocolate layer and   55 then go to the Sunset and still have plenty money for potato chips and ice cream sodas."

"Uh hunh."   56

"Race you to Hascombs," she say.   57

We start down the block and she gets ahead which is O.K. by me   58 cause I'm going to the West End and then over to the Drive to think this day through. She can run if she want to and even run faster. But ain't nobody gonna beat me at nuthin.

THE SPAN
OF LIFE

The Span of Life: Preview

E. B. WHITE Once More to the Lake 823

I would be in the middle of some simple act, I would be picking up a bait box or laying down a table fork, or I would be saying something, and suddenly it would be not I but my father who was saying the words or making the gesture.

SIMONE DE BEAUVOIR The Coming of Age 829

Buddha recognized his own fate in the person of a very aged man, because, being born to save humanity, he chose to take upon himself the entirety of the human state. In this he differed from the rest of mankind, for they evade those aspects of it that distress them. And above all they evade old age. The Americans have struck the word death out of their vocabulary.

WILLIAM MANCHESTER My Old Man: The Last Years of H. L. Mencken 835

In that first year of his disability he refused to allow anyone to read to him, refused to look at magazines with enlarged print, and wouldn't even listen to phonograph records. In one of his few remaining flashes of humor he hoarsely told me, "When I get to heaven, I'm going to speak to God very sharply."

MALCOLM COWLEY The View from Eighty 851

The new octogenarian feels as strong as ever when he is sitting back in a comfortable chair. He ruminates, he dreams, he remembers. He doesn't want to be disturbed by others. It seems to him that old age is only a costume assumed for those others; the true, the essential self is ageless.

PATRICIA HAMPL Teresa 862

There are several indications that she went through the spiritual cleansing that saints and mystics describe. I was most struck when my father told me that she had said, apropos of nothing (not even of pain: there wasn't a lot of pain at the end), "Well, I think it's time to die tonight." And she did.

Overview and Ideas for Writing

The summer I turned twenty-three I spent two weeks doing
practically nothing except reading the poetry and sermons of John
Donne, one of Shakespeare's most famous contemporaries. It was
an alarming experience. The poetry is so filled with plagues, funeral shrouds, cemeteries, and worm-riddled carcasses that I once
found myself reading with my hand on my throat, subconsciously
checking my carotid pulse. The last straw was Isaak Walton's description of Donne's final days, including the painting of his funeral
portrait. From his sickbed, Donne had ordered a carver to make a
wooden pedestal in the shape of a burial urn. When it was finished,
he had several fires lit to keep the chill out of his study, then

> . . . he brought with him into that place his winding-sheet in his hand,
> and having put off all his clothes, had this sheet put on him, and so
> tied with knots at his head and feet, and his hands so placed as dead
> bodies are usually fitted, to be shrowded and put into their coffin, or
> grave. Upon this Urn he thus stood, with his eyes shut, and with so
> much of the sheet turned aside as might shew his lean, pale, and
> death-like face, which was purposely turned toward the East, from
> whence he expected the second coming of his and our Saviour Jesus.
> In this posture he was drawn at this just height; and when the picture
> was fully finished, he caused it to be set by his bedside, where it
> continued and became his hourly object till his death. . . .

All this was too much for me, and I wrote an essay that was supposed to be about Donne the poet but was really about Donne the morbid neurotic.

My teacher quietly dismantled my thesis at our next meeting. He reminded me that as a baby-boom American I was part of the first generation on earth to concern itself seriously with tooth decay. He guessed (quite rightly) that my health was robust, that all my siblings were alive, that my father was still capable of beating me at tennis, that my mother could nearly pass for a college student, and that my grandparents were aging quietly in some distant city and would die under professional supervision in a hospital. Donne, on the other hand, experienced life and death the old-fashioned way. Two of his siblings died in infancy, and three others in childhood. His father died when he was four. Of Donne's own twelve children, three died in childhood and two were stillborn. His wife died in childbirth. When Donne was in his fifties, the plague, which had killed his brother thirty years earlier, returned. Donne buried hundreds of his parishioners and reported that in the summer of 1625 a thousand people per day were dying of the disease. To have lived almost six decades in so perilous a world had made Donne very familiar with death and trained him to face his own. A young person of my generation, my teacher said, might try to avoid death by looking the other way: For most of human history there had been no other way to look.

Looking the other way, he added, would only serve so long. He smiled and turned around to show me the bald spot on his head: his *memento mori*, the equivalent of the skull that scholars of Donne's time kept on their writing tables.

This unit, inspired by the memory of my conversation with Dr. Wilders, is dominated by other memories of encounters between people at different points in the span of life. Time spent with their children remind E. B. White and Annie Dillard that they have lived through a turn of generations. Patricia Hampl remembers the last years of her grandmother, William Manchester the last years of the man whose example shaped his life. Malcolm Cowley gives us "a road map and guide" to life at eighty, and Alice Walker, in a story based on her own experience, remembers with fondness a man "revived" so often that he lived to be ninety.

Clearly, the broadest invitation the unit opens to you is to write about your own memories of your relationship with someone from another generation. But there is another invitation as well. Simone de Beauvoir's essay, written in 1970, condemns society's attitudes toward the very old. A generation has now passed, and you might fruitfully compare our attitudes today toward "the old person that we must become."

E. B. WHITE

Once More to the Lake

E(lwyn) B(rooks) White (1899–1985) was a brilliant writer for
The New Yorker and *Harper's Magazine* (see "Twins" p. 147, and
"Progress and Change," p. 269). Though he was a man with an
almost proverbial sunny disposition, he had from middle age
forward fears of a premature death. Despite "a few noisy and ill-
timed farewells," however, he compared himself to "a drunk at a
wedding he is enjoying to the hilt and has no real intention of
leaving." In his eighty-fourth year he wrote to a friend, "I have
first degree heart block, have lost the sight of my right eye because of a degenerated retina, can't wind my wrist watch because
my fingers have knuckled under to arthritis. . . . On the other
hand, I am camped alone, here at Bert Mosher's Camps on the
shore of the Great Pond I first visited in 1904." When White's
death came two years later, William Shawn, editor of *The New
Yorker*, issued a memorable tribute: "His literary style was as
pure as any in our language. It was singular, colloquial, clear,
unforced, thoroughly American and utterly beautiful. Because of
his gentle influence, several generations of this country's writers
will write better than they might have. He never wrote a mean or
careless sentence." "Once More to the Lake" was published in
Harper's Magazine in August 1941.

One summer, along about 1904, my father rented a camp on a   1
lake in Maine and took us all there for the month of August. We all
got ringworm from some kittens and had to rub Pond's Extract on
our arms and legs night and morning, and my father rolled over in
a canoe with all his clothes on; but outside of that the vacation was
a success and from then on none of us ever thought there was any
place in the world like that lake in Maine. We returned summer
after summer—always on August 1st for one month. I have since
become a salt-water man, but sometimes in summer there are days
when the restlessness of the tides and the fearful cold of the sea
water and the incessant wind which blows across the afternoon
and into the evening make me wish for the placidity of a lake in the
woods. A few weeks ago this feeling got so strong I bought myself a
couple of bass hooks and a spinner and returned to the lake where
we used to go, for a week's fishing and to revisit old haunts.

I took along my son, who had never had any fresh water up his   2
nose and who had seen lily pads only from train windows. On the
journey over to the lake I began to wonder what it would be like.

I wondered how time would have marred this unique, this holy spot—the coves and streams, the hills that the sun set behind, the camps and the paths behind the camps. I was sure the tarred road would have found it out and I wondered in what other ways it would be desolated. It is strange how much you can remember about places like that once you allow your mind to return into the grooves which lead back. You remember one thing, and that suddenly reminds you of another thing. I guess I remembered clearest of all the early mornings, when the lake was cool and motionless, remembered how the bedroom smelled of the lumber it was made of and of the wet woods whose scent entered through the screen. The partitions in the camp were thin and did not extend clear to the top of the rooms, and as I was always the first up I would dress softly so as not to wake the others, and sneak out into the sweet outdoors and start out in the canoe, keeping close along the shore in the long shadows of the pines. I remembered being very careful never to rub my paddle against the gunwale for fear of disturbing the stillness of the cathedral.

The lake had never been what you would call a wild lake. There were cottages sprinkled around the shores, and it was in farming country although the shores of the lake were quite heavily wooded. Some of the cottages were owned by nearby farmers, and you would live at the shore and eat your meals at the farmhouse. That's what our family did. But although it wasn't wild, it was a fairly large and undisturbed lake and there were places in it which, to a child at least, seemed infinitely remote and primeval.

I was right about the tar: it led to within half a mile of the shore. But when I got back there, with my boy, and we settled into a camp near a farmhouse and into the kind of summertime I had known, I could tell that it was going to be pretty much the same as it had been before—I knew it, lying in bed the first morning, smelling the bedroom, and hearing the boy sneak quietly out and go off along the shore in a boat. I began to sustain the illusion that he was I, and therefore, by simple transposition, that I was my father. This sensation persisted, kept cropping up all the time we were there. It was not an entirely new feeling, but in this setting it grew much stronger. I seemed to be living a dual existence. I would be in the middle of some simple act, I would be picking up a bait box or laying down a table fork, or I would be saying something, and suddenly it would be not I but my father who was saying the words or making the gesture. It gave me a creepy sensation.

We went fishing the first morning. I felt the same damp moss covering the worms in the bait can, and saw the dragonfly alight on the tip of my rod as it hovered a few inches from the surface of the water. It was the arrival of this fly that convinced me beyond any doubt that everything was as it always had been, that the years were a mirage and there had been no years. The small waves were the same, chucking the rowboat under the chin as we fished at anchor, and the boat was the same boat, the same color green and the ribs broken in the same places, and under the floor-boards the same fresh-water leavings and débris—the dead helgramite,[1] the wisps of moss, the rusty discarded fishhook, the dried blood from yesterday's catch. We stared silently at the tips of our rods, at the dragonflies that came and went. I lowered the tip of mine into the water, tentatively, pensively dislodging the fly, which darted two feet away, poised, darted two feet back, and came to rest again a little farther up the rod. There had been no years between the ducking of this dragonfly and the other one—the one that was part of memory. I looked at the boy, who was silently watching his fly, and it was my hands that held his rod, my eyes watching. I felt dizzy and didn't know which rod I was at the end of.

We caught two bass, hauling them in briskly as though they were mackerel, pulling them over the side of the boat in a businesslike manner without any landing net, and stunning them with a blow on the back of the head. When we got back for a swim before lunch, the lake was exactly where we had left it, the same number of inches from the dock, and there was only the merest suggestion of a breeze. This seemed an utterly enchanted sea, this lake you could leave to its own devices for a few hours and come back to, and find that it had not stirred, this constant and trustworthy body of water. In the shallows, the dark, water-soaked sticks and twigs, smooth and old, were undulating in clusters on the bottom against the clean ribbed sand, and the track of the mussel was plain. A school of minnows swam by, each minnow with its small individual shadow, doubling the attendance, so clear and sharp in the sunlight. Some of the other campers were in swimming, along the shore, one of them with a cake of soap, and the water felt thin and clear and unsubstantial. Over the years there had been this person with the cake of soap, this cultist, and here he was. There had been no years.

Up to the farmhouse to dinner through the teeming, dusty field, the road under our sneakers was only a two-track road. The middle track was missing, the one with the marks of the hooves and the splotches of dried, flaky manure. There had always been three tracks to choose from in choosing which track to walk in; now the choice was narrowed down to two. For a moment I missed terribly

6

7

---

1. An insect larva used for bait.

the middle alternative. But the way led past the tennis court and something about the way it lay there in the sun reassured me; the tape had loosened along the backline, the alleys were green with plantains and other weeds, and the net (installed in June and removed in September) sagged in the dry noon, and the whole place steamed with midday heat and hunger and emptiness. There was a choice of pie for dessert, and one was blueberry and one was apple, and the waitresses were the same country girls, there having been no passage of time, only the illusion of it as in a dropped curtain—the waitresses were still fifteen; their hair had been washed, that was the only difference—they had been to the movies and seen the pretty girls with the clean hair.

Summertime, oh summertime, pattern of life indelible, the fade- 8 proof lake, the woods unshatterable, the pasture with the sweet-fern and the juniper forever and ever, summer without end; this was the background, and the life along the shore was the design, the cottages with their innocent and tranquil design, their tiny docks with the flagpole and the American flag floating against the white clouds in the blue sky, the little paths over the roots of the trees leading from camp to camp and the paths leading back to the outhouses and the can of lime for sprinkling, and at the souvenir counters at the store the miniature birch-bark canoes and the post cards that showed things looking a little better than they looked. This was the American family at play, escaping the city heat, wondering whether the newcomers in the camp at the head of the cove were "common" or "nice," wondering whether it was true that the people who drove up for Sunday dinner at the farm-house were turned away because there wasn't enough chicken.

It seemed to me, as I kept remembering all this, that those times 9 and those summers had been infinitely precious and worth saving. There had been jollity and peace and goodness. The arriving (at the beginning of August) had been so big a business in itself, at the railway station the farm wagon drawn up, the first smell of the pine-laden air, the first glimpse of the smiling farmer, and the great importance of the trunks and your father's enormous authority in such matters, and the feel of the wagon under you for the long ten-mile haul, and at the top of the last long hill catching the first view of the lake after eleven months of not seeing this cherished body of water. The shouts and cries of the other campers when they saw you, and the trunks to be unpacked, to give up their rich burden. (Arriving was less exciting nowadays, when you sneaked up in your car and parked it under a tree near the camp and took out the bags and in five minutes it was all over, no fuss, no loud wonderful fuss about trunks.)

Peace and goodness and jollity. The only thing that was wrong   10
now, really, was the sound of the place, an unfamiliar nervous
sound of the outboard motors. This was the note that jarred, the
one thing that would sometimes break the illusion and set the years
moving. In those other summertimes all motors were inboard;
and when they were at a little distance, the noise they made was a
sedative, an ingredient of summer sleep. They were one-cylinder
and two-cylinder engines, and some were make-and-break and
some were jump-spark, but they all made a sleepy sound across
the lake. The one-lungers throbbed and fluttered, and the twin-
cylinder ones purred and purred, and that was a quiet sound too.
But now the campers all had outboards. In the daytime, in the hot
mornings, these motors made a petulant, irritable sound; at night,
in the still evening when the afterglow lit the water, they whined
about one's ears like mosquitoes. My boy loved our rented outboard, and his great desire was to achieve singlehanded mastery
over it, and authority, and he soon learned the trick of choking it a
little (but not too much), and the adjustment of the needle valve.
Watching him I would remember the things you could do with the
old one-cylinder engine with the heavy flywheel, how you could
have it eating out of your hand if you got really close to it spiritually. Motor boats in those days didn't have clutches, and you
would make a landing by shutting off the motor at the proper time
and coasting in with a dead rudder. But there was a way of reversing them, if you learned the trick, by cutting the switch and putting
it on again exactly on the final dying revolution of the flywheel, so
that it would kick back against compression and begin reversing.
Approaching a dock in a strong following breeze, it was difficult to
slow up sufficiently by the ordinary coasting method, and if a boy
felt he had complete mastery over his motor, he was tempted to
keep it running beyond its time and then reverse it a few feet from
the dock. It took a cool nerve, because if you threw the switch a
twentieth of a second too soon you would catch the flywheel when
it still had speed enough to go up past center, and the boat would
leap ahead, charging bull-fashion at the dock.

We had a good week at the camp. The bass were biting well and   11
the sun shone endlessly, day after day. We would be tired at night
and lie down in the accumulated heat of the little bedrooms after
the long hot day and the breeze would stir almost imperceptibly
outside and the smell of the swamp drift through the rusty screens.
Sleep would come easily and in the morning the red squirrel would
be on the roof, tapping out his gay routine. I kept remembering
everything, lying in bed in the mornings—the small steamboat that
had a long rounded stern like the lip of a Ubangi, and how quietly

she ran on the moonlight sails, when the older boys played their mandolins and the girls sang and we ate doughnuts dipped in sugar, and how sweet the music was on the water in the shining night, and what it had felt like to think about girls then. After breakfast we would go up to the store and the things were in the same place—the minnows in a bottle, the plugs and spinners disarranged and pawed over by the youngsters from the boys' camp, the fig newtons and the Beeman's gum. Outside, the road was tarred and cars stood in front of the store. Inside, all was just as it had always been, except there was more Coca-Cola and not so much Moxie and root beer and birch beer and sarsaparilla. We would walk out with a bottle of pop apiece and sometimes the pop would backfire up our noses and hurt. We explored the streams, quietly, where the turtles slid off the sunny logs and dug their way into the soft bottom; and we lay on the town wharf and fed worms to the tame bass. Everywhere we went I had trouble making out which was I, the one walking at my side, the one walking in my pants.

One afternoon while we were there at that lake a thunderstorm   12 came up. It was like the revival of an old melodrama that I had seen long ago with childish awe. The second-act climax of the drama of the electrical disturbance over a lake in America had not changed in any important respect. This was the big scene, still the big scene. The whole thing was so familiar, the first feeling of oppression and heat and a general air around camp of not wanting to go very far away. In midafternoon (it was all the same) a curious darkening of the sky, and a lull in everything that had made life tick; and then the way the boats suddenly swung the other way at their moorings with the coming of a breeze out of the new quarter, and the premonitory rumble. Then the kettle drum, then the snare, then the bass drum and cymbals, then crackling light against the dark, and the gods grinning and licking their chops in the hills. Afterward the calm, the rain steadily rustling in the calm lake, the return of light and hope and spirits, and the campers running out in joy and relief to go swimming in the rain, their bright cries perpetuating the deathless joke about how they were getting simply drenched, and the children screaming with delight at the new sensation of bathing in the rain, and the joke about getting drenched linking the generations in a strong indestructible chain. And the comedian who waded in carrying an umbrella.

When the others went swimming my son said he was going in   13 too. He pulled his dripping trunks from the line where they had hung all through the shower, and wrung them out. Languidly, and with no thought of going in, I watched him, his hard little body, skinny and bare, saw him wince slightly as he pulled up around his vitals the small, soggy, icy garment. As he buckled the swollen belt suddenly my groin felt the chill of death.

SIMONE DE BEAUVOIR

The Coming of Age

Simone de Beauvoir (1908–1986) attended Catholic schools in Paris before studying philosophy at the Sorbonne. There she met Jean-Paul Sartre, her life-long companion, who later became the most famous of the existentialist philosophers. Herself a member of a privileged class, de Beauvoir was a left-wing individualist committed to equality for those struggling with economic and social disadvantages. Her analysis of the position of women in *The Second Sex* (1949; translation, 1954) made her a leader of the radical feminist movement. Her philosophical work *The Ethics of Ambiguity* (1947; translation, 1949) established her as one of the most lucid and persuasive advocates of existentialism. After a series of novels, travel narratives, and a three-part autobiography, de Beauvoir set to work on her twenty-first book, *La Vieillesse* (1970). The book's title can be directly translated as *Old Age*, though her American publisher initially chose to call it *The Coming of Age* (1972). This renaming seems to offer further proof of the book's thesis: that in modern capitalistic societies (which are committed to optimism, productivity, and progress) old age is a taboo topic.

When Buddha was still Prince Siddartha he often escaped from the splendid palace in which his father kept him shut up and drove about the surrounding countryside. The first time he went out he saw a tottering, wrinkled, toothless, white-haired man, bowed, mumbling and trembling as he propped himself along on his stick. The sight astonished the prince and the charioteer told him just what it meant to be old. "It is the world's pity," cried Siddartha, "that weak and ignorant beings, drunk with the vanity of youth, do not behold old age! Let us hurry back to the palace. What is the use of pleasures and delights, since I myself am the future dwelling-place of old age?"

Buddha recognized his own fate in the person of a very aged man, because, being born to save humanity, he chose to take upon himself the entirety of the human state. In this he differed from the rest of mankind, for they evade those aspects of it that distress them. And above all they evade old age. The Americans have struck the word death out of their vocabulary—they speak only of "the dear departed": and in the same way they avoid all reference to great age. It is a forbidden subject in present-day France, too. What a furious outcry I raised when I offended against this taboo at the end of *La Force des choses*! Acknowledging that I was on the threshold of old age was tantamount to saying that old age was lying there in wait for every woman, and that it had already laid hold upon many of them. Great numbers of people, particularly old people, told me, kindly or angrily but always at great length and again and again, that old age simply did not exist! There were some who were less young than others, and that was all it amounted to. Society looks upon old age as a kind of shameful secret that it is unseemly to mention. There is a copious literature dealing with women, with children, and with young people in all their aspects: but apart from specialized works we scarcely ever find any reference whatsoever to the old. A comic-strip artist once had to re-draw a whole series because he had included a pair of grandparents among his characters. "Cut out the old folks," he was ordered.[1] When I say that I am working on a study of old age people generally exclaim, "What an extraordinary notion! . . . But you aren't old! . . . What a dismal subject."

And that indeed is the very reason why I am writing this book. I mean to break the conspiracy of silence. Marcuse[2] observes that the consumers' society has replaced a troubled by a clear conscience and that it condemns all feelings of guilt. But its peace of mind has to be disturbed. As far as old people are concerned this society is not only guilty but downright criminal. Sheltering behind the myths of expansion and affluence, it treats the old as outcasts. In France, where twelve per cent of the population are over sixty-five and where the proportion of old people is the highest in the world, they are condemned to poverty, decrepitude, wretchedness and despair. In the United States their lot is no happier. To reconcile this barbarous treatment with the humanist morality they profess to follow, the ruling class adopts the convenient plan of refusing to consider them as real people: if their voices were heard, the hearers would be forced to acknowledge that these were human voices. I shall compel my readers to hear them. I shall describe the position

1. Reported by François Garrigue in *Dernières Nouvelles d'Alsace*, October 12, 1968. [author's note]
2. Herbert Marcuse (1898–1979), a German-American philosopher, opponent of both capitalism and communism, advocate of democratic socialism.

that is allotted to the old and the way in which they live: I shall tell
what in fact happens inside their minds and their hearts; and what
I say will not be distorted by the myths and the clichés of bourgeois
culture.

Then again, society's attitude towards the old is deeply ambiva- 4
lent. Generally speaking, it does not look upon the aged as belonging to one clearly-defined category. The turning-point of puberty
allows the drawing of a line between the adolescent and the
adult—a division that is arbitrary only within narrow limits; and at
eighteen or perhaps twenty-one youths are admitted to the community of grown men. This advancement is nearly always accompanied by initiation rites. The time at which old age begins is ill-
defined; it varies according to the era and the place, and nowhere
do we find any initiation ceremonies that confirm the fresh status.[3]
Throughout his life the individual retains the same political rights
and duties: civil law makes not the slightest difference between a
man of forty and one of a hundred. For the lawyers an aged man is
as wholly responsible for his crimes as a younger one, except in
pathological cases.[4] In practice the aged are not looked upon as a
class apart, and in any case they would not wish so to be regarded.
There are books, periodicals, entertainments, radio and television
programmes for children and young people: for the old there are
none.[5] Where all these things are concerned, they are looked upon
as forming part of the body of adults less elderly than themselves.
Yet on the other hand, when their economic status is decided
upon, society appears to think that they belong to an entirely different species: for if all that is needed to feel that one has done
one's duty by them is to grant them a wretched pittance, then they
have neither the same needs nor the same feelings as other men.
Economists and legislators endorse this convenient fallacy when
they deplore the burden that the "non-active" lay upon the shoulders of the active population, just as though the latter were not
potential non-actives and as though they were not insuring their
own future by seeing to it that the aged are taken care of. For their
part, the trades-unionists do not fall into this error: whenever they

---

3. The feasts with which some societies celebrate people's sixtieth or eightieth birth-
days are not of an initiatory character. [author's note]
4. Mornet, the public prosecutor, began his indictment of Pétain by reminding his
hearers that the law takes no account of age. In recent years the "inquiry into
personality" that comes before the trial can emphasize the age of the accused: but
only as one feature among all the rest. [author's note]
5. La Bonne Presse has recently launched a periodical intended for old people. It
confines itself to giving information and practical advice. [author's note]

put forward their claims the question of retirement always plays an important part in them.

The aged do not form a body with any economic strength whatsoever and they have no possible way of enforcing their rights: and it is to the interest of the exploiting class to destroy the solidarity between the workers and the unproductive old so that there is no one at all to protect them. The myths and the clichés put out by bourgeois thought aim at holding up the elderly man as someone who is different, as *another being.* "Adolescents who last long enough are what life makes old men out of," observes Proust.[6] They still retain the virtues and the faults of the men they were and still are: and this is something that public opinion chooses to overlook. If old people show the same desires, the same feelings and the same requirements as the young, the world looks upon them with disgust: in them love and jealousy seem revolting or absurd, sexuality repulsive and violence ludicrous. They are required to be a standing example of all the virtues. Above all they are called upon to display serenity: the world asserts that they possess it, and this assertion allows the world to ignore their unhappiness. The purified image of themselves that society offers the aged is that of the white-haired and venerable Sage, rich in experience, planing high above the common state of mankind: if they vary from this, then they fall below it. The counterpart of the first image is that of the old fool in his dotage, a laughing-stock for children. In any case, either by their virtue or by their degradation they stand outside humanity. The world, therefore, need feel no scruple in refusing them the minimum of support which is considered necessary for living like a human being.

We carry this ostracism so far that we even reach the point of turning it against ourselves: for in the old person that we must become, we refuse to recognize ourselves. "Of all realities [old age] is perhaps that of which we retain a purely abstract notion longest in our lives," says Proust with great accuracy. All men are mortal: they reflect upon this fact. A great many of them become old: almost none ever foresees this state before it is upon him. Nothing should be more expected than old age; nothing is more unforeseen. When young people, particularly girls, are asked about their future, they set the utmost limit of life at sixty. Some say, "I shan't get that far: I'll die first." Others even go so far as to say, "I'll kill myself first." The adult behaves as though he will never grow old. Working men are often amazed, stupefied when the day of retirement comes. Its date was fixed well beforehand; they knew it; they

6. Marcel Proust (1871–1922), French novelist.

ought to have been ready for it. In fact, unless they have been thoroughly indoctrinated politically, this knowledge remains entirely outside their ken.

When the time comes nearer, and even when the day is at hand, people usually prefer old age to death. And yet at a distance it is death that we see with a clearer eye. It forms part of what is immediately possible for us: at every period of our lives its threat is there: there are times when we come very close to it and often enough it terrifies us. Whereas no one ever becomes old in a single instant: unlike Buddha, when we are young or in our prime we do not think of ourselves as already being the dwelling-place of our own future old age. Age is removed from us by an extent of time so great that it merges with eternity: such a remote future seems unreal. Then again the dead are *nothing*. This nothingness can bring about a metaphysical vertigo, but in a way it is comforting— it raises no problems. "I shall no longer exist." In a disappearance of this kind I retain my identity.[7] Thinking of myself as an old person when I am twenty or forty means thinking of myself as someone else, as *another* than myself. Every metamorphosis has something frightening about it. When I was a little girl I was amazed and indeed deeply distressed when I realized that one day I should turn into a grown-up. But when one is young the real advantages of the adult status usually counterbalance the wish to remain oneself, unchanged. Whereas old age looms ahead like a calamity: even among those who are thought well preserved, age brings with it a very obvious physical decline. For of all species, mankind is that in which the alterations caused by advancing years are the most striking. Animals grow thin; they become weaker: they do not undergo a total change. We do. It wounds one's heart to see a lovely young woman and then next to her her reflection in the mirror of the years to come—her mother. Lévi-Strauss[8] says that the Nambikwara Indians have a single word that means "young and beautiful" and another that means "old and ugly." When we look at the image of our own future provided by the old we do not believe it: an absurd inner voice whispers that *that* will never happen to us—when *that* happens it will no longer be ourselves that it happens to. Until the moment it is upon us old age is something that only affects other people. So it is understandable that society should manage to prevent us from seeing our own kind, our fellow-men, when we look at the old.

7. This identity is all the more strongly guaranteed to those who believe they have an immortal soul. [author's note]
8. Claude Lévi-Strauss (1908–   ), French anthropologist.

We must stop cheating: the whole meaning of our life is in   8
question in the future that is waiting for us. If we do not know
what we are going to be, we cannot know what we are: let us
recognize ourselves in this old man or in that old woman. It must
be done if we are to take upon ourselves the entirety of our human
state. And when it is done we will no longer acquiesce in the
misery of the last age: we will no longer be indifferent, because we
shall feel concerned, as indeed we are. This misery vehemently
indicts the system of exploitation in which we live. The old person
who can no longer provide for himself is always a burden. But in
those societies where there is some degree of equality—within a
rural community, for example, or among certain primitive nations—the middle-aged man is aware, in spite of himself, that his
state tomorrow will be the same as that which he allots to the old
today. That is the meaning of Grimm's tale, versions of which are
to be found in every countryside. A peasant makes his old father
eat out of a small wooden trough, apart from the rest of the family:
one day he finds his son fitting little boards together. "It's for you
when you are old," says the child. Straight away the grandfather is
given back his place at the family table. The active members of the
community work out compromises between their long-term and
their immediate interests. Imperative necessity compels some
primitive tribes to kill their aged relatives, even though they themselves have to suffer the same fate later on. In less extreme cases
selfishness is moderated by foresight and by family affection. In the
capitalist world, long-term interests no longer have any influence:
the ruling class that determines the fate of the masses has no fear of
sharing that fate. As for humanitarian feelings, they do not enter
into account at all, in spite of the flood of hypocritical words. The
economy is founded upon profit; and in actual fact the entire civilization is ruled by profit. The human working stock is of interest
only in so far as it is profitable. When it is no longer profitable it is
tossed aside. At a congress a little while ago, Dr. Leach, a Cambridge anthropologist, said, in effect, "In a changing world, where
machines have a very short run of life, men must not be used too
long. Everyone over fifty-five should be scrapped."[9]

The word "scrap" expresses his meaning admirably. We are told   9
that retirement is the time of freedom and leisure: poets have sung
"the delights of reaching port."[10] These are shameless lies. Society
inflicts so wretched a standard of living upon the vast majority of

9. This was written in December 1968. [author's note]
10. Racan's phrase. [author's note]

old people that it is almost tautological to say "old and poor": again, most exceedingly poor people are old. Leisure does not open up new possibilities for the retired man; just when he is at last set free from compulsion and restraint, the means of making use of his liberty are taken from him. He is condemned to stagnate in boredom and loneliness, a mere throw-out. The fact that for the last fifteen or twenty years of his life a man should be no more than a reject, a piece of scrap, reveals the failure of our civilization: if we were to look upon the old as human beings, with a human life behind them, and not as so many walking corpses, this obvious truth would move us profoundly. Those who condemn the maiming, crippling system in which we live should expose this scandal. It is by concentrating one's efforts upon the fate of the most unfortunate, the worst-used of all, that one can successfully shake a society to its foundations. In order to destroy the caste system, Gandhi tackled the status of the pariahs: in order to destroy the feudal family, Communist China liberated the women. Insisting that men should remain men during the last years of their life would imply a total upheaval of our society. The result cannot possibly be obtained by a few limited reforms that leave the system intact: for it is the exploitation of the workers, the pulverization of society, and the utter poverty of a culture confined to the privileged, educated few that leads to this kind of dehumanized old age. And it is this old age that makes it clear that everything has to be reconsidered, recast from the very beginning. That is why the whole problem is so carefully passed over in silence: and that is why this silence has to be shattered. I call upon my readers to help me in doing so.

Translated by Patrick O'Brien.

WILLIAM MANCHESTER

My Old Man: The Last Years of H. L. Mencken

William Manchester (1922–   ) began his long and controversial career as a journalist and historian after serving as a Marine in World War II (see "Okinawa: The Bloodiest Battle of All," p. 461) and completing an M.A. in English at the University of Missouri. The subject of his thesis was H. L. Mencken, the Baltimore journalist whose essays and reviews helped set the tone of

American literature and thought in the 1920s. Mencken, opponent of business, religion, and middle-class values, once described Americans as "the most timorous, sniveling, poltroonish,
ignominious mob of serfs and goose-steppers ever gathered
under one flag in Christendom since the end of the Middle
Ages." The ferocity of Mencken's opinions contrasts sharply with
the kindness he showed Manchester: he found his young admirer
a job on the Baltimore *Sun* and became his mentor. A colleague
at the paper reported that "Bill talked the way Mencken talked,
wrote the way Mencken wrote. I guess he was Bill's first hero."
In 1951 Manchester published Mencken's biography, *Disturber
of the Peace.* In 1954 he left the *Sun* to become Mencken's
confidential secretary. The following account of this experience
appeared in *Controversy and Other Essays in Journalism* (1976).

"The cooks here do a swell job with soft-shell crabs," Mencken   1
said in a gravelly voice, peering at me over his spectacles. Beneath
the old-fashioned center part of his white hair his pot-blue eyes
gleamed like twin gas jets. "They fry them in the altogether," he
rasped. "Then they add a small jockstrap of bacon."

It was June 2, 1947. We were in the dining room of the Mary-   2
land Club. The meeting was our first—I had just flown in from a
Midwestern graduate school, where I was writing my dissertation
on his early literary criticism—and it was the beginning of a seven-
year friendship, an April–December relationship which I cherished, and cherish still, despite the dirty tricks fate began to play on
him eighteen months after it began.

"This is a very high-toned club," he said over the crabs. "Noth-   3
ing but men. Any member who suffers a heart attack must be
carried outside to the front steps before a nurse can attend him."

He was in fine form that Monday noon. The thought that he   4
himself might fall the victim of a seizure and wind up in the hands
of nurses was very far away. At sixty-six he was still at the height
of his remarkable powers and had, in fact, just completed the most
productive period in his career. Since 1940 he had been feuding
with his paper, the Baltimore *Sun*, as a result of the *Sun*'s support of
what he had called "Roosevelt's War." Holed up in his study at
1524 Hollins Street, he had written *Happy Days, Newspaper Days,
Heathen Days, A Christmas Story, A New Dictionary of Quotations,* and
two massive supplements to *The American Language* and was, when
we met, at work on *A Mencken Chrestomathy.* His machete was still
long and sharp and heavy, and he had never swung it with greater
gusto.

Face-to-face with the man himself, I was enormously impressed.   5
Alistair Cooke once observed that Mencken had "the longest torso

on the shortest legs in the entire history of legmen," and Mencken himself said there would be no point in erecting a statue to him, because it would just look like a monument to a defeated alderman, but actually he was a man of great physical presence. To be sure, his torso was ovoid, his ruddy face homely, and his legs not only stubby but also thin and bowed. Nevertheless there was a sense of dignity and purpose about all his movements, and when you were with him it was impossible to forget that you were watching a great original. Nobody else could stuff Uncle Willie stogies into a seersucker jacket with the flourish of Mencken, or wipe a blue bandanna across his brow so dramatically. His friends treasured everything about him, because the whole of the man was manifest in each of his aspects—the tilt of his head, his close-fitting clothes, his high-crowned felt hat creased in the distinct fashion of the 1920's, his strutting walk, his abrupt gestures, his habit of holding a cigar between his thumb and forefinger like a baton, the roupy inflection of his voice, and, most of all, those extraordinary eyes: so large, and intense, and merry. He was sui generis in all ways, and the instant I saw him I wanted to write his biography.

After reading my thesis the following summer, he agreed. ("I 6 marvel at the hard work you put into it," he wrote me. "It tells me many things about my own self that I didn't know myself. . . . You will be rewarded in Heaven throughout eternity.") He did more. Swallowing his pride, he asked the *Sun* to give me a job, so that I could support myself while working on the book. My journalistic career was launched that September, and while I was unlikely to match the trajectory of his soaring star—at my age, twenty-five, he had been a managing editor—it did give us something else to talk about.

Beginning that autumn, we talked a great deal, sometimes at the 7 *Sun*, which he now began visiting with growing frequency; other times in his club, his home, the Enoch Pratt Free Library, Miller Brothers' restaurant, and on long walks through downtown Baltimore. There was, of course, no pretense to conversation between equals; I regarded him with the special deference of the fledgling writer for the master. The high-ceilinged Hollins Street sitting room, with its cheery fireplace, dark rosewood furniture, and Victorian bric-a-brac became a kind of shrine to me. I treasured his letters to me, which were even more frequent than our talks, for he loved correspondence, always preferring the written word to the telephone. And I kept elaborate notes on all our contacts, which, he being Mencken, really were notable.

One warm day I covered a fire in his neighborhood. He appeared 8 friskily at the height of it, carrying a pencil and perspiring happily.

"I'm like the hippopotamus," he said in greeting, "an essentially tropical animal." Like the hippo, he was also a creature of exaggeration. He never asked me just to join him for a beer; I was invited to "hoist a schooner of malt." He couldn't order sweetbreads at Miller's without explaining that they were taken from "the pancreases of horned cattle, the smaller intestines of swine, and the vermiform appendix of the cow"—thereby causing me to choose something else. Anthony Comstock hadn't merely been a censor; he had been "a great smeller." Mencken was forever stuffing letters to me with advertisements for chemical water closets, quack-remedy broadsides, and religious pamphlets. Once, while showing me his manuscript collection in the Pratt Library, he said he was worried about its security; the stack containing it was locked, but he wanted a sign, too. "Saying 'KEEP OUT'?" I asked. "No," he said. "Saying: 'WARNING: TAMPERING WITH THIS GATE WILL RELEASE CHLORINE GAS UNDER 250 POUNDS PRESSURE.' "

By the spring of 1948 he was a daily visitor to the *Sun*. In the 9 paper's morgue he advised a man updating the Mencken obituary to "Leave it as it is. Just add one line: 'As he grew older, he grew worse.' " One afternoon on Charles Street we encountered two sedate women from the *Sun*'s library coming the other way, and Mencken cried out heartily, "Hello, girls! How's the profession?" Later one of them said to me, "Of course, he didn't mean it the way it sounded." I knew that was exactly how he had meant it. By then, though, it was clear that he was yearning for a consummation of his rapprochement with the paper. The feud formally ended the following summer, when he arrived in Philadelphia to join the *Sun* men covering that year's presidential nominations and write happily of "the traditional weather of a national convention . . . a rising temperature, very high humidity, and lazy puffs of gummy wind from the mangrove swamps surrounding the city." Of the three political parties then taking the field, he preferred the Progressives, because they were the most preposterous. After Wallace had been nominated, he received a delegation of young Progressives in the hotel suite housing the *Sun* delegation and proposed that they join him in singing "The Star-Spangled Banner." He deliberately picked the impossible key of F Major. After crooning a few bars in his rasping tenor, he dropped out, waiting to hear his guests crack up, as was inevitable, on the impossible high E. When it happened, they looked appealingly to him for help. He just stuck his cigar in his mouth and beamed back at them.

My best recollection of the campaign which followed is of a 10 Wallace rally in Baltimore's Fifth Regiment Armory which I covered with Mencken. By then everyone in the audience had read the old man's *Sun* articles taunting their hero, and they knew the old man would be there that night. After the speeches, a mob of them crowded around the press bench, where, incredibly, he had un-sheathed his portable typewriter and set to work. He had decided to knock out his piece with them watching. I know of no other writer who could have performed under the circumstances. There were perhaps a score of hostile, humorless men and women in an arc behind him, peering over his shoulder, and behind them were others who were calling out, "What's he saying about us?" The outrageous phrases were called back, the crowd growled—and the old man hunted and pecked on, enjoying himself hugely. He even hummed that catchy little ditty, "Friendly Henry Wallace."

Mencken was immensely amused, as the *Sun* hierarchy was not, by Truman's unexpected victory. He felt that it justified his assess-ment of democracy as a comic spectacle. He returned to Hollins Street, refreshed, to tackle a new book. Meantime I had written the opening sections of my biography, and he had read them. On September 27 he had written me, "It seems to me that, as they stand, the first two chapters are excellent. Some of your generaliza-tions surprise me, and even horrify me, but they are yours, not mine. Don't let anyone tell you how to write it. Do it in your own way. You are obviously far ahead of most young writers, and I have every confidence in you." Thus we were both busy with thickening manuscripts as winter approached. On Wednesday, November 24, we were to take a break. A luncheon reservation had been made at the Maryland Club for four—Mencken, Evelyn Waugh, a Jesuit priest, and me. Waugh and Mencken had never met; the priest and I had arranged everything, like seconds before a duel. The en-counter never took place, however, because disaster struck the old man the evening before.

Mencken was fascinated by the frailties of the human body, his own and everybody else's. He was constantly studying medical journals, reading up on diseases of the bronchial tubes, gall blad-der, etc., and he was the most considerate visitor of the sick in Baltimore. Acquaintances who, in health, would not see him for weeks, found him at their hospital doors each evening, as long as they remained bedridden, fascinated by their progress, or, even more, by their lack of it. His letters to me and to others reflected his preoccupation with illness and anatomy. "Imagine," he wrote typ-ically, "hanging the stones of a man *outside,* where they are forever getting themselves knocked, pinched and bruised. Any decent mechanic would have put them in the exact center of the body, protected by a body envelope twice as thick as even a Presbyterian's skull. Moreover, consider certain parts of the female—always too large or too small. The elemental notion of standardization seems to have never presented itself to the celestial Edison."

He ended another note: "As for me, I am enjoying my usual [13] decrepitude. A new disease has developed, hitherto unknown to the faculty: a dermatitis caused by the plates I wear for my arches. No one knows how to cure it. I shall thus go limping to the crematory." He was always having a tumor dug out of his foot, or entering St. Agnes Hospital to have a folded membrane in his rectum investigated, or, depressed, shipping out samples of his body wastes to all the Baltimore pathologists he knew, which meant all the pathologists in the city. (A note of desperation here: "I begin to believe that in the end, as the hearse approaches the cemetery, I shall rise up and give three cheers.") Some weeks not a screed would go into the mailbox without some complaint, such as, "I have a sore mouth, can't smoke, it is 90 degrees, and at least twenty pests are in town," or, "My liver is swelled to a thickness of seven inches, and there are spiders in my urine." Other times he would audit his agonies—"an onslaught of pimples, aches, razor cuts, arch pains, and asthma," or, "asthma, piles, tongue trouble, hay fever, alcoholic liver, weak heels, dandruff, etc." Once he wrote George Jean Nathan:

> My ailments this morning come to the following:
> a. A burn on the tongue (healing)
> b. A pimple inside the jaw
> c. A sour stomach
> d. Pain in the prostate
> e. Burning in the gospel pipe (always a preliminary of the hay fever season)
> f. A cut finger
> g. A small pimple inside the nose (going away)
> h. A razor cut, smarting
> i. Tired eyes

Nathan, feeling that this was too much, sent him a set of false [14] teeth, a hairpiece, a cork leg, six bottles of liniment, and a copy of *What Every Boy Should Know*. In the return mail he received a querulous note asking why a bottle of asthma medicine had been omitted. "I am hacking and wheezing like Polonius."

It seemed to me that his hay fever sufferings were no greater [15] than those of other victims, though they may have been exacerbated by his willingness to try every nostrum on the market. ("My carcass is a battleground, and I am somewhat rocky. Hay fever pollen is pouring into my nose by the quart, but in my arteries it encounters the violent opposition of hay fever vaccine, and as a result there is a considerable boiling and bubbling.") This tendency had increased with the years and the advent of other complaints. In his preface to *Supplement Two,*[1] published in the spring of 1948, he wrote that his readers must not expect a third supplement, because "at my age a man encounters frequent reminders, some of them disconcerting, that his body is no more than a highly unstable congeries of the compounds of carbon."

By that autumn he was convinced that the end was near—with some reason. His friends had long ago written him off as a hypochondriac, for he had been crying "Wolf!" as long as they could remember, but a real wolf had been quietly stalking him for ten years. On April 12, 1938, he had suffered a slight stroke. Two years later his doctor had found evidence that his cerebral circulation had been impaired. Mencken immediately started a journal to document the stages in his disintegration. By the evening of November 23, 1948, when he called at the apartment of his secretary, Rosalind C. Lohrfinck, preparatory to taking her to dinner, his deathwatch on himself amounted to a thick sheaf of typescript, some fifty pages in all. There were to be no entries after that, for that was the night his preoccupation with afflictions stopped being funny. 16

He was having a cocktail with Mrs. Lohrfinck when, in the middle of a lucid sentence, he began to babble incoherently. Alarmed, she called his physician. When the doctor arrived, Mencken was pacing back and forth, ranting. At Johns Hopkins Hospital it was found that he had again been stricken by a cerebral thrombosis affecting his speech center and paralyzing his entire right side. He hovered for days at the threshold of death; then, slowly, he began to improve. The disability in his right side eased gradually and, after a month and a half of extensive treatment, left his arm and leg completely. But his speech center remained affected, and he could neither write nor read. Since boyhood his life had been built around the reading of the written word and the expression of his reflections. Now everything which had given meaning to his existence was gone. 17

The burden of caring for him—and it was to be a heavy one—fell on his unmarried younger brother August, a retired engineer who looked and sounded uncannily like him and with whom he shared the Hollins Street house. After Mencken's fifth week of hospitalization August brought the old man home. His condition was appalling. In conversation he tried again and again to summon the right word, and failed. Sometimes he would resort to pan- 18

1. Of *The American Language.*

tomime, raising an imaginary cup to his lips when he could not recall the word for drinking. Other times he would try circumlocutions, saying "the thing you cut with," for example, when he meant "scissors." And occasionally nonsense words came forth: "yarb" for "yard," "ray" for "rain," "scoot" for "coat," etc.

It was a bitter blow for the author of *The American Language,* and the worst of it was that he was fully aware of what was happening, understood the extent of the brain damage, and knew that his aphasia was incurable. In the Hopkins he had threatened to kill himself, but for all his thundering prose he had never been, and was not now, capable of violence. What actually happened was that he sank into a dreadful depression. He would stand in his study window, looking across at Union Square, on the opposite side of Hollins Street, saying almost inaudibly, "I wish this hideous existence would stop," saying, "How can anyone so stupid live," saying, "That a man like me, able to produce something, with the drive I had. . . . It's comic; it's just comic." In that first year of his disability he refused to allow anyone to read to him, refused to look at magazines with enlarged print, and wouldn't even listen to phonograph records. In one of his few remaining flashes of humor he hoarsely told me, "When I get to heaven, I'm going to speak to God very sharply."

Each time I called at his home I thought it was the last time, but he lingered and lingered. The 1940's became the 1950's; my biography, *Disturber of the Peace,* was published—in an act of conspicuous gallantry, he had managed to initial his approval of every quotation from his correspondence—and still his agony continued undiminished. Late in 1951 he suffered a massive heart attack. Again the Hopkins put him on the critical list, but after five months in the hospital he was released once more. August asked me to lend a hand, and together we brought his brother back to Hollins Street.

During the next two years I rarely saw the Menckens, for I was moving up at the *Sun,* which meant assignments farther and farther from home. The ultimate outpost, for me, was New Delhi. After the better part of a year as the paper's Indian correspondent, I returned to Baltimore, and I had just finished covering the Army-McCarthy hearings when August told me that his brother's mood had changed slightly. He was now willing to be read to. Did I know anyone who could spend mornings as his companion? I hesitated for a moment. By then love had died between me and the *Sun,* and there was no hope of a reconciliation. So I answered August: "Yes. Me."

In those twilight years Mencken's day began at 8 A.M., when   22
Renshaw, a hospital orderly, arrived at the house after an all-night
shift in the Johns Hopkins accident room. "Rancho," as the old
man always called him, gave him a rubdown in his third-floor
bedroom, helped him wash and dress, and entertained him with
vivid stories of colorful cases he had seen during the night. Meanwhile August was preparing his brother's breakfast downstairs—
fruit juice, two soft-boiled eggs, and a slice of bread. Mencken ate
this in his second-floor study, swiveling his chair around to the
window so he could watch elementary school pupils trooping to
school while he drank his coffee.

Children had become dear to him; unlike their parents they were   23
natural in his presence, unembarrassed by his condition. He enjoyed trips to the barber because he could admire a kindergarten
class playing across the street while his hair was cut, and two small
boys who saw him almost every day were five-year-old Butch,
who lived in the house next to his, and Alvin, a six-year-old Negro
from down the street. He would stroke Butch's rather emaciated
little dog—all pets look starved on Hollins Street; since Mencken's
own childhood the neighborhood had gone downhill and was, his
own home apart, virtually a slum—and congratulated Alvin on
the racing speed of his pet turtle. Emma, the Mencken cook, nearly
always had cookies for the boys. And each Christmas the old man
distributed huge sacks of candy to all the children who lived
around Union Square.

After breakfast Mrs. Lohrfinck came in. Together the two of   24
them went through the morning mail; painful though all communication had become for him, he insisted that everyone who
wrote him receive some sort of answer. Then she would riffle
through miscellaneous notes in his files, reading them to him, and
he would make a simple editorial judgment over the suitability of
each. (The resulting collection was published four months after his
death as *Minority Report.*) At ten o'clock she left. Her employer
accompanied her downstairs to the front door. Then, unless the
weather was impossible for him, he turned, trudged through the
house, took his cap from a peg in the dining room, and went
outside.

For Mencken admirers, the geography of the backyard at 1524   25
Hollins Street is often clearer than scenes from their own childhood. To the left, as you came out the kitchen door, stood a high
brick wall which he had begun building after the First World War.
In it were set various tiles, with a concrete replica of Beethoven's
life mask and the first five bars of his Fifth Symphony at the far end.

To the right of the back gate was a green-and-white shed which had sheltered Mencken's pony when he was a boy, and which now housed August's tools. In warm seasons morning glories blossomed over the shed, raising their lovely green fingers against the West Baltimore sky. Beside the shed, sloping toward the house, was a workbench and a woodpile splashed with outrageously bright colors. Nearby stood a child's wagon; an unsuccessful thief had left it behind one night, and it, too, was splotched with purples, yellows, greens, and reds. Between these giddy hues and the kitchen was a brick terrace over which, on sunny mornings, the devoted August would hoist an awning. He would work at the bench, puffing a pipe and glancing up at the sky from time to time while his brother sat on a canvas chair, his hands lying in his lap like weapons put to rest.

When the noon whistle blew, they reentered the house and   26
Emma prepared lunch. Afterward they sat in the yard again until the children returned from school. Mencken then napped, and after an early supper they drank two martinis and retired. Often friends joined them for the evening cocktails. August controlled the social calendar. He excluded those who he thought might upset the old man and everyone he regarded as trivial—which, August being a misogynist, included all women except Blanche Knopf. The most frequent visitors were Louis Cheslock, Dr. Arnold Rich, Hamilton Owens of the *Sun*, and me.

There were variations in this routine. On sultry mornings, for   27
example, Mencken went through an elaborate stage business with the backyard thermometer, inspecting it and denouncing it. The brothers had no use for dry cleaning, and once I found them in the yard washing their suits and coats with a garden hose. Saturday afternoons Mencken listened to the Metropolitan broadcasts. Saturday evenings the brothers called on the Cheslocks. And at least once a week they went to a movie. This was a new medium for Mencken. Had he retained his ability to read, he would have finished life without having seen more than a half-dozen films, but now his disability left him with little choice. Despite his disability he retained his scorn for artistic dishonesty; he enjoyed Walt Disney full-length cartoon features, Alec Guinness comedies, *Show Boat*, and *Lili*, but he despised melodrama or mawkishness in any form, and positively loathed anything about sports.

Starting in June of 1954 I arrived each morning as Mrs.   28
Lohrfinck was leaving. Usually Mencken was ready for me. If he wasn't, and the sun was shining, I would wait in the yard. Balmy weather was a good sign; he would greet me cheerily, saying, "Well, it's very nice out today; that should make us feel good," or

"It's not too bad, we might be able to do a little work today." Even
if rain was falling, we could sit in the shed, provided the day wasn't
actually raw. When the weather was impossible—when it was
sleeting, say—I would approach Hollins Street with dread, knowing that his mood would be grim. "Did you ever see anything like
this? Isn't it ghastly?" he would groan, or "I feel very wobbly this
morning; I'm going to pieces." At such times August would inter-
vene, raising a hand like a traffic policeman and growling back at
him, "Look, you don't feel any worse than I do." And his brother,
instantly concerned, would say, "Is that right? Don't you feel well,
August?"

Our sessions always began with the *Sun*. If it was the hay fever   29
season we always started with the report of the pollen count.
Otherwise, as I leafed through the paper, he would ask, "Well,
what's been happening? Any good stuff there, anything rich? Any
murders or rapes? Any robberies?" Complex events—Germany's
entry into NATO; McCarthyism—were beyond him now. He tried
to grasp the tumultuous changes in China, but he couldn't, so we
settled for small calamities. Sometimes there were none, and I
would tell him so. He would stare at me, his eyes wide with amazement. "What?" he would say. "It's hard to believe. I don't know
what's wrong with people nowadays. They're not killing one another any more. August, did you hear that?" And his brother,
usually in the midst of painting some object a ghastly orange, or
repairing a model boat for Alvin, would lay down his brush to echo
his astonishment.

One day the *Sun* carried a story about a husband who had killed   30
his wife, her lover and himself. "You know," Mencken said, "it's
probably the only decent thing he did in his life." Another high
point was Dr. Samuel Shepard's trial for the murder of his wife. For
Mencken it had everything: high theater, the physician who wasn't
really a physician, the pillar of the community exposed as a hypocrite. Of Mrs. Shepard, Mencken said with a deep sigh, "Well, she's
a goner now. She's up there with the angels." We sat for a moment
in meditation, contemplating the sublime fate of the doctor's victim. Then Mencken gestured impatiently at the paper. "Come on,"
he rasped. "How the hell did he croak her?"

On less favored days we turned to serious reading, and in retro-   31
spect I marvel on how much we got through that year: all of Twain
and most of Conrad. I was struck by his observation that *Huckleberry Finn* breaks down at the point where Huck is reunited with
Tom; Hemingway had said the same thing. Apart from that, both
felt, it was a perfect novel. The most moving book we read, however, was Conrad's *Youth*. Conrad never mastered our idiom,

Mencken said; he was translating Polish into English. Yet he admired the Pole more than any other writer of his time. The rich prose of *Youth* evoked memories of his own youth. I too was deeply affected. I had first read the book in college and hadn't understood it at all. Now in my early thirties the torrent of energy with which I had written my first two books was beginning to slacken. I glimpsed what lay ahead—literally glimpsed it, for there was Mencken beside me—and deeply felt a profound sense of sadness for the irretrievable stamina of the receding past.

One morning I stumbled over a hi-fi set in the front vestibule. It had arrived the previous afternoon, a present from Alfred Knopf, and the thoughtful dealer had included the latest Liberace record. Both brothers were exasperated. They didn't know how the thing worked. My own mechanical IQ is very low, but I can remove an appliance from a carton, stick a plug into the wall, lay a plastic disc on a turntable, and flip a switch—which was all that was necessary. We played perhaps thirty seconds of Liberace; then Mencken muttered something obscene and I switched it off. That evening I loaned him my Gilbert and Sullivan collection, however, and he was pathetically pleased by a new source of pleasure. Later, because *The Mikado* was his favorite, I bought him the album. I also introduced him to FM music. He had begun listening to AM stations before retiring and had been complaining sourly about their programing. August and I found the best FM stations for him, and that helped.

Apart from the reading, there was no fixed schedule for our mornings, but certain patterns recurred. Twice a week, after we had left the kitchen to Emma and settled in the yard beneath the gaudy awning, we would hear the distant clatter of garbage can lids. "Ah!" Mencken would breathe, brightening visibly; "here come the professors!" Watching the trash men empty his own cans—each of which was gaily painted "1524 Hollins Street" in red and yellow—he would remark, "You know, they do that very well. The professors are really very elegant men." Now and then visitors came to the front door. They rarely saw him. He ordered William Randolph Hearst, Jr., turned away, and shook his head when I suggested that I ask John Dos Passos to come in from the York Road and visit him. He still had his pride; he didn't want strangers or slight acquaintances to see him in this condition.

Often he was even uncomfortable with August and me. His aphasia came and went. When it was bad, he couldn't remember simple words or terms. He always recalled his brother's name, but there were times when he couldn't think of Mrs. Lohrfinck's,

Emma's, Rancho's, Butch's, Alvin's, or mine; and he despaired. Those sessions were grim for all of us, most of all for him. At his best, however, he was very like his old self. He described with gusto his vasectomy at Johns Hopkins when he was younger, and the fecund woman in New York who had voluntarily tested the success of the operation from time to time over the next year. He also told me that he knew twenty men, none of them braggarts, who had told him in confidence that they had bedded a famous Baltimore beauty during what she herself had called her "fast" youth. To him all women were either ladies, to be treated with elaborate chivalry, or sex objects. There was no third category. He was particularly hard on female journalists. He would dismiss them with a snort or a few corrosive phrases. ("God, what an elephant," he said of one. "She makes you want to burn every bed in the world.")

Occasionally he would talk of two books he had planned to   35
write, which would now remain unwritten; the first on the human condition, for which he had completed two chapters, and the second on American politics. And sometimes he spoke of other writers: of James T. Farrell, who was a good friend to the end; of Scott Fitzgerald, whose alcoholism had disgusted him; of Nathan, whose late marriage he regarded as highly comic; and of Sinclair Lewis's dermatological problems—"The only thing to do with Red," he reflected one morning, "was to skin him."

After reading and talking we would sit a while watching August   36
wield his bright paint brush, dabbing it dry from time to time on the outside of the woodpile. "Isn't that gorgeous work my brother's doing?" the old man would say from time to time. But he rarely sat idle through an entire session. He had to be doing something; even make-work was preferable to no work at all. Heaving up from his canvas chair, he would drop to his knees among the shrubs, stripping leaves from fallen branches for his compost heap and binding the twigs into fagots for the fireplace. On hot days he would periodically mutter, "Here, I'd better quit this or I'll fall to pieces, this is knocking me out." But after an interval he would start groping among the bushes again.

Our most strenuous activity—I shared in it—was adding to the   37
woodpile. On bitter days his fireplace was his chief solace. Cutting wood for it, and burning the wood, gave him extraordinary pleasure; it appealed, he said, to the boyhood love of vandalism which lingered in every man. The gathering of the fuel was as important to him as feeding it to the flames. His friends ordered seasoned cords over the telephone. In his view it was far nobler to scavenge neighborhood alleys and then saw up the loot.

Rising from his chair he would say to me, "Let's see what we can   38 find outside. You can't tell—we might turn up something really superb." Strolling down the narrow lanes with the child's wagon and poking among the trash cans, we would uncover a variety of burnable junk—piano stools, fence posts, broom handles, discarded chairs, hatracks, broken coffee tables, ancient lounge chairs. If I spotted a particularly hideous specimen of Grand Rapids golden oak, he would gape and say, "Wow! *Look* at that, will you!" As we returned from patrol, he would call ahead, "August, I found something really rich. Isn't that beautiful? It's simply exquisite." Then a shade of comic doubt would cross his ruddy face. He would ask us gravely, "But don't you think it's a shame to burn a lovely piece like that?" After deliberation his brother would say, "It's a shame, all right, Harry, but we've got a long winter ahead." "It seems hard," the old man would say worriedly, and August would make a great show of winning him over by promising to save it for a very special occasion. This was the quintessential Mencken, clothing the preposterous in the robes of high seriousness. A passing stranger would have taken him literally, and he would have been in good company; Mencken had misled humorless critics thus for a half-century.

He himself wasn't well enough to do much sawing, so he sat by   39
the end of the workbench, making outrageous comments while August and I took turns sinking the blade deep. We had a ritual; the length of each piece cut was determined by a measuring stick which was the exact width of the fireplace within. A certain percentage of our output had to be backlogs, and if our alley loot didn't include lengths of the proper thickness, we would nail odds and ends together—two mop handles, say, affixed to a broken crucifix, the base of a peach basket, and the wooden remains of a dilapidated plumber's helper. The more absurd the result, the uneasier Mencken grew over the propriety of feeding it to the flames. When its turn came at the hearth, he would wrestle audibly with his conscience before flinging it on the grate.

Eventually everything combustible went up in smoke, with one   40
memorable exception. One morning we were prowling in an alley, furtively lifting galvanized lids and looking, I'm sure, like refugees in postwar Europe searching for a scrap of meat, when he saw, standing against a fence, a shabby chest of drawers. The rats had been at it; we were far from Mencken's back gate; whether it was worth dragging all that way was questionable. As we were debating, a third figure joined us—a short, swart man in seedy khaki. He asked us whether we wanted the dresser. We told him we didn't know. He explained: his little daughter needed a place to store her clothes. If we weren't going to take it, he would.

Disconcerted, and beset this time by genuine pangs, Mencken 41
stammered that we were merely hunting for firewood; by all
means the child should have it. The young man brightened with
gratitude. He would be back shortly, he said. His car was parked
across the street; he would fetch it and whisk the dresser home. As
he dashed off we reexamined the rat holes. They were really enormous. It was a marvel that the thing stood. It had seemed worthless; it still did.

"Poor fellow," Mencken said.   42

In the long silence that followed we contemplated the plight of a 43
father reduced to scrounging among castoffs for his children's furniture.

Then the hush was broken by the deep-throated roar of a finely 44
tuned engine, and into the lane backed the longest, fattest, shiniest
pink Cadillac I had ever seen. The man leaped out, the chest of
drawers disappeared into its cavernous trunk, and then the Cadillac vanished, too, gone in a cloud of exhaust.

Mencken's mouth fell open in amazement. *"Jesus Christ!"* he 45
gasped. "Did you see *that*?" I told him I could hardly have missed
it. "Think of it," he mused. "Imagine that man raising a family,
sending his children off to learn the principles of Americanism,
keeping his mother off the poor farm, raising money to cure his
wife of gallstones—and driving around in a rose-colored hearse!
August!" he hoarsed as we neared home. "We just saw the god-
damndest animal in Baltimore!"

As the noon whistle sounded he would methodically measure 46
the wood sawed. "Say, we got a lot of work done today," he would
say, standing back and admiring the stack. "Look how high that
pile is now." As winter deepened it shrank again, for unless there
was a thaw the brothers laid a fire every night. Evenings when I
dropped in to listen to their growing collection of LP classics, the
three of us would stare into the vivid coals. Like everything else
about Mencken, his fires were unique. Their colors ranged all over
the spectrum, for he cherished a hoard of chemically treated wood
which, when ignited, matched the rainbow. I never learned to
share his taste for after-dinner martinis, but I was tremendously
impressed by those spectacular flames, and I said so.

When warm weather returned in the spring of 1955, Gertrude 47
Mencken arrived from her farm and joined us for two nerve-
wracking hours. I had never met the brothers' sister before, and I
think I came to understand something of their attitude toward
women that evening. She was pleasant enough, but she couldn't
seem to stop talking. The monologue went on and on, while Au-

gust stared gloomily into the purple and orange fire and Mencken swelled with frustration. When she had departed the old man turned to his brother. In a slurred, gritty voice he demanded, "Where's the thing that makes music?" August replied, "You mean the gramophone, Harry?" Mencken nodded grimly. He said, "I want the ghastly one. Lib—Lib—" "Liberace," I supplied, and August brought it from across the room. Mencken ordered, "Throw it on the fire." For once August hesitated. "It will make a terrible stink," he said. "Baloney," said Mencken. "It will be elegant. We need it to finish off this classy occasion." Into the flames it went. The stench was dreadful; after a while the old man stalked wordlessly off to bed and August removed the record with tongs. Even so, the odor was evident the next morning, and Emma had to air the house all day.

When summer arrived I said my last good-bye at Hollins Street. I was leaving Baltimore for New England and had found a Hopkins graduate student who would come in mornings and read the paper to Mencken. It was a wrench for me; he obviously didn't want me to go, and at first he said so vehemently. That evening August reminded him that I had my own writing to do, and the next morning the old man had swung around completely; he offered his congratulations and said he expected me to write some swell books. His generosity, and his pretense that he had changed his mind, were typical of him. I have never known a public figure who was so different from his reputation. His readers thought of him as bigoted, cantankerous, wrathful, and rude, and he was none of those things. He was the elderly friend of Butch and Alvin. He was the cripple who was always solicitous about his brother's health. He was the stricken man who forced himself to initial the pages of my first manuscript, who always asked me in the shed whether I was properly clad; who, when he was in the depth of his worst depressions, would excuse himself and retire to his bedroom because he didn't want to burden me with his troubles. 48

We both knew we would never meet again, for all our talk of reunions. He was failing rapidly now. Yet he rallied gallantly that last afternoon, and as I turned to leave through the vestibule he struck a pose, one foot in front of the other, one hand on the banister and the other, fisted, on his hip. "You know, I had a superb time while it lasted," he said in that inimitable voice. "Very soon it will stop, and I will go straight to heaven. Won't that be exquisite? It will be very high-toned." 49

We shook hands; he trudged up the stairs into shadow, and I departed carrying two farewell gifts, an Uncle Willie stogie and a piece of the treated firewood. Seven months later an Associated 50

Press reporter called me in Connecticut to tell me that Mencken had died in his sleep. His ashes were deposited in Baltimore's Loudon Park Cemetery. Long afterward I read of his brother's death, and later word reached me that the Hollins Street house— "as much a part of me as my two hands," Mencken had once said of it—was now occupied by the University of Maryland's School of Social Work. That evening I carefully laid the piece of treated firewood in my own fireplace. I didn't expect much; after all that time, I thought, the chemicals would have lost their potency. But I was wrong. Instantly a bright blue flame sprang up. Blue changed to crimson, and after a few minutes there was another change. It was eerie. From end to end the wood blazed up in a deep green which would have been familiar to anyone who had ever held a copy of *The American Mercury*.

Fleetingly I thought: *If only the Mercury were still being published!* 51 And: *If only he were still alive!* I remembered him lamenting the fact that there was no decent memorial service for nonbelievers. This little fire, I realized, was the closest I would ever come to one for him. Now his home had become a headquarters for a profession he had ridiculed. Miller Brothers' eating house, where we had drained steins of pilsener, was being torn down; the name of the restaurant lived on ignominiously in a sterile new Hilton Hotel. The Baltimore which delighted Mencken as a young reporter, when, he wrote, "the days chased one another like kittens chasing their tails," was swiftly vanishing, as the flames on my andirons were vanishing; soon the Baltimore I had known would disappear, too. Briefly I was near tears. And then I checked myself. I realized what Mencken's reaction to the maudlin fireside scene would have been. He would have split it into sentimental flinders with one vast gravelly chuckle.

MALCOLM COWLEY

The View from Eighty

Malcolm Cowley (1898–1989) grew up in Pittsburgh and entered Harvard University in 1915. His college career was interrupted twice by World War I: he drove a munitions truck for the French Army and later trained as an artillery officer for the U.S. Army. After graduating in 1920, he studied French literature and history at the Université de Montpellier. He had, meanwhile,

begun to support himself by writing clear, logical prose that delighted editors because it needed no revising: one magazine paid
him a penny per word. In 1929 his first volume of poems, *Blue
Juniata*, was published and he became literary editor of *The New
Republic*, where his weekly book reviews were eagerly read and
influential. In 1934 he published *Exile's Return*, a book explaining the influences that shaped his life and the lives of other
members of America's "lost generation." The book established
Cowley as a literary historian and led to several other books.
"Being a literary historian," he once remarked, "is a rewarding
but not a lucrative profession." He supplemented his income by
teaching at several universities. "The View from Eighty" was first
published in *Life* (December 1978) and in 1980 expanded into a
book with the same name.

They gave me a party on my 80th birthday in August 1978. First   1
there were cards, letters, telegrams, even a cable of congratulation
or condolence; then there were gifts, mostly bottles; there was
catered food and finally a big cake with, for some reason, two
candles (had I gone back to very early childhood?). I blew the
candles out a little unsteadily. Amid the applause and clatter I
thought about a former custom of the Northern Ojibwas when they
lived on the shores of Lake Winnipeg. They were kind to their old
people, who remembered and enforced the ancient customs of the
tribe, but when an old person became decrepit, it was time for him
to go. Sometimes he was simply abandoned, with a little food, on
an island in the lake. If he deserved special honor, they held a tribal
feast for him. The old man sang a death song and danced, if he
could. While he was still singing, his son came from behind and
brained him with a tomahawk.

That was quick, it was dignified, and I wonder whether it was   2
any more cruel, essentially, than some of our civilized customs or
inadvertences in disposing of the aged. I believe in rites and ceremonies. I believe in big parties for special occasions such as an 80th
birthday. It is a sort of belated bar mitzvah, since the 80-year-old,
like a Jewish adolescent, is entering a new stage of life; let him (or
her) undergo a *rite de passage*, with toasts and a cantor. Seventy-
year-olds, or septuas, have the illusion of being middle-aged, even
if they have been pushed back on a shelf. The 80-year-old, the
octo, looks at the double-dumpling figure and admits that he is old.
The last act has begun, and it will be the test of the play.

He has joined a select minority that numbers, in this country,   3
4,842,000 persons (according to Census Bureau estimates for
1977), or about two percent of the American population. Two-
thirds of the octos are women, who have retained the good habit of

living longer than men. Someday you, the reader, will join that
minority, if you escape hypertension and cancer, the two killers,
and if you survive the dangerous years from 75 to 79, when half
the survivors till then are lost. With advances in medicine, the
living space taken over by octos is growing larger year by year.

To enter the country of age is a new experience, different from   4
what you supposed it to be. Nobody, man or woman, knows the
country until he has lived in it and has taken out his citizenship
papers. Here is my own report, submitted as a road map and guide
to some of the principal monuments.

The new octogenarian feels as strong as ever when he is sitting   5
back in a comfortable chair. He ruminates, he dreams, he remembers. He doesn't want to be disturbed by others. It seems to him
that old age is only a costume assumed for those others; the true,
the essential self is ageless. In a moment he will rise and go for a
ramble in the woods, taking a gun along, or a fishing rod, if it is
spring. Then he creaks to his feet, bending forward to keep his
balance, and realizes that he will do nothing of the sort. The body
and its surroundings have their messages for him, or only one
message: "You are old." Here are some of the occasions on which
he receives the message:

- when it becomes an achievement to do thoughtfully, step by step,
  what he once did instinctively
- when his bones ache
- when there are more and more little bottles in the medicine
  cabinet, with instructions for taking four times a day
- when he fumbles and drops his toothbrush (butterfingers)
- when his face has bumps and wrinkles, so that he cuts himself
  while shaving (blood on the towel)
- when year by year his feet seem farther from his hands
- when he can't stand on one leg and has trouble pulling on his
  pants
- when he hesitates on the landing before walking down a flight of
  stairs
- when he spends more time looking for things misplaced than he
  spends using them after he (or more often his wife) has found
  them
- when he falls asleep in the afternoon
- when it becomes harder to bear in mind two things at once
- when a pretty girl passes him in the street and he doesn't turn his
  head
- when he forgets names, even of people he saw last month ("Now

I'm beginning to forget nouns," the poet Conrad Aiken said at
80)
• when he listens hard to jokes and catches everything but the
snapper
• when he decides not to drive at night anymore
• when everything takes longer to do—bathing, shaving, getting
dressed or undressed—but when time passes quickly, as if he
were gathering speed while coasting downhill. The year from 79
to 80 is like a week when he was a boy.

Those are some of the intimate messages. "Put cotton in your 6
ears and pebbles in your shoes," said a gerontologist, a member of
that new profession dedicated to alleviating all maladies of old
people except the passage of years. "Pull on rubber gloves. Smear
Vaseline over your glasses, and there you have it: instant aging."
Not quite. His formula omits the messages from the social world,
which are louder, in most cases, than those from within. We start
by growing old in other people's eyes, then slowly we come to
share their judgment.

I remember a morning many years ago when I was backing out 7
of the parking lot near the railroad station in Brewster, New York.
There was a near collision. The driver of the other car jumped out
and started to abuse me; he had his fists ready. Then he looked
hard at me and said, "Why, you're an old man." He got back into
his car, slammed the door, and drove away, while I stood there
fuming. "I'm only 65," I thought. "He wasn't driving carefully. I
can still take care of myself in a car, or in a fight, for that matter."

My hair was whiter—it may have been in 1974—when a young 8
woman rose and offered me her seat in a Madison Avenue bus.
That message was kind and also devastating. "Can't I even stand
up?" I thought as I thanked her and declined the seat. But the same
thing happened twice the following year, and the second time I
gratefully accepted the offer, though with a sense of having diminished myself. "People are right about me," I thought while wondering why all those kind gestures were made by women. Do men
now regard themselves as the weaker sex, not called upon to show
consideration? All the same it was a relief to sit down and relax.

A few days later I wrote a poem, "The Red Wagon," that be- 9
longs in the record of aging:

> *For his birthday they gave him a red express wagon*
> *with a driver's high seat and a handle that steered.*
> *His mother pulled him around the yard.*
> *"Giddyap," he said, but she laughed and went off*
> *to wash the breakfast dishes.*

"I wanta ride too," his sister said,
and he pulled her to the edge of a hill.
"Now, sister, go home and wait for me,
but first give a push to the wagon."

He climbed again to the high seat,
this time grasping that handle-that-steered.
The red wagon rolled slowly down the slope,
then faster as it passed the schoolhouse
and faster as it passed the store,
the road still dropping away.
Oh, it was fun.

But would it ever stop?
Would the road always go downhill?

The red wagon rolled faster.
Now it was in strange country.
It passed a white house he must have dreamed about,
deep woods he had never seen,
a graveyard where, something told him, his sister was buried.

Far below
the sun was sinking into a broad plain.

The red wagon rolled faster.
Now he was clutching the seat, not even trying to steer.
Sweat clouded his heavy spectacles.
His white hair streamed in the wind.

Even before he or she is 80, the aging person may undergo 10 another identity crisis like that of adolescence. Perhaps there had also been a middle-aged crisis, the male or the female menopause, but the rest of adult life he had taken himself for granted, with his capabilities and failings. Now, when he looks in the mirror, he asks himself, "Is this really me?"—or he avoids the mirror out of distress at what it reveals, those bags and wrinkles. In his new makeup he is called upon to play a new role in a play that must be improvised. André Gide, that long-lived man of letters, wrote in his journal, "My heart has remained so young that I have the continual feeling of playing a part, the part of the 70-year-old that I certainly am; and the infirmities and weaknesses that remind me of my age act like a prompter, reminding me of my lines when I tend to stray. Then, like the good actor I want to be, I go back into my role, and I pride myself on playing it well."

In his new role the old person will find that he is tempted by new 11 vices, that he receives new compensations (not so widely known), and that he may possibly achieve new virtues. Chief among these is the heroic or merely obstinate refusal to surrender in the face of time. One admires the ships that go down with all flags flying and the captain on the bridge.

Among the vices of age are avarice, untidiness, and vanity, which last takes the form of a craving to be loved or simply admired. Avarice is the worst of those three. Why do so many old persons, men and women alike, insist on hoarding money when they have no prospect of using it and even when they have no heirs? They eat the cheapest food, buy no clothes, and live in a single room when they could afford better lodging. It may be that they regard money as a form of power; there is a comfort in watching it accumulate while other powers are dwindling away. How often we read of an old person found dead in a hovel, on a mattress partly stuffed with bankbooks and stock certificates! The bankbook syndrome, we call it in our family, which has never succumbed. 12

Untidiness we call the Langley Collyer syndrome. To explain, Langley Collyer was a former concert pianist who lived alone with his 70-year-old brother in a brownstone house on upper Fifth Avenue. The once fashionable neighborhood had become part of Harlem. Homer, the brother, had been an admiralty lawyer, but was now blind and partly paralyzed; Langley played for him and fed him on buns and oranges, which he thought would restore Homer's sight. He never threw away a daily paper because Homer, he said, might want to read them all. He saved other things as well and the house became filled with rubbish from roof to basement. The halls were lined on both sides with bundled newspapers, leaving narrow passageways in which Langley had devised booby traps to catch intruders. 13

On March 21, 1947, some unnamed person telephoned the police to report that there was a dead body in the Collyer house. The police broke down the front door and found the hall impassable; then they hoisted a ladder to a second-story window. Behind it Homer was lying on the floor in a bathrobe; he had starved to death. Langley had disappeared. After some delay, the police broke into the basement, chopped a hole in the roof, and began throwing junk out of the house, top and bottom. It was 18 days before they found Langley's body, gnawed by rats. Caught in one of his own booby traps, he had died in a hallway just outside Homer's door. By that time the police had collected, and the Department of Sanitation had hauled away, 120 tons of rubbish, including, besides the newspapers, 14 grand pianos and the parts of a dismantled Model T Ford. 14

Why do so many old people accumulate junk, not on the scale of 15

Langley Collyer, but still in a dismaying fashion? Their tables are
piled high with it, their bureau drawers are stuffed with it, their
closet rods bend with the weight of clothes not worn for years. I
suppose that the piling up is partly from lethargy and partly from
the feeling that everything once useful, including their own bodies,
should be preserved. Others, though not so many, have such a fear
of becoming Langley Collyers that they strive to be painfully neat.
Every tool they own is in its place, though it will never be used
again; every scrap of paper is filed away in alphabetical order. At
last their immoderate neatness becomes another vice of age, if a
milder one.

The vanity of older people is an easier weakness to explain, and 16
to condone. With less to look forward to, they yearn for recognition of what they have been: the reigning beauty, the athlete, the
soldier, the scholar. It is the beauties who have the hardest time. A
portrait of themselves at twenty hangs on the wall, and they try to
resemble it by making an extravagant use of creams, powders, and
dyes. Being young at heart, they think they are merely revealing
their essential persons. The athletes find shelves for their silver
trophies, which are polished once a year. Perhaps a letter sweater
lies wrapped in a bureau drawer. I remember one evening when a
no-longer athlete had guests for dinner and tried to find his sweater. "Oh, that old thing," his wife said. "The moths got into it and I
threw it away." The athlete sulked and his guests went home early.

Often the yearning to be recognized appears in conversation as 17
an innocent boast. Thus, a distinguished physician, retired at 94,
remarks casually that a disease was named after him. A former
judge bursts into chuckles as he repeats bright things that he said
on the bench. Aging scholars complain in letters (or one of them
does), "As I approach 70 I'm becoming avid of honors, and such
things—medals, honorary degrees, etc.—are only passed around
among academics on a *quid pro quo* basis (one hood capping another)." Or they say querulously, "Bill Underwood has ten honorary doctorates and I have only three. Why didn't they elect me
to . . .?" and they mention the name of some learned society. That
search for honors is a harmless passion, though it may lead to
jealousies and deformations of character, as with Robert Frost in
his later years. Still, honors cost little. Why shouldn't the very old
have more than their share of them?

To be admired and praised, especially by the young, is an autum- 18
nal pleasure enjoyed by the lucky ones (who are not always the
most deserving). "What is more charming," Cicero[1] observes in his

1. Roman statesman and philosopher, 106–43 B.C.

famous essay *De Senectute,* "than an old age surrounded by the enthusiasm of youth! . . . Attentions which seem trivial and conventional are marks of honors—the morning call, being sought after, precedence, having people rise for you, being escorted to and from the forum. . . . What pleasures of the body can be compared to the prerogatives of influence?" But there are also pleasures of the body, or the mind, that are enjoyed by a greater number of older persons.

Those pleasures include some that younger people find hard to   19
appreciate. One of them is simply sitting still, like a snake on a sun-warmed stone, with a delicious feeling of indolence that was seldom attained in earlier years. A leaf flutters down; a cloud moves by inches across the horizon. At such moments the older person, completely relaxed, has become a part of nature—and a living part, with blood coursing through his veins. The future does not exist for him. He thinks, if he thinks at all, that life for younger persons is still a battle royal of each against each, but that now he has nothing more to win or lose. He is not so much above as outside the battle, as if he had assumed the uniform of some small neutral country, perhaps Liechtenstein or Andorra. From a distance he notes that some of the combatants, men or women, are jostling ahead—but why do they fight so hard when the most they can hope for is a longer obituary? He can watch the scrounging and gouging, he can hear the shouts of exultation, the moans of the gravely wounded, and meanwhile he feels secure; nobody will attack him from ambush.

Age has other physical compensations besides the nirvana of   20
dozing in the sun. A few of the simplest needs become a pleasure to satisfy. When an old woman in a nursing home was asked what she really liked to do, she answered in one word: "Eat." She might have been speaking for many of her fellows. Meals in a nursing home, however badly cooked, serve as climactic moments of the day. The physical essence of the pensioners is being renewed at an appointed hour; now they can go back to meditating or to watching TV while looking forward to the next meal. They can also look forward to sleep, which has become a definite pleasure, not the mere interruption it once had been.

Here I am thinking of old persons under nursing care. Others   21
ferociously guard their independence, and some of them suffer less than one might expect from being lonely and impoverished. They can be rejoiced by visits and meetings, but they also have company inside their heads. Some of them are busiest when their hands are still. What passes through the minds of many is a stream of per-

sons, images, phrases, and familiar tunes. For some that stream has continued since childhood, but now it is deeper; it is their present and their past combined. At times they conduct silent dialogues with a vanished friend, and these are less tiring—often more rewarding—than spoken conversations. If inner resources are lacking, old persons living alone may seek comfort and a kind of companionship in the bottle. I should judge from the gossip of various neighborhoods that the outer suburbs from Boston to San Diego are full of secretly alcoholic widows. One of those widows, an old friend, was moved from her apartment into a retirement home. She left behind her a closet in which the floor was covered wall to wall with whiskey bottles. "Oh, those empty bottles!" she explained. "They were left by a former tenant."

Not whiskey or cooking sherry but simply giving up is the greatest temptation of age. It is something different from a stoical acceptance of infirmities, which is something to be admired. At 63, when he first recognized that his powers were failing, Emerson wrote one of his best poems, "Terminus": 22

> It is time to be old,
> To take in sail:—
> The god of bounds,
> Who sets to seas a shore,
> Came to me in his fatal rounds,
> And said: "No more!
> No farther shoot
> Thy broad ambitious branches, and thy root.
> Fancy departs: no more invent;
> Contract thy firmament
> To compass of a tent."

Emerson lived in good health to the age of 79. Within his narrowed firmament, he continued working until his memory failed; then he consented to having younger editors and collaborators. The givers-up see no reason for working. Sometimes they lie in bed all day when moving about would still be possible, if difficult. I had a friend, a distinguished poet, who surrendered in that fashion. The doctors tried to stir him to action, but he refused to leave his room. Another friend, once a successful artist, stopped painting when his eyes began to fail. His doctor made the mistake of telling him that he suffered from a fatal disease. He then lost interest in everything except the splendid Rolls-Royce, acquired in his prosperous days, that stood in the garage. Daily he wiped the dust from its hood. He couldn't drive it on the road any longer, but he used to sit in the 23

driver's seat, start the motor, then back the Rolls out of the garage
and drive it in again, back twenty feet and forward twenty feet;
that was his only distraction.

I haven't the right to blame those who surrender, not being able   24
to put myself inside their minds or bodies. Often they must have
compelling reasons, physical or moral. Not only do they suffer from
a variety of ailments, but also they are made to feel that they no
longer have a function in the community. Their families and neighbors don't ask them for advice, don't really listen when they speak,
don't call on them for efforts. One notes that there are not a few
recoveries from apparent senility when that situation changes. If it
doesn't change, old persons may decide that efforts are useless. I
sympathize with their problems, but the men and women I envy
are those who accept old age as a series of challenges.

For such persons, every new infirmity is an enemy to be out-   25
witted, an obstacle to be overcome by force of will. They enjoy each
little victory over themselves, and sometimes they win a major
success. Renoir was one of them. He continued painting, and
magnificently, for years after he was crippled by arthritis; the brush
had to be strapped to his arm. "You don't need your hand to
paint," he said. Goya was another of the unvanquished. At 72 he
retired as an official painter of the Spanish court and decided to
work only for himself. His later years were those of the famous
"black paintings" in which he let his imagination run (and also of
the lithographs, then a new technique). At 78 he escaped a reign of
terror in Spain by fleeing to Bordeaux. He was deaf and his eyes
were failing; in order to work he had to wear several pairs of
spectacles, one over another, and then use a magnifying glass; but
he was producing splendid work in a totally new style. At 80 he
drew an ancient man propped on two sticks, with a mass of white
hair and beard hiding his face and with the inscription "I am still
learning."

Giovanni Papini said when he was nearly blind, "I prefer mar-   26
tyrdom to imbecility." After writing sixty books, including his famous *Life of Christ,* he was at work on two huge projects when he
was stricken with a form of muscular atrophy. He lost the use of his
left leg, then of his fingers, so that he couldn't hold a pen. The two
big books, though never to be finished, moved forward slowly by
dictation; that in itself was a triumph. Toward the end, when his
voice had become incomprehensible, he spelled out a word, tapping on the table to indicate letters of the alphabet. One hopes
never to be faced with the need for such heroic measures.

"Eighty years old!" the great Catholic poet Paul Claudel wrote in   27
his journal. "No eyes left, no ears, no teeth, no legs, no wind! And

when all is said and done, how astonishingly well one does without them!"

Yeats is the great modern poet of age, though he died—I am now   28
tempted to say—as a mere stripling of 73. His reaction to growing
old was not that of a stoic like Emerson or Cicero, bent on obeying
nature's laws and the edicts of Terminus, the god "Who sets to seas
a shore"; it was that of a romantic rebel, the Faustian[2] man. He was
only 61 when he wrote (in "The Tower"):

> What shall I do with this absurdity—
> O heart, O troubled heart—this caricature,
> Decrepit age that has been tied to me
> As to a dog's tail?

At 68 he began to be worried because he wasn't producing   29
many new poems. Could it be, he must have wondered, that his
libido had lost its force and that it was somehow connected with
his imagination? He had the Faustian desire for renewed youth, felt
almost universally, but in Yeats's case with a stronger excuse, since
his imagination was the center of his life. A friend told him, with
gestures, about Dr. Steinach's then famous operation designed to
rejuvenate men by implanting new sex glands. The operation has
since fallen into such medical disfavor that Steinach's name is nowhere mentioned in the latest edition of *The Encyclopaedia Britan-
nica*. But Yeats read a pamphlet about it in the Trinity College
library, in Dublin, and was favorably impressed. After consulting a
physician, who wouldn't say yes or no, he arranged to have the
operation performed in a London clinic; that was in May 1934.

Back in Dublin he felt himself to be a different man. Oliver St.   30
John Gogarty, himself a physician, reports a conversation with
Yeats that took place the following summer. "I was horrified," he
says, "to hear when it was too late that he had undergone such an
operation. 'On both sides?' I asked.

" 'Yes,' he acknowledged.   31
" 'But why on earth did you not consult anyone?'   32
" 'I read a pamphlet.'   33
" 'What was wrong with you?'   34
" 'I used to fall asleep after lunch.' "   35

It was no use making a serious answer to Gogarty the jester. He   36
tells us in his memoir of Yeats that the poet claimed to have been
greatly benefitted by the operation, but adds, "I have reason to
believe that this was not so. He had reached the age when he

2. So called after Faust, the hero of *Faust*, by the German poet Goethe (1749–1832).

would not take 'Yes' for an answer." Gogarty's judgment as a physician was probably right; the poet's physical health did not improve and in fact deteriorated. One conjectures that the operation may have put an added strain on his heart and thus may have shortened his life by years. Psychologically, however, Yeats was transformed. He began to think of himself as "the wild old wicked man," and in that character he wrote dozens of poems in a new style, direct, earthy, and passionate. One of them reads:

> *You think it horrible that lust and rage*
> *Should dance attention upon my old age;*
> *They were not such a plague when I was young;*
> *What else have I to spur me into song?*

False remedies are sometimes beneficial in their own fashion. ₃₇ What artists would not sacrifice a few years of life in order to produce work on a level with Yeats's *Last Poems*? Early in January 1939, he wrote to his friend Lady Elizabeth Pelham:

> I know for certain that my time will not be long. . . . I am happy, and I think full of energy, of an energy I had despaired of. It seems to me that I have found what I wanted. When I try to put all into a phrase I say, "Man can embody truth but he cannot know it." I must embody it in the completion of my life.

His very last poem, and one of the best, is "The Black Tower," ₃₈ dated the 21st of that month. Yeats died a week after writing it.

PATRICIA HAMPL

Teresa

Patricia Hampl (1946–   ) lives in St. Paul and teaches at the University of Minnesota. She is a poet and the author of *A Romantic Education* (1981), a memoir of her childhood and coming of age. (For Hampl's reflections on writing about one's own life, see "Memory and Imagination, p. 93.) In her memoir, Hampl recalls standing on a grade-school playground talking about her ancestry: " 'I'm half Irish,' I said, sweeping my hand like a cleaver exactly across my midriff, 'and half Czech.' " The most significant representative of the Czech half was Hampl's paternal grandmother, who owned and cried over an album of nineteenth-century views of Prague and who hung above her horsehair sofa a painting of a girl playing a lute: "The girl's mouth was parted slightly. . . . I always thought the song had just ended. Her gaze was not directed at me as I lay on the sofa, looking up at her in the midafternoon half-light of the parlor. Her gaze was higher, above me, pure and direct, undeflected." The girl in the painting resembled the grandmother in her youth, and both the picture and person had for Hampl the fascination of association with the old world. The album and the painting figure in the chapter that follows.

And my grandmother, the elderly art nouveau figure, finally 1 disappeared. She ended up in a nursing home, in the modern way. We all hated it. My father cried and made a fist in his pocket. My mother, who got her household back after years of the ignorant lowness ruining her roses, ruining her role as chatelaine, was not happy and wanted her back, and did not root up the chive plant in the back yard but allowed it to take over so that even today there are chives everywhere, even in the chinks of the sidewalk. My aunts said, "What else can we do?" And what else could we.

I wasn't living at home anymore, but I got letters from my 2 mother. The card parties and Czech lodge meetings with other old ladies who spoke some nineteenth-century version of Czech known only to themselves had come to an end. There weren't even any wakes or funerals for my grandmother to go to anymore; apparently everyone was dead, except for her. She had kept up her relentless cooking and the deep concern for her looks, a discipline held so long it had become a kind of honor. But slowly, steadily, as if they followed a plot, my mother's letters led to the nursing home: Grandma had burned herself one day when she didn't notice she'd left the gas flame on the stove. Her housedresses, cotton flower-print dresses with rickrack trim (her uniform at home), were often not clean: unbelievable.

Then an account of how Grandma had gotten into the bathtub 3 and couldn't hoist herself out; she had sat there, her skin puckering in the water for three hours until my mother heard strange heave-ho noises in the apartment and came in to pull her out. Later, another report that Aunt Sylvia had decided to come every week to clean the apartment ("the kitchen is filthy"). Then Aunt Sylvia suggested that my grandmother should take a bath only when someone was with her. There was a follow-up report that Aunt Sylvia, cleaning the apartment, had been unable to pull Grandma out of the tub and had started to cry. My grandmother began to laugh. It was a stand-off, one of them too weak from crying, the other from laughing. Finally, my aunt called in my mother from next door, and the hoist was accomplished, their big elderly baby laughing because there was nothing else to do.

Then a letter came saying Grandma had fallen down the base-   4
ment stairs. It might be a stroke. She would have to go to a nursing
home: for a while, maybe for longer. She couldn't take care of
herself. My mother and father both worked; no one was at home
during the day.

A few days later I got a brief note from my mother saying my   5
grandmother was in the nursing home (address included, suggestion that I send a card) and was confined to a wheelchair. She of
the endless avidity and the boundless faith that work was life. My
grandmother *sitting*—it was a contradiction in terms. Maybe it was
an effect of the stroke, no one seemed sure. But she said she
couldn't walk and sank into the wheelchair with no apparent intention of walking again.

For several months she was taken to physical therapy, but finally   6
the head nurse told my father he might as well buy a wheelchair;
the rented one was not economical for long-term cases. Then the
therapy ended and she had a catheter as a permanent appendage,
and showed it to her visitors, unasked, with a kind of wonder at its
obvious functionalism. There was no more talk of her walking.

I think she went through some kind of nervous breakdown. It's   7
strange to think of a dark night of the soul coming to someone
eighty-seven or eighty-eight. By then it would seem that the husk
of the personality has rigidified so that if it splits apart at all, it is
only into the splinters of senility. I would not have thought of a
very old person cracking the personality open and hurling out its
pain and experience in sorrow and then, as if there were a future,
turning upward in a huge cleansing wave, leaving the soul spent
but free and wise at the last shore of its life. But something like that
happened to my grandmother.

It took about two years. There are several indications that she   8
went through the spiritual cleansing that saints and mystics describe. I was most struck when my father told me that she had said,
apropos of nothing (not even of pain: there wasn't a lot of pain at
the end), "Well, I think it's time to die tonight." And she did. Her
body and soul were that finely meshed by the end. As my aunt
said, she knew *what she was.* She knew she was about to be dead.

At first, in the nursing home, she fought like a tiger. She did not   9
fight the good fight the physical therapy people wanted her to fight.
She must have sensed that there was no future in being a goody-
goody. She was out to break the joint. She fought her roommates
who, each in turn, asked to be moved out. She fought the medication. She fought being put in bed and then snarled when she was
taken out again and put in her wheelchair. She hated the food, but
complained that she didn't get enough. She cried and demanded to

go home; she sulked and then said casually that when she got home she intended to buy herself a new bed like the one she had in the nursing home—the best bed of her life, she said. She spoke authoritatively, as if acquisition implied mobility. And when no one, out of kindness, reminded her that she wouldn't be going back to her apartment, she reported to her next visitor that she was soon going home.

Her children or grandchildren and their children came every day   10
to visit. Everyone talked to her, to each other, about what a nice place the nursing home was, how friendly the staff was, how clean the rooms were, how there were lots of people around to play cards with, and that the best part was that they could take her home anytime for dinners, picnics, holidays. And then they left, and hardly got out of the front door before they burst into tears and cried aloud: why did their mother have to be there, in that nice, clean, friendly place?

This was not one of the miserable holes for the aged, gigantic and   11
crowded, with loudspeakers blatting endless messages, not one of the sleazy places that is marginally in the news because of some legislative inquiry about mishandling of public funds. It was what we told her, told each other: a nice, clean, friendly place, modern and light with lots of windows, a yard too small and too near busy traffic perhaps, but the staff was competent, not cruelly over-worked, often affectionate. The rooms were not large but were bigger than hospital rooms, and there were only two beds in each one, with a certain commitment to privacy. Large windows, a bath for each room, bright and tiled. I never saw or tasted the food, but my aunts said it was all right. My grandmother was diagnosed as a diabetic soon after arriving so her diet was restricted, probably bland. My family, always clannish, liked to visit her, liked to be with her, and it was generally agreed that even though the place was *very nice*, it didn't do any harm to make it clear that Mrs. Hampl in 106 had four children, innumerable other relatives, and that they came, one or another of them, every day to visit her. *If* the staff merely put on an act for visitors, our endless parade would keep them busily at it. This was the watchful thought.

In an effort to get her interested in the world around her, away   12
from the apartment she kept refurnishing in her mind and conver-sation, her children and the staff tried to introduce her to other people. They got her to play cards, always her favorite pastime. But years of playing five hundred with indulgent children who let her cheat without much comment had blunted her technique, of play-ing and of cheating. She was hurt and angry, as chronic cheaters always are, when her new companions bluntly told her to cut it

out. Besides, she said, some of them didn't talk right. This was the
beginning of her acquaintance with those who, as she put it, were
touched. Eventually, if she saw one of her visitors foolishly attempting conversation with someone woefully touched, she discreetly tapped her finger on her own forehead and shook her head,
more savvy than her children about the signs around her.

Her wild-tiger time, when she fought the place, lasted less than a   13
year, but it continued in occasional energetic jags for two years. It
was a denial of the place and its purpose. She never talked about
death or dying. Nor about illness or infirmity. She wanted to go
home.

One of the last times I visited her, while I was home for a vaca-   14
tion, I noticed a change. It frightened me; I thought she was going
to become one of the touched. She was sitting in her wheelchair
moaning when I came in. This was something I hadn't seen her do
before. She didn't stop or try to cover her tears. I thought she might
be in physical pain, might need a nurse. But that wasn't it. She kept
moaning and crying, rocking herself back and forth, not oblivious
to my presence, but somewhere out of reach of the conventions of
etiquette, the charm that had been one of her enduring principles,
deep in her own anguish, not about to abandon her intimacy with
it. She took my hand (any hand), stroked her own cheek with it,
cried that she was lonely, lonely, looonely, hanging on to the *o*
sound. She wanted to die. She made me promise I would come to
her funeral. But mostly she did not talk. She moaned and rocked
back and forth, like one of the anonymous touched. She wouldn't
talk and acknowledged my inept affection (I held her hand, stroked
her hair) only from a great distance. That is when she said, more
greenhorn than grandmother, "You're good, you're kind."

When I left she didn't have me wheel her down to the big lounge   15
picture window, as she had every other time, so that she could
wave to me as I drove off—a procedure that always made me feel
like a culprit and, really a culprit, made me glad to get away fast.
This time she stayed where she was and continued to moan. I felt
guilty, I still feel wrong, but I left her moaning there. Anything to
get away from that mantra of sorrow, that awful moaning, tone-
less, impersonal, not *her*. It—if not she—seemed prepared to go on
moaning endlessly. That was the worst part: the eternity in that
moan.

When I got home one of my aunts was visiting my mother;   16
everybody was glad to see me: coffee, Christmas cookies, kisses
around. I didn't want to tell them about the moaning. In some odd,
callous way, I was already seeing it as less important than it had

seemed at the time. And then my aunt said—mostly to my mother, for my mother—how good I was to take time during my vacation to visit my grandmother, and I began to focus, by degrees, on that aspect of the visit: my kindness. It had been my grandmother's comment too.

I thought this was the beginning of her descent into senility and mindlessness. And that the next time I went to visit her she would be babbling and incoherent, her mind woolly with bent memories. I thought her sadness had no bottom, or that there was no trap door to that moan, no escape but death. It occurred to me that she might arrive, in senility, back in Bohemia, the life and country she had had so little memory of, and that she would live there alone in her antiquated, mashed form of the language, mumbling, back in the embrace of the peasantry, lumpen. I didn't want to visit her again. I only saw her once or twice more.

But she wasn't senile and she didn't, ever again, moan that way. The curtain in her heart that split in half from top to bottom that day had mended—or hadn't been rent? I almost wondered if I had imagined it. She had become calm and humorous, patient, not the same as before—she had always been feisty—but not senile. After her death, my father wrote me about the end. There was a tone of wonder in his letter. The last six months of her life, he wrote, something strange had happened. He didn't know what to call it, he wrote. She just became, after her tiger period, very *kind*. It was she who talked sensibly and naturally to those who were touched in the worst, most unreachable ways; she who held a hand, wheeled herself over to someone sitting vacant and weird in a corner. She cheered the nurses (the nurses said; it was beyond a polite remark, my father wrote). She seemed to understand everybody's troubles, asked for nothing, gave amazing light. Everyone wanted to be around her. Teresa, they called her: her name, of course, but unusual to be called by one's most personal, authentic name in these end-of-the-line places where false affection makes everyone Grandma or, more courteously, more coolly, Mrs. this or that. She died Teresa, a person.

I didn't see any of this. I wasn't around during those last months. I know it from my father who was amazed, bemused by this turn of events. She had gone down and down, and, then, when everyone had every reason to expect her to go even more desperately down—into senility, into woeful bitterness—she made that strange, luminous turn. She glittered at the end not with charm, but with pure spirit, more than a brave salute. Our immigrant became a noble.

I did not go home for her funeral. I was living in a tiny river town   20
in Illinois, right on the river in fact, so close to the bank that in
spring the channel flooded the narrow frontage road and almost
reached the strand of houses facing the water. There was no getting
away from St. Paul; we were still connected, in a direct line, by the
river. In St. Paul the Mississippi is not the Father of Waters; it is
narrow and threads its unromantic way past industrial plants. But
in Illinois where it begins to become the river of Mark Twain and
billows out in a wider, plainlike channel, it becomes aloof and
serious.

After my mother called with the news of my grandmother's   21
death—it hadn't been expected—I went outside by the river. I felt
a satisfying finality, what I took to be acceptance. The river glided
by, still, grand, metaphoric. I didn't go home for the funeral because a friend of mine had just had twin babies and I felt, solemnly
and sincerely, that I was choosing life over death, staying near my
friend who wanted me there. My grandmother, who had had twins
herself, would have approved, I thought.

She would not have approved. But I was impervious to the last   22
to her personality. I considered, philosophically, the misty middle
ground between life and death that old people inhabit at the end. It
was almost pleasant, this idea of fading. I thought I had probably
already said my good-bye to her years before when she first began
to get really old, or when she went to the nursing home. Or maybe
the day in her room when she had moaned and moaned, as if she
were no one in particular, just that grievous sound. She died a long
time ago, I thought, as I stood by the wide river, and this recent
death is just the expression of it. She had just made it into her tenth
decade: she had been ninety on Columbus Day and she died in
November. A long life, such a long life as hers, cannot end all of a
sudden, I felt. She is at peace, I thought. And so am I.

Several weeks later I woke, jolted out of deep sleep in the middle   23
of the night by nothing at all. I was drenched in sweat. I hadn't
been dreaming, or hadn't remembered that I was. I was sobbing—I
had no idea why at first. Then I focused: I had made a *terrible
mistake* and should have gone to her funeral. This was the knowledge—not a dream—that had awakened me. And not having
gone, there was no way to undo it.

I cried at sudden, unpredictable moments for two weeks after   24
that, sobbing as I drove home, hunched over the steering wheel,
unable to see through the tears, as if I were beating my way
through a Minnesota blizzard. I moaned aloud in the public library
stacks one day, again to my utter surprise. There was an elderly

man on the other side of the stacks who peered through a chink in the wall of books to see what the matter was. He was wearing rimless glasses. Those are the cleanest glasses I've ever seen, I thought, and stared at them, fascinated, as if he were the apparition and not I.

I must have looked more astonished than miserable; my attacks (as I thought of them) were the advance guard of my emotions. I sobbed, I moaned stupidly, and only after the sound did I think, "Oh, it's Grandma. Because she's dead." The sobbing and moaning were acts dissociated from feeling. It was a weird sensation: to moan aloud in a supermarket check-out line, and then to look sheepishly at the bemused, unsobbing people around me. Yet I didn't miss her. And after a while the sobbing and my sudden public moans diminished and finally, left me entirely.

The picture of the luscious art nouveau girl[1] with her lute went to my Aunt Therese. There was no will, nothing that self-conscious. Things just went, of their own accord, to the family members who wanted or needed them. My cousin ended up with the purple satin eiderdown, perhaps the most Bohemian of my grandmother's possessions: the great goose-down quilt of middle Europe. My father wrote in his letter that it seemed as if Grandma had everything beautifully timed: her savings left exactly enough for her burial and for checks of $500 to each of her four children and to Frank's daughter: she had left heirs. If she had lived a few more months, her money would have run out. Nothing would have changed, but welfare—or some version of it—would have paid her way. Ever the housekeeper, she had arranged to the end, tidily. She stopped on a dime.

I asked for the album of Prague views. My aunt wrote back that nobody could find it; somehow or other it was lost. She sent me instead my grandmother's ring, a Bohemian garnet set in white gold with an art nouveau design. I felt someone else should have had it, Frank's daughter perhaps, but this was the object that came to me, apparently it was what I was meant to have. I put it on my finger, the one on which the other women in the family wear their wedding rings; I was the only unmarried one among them.

Then, our personal Europe dead and buried, I decided I must go there.

1. See the description of this picture in the headnote.

ANNIE DILLARD

Aces and Eights

Annie Dillard (1945–   ) grew up in Pittsburgh, Pennsylvania,
with two sisters, a mother who fretted in her role as a housewife
like "Samson in chains," and a father who was such an avid
reader of Mark Twain that he quit his job to float downriver to
New Orleans. Dillard herself, at about the same time (1955),
discovered *The Field Book of Ponds and Streams* in her neighborhood library and embarked on a lifetime of discoveries about the
natural world (see "The Fixed," p. 171). When she was a senior
in high school, she rebelled briefly against her Christian upbringing, a rebellion her minister countered by filling her arms with
books by C. S. Lewis. At Hollins College in Virginia, she majored
in English and creative writing, but also studied theology "because of the great beauty of it." Like all theologians, Dillard is
concerned about questions of pain, death, communion, rebirth,
and renewal (see "Singing with the Fundamentalists," p. 705).
Like all parents, she feels these questions acutely in the presence
of a child. "Aces and Eights" is from *Teaching a Stone to Talk*
(1982), a book that followed eight years after her Pulitzer Prize–
winning *Pilgrim at Tinker Creek*.

I

I am here against my good judgment. I understood long ago just   1
what it would be like; I knew that the weekend would be, above
all, over. At home at my desk I doodled on tablets and imagined
myself and the child standing side by side on the riverbank behind
the cottage in the woods, standing on the riverbank and watching
the blossoms float down, or the dead leaves float down, or just the
water—whatever it would be—and thinking, each of us: remember this, remember this now, this weekend in the country. And I
knew that instead of seeing (let alone remembering) the blossoms,
or the leaves, or whatever, the child and I would each see and
remember some dim picture of our own selves as figures side by
side on the riverbank, as figures in our own future memories, as
focal points for some absurd, manufactured nostalgia.

There was no use going. At best, we would miss the whole thing.   2
If any part of the weekend should prove in the least pleasant, and
worth trying to remember on that account, or on account of its
never-to-be-repeated quality, it would be unbearable. Who would
subject a child to such suffering? On the other hand, maybe it
would rain.

I decided, in short, not to go. The child is nine, and already   3
morbidly nostalgic and given to wringing meaningful moments out
of our least occasions. I am thirty-five; my tolerance for poignancy
has diminished to the vanishing point. If I wish, and I do not, I can
have never-to-be-repeated moments, however dreadful, anywhere
and anytime, simply by calling that category to mind.

But we are here: the child, and I, and the dog. It is a weekend in   4
mid-July. We will leave here Sunday morning early.

The cottage is in the Appalachians, in a long-settled river valley.   5
The forest is in its ninth or twelfth growth: oak-maple-hickory,
with hemlock and laurel in the mountain gorges. It is the same
everywhere in the Appalachians, from Maine to Georgia. There is
no place else in the fifty states where you could build a 2,050-mile
linear trail through country that changes so little.

The ridges are dry—blackjack oak, berry bushes, and pine—and   6
steep. Near here there is a place on a steep mountain called Carson's Castle. One summer many years ago a neighbor, Noah Very,
took me and my cousins on an outing to this Carson's Castle. It is
nothing but a cave in the mountaintop with a stone ledge in front
of it. The ledge overhangs the next valley so far that you have to
look behind you, between your feet, to see the stream far below. In
the eighteenth century, this stream became part of the state line.

Mr. Very walked us children up there and told us that when the   7
Indians chased Mr. Carson—some time ago—he ran up the mountain and hid in the cave. And when the Indians, who were naturally conducting their chase Indian file, attained the cliff edge, each
paused to wonder where Mr. Carson might have gone. Mr. Carson
took advantage of their momentary confusion by pushing them,
one by one, from the ledge—from the ledge, from the mountain,
and as it would happen, out of state. He pushed them until there
were none. That, at any rate, is the legend. An old Indian legend, I
believe.

Literalist and begrudger as I was and am, I expected to see a   8
rather fancy castle on the mountaintop that day, and was disappointed. But now I choose to remember this outing as a raging
success, and am grateful to "Count" Noah Very, and intend to bake
him a cake while we are here, although he has long since turned
into an old, disgreeable coot.

The ridges are dry, I say, and the bottomlands are wet. There are   9
sycamores on the riverbanks, and tulip poplars, willows, and silver
maples; there is jewelweed in the sun and rhododendron in the

shade. The cottage is in a small clearing in the woods on a river-bank.

The child has discovered the blackboard in the children's room. 10 She wheels it into the living room where I sit and writes on it, "I love Francis Burn." She says that Francis Burn is a boy in her school, going into the sixth grade. When I ask her what it is about Francis Burn that she loves, she answers that he is cute.

Once I knew a woman, who has since died, whose field was 11 German philosophy. When I knew her she had just been widowed. Her husband—an old man, remote and stern—had held a university chair in intellectual history; between them they had written a dozen books. Once, when the woman and I were alone, she broke down. She broke down in grief, and cried in my arms, and repeated into my shoulder, "He was so cute!"

The child wheels the blackboard against a bare wall, to serve as 12 our mural or graffito for the weekend. She is nine, beloved, as open-faced as the sky and as self-contained. I have watched her grow. As recently as three or four years ago, she had a young child's perfectly shallow receptiveness; she fitted into the world of time, it fitted into her, as thoughtlessly as sky fits its edges, or a river its banks. But as she has grown, her smile has widened with a touch of fear and her glance has taken on depth. Now she is aware of some of the losses you incur by being here—the extortionary rent you have to pay as long as you stay. We have lived together so often, and parted so many times, that the very sight of each other means loss. The ever-taller embrace of our hellos is a tearful affair, aware as we are of our imminent parting; fortunately the same anticipation cancels our good-byes, and we embrace cheerfully, like long-lost kin at a reunion.

I have not been here in years. I think of it, though, when I 13 cannot sleep; I stand on the bank and watch the river move, and watch the water's speckled reflections jiggle on the overarching boughs of sycamore, and jiggle on the sycamore's trunk, and on the bottoms of its leaves. Across the river I see pasture veined by the thin paths of cows. The cowpaths wobble over the floodplain and cut around the junipers and clumps of thistle or rose; they climb a close-cropped slope whose every bump and ripple shows, a slope which is actually the foot of a wooded mountain. The pasture ends, and the forest begins, in a saggy wooden fence.

Personally, I find the keeping of golden Guernseys rather an 14 affectation. But the actual cows themselves, I allow, are innocent. The actual cows themselves, in this soporific vision of mine, are splayed about the landscape, lending solid areas of warm color to a field otherwise pallidly, sentimentally, green. Behind their pasture is a border of woods, a sloping cornfield, and beyond, rolling ridges.

When we opened the cottage over an hour ago, I found a note   15
taped to the icebox door. It read: "Matches in the tin box on mantel. Do not eat purple berries from bush by porch. Bulbs of creek grass OK, good boiled. Blue berries in woods make you sick." Accompanying the text were careful schematic drawings of the plants in question: pokeberry, something I do not recognize, huckleberry. Huckleberries are perfectly edible. Many people have used this cottage over the years—including, I suppose, grouches with sour stomachs, and hoaxers. If I were interested in such things, I would have to do all the research again. I am not interested in such things. It has been quite a while since I sampled bits of the landscape. I have brought a box of groceries from home.

It is all woods on this side of the river—woods, and a surprising   16
number of paved roads. A steep driveway leads from a hill down to the cottage; you park beside the cottage on the grass, on that thin, round-bladed, bluish grass that grows under trees. The cottage rests on cinder blocks; a sort of yard slopes to the river's edge.

In the 1920s, American manufacturers started prefabricating   17
summer cottages; this cottage is one of the first of those. It does not look prefabricated. It is just on the fussy side of idyllic—white frame, two bedrooms, a big screened porch, and lots of painted latticework. When you lie in bed you can see the big bolts in the ceiling that hold the house together. The bolts are painted white, like everything else.

You know what it is to open up a cottage. You barge in with   18
your box of groceries and your duffelbag full of books. You drop them on a counter and rush to the far window to look out. I would say that coming into a cottage is like being born, except we do not come into the world with a box of groceries and a duffelbag full of books—unless you want to take these as metonymic symbols for culture. Opening up a summer cottage is like being born in this way: at the moment you enter, you have all the time you are ever going to have.

The child maintains—she has always maintained—that she re-   19
members being born. It is a surefire attention-getter. "I remember," she says, "the light hurt my eyes." Many of her anecdotes are

literary like this, and more than a little self-pitying. Should I stop hugging her so much?

Filling the window's frame, crowding each of its nine square 20 panes, is the river, moving down.

The yellow afternoon light has faded from the water and the blue 21 evening light is fading; the sycamore branches over the bank are flattening and growing dark. I see the sky on the running river. Blue, it shatters and pulls; blue, it catches and pools behind a rock. The sun is down behind the mountains, but not yet down behind the world.

The child and I go to play in the water. We leave the cottage, 22 crouch on the bank, and send sticks down the river. Soon the night is too dark for us to see. We fetch some candle stubs from the house; we fetch some flat kindling from the woodpile; we light the candles, stick them to the flat wood, and launch them into the river. The river and the sky are just visible as blueness, bordered everywhere by indecipherable black. Now we can see the candle flames mark their own passage. We watch them wander above the water; we watch them wobble downstream and gutter out, one by one, just before they would have rounded the black, invisible bend.

"You cannot kill time," I read once, "without injuring eternity." 23 Our setting the candles afloat down the river—was this not a pretty thing to do? Why, when we were actually seeing the candles wobble down the river, did I think, this should be better? It seemed both to take too long and end too soon. As a memory, however, it is already looking good.

In bed I stare at the painted bolts in the walls. I hear the river 24 outside the window, if I remember to listen. I read a magazine which contains instructions for jumping from a moving train:

> If for some extraordinary reason you have to jump off a moving train, look ahead and try to pick a spot that looks soft. Throw your pack and, as you jump, lean way back (this is the hard part) and take huge, leaping steps in the air. If you lean back far enough, and don't trip as you touch the ground, you will experience the rare thrill of running 35 to 40 miles an hour.

I cannot remember to listen for the river. Some elation keeps me 25 from sleeping. I leave the bed and move to the porch, and stand in the open back door. There is a whippoorwill; there are stars over the pasture. It occurs to me to try to step down from the porch, which is moving in orbit at 68,400 miles an hour. I plan to take huge, leaping steps in the air. It will be, I realize, a rare thrill, but unfortunately I cannot find a landing space that looks soft.

II

Saturday morning, and all is changed. Sunlight on the table and   26
on the shining wood floor is bright; the child and I walk around
squinting and eager for action. How could I ever have wanted to
read? I can scarcely credit that we played cards on this table last
night, almost whispering, in a circle of lamplight not four feet
across. Who, on a Saturday morning, would think of reading or
playing cards? We are as changed from evening to morning, and as
careless of yesterday, as if we had flown overnight to Nepal.

The child has found a bicycle under the porch; she wants to ride   27
it. Incredibly, there is a bicycle pump half buried in the dry dirt
beside it—a pump which works, once I scour and oil the shaft and
screw dirt from the nozzle with a paperclip. I drag the bike out and
stand it in the bluish grass at the foot of the driveway next to an
apple tree. Pump the tires. I find a wrench to adjust the seat, find
some WD-40 to loosen the bolt; lower the seat. Adjust the han-
dlebars. Oil the chain and the steering column. Wash the seat, the
handgrips, the fenders while I'm at it.

Throughout these tasks, which occupy the morning, the child   28
and I are singing some old Dixieland standards: "The World Is
Waiting for the Sunrise," "Cherokee," "Basin Street Blues"—most
of which we have sung often before. When the bicycle is ready to
roll, it is almost time for lunch. The child mounts the bike and
wobbles up the driveway. She takes a right, turns down the hill,
and vanishes, singing at the top of her lungs.

On the bluish grass under the apple tree are two wrenches, a can   29
of WD-40, a hammer, a scouring pad, a straightened paperclip, a
pile of dirty paper towels and sponges, a pail of dirty water, and the
child's sweater. I am hungry. In all the history of the world, it has
never been so late.

I do not know when the child will be back, or if she will want to   30
take a walk. I haul out my notebooks and sit at the table.

The child bursts in, hale and enthusiastic. She has discovered a   31
long loop route around which to ride. While she talks she reaches
into the table's drawer and finds the deck of cards we brought. She
sits at the table, rummages through the deck, and asks if we have
any clothespins.

I am always amazed at how straight she sits in a chair, at how   32
touching is the sight of her apparently boneless hands, and at how
pleased she herself is with those hands, how conscious of them.
She asked me once if she could insure them. Do we have any
clothespins?

She wants clothespins to fasten some cards to her bicycle so that   33 when the wheels turn the cards will slap in the spokes. She pulls from the deck a pair of aces and a pair of eights.

Last night we played poker, the two of us. We got popcorn butter   34
on the cards; we used aspirin tablets as chips. In the course of the play I showed aces and eights—"dead man's hand"—so I told her about that. I told her we call aces and eights "dead man's hand" because Wild Bill Hickok was holding them in a poker game when he was shot in the back. I no longer remember precisely why someone shot Wild Bill Hickok in the back, but I made up something I hope she forgets before she passes it on.

I find her some spring clothespins in this pre-equipped cottage   35
which apparently has everything needed for life on earth except poker chips. I make her a sandwich, and put it in a knapsack with a jar of milk, a banana, and a funny little riddle book I found last night. Off she goes.

Once, many years ago, there was a child of nine who loved   36
Walter Milligan. One Saturday morning she was walking in the neighborhood of her school. She walked and thought, "The plain fact is—as I have heard so many times—that in several years' time I will not love Walter Milligan. I will very probably marry someone else. I will be untrue; I will forget Walter Milligan."

Deeply, unforgettably, she thought that if what they said about   37
Walter Milligan was true, then the rest went with it: that she would one day like her sister, and that she would be glad she had taken piano lessons. She was standing at the curb, waiting for the light to change. It was all she could do to remember not to get run over, so she would live to betray herself. For a series of connected notions presented themselves: if all these passions of mine be overturned, then what will become of me? Then what am I now?

She seemed real enough to herself, willful and conscious, but she   38
had to consider the possibility—the likelihood, even—that she was a short-lived phenomenon, a fierce, vanishing thing like a hard shower, or a transitional form like a tadpole or winter bud—not the thing in itself but a running start on the thing—and that she was being borne helplessly and against all her wishes to suicide, to the certain loss of self and all she held dear. Herself and all that she held dear—this particular combination of love for Walter Milligan, hatred of sister and piano lessons, etc.—would vanish, destroyed against her wishes by her own hand.

When she changed, where will that other person have gone?   39
Could anyone keep her alive, this person here on the street, and her passions? Will the unthinkable adult that she would become remember her? Will she think she is stupid? Will she laugh at her?

She was a willful one, and she made a vow. The light changed;   40
she crossed the street and set off up the sloping sidewalk by the
school. I must be loyal, for no one else is. If this is the system, then I
will buck it. I will until I die ride my bike and walk along these very
streets, where I belong. I will until I die love Walter Milligan and
hate my sister and read and walk in the woods. And I will never,
not I, sit and drink and smoke and do nothing but talk.

Foremost in her vow was this, that she would remember the   41
vow itself. She woke to her surroundings; it was cold. Even walking so fiercely uphill, she was cold, and illuminated by a powerful
energy. To her left was the stone elementary school, deserted on
Saturday. Across the street was a dark row of houses, stone and
brick, with their pillared porches. The porch floors were painted
red or gray or green. This was not her own neighborhood, but it
was her turf. She pushed uphill to the next corner. She committed
to memory the look of that block, that neighborhood: the familiar
cracked sidewalk, how pale it was, how sand collected in its cracks;
the sycamores; the muffled sky.

Now it is early Saturday afternoon—the center of the weekend.   42
I am sitting under the sycamore on the riverbank below the   43
cottage, just below the driveway. The dog and I have returned from
a walk through the woods by the river upstream. Now I sit and
look around and try to comfort the dog, who, on his part, is trying
to persuade me to continue our walk downstream to New Orleans.

It is the height of day in the height of summer—mid-July. This   44
means that the sky essentially does not exist, or is not, at any rate, a
thing you would care to examine. Under the sky in the distance
ahead roll some hazy wooded ridges—the mountains. Below them
are crowded slopes of field corn. In their floodplain pasture a dozen
brown cows are drowsing on their feet, heads down, or browsing
near the fence on slopes where the woods' shadow falls. I watch a
flycatcher on a limb across the river. The air is so fat with food that
this flycatcher never leaves its perch; it simply turns its head, snaps
its beak, and dines.

Two things are distracting me. One is a gang of carp on the river   45
bottom; I can see the carp where the sycamore boughs cast shade.
During times of excess leisure like this, you can see not only fish,
but also a loose-knit network of sunlight on fishes' backs. The same
moving pattern falls on the stony river bottom. It looks as though
someone has cast over the fish a throw net made of sunlight. Some
people eat carp.

Near the bank at my feet is a sunny backwater upon which   46
dozens of water striders are water striding about: They seem to be

rushing so they don't fall in. I soon discover that these insects are actually skidding along on the underside of a cloud. The water here is reflecting a patch of sky and a complete cumulus cloud. It is on the bottom of this cloud that the water striders are foraging. They are the size of biplanes or prehistoric birds. They scrabble all unawares on a cloud bottom, clinging to this delicate stuff upside down, like lizards on a ceiling.

While these complexities are narrowing the focus of my attention, the dog looks up. I look up. The wide world swings into view and fades at once while I listen for a sound. The dog and I are both hearing it. We hear a slow series of clicks up on the road. It is the child, riding her bicycle up the hill. 47

The child is riding her bicycle up the hill. I stand and look around; the thick summer foliage blocks the road from view. I turn back toward the river and hear the playing cards slap in the spokes. They click and slap slowly, for the hill is steep. Now the pushing grows suddenly easier, evidently; the cards click and slap. At once, imperceptibly, she starts down. The pace increases. The cards are slapping and she is rolling; the pace speeds up, she is rolling, and the cards are slapping so fast the sounds blur. And so she whirs down the hill. I can see her through the woods downstream where the road evens out. She is fine, still coasting, and leaning way back. 48

We do love scaring ourselves silly—but less every year. Have I mentioned that my classmates and I are now thirty-five? 49

There is an old Pawnee notion that when you are in your thirties and forties you are "on top." The idea is that at this age you can view grandly, in the fullness of your strength, both the uphill struggle of youth and the downhill slide of age. I suggest that this metaphor is inaccurate. If there is such a place as "on top"—if there is a sensation of riding a life span's crest—it does not last ten or twenty years. On the contrary, the crest is so small that I, for one, missed it altogether. 50

You are young, you are on your way up, when you cannot imagine how you will save yourself from death by boredom until dinner, until bed, until the next day arrives to be outwaited, and then, slow slap, the next. You read in despair all the titles of the books on the bookshelf; you play with your fingers; you revolve in your upholstered chair, slide out of the chair upside down onto your head, hope you will somehow damage your heart by waiting for dinner in that position, and think that life by its mere appalling length is a feat of endurance for which you haven't the strength. 51

But momentum propels you over the crest. Imperceptibly, you 52 start down. When do the days start to blur and then, breaking your heart, the seasons? The cards click faster in the spokes; you pitch forward. You roll headlong, out of control. The blur of cards makes one long sound like a bomb's whine, the whine of many bombs, and you know your course is fatal.

Now the world swings into view again. I shift my weight. The cumulus cloud has dissolved in the river. The water striders have lost their grip on the heavens. One by one they seemed to have slipped from the sky, somersaulted in the air, and landed on their feet in this backwater under the sycamore. The carp are stirring up silt from the bottom. The cows are apparently moribund; the dog is at standby alert. 53

Here it comes again. The child has gone around the loop of roads and is climbing the hill once more. I turn toward the cottage, thinking she might be coming down the drive. But there she goes again, down the hill. She really does sound like the London blitz. 54

This is limestone country. That means the dairy farmers lose a cow every few years; the cows, poor things, fall through their pastures when the underground roofs collapse. They break their legs or worse and die there of shock, I guess, or blood loss, or thirst, or else the farmers shoot them there. I once saw one of these cows which had fallen through. 55

Many years ago, walking far downstream where the land is clear, I came across one of these cows, a golden Guernsey lying down in a pasture with her back toward me. I only discovered that she was in fact *in absentia* by walking around to her front and seeing that she had no insides. She had not so much as *one* inside that I could see. Her eyes were gone down to the bone, and her udder and belly were opened and empty; there was her backbone. She was dry leather on a frame, like a kettledrum. Her mouth was open and there was nothing in it but teeth. Instead of the roof of her mouth I saw the dark, dry pan of her skull. Both her front legs were broken. They were stuck in the same hole in the ground—a hole two feet across, limestone shards with grass growing on them. The hole was as jagged as a poked egg. How could she have known which step was the false one? 56

I backed away. Trying to spread my weight, I made a wide circle around her, the way I had come, hoping the ground would hold me and not having the faintest idea what I would do if it did not, or how far I would fall. Back on the riverside path, I turned. Once again, from the back, that hollow golden Guernsey—old skin-and-bones—looked, as the saying goes, as though she were only sleeping. 57

It is limestone country, and toward the town is a mineral springs.   58
Before the turn of the century, people from several cities bought
farms here, or built summer houses, so they could take vacations
near the mineral springs. Some of these summer people retired
here and took to farming. The local farmers, a passive lot, accepted
the new gentry—so easily distinguishable in town by their plaid
shirts and rubber boots. This was, as I say, around the turn of the
century.

Soon the valley became, like so many places, the height of fash-   59
ion among its own inhabitants. The children of the original summer folk moved here, some of them, and raised their own families
here. Then the back-to-the-landers of my generation came, and
began clearing land for starveling farms. By then, most of the original farmers had moved to the cities.

The old gentry families and the newcomers got together. They   60
talked about community. They raised barns; they built a Quaker
meeting house and used it to organize the blocking of a power
project. They held square dances; they blocked a proposal to widen
the highway.

They are a people of profound beliefs. They treat cancer with tea.   61
They have come here to abandon society to its own foolishness.
They believe in wood heat, unpasteurized milk, and whales. To
everyone they are unfailingly helpful.

I meant to accomplish a good bit today. Instead I keep thinking: 62
Will the next generation of people remember to drain the pipes in
the fall? I will leave them a note.

Late afternoon: we are inside the cottage now, and baking. I am   63
trying to tell the child a few of the principles by which I live: A
good gag is worth any amount of time, money, and effort; never
draw to fill an inside straight; always keep score in games, never in
love; never say "Muskrat Ramble"; always keep them guessing;
never listen to the same conversation twice; and (this is the hard
part) listen to no one. I must be shouting—listen to no one! At this
the child walks out of the kitchen, goes into her room, and shuts
the door. She is this obedient. I have never detected a jot of rebellion in her. If she stays this way she is doomed. On the other hand,
I wonder: did she do it for the gag? Even so.

We are baking a cake for Count Noah Very, the neighbor. Here a   64
concern for truth forces me to confess that although I am writing in
the present tense, actually some years have elapsed since this
weekend in the country. In the course of those years, Noah Very

has died. He died of a stroke, and, sadly, was not mourned by kin. His death, of course, makes me recall him with more fondness than I felt for him while he lived, for in truth he was a grouch who despised everyone.

It has been almost thirty years since Noah Very walked us chil- 65 dren up to Carson's Castle. Now Noah is in his seventies. He is a hermit who hides in the woods. He is a direct descendant of Jones Very, the transcendentalist poet who composed "The Spirit Land" and other abstracting sonnets.

When Noah was in his twenties, with a degree in English litera- 66 ture from Yale, he had one of his parents' servants' cottages moved to its present location in the woods downstream. He intended, he told me once, to spend a year or two there writing a novel. Some- where in there he took a false step, like the cow. He got involved milling lumber with which to build bookcases. In his thirties he made a desk. He inlaid the desk's surface with multicolored ve- neers in elaborate patterns; he carved the drawer pulls in the shape of veined oak leaves. God knows it is your human obligation to admire this desk if you ever visit him and get past the door—and in fact, I never did see such a wonderful desk.

Many years ago his wife renounced him for his adulteries; he 67 renounced their children, who are now variously spoused and dis- persed. Over the years he renounced meat, obligation, soap, work, pleasure, ambition, and other people. When the child delivered to him an invitation just before dinner, he was asleep. Like almost everyone, he considers himself an intellectual. He does his shop- ping when the store opens; if he sees another car parked at the store, he drives around in a rage until it goes away.

He refuses all visitors but young women and girls. When other 68 people come into his woods, he hides and watches them. He hides in the hemlocks; he hides in a silver maple; he hides among clumps of witch hazel. He hides and watches the people knock on his door. He told me all this. The interesting part is why people visit him at all. Because he is hiding in the woods, he cannot refuse zucchini squash. He is the valley's sole outlet for zucchini squash.

One woman, incidentally, who brings him gifts of food weekly, 69 and who has not laid eyes on him in four years, told me she likes this feeling of being watched.

Inside the cottage, Noah accepts sherry and cake. He has aged. 70 The bones of his skull are tent poles from which his skin hangs in catenary curves. The back of his skull is small, but his face is large. He is clean-shaven. His bluish mouth usually has a whining or peeved expression, but tonight the mouth, and the man, look pleased. The child, who is feeling particularly charming, has got herself up in a yellow dress; she arranges herself attractively and temporarily on the couch under a side window. Noah sits in a wicker chair by the magazines and explains how he views various magazines. I haven't seen him in years. I notice with some shock that he is wearing a silk shirt.

It is dark. Outside the whippoorwill is loosening up for a 71 marathon. Actually, I know why the child loves Francis Burn. It is because he is the one to whom she has given her love. But why were we given this fierce love? It beats me. I, too, love one. The child writes poems about Francis Burn and leaves them around for me to find.

"How old are you?" Noah asks the child.   72
"Nine."   73
"And what grade are you going into?"   74
"Fourth." She cannot hide a look of contempt. Her whole class   75
is going into fourth grade.
"Do you know I can't keep track of how old I am? I started   76
losing track of my own age many, many years ago, long before you were even born." If there is anything the child cannot grasp, it is why some adults try to impress her, and why, even if there were a good reason for it, they go about it so badly.
"My children used to think that was the funniest thing, that   77
someone wouldn't know how old he was. Do you think it is funny?"
The child says, "I think it is completely ridiculous."   78

I am sitting opposite the child, with an ashtray on my lap. Noah, 79
relaxed, is resting his legs on the low wicker table between us.
"One time," Noah is saying, "when my children were little, and   80
we were all living where I live now, I looked out of the window and saw the children playing by the river. There is a little patch of sand on the bank there. The children were all very young, very small, and they were playing with buckets, and pouring water, and piling sand on each other's feet. I remember thinking, 'This is it, now, when the children are little. This will be a time called "when the children were little." ' I couldn't hear anything through the window; I just saw them. It was morning. They were all three blond and still curly-headed then, and the sun was behind them."
I looked closely at Noah, who was looking at the child.   81
"I said to myself, 'Noah, now you remember this sight, the chil- 82
dren being so young together and playing by the river this particu-

lar morning. You remember it.' And I remember it as if it happened this morning. It must have been summer. There are another twenty years in there I don't remember at all."

He asks how it feels to be here for just a weekend. He explains   83 how well he knows this land and cottage; his grandfather used to own it all. His grandfather planted the apple tree beside the driveway, the apple tree under which we fixed the bike this morning. Now he is addressing the child overheartily, as if she were three. She encourages this. Later she tells me she thinks he is "stupid." But he catches her off guard. He is lecturing her about his grandfather's apple tree, in which she has not the slightest interest.

He indicates the window behind her—the yard where his grand-   84 father planted the apple tree. The child, to escape his overexcited gaze, turns on the couch, kneels up against its back, and pretends to look through the window at the apple tree—which, however, she cannot see, because it is dark. She is looking instead at her own reflection. I am just across from her, and can see her in the window.

"Do you know how long it takes to grow an apple tree?"   85

Noah is leaning forward, and all but singing. "Do you know how   86 long it takes to grow an apple tree?

> *You'd have to wait*
> *until you were ALL grown up . . .*
> *and married . . .*
> *and had FOUR children. . . .''*

She is listening. She hears the hard part, about being all grown   87 up, and married, and having four children. . . . And as he speaks, her eyes slide out of focus, leave the room, and fill with the blank, impossible figures of these strangers. There is a strange, unthinkable female in a yellow dress, and a tall, blank husband beside her. There are these four children of hers. And she thinks, I swear she thinks, I see her eyes widen as she thinks, seeing these blurred children all in a row: The oldest would be older than I am!

I laugh. The child's eyes snap into focus, and abruptly, delighted,   88 meet my gaze in the window. The woman, husband, and four children vanish. The child sees this: inside the near, shadowed outline of her own reflection in the window, a smaller, distant reflection under a lamp—just me, a woman in her thirties, drinking sherry and smoking a cigarette.

The child is holding my eye, which she sees inside the lighted   89 scene inside the breast of her dress. She is laughing because I laughed and she knows why. She looks at me deeply, the way she does, smiling enormously. I put out my cigarette. The child turns

herself around on the couch, and together we resume listening to
Noah.

Later, when Noah leaves, I am sad not to be seeing him again for   90
what will likely be such a long time. But Noah says, shaking my
hand, that I am silly, that at "our age" there is no such thing as a
long time. We are saying good-bye on the grass outside the porch;
Noah is taking the path through the woods back home. He has
refused a flashlight; he has accepted the cake and several books,
among them a Fowler's *English Usage*.

Before bed the child and I play several games of spit. She shows   91
no sign of flagging, and it is, after all, Saturday night in this hemisphere, and we are leaving first thing in the morning, so we get out
the aspirin again, and find a full deck, and I teach her the pyramid
system of betting at blackjack. She likes it. Although it takes many
hours of working this system, and much caution, to beat the house
by even a little, as I stress, she nevertheless wins six hundred dollars in forty-five minutes, for which the house, by prearrangement,
pays sixty cents. Wasn't there something I wanted to write down?

III

Now it is Sunday morning, mid-July, hotter than blazes, the   92
birds half dead and hushed. We are on our way; we are taking a
last look at the river. The water seems lower. The water seems
lower, and there's a bit of chalk moon over the woods downstream. On the way back we will visit my sister, as we did on the
way—my sister, whom I love. We have eaten and packed the car.

It is funny how the occasion imperceptibly changes, like the   93
light, at an inconstant rate. At any given glance you may see that
the dog has rolled over in his sleep, or the trees have lost their
leaves. Morning drains inexpressibly into lunchtime, or Christmastime. Overhead the geese are migrating, just as they were the last
time you looked. You wash the dishes, turn around, and it is summer again, or some other time, or time to go.

The child and I are standing by the river. Circling us is the dog, 94
who has been disconsolate since we packed the car. He keeps
coming up with the idea of hiding in the woods, and keeps rejecting the idea. The child and I are standing side by side. Beyond the
pasture, the mountains have vanished in haze. The cows are absent. Over the river the sycamore branches hang wooden without
wavering; light from the water wobbles around the branches'
undersides and flat across the bottoms of their leaves.

"I'm not going," the child says. "I'm staying here." Some specu- 95
lation ensues about who is in charge of granting wishes. We watch
the water striders. We are, alas, imagining ourselves in the future
remembering standing here now, the morning light on the green
valley and on the clear river, the child playing with the woman's
fingers. I had not thought of that before we came, that she would
be playing with my fingers, or that we would hear trucks shifting
down to climb the hill behind the cottage. We turn to leave.

And leaving—let me add by way of epilogue—we find ourselves 96
on the receiving end of a tiny, final event, a piece of unexpected
wind.

A ripple of wind comes down from the woods and across the 97
clearing toward us. We see a wave of shadow and gloss where the
short grass bends and the cottage eaves tremble. It hits us in
the back. It is a single gust, a sport, a rogue breeze out of the north,
as if some reckless, impatient wind has bumped the north door
open on its hinges and let out this acre of scent familiar and forgotten, this cool scent of tundra, and of November. Fall! Who authorized this intrusion? Stop or I'll shoot. It is an entirely misplaced
air—fall, that I have utterly forgotten, that could be here again,
another fall, and here it is only July. I thought I was younger, and
would have more time. The gust crosses the river and blackens the
water where it passes, like a finger closing slats.

ALICE WALKER

To Hell with Dying

Alice Walker (1944–   ), poet, essayist, and Pulitzer Prize–
winning novelist, grew up in rural Georgia in a four-room house
with seven older brothers. When she was eight, one of her
brothers accidentally shot her in the eye with a BB gun, and
because the Walkers had no car to reach the hospital, the wound
resulted in permanent blindness on one side. Walker was the
valedictorian of her high school class, and her partial blindness
allowed her to win a scholarship for handicapped students to
Spelman College in Atlanta; her neighbors raised the $75 she
needed for bus fare. At Spelman, Walker became involved in the
civil rights movement, an involvement that led to her first published essay, in *The American Scholar* in 1967. "To Hell with

Dying," her first published story, appeared the same year. The story, based on Walker's own experience with an elderly neighbor, was written on the day of his funeral. Walker's short stories are collected in *In Love and Trouble* (1973) and *You Can't Keep a Good Woman Down* (1981). Her novels to date are *The Third Life of Grange Copeland* (1970), *Meridian* (1976), and *The Color Purple* (1982). *The Temple of My Familiar* (1989) is a reimagination of human history through the eyes of a series of storytellers.

"To hell with dying," my father would say. "These children want Mr. Sweet!" 1

Mr. Sweet was a diabetic and an alcoholic and a guitar player and lived down the road from us on a neglected cotton farm. My older brothers and sisters got the most benefit from Mr. Sweet, for when they were growing up he had quite a few years ahead of him and so was capable of being called back from the brink of death any number of times—whenever the voice of my father reached him as he lay expiring. "To hell with dying, man," my father would say, pushing the wife away from the bedside (in tears although she knew the death was not necessarily the last one unless Mr. Sweet really wanted it to be). "These children want Mr. Sweet!" And they did want him, for at a signal from Father they would come crowding around the bed and throw themselves on the covers, and whoever was the smallest at the time would kiss him all over his wrinkled brown face and tickle him so that he would laugh all down in his stomach, and his mustache, which was long and sort of straggly, would shake like Spanish moss and was also that color.

Mr. Sweet had been ambitious as a boy, wanted to be a doctor or lawyer or sailor, only to find that black men fare better if they are not. Since he could become none of these things he turned to fishing as his only earnest career and playing the guitar as his only claim to doing anything extraordinarily well. His son, the only one that he and his wife, Miss Mary, had, was shiftless as the day is long and spent money as if he were trying to see the bottom of the mint, which Mr. Sweet would tell him was the clean brown palm of his hand. Miss Mary loved her "baby," however, and worked hard to get him the "li'l necessaries" of life, which turned out mostly to be women.

Mr. Sweet was a tall, thinnish man with thick kinky hair going dead white. He was dark brown, his eyes were squinty and sort of bluish, and he chewed Brown Mule tobacco. He was constantly on the verge of being blind drunk, for he brewed his own liquor and was not in the least a stingy sort of man, and was always very melancholy and sad, though frequently when he was "feelin' good" he'd dance around the yard with us, usually keeling over just as my mother came to see what the commotion was.

Toward all of us children he was very kind, and had the grace to be shy with us, which is unusual in grown-ups. He had great respect for my mother for she never held his drunkenness against him and would let us play with him even when he was about to fall in the fireplace from drink. Although Mr. Sweet would sometimes lose complete or nearly complete control of his head and neck so that he would loll in his chair, his mind remained strangely acute and his speech not too affected. His ability to be drunk and sober at the same time made him an ideal playmate, for he was as weak as we were and we could usually best him in wrestling, all the while keeping a fairly coherent conversation going.

We never felt anything of Mr. Sweet's age when we played with him. We loved his wrinkles and would draw some on our brows to be like him, and his white hair was my special treasure and he knew it and would never come to visit us just after he had had his hair cut off at the barbershop. Once he came to our house for something, probably to see my father about fertilizer for his crops because, although he never paid the slightest attention to his crops, he liked to know what would be best to use on them if he ever did. Anyhow, he had not come with his hair since he had just had it shaved off at the barbershop. He wore a huge straw hat to keep off the sun and also to keep his head away from me. But as soon as I saw him I ran up and demanded that he take me up and kiss me with his funny beard which smelled so strongly of tobacco. Looking forward to burying my small fingers into his woolly hair I threw away his hat only to find he had done something to his hair, that it was no longer there! I let out a squall which made my mother think that Mr. Sweet had finally dropped me in the well or something and from that day I've been wary of men in hats. However, not long after, Mr. Sweet showed up with his hair grown out and just as white and kinky and impenetrable as it ever was.

Mr. Sweet used to call me his princess, and I believed it. He made me feel pretty at five and six, and simply outrageously devastating at the blazing age of eight and a half. When he came to our house with his guitar the whole family would stop whatever they were doing to sit around him and listen to him play. He liked to play "Sweet Georgia Brown," that was what he called me sometimes, and also he liked to play "Caldonia" and all sorts of sweet, sad, wonderful songs which he sometimes made up. It was from one of these songs that I heard that he had had to marry Miss Mary when he had in fact loved somebody else (now living in Chi-ca-go, or De-stroy, Michigan). He was not sure that Joe Lee, her "baby," was also his baby. Sometimes he would cry and that was an indication that he was about to die again. And so we would all get prepared, for we were sure to be called upon.

I was seven the first time I remember actually participating in one of Mr. Sweet's "revivals"—my parents told me I had participated before, I had been the one chosen to kiss him and tickle him long before I knew the rite of Mr. Sweet's rehabilitation. He had come to our house, it was a few years after his wife's death, and was very sad, and also, typically, very drunk. He sat on the floor next to me and my older brother, the rest of the children were grown up and lived elsewhere, and began to play his guitar and cry. I held his woolly head in my arms and wished I could have been old enough to have been the woman he loved so much and that I had not been lost years and years ago.

When he was leaving, my mother said to us that we'd better sleep light that night for we'd probably have to go over to Mr. Sweet's before daylight. And we did. For soon after we had gone to bed one of the neighbors knocked on our door and called my father and said that Mr. Sweet was sinking fast and if he wanted to get in a word before the crossover he'd better shake a leg and get over to Mr. Sweet's house. All the neighbors knew to come to our house if something was wrong with Mr. Sweet, but they did not know how we always managed to make him well, or at least stop him from dying, when he was so often near death. As soon as we heard the cry we got up, my brother and I and my mother and father, and put on our clothes. We hurried out of the house and down the road for we were always afraid that we might someday be too late and Mr. Sweet would get tired of dallying.

When we got to the house, a very poor shack really, we found   10
the front room full of neighbors and relatives and someone met us at the door and said it was all very sad that old Mr. Sweet Little (for Little was his family name, although we mostly ignored it) was about to kick the bucket. My parents were advised not to take my brother and me into the "death room," seeing we were so young and all, but we were so much more accustomed to the death room than he that we ignored him and dashed in without giving his warning a second thought. I was almost in tears, for these deaths upset me fearfully, and the thought of how much depended on me and my brother (who was such a ham most of the time) made me very nervous.

The doctor was bending over the bed and turned back to tell us for at least the tenth time in the history of my family that, alas, old Mr. Sweet Little was dying and that the children had best not see the face of implacable death (I didn't know what "implacable" was, but whatever it was, Mr. Sweet was not!). My father pushed him rather abruptly out of the way saying, as he always did and very loudly for he was saying it to Mr. Sweet, "To hell with dying, man, these children want Mr. Sweet"—which was my cue to throw myself upon the bed and kiss Mr. Sweet all around the whiskers and under the eyes and around the collar of his nightshirt where he smelled so strongly of all sorts of things, mostly liniment.

I was very good at bringing him around, for as soon as I saw that he was struggling to open his eyes I knew he was going to be all right, and so could finish my revival sure of success. As soon as his eyes were open he would begin to smile and that way I knew that I had surely won. Once, though, I got a tremendous scare, for he could not open his eyes and later I learned that he had had a stroke and that one side of his face was stiff and hard to get into motion. When he began to smile I could tickle him in earnest because I was sure that nothing would get in the way of his laughter, although once he began to cough so hard that he almost threw me off his stomach, but that was when I was very small, little more than a baby, and my bushy hair had gotten in his nose.

When we were sure he would listen to us we would ask him why he was in bed and when he was coming to see us again and could we play his guitar, which more than likely would be leaning against the bed. His eyes would get all misty and he would some-times cry out loud, but we never let it embarrass us, for he knew that we loved him and that we sometimes cried too for no reason. My parents would leave the room to just the three of us; Mr. Sweet, by that time, would be propped up in bed with a number of pillows behind his head and with me sitting and lying on his shoul-der and along his chest. Even when he had trouble breathing he would not ask me to get down. Looking into my eyes he would shake his white head and run a scratchy old finger all around my hairline, which was rather low down, nearly to my eyebrows, and made some people say I looked like a baby monkey.

My brother was very generous in all this, he let me do all the revivaling—he had done it for years before I was born and so was glad to be able to pass it on to someone new. What he would do while I talked to Mr. Sweet was pretend to play the guitar, in fact pretend that he was a young version of Mr. Sweet, and it always made Mr. Sweet glad to think that someone wanted to be like him—of course, we did not know this then, we played the thing by ear, and whatever he seemed to like, we did. We were desperately afraid that he was just going to take off one day and leave us.

It did not occur to us that we were doing anything special; we had not learned that death was final when it did come. We thought

nothing of triumphing over it so many times, and in fact became a
trifle contemptuous of people who let themselves be carried away.
It did not occur to us that if our father had been dying we could not
have stopped it, that Mr. Sweet was the only person over whom we
had power.

When Mr. Sweet was in his eighties I was studying in the university many miles from home. I saw him whenever I went home, but
he was never on the verge of dying that I could tell and I began to
feel that my anxiety for his health and psychological well-being
was unnecessary. By this time he not only had a mustache but a
long flowing snow-white beard, which I loved and combed and
braided for hours. He was very peaceful, fragile, gentle, and the
only jarring note about him was his old steel guitar, which he still
played in the old sad, sweet, down-home blues way.

On Mr. Sweet's ninetieth brithday I was finishing my doctorate
in Massachusetts and had been making arrangements to go home
for several weeks' rest. That morning I got a telegram telling me
that Mr. Sweet was dying again and could I please drop everything
and come home. Of course I could. My dissertation could wait and
my teachers would understand when I explained to them when I
got back. I ran to the phone, called the airport, and within four
hours I was speeding along the dusty road to Mr. Sweet's.

The house was more dilapidated than when I was last there,
barely a shack, but it was overgrown with yellow roses which my
family had planted many years ago. The air was heavy and sweet
and very peaceful. I felt strange walking through the gate and up
the old rickety steps. But the strangeness left me as I caught sight of
the long white beard I loved so well flowing down the thin body
over the familiar quilt coverlet. Mr. Sweet!

His eyes were closed tight and his hands, crossed over his
stomach, were thin and delicate, no longer scratchy. I remembered
how always before I had run and jumped up on him just anywhere; now I knew he would not be able to support my weight. I
looked around at my parents, and was surprised to see that my
father and mother also looked old and frail. My father, his own hair
very gray, leaned over the quietly sleeping old man, who, incidentally, smelled still of wine and tobacco, and said, as he'd done so
many times, "To hell with dying, man! My daughter is home to see
Mr. Sweet!" My brother had not been able to come as he was in
the war in Asia. I bent down and gently stroked the closed eyes and
gradually they began to open. The closed, wine-stained lips
twitched a little, then parted in a warm, slightly embarrassed smile.
Mr. Sweet could see me and he recognized me and his eyes looked
very spry and twinkly for a moment. I put my head down on the

pillow next to his and we just looked at each other for a long time. Then he began to trace my peculiar hairline with a thin, smooth finger. I closed my eyes when his finger halted above my ear (he used to rejoice at the dirt in my ears when I was little), his hand stayed cupped around my cheek. When I opened my eyes, sure that I had reached him in time, his were closed.

Even at twenty-four how could I believe that I had failed? that [20] Mr. Sweet was really gone? He had never gone before. But when I looked at my parents I saw that they were holding back tears. They had loved him dearly. He was like a piece of rare and delicate china which was always being saved from breaking and which finally fell. I looked long at the old face, the wrinkled forehead, the red lips, the hands that still reached out to me. Soon I felt my father pushing something cool into my hands. It was Mr. Sweet's guitar. He had asked them months before to give it to me; he had known that even if I came next time he would not be able to respond in the old way. He did not want me to feel that my trip had been for nothing.

The old guitar! I plucked the strings, hummed "Sweet Georgia Brown." The magic of Mr. Sweet lingered still in the cool steel box. Through the window I could catch the fragrant delicate scent of tender yellow roses. The man on the high old-fashioned bed with the quilt coverlet and the flowing white beard had been my first love.

THREE
ESSAYISTS

Three Essayists: Preview

When I sit down to write a book, I do not say to myself, "I am going to produce a work of art." I write it because there is some lie that I want to expose, some fact to which I want to draw attention, and my initial concern is to get a hearing. But I could not do the work of writing a book . . . if it were not also an aesthetic experience.

With one part of my mind I thought of the British Raj as an unbreakable tyranny, as something clamped down, in *saecula saeculorum,* upon the will of prostrate peoples; with another part I thought that the greatest joy in the world would be to drive a bayonet into a Buddhist priest's guts.

In a tropical landscape one's eye takes in everything except the human beings. It takes in the dried-up soil, the prickly pear, the palm tree and the distant mountain, but it always misses the peasant hoeing at his patch. He is the same colour as the earth, and a great deal less interesting to look at.

A man may take to drink because he feels himself to be a failure, and then fail all the more completely because he drinks. It is rather the same thing that is happening to the English language. It becomes ugly and inaccurate because our thoughts are foolish, but the slovenliness of our language makes it easier for us to have foolish thoughts.

. . . the most crucial time in my own development came when I was forced to recognize that I was a kind of bastard of the West; when I followed the line of my past I did not find myself in Europe but in Africa. And this meant that in some subtle way, in a really profound way, I brought to Shakespeare, Bach . . . to the cathedral at Chartres, and to the Empire State Building, a special attitude.

> Terror is the given of the place. Black-and-white police cars cruise in pairs, each with the barrel of a rifle extruding from an open window. Roadblocks materialize at random, soldiers fanning out from trucks and taking positions, fingers always on triggers, safeties clicking on and off. Aim is taken as if to pass the time.

Overview and Ideas for Writing

All the other units in *The Dolphin Reader* are built on the assumption that we read an essay better if we see it in the context of essays by other authors with contrasting attitudes and styles. "Three Essayists" is put together quite differently. It assumes that there is also an advantage in looking at an individual essayist in enough depth to recognize the writer's themes and become familiar with his or her style. There may also be an advantage in learning enough about the writer's life and motives to understand the connection between the person and the work. George Orwell, James Baldwin, and Joan Didion particularly reward this kind of study because they have written fine essays about how and why they write.

The three vary enough that you could write interesting papers comparing them. George Orwell's essays of the 1930s and 1940s, committed to political reform and written in prose "like a window-pane," set a standard many of our best writers still strive to reach. Richard Rodriguez, whose first essay was published a quarter century after Orwell died, says that his model for the "marriage of journalism and literature is, of course, George Orwell."

James Baldwin began to make his mark as an essayist in the 1950s. He was, like Orwell, a deeply political writer whose life and writing are intertwined, yet he does not count Orwell among the influences that shaped his style. Instead he lists "the King James Bible, the rhetoric of the store-front church, something ironic and violent and perpetually understated in Negro speech—and something of Dickens' love for bravura." The result, as Eldridge Cleaver once remarked, is a style "full of sound, but not noisy" that you might contrast with Orwell's.

Joan Didion, who won a readership in the 1960s, once wrote that she had spent a summer reading all of Orwell, and we see his influence not only in her choice of the title "Why I Write," but in her reporting of the politics of El Salvador and Miami in the 1980s. Nonetheless, no page of hers could be confused with a page of Orwell's. A product of a society in flux and an accomplished screenwriter as well as novelist, Didion changes perspectives (''camera angles'') in a way that Orwell would have found dizzying.

If you decide to study Orwell, Baldwin, or Didion, remember that there are ways to extend your reading and research beyond the essays here. The headnote for each author provides you with a list of his or her works. *Current Biography, Contemporary Authors,* and a good encyclopedia will give you some information about the author's life and reputation and will point to sources where you can find more. As you read these, you will discover a number of questions to explore. How did the politically committed Orwell respond to the idea of art for art's sake? How are the ideas in "Politics and the English Language" developed in his fiction? How did Baldwin react to the political and social changes of the last three decades? How have other writers, white and black, responded to his analysis of the racial situation in the United States? Was he freer in Europe than he was in America? What political and moral commitments underlie Didion's writing? Is she essentially liberal or conservative? Is she a feminist? What is the connection between her style as a novelist and screenwriter and her style as an essayist? The questions you cannot answer easily may be the ones you should explore in your essay.

Of course, you need not confine such questions to the writers collected in this unit. There are eighty-three writers in *The Dolphin Reader,* several of them represented by more than one essay. Didion points out that writing is "the act of saying *I,* of imposing oneself on other people, of saying *listen to me, see it my way, change your mind.*" It is always best to know who is talking.

GEORGE ORWELL

George Orwell (1903–1950), originally named Eric Arthur Blair, was born in Bengal, India. His father was a minor British colonial officer and his mother the daughter of a French merchant. When his family moved to England in 1911, Orwell spent six unpleasant years in a snobbish preparatory school before winning a scholarship to Eton, a still more exclusive school where his relative poverty made him feel like an outsider. On the advice of one of his tutors, he elected not to enter Cambridge University, but instead to join the Indian Imperial Police in Burma, a job he held until 1927, when guilt at being "part of that evil despotism" drove him out. To experience a life unprotected by the privileges of the British middle class, he then lived among the poor in Paris and London, working as a dishwasher and day laborer. In 1933 he published an account of this life in *Down and Out in Paris and London* under the pseudonym by which he has been known ever since. From that point forward, Orwell plunged into a series of political and social investigations. He lived with unemployed coal miners while he worked on *The Road to Wigan Pier* (1937) and fought with the Republican army in the Spanish Civil War before writing *Homage to Catalonia* (1938). Rejected for military service in World War II, he worked tirelessly in the British Broadcasting Corporation's propaganda war in Asia. Though Orwell's fame in his own time was made largely by his novels—especially the satirical *Animal Farm* (1945) and the gloomy *1984* (1949)—his long-lasting influence has come from his nonfiction, collected in *Inside the Whale* (1940), *Dickens, Dali and Others* (1946), *Shooting an Elephant* (1950), and *Such, Such were the Joys* (1953).

GEORGE ORWELL

Why I Write[1]

From a very early age, perhaps the age of five or six, I knew that   1
when I grew up I should be a writer. Between the ages of about
seventeen and twenty-four I tried to abandon this idea, but I did so

1. First published in *Gangrel*, Summer 1946.

with the consciousness that I was outraging my true nature and that sooner or later I should have to settle down and write books.

I was the middle child of three, but there was a gap of five years on either side, and I barely saw my father before I was eight. For this and other reasons I was somewhat lonely, and I soon developed disagreeable mannerisms which made me unpopular throughout my schooldays. I had the lonely child's habit of making up stories and holding conversations with imaginary persons, and I think from the very start my literary ambitions were mixed up with the feeling of being isolated and undervalued. I knew that I had a facility with words and a power of facing unpleasant facts, and I felt that this created a sort of private world in which I could get my own back for my failure in everyday life. Nevertheless the volume of serious—*i.e.* seriously intended—writing which I produced all through my childhood and boyhood would not amount to half a dozen pages. I wrote my first poem at the age of four or five, my mother taking it down to dictation. I cannot remember anything about it except that it was about a tiger and the tiger had "chair-like teeth"—a good enough phrase, but I fancy the poem was a plagiarism of Blake's "Tiger, Tiger." At eleven, when the war of 1914–18 broke out, I wrote a patriotic poem which was printed in the local newspaper, as was another, two years later, on the death of Kitchener.[2] From time to time, when I was a bit older, I wrote bad and usually unfinished "nature poems" in the Georgian style. I also, about twice, attempted a short story which was a ghastly failure. That was the total of the would-be serious work that I actually set down on paper during all those years.

However, throughout this time I did in a sense engage in literary activities. To begin with there was the made-to-order stuff which I produced quickly, easily and without much pleasure to myself. Apart from school work, I wrote *vers d'occasion*, semi-comic poems which I could turn out at what now seems to me astonishing speed—at fourteen I wrote a whole rhyming play, in imitation of Aristophanes,[3] in about a week—and helped to edit school magazines, both printed and in manuscript. These magazines were the most pitiful burlesque stuff that you could imagine, and I took far less trouble with them than I now would with the cheapest journalism. But side by side with all this, for fifteen years or more, I was carrying out a literary exercise of a quite different kind: this was the making up of a continuous "story" about myself, a sort of diary

2. Herbert Horatio Kitchener (1850–1916), British general and politician, lost at sea in military action.
3. Greek playwright (ca. 448–380 B.C.).

existing only in the mind. I believe this is a common habit of children and adolescents. As a very small child I used to imagine that I was, say, Robin Hood, and picture myself as the hero of thrilling adventures, but quite soon my "story" ceased to be narcissistic in a crude way and became more and more a mere description of what I was doing and the things I saw. For minutes at a time this kind of thing would be running through my head: "He pushed the door open and entered the room. A yellow beam of sunlight, filtering through the muslin curtains, slanted on to the table, where a match-box, half open, lay beside the inkpot. With his right hand in his pocket he moved across to the window. Down in the street a tortoiseshell cat was chasing a dead leaf," etc., etc. This habit continued till I was about twenty-five, right through my non-literary years. Although I had to search, and did search, for the right words, I seemed to be making this descriptive effort almost against my will, under a kind of compulsion from outside. The "story" must, I suppose, have reflected the styles of the various writers I admired at different ages, but so far as I remember it always had the same meticulous descriptive quality.

When I was about sixteen I suddenly discovered the joy of mere   4
words, *i.e.*, the sounds and associations of words. The lines from *Paradise Lost*—

> *So hee with difficulty and labour hard*
> *Moved on: with difficulty and labour hee,*

which do not now seem to me so very wonderful, sent shivers down my backbone; and the spelling "hee" for "he" was an added pleasure. As for the need to describe things, I knew all about it already. So it is clear what kind of books I wanted to write, in so far as I could be said to want to write books at that time. I wanted to write enormous naturalistic novels with unhappy endings, full of detailed descriptions and arresting similes, and also full of purple passages in which words were used partly for the sake of their sound. And in fact my first completed novel, *Burmese Days*, which I wrote when I was thirty but projected much earlier, is rather that kind of book.

I give all this background information because I do not think one   5
can assess a writer's motives without knowing something of his early development. His subject matter will be determined by the age he lives in—at least this is true in tumultuous, revolutionary ages like our own—but before he ever begins to write he will have acquired an emotional attitude from which he will never completely escape. It is his job, no doubt, to discipline his temperament and avoid getting stuck at some immature stage, or in some per-

verse mood: but if he escapes from his early influences altogether, he will have killed his impulse to write. Putting aside the need to earn a living, I think there are four great motives for writing, at any rate for writing prose. They exist in different degrees in every writer, and in any one writer the proportions will vary from time to time, according to the atmosphere in which he is living. They are:

(1) Sheer egoism. Desire to seem clever, to be talked about, to be   6
remembered after death, to get your own back on grown-ups who snubbed you in childhood, etc., etc. It is humbug to pretend that this is not a motive, and a strong one. Writers share this character-istic with scientists, artists, politicians, lawyers, soldiers, successful businessmen—in short, with the whole top crust of humanity. The great mass of human beings are not acutely selfish. After the age of about thirty they abandon individual ambition—in many cases, indeed, they almost abandon the sense of being individuals at all—and live chiefly for others, or are simply smothered under drudgery. But there is also the minority of gifted, wilful people who are determined to live their own lives to the end, and writers be-long in this class. Serious writers, I should say, are on the whole more vain and self-centered than journalists, though less interested in money.

(2) Aesthetic enthusiasm. Perception of beauty in the external   7
world, or, on the other hand, in words and their right arrangement. Pleasure in the impact of one sound on another, in the firmness of good prose or the rhythm of a good story. Desire to share an experi-ence which one feels is valuable and ought not to be missed. The aesthetic motive is very feeble in a lot of writers, but even a pam-phleteer or a writer of textbooks will have pet words and phrases which appeal to him for non-utilitarian reasons; or he may feel strongly about typography, width of margins, etc. Above the level of a railway guide, no book is quite free from aesthetic considera-tions.

(3) Historical impulse. Desire to see things as they are, to find out   8
true facts and store them up for the use of posterity.

(4) Political purpose—using the word "political" in the widest   9
possible sense. Desire to push the world in a certain direction, to alter other people's idea of the kind of society that they should strive after. Once again, no book is genuinely free from political bias. The opinion that art should have nothing to do with politics is itself a political attitude.

It can be seen how these various impulses must war against one   10
another, and how they must fluctuate from person to person and from time to time. By nature—taking your "nature" to be the state you have attained when you are first adult—I am a person in

whom the first three motives would outweigh the fourth. In a peaceful age I might have written ornate or merely descriptive books, and might have remained almost unaware of my political loyalties. As it is I have been forced into becoming a sort of pamphleteer. First I spent five years in an unsuitable profession (the Indian Imperial Police, in Burma), and then I underwent poverty and the sense of failure. This increased my natural hatred of authority and made me for the first time fully aware of the existence of the working classes, and the job in Burma had given me some understanding of the nature of imperialism: but these experiences were not enough to give me an accurate political orientation. Then came Hitler, the Spanish civil war, etc. By the end of 1935 I had still failed to reach a firm decision. I remember a little poem that I wrote at that date, expressing my dilemma:

> *A happy vicar I might have been*
> *Two hundred years ago,*
> *To preach upon eternal doom*
> *And watch my walnuts grow;*
>
> *But born, alas, in an evil time,*
> *I missed that pleasant haven,*
> *For the hair has grown on my upper lip*
> *And the clergy are all clean-shaven.*
>
> *And later still the times were good,*
> *We were so easy to please,*
> *We rocked our troubled thoughts to sleep*
> *On the bosoms of the trees.*
>
> *All ignorant we dared to own*
> *The joys we now dissemble;*
> *The greenfinch on the apple bough*
> *Could make my enemies tremble.*
>
> *But girls' bellies and apricots,*
> *Roach in a shaded stream,*
> *Horses, ducks in flight at dawn,*
> *All these are a dream.*
>
> *It is forbidden to dream again;*
> *We maim our joys or hide them;*
> *Horses are made of chromium steel*
> *And little fat men shall ride them.*
>
> *I am the worm who never turned,*
> *The eunuch without a harem;*

Between the priest and the commissar
I walk like Eugene Aram;

And the commissar is telling my fortune
While the radio plays,
But the priest has promised an Austin Seven,
For Duggie always pays.

I dreamed I dwelt in marble halls,
And woke to find it true;
I wasn't born for an age like this;
Was Smith? Was Jones? Were you?

The Spanish war and other events in 1936–7 turned the scale and thereafter I knew where I stood. Every line of serious work that I have written since 1936 has been written, directly or indirectly, *against* totalitarianism and *for* democratic socialism, as I understand it. It seems to me nonsense, in a period like our own, to think that one can avoid writing of such subjects. Everyone writes of them in one guise or another. It is simply a question of which side one takes and what approach one follows. And the more one is conscious of one's political bias, the more chance one has of acting politically without sacrificing one's aesthetic and intellectual integrity.

What I have most wanted to do throughout the past ten years is   11
to make political writing into an art. My starting point is always a feeling of partisanship, a sense of injustice. When I sit down to write a book, I do not say to myself, "I am going to produce a work of art." I write it because there is some lie that I want to expose, some fact to which I want to draw attention, and my initial concern is to get a hearing. But I could not do the work of writing a book, or even a long magazine article, if it were not also an aesthetic experience. Anyone who cares to examine my work will see that even when it is downright propaganda it contains much that a full-time politician would consider irrelevant. I am not able, and I do not want, completely to abandon the world view that I acquired in childhood. So long as I remain alive and well I shall continue to feel strongly about prose style, to love the surface of the earth, and to take a pleasure in solid objects and scraps of useless information. It is no use trying to suppress that side of myself. The job is to reconcile my ingrained likes and dislikes with the essentially public, non-individual activities that this age forces on all of us.

It is not easy. It raises problems of construction and of language,   12
and it raises in a new way the problem of truthfulness. Let me give just one example of the cruder kind of difficulty that arises. My

book about the Spanish civil war, *Homage to Catalonia*, is, of course, a frankly political book, but in the main it is written with a certain detachment and regard for form. I did try very hard in it to tell the whole truth without violating my literary instincts. But among other things it contains a long chapter, full of newspaper quotations and the like, defending the Trotskyists who were accused of plotting with Franco. Clearly such a chapter, which after a year or two would lose its interest for any ordinary reader, must ruin the book. A critic whom I respect read me a lecture about it. "Why did you put in all that stuff?" he said. "You've turned what might have been a good book into journalism." What he said was true, but I could not have done otherwise. I happened to know, what very few people in England had been allowed to know, that innocent men were being falsely accused. If I had not been angry about that I should never have written the book.

In one form or another this problem comes up again. The problem of language is subtler and would take too long to discuss. I will only say that of late years I have tried to write less picturesquely and more exactly. In any case I find that by the time you have perfected any style of writing, you have always outgrown it. *Animal Farm* was the first book in which I tried, with full consciousness of what I was doing, to fuse political purpose and artistic purpose into one whole. I have not written a novel for seven years, but I hope to write another fairly soon. It is bound to be a failure, every book is a failure, but I do know with some clarity what kind of book I want to write. Looking back through the last page or two, I see that I have made it appear as though my motives in writing were wholly public-spirited. I don't want to leave that as the final impression. All writers are vain, selfish, and lazy, and at the very bottom of their motives there lies a mystery. Writing a book is a horrible, exhausting struggle, like a long bout of some painful illness. One would never undertake such a thing if one were not driven on by some demon whom one can neither resist nor understand. For all one knows that demon is simply the same instinct that makes a baby squall for attention. And yet it is also true that one can write nothing readable unless one constantly struggles to efface one's own personality. Good prose is like a windowpane. I cannot say with certainty which of my motives are the strongest, but I know which of them deserve to be followed. And looking back through my work, I see that it is invariably where I lacked a *political* purpose that I wrote lifeless books and was betrayed into purple passages, sentences without meaning, decorative adjectives, and humbug generally.

GEORGE ORWELL

Shooting an Elephant[1]

In Moulmein, in Lower Burma, I was hated by large numbers of   1
people—the only time in my life that I have been important
enough for this to happen to me. I was sub-divisional police officer
of the town, and in an aimless, petty kind of way anti-European
feeling was very bitter. No one had the guts to raise a riot, but if a
European woman went through the bazaars alone somebody
would probably spit betel juice over her dress. As a police officer I
was an obvious target and was baited whenever it seemed safe to
do so. When a nimble Burman tripped me up on the football field
and the referee (another Burman) looked the other way, the crowd
yelled with hideous laughter. This happened more than once. In
the end the sneering yellow faces of young men that met me
everywhere, the insults hooted after me when I was at a safe distance, got badly on my nerves. The young Buddhist priests were
the worst of all. There were several thousands of them in the town
and none of them seemed to have anything to do except stand on
street corners and jeer at Europeans.

All this was perplexing and upsetting. For at that time I had   2
already made up my mind that imperialism was an evil thing and
the sooner I chucked up my job and got out of it the better. Theoretically—and secretly, of course—I was all for the Burmese and
all against their oppressors, the British. As for the job I was doing, I
hated it more bitterly than I can perhaps make clear. In a job like
that you see the dirty work of Empire at close quarters. The
wretched prisoners huddling in the stinking cages of the lockups,
the grey, cowed faces of the long-term convicts, the scarred buttocks of the men who had been flogged with bamboos—all these
oppressed me with an intolerable sense of guilt. But I could get
nothing into perspective. I was young and ill-educated and I had to
think out my problems in the utter silence that is imposed on every
Englishman in the East. I did not even know that the British Empire is dying, still less did I know that it is a great deal better than
the younger empires that are going to supplant it. All I knew was
that I was stuck between my hatred of the empire I served and my
rage against the evil-spirited little beasts who tried to make my job
impossible. With one part of my mind I thought of the British Raj
as an unbreakable tyranny, as something clamped down, in *saecula*

1. First published in *New Writing*, Autumn 1936.

saeculorum,[2] upon the will of prostrate peoples; with another part I thought that the greatest joy in the world would be to drive a bayonet into a Buddhist priest's guts. Feelings like these are the normal by-products of imperialism; ask any Anglo-Indian official, if you can catch him off duty.

One day something happened which in a roundabout way was enlightening. It was a tiny incident in itself, but it gave me a better glimpse than I had had before of the real nature of imperialism— the real motives for which despotic governments act. Early one morning the sub-inspector at a police station the other end of the town rang me up on the 'phone and said that an elephant was ravaging the bazaar. Would I please come and do something about it? I did not know what I could do, but I wanted to see what was happening and I got on to a pony and started out. I took my rifle, an old .44 Winchester and much too small to kill an elephant, but I thought the noise might be useful *in terrorem.* Various Burmans stopped me on the way and told me about the elephant's doings. It was not, of course, a wild elephant, but a tame one which had gone "must." It had been chained up, as tame elephants always are when their attack of "must" is due, but on the previous night it had broken its chain and escaped. Its mahout, the only person who could manage it when it was in that state, had set out in pursuit, but had taken the wrong direction and was now twelve hours' journey away, and in the morning the elephant had suddenly reappeared in the town. The Burmese population had no weapons and were quite helpless against it. It had already destroyed somebody's bamboo hut, killed a cow and raided some fruit-stalls and devoured the stock; also it had met the municipal rubbish van and, when the driver jumped out and took to his heels, had turned the van over and inflicted violences upon it.

The Burmese sub-inspector and some Indian constables were waiting for me in the quarter where the elephant had been seen. It was a very poor quarter, a labyrinth of squalid bamboo huts, thatched with palm-leaf, winding all over a steep hillside. I remember that it was a cloudy, stuffy morning at the beginning of the rains. We began questioning the people as to where the elephant had gone and, as usual, failed to get any definite information. That is invariably the case in the East; a story always sounds clear enough at a distance, but the nearer you get to the scene of events the vaguer it becomes. Some of the people said that the elephant had gone in one direction, some said that he had gone in another, some professed not even to have heard of any elephant. I had

2. "For ages of ages"; until the end of time.

almost made up my mind that the whole story was a pack of lies, when we heard yells a little distance away. There was a loud, scandalized cry of "Go away, child! Go away this instant!" and an old woman with a switch in her hand came round the corner of a hut, violently shooing away a crowd of naked children. Some more women followed, clicking their tongues and exclaiming; evidently there was something that the children ought not to have seen. I rounded the hut and saw a man's dead body sprawling in the mud. He was an Indian, a black Dravidian coolie, almost naked, and he could not have been dead many minutes. The people said that the elephant had come suddenly upon him round the corner of the hut, caught him with its trunk, put its foot on his back and ground him into the earth. This was the rainy season and the ground was soft, and his face had scored a trench a foot deep and a couple of yards long. He was lying on his belly with arms crucified and head sharply twisted to one side. His face was coated with mud, the eyes wide open, the teeth bared and grinning with an expression of unendurable agony. (Never tell me, by the way, that the dead look peaceful. Most of the corpses I have seen look devilish.) The friction of the great beast's foot had stripped the skin from his back as neatly as one skins a rabbit. As soon as I saw the dead man I sent an orderly to a friend's house nearby to borrow an elephant rifle. I had already sent back the pony, not wanting it to go mad with fright and throw me if it smelt the elephant.

The orderly came back in a few minutes with a rifle and five   5 cartridges, and meanwhile some Burmans had arrived and told us that the elephant was in the paddy fields below, only a few hundred yards away. As I started forward practically the whole population of the quarter flocked out of the houses and followed me. They had seen the rifle and were all shouting excitedly that I was going to shoot the elephant. They had not shown much interest in the elephant when he was merely ravaging their homes, but it was different now that he was going to be shot. It was a bit of fun to them, as it would be to an English crowd; besides they wanted the meat. It made me vaguely uneasy. I had no intention of shooting the elephant—I had merely sent for the rifle to defend myself if necessary—and it is always unnerving to have a crowd following you. I marched down the hill, looking and feeling a fool, with the rifle over my shoulder and an ever-growing army of people jostling at my heels. At the bottom, when you got away from the huts, there was a metalled road and beyond that a miry waste of paddy fields a thousand yards across, not yet ploughed but soggy from the first rains and dotted with coarse grass. The elephant was standing eight yards from the road, his left side towards us. He took not the slightest notice of the crowd's approach. He was tearing up bunches of grass, beating them against his knees to clean them and stuffing them into his mouth.

I had halted on the road. As soon as I saw the elephant I knew with perfect certainty that I ought not to shoot him. It is a serious matter to shoot a working elephant—it is comparable to destroying a huge and costly piece of machinery—and obviously one ought not to do it if it can possibly be avoided. And at that distance, peacefully eating, the elephant looked no more dangerous than a cow. I thought then and I think now that his attack of "must" was already passing off; in which case he would merely wander harmlessly about until the mahout came back and caught him. Moreover, I did not in the least want to shoot him. I decided that I would watch him for a little while to make sure that he did not turn savage again, and then go home. 6

But at that moment I glanced round at the crowd that had followed me. It was an immense crowd, two thousand at the least and growing every minute. It blocked the road for a long distance on either side. I looked at the sea of yellow faces above the garish clothes—faces all happy and excited over this bit of fun, all certain that the elephant was going to be shot. They were watching me as they would watch a conjurer about to perform a trick. They did not like me, but with the magical rifle in my hands I was momentarily worth watching. And suddenly I realized that I should have to shoot the elephant after all. The people expected it of me and I had got to do it; I could feel their two thousand wills pressing me forward, irresistibly. And it was at this moment, as I stood there with the rifle in my hands, that I first grasped the hollowness, the futility of the white man's dominion in the East. Here was I, the white man with his gun, standing in front of the unarmed native crowd—seemingly the leading actor of the piece; but in reality I was only an absurd puppet pushed to and fro by the will of those yellow faces behind. I perceived in this moment that when the white man turns tyrant it is his own freedom that he destroys. He becomes a sort of hollow, posing dummy, the conventionalized figure of a sahib. For it is the condition of his rule that he shall spend his life in trying to impress the "natives," and so in every crisis he has got to do what the "natives" expect of him. He wears a mask, and his face grows to fit it. I had got to shoot the elephant. I had committed myself to doing it when I sent for the rifle. A sahib has got to act like a sahib; he has got to appear resolute, to know his own mind and do definite things. To come all that way, rifle 7 in hand, with two thousand people marching at my heels, and then to trail feebly away, having done nothing—no, that was impossible. The crowd would laugh at me. And my whole life, every white man's life in the East, was one long struggle not to be laughed at.

But I did not want to shoot the elephant. I watched him beating   8
his bunch of grass against his knees, with that preoccupied grand-motherly air that elephants have. It seemed to me that it would be murder to shoot him. At that age I was not squeamish about killing animals, but I had never shot an elephant and never wanted to. (Somehow it always seems worse to kill a *large* animal.) Besides, there was the beast's owner to be considered. Alive, the elephant was worth at least a hundred pounds; dead, he would only be worth the value of his tusks, five pounds, possibly. But I had got to act quickly. I turned to some experienced-looking Burmans who had been there when we arrived, and asked them how the elephant had been behaving. They all said the same thing; he took no notice of you if you left him alone, but he might charge if you went too close to him.

It was perfectly clear to me what I ought to do. I ought to walk   9
up to within, say, twenty-five yards of the elephant and test his behavior. If he charged, I could shoot; if he took no notice of me, it would be safe to leave him until the mahout came back. But also I knew that I was going to do no such thing. I was a poor shot with a rifle and the ground was soft mud into which one would sink at every step. If the elephant charged and I missed him, I should have about as much chance as a toad under a steamroller. But even then I was not thinking particularly of my own skin, only of the watch-ful yellow faces behind. For at that moment, with the crowd watching me, I was not afraid in the ordinary sense, as I would have been if I had been alone. A white man mustn't be frightened in front of "natives"; and so, in general, he isn't frightened. The sole thought in my mind was that if anything went wrong those two thousand Burmans would see me pursued, caught, trampled on and reduced to a grinning corpse like that Indian up the hill. And if that happened it was quite probable that some of them would laugh. That would never do. There was only one alternative. I shoved the cartridges into the magazine and lay down on the road to get a better aim.

The crowd grew very still, and a deep, low, happy sigh, as of   10
people who see the theatre curtain go up at last, breathed from innumerable throats. They were going to have their bit of fun after all. The rifle was a beautiful German thing with cross-hair sights. I did not then know that in shooting an elephant one would shoot to

cut an imaginary bar running from ear-hole to ear-hole. I ought, therefore, as the elephant was sideways on, to have aimed straight at his ear-hole; actually I aimed several inches in front of this, thinking the brain would be further forward.

When I pulled the trigger I did not hear the bang or feel the 11 kick—one never does when a shot goes home—but I heard the devilish roar of glee that went up from the crowd. In that instant, in too short a time, one would have thought, even for the bullet to get there, a mysterious, terrible change had come over the elephant. He neither stirred nor fell, but every line of his body had altered. He looked suddenly stricken, shrunken, immensely old, as though the frightful impact of the bullet had paralysed him without knocking him down. At last, after what seemed a long time—it might have been five seconds, I dare say—he sagged flabbily to his knees. His mouth slobbered. An enormous senility seemed to have settled upon him. One could have imagined him thousands of years old. I fired again into the same spot. At the second shot he did not collapse but climbed with desperate slowness to his feet and stood weakly upright, with legs sagging and head drooping. I fired a third time. That was the shot that did for him. You could see the agony of it jolt his whole body and knock the last remnant of strength from his legs. But in falling he seemed for a moment to rise, for as his hind legs collapsed beneath him he seemed to tower upward like a huge rock toppling, his trunk reaching skywards like a tree. He trumpeted, for the first and only time. And then down he came, his belly towards me, with a crash that seemed to shake the ground even where I lay.

I got up. The Burmans were already racing past me across the 12 mud. It was obvious that the elephant would never rise again, but he was not dead. He was breathing very rhythmically with long rattling gasps, his great mound of a side painfully rising and falling. His mouth was wide open—I could see far down into caverns of pale pink throat. I waited a long time for him to die, but his breathing did not weaken. Finally I fired my two remaining shots into the spot where I thought his heart must be. The thick blood welled out of him like red velvet, but still he did not die. His body did not even jerk when the shots hit him, the tortured breathing continued without a pause. He was dying, very slowly and in great agony, but in some world remote from me where not even a bullet could damage him further. I felt that I had got to put an end to that dreadful noise. It seemed dreadful to see the great beast lying there, powerless to move and yet powerless to die, and not even to be able to finish him. I sent back for my small rifle and poured shot after shot into his heart and down his throat. They seemed to make no impression. The tortured gasps continued as steadily as the ticking of a clock.

In the end I could not stand it any longer and went away. I heard 13 later that it took him half an hour to die. Burmans were bringing dahs and baskets even before I left, and I was told they had stripped his body almost to the bones by the afternoon.

Afterwards, of course, there were endless discussions about the 14 shooting of the elephant. The owner was furious, but he was only an Indian and could do nothing. Besides, legally I had done the right thing, for a mad elephant has to be killed, like a mad dog, if its owner fails to control it. Among the Europeans opinion was divided. The older men said I was right, the younger men said it was a damn shame to shoot an elephant for killing a coolie, because an elephant was worth more than any damn Coringhee coolie. And afterwards I was very glad that the coolie had been killed; it put me legally in the right and it gave me a sufficient pretext for shooting the elephant. I often wondered whether any of the others grasped that I had done it solely to avoid looking a fool.

GEORGE ORWELL

Marrakech[1]

As the corpse went past, the flies left the restaurant table in a 1 cloud and rushed after it, but they came back a few minutes later.

The little crowd of mourners—all men and boys, no women— 2 threaded their way across the market-place between the piles of pomegranates and the taxis and the camels, wailing a short chant over and over again. What really appeals to the flies is that the corpses here are never put into coffins, they are merely wrapped in a piece of rag and carried on a rough wooden bier on the shoulders of four friends. When the friends get to the burying-ground they hack an oblong hole a foot or two deep, dump the body in it and fling over it a little of the dried-up, lumpy earth, which is like broken brick. No gravestone, no name, no identifying mark of any kind. The burying-ground is merely a huge waste of hummocky

1. First published in *New Writing*, Christmas 1939.

earth, like a derelict building-lot. After a month or two no one can even be certain where his own relatives are buried.

When you walk through a town like this[2]—two hundred thousand inhabitants, of whom at least twenty thousand own literally nothing except the rags they stand up in—when you see how the people live, and still more how easily they die, it is always difficult to believe that you are walking among human beings. All colonial empires are in reality founded upon that fact. The people have brown faces—besides, there are so many of them! Are they really the same flesh as yourself? Do they even have names? Or are they merely a kind of undifferentiated brown stuff, about as individual as bees or coral insects? They rise out of the earth, they sweat and starve for a few years, and then they sink back into the nameless mounds of the graveyard and nobody notices that they are gone. And even the graves themselves soon fade back into the soil. Sometimes, out for a walk, as you break your way through the prickly pear, you notice that it is rather bumpy underfoot, and only a certain regularity in the bumps tells you that you are walking over skeletons.

I was feeding one of the gazelles in the public gardens. 4

Gazelles are almost the only animals that look good to eat when 5 they are still alive, in fact, one can hardly look at their hindquarters without thinking of mint sauce. The gazelle I was feeding seemed to know that this thought was in my mind, for though it took the piece of bread I was holding out it obviously did not like me. It nibbled rapidly at the bread, then lowered its head and tried to butt me, then took another nibble and then butted again. Probably its idea was that if it could drive me away the bread would somehow remain hanging in mid-air.

An Arab navvy working on the path nearby lowered his heavy 6 hoe and sidled slowly towards us. He looked from the gazelle to the bread and from the bread to the gazelle, with a sort of quiet amazement, as though he had never seen anything quite like this before. Finally he said shyly in French:

"I could eat some of that bread." 7

I tore off a piece and he stowed it gratefully in some secret place 8 under his rags. This man is an employee of the Municipality.

When you go through the Jewish quarters you gather some idea 9 of what the medieval ghettoes were probably like. Under their Moorish rulers the Jews were only allowed to own land in certain

2. Marrakech is a city in the northern African country of Morocco.

restricted areas, and after centuries of this kind of treatment they have ceased to bother about overcrowding. Many of the streets are a good deal less than six feet wide, the houses are completely windowless, and sore-eyed children cluster everywhere in unbelievable numbers, like clouds of flies. Down the centre of the street there is generally running a little river of urine.

In the bazaar huge families of Jews, all dressed in the long black robe and little black skull-cap, are working in dark fly-infested booths that look like caves. A carpenter sits crosslegged at a prehistoric lathe, turning chair-legs at lightning speed. He works the lathe with a bow in his right hand and guides the chisel with his left foot, and thanks to a lifetime of sitting in this position his left leg is warped out of shape. At his side his grandson, aged six, is already starting on the simpler parts of the job.   10

I was just passing the coppersmiths' booths when somebody noticed that I was lighting a cigarette. Instantly, from the dark holes all round, there was a frenzied rush of Jews, many of them old grandfathers with flowing grey beards, all clamouring for a cigarette. Even a blind man somewhere at the back of one of the booths heard a rumour of cigarettes and came crawling out, groping in the air with his hand. In about a minute I had used up the whole packet. None of these people, I suppose, works less than twelve hours a day, and every one of them looks on a cigarette as a more or less impossible luxury.   11

As the Jews live in self-contained communities they follow the same trades as the Arabs, except for agriculture. Fruit-sellers, potters, silversmiths, blacksmiths, butchers, leatherworkers, tailors, water-carriers, beggars, porters—whichever way you look you see nothing but Jews. As a matter of fact there are thirteen thousand of them, all living in the space of a few acres. A good job Hitler wasn't here. Perhaps he was on his way, however. You hear the usual dark rumours about the Jews, not only from the Arabs but from the poorer Europeans.   12

"Yes, mon vieux, they took my job away from me and gave it to a Jew. The Jews! They're the real rulers of this country, you know. They've got all the money. They control the banks, finance—everything."   13

"But," I said, "isn't it a fact that the average Jew is a labourer working for about a penny an hour?"   14

"Ah, that's only for show! They're all moneylenders really. They're cunning, the Jews."   15

In just the same way, a couple of hundred years ago, poor old women used to be burned for witchcraft when they could not even work enough magic to get themselves a square meal.   16

All people who work with their hands are partly invisible, and the more important the work they do, the less visible they are. Still, a white skin is always fairly conspicuous. In northern Europe, when you see a labourer ploughing a field, you probably give him a second glance. In a hot country, anywhere south of Gibraltar or east of Suez, the chances are that you don't even see him. I have noticed this again and again. In a tropical landscape one's eye takes in everything except the human beings. It takes in the dried-up soil, the prickly pear, the palm tree and the distant mountain, but it always misses the peasant hoeing at his patch. He is the same colour as the earth, and a great deal less interesting to look at.

It is only because of this that the starved countries of Asia and Africa are accepted as tourist resorts. No one would think of running cheap trips to the Distressed Areas. But where the human beings have brown skins their poverty is simply not noticed. What does Morocco mean to a Frenchman? An orange-grove or a job in Government service. Or to an Englishman? Camels, castles, palm trees, Foreign Legionnaires, brass trays, and bandits. One could probably live there for years without noticing that for nine-tenths of the people the reality of life is an endless, back-breaking struggle to wring a little food out of an eroded soil.

Most of Morocco is so desolate that no wild animal bigger than a hare can live on it. Huge areas which were once covered with forest have turned into a treeless waste where the soil is exactly like broken-up brick. Nevertheless a good deal of it is cultivated, with frightful labour. Everything is done by hand. Long lines of women, bent double like inverted capital L's, work their way slowly across the fields, tearing up the prickly weeds with their hands, and the peasant gathering lucerne for fodder pulls it up stalk by stalk instead of reaping it, thus saving an inch or two on each stalk. The plough is a wretched wooden thing, so frail that one can easily carry it on one's shoulder, and fitted underneath with a rough iron spike which stirs the soil to a depth of about four inches. This is as much as the strength of the animals is equal to. It is usual to plough with a cow and a donkey yoked together. Two donkeys would not be quite strong enough, but on the other hand two cows would cost a little more to feed. The peasants possess no harrows, they merely plough the soil several times over in different directions, finally leaving it in rough furrows, after which the whole field has to be shaped with hoes into small oblong patches to conserve water. Except for a day or two after the rare rainstorms there is never enough water. Along the edges of the fields channels are hacked out to a depth of thirty or forty feet to get at the tiny trickles which run through the subsoil.

17

18

19

Every afternoon a file of very old women passes down the road   20
outside my house, each carrying a load of firewood. All of them are
mummified with age and the sun, and all of them are tiny. It seems
to be generally the case in primitive communities that the women,
when they get beyond a certain age, shrink to the size of children.
One day a poor old creature who could not have been more than
four feet tall crept past me under a vast load of wood. I stopped her
and put a five-sou piece (a little more than a farthing) into her
hand. She answered with a shrill wail, almost a scream, which was
partly gratitude but mainly surprise. I suppose that from her point
of view, by taking any notice of her, I seemed almost to be violating
a law of nature. She accepted her status as an old woman, that is to
say as a beast of burden. When a family is travelling it is quite usual
to see a father and a grown-up son riding ahead on donkeys, and
an old woman following on foot, carrying the baggage.

But what is strange about these people is their invisibility. For   21
several weeks, always at about the same time of day, the file of old
women had hobbled past the house with their firewood, and
though they had registered themselves on my eyeballs I cannot
truly say that I had seen them. Firewood was passing—that was
how I saw it. It was only that one day I happened to be walking
behind them, and the curious up-and-down motion of a load of
wood drew my attention to the human being beneath it. Then for
the first time I noticed the poor old earth-coloured bodies, bodies
reduced to bones and leathery skin, bent double under the crushing weight. Yet I suppose I had not been five minutes on Moroccan
soil before I noticed the overloading of the donkeys and was in-
furiated by it. There is no question that the donkeys are damnably
treated. The Moroccan donkey is hardly bigger than a St. Bernard
dog, it carries a load which in the British Army would be considered too much for a fifteen-hands mule, and very often its pack-
saddle is not taken off its back for weeks together. But what is
peculiarly pitiful is that it is the most willing creature on earth, it
follows its master like a dog and does not need either bridle or
halter. After a dozen years of devoted work it suddenly drops dead,
whereupon its master tips it into the ditch and the village dogs have
torn its guts out before it is cold.

This kind of thing makes one's blood boil, whereas—on the   22
whole—the plight of the human beings does not. I am not com-
menting, merely pointing to a fact. People with brown skins are
next door to invisible. Anyone can be sorry for the donkey with its
galled back, but it is generally owing to some kind of accident if
one even notices the old woman under her load of sticks.

As the storks flew northward the Negroes were marching south-   23
ward—a long, dusty column, infantry, screw-gun batteries, and
then more infantry, four or five thousand men in all, winding up
the road with a clumping of boots and a clatter of iron wheels.

They were Senegalese, the blackest Negroes in Africa, so black   24
that sometimes it is difficult to see whereabouts on their necks the
hair begins. Their splendid bodies were hidden in reach-me-down
khaki uniforms, their feet squashed into boots that looked like
blocks of wood, and every tin hat seemed to be a couple of sizes too
small. It was very hot and the men had marched a long way. They
slumped under the weight of their packs and the curiously sensitive
black faces were glistening with sweat.

As they went past a tall, very young Negro turned and caught   25
my eye. But the look he gave me was not in the least the kind of
look you might expect. Not hostile, not contemptuous, not sullen,
not even inquisitive. It was the shy, wide-eyed Negro look, which
actually is a look of profound respect. I saw how it was. This
wretched boy, who is a French citizen and has therefore been
dragged from the forest to scrub floors and catch syphilis in garri-
son towns, actually has feelings of reverence before a white skin.
He has been taught that the white race are his masters, and he still
believes it.

But there is one thought which every white man (and in this   26
connection it doesn't matter twopence if he calls himself a socialist)
thinks when he sees a black army marching past. "How much
longer can we go on kidding these people? How long before they
turn their guns in the other direction?"

It was curious, really. Every white man there had this thought   27
stowed somewhere or other in his mind. I had it, so had the other
onlookers, so had the officers on their sweating chargers and the
white N.C.O.'s marching in the ranks. It was a kind of secret which
we all knew and were too clever to tell; only the Negroes didn't
know it. And really it was like watching a flock of cattle to see the
long column, a mile or two miles of armed men, flowing peacefully
up the road, while the great white birds drifted over them in the
opposite direction, glittering like scraps of paper.

GEORGE ORWELL

Politics and the English Language [1]

Most people who bother with the matter at all would admit that   1
the English language is in a bad way, but it is generally assumed
that we cannot by conscious action do anything about it. Our
civilization is decadent and our language—so the argument runs—
must inevitably share in the general collapse. It follows that any
struggle against the abuse of language is a sentimental archaism,
like preferring candles to electric light or hansom cabs to aeroplanes. Underneath this lies the half-conscious belief that language
is a natural growth and not an instrument which we shape for our
own purposes.

Now, it is clear that the decline of a language must ultimately   2
have political and economic causes: it is not due simply to the bad
influence of this or that individual writer. But an effect can become
a cause, reinforcing the original cause and producing the same
effect in an intensified form, and so on indefinitely. A man may
take to drink because he feels himself to be a failure, and then fail
all the more completely because he drinks. It is rather the same
thing that is happening to the English language. It becomes ugly
and inaccurate because our thoughts are foolish, but the slovenliness of our language makes it easier for us to have foolish
thoughts. The point is that the process is reversible. Modern English, especially written English, is full of bad habits which spread by
imitation and which can be avoided if one is willing to take the
necessary trouble. If one gets rid of these habits one can think more
clearly, and to think clearly is a necessary first step towards political
regeneration: so that the fight against bad English is not frivolous
and is not the exclusive concern of professional writers. I will come
back to this presently, and I hope that by that time the meaning of
what I have said here will have become clearer. Meanwhile, here
are five specimens of the English language as it is now habitually
written.

These five passages have not been picked out because they are   3
especially bad—I could have quoted far worse if I had chosen—but
because they illustrate various of the mental vices from which we
now suffer. They are a little below the average, but are fairly representative samples. I number them so that I can refer back to them
when necessary:

1. First published in *Horizon*, April 1946.

"(1) I am not, indeed, sure whether it is not true to say that the Milton who once seemed not unlike a seventeenth-century Shelley had not become, out of an experience ever more bitter in each year, more alien [sic] to the founder of that Jesuit sect which nothing could induce him to tolerate."

Professor Harold Laski (Essay in *Freeedom of Expression*).

"(2) Above all, we cannot play ducks and drakes with a native battery of idioms which prescribes such egregious collocations of vocables as the Basic *put up with* for *tolerate* or *put at a loss* for *bewilder*."

Professor Lancelot Hogben (*Interglossa*).

"(3) On the one side we have the free personality: by definition it is not neurotic, for it has neither conflict nor dream. Its desires, such as they are, are transparent, for they are just what institutional approval keeps in the forefront of consciousness; another institutional pattern would alter their number and intensity; there is little in them that is natural, irreducible, or culturally dangerous. But *on the other side*, the social bond itself is nothing but the mutual reflection of these self-secure integrities. Recall the definition of love. Is not this the very picture of a small academic? Where is there a place in this hall of mirrors for either personality or fraternity?"

Essay on psychology in *Politics* (New York).

"(4) All the 'best people' from the gentlemen's clubs, and all the frantic fascist captains, united in common hatred of Socialism and bestial horror of the rising tide of the mass revolutionary movement, have turned to acts of provocation, to foul incendiarism, to medieval legends of poisoned wells, to legalize their own destruction of proletarian organizations, and rouse the agitated petty-bourgeoisie to chauvinistic fervour on behalf of the fight against the revolutionary way out of the crisis."

Communist pamphlet.

"(5) If a new spirit *is* to be infused into this old country, there is one thorny and contentious reform which must be tackled, and that is the humanization and galvanization of the B.B.C. Timidity here will bespeak cancer and atrophy of the soul. The heart of Britain may be sound and of strong beat, for instance, but the British lion's roar at present is like that of Bottom in Shakespeare's *Midsummer Night's Dream*—as gentle as any sucking dove. A virile new Britain cannot continue indefinitely to be traduced in the eyes or rather ears, of the world by the effete languors of Langham Place, brazenly masquerading as 'standard English'. When the Voice of Britain is heard at nine o'clock, better far and infinitely less ludicrous to hear aitches hon-

estly dropped than the present priggish, inflated, inhibited, school-
ma'amish arch braying of blameless bashful mewing maidens!"

Letter in *Tribune*.

Each of these passages has faults of its own, but, quite apart from   4
avoidable ugliness, two qualities are common to all of them. The
first is staleness of imagery: the other is lack of precision. The writer
either has a meaning and cannot express it, or he inadvertently
says something else, or he is almost indifferent as to whether his
words mean anything or not. This mixture of vagueness and sheer
incompetence is the most marked characteristic of modern English
prose, and especially of any kind of political writing. As soon as
certain topics are raised, the concrete melts into the abstract and no
one seems able to think of turns of speech that are not hackneyed:
prose consists less and less of *words* chosen for the sake of their
meaning, and more and more of *phrases* tacked together like the
sections of a prefabricated hen-house. I list below, with notes and
examples, various of the tricks by means of which the work of
prose-construction is habitually dodged:

DYING METAPHORS

A newly invented metaphor assists thought by evoking a visual   5
image, while on the other hand a metaphor which is technically
"dead" (e.g. *iron resolution*) has in effect reverted to being an ordinary word and can generally be used without loss of vividness. But
in between these two classes there is a huge dump of worn-out
metaphors which have lost all evocative power and are merely
used because they save people the trouble of inventing phrases for
themselves. Examples are: *Ring the changes on, take up the cudgels
for, toe the line, ride roughshod over, stand shoulder to shoulder with,
play into the hands of, no axe to grind, grist to the mill, fishing in
troubled waters, on the order of the day, Achilles' heel, swan song,
hotbed.* Many of these are used without knowledge of their meaning (what is a "rift," for instance?), and incompatible metaphors
are frequently mixed, a sure sign that the writer is not interested in
what he is saying. Some metaphors now current have been twisted
out of their original meaning without those who use them even
being aware of the fact. For example, *toe the line* is sometimes
written *tow the line*. Another example is *the hammer and the anvil*,
now always used with the implication that the anvil gets the worst
of it. In real life it is always the anvil that breaks the hammer, never
the other way about: a writer who stopped to think what he was
saying would be aware of this, and would avoid perverting the
original phrase.

OPERATORS OR VERBAL FALSE LIMBS

These save the trouble of picking out appropriate verbs and   6
nouns, and at the same time pad each sentence with extra syllables
which give it an appearance of symmetry. Characteristic phrases
are: *render inoperative, militate against, make contact with, be subjected
to, give rise to, give grounds for, have the effect of, play a leading part
(role) in, make itself felt, take effect, exhibit a tendency to, serve the
purpose of, etc., etc.* The keynote is the elimination of simple verbs.
Instead of being a single word, such as *break, stop, spoil, mend, kill,*
a verb becomes a *phrase*, made up of a noun or adjective tacked on
to some general-purposes verb such as *prove, serve, form, play, render.* In addition, the passive voice is wherever possible used in
preference to the active, and noun constructions are used instead of
gerunds (*by examination of* instead of *by examining*). The range of
verbs is further cut down by means of the *-ize* and *de-* formation,
and the banal statements are given an appearance of profundity by
means of the *not un-* formation. Simple conjunctions and prepo-
sitions are replaced by such phrases as *with respect to, having regard
to, the fact that, by dint of, in view of, in the interests of, on the hypothesis that;* and the ends of sentences are saved from anticlimax
by such resounding commonplaces as *greatly to be desired, cannot be
left out of account, a development to be expected in the near future,
deserving of serious consideration, brought to a satisfactory conclusion,*
and so on and so forth.

PRETENTIOUS DICTION

Words like *phenomenon, element, individual* (as noun), *objective,*   7
*categorical, effective, virtual, basic, primary, promote, constitute, exhibit,
exploit, utilize, eliminate, liquidate,* are used to dress up simple statements and give an air of scientific impartiality to biased judgments.
Adjectives like *epoch-making, epic, historic, unforgettable, triumphant,
age-old, inevitable, inexorable, veritable,* are used to dignify the sordid
processes of international politics, while writing that aims at
glorifying war usually takes on an archaic colour, its characteristic
words being: *realm, throne, chariot, mailed fist, trident, sword, shield,
buckler, banner, jackboot, clarion.* Foreign words and expressions
such as *cul de sac, ancien régime, deus ex machina, mutatis mutandis,
status quo, gleichschaltung, weltanschauung,* are used to give an air of
culture and elegance. Except for the useful abbreviations *i.e., e.g.,*
and *etc.,* there is no real need for any of the hundreds of foreign
phrases now current in English. Bad writers, and especially
scientific, political and sociological writers, are nearly always
haunted by the notion that Latin or Greek words are grander than
Saxon ones, and unnecessary words like *expedite, ameliorate, pre-*

dict, extraneous, deracinated, clandestine, subaqueous and hundreds of others constantly gain ground from their Anglo-Saxon opposite numbers.[2] The jargon peculiar to Marxist writing (*hyena, hangman, cannibal, petty bourgeois, these gentry, lacquey, flunkey, mad dog, White Guard,* etc.) consists largely of words and phrases translated from Russian, German or French; but the normal way of coining a new word is to use a Latin or Greek root with the appropriate affix and, where necessary, the *-ize* formation. It is often easier to make up words of this kind (*deregionalize, impermissible, extramarital, non-fragmentatory* and so forth) than to think up the English words that will cover one's meaning. The result, in general, in an increase in slovenliness and vagueness.

MEANINGLESS WORDS

In certain kinds of writing, particularly in art criticism and literary criticism, it is normal to come across long passages which are almost completely lacking in meaning.[3] Words like *romantic, plastic, values, human, dead, sentimental, natural, vitality,* as used in art criticism, are strictly meaningless in the sense that they not only do not point to any discoverable object, but are hardly ever expected to do so by the reader. When one critic writes, "The outstanding feature of Mr. X's work is its living quality", while another writes, "The immediately striking thing about Mr. X's work is its peculiar deadness", the reader accepts this as a simple difference of opinion. If words like *black* and *white* were involved, instead of the jargon words *dead* and *living,* he would see at once that language was being used in an improper way. Many political words are similarly abused. The word *Fascism* has now no meaning except in so far as it signifies "something not desirable." The words *democracy, socialism, freedom, patriotic, realistic, justice,* have each of them several different meanings which cannot be reconciled with one another. In the case of a word like *democracy,* not only is there no agreed definition, but the attempt to make one is resisted from all

8

2. An interesting illustration of this is the way in which the English flower names which were in use till very recently are being ousted by Greek ones, *snapdragon* becoming *antirrhinum, forget-me-not* becoming *myosotis,* etc. It is hard to see any practical reason for this change of fashion: it is probably due to an instinctive turning-away from the more homely word and a vague feeling that the Greek word is scientific. [author's note]

3. Example: "Comfort's catholicity of perception and image, strangely Whitman-esque in range, almost the exact opposite in aesthetic compulsion, continues to evoke that trembling atmospheric accumulative hinting at a cruel, an inexorably serene timelessness . . . Wrey Gardiner scores by aiming at simple bull's-eyes with precision. Only they are not so simple, and through this contented sadness runs more than the surface bitter-sweet of resignation" (*Poetry Quarterly*). [author's note]

sides. It is almost universally felt that when we call a country democratic we are praising it: consequently the defenders of every kind of régime claim that it is a democracy, and fear that they might have to stop using the word if it were tied down to any one meaning. Words of this kind are often used in a consciously dishonest way. That is, the person who uses them has his own private definition, but allows his hearer to think he means something quite different. Statements like *Marshal Pétain was a true patriot, The Soviet Press is the freest in the world, The Catholic Church is opposed to persecution,* are almost always made with intent to deceive. Other words used in variable meanings, in most cases more or less dishonestly, are: *class, totalitarian, science, progressive, reactionary, bourgeois, equality.*

Now that I have made this catalogue of swindles and perversions, let me give another example of the kind of writing that they lead to. This time it must of its nature be an imaginary one. I am going to translate a passage of good English into modern English of the worst sort. Here is a well-known verse from *Ecclesiastes*:   9

> "I returned and saw under the sun, that the race is not to the swift, nor the battle to the strong, neither yet bread to the wise, nor yet riches to men of understanding, nor yet favour to men of skill; but time and chance happeneth to them all."

Here it is in modern English: 10

> "Objective consideration of contemporary phenomena compels the conclusion that success or failure in competitive activities exhibits no tendency to be commensurate with innate capacity, but that a considerable element of the unpredictable must invariably be taken into account."

This is a parody, but not a very gross one. Exhibit (3), above, for instance, contains several patches of the same kind of English. It will be seen that I have not made a full translation. The beginning and ending of the sentence follow the original meaning fairly closely, but in the middle the concrete illustrations—race, battle, bread—dissolve into the vague phrase "success or failure in competitive activities." This had to be so, because no modern writer of the kind I am discussing—no one capable of using phrases like "objective consideration of contemporary phenomena"—would ever tabulate his thoughts in that precise and detailed way. The whole tendency of modern prose is away from concreteness. Now analyse the two sentences a little more closely. The first contains forty-nine words but only sixty syllables, and all its words are those of everyday life. The second contains thirty-eight words of ninety syllables: eighteen of its words are from Latin roots, and one from   11

Greek. The first sentence contains six vivid images, and only one phrase ("time and chance") that could be called vague. The second contains not a single fresh, arresting phrase, and in spite of its ninety syllables it gives only a shortened version of the meaning contained in the first. Yet without a doubt it is the second kind of sentence that is gaining ground in modern English. I do not want to exaggerate. This kind of writing is not yet universal, and outcrops of simplicity will occur here and there in the worst-written page. Still, if you or I were told to write a few lines on the uncertainty of human fortunes, we should probably come much nearer to my imaginary sentence than to the one from *Ecclesiastes.*

As I have tried to show, modern writing at its worst does not 12 consist in picking out words for the sake of their meaning and inventing images in order to make the meaning clearer. It consists in gumming together long strips of words which have already been set in order by someone else, and making the results presentable by sheer humbug. The attraction of this way of writing is that it is easy. It is easier—even quicker, once you have the habit—to say *In my opinion it is a not unjustifiable assumption that* than to say *I think.* If you use ready-made phrases, you not only don't have to hunt about for words; you also don't have to bother with the rhythms of your sentences, since these phrases are generally so arranged as to be more or less euphonious. When you are composing in a hurry—when you are dictating to a stenographer, for instance, or making a public speech—it is natural to fall into a pretentious, Latinized style. Tags like *a consideration which we should do well to bear in mind* or *a conclusion to which all of us would readily assent* will save many a sentence from coming down with a bump. By using stale metaphors, similes and idioms, you save much mental effort, at the cost of leaving your meaning vague, not only for your reader but for yourself. This is the significance of mixed metaphors. The sole aim of a metaphor is to call up a visual image. When these images clash—as in *The Fascist octopus has sung its swan song, the jackboot is thrown into the melting pot*—it can be taken as certain that the writer is not seeing a mental image of the objects he is naming; in other words he is not really thinking. Look again at the examples I gave at the beginning of this essay. Professor Laski (1) uses five negatives in fifty-three words. One of these is superfluous, making nonsense of the whole passage, and in addition there is the slip *alien* for akin, making further nonsense, and several avoidable pieces of clumsiness which increase the general vagueness. Professor Hogben (2) plays ducks and drakes with a battery which is able to write prescriptions, and, while disapproving of the everyday phrase *put up with*, is unwilling to look *egregious* up in the dictionary and see what it means. (3), if one takes an uncharitable attitude towards it, is simply meaningless: probably one could work out its intended meaning by reading the whole of the article in which it occurs. In (4), the writer knows more or less what he wants to say, but an accumulation of stale phrases chokes him like tea leaves blocking a sink. In (5), words and meaning have almost parted company. People who write in this manner usually have a general emotional meaning—they dislike one thing and want to express solidarity with another—but they are not interested in the detail of what they are saying. A scupulous writer, in every sentence that he writes, will ask himself at least four questions, thus: What am I trying to say? What words will express it? What image or idiom will make it clearer? Is this image fresh enough to have an effect? And he will probably ask himself two more: Could I put it more shortly? Have I said anything that is avoidably ugly? But you are not obliged to go to all this trouble: You can shirk it by simply throwing your mind open and letting the ready-made phrases come crowding in. They will construct your sentences for you—even think your thoughts for you, to a certain extent—and at need they will perform the important service of partially concealing your meaning even from yourself. It is at this point that the special connection between politics and the debasement of language becomes clear.

In our time it is broadly true that political writing is bad writing. 13 Where it is not true, it will generally be found that the writer is some kind of rebel, expressing his private opinions and not a "party line." Orthodoxy, of whatever colour, seems to demand a lifeless, imitative style. The political dialects to be found in pamphlets, leading articles, manifestos, White Papers and the speeches of under-secretaries do, of course, vary from party to party, but they are all alike in that one almost never finds in them a fresh, vivid, home-made turn of speech. When one watches some tired hack on the platform mechanically repeating the familiar phrases —*bestial atrocities, iron heel, bloodstained tyranny, free peoples of the world, stand shoulder to shoulder*—one often has a curious feeling that one is not watching a live human being but some kind of dummy: a feeling which suddenly becomes stronger at moments when the light catches the speaker's spectacles and turns them into blank discs which seem to have no eyes behind them. And this is not altogether fanciful. A speaker who uses that kind of phraseology has gone some distance towards turning himself into a machine. The appropriate noises are coming out of his larynx, but his brain is not involved as it would be if he were choosing his words for himself. If the speech he is making is one that he is accustomed to make over and over again, he may be almost unconscious of what he is saying, as one is when one utters the responses in church. And this reduced state of consciousness, if not indispensable, is at any rate favourable to political conformity.

In our time, political speech and writing are largely the defence 14 of the indefensible. Things like the continuance of British rule in India, the Russian purges and deportations, the dropping of the atom bombs on Japan, can indeed be defended, but only by arguments which are too brutal for most people to face, and which do not square with the professed aims of political parties. Thus political language has to consist largely of euphemism, question-begging and sheer cloudy vagueness. Defenceless villages are bombarded from the air, the inhabitants driven out into the countryside, the cattle machine-gunned, the huts set on fire with incendiary bullets: this is called *pacification*. Millions of peasants are robbed of their farms and sent trudging along the roads with no more than they can carry: this is called *transfer of population* or *rectification of frontiers*. People are imprisoned for years without trial, or shot in the back of the neck or sent to die of scurvy in Arctic lumber camps: this is called *elimination of unreliable elements*. Such phraseology is needed if one wants to name things without calling up mental pictures of them. Consider for instance some comfortable English professor defending Russian totalitarianism. He cannot say outright, "I believe in killing off your opponents when you can get good results by doing so." Probably, therefore, he will say something like this:

"While freely conceding that the Soviet régime exhibits certain 15 features which the humanitarian may be inclined to deplore, we must, I think, agree that a certain curtailment of the right to political opposition is an unavoidable concomitant of transitional periods, and that the rigours which the Russian people have been called upon to undergo have been amply justified in the sphere of concrete achievement."

The inflated style is itself a kind of euphemism. A mass of Latin 16 words falls upon the facts like soft snow, blurring the outlines and covering up all the details. The great enemy of clear language is insincerity. When there is a gap between one's real and one's declared aims, one turns as it were instinctively to long words and exhausted idioms, like a cuttlefish squirting out ink. In our age there is no such thing as "keeping out of politics." All issues are political issues, and politics itself is a mass of lies, evasions, folly, hatred and schizophrenia. When the general atmosphere is bad, language must suffer. I should expect to find—this is a guess which

I have not sufficient knowledge to verify—that the German, Russian and Italian languages have all deteriorated in the last ten or fifteen years, as a result of dictatorship.

But if thought corrupts language, language can also corrupt 17 thought. A bad usage can spread by tradition and imitation, even among people who should and do know better. The debased language that I have been discussing is in some ways very convenient. Phrases like *a not unjustifiable assumption, leaves much to be desired, would serve no good purpose, a consideration which we should do well to bear in mind*, are a continuous temptation, a packet of aspirins always at one's elbow. Look back through this essay, and for certain you will find that I have again and again committed the very faults I am protesting against. By this morning's post I have received a pamphlet dealing with conditions in Germany. The author tells me that he "felt impelled" to write it. I open it at random, and here is almost the first sentence that I see: "(The Allies) have an opportunity not only of achieving a radical transformation of Germany's social and political structure in such a way as to avoid a nationalistic reaction in Germany itself, but at the same time of laying the foundations of a co-operative and unified Europe." You see, he "feels impelled" to write—feels, presumably, that he has something new to say—and yet his words, like cavalry horses answering the bugle, group themselves automatically into the familiar dreary pattern. This invasion of one's mind by ready-made phrases (*lay the foundations, achieve a radical transformation*) can only be prevented if one is constantly on guard against them, and every such phrase anesthetizes a portion of one's brain.

I said earlier that the decadence of our language is probably 18 curable. Those who deny this would argue, if they produced an argument at all, that language merely reflects existing social conditions, and that we cannot influence its development by any direct tinkering with words and constructions. So far as the general tone or spirit of a language goes, this may be true, but it is not true in detail. Silly words and expressions have often disappeared, not through any evolutionary process but owing to the conscious action of a minority. Two recent examples were *explore every avenue* and *leave no stone unturned*, which were killed by the jeers of a few journalists. There is a long list of flyblown metaphors which could similarly be got rid of if enough people would interest themselves in the job; and it should also be possible to laugh the *not un-* formation out of existence,[4] to reduce the amount of Latin and

---

4. One can cure oneself of the *not un-* formation by memorizing this sentence: *A not unblack dog was chasing a not unsmall rabbit across a not ungreen field.* [author's note]

Greek in the average sentence, to drive out foreign phrases and strayed scientific words, and, in general, to make pretentiousness unfashionable. But all these are minor points. The defence of the English language implies more than this, and perhaps it is best to start by saying what it does *not* imply.

To begin with it has nothing to do with archaism, with the salvaging of obsolete words and turns of speech, or with the setting up of a "standard English" which must never be departed from. On the contrary, it is especially concerned with the scrapping of every word or idiom which has outworn its usefulness. It has nothing to do with correct grammar and syntax, which are of no importance so long as one makes one's meaning clear, or with the avoidance of Americanisms, or with having what is called a "good prose style." On the other hand it is not concerned with fake simplicity and the attempt to make written English colloquial. Nor does it even imply in every case preferring the Saxon word to the Latin one, though it does imply using the fewest and shortest words that will cover one's meaning. What is above all needed is to let the meaning choose the word, and not the other way about. In prose, the worst thing one can do with words is to surrender to them. When you think of a concrete object, you think wordlessly, and then, if you want to describe the thing you have been visualizing you probably hunt about till you find the exact words that seem to fit. When you think of something abstract you are more inclined to use words from the start, and unless you make a conscious effort to prevent it, the existing dialect will come rushing in and do the job for you, at the expense of blurring or even changing your meaning. Probably it is better to put off using words as long as possible and get one's meaning as clear as one can through pictures or sensations. Afterwards one can choose—not simply *accept*—the phrases that will best cover the meaning, and then switch round and decide what impression one's words are likely to make on another person. This last effort of the mind cuts out all stale or mixed images, all prefabricated phrases, needless repetitions, and humbug and vagueness generally. But one can often be in doubt about the effect of a word or a phrase, and one needs rules that one can rely on when instinct fails. I think the following rules will cover most cases:

(i) Never use a metaphor, simile or other figure of speech which you are used to seeing in print.

(ii) Never use a long word where a short one will do.

(iii) If it is possible to cut a word out, always cut it out.

(iv) Never use the passive where you can use the active.

(v) Never use a foreign phrase, a scientific word or a jargon word if you can think of an everyday English equivalent.

(vi) Break any of these rules sooner than say anything outright barbarous.

These rules sound elementary, and so they are, but they demand a deep change of attitude in anyone who has grown used to writing in the style now fashionable. One could keep all of them and still write bad English, but one could not write the kind of stuff that I quoted in those five specimens at the beginning of this article.

I have not here been considering the literary use of language, but   20
merely language as an instrument for expressing and not for concealing or preventing thought. Stuart Chase and others have come near to claiming that all abstract words are meaningless, and have used this as a pretext for advocating a kind of political quietism. Since you don't know what Fascism is, how can you struggle against Fascism? One need not swallow such absurdities as this, but one ought to recognize that the present political chaos is connected with the decay of language, and that one can probably bring about some improvement by starting at the verbal end. If you simplify your English, you are freed from the worst follies of orthodoxy. You cannot speak any of the necessary dialects, and when you make a stupid remark its stupidity will be obvious, even to yourself. Political language—and with variations this is true of all political parties, from Conservatives to Anarchists—is designed to make lies sound truthful and murder respectable, and to give an appearance of solidity to pure wind. One cannot change this all in a moment, but one can at least change one's own habits, and from time to time one can even, if one jeers loudly enough, send some worn-out and useless phrase—some *jackboot, Achilles' heel, hotbed, melting pot, acid test, veritable inferno* or other lump of verbal refuse—into the dustbin where it belongs.

JAMES BALDWIN

James [Arthur] Baldwin (1924–1987) was born and raised in Harlem, the stepson of an evangelical preacher. Baldwin himself underwent a dramatic religious conversion when he was fourteen years old and later realized that involvement with the church had sheltered him from the despair and bitterness many of his classmates felt as they grew up in a segregated society. For three years a junior minister, he separated from the church because he felt that Christianity had become a tool to encourage black quietism. After graduating from high school, Baldwin worked as a handyman, dishwasher, waiter, and office boy before Richard Wright helped him win the first of a series of literary fellowships that allowed him to write his novel *Go Tell It on the Mountain* (1953). From 1948 to 1957, unable to find his individual voice and perspective in the segregated United States, he lived in Paris. When he returned, he threw himself into his writing and into the civil rights struggle, writing novels, short stories, and plays exploring the psychology of race and the position of the homosexual in a heterosexual society. It was Baldwin's essays, however, that established his stature as a writer. Critic Irving Howe placed Baldwin among "the two or three greatest essayists this country has ever produced." His earliest and most famous essays are collected in *Notes of a Native Son* (1955), *Nobody Knows My Name* (1961), and *The Fire Next Time* (1963). His later and less well known essays have dealt with such topics as national and regional politics, the representation of blacks in motion pictures, and sexual attitudes in the United States. His collected essays were published in *The Price of the Ticket* (1985).

JAMES BALDWIN

Autobiographical Notes[1]

I was born in Harlem thirty-one years ago. I began plotting   1
novels at about the time I learned to read. The story of my childhood is the usual bleak fantasy, and we can dismiss it with the restrained observation that I certainly would not consider living it again. In those days my mother was given to the exasperating and mysterious habit of having babies. As they were born, I took them over with one hand and held a book with the other. The children probably suffered, though they have since been kind enough to deny it, and in this way I read *Uncle Tom's Cabin* and *A Tale of Two Cities* over and over and over again; in this way, in fact, I read just about everything I could get my hands on—except the Bible, prob-

---

1. First published in *Notes of a Native Son* (1955).

ably because it was the only book I was encouraged to read. I must also confess that I wrote—a great deal—and my first professional triumph, in any case, the first effort of mine to be seen in print, occurred at the age of twelve or thereabouts, when a short story I had written about the Spanish revolution won some sort of prize in an extremely short-lived church newspaper. I remember the story was censored by the lady editor, though I don't remember why, and I was outraged.

Also wrote plays, and songs, for one of which I received a letter   2
of congratulations from Mayor La Guardia, and poetry, about which the less said, the better. My mother was delighted by all these goings-on, but my father wasn't; he wanted me to be a preacher. When I was fourteen I became a preacher, and when I was seventeen I stopped. Very shortly thereafter I left home. For God knows how long I struggled with the world of commerce and industry—I guess they would say they struggled with *me*—and when I was about twenty-one I had enough done of a novel to get a Saxton Fellowship. When I was twenty-two the fellowship was over, the novel turned out to be unsalable, and I started waiting on tables in a Village[2] restaurant and writing book reviews—mostly, as it turned out, about the Negro problem, concerning which the color of my skin made me automatically an expert. Did another book, in company with photographer Theodore Pelatowski, about the storefront churches in Harlem. This book met exactly the same fate as my first—fellowship, but no sale. (It was a Rosenwald Fellowship.) By the time I was twenty-four I had decided to stop reviewing books about the Negro problem—which, by this time, was only slightly less horrible in print than it was in life—and I packed my bags and went to France, where I finished, God knows how, *Go Tell It on the Mountain.*

Any writer, I suppose, feels that the world into which he was   3
born is nothing less than a conspiracy against the cultivation of his talent—which attitude certainly has a great deal to support it. On the other hand, it is only because the world looks on his talent with such a frightening indifference that the artist is compelled to make his talent important. So that any writer, looking back over even so short a span of time as I am here forced to assess, finds that the things which hurt him and the things which helped him cannot be divorced from each other; he could be helped in a certain way only because he was hurt in a certain way; and his help is simply to be enabled to move from one conundrum to the next—one is tempted to say that he moves from one disaster to the next. When one

2. Manhattan's Greenwich Village, a neighborhood popular with artists and writers.

begins looking for influences one finds them by the score. I haven't thought much about my own, not enough anyway; I hazard that the King James Bible, the rhetoric of the storefront church, something ironic and violent and perpetually understated in Negro speech—and something of Dickens' love for bravura—have something to do with me today; but I wouldn't stake my life on it. Likewise, innumerable people have helped me in many ways; but finally, I suppose, the most difficult (and most rewarding) thing in my life has been the fact that I was born a Negro and was forced, therefore, to effect some kind of truce with this reality. (Truce, by the way, is the best one can hope for.)

One of the difficulties about being a Negro writer (and this is not   4
special pleading, since I don't mean to suggest that he has it worse than anybody else) is that the Negro problem is written about so widely. The bookshelves groan under the weight of information, and everyone therefore considers himself informed. And this information, furthermore, operates usually (generally, popularly) to reinforce traditional attitudes. Of traditional attitudes there are only two—For or Against—and I, personally, find it difficult to say which attitude has caused me the most pain. I am speaking as a writer; from a social point of view I am perfectly aware that the change from ill-will to good-will, however motivated, however imperfect, however expressed, is better than no change at all.

But it is part of the business of the writer—as I see it—to exam-   5
ine attitudes, to go beneath the surface, to tap the source. From this point of view the Negro problem is nearly inaccessible. It is not only written about so widely; it is written about so badly. It is quite possible to say that the price a Negro pays for becoming articulate is to find himself, at length, with nothing to be articulate about. ("You taught me language," says Caliban to Prospero,[3] "and my profit on't is I know how to curse.") Consider: the tremendous social activity that this problem generates imposes on whites and Negroes alike the necessity of looking forward, of working to bring about a better day. This is fine, it keeps the waters troubled; it is all, indeed, that has made possible the Negro's progress. Nevertheless, social affairs are not generally speaking the writer's prime concern, whether they ought to be or not; it is absolutely necessary that he establish between himself and these affairs a distance which will allow, at least, for clarity, so that before he can look forward in any meaningful sense, he must first be allowed to take a long look back.

3. In Shakespeare's play *The Tempest,* the magician Prospero educates the savage Caliban.

In the context of the Negro problem neither whites nor blacks, for excellent reasons of their own, have the faintest desire to look back; but I think that the past is all that makes the present coherent, and further, that the past will remain horrible for exactly as long as we refuse to assess it honestly.

I know, in any case, that the most crucial time in my own development came when I was forced to recognize that I was a kind of bastard of the West; when I followed the line of my past I did not find myself in Europe but in Africa. And this meant that in some subtle way, in a really profound way, I brought to Shakespeare, Bach, Rembrandt, to the stones of Paris, to the cathedral at Chartres, and to the Empire State Building, a special attitude. These were not really my creations, they did not contain my history; I might search in them in vain forever for any reflection of myself. I was an interloper; this was not my heritage. At the same time I had no other heritage which I could possibly hope to use—I had certainly been unfitted for the jungle or the tribe. I would have to appropriate these white centuries, I would have to make them mine—I would have to accept my special attitude, my special place in this scheme—otherwise I would have no place in *any* scheme. What was the most difficult was the fact that I was forced to admit something I had always hidden from myself, which the American Negro has had to hide from himself as the price of his public progress; that I hated and feared white people. This did not mean that I loved black people; on the contrary, I despised them, possibly because they failed to produce Rembrandt. In effect, I hated and feared the world. And this meant, not only that I thus gave the world an altogether murderous power over me, but also that in such a self-destroying limbo I could never hope to write.

One writes out of one thing only—one's own experience. Everything depends on how relentlessly one forces from this experience the last drop, sweet or bitter, it can possibly give. This is the only real concern of the artist, to recreate out of the disorder of life that order which is art. The difficulty then, for me, of being a Negro writer was the fact that I was, in effect, prohibited from examining my own experience too closely by the tremendous demands and the very real dangers of my social situation.

I don't think the dilemma outlined above is uncommon. I do think, since writers work in the disastrously explicit medium of language, that it goes a little way towards explaining why, out of the enormous resources of Negro speech and life, and despite the example of Negro music, prose written by Negroes has been generally speaking so pallid and so harsh. I have not written about being a Negro at such length because I expect that to be my only subject, but only because it was the gate I had to unlock before I could hope to write about anything else. I don't think that the Negro problem in America can be even discussed coherently without bearing in mind its context; its context being the history, traditions, customs, the moral assumptions and preoccupations of the country; in short, the general social fabric. Appearances to the contrary, no one in America escapes its effects and everyone in America bears some responsibility for it. I believe this the more firmly because it is the overwhelming tendency to speak of this problem as though it were a thing apart. But in the work of Faulkner, in the general attitude and certain specific passages in Robert Penn Warren, and, most significantly, in the advent of Ralph Ellison,[4] one sees the beginnings—at least—of a more genuinely penetrating search. Mr. Ellison, by the way, is the first Negro novelist I have ever read to utilize in language, and brilliantly, some of the ambiguity and irony of Negro life.

About my interests: I don't know if I have any, unless the mor- 9
bid desire to own a sixteen-millimeter camera and make experimental movies can be so classified. Otherwise, I love to eat and drink—it's my melancholy conviction that I've scarcely ever had enough to eat (this is because it's *impossible* to eat enough if you're worried about the next meal)—and I love to argue with people who do not disagree with me too profoundly, and I love to laugh. I do *not* like bohemia, or bohemians, I do not like people whose principal aim is pleasure, and I do not like people who are *earnest* about anything. I don't like people who like me because I'm a Negro; neither do I like people who find in the same accident grounds for contempt. I love America more than any other country in the world, and, exactly for this reason, I insist on the right to criticize her perpetually. I think all theories are suspect, that the finest principles may have to be modified, or may even be pulverized by the demands of life, and that one must find, therefore, one's own moral center and move through the world hoping that this center will guide one aright. I consider that I have many responsibilities, but none greater than this: to last, as Hemingway says, and get my work done.

I want to be an honest man and a good writer.   10

4. William Faulkner (1897–1962) and Robert Penn Warren (1905–1989) were white Southern novelists. Ralph Ellison (1914–   ), a black novelist, published *Invisible Man* in 1952.

JAMES BALDWIN

Stranger in the Village[1]

From all available evidence no black man had ever set foot in   1
this tiny Swiss village before I came. I was told before arriving that I
would probably be a "sight" for the village; I took this to mean that
people of my complexion were rarely seen in Switzerland, and also
that city people are always something of a "sight" outside of the
city. It did not occur to me—possibly because I am an American—
that there could be people anywhere who had never seen a Negro.

It is a fact that cannot be explained on the basis of the inaccessi-   2
bility of the village. The village is very high, but it is only four hours
from Milan and three hours from Lausanne. It is true that it is
virtually unknown. Few people making plans for a holiday would
elect to come here. On the other hand, the villagers are able, presumably, to come and go as they please—which they do: to another town at the foot of the mountain, with a population of approximately five thousand, the nearest place to see a movie or go to
the bank. In the village there is no movie house, no bank, no
library, no theater; very few radios, one jeep, one station wagon;
and, at the moment, one typewriter, mine, an invention which the
woman next door to me here had never seen. There are about six
hundred people living here, all Catholic—I conclude this from the
fact that the Catholic church is open all year round, whereas the
Protestant chapel, set off on a hill a little removed from the village,
is open only in the summertime when the tourists arrive. There are
four or five hotels, all closed now, and four or five *bistros*,[2] of
which, however, only two do any business during the winter.
These two do not do a great deal, for life in the village seems to end
around nine or ten o'clock. There are a few stores, butcher, baker,
épicerie,[3] a hardware store, and a money-changer—who cannot
change travelers' checks, but must send them down to the bank, an
operation which takes two or three days. There is something called
the *Ballet Haus*, closed in the winter and used for God knows what,
certainly not ballet, during the summer. There seems to be only one
schoolhouse in the village, and this for the quite young children; I

1. First published in *Harper's*, October 1953.
2. Small taverns.
3. Grocery store.

suppose this to mean that their older brothers and sisters at some point descend from these mountains in order to complete their education—possibly, again, to the town just below. The landscape is absolutely forbidding, mountains towering on all four sides, ice and snow as far as the eye can reach. In this white wilderness, men and women and children move all day, carrying washing, wood, buckets of milk or water, sometimes skiing on Sunday afternoons. All week long boys and young men are to be seen shoveling snow off the rooftops, or dragging wood down from the forest in sleds.

The village's only real attraction, which explains the tourist sea-   3
son, is the hot spring water. A disquietingly high proportion of these tourists are cripples, or semicripples, who come year after year—from other parts of Switzerland, usually—to take the waters. This lends the village, at the height of the season, a rather terrifying air of sanctity, as though it were a lesser Lourdes.[4] There is often something beautiful, there is always something awful, in the spectacle of a person who has lost one of his faculties, a faculty he never questioned until it was gone, and who struggles to recover it. Yet people remain people, on crutches or indeed on deathbeds; and wherever I passed, the first summer I was here, among the native villagers or among the lame, a wind passed with me—of astonishment, curiosity, amusement, and outrage. That first summer I stayed two weeks and never intended to return. But I did return in the winter, to work; the village offers, obviously, no distractions whatever and has the further advantage of being extremely cheap. Now it is winter again, a year later, and I am here again. Everyone in the village knows my name, though they scarcely ever use it, knows that I come from America—though, this, apparently, they will never really believe: black men come from Africa—and everyone knows that I am the friend of the son of a woman who was born here, and that I am staying in their chalet. But I remain as much a stranger today as I was the first day I arrived, and the children shout *Neger! Neger!* as I walk along the streets.

It must be admitted that in the beginning I was far too shocked to   4
have any real reaction. In so far as I reacted at all, I reacted by trying to be pleasant—it being a great part of the American Negro's education (long before he goes to school) that he must make people "like" him. This smile-and-the-world-smiles-with-you routine worked about as well in this situation as it had in the situation for which it was designed, which is to say that it did not work at all. No

4. French town frequented by pilgrims as a result of a young girl's miraculous visions in 1858.

one, after all, can be liked whose human weight and complexity cannot be, or has not been, admitted. My smile was simply another unheard-of phenomenon which allowed them to see my teeth— they did not, really, see my smile and I began to think that, should I take to snarling, no one would notice any difference. All of the physical characteristics of the Negro which had caused me, in America, a very different and almost forgotten pain were nothing less than miraculous—or infernal—in the eyes of the village people. Some thought my hair was the color of tar, that it had the texture of wire, or the texture of cotton. It was jocularly suggested that I might let it all grow long and make myself a winter coat. If I sat in the sun for more than five minutes some daring creature was certain to come along and gingerly put his fingers on my hair, as though he were afraid of an electric shock, or put his hand on my hand, astonished that the color did not rub off. In all of this, in which it must be conceded there was the charm of genuine wonder and in which there was certainly no element of intentional unkindness, there was yet no suggestion that I was human: I was simply a living wonder.

I knew that they did not mean to be unkind, and I know it now;   5 it is necessary, nevertheless, for me to repeat this to myself each time that I walk out of the chalet. The children who shout *Neger!* have no way of knowing the echoes this sound raises in me. They are brimming with good humor and the more daring swell with pride when I stop to speak with them. Just the same, there are days when I cannot pause and smile, when I have no heart to play with them; when, indeed, I mutter sourly to myself, exactly as I muttered on the streets of a city these children have never seen, when I was no bigger than these children are now: *Your* mother *was a nigger.* Joyce[5] is right about history being a nightmare—but it may be the nightmare from which no one *can* awaken. People are trapped in history and history is trapped in them.

There is a custom in the village—I am told it is repeated in many   6 villages—of "buying" African natives for the purpose of converting them to Christianity. There stands in the church all year round a small box with a slot for money, decorated with a black figurine, and into this box the villagers drop their francs. During the *carnaval* which precedes Lent, two village children have their faces blackened—out of which bloodless darkness their blue eyes shine like ice—and fantastic horsehair wigs are placed on their blond heads; thus disguised, they solicit among the villagers for money for the missionaries in Africa. Between the box in the church and the

5. James Joyce (1882–1941), Irish novelist and poet.

blackened children, the village "bought" last year six or eight African natives. This was reported to me with pride by the wife of one of the *bistro* owners and I was careful to express astonishment and pleasure at the solicitude shown by the village for the souls of black folk. The *bistro* owner's wife beamed with a pleasure far more genuine than my own and seemed to feel that I might now breathe more easily concerning the souls of at least six of my kinsmen.

I tried not to think of these so lately baptized kinsmen, of the   7
price paid for them, or the peculiar price they themselves would pay, and said nothing about my father, who having taken his own conversion too literally never, at bottom, forgave the white world (which he described as heathen) for having saddled him with a Christ in whom, to judge at least from their treatment of him, they themselves no longer believed. I thought of white men arriving for the first time in an African village, strangers there, as I am a stranger here, and tried to imagine the astounded populace touching their hair and marveling at the color of their skin. But there is a great difference between being the first white man to be seen by Africans and being the first black man to be seen by whites. The white man takes the astonishment as tribute, for he arrives to conquer and to convert the natives, whose inferiority in relation to himself is not even to be questioned; whereas I, without a thought of conquest, find myself among a people whose culture controls me, has even, in a sense, created me, people who have cost me more in anguish and rage than they will ever know, who yet do not even know of my existence. The astonishment with which I might have greeted them, should they have stumbled into my African village a few hundred years ago, might have rejoiced their hearts. But the astonishment with which they greet me today can only poison mine.

And this is so despite everything I may do to feel differently,   8
despite my friendly conversations with the *bistro* owner's wife, despite their three-year-old son who has at last become my friend, despite the *saluts*[6] and *bonsoirs*[7] which I exchange with people as I walk, despite the fact that I know that no individual can be taken to task for what history is doing, or has done. I say that the culture of these people controls me—but they can scarcely be held responsible for European culture. America comes out of Europe, but these people have never seen America, nor have most of them seen more of Europe than the hamlet at the foot of their mountain. Yet they move with an authority which I shall never have; and they regard me, quite rightly, not only as a stranger in their village but as

6. *Salut* is used as a greeting, wishing a person good health.
7. "Good-evenings."

a suspect latecomer, bearing no credentials, to everything they have—however unconsciously—inherited.

For this village, even were it incomparably more remote and incredibly more primitive, is the West, the West onto which I have been so strangely grafted. These people cannot be, from the point of view of power, strangers anywhere in the world; they have made the modern world, in effect, even if they do not know it. The most illiterate among them is related, in a way that I am not, to Dante, Shakespeare, Michelangelo, Aeschylus, Da Vinci, Rembrandt, and Racine; the cathedral at Chartres says something to them which it cannot say to me, as indeed would New York's Empire State Building, should anyone here ever see it. Out of their hymns and dances come Beethoven and Bach. Go back a few centuries and they are in their full glory—but I am in Africa, watching the conquerors arrive.

The rage of the disesteemed is personally fruitless, but it is also absolutely inevitable; this rage, so generally discounted, so little understood even among the people whose daily bread it is, is one of the things that makes history. Rage can only with difficulty, and never entirely, be brought under the domination of the intelligence and is therefore not susceptible to any arguments whatever. This is a fact which ordinary representatives of the *Herrenvolk*,[8] having never felt this rage and being unable to imagine it, quite fail to understand. Also, rage cannot be hidden, it can only be dissembled. This dissembling deludes the thoughtless, and strengthens rage and adds, to rage, contempt. There are, no doubt, as many ways of coping with the resulting complex of tensions as there are black men in the world, but no black man can hope ever to be entirely liberated from this internal warfare—rage, dissembling, and contempt having inevitably accompanied his first realization of the power of white men. What is crucial here is that, since white men represent in the black man's world so heavy a weight, white men have for black men a reality which is far from being reciprocal; and hence all black men have toward all white men an attitude which is designed, really, either to rob the white man of the jewel of his naïveté, or else to make it cost him dear.

The black man insists, by whatever means he finds at his disposal, that the white man cease to regard him as an exotic rarity and recognize him as a human being. This is a very charged and difficult moment, for there is a great deal of will power involved in the white man's naïveté. Most people are not naturally reflective any more than they are naturally malicious, and the white man

8. The group believed to be racially superior.

prefers to keep the black man at a certain human remove because it is easier for him thus to preserve his simplicity and avoid being called to account for crimes committed by his forefathers, or his neighbors. He is inescapably aware, nevertheless, that he is in a better position in the world than black men are, nor can he quite put to death the suspicion that he is hated by black men therefore. He does not wish to be hated, neither does he wish to change places, and at this point in his uneasiness he can scarcely avoid having recourse to those legends which white men have created about black men, the most usual effect of which is that the white man finds himself enmeshed, so to speak, in his own language which describes hell, as well as the attributes which lead one to hell, as being as black as night.

Every legend, moreover, contains its residuum of truth, and the   12
root function of language is to control the universe by describing it. It is of quite considerable significance that black men remain, in the imagination, and in overwhelming numbers in fact, beyond the disciplines of salvation; and this despite the fact that the West has been "buying" African natives for centuries. There is, I should hazard, an instantaneous necessity to be divorced from this so visibly unsaved stranger, in whose heart, moreover, one cannot guess what dreams of vengeance are being nourished; and, at the same time, there are few things on earth more attractive than the idea of the unspeakable liberty which is allowed the unredeemed. When, beneath the black mask, a human being begins to make himself felt one cannot escape a certain awful wonder as to what kind of human being it is. What one's imagination makes of other people is dictated, of course, by the laws of one's own personality and it is one of the ironies of black-white relations that, by means of what the white man imagines the black man to be, the black man is enabled to know who the white man is.

I have said, for example, that I am as much a stranger in this   13
village today as I was the first summer I arrived, but this is not quite true. The villagers wonder less about the texture of my hair than they did then, and wonder rather more about me. And the fact that their wonder now exists on another level is reflected in their attitudes and in their eyes. There are the children who make those delightful, hilarious, sometimes astonishingly grave overtures of friendship in the unpredictable fashion of children; other children, having been taught that the devil is a black man, scream in genuine anguish as I approach. Some of the older women never pass without a friendly greeting, never pass, indeed, if it seems that they will be able to engage me in conversation; other women look down or look away or rather contemptuously smirk. Some of the men drink

with me and suggest that I learn how to ski—partly, I gather, because they cannot imagine what I would look like on skis—and want to know if I am married, and ask questions about my *métier*.[9] But some of the men have accused *le sale nègre*[10]—behind my back—of stealing wood and there is already in the eyes of some of them that peculiar, intent, paranoiac malevolence which one sometimes surprises in the eyes of American white men when, out walking with their Sunday girl, they see a Negro male approach.

There is a dreadful abyss between the streets of this village and the streets of the city in which I was born, between the children who shout *Neger!* today and those who shouted *Nigger!* yesterday— the abyss is experience, the American experience. The syllable hurled behind me today expresses, above all, wonder: I am a stranger here. But I am not a stranger in America and the same syllable riding on the American air expresses the war my presence has occasioned in the American soul. 14

For this village brings home to me this fact: that there was a day, and not really a very distant day, when Americans were scarcely Americans at all but discontented Europeans, facing a great unconquered continent and strolling, say, into a marketplace and seeing black men for the first time. The shock this spectacle afforded is suggested, surely, by the promptness with which they decided that these black men were not really men but cattle. It is true that the necessity on the part of the settlers of the New World of reconciling their moral assumptions with the fact—and the necessity—of slavery enhanced immensely the charm of this idea, and it is also true that this idea expresses, with a truly American bluntness, the attitude which to varying extents all masters have had toward all slaves. 15

But between all former slaves and slave-owners and the drama which begins for Americans over three hundred years ago at Jamestown, there are at least two differences to be observed. The American Negro slave could not suppose, for one thing, as slaves in past epochs had supposed and often done, that he would ever be able to wrest the power from his master's hands. This was a supposition which the modern era, which was to bring about such vast changes in the aims and dimensions of power, put to death; it only begins, in unprecedented fashion, and with dreadful implications, to be resurrected today. But even had this supposition persisted with undiminished force, the American Negro slave could not have used it to lend his condition dignity, for the reason that this suppo- 16

9. Vocation; area of special knowledge.
10. "The dirty nigger."

sition rests on another: that the slave in exile yet remains related to his past, has some means—if only in memory—of reversing and sustaining the forms of his former life, is able, in short, to maintain his identity.

This was not the case with the American Negro slave. He is unique among the black men of the world in that his past was taken from him, almost literally, at one blow. One wonders what on earth the first slave found to say to the first dark child he bore. I am told that there are Haitians able to trace their ancestry back to African kings, but any American Negro wishing to go back so far will find his journey through time abruptly arrested by the signature on the bill of sale which served as the entrance paper for his ancestor. At the time—to say nothing of the circumstances—of the enslavement of the captive black man who was to become the American Negro, there was not the remotest possibility that he would ever take power from his master's hands. There was no reason to suppose that his situation would ever change, nor was there, shortly, anything to indicate that his situation had ever been different. It was his necessity, in the words of E. Franklin Frazier, to find a "motive for living under American culture or die." The identity of the American Negro comes out of this extreme situation, and the evolution of this identity was a source of the most intolerable anxiety in the minds and the lives of his masters.

For the history of the American Negro is unique also in this: that the question of his humanity, and of his rights therefore as a human being, became a burning one for several generations of Americans, so burning a question that it ultimately became one of those used to divide the nation. It is out of this argument that the venom of the epithet *Nigger!* is derived. It is an argument which Europe has never had, and hence Europe quite sincerely fails to understand how or why the argument arose in the first place, why its effects are so frequently disastrous and always so unpredictable, why it refuses until today to be entirely settled. Europe's black possessions remained—and do remain—in Europe's colonies, at which remove they represented no threat whatever to European identity. If they posed any problem at all for the European conscience, it was a problem which remained comfortingly abstract: in effect, the black man, *as a man*, did not exist for Europe. But in America, even as a slave, he was an inescapable part of the general social fabric and no American could escape having an attitude toward him. Americans attempt until today to make an abstraction of the Negro, but the very nature of these abstractions reveals the tremendous effects the presence of the Negro has had on the American character.

When one considers the history of the Negro in America it is of   19
the greatest importance to recognize that the moral beliefs of a
person, or a people, are never really as tenuous as life—which is
not moral—very often causes them to appear; these create for
them a frame of reference and a necessary hope, the hope being
that when life has done its worst they will be enabled to rise above
themselves and to triumph over life. Life would scarcely be bear-
able if this hope did not exist. Again, even when the worst has
been said, to betray a belief is not by any means to have put oneself
beyond its power; the betrayal of a belief is not the same thing as
ceasing to believe. If this were not so there would be no moral
standards in the world at all. Yet one must also recognize that
morality is based on ideas and that all ideas are dangerous—
dangerous because ideas can only lead to action and where the
action leads no man can say. And dangerous in this respect: that
confronted with the impossibility of remaining faithful to one's
beliefs, and the equal impossibility of becoming free of them, one
can be driven to the most inhuman excesses. The ideas on which
American beliefs are based are not, though Americans often seem
to think so, ideas which originated in America. They came out of
Europe. And the establishment of democracy on the American
continent was scarcely as radical a break with the past as was the
necessity, which Americans faced, of broadening this concept to
include black men.

This was, literally, a hard necessity. It was impossible, for one   20
thing, for Americans to abandon their beliefs, not only because
these beliefs alone seemed able to justify the sacrifices they had
endured and the blood that they had spilled, but also because these
beliefs afforded them their only bulwark against a moral chaos as
absolute as the physical chaos of the continent it was their destiny
to conquer. But in the situation in which Americans found themselves, these beliefs threatened an idea which, whether or not one
likes to think so, is the very warp and woof of the heritage of the
West, the idea of white supremacy.

Americans have made themselves notorious by the shrillness   21
and the brutality with which they have insisted on this idea, but
they did not invent it; and it has escaped the world's notice that
those very excesses of which Americans have been guilty imply a
certain, unprecedented uneasiness over the idea's life and power, if
not, indeed, the idea's validity. The idea of white supremacy rests
simply on the fact that white men are the creators of civilization
(the present civilization, which is the only one that matters; all
previous civilizations are simply "contributions" to our own) and
are therefore civilization's guardians and defenders. This it was

impossible for Americans to accept the black man as one of themselves, for to do so was to jeopardize their status as white men. But not so to accept him was to deny his human reality, his human weight and complexity, and the strain of denying the overwhelmingly undeniable forced Americans into rationalizations so fantastic that they approached the pathological.

At the root of the American Negro problem is the necessity of 22 the American white man to find a way of living with the Negro in order to be able to live with himself. And the history of this problem can be reduced to the means used by Americans—lynch law and law, segregation and legal acceptance, terrorization and concession—either to come to terms with this necessity, or to find a way around it, or (most usually) to find a way of doing both these things at once. The resulting spectacle, at once foolish and dreadful, led someone to make the quite accurate observation that "the Negro-in-America is a form of insanity which overtakes white men."

In this long battle, a battle by no means finished, the unforesee- 23 able effects of which will be felt by many future generations, the white man's motive was the protection of his identity; the black man was motivated by the need to establish an identity. And despite the terrorization which the Negro in America endured and endures sporadically until today, despite the cruel and totally inescapable ambivalence of his status in his country, the battle for his identity has long ago been won. He is not a visitor to the West, but a citizen there, an American; as American as the Americans who despise him, the Americans who fear him, the Americans who love him—the Americans who became less than themselves, or rose to be greater than themselves by virtue of the fact that the challenge he represented was inescapable. He is perhaps the only black man in the world whose relationship to white men is more terrible, more subtle, and more meaningful than the relationship of bitter possessed to uncertain possessor. His survival depended, and his development depends, on his ability to turn his peculiar status in the Western world to his own advantage and, it may be, to the very great advantage of that world. It remains for him to fashion out of his experience that which will give him sustenance, and a voice.

The cathedral at Chartres, I have said, says something to the 24 people of this village which it cannot say to me; but it is important to understand that this cathedral says something to me which it cannot say to them. Perhaps they are struck by the power of the spires, the glory of the windows; but they have known God, after all, longer than I have known him, and in a different way, and I am terrified by the slippery bottomless well to be found in the crypt, down which heretics were hurled to death, and by the obscene, inescapable gargoyles jutting out of the stone and seeming to say that God and the devil can never be divorced. I doubt that the villagers think of the devil when they face a cathedral because they have never been identified with the devil. But I must accept the status which myth, if nothing else, gives me in the West before I can hope to change the myth.

Yet, if the American Negro has arrived at his identity by virtue of   25
the absoluteness of his estrangement from his past, American white men still nourish the illusion that there is some means of recovering the European innocence, of returning to a state in which black men do not exist. This is one of the greatest errors Americans can make. The identity they fought so hard to protect has, by virtue of that battle, undergone a change: Americans are as unlike any other white people in the world as it is possible to be. I do not think, for example, that it is too much to suggest that the American vision of the world—which allows so little reality, generally speaking, for any of the darker forces in human life, which tends until today to paint moral issues in glaring black and white— owes a great deal to the battle waged by Americans to maintain between themselves and black men a human separation which could not be bridged. It is only now beginning to be borne in on us—very faintly, it must be admitted, very slowly, and very much against our will—that this vision of the world is dangerously inaccurate, and perfectly useless. For it protects our moral highmindedness at the terrible expense of weakening our grasp of reality. People who shut their eyes to reality simply invite their own destruction, and anyone who insists on remaining in a state of innocence long after that innocence is dead turns himself into a monster.

The time has come to realize that the interracial drama acted out   26
on the American continent has not only created a new black man, it has created a new white man, too. No road whatever will lead Americans back to the simplicity of this European village where white men still have the luxury of looking on me as a stranger. I am not, really, a stranger any longer for any American alive. One of the things that distinguishes Americans from other people is that no other people has ever been so deeply involved in the lives of black men, and vice versa. This fact faced, with all its implications, it can be seen that the history of the American Negro problem is not merely shameful, it is also something of an achievement. For even when the worst has been said, it must also be added that the perpetual challenge posed by this problem was always, somehow,

perpetually met. It is precisely this black-white experience which may prove of indispensable value to us in the world we face today. This world is white no longer, and it will never be white again.

JAMES BALDWIN

Notes of a Native Son[1]

On the 29th of July, in 1943, my father died. On the same day, a   1
few hours later, his last child was born. Over a month before this, while all our energies were concentrated in waiting for these events, there had been, in Detroit, one of the bloodiest race riots of the century. A few hours after my father's funeral, while he lay in state in the undertaker's chapel, a race riot broke out in Harlem. On the morning of the 3rd of August, we drove my father to the graveyard through a wilderness of smashed plate glass.

The day of my father's funeral had also been my nineteenth   2
birthday. As we drove him to the graveyard, the spoils of injustice, anarchy, discontent, and hatred were all around us. It seemed to me that God himself had devised, to mark my father's end, the most sustained and brutally dissonant of codas. And it seemed to me, too, that the violence which rose all about us as my father left the world had been devised as a corrective for the pride of his eldest son. I had declined to believe in that apocalypse which had been central to my father's vision; very well, life seemed to be saying, here is something that will certainly pass for an apocalypse until the real thing comes along. I had inclined to be contemptuous of my father for the conditions of his life, for the conditions of our lives. When his life had ended I began to wonder about that life and also, in a new way, to be apprehensive about my own.

I had not known my father very well. We had got on badly,   3
partly because we shared, in our different fashions, the vice of stubborn pride. When he was dead I realized that I had hardly ever spoken to him. When he had been dead a long time I began to wish I had. It seems to be typical of life in America, where opportunities, real and fancied, are thicker than anywhere else on the globe, that the second generation has no time to talk to the first. No one,

1. First published in *Harper's*, November 1955.

including my father, seems to have known exactly how old he was, but his mother had been born during slavery. He was of the first generation of free men. He, along with thousands of other Negroes, came North after 1919 and I was part of that generation which had never seen the landscape of what Negroes sometimes call the Old Country.

He had been born in New Orleans and had been a quite young   4
man there during the time that Louis Armstrong, a boy, was running errands for the dives and honky-tonks of what was always presented to me as one of the most wicked of cities—to this day, whenever I think of New Orleans, I also helplessly think of Sodom and Gomorrah. My father never mentioned Louis Armstrong, except to forbid us to play his records; but there was a picture of him on our wall for a long time. One of my father's strong-willed female relatives had placed it there and forbade my father to take it down. He never did, but he eventually maneuvered her out of the house and when, some years later, she was in trouble and near death, he refused to do anything to help her.

He was, I think, very handsome. I gather this from photographs   5
and from my own memories of him, dressed in his Sunday best and on his way to preach a sermon somewhere, when I was little. Handsome, proud, and ingrown, "like a toe-nail," somebody said. But he looked to me, as I grew older, like pictures I had seen of African tribal chieftains: he really should have been naked, with war-paint on and barbaric mementos, standing among spears. He could be chilling in the pulpit and indescribably cruel in his personal life and he was certainly the most bitter man I have ever met; yet it must be said that there was something else in him, buried in him, which lent him his tremendous power and, even, a rather crushing charm. It had something to do with his blackness, I think—he was very black—with his blackness and his beauty, and with the fact that he knew that he was black but did not know that he was beautiful. He claimed to be proud of his blackness but it had also been the cause of much humiliation and it had fixed bleak boundaries to his life. He was not a young man when we were growing up and he had already suffered many kinds of ruin; in his outrageously demanding and protective way he loved his children, who were black like him and menaced, like him; and all these things sometimes showed in his face when he tried, never to my knowledge with any success, to establish contact with any of us. When he took one of his children on his knee to play, the child always became fretful and began to cry; when he tried to help one of us with our homework the absolutely unabating tension which emanated from him caused our minds and our tongues to become

paralyzed, so that he, scarcely knowing why, flew into a rage and the child, not knowing why, was punished. If it ever entered his head to bring a surprise home for his children, it was, almost unfailingly, the wrong surprise and even the big watermelons he often brought home on his back in the summertime led to the most appalling scenes. I do not remember, in all those years, that one of his children was ever glad to see him come home. From what I was able to gather of his early life, it seemed that this inability to establish contact with other people had always marked him and had been one of the things which had driven him out of New Orleans. There was something in him, therefore, groping and tentative, which was never expressed and which was buried with him. One saw it most clearly when he was facing new people and hoping to impress them. But he never did, not for long. We went from church to smaller and more improbable church, he found himself in less and less demand as a minister, and by the time he died none of his friends had come to see him for a long time. He had lived and died in an intolerable bitterness of spirit and it frightened me, as we drove him to the graveyard through those unquiet, ruined streets, to see how powerful and overflowing this bitterness could be and to realize that this bitterness now was mine.

When he died I had been away from home for a little over a year.   6 In that year I had had time to become aware of the meaning of all my father's bitter warnings, had discovered the secret of his proudly pursed lips and rigid carriage: I had discovered the weight of white people in the world. I saw that this had been for my ancestors and now would be for me an awful thing to live with and that the bitterness which had helped to kill my father could also kill me.

He had been ill a long time—in the mind, as we now realized,   7 reliving instances of his fantastic intransigence in the new light of his affliction and endeavoring to feel a sorrow for him which never, quite, came true. We had not known that he was being eaten up by paranoia, and the discovery that his cruelty, to our bodies and our minds, had been one of the symptoms of his illness was not, then, enough to enable us to forgive him. The younger children felt, quite simply, relief that he would not be coming home any more. My mother's observation that it was he, after all, who had kept them alive all these years meant nothing because the problems of keeping children alive are not real for children. The older children felt, with my father gone, that they could invite their friends to the house without fear that their friends would be insulted or, as had sometimes happened with me, being told that their friends were in

league with the devil and intended to rob our family of everything
we owned. (I didn't fail to wonder, and it made me hate him, what
on earth we owned that anybody else would want.)

His illness was beyond all hope of healing before anyone realized   8
that he was ill. He had always been so strange and had lived, like a
prophet, in such unimaginably close communion with the Lord
that his long silences which were punctuated by moans and hal-
lelujahs and snatches of old songs while he sat at the living-room
window never seemed odd to us. It was not until he refused to eat
because, he said, his family was trying to poison him that my
mother was forced to accept as a fact what had, until then, been
only an unwilling suspicion. When he was committed, it was discovered that he had tuberculosis and, as it turned out, the disease
of his mind allowed the disease of his body to destroy him. For the
doctors could not force him to eat, either, and, though he was fed
intravenously, it was clear from the beginning that there was no
hope for him.

In my mind's eye I could see him, sitting at the window, locked   9
up in his terrors; hating and fearing every living soul including his
children who had betrayed him, too, by reaching toward the world
which had despised him. There were nine of us. I began to wonder
what it could have felt like for such a man to have had nine
children whom he could barely feed. He used to make little jokes
about our poverty, which never, of course, seemed very funny to
us; they could not have seemed very funny to him, either, or else
our all too feeble response to them would never have caused such
rages. He spent great energy and achieved, to our chagrin, no small
amount of success in keeping us away from the people who surrounded us, people who had all-night rent parties to which we
listened when we should have been sleeping, people who cursed
and drank and flashed razor blades on Lenox Avenue. He could
not understand why, if they had so much energy to spare, they
could not use it to make their lives better. He treated almost
everybody on our block with a most uncharitable asperity and
neither they, nor, of course, their children were slow to reciprocate.

The only white people who came to our house were welfare   10
workers and bill collectors. It was almost always my mother who
dealt with them, for my father's temper, which was at the mercy of
his pride, was never to be trusted. It was clear that he felt their very
presence in his home to be a violation: this was conveyed by his
carriage, almost ludicrously stiff, and by his voice, harsh and vin-
dictively polite. When I was around nine or ten I wrote a play
which was directed by a young, white schoolteacher, a woman,

who then took an interest in me, and gave me books to read and, in order to corroborate my theatrical bent, decided to take me to see what she somewhat tactlessly referred to as "real" plays. Theatergoing was forbidden in our house, but, with the really cruel intuitiveness of a child, I suspected that the color of this woman's skin would carry the day for me. When, at school, she suggested taking me to the theater, I did not, as I might have done if she had been a Negro, find a way of discouraging her, but agreed that she should pick me up at my house one evening. I then, very cleverly, left all the rest to my mother, who suggested to my father, as I knew she would, that it would not be very nice to let such a kind woman make the trip for nothing. Also, since it was a schoolteacher, I imagine that my mother countered the idea of sin with the idea of "education," which word, even with my father, carried a kind of bitter weight.

Before the teacher came my father took me aside to ask *why* she 11 was coming, what *interest* she could possibly have in our house, in a boy like me. I said I didn't know but I, too, suggested that it had something to do with education. And I understood that my father was waiting for me to say something—I didn't quite know what; perhaps that I wanted his protection against this teacher and her "education." I said none of these things and the teacher came and we went out. It was clear, during the brief interview in our living room, that my father was agreeing very much against his will and that he would have refused permission if he had dared. The fact that he did not dare caused me to despise him: I had no way of knowing that he was facing in that living room a wholly unprecedented and frightening situation.

Later, when my father had been laid off from his job, this woman 12 became very important to us. She was really a very sweet and generous woman and went to a great deal of trouble to be of help to us, particularly during one awful winter. My mother called her by the highest name she knew: she said she was a "christian." My father could scarcely disagree but during the four or five years of our relatively close association he never trusted her and was always trying to surprise in her open, Midwestern face the genuine, cunningly hidden, and hideous motivation. In later years, particularly when it began to be clear that this "education" of mine was going to lead me to perdition, he became more explicit and warned me that my white friends in high school were not really my friends and that I would see, when I was older, how white people would do anything to keep a Negro down. Some of them could be nice, he admitted, but none of them were to be trusted and most of them were not even nice. The best thing was to have as little to do with them as possible. I did not feel this way and I was certain, in my innocence, that I never would.

But the year which preceded my father's death had made a great 13 change in my life. I had been living in New Jersey, working in defense plants, working and living among southerners, white and black. I knew about the south, of course, and about how southerners treated Negroes and how they expected them to behave, but it had never entered my mind that anyone would look at me and expect *me* to behave that way. I learned in New Jersey that to be a Negro meant, precisely, that one was never looked at but was simply at the mercy of the reflexes the color of one's skin caused in other people. I acted in New Jersey as I had always acted, that is as though I thought a great deal of myself—I had to *act* that way— with results that were, simply, unbelievable. I had scarcely arrived before I had earned the enmity, which was extraordinarily ingenious, of all my superiors and nearly all my co-workers. In the beginning, to make matters worse, I simply did not know what was happening. I did not know what I had done, and I shortly began to wonder what *anyone* could possibly do, to bring about such unanimous, active, and unbearably vocal hostility. I knew about jim-crow[2] but I had never experienced it. I went to the same self-service restaurant three times and stood with all the Princeton boys before the counter, waiting for a hamburger and coffee; it was always an extraordinarily long time before anything was set before me; but it was not until the fourth visit that I learned that, in fact, nothing had ever been set before me: I had simply picked something up. Negroes were not served there, I was told, and they had been waiting for me to realize that I was always the only Negro present. Once I was told this, I determined to go there all the time. But now they were ready for me and, though some dreadful scenes were subsequently enacted in that restaurant, I never ate there again.

It was the same story all over New Jersey, in bars, bowling alleys, 14 diners, places to live. I was always being forced to leave, silently, or with mutual imprecations. I very shortly became notorious and children giggled behind me when I passed and their elders whispered or shouted—they really believed that I was mad. And it did begin to work on my mind, of course; I began to be afraid to go anywhere and to compensate for this I went places to which I really should not have gone and where, God knows, I had no

2. Systematic suppression and segregation of blacks. See Richard Wright's "The Ethics of Living Jim Crow" (p. 444).

desire to be. My reputation in town naturally enhanced my reputation at work and my working day became one long series of acrobatics designed to keep me out of trouble. I cannot say that these acrobatics succeeded. It began to seem that the machinery of the organization I worked for was turning over, day and night, with but one aim: to eject me. I was fired once, and contrived, with the aid of a friend from New York, to get back on the payroll; was fired again, and bounced back again. It took a while to fire me for the third time, but the third time took. There were no loopholes anywhere. There was not even any way of getting back inside the gates.

That year in New Jersey lives in my mind as though it were the   15
year during which, having an unsuspected predilection for it, I first contracted some dread, chronic disease, the unfailing symptom of which is a kind of blind fever, a pounding in the skull and fire in the bowels. Once this disease is contracted, one can never be really carefree again, for the fever, without an instant's warning, can recur at any moment. It can wreck more important things than race relations. There is not a Negro alive who does not have this rage in his blood—one has the choice, merely, of living with it consciously or surrendering to it. As for me, this fever has recurred in me, and does, and will until the day I die.

My last night in New Jersey, a white friend from New York took   16
me to the nearest big town, Trenton, to go to the movies and have a few drinks. As it turned out, he also saved me from, at the very least, a violent whipping. Almost every detail of that night stands out very clearly in my memory. I even remember the name of the movie we saw because its title impressed me as being so patly ironical. It was a movie about the German occupation of France, starring Maureen O'Hara and Charles Laughton and called *This Land Is Mine*. I remember the name of the diner we walked into when the movie ended: it was the "American Diner." When we walked in the counterman asked what we wanted and I remember answering with the casual sharpness which had become my habit: "We want a hamburger and a cup of coffee, what do you think we want?" I do not know why, after a year of such rebuffs, I so completely failed to anticipate his answer, which was, of course, "We don't serve Negroes here." This reply failed to discompose me, at least for the moment. I made some sardonic comment about the name of the diner and we walked out into the streets.

This was the time of what was called the "brown-out," when the   17
lights in all American cities were very dim. When we re-entered the streets something happened to me which had the force of an optical illusion, or a nightmare. The streets were very crowded and

I was facing north. People were moving in every direction but it seemed to me, in that instant, that all of the people I could see, and many more than that, were moving toward me, against me, and that everyone was white. I remember how their faces gleamed. And I felt, like a physical sensation, a *click* at the nape of my neck as though some interior string connecting my head to my body had been cut. I began to walk. I heard my friend call after me, but I ignored him. Heaven only knows what was going on in his mind, but he had the good sense not to touch me—I don't know what would have happened if he had—and to keep me in sight. I don't know what was going on in my mind, either; I certainly had no conscious plan. I wanted to do something to crush these white faces, which were crushing me. I walked for perhaps a block or two until I came to an enormous, glittering, and fashionable restaurant in which I knew not even the intercession of the Virgin would cause me to be served. I pushed through the doors and took the first vacant seat I saw, at a table for two, and waited.

I do not know how long I waited and I rather wonder, until 18
today, what I could possibly have looked like. Whatever I looked like, I frightened the waitress who shortly appeared, and the moment she appeared all of my fury flowed toward her. I hated her for her white face, and for her great, astounded, frightened eyes. I felt that if she found a black man so frightening I would make her fright worth-while.

She did not ask me what I wanted, but repeated, as though she 19
had learned it somewhere, "We don't serve Negroes here." She did not say it with the blunt, derisive hostility to which I had grown so accustomed, but, rather, with a note of apology in her voice, and fear. This made me colder and more murderous than ever. I felt I had to do something with my hands. I wanted her to come close enough for me to get her neck between my hands.

So I pretended not to have understood her, hoping to draw her 20
closer. And she did step a very short step closer, with her pencil poised incongruously over her pad, and repeated the formula: ". . . don't serve Negroes here."

Somehow, with the repetition of that phrase, which was already 21
ringing in my head like a thousand bells of a nightmare, I realized that she would never come any closer and that I would have to strike from a distance. There was nothing on the table but an ordinary water-mug half full of water, and I picked this up and hurled it with all my strength at her. She ducked and it missed her and shattered against the mirror behind the bar. And, with that sound, my frozen blood abruptly thawed, I returned from wherever I had been, I *saw*, for the first time, the restaurant, the people

with their mouths open, already, as it seemed to me, rising as one man, and I realized what I had done, and where I was, and I was frightened. I rose and began running for the door. A round, potbellied man grabbed me by the nape of the neck just as I reached the doors and began to beat me about the face. I kicked him and got loose and ran into the streets. My friend whispered, *"Run!"* and I ran.

My friend stayed outside the restaurant long enough to misdirect   22
my pursuers and the police, who arrived, he told me, at once. I do not know what I said to him when he came to my room that night. I could not have said much. I felt, in the oddest, most awful way, that I had somehow betrayed him. I lived it over and over and over again, the way one relives an automobile accident after it has happened and one finds oneself alone and safe. I could not get over two facts, both equally difficult for the imagination to grasp, and one was that I could have been murdered. But the other was that I had been ready to commit murder. I saw nothing very clearly but I did see this: that my life, my *real* life, was in danger, and not from anything other people might do but from the hatred I carried in my own heart.

II

I had returned home around the second week in June—in great   23
haste because it seemed that my father's death and my mother's confinement were both but a matter of hours. In the case of my mother, it soon became clear that she had simply made a miscalculation. This had always been her tendency and I don't believe that a single one of us arrived in the world, or has since arrived anywhere else, on time. But none of us dawdled so intolerably about the business of being born as did my baby sister. We sometimes amused outselves, during those endless, stifling weeks, by picturing the baby sitting within in the safe, warm dark, bitterly regretting the necessity of becoming a part of our chaos and stubbornly putting it off as long as possible. I understood her perfectly and congratulated her on showing such good sense so soon. Death, however, sat as purposefully at my father's bedside as life stirred within my mother's womb and it was harder to understand why he so lingered in that long shadow. It seemed that he had bent, and for a long time, too, all of his energies toward dying. Now death was ready for him but my father held back.

All of Harlem, indeed, seemed to be infected by waiting. I had   24
never before known it to be so violently still. Racial tensions throughout this country were exacerbated during the early years of

the war, partly because the labor market brought together hundreds of thousands of ill-prepared people and partly because Negro soldiers, regardless of where they were born, received their military training in the south. What happened in defense plants and army camps had repercussions, naturally, in every Negro ghetto. The situation in Harlem had grown bad enough for clergymen, policemen, educators, politicians, and social workers to assert in one breath that there was no "crime wave" and to offer, in the very next breath, suggestions as to how to combat it. These suggestions always seemed to involve playgrounds, despite the fact that racial skirmishes were occurring in the playgrounds, too. Playground or not, crime wave or not, the Harlem police force had been augmented in March, and the unrest grew—perhaps, in fact, partly as a result of the ghetto's instinctive hatred of policemen. Perhaps the most revealing news item, out of the steady parade of reports of muggings, stabbings, shootings, assaults, gang wars, and accusations of police brutality, is the item concerning six Negro girls who set upon a white girl in the subway because, as they all too accurately put it, she was stepping on their toes. Indeed she was, all over the nation.

I had never before been so aware of policemen, on foot, on   25 horseback, on corners, everywhere, always two by two. Nor had I ever been so aware of small knots of people. They were on stoops and on corners and in doorways, and what was striking about them, I think, was that they did not seem to be talking. Never, when I passed these groups, did the usual sound of a curse or a laugh ring out and neither did there seem to be any hum of gossip. There was certainly, on the other hand, occurring between them communication extraordinarily intense. Another thing that was striking was the unexpected diversity of the people who made up these groups. Usually, for example, one would see a group of sharpies standing on the street corner, jiving the passing chicks; or a group of older men, usually, for some reason, in the vicinity of a barber shop, discussing baseball scores, or the numbers, or making rather chilling observations about women they had known. Women, in a general way, tended to be seen less often together— unless they were church women, or very young girls, or prostitutes met together for an unprofessional instant. But that summer I saw the strangest combinations: large, respectable, churchly matrons standing on the stoops or the corners with their hair tied up, together with a girl in sleazy satin whose face bore the marks of gin and the razor, or heavy-set, abrupt, no-nonsense older men, in company with the most disreputable and fanatical "race" men, or these same "race" men with the sharpies, or these sharpies with the churchly women. Seventh Day Adventists and Methodists and Spiritualists seemed to be hobnobbing with Holyrollers and they were all, alike, entangled with the most flagrant disbelievers; something heavy in their stance seemed to indicate that they had all, incredibly, seen a common vision, and on each face there seemed to be the same strange, bitter shadow.

The churchly women and the matter-of-fact, no-nonsense men   76
had children in the Army. The sleazy girls they talked to had lovers there, the sharpies and the "race" men had friends and brothers there. It would have demanded an unquestioning patriotism, happily as uncommon in this country as it is undesirable, for these people not to have been disturbed by the bitter letters they received, by the newspaper stories they read, not to have been enraged by the posters, then to be found all over New York, which described the Japanese as "yellow-bellied Japs." It was only the "race" men, to be sure, who spoke ceaselessly of being revenged— how this vengeance was to be exacted was not clear—for the indignities and dangers suffered by Negro boys in uniform; but everybody felt a directionless, hopeless bitterness, as well as that panic which can scarcely be suppressed when one knows that a human being one loves is beyond one's reach, and in danger. This helplessness and this gnawing uneasiness does something, at length, to even the toughest mind. Perhaps the best way to sum all this up is to say that the people I knew felt, mainly, a peculiar kind of relief when they knew that their boys were being shipped out of the south, to do battle overseas. It was, perhaps, like feeling that the most dangerous part of a dangerous journey had been passed and that now, even if death should come, it would come with honor and without the complicity of their countrymen. Such a death would be, in short, a fact with which one could hope to live.

It was on the 28th of July, which I believe was a Wednesday,   27
that I visited my father for the first time during his illness and for the last time in his life. The moment I saw him I knew why I had put off this visit so long. I had told my mother that I did not want to see him because I hated him. But this was not true. It was only that I *had* hated him and I wanted to hold on to this hatred. I did not want to look on him as a ruin: it was not a ruin I had hated. I imagine that one of the reasons people cling to their hates so stubbornly is because they sense, once hate is gone, that they will be forced to deal with pain.

We traveled out to him, his older sister and myself, to what   28
seemed to be the very end of a very Long Island. It was hot and dusty and we wrangled, my aunt and I, all the way out, over the fact that I had recently begun to smoke and, as she said, to give

myself airs. But I knew that she wrangled with me because she could not bear to face the fact of her brother's dying. Neither could I endure the reality of her despair, her unstated bafflement as to what had happened to her brother's life, and her own. So we wrangled and I smoked and from time to time she fell into a heavy reverie. Covertly, I watched her face, which was the face of an old woman; it had fallen in, the eyes were sunken and lightless; soon she would be dying, too.

In my childhood—it had not been so long ago—I had thought   29 her beautiful. She had been quick-witted and quick-moving and very generous with all the children and each of her visits had been an event. At one time one of my brothers and myself had thought of running away to live with her. Now she could no longer produce out of her handbag some unexpected and yet familiar delight. She made me feel pity and revulsion and fear. It was awful to realize that she no longer caused me to feel affection. The closer we came to the hospital the more querulous she became and at the same time, naturally, grew more dependent on me. Between pity and guilt and fear I began to feel that there was another me trapped in my skull like a jack-in-the-box who might escape my control at any moment and fill the air with screaming.

She began to cry the moment we entered the room and she saw   30 him lying there, all shriveled and still, like a little black monkey. The great, gleaming apparatus which fed him and would have compelled him to be still even if he had been able to move brought to mind, not beneficence, but torture; the tubes entering his arm made me think of pictures I had seen when a child, of Gulliver, tied down by the pygmies on that island. My aunt wept and wept, there was a whistling sound in my father's throat; nothing was said; he could not speak. I wanted to take his hand, to say something. But I do not know what I could have said, even if he could have heard me. He was not really in that room with us, he had at last really embarked on his journey; and though my aunt told me that he said he was going to meet Jesus, I did not hear anything except that whistling in his throat. The doctor came back and we left, into that unbearable train again, and home. In the morning came the telegram saying that he was dead. Then the house was suddenly full of relatives, friends, hysteria, and confusion and I quickly left my mother and the children to the care of those impressive women, who, in Negro communities at least, automatically appear at times of bereavement armed with lotions, proverbs, and patience, and an ability to cook. I went downtown. By the time I returned, later the same day, my mother had been carried to the hospital and the baby had been born.

III

For my father's funeral I had nothing black to wear and this   31
posed a nagging problem all day long. It was one of those problems, simple, or impossible of solution, to which the mind insanely
clings in order to avoid the mind's real trouble. I spent most of that
day at the downtown apartment of a girl I knew, celebrating my
birthday with whiskey and wondering what to wear that night.
When planning a birthday celebration one naturally does not expect that it will be up against competition from a funeral and this
girl had anticipated taking me out that night, for a big dinner and a
night club afterwards. Sometime during the course of that long day
we decided that we would go out anyway, when my father's funeral service was over. I imagine *I* decided it, since, as the funeral
hour approached, it became clearer and clearer to me that I would
not know what to do with myself when it was over. The girl,
stifling her very lively concern as to the possible effects of the
whiskey on one of my father's chief mourners, concentrated on
being conciliatory and practically helpful. She found a black shirt
for me somewhere and ironed it and, dressed in the darkest pants
and jacket I owned, and slightly drunk, I made my way to my
father's funeral.

The chapel was full, but not packed, and very quiet. There were,   32
mainly, my father's relatives, and his children, and here and there I
saw faces I had not seen since childhood, the faces of my father's
one-time friends. They were very dark and solemn now, seeming
somehow to suggest that they had known all along that something
like this would happen. Chief among the mourners was my aunt,
who had quarreled with my father all his life; by which I do not
mean to suggest that her mourning was insincere or that she had
not loved him. I suppose that she was one of the few people in the
world who had, and their incessant quarreling proved precisely
the strength of the tie that bound them. The only other person in
the world, as far as I knew, whose relationship to my father rivaled
my aunt's in depth was my mother, who was not there.

It seemed to me, of course, that it was a very long funeral. But it   33
was, if anything, a rather shorter funeral than most, nor, since
there were no overwhelming, uncontrollable expressions of grief,
could it be called—if I dare to use the word—successful. The
minister who preached my father's funeral sermon was one of the
few my father had still been seeing as he neared his end. He presented to us in his sermon a man whom none of us had ever seen—
a man thoughtful, patient, and forbearing, a Christian inspiration
to all who knew him, and a model for his children. And no doubt

the children, in their disturbed and guilty state, were almost ready
to believe this; he had been remote enough to be anything and,
anyway, the shock of the incontrovertible, that it was really our
father lying up there in that casket, prepared the mind for anything.
His sister moaned and this grief-stricken moaning was taken
as corroboration. The other faces held a dark, non-committal
thoughtfulness. This was not the man they had known, but they
had scarcely expected to be confronted with *him*; this was, in a
sense deeper than questions of fact, the man they had not known,
and the man they had not known may have been the real one. The
real man, whoever he had been, had suffered and now he was
dead: this was all that was sure and all that mattered now. Every
man in the chapel hoped that when his hour came he, too, would
be eulogized, which is to say forgiven, and that all of his lapses,
greeds, errors, and strayings from the truth would be invested with
coherence and looked upon with charity. This was perhaps the last
thing human beings could give each other and it was what they
demanded, after all, of the Lord. Only the Lord saw the midnight
tears, only He was present when one of His children, moaning and
wringing hands, paced up and down the room. When one slapped
one's child in anger the recoil in the heart reverberated through
heaven and became part of the pain of the universe. And when the
children were hungry and sullen and distrustful and one watched
them, daily, growing wilder, and further away, and running headlong into danger, it was the Lord who knew what the charged heart
endured as the strap was laid to the backside; the Lord alone who
knew what one *would* have said if one had had, like the Lord, the
gift of the living word. It was the Lord who knew of the impossibility every parent in that room faced: how to prepare the child for the
day when the child would be despised and how to *create* in the
child—by what means?—a stronger antidote to this poison than
one had found for oneself. The avenues, side streets, bars, billiard
halls, hospitals, police stations, and even the playgrounds of Harlem—not to mention the houses of correction, the jails, and the
morgue—testified to the potency of the poison while remaining
silent as to the efficacy of whatever antidote, irresistibly raising the
question of whether or not such an antidote existed; raising, which
was worse, the question of whether or not an antidote was desirable; perhaps poison should be fought with poison. With these
several schisms in the mind and with more terrors in the heart than
could be named, it was better not to judge the man who had gone
down under an impossible burden. It was better to remember:
Thou knowest this man's fall; but thou knowest not his wrassling.

While the preacher talked and I watched the children—years of   34
changing their diapers, scrubbing them, slapping them, taking
them to school, and scolding them had had the perhaps inevitable
result of making me love them, though I am not sure I knew this
then—my mind was busily breaking out with a rash of disconnected impressions. Snatches of popular songs, indecent jokes, bits
of books I had read, movie sequences, faces, voices, political issues—I thought I was going mad; all these impressions suspended,
as it were, in the solution of the faint nausea produced in me by the
heat and liquor. For a moment I had the impression that my alcoholic breath, inefficiently disguised with chewing gum, filled the
entire chapel. Then someone began singing one of my father's
favorite songs and, abruptly, I was with him, sitting on his knee, in
the hot, enormous, crowded church which was the first church we
attended. It was the Abyssinian Baptist Church on 138th Street.
We had not gone there long. With this image, a host of others
came. I had forgotten, in the rage of my growing up, how proud
my father had been of me when I was little. Apparently, I had had
a voice and my father had liked to show me off before the members
of the church. I had forgotten what he had looked like when he
was pleased but now I remembered that he had always been grinning with pleasure when my solos ended. I even remembered certain expressions on his face when he teased my mother—had he
loved her? I would never know. And when had it all begun to
change? For now it seemed that he had not always been cruel. I
remembered being taken for a haircut and scraping my knee on the
footrest of the barber's chair and I remembered my father's face as
he soothed my crying and applied the stinging iodine. Then I remembered our fights, fights which had been of the worst possible
kind because my technique had been silence.

I remembered the one time in all our life together when we had   35
really spoken to each other.

It was on a Sunday and it must have been shortly before I left   36
home. We were walking, just the two of us, in our usual silence, to
or from church. I was in high school and had been doing a lot of
writing and I was, at about this time, the editor of the high school
magazine. But I had also been a Young Minister and had been
preaching from the pulpit. Lately, I had been taking fewer engagements and preached as rarely as possible. It was said in the church,
quite truthfully, that I was "cooling off."

My father asked me abruptly, "You'd rather write than preach,   37
wouldn't you?"

I was astonished at his question—because it was a real question.   38
I answered, "Yes."

That was all we said. It was awful to remember that that was all   39
we had *ever* said.

The casket now was opened and the mourners were being led up   40
the aisle to look for the last time on the deceased. The assumption
was that the family was too overcome with grief to be allowed to
make this journey alone and I watched while my aunt was led to
the casket and, muffled in black, and shaking, led back to her seat. I
disapproved of forcing the children to look on their dead father,
considering that the shock of his death, or, more truthfully, the
shock of death as a reality, was already a little more than a child
could bear, but my judgment in this matter had been overruled and
there they were, bewildered and frightened and very small, being
led, one by one, to the casket. But there is also something very
gallant about children at such moments. It has something to do
with their silence and gravity and with the fact that one cannot
help them. Their legs, somehow, seem *exposed*, so that it is at once
incredible and terribly clear that their legs are all they have to hold
them up.

I had not wanted to go to the casket myself and I certainly had   41
not wished to be led there, but there was no way of avoiding either
of these forms. One of the deacons led me up and I looked on my
father's face. I cannot say that it looked like him at all. His blackness had been equivocated by powder and there was no suggestion
in that casket of what his power had or could have been. He was
simply an old man dead, and it was hard to believe that he had ever
given anyone either joy or pain. Yet, his life filled that room. Further up the avenue his wife was holding his newborn child. Life
and death so close together, and love and hatred, and right and
wrong, said something to me which I did not want to hear concerning man, concerning the life of man.

After the funeral, while I was downtown desperately celebrating   42
my birthday, a Negro soldier, in the lobby of the Hotel Braddock,
got into a fight with a white policeman over a Negro girl. Negro
girls, white policemen, in or out of uniform, and Negro males—in
or out of uniform—were part of the furniture of the lobby of the
Hotel Braddock and this was certainly not the first time such an
incident had occurred. It was destined, however, to receive an
unprecedented publicity, for the fight between the policeman and
the soldier ended with the shooting of the soldier. Rumor, flowing
immediately to the streets outside, stated that the soldier had been
shot in the back, an instantaneous and revealing invention, and
that the soldier had died protecting a Negro woman. The facts were
somewhat different—for example, the soldier had not been shot in
the back, and was not dead, and the girl seems to have been as

dubious a symbol of womanhood as her white counterpart in Georgia usually is, but no one was interested in the facts. They preferred the invention because this invention expressed and corroborated their hates and fears so perfectly. It is just as well to remember that people are always doing this. Perhaps many of those legends, including Christianity, to which the world clings began their conquest of the world with just some such concerted surrender to distortion. The effect, in Harlem, of this particular legend was like the effect of a lit match in a tin of gasoline. The mob gathered before the doors of the Hotel Braddock simply began to swell and to spread in every direction, and Harlem exploded.

The mob did not cross the ghetto lines. It would have been easy, 43 for example, to have gone over Morningside Park on the west side or to have crossed the Grand Central railroad tracks at 125th Street on the east side, to wreak havoc in white neighborhoods. The mob seems to have been mainly interested in something more potent and real than the white face, that is, in white power, and the principal damage done during the riot of the summer of 1943 was to white business establishments in Harlem. It might have been a far bloodier story, of course, if, at the hour the riot began, these establishments had still been open. From the Hotel Braddock the mob fanned out, east and west along 125th Street, and for the entire length of Lenox, Seventh, and Eighth avenues. Along each of these avenues, and along each major side street—116th, 125th, 135th, and so on—bars, stores, pawnshops, restaurants, even little luncheonettes had been smashed open and entered and looted—looted, it might be added, with more haste than efficiency. The shelves really looked as though a bomb had struck them. Cans of beans and soup and dog food, along with toilet paper, corn flakes, sardines, and milk tumbled every which way, and abandoned cash registers and cases of beer leaned crazily out of the splintered windows and were strewn along the avenues. Sheets, blankets, and clothing of every description formed a kind of path, as though people had dropped them while running. I truly had not realized that Harlem *had* so many stores until I saw them all smashed open; the first time the word *wealth* ever entered my mind in relation to Harlem was when I saw it scattered in the streets. But one's first, incongruous impression of plenty was countered immediately by an impression of waste. None of this was doing anybody any good. It would have been better to have left the plate glass as it had been and the goods lying in the stores.

It would have been better, but it would also have been intol- 44 erable, for Harlem had needed something to smash. To smash something is the ghetto's chronic need. Most of the time it is the members of the ghetto who smash each other, and themselves. But as long as the ghetto walls are standing there will always come a moment when these outlets do not work. That summer, for example, it was not enough to get into a fight on Lenox Avenue, or curse out one's cronies in the barber shops. If ever, indeed, the violence which fills Harlem's churches, pool halls, and bars erupts outward in a more direct fashion, Harlem and its citizens are likely to vanish in an apocalyptic flood. That this is not likely to happen is due to a great many reasons, most hidden and powerful among them the Negro's real relation to the white American. This relation prohibits, simply, anything as uncomplicated and satisfactory as pure hatred. In order really to hate white people, one has to blot so much out of the mind—and the heart—that this hatred itself becomes an exhausting and self-destructive pose. But this does not mean, on the other hand, that love comes easily: the white world is too powerful, too complacent, too ready with gratuitous humiliation, and, above all, too ignorant and too innocent for that. One is absolutely forced to make perpetual qualifications and one's own reactions are always canceling each other out. It is this, really, which has driven so many people mad, both white and black. One is always in the position of having to decide between amputation and gangrene. Amputation is swift but time may prove that the amputation was not necessary—or one may delay the amputation too long. Gangrene is slow, but it is impossible to be sure that one is reading one's symptoms right. The idea of going through life as a cripple is more than one can bear, and equally unbearable is the risk of swelling up slowly, in agony, with poison. And the trouble, finally, is that the risks are real even if the choices do not exist.

"But as for me and my house," my father had said, "we will serve the Lord." I wondered, as we drove him to his resting place, what this line had meant for him. I had heard him preach it many times. I had preached it once myself, proudly giving it an interpretation different from my father's. Now the whole thing came back to me, as though my father and I were on our way to Sunday school and I were memorizing the golden text: *And if it seem evil unto you to serve the Lord, choose you this day whom you will serve; whether the gods which your fathers served that were on the other side of the flood, or the gods of the Amorites, in whose land ye dwell: but as for me and my house, we will serve the Lord.* I suspected in these familiar lines a meaning which had never been there for me before. All of my father's texts and songs, which I had decided were meaningless, were arranged before me at his death like empty bottles, waiting to hold the meaning which life would give them for me. This was his legacy: nothing is ever escaped. That bleakly memorable morning I

45

hated the unbelievable streets and the Negroes and whites who had, equally, made them that way. But I knew that it was folly, as my father would have said, this bitterness was folly. It was necessary to hold on to the things that mattered. The dead man mattered, the new life mattered; blackness and whiteness did not matter; to believe that they did was to acquiesce in one's own destruction. Hatred, which could destroy so much, never failed to destroy the man who hated and this was an immutable law.

It began to seem that one would have to hold in the mind forever   46
two ideas which seemed to be in opposition. The first idea was acceptance, the acceptance, totally without rancor, of life as it is, and men as they are: in the light of this idea, it goes without saying that injustice is a commonplace. But this did not mean that one could be complacent, for the second idea was of equal power: that one must never, in one's own life, accept these injustices as commonplace but must fight them with all one's strength. This fight begins, however, in the heart and it now had been laid to my charge to keep my own heart free of hatred and despair. This intimation made my heart heavy and, now that my father was irrecoverable, I wished that he had been beside me so that I could have searched his face for the answers which only the future would give me now.

JAMES BALDWIN

Fifth Avenue, Uptown: A Letter from Harlem[1]

There is a housing project standing now where the house in   1
which we grew up once stood, and one of those stunted city trees is snarling where our doorway used to be. This is on the rehabilitated side of the avenue. The other side of the avenue—for progress takes time—has not been rehabilitated yet and it looks exactly as it looked in the days when we sat with our noses pressed against the windowpane, longing to be allowed to go "across the street." The grocery store which gave us credit is still there, and there can be no doubt that it is still giving credit. The people in the project certainly need it—far more, indeed, than they ever needed the project. The

1. First published in *Esquire,* July 1960.

last time I passed by, the Jewish proprietor was still standing among his shelves, looking sadder and heavier but scarcely any older. Farther down the block stands the shoe-repair store in which our shoes were repaired until reparation became impossible and in which, then, we bought all our "new" ones. The Negro proprietor is still in the window, head down, working at the leather.

These two, I imagine, could tell a long tale if they would (per-   2 haps they would be glad to if they could), having watched so many, for so long, struggling in the fishhooks, the barbed wire, of this avenue.

The avenue is elsewhere the renowned and elegant Fifth. The   3 area I am describing, which, in today's gang parlance, would be called "the turf," is bounded by Lenox Avenue on the west, the Harlem River on the east, 135th Street on the north, and 130th Street on the south. We never lived beyond these boundaries; this is where we grew up. Walking along 145th Street—for example— familiar as it is, and similar, does not have the same impact because I did not know any of the people on the block. But when I turn east on 131st Street and Lenox Avenue, there is first a soda-pop joint, then a shoeshine "parlor," then a grocery store, then a dry clean- ers', then the houses. All along the street there are people who watched me grow up, people who grew up with me, people I watched grow up along with my brothers and sisters; and, some- times in my arms, sometimes underfoot, sometimes at my shoul- der—or on it—their children, a riot, a forest of children, who include my nieces and nephews.

When we reach the end of this long block, we find ourselves on   4 wide, filthy, hostile Fifth Avenue, facing that project which hangs over the avenue like a monument to the folly, and the cowardice, of good intentions. All along the block, for anyone who knows it, are immense human gaps, like craters. These gaps are not created merely by those who have moved away, inevitably into some other ghetto; or by those who have risen, almost always into a greater capacity for self-loathing and self-delusion; or yet by those who, by whatever means—War II, the Korean war, a policeman's gun or billy, a gang war, a brawl, madness, an overdose of heroin, or, simply, unnatural exhaustion—are dead. I am talking about those who are left, and I am talking principally about the young. What are they doing? Well, some, a minority, are fanatical churchgoers, members of the more extreme of the Holy Roller sects. Many, many more are "moslems," by affiliation or sympathy, that is to say that they are united by nothing more—and nothing less—than a hatred of the white world and all its works. They are present, for example,

at every Buy Black street-corner meeting—meetings in which the
speaker urges his hearers to cease trading with white men and
establish a separate economy. Neither the speaker nor his hearers
can possibly do this, of course, since Negroes do not own General
Motors or RCA or the A & P, nor, indeed, do they own more than a
wholly insufficient fraction of anything else in Harlem (those who
do own anything are more interested in their profits than in their
fellows). But these meetings nevertheless keep alive in the partic-
ipators a certain pride of bitterness without which, however
futile this bitterness may be, they could scarcely remain alive at all.
Many have given up. They stay home and watch the TV screen,
living on the earnings of their parents, cousins, brothers, or uncles,
and only leave the house to go to the movies or to the nearest bar.
"How're you making it?" one may ask, running into them along
the block, or in the bar. "Oh, I'm TV-ing it"; with the saddest,
sweetest, most shame-faced of smiles, and from a great distance.
This distance one is compelled to respect; anyone who has traveled
so far will not easily be dragged again into the world. There are
further retreats, of course, than the TV screen or the bar. There are
those who are simply sitting on their stoops, "stoned," animated
for a moment only, and hideously, by the approach of someone
who may lend them the money for a "fix." Or by the approach of
someone from whom they can purchase it, one of the shrewd ones,
on the way to prison or just coming out.

   And the others, who have avoided all of these deaths, get up in   5
the morning and go downtown to meet "the man." They work in
the white man's world all day and come home in the evening to
this fetid block. They struggle to instill in their children some private sense of honor or dignity which will help the child survive.
This means, of course, that they must struggle, stolidly, incessantly,
to keep this sense alive in themselves, in spite of the insults, the
indifference, and the cruelty they are certain to encounter in their
working day. They patiently browbeat the landlord into fixing the
heat, the plaster, the plumbing; this demands prodigious patience;
nor is patience usually enough. In trying to make their hovels
habitable, they are perpetually throwing good money after bad.
Such frustration, so long endured, is driving many strong, admirable men and women whose only crime is color to the very gates of
paranoia.

   One remembers them from another time—playing handball in   6
the playground, going to church, wondering if they were going to
be promoted at school. One remembers them going off to war—
gladly, to escape this block. One remembers their return. Perhaps
one remembers their wedding day. And one sees where the girl is

now—vainly looking for salvation from some other embittered, trussed, and struggling boy—and sees the all-but-abandoned children in the streets.

Now I am perfectly aware that there are other slums in which 7 white men are fighting for their lives, and mainly losing. I know that blood is also flowing through those streets and that the human damage there is incalculable. People are continually pointing out to me the wretchedness of white people in order to console me for the wretchedness of blacks. But an itemized account of the American failure does not console me and it should not console anyone else. That hundreds of thousands of white people are living, in effect, no better than the "niggers" is not a fact to be regarded with complacency. The social and moral bankruptcy suggested by this fact is of the bitterest, most terrifying kind.

The people, however, who believe that this democratic anguish 8 has some consoling value are always pointing out that So-and-So, white, and So-and-So, black, rose from the slums into the big time. The existence—the public existence—of, say, Frank Sinatra and Sammy Davis, Jr. proves to them that America is still the land of opportunity and that inequalities vanish before the determined will. It proves nothing of the sort. The determined will is rare—at the moment, in this country, it is unspeakably rare—and the inequalities suffered by the many are in no way justified by the rise of a few. A few have always risen—in every country, every era, and in the teeth of regimes which can by no stretch of the imagination be thought of as free. Not all of these people, it is worth remembering, left the world better than they found it. The determined will is rare, but it is not invariably benevolent. Furthermore, the American equation of success with the big times reveals an awful disrespect for human life and human achievement. This equation has placed our cities among the most dangerous in the world and has placed our youth among the most empty and most bewildered. The situation of our youth is not mysterious. Children have never been very good at listening to their elders, but they have never failed to imitate them. They must, they have no other models. That is exactly what our children are doing. They are imitating our immorality, our disrespect for the pain of others.

All other slum dwellers, when the bank account permits it, can 9 move out of the slum and vanish altogether from the eye of persecution. No Negro in this country has ever made that much money and it will be a long time before any Negro does. The Negroes in Harlem, who have no money, spend what they have on such gimcracks as they are sold. These include "wider" TV screens, more "faithful" hi-fi sets, more "powerful" cars, all of which, of course, are obsolete long before they are paid for. Anyone who has ever struggled with poverty knows how extremely expensive it is to be poor; and if one is a member of a captive population, economically speaking, one's feet have simply been placed on the treadmill forever. One is victimized, economically, in a thousand ways— rent, for example, or car insurance. Go shopping one day in Harlem—for anything—and compare Harlem prices and quality with those downtown.

The people who have managed to get off this block have only got   10 as far as a more respectable ghetto. This respectable ghetto does not even have the advantages of the disreputable one—friends, neighbors, a familiar church, and friendly tradesmen; and it is not, moreover, in the nature of any ghetto to remain respectable long. Every Sunday, people who have left the block take the lonely ride back, dragging their increasingly discontented children with them. They spend the day talking, not always with words, about the trouble they've seen and the trouble—one must watch their eyes as they watch their children—they are only too likely to see. For children do not like ghettos. It takes them nearly no time to discover exactly why they are there.

The projects in Harlem are hated. They are hated almost as much   11 as policemen, and this is saying a great deal. And they are hated for the same reason: both reveal, unbearably, the real attitude of the white world, no matter how many liberal speeches are made, no matter how many lofty editorials are written, no matter how many civil-rights commissions are set up.

The projects are hideous, of course, there being a law, apparently   12 respected throughout the world, that popular housing shall be as cheerless as a prison. They are lumped all over Harlem, colorless, bleak, high, and revolting. The wide windows look out on Harlem's invincible and indescribable squalor: the Park Avenue railroad tracks, around which, about forty years ago, the present dark community began; the unrehabilitated houses, bowed down, it would seem, under the great weight of frustration and bitterness they contain; the dark, the ominous schoolhouses from which the child may emerge maimed, blinded, hooked, or enraged for life; and the churches, churches, block upon block of churches, niched in the walls like cannon in the walls of a fortress. Even if the administration of the projects were not so insanely humiliating (for example: one must report raises in salary to the management, which will then eat up the profit by raising one's rent; the management has the right to know who is staying in your apartment; the management can ask you to leave, at their discretion), the projects would still be hated because they are an insult to the meanest intelligence.

Harlem got its first private project, Riverton[2]—which is now, naturally, a slum—about twelve years ago because at that time Negroes were not allowed to live in Stuyvesant Town. Harlem watched Riverton go up, therefore, in the most violent bitterness of spirit, and hated it long before the builders arrived. They began hating it at about the time people began moving out of their condemned houses to make room for this additional proof of how thoroughly the white world despised them. And they had scarcely moved in, naturally, before they began smashing windows, defacing walls, urinating in the elevators, and fornicating in the playgrounds. Liberals, both white and black, were appalled at the spectacle. I was appalled by the liberal innocence—or cynicism, which comes out in practice as much the same thing. Other people were delighted to be able to point to proof positive that nothing could be done to better the lot of the colored people. They were, and are, right in one respect: that nothing can be done as long as they are treated like colored people. The people in Harlem know they are living there because white people do not think they are good enough to live anywhere else. No amount of "improvement" can sweeten this fact. Whatever money is now being earmarked to improve this, or any other ghetto, might as well be burnt. A ghetto can be improved in one way only: out of existence. 13

Similarly, the only way to police a ghetto is to be oppressive. None of the Police Commissioner's men, even with the best will in the world, have any way of understanding the lives led by the people they swagger about in twos and threes controlling. Their very presence is an insult, and it would be, even if they spent their entire day feeding gumdrops to children. They represent the force of the white world, and the world's real intentions are, simply, for the world's criminal profit and ease, to keep the black man corraled up here, in his place. The badge, the gun in the holster, and the swinging club make vivid what will happen should his rebellion 14

2. The inhabitants of Riverton were much embittered by this description; they have, apparently, forgotten how their project came into being; and have repeatedly informed me that I cannot possibly be referring to Riverton, but to another housing project which is directly across the street. It is quite clear, I think, that I have no interest in accusing any individuals or families of the depredations herein described: but neither can I deny the evidence of my own eyes. Nor do I blame anyone in Harlem for making the best of a dreadful bargain. But anyone who lives in Harlem and imagines that he has *not* struck this bargain, or that what he takes to be his status (in whose eyes?) protects him against the common pain, demoralization, and danger, is simply self deluded. [author's note]

become overt. Rare, indeed, is the Harlem citizen, from the most
circumspect church member to the most shiftless adolescent, who
does not have a long tale to tell of police incompetence, injustice,
or brutality. I myself have witnessed and endured it more than
once. The businessmen and racketeers also have a story. And so do
the prostitutes. (And this is not, perhaps, the place to discuss Harlem's very complex attitude toward black policemen, nor the reasons, according to Harlem, that they are nearly all downtown.)

It is hard, on the other hand, to blame the policeman, blank,   15
good-natured, thoughtless, and insuperably innocent, for being
such a perfect representative of the people he serves. He, too, believes in good intentions and is astounded and offended when they
are not taken for the deed. He has never, himself, done anything
for which to be hated—which of us has?—and yet he is facing,
daily and nightly, people who would gladly see him dead, and he
knows it. There is no way for him not to know it: there are few
things under heaven more unnerving than the silent, accumulating
contempt and hatred of a people. He moves through Harlem, therefore, like an occupying soldier in a bitterly hostile country; which is
precisely what, and where, he is, and is the reason he walks in twos
and threes. And he is not the only one who knows why he is
always in company: the people who are watching him know why,
too. Any street meeting, sacred or secular, which he and his colleagues uneasily cover has as its explicit or implicit burden the
cruelty and injustice of the white domination. And these days, of
course, in terms increasingly vivid and jubilant, it speaks of the end
of that domination. The white policeman standing on a Harlem
street corner finds himself at the very center of the revolution now
occurring in the world. He is not prepared for it—naturally, nobody is—and, what is possibly much more to the point, he is
exposed, as few white people are, to the anguish of the black
people around him. Even if he is gifted with the merest mustard
grain of imagination, something must seep in. He cannot avoid
observing that some of the children, in spite of their color, remind
him of children he has known and loved, perhaps even of his own
children. He knows that he certainly does not want *his* children
living this way. He can retreat from his uneasiness in only one
direction: into a callousness which very shortly becomes second
nature. He becomes more callous, the population becomes more
hostile, the situation grows more tense, and the police force is
increased. One day, to everyone's astonishment, someone drops a
match in the powder keg and everything blows up. Before the dust
has settled or the blood congealed, editorials, speeches, and civil-
rights commissions are loud in the land, demanding to know what

happened. What happened is that Negroes want to be treated like men.

Negroes want to be treated like men: a perfectly straightforward 16 statement, containing only seven words. People who have mastered Kant, Hegel, Shakespeare, Marx, Freud, and the Bible find this statement utterly impenetrable. The idea seems to threaten profound, barely conscious assumptions. A kind of panic paralyzes their features, as though they found themselves trapped on the edge of a steep place. I once tried to describe to a very well-known American intellectual the conditions among Negroes in the South. My recital disturbed him and made him indignant; and he asked me in perfect innocence, "Why don't all the Negroes in the South move North?" I tried to explain what *has* happened, unfailingly, whenever a significant body of Negroes move North. They do not escape Jim Crow: they merely encounter another, not-less-deadly variety. They do not move to Chicago, they move to the South Side; they do not move to New York, they move to Harlem. The pressure within the ghetto causes the ghetto walls to expand, and this expansion is always violent. White people hold the line as long as they can, and in as many ways as they can, from verbal intimidation to physical violence. But inevitably the border which has divided the ghetto from the rest of the world falls into the hands of the ghetto. The white people fall back bitterly before the black horde; the landlords make a tidy profit by raising the rent, chopping up the rooms, and all but dispensing with the upkeep; and what has once been a neighborhood turns into a "turf." This is precisely what happened when the Puerto Ricans arrived in their thousands—and the bitterness thus caused is, as I write, being fought out all up and down those streets.

Northerners indulge in an extremely dangerous luxury. They 17 seem to feel that because they fought on the right side during the Civil War, and won, they have earned the right merely to deplore what is going on in the South, without taking any responsibility for it; and that they can ignore what is happening in Northern cities because what is happening in Little Rock or Birmingham is worse. Well, in the first place, it is not possible for anyone who has not endured both to know which is "worse." I know Negroes who prefer the South and white Southerners, because "At least there, you haven't got to play any guessing games!" The guessing games referred to have driven more than one Negro into the narcotics ward, the madhouse, or the river. I know another Negro, a man very dear to me, who says with conviction and with truth, "The spirit of the South is the spirit of America." He was born in the North and did his military training in the South. He did not, as far as I can gather, find the South "worse"; he found it, if anything, all too familiar. In the second place, though, even if Birmingham *is* worse, no doubt Johannesburg, South Africa, beats it by several miles, and Buchenwald was one of the worst things that ever happened in the entire history of the world. The world has never lacked for horrifying examples; but I do not believe that these examples are meant to be used as justification for our own crimes. This perpetual justification empties the heart of all human feeling. The emptier our hearts become, the greater will be our crimes. Thirdly, the South is not merely an embarrassingly backward region, but a part of this country, and what happens there concerns every one of us.

As far as the color problem is concerned, there is but one difference between the Southern white and the Northerner: the Southerner remembers, historically and in his own psyche, a kind of Eden in which he loved black people and they loved him. Historically, the flaming sword laid across this Eden is the Civil War. Personally, it is the Southerner's sexual coming of age, when, without any warning, unbreakable taboos are set up between himself and his past. Everything, thereafter, is permitted him except the love he remembers and has never ceased to need. The resulting, indescribable torment affects every Southern mind and is the basis of the Southern hysteria.   18

None of this is true for the Northerner. Negroes represent nothing to him personally, except, perhaps, the dangers of carnality. He never sees Negroes. Southerners see them all the time. Northerners never think about them whereas Southerners are never really thinking of anything else. Negroes are, therefore, ignored in the North and are under surveillance in the South, and suffer hideously in both places. Neither the Southerner nor the Northerner is able to look on the Negro simply as a man. It seems to be indispensable to the national self-esteem that the Negro be considered either as a kind of ward (in which case we are told how many Negroes, comparatively, bought Cadillacs last year and how few, comparatively, were lynched), or as a victim (in which case we are promised that he will never vote in our assemblies or go to school with our kids). They are two sides of the same coin and the South will not change—*cannot* change—until the North changes. The country will not change until it re-examines itself and discovers what it really means by freedom. In the meantime, generations keep being born, bitterness is increased by incompetence, pride, and folly, and the world shrinks around us.   19

It is a terrible, an inexorable, law that one cannot deny the humanity of another without diminishing one's own: in the face of   20 one's victim, one sees oneself. Walk through the streets of Harlem and see what we, this nation, have become.

JOAN DIDION

Joan Didion (1934–   ) was born in Sacramento. She is sixth-generation Californian whose great-great-great grandmother reached the Sacramento Valley in 1847, the year starving members of Donner party (with whom she had traveled for a time) turned to cannibalism to survive. In 1956 Didion graduated from the University of California at Berkeley with a B.A. in English and won *Vogue* magazine's essay contest for young writers. The prize took her to New York to work for *Vogue,* first as a writer of advertising copy and later as an editor. During this period she also did free-lance work for *Mademoiselle* and *National Review* and wrote her first novel, *River Run* (1963). In 1964 she and her husband, John Gregory Dunne, moved to Southern California, where they continued to free-lance for several magazines. From 1967 to 1969, Didion and Dunne alternately wrote "Points West," a column for *The Saturday Evening Post.* Didion's West in these essays seems to be a society disintegrating or frantically attempting to reassemble itself without a blueprint: She chose as her epigraph for her first collection of essays, *Slouching Towards Bethlehem* (1968), an appropriate quotation from William Butler Yeats—"Things fall apart; the centre cannot hold." Didion's geographical range has expanded since the sixties, but she continues to investigate societies torn by internal pressures or strained by social and political changes. Her books include *Play It as It Lays* (novel, 1970), *A Book of Common Prayer* (novel, 1977), *The White Album* (essays, 1979), *Salvador* (reportage, 1983), *Democracy* (novel, 1984), and *Miami* (reportage, 1987). She and her husband have also co-authored screenplays, including *Panic in Needle Park* (1971), *Play It as It Lays* (1972, based on Didion's novel), and *True Confessions* (1981, based on Dunne's novel).

JOAN DIDION

Why I Write[1]

Of course I stole the title for this talk, from George Orwell. One   1
reason I stole it was that I like the sound of the words: Why I Write.
There you have three short unambiguous words that share a
sound, and the sound they share is this:

I   2

I   3

I   4

In many ways writing is the act of saying *I*, of imposing oneself   5
upon other people, of saying *listen to me, see it my way, change your
mind*. It's an aggressive, even a hostile act. You can disguise its
aggressiveness all you want with veils of subordinate clauses and
qualifiers and tentative subjunctives, with ellipses and evasions—
with the whole manner of intimating rather than claiming, of alluding rather than stating—but there's no getting around the fact
that setting words on paper is the tactic of a secret bully, an invasion, an imposition of the writer's sensibility on the reader's most
private space.

I stole the title not only because the words sounded right but   6
because they seemed to sum up, in a no-nonsense way, all I have
to tell you. Like many writers I have only this one "subject," this
one "area": the act of writing. I can bring you no reports from any
other front. I may have other interests: I am "interested," for example, in marine biology, but I don't flatter myself that you would
come out to hear me talk about it. I am not a scholar. I am not in
the least an intellectual, which is not to say that when I hear the
word "intellectual" I reach for my gun, but only to say that I do not
think in abstracts. During the years when I was an undergraduate
at Berkeley I tried, with a kind of hopeless late-adolescent energy,
to buy some temporary visa into the world of ideas, to forge for
myself a mind that could deal with the abstract.

In short I tried to think. I failed. My attention veered inexorably   7
back to the specific, to the tangible, to what was generally considered, by everyone I knew then and for that matter have known
since, the peripheral. I would try to contemplate the Hegelian
dialectic and would find myself concentrating instead on a flowering pear tree outside my window and the particular way the petals
fell on my floor. I would try to read linguistic theory and would

1. First published in the *New York Times Book Review*, December 5, 1976.

find myself wondering instead if the lights were on in the bevatron up the hill. When I say that I was wondering if the lights were on in the bevatron you might immediately suspect, if you deal in ideas at all, that I was registering the bevatron as a political symbol, thinking in shorthand about the military-industrial complex and its role in the university community, but you would be wrong. I was only wondering if the lights were on in the bevatron, and how they looked. A physical fact.

I had trouble graduating from Berkeley, not because of this inability to deal with ideas—I was majoring in English, and I could locate the house-and-garden imagery in *The Portrait of a Lady* as well as the next person, "imagery" being by definition the kind of specific that got my attention—but simply because I had neglected to take a course in Milton. For reasons which now sound baroque I needed a degree by the end of that summer, and the English department finally agreed, if I would come down from Sacramento every Friday and talk about the cosmology of *Paradise Lost*, to certify me proficient in Milton. I did this. Some Fridays I took the Greyhound bus, other Fridays I caught the Southern Pacific's City of San Francisco on the last leg of its transcontinental trip. I can no longer tell you whether Milton put the sun or the earth at the center of his universe in *Paradise Lost*, the central question of at least one century and a topic about which I wrote 10,000 words that summer, but I can still recall the exact rancidity of the butter in the City of San Francisco's dining car, and the way the tinted windows on the Greyhound bus cast the oil refineries around Carquinez Straits into a grayed and obscurely sinister light. In short my attention was always on the periphery, on what I could see and taste and touch, on the butter, and the Greyhound bus. During those years I was traveling on what I knew to be a very shaky passport, forged papers: I knew that I was no legitimate resident in any world of ideas. I knew I couldn't think. All I knew then was what I couldn't do. All I knew then was what I wasn't, and it took me some years to discover what I was.

Which was a writer.

By which I mean not a "good" writer or a "bad" writer but simply a writer, a person whose most absorbed and passionate hours are spent arranging words on pieces of paper. Had my credentials been in order I would never have become a writer. Had I been blessed with even limited access to my own mind there would have been no reason to write. I write entirely to find out what I'm thinking, what I'm looking at, what I see and what it means. What I want and what I fear. Why did the oil refineries around Carquinez Straits seem sinister to me in the summer of 1956? Why have the night lights in the bevatron burned in my mind for twenty years? *What is going on in these pictures in my mind?*

When I talk about pictures in my mind I am talking, quite specif-   11
ically, about images that shimmer around the edges. There used to be an illustration in every elementary psychology book showing a cat drawn by a patient in varying stages of schizophrenia. This cat had a shimmer around it. You could see the molecular structure breaking down at the very edges of the cat: the cat became the background and the background the cat, everything interacting, exchanging ions. People on hallucinogens describe the same perception of objects. I'm not a schizophrenic, nor do I take hallucinogens, but certain images do shimmer for me. Look hard enough, and you can't miss the shimmer. It's there. You can't think too much about these pictures that shimmer. You just lie low and let them develop. You stay quiet. You don't talk to many people and you keep your nervous system from shorting out and you try to locate the cat in the shimmer, the grammar in the picture.

Just as I meant "shimmer" literally I mean "grammar" literally.   12
Grammar is a piano I play by ear, since I seem to have been out of school the year the rules were mentioned. All I know about grammar is its infinite power. To shift the structure of a sentence alters the meaning of that sentence, as definitely and inflexibly as the position of a camera alters the meaning of the object photographed. Many people know about camera angles now, but not so many know about sentences. The arrangement of the words matters, and the arrangement you want can be found in the picture in your mind. The picture dictates the arrangement. The picture dictates whether this will be a sentence with or without clauses, a sentence that ends hard or a dying-fall sentence, long or short, active or passive. The picture tells you how to arrange the words and the arrangement of the words tells you, or tells me, what's going on in the picture. *Nota bene.*[2]

It tells you.   13

You don't tell it.   14

Let me show you what I mean by pictures in the mind. I began   15
Play It as It Lays just as I have begun each of my novels, with no notion of "character" or "plot" or even "incident." I had only two pictures in my mind, more about which later, and a technical intention, which was to write a novel so elliptical and fast that it would be over before you noticed it, a novel so fast that it would scarcely exist on the page at all. About the pictures: the first was of white space. Empty space. This was clearly the picture that dictated

2. "Note well."

the narrative intention of the book—a book in which anything that happened would happen off the page, a "white" book to which the reader would have to bring his or her own bad dreams—and yet this picture told me no "story," suggested no situation. The second picture did. This second picture was of something actually witnessed. A young woman with long hair and a short white halter dress walks through the casino at the Riviera in Las Vegas at one in the morning. She crosses the casino alone and picks up a house telephone. I watch her because I have heard her paged, and recognize her name: she is a minor actress I see around Los Angeles from time to time, in places like Jax and once in a gynecologist's office in the Beverly Hills Clinic, but have never met. I know nothing about her. Who is paging her? Why is she here to be paged? How exactly did she come to this? It was precisely this moment in Las Vegas that made *Play It as It Lays* begin to tell itself to me, but the moment appears in the novel only obliquely, in a chapter which begins:

"Maria made a list of things she would never do. She would never: walk through the Sands or Caesar's alone after midnight. She would never: ball at a party, do S-M unless she wanted to, borrow furs from Abe Lipsey, deal. She would never: carry a Yorkshire in Beverly Hills." 16

That is the beginning of the chapter and that is also the end of the chapter, which may suggest what I meant by "white space." 17

I recall having a number of pictures in my mind when I began the novel I just finished, *A Book of Common Prayer*. As a matter of fact one of these pictures was of that bevatron I mentioned, although I would be hard put to tell you a story in which nuclear energy figures. Another was a newspaper photograph of a hijacked 707 burning on the desert in the Middle East. Another was the night view from a room in which I once spent a week with paratyphoid, a hotel room on the Colombian coast. My husband and I seemed to be on the Colombian coast representing the United States of America at a film festival (I recall invoking the name "Jack Valenti" a lot, as if its reiteration could make me well), and it was a bad place to have fever, not only because my indisposition offended our hosts but because every night in this hotel the generator failed. The lights went out. The elevator stopped. My husband would go to the event of the evening and make excuses for me and I would stay alone in this hotel room, in the dark. I remember standing at the window trying to call Bogotá (the telephone seemed to work on the same principle as the generator) and watching the night wind come up and wondering what I was doing eleven degrees off the equator with a fever of 103. The view from 18

that window definitely figures in *A Book of Common Prayer*, as does
the burning 707, and yet none of these pictures told me the story I
needed.

The picture that did, the picture that shimmered and made these   19
other images coalesce, was the Panama airport at 6 A.M. I was in
this airport only once, on a plane to Bogotá that stopped for an
hour to refuel, but the way it looked that morning remained
superimposed on everything I saw until the day I finished *A Book of
Common Prayer*. I lived in that airport for several years. I can still
feel the hot air when I step off the plane, can see the heat already
rising off the tarmac at 6 A.M. I can feel my skirt damp and wrinkled on my legs. I can feel the asphalt stick to my sandals. I remember the big tail of a Pan American plane floating motionless down
at the end of the tarmac. I remember the sound of a slot machine in
the waiting room. I could tell you that I remember a particular
woman in the airport, an American woman, *a norteamericana*, a
thin *norteamericana* about forty who wore a big square emerald in
lieu of a wedding ring, but there was no such woman there.

I put this woman in the airport later. I made this woman up, just   20
as I later made up a country to put the airport in, and a family to
run the country. This woman in the airport is neither catching a
plane nor meeting one. She is ordering tea in the airport coffee
shop. In fact she is not simply "ordering" tea but insisting that the
water be boiled, in front of her, for twenty minutes. Why is this
woman in this airport? Why is she going nowhere, where has she
been? Where did she get that big emerald? What derangement, or
disassociation, makes her believe that her will to see the water
boiled can possibly prevail?

"She had been going to one airport or another for four months,   21
one could see it, looking at the visas on her passport. All those
airports where Charlotte Douglas's passport had been stamped
would have looked alike. Sometimes the sign on the tower would
say "Bienvenidos" and sometimes the sign on the tower would say
"Bienvenue," some places were wet and hot and others dry and
hot, but at each of these airports the pastel concrete walls would
rust and stain and the swamp off the runway would be littered with
the fuselages of cannibalized Fairchild F-227's and the water
would need boiling.

"I knew why Charlotte went to the airport even if Victor did not.   22

"I knew about airports."   23

These lines appear about halfway through *A Book of Common*   24
Prayer, but I wrote them during the second week I worked on the
book, long before I had any idea where Charlotte Douglas had
been or why she went to airports. Until I wrote these lines I had no

character called "Victor" in mind: the necessity for mentioning a name, and the name "Victor," occurred to me as I wrote the sentence. *I knew why Charlotte went to the airport* sounded incomplete. *I knew why Charlotte went to the airport even if Victor did not* carried a little more narrative drive. Most important of all, until I wrote these lines I did not know who "I" was, who was telling the story. I had intended until then that the "I" be no more than the voice of the author, a nineteenth-century omniscient narrator. But there it was:

"I knew why Charlotte went to the airport even if Victor did not.   25
"I knew about airports."   26

This "I" was the voice of no author in my house. This "I" was   27
someone who not only knew why Charlotte went to the airport but also knew someone called "Victor." Who was Victor? Who was this narrator? Why was this narrator telling me this story? Let me tell you one thing about why writers write: had I known the answer to any of these questions I would never have needed to write a novel.

JOAN DIDION

On Going Home[1]

I am home for my daughter's first birthday. By "home" I do not   1
mean the house in Los Angeles where my husband and I and the baby live, but the place where my family is, in the Central Valley of California. It is a vital although troublesome distinction. My husband likes my family but is uneasy in their house, because once there I fall into their ways, which are difficult, oblique, deliberately inarticulate, not my husband's ways. We live in dusty houses ("D-U-S-T," he once wrote with his finger on surfaces all over the house, but no one noticed it) filled with mementos quite without value to him (what could the Canton[2] dessert plates mean to him? how could he have known about the assay scales,[3] why should he care if he did know?), and we appear to talk exclusively about people we know who have been committed to mental hospitals, about people we know who have been booked on drunk-driving

---

1. First published in *The Saturday Evening Post*, June 3, 1967.
2. Fine Chinese porcelain.
3. Scales used to determine the proportion of metal in ore.

charges, and about property, particularly about property, land, price per acre and C-2 zoning and assessments and freeway access. My brother does not understand my husband's inability to perceive the advantage in the rather common real-estate transaction known as "sale-leaseback," and my husband in turn does not understand why so many of the people he hears about in my father's house have recently been committed to mental hospitals or booked on drunk-driving charges. Nor does he understand that when we talk about sale-leasebacks and right-of-way condemnations we are talking in code about things we like best, the yellow fields and the cottonwoods and the rivers rising and falling and the mountain roads closing when the heavy snow comes in. We miss each other's points, have another drink and regard the fire. My brother refers to my husband, in his presence, as "Joan's husband." Marriage is the classic betrayal.

Or perhaps it is not any more. Sometimes I think that those of us 2 who are now in our thirties were born into the last generation to carry the burden of "home," to find in family life the source of all tension and drama. I had by all objective accounts a "normal" and a "happy" family situation, and yet I was almost thirty years old before I could talk to my family on the telephone without crying after I had hung up. We did not fight. Nothing was wrong. And yet some nameless anxiety colored the emotional charges between me and the place that I came from. The question of whether or not you could go home again was a very real part of the sentimental and largely literary baggage with which we left home in the fifties; I suspect that it is irrelevant to the children born of the fragmentation after World War II. A few weeks ago in a San Francisco bar I saw a pretty young girl on crystal take off her clothes and dance for the cash prize in an "amateur-topless" contest. There was no particular sense of moment about this, none of the effect of romantic degradation, of "dark journey," for which my generation strived so assiduously. What sense could that girl possibly make of, say *Long Day's Journey into Night?*[4] Who is beside the point?

That I am trapped in this particular irrelevancy is never more 3 apparent to me than when I am home. Paralyzed by the neurotic lassitude engendered by meeting one's past at every turn, around every corner, inside every cupboard, I go aimlessly from room to room. I decide to meet it head-on and clean out a drawer, and I spread the contents on the bed. A bathing suit I wore the summer I was seventeen. A letter of rejection from *The Nation,* an aerial

___

4. Play by American dramatist Eugene O'Neill (1888–1953); his tragic autobiographical masterpiece.

photograph of the site for a shopping center my father did not build in 1954. Three teacups hand-painted with cabbage roses and signed "E.M.," my grandmother's initials. There is no final solution for letters of rejection from *The Nation* and teacups hand-painted in 1900. Nor is there any answer to snapshots of one's grandfather as a young man on skis, surveying around Donner Pass in the year 1910. I smooth out the snapshot and look into his face, and do and do not see my own. I close the drawer, and have another cup of coffee with my mother. We get along very well, veterans of a guerrilla war we never understood.

Days pass. I see no one. I come to dread my husband's evening call, not only because he is full of news of what by now seems to me our remote life in Los Angeles, people he has seen, letters which require attention, but because he asks what I have been doing, suggests uneasily that I get out, drive to San Francisco or Berkeley. Instead I drive across the river to a family graveyard. It has been vandalized since my last visit and the monuments are broken, overturned in the dry grass. Because I once saw a rattle-snake in the grass I stay in the car and listen to a country-and-Western station. Later I drive with my father to a ranch he has in the foothills. The man who runs his cattle on it asks us to the roundup, a week from Sunday, and although I know that I will be in Los Angeles I say, in the oblique way my family talks, that I will come. Once home I mention the broken monuments in the graveyard. My mother shrugs.

I go to visit my great-aunts. A few of them think now that I am my cousin, or their daughter who died young. We recall an anecdote about a relative last seen in 1948, and they ask if I still like living in New York City. I have lived in Los Angeles for three years, but I say that I do. The baby is offered a horehound drop, and I am slipped a dollar bill "to buy a treat." Questions trail off, answers are abandoned, the baby plays with the dust motes in a shaft of afternoon sun.

It is time for the baby's birthday party: a white cake, strawberry-marshmallow ice cream, a bottle of champagne saved from another party. In the evening, after she has gone to sleep, I kneel beside the crib and touch her face, where it pressed against the slats, with mine. She is an open and trusting child, unprepared for and unaccustomed to the ambushes of family life, and perhaps it is just as well that I can offer her little of that life. I would like to give her more. I would like to promise her that she will grow up with a sense of her cousins and of rivers and of her great-grandmother's teacups, would like to pledge her a picnic on a river with fried chicken and her hair uncombed, would like to give her *home* for

her birthday, but we live differently now and I can promise her
nothing like that. I give her a xylophone and a sundress from
Madeira, and promise to tell her a funny story.

JOAN DIDION

Marrying Absurd[1]

To be married in Las Vegas, Clark County, Nevada, a bride must   1
swear that she is eighteen or has parental permission and a bridegroom that he is twenty-one or has parental permission. Someone
must put up five dollars for the license. (On Sundays and holidays,
fifteen dollars. The Clark County Courthouse issues marriage licenses at any time of the day or night except between noon and
one in the afternoon, between eight and nine in the evening, and
between four and five in the morning.) Nothing else is required.
The State of Nevada, alone among these United States, demands
neither a premarital blood test nor a waiting period before or after
the issuance of a marriage license. Driving in across the Mojave
from Los Angeles, one sees the signs way out on the desert, looming up from that moonscape of rattlesnakes and mesquite, even
before the Las Vegas lights appear like a mirage on the horizon:
"GETTING MARRIED? Free License Information First Strip Exit." Perhaps the Las Vegas wedding industry achieved its peak operational
efficiency between 9:00 P.M. and midnight of August 26, 1965, an
otherwise unremarkable Thursday which happened to be, by Presidential order, the last day on which anyone could improve his draft
status merely by getting married. One hundred and seventy-one
couples were pronounced man and wife in the name of Clark
County and the State of Nevada that night, sixty-seven of them by
a single justice of the peace, Mr. James A. Brennan. Mr. Brennan
did one wedding at the Dunes and the other sixty-six in his office,
and charged each couple eight dollars. One bride lent her veil to six
others. "I got it down from five to three minutes," Mr. Brennan
said later of his feat. "I could've married them *en masse*, but they're
people, not cattle. People expect more when they get married."

What people who get married in Las Vegas actually do expect—   2
what, in the largest sense, their "expectations" are—strikes one as

1. First published in *The Saturday Evening Post*, December 16, 1967.

a curious and self-contradictory business. Las Vegas is the most extreme and allegorical of American settlements, bizarre and beautiful in its venality and in its devotion to immediate gratification, a place the tone of which is set by mobsters and call girls and ladies' room attendants with amyl nitrite poppers in their uniform pockets. Almost everyone notes that there is no "time" in Las Vegas, no night and no day and no past and no future (no Las Vegas casino, however, has taken the obliteration of the ordinary time sense quite so far as Harold's Club in Reno, which for a while issued, at odd intervals in the day and night, mimeographed "bulletins" carrying news from the world outside); neither is there any logical sense of where one is. One is standing on a highway in the middle of a vast hostile desert looking at an eighty-foot sign which blinks "STARDUST" or "CAESAR'S PALACE." Yes, but what does that explain? This geographical implausibility reinforces the sense that what happens there has no connection with "real" life; Nevada cities like Reno and Carson are ranch towns, Western towns, places behind which there is some historical imperative. But Las Vegas seems to exist only in the eye of the beholder. All of which makes it an extraordinarily stimulating and interesting place, but an odd one in which to want to wear a candlelight satin Priscilla of Boston wedding dress with Chantilly lace insets, tapered sleeves and a detachable modified train.

And yet the Las Vegas wedding business seems to appeal to   3 precisely that impulse. "Sincere and Dignified Since 1954," one wedding chapel advertises. There are nineteen such wedding chapels in Las Vegas, intensely competitive, each offering better, faster, and, by implication, more sincere services than the next: Our Photos Best Anywhere, Your Wedding on A Phonograph Record, Candlelight with Your Ceremony, Honeymoon Accommodations, Free Transportation from Your Motel to Courthouse to Chapel and Return to Motel, Religious or Civil Ceremonies, Dressing Rooms, Flowers, Rings, Announcements, Witnesses Available, and Ample Parking. All of these services, like most others in Las Vegas (sauna baths, payroll-check cashing, chinchilla coats for sale or rent) are offered twenty-four hours a day, seven days a week, presumably on the premise that marriage, like craps, is a game to be played when the table seems hot.

But what strikes one most about the Strip chapels, with their   4 wishing wells and stained-glass paper windows and their artificial bouvardia, is that so much of their business is by no means a matter of simple convenience, of late-night liaisons between show girls and baby Crosbys. Of course there is some of that. (One night about eleven o'clock in Las Vegas I watched a bride in an orange mini-

dress and masses of flame-colored hair stumble from a Strip chapel
on the arm of her bridegroom, who looked the part of the expend-
able nephew in movies like *Miami Syndicate*. "I gotta get the kids,"
the bride whimpered. "I gotta pick up the sitter, I gotta get to the
midnight show." "What you gotta get," the bridegroom said,
opening the door of a Cadillac Coupe de Ville and watching her
crumple on the seat, "is sober.") But Las Vegas seems to offer
something other than "convenience"; it is merchandising "niceness," the facsimile of proper ritual, to children who do not know
how else to find it, how to make the arrangements, how to do it
"right." All day and evening long on the Strip, one sees actual
wedding parties, waiting under the harsh lights at a crosswalk,
standing uneasily in the parking lot of the Frontier while the photographer hired by The Little Church of the West ("Wedding Place
of the Stars") certifies the occasion, takes the picture: the bride in a
veil and white satin pumps, the bridegroom usually in a white
dinner jacket, and even an attendant or two, a sister or a best friend
in hot-pink *peau de soie*, a flirtation veil, a carnation nosegay.
"When I Fall in Love It Will Be Forever," the organist plays, and
then a few bars of Lohengrin. The mother cries; the stepfather,
awkward in his role, invites the chapel hostess to join them for a
drink at the Sands. The hostess declines with a professional smile;
she has already transferred her interest to the group waiting outside. One bride out, another in, and again the sign goes up on the
chapel door: "One moment please—Wedding."

I sat next to one such wedding party in a Strip restaurant the last   5
time I was in Las Vegas. The marriage had just taken place; the
bride still wore her dress, the mother her corsage. A bored waiter
poured out a few swallows of pink champagne ("on the house")
for everyone but the bride, who was too young to be served.
"You'll need something with more kick than that," the bride's
father said with heavy jocularity to his new son-in-law; the ritual
jokes about the wedding night had a certain Panglossian character,
since the bride was clearly several months pregnant. Another
round of pink champagne, this time not on the house, and the
bride began to cry. "It was just as nice," she sobbed, "as I hoped
and dreamed it would be."

JOAN DIDION

Salvador[1]

The three-year-old El Salvador International Airport is glassy   1
and white and splendidly isolated, conceived during the waning of
the Molina[2] "National Transformation" as convenient less to the
capital (San Salvador is forty miles away, until recently a drive of
several hours) than to a central hallucination of the Molina and
Romero[3] regimes, the projected beach resorts, the Hyatt, the Pacific
Paradise, tennis, golf, water-skiing, condos, *Costa del Sol;*[4] the visionary invention of a tourist industry in yet another republic
where the leading natural cause of death is gastrointestinal infection. In the general absence of tourists these hotels have since been
abandoned, ghost resorts on the empty Pacific beaches, and to land
at this airport built to service them is to plunge directly into a state
in which no ground is solid, no depth of field reliable, no perception so definite that it might not dissolve into its reverse.

The only logic is that of acquiescence. Immigration is negotiated   2
in a thicket of automatic weapons, but by whose authority the
weapons are brandished (Army or National Guard or National
Police or Customs Police or Treasury Police or one of a continuing
proliferation of other shadowy and overlapping forces) is a blurred
point. Eye contact is avoided. Documents are scrutinized upside
down. Once clear of the airport, on the new highway that slices
through green hills rendered phosphorescent by the cloud cover of
the tropical rainy season, one sees mainly underfed cattle and
mongrel dogs and armored vehicles, vans and trucks and Cherokee
Chiefs fitted with reinforced steel and bulletproof Plexiglas an inch
thick. Such vehicles are a fixed feature of local life, and are popularly associated with disappearance and death. There was the
Cherokee Chief seen following the Dutch television crew killed in
Chalatenango province in March of 1982. There was the red
Toyota three-quarter-ton pickup sighted near the van driven by the
four American-Catholic workers on the night they were killed in
1980. There were, in the late spring and summer of 1982, the three

1. First published in the *New York Review of Books*, November 4, 1982.
2. Arturo Armando Molina (1927–   ), a military strongman and president of El
Salvador from 1972 to 1977.
3. Carlos Humberto Romero (1925–   ), a military strongman and president of El
Salvador from 1977 to 1979.
4. Coast of the sun.

Toyota panel trucks, one yellow, one blue, and one green, none
bearing plates, reported present at each of the mass detentions (a
"detention" is another fixed feature of local life, and often precedes
a "disappearance") in the Amatepec district of San Salvador. These
are the details—the models and the colors of armored vehicles, the
makes and calibers of weapons, the particular methods of dismem-
berment and decapitation used in particular instances—on which
the visitor to Salvador learns immediately to concentrate, to the
exclusion of past or future concerns, as in a prolonged amnesiac
fugue.

Terror is the given of the place. Black-and-white police cars   3
cruise in pairs, each with the barrel of a rifle extruding from an
open window. Roadblocks materialize at random, soldiers fanning
out from trucks and taking positions, fingers always on triggers,
safeties clicking on and off. Aim is taken as if to pass the time.
Every morning *El Diario de Hoy* and *La Prensa Gráfica* carry cau-
tionary stories. *"Una madre y sus dos hijos fueron asesinados con arma
cortante (corvo) por ocho sujetos desconocidos el lunes en la noche"*: A
mother and her two sons hacked to death in their beds by eight
desconocidos, unknown men. The same morning's paper: the unidentified body of a young man, strangled, found on the shoulder
of a road. Same morning, different story: the unidentified bodies of
three young men, found on another road, their faces partially destroyed by bayonets, one face carved to represent a cross.

It is largely from these reports in the newspapers that the United   4
States embassy compiles its body counts, which are transmitted to
Washington in a weekly dispatch referred to by embassy people as
"the grim-gram." These counts are presented in a kind of tortured
code that fails to obscure what is taken for granted in El Salvador,
that government forces do most of the killing. In a January 15
1982 memo to Washington, for example, the embassy issued a
"guarded" breakdown on its count of 6,909 "reported" political
murders between September 16 1980 and September 15 1981. Of
these 6,909, according to the memo, 922 were "believed committed by security forces," 952 "believed committed by leftist terrorists," 136 "believed committed by rightist terrorists," and 4,889
"committed by unknown assailants," the famous *desconocidos*
favored by those San Salvador newspapers still publishing. (The
figures actually add up not to 6,909 but to 6,899, leaving ten in a
kind of official limbo.) The memo continued:

> "The uncertainty involved here can be seen in the fact that reponsibil-
> ity cannot be fixed in the majority of cases. We note, however, that it is
> generally believed in El Salvador that a large number of the unex-

plained killings are carried out by the security forces, officially or unofficially. The Embassy is aware of dramatic claims that have been made by one interest group or another in which the security forces figure as the primary agents of murder here. El Salvador's tangled web of attack and vengeance, traditional criminal violence and political mayhem make this an impossible charge to sustain. In saying this, however, we make no attempt to lighten the responsibility for the deaths of many hundreds, and perhaps thousands, which can be attributed to the security forces. . . ."

The body count kept by what is generally referred to in San Salvador as "the Human Rights Commission" is higher than the embassy's, and documented periodically by a photographer who goes out looking for bodies. These bodies he photographs are often broken into unnatural positions, and the faces to which the bodies are attached (when they are attached) are equally unnatural, sometimes unrecognizable as human faces, obliterated by acid or beaten to a mash of misplaced ears and teeth or slashed ear to ear and invaded by insects. *"Encontrado en Antiguo Cuscatlán el día 25 de Marzo 1982: camison de dormir celeste,"* the typed caption reads on one photograph: found in Antiguo Cuscatlán March 25 1982 wearing a sky-blue nightshirt. The captions are laconic. Found in Soyapango May 21 1982. Found in Mejicanos June 11 1982. Found at El Playón May 30, 1982, white shirt, purple pants, black shoes.

The photograph accompanying that last caption shows a body with no eyes, because the vultures got to it before the photographer did. There is a special kind of practical information that the visitor to El Salvador acquires immediately, the way visitors to other places acquire information about the currency rates, the hours for the museums. In El Salvador one learns that vultures go first for the soft tissue, for the eyes, the exposed genitalia, the open mouth. One learns that an open mouth can be used to make a specific point, can be stuffed with something emblematic; stuffed, say, with a penis, or, if the point has to do with land title, stuffed with some of the dirt in question. One learns that hair deteriorates less rapidly than flesh, and that a skull surrounded by a perfect corona of hair is a not uncommon sight in the body dumps.

All forensic photographs induce in the viewer a certain protective numbness, but dissociation is more difficult here. In the first place these are not, technically, "forensic" photographs, since the evidence they document will never be presented in a court of law. In the second place the disfigurement is too routine. The locations are too near, the dates too recent. There is the presence of the relatives of the disappeared: the women who sit every day in this

cramped office on the grounds of the archdiocese, waiting to look
at the spiral-bound photo albums in which the photographs are
kept. These albums have plastic covers bearing soft-focus color
photographs of young Americans in dating situations (strolling
through autumn foliage on one album, recumbent in a field of
daisies on another), and the women, looking for the bodies of their
husbands and brothers and sisters and children, pass them from
hand to hand without comment or expression.

> "One of the more shadowy elements of the violent scene here [is] the
> death squad. Existence of these groups has long been disputed, but not
> by many Salvadorans. . . . Who constitutes the death squads is yet
> another difficult question. We do not believe that these squads exist as
> permanent formations but rather as ad hoc vigilante groups that
> coalesce according to perceived need. Membership is also uncertain,
> but in addition to civilians we believe that both on- and off-duty
> members of the security forces are participants. This was unofficially
> confirmed by right-wing spokesman Maj. Roberto D'Aubuisson who
> stated in an interview in early 1981 that security force members utilize
> the guise of the death squad when a potentially embarrassing or odius
> task needs to be performed."
>
> —*From the confidential but later declassified January 15, 1982, memo
> previously cited, drafted for the State Department by the political section
> at the embassy in San Salvador.*

The dead and pieces of the dead turn up in El Salvador every-   8
where, every day, as taken for granted as in a nightmare, or a
horror movie. Vultures of course suggest the presence of a body. A
knot of children on the street suggests the presence of a body.
Bodies turn up in the brush of vacant lots, in the garbage thrown
down ravines in the richest districts, in public rest rooms, in bus
stations. Some are dropped in Lake Ilopango, a few miles east of
the city, and wash up near the lakeside cottages and clubs frequented by what remains in San Salvador of the sporting bourgeoisie. Some still turn up in El Playón, the lunar lava field of rotting
human flesh visible at one time or another on every television
screen in America but characterized in June of 1982 in the *El
Salvador News Gazette,* an English-language weekly edited by an
American named Mario Rosenthal, as an "uncorroborated story
. . . dredged up from the files of leftist propaganda." Others turn up
at Puerta del Diablo, above Parque Balboa, a national *Turicentro*
described as recently as the April-July 1982 issue of *Aboard TACA,*
the magazine provided passengers on the national airline of El
Salvador, as "offering excellent subjects for color photography."

I drove up to Puerta del Diablo one morning in June of 1982,   9
past the Casa Presidencial and the camouflaged watch towers and

heavy concentrations of troops and arms south of town, on up a
narrow road narrowed further by landslides and deep crevices in
the roadbed, a drive so insistently premonitory that after a while I
began to hope that I would pass Puerta del Diablo without knowing it, just miss it, write it off, turn around and go back. There was
however no way of missing it. Puerta del Diablo is a "view site" in
an older and distinctly literary tradition, nature as lesson, an immense cleft rock through which half of El Salvador seems framed, a
site so romantic and "mystical," so theatrically sacrificial in aspect,
that it might be a cosmic parody of nineteenth-century landscape
painting. The place presents itself as pathetic fallacy: the sky
"broods," the stones "weep," a constant seepage of water weighting the ferns and moss. The foliage is thick and slick with moisture.
The only sound is a steady buzz, I believe of cicadas.

Body dumps are seen in El Salvador as a kind of visitors' must-   10
do, difficult but worth the detour. "Of course you have seen El
Playón," an aide to President Alvaro Magaña said to me one day,
and proceeded to discuss the site geologically, as evidence of the
country's geothermal resources. He made no mention of the bodies. I was unsure if he was sounding me out or simply found the
geothermal aspect of overriding interest. One difference between El
Playón and Puerta del Diablo is that most bodies at El Playón
appear to have been killed somewhere else, and then dumped; at
Puerta del Diablo the executions are believed to occur in place, at
the top, and the bodies thrown over. Sometimes reporters will
speak of wanting to spend the night at Puerta del Diablo, in order
to document the actual execution, but at the time I was in Salvador
no one had.

The aftermath, the daylight aspect, is well documented. "Noth-   11
ing fresh today, I hear," an embassy officer said when I mentioned
that I had visited Puerta del Diablo. "Were there any on top?"
someone else asked. "There were supposed to have been three on
top yesterday." The point about whether or not there had been any
on top was that usually it was necessary to go down to see bodies.
The way down is hard. Slabs of stone, slippery with moss, are set
into the vertiginous cliff, and it is down this cliff that one begins the
descent to the bodies, or what is left of the bodies, pecked and
maggoty masses of flesh, bone, hair. On some days there have been
helicopters circling, tracking those making the descent. Other days
there have been militia at the top, in the clearing where the road
seems to run out, but on the morning I was there the only people
on top were a man and a woman and three small children, who
played in the wet grass while the woman started and stopped a
Toyota pickup. She appeared to be learning how to drive. She

drove forward and then back toward the edge, apparently following the man's signals, over and over again.

We did not speak, and it was only later, down the mountain and   12
back in the land of the provisionally living, that it occurred to me
that there was a definite question about why a man and a woman
might choose a well-known body dump for a driving lesson. This
was one of a number of occasions, during the two weeks my husband and I spent in El Salvador, on which I came to understand, in
a way I had not understood before, the exact mechanism of terror.

Whenever I had nothing better to do in San Salvador I would   13
walk up in the leafy stillness of the San Benito and Escalón districts, where the hush at midday is broken only by the occasional
crackle of a walkie-talkie, the click of metal moving on a weapon. I
recall a day in San Benito when I opened my bag to check an
address, and heard the clicking of metal on metal all up and down
the street. On the whole no one walks up here, and pools of blossoms lie undisturbed on the sidewalks. Most of the houses in San
Benito are more recent than those in Escalón, less idiosyncratic and
probably smarter, but the most striking architectural features in
both districts are not the houses but their walls, walls built upon
walls, walls stripped of the usual copa de oro and bougainvillea,
walls that reflect successive generations of violence: the original
stone, the additional five or six or ten feet of brick, and finally the
barbed wire, sometimes concertina, sometimes electrified; walls
with watch towers, gun ports, closed-circuit television cameras,
walls now reaching twenty and thirty feet.

San Benito and Escalón appear on the embassy security maps as   14
districts of relatively few "incidents," but they remain districts in
which a certain oppressive uneasiness prevails. In the first place
there are always "incidents"—detentions and deaths and disap-
pearances—in the *barrancas,* the ravines lined with shanties that
fall down behind the houses with the walls and the guards and the
walkie-talkies; one day in Escalón I was introduced to a woman
who kept the lean-to that served as a grocery in a *barranca* just
above the Hotel Sheraton. She was sticking prices on bars of
Camay and Johnson's baby soap, stopping occasionally to sell a
plastic bag or two filled with crushed ice and Coca-Cola, and all the
while she talked in a low voice about her fear, about her eighteen-
year-old son, about the boys who had been taken out and shot on
successive nights recently in a neighboring *barranca.*

In the second place there is, in Escalón, the presence of the   15
Sheraton itself, a hotel that has figured rather too prominently
in certain local stories involving the disappearance and death of

Americans. The Sheraton always seems brighter and more mildly festive than either the Camino Real or the Presidente, with children in the pool and flowers and pretty women in pastel dresses, but there are usually several bulletproofed Cherokee Chiefs in the parking area, and the men drinking in the lobby often carry the little zippered purses that in San Salvador suggest not passports or credit cards but Browning 9-mm. pistols.

It was at the Sheraton that one of the few American *desaparecidos*, a young free-lance writer named John Sullivan, was last seen, in December of 1980. It was also at the Sheraton, after eleven on the evening of January 3 1981, that the two American advisers on agrarian reform, Michael Hammer and Mark Pearlman, were killed, along with the Salvadoran director of the Institute for Agrarian Transformation, José Rodolfo Viera. The three were drinking coffee in a dining room off the lobby, and whoever killed them used an Ingram MAC-10, without sound suppressor, and then walked out through the lobby, unapprehended. The Sheraton has even turned up in the investigation into the December 1980 deaths of the four American churchwomen, Sisters Ita Ford and Maura Clarke, the two Maryknoll nuns; Sister Dorothy Kazel, the Ursuline nun; and Jean Donovan, the lay volunteer. In *Justice in El Salvador: A Case Study*, prepared and released in July of 1982 in New York by the Lawyers' Committee for International Human Rights, there appears this note:

> "On December 19, 1980, the [Duarte government's] Special Investigative Commission reported that 'a red Toyota ¾-ton pickup was seen leaving (the crime scene) at about 11:00 P.M. on December 2' and that 'a red splotch on the burned van' of the churchwomen was being checked to determine whether the paint splotch 'could be the result of a collision between that van and the red Toyota pickup.' By February 1981, the Maryknoll Sisters' Office of Social Concerns, which has been actively monitoring the investigation, received word from a source which it considered reliable that the FBI had matched the red splotch on the burned van with a red Toyota pickup belonging to the Sheraton hotel in San Salvador. . . . Subsequent to the FBI's alleged matching of the paint splotch and a Sheraton truck, the State Department has claimed, in a communication with the families of the churchwomen, that 'the FBI could not determine the source of the paint scraping.'"

There is also mention in this study of a young Salvadoran businessman named Hans Christ (his father was a German who arrived in El Salvador at the end of World War II), a part owner of the Sheraton. Hans Christ lives now in Miami, and that his name should have even come up in the Maryknoll investigation made many people uncomfortable, because it was Hans Christ, along with his brother-in-law, Ricardo Sol Meza, who, in April of 1981, was first charged with the murders of Michael Hammer and Mark Pearlman and José Rodolfo Viera at the Sheraton. These charges were later dropped, and were followed by a series of other charges, arrests, releases, expressions of "dismay" and "incredulity" from the American embassy, and even, in the fall of 1982, confessions to the killings from two former National Guard corporals, who testified that Hans Christ had led them through the lobby and pointed out the victims. Hans Christ and Ricardo Sol Meza have said that the dropped case against them was a government frame-up, and that they were only having drinks at the Sheraton the night of the killings, with a National Guard intelligence officer. It was logical for Hans Christ and Ricardo Sol Meza to have drinks at the Sheraton because they both had interests in the hotel, and Ricardo Sol Meza had just opened a roller disco, since closed, off the lobby into which the killers walked that night. The killers were described by witnesses as well dressed, their faces covered. The room from which they walked was at the time I was in San Salvador no longer a restaurant, but the marks left by the bullets were still visible, on the wall facing the door.

Whenever I had occasion to visit the Sheraton I was apprehensive, and this apprehension came to color the entire Escalón district for me, even its lower reaches, where there were people and movies and restaurants. I recall being struck by it on the canopied porch of a restaurant near the Mexican embassy, on an evening when rain or sabotage or habit had blacked out the city and I became abruptly aware, in the light cast by a passing car, of two human shadows, silhouettes illuminated by the headlights and then invisible again. One shadow sat behind the smoked glass windows of a Cherokee Chief parked at the curb in front of the restaurant; the other crouched between the pumps at the Esso station next door, carrying a rifle. It seemed to me unencouraging that my husband and I were the only people seated on the porch. In the absence of the headlights the candle on our table provided the only light, and I fought the impulse to blow it out. We continued talking, carefully. Nothing came of this, but I did not forget the sensation of having been in a single instant demoralized, undone, humiliated by fear, which is what I meant when I said that I came to understand in El Salvador the mechanism of terror. . . .

The place brings everything into question. One afternoon when I had run out of the Halazone tablets I dropped every night in a pitcher of tap water (a demented *gringa*[5] gesture, I knew even then, in a country where everyone not born there was at least mildly ill, including the nurse at the American embassy), I walked across the street from the Camino Real to the Metrocenter, which is referred to locally as "Central America's Largest Shopping Mall." I found no Halazone at the Metrocenter but became absorbed in making notes about the mall itself, about the Muzak playing "I Left My Heart in San Francisco" and "American Pie" ("*. . . singing this will be the day that I die . . .*") although the record store featured a cassette called *Classics of Paraguay,* about the *pâté de foie gras* for sale in the supermarket, about the guard who did the weapons check on everyone who entered the supermarket, about the young matrons in tight Sergio Valente jeans, trailing maids and babies behind them and buying towels, big beach towels printed with maps of Manhattan that featured Bloomingdale's; about the number of things for sale that seemed to suggest a fashion for "smart drinking," to evoke modish cocktail hours. There were bottles of Stolichnaya vodka packaged with glasses and mixer, there were ice buckets, there were bar carts of every conceivable design, displayed with sample bottles.

This was a shopping center that embodied the future for which 20 El Salvador was presumably being saved, and I wrote it down dutifully, this being the kind of "color" I knew how to interpret, the kind of inductive irony, the detail that was supposed to illuminate the story. As I wrote it down I realized that I was no longer much interested in this kind of irony, that this was a story that would not be illuminated by such details, that this was a story that would perhaps not be illuminated at all, that this was perhaps even less a "story" than a true *noche obscura.*[6] As I waited to cross back over the Boulevard de los Heroes to the Camino Real I noticed soldiers herding a young civilian into a van, their guns at the boy's back, and I walked straight ahead, not wanting to see anything at all.

---

5. Foreign.
6. Dark night. Didion is thinking of *los noches oscuras del alma,* "dark nights of the soul."

AUTHOR/
TITLE INDEX

ACKNOWLEDGMENTS
(continued from p. iv)

WENDELL BERRY: "Against PCs," *Harper's*, September 1988, is excerpted from forthcoming book of essays by Wendell Berry, to be published by North Point Press in 1990. Copyright © 1990 by Wendell Berry.
Letters to *Harper's* in response to "Against PCs" by Nathaniel S. Borenstein, Gordon Inkeles, Bradley C. Johnson, Toby Koosman, and James Rhoads are reprinted by permission.
Wendell Berry's rejoinder reprinted courtesy of the author.
ALICE BLOOM: "On a Greek Holiday," by Alice Bloom. Reprinted by permission of *The Hudson Review*, Vol. XXXVI, No. 3 (Autumn 1983). Copyright © 1983 by Alice Bloom.
DANIEL J. BOORSTIN: "Technology and Democracy." Copyright, 1974, by Daniel J. Boorstin. From *Democracy and Its Discontents* (Random House, New York, 1974).
DAVID BRADLEY: "The Faith" by David Bradley, from *In Praise of What Persists* (Stephen Berg, ed., 1984). Copyright © 1984 by David Bradley. Reprinted by permission of The Wendy Weil Agency, Inc.
JACOB BRONOWSKI: "The Creative Mind," from *Science and Human Values* by Jacob Bronowski. Copyright © 1956, 1965 by J. Bronowski. Reprinted by permission of Julian Messner, a division of Simon & Schuster, Inc.
BRIGID BROPHY: "The Menace of Nature" and "Women" from *Don't Never Forget*. Copyright 1966 by Brigid Brophy. All rights reserved. Reprinted by kind permission of the author.
SUSAN BROWNMILLER: "Prologue" from *Femininity* by Susan Brownmiller. Copyright © 1984 by Susan Brownmiller. Reprinted by permission of Linden Press, a division of Simon & Schuster, Inc.
JAMES BRUCHAC III: "Turtle Meat" reprinted with permission from *Earth Power Coming: Short Fiction in Native American Literature*, edited by Simon J. Ortiz, Navajo Community College Press, 1983.
NAPOLEON A. CHAGNON: "Yanomamö: The Fierce People" reprinted with permission from *Natural History*, January 1967. Copyright the American Museum of Natural History, 1966.
MALCOLM COWLEY: "The View from 80," *The View from 80* by Malcolm Cowley. Copyright © 1978, 1980 by Malcolm Cowley. All rights reserved. Reprinted by permission of Viking Penguin, a division of Penguin Books USA, Inc.
HARRY CREWS: "Pages from the Life of a Georgia Innocent." Copyright © 1976 by Harry Crews. Reprinted by permission of John Hawkins & Associates, Inc.
SIMONE DE BEAUVOIR: Reprinted by permission of The Putnam Publishing Group and Andre Deutsch Ltd from *Old Age* by Simone de Beauvoir. Copyright © 1970 by Editions Gallimard. English translation *Coming of Age* © 1972 by Andre Deutsch.
JOAN DIDION: "On Going Home" and "Marrying Absurd" from *Slouching Towards Bethlehem* by Joan Didion. Copyright © 1967, 1968 by Joan Didion. Reprinted by permission of Farrar, Straus and Giroux, Inc. "Salvador" from *Salvador* by Joan Didion. Copyright © 1983 by Joan Didion. Reprinted by permission of Simon & Schuster, Inc. "Why I Write" by Joan Didion. Reprinted by permission of Wallace Literary Agency, Inc. Copyright © 1976 by Joan Didion. First published in *The New York Times Book Review*.
ANNIE DILLARD: "Aces and Eights" from *Teaching a Stone to Talk* by Annie

Dillard. Copyright © 1982 by Annie Dillard. Reprinted by permission of Harper & Row, Publishers, Inc. "The Fixed" from *Pilgrim at Tinker Creek* by Annie Dillard. Copyright © 1974 by Annie Dillard. Reprinted by permission of Harper & Row, Publishers, Inc. "Singing with the Fundamentalists" by Annie Dillard. Reprinted by permission of the author and her agent Blanche C. Gregory, Inc. Copyright © 1984 by Annie Dillard.

JOSÉ DONOSO: "Paseo" from *Cuentos* by José Donoso. Copyright © José Donoso, 1971. Reprinted by permission of Agencia Literaria Carmen Balcells, S. A., Barcelona.

BARBARA EHRENREICH: "Iranscam: The Real Meaning of Oliver North," *Ms.*, May 1987, is reprinted by permission of the author.

GRETEL EHRLICH: "Looking for a Lost Dog" is reprinted by permission of the author.

LOREN EISELEY: Reprinted by permission of Charles Scribner's Sons, an imprint of Macmillan Publishing Company from "The Brown Wasps" in *The Night Country* by Loren Eiseley. Copyright © 1971 Loren Eiseley.

E. M. FORSTER: "My Wood" from *Abinger Harvest*, copyright 1936 and renewed 1964 by Edward Morgan Forster, reprinted by permission of Harcourt Brace Jovanovich, Inc. and Edward Arnold Publishers. "What I Believe" and "Jew Consciousness" from *Two Cheers for Democracy*, by E. M. Forster, copyright 1939 by E. M. Forster and renewed 1967 by E. M. Forster, reprinted by permission of Harcourt Brace Jovanovich, Inc. and Edward Arnold Publishers.

ROBERT FROST: "Education of Poetry" from *Selected Prose of Robert Frost* edited by Hyde Cox and Edward Connery Lathem. Copyright © 1966 by Holt, Rinehart and Winston. Reprinted by permission of Henry Holt and Company, Inc.

JOHN KENNETH GALBRAITH: "How to Get the Poor Off Our Conscience" by John Kenneth Galbraith, from *Harper's* magazine, November 1985. Reprinted by permission of the author.

SUSAN GLASPELL: "Trifles," by Susan Glaspell. Copyright 1916 by Frank Shay; Copyright 1920 by Dodd, Mead & Company, Inc. Copyright renewed 1948 by Susan Glaspell; Text revised, prompt book added and new material, Copyright, 1951 by Walter H. Baker Company. For production rights contact Baker's Plays, Boston, MA 02111.

HARRY GOLDEN: "The Vertical Negro Plan" from *The Best of Harry Golden* by Harry Golden. Copyright © 1967 by Harry Golden. Reprinted by permission of Harper & Row, Publishers, Inc.

JANE GOODALL: see Jane Van Lawick-Goodall

NADINE GORDIMER: "Which New Era Would That Be?" *Selected Stories* by Nadine Gordimer. Copyright © 1956, 1975 by Nadine Gordimer. All rights reserved. Reprinted by permission of Viking Penguin, a division of Penguin Books USA, Inc.

MELISSA GREENE: Excerpts from "No Rms, Jungle Vu" by Melissa Greene. Reprinted by permission of the author. First published in *The Atlantic*, December 1987.

PATRICIA HAMPL: "Teresa" from *A Romantic Education* by Patricia Hampl. Copyright © 1981 by Patricia Hampl. "Memory and Imagination," copyright © 1985 by Patricia Hampl. Reprinted by permission of The Rhoda Weyr Agency, Chapel Hill, NC.

GARRETT HARDIN: "The Tragedy of the Commons" by Garrett Hardin. *Science*, Vol. 162, pp. 1243–1248, 13 December 1968. Reprinted by permission of the author and the American Association for the Advancement of Science.

EDWARD HOAGLAND: "Dogs, and the Tug of Life." Copyright © 1976 by Edward

Hoagland. Reprinted from *The Edward Hoagland Reader*, edited by Geoffrey Wolff, by permission of Random House, Inc.

SUE HUBBELL: From *A Country Year: Living the Questions* by Sue Hubbell. Copyright © 1983, 1984, 1985, 1986 by Sue Hubbell. Reprinted by permission of Random House, Inc.

ALDOUS HUXLEY: "Hyperion to a Satyr," from *Tomorrow and Tomorrow and Tomorrow and Other Stories* by Aldous Huxley. Copyright 1953 by Aldous Huxley. Reprinted by permission of Harper & Row, Publishers, Inc. "Hyperion to a Satyr" from *Adonis and the Alphabet* (British title) by Aldous Huxley. Reprinted by permission of Mrs. Laura Ashley and Chatto & Windus.

RANDALL JARRELL: "A Sad Heart at the Supermarket" from *A Sad Heart at the Supermarket*, copyright © 1962. Reprinted by permission of Mary Jarrell.

JOMO KENYATTA: "Gikuyu Industries" from *Facing Mt. Kenya* by Jomo Kenyatta. Copyright 1938 by Jomo Kenyatta. Reprinted by permission of Random House, Inc. and Martin Secker & Warburg Limited.

MARTIN LUTHER KING, JR: "Letter from Birmingham Jail" from *Why We Can't Wait* by Martin Luther King, Jr. Copyright © 1963, 1964 by Martin Luther King, Jr. Reprinted by permission of Harper & Row, Publishers, Inc.

PERRI KLASS: "Learning the Language" reprinted by permission of The Putnam Publishing Group from *A Not Entirely Benign Procedure* by Perri Klass. Copyright © 1987 by Perri Klass. "Are Women Better Doctors?", *The New York Times Magazine*, April 10, 1988. Copyright © 1988 by Perri Klass. Reprinted by permission of the author.
Letters to the *New York Times Magazine* in response to "Are Women Better Doctors?" by Deborah Curtis Donovan, David M. Lans, Ruth Kahan Kaminer, and Jeff Ecker are reprinted by permission.

MARK KRAMER: "The Ruination of the Tomato," from *The Atlantic Monthly*, January 1980. Copyright © 1980 by Mark Kramer. Reprinted by permission of the author.

JOSEPH WOOD KRUTCH: "No Essays, Please!" © 1964 from *A Krutch Omnibus* by Joseph Wood Krutch. Copyright © 1980 by Joseph Wood Krutch. By permission of William Morrow and Company, Inc.

GEORGE LEONARD: "The Warrior" by George Leonard, from *Esquire Magazine*, July 1986. Reprinted by permission of Sterling Lord Literistic, Inc. Copyright © 1986 by George Leonard.

C. S. LEWIS: "The Inner Ring" from *Screwtape Proposes a Toast—and other pieces* and "Vivisection" from *God in the Dock* by C. S. Lewis reprinted by permission of William Collins Sons & Co. Ltd.

KONRAD LORENZ: "The Language of Animals" from *King Solomon's Ring* by Konrad Lorenz. Copyright 1952 by Konrad Lorenz. Reprinted by permission of Harper & Row, Publishers, Inc. Excerpt from *On Aggression* by Konrad Lorenz, copyright © 1963 by Dr. G. Borotha-Schoder Verlag, Wien, English translation copyright © 1966 by Konrad Lorenz, reprinted by permission of Harcourt Brace Jovanovich, Inc.

MYRON MAGNET: "The Rich and the Poor," *Fortune*, June 6, 1988. Copyright © 1988 Time Inc. All rights reserved.

WILLIAM MANCHESTER: "My Old Man: The Last Years of H. L. Mencken" from *Controversy and Other Essays in Journalism, 1950–1975* by William Manchester. Copyright 1952, © 1956, 1957, 1959, 1960, 1961, 1962, 1974, 1975, 1976 by William Manchester. By permission of Little, Brown and Company. "Okinawa: The Bloodiest Battle of Them All" by William Manchester. Reprinted by permission of Don Congdon Associates, Inc. Copyright © 1987 by William Manchester.

JERRY MANDER: "The Walling of Experience," pp. 53–68 from *Four Arguments for the Elimination of Television* by Jerry Mander. Copyright © 1977, 1978 by Jerry Mander. By permission of William Morrow and Company, Inc.

MARGARET MEAD: "Warfare Is Only an Invention—Not a Biological Necessity," is reprinted from *Asia*, Vol. 40, No. 8, August 1940, pp. 402–405, by permission of the author's estate.

STANLEY MILGRAM: Excerpt from *Obedience to Authority* by Stanley Milgram. Copyright © 1974 by Stanley Milgram. Reprinted by permission of Harper & Row, Publishers, Inc.

N. SCOTT MOMADAY: "The Way to Rainy Mountain" by N. Scott Momaday. First published in *The Reporter*, January 26, 1967. Reprinted by permission of the University of New Mexico Press.

ELAINE MORGAN: Excerpts from "Primate Politics" from *The Descent of Woman* by Elaine Morgan. Reprinted by permission of Souvenir Press Ltd.

JAN MORRIS: "To Everest," by Jan Morris, from *Conundrum*, copyright © 1974 by Jan Morris. Reprinted by permission of Harcourt Brace Jovanovich, Inc., and by kind permission of Jan Morris.

CHARLES MURRAY: "What's So Bad About Being Poor?" from *In Pursuit: Of Happiness and Good Government* by Charles Murray. Copyright © 1988 by Cox and Murray, Inc. Reprinted by permission of Simon & Schuster, Inc.

MICHAEL NORMAN: "Standing His Ground" by Michael Norman, April 1, 1984. *The New York Times Magazine*. Copyright © 1984 by The New York Times Company. Reprinted by permission.

FLANNERY O'CONNOR: "Revelation" from *Everything That Rises Must Converge* by Flannery O'Connor. Copyright © 1964, 1965 by the Estate of Flannery O'Connor. Reprinted by permission of Farrar, Straus and Giroux, Inc.

FRANK O'CONNOR: From *Collected Stories*, by Frank O'Connor. Copyright © 1981 by Harriet O'Donovan Sheehy, Executrix of the Estate of Frank O'Connor. Reprinted by permission of Alfred A. Knopf, Inc. and Joan Daves.

GEORGE ORWELL: "Shooting an Elephant" from *Shooting an Elephant and Other Essays*, by George Orwell, copyright 1950 by Sonia Brownell Orwell and renewed 1978 by Sonia Pitt-Rivers, reprinted by permission of Harcourt Brace Jovanovich, Inc. and the estate of the late Sonia Brownell Orwell and Martin Secker & Warburg Ltd. "Politics and the English Language" from *Shooting an Elephant and Other Essays*, by George Orwell, copyright 1946 by Sonia Brownell Orwell and renewed 1974 by Sonia Brownell Orwell, reprinted by permission of Harcourt Brace Jovanovich, Inc. and the estate of the late Sonia Brownell Orwell and Martin Secker and Warburg Ltd. "Marrakech" and "Why I Write" from *Such, Such Were the Joys*, by George Orwell, copyright 1953 by Sonia Brownell Orwell, renewed 1981 by Mrs. George K. Perutz, Mrs. Miriam Gross, Dr. Michael Dickson, Executors of the Estate of Sonia Brownell Orwell, reprinted by permission of Harcourt Brace Jovanovich, Inc., and Martin Secker & Warburg Ltd.

CYNTHIA OZICK: "We Are the Crazy Lady" by Cynthia Ozick from *The First Ms. Reader*. Reprinted by permission of Cynthia Ozick and her agents, Raines & Raines, 71 Park Avenue, New York, NY 10016. Copyright © 1972 by Majority Enterprise, Inc.

NOEL PERRIN: "The Androgynous Man" by Noel Perrin, February 5, 1984, *The New York Times Magazine*. Copyright © 1984 by The New York Times Company. Reprinted by permission.

WILLIAM G. PERRY: "Examsmanship and the Liberal Arts" by William G. Perry, from *Examining in Harvard College*. Reprinted by permission of Harvard University Press.

ADRIENNE RICH: "Claiming an Education" is reprinted from *On Lies, Secrets, and Silence, Selected Prose 1966–1978*, by Adrienne Rich, by permission of

W. W. Norton & Company, Inc. Copyright © 1979 by W. W. Norton & Company, Inc.

LEONARD L. RISKIN: "Unsportsmanlike Conduct" by Leonard L. Riskin, January 22, 1989, *The New York Times*. Copyright © 1989 by The New York Times Company. Reprinted by permission.

RICHARD RODRIGUEZ: "Going Home Again: The New American Scholarship Boy" by Richard Rodriguez. Reprinted by permission of Georges Borchardt, Inc. and the author. Copyright © 1975 by Richard Rodriguez.

D. L. ROSENHAN: "On Being Sane in Insane Places." *Science*, Vol. 179, pp. 250–257, 19 January 1973. Reprinted by permission of the author and the American Association for the Advancement of Science.

SCOTT RUSSELL SANDERS: "At Play in the Paradise of Bombs" from *At Play in the Paradise of Bombs* by Scott Russell Sanders. Copyright © 1987 by Scott Russell Sanders; reprinted by permission of the author and the author's agent, Virginia Kidd.

DOROTHY SAYERS: "Are Women Human?" from *Unpopular Opinions* by Dorothy Sayers, 1947, Gollancz. Reprinted by permission of David Higham Associates Limited, London.

LESLIE MARMON SILKO: "Lullaby" copyright © 1981 by Leslie Marmon Silko. Reprinted from *Storyteller* by Leslie Marmon Silko, published by Seaver Books, New York, New York, 1981.

JOHN STEINBECK: "The Chrysanthemums," from *The Long Valley* by John Steinbeck. Copyright 1938, renewed © 1966 by John Steinbeck. All rights reserved. Reprinted by permission of Viking Penguin, a division of Penguin Books USA, Inc.

LEWIS THOMAS: "Ponds" from *The Medusa and the Snail* by Lewis Thomas. Copyright © 1978 by Lewis Thomas. All rights reserved. Reprinted by permission of Viking Penguin, a division of Penguin Books USA, Inc. "House Calls: Medicine Before 1937" from *The Youngest Science* by Lewis Thomas. Copyright © 1983 by Lewis Thomas. All rights reserved. Reprinted by permission of Viking Penguin, a division of Penguin Books USA, Inc. Titled originally "House Calls," and "1911 and 1933 Medicine."

JANE VAN LAWICK-GOODALL: From *In The Shadow of Man* by Jane Van Lawick-Goodall. Copyright © 1971 by Hugo and Jane Van Lawick-Goodall. Reprinted by permission of Houghton Mifflin Company and George Weidenfeld & Nicolson Limited.

ALICE WALKER: "Brothers and Sisters" from *In Search of Our Mothers' Gardens*, copyright © 1975 by Alice Walker, reprinted by permission of Harcourt Brace Jovanovich, Inc. "To Hell With Dying" from *In Love & Trouble: Stories of Black Women*, by Alice Walker, copyright © 1967 by Alice Walker, reprinted by permission of Harcourt Brace Jovanovich, Inc.

E. B. WHITE: "Progress and Change" from *One Man's Meat* by E. B. White. Copyright 1939 by E. B. White. "Twins" from *Poems and Sketches of E. B. White*. Copyright 1948 by E. B. White. "Once More to the Lake" from *Essays of E. B. White*. Copyright 1941 by E. B. White. Reprinted by permission of Harper & Row, Publishers, Inc.

ROGER WILKINS: "Confessions of a Blue-Chip Black" by Roger Wilkins. Reprinted by permission of International Creative Management. Copyright © 1982 by Roger Wilkins.

TOM WOLFE: Excerpt from *The Right Stuff* by Tom Wolfe. Copyright © 1979 by Tom Wolfe. Reprinted by permission of Farrar, Straus and Giroux, Inc.

VIRGINIA WOOLF: "The Society of Outsiders and the Prevention of War," excerpt from *The Three Guineas* by Virginia Woolf, copyright 1938 by Harcourt Brace Jovanovich, Inc. and renewed 1966 by Leonard Woolf, reprinted by permission of the publisher. "The Patriarchy," Chapter 2 from *A Room of One's Own* by Virginia Woolf; copyright 1929 by Harcourt Brace Jovanovich, Inc. and renewed 1957 by Leonard Woolf. Reprinted by permission of the publisher and The Hogarth Press. "Professions for Women," from *The Death of the Moth and Other Essays* by Virginia Woolf, copyright 1942 by Harcourt Brace Jovanovich, Inc. and renewed 1970 by Marjorie T. Parsons, Executrix. Reprinted by permission of the publisher and The Hogarth Press.

RICHARD WRIGHT: "The Ethics of Living Jim Crow" from *Uncle Tom's Children* by Richard Wright. Copyright 1937 by Richard Wright. Renewed 1964 by Ellen Wright. Reprinted by permission of Harper & Row, Publishers, Inc.

W. B. YEATS: "The Spur" reprinted with permission of Macmillan Publishing Company from *The Poems of W. B. Yeats: A New Edition*, edited by Richard J. Finneran. Copyright © 1940 by Georgie Yeats, renewed 1968 by Bertha Georgie Yeats, Michael Butler Yeats, and Anne Yeats. Four lines from "The Tower" reprinted with permission of Macmillan Publishing Company from *The Poems of W. B. Yeats: A New Edition*, edited by Richard J. Finneran. Copyright 1928 by Macmillan Publishing Company, renewed 1956 by Georgie Yeats.

W. B. YEATS: "The Spur" and "The Tower" taken from *The Collected Poems of W. B. Yeats* and reprinted by permission of A P Watt Limited, on behalf of Michael B. Yeats and Macmillan London Ltd.